DATE DUE

05-15-03			

DEMCO 38-296

The Cambridge Survey of World Migration begins in the sixteenth century with the establishment of European colonies overseas and covers the history of migration to the late twentieth century, when political conflict, global communications and transport systems stimulated immense and complex flows of displaced persons, labour migrants and skilled professionals. In ninety-five contributions, leading scholars from twenty-seven different countries consider a wide variety of issues including regional migration patterns, the flights of refugees and illegal migration. Each entry constitutes a substantive essay, supported by up-to-date bibliographies, tables, plates, maps and figures. As the most wide-ranging coverage of migration in a single volume, the book will be an indispensable reference tool for scholars and students in the field.

THE CAMBRIDGE SURVEY OF WORLD MIGRATION

THE CAMBRIDGE SURVEY OF WORLD MIGRATION

Edited by

ROBIN COHEN
University of Warwick

CAMBRIDGE
UNIVERSITY PRESS

Published by the Press Syndicate of the University of Cambridge
The Pitt Building, Trumpington Street, Cambridge, CB2 1RP
40 West 20th Street, New York, NY 10011–4211, USA
10 Stamford Road, Oakleigh, Victoria 3166, Australia

First published 1995

Printed in Great Britain at the University Press, Cambridge

A catalogue record for this book is available from the British Library

Library of Congress cataloging-in-publication data

The Cambridge survey of world migration / edited by Robin Cohen.
     p.   cm.
  Includes index.
  ISBN 0 521 44405 5
  1. Emigration and immigration – History.   I. Cohen, Robin, 1944–

JV6021.C35   1995
304.8'09 – dc20   95–16842 CIP

ISBN 0 521 44405 5 hardback

Contents

Illustrations

Tables

Notes on contributors

The editor

COHEN, Robin. Professor of sociology at the University of Warwick. Author of *The new helots: migrants in the international division of labour* (1987), *Frontiers of identity: the British and the others* (1994) and co-editor of *Reluctant hosts: Europe and its refugees* (1989).

The contributors

ABADAN-UNAT, Nermin. Professor of political science and director of the Unit for Migration and Refugee Studies, Bosporus University, Istanbul, Turkey. Author, with others, of *Migration and development* (1976), 'The effect of international labour migration on women's roles' in C. Kagitcibasi (ed.) *Sex roles: family and community in Turkey* (1982) and 'The socio-economic aspects of return migration in Turkey', *Migration* (1988).

ABELLA, Manolo I. Regional adviser on migrant workers, International Labor Office, Regional Office for Asia and Pacific, Bangkok. Author of 'Labour migration from south and southeast Asia: some policy issues', *International Labor Review* (1984), 'Contemporary labour migration from Asia: policies and perspectives of sending countries' in M. Kritz et al. (eds) *Global interactions: international migration systems in an interdependent world* (1991) and co-editor of *Middle East interlude: Asian workers abroad: a comparative study of four countries* (1986).

ADELMAN, Howard. Professor of philosophy and director of the Centre for Refugee Studies, York University, Toronto. Author of 'Palestinian refugees', *World Refugee Survey* (1983), 'Palestinian refugees and the peace process' in P. Marantz and J. Stein (eds) *Peace-making in the Middle East* (1985) and, with others, editor of *Palestinian refugee and demographic report* (1992).

ADELMAN, Jeremy. Assistant professor of history at Princeton University. Editor of *Essays in Argentine labor history, 1870–1930* (1992) and author of *Frontier development, land, labour and capital on the wheatlands of Argentina and Canada, 1890–1914* (1993).

ADEPOJU, Aderanti. Professor of demography, United Nations African Institute for Economic Development and Planning, Dakar, Senegal. Author of 'The dimension of the refugee problem in Africa', *African Affairs* (1982), 'International migration in Africa south of the Sahara' in R. Appleyard (ed.) *International migration today vol. 1: trends and prospects* (1988) and 'South–north migration: the African experience', *International Migration* (1991).

ALTMAN, Ida. Professor of history at the University of New Orleans. Author of *Emigrants and society: Extremadura and Spanish America in the sixteenth century* (1989), co-editor of *'To make America': European emigration in the early modern period* (1991) and *Provinces of early Mexico* (1976).

ANWAR, Muhammad. Professor in the Centre for Research in Ethnic Relations, University of Warwick. Author of *The myth of return* (1979), *Race and politics* (1986) and co-editor of *Black and ethnic leaderships* (1991).

BADE, Klaus J. Professor of contemporary history and director of the Institute for Migration and Intercultural Studies at the University of Osnabrück in Germany. Author of *Friedrich Fabri unde de imperialismus in der Bismarckzeit: revolution, depression, expansion* (1975), editor of *Population, labor* *and migration in nineteenth- and twentieth-century Germany* (1987) and *Deutsche im Ausland: fremde in Deutschland: migration in Geschichte und Gegenwart* (1992).

BAGANHA, María Ioannis B. Formerly with the Universidade Aberta, now professor of quantitative methods for the social sciences at the sociology department of the Universidade de Coimbra. Author of *Portuguese emigration to the United States, 1820–1930* (1990), 'Social mobility in the receiving society: Portuguese immigrants in the United States', *International Migration Review* (1991) and other publications in Portuguese on migration issues.

BASOK, Tanya. Assistant professor in the department of sociology at the University of Windsor in Canada. Author of *Keeping heads above water: Salvadorean refugees in Costa Rica* (1993), co-editor of *Soviet-Jewish emigration and resettlement in the 1990s* (1992) and 'Individual, household and cooperative production: the case of Salvadorean refugees in Costa Rica', *Canadian Journal of Latin American and Caribbean Studies* (1993).

BAUBÖCK, Rainer. Assistant professor of political science at the Institute for Advanced Studies in Vienna. Author of *Immigration and the boundaries of citizenship* (1992), 'Optional citizenship: articulation of interests and identities in naturalisations', *Innovations* (1992) and 'Legitimate immigration control' in H. Adelman (ed.) *Legitimate and illegitimate discrimination: new directions in migration* (1993).

BENIFAND, Alexander. Research fellow, Centre for Refugee Studies at York University, Toronto. Author of many works in Russian and 'Jewish emigration from the USSR in the 1990s' in T. Basok and R. Brym (eds) *Soviet-Jewish emigration and resettlement in the 1990s* (1992), 'Troubled settlement of refugees in Russia' and 'Ethnic purification and its three types of refugees', both in *Refuge* (1993).

BIGMAN, Laura. Until her death in 1995 was director, Africans in Washington Project, Washington DC and research associate at Howard University. Author of *History and hunger in West Africa* (1993) and *Connections: Africans in Washington* (1990).

BOTTOMLEY, Gillian. Professor of anthropology at Macquarie University, Australia. Author of *After the Odyssey: a study of Greek Australians* (1979), *From another place: migration and the politics of culture* (1992) and co-author and co-editor of *Intersexions: gender/class/culture/ethnicity* (1991).

CALAVITA, Kitty. Associate professor of criminology, law and society at the University of California, Irvine. Author of *Inside the state: the Bracero Program, immigration and the INS* (1992), 'Employer sanctions violations', *Law and Society Review* (1990), and 'The contradictions of immigration law-making', *Law and Policy* (1989).

CAMMACK, Diana. SSRC-MacArthur fellow and senior associate member at St Antony's College, Oxford. Author of 'The "human face" of destabilization: the war in Mozambique', *Review of African Political Economy* (1987), *The Rand at war: 1899–1902: the Witwatersrand and the Anglo-Boer War* (1990) and 'African refugees: a failure of development', *Refuge* (1987).

CAMPANI, Giovanna. Professor of comparative education at the University of Florence. Author of 'Intercultural education: an international perspective', *Tecnodid*, Rome (1993), 'Immigration and racism in Italy', *Ethnic and Racial Studies* (1993) and joint guest editor of two special issues of *European Journal of Intercultural Studies* on intercultural education in Europe (1993/4).

CASTLES, Stephen. Director of the Centre for Multicultural Studies, University of Wollongong, Australia. Author of *Australia's Italians: culture and community in a changing society* (1992) and co-author of *Immigrant workers in the class structure in Europe* (1973 and 1985) and *The age of migration: international population movements in the modern world* (1993).

CHAN Kwok Bun. Senior lecturer in sociology at the National University of Singapore. Author of *Smoke and fire: the Chinese in Montreal* (1991), co-author of *Stepping out: the making of Chinese entrepreneurs* (1993) and co-editor of *Asian transmigration* (1993).

COLLINS, Jock. Associate professor of economics and director of research and planning in the School of Finance and Economics at the University of Technology, Sydney. Author of *Migrant hands in a distant land: Australia's post-war immigration* (1988, with subsequent editions) and 'Australian immigration: an issue of class', *Journal of Intercultural Studies* (1984).

CRUSH, Jonathan. Professor of geography, Queen's University in Canada. Author of *The struggle for Swazi labour, 1890–1920* (1987), co-author of *South Africa's labor empire: a history of black migrancy to the gold mines* (1991) and co-editor of *Liquor and labor in southern Africa* (1992).

DANIELS, Roger. Professor of history at the University of Cincinnati, USA. Author of *Coming to America: a history of immigration and ethnicity in American life* (1990), *Asian America: Chinese and Japanese in the United States since 1850* (1988) and 'On the comparative study of immigrant and ethnic groups in the new world: a note', *Comparative Studies in Society and History* (1983).

DÍAZ, Luz Marina. Director of the population section at the Corporación Centro Regional de Población in Bogotá, Colombia. Author of 'Labour migrations from Colombia to Venezuela during the last two decades' in *Opciones para las integración, migración y desarrollo* (1991), co-author of *Economic recession, labor migration and their effects on the Colombo-Venezuelan border area* (1985) and *Illegal Colombians in Venezuela* (1983).

DUMMETT, Ann. Former director of the Runnymede Trust and now consultant to the Commission for Racial Equality, London. Author of *A new immigration policy* (1978), *A portrait of English racism* (1973) and co-author of *Subjects, citizens, aliens and others* (1990).

ENTZINGER, Han. Professor of multi-ethnic studies at Utrecht University and academic director of the Netherlands School for Social and Economic Policy Research. Co-editor of *Lost illusions: Caribbean minorities in Britain and the Netherlands* (1988), author of 'The lure of integration', *European Journal of International Affairs* (1990) and 'Shifting paradigms: the appraisal of immigration in the Netherlands', *European Migration* (1993).

FAKIOLAS, Rossetos. Professor of Economics and director of the Division of Humanities at the National Technical University, Athens. Author of many publications (in Greek) on migratory movements to and from Greece and on the trade union movement in that country.

FASSMANN, Heinz. Director of the Institute of Urban and Regional Research of the Austrian Academy of Sciences and senior lecturer at the University of Vienna. Author of *Arbeitsmarktsegmentation und berufslaufbahnen* (Labour market segmentation and occupational career) (1993), co-author of *Einwanderungsland Österreich* (1992) and *European migration in the late 20th century* (1992).

FERRIS, Elizabeth G. Director of the immigration and refugee programme of the Church World Service, New York. Editor of *Refugees and world politics* (1985), author of *The Central American refugees* (1987) and *Beyond borders: refugees, migrants and human rights in the post-cold war era* (1993).

FINCH, Henry. Senior lecturer in economic and social history at the University of Liverpool. Author of *Historia económica del Uruguay contemporáneo* (1980), *A political economy of Uruguay since 1870* (1981) and *Contemporary Uruguay: problems and prospects* (1989).

FINDLAY, Allan M. Professor of geography at the University of Dundee, Scotland. Author of *Population and development in the Third World* (1987), 'From settlers to skilled transients', *Geoforum* (1988) and co-editor of *Population migration and the changing world order* (1994).

GJERDE, Jon. Associate professor of history at the University of California, Berkeley. Author of *From peasants to farmers: the migration from Balestrand, Norway, to the upper Middlewest* (1985) and numerous articles on immigrants in the USA.

GOULD, W. T. S. Reader in geography at the University of Liverpool. Author of *People and education in the Third World* (1993), 'Population mobility' in M. B. Gleave (ed.) *Tropical African development:*

geographical perspectives (1992) and co-editor of *Population migration and the changing world order* (1994).

GUGLER, Josef. Professor of sociology at the University of Connecticut. Co-author of *Cities, poverty and development: urbanization in the Third World* (1992), editor of *The urban transformation in Asia, Africa and Latin America: regional trajectories* (1995) and *Cities in Asia, Africa and Latin America: multiple perspectives* (1995).

HAMMAR, Tomas. Professor of political science and formerly director of the Centre for Research in International Migration and Ethnicity, University of Stockholm, Sweden. Author of *Democracy and the nation state: aliens, denizens and citizens in a world of international migration* (1990) and editor of *European immigration policy: a comparative study* (1985).

HEFFERNAN, Michael. Lecturer in geography at Loughborough University. Co-author of *Colonialism and development in the contemporary world* (1991), *French and Algerian identities from colonial times to the present: a century of interaction* (1993) and *Geographical knowledge and imperial power* (1994).

HERNÁNDEZ-CRUZ, Juan E. Professor of sociology at the Inter-American University of Puerto Rico, San Germán campus, and director of the Caribbean Institute and Study Center for Latin America (CISLA). Author of 'Las migraciones en el Caribe: el caso de Puerto Rico y Santo Domingo' in E. García Zarza (ed.) *Las migraciones en Iberoamérica* (1993), *Migratory currents in contemporary Puerto Rico* (1992) and 'Reintegration of circulating families in southwestern Puerto Rico', *International Migration Review* (1986).

HOFFMAN-NOWOTNY, Hans-Joachim. Professor of sociology and director of the Sociological Institute, University of Zurich. Co-author of 'International and internal migration: towards a new paradigm' in Tom Bottomore et al. *Sociology: the state of the art* (1982), 'Social integration and cultural pluralism: structural and cultural problems of immigration in European industrial countries' in W. Alonso (ed.) *Population in an interacting world* (1986) and 'Integration, assimilation und "plurale gesellschaft": konzeptuelle theoretische und praktische überlegungen' in C. Höhn and D. B. Rain (eds) *Ausländer in der Bundesrepublik Deutschland* (1990).

HOLMES, Colin. Professor of history at the University of Sheffield. Author of *Anti-Semitism in British society 1876–1939* (1979), *John Bull's island* (1988) and *A tolerant country?* (1991). He is joint-editor of the journal *Immigrants and Minorities*.

HU-DEHART, Evelyn. Professor of history and director of the Center for Studies of Ethnicity and Race in America, University of Colorado, Boulder. Author of 'From yellow peril to model minority: the Columbus legacy and Asians in America', *The New World* (1992), 'Chinese coolie labor in Cuba in the nineteenth century', *Slavery and Abolition* (1992) and 'Latin America in Asia-Pacific perspective' in A. Dirlik (ed.) *What is in a rim? critical perspectives on the Pacific rim* (1993).

HUGO, Graeme. Professor of geography at the University of Adelaide. Author, among many works, of *Population mobility in West Java* (1978), *Australia's changing population: trends and implications* (1986) and co-author of *The demographic dimension in Indonesian development* (1987).

ISHEMO, Shubi L. Senior lecturer in the School of Humanities, Trinity and All Saints College, Leeds. Co-editor of *Forced labour, migration and patterns of movement within Africa* (1989) and *Lower Zambezi basin in Mozambique, 1850–1920: a study in economy and society* (1995).

ISLAM, Muinul. Professor of economics at the University of Chittagong, Bangladesh. Co-author of *Overseas migration from rural Bangladesh: a micro study* (1987) and *Illegal international trade in Bangladesh: impact on the domestic economy* (1991).

JEEVES, Alan H. Professor of history at Queen's University at Kingston, Canada. Author of *Migrant labour in South Africa's mining economy: the struggle for the gold mines' labour supply, 1890–1920* (1985), 'Sugar and gold in the making of the South African labour system: the crisis of supply on the

Zululand sugar estates, 1906–39', *South African Journal of Economic History* (1992) and co-author of *South Africa's labor empire: a history of black migrancy to the gold mines* (1991).

JOLY, Danièle. Senior research fellow at the Centre for Research in Ethnic Relations, University of Warwick, UK. Co-editor of *Reluctant hosts: Europe and its refugees* (1989), author of *The French Communist Party and the Algerian war* (1991) and *Refugees: asylum in Europe?* (1992).

KANAPATHIPILLAI, Valli. Consultant/researcher at the International Centre for Ethnic Studies, Colombo, Sri Lanka. Author of 'Victims of July '83' in V. Das (ed.) *Mirrors of violence* (1990) and *A decade of change in the plantations: implications for women workers* (1991).

KARLSSON, Klas-Göran. Associate professor in the department of history at the University of Lund, Sweden. Author (in Swedish) of *Armenia: from Mount Ararat to mountainous Karabakh* (1990) and *History teaching in a classical frame: the objectives of history in the Russian and Soviet school, 1900–1940* (1987).

KAY, Diana. Sociologist currently living in the Netherlands. Author, with Robert Miles, of *Refugees or migrant workers? European volunteer workers in Britain 1946–1951* (1992), *Chileans in exile: private struggles, public lives* (1987) and, also with Robert Miles, 'The TUC, foreign labour and the Labour government 1945–1951', *Immigrants and Minorities* (1990).

KIERNAN, Victor. Emeritus professor of modern history at Edinburgh University. Author of *The lords of human kind* (1988), 'Britons old and new' in C. Holmes (ed.) *Immigrants and minorities in British society* (1978) and *State and society in Europe 1550–1650* (1980).

KLEIN, Herbert S. Professor of history at Columbia University, New York. Author of *The middle passage: comparative studies in the Atlantic slave trade* (1978), 'The social and economic integration of Portuguese immigrants in Brazil in the late nineteenth and twentieth centuries', *Journal of Latin American Studies* (1991) and 'The social and economic integration of Spanish immigrants in 19th and 20th century Brazil', *Journal of Social History* (1992).

KOEHN, Peter. Director of the Office of International Programs at the University of Montana. Author of *Refugees from revolution: US policy and Third World migration* (1991), *Public policy and administration in Africa: lessons from Nigeria* (1990) and co-author of *Resettled refugees and asylum applicants: implications of the case of migrants from Ethiopia for United States policy* (1987).

LAM, Lawrence. Assistant professor of sociology and associate director of the Centre for Refugee Studies, York University, Toronto. Author of 'Target for hate: the impact of the Zundel and Keegstra trials on a Jewish Canadian audience', *Canadian Ethnic Studies* (1993), 'The impact of migration on the sexual division of family work: a case study of Italian immigrant couples', *Journal of Comparative Family Studies* (1994) and 'Life in refugee camps: Hong Kong' in B. Matthews (ed.) *The quality of life in southeast Asia* (1992).

LIAN Kwen Fee. Lecturer in sociology at the National University of Singapore. Author of 'The socio-political process of identity formation in an ethnic community: the Chinese in New Zealand', *Ethnic and Racial Studies* (1988), 'The state and tribal political development in a settler society', *Plural Societies* (1990) and co-author of 'The ethnic mosaic' in G. Evans (ed.) *Asia's cultural mosaic: an anthropological introduction* (1993).

LIPPMAN ABU-LUGHOD, Janet. Professor of sociology and historical studies at the graduate faculty of the New School for Social Research, New York. Author of 'The demographic transformation of Palestine' in I. Abu-Lughod (ed.) *Transformation of Palestine* (1971), 'Exiles at home and abroad', *Current Sociology* (1988) and *The demographic characteristics of the Palestine population* (1980).

LIU, John M. Associate professor in Asian American studies and social sciences, University of California, Irvine. Author of 'The contours of Asian professional, technical and kindred migration', *Sociological Perspectives* (1992), 'The relationship of migration research to Asian American studies' in

G. Y. Okihiro (ed.) *Reflections on Shattered Windows* (1988) and co-author of 'Pacific Rim development and the duality of post-1965 Asian immigration to the United States' in P. Ong et al. (eds) *The new Asian immigration in Los Angeles and global restructuring* (1994).

LLAMBIAS-WOLFF, Jaime. Associate professor of social science at the University of York, Toronto. Author of *Notre exil pour parler: les Chiliens au Québec* (1988), co-author of *¿Con qué sueñas tú?* (1983) and co-editor of *Médecine et société: les années 80* (1981).

LOESCHER, Gil. Professor of international relations at the University of Notre Dame, Indiana. Co-author of *Calculated kindness: refugees and America's half open door, 1945 to present* (1986), co-editor of *Refugees and international relations* (1989) and author of *Beyond charity: international cooperation and the global refugee problem* (1993).

LOISKANDL, Helmut. Professor of comparative sociology at Tokiwa University, Mito, Japan. Author of 'Temporal Japanese business migrants in Brisbane', *Tokiwa Journal of Human Science* (1993), 'The problem of foreign workers in international perspective' (in Japanese), *Symposium: Gaikokkujin Rodosha Nihon to Doitsu* (1991) and *Georg Simmel: Schopenhauer and Nietzsche* (1986).

LUCASSEN, Jan. Head of the department of research and publications of the International Institute of Social History, Amsterdam and professor of social history at the Free University, Amsterdam. Author of *Migrant labour in Europe 1600–1900* (1987).

LUCASSEN, Leo. Fellow of the Royal Netherlands Academy of Arts and Sciences and of the department of history at Leiden University. Author of *En men noemde hen zigeuners* (1990), 'Under the cloak of begging', *Ethnologia Europaea* (1993), 'A blind spot', *International Review of Social History* (1993) and co-author of 'Justice or injustice', *Immigrants and Minorities* (1992).

LUCIUK, Lubomyr Y. Associate professor in the department of politics and economics at the Royal Military College of Canada and an adjunct professor in the department of geography at Queen's University. Co-author of *Creating a landscape: a geography of Ukrainians in Canada* (1989), co-editor of *Canada's Ukrainians: negotiating an identity* (1991) and *Searching for place: Canada's Ukrainians and their encounter with the displaced persons of Europe* (forthcoming).

MacMASTER, Neil. Lecturer in modern French history at the University of East Anglia. Author of *Spanish fighters: an oral history of civil war and exile* (1990), 'The "Seuil de tolérance": the uses of a "scientific" racist concept' in M. Silverman (ed.) *Race, discourse and power in France* (1991) and 'Patterns of emigration, 1905–1954: "Kabyles" and "Arabs"' in A. G. Hargreaves and M. J. Heffernan (eds) *French and Algerian identities from colonial times to the present* (1993).

MIGNOT, Michel. Anthropologist at the CNRS, Paris (1979–90) and assistant secretary of the Commission on Migration, Refugees and Demography at the Council of Europe. Author of 'Secondary migration of southeast Asian refugees' in P. J. Ruledge (ed.) *In search of tradition and adaption* (1993), *Kampuchean, Laotian and Vietnamese Refugees in Australia, New Zealand, Canada, France and the United Kingdom* (1988) and 'La contribution des réfugiés à l'enrichissement et à l'évolution des pays d'accueil', *AWR Bulletin* (1987).

MILLER, Mark J. Professor of political science at the University of Delaware and assistant editor of *International Migration Review*. Co-author of *The age of migration* (1993), *The unavoidable issue: US immigration policy in the 1980s* (1982) and *Administering foreign worker programs: lessons from Europe* (1982).

MOCH, Leslie Page. Professor of history at the University of Michigan-Flint. Author of *Moving Europeans: migration in Western Europe since 1650* (1993), *Paths to the city: regional migration in nineteenth century France* (1983) and, with R. G. Fuchs, 'Pregnant, single, and far from home: migrant women in nineteenth-century Paris', *American Historical Review* (1990).

MORAWSKA, Ewa. Professor of sociology and history at the University of Pennsylvania. Author of *Insecure prosperity: small-town Jews in industrial America, 1880–1940* (forthcoming), *For bread with butter: lifeworlds of the east central Europeans in Johnstown, Pennsylvania, 1890–1940* (1985) and 'The sociology and historiography of immigration' in V. Yans-McLaughlin (ed.) *Immigration reconsidered: history, sociology and politics* (1990).

MÜNZ, Rainer. Professor of demography at Humboldt University, Berlin and former director of the demographic institute of the Austrian Academy of Science, Vienna. Co-author (all in German) of *Old age and care* (1992), *Austria as an immigration country* (1992) and *Changing trends: language and ethnicity in Burgenland* (1993).

NOIRIEL, Gérard. Professor of social history at the Ecole Normale Supérieure in Paris. Author of *Le creuset français: histoire de l'immigration* (1988), *La tyrannie du national: le droit d'asile en Europe (1793–1993)* (1991) and co-editor of *Immigrants in two democracies: French and American experiences* (1992).

NUGENT, Walter. Tackes professor of history at the University of Notre Dame, Indiana. Author of *Crossings: the great transatlantic migrations, 1870–1914* (1992), *Structures of American social history* (1981) and *Money and American society: 1865–1880* (1968).

OGDEN, Philip E. Reader in geography at Queen Mary and Westfield College, University of London, UK. Author of *Migration and geographical change* (1984) and co-editor of *Migrants in modern France: population mobility in the later nineteenth and twentieth centuries* (1989).

ONG Jin Hui. Head of the department of sociology at the National University of Singapore and former director of the Centre of Advanced Studies. His recent works include *Prostitution: the interaction of social and legal control* and *Crossing borders: transmigration in the Asia-Pacific*.

PEACH, Ceri. Professor of social geography at the University of Oxford. Author of *West Indian migration* (1968), co-editor and contributor to *Ethnic segregation in cities* (1968) and co-editor and contributor to *South Asians overseas* (1990).

POLYAKOV, Alexei. Scientific coordinator, Institute of International Economic and Political Studies, Russian Academy of Sciences, Moscow. Author of paper on 'Labour emigration from the former USSR: challenges for the European labour markets and cooperation' (1992) and co-author of paper on 'Labour market and migration trends in Russia' (1993).

RICHMOND, Anthony H. Emeritus professor and senior scholar, department of sociology, York University, Toronto, Canada. Author of numerous articles and books on migration and ethnic relations, including *Immigration and ethnic conflict* (1988) and *Global apartheid: refugees, racism and the new world order* (1994).

ROBINSON, Vaughan. Senior lecturer in geography and director of the Migration Unit, at University College, Swansea. Author of *Transients, settlers and refugees: Asians in Britain* (1986), editor of *The international refugee crisis: British and Canadian responses* (1992) and co-editor of *Geography and refugees: patterns and processes of change* (1993).

ROCHA-TRINDADE, Maria Beatriz. Professor of sociology at the Centro de Estudos das Migrações e das Relações Interculturais, Aberta University, Lisbon. Author of 'La sociologie des migrations au Portugal', *Current Sociology* (1984), 'Towards the reintegration of migrants' in Verlag Breitentach Pub. (ed.) *Closing the migratory cycle: the case of Portugal* (1985) and 'Portuguese migration to Brazil in the 19th and 20th centuries: an international cultural exchange' in The Multicultural History Society of Ontario (ed.) *Portuguese migration in global perspective* (1990).

SCALLY, Robert. Professor of history and director of the Glucksman Ireland House, New York University. Author of *The origins of the Lloyd George coalition: the politics of social imperialism, 1900–*

1918 (1975), 'Liverpool ships and Irish emigrants in the age of sail', *Social History* (1984) and *The end of hidden Ireland: rebellion, famine and emigration* (1995).

SCHIERUP, Carl-Ulrik. Associate professor and reader in sociology at the University of Umeå, Sweden. Author of *Migration, socialism and the international division of labour* (1990), co-author, with Aleksandra Ålund of *Will they still be dancing? integration and ethnic transformation among Yugoslav immigrants in Scandinavia* (1987) and, again with Aleksandra Ålund, *Paradoxes of multiculturalism* (1991).

SEDDON, David. Professor in the School of Development Studies, University of East Anglia, UK. Author of *Nepal: a state of poverty* (1993), co-author of *Nepal in crisis* (1980) and *Peasants and workers in Nepal* (1979).

SHAFIR, Gershon. Associate professor of sociology at the University of California, San Diego. Author of 'Israel's "open frontier" on the West Bank', *Theory and Society* (1984), *Land, labour and the origins of the Israeli–Palestinian conflict 1882–1914* (1989) and 'Ideological politics or the politics of demography' in I. S. Lustick and B. Rubin (eds) *Critical essays in Israeli society, politics and culture* (1991).

SHIMPO, Mitsuru. Professor of sociology at Japan Women's University in Japan. Author (in Japanese) of *Immigrants from Japan* (1986), *The history of the Japanese Canadian fishermen in British Columbia* (1985) and *The social history of Japanese Canadians* (1975).

SKELDON, Ronald. Reader in geography at the University of Hong Kong. Author of *Population mobility in developing countries: a reinterpretation* (1990), editor of *Reluctant exiles? Migration from Hong Kong and the new overseas Chinese* (1994) and author of numerous articles on migration in professional journals.

SOLÉ, Carlota. Professor of sociology at the Universitat Autònoma of Barcelona, Spain. Among her many publications are *Trabajadores extranjeros en Cataluña: integración o racismo?* (1991), *La realitat social de les minories ètniques a Barcelona* (1993) and 'The integration of immigrants in an industrialised society' in R. Gunther (ed.) *Politics, society and democracy* (1992).

SUHRKE, Astri. Professor and director of research at The Chr. Michelsen Institute of Development and Human Rights Studies in Norway. Co-author of *Escape from violence: conflict and the refugee crisis in the developing world* (1989), *Pressure points: environmental degradation, migration and conflict* (1993) and 'Migration, state and civil society in southeast Asia' in M. Weiner (ed.) *International migration and security* (1993).

SWINDELL, Kenneth. Former reader in geography at the University of Birmingham, UK. Author of *Farm labour* (1985), 'Farmers, labourers and traders: dry season migration from northwestern Nigeria, 1900–33', *Africa* (1984) and 'International labour migration in Nigeria, 1976–86', *Migration* (1990).

SWORD, Keith. Research fellow at the School of Slavonic and East European Studies, University of London, UK. Co-author of *The formation of the Polish community in Great Britain, 1939–50* (1989), editor of and contributor to *The Times guide to Eastern Europe* (1990, 1991) and editor of *The Soviet takeover of the Polish eastern provinces, 1939–41* (1991).

TATLA, Darshan Singh. Lecturer in the department of languages and community studies, South Birmingham College, Birmingham. Author of *Sikhs in North America: an annotated bibliography* (1991), 'Nurturing the faithful: the role of *Sant* among Britain's Sikhs', *Religion* (1992) and co-author of *Sikhs in Britain* (1994).

THIARA, Ravinder K. Research associate in continuing education, University of Warwick. Her doctoral thesis is titled 'Migration, organization and inter-ethnic relations: Indian South Africans, 1860–1990' (University of Warwick, 1994).

TINKER, Hugh. Emeritus professor of politics at the University of Lancaster, UK. Author of *A new system of slavery* (1974), *The banyan tree* (1979) and *Race, conflict and the international order* (1977).

TWADDLE, Michael. Institute of Commonwealth Studies, University of London, UK. Editor of *Expulsion of a minority: essays on Ugandan Asians* (1975) and many writings on Uganda.

USHKALOV, Igor. Professor and head of the section on social problems of international cooperation at the Institute of International Economic and Political Sciences in Moscow. Author, in Russian, of *The human factor in international cooperation* (1990), *Emigration: as it looks from East and West* (1991) and, in English, 'Inter-state migrations in the former Soviet Union', *Migration* (1991).

VAN AMERSFOORT, Hans. Professor at the Institute of Social Geography, University of Amsterdam, Netherlands. Author of *Immigration and the formation of minority groups* (1982), co-editor of *States and nations: the rebirth of the nationality question in Europe* (1991) and 'Ethnic residential patterns in a welfare state: lessons from Amsterdam 1970–1990', *New Community* (1992).

VAN HEAR, Nicholas. Researcher at the Refugee Studies Programme, Queen Elizabeth House, University of Oxford. Co-author of *Refugees: dynamics of displacement* (1986), author of *Consequences of the forced mass repatriation of migrant communities: recent cases from West Africa and the Middle East* (1992) and 'Mass flight in the Middle East: involuntary migration and the Gulf conflict, 1990–91' in R. Black and V. Robinson (eds) *Geography and refugees: patterns and processes of change* (1993).

VECOLI, Rudolph J. Professor of history and director of the Immigration History Research Center, University of Minnesota, St Paul, USA. Author, with others, of 'The invention of ethnicity', *Journal of American Ethnic History* (1992), 'Problems in comparative studies of international emigrant communities' in A. Hourani and N. Shehadi (eds) *The Lebanese in the world: a century of emigration* (1992) and co-editor of *A century of European migrations, 1830–1930* (1991).

VERTOVEC, Steven. Principal research fellow at the Centre for Research in Ethnic Relations, University of Warwick. Author of *Hindu Trinidad: religion, ethnicity and socio-economic change* (1992), editor of *Aspects of the South Asian diaspora* (1991) and co-editor of *South Asians overseas: migration and ethnicity* (1990).

WILLEMS, Wim. Research fellow at the Leiden Institute of Social Scientific Research, Leiden University. Co-author of *Ongewenste vreemdelingen* (1990), 'Justice or injustice', *Immigrants and Minorities* (1992) and, with Leo Lucassen, *Het onbekende vaderland: de repatriëring van Indische Nederlanders, 1945–1964* (1995).

WILSON, K. B. Research officer at the Refugee Studies Programme, Queen Elizabeth House, Oxford. Co-author of 'Dealing with dying: anthropological reflections on the need for assistance by African relief programmes for bereavement and burial', *Journal of Refugee Studies* (1990), 'Repatriation to Mozambique: refugee initiatives and agency planning: the case of Milange District, 1982–1991' in Allen and Morsink (eds) *When refugees go home* (1993) and author of *A state of the art review of research on internally displaced, refugees and returnees from and in Mozambique* (1992).

ZEGEYE, Abebe. Director of the Centre for Modern African Studies, University of Warwick. Co-editor of *Forced labour and migration: patterns of movements within Africa* (1989), *Repression and resistance: insider accounts of apartheid* (1990) and *Ethiopia in change: peasantry, nationalism and democracy* (1994).

ZUCKER, Norman L. and Naomi Flink Zucker. Norman L. Zucker is professor of political science and Naomi Flink Zucker is a lecturer in writing at the University of Rhode Island (USA). Among the many works they have co-authored are *The coming crisis in Israel: private faith and public policy* (1973), *The guarded gate: the reality of American refugee policy* (1987) and 'From immigration to refugee redefinition: a history of refugee and asylum policy in the United States' in G. Loescher (ed.) *Refugees and the asylum dilemma in the West* (1992).

PART ONE

PROLOGUE

As each of the 15 sections of this *Survey* opens with an editorial introduction, the prologue is more limited in intention. I want principally to provide some justification for the selection of topics, regions and periods. In this respect, it is only proper to start with a modicum of modesty. Despite this being a very ambitious project, no one editor and no one volume can hope to encompass all the manifold aspects and all the major examples of human migration. It is simply too vast a subject. The description 'survey', rather than 'encyclopaedia', has been used to indicate that neither the publishers nor the editor claim complete comprehensiveness. At the same time, we *have* covered a good deal of ground. The *Survey* contains 95 contributions by 99 authors from 27 countries. The authors' home disciplines range across most of the humanities and social sciences. We can thus legitimately claim that this book provides the most representative and wide-ranging coverage of migration ever attempted in a single volume.

However, comprehensiveness alone was regarded as insufficient. We rejected the short anodyne entries typical of a one-volume encyclopaedia in favour of 'midi-sized' contributions (of 2000 to 5000 words) which allowed authors to develop an argument without being too prolix. This inevitably involved fewer, but more targeted, topics. How then were editorial decisions made? After wrestling with a number of alternatives, the overriding conclusion reached was that no single criterion for selection would work. In practice, to reflect the complexity of the phenomenon of migration itself, a number of organizing principles had necessarily to go hand in hand. I will discuss, in turn, issues of period, place, forms of migration and differing approaches.

Historical
Population shifts are present at the dawn of human history – the phenomena of hunting and gathering, transhumance (seeking seasonal pasture) and nomadism being as old as human social organization itself. Flights from natural disasters, adverse climatic changes, famine and territorial aggression by other communities or other species are also common occurrences. The biblical legend of the exodus of the Jews and Homer's epic poem of the wanderings of Odysseus are interwoven into western consciousness. We talk of 'a promised land' and 'an odyssey' without being particularly aware of the origins of these expressions. Other ancient civilizations uninfluenced by the Judaeo-Hellenist world – notably the Mesopotamian, Inca, Indus and Zhou empires – also generated their own migratory myths and their own population flows, often occasioned by the construction of immense monuments. The hanging gardens of Babylon, and the temples, palaces and pyramids of other cultures were built by subordinated peoples dragooned to work, often from long distances. Pre-modern trading diasporas of migrating merchants were established in Africa, Asia, across the Indian Ocean and the Mediterranean.

Despite the existence and variety of these pre-modern forms of migration it seems sensible to begin a survey of world migration in the 'modern' period, marked by the flourishing of long-distance trade and the opening up of global lines of communication. In Wallerstein's (1974: 15) well-known formulation, 'In the late fifteenth and early sixteenth century, there came into existence what we might call a European world economy. … It was different and new.' It was different, he argues, in that, unlike the prior 'world economies' of China, Persia and Rome, the European-dominated world system was dominated by trade, not by the construction of an empire. What is generally under-emphasized by the world system theorists, however, is that along the newly constructed trade arteries flowed not only commodities like gold, furs, spices and ivory but seamen, settlers, merchants and slaves. In particular, European mercantilism initiated the hitherto largest process of forced migration – the shipment of ten million slaves from western Africa to the New World. It was a difficult editorial decision not to include a separate section on African slave migration. However, I finally concluded that this terrible event has already been extensively chronicled by a prodigious and easily accessible literature to which a volume of this kind could add little.[1]

Slavery and indentureship were two predominant forms of migration in the first 300 years of the world system. After the collapse of slavery, indentured labour from China, India and Japan worked the plantations of the European powers. The entries in Part 3 of this *Survey* cover both Asian indentured and more voluntary colonial migration. The persistence of unfree migrant labour into the twentieth century – indentureship, for example, lingered on until 1941 in the Dutch East Indies – has led some authors (Cohen 1987; Miles 1987; Potts 1991) to conclude that it was an intrinsic part of the evolution of capitalism on a global scale.

European expansion was also associated with voluntary settlement from Europe, particularly to the colonies of settlement, the dominions and the Americas. There is considerable room for disagreement as to how much this movement was fuelled by local and personal decisions and how much, on the other hand, it was state sponsored. Certainly, all the great mercantile powers – Britain, the Netherlands, Spain and France – were involved in promoting settlement of their nationals abroad, as the contributions in Part 2 of this *Survey* demonstrate. Nationalists and imperialists in Portugal, Germany and Italy also sought to emulate their European neighbours, though German ambitions were thwarted by defeat in the First World War and Portugal and Italy both got off to a late start. Britain was the only mercantile power to have made an unambiguous success of colonial settlement – if we understand success to be the establishment of a hegemonic presence. Other than in Quebec the French abroad were never concentrated in sufficient numbers. Even in Algeria and Indo-China, where there were substantial settlements, they were driven out by powerful anti-colonial movements. The variable but often mediocre accomplishments of the Portuguese, Spanish, Dutch and German colonists are discussed in my introduction to Part 2. Essentially, this form of migration coincided with the period of European expansion and imperialism, and came to an end with the rise of the anti-colonial nationalist movements.

The next period of migration (covered in Part 4) is marked by the rise of the industrial power of the USA. Although it was already significant by the mid-nineteenth century, US manufacturing output dramatically accelerated at the turn of the century. The USA's share of world manufacturing moved from 14.7 per cent (1880), to 23.6 per cent (1900), to 32.0 per cent (1913), to a staggering 39.3 per cent in 1928 (Kennedy 1987: 202). Millions of workers from the stagnant economic regions and repressive polities of northern, southern and eastern Europe poured into the USA over the period 1880–1933. Thereafter immigration restrictions – directed particularly at Asian workers – and then the Great Depression significantly slowed the flow. Labour migration to the buoyant parts of Europe, like turn-of-the-century Germany (see the entry in Part 5), and to the economies like Brazil and Argentina (see entries in Part 7) also followed a similar rhythm and often drew workers from the same source countries.

The next major period of migration was after the Second World War. It is perhaps worth making the obvious point that voluntary international migration was much reduced in both world wars when borders became more impermeable (passport checks were only generally introduced in 1914), merchant ships were commandeered and nation states demanded conscripts and enforced exclusive loyalties on their citizenries. Naturally, wars also produce much involuntary migration, as minorities whose loyalties are seen as suspect are victimized and populations seek to escape the path of marching armies and aerial bombardment. I will further discuss involuntary migration in due course. Meanwhile, we can note that by the end of the Second World War the strong propensity to migrate in search of work could now reassume its customary importance.

In the USA and in the victorious Allied states, powerful 'vents for surplus' were created as governments created hothouse consumer economies and provided massive extensions to social security, health and welfare services. The raw labour power to sustain these boom economies was provided by illegal and legal labour from many countries (see the contributions in Parts 8 and 9). In the defeated Axis powers similar economic imperatives were underpinned by internal rural labour in the cases of Japan and Italy, and by East German refugees in the German case, until that economy grew so fast that it could only be sustained by additional supplies of labour from Italy, Turkey and Yugoslavia.

By the mid-1970s the international migrant labour boom was over in Europe, though it continued until the early 1990s in the USA. Even where there was some sectoral demand for imported migrants, nativist movements ensured that governments could not sanction open, legal, international migration. By this time too, the engine-room of the global economy had begun to shift to the Asia-Pacific region. In Part 11, a number of contributions are focused on the patterns of contemporary legal and illegal migration to Japan and the other powerful Asia-Pacific economies. Even the Australian and New Zealand politicians, who had resisted Asian migration for generations, were forced into accepting the new geo-political realties.

As the twenty-first century approaches, migration flows are becoming more global in scope and more complex and diverse in character. For example, the post-cold war period triggered movements of displaced peoples and refugees on a scale not seen since the chaos immediately following the end of the Second World War. This complexity will gain discussion at a number of points throughout the *Survey*, but I need to turn now to the more limited question of how regional migration histories on the one hand remain distinctive or, on the other hand, relate to emerging global patterns. In other words, what are the geographical limits to world migration flows.

Geographical

All the world's major geographical regions are represented in the volume, but not in a mechanically egalitarian way. This is because it is important to give some weight to the salience as well as to the volume of the various migratory flows. If we start by considering intercontinental movements, Europe's historical centrality in the global picture becomes apparent. In the period from 1500 to 1914 somewhere between 60 and 65 million Europeans participated in international migration, compared with a combined total of about 15 million African and Asian intercontinental migrants (Emmer 1992: 5,6). Even in the period 1945 to 1975, when Europe became a major destination zone, the numbers leaving Europe for other continents probably constituted about half the global total of intercontinental migrants. This centrality is, of course, somewhat ironic as the nativist and racist movements that have mushroomed in European countries during the past decade seek to represent Europe as a timeless, stable, undisturbed continent threatened by hordes of restless foreign immigrants, particularly those with black, brown and yellow skins (Cohen 1994: 161–91).

Intercontinental migration from Asia across the Pacific was inhibited by fierce anti-Asian legislation in North America, dramatized by the Chinese Exclusion Art of 1882. The internment of Japanese-Americans in the Second World War also provided a brutal proclamation that the USA was still not ready to embrace Asian migration. In the past 20 years, however, the climate for acceptance of Asians in the USA and Canada has changed in a positive direction, particularly as the recognition of the Pacific basin as a crucial economic zone gained ground. As one writer puts it, Asians in America have been turned in one hundred years 'From a Yellow Peril to a Model

Minority' (Hu-DeHart 1992). This does not mean that xenophobic white Californians have suddenly become angels, but rather that they have had to recognize their place in the Pacific regional economy and are, in any event, currently directing their fire at other victims, principally undocumented Mexicans (see the contribution on this theme in Part 8). The possibilities and pressures to emigrate from Asia to North America are also now greater than in the period up to the 1970s, especially in one or two dramatic cases. For example, the thriving economy of Hong Kong is threatened by the restoration of the territory to China in 1997 and many Hong Kong professionals have sought a second chance (or at least a bolt hole) in cities like Vancouver and San Francisco in anticipation of this event.

If we turn to African intercontinental migration, from the fifteenth to the nineteenth century, much of it was of a forced kind. Now three forms of intercontinental migration are predominant. The first, from South Africa, has some similarity with the repatriate migration of French and Portuguese settlers at the end of their colonial empires (see Part 10) in that settlers of European descent are leaving in anticipation of violence following African majority rule. It is different, however, in that no one European power has responsibility for accepting South African repatriates and many are, in any case, skilled voluntary migrants leaving for countries like Canada, the USA and Australia. The second form of contemporary African intercontinental migration comprises black Africans fleeing from civil wars, political strife and governmental breakdowns. (The 'second diaspora' phenomenon in the USA is described by a contributor in Part 8 of the *Survey*.) The third important flow from Africa is from North (and, to a lesser degree, West) Africa into southern Europe. Although this is *stricto sensu* intercontinental migration one can, alternatively, follow Braudel's (1949) lead in his acclaimed book on the Mediterranean. He argues there that all the countries bordering on the Mediterranean, including those in North Africa, are part of a single economic and cultural area, with a vital, interdependent historical experience. In particular, the single Hellenic and Roman worlds, the Islamic penetration of Spain or, for that matter, Hannibal's invasion may all be historical pointers to explaining why it will ultimately be impossible in migration terms to affix southern Europe to the European Union while simultaneously detaching it from its intimate past association with North Africa, Turkey and the eastern Mediterranean.

The sections in the *Survey* on intercontinental migration from Europe, Asia and Africa are paralleled by studies of regional migration *within* each continent – Europe (Part 5), Asia and Oceania (Part 11) and Africa (Part 6.) These three regional sections are supplemented by sections on Latin and Central America (Part 7) and the Middle East (Part 12). It proved impossible to be a classificatory purist in establishing these regional sections. In the case of Europe between 1800 and 1950 we are dealing almost entirely with migration that originated and ended in Europe. This applies too, with some minor reservations, to the African section. But it would be absurd to consider Middle Eastern migration without considering the case of exogenous Zionist settler immigration to Palestine, a phenomenon indeed that our contributor links firmly to the model of European colonization and settlement considered earlier in the volume. Again, Latin and Central American migration history cannot be understood without reference to the European and Asian origins of many of the migrants. Finally, while it may now look odd in regional terms to have included a contribution on southern Europeans migrating to Australia in the section on Asia and Oceania, I wanted to give some recognition to Australasia's long-held identity as a European, particularly British, settlement zone. A more contemporaneous use of the expression 'Oceania' alludes rather to the Pacific islands *and* Australasia. This contemporary use, which I have adopted in the book, has the advantage of signalling Australasia's reorientation to the immediate zones around it and away from its traditional migration supply zones.

So what, geographically, is omitted? Unfortunately, all too much. Within each region, numerous eddies and currents that feed into the main migration flows have not gained recognition in this volume. Even fairly significant flows could not find space. To take a few examples more or less at random: the intricate migration patterns of Polynesia, Micronesia and Melanesia are only considered *en passant*; the settlement of Manchuria by the Russians, the Japanese, then the Chinese – all largely for strategic reasons – has not found space; the enforced Europeanization of Siberia was significant in numerical and cultural terms, yet is not covered here; nor are the immense and complex rural–urban migrations within China and India, except as part of a general treatment on the urbanization of the globe (see the contribution in Part 15). However, an editorial decision had to be made as to the broad bias of the volume. This was made in favour of international and intercontinental migrations, while fully recognizing that internal migration is separated only by a thin and often permeable membrane from these other, characteristically more visible, forms of migration.

Forms of migration
It is perhaps useful to start a discussion of the different forms of migration with the distinction just mentioned between internal migration on the one hand, and international and intercontinental migration on the other. In the established literature a number of eminent migration scholars have sought to dispense with or minimize this distinction in favour of generalized typologies (Lee 1966; Petersen 1958), or theories of circulation (Zelinsky 1971). The earliest systematic studies of migration (Ravenstein 1895; 1889) were totally oblivious of the distinction. For those, like the present author, who wish to maintain that the separation is often important, it needs to be conceded straight away that in some circumstances it is irrelevant. For example, where state frontiers are imperfectly respected and policed or where particular ethnic groups are settled across boundaries, migration tends to go on in defiance or ignorance of the nation state. For this reason, for instance, migration flows in West or East Africa have had to be analysed with little reference to recognized polities (see the contributions in Part 6). In other circumstances it is virtually impossible to delineate whether we are observing internal or international migration. Take, for instance, the case of 'former Yugoslavia', as that infelicitous description goes. 'Why be a minority in someone else's country, when you can be a majority in your own?' This seems to be the only compelling logic in the multiple splits and shifts in boundaries following the collapse of the communist regime. Who is from Bosnia, Herzegovena, Croatia or Serbia, and therefore who is an internal or international migrant, is likely to depend as much upon the fortunes of war as upon strict definitions of citizenship and nationality.

   Given all these objections and uncertainties, why do I insist on maintaining the division between internal and international migration? My reason for doing so is that the overwhelming number of states from the turn of the century, and increasingly at the end of the twentieth century, make enormous efforts to try to fence off their countries from unwanted foreign migrants. Some states (see the contribution on Soviet Jewish emigration in Part 14) even seek to control exit as well as entry policies. Without firmly grasping the importance of this political intervention into the international migrant market, one loses such important issues as the analysis of xenophobia and racism, the selectivity of certain migration channels, the determining influence of international migration on ethnic relations in the receiving country and the switch in destinations as one outlet for a migration stream closes or another opens up. In other words one is in danger of losing the *meaning* of migration by providing only a desiccated statistical profile of migratory movements. Throughout the *Survey*, therefore, our contributors have been invited to be sensitive to the international context of their studies, to interpret the consequences of migration for source and destination areas, as well as to describe the nature of migratory movements.

   The paired contrast between internal and international migration is paralleled by five other dyads, which usefully summarize most of the forms of migration covered in the *Survey*. These are:

- forced versus free migration
- settler versus labour migration
- temporary versus permanent migration
- illegal versus legal migration
- planned versus flight migration

Again, there are many occasions when each side of these linked dyads merges with its opposite. If a migrant's economic circumstances are so adverse as to leave little opportunity for gainful employment or self-employment, in a sense that person's migration becomes impelled, even if legally 'free'. The dream of many nineteenth-century migrants going to the New World (and those now bound for Europe, the USA and the richer countries of the Asia-Pacific) was to establish themselves as independent proprietors, even if they had, in the first instance, to work for others. Were they settlers or labour migrants? Is intent the significant criterion, or outcome? How temporary is temporary migration? A legally binding contract may specify a limited period of residence and work, but an employer may extend a contract, new horizons could open out, and the migrant's situation may change in the country of origin. In other words, temporary migration could easily become long-term residence or even permanent settlement. The reverse process also occurs, though no doubt this is a rarer phenomenon. The distinction between illegal and legal migration is, on the surface, much easier to sustain, though even here there are many ambiguities. Because a migrant is undocumented does not make him or her illegal. States may choose to ignore long-established circulatory zones rather than invite controversy, expense or ridicule if they fail to police their frontier effectively. Amnesty programmes (discussed, for example, in the contribution on Mexican migration in Part 8) may suddenly and retrospectively make illegal migration, legal. Finally, even in the strong contrast between planned and flight (i.e. refugee) migration, some scholars (for example, Kunz 1973) have noticed strong regularities in apparently spontaneous movements.

These antinomies are therefore not to be regarded as pure categories imprisoning all reality, but are more akin to Weber's 'ideal types', which can be briefly defined as archetypes used for analytical, evaluative and comparative purposes.[2] One cannot judge how 'free' is 'free migration', or how 'illegal' is 'illegal migration' until the logical possibilities are established and the range of cognate phenomena described. Naturally, there were space limitations on how far all forms of migration could be covered in the *Survey* either as typology or as range, but a glance at the list of contents will indicate that there is a good sample of contributions in all the dyads I have highlighted.

I was particularly concerned to ensure that there was a good sprinkling of material on flight and refugee migrations in the light of the current political salience, extent and volume of this form of migration. Of course the definitions of 'refugees' or 'immigrants' assigned by the immigration authorities are here very important. When (as, for example, in turn-of-the-century USA) immigrants are positively welcomed, it mattered little to the authorities at Ellis Island whether the people presenting themselves were fleeing poverty in Ireland or pogroms in Russia. Later, when entry policies were determined by foreign policy, those escaping from Cuba's communist regime were deemed 'refugees' while those taking to leaky boats to evade Haiti's brutal dictatorship were considered 'economic migrants' (see the relevant contribution in Part 13). Currently, many western European countries are paying little but lip-service to the legal conventions they had signed compelling them to assess properly the claims of those demanding asylum.

Part 15 of the *Survey* has been used partly to pick up forms of migration that did not easily fall within the planned dyads as well as to spot new trends. Modern contract labour (a new form of 'unfree' labour), the migration of skilled transients, entrepreneurial migration and the new importance of women as independently motivated migrants are all given consideration in this section of the volume. The emergence of trans-Pacific migration and an evaluation of the extent of illegal migration are also included.

An assiduous reviewer will probably catch me out on my next statement, but I can think only of three main forms of migration that, rather too late in the day, I felt should have gained separate treatment. The first is military migration, which is discussed in the contribution on Sikhs in Part 3, but might have gained specialized discussion in respect of the extraordinary importance of soldiers returning from abroad to the politics of their home countries. This point can be quickly underlined by pointing to the Labour Party's victory over the British war hero, Churchill, in the national elections in 1945, while Eisenhower's election to the US presidency and the role of ex-servicemen in the development of African nationalism provide further illustrations. The second is return migration. This theme gains considerable attention in the cases of Turkey and Puerto Rico, but receives little systematic treatment elsewhere. On the other hand the return of repatriates, a type of migration that is often overlooked, gets generous coverage. The remaining, glaringly omitted, form of migration is movement for religious purposes. The proselytizing religions of Christianity and Islam, in particular, sent priests, missionaries and imams out of their natal religious areas and often received pilgrims, crusaders and hadjis in return. The Black Stone (the *qibla*) set into the wall of the most sacred part of the Grand Mosque in Mecca now cannot be touched for fear that it might be worn away by the hands of the multitude of hadjis (nearly two million annually) who reverentially file past on their spiritual quest. However, religious migration to holy sites and to places like Lourdes shades rather uncomfortably into travel and tourism which, for fairly self-evident reasons, are not normally considered as migratory movements.

Differing approaches

As Richardson (1967: 3) has observed, migration has attracted the attention of all the social and human sciences: 'it has been studied by demographers and economists, by sociologists and anthropologists, by historians and political scientists and by psychiatrists and psychologists. Each has focused on a different aspect of migratory behaviour and utilized a somewhat different class of data.' This comment is inadequate only in that it *understates* the degree to which migration has been a subject considered by scholars in many disciplines. The most obvious omission to Richardson's statement is that geographers, particularly human or social geographers, have made fundamental contributions to migration studies. In addition, and more recently, international relations specialists have become concerned with migration in that 'south–north' migration and 'east–west' migration – especially to Europe – are perceived as threats to the social and political order of the rich nation states (see the contribution on population movements and international security in Part 15). Philosophers have also started to write on migration insofar as the vigorous attempts to exclude most forms of migration by state authorities have raised difficult moral dilemmas (see the contribution on the ethical problems of immigration control, again in Part 15). Finally, scholars in cultural studies have begun to make important connections between migration and emergent forms of identity (Bammer 1994; Chambers 1994; Gilroy 1994).

For the record, the disciplinary breakdown of the ninety-nine contributors to this volume is (in descending order) as follows: twenty-one sociologists, twenty historians, eleven geographers, ten general social scientists, nine political scientists, four economists, four general humanities scholars, three demographers, two anthropologists, two educationalists, two philosophers, one criminologist and one scholar of international relations. Nine scholars failed to disclose their home disciplines. No doubt some hidden biases in my selection of contributors can be discerned, but with one exception, they were not conscious. The exception is that I was reluctant to represent the work of a number of economists who, although engaged in important and relevant research, use algebraic formulae and mathematical models that are not – 'as yet' they might say – accessible to most scholars in the humanities and social sciences.[3] I have, of course, included the work of other economists whose work is readily understood. I emphasize also that this self-confessed bias should not be seen as an attack on quantitative work as such: as the many tables and figures show I was only too pleased to include statistical and graphical material that was illustrative and demonstrative of the text.

More important to my selection than this disciplinary breakdown was my conviction that the study of migration confirms, *par excellence*, the newer emphasis in the social sciences and humanities on commensurability and mutual intelligibility across disciplines. This is witnessed in the increasing number of scholars who work comfortably across disciplinary divides. The emerging dialogue is best summed up in the expression 'unidisciplinarity' – a notion that goes well beyond the more conventional ideas of interdisciplinarity (essentially meeting on neutral ground) and multi-disciplinarity (attacking a problem from several sides, thus illustrating its multifaceted character). The limit to these two earlier notions is that the participants essentially remain in their backyards (or should that be 'back fields') except for the limited projects for which they are required to court danger.

The newer notion assumes that a consensus is emerging around social and cultural anthropology, law (dispensing with 'black letter' law), sociology, politics, philosophy, economics (where humans still matter), history, human and population geography, social psychology and other cognate fields too numerous to mention[4] – in short, around a list of established disciplines not unlike those represented by the contributors to this book. But, as I hope is demonstrated by our contributors, this new-found transparency should not be a licence for an 'anything goes' type of scholarship. Instead, systematic investigation, rigorous method, appropriate language skills, a combination of empathy for and critical distance from the subject, attention to sources and to related research all acquire a renewed importance.

Those of us who have the migration 'bug' recognize each other across disciplines and across nations, languages and cultures. We are part of the webbing that binds an emerging global society. This may be partly because many of the scholars interested in migration are international migrants themselves or the children of those who migrated. We have normally found that our research is inadequate without moving to history and to other social science disciplines with which we had previously been unfamiliar. Above all, perhaps, we recognize that the study of world migration connects biography with history and with lived social experience. The well-established (see Archer 1992: ix–x) dualism in social theory of agency versus structure, subjective versus objective factors, micro versus macro perspectives, voluntarism versus determinism, feeling free and also constrained – these contradictory tensions are rehearsed, reflected and occasionally resolved in the migration experience. As the editor of this volume I was pleasantly surprised by how many authors made insightful contributions to understanding the old dualism. This led me to conclude that much larger questions pertaining to the nature and variety of the human condition are tangibly grasped through the study of migration. I can only hope that our readers will also share this gratifying sense of serendipity and the feeling of empathy with migrants all over the world.

Notes

1. Among the more significant and representative works on the African slave trade and settlement in the New World are works by Anstey (1975), Bonnet and Watson (1990), Bush (1990), Curtin (1970), Inkori and Engerman (1992), Irwin (1977), Thompson (1987) and Unesco (1979).
2. The concept is discussed more elaborately in Gerth and Mills (1948: Chapter 8).
3. Particularly noteworthy in this group is Stark's (1991) book which is a useful state-of-the-art statement by a mathematical economist interested in migration.
4. I first saw the notion of 'unidisciplinarity' discussed in the *Bulletin of the Braudel Center for the Study of Economies, Historical Systems and Civilizations*, State University of New York, Binghamton. Although anonymously authored it was certainly the work of the redoubtable Immanuel Wallerstein, who has also carried articles on the theme in *Review*, the Center's journal. He has persuaded the Gulbenkian Foundation to fund a high-powered commission looking at the emerging intellectual disciplines of

the twenty-first century. The expression 'the historical social sciences' is the proposed grouping of the cognate disciplines I have listed.

References

Anstey, Roger (1975) *The Atlantic Slave Trade and British Abolition, 1760–1810*, London: Macmillan

Archer, Margaret (1992), *Culture and Agency*, Cambridge: Cambridge University Press

Bammer, Angelika (ed.) (1994) *Displacements: Cultural Identities in Question*, Bloomington: Indiana University Press

Bonnet, Aubrey W. and C. Llewellyn Watson (eds) (1990) *Emerging Perspectives on the Black Diaspora*, Lanham, MD: University Press of America

Braudel, Fernand (1949) *La Méditerranée et la monde méditerraneen à l'époque de Philippe II*, Paris: Colin

Bush, B. (1990) *Slave Women in Caribbean Society, 1650–1832*, Bloomington: Indiana University Press

Chambers, Iain (1994) *Migrancy, Culture, Identity*, London: Routledge

Cohen, Robin (1987) *The New Helots: Migrants in the International Division of Labour*, Aldershot: Gower
   (1994) *Frontiers of Identity: The British and the Others*, London: Longman

Curtin, Philip D. (1970) *The Atlantic Slave Trade: A Census*, Madison: University of Wisconsin Press

Emmer, P. C. (1992) 'European Expansion and Migration: The European Colonial Past and Intercontinental Migration; An Overview', in P. C. Emmer and M. Mörner (eds) *European Expansion and Migration: Essays on the Intercontinental Migration from Africa, Asia and Europe*, New York: Berg, 1–12

Gerth, H. H. and C. Wright Mills (1948) *From Max Weber: Essays in Sociology*, New York: Oxford University Press

Gilroy, Paul (1994) *The Black Atlantic: Modernity and Double Consciousness*, London: Verso

Hu-DeHart, Evelyn (1992) 'From Yellow Peril to Model Minority: The Columbus Legacy and Asians in America', *The New World*, 3, Spring/Summer

Inkori, Joseph and Stanley L. Engerman (eds) (1992) *The Atlantic Slave Trade: Effects on Economies, Societies and Peoples in Africa, the Americas, and Europe*, Durham, NC: Duke University Press

Irwin, G. W. (ed.) (1977) *Africans Abroad: a Documentary History of the Black Diaspora in Asia, Latin America and the Caribbean During the Age of Slavery*, New York: Columbia University Press

Kennedy, Paul (1987) *The Rise and Fall of the Great Powers: Economic Change and Military Conflict from 1500 to 2000*, New York: Random House

Kunz, E. F. (1973) 'The Refugee as Flight: Kinetic Models and Forms of Displacement', *International Migration*, 7 (3) 125–46

Lee, Everett (1966) 'A Theory of Migration', *Demography*, 3 (1) 47–57

Miles, Robert (1987) *Capitalism and Unfree Labour: Anomaly or Necessity?*, London: Tavistock

Petersen, William (1958) 'A General Typology of Migration', *American Sociological Review*, 23, 256–66

Potts, L. (1991) *The World Labour Market*, London: Zed Press

Ravenstein, E. G. (1885) 'The Laws of Migration', *Journal of the Statistical Society*, 48, 167–235
   (1889) 'The Laws of Migration', *Journal of the Statistical Society*, 82, 214–301

Richardson, A. (1967) 'A Theory and a Method for the Psychological Study of Assimilation', *International Migration Review*, 2 (4)

Stark, Oded (1991) *The Migration of Labour*, Oxford: Blackwell

Thompson, Vincent Bakpetu (1987) *The Making of the African Diaspora in the Americas 1441–1900*, Harlow: Longman

Unesco (1979) *The African Slave Trade from the Fifteenth to the Nineteenth Century: Reports and Papers of a Meeting of Experts Organised by Unesco at Port-au-Prince, Haiti 31 January–4 February 1978*, Paris: Unesco

Wallerstein, Immanuel (1974) *The Modern World System: Capitalist Agriculture and the Origins of the European World-Economy in the Sixteenth Century*, New York: Academic Press

Zelinsky, W. (1971) 'The Hypothesis of the Mobility Transition', *Geographical Review*, 61 (2) 219–49

PART TWO

EUROPEAN COLONIZATION AND SETTLEMENT

The major European colonial powers were Britain, the Netherlands, Portugal, France and Spain, but Britain was to prove the most successful by far in using the export of population to establish its imperial hegemony. As *Tinker*[1] notes, this was far from accidental, as popular myth held. Emigration to the settler countries was systematically planned as a solution to social problems at home and a means of expanding English (then British) interests abroad. This notion was first advanced in a state paper delivered to James I by Bacon in 1606. He suggested that by emigration England would gain, 'a double commodity, in the avoidance of people here, and in making use of them there' (cited Williams 1964: 10). The poor rates and overpopulation would be relieved and idlers, vagrants and criminals would be put to good use elsewhere.

Once established, the principle was extended laterally. Scottish crofters, troublesome Irish peasants, dissident soldiers (like the Levellers), convicts, victims of the Great Fire of London – all were shipped out to the colonies of settlement. Indigent and orphaned children also met the same fate. Under various child migration schemes, the first batch was sent to Richmond, Virginia, in 1617, while the last group left for Canada as late as 1967. The scale of these schemes can be indicated by noting that 11 per cent of Canada's population is derived from destitute British children (Bean and Melville 1989). The numbers from all sources (free and induced) were greater than in the case of any other European power, but just as significant was the intent of the emigration. A typical licence from the Crown, as in the case of the Virginia Company of London, granted 'all Liberties, Franchises and Immunities' to the settlers *and* their offspring 'as if they had been abiding and born within this our Realm of England' (cited Ringer 1983: 39).

The bulk of British migrants went to the USA, New Zealand, Canada, Australia, Rhodesia and South Africa. In each case, British legal, social and political institutions became dominant while, just as the proponents of colonization had promised, trade and commerce with the motherland flourished. This great success story was slow to collapse. But, under slogans like the famous 'no taxation without representation', the nationalist bourgeoisie in each territory was ultimately numerous enough and powerful enough to assert, or try to assert, independence from the motherland and hegemony over the indigenous populations.

Unlike the British, the Dutch were unable to reap all the rewards of colonial settlement. The potential prizes were just as great and their trading network was extensive, but the Dutch had the misfortune to strike less temperate climes. As *Lucassen* shows, nearly half a million Dutch settlers and their allies died in the East Indies, while even the successful settlements were very thinly populated with free Dutch burghers. Before 1835, Dutch emigrants to the settlements in the West Indies and the Americas comprised probably no more than 25,000 people. Thereafter, both for religious reasons and in response to the favourable land prices in the USA, a significant number of Dutch farmers left for North America. However, the political and cultural die had already been cast: to all intents and purposes the Dutch were migrating to a country which could no longer be subordinated to Dutch hegemony.

Were the intentions of the British and the Dutch simply different? This is argued strongly by Frederickson (1981: 20ff.), who suggested that the English ideology of colonization implied the seizure of land, the expulsion of those occupying it and the establishment of a territorial claim. The Dutch ideology on the other hand meant trade with the local peoples and an acceptance of cultural differences without large-scale conquest of territory. Although *Lucassen* does not address this view directly, his authoritative figures of the numbers of soldiers killed in pursuit of Dutch interests in the East Indies, suggest that the Dutch were not simply non-interventionist mercantilists; the benign ideology of pluralism was probably constructed after the event.

As this *Survey* does not explicitly contain a discussion of Portuguese colonization,[2] I will need to add some remarks here. Perhaps the greatest contrast with Britain is with respect to Portuguese attitudes to emigration. The numbers were often very large in relation to the home population and much greater than the comparable figures for the British Isles, with the possible exception of Ireland. But the great propensity of Portuguese to migrate was not strongly directed by the state. So large was the outflow that emigration was seen as a 'drain' and a threat to the home country, not an opportunity. Moreover, although many migrants went to Brazil and other parts of the Portuguese empire, a substantial proportion did not confine themselves to the empire and most of the migrants to Brazil went there *after* independence when Portugal's hold on its former colony was attenuated. As Godinho (1992: 29–30) comments:

> The Portuguese emigrants have never succeeded in contenting themselves with the territories governed by Portugal, but they have always broken away to foreign lands. It is true they have built up the Atlantic archipelagos and Brazil, but they have too often shown their preference to go and fit into the framework of societies that already existed and were of a superior level of development – India in the sixteenth century, the industrialized nations and even those of the tertiary revolutions, during our times.

The nature of Portuguese emigration was perhaps less to do with the disinclination of the migrants to clear virgin land, as it was to do with the underdeveloped state of Portugal itself – which, because of its enduring feudalism, was unable to turn its mercantilist advantage into industrial power. When the decisive challenge to feudalism finally arrived in the form of Salazar's long dictatorship (1932–68), schemes for a settler-based colonization of Portugal's African colonies were instituted. But it was already too late. By 1950 the total population of the African territories was 12,113,000. However, only 185,609 Portuguese emigrants (and 171,693 mixed-race *assimilados*) had established themselves. With the advancing pace of African nationalism in the 1970s and 1980s most of the settlers re-migrated to Portugal.

What then of Spanish and French colonial migration? As in Portugal, emigration took place largely from private motivation, rather than being regulated by church or state. None the less, the character of Spanish migration to the Americas was closer to the British model. Throughout the Americas, but particularly in Mexico and Peru, migrants followed conquests and they brought strong cultural predilections with them. Catholicism and the Spanish language soon became dominant in most parts of South America (excluding Brazil), and in Central and North America as far as the Spanish city of San Francisco. However, unlike most British settler colonies, the *conquistadores* and their successors had few inhibitions about marrying or having sexual relations with the locals. This may have been a result of the more restricted opportunities for migration by Spanish women which, *Altman* suggests, was largely confined to family migration in the later phases of the movement. The Spanish in short became localized (or 'creolized') with attachments to the old country being more sporadic and tenuous than in the case of their British counterparts.

As for the French, the constant rivalry with the British was also to find expression in plans to set up colonies in the Americas (in the first phase of expansion), then in Africa, the Middle East and Indo-China, where the second phase of French colonial ambitions were centred. In the Americas the problem was not the intention to colonize, but the number of willing settlers. Indeed, French schemes for colonization were, as *Heffernan* demonstrates, if anything more ambitious than their British equivalents. Free passages, grants of land, the press-ganging of criminals and orphan girls – all this directly paralleled the measures taken by the arch-rival across the Channel. But all this pump-priming was to little avail. The European population in American New France was only 55,000 by 1750, about the same as the Anglo-Saxon population in Massachusetts alone (*Heffernan*). Moreover the draining effects of the Revolutionary and Napoleonic wars as well as the slave revolt in Saint Domingue severely weakened military support for French colonists on the American mainland.

The French did much better in Algeria where nearly two million French settlers proclaimed that Algeria was French, indeed that it was *France*. Unfortunately for the French, some 18 million Islamicized Berbers and Arabs did not agree. Under de Gaulle, the French were forced to withdraw from their most populous territory. By 1939 France had ended up with an empire large in extent (12 million square kilometres), but one which could not compare with the British dominions and empire in population, economic strength or cultural affinity to the homeland.

The European colonies of settlement were extensive, but many also sought to be exclusive. This dismissal of 'the other' was at first directed to the indigenous peoples. The British in Australia killed the Aborigines and virtually destroyed their way of life; the British in New Zealand crippled Maori culture; the Canadians forced the Inuit peoples into reservations. (Not that the British were uniquely wicked. The Germans massacred the Herero, the Belgians the Congolese, the Dutch in the Cape the San and the Khoi-khoi.) But having founded their New Jerusalems in the New World, the settlers were all too prone to legislate against others joining in. At first, as *Daniels* notes, it was the Asian 'horde' (and especially the 'Yellow Peril' from China) that the settlers feared. Later the colonists' 'nativism' (the expression used by *Daniels*) was directed against southern and eastern Europeans, though these anti-immigration campaigns were not always sustained or successful.

The intensity of the link with the home country also varied greatly and in several cases (the USA compared with Great Britain, Brazil compared with Portugal) the settlers soon could command military, commercial and economic power vastly in excess of the countries that provided the bulk of their European migrants. At an individual level the migrants lived longer and better than their fellow Europeans who did not migrate (Emmer 1992: 11). But, perhaps more important than individual good fortune or social mobility was the fact that large parts of the world were brought into the European spheres of influence and became Europeanized in language, religion, ideologies, and political and judicial institutions. The modern world – with some important, but partial exceptions in China, Egypt, Japan and Turkey – had been transformed by European migration.

Notes

1. All references to authors' contributions appearing in this *Survey* will be italicized.
2. But see *Baganha* in Part 4, *Ishemo* in Part 6, *Klein* in Part 7 and *Rocha-Trinidade* in Part 10 for related contributions.

References

Bean, Philip and Joy Melville (1989) *Lost Children of the Empire*, London: Allen and Unwin

Emmer, P. C. (1992) 'European Expansion and Migration: The European Colonial Past and Intercontinental Migration; an Overview' in P. C. Emmer and M. Mörner (eds) *European Expansion and Migration: Essays on the Intercontinental Migration from Africa, Asia and Europe*, New York: Berg, 1–12

Frederickson, George M. (1981) *White Supremacy: A Comparative Study in American and South African History*, New York: Oxford University Press

Godinho, Vitorino Magalhães (1992) 'Portuguese Immigration from the Fifteenth to the Twentieth Century: Constants and Changes', in P. C. Emmer and M. Mörner (eds) *European Expansion and Migration: Essays on the Intercontinental Migration from Africa, Asia and Europe*, New York: Berg, 13–48

Ringer, Benjamin B. (1983) *'We the People' and Others: Duality and America's Treatment of its Racial Minorities*, New York: Tavistock Publications

Williams, Eric (1964) *Capitalism and Slavery*, London: André Deutsch

THE BRITISH COLONIES OF SETTLEMENT

HUGH TINKER

When Sir John Seeley (1883) wrote, 'We seem, as it were, to have conquered and peopled half the world in a fit of absence of mind', there may have been a note of irony in his tone but many of his readers took this as a literal statement. *Laissez-faire* may have been the dominant philosophy of industrial Britain, but it played no part in colonial emigration. The peopling of the British empire was a highly organized business, beginning with the first major migration in Canada. The fact that far more emigrants continued to settle in the USA without any assistance or encouragement was a challenge to all who believed in settlement under the Crown.

The first big movement into Canada came with the arrival of the United Empire Loyalists – incomers from the Thirteen Colonies who repudiated the legitimacy of the new republic. Although Americans, they still regarded themselves as British to the core. Some settled in the region of the Bay of Fundy; others moved on into the interior into what was to become Upper Canada or Ontario. Most were townspeople, but they confronted the task of opening up the wilderness. Conscious of its obligations to the Loyalists the home government exerted itself to make their new life tolerable with rations to tide them over the period in which they planted their crops, and building materials with which to construct new homes. The Loyalists were the creatures of the same social forces as those who had remained in the USA, but they began to diverge widely from those who had not moved. The climacteric experience was the war of 1812 in which the American invasion was repulsed, mainly by militia assembled by the Loyalists, though the French Canadians led by Bishop Plessis of Quebec also rallied in support. The war of 1812 was what first gave Canada the sense of a separate identity.

The Loyalists had to penetrate the wilderness and the rationale of colonization elsewhere was of the occupation of empty lands scantily peopled by savages. As the Darwinian philosophy became dominant it was assumed that the 'inferior races' would give way to the white man wherever he went. The first Africans the white immigrants in South Africa encountered were the Khoi-khoi (Hottentots), who

seemed incapable of offering resistance. Many withdrew to areas beyond white settlement. The belief that the white settlers were taking over empty lands encouraged the rationale of white occupation of the country from the Cape up to Kenya, claimed by Lord Delamere as White Man's Country. Although conditions in the temperate lands being opened up by British settlers were very different from Africa the pioneers also acted as if only they had a right to the whole land and any existing inhabitants were brushed aside.[1]

The emigrants to the temperate lands were mainly from the 'respectable' working class, determined to better themselves, to get away from an England in which there was a governing class which combined social position and political power – especially in rural society. The emigrants were seeking a country where they could attain their full potential.

Migration to Canada was on a tiny scale compared with the massive movement to the USA. The earliest arrivals were after the fur trade. Many (most?) were Scots. Among them was James McGill (1744–1813) from Glasgow. He made a fortune, with his headquarters at Montreal. During the war of 1812 he was Colonel of the Montreal Volunteers. After his death the bulk of his fortune went into the endowment of McGill University which received its Charter in 1821. Because so many Canadians were of Scottish origin, education, the church and the law were highly respected.

Many of the Scots who arrived after 1815 were Highlanders who had lost their crofts in the 'clearances'. They arrived at small ports to embark upon small craft: sometimes in recognition of all they had lost their laird chartered the ship himself, but when they arrived in the St Lawrence river they had to fend for themselves. Mortality was high. This enforced migration continued through most of the nineteenth century. Some leaders were thrown up by the emigrant Scots, notably Sir John MacDonald (1815–91), born in Glasgow. He arrived at the age of five, was elected to the legislature in 1844 and became prime minister in 1854. He saw the USA as a massive threat to his country and led the movement

PLATE 1: Scottish boys photographed at Ellis Island, New York, c. 1910, where ultimately over 12 million immigrants to the USA were processed. Cabin passengers alighted at Manhattan, so many of those in steerage who were to be examined at Ellis Island were anxious to impress the inspectors with their respectable best, often their national costumes.

for the union of the different provinces in a con-federation (1867). The original founding provinces were joined by Manitoba in 1870 when its total popu-lation was 1563, though one year later this had increased to 25,268. British Columbia followed in the next year and Prince Edward Island joined the new entity in 1873. MacDonald continued in power with one brief interregnum until his death and his greatest achievement was the completion of the epic trans-continental railway. Despite his contribution to Canadian nationhood, he frequently repeated the maxim, 'A British subject I was born; a British sub-ject I will die.'

MacDonald's successor was a French Canadian, Sir Wilfred Laurier (1841–1919). Unlike the vast major-ity of his community, Laurier received a bi-cultural education, taught first by a Scottish teacher at New Glasgow, Nova Scotia, and completing his studies at McGill University. He was fortunate in presiding during a boom period, 1896–1911, when Canada at last emerged from its subordination to the USA. Laurier came up with the slogan, 'the twentieth century will be Canada's century'. Foreign immi-grants joined the British in the prairie provinces: expansion was encouaged by the introduction of early maturing varieties of wheat. Immigration boomed; the annual intake of new settlers rose from 16,835 in 1896 to 400,870 in 1913; predominantly British, they also included people from central and eastern Europe. The total population of Canada rose from 5,371,315 in 1901 to 7,206,643 in 1911.

Early settlement in Australia was of slow growth. While those entering Australia were convicts the dis-tance was no deterrent: the further away the better. Because the penal system in the eighteenth century was so haphazard not all the arrivals were hardened criminals (the Tolpuddle martyrs at once come to mind) and they included men of education, including the architects of some of Australia's early public buildings. If free emigrants were to be attracted to the lands of the southern hemisphere (and European colonial rivalry, especially from France, gave this some urgency), then something more was required than the purely commercial traffic of the North Atlantic. And so, in an environment increasingly dominated by *laissez-faire*, Australian migration slowly built up as a managed system. Various controls were instituted until, in 1839, the Land and Emigration Board was set up. Operating as part of the Colonial Office, the board was charged with selecting and transporting emigrants to Australia. It was to be financed by the sale of virgin land in the outback at a viable price. The board gradually evolved a systematic emigration. In contrast to the North Atlantic run with its high mortality due to shipboard fevers, on the voyage to Australia mortality was brought down to 0.5 per cent. This was partly due to strict regulation (an emigrant family was limited to embarking two children under seven years of age) and partly to care-ful medical supervision on board: the surgeon superin-tendent was paid according to the number of emigrants 'landed alive'.

Convict transportation continued until 1840 in New South Wales, but increasingly the free emigrants were in the majority. In 1842, New South Wales achieved self-government; the voters included 'emancipists', that is time-expired convicts, along with the free emigrants. There was much bad feeling between ex-convict and free. The system of land grants encour-aged the growth of large sheep runs, yet a majority of the settlers remained in the coastal towns – soon to become cities.

The slow growth of population received a boost with the discovery of gold in 1851 in what became the state of Victoria. The total population grew from 405,356 in 1850 to 1,455,585 in 1860. The great majority of the 'diggers' (the name subsequently adopted by all Australians) came from the United Kingdom, though some were disappointed prospectors from California. The social mix was explosive: among the Irish there were militants. Prospecting centred on Ballarat where in 1854 there was a revolt, known by the name of its most dramatic event, the siege of the Eureka Stockade in which twenty-five miners were shot down.

The Eureka Stockade was one of the factors in the democratization of politics going much further than in contemporary Britain. The secret ballot was intro-duced in 1856, and the first Labour member was elected to the Victoria Assembly. Social legislation followed whereby trade unions became powerful. The negative side of this proletarian advance was the ban on the entry of Asiatics as competitors in the labour market, although Chinese miners had arrived in the 1850s. In the 1880s there was another boom, followed by a slump in the 1890s as the price of wool fell from over 12 pence per bale in 1884 to 6½ pence in 1890. Australian finances were largely dependent on trends in Britain.

How far did all this affect Australia's relationship with the 'mother country'? A leading New South Wales politician, Sir Henry Parkes, born in Warwick-shire, spoke of 'the crimson thread of kinship which runs through us all'. This belief led him to advocate the joining together of the colonies in a federation. There were problems: some colonies wanted free trade and some protectionism, while the railways were of different gauges, entailing a complicated transfer between states. The New Federation came into being in 1901, though New Zealand, hopefully included, declined to enter. New South Wales and Western Australia both had to be cajoled into entry against serious opposition. In 1934 Western Australia petitioned Westminster to get back its separate status.

South Africa did not attract British emigrants, even to the extent that the other dominions succeeded, although the administration was almost wholly provided by Britain. The most serious attempt to introduce immigrants was made in 1820 when a settlement scheme was planned for the eastern Cape, to be made up of soldiers discharged after the Napoleonic wars, including veterans of the King's German Legion: but the land was harsh and little came of the scheme. After diamonds were discovered in Kimberley there was an influx there, then to the Transvaal gold fields by Uitlanders, mainly British. Immigration raised the white population from 328,000 in 1875 to 1,117,000 in 1904, but the hope that South Africa would become an English-speaking country was not realized. The Afrikaners remained the majority. Though their share in business and industry was restricted, they became predominant in the public services like the railways, excluding others such as Indians who had held the jobs before. From being an almost wholly rural community, Afrikaners infiltrated the cities, even in Natal, the most British of the provinces.

The smallest of the dominions, New Zealand, was also the most British. True, the immigrants had to come to terms with an already settled population, the Maori, a Polynesian race who had themselves migrated to New Zealand in past centuries, the most important movement being that of 'the Great Fleet' in about 1350 AD. The Maori had settled in the fertile North Island where they offered fierce resistance to the whites (pakeha). The new white settlements received support from religious bodies: at Christchurch from the Anglicans and at Dunedin from Scottish Presbyterians (both these settlements being on the South Island). When white settlement began in 1840 the population was perhaps 1,000; by 1900 numbers were 750,000. New Zealand had some leaders of vision, the most notable being Edward Gibbon Wakefield (1796–1862) who virtually compelled the British government to annex New Zealand in the face of French ambitions. He was only the first of some notable reformers who led the world in social

legislation: women's suffrage was introduced in 1893, followed by old age pensions (1898), state ownership of the railways and other innovations, some of which were imitated in Australia. Accepted as a dominion in 1907, New Zealand remained strongly attached to Britain, partly through self-interest: the bulk of its exports went to the 'mother country'.

When war broke out in Europe in 1914 the dominions all pledged support to Britain: in many ways they came of age on the battlefield. Australia and New Zealand were virtually unanimous in their support. British Canada was also wholly committed: French Canada was at first supportive but resisted the policy of conscription. South Africa was divided; it was only twelve years since the war between British and Boers had ended. Botha and Smuts warmly supported the war effort (they were to receive the reward of mandates over German colonial territory) but some Boer dissidents saw this as the opportunity to restore the Boer republics. The main figure was De Wet, the foremost guerrilla leader of the Boer War. He planned a rising, which was unsuccessful; he was captured in December 1914.

In Canada, from a population of about 7.5 million, 628,000 enlisted in the armed forces, of whom 450,000 served overseas. Canada insisted that the troops be formed into a separate army corps under their own officers. Lieutenant-General Sir Arthur Currie was appointed the commander in 1917, proving himself an outstanding leader. The corps was acknowledged as an elite force; used as shock troops, it endured heavy casualties: Canadian losses were heavier than those of the USA (despite the wasteful battles in the Argonne).

Australia also raised a highly efficient military force, putting 329,000 soldiers into the field from a population of less than 5 million. Combined with the soldiers of New Zealand they formed the famous ANZACs, a corps which fought first at Gallipoli and then on the western front. They too served under their own commander, Sir John Monash, a brilliant planner who came into his own in the last great Allied offensive of August 1918.

The camaraderie of men at war was given the peculiarly Australian name of 'mateship' and formed an important element in folklore: a way of getting through the bad times and enjoying the good times. A wholly masculine phenomenon, mateship remains embedded in the Australian psyche. The returned servicemen remained an important force in post-war politics.

The 1930s halted the massive exodus to the

dominions and some emigrants actually returned to Britain. Although conditions were bad at home, at any rate they would be in familiar surroundings. The world slump brought about an interesting Anglo-Canadian response. A British engineer and economist, C. H. Douglas evolved a political philosophy that he called Social Credit, intended to counter the depression by compulsory saving. Social Credit attracted a good deal of interest in Britain in the 1920s, but it was left to Canada to bring it into action. A high school principal and radio commentator, William Aberhart of Calgary (1878–1943) popularized the idea and won the Alberta provincial election in 1935, going on to win five more times and electing a bloc of MPs in the Canadian House of Commons. The name, Social Credit, was attached to a political movement in British Columbia which won power in 1952, giving way to the New Democratic Party in 1972. Social Credit gained a name for efficiency, especially in Alberta; counterparts emerged in four other provinces without achieving power.

The First World War evoked a strong feeling of empire solidarity. When peace returned, many in Britain were restless and the idea of emigration was attractive. The Lloyd George government responded with the Empire Settlement Act of 1922 to aid 'settlement in, or migration to any part of His Majesty's Overseas Dominions by assistance with passages, initial allowances, training or otherwise' (UK Government 1921). During the 1920s about two-thirds of Britons going to other empire countries were assisted under the act, many of them being ex-servicemen. Nearly four-fifths of the emigrants remained within the empire: only 18 per cent now went to the USA.[2] Canada was the most popular destination (45 per cent of the total) followed by Australia (30 per cent).[3] Kenya took in large numbers of people, mainly from the upper classes, especially during the energetic governorship of Sir Edward Grigg. At the Colonial Office they pronounced that Grigg was 'thoroughly infected with Kenyitis'.

The policy of British government support for emigration was continued. The Statute of Westminster (1931) gave legal recognition to dominion autonomy along lines which Eire, South Africa and Canada deemed essential though, for some, its implications were too much. New Zealand did not introduce the measure until 1947. In 1943, the colonial under-secretary, Lord Devonshire, told the House of Lords, 'Migration is not a matter which concerns only the migrant's own country. It is also very closely (and perhaps even more closely) the concern of the government of the country to which he desires to emigrate' (UK Government 1945).

The Second World War put strains on imperial unity in ways never expected before. This particularly affected Australia which had always looked to the Royal Navy for protection: now the Japanese almost reached its borders. Of a population of 7,229,864 in 1943 nearly one million Australians put on uniform: there was conscription for home defence, although not for service overseas, and 95,561 casualties were suffered. This experience convinced Australian leaders of all parties that a substantial increase in population was necessary. They planned a more positive immigration policy.

Soon after the war, Canada enacted the Canada Citizenship Act (1946) which introduced a separate status for its own citizens in place of the old imperial 'common code'. The new act provided that new immigrants who were British citizens (i.e. from Great Britain) could vote after one year's residence and could apply for a certificate of Canadian citizenship after five years: aliens residing in Canada could not vote. The 'common code' was generally acknowledged to be out of date and a conference of the dominions and those *en route* to dominionhood was held in London in February 1947. A draft bill was laid before them, but it proved impossible to obtain general agreement. Eire, on the point of withdrawing from the Commonwealth, resisted any more specific definition, while Australia and New Zealand both emphasized that in their countries British immigrants were 'on the same footing' as the native born. The conference was followed by the British Nationality Act of 1948, which defined Commonwealth citizenship for Great Britain and the colonies and recognized an open door for all entering from any Commonwealth country. Apart from Britain, the white dominions were reluctant to admit non-Europeans. Introducing the Bill in the Lords the Lord Chancellor commented, 'common nationality does not necessarily confer rights in other member states': Australia's immigration policy was Australia's own affair, he declared. The older dominions left everything as it was. New Zealand brought in legislation under the title of the British Nationality and New Zealand Citizenship Act (1948), and Australia took similar measures; both made their own citizenship interchangeable with British nationality. Matters remained unchanged during the next two decades.[4]

The rhythm of emigration from Britain was resumed soon after the war ended: during the five years from 1946 to 1951 nearly 900,000 emigrants left

Britain. In the immediate post-war years Canada, South Africa and Rhodesia were all important destinations, but from 1949 Australia emerged as the Mecca of British emigrants, absorbing almost 40 per cent of those who left. The 'Ten Pound Passage Scheme' played a major part in this attraction. By comparison, Canada had to turn to Germany, the Netherlands, Italy and other European countries. After the fall of Smuts in South Africa that country lost its appeal for British immigrants. New Zealand, the most British of all the dominions, felt unable to afford mass immigration. There was a scheme of assistance, but by 1952 only 12,079 British people had been attracted with 1155 from the Netherlands (with help from the Dutch government). Kenya enjoyed a generous scheme promoted by the UK's Labour government: £950,000 was invested in the settlement of British ex-servicemen, mainly to start farming. Immediately after the war 500 settlers were given land in the White Highlands. Between 1949 and 1953 admission was granted to 12,500 Europeans. The white population numbered 16,812 in 1931; it rose to 29,660 in 1948 and 55,759 by 1962. In the same period the numbers entering South Africa declined after the rise to power of the Nationalists. In 1960 there was a substantial white population shrinkage. There were nearly 9800 white immigrants (many from southern Europe) and 12,600 emigrants, most being professional people. This became the pattern in subsequent years.

Meanwhile the Assisted Passage scheme to Australia continued to flourish: from 33,447 arrivals in 1960, the total rose to 73,501 in 1965 (the election of a Labour government in Britain in 1964 after an interval of thirteen years seemed to stimulate emigration). The Ten Pound scheme flourished until the election of the Gough Whitlam government in 1975 raised a question over the 'white Australia' philosophy: subsequent prime ministers have not gone back to the old exclusive policy. By 1988 the total population had risen to 16,700,000, a phenomenal increase from the pre-war total. Despite the more liberal immigration policy, the white population still formed over 94 per cent of the total, with 77.6 per cent being native born and 22.4 per cent born overseas (1986). The United Kingdom still predominated, providing over half those of European origin; Italy, Greece and Yugoslavia followed, in that order, though far behind the British figure.

Although Canada pursued a less vigorous immigration policy than Australia, its population continued to expand, despite a constant haemorrhage to the USA (J. K. Galbraith and Zbigniew Brzezinski are two public men who grew up as Canadians but achieved prominence as Americans). The total Canadian population grew almost as rapidly as that of Australia. By 1988 the total was 25,880,000: over 40 per cent were shown as British in origin and 27 per cent as French. The next group in size were those of German origin (4 per cent), with Italians (3 per cent) and Ukrainians (2.2 per cent) also significant. South Africa's population of 29,628,000 included 18 per cent of whites. The proportion shrank as more Afrikaners moved into the towns and had smaller families. English speakers formed less than 40 per cent of the whites; their numbers also diminished as they steadily migrated, mainly to Britain and America. New Zealand remains 'Little Britain' in the Antipodes, with a total population of only 3,666,000 in 1988, of which 82 per cent are white (overwhelmingly British in origin). The Maori formed 9 per cent and other Polynesians (mainly Cook Islanders) another 3 per cent. New Zealand was more a WASP (white Anglo-Saxon Protestant) society than Britain in the 1980s.

The growth of the British colonies of settlement formed an overspill from the home country. Not until the mid-twentieth century did the dominions become free of the colonial ethos, and then they still seemed very British to those in the society whose origins were separate. The British emigrant had many advantages over the others. The British arrived knowing the language, in their own estimation knowing it better than the colonials. The institutions they now encountered were already familiar – the legislature, the law, the church were clones of the institutions they had left behind. The British emigrant did not have to go through an adaptive phase like others in which safety was sought and found in 'ethnic' institutions and customs reminiscent of the old country. Definitely otherwise: it was reassuring to discover places and people similar to those left behind. What was different – emigrants hoped – was that in the new country people's opportunities were not limited by who their parents and grandparents were. This was a different Britain (they hoped) in which people could go to the limit according to their own ability. There were just a few who stood apart, the so-called 'Remittance Men', upper-class misfits who had disgraced their homes and families, and received an allowance in some distant place on condition that they stayed away. But most of the emigrants were endowed with more than average initiative and energy.

The ability of British migrants to get to the top was illustrated by the rise of two prime ministers of New Zealand and one of Australia. R. J. Seddon, born in

Lancashire, was five times premier of New Zealand, and Walter Nash, born in Worcestershire, became deputy prime minister in 1940 holding the supreme post between 1957 and 1960. A more colourful character was Billy Hughes, born in London, the cockney prime minister of Australia from 1915 to 1922. He successfully opposed a Japanese proposal to the League of Nations to outlaw racial discrimination ('nonsense'). The latest example of a British emigrant attaining an unusual distinction is provided by the woman who became the first female Anglican diocesan bishop anywhere, in Christchurch, New Zealand. She was born and educated in England.

Their special status enables British emigrants to avoid the label of a 'hyphenated' citizen, so hard for most minorities to escape, especially in the USA. The privileges enjoyed by the British are often resented by immigrants from other cultures. Thus, 'the attempts in every way — militarily, politically, economically, and in literature, by English Canadians to dominate Canada and make it one homogeneous state modelled after Britain are perhaps the most significant internal events in its history' (Craig 1987: 149).

However, with the passage of time, the 'colonial' status of the former white dominions grows ever less. Even Australia, with a population overwhelmingly British in origin, has reacted against the mother country: the process seemed almost complete when Paul Keating became prime minister. With his Irish origin, Keating takes up what often seems almost an anti-British posture.

Notes

1. A French colonial historian observed that if Britain had not transported convicts to Australia the only inhabitants would have been kangaroos (Leroy-Beaulieu 1902: 107).
2. In 1924 the USA introduced a quota system for immigrants based upon the ethnic composition of the population in 1890. Great Britain received by far the largest quota. Although most countries rapidly exhausted their quotas, the British never took theirs up in full.
3. Emigration to Australia reached a peak in the mid-1920s: 1922 (84,263), 1923 (85,440), 1924 (88,335) and 1925 (82,662). See Isaac (1954).
4. Fuller treatment of this subject is given in Tinker (1976: Chapter 10, 'The Moment of Equality').

References

Craig, Terence (1987) *Racial Attitudes in English Canadian Fiction*, Waterloo: Ontario University Press

Isaac, J. (1954) *British Post-War Migration*, Cambridge: Cambridge University Press

Leroy-Beaulieu, Paul (1902) *De la colonisation chez les peuples modernes*, vol. II, 5th edition, Paris: Guilaumin et Cie

Seeley, Sir John (1883) *The Expansion of England*, Lecture I, Cambridge: Cambridge University Press

Tinker, Hugh (1976) *Separate and Unequal*, London: C. Hurst

UK Government (1921) *Conference of Prime Ministers ... Summary of Proceedings and Documents*, London: HMSO, Cmd. 1747

—— (1945) *Migration within the British Commonwealth*, London: HMSO, Cmd. 6658

EMIGRATION TO THE DUTCH COLONIES AND THE USA

JAN LUCASSEN

The migration history of the Netherlands was as much a history of immigration as emigration (Lucassen 1991, 1994; Lucassen and Penninx 1994). But if the attractions of the Netherlands were so great as to encourage millions to move there, why did any of the indigenous Dutch population wish to leave? I shall give special consideration to the migrants' motives later in this contribution. In studying outward movement from the Netherlands I shall also make use of a distinction between emigrants, 'labour migrants' and 'seasonal labourers', though I will deal mostly with the first group. With the collapse of the North Sea system at the end of the nineteenth century, seasonal migrant labourers switched their destination from the North Sea coastal region to places like the Ruhr. Labour migrants employed as sailors or soldiers leaving for the colonies will be discussed briefly, and particular attention will be paid to the soldiers recruited for the Dutch East India Army. Most other emigrant groups large enough to be discussed here must be considered to have been emigrants, i.e. people intending to leave for good. In my treatment of emigrant groups I shall take a more or less chronological order, considering, first, migration to the Dutch colonies in Asia and the Americas, then those leaving for the USA between 1835 and 1914. The smaller emigrant groups, not to be discussed here, included merchants, artisans, industrialists and artists, who helped to spread culture, knowledge and skills throughout the Netherlands and from there all over Europe. In the nineteenth century there were many other small flows of mostly economic emigrants, particularly those who migrated to Belgium and to some countries in South America and South Africa during the course of the nineteenth century.[1]

Emigration and labour migration 1600–1914

A preliminary answer has to be given to the question as to why significant numbers of Dutch men and women migrated to the colonies. In a sense, of course, they remained part of the Dutch sphere of influence and the Dutch economy. On the other hand, the risks involved in going to the tropics were widely acknowledged. The problem remains therefore to identify the factors that led migrants to exchange a life in one of the richest countries of the world for the dangers of the sea and tropical diseases.

The Dutch East India Company 1600–1800

Since the Dutch East India Company depended so heavily on the recruitment of foreign labour migrants, many of its employees were neither immigrants to the Netherlands nor emigrants from the Netherlands, but rather transmigrants, using Amsterdam as a stepping stone between poor inland Germany and the promise offered by the Indies. Of course, apart from being driven by sheer poverty, those signing up with the Dutch East India Company also had positive reasons for so doing. It was not so much that the wages were attractive as the fact that seamen were allowed to take merchandise back to Europe and sell it themselves, if they were lucky enough to survive their years in the Indies (Bruijn and Gaastra 1994). Some of the 235,000 Dutchmen and 255,000 foreigners who did not return — the majority of them died during their years in the Indies[2] — tried to settle down at one of the trading posts established by the Dutch East India Company. By the time the company was dissolved, however, there was only a handful of settlements with a substantial European population. Most were at the Cape of Good Hope, where 150 years after its establishment the free burgher population numbered 16,000 (Marquard 1968: 56). In the more tropical climate of Batavia, the centre of the Dutch East India Company empire in the East Indies, there were only 2037 inhabitants of European origin in 1811, and of these only 552 were born in Europe (Taylor 1983: 97).[3] The settlements in Ceylon contained even fewer Europeans (van Goor 1978: 16–18). In all other Dutch East India Company outposts the number of European settlers was insignificant.[4]

The Dutch East Indies 1800–1900

For the nineteenth and early twentieth centuries we have to distinguish two different kinds of migration to the Dutch East Indies: military and civilian. For most

of the time military emigration was the most important; it is certainly the better documented (Bossenbroek 1986; Curtin 1989). The Dutch East India Army
was engaged in almost permanent conflict between
1815 and 1910, the most important being the so-called
Java and Achin wars (of 1825–30 and 1873–1903
respectively). The war against the principality of
Achin on the northern tip of Sumatra led to the
dispatch of two major expeditionary forces in the
early years and engagement in a long period of continuous guerrilla warfare in the years that followed.
We are not so interested here in the military outcome
of these wars; what concerns us is how they affected
the labour market for soldiers, particularly European
soldiers.[5]

In the years between 1815 and 1910 over 150,000
men left Europe to serve in the Dutch East India
Army. The losses on the outward voyage may have
amounted to around a thousand for the total period,
low in comparison with those in the preceding centuries.[6] It is difficult to say, given the current state of
research, how many soldiers died during the whole
period under consideration after they arrived in the
East Indies. The data suggest, however, that on the
Dutch side the Java War cost the lives of 7000 Indonesian and 8000 European soldiers. The Achin War
led to the loss of a further 12,500 lives (again on the
Dutch side), more than half of which may have been
European (Bossenbroek 1986: 24).[7] Disease, of
course, was also a peacetime phenomenon. In the
years preceding the Achin War the annual death rate
among European soldiers was 2.5 per cent, a figure
that implies the death of more than 22,000 soldiers
during the period under consideration.[8] In the nineteenth century at least 35,000 to 40,000, or a quarter
of those sailing as soldiers or officers to the Dutch
East Indies, did not see Europe again.

On the basis of Dutch migration statistics on the
flow between the Netherlands and the colonies, I
reach the unexpected conclusion that there was a net
out-migration of females from the East Indies to the
Netherlands. This means that in the nineteenth and
early twentieth centuries more women were returning
from the East Indies than had sailed there. One possible explanation for this is that a number of the men
migrating to the colonies married there and returned
home with their Eurasian or Indonesian wives and
daughters.

It is hard to say if there was also a net out-migration
of civilian males from the colonies.[9] Since the Euro-
pean-born population of the colonies was growing
only slowly in the nineteenth century, from a few

thousand in the first half of the nineteenth century to
more than ten thousand at the end, some migration
losses among European male civilians are more than
likely.[10]

In 1905, 35 per cent of the Europeans in the Indies
with a profession were engaged in agriculture, 20 per
cent in commerce and 20 per cent in industry. The
important agricultural sector boomed after the opening of the Suez Canal in 1869 and the Indies were
'opened up' to European enterprise. After the economic depression of the 1880s, economic development
in the Indies was further stimulated by the restructuring of the plantations on Sumatra and Java and their
establishment as limited companies based in the
Netherlands. Nevertheless, the mestizo culture, which
has been so well described by Taylor, began to change
only very slowly at the end of our period, when
society became much more stratified, with a stronger
and more insular European population at the top
(Kossmann 1978: 398–412; Spooner 1986; Taylor
1983).

We might conclude then that, with the important
exception of the labour migration of soldiers and sailors, the Dutch empire in Asia in the nineteenth
century, despite its size and undoubted economic
importance, was dependent on surprisingly few
settlers from the Netherlands and Europe.

The Dutch West Indies 1600–1900

Dutch involvement in the Americas and Africa was of
a completely different nature from its involvement in
East Asia. It was, for example, to a great extent the
concern of one province – Zeeland. Just as the Dutch
East India Company had dominated activities in the
East Indies, Zeeland (and of course Holland) had the
major stake in Dutch Atlantic enterprises. Unlike the
Dutch East India Company, however, the Dutch West
India Company (which was established only in 1621,
reorganized in 1674 and abolished in 1795) failed to
gain a monopoly of trade from Holland. Second, the
West India Company was more restricted in its
activities, spending most of its early years warring
with the Spanish and the Portuguese, and much of its
later life involved in the slave trade. Apart from its
settlements in North America, which I shall consider
later, the north-east coast of Brazil was the most
important area colonized by the West India Company
in the first half of the seventeenth century. Nieuw
Holland, as it was named by the Dutch, was taken in
1630 and, despite challenges from the Portuguese,
was held for a quarter of a century. At the beginning
of the period of Dutch rule the total white, mestizo

and mulatto population was around 40,000 (there are few population data available, but see van den Boogaart 1980; Israel 1989). Although the West India Company had 10,000 employees based in Brazil in 1639, a figure that fell to 4000 by 1642, there was little permanent immigration from the Netherlands. The number of *vrijlieden* (ex-West India Company employees and other immigrants) grew from an original 1100 to 3000 in 1645; a quarter of them were accompanied by their families. The West India Company tried to encourage immigration by offering immigrants land on favourable conditions and also by accepting Jewish immigrants from Amsterdam; though these Jewish immigrants were ultimately to form one-third of the *vrijlieden*, there was little permanent settlement. When Dutch rule collapsed in 1654, many Dutch immigrants left, some to go to Dutch colonies in the Caribbean and North America. The net result of Dutch involvement in Brazil was the loss of several thousand lives.

By the time the Dutch conquered Surinam in 1667, most of the Europeans who had already settled there were English; at most there were also 150 Jewish settlers, who had come either directly or indirectly from Amsterdam. The number migrating to Surinam, which had the oldest surviving Jewish settlement in the Americas, may have amounted to 1000; most migrated during the seventeenth and eighteenth centuries (Cohen 1982 and 1992; van Lier 1982; Rens 1982). Population data further suggest that European settlement in this slave-plantation colony was never extensive. Dutch-owned plantations, which sometimes had hundreds of West African slaves working on them, were run by a handful of whites, the majority of whom (the chief exception being the Jewish settlers) intended to return to the Netherlands rather than settle permanently in the Americas.[11] Consequently, net emigration from the Netherlands among this group, and incidentally among missionaries and civil servants too, was largely a result of death during the voyage or a consequence of tropical diseases. Those losses could be heavy indeed. Of the 426 Herrnhuters who travelled from the Netherlands as missionaries between 1735 and 1882, 166 or 40 per cent died in Surinam and a further 167 were forced to return; only 93 stayed as long as had been intended, before returning to the Dutch village of Zeist where they were based (Cohen 1992: 36–65; Kleinschmidt 1914–17).

Apart from the civilian population there were also military personnel, whose functions were to maintain order, particularly on the plantations, and to ensure the defence of Dutch interests in the face of foreign competition (van Lier 1972: 26; van der Sande Lacoste 1914–17). The numbers involved were small, probably in the region of 300, but, particularly during the century between 1763 (the date of the Berbice slave revolt) and 1863 (when slavery in Surinam was abolished), many more than 300 soldiers were needed. When attempts were made to recapture the *bosnegers* (bush negroes) in 1773, there may have been as many as 2300 professional soldiers in Surinam.

Until the beginning of the nineteenth century the Dutch were also in command of the western parts of Guyana (Essequibo, Berbice and Demerara) which later became British Guiana (for population data on this region see Adamson 1972; Menezes 1977; Netscher 1888). Although in 1800 the population of these colonies was around 10,000 (excluding the slave population), nearly double that of Surinam, much of this was the result of recent population growth, especially in Demerara, and most of the colonists were of British descent, moving there from the British-controlled Caribbean islands. Ten years after the end of nearly two centuries of Dutch rule, 95 per cent of the white settlers were British (Adamson 1972: 22; Netscher 1888: 281–2, 290, 292, 301).

Civilian migration from the Netherlands to the Dutch Caribbean islands resembles that to the Guianas in several respects (see the articles on the separate islands of Aruba, Bonaire, Curaçao, St Martin, St Eustatius and Saba in the *Encyclopaedie van Nederlandsch West-Indië* 1914–17). In the seventeenth century hundreds of emigrants from Zeeland settled on the Dutch Windward Islands of Saba, St Eustatius and St Martin. These settlements remained small scale, however, and they gradually lost their Dutch character. Though these islands continue to be part of the kingdom of the Netherlands, it is English that is spoken there.

It is clear that migration from the Netherlands to the Dutch Caribbean islands took place on a very limited scale, and mostly during the course of the seventeenth century. As many as 15,000 in total may have migrated from the Netherlands to the colonies in South America and the Caribbean, to West Africa,[12] half of them during the second half of the eighteenth century and probably around one quarter before and one quarter after that date; most went to the Guianas. While the quality of the data available warrants a degree of scepticism, they are nonetheless of sufficient reliability to enable us to illustrate the differences in the order of magnitude between migration flows to the Dutch West Indies and the Dutch East

Indies, and I can confidently conclude that migration to the West Indies was but a fraction of that to the East.

North America 1624–1830s

'Dutch settlement in North America antedates that of almost every European nation, except the English' (Swierenga 1982: 517). Yet the total number of emigrants from the Netherlands to North America during the seventeenth and eighteenth centuries may not have exceeded 10,000. Only after the mid-1840s did significant numbers leave the Netherlands for North America.

The establishment by the West India Company of Nieuw Amsterdam on Manhattan Island in 1625, sixteen years after its discovery by the English Dutch East India Company agent Henry Hudson, did not lead to mass immigration, at least not during the first few decades of the century (Rink 1986: 139–71). It was a period marked by mismanagement and savage Indian wars, and the population of Nieuw Nederland amounted to little more than 2500 in 1645; 500 of them lived in the capital, Nieuw Amsterdam. It was only after a municipal charter was granted in 1653 and the *burgherrecht* introduced in 1657 that the town became more prosperous; by 1660 Nieuw Amsterdam had a population of 1500 inhabitants. The late 1650s and early 1660s also saw a reappraisal by the West India Company and the government of the republic of their policy regarding Nieuw Nederland after the loss of Brazil, the first Anglo–Dutch War and the Navigation Acts. The total population of the colony grew from between 2000 and 3500 in 1655 to around 9000 in 1664. Much of this increase can be accounted for by the influx of as many as 4000 immigrants from the United Provinces; significantly for the future growth of the settlements, most of them migrated as families. In addition, the influx of refugees from Recife in Brazil in 1654, the conquest of a Swedish colony on the Delaware (1638–55) and the influx of English settlers from neighbouring colonies contributed to this growth.

Not all those emigrating from the Netherlands to Nieuw Nederland were Dutch, though those who were not had usually succeeded in assimilating to the Dutch language and culture either before or after their arrival in Nieuw Nederland. Many were English or Scottish dissenters or German Lutherans who migrated with the Dutch after staying for a short period in the republic. Despite the personal opposition of the last Dutch governor of Nieuw Nederland, Peter Stuyvesant, the West India Company advocated a liberal policy with regard to immigration, and it encouraged thousands of Dutch Quakers, Mennonites and Jews to settle.

By then, however, Dutch possessions in North America, which had stretched from the Delaware River in the south to Cape Cod in the north, had been progressively lost to English colonists. Nieuw Nederland fell in 1664, and a treaty of 1667 officially marked the end of Dutch imperialist ambitions in North America. New York and its surroundings continued to have a Dutch character though. The important Dutch Reformed Church in America acquired its independence from Amsterdam only in 1772, and until the provision of its own theological education at Queens' College, now Rutgers University, New Jersey, all candidates for the ministry were expected to return to the Netherlands for their final training and ordination; this continued up until 1771 (Tanis 1982). It was not until 1867 indeed that the Dutch Reformed Church in America dropped the antecedent 'Dutch'. Further, the Dutch language continued to be spoken by many families until the nineteenth century.

Emigration to the USA 1845–1914

From the mid-1840s onwards around a quarter of a million people emigrated from the Netherlands to the USA. We are bound to ask why. The first wave of emigration from the Netherlands occurred in the period between 1847 and 1857 and it tended to consist of well-defined groups. Nearly half of those departing between 1845 and 1849 belonged to a dissenting Protestant denomination called the *Afgescheidenen*, or Seceders. These Seceders, never large in number (they constituted only 1.3 per cent of the total population), had broken away from the national Reformed Church. A period of suppression by the state led many to flee to North America. But this is only a partial explanation. It does not account for the majority of emigrants, for whom religious oppression played no role, nor for emigration in later years.

It is necessary to look to regional economic characteristics in order to obtain a more general explanation for the patterns of emigration that can be observed. Most emigrants (55 per cent before 1855) originated from those parts of the rich marine clay-soil areas specializing in crop growing in the provinces of Zeeland, Groningen and later on also Friesland. Emigrants from these regions, for example from the grain growing western part of Zeeuws-Vlaanderen, were for the most part day labourers working on the farms. Another important group (accounting for 31 per cent of emigrants) were mainly small farmers from the light sandy-soil areas in the east and the south of the country. Common to both groups was their need for land. Just like the areas from which they came, the areas to which they migrated were rural, concentrated mainly to the east of Lake Michigan. As Swierenga (1982) has shown, the majority of these people successfully managed to establish themselves as farmers upon emigrating to the New World.

The explanation for this overrepresentation of rural areas in general, and of the Zeeland and Groningen crop growing marine clay-soil areas in particular, lies partly in the consequences of agricultural crises. The wave of emigration between 1847 and 1857 may be attributed to the failures of three consecutive potato and rye harvests in the mid-1840s. The failure of the potato harvest particularly hit the farm labourers, who were already heavily dependent for their daily food on their small garden plots; many of these labourers chose to emigrate. Again, the great agricultural crises of the 1880s and 1890s, and the agricultural restructuring they entailed, is mirrored in the wave of emigration that occurred between 1880 and 1893.

But this explanation is less convincing in accounting for two other great upswings in emigration, those occurring in the years 1865–73 and 1903–13. Nor does it, as Wintle (1990) has shown, account for the exact timing of the peak in emigration. He suggests that, unless they were being influenced by the threat or fear of epidemics like cholera, smallpox and rinderpest, those wanting to migrate in response to the structural changes occurring in rural society did so only in particular periods. These periods were ones when farming was once again prosperous. Then labourers (particularly in the south-west and north-east) and farmers (particular in the south and the east) were able to acquire enough money to enable them to emigrate. Wintle (1990) remarks that: 'The successful agricultural entrepreneur is just as much part of the emigration movement as the starving persecuted farmer.' This conclusion is fully supported by Swierenga (1986). Probably of even greater significance in accounting for the timing of the peaks in emigration in 1847–57, 1865–73 and 1880–93, however, was the American domestic economy: in the words of Swierenga, 'prospective Dutch emigrants ... responded directly to American conditions. "Land booms" stimulated the immigration of the Dutch while economic depression discouraged migration.'

For the last few decades of the nineteenth and the early part of the twentieth centuries there is evidence of high levels of emigration not only to the USA, but also, increasingly, to Germany. That there continued to be a preference for America may be attributable to the phenomenon known as chain migration. And right up to the end of our period the regional particularities of Dutch migration to the USA were maintained.

Conclusion: migration from the Netherlands

During the seventeenth and eighteenth centuries migrant labourers based in the western parts of Germany and also in the southern and eastern parts of the country went to 'pull' areas within the Netherlands. In addition, migrant labourers and emigrants travelled within the Dutch sphere of influence. They were attracted by the prospect of work in the republic, in the army and navy, wherever needed, and in the Dutch empire in Asia and America. The numbers going to Asia were large: half a million migrated permanently to the East Indies, compared with maybe 15,000 to South America and the Caribbean, and another 10,000 to North America.

It is clear from this study that terms like emigration and immigration are inadequate. Before 1800 more than half of these transatlantic migrants were born outside the Netherlands. Most of them should therefore be considered to be transmigrants, who used the republic as a stopping-off point prior to seeking work in its empire overseas.

This peculiar pattern of a worldwide Dutch labour market vanished in the nineteenth century, though there was still a significant level of migration to the Dutch East Indies – another 35,000 to 40,000 soldiers, many of them foreign born, died in the East Indies.

Just before the second half of the nineteenth century a completely new phenomenon emerged: emigration from the Netherlands not to the empire, but to areas outside (see Stokvis 1985). In this the Netherlands was beginning to follow a pattern that already characterized a number of other European countries. Within a few decades the Netherlands had lost its age-old seasonal *Hollandsgänger*, and by the end of the century significant numbers of Dutch men and women were migrating to Germany.

In the long-term history of Dutch migration the period 1600–1800/50 might be regarded as exceptional. This becomes clear not only when I contrast the insignificant level of emigration during this period with subsequent emigration to the USA and Germany, but also in comparing the Dutch Golden Age with the late Middle Ages and the beginning of the early modern period. There were important mass emigrations before 1600, especially of farmers from the provinces of Holland and Friesland to Germany, Poland and the Baltic in the late Middle Ages. In addition, significant numbers left the Netherlands in the early sixteenth century for ideological reasons: many Baptists fled to Münster, and Calvinists to London and East Anglia and to German towns like Emden and Frankfurt. Only a reversal of fortunes in the war against Spain encouraged these Calvinists to return (see Schilling 1972). The Netherlands as a country characterized by immigration was reaffirmed after the First World War. It remains an immigrant society today.

Notes

1. Excluding those going to the colonies there were a further 400,000 emigrants leaving the Netherlands between 1840 and 1920; 250,000 of these went to the USA, more than 100,000 to Germany and around 50,000 to other countries (around 1914, in addition to those living in Belgium, 10,000 Netherlanders lived in South America, 5000 in South Africa and 4000 in Canada). See, for example, Ganzevoort and Boekelman (1983), and Ploeger (1985/6).
2. Nearly 95,000 European employees of the Dutch East India Company died in the hospital in Batavia between 1725 and 1786, an average of over 1500 a year. See Bruijn (1976: 25).
3. Taylor's figure of 2028 seems to be incorrect. See Spooner (1986: 13) for data relating to the period 1691–1790 that show that the figure of 2034 for 1760 was nearly halved by 1790.
4. See Gaastra (1980: 443), who suggests that in 1780 Dutch East India Company employees were distributed as follows: 20 per cent in Ceylon, 19 per cent in Batavia, 10 per cent on the eastern coast of Java and 9 per cent at the Cape, leaving 7 per cent on ships and 35 per cent in twenty-one other settlements and trading posts.
5. The non-European component of the army was growing more rapidly than the European one: whereas there were equal numbers of each (5000) in the army at the beginning of the nineteenth century, and as late as 1880, at the beginning of the twentieth century the army contained 12,500 Europeans and 23,000 Asians (cf. Bossenbroek 1986 and 1992.)
6. The death rate on outward voyages on Dutch East India Company ships was normally around 4 per cent. See Bruijn et al. (1987: 162).
7. This assertion is based on the fact that in the first years of this war, when casualties were highest, death rates for the Europeans in the military expeditions of 1873 and 1874 averaged 9.34 per cent and 15.44 per cent, compared with a total average of 6.79 per cent and 11.53 per cent (2205 Europeans out of a total of 3105 deceased).
8. If I assume that the average length of stay for a European soldier in the East Indies was six years, then I can assume that 15 per cent, or at least 22,000, died in the East Indies. See Curtin (1989: 81–2, 86–93, 201–2) on mortality levels for European troops in the Dutch East Indies 1859–1914.
9. This depends on the proportion of soldiers among those dying. Net migration to the East Indies among males may have been something in the region of 85,000. If the loss of life among the military did indeed amount to at least 40,000, then the rest of this 85,000 is accounted for by the loss of civilian lives. If 40,000 is an underestimate, then it follows that the numbers of civilians returning to Europe was lower.
10. For data on population by place of birth in the nineteenth century see Taylor (1983: 97) for 1811, van Marle (1951/2: 187) for 1854, and Methors (1911: 87) for 1880–1905. It is

not clear whether these figures include civil servants (of whom there were 9000 of European origin in 1905); the *Encyclopaedie voor Nederlandsch Indië* I (1917: 299) seems to suggest that they do not.
11. Van Lier (1972: 21) gives some population data for Surinam. In 1675 there were 123 Dutch and 58 adult Jewish men; in 1787 there were 3360 whites, of whom 1311 were Jews; in 1811 there were 2029 whites, of whom 1292 were Jews; and in 1830 there were 2638 whites, of whom 1324 were Jews. See also Cohen (1992).
12. For nearly two and a half centuries, until 1871, the Dutch also had a number of settlements on the Gold Coast. By the time the English abolished the slave trade in 1814, however, these settlements had long ceased to be of any significance. It is doubtful if there were ever more than a few European settlers there: they seldom amounted to more than 280 people, of whom at least 10 per cent were non-Dutch nationals. See van den Boogaart (1980: 235); Emmer (1973 and 1974); Postma (1973: 67); Unger (1961).

References

Adamson, A. H. (1972) *Sugar Without Slaves: The Political Economy of British Guiana, 1838–1904*, New Haven: Yale University Press

Boogaart, E. van den (1980) 'De Nederlandse expansie in het atlantisch gebied 1590–1674', *Algemene Geschiedenis der Nederlanden*, (7), 220–54

Bossenbroek, M. P. (1986) *Van Holland naar Indië. Het transport van koloniale troepen voor het Oost-Indisch leger 1815–1909*, Amsterdam: De Hollandsche Leeuw

—— (1992) *Volk voor Indië, de werring van Europese militairen voor de Nederlandse koloniale dienst, 1814–1909*, Amsterdam: Van Soeren & Company

Bruijn, J. R. (1976) 'De personeelsbehoefte van de VOC overzee en aan boord, bezien in Aziatisch en Nederlands perspectief', *Bijdragen en Mededelingen betreffende de Geschiedenis der Nederlanden*, (91), 218–48

Bruijn, J. R. et al. (1987) *Dutch-Asiatic Shipping in the 17th and 18th Centuries*, vol. I, The Hague: Martinus Nijhoff

Bruijn, J. R. and F. S. Gaastra (eds) (1994) *Ships, Sailors and Spices: East India Companies and their Shipping in the 16th, 17th and 18th Centuries*, Amsterdam: NEHA

Cohen, R. (1982) 'Patterns of Marriage and Remarriage among the Sephardi Jews of Surinam, 1788–1818', in R. Cohen (ed.) *The Jewish Nation in Surinam: Historical Essays*, Amsterdam: Emmering, 89–100

—— (1992) *Jews in another Environment: Surinam in the Second Half of the Eighteenth Century*, Leiden: Brill

Curtin, P. D. (1989) *Death by Migration: Europe's Encounter with the Tropical World in the Nineteenth Century*, Cambridge: Cambridge University Press

Emmer, P. C. (1973 and 1974) 'Engeland, Nederland. Afrika en de slavenhandel un de negentiende eeuw', *Economisch- en Sociaal Historisch Jaarboek*, 36 (1973: 146–215) and 37 (1974: 44–144)

Encyclopaedie van Nederlandsch Indië I (1917), The Hague and Leiden: Nijhoff

Encyclopaedie van Nederlandsch West-Indië (1914–17), The Hague and Leiden: Nijhoff

Gaastra, F. S. (1980) 'De VOC in Azie', *Algemene Geschiedenis der Nederlanden*, (9), 24–67

Ganzevoort, H. and M. Boekelman (eds) (1983) *Dutch Immigration to North America*, Toronto: Multicultural Society of Ontario

Goeje, C. H. de (1914–17) 'Suriname I. Aardrijkskundig overzicht, *Encyclopaedie van Nederlandsch West-Indië*, The Hague and Leiden: Nijhoff

Goor, J. van (1978) 'Jan Kompenie as Schoolmaster: Dutch Education in Ceylon 1690–1795', *Historische Studies*, 34

Israel. J. I. (1989) *European Jewry in the Age of Mercantilism 1550–1750*, Oxford: Oxford University Press

Kleinschmidt, E. A. (1914–17) 'Broedergemeente', *Encyclopaedie van Nederlandsch West-Indië*, The Hague and Leiden: Nijhoff, 178–82

Kossman, E. H. (1978) *The Low Countries 1780–1940*, Oxford: Oxford University Press

Lier, R. A. J. van (1972) *Samenleving in een grensgebied. Een sociaal-historische studie van Suriname*, Deventer: Van Loghum Slaterus

—— (1982) 'The Jewish Community in Surinam: A Historical Survey', in R. Cohen (ed.) *The Jewish Nation in Surinam: Historical Essays*, Amsterdam: Emmering, 19–27

Lucassen, J. (1991) *Dutch Long Distance Migration: A Concise History 1600–1900*, Amsterdam: IISG, Research Papers 3

—— (1994) 'The Netherlands, the Dutch and Long-distance Migration in the Late Sixteenth to Early Nineteenth Centuries', in N. Canny (ed.) *Europeans on the Move: Studies on European Migration, 1500–1800*, Oxford: Oxford University Press, 153–91

Lucassen, J. and R. Penninx (1994) *Nieuwkomers, nakomelingen, Nederlanders: Immigranten in Nederland 1550–1993*, Amsterdam: Het Spinhuis

Marle, A. van (1951/2) 'De groep der Europeanen in Nederlands-Indië, iets over onstaan en groei', *Indonesië*, (5), 97–121, 314–41, 483–509

Marquard, L. (1968) *The Story of South Africa*, London: Faber and Faber

Menezes, M. N. (1977) *British Policy towards the Amerindians in British Guiana 1803–1873*, Oxford: Oxford University Press

Methors, M. H. W. (1911) *Résumé rétrospectif de l'Annuaire Statistique des Pays-Bas*, The Hague: Belinfante

Netscher, P. M. (1888) *Geschiedenis van de koloniën Essequebo, Demerary en Berbice, van de vestiging der Nederlanders aldaar tot op onzen tijd*, The Hague: Prov. Utrechtich Gen. van Kunsten en Wetenschappen

Ploeger, J. (1985/6) *Nederlandse Landsverhuising na Suid-Afrika 1849–1862*, 2 vols, Cape Town: Supplementa en Familia

Postma, J. (1973), 'West African Exports and the Dutch West India Company, 1675–1731', *Economisch- en Sociaal-Historisch Jaarboek*, (36), 53–74

Rens, L. L. E. (1982) 'Analysis of Annals relating to Early Jewish Settlement in Surinam', in R. Cohen (ed.) *The Jewish Nation in Surinam: Historical Essays*, Amsterdam: Emmering, 29–46

Rink, O. A. (1986) *Holland on the Hudson: An Economic and Social History of Dutch New York*, Ithica: Cornell University Press

Roos, J. S. (1914–17) 'Israëlietische gemeenten', *Encyclopaedie van Nederlandsch West-Indië*, The Hague and Leiden: Nijhoff, 385–90

Sande Lacoste, A. C. van der (1914–17) 'Krijgsmach', *Encyclopaedie van Nederlandsch West-Indië,* The Hague and Leiden: Nijhoff, 420–32

Schilling, H. (1972) *Niederländische Exulanten im 16 Jahrhundert. Ihre Stellung im sozialgefüge und im religiösen Leben deutscher und englischer Städte*, Gütersloh: Mohn

Spooner. F. (1986) 'Batavia 1673–1790: A City of Colonial Growth and Migration', in I. A. Glazier and L. de Rosa, *Migration across Time and Nations: Population Mobility in Historical Contexts*, New York and London: Holmes and Meier, 30–57

Stokvis, P. R. D. (1985) Dutch International Migration 1815–1910', in R. P. Swierenga (ed.) *The Dutch in America: Immigration, Settlement and Cultural Change*, New Brunswick NJ: Rutgers University Press, 43–63

Swierenga, R. P. (1982) 'Exodus Netherlands, Promised Land America: Dutch Immigration and Settlement in the United States', *Bijdragen en Mededelingen betreffende de Geschiedenis der Nedelanden*, (97), 517–47

—— (1986) 'Dutch International Migration and Occupational Change: A Structural Analysis of Multinational Linked Files', in I. A. Glazier and L. de Rosa (eds), *Migration across Time and Nations: Population Mobility in Historical Contexts*, New York and London: Holmes and Meier, 95–124

Tanis, J. (1982) 'The American Dutch: Their Church and the Revolution', *Bijdragen en Mededelingen betreffende de Geschiedenis der Nederlanden*, (97), 505–16

Taylor, J. G (1983) *The Social World of Batavia: European and Eurasian in Dutch Asia*, Wisconsin: The University of Wisconsin Press

Unger, W. S. (1961) 'Bijdragen tot de geschiedenis van de Nederlandse slavenhandel', *Economisch-Historisch Jaarboek*, (28), 3–148

Wintle, M. (1990) 'Push-Factors in Emigration: The Case of the Province of Zeeland in the Nineteenth Century', paper presented to the Colloquium on Long Distance Migrations (1500–1900), Madrid, 29–30 August

SPANISH MIGRATION TO THE AMERICAS

IDA ALTMAN

Spanish migration to the Americas began with the second voyage of Columbus in 1493. Spaniards and other Europeans who accompanied them (in addition to Columbus a number of Italians participated in the early phase of colonization) spent more than twenty years in the Caribbean; in fact it was more than fifteen years before Spaniards moved from Hispaniola, the first focus of European activity and settlement, to the other islands of the Greater Antilles. In these years a relatively small number of migrants left Castile for the Indies, as the new possessions most commonly were known. The movement only gained significantly in size and momentum following the conquests of Mexico (1521) and Peru (1532). These two regions, with their dense indigenous populations, productive agriculture and mineral wealth, would become the major centres of Spanish colonization in the Americas and the principal destinations of emigrants in the sixteenth century. This pattern obtained through most of the rest of the colonial period, although in the latter part of the eighteenth century rapidly developing centres such as Buenos Aires (which became the capital of the viceroyalty of the Río de la Plata created in 1776), Havana and Caracas, which formerly had been quite unimportant in the Spanish empire, began to attract substantial numbers of migrants.

Between such marginal places and the central areas of New Spain (Mexico) and Peru were secondary centres of development which all through the colonial period either attracted emigrants in their own right (in New Granada – modern Colombia – the long-term success of gold mining helped to sustain an economy based on mining, agriculture and trade) or in effect received a spillover from the central regions to which they were adjacent and in some ways economically tied (Guatemala, Chile). Santo Domingo, the first Spanish city established in the Indies, by virtue of its location and administrative functions (it was the site of the first *Audiencia*, or high court, which acted as the highest governing body wherever there was no viceroy) continued to be a destination for emigrants, despite an early decline in the island's economy and importance. Over time, however, Havana to a great extent displaced Santo Domingo as a strategic and commercial point and a centre for population. After the very earliest years in the Caribbean migration to these primary and secondary centres of colonization and development flowed more or less spontaneously, largely organized on a private basis (rather than by officials of church or state) and relatively unregulated. There did exist a body of legislation that in principle would have deterred people judged undesirable (gypsies, *moriscos*, *conversos*) from going to the Indies (Spain never used its American territories as dumping grounds for troublemakers or criminals) and a cumbersome procedure by which migrants had to obtain licences to depart (Jacobs 1991), with the House of Trade in Seville (created in 1503) acting as the checkpoint for the traffic in both people and commerce.

Very remote or seemingly risky destinations did not attract the same kind of self-generated and self-sustaining migration that took people to the fastest-developing centres of colonization, so that official or quasi-official recruitment efforts originating in Spain continued to figure throughout the sixteenth century in attempts to settle places like the Río de la Plata region, the Philippines or Florida (Hoffman 1990). More common, however, was the organization of *entradas* (expeditions) from places that were already at least partially established to less known, more peripheral ones – hence the settlement of New Mexico from central Mexico or of Chile from Peru. The conquest and early Spanish occupation of central Mexico itself had been essentially a Cuban enterprise. In the period up to around 1560 or 1570, during which Spain successfully laid claim to most of what would constitute its American empire until the early nineteenth century, the leap-frogging progress of settlement in which one area became the base from which Spaniards reconnoitred and conquered others meant that not only the material but also the human resources of one place would be transferred to another. This process linked the foci of settlement and complicates discussion of migrants' destinations, since it was common, most especially perhaps in the first two or three generations of Spanish movement to the Indies, for people to move on from their initial destination, often more than once (Robinson 1990). Overall Mexico and Peru received the largest volume of both primary and secondary migration, with Mexico attracting the highest numbers of migrants in every decade after the conquest through the sixteenth century with one exception (Boyd-Bowman 1976a). Although lacking the spectacular wealth of early Peru, Mexico for the most part escaped Peru's conflict and instability (probably for that very reason) which, together with its greater geographic accessibility, probably accounts in large part for its success in attracting migrants.

Despite the importance of the movement of people from Spain – really from the realms of the crown of Castile, since until the eighteenth century there was virtually no migration from the crown of Aragón – scholarship on early modern migration until recently has been limited, so that notwithstanding a recent growing interest in the subject (especially in Spain itself and focusing more on particular localities than in the past) global figures scarcely exist. Magnus Mörner (1991: 1–2) recently has noted that his earlier estimate of 437,669 emigrants to the Indies between 1500 and 1650 (Mörner 1976) has yet to be tested and for the subsequent years to the end of the colonial period there are essentially no reliable figures at all. Despite the lack of specific data at the most general level, however, Peter Boyd-Bowman and scholars who have studied migrant groups in Spanish America (see Boyd-Bowman 1964/1968; Lockhart 1972; Otte 1988) have uncovered clear regional, demographic and socio-economic patterns in the movement. Boyd-Bowman's work shows that southern Spain – Andalusia (especially Seville and its hinterland) – consistently provided the largest number of emigrants of any single region, although its early predominance diminished and over time the movement changed from being essentially an Andalusian enterprise to a more generally Castilian one. He also has documented the growing presence of women, whose representation in the movement increased from 5.6 per cent in the period up to 1519 to between 25 and 35 per cent of migrants in the last third of the sixteenth century (Boyd-Bowman 1973: 25, 49, 72) and of family groups, as well as the shifts in migrants' destinations over time. For subsequent centuries of migration we have virtually no comparable demographic or regional data.

If quantitative data remain elusive, research to date none the less has revealed much about the social and demographic aspects of the transatlantic movement, in particular the extent to which it reflected and incorporated a range of socio-economic and occupational groups that constituted the broad middle sectors of Castilian society, already-existing forms of social organization, the strong localism of early modern Castilian society, the predisposition of people at practically all levels of society to move around (often several times in a lifetime), mainly in search of economic opportunity, and the importance of Seville in funnelling emigrants and mediating the entire Indies enterprise.

The social and occupational composition of migrant groups varied over time and also according to particular place of origin; thus, for example, the proportion of *hidalgo*s leaving the Extremaduran city of Cáceres for the Indies in the sixteenth century was notably higher than in the group departing from the neighbouring city of Trujillo (Altman 1989: 196–7), and among the several hundred migrants who left the textile-manufacturing Castilian town of Brihuega during several decades after 1560 no one claimed *hidalgo* status, although certainly the group encompassed different levels of wealth (Altman 1994). Notwithstanding these kinds of variations in the make-up of specific groups, however, studies of immigrants and of Spanish society in the Indies reflect a wide socio-economic representation in the settlement of the New World (Boyd-Bowman 1976b: 729–32; Lockhart 1968, 1972); only the extremes of Spanish society – the highest nobles who commanded great wealth and resources, and the true paupers – scarcely participated in the movement.

Many people who lacked the means to acquire a licence and purchase a passage travelled as servants or employees (Altman 1989; Jacobs 1991); Boyd-Bowman (1976b: 729) found that over half the men identified in a group of 1595–98 emigrated as *criados*. The term *criado* did not necessarily imply a particular social status; rather it could be used for people at many social levels and individuals moved in and out of this category, especially on reaching the Indies, which afforded many opportunities to work on one's own. In contrast to the British or French movements, there was no Spanish 'servant' migration as such, if one takes the term to mean that people arrived in the New World under obligation to perform a fixed term of labour service (Altman and Horn 1991). Migrants from Spain, with the exception of African (and a very small number of *morisco*) slaves, were free.

Family and kinship relationships and considerations played a key role in the migration process. Position in the family could help determine who would leave home and who would stay, and family members on either or both sides of the Atlantic often provided both the impetus and the material wherewithal for a person to emigrate (Altman 1989). People commonly went to the Indies accompanied by relatives or expecting to join them, and all through the colonial period they sought out their kin and people from their home towns (Brading 1971: 106–8, 112–13; Socolow 1978: 17–21). Cycles and networks based on family, patronage ties and common origin linked people and places in Spain and America, creating multiple and enduring connections that fostered continuing emigration, often directed to particular places. These networks of association and kinship, present from the very outset, shaped not only the migration movement but patterns of social organization in Spanish America as well. Reliance on friends and relatives, collective decision making and patron–client relations – all notable in the activities of migrants – also were basic to the functioning of early modern Spanish society. Hence emigration can be seen as the extension of, rather than a deviation from, normal and customary social and familial relations and structures.

Patterns of mobility which propelled substantial numbers of migrants to leave Castile also were strongly rooted in the home society. Much of the internal movement in early modern society was local or cyclical – that is, from smaller places to larger ones, or conversely from central to more outlying parts of municipal jurisdictions where land was available, or seasonally in conjunction with transport, marketing or agricultural work. There also was movement over longer distances, directed in particular towards the fastest-growing urban centres, especially Seville, which grew to over 100,000 inhabitants by the end of the sixteenth century and attracted people from all over the peninsula (Molinié-Bertrand 1985 on the growth of cities; Reher 1990 on rural to urban mobility). Domestic service by children and adolescents took both girls and boys away from their villages, usually to neighbouring ones but sometimes much further away (Reher 1990: 255–6; Vassberg 1992). Relatives and acquaintances often played a part in making these arrangements. Career mobility was common among the upper middle and noble (*hidalgo*) groups, with young men (especially those whose inheritance might be limited) leaving home to study at the university, enter religious orders or serve in the military (Altman 1989: 79–86). These forms of mobility suggest that leaving home and family was a commonly accepted, and for many even an expected, occurrence, frequently connected with the achievement of economic independence and formation of new households through marriage. Emigration to the Indies

functioned in much the same way, as a life-stage and career choice that took people away from home, temporarily or permanently, to places offering greater economic opportunities and greater social flexibility as well. The latter meant an escape from the social constraints that at home made it nearly impossible for a young man of the *hidalgo* group to pursue economic opportunities (whether active participation in commerce or marriage to a wealthy non-*hidalgo* woman) that would have been considered radically at odds with his social rank.

Thus forms of physical mobility reflected and depended upon a number of factors, including age, marital status, social rank, occupation and gender. The emigration of families, which became more common as migration cycles reached a point of maturity (Altman 1994) and society in the Indies stabilized and consolidated, responded to a somewhat different set of variables than that of single young people. A married man of the working classes who decided to relocate with his family probably either had been working already in a given occupation and expected to continue doing the same (even more profitably) in America, or found himself in such straitened circumstances at home in Castile that migration might offer the only remaining option. Unmarried young men usually had fewer if any familial obligations and hence enjoyed greater freedom of movement; it was not uncommon for men to spend some years in the Indies amassing at least a modest stake and then return to establish themselves at home (Altman 1989: 251–2).

The migration patterns of women again differed notably. Within Spain women and girls appear to have moved principally to prearranged destinations where they would marry or be received in a specific household (of an employer or relative), or they moved with their husbands, fathers or other male relatives. Similarly few women of any social rank travelled alone to the Indies; they moved under circumstances very similar to those under which they relocated within Spain itself. Among the sixteenth-century emigrants from Trujillo, for example, in those cases where it was possible to determine modes of travel, only seven women seem to have undertaken the journey alone (none of them before 1530); in contrast fourteen travelled as *criadas* (servants), almost sixty with husbands or children, eighty-two with parents, siblings or other relatives, and thirteen went to join relatives (Altman 1989: Table 9, 177).

From the work that has been done on migration from specific places it is clear that the emigration movement from Castile really was an aggregate of movements from separate localities where particular economic, social and familial factors strongly influenced the nature and timing of migration and determined who would leave (and return) with whom, and to what destinations. Certainly these local movements shared many elements in common in terms of timing, composition and organization; yet the study of particular migrant groups and the contexts in which they functioned sheds considerable light on the nature of the movement and how it affected society in both Spain and the Indies.

To date the most detailed study of emigration in the context of local society focuses on the small Extremaduran cities of Cáceres and Trujillo (Altman 1989). In the late 1520s Francisco Pizarro recruited his four half-brothers and a number of other men from his home town of Trujillo and the surrounding area (including Cáceres) for the enterprise (Lockhart 1972). The result was that people from these cities forged strong connections with events and people in Peru. Nearly half the Trujillo emigrants and a third of the people from Cáceres went there directly, and, since people often moved on from their initial destination, probably well over half of the emigrants from the area ended up in Peru. Thus the general thrust of the movement from these cities was similar, and the cities resembled each other politically, economically and socially, as well as being approximately the same size.

The migrant groups differed, however. Emigration from Cáceres got going earlier (until 1520 emigrants from Cáceres were almost twice as numerous as from Trujillo, doubtless due to the appointment of Fray Nicolás de Ovando, member of a *cacereño* noble family, as governor of Hispaniola in 1502). Yet in the sixteenth century Trujillo produced more than twice as many emigrants as Cáceres (921 known emigrants compared with 410). The early strong participation of *hidalgo*s in the movement from Cáceres had a lasting influence on the composition of its emigrant group (Altman 1987). The larger Trujillo group was more plebeian and more familial in nature (around 27 per cent of the Trujillo people emigrated in nuclear family groups, compared with 14 per cent of the *cacereños*). Doubtless the larger size of the Trujillo group helped to account for the greater variety in occupation, status and even motivation.

Analysis of return migration also suggests differences that hinged on a number of factors, such as social and economic status, position within the family and timing of arrival in the Indies. While the rates of both temporary and permanent return to the two places might have been approximately the same – perhaps 10 per cent – the *cacereños* on the whole stayed away longer. Whereas fully half of the 45 permanent returnees to Trujillo whose length of absence can be determined spent ten years or less in the Indies, 75 per cent of the returnees to Cáceres remained in the Indies for more than ten years (Altman 1989: 251). These longer sojourns in the New World are consistent with the presumption that higher-ranking individuals (of whom there were more in the Cáceres group) would want to accumulate substantial wealth before returning home permanently, which normally took many years (Lockhart 1976: 791). The more varied lengths of absence of the *trujillanos* suggest that more of them went to the Indies with finite objectives and expectations.

Return migration has received little scholarly attention (Fair 1972), but study of returnees to Trujillo and Cáceres shows that, since most returnees went back to their places of origin, return migration played a crucial role in stimulating the subsequent departure of their relatives and fellow townspeople, and in maintaining connections with people and events in the Indies. The importance of this phenomenon also underscores the complexity that from the start characterized early modern Castilian migration. It was a movement that encompassed chain migration, second time and re-emigration, circulation (moving back and forth) and forms of labour migration, as well as temporary and permanent return.

References

Altman, Ida (1987) 'Spanish Hidalgos and America: The Ovandos of Cáceres', *The Americas*, 43 (3), 323–44

  (1989) *Emigrants and Society: Extremadura and Spanish America in the Sixteenth Century*, Berkeley: University of California Press

  (1994) 'Moving Around and Moving On: Spanish Emigration in the Age of Expansion', University of Maryland Department of Spanish and Portuguese, Working Papers on Discovery of the Americas

Altman, Ida and James Horn (eds) (1991) '*To Make America': European Emigration in the Early Modern Period*, Berkeley: University of California Press

Boyd-Bowman, Peter (1964/1968) *Indice geobiográfico de cuarenta mil pobladores españoles de América en el siglo XVI*, 2 vols, Bogota and Mexico

  (1973) *Patterns of Spanish Emigration to the New World (1492–1580)*, Buffalo: State University of New York

  (1976a) 'Patterns of Spanish Emigration to the Indies until 1600', *Hispanic American Historical Review*, 56, 580–604

  (1976b) 'Spanish Emigrants to the Indies, 1595–98: A Profile', in F. Chiappelli (ed.) *First Images of America*, Berkeley: University of California Press, vol. II, 723–35

Brading, D. A. (1971) *Miners and Merchants in Bourbon*

Mexico, 1763–1810, Cambridge: Cambridge University Press

Fair, Theopolis (1972) 'The *Indiano* during the Spanish Golden Age from 1550–1650', Ph.D. dissertation, Temple University

Hoffman, Paul E. (1990) *A New Andalucía and a Way to the Orient*, Baton Rouge: Louisiana State University Press

Jacobs, Pieter (1991) 'Legal and Illegal Emigration from Seville, 1550–1650', in I. Altman and J. Horn (eds) '*To Make America': European Emigration in the Early Modern Period*, Berkeley: University of California Press, 59–84

Lockhart, James (1968) *Spanish Peru, 1532–1560*, Madison: University of Wisconsin Press

(1972) *The Men of Cajamarca*, Austin: University of Texas Press

(1976) 'Letters and People to Spain', in F. Chiappelli (ed.) *First Images of America*, Berkeley: University of California Press, vol. II, 783–90

Molinié-Bertrand, Annie (1985) *Au siècle d'or: L'Espagne et ses Hommes. La population du Royaume de Castille au XVIe siècle*, Paris: Económica

Mörner, Magnus (1976) 'Spanish Migration to the New World prior to 1810: A Report on the State of Research', in F. Chiappelli (ed.) *First Images of America*, Berkeley: University of California Press, vol. II, 737–82, 797–804

(1991) 'Migraciones a Hispanoamérica durante la época colonial', Suplemento de *Anuario de Estudios Americanos*, 43 (2), 3–25

Otte, Enrique (1988) *Cartas privadas de Emigrantes a Indias*, Seville: Consejería de Cultura – Junta de Andalucía

Reher, David S. (1990) *Town and Country in Pre-industrial Spain: Cuenca, 1550–1870*, Cambridge: Cambridge University Press

Robinson, David J. (ed.) (1990) *Migration in Colonial Spanish America*, Cambridge: Cambridge University Press

Socolow, Susan M. (1978) *The Merchants of Buenos Aires, 1778–1811*, Cambridge: Cambridge University Press

Vassberg, David E. (1992) 'Mobility and Migration in Sixteenth-Century Spanish Villages', presented at the 1992 meeting of the American Historical Association

FRENCH COLONIAL MIGRATION

MICHAEL HEFFERNAN

France's imperial history can be divided in two distinct phases. The first extended from the sixteenth to the eighteenth centuries, the second from the 1830s to the 1960s. During the first period, French interests were focused on the Americas (Eccles 1990; Meinig 1986). French commerce expanded along the St Lawrence river from the mid-sixteenth century and ultimately dominated a large area known as New France, stretching from Acadia (Nova Scotia) to the Great Lakes. Fur trading was the dominant activity, coordinated through a series of fortified settlements at Quebec (1608), Ville-Marie (Montréal) (1642) and Detroit (1701). French influence gradually expanded southwards along the Mississippi to the Gulf of Mexico where settlements were established at Mobile (1701) and New Orleans (1718). French merchants also established tobacco plantations on several Caribbean islands and gained a strategic foothold on the South American coast at Guiana. Under the mercantilist policies of Jean-Baptiste Colbert, Louis XIV's finance minister, Caribbean tobacco was superseded by more lucrative sugar, indigo and cotton production (Galloway 1989: 84–119).

A bitter Anglo-French struggle for American supremacy was underway by the mid-1600s. The Treaty of Utrecht (1713) handed Acadia (Nova Scotia) and Newfoundland to Britain, though France retained Louisiana and the highly-profitable sugar islands in the Caribbean. Between 1710 and 1750, the value of French colonial trade grew by a factor of six and Saint Domingue (Haiti) became the world's most valuable colony with more than 600 sugar plantations (Boucher 1989: 71).

The Seven Years War (1756–63) destroyed French aspirations in the Americas (as well as in other colonial arenas like India). Britain's naval power and dominance of the eastern American seaboard were critical advantages. British forces captured Louisbourg in 1758, Quebec, Guadeloupe, Tobago and Grenada in 1759, Montreal in 1760 and Martinique in 1762. Louisiana was also offered to Spain in return for support against Britain. The Treaty of Paris (1763) gave Canada and land east of the Mississippi to

Britain but returned the major sugar islands to France. Few mourned the loss of mainland territory which was a drain on the French economy. The Caribbean islands were, by contrast, extremely valuable. By 1789, Saint Domingue, the jewel in the French Caribbean crown, provided 40 per cent of the world's sugar through a flotilla of nearly 700 cargo ships.

France's overseas empire effectively collapsed during the Revolutionary and Napoleonic eras (1789–1815), partly through British efforts but also because of the great slave revolt on Saint Domingue, led by Toussaint L'Ouverture (Benot 1988; James 1938; Lokke 1932). France emerged from the Treaty of Vienna (1815) with only Guadeloupe, Martinique, Guiana, the islands of Saint Pierre and Miquelon off Newfoundland and a few coastal enclaves in India.

The second period of French imperial expansion, based on Africa and Indo-China, began in 1830 with the seizure of the Ottoman city of Algiers. Subsequent imperial expansion was mainly a military affair. Political leaders in Paris were often reduced to impotent onlookers as army commanders acquired ever larger portions of African territory in flagrant opposition to official policy. After 1870, the imperial centre of gravity shifted from the colonial periphery to the metropolitan core and from the army to a small group of colonialists within the French middle class. The bourgeois membership of the *Parti Colonial* – a loosely-structured pressure group – was able to exploit France's chronic governmental instability to promote ambitious colonial projects despite public apathy and occasional antipathy. Preoccupied by domestic and European questions, successive French governments abdicated their responsibility for colonial affairs to civil servants and political advisers with an interest in the empire – in short, to the leading members of the *Parti Colonial*. The 'second' French overseas empire in Africa, Indo-China and the Middle East was carved out by a handful of unelected imperialists operating first in the colonial army and subsequently in a small, unrepresentative pressure group (Andrew and Kanya-Forstner 1988; Brunschwig 1966; Ganiage 1968; Girardet 1972).

By 1939, the French empire covered nearly 12 million square kilometres and was inhabited by 69 million people (Ansprenger 1989: 305–6). Colonial administration was complex. Algeria was theoretically not a colony at all but an extension of metropolitan France. Tunisia and Morocco, occupied in the 1880s and early twentieth century, were both protectorates. There were three giant African federations – French West Africa based on Dakar (including modern Mauritania, Senegal, Guinea, Mali, Ivory Coast, Upper Volta, Benin and Niger), French Equatorial Africa based on Brazzaville (Chad, Central African Republic, Congo and Gabon), and Madagascar and the Comoro Islands based on Tananarivo. The fourth federation was French Indo-China (Vietnam, Laos and Cambodia) centred on Hanoi and the product of French military expansion dating back to the 1860s. The tricolour also fluttered over islands in the Caribbean and in the Indian and Pacific Oceans such as Réunion, Tahiti and New Caledonia (Aldrich 1990). The strategic East African port of Djibouti was also in French hands. After 1918, the League of Nations mandates for Syria and Lebanon passed to France.

France's retreat from empire after 1945 was as uncoordinated as the earlier phases of imperial expansion. Compared with British decolonization, the French experience was extremely violent. Indo-China was lost in 1954 after military defeat by communist-backed nationalists. No sooner was this resolved than French Algeria erupted into a bitter eight-year struggle for independence which claimed over a million lives. The remaining colonies in North and West Africa had gained independence by the time Algeria freed itself from French rule in July 1962 (Betts 1991).

French colonial settlement and migration

France's success in exploration and imperial conquest was not matched by achievements in the more mundane business of colonial settlement. While other Europeans emigrated in huge numbers, the French remained closely attached to their homeland. This was partly due to the country's size and comparatively modest population growth after 1789. Insofar as overseas emigration was a response to economic and social problems created by rapid population growth, French men and women had less incentive to move.

During the French American empire transoceanic settlement was modest. Despite the efforts of pioneering religious communities such as the Huguenots and the Jesuits, the number of French colonists remained small, partly because the all-important fur trade, with its widely-dispersed army of trappers, was not conducive to a settled agricultural economy. Under Colbert, civilian colonization was encouraged to consolidate the tenuous grip on the American colonies. Free passage and generous allocations of land and accommodation were offered to army veterans; official propaganda was circulated celebrating the richness of the colonies; orphan girls were forcibly transported to redress the colonial gender imbalance; and press gangs roamed the streets of French cities 'recruiting' petty criminals and the unemployed as pioneer colonists. Between 1665 and 1672, the number of settlers more than doubled from 3200 to 7000 (Boucher 1989: 54). After the 1670s incentives were reduced, though high fertility rates in the colonies maintained population increase. Between 1725 and 1750, the European population of New France increased from about 20,000 to 55,000. But this was tiny compared with the Anglo-Saxon population. By the late 1600s, there were 250,000 settlers in the British colonies and by 1750, Massachusetts alone had a larger European population than the whole of New France.

Official French enthusiasm for American settlement periodically returned. After the Treaty of Utrecht (1713) deprived France of Acadia and Newfoundland, a propaganda campaign was launched to raise colonists for Louisiana. Some 4000 convicts and volunteer *colons* arrived between 1718 and 1721. The wildly optimistic claims about the region were soon evident and most of those who survived the harsh realities of American life returned to France (Allain 1988). French Guiana, which had about 600 settlers in 1760, was the focus of a similar propaganda campaign after the Treaty of Paris (1763). Cayenne, a squalid and miserable outpost, was depicted as an earthly paradise of richness and abundance. In the mid-1760s, 15,000 colonists, mainly from Alsace-Lorraine, set sail for Guiana; 9000 died of disease within months.

Despite their tiny size, the Caribbean islands were more attractive to French migrants. In 1645, there were 8500 settlers in the Caribbean compared with just 300 in New France (Boucher 1989: 37). Numbers increased steadily thereafter. On Martinique, for example, the white population rose from 4,770 in 1683 to 14,000 in 1756. However, the island economies were increasingly dependent on African slave labour. During the eighteenth century, a million Africans were transported by French slave-traders to the Caribbean, 270,000 arriving in the 1780s alone. Between 1713 and 1753, the slave population of Martinique and Guadeloupe rose from 14,500 to

65,000. On Saint Domingue, there were 9,000 slaves in 1700, 172,000 in 1752 and 480,000 in 1790, more than six to every European (Boucher 1989: 71, 90). A rigid social and racial pyramid emerged characterized by a small number of plantation owners and increasing numbers of *petits blancs* (small white farmers), *engagés* (descendants of forcibly transported Europeans who arrived before the slave trade commenced), mulattos of mixed race and African slaves.

During the second period of French expansion, beginning in 1830, settlement was concentrated in North Africa, particularly Algeria (Ageron 1991; Heffernan and Sutton 1991; Ruedy 1992). Small European villages appeared from the late 1830s on newly drained land in the hinterland of Algiers. Built by the army to a standard grid-iron pattern, these were initially occupied by demobilized veterans and their families. After 1841, civilian colonization was encouraged on territory seized by the French army. Colonists were offered free passage, land and accommodation. Propaganda was circulated in France and throughout central and southern Europe to recruit non-French Europeans who, once in Algeria, became French citizens. Life in early colonial Algeria contrasted starkly with official images of a bucolic idyll on the edge of a new continent. The number of *colons* increased nevertheless from 38,000 in 1841, concentrated mainly in the larger towns, to 110,000 by 1847, a fifth living in agricultural villages. Only 43 per cent were of French origin. The remainder came from Spain, Italy, Malta, Switzerland and central Europe.

After the 1848 revolution, the republican government offered unemployed Parisian workers a chance to emigrate to rural Algeria at the state's expense in an attempt to reduce tension in the aftermath of the June insurrections. It was hoped that 100,000 Parisians (10 per cent of the city's population) would leave over a three-year period. Like earlier attempts to populate Guiana and Louisiana, this rash and ill-considered experiment ended in misery and death. Of the 15,000 colonists who left in 1848–49, a third died and a third returned to France within a year (Heffernan 1989).

Despite these failures, 170,000 Europeans had settled in Algeria by 1856. After 1870, the pace of emigration increased. Nearly a thousand refugee families from Alsace and Lorraine, their homes now under German rule, accepted an offer of Algerian land in the early 1870s. Between 1872 and 1882, the number of Europeans increased from 260,000 to more than 412,000. By 1900, there were 630,000 and by 1936, 950,000. The indigenous population, over 4 million strong, owned less than 15 per cent of the land.

Migration to Tunisia was also encouraged and often sponsored by the state. There were 250,000 Europeans in the country on the eve of independence. In Morocco, the European population increased from less than 10,000 in 1911 to 100,000 by the late 1920s and over 500,000 by the mid-1950s (out of a total population of 10 million). A large proportion were of Spanish or Italian origin. Originally, four out of five Europeans lived in the coastal towns. There were 35,000 in Casablanca alone, a third of the city's population. Gradually, European settlement spread inland as part of an ambitious attempt to develop the agricultural sector. By 1952, a third lived in the rural interior (Rivet 1988, III: 7–33; Swearingen 1987). The 1.75 million North African whites (or *pieds noirs* as they were called) began to leave during the Algerian war and most fled after 1962. Their dispersion during the early 1960s to France, Latin America and Spain represents one of the largest population movements in post-war European history.

The rest of the French empire experienced little civilian colonization. In Indo-China, one of the most productive parts of the French empire, there were never more than 3000 European settlers in Cochin-China (former South Vietnam), 1000 in Amman-Tonkin (former North Vietnam) and about 800 in Cambodia (Meyer 1985). The tropical African federations, temporary home to thousands of French troops and civil servants, were relatively untouched by permanent European settlement.

Other parts of the empire experienced immigration of a highly specific kind. New Caledonia was the focus for large-scale penal resettlement beginning in 1865. After the upheavals of 1870–71, around 4000 supporters of the Paris Commune were transported to the island. By the mid-1880s, 500 convicts a year were arriving. By 1886, the European population reached 10,500. Despite hopes that transportees would settle and develop the island's economy after serving their sentences, few did so. By 1891, there were only 6500 free settlers left, though numbers increased to 54,000 by 1983 (a third of the island's population) (Lyons 1986: 68–85).

Colonial settlement and colonial debate

The nature and scale of French colonial migration, while ultimately determined by fundamental economic and demographic factors, was significantly influenced by domestic political upheavals and shifts in colonial policy.

Emigration was thus an intensely political matter and the subject of considerable debate. There were several schools of thought which all, at various times, influenced official policy.

Among the earliest advocates of colonial emigration were army commanders. The military view of colonial settlement, derived from the Roman model, was best represented by Thomas-Robert Bugeaud, governor-general of Algeria from 1841 to 1847 (Julien 1947; Sullivan 1983). Bugeaud believed settlement would consolidate colonial authority against internal threats from indigenes and external challenges from rival colonial powers. However, he insisted the only viable colonists were veteran colonial soldiers accustomed to a strict military regime and acclimatized to the rigours of a non-European environment. Colonists drawn from the army could defend themselves and reduce the burden on the regular colonial forces. As they had themselves cleared and drained land and constructed villages, they had a vested interest in colonial life. Civilian emigration should only be considered once colonies were 'pacified' and after the families of former soldiers had spawned a significant pioneer population.

Other proponents of colonial emigration disagreed with this view. Some saw colonies as far-flung places where the unwanted, the unruly and the dispossessed could profitably be relocated to the benefit, not of the colonies, but of the social and political order of metropolitan France. In times of domestic economic and political crisis, such as 1848–49, official support for colonial emigration was undeniably inspired by this simple rationale. If transportees ultimately helped create profitable colonial economies this would be an added, but unexpected, advantage. The persistence into the twentieth century of penal resettlement to New Caledonia and Devil's Island, the infamous penal colony off the Guiana coast, is a painful reminder that this primitive brand of colonial thinking retained some influence on official policy.

More sophisticated arguments in favour of colonial emigration emerged during the nineteenth century. The idea of overseas colonization as a means of spreading French language and culture became a peculiarly insistent leitmotif in colonial debates. During the 1830s, the Saint-Simonian thinker Prosper Enfantin developed a radical, crypto-socialist justification for large-scale colonial emigration to Africa and Asia. Enfantin contrasted the dynamic, secular, technologically advanced and 'male' world of Europe with a passive, spiritual and 'female' non-European sphere. The colonization of the latter by the former

would produce, he predicted, a perfect union between these two gendered civilizations. This would create, following interbreeding and hybridization, a new world civilization containing the best elements of both 'parent' cultures. If properly administered, the civilian colonization of Algeria would be the first step towards a utopian fusion of Europe and Africa (Enfantin 1843).

Variations on Enfantin's theme resurfaced in later years. In 1868, the nationalist prophet Anatole Prévost-Paradol produced an influential book, *La France Nouvelle*, which painted a gloomy picture of a decadent and stagnant French culture. The only cure, he claimed (Prévost-Paradol 1981: 286), was aggressive overseas colonization, particularly into Africa: 'If our population, obstinately attached to our native soil, continues to grow so slowly, then we shall inevitably become as Greece is now – an ancient though dead civilization, an historical and cultural artefact.' France's slow population growth was evidence that the nation had become insular, sick and impotent. To counter the logical argument that if there were too few French people there was little point in encouraging them to colonize distant regions of the globe, Prévost-Paradol insisted that it was only through colonization that national vigour and psychological pride would return. The Anglo-Saxon experience was illuminating: Britain had not become a great imperial power because of its rapid population growth, as was often claimed. Rather, the demographic vitality of the British, both domestically and in the colonies, was the result of the cultural prestige and moral power brought by empire. If France could colonize energetically, it could replicate the success of Britain. By spreading French language, culture and civilization around the world, it would also challenge the growing cultural (and therefore political) hegemony of the British. Prévost-Paradol, like Jules Michelet, saw France not as a single, declining European country but rather as a universal spiritual idea which all men and women could embrace. Under a benign French colonial system, the indigenous peoples of the empire could be incorporated into a greater, global France.

The disasters of 1870–71 – defeat by the Prussian army, the loss of Alsace-Lorraine to the new German empire and the bloody interlude of the Paris Commune – seemed to confirm Prévost-Paradol's prognosis. Many of the leading prophets in the colonial lobby argued in favour of colonial emigration on similar cultural and nationalist grounds (Dubois 1895; Hardy 1947; Piolet 1900). An influential statement was Paul Leroy-Beaulieu's *De la colonisation chez les peuples modernes* (1874), which expanded on the idea of cultural reciprocity (Gemie 1992; Murphy 1948: 103–38). France's civilization was enhanced by interaction with the colonies. At the same time, the colonial system allowed France's unique culture and language to be disseminated among 'less fortunate' non-European peoples. The central elements of French colonial policy after the 1880s – the ideas of *mission civilisatrice*, assimilation and association – were all inspired by this school of thought (Betts 1961; Burrows 1986; Lewis 1961/2).

Those advocating colonial emigration often clashed with economic imperialists who sought a commercially profitable empire based on trade. From their perspective, colonies should be seen in purely economic terms. The use of scarce European labour to develop colonies was senseless. This could easily be undertaken by indigenous people under European guidance. Civilian colonization was at best a diversion and at worst a costly drain on metropolitan and colonial resources. Far from increasing French vigour, emigration would inevitably diminish it (Marseille 1984).

Conclusion

It is important to note that French colonial emigration, particularly during the 'second' overseas empire, was only part of a broader pattern of population movement. Migrants to non-colonial areas in Europe, North America and Latin America normally outnumbered those leaving for the colonies. Of the 26,000 people who left France each year during the 1840s, for example, 8000 were bound for other European destinations, 7700 for the USA, 5500 for South America and only 4500 for Algeria (Chevalier 1947).

Although France was a less significant source of colonial migrants than other countries, its importance as a colonizing power should not be overlooked. Seven million Canadians (27 per cent of the population) and fourteen million US citizens are of French origin (Boucher 1989: 1). Over a million French-speaking people of European descent still live on islands in the Caribbean and in the Pacific and Indian Oceans known collectively as the DOM–TOMs (*départements et territoires d'outre-mer*) (Aldrich and Connell 1992).

References

Ageron, Charles-Robert (1991) *Modern Algeria: A History from 1830 to the Present*, London: Hurst
Aldrich, Robert (1990) *The French Presence in the South Pacific 1842–1940*, London: Macmillan
Aldrich, Robert and John Connell (1992) *France's Overseas Frontier: Départements et Territoires d'outre-mer*, Cambridge: Cambridge University Press
Allain, Mathé (1988) *'Not Worth a Straw': French Colonial Policy and the Early Years of Louisiana*, Lafayette: University of Southwestern Louisiana Press
Andrew, C. M. and A. S. Kanya-Forstner (1988) 'Centre and Periphery in the Making of the Second French Colonial Empire, 1815–1920', *Journal of Imperial and Commonwealth History*, 16 (3), 9–34
Ansprenger, Franz (1989) *The Dissolution of the Colonial Empires*, London: Routledge
Benot, Yves (1988) *La Révolution française et la Fin des Colonies*, Paris: Éditions de la Découverte
Betts, Raymond F. (1961) *Assimilation and Association in French Colonial Theory, 1890–1914*, New York: Columbia University Press
—— (1991) *France and Decolonisation 1900–1960*, London: Macmillan
Boucher, Philip P. (1989) *Les Nouvelles Frances: France in America, 1500–1815 – An Imperial Perspective*, Providence: John Carter Brown Library
Brunschwig, Henri (1966) *French Colonialism, 1871–1914: Myths and Realities*, London: Pall Mall Press
Burrows, Mathew (1986) ' "Mission civilisatrice": French Cultural Policy in the Middle East, 1860–1914', *The Historical Journal*, 29 (1), 109–35
Chevalier, Louis (1947) 'L'Émigration française au XIXe Siècle', *Études d'Histoire Moderne et Contemporaine*, 1, 127–71
Dubois, Marcel (1895) *Systèmes coloniaux et Peuple colonisateurs: Dogmes et Faits*, Paris: Plon
Eccles, W. J. (1990) *France in America*, East Lansing: Michigan State University Press
Enfantin, B.-P. (1843) *Colonisation de l'Algérie*, Paris: Bertrand
Galloway, Jock (1989) *The Sugar Cane Industry: An Historical Geography from its Origins to 1914*, Cambridge: Cambridge University Press
Ganiage, Jean (1968) *L'Expansion coloniale de la France sous la Troisième République 1871–1914*, Paris: Payot
Gemie, Sharif (1992) 'Politics, Morality and the Bourgeoisie: The Work of Paul Leroy-Beaulieu (1843–1916)', *Journal of Contemporary History*, (27), 345–62
Girardet, Raoul (1972) *L'Idée coloniale en France de 1871 à 1962*, Paris: La Table Ronde
Hardy, Georges (1947) *Histoire de la Colonisation française*, Paris: Librairie Larose
Heffernan, Michael J. (1989) 'The Parisian Poor and the Colonization of Algeria during the Second Empire', *French History*, 3 (4), 377–403
Heffernan, Michael J. and Keith Sutton (1991) 'The Landscape of Colonialism: The Impact of French Colonial Rule on the Algerian Rural Settlement Pattern, 1830–1987', in Chris Dixon and Michael Heffernan (eds) *Colonialism and Development in the Contemporary World*, London: Mansell, 121–52
James, C. L. R. (1938) *The Black Jacobins: Toussaint L'Ouverture and the San Domingo Revolution*, London: Secker & Warburg
Julien, C. A. (1947) 'Bugeaud', in C.-A. Julien (ed.) *Les Techniciens de la Colonisation (XIXe–XXe Siècles)*, Paris: Presses Universitaires de France, 55–74
Leroy-Beaulieu, Paul (1874) *De la Colonisation chez les Peuples modernes*, Paris: Guillaumin

Lewis, M. D. (1961/2) "One Hundred Million Frenchmen": The Assimilation Theory in French Colonial Policy', *Comparative Studies in Society and History*, 4, 129–53

Lokke, Carl Ludwig (1932) *France and the Colonial Question: A Study of Contemporary French Opinion, 1763–1801*, New York: Columbia University Press

Lyons, Martyn (1986) *The Totem and the Tricoleur: A Short History of New Caledonia since 1774*, Kensington, New South Wales: New South Wales University Press

Marseille, J. (1984) *Empire colonial et Capitalisme française: Histoire d'un Divorce*, Paris: Albin Michel

Meinig, Donald W. (1986) *The Shaping of America: A Geographical Perspective on 500 Years of History. Volume I: Atlantic America, 1492–1800*, New Haven: Yale University Press

Meyer, Charles (1985) *La Vie quotidienne des Français en Indochine 1860–1910*, Paris: Hachette

Murphy, Agnes (1948) *The Ideology of French Imperialism 1871–1881*, Washington DC: The Catholic University of America Press

Piolet, J.-B. (1900) *La France hors de France: Notre Émigration – Sa Nécessité, ses Conditions*, Paris: Gernier Baillière

Prévost-Paradol, L.-A. (1981) *La France nouvelle et Pages choisis*, Paris: Garnier

Rivet, Daniel (1988) *Lyautey et l'Institution du Protectorat français au Maroc 1912–1925*, 3 vols, Paris: L'Harmattan

Ruedy, John (1992) *Modern Algeria: The Origins and Development of a Nation*, Bloomington: University of Indiana Press

Sullivan, A. T. (1983) *Thomas-Robert Bugeaud, France and Algeria, 1789–1849: Power and the Good Society*, Hamden, Connecticut: Archon Books

Swearingen, Will D. (1987) *Moroccan Mirages: Agrarian Dreams and Deceptions, 1912–1986*, London: I.B. Tauris

THE GROWTH OF RESTRICTIVE IMMIGRATION POLICIES IN THE COLONIES OF SETTLEMENT

ROGER DANIELS

Ironically, colonies that were established in the New World, the Antipodes and southern Africa from the sixteenth to the eighteenth centuries, in part to provide for the settlement of Europeans, were, in the late nineteenth and early twentieth centuries, pioneers in developing restrictive immigration policies, policies which were first directed against Asians but, in almost every case, soon broadened to include Europeans as well. To be sure, colonial powers enacted all kinds of restrictive immigration laws in the earlier period (see, for example, Din 1973 and Proper 1900), but they were largely ineffectual, for they had created no apparatus capable of enforcing them.

The suppression of the slave trade, which was, of course, a control of immigration, spurred the recruitment of Asians into what Hugh Tinker (1974) has called 'a new system of slavery' in various parts of the plantation world. Soon after indentured Indian labourers were imported to work sugar plantations on Mauritius in 1830, they were brought to the Caribbean, to East and South Africa, and to Pacific islands, particularly Fiji (see, for example, Bhana 1993: 186–94; Chandrasekhar 1992; Look Lai 1993). The 'success', from the plantation owners' point of view, of Indian labour soon led to a similar use of Chinese indentured labour in the Caribbean, in South America and, in time, in South Africa.[1] In addition, free migrants from China began by mid-century to find their way first to North America and then to Australia, spurred by discoveries of gold in each place (Tsai 1986; Yarwood 1964). (The Chinese characters for California can be read as 'Gold Mountain', those for Australia as 'New Gold Mountain'.) In the USA large numbers of Chinese were employed in the construction of the transcontinental railroads from the mid-1860s, a practice Canada emulated from the 1880s. Both in what Huttenback calls the 'Empire of Settlement' and in the USA working men and their organizations quickly created movements to protest against Asian immigrants, but these movements ran afoul of laws and traditions that favoured immigration. Anti-Asian worker movements, which quickly gained middle-class adherents, were an amalgam of class

economic interest and naked racism (Markus 1979; Saxton 1971). Although there was much legal and extra-legal anti-Asian harassment, much of it accompanied by violence, 'solutions' satisfactory to the bulk of the white settlers were not achieved until late in the century (Huttenback 1976; Price 1974; Sandmeyer 1939).

The first legislative restriction of immigration was the Chinese Exclusion Act, which the USA put into effect in 1882. Passed as an 'experiment' for a ten-year term, it was re-enacted in 1892, made 'permanent' in 1901 and was not repealed until 1943 (Daniels 1988). It barred the entry of Chinese 'labourers', but established stringent conditions under which Chinese 'merchants', their families and certain others could enter. This act can now be seen as the hinge on which all US immigration policy would turn and one that set a kind of example for other countries of settlement. When Japanese immigrants began to enter the USA in significant numbers in the first decade of the twentieth century, a parallel 'Japanese Exclusion Act' was forestalled by the Gentlemen's Agreement of 1907–8, under which the USA and Japan agreed that Tokyo, not Washington, would set limits on passports issued to Japanese; half a century later the two countries would make similar agreements about export controls for automobiles. In 1917 the USA, by means of a 'barred zone act', excluded all other Asian immigrants, save Filipinos, who, as US nationals – not citizens – could not be excluded. Finally, in 1924, when the USA enacted a severe general restriction on immigration (see below), it also abrogated the Gentlemen's Agreement and totally barred Japanese and Chinese immigrants (Daniels 1990).[2]

In Canada the Chinese question was dealt with differently. Although the vast majority of white British Columbians wanted Chinese 'exclusion' in the 1880s, Ottawa would not countenance such a measure. In 1885 the Canadian parliament put a $50 head tax on each entering Chinese; this was raised to $100 in 1900 and to $500 in 1904. This slowed but did not stop Chinese immigration. Only in 1923 did Canada pass a

Chinese Immigration Act that effectively ended Chinese immigration into Canada until after the Second World War.

In the USA it was necessary for Californians and other westerners to convince a majority of the US Congress of the justice of its anti-Asian cause. Since the British empire had pretensions of racial equality within and between its members, the approval of London was necessary to effect exclusion. Had the colonies of settlement, or California and other western states for that matter, been independent, restriction would have come decades earlier. After a number of unsuccessful expedients within the empire – such as limiting the number of passengers per ship and the poll tax – a successful method of limiting 'undesirable' immigration that did not offend the sensibilities of London officialdom was hit upon by officials in Natal in 1897.

The immediate target was free Indian immigration. After a first nakedly racial attempt was disallowed, the Natal authorities produced Act 14 of 1897, which was, technically, colour-blind. All new immigrants into Natal were required to have £25 and a knowledge of a European language. The evaluation of language ability was to depend on the judgement of the immigration inspector, rather than upon a set examination. Natal's prime minister openly told the legislature that: 'It never occurred to me for a single minute that [the act] should [apply] to English immigrants. ... The object of the bill is to deal with Asiatic immigrants [25 March 1897].'[3]

Despite this frankness, Joseph Chamberlain, speaking for the British government, claimed that the act did not 'affect British Indians as such' (12 November 1897).

Privately the Colonial Office had explained to the India Office that: 'Some form of legislation in restriction of Indian immigration was inevitable in Natal; and the Secretary of State was of [the] opinion that it was desirable that a law should be passed which was not open to objection that it persecuted persons of a particular race [2 October 1897].' An internal Colonial Office minute earlier that year was franker: 'The whole subject is perhaps the most difficult we have to deal with. The Colonies wish to exclude the Indians from spreading themselves all over the empire. If we agree, we are liable to forfeit the loyalty of the Indians. If we do not agree we forfeit the loyalty of the Colonists [6 March 1897].' The operation of the law did allow a few Indians in – twelve in the first year of its operation – but it served the purpose the white settler government desired.

The Natal act formula, with variations, was soon used elsewhere in Africa, the Antipodes and, two decades later, in the USA. The several Australian states had discriminated and legislated against Chinese in various ways prior to 1901,[4] when the newly federated Australia instituted its 'white Australia' policy, using an extreme variant of the Natal act or literacy test formula. The key passages of Act 17 of 1901, 'to place certain restrictions on Immigration and to provide for the removal from the Commonwealth of prohibited immigrants', provided that a prohibited immigrant was 'any person who when asked to do so by an officer fails to write out at dictation and sign in the presence of the officer a passage of fifty words in length in a European language dictated by the officer.' Other parts of the original act, which was refined but stayed intact until well after the Second World War, allowed the government to compel any individual to take the test within a year of immigrating to Australia and to require persons who were not citizens of Australia or the United Kingdom to take the test after a term of imprisonment. New Zealand, which had previously passed several measures to restrict Chinese immigration, used a variant of the Natal act in 1907, but restricted its operation to Chinese immigrants. A final significant use of a watered down Natal act was in the USA. After decades of debate and three presidential vetoes a literacy test was enacted in 1917 over a fourth presidential veto. It was, however, a fairly innocuous measure, requiring literacy in 'any recognized language (including Yiddish)' for adult immigrants, but allowing families to enter if the head was literate and providing exemptions for persons joining family members already resident.

Canada dealt with non-Chinese Asian immigrants in different ways. Japanese immigration was never entirely prohibited, and Canada, especially during the years of the Anglo-Japanese Alliance (1902–22), was restrained by London from anti-Japanese actions it might otherwise have taken. Indian immigration to Canada, which began in about 1900, was largely excluded by an 1908 Order in Council, which made excludable any immigrant to Canada who did not arrive by 'a continuous voyage'. Since there was no direct passenger service between India and Canada (most had come via Hong Kong and/or Japan) Indians could be excluded without being specified (Buchignani et al. 1985).

As the foregoing sketch has indicated, by the time of the First World War most of the colonies of settlement had effectively barred their doors to immigrants from Asia. The major exceptions, not previously discussed here, were the South American nations of Peru and Brazil, each of which had a relatively large immigration of Japanese, most of whom arrived after the North American nations had been closed to them.[5] Prior to the war none of the colonies of settlement had meaningful restrictions on European immigrants, although there was a clear bias in favour of British immigrants within the empire.

The First World War changed all that. The combination of resurgent nationalism, economic dislocation and the long-present fear of foreign radicalism, exacerbated by the success of the Bolshevik Revolution, created higher barriers, both formal and informal, against immigration of any kind in most countries of settlement. The USA led the way. By the time it had entered the First World War, its once free and unrestricted immigration policy had been limited in eight major ways: slaves, all Asians except Japanese and Filipinos, some criminals, persons who failed to meet certain moral standards, those with various diseases, paupers, certain radicals and illiterates had all been denied admission. However, nothing had been done to regulate the volume of immigration, which, despite fluctuations, had increased from an annual average of fewer than 300,000 in the 1870s to one of just over a million a year in the ten years before the outbreak of war. Although fewer than 200,000 came in during each of the last two wartime years, many Americans feared a post-war surge of refugees. In addition, there was an increasing intolerance among most leading US politicians towards immigrants from southern and eastern Europe, who had predominated among immigrants since about 1890. The immediate post-war Congresses were concerned both with the volume and the European sources of US immigration.

The result was a series of statutes culminating in the Immigration Act of 1924, which tried to put a numerical cap on immigration and instituted a deliberately discriminatory system of annual national origin quotas based, initially, on the composition of the US population as recorded in the census of 1890, the last census prior to the shift to immigration from southern and eastern Europe. Total quota immigration was limited to fewer than 300,000 a year. In 1921, the last year before there were any quotas, 95,000 persons from Poland and 222,000 persons from Italy entered; they represented about two-fifths of all entrants. For the period 1925–30, about 8000 persons from Poland and 15,000 persons from Italy entered; they represented about a twelfth of all entrants. It should be noted that there were no quotas on western hemisphere migrants: Canadians had virtually free entry;

Mexicans and others from Latin America and the Caribbean were often kept out administratively under statutory provisions barring persons 'likely to become a public charge' (Daniels 1990).

This drastic change in policy had its roots in fears held by many Americans, some rational, some not. Both the unstable nature of the post-war world and socio-economic changes taking place within the USA suggested that some kind of lessening of the volume of immigration was in order. But in addition to these rational concerns US policy – and the policies of most other former colonies of settlement – was shaped by what historians have come to call nativism. In his classic work, *Strangers in the Land*, the historian John Higham defined nativism as 'intense opposition to an internal minority on the ground of its foreign (i.e. "un-American") connections' (Higham 1955: 4). Other historians, such as the Canadian Howard Palmer, have argued that nativism is not just an artefact of American exceptionalism, but that it exists in other areas of settlement.[6] In the USA in the 1920s nativism was directed at foreigners in general, and particularly at those who were Catholics, Jews and Greek Orthodox and/or those who held radical views, real or imagined. One sample of nativist rhetoric will suffice here. Albert Johnson (1869–1957), a Republican congressman from the state of Washington who co-authored the 1924 bill, justified his handiwork three years later:

[O]ur capacity to maintain our cherished institutions stands diluted by a stream of alien blood, with all its inherited misconceptions respecting the relations of the governing power to the governed. ... the American people have seen, patent and plain, the encroachments of the foreign-born flood upon their own lives. They have come to realize that such a flood ... can not fail likewise to affect the institutions which have made and preserved American liberties. ... the myth of the melting pot has been discredited. ... The United States is our land. ... We intend to maintain it so. The day of unalloyed welcome to all peoples, the day of indiscriminate welcome to all peoples, the day of indiscriminate acceptance of all races, has definitely ended.

Most of the other nations of settlement kept their doors somewhat open to Europeans during the 1920s, but the worldwide depression of the 1930s caused barriers to go up everywhere. But as fascist persecution, and then war, developed in Europe, pressures for admission of refugees rose. Those pressures were largely resisted by the USA, other nations of settlement, and the West generally. As US Vice-President

Walter Mondale observed in 1979, the nations of the West simply failed the test of civilization. As awareness of this failure grew and the enormity of the Holocaust began to seep into the consciousness of the West in the decades after the war, the policies of restriction were somewhat relaxed, especially for Europeans. Later, during the cold war, ideological imperatives other than nativism began to shape immigration policies (Abella and Troper 1982; Daniels 1983; Dinnerstein 1982; Laikin 1983).

Notes

1. For aspects of Chinese indentured labour see Campbell (1923); Clarence-Smith (1984); Jiménez Pastrana (1983); Meagher (1978); Stewart (1951). For the Chinese government reaction see Irick (1977). Some 30,000 Indonesians were brought to the Dutch Caribbean between 1890 and 1939 (Ismael 1949).
2. All immigrants 'ineligible to citizenship' were barred, which meant Asians, for US law limited naturalization to 'white persons and persons of African descent'. It should be noted that the XIV Amendment to the American Constitution (1870) made 'all persons born or naturalized in the United States' citizens, so there was no hereditary caste of noncitizens. In Canada, conversely, Asian immigrants could be naturalized under federal law, but in British Columbia, where most Asian Canadians lived before the Second World War, provincial law barred Asians from voting regardless of their citizenship status.
3. This and the next three quotations are from Huttenback (1976: 141 ff).
4. See Price (1974) and Markus (1979) for the complex details.
5. For Brazil there is a large literature; see, for example, Suzuki (1969). Tigner (1981) is comprehensive but dated.
6. Palmer (1882: 6–10). Other scholars have extended the concept of nativism even further afield. See, for example, Harootunian (1988), Nosco (1990) and Appiah (1992). I am not aware of the term nativism being used in a European context, but surely that will come.

References

Abella, Irving and Harold Troper (1982) *None is too Many: Canada and the Jews of Europe, 1933–1948*, Toronto: Lester & Orpen Dennys

Appiah, Anthony (1992) 'Topologies of Nativism', in A. Appiah, *My Father's House: Africa in the Philosophy of Culture*, New York: Oxford University Press

Bhana, Surendra (1993) 'Indentured Labor Migration: Indian Migrants to Natal, South Africa, 1860–1902', in Carl Strikwerda and Camille Guerin-Gonzales (eds) *The Politics of Immigrant Workers: Labor Activism and Migration in the World Economy since 1830*, New York: Holmes & Meier

Buchignani, Norman et al. (1985) *Continuous Journey: A Social History of South Asians in Canada*. Toronto: McClelland & Stewart

Campbell, Persia Crawford (1923) *Chinese Coolie Emigration to Countries within the British Empire*, London: P. S. King

Chandrasekhar, S. (ed.) (1992) *From India to Australia*, La Jolla: Population Review

Clarence-Smith, Gervase (1984) 'The Portuguese Contribution to the Cuban Slave and Coolie Trades in the 19th Century', *Slavery and Abolition*, (5) May

Daniels, Roger (1983) 'American Refugee Policy in Historical Perspective', in J. C. Jackman and C. M. Borden (eds) *The Muses Flee Hitler: Cultural Transfer and Adaptation, 1930–1945*, Washington: Smithsonian Institution Press

—— (1988) *Asian America: Chinese and Japanese in the United States since 1850*, Seattle: University of Washington Press

—— (1990) *Coming to America: A History of Immigration and Ethnicity in American Life*, New York: Harper Collins

Din, Gilbert C. (1973) 'Spain's Immigration Policy in Louisiana and the American Penetration, 1792–1803', *Southwestern Historical Quarterly*, (76), 255–76

Dinnerstein, Leonard (1982) *America and the Survivors of the Holocaust*, New York: Columbia University Press

—— (1975) *The Japanese and Peru, 1873–1973*, Albuquerque: University of New Mexico Press

—— (1981) *Pawns in a Triangle of Hate: The Peruvian Japanese and the United States*, Seattle: University of Washington Press

Harootunian, Harry D. (1988) *Things Seen and Unseen: Discourse and Ideology in Tokugawa Nativism*, Chicago: University of Chicago Press

Higham, John (1955) *Strangers in the Land: Patterns of American Nativism, 1860–1925*, 2nd edition, New Brunswick, NJ: Rutgers University Press

Huttenback, Robert A. (1976) *Racism and Empire: White Settlers and Colored Immigrants in the British Self-Governing Colonies 1830–1910*, Ithaca, NY: Cornell University Press

Irick, Robert L. (1977) *Ch'ing Policy toward the Coolie Trade, 1847–1878*, San Francisco: Chinese Materials Center

Ismael, Joseph (1949) 'De immigratie van Indonesiërs in Suriname', doctoral dissertation, University of Leiden

Jiménez Pastrana, Juan (1983) *Los Chinos en la Historia de Cuba, 1847–1930*, Havana: Ediciones Politicas

Laikin, Judith Elkin (1983) 'The Reception of the Muses in the Circum-Caribbean', in J. C. Jackman and C. M. Borden (eds) *The Muses Flee Hitler: Cultural Transfer and Adaptation, 1930–1945*, Washington: Smithsonian Institution Press

Look Lai, W. (1993) *Indentured Labor, Caribbean Sugar: Chinese and Indian Migrants to the British West Indies*, Baltimore: Johns Hopkins

Markus, Andrew (1979) *Fear and Hatred: Purifying Australia and California, 1850–1901*, Sydney: Hale & Iremonger

Meagher, Arnold Joseph (1978) *The Introduction of Chinese Laborers to Latin America: The 'Coolie Trade', 1847–1874*, San Francisco: Chinese Materials Center

Nosco, Peter (1990) *Remembering Paradise: Nativism and Nostalgia in Eighteenth Century Japan*, Cambridge: Harvard University Press

Palmer, Howard (1882) *Patterns of Prejudice: A History of Nativism in Alberta*, Toronto: McClelland & Stewart

Price, Charles A. (1974) *The Great White Walls Are Built: Restrictive Immigration to North America and Australasia, 1836–1888*, Canberra: Australian National University Press

Proper, Emberson E. (1900) *Colonial Immigration Laws: A Study of the Regulation of Immigration by the English Colonies in America*, New York: Columbia University Press

Sandmeyer, Elmer C. (1939) *The Anti-Chinese Movement in California*, Urbana: University of Illinois Press

Saxton, Alexander (1971) *The Indispensable Enemy: Labor and the Anti-Chinese Movement in California*, Berkeley: University of California Press

Stewart, Watt (1951) *Chinese Bondage in Peru: A History of the*

Chinese Coolie in Peru, Durham: Duke University Press

Suzuki, T. (1969) *The Japanese Immigrant in Brazil*, 2 vols, Tokyo: University of Tokyo Press

Tigner, James (1981) 'Japanese Immigration into Latin America: A Survey', *Journal of Inter-American Studies and World Affairs*, (23), 457–82

Tinker, Hugh (1974) *A New System of Slavery: The Export of Indian Labour Overseas, 1830–1920*, London: Oxford University Press

Tsai, Shih-shan Henry (1986) *The Chinese Experience in America*, Bloomington: Indiana University Press

Yarwood, Alexander T. (1964) *Asian Migration to Australia*, Melbourne: Melbourne University Press

PART THREE

ASIAN INDENTURED AND COLONIAL MIGRATION

Viewed on a global scale, unfree labour was the predominant form of labour control until a date much later than many might suppose. Even in Europe, Steinfield (cited Brass et al. 1993: 8) suggests that free labour, conceived in the sense of the freedom to choose one's employer, did not become a dominant legal ideal until the later eighteenth century and not the dominant paradigm until the nineteenth. Lucassen (in Brass et al. 1993: 10–18) alludes to three forms of productive unfree labour in the Old World and the Atlantic system – small-scale household, farm and artisan labour; large-scale plantation and mining labour; and unfree service as soldiers and sailors. As the same author notes, a number of scholars (for example, Paterson 1982, 1991; Curtin 1990) have demonstrated considerable continuities in the deployment of unfree labour. Moreover, a link between classical slavery and modern slavery has been established via Syria and Palestine, Cyprus, Sicily, Spain, the Azores and thence to the Americas.

Slavery disappeared in north-west Europe only to be replaced by servitude. The gradual progress to free labour and to independent economic activity in that part of Europe was, however, in marked contrast to the reintroduction of serfdom (the so-called 'second serfdom') in eastern Europe. Serfdom was only formally abolished in Poland in 1800 and in Russia in 1861. Naturally, legal prohibition concealed the continuation of other forms of unfree labour, including the 'industrial slaves' of the late nineteenth-century. While I have mentioned the best-documented case of Europe to illustrate the persistence of unfree labour, similar or more graphic accounts of unfree labour are found in studies of Africa, India, China and South America. Even in the late twentieth century bonded and child labour worldwide numbers many millions.[1]

Unfree labour was of intrinsic importance to the evolution of the modern world system. This, of course, is where unfree labour and world migration connect. The key European mercantile powers underwrote their trading empires by the production of tropical commodities and precious metals. The means that they chose was the introduction of mass slavery and coerced labour to the Americas. The 'triangular trade' between Europe, Africa and the Americas was the lusty infant that was to mature as modern world capitalism. Slave labour in the plantations of the Caribbean, the southern states of the USA and Brazil, and *repartimiento* labour in Spanish America provided the mother's milk to the newborn baby. In this section of the *Survey,* we are concerned with the main successor form to modern slavery, namely indentured labour. The switch in forms of labour also involved a switch in the sourcing of the labour supply, from Africa to Asia. With this switch in location another continent, hitherto linked only by trade, was more firmly bolted onto the modern world system.

Most indentured labourers (perhaps about 1.5 million in all) were recruited from India, their story being notably documented in Tinker's (1974) influential account. The movement of Indians to the tropical plantations provides an instructive reminder of how far the planters were prepared to go in keeping their two desiderata – abundant land and cheap labour. As *Vertovec* reminds us, the recruiters were ruthless, the journey was horrific and the arrangements made for the legal protection of the workers were inadequate. Many of the indentured Indians were physically moved into the slave barracks of the former African slaves – a poignant reminder of why they were there.

Despite this strong evidence of continuity, I maintain that the analogy with slavery can be taken too far. Just as in early modern Europe, the predominant domestic forms of labour control in India itself included a high level of servitude and repression. For some, intercontinental migration provided a window of opportunity for social mobility that the rigid caste system inhibited, if not totally prevented. A common in-group joke among contemporary Indo-Trinidadans is that there were no Brahmins when the ships set out from Calcutta, but by the time they arrived in Port of Spain (Trinidad) several gentlemen had assumed a haughty, priestly mien. Indenture also offered a free return passage at the end of the contract, an option only taken up by 25 per cent of the Indians taken to the Caribbean. The majority seized the opportunity to acquire land – a possibility which was very remote if they remigrated to India.

As *Thiara* shows, the issue of land for the former indentured workers was a crucial issue in the case of those Indians who were recruited for the plantations in the Indian Ocean area. In Mauritius, Indians were able to extend their land claims and to promote a sizeable educated, professional class that was to inherit state power at independence. In Fiji, when indenture came to an end in 1916, 83 per cent of the land was owned by indigenous Fijians, 10 per cent was Crown land and only 7 per cent was freehold. Indians were regarded as intruders for whom short-term leases were the most that could be conceded. In the post-independence period they suffered extensive discrimination at the hands of the Fijian political elite. In a 'consultation' conference on the 1990 constitution one of the Indo-Fijian delegates, Krishna Datt (1994: 90–1), made an impassioned plea to be allowed a permanent relationship to the Fijian soil:

Land has been raised as an issue very close to the hearts of Fijians. We have been told of the very special, almost spiritual, ties of the Fijian with land. For the Indo-Fijian the tie is no less. ... A symbiotic relationship of love and balance develops between the Indo-Fijian household and the land. For four generations of Indo-Fijians, that land has now acquired a very special, sentimental and religious significance. ... The Indo-Fijians have a saying about one's roots: 'One's roots are where one's umbilical cord is buried'. Mine is buried in that block of land in Mateniwai. Half of it is now 'reserved', but we continue to use it. ... The other half of the land is now on tenancy at will. If ever we were to lose that piece, something within me will have died. I will have lost my roots. That piece of land holds me here, provides me with a sense of identity.

The preoccupation of Indo-Fijians can, with modifications, be observed in the other overseas Indian communities of the Indian Ocean area. Those who found themselves in Natal were desperate to acquire a stake in urban property in Durban and Pietermaritzburg, a trajectory that was vigorously resisted by the white authorities. This was the issue on which the young lawyer, Mahatma Gandhi, first cut his political teeth. While the Indian South Africans slowly secured a more agreeable economic situation, they were excluded from white political power and their relationship with indigenous Africans deteriorated, resulting in an outbreak of intercommunal violence in 1949.

The 1949 riots in Natal, serious as they were, were something of a picnic compared with the radical measures taken by President Idi Amin's regime in post-independence Uganda. As is shown by *Twaddle's* account of South Asians in East Africa, Amin wielded a very blunt instrument. South Asians there were much more diverse in their origins than in the case of the plantation societies previously discussed. Baluchis, Sunni and Shia Muslims, Ismaelis, Hindu traders, Jains, Gaons and Sikhs were all lumped together in an undiscriminating way into the category of 'East African Asian'. To be sure, the category acquired some political meaning, first, when the British colonial administration restricted Indian immigration and, second, when Amin turned his fire on all Asians and expelled them. One particular group, the Sikhs, who were also part of the free migrant communities of East Africa, was to acquire a special significance for the British colonial administration. As *Tatla* shows, Punjabi emigrants escaped the worst of the indentured system, but only by enlisting in quite remarkable numbers in the British army. They were deployed in Africa, Malaya, the Mediterranean and Europe. By the time of the First World War there were 150,000 Sikhs under arms. Their role as loyal colonial auxiliaries was gradually to fade as the empire itself collapsed. However, the migrating genie had been let out of the Punjab bottle. About one million Sikhs now find themselves abroad, mainly in the USA, Canada and the UK.

While discussions of Asian indentured and colonial migrants have rightly focused on the numerically most important case of the Indian subcontinent, there were significant contingents of indentured workers recruited from China and Japan too, perhaps half a million in the first case and one million in the second. The story of these indentured workers has received limited attention from Japanese and Chinese scholars, partly because of the great sensitivity of the issue in both countries. The assertive nationalism of the post-Second World War years led to a sense of unease about those fellow nationals who were taken by force or deception by the European powers when Japan and China were weak. The acceptance of the Japanese diaspora in Brazil and Peru by Japanese politicians and the public has indeed been quite recent – with the recruitment of Japanese Brazilians to the labour-hungry factories in Japan and the rise to celebrity of some Japanese Peruvians (Peru's president, Fujimori, is of Japanese origin). For China too, the 'coolie trade' was an ugly stain on its history. Nonetheless, as *Ong* recognizes in a very apt sociological phrase, the patience of the indentured Chinese abroad was a marvellous display of 'deferred gratification'. Despite tremendous hardship, they staked out the occupations (in restaurants, laundries and merchandising) and established the Chinatowns that were subsequently to be populated by much more significant numbers of free workers, traders and entrepreneurs.

Indentured labour was the bridge between slavery and modern forms of contract labour (see Cohen 1987: 4–32; Potts 1990: 199–207). Its political significance far outweighed the numbers involved. At the level of global capitalism, its deployment demonstrated that (contrary to Marx's assumptions) free and unfree forms of labour could successfully and highly profitably be combined. This principle was extended to many forms of migrant labour including, for example, the *gastarbeiters* in post-war Germany and mine labourers in the period of classical apartheid in South Africa. At the national level, indentured labourers and their offspring developed a troubled and often hostile relationship with the indigenous people and other migrant groups. The inter-ethnic tensions in countries like Guyana, Fiji and South Africa provide cases in point. At the same time, both indentured and free colonial migrants constituted an advance guard for later Asia migration to Europe, Africa and the Americas. As is explained in later sections of this *Survey*, in the contemporary world the renewed link between the Asian communities abroad and their places of origin is also of notable cultural and economic importance.

Note
1. The UN estimates that by the end of the twentieth century there will be 375 million child labourers worldwide, 175 million of whom will be working in India alone.

References
Brass, T. et al. (1993) *Free and Unfree Labour*, Amsterdam: International Institute for Social History
Cohen, Robin (1987) *The New Helots: Migrants in the Internatonal Divsion of Labour*, Aldershot: Gower
Curtin, Philip (1990) *The Rise and Fall of the Plantation Complex: Essays in Atlantic History*, Cambridge: Cambridge University Press
Datt, Krishna (1994) 'Indo-Fijian Concerns', *Report on Consultation on Fiji's Constitutional Review*, Suva, Fiji: International Alert and the School of Social and Economic Development, University of South Pacific, 89–91
Paterson, Orlando (1982) *Slavery and Social Death*, Cambridge, MA: Harvard University Press
(1991) *Freedom: Freedom in the Making of Western Culture*, vol. I, New York: Basic Books
Potts, Lydia (1990) *The World Labour Market: A History of Migration*, London: Zed Books
Tinker, Hugh (1974) *A New System of Slavery: The Export of Indian Labour Overseas, 1820–1920*, London: Oxford University Press

INDENTURED MIGRANTS FROM JAPAN

MITSURU SHIMPO

Between 1815 and 1932, 60 million people migrated from Europe to the American continents. During the same period, the number of migrants from Japan was limited to much less than one million for several reasons. First, the government of Japan did not have the political power to ensure the welfare of overseas Japanese. Second, considering the difficulties in travelling long distances at that time, the new continents were geographically distant from Japan. Third, the new continents were under the dominance of European cultures, which were vastly different from Japanese culture. Finally, after the Russo-Japanese War (1904–1905), strong exclusion movements prevented further migration from Japan (Ministry of Foreign Affairs 1971 (I) 52–3).

This entry is a brief discussion of indentured migration from Japan to Hawaii and the USA, and to Peru and Brazil before the end of the Second World War. The term 'indentured migration' indicates immigration of a Japanese national to a specific country under a contractual agreement between the respective governments and/or between private organizations in the respective countries.

Indentured migration to Hawaii and the USA

Hawaii was the first destination for migrants from Japan. In 1868, 147 men and 6 women crossed the Pacific Ocean on the *SS Scioto*. This migration was arranged by Eugene M. Van Reed, the general consular of the kingdom of Hawaii. The migrants suffered greatly on the sugar-cane plantations because of the lack of support from the Japanese government. A similar incident in 1871 hardened the attitude of the Japanese government toward international migration until 1883 (Ministry of Foreign Affairs 1971 (I) 88–8).

The kingdom of Hawaii reopened inter-governmental negotiations in 1884, and the Japanese government consented to send migrants to Hawaii under official agreement. Between 1885 and 1894, under these terms, ships set sail 26 times, carrying a total of 29,132 Japanese to Hawaii.

As the destinations for migration diversified, small-scale private recruiting agencies called *Imin-Kaisha*

started active operation. They arranged contracts with private organizations such as plantations in a specific country and recruited Japanese workers under specific terms. Many of them tended to exaggerate favourably the terms of the contract while neglecting the responsibilities to keep them.

Japan was engaged in a war against China (1894–95), and the government, concentrating all its efforts on the war, was not properly able to look after the welfare of the overseas Japanese. In 1894 it passed protective regulations for migrants in which the first official definitions of 'immigration' and 'recruiting agent' appeared. It then transferred to these agencies the responsibilities for recruiting activities as well as protection of the clients (Ministry of Foreign Affairs 1971 (II) 91).

Competition among recruiting agencies was fierce: in order to get contracts from plantations, some of them revealed the weak points of the Japanese migrants, resulting in disadvantageous contracts for clients. Generally, migrants suffered under these contracts. Both their living and working conditions were poor. The language barriers made basic communication between the migrants and plantation managers incomplete. The latter regarded the former as a kind of slave, a situation which provoked numerous problems. As will be illustrated with the Peruvian cases later, this pattern was widely observed throughout the American continents.

The first Japanese to emigrate to the USA were a group of about forty, who were led by Dutchman Edward W. Schnell in 1869 to establish a colony in California. Several similar parties followed in later years. In 1898, the kingdom of Hawaii was absorbed into the USA, and the Japanese migrants to Hawaii came to be counted as immigrants to the USA.

By 1899, Japanese migrants on the mainland totalled 35,000. Around this time, particularly in California, exclusion movements against orientals gained momentum, culminating in the New Immigration Act of 1924, which completely halted migration from Japan. Because of this, the Japanese government had to reroute migrants bound for the USA to Brazil. By

1940, a total of 277,591 Japanese had migrated to the USA (Ministry of Foreign Affairs 1971 (II) 218). In 1990, the total number of Japanese Americans reached 671,661 and Japanese permanent residents 73,533.

Indentured migrants to Peru

Indentured migration for Peru through recruiting agencies started in 1899 and ceased in 1923. During this period 82 ships brought a total of 17,764 immigrants to Peru (Editorial Peru Shimpo 1974: 67). After 1923, migration from Japan continued through more informal channels. The last boatload of migrants was discharged at Callao in 1939. In total 33,070 Japanese migrated to Peru by 1940, although as with other countries many of the migrants returned to Japan.

When orientals in the USA were faced with exclusion movements the Japanese government had to set its sights on alternative destinations. Peru was one such possibility (Morimoto 1992: 21). Sugar plantations in Peru needed an ample supply of cheap labour from overseas, and Japanese recruiting agents signed a series of contracts with them.

From the outset, however, Peru was not a very tolerant society. At the outbreak of the Second World War in the Pacific, for example, the Japanese population was about 25,000, but the Peruvian government attempted to reduce it to 15,000. In keeping with this policy, fifteen arrests were made and 1771 people were sent to relocation camps in the USA (Japanese Immigration 80th Anniversary Committee 1991: 42). This happened prior to the official Peruvian declaration of war against Japan on 12 February 1945.

The same government attempted to dispose of all commercial facilities and property possessed by 'enemy aliens'. Some second generation Japanese Peruvians insisted on their rights as Peruvian citizens and were able to protect their parents' property (Japanese Immigration 80th Anniversary Committee 1991: 42). Only 50 or so Japanese who had been naturalized prior to the war were allowed to return to Peru after the hostilities had ended (Ministry of Foreign Affairs 1971 (II) 176). This kind of social ethos was revealed in plantation owners' treatment of oriental labourers and workers.

The first party of 790 migrants was sent to several plantations. Each plantation was almost autonomous. Often Peruvian law was not recognized, and the owners tended to regard Japanese labourers as little more than slaves (Editorial Peru Shimpo 1974: 23). The labourers' living and working conditions were extremely poor. They were economically exploited by the compulsory use of on-plantation stores which were more expensive than those off the plantation. Their wages were curtailed and often not paid. Many owners did not seem to have considered the migrants' contracts to be binding. On the other hand, if they considered their own contract to have been violated, they demanded considerable compensation from the recruiting agency. If workers were disobedient, the owners did not hesitate to threaten them with flogging. Worse, none of the Japanese were Spanish-speaking. Mutual misunderstandings exacerbated already deteriorating working relationships (Morimoto 1992: 36–43). Some migrants organized strikes while others ran away, leaving everything behind. Under these circumstances, 124 able-bodied workers died in one year (Editorial Peru Shimpo 1974: 24).

Japanese migrants gradually settled in urban areas and started small-scale commercial activities. Under strong political and social oppression, they formed families and obtained good educations for their children. When the hostilities were over, the first generation was young enough to be able to recover economically. The well-educated second and third generations enabled them to raise their group status in Peru. Since about 1979, Japanese Peruvians have taken an active part in politics. Many MPs, mayors and aldermen/women were elected from this ethnic group. In 1990, a Japanese Peruvian, Alberto Fujimori, was elected as president (Morimoto 1992: 172–80). The Japanese Peruvian population in 1990 was 52,300 and Japanese permanent residents 3035.

Indentured migrants to Brazil

The first group of 781 Japanese migrants arrived at Santos in June 1908. This was a consequence of the closed door policies in the USA and Canada.

Between 1908 and 1914, ten boats brought 3734 families (14,886 people) under specific contracts. Family migration is said to be one of the distinct characteristics of Japanese migration to Brazil.

After a one-year interruption, indentured migration recommenced in 1916. The post-war economic recession started in 1918, and the governments at municipal, provincial and national levels propagated the need for emigration. From 1921, the Japanese government provided subsidies for indentured migration (Ministry of Foreign Affairs 1971 (II) 95). The peak of emigration to Brazil was in 1933 when 23,299 Japanese landed at Brazilian ports. In 1934, the Brazilian government introduced the quota system, which resulted in a sharp decline in the number of migrants from Japan. The last boat for Brazil prior to the outbreak of the Pacific War left Japan in June 1941.

According to the official statistics, 188,986 people migrated to Brazil between 1908 and 1941 (Ministry of Foreign Affairs (ed.) 1971 (II) 149). The total number of Japanese Brazilians in 1990 was 529,310, and Japanese permanent residents 105,046.

At the outset, recruiting agencies were deeply involved in the conflicts between plantation owners and Japanese workers. Not all the recruiting agencies were deliberate in favourably exaggerating the terms of the contracts: they did not know the real situation on the coffee plantations nor did they have sound judgement in reading the fluctuations of the international coffee market (Ministry of Foreign Affairs (ed.) 1971 (II) 64). Frustrated Japanese migrants changed their place of work frequently, and consequently were labelled as an unstable labour force.

The migrants' hard working habits, together with improvements in the international coffee market and domestic coffee and vegetable production, as well as the development of ethnic colonies and the tolerant ethos of Brazilian society (Okazaki 1975: 44), all contributed to an improvement in the economic status of Japanese migrants. This improvement was one of the major reasons why the Japanese government favoured emigration to Brazil.

A brief explanation of 'ethnic colonies' may be helpful in understanding the aforementioned development. Both in Brazil and in Japan, private and official agencies organized 'unions of migrants', which were to establish 'colonies'. (The first such colony appeared in 1913.) According to ethnic historians, these colonies became the basis for development of the Japanese Brazilian community in the São Paulo region. It was the fruit of cooperation between migrants with limited resources and business firms which did not have an adequate labour force (Ministry of Foreign Affairs (ed.) 1971 (II) 66–7).

Ethnic colonies certainly helped in ameliorating the migrants' economic status, but by the same token, they prevented their social integration. These colonies culturally insulated their members so that the migrants were slow to learn the language of their host society — Portuguese. They overlooked the significance of educating their children in the public education system, further ostracizing themselves. After the Second World War, the Japanese Brazilian community was split into two factions and bitter quarrels ensued. The problems were partly due to their socio-cultural isolation; the outside world had little effect on their inner politics.

Summary

Migration from Japan to other countries started in the middle of the nineteenth century, but did not develop as expected. Japan was a slow starter and the new continents were already 'full'. Anti-oriental exclusion movements set low ceilings for migrants from Asian countries. The still underdeveloped Japanese government did not have the power to look after its overseas nationals.

Recruiting agencies mediated between foreign plantations and other firms, and Japanese workers. These agencies did not have accurate information on foreign organizations and they exaggerated contract terms to their clients. Consequently, the migrants were exposed to unexpectedly poor working environments.

The cultural gap between the two sides precipitated deterioration of working relationships. Plantation owners had a paternalistic attitude, while Japanese workers could not adequately communicate their frustrations. The violation of contracts on both sides caused political turmoil in the host societies.

Japanese migrants, who had a cultural heritage different from those of the host societies, flocked together. They tended to be nationalistic and initially educated their children along these lines. This cultural isolation delayed their integration into the host society and invited criticisms from non-Japanese. The second generation, which was better educated, managed to advance the social status of their community.

References

(Original titles are all in Japanese.)

Editorial Peru Shimpo (1974) *A 75-Year History of the Japanese in Peru, 1899–1974*, Lima: Editorial Peru Shimpo S.A.

Japanese Immigration 80th Anniversary Committee (ed.) (1991) *An 80-Year History of Japanese Immigrants to Brazil*, São Paulo: Japanese Immigration 80th Anniversary Committee

Ministry of Foreign Affairs (ed.) (1971) *Development of Overseas Japanese*, 2 vols, Tokyo: Ministry of Foreign Affairs

Morimoto, Amelia, (1992) *Japanese Immigrants in Peru*, Tokyo: Nihon Hyouronsha

Okazaki, Ayanori (1975) *Problems of International Migration*, Tokyo: Japan Association of Foreign Policy Studies

CHINESE INDENTURED LABOUR: COOLIES AND COLONIES

ONG JIN HUI

The period of the coolie trade extends from approximately the early 1840s to the 1920s. The idea behind the coolie trade was a simple one. It sought to extract labour from China and to bring it to locations where it was in short supply through a system of indenture. However, the system that developed was defective and exploitative from the beginning. In the process, all the nations involved in this episode of human migration must accept blame for the misery it caused. W. P. Reeves in his preface to Campbell (1923) wondered how such 'sinister experiments, so unattractive at their best, so repulsive at their worst, came to be tried in civilized countries in the nineteenth and twentieth centuries'. Looking at the phenomenon with the passage of time, it may be fairer to say that the processes and outcomes of this attempt at indentured labour was less a 'sinister experiment' than the unfortunate result of different strands of social, political and economic realities being woven together into an ugly pattern. As Irick's (1982: 2–7) discussion of the origin of the word coolie shows, the term (probably of Indian origin) has come to denote labourers who have been 'taken abroad by deception or by force'. The trade in *chu-tsai* (human pigs) was 'intended to and does in most respects equate to a slave trade in Chinese labourers'.

The coolie trade was driven and funded by the overpowering demands of the economic opportunities created by the European colonial expansions of earlier decades. A desire to gain the economic advantage and to fulfil the promise of European-controlled colonies made the exploitation of Chinese coolies almost inevitable. The stimulus for migration in this context of an international demand for labour was provided by socio-economic conditions in China. The Ch'ing court's inability to handle such demands in a period of dynastic decay contributed to the phenomenon that came to be known as the coolie trade.

The foundations of the coolie trade

Several causal factors have been cited to explain the migratory impulse. Over-population was a major one. As Yen (1985: 33) notes, China's population tripled between 1700 and 1850, resulting in heavy pressure on land-use and an inflationary spiral. Drought and floods both contributed to periodic internal migration, which further unbalanced the regional production and consumption patterns of Fukien and Kwangtung. China in the years preceding the coolie trade was also in political turmoil (Wang 1978: 12–13). The Taiping rebellion was instrumental in destabilizing central and southern China. The resultant chaos and disruption of the socio-economic fabric produced large rural–urban migrations and an over-supply of labour in the coastal cities (Chen 1923: 4–17).

The interactive effects of these and other social factors, rather than any single cause, explain much of the readiness to seek new livelihoods overseas. The significance of these economic and demographic factors as motivating forces for emigration were probably enhanced by the fact that, in the two provinces of Fukien and Kwangtung, early contact with Nanyang (the Southseas) had already established a tradition of seeking fortunes elsewhere. Comparing communities that had large emigrant populations with those that did not, Chen (1940) found that those who left were important to the economic development of their villages and provided a catalyst for attitudinal change. The example of the successful migrant was an important factor in the migration equation.

Internationally, probably the most significant trigger for the development of the coolie trade was the end of slavery, which threatened the plantation economies and the colonial infrastructure of the European powers with collapse. The labour-intensive plantations and mining developments were important to the economies of both the colonies and the home country. And the Chinese coolie, as a surrogate slave, became an important economic resource. Unlike the subsistence agriculture of the native economies, organized plantation production, the exploitation of mines, and the development of transport and communications through rail and roads, required large quantities of labour to be focused on a major activity. The social organization of the tight-knit Chinese coolie labour gang was made to order for the colonies.

Despite the migratory impulses, however, countervailing and contradictory social and psychological elements made the development of the coolie trade a paradox. Although local factors promoted migration, not every individual, village or city was similarly affected. Some accepted the idea of indentured labour and were prepared to face the unknown, while others preferred to suffer where they were. The tradition of ancestral worship and the need to maintain familial links were also important disincentives (Chan 1991: 23–8). In fact there was so much social and cultural resistance to migration that the coolie brokers had to resort to force to obtain sufficient labour.

Contradictory expectations also operated at the national level. Imperial edicts and strict policies forbade migration over two dynasties, but these were disregarded by local officials and citizens alike when convenient. The exploitative aspects of the trade were well known after the first waves of coolie recruitment, yet many Chinese willingly participated in it, especially in the later decades. Despite having experienced the exploitation and discrimination themselves, receiving communities often acted as middlemen to the host society. Although the economics of the coolie trade comprised a compelling factor, the participation of Chinese nationals in China and abroad in the development of the trade was a paradox in many ways.

The end of the trade also contradicted its beginning. The very same cultural attributes and attitudes towards work and sacrifice that made coolies an attractive resource, also made them a threat. The paradox was that the very advantage of a hardworking Chinese labour force became a disadvantage when its members entered the open market. And this partly accounted for the resistance to further entry of indentured labour and migrants.

These contrary processes and outcomes should be borne in mind in trying to understand the evolution and termination of the trade, as well as its characteristics. At the micro level of individuals and families and the macro levels of national policies and international diplomacy, the motivating factors were often in conflict with each other and seemingly irresolvable. The voluntary and involuntary movement of Chinese coolies was a complicated sociological phenomenon.

Development of the coolie trade

Recruitment into the coolie trade consisted of several parallel forms of labour exchange arrangements. The induction of coolies into the system was through a contractual agreement, an indenture. The period of service and the form of labour would be agreed upon, even though the indenture was not formalized in any documentary form in the earlier phases. The coolie agent covered all the costs involved on behalf of the coolie who would be committed to a fixed term of labour. A second form of the trade was the credit-ticket system. The cost of the passage was advanced to the coolie by brokers acting as agents for large European trading houses, or for coolie ships recruiting on contract to planters and others. Repayment was through earnings and/or labour for a fixed period. Repayment through earnings gave the coolie more control over the period during which he provided his labour. The line between this and contract labour was, however, often blurred. A third form of migration was as free-migrants who paid their own way. Although a number did pay their own way, this was often another form of the credit-ticket system, the difference being that the sponsors might be kinfolk or clan associates. In all cases, the coolie was committing several years of labour to the arrangement (see Wang 1978: 39–118 for a comparison).

The trade would have been quite innocuous in the form in which it was first conceived. The problem lay in the high demand for labour. Given the high profits possible, Chinese brokers working with coolie agents resorted to illegal means to fill their quotas. Many 'coolies' did not intend to become indentured labourers, but were deceived or forced into the system. Many were kidnapped and sold into bondage to repay debts. Others were simply captives from Triad wars or victims of rigged gaming halls. Given the amount of fraud, force and fear generated by such activities and the need to maintain a hold over the recruits (whatever the means of induction), abuse and violence became necessary means of control. The treatment of coolies was comparable to that of slaves in earlier decades and mutinies were common in the barracoons (coolie stockades) and on board ship, justifying further repressive actions (Wang 1978; Yen 1985).

The socio-cultural and political situation in China at the inception of the coolie trade accounts for much of the imperial court's failure to pay attention to what was in effect western imperialism at its worst. Migration had been forbidden on pain of death since the early Ming dynasty. Migrants were considered unfilial and were treated as fugitives and traitors. The negative view of Chinese traders stems from this socio-political frame of reference. Instead of being regarded as potential contributors to the nation's wealth and prestige, as in the case of their European counterparts, Chinese traders were persecuted. Those who left China were not treated sympathetically and even less so the coolies. Being at the bottom of the social stratification ladder they were easily ignored or dismissed.

To understand why the coolie trade developed to the extent that it did, given such a negative attitude to migration, it is necessary to look at the forces overwhelming China during this period. Using the available data, Wang (1978: 11) estimated the total number of migrants in this era at about 2.35 million. That the trade lasted so long suggests there was a failure to appreciate the impact of new international realities. The approach of the court was to contain the western intrusion in selected treaty ports and to assign responsibility for keeping it in check to the officials. The structure provided a buffer for the court, but the realities of the trade were also kept from it by layers of bureaucracy. One of the consequences of this failure to meet the demands and challenges at the centre was that two decades passed before the issues were seriously addressed. This was a manifestation of xenophobia, if not an implied snub of the western powers. The court seemed more interested in maintaining the status quo than in coping with the social and political changes forced on China by the West.

With supply and demand factors operating in tandem to create the need for a cheap and viable labour force, all that was required was an opportunity to activate the process. After the Opium War the Treaty of Nanking (1842) gave the European powers extraterritorial rights in five treaty ports (Amoy, Canton, Foochow, Ningpo and Shanghai), but gave nothing to China in return. It provided the western powers with the infrastructure to develop the coolie trade. Taking advantage of their new freedom and influence in the treaty ports, the foreign merchants developed coolie agencies to meet the international demand. As they were not able to penetrate the hinterland easily they depended on Chinese coolie brokers. These brokers were mainly responsible for filling the quotas and their activities within the surrounds of the treaty ports caused much concern and consternation. Their Triad connections added a violent aspect to the organization of migration. The exploitation of Chinese labour was thus facilitated by dovetailing international needs with those of local power brokers.

Except for a conscientious few, Chinese officials in the ports were basically ineffective. Decentralization of authority gave them responsibility but insufficient military force to maintain control. Foreigners, and the Chinese in their employ, blatantly went against the anti-migration policy. Given the conflicting norms and the inability to hold the line, the officials often became part of the coolie network, either actively or through negligence or inattention.

The population in the coastal provinces of the treaty ports was another matter. With the support of the gentry and the Chinese traders who had much to lose from the increasing strength of the foreigners, they mounted demonstrations (sometimes violent) to publicize and prevent the illegal activities. Those officials who were concerned about the trade were able to use the popular unrest to curtail the worst of the activities of the agents and brokers (Irick 1982: 396). Peer pressure and the publicity generated by the populace also made it difficult for corrupt officials to be entirely unconcerned.

The most important aspect of the protests was that they were as much against foreigners as they were against the coolie trade. Racism was always just under the surface and what occurred should be characterized as racial riots. The violence and protests against the excesses of the coolie agencies were making inroads into the legitimate trade and constantly trying to force a solution to the issue. If colonial economic interest was a factor in promoting the coolie trade, the consequences of the trade were fast making an impact on the economics of the Chinese trade.

The provinces and ports that had to deal with the effects of the trade very quickly became conversant with its consequences and the difficulty of finding individual solutions at the regional level. However, the problem remained at the periphery because the court insisted on the reality of its anti-migration edicts and would not deal with the regional issues as a totality. Its definition of the problem as a strictly regional issue left it to the provincial officials to find a viable *modus vivendi* with the agents and coolies. By keeping to a normative system long shattered by reality, the court was forcing deviance on its citizens and officials. The coolie system that developed was, thus, a most unusual social phenomenon. The social organization for the recruitment and exploitation of coolies spanned many cultures and political systems. The social actors spanned the entire stratificational spectrum. This included diplomats on one end and criminals on the other; it integrated Chinese social organizational forms and western industrial expertise; it involved the corrupt as well as the moral and the religious; it involved individuals, families and communities from various cultural and racial groups in a network that functioned with unexpected efficiency. The one factor capable of keeping the diverse social actors integrated within such a confused mosaic of perceptions, attitudes and expectations, was money. It held together a system that should have been broken apart by its inherent conflicting forces.

Despite the protests, the coolie trade expanded greatly. Coolie ships left China in convoys and, in some cases, cargo was brought to its destination on a purely speculative basis (McNair 1924: 228). The economic gains from the coolie trade have been very well documented by Wang (1978: 74–87). The wealth and power to be gained made it that much easier to ignore the abuses found in all phases of the trade.

Contradictions of the coolie trade
In the final analysis, the coolie trade was conceived of, and conducted as, a commodity trade. There have been many comparisons with the slave trade of the earlier century and the conditions of shipment equated to those found on slave ships (Irick 1982: 201–33; McNair 1924: 209–10; Wang 1978: 165–255). When the trade is reduced to the lowest common denominator, humanity becomes a very insignificant aspect of the reality, and abuse a foregone conclusion.

Whatever the reason – racism, cultural indifference or tolerance of suffering – the ill-treatment of the coolies can only be explained by the owners' desire for a return on their investment in the shortest possible time. Given that replacements for losses seemed inexhaustible, the treatment of these 'living machines' (Yen 1985: 69) was dictated by the profit margin and coloured by strong racist undertones. The treatment of the coolies required justification and this, in turn, provided a foundation for many stereotypes and prejudices. The coolie trade, like slavery, engendered many of the stereotypes that were to make ethnic stratification and integration in the host societies so much more problematic in the following century.

The dilemma for the more humanitarian western powers such as Britain and the USA was that, while recognizing the extreme exploitation of the Chinese, they were caught up in the economic needs of their colonies. British Hong Kong, for example, needed foreign trade in order to develop. And, to realize their expectations, these powers also needed the coolie trade. Their colonies depended on coolies as much as did those of other European powers. On the other hand, their public stance on slavery made the slave-like trade in coolies an embarrassment.

The first twenty years of the coolie trade created a socio-political climate which pushed it into the next phase of its evolution. In many respects the contradictions of the trade created the new developments. The coolies' economic contribution made it necessary to import more of them. But, given the public outcry in Britain and Europe about the iniquities of the trade, a more humane means of obtaining cheap labour had to be developed. The need to balance public opinion against economic gain was now added to the negative reaction to the trade in the ports.

To defuse the situation the British and French proposed a new recruitment procedure – the canton system (Yen 1985: 87–98). Significantly, its implementation was supported by local officials and even the local gentry. A new socio-political system was evolving in the treaty ports which sought, consciously or unconsciously, to bypass the Ch'ing court. The centre was in danger of losing its control. Although the canton system worked quite well the emperor denounced it as illegal and issued edicts against it. Only when the allies entered Peking in 1860, threatening the emperor himself, was the Tsungli Yamen (Foreign Ministry) instructed to negotiate the terms for peace and also to deal with the demands on the coolie trade. It had taken twenty years for the court to become directly involved with the trade. It began a new era in China's foreign affairs and a new phase of the coolie trade. The negotiations were now being pursued in Peking instead of the provincial ports of embarkation, where the realities of the trade had long been recognized.

The negotiations preceding the Peking regulations sought to put right the troublesome issues related to the trade (Yen 1985: 103–14). The foreign powers held the key to the success of the regulations and their support was vital. Even with the best of motivations on their part, the Yamen faced difficulties in getting them to ratify the negotiated regulations. The delays were caused by the refusal of the colonies to accept the terms and conditions on which their negotiators had agreed. The power of the colonies was a factor even their home governments failed to recognize. A liberal ideology was still being deflected by the economic moment. It delayed the acceptance of the regulations by Britain and the other powers (except Spain and Portugal) for another thirteen years. The exclusion of Spain and Portugal from regulated migrations was, presumably, to underline the new framework of diplomatic negotiations and agreements. But it served only to give a stronger impetus to their illegal activities through Macau. Excluding key actors from the definition of the situation was unlikely to lead to a successful scheme for control. Imperial China had yet to learn consensus building. There were other lessons in the sociology of power that were missed by the Yamen. The West was not a monolithic block and it had not taken that into consideration. It failed to utilize the power and self-interest of the various countries to provide them with leverage in the negotiations. The resolution of the issue required the mediation and influence of five western powers (Britain, France, Germany, Russia and the USA). The Spanish finally agreed to a fact-finding trip by the Cuba Commission (which included British and French appointees) in 1874. The findings were a foregone conclusion but it gave China the leverage needed. Britain and the USA exerted pressure on the Portuguese to abolish the illegal trade in 1874. That they had to operate within the Peking regulations, while Macau did not, was probably an important consideration.

The Yamen had finally won recognition for the Chinese coolies. In the process, it established and emphasized the need for centralization of the dealings with the western powers. Until then, the coolies were regarded as nothing more than units of labour by the western powers and as a troublesome distraction by the court. The coolies were stateless entities, without a defender for their most basic rights. They were criminalized by the court's prohibitions against migration and marginalized by the host society's perception of them as purely economic animals. They were social and political nonentities at home and abroad. In fact McNair (1924: 146) notes that, in all the treaties signed during this era, there was never a clause that protected Chinese nationals. This is especially telling in a context where the rights of foreigners were protected by the concept of extra-territoriality.

In trying to come to terms with the coolie issue, the Ch'ing government was compelled to question its traditional policy towards overseas subjects and the issue of emigration in general (Yen 1985: 32). The protection of the coolies and migrants, which formed the main part of late Ch'ing policy towards its overseas subjects, was a major change. The new regulations, however, focused only on contract coolie labour and excluded the so-called 'free emigrants' who were migrating without registering at the emigration houses. The Yamen considered these migrants undeserving of protection because they were not within the government-sponsored programme. In this, the old prohibitive edicts were still haunting the policies of the day. Although attitudes did change, the Yamen was still constrained by tradition.

The change that did occur may have been accelerated by a recognition of the accomplishments of the migrants themselves. Increasingly, their contribution

to China's economy was being felt (Chen 1940). It was now conceivable that they could be the vanguard of the modernization of China. The idea of imitating the West by supporting commercialism was being championed by a new group of officials who saw the potential of the overseas Chinese in this new light. The approach taken by China was now more integrated and coherent than when the coolie trade first started. The socialization process was, however, not without cost. In trying to explain the Ch'ing court's slow start in the defence of Chinese migrants, Irick (1982: 414) suggested that 'the Chinese were not so much unaware of what should be done as they were painfully aware of what could not be done'. Within the context of western imperialism the coolies were pawns who may have been sacrificed to keep the powers at bay.

In 1893, the prohibitive edicts that criminalized those who ventured abroad were finally repealed by the imperial court. But, by that time, the coolie trade was a lesser aspect of migratory labour for the Chinese. It did, however, serve to promote trade and other opportunities that were opening up based on the foundations created by the coolie and free migrant communities.

The end of the coolie era

Coolies who left China did not see themselves as permanent migrants. They had committed themselves to working for a limited period of time and transiency was an important factor in their calculations. Because they saw indenture as temporary, they were willing to undergo many of the hardships they had to face under the system. They accepted the discomforts of the frontier and the meanness of the cities because they were making relatively good wages compared with starvation in China. Indentured labour was a most dramatic example of deferred gratification.

The early Chinatowns were the solution to the need for social organization by a semi-transient community (Lee 1960: 52–68; McNair 1924: 304–5; Tsai 1986: 33–45). And they served the migrants by providing them with the social form and function of the communities they had given up. The crucial social psychological factor was then the acceptance of the fact of settlement. Once this was part of the cognitive map, a migrant became a new socio-economic and political entity – a settled migrant.

A more stable community and inroads into the regular economy resulted in new economic relationships between the Chinese communities and their hosts. The new developments were met with resistance. When the coolies had made their contributions towards building the infrastructures of the colonies (by developing their railways, mines, plantations and hinterlands) and had become a factor in the free labour market, the exclusionary acts quickly came into force to prevent further migrations. Cheap labour was no longer needed and the anti-Chinese movement frequently took on violent forms. The earlier waves of migrants from Europe organized to protect their interests and the classic conflict between new and older waves of migrants became the new context for interracial relations.

The Chinese communities were not, initially, politically organized to resist the challenges mounted by the labour unions and exclusionary organizations (Yen 1985: 210). They were not socially integrated into the host communities and only unwillingly so at the economic level. The social insulation provided by the community meant also that they had few opportunities to become part of the social and political life of the host society. Local politics were unimportant because migrants never expected to stay long enough for them to matter. In order to protect the communities that developed they had to learn to work within the political structures of their host societies. Within this context, the coolie trade limped on into the early twentieth century. The end of the coolie era was a passing which was probably noted only by a few, and even fewer viewed its passing with regret.

References

Campbell, P. C. (1923) *Chinese Coolie Emigration*, London: P. S. King & Son

Chan, K. B. (1991) *Smoke and Fire: The Chinese in Montreal*, Hong Kong: The Chinese University of Hong Kong

Chen, Ta (1923) *Chinese Migrations With Special Reference to Labor Conditions*, Washington: Government Printing Office

—— (1940) *Emigrant Communities in South China*, New York: Institute of Pacific Relations

Irick, R. L. (1982) *Ch'ing Policy Toward the Coolie Trade 1847–1878*, China: Chinese Materials Centre

Lee, R. H. (1960) *The Chinese in the United States of America*, Hong Kong: Hong Kong University Press

McNair, H. F. (1924) *The Chinese Abroad*, China: The Commercial Press

Tsai, S. H. (1986) *The Chinese Experience in America*, Bloomington: Indiana University Press

Wang, S. W. (1978) *The Organization of Chinese Emigration 1848–1888*, China: Chinese Materials Centre

Yen, C. H. (1985) *Coolies and Mandarins*, Singapore: Singapore University Press

INDIAN INDENTURED MIGRATION
TO THE CARIBBEAN

STEVEN VERTOVEC

The abolition of slavery and the emancipation of the slave population marked a turning point in the history of the West Indies. The British government passed the Act of Emancipation in 1833 and declared it law in the following year, freeing a slave population of around 665,000 in the British Caribbean (Higman 1984). In the years to follow, slavery was similarly abolished in the French (1848), Danish (1848) and Dutch (1863) Caribbean. The regional economy – which, in turn, held a key position in each respective imperial political economy – centred on labour-intensive plantation agriculture, especially devoted to the production of sugar. While the emancipation of slaves was brought about by growing humanitarian and liberal sentiments in Europe, in the tropics it caused an immediate crisis among planters. They perceived their success as hinged upon a kind of critical ratio between abundant land and cheap labour (Saunders 1984), a ratio which slavery had served and which, after abolition, they felt needed replacement by 'a new system of slavery' (Tinker 1974).

Initially, the planters feared that the African ex-slaves would flee to the hinterlands, leaving the plantations without a labour force. For a time, planters attempted to keep the ex-slaves labouring on estates through many means, including offers of huts, provision grounds and wages. But high rents, a restricted economy and planters' unchanged attitudes towards the ex-slaves ensured that a post-emancipation movement of Africans away from estates indeed occurred – which was not a flight from the horrors of slavery, but 'a protest against the inequalities of early "freedom"' (Hall 1978: 23).

After abolition, sugar production dramatically decreased and the market value of West Indian estates declined. Caribbean planters argued that a labour shortage was at the heart of the problem. Various immigration schemes were soon initiated in parts of the British Caribbean, including the introduction of African peoples liberated from other nations' slave ships, brought directly from the African continent or from other Caribbean islands. Portuguese, Madeirans and Chinese were also induced to immigrate to West Indian plantations. The influx of such peoples added considerable heterogeneity to already multicultural colonial societies. But for various reasons, none of these groups were found to be suitable by planters, who demanded a wholly controllable, extremely cheap workforce that was used to agricultural labour.

Indian migration and indenture

From the 1820s, sugar planters in Réunion and Mauritius had experienced some success in importing labourers from India. Learning of such success, John Gladstone, a planter in British Guiana (and father of the famous British statesman) wrote to the firm of Gillanders, Arbuthnot & Co. in Calcutta – which had recruited and shipped labourers to Mauritius – in order to enquire as to the possibility of similarly obtaining labourers for the Caribbean. The firm replied, 'We are not aware that any greater difficulty would present itself in sending men to the West Indies, the natives being perfectly ignorant of the place they go to or the length of the voyage they are undertaking' (in Tinker 1974: 63). To arrange for such, numerous legislative and administrative measures were subsequently taken in Britain, India and the Caribbean colonies. These measures were closely overseen and occasionally modified over the next eighty years (Erickson 1930, 1934; Tinker 1974).

In 1838, British Guiana was the first Caribbean territory to receive indentured Indians; several other Caribbean colonies began importing Indian labour in following years (Table 3. 1). Between 1838 and 1917, more than half a million Indians were brought to the Caribbean. Throughout this period, shipment to various colonies often temporarily ceased following evidence of abuses involving labourers' recruitment in India, their transport and their treatment on overseas estates (Protector of Emigrants 1875–1918). Accounts of Indian migration to the Danish colony of St Croix, for example, were so harsh that the government of India cancelled its permission to obtain labourers after only a single shipment. The system of indentured

PLATE 2: Indian children at breakfast on board a 'coolie ship' bound for the Caribbean, some time between 1900 and 1914.

Table 3.1: *Indentured Indian migration to the Caribbean*

Colony	Period	Immigrants
British Guiana	1838–1917	238,909
Trinidad	1845–1917	143,939
Guadeloupe	1854–1889	42,326
Jamaica	1854–1885	36,420
Dutch Guiana	1873–1916	34,304
Martinique	1854–1889	25,509
French Guiana	1856–1877	6,551
St Lucia	1858–1895	4,354
Grenada	1857–1885	3,200
St Vincent	1860–1880	2,472
St Kitts	1860–1865	337
St Croix	1862	321
Total		538,642

Sources: Roberts and Byrne (1966); Singaravelou (1990); Tinker (1974)

migration was brought to a halt mainly through pressures in India by middle-class and nascent nationalist Indians (Emmer 1986; Tinker 1974).

The considerable expense of recruiting and shipping labourers from India to the British West Indies was originally met in its entirety by local colonial governments; over subsequent years, however, planters were required to pay an increasing share of these costs. Under licence from the Protector of Emigrants in Calcutta or Madras, emigration agencies sought recruits throughout the Indian countryside. Although many Indians in the Caribbean today believe their forebears were tricked into leaving India, the historical record surrounding bureaucratic processes in Calcutta shows little evidence of fraud, deception or kidnapping ever being widely used to gain indentured migrants (Erickson 1930; Emmer 1986). However, the Sanderson Committee reported to the British parliament that many Indian emigrants did not fully understand all of the implications of indentureship and migration (BPP 1910).

So-called 'push factors' probably had more to do with migrants' decisions to indenture themselves abroad than did 'pull' factors of promised opportunities. In the second half of the nineteenth century, throughout India peasants faced famines and a massive disruption to livelihoods with the demise of traditional industries, relocated local economies, new demands of cash payments for upwardly spiralling rents, a high incidence of evictions, and widespread unemployment (Vertovec 1992). Indentured migration represented only a small part of consequent total labour migration flows within the subcontinent.

The wide range of indentured emigrants' geographic origins was mainly a function of recruiters' ever-broader excursions, from urban peripheries and tribal areas in the early years of the system to rural hinterlands in later decades. Although migrants originally came from both north-east and southern India, emigration through Madras to the British Caribbean ceased between 1861 and 1906 – largely due to a variety of planters' prejudices against southern Indians (de Verteuil 1990; Mangru 1983). The bulk of Indian migrants to the British and Dutch colonies came from what is now western Bihar and eastern Uttar Pradesh (Vertovec 1994). The great majority of Indians who migrated to the French colonies were Tamil-speaking south Indians (Singaravelou 1990). Regardless of geographic origins, migrants were drawn from a wide variety of social, religious and caste backgrounds. Most were aged in their twenties, with an average sex ratio of three males to one female.

The voyage from Calcutta to the Caribbean took three to four months (reduced to six weeks by the turn of the century) on ships carrying between 270 and 510 migrants. Cholera was the 'terror of the Indian coolie trade', dysentery was rife, sanitation was inadequate, and the sailing was perilous, especially around the Cape of Good Hope. Mortality on board ship was high – up to 18 per cent – including numerous suicides.

Indenture contracts agreed upon by Indian migrants to the Caribbean involved a five-year period of indenture with provision of return passage, free housing, medical attention and standard rations, in return for work of around nine hours per day, six days per week. Certain aspects of such contracts varied in minor ways between colonies and changed only slightly throughout the period of indentured migration (Protector of Emigrants 1875–1918). However, other aspects differed considerably such as rates of pay – from as little as 1*s*. 6*d*. per week in 1860s' Jamaica to 6*s*. 3*d*. in 1880s' British Guiana (Tinker 1974: 185). There was great disparity in arrangements for return passage, too. In Surinam, for instance, migrants were entitled to free return passage immediately upon expiration of their five-year indenture contracts (Emmer 1984). For most of the period of indentured migration to Trinidad, the government paid all return transport costs for labourers after they had worked an additional five years in the colony following expiration of their contracts. But by 1898, males were required to pay half the cost of return passage, females one-third of the cost (Brereton 1981; Wood 1968).

Plantation life and labour

Caribbean plantation estates were austere, and the lifestyle was highly regimented. The labourers were housed in lines of wooden barracks, which were in fact the previous slaves' quarters. Sometimes labourers were allowed to cultivate a small patch of ground or to keep a cow or pig; but despite this and the rationing of food, vitamin deficiency plagued the estates, as did malaria and hookworm. The absence of latrines was perhaps the worst defect of estate conditions, along with leaky roofs, bad ventilation and poor drainage. Colonial authorities, however, often justified the poor environment of estate Indians by claiming that 'the general condition of the dwellings and their surroundings was much more sanitary than that of the houses in an ordinary Indian village' (MacNeill and Lal 1914, Part I: 4). Inspectors under the Protector of Immigrants were expected to visit each estate at least once in every six weeks, and owners were required to have regular times when labourers could voice their grievances. Estates with excessive mortality (over 7 per cent) or those found to be mistreating workers could be penalized or have further shipments

of indentured Indians denied. However, as Tinker (1974: 178) notes: 'The watch-dogs – the Protectors and the Magistrates – supposedly set by the government to ensure that the harsh laws were not exceeded, were in most cases themselves involved in the system: they identified with the interests of the planters, not with those of a benevolent government, still less those of the coolies.'

By law Indian workers were confined to estates, where discipline was maintained by whips and stocks. Sporadic and spontaneous protests and strikes still took place, however.

The work performed by Indians on sugar plantations varied according to sex, age, ability and experience. The primary tasks of forking and cutting cane dominated the labour of men, who were organized into gangs under a driver or overseer (often an Indian himself). Women concentrated on weeding, while young boys were expected to tend livestock. The most skilled estate workers were in the sugar mill. Heavy labour, such as trenching and hill banking, was given to African workers, many of whom still lived on estates in quarters separate from the Indians. Indians, indentured and unindentured, also served estates as carpenters, stockkeepers, grooms and watchmen.

Indian labour stimulated a major upswing in the British West Indies sugar trade. The period 1865–84 was an unprecedented period of prosperity for West Indian sugar, facilitated not only by cheap labour, but by increased overseas consumption, low duties and high prices, and the introduction of new technologies (Beachey 1957). Yet the 1880s saw a rapid demise of West Indian cane sugar, due primarily to a boom in European beet sugar production. The price of West Indian cane sugar consequently plummeted. This meant the failing of many plantations, or the amalgamation of estates and their concentration in the hands of a few individuals or firms. Given the drastic constriction of the sugar industry, there was little question of a labour shortage. In addition to the local African part-time labourers and the estate Indian labour force, steamship services within the Caribbean carried large numbers of immigrants between colonies. Still, Caribbean planters continued to press the colonial authorities for more and more indentured Indian immigrants. Their primary motivation was to suppress agricultural wages; as long as there was an indentured labour force, free labour could make no demands on the plantocracy. While indentured labourers continued to arrive from India, migrants who had finished their contracts tended to remain in the Caribbean.

Post-indenture settlement

On average, no more than a quarter of the Indian immigrants to the Caribbean returned to India (Roberts and Byrne 1966). The vast majority who chose to remain in the Caribbean did so for a combination of reasons: work was virtually guaranteed and opportunities for gaining land were usually opening up, while conditions back in India were known to be dire and unpredictable; many migrants disliked the idea of returning to an ascribed low position in the traditional caste hierarchy, whereas overseas social position could be more readily achieved; and many who did return to India for a time found that they had lost their family, were rejected by their villages or were regarded as exceptionally polluted because they had crossed the ocean, lived with inferior castes or disregarded caste restrictions while abroad. Of those who did return to India, some took substantial savings; others who found resettling in India too difficult subsequently re-indentured themselves once again as migrant labourers abroad.

In order to keep seasoned, ex-indentured labourers on their estates, owners had long offered land or cash to Indians whose indenture contracts had finished. Many free Indians soon realized they could sell their labour at higher prices elsewhere, such as on cocoa plantations. Others gradually took up occupations as grass sellers, pedlars and shopkeepers. Yet the greatest number continued to work, part-time at least, on the familiar sugar estates. As early as the 1860s, the free Indian population had spilled over to areas outside established plantations. Together with Africans and Venezuelans, they squatted on Crown lands in adjacent areas. By the turn of the century in Trinidad and British Guiana, ex-indentured labourers far outnumbered those still under contract. Seeing the opportunity to save the government transport costs, relieve the squatter situation, settle undeveloped land and provide the burgeoning Indian community with some stability, colonial governments offered many ex-indentured Indians grants of Crown lands in lieu of their return passage to India. Indians became independent farmers themselves, and were soon the largest producers of sugar cane in the larger territories as well as almost exclusively the producers of rice. Thus Indians gained the key positions in southern Caribbean agricultural sectors that they still maintain today.

From the time of their introduction to the region, Indians had a generally rather uneasy relationship with whites, who looked upon them as a 'heathen' population, and with Africans, who often regarded them as a kind of 'scab' labour force (Brereton 1979; Moore 1970; Shepherd 1988). In Trinidad, British Guiana (Guyana) and Surinam, ethnic tensions eventually manifested in political confrontations in the wake of decolonization (see, for instance, Dew 1978; Hintzen 1989). In social and cultural spheres, many kinds of modification and change have affected traditional Indian forms and practices over their 150-year presence (Vertovec 1992, 1994), yet these remain a notable feature of numerous, complex Caribbean societies today.

References

BPP (British Parliamentary Papers) (1910) 'Report of the Committee on Emigration from India to the Crown Colonies and Protectorates' (a.k.a. the Sanderson Report) XXVII (c. 5194)

Beachey, R. W. (1957) *The British West Indies Sugar Industry in the Late 19th Century*, Oxford: Blackwell

Brereton, B. (1979) *Race Relations in Colonial Trinidad, 1870–1900*, Cambridge: Cambridge University Press

— (1981) *A History of Modern Trinidad 1783–1962*, London: Heinemann

de Verteuil, A. (1990) 'Madrasi Emigration to Trinidad, 1846–1916', paper to the 22nd Annual Conference of the Association of Caribbean Historians, St Augustine, Trinidad

Dew, E. (1978) *The Difficult Flowering of Surinam*, The Hague: Martinus Nijhoff

Emmer, P. C. (1984) 'The Importation of British Indians into Surinam (Dutch Guiana), 1873–1916', in S. Marks and P. Richardson (eds) *International Labour Migration*, London: Temple Smith, 90–111

— (1986) 'The Meek Hindu: The Recruitment of Indian Indentured Labourers for Service Overseas, 1870–1916', in P. C. Emmer (ed.) *Colonialism and Migration: Indentured Labour Before and After Slavery*, Dordrecht: Martinus Nijhoff, 187–207

Erickson, E. (1930) 'East Indian Coolies in the West Indies 1838–1870', unpublished Ph.D. dissertation, University of Wisconsin

— (1934) 'The Introduction of East Indian Coolies into the British West Indies', *Journal of Modern History*, 6: 127–46

Hall, D. (1978) 'The Flight from the Estates Reconsidered: The British West Indies, 1838–42', *Journal of Caribbean History*, 10 (11), 7–24

Higman, B. W. (1984) *Slave Population of the British Caribbean 1807–1834*, Baltimore: Johns Hopkins University Press

Hintzen, P. (1989) *The Costs of Regime Survival: Racial Mobilization, Elite Domination and Control of the State in Guyana and Trinidad*, Cambridge: Cambridge University Press

MacNeill, J. and C. Lal (1914) *Report on the Condition of Indian Immigrants in the Four British Colonies: Trinidad, British Guiana or Demerara, Jamaica and Fiji, and in the Dutch Colony of Surinam or Dutch Guiana*, Simla: Government Central Press

Mangru, B. (1983) 'Disparity in Bengal and Madras Emigration to British Guiana in the Nineteenth Century', *Revista Interamericana*, 13, 99–107

Moore, R. J. (1970) 'East Indians and Negroes in British Guiana 1838–1880', D.Phil. thesis, University of Sussex

Protector of Emigrants, Government of Bengal (1875–1918) *Annual Report[s] on Emigration to British and Foreign Colonies from the Port of Calcutta*, Calcutta: Bengal Secretariat

Roberts, G. W. and J. Byrne (1966) 'Summary Statistics on Indenture and Associated Migration affecting the West Indies, 1834–1918', *Population Studies*, 20, 125–34

Saunders, K. (ed.) (1984) *Indentured Labour in the British Empire 1834–1920*, London: Croom Helm

Shepherd, V. (1988) 'Indians and Blacks in Jamaica in the Nineteenth and Early Twentieth Centuries: A Micro-Study of the Foundation of Race Antagonisms', *Immigrants and Minorities*, 7, 95–112

Singaravelou (1990) 'Indians in the French Overseas Departements: Guadeloupe, Martinique, Réunion', in C. Clarke et al. (eds) *South Asians Overseas: Migration and Ethnicity*, Cambridge: Cambridge University Press, 75–87

Tinker, H. (1974) *A New System of Slavery: The Export of Indian Labour Overseas 1830–1920*, London: Oxford University Press

Vertovec, S. (1992) *Hindu Trinidad: Religion, Ethnicity and Socio–Economic Change*, London: Macmillan

—— (1994) '"Official" and "Popular" Hinduism in the Diaspora: Historical and Contemporary Trends in Surinam, Trinidad and Guyana', *Contributions to Indian Sociology*, 28 (1)

Wood, D. (1968) *Trinidad in Transition: The Years after Slavery*, London: Oxford University Press

INDIAN INDENTURED WORKERS IN MAURITIUS, NATAL AND FIJI

RAVINDER K. THIARA

Indentured migration to Mauritius, Natal and Fiji, the focus of this paper, was part of a global process of labour migration from India which began after the abolition of slavery. During this period, the demand for a cheap, unskilled and pliant labour force in colonies primarily engaged in sugar production was heightened and, as noted by Vertovec elsewhere in this volume, indentured labour from India significantly filled this labour vacuum in numerous colonial settlements. During the eighty years of its existence, the system of indenture, which formally survived from 1830 to 1916, was responsible for the transportation of over one million Indians who provided the necessary cheap labour required for the global development of British capitalism (Tinker 1974). Indeed, the sale of southern Indian slaves by the Dutch in the latter part of the eighteenth century to French planters in Mauritius and Réunion was a precursor of indenture; in 1800 there were an estimated 6000 Indian slaves in the Mauritian estates while thousands were enslaved in Réunion (Tinker 1974). Later, Mauritius, having partly solved its labour shortage through the importation of Indians in the early nineteenth century, set a precedent which led to the formalization of the indenture system. Thereafter, indentured labour was crucial both in facilitating the expansion of local colonial economies by cutting labour costs and in the global process of capital accumulation, until the early twentieth century. The experience and fate of indentured Indians, however, were determined by the local economic and political conditions prevalent in each colony.

A historical assessment of the conditions prevailing in India during British rule reveals a crucial connection between British expansionism and the international commoditization of Indian labour (Thiara 1994). The transportation *en masse* of Indians through the indenture system was a direct consequence of British penetration into the entire economic and social fabric of Indian society. The introduction of landlordism, excessive revenue demands, commercialization of agriculture, change in rent in kind to cash, decline of indigenous handicrafts, discriminatory taxation on Indian goods, and persistent famines and pestilence were among the many reasons for migration, which offered the only avenue of hope to many. While all sectors of Indian society were affected by these profound changes, the lower agricultural classes, who predominated among the recruits, were the worst affected.

During the period 1834–1910, over half a million indentured migrants entered Mauritius; in Natal, 152,189 arrived between 1860 and 1911; while a total of 60,965 Indians landed in Fiji between 1879 and 1916 (Gillion 1962). Unlike Natal, the majority of the Fiji labourers originated from the United Provinces, Bihar and Central Provinces; 75 per cent of the total number of recruits boarded from Calcutta and, after 1903, 25 per cent left from Madras (Lal 1984). Of those transported to Natal, two-thirds embarked from Madras and a third from Calcutta; nearly 60 per cent of the Tamil-speaking migrants came from three districts in Madras, North and South Arcot, and Chingleput (Beall 1982). Compared with other colonies, the average age of the Fiji migrants was low; 42 per cent of the men and 45 per cent of the women were under 20, the remainder being under 30 (Tinker 1974). In all three colonies, numerous experiments with labour were tried before indentured Indians were secured. Recruits were predominantly male (a ratio of 3.3:1 for Mauritius and 2.2:1 for Natal), until problems caused by the unequal sex ratio were highlighted and efforts made to enforce a ratio of 40 women for every 100 men (Tinker 1974). Unprohibited by caste, religious and dietary restrictions, Dhangars (hill people) from Chota Nagpur predominated among those initially recruited until increased demand for labour in India together with a high death rate among them during the voyage led to a decrease in their number in the 1850s (Tinker 1974). Thereafter, the majority of recruits were 'simple country folk who had been attracted to the big city in search of casual work', many others were unemployed cooks, footmen, washermen, grooms and entertainers (Tinker 1974: 51). Calcutta remained the main 'coolie catchment' centre and port of embarkation until 1870 after which the recruiters cast their net towards the United Provinces and Bihar. Increased demand for labour also resulted in the resumption of migration from Madras and Bombay in the 1840s (Tinker 1974). Often colonies expressed a preference for recruits from particular geographical areas of India, as illustrated by the Caribbean, where a prejudice existed against workers from south India (Tinker 1974). After 1880, the flow of indentured labour migration was deflected away from Mauritius, which by 1871 had an Indian population of 216,258 compared with 99,784 Creoles, constituting approximately 70 per cent of the population, a figure which has remained constant thereafter (Tinker 1974). After 1880, the scale of migration became smaller and was mainly directed towards Natal and the Caribbean. Migration to Fiji became significant only in the twentieth century and, while it was small in scale, the Indian population equalled the indigenous Fijians.

While labour in the colonies of the Pacific and Indian oceans was also required for construction work, it was predominantly engaged in agricultural production. In Mauritius, sugar production began in the 1790s and rapid expansion was maintained after the British conquest as further links were facilitated by British merchant capitalists (Hazareesingh 1975). With an economy heavily reliant on sugar monoculture for export where plantation agricultural production was crucial, Mauritius was the first colony to receive indentured Indians in 1834. By 1838, around 25,000 Indians, halving the cost of slaves, had arrived in Mauritius (Tinker 1974). Unlike the Caribbean, foreign capital played a less vital role in the sugar industry of Mauritius, where ownership by colonial families was pronounced and absentee ownership rare. The plantocracy's monopoly of access to the colonial state, which acted as its instrument, was ensured by a narrow franchise; colonial officials were often tied to sugar plantations either through marriage or investment. Given that the sugar industry was the main generator of public finances, its continued prosperity was vital and the colonial state maintained conditions for profitable sugar production, primarily by guaranteeing a cheap and docile labour supply. Aided by Indian labour, after a brief depression immediately following abolition, sugar production expanded rapidly, rising from an annual average of 36,000 short tons during apprenticeship to 136,000 in the early 1860s (North-Coombes 1990). Technical advances, the centralization of sugar milling, an expansion of the cane growing area achieved by Indian labourers and a restructuring of the labour

force were factors responsible for this expansion. Plantations became the dominant form of enterprise in Mauritius and in 1913, 94 per cent of cultivated acreage was committed to sugar cane, up to 98 per cent of which was exported (North-Coombes 1990). From the 1860s to 1914, for instance, Mauritius sugar exports were directed towards the Indian market. Consequently, consumer items required on the island were imported including rice, dhal and salt fish, the staple plantation diet.

In Natal, sugar production, which began in 1852 with the assistance of experienced planters and Indian workers from Mauritius, was smaller in scale and the sugar industry, marked by lack of capital and technological backwardness, was limited in its significance (Brain 1985). While Natal planters had political influence, they received little help from the colonial state, lacking the political leverage enjoyed by Mauritian planters. Less reliant on plantation production and monoculture, Natal was marked by greater diversity in agricultural production, with mining and the urban sector also being crucial to the economy. Containing a greater extent of natural and human resources, Natal had more potential for economic growth and structural change than Mauritius. This later facilitated greater diversification and a higher rate of Indian urbanization. With the assistance of indentured labour, as in Mauritius, production also doubled in Natal from 1860 to 1864 and again from 1890 to 1894 (North-Coombes 1990).

In Fiji, annexation of the islands by Britain in 1874, together with changing policies by the imperial government and general economic difficulties, led to the promotion of plantation agriculture. Sir Arthur Hamilton Gordon, Fiji's first governor, invited the Australian Colonial Sugar Refining Company (CSR), which predominated until the 1970s, to extend its activities to Fiji; all that remained thereafter was to secure a supply of cheap labour (Lal 1984). After numerous experiments with labour from the Pacific islands, Gordon turned to the reservoir of labour in India.

Conditions and life under indenture

While Act V of 1837 laid out specific conditions for the regulation of emigration, in reality conditions varied greatly and were frequently modified throughout the life of the system (Tinker 1974). Legislation passed in Mauritius acted as a model for Natal and Fiji where, for instance, five-year contracts were the norm from the beginning. Although the sale of their labour away from the homeland was a reality for many Indians, under indenture this assumed rather

PLATE 3: Sugar was the normal commodity harvested by Indian indentured workers outside Ceylon, but here Indian women are harvesting Golden Pekoe tea at a plantation in Kearsney, about 80 km north of Durban, Natal, c. 1900.

different dimensions. Recruiters and their *arkatis*, who exploited local knowledge and contacts, provided to the vulnerable embellished tales of opportunities waiting to be exploited. Forced banishments, kidnapping and deception were an entrenched part of the indenture system (Tinker 1974).

A common assumption made by colonial officials and later writers is that indentured migrants consisted of the lowest and least desirable elements of the Indian population. In reality, migrants represented a cross-section of the population, as reflected in the recruits for Mauritius, Natal and Fiji. In the latter, 34.8 per cent were from middle castes, 26.2 per cent from lower castes, while 3.7 per cent were from high castes, with the remainder being made up of a range of higher castes (Lal 1984). Given the need to fill their quotas, recruiting agents often failed to check the migrants' backgrounds. For instance in 1891/2, workers dispatched to Natal included travellers, weavers, shopkeepers, palaquin bearers, beggars and policemen, all of whom were generally unsuited to unskilled agricultural labour (Tinker 1974). Rather than being an avenue of opportunity, for the majority of Indians indenture was an 'exile into bondage' as 'many found they had exchanged one form of poverty

and servitude for another, and many more found only death and disease' (Tinker 1974: 60).

Traditional barriers of caste, religion and language were eroded during the traumatic journey, which to Fiji could take up to three months, and to Natal and Mauritius twelve weeks and ten weeks respectively (Tinker 1974). Unlike those of Natal and Mauritius, the Fiji planters showed little enthusiasm for Indian labourers, the majority of whom were initially employed by the government. Like the Africans in Natal, the indigenous Fijians had little say in the introduction of Indian labour; in both colonies this was to have a profound effect on future inter-group relations.

The cost of transporting workers was met, in the main, by employers in Natal and Fiji, while planters in Mauritius paid a quarter of the costs. The colonial authorities regulated the recruitment, importation, allocation and employment of labour; control over the repressive apparatus, like the courts, police and prisons, all of which acted to repress workers, was also in their hands. Despite regional variation, it is possible to build up a general picture of plantation life, which remained unchanged from the days of slavery. Indenture, like slavery, was premised on an elaborate

PLATE 4: Indian women trenching and planting sugar cane in Natal, c. 1900.

system of coercion which restricted the free movement of labourers outside the estates; it not only regulated their labour power but isolated them on plantations. Many formal and informal systems of control were used not only to confine workers on the estates but also in indenture (Swan 1990). In Natal and Mauritius, an annual tax (£3 and £2 18s. respectively) was introduced to force workers to reindenture; vagrancy laws and licences were further imposed to restrict worker mobility outside the plantation and to reduce the alternatives available upon termination of contracts (North-Coombes 1990).

While the stipulated conditions of work, pay, housing and medical facilities were similar for all the colonies, in reality their interpretation was left to the discretion of the employers, overseers and managers. The everyday reality for workers was marked by grinding overwork, low wages, malnutrition, persistent illness, and poor housing, social and medical facilities, as well as a range of punitive measures, including beatings, fines and imprisonment. Little attention was paid to their mental and emotional needs since workers were viewed as little more than vehicles of labour.

The official apparatus functioned in the interests of employers rather than to protect workers; in 1849 and 1862 in Mauritius, it acted on the planters' behalf by reducing wages through lengthening contracts from one to three and then to five years, thus effectively reducing worker choice (North-Coombes 1990). Conditions of contracts were also harshly enforced

through labour-coercive techniques (Swan 1985) as illustrated by Mauritius, where workers could be gaoled for up to six months for desertion, neglect of work and indolence, and where refusal to obey an order could result in the loss of two weeks' pay or imprisonment with hard labour (North-Coombes 1990). Legislation introduced to improve the workers' lot was often ineffectual and commissions investigating planter abuse rarely made recommendations detrimental to them. The protectors of immigrants, sharing the same class background and interests, were frequently the friends of employers (Emmer 1984). Thus colonial authorities and sugar planters colluded to draw 'a cloak of secrecy over actual conditions on the estates and in whitewashing the system' (North-Coombes 1990: 39).

Indian managers (*sirdar*s), speaking the workers' language, were appointed to ensure the effective running of the estates and many gained notoriety among the workers. Assaults on both men and women by overseers and *sirdar*s were commonplace; women particularly were forced to provide sexual services. Workers in turn found it difficult to prove assaults and, when found guilty, overseers and *sirdar*s escaped with light sentences. As a result, few workers registered complaints for fear of reprisal from employers.

Rigorous labour and harsh conditions took their toll on the health of indentured workers, leading to high rates of occupationally and environmentally related diseases and mortality (Brain and Brain 1982). Illness was often treated as malingering or blamed on the carelessness of the Indians (Brain and Brain 1982). Disease was responsible for the greatest number of deaths, diarrhoea and dysentery being the most common. Infant mortality caused by bronchitis, pneumonia and malnutrition was also high, in Fiji averaging around 20 per cent compared with around 5 per cent for adults (Lal 1984). Of the three colonies, mortality rates in Mauritius were the highest (North-Coombes 1990). Worker attempts to maintain a system of family and religious support were frustrated though not entirely prevented by life in the barracks. Some employers required their consent to be obtained before marriages could take place; further problems of access arose when one party had completed indenture while the other remained. Religion played an integral role in the adjustment of indentured workers to a new environment; the performance of religious ceremonies and rites helped to create a sense of security and solidarity. For many, however, ill treatment and lack of sympathy became intolerable and drove them over the edge. The rate of suicides, a third of which took place in the first year of indenture, among Natal's workers was second only to Fiji, at 64 per 1000 (Brain and Brain 1982).

While the experiences of Indian women under indenture have been under-explored, it is possible to make some generalizations about their situation based on available information. Although they performed many crucial productive and reproductive functions, women were recruited reluctantly by employers who viewed them as a burden. They were often left to the mercy of their male partners or forced into dependent relationships with men. Indian women initially performed tasks such as hoeing, planting, weeding, cutting and tea-picking. They worked eight to ten hours, were paid a fraction of the male wage and received half of the rations allotted to men (Beall 1990). In Natal, Indian women were gradually replaced by African workers, leading them into destitution and dependency on men. Women also played a critical sexual role and many were subjected to intense oppression. Rather than passively accepting their lot, however, many women resisted both individually and through participation in collective resistance. In Natal, for instance, Indian women played a critical role in the 1913 passive resistance campaign (Beall 1990). The paucity of women (the ratio of women to men was 40:100 in Natal and 33:100 in Mauritius) led to much sexual harassment and even murder of 'unfaithful' wives. In Fiji, between 1885 and 1920, there were 230 cases of murder due to 'sexual jealousy' (Lal 1984: 148).

Labour and resistance

Although collective worker organization beyond individual estates was highly frustrated, given the structural conditions of indenture, adverse working conditions and persistent abuse frequently led to worker action, which manifested itself in a variety of passive and active ways through informal and formal acts. Most protest was expressed through day to day actions, in the main individualistic and spontaneous, directed against the overseer or driver. In Fiji, for instance, Indians acquired a reputation for their 'murderous intent': thirty-two charges of assault on overseers and *sirdar*s were laid against workers in 1900 resulting in eleven convictions; in 1902, there were thirty-five charges with twenty-eight convictions (Lal 1984). Mass worker protests also took place in Mauritius in 1872 (North-Coombes 1990), but the most significant occurred in Natal. Here, since 75 per cent of indentured workers were employed in agriculture, marked by the worst working conditions, this

ultimately led between 5000 and 20,000 workers to strike in October 1913 (Bhana 1990). In Fiji, the most serious strike took place in 1886 in Koronivia when 132 workers, carrying their work instruments, marched to the agent general of immigration in Suva (Lal 1984).

Workers developed an array of devices to strike back at their exploitation, including absenteeism, idleness, petty larceny, desertion, destruction of employers' property and tools, and drunkenness. Workers also established a system of self-help; they set up funds based on voluntary subscriptions which were used to pay fines. Free Indians also frequently harboured deserters. Resistance rarely posed a threat to planter dominance, however, and may even have enhanced the methods of social control as resistance was often met with stringent labour legislation aimed at deterring collective action (Lal 1984). In Fiji, it was stated that 'it is desirable to break up a gang of men who have caused or are likely to cause serious disturbance of the peace' (Lal 1984: 138). Leaders were invariably criminalized and banished. Resistance, however expressed, persisted and grew stronger as labourers became more accustomed to their new environment (Haraksingh 1987).

Post-indenture settlement and incorporation

Natal and Mauritius contain two of the three largest overseas communities of South Asian origin. In Mauritius, where their settlement was actively encouraged, Indians constituted two-thirds of the total population as early as 1860 (North-Coombes 1990); in Natal, they were numerically significant in the borough of Durban and in Pietermaritzburg. In Fiji, Indians constituted around half of the population by the end of indenture (Lal 1990). In all three colonies, Indians played a crucial role in uplifting the local economies. Differences in economic contexts not only determined the role of indentured labour but also played a vital role in its termination. As argued by North-Coombes, in both Mauritius and Natal, 'the phasing out of indenture had more to do with the internal dissolution of the system in the context of a crisis in the world sugar economy than to the opposition of pressure groups, whether located within the colonies or outside them' (North-Coombes 1990: 43).

While one of the conditions of indenture was to make an optional return passage available to all labourers after ten years, Mauritius relinquished this responsibility in 1851 (Tinker 1974). Natal, under obligation to offer this, often failed to do so, arguing that migrants had the option of obtaining land for settlement, though land was rarely granted (Bhana and Brain 1990). Unlike Mauritius, in the 1880s the waning political influence of planters in Natal and heightened opposition to permanent Indian settlement created great acrimony on the subject of Indian migration. The £3 tax imposed in 1885 reduced the status of Indians to mere labour providers, faced either with reindenture or repatriation (Swan 1990).

Although most of the Indian migrants enlisting for indenture believed they would return to India after five or ten years, in reality only a small percentage were to realize this goal. Despite efforts to retain labourers, the rate of return remained fairly constant; by 1910, 31 per cent of the labourers imported to Mauritius returned to India, whereas in Natal this figure stood at 14 per cent until 1893 and at 43 per cent thereafter (North-Coombes 1990).

The majority who set their roots in receiving colonies were to face differing prospects depending on the local economic context. While the reliance on sugar production limited the extent of economic and social change, the parcellization of land resulted in a class of small cane-growers in Mauritius, where modern technology, wage labour and centralization slowly eroded the previously integrated plantation units (North-Coombes 1990). In Natal, the diversification of the economy created greater opportunities for ex-indentured workers to enter the urban space, though the anti-Indianism of whites gradually restricted their economic activities (Bhana and Brain 1990). In Fiji, the majority of free Indians set up on their own, on land leased from employers, trying market gardening, banana cultivation, poultry farming and mainly sugar cane farming, which was encouraged by the CSR (Lal 1984). As settlement proceeded, Indians moved into a variety of commercial, industrial and professional occupations in all three colonies. The move out of indenture also facilitated the reconstitution of culture and communities. With the exception of Mauritius where they constituted a majority, Indians were to occupy an uneasy political position in Natal and Fiji, where relations with the indigenous people were marked by hostility and mistrust.

References

Beall, J. D. (1982) 'Class, Race and Gender: The Political Economy of Women in Colonial Natal', M.A. dissertation, University of Natal

—— (1990) 'Women Under Indenture in Natal', in S. Bhana (ed.) *Essays on Indentured Indians in Natal*, Leeds: Peepal Tree Press, 89–116

Bhana, S. (ed.) (1990) *Essays on Indentured Indians in Natal*, Leeds: Peepal Tree Press

Bhana, S. and J. Brain (eds) (1990) *Setting Down Roots: Indian Migrants in South Africa 1860–1911*, Johannesburg: Witwatersrand University Press

Brain, J. (1985) 'Indentured and Free Indians in the Economy of Colonial Natal', in B. Guest and J. M. Sellers (eds) *Enterprise and Exploitation in a Victorian Colony*, Pietermaritzburg: University of Natal Press, 199–234

Brain, J. B. and P. Brain (1982) 'The Health of Indentured Indian Migrants to Natal, 1860–1911', *South African Medical Journal*, 62, 739–42

Emmer, P. (1984) 'The Importation of British Indians into Surinam, 1873–1916', in S. Marks and P. Richardson (eds) *International Labour Migration*, London: Temple Smith, 90–111

Gillion, K. L. (1962) *Fiji's Indian Migrants: A History to the End of Indenture in 1920*, Melbourne: Oxford University Press

Haraksingh, K. (1987) 'Control and Resistance among Indian Workers: A Study of Labour on the Sugar Plantations of Trinidad, 1875–1917', in D. Dabydeen and B. Samaroo (eds) *India in the Caribbean*, London: Hansib, 61–80

Hazareesingh, K. (1975) *History of Indians in Mauritius*, London: Macmillan

Lal, B. (1984) 'Labouring Men and Nothing More: Some Problems of Indian Indenture in Fiji', in K. Saunders (ed.) *Indentured Labour in the British Empire 1834–1920*, London: Croom Helm, 126–57

Lal, V. (1990) 'The Fiji Indians: Marooned at Home', in C. Clarke et al. (eds) *South Asians Overseas: Migration and Ethnicity*, Cambridge: Cambridge University Press, 113–30

Marks, S. and P. Richardson (eds) (1984), *International Labour Migration*, London: Temple Smith

North-Coombes, M. D. (1990) 'Indentured Labour in the Sugar Industries of Natal and Mauritius, 1834–1910', in S. Bhana (ed.) *Essays on Indentured Indians in Natal*, Leeds: Peepal Tree Press, 12–88

Swan, M. (1985) *Gandhi: The South African Experience*, Johannesburg: Ravan Press

—— (1990) 'Indentured Indians: Accommodation and Resistance, 1890–1913', in S. Bhana (ed.) *Essays on Indentured Indians in Natal*, Leeds: Peepal Tree Press, 117–36

Thiara, R. K. (1994) 'Migration, Organization and Inter-Ethnic Relations: Indian South Africans 1860–1990', Ph.D. thesis, University of Warwick

Tinker, H. (1974) *A New System of Slavery: The Export of Indian Labour Overseas 1830–1920*, London: Oxford University Press

SIKH FREE AND MILITARY MIGRATION DURING THE COLONIAL PERIOD

DARSHAN SINGH TATLA

At the end of the annual Remembrance Day parade in London a small contingent of former Sikh soldiers of the former Indian Army can be seen paying their respects. Most of them experienced service in Europe during the Second World War and the majority then settled in Britain in the 1950s and 1960s. This association symbolizes not only the enduring links with the former Indian Army but ties with colonial Punjab that date from the middle of the nineteenth century.

The imposition of British rule in the Punjab in 1849 had a profound effect on Punjabi society. Major irrigation projects were started in west Punjab and the Indian mutiny in 1857 led to a policy of preferential recruitment of Punjabi 'martial races' into the Indian Army. Both these developments prepared the ground for Punjabis to venture out, at first to the outlying areas, and then abroad. During the late nineteenth century the integration of the Punjab economy into the colonial economic system proceeded briskly. Between 1873 and 1903 Punjab's rail system was extended from 400 miles to over 3000 and its irrigation canals from 2744 miles to 16,893. In 1904 Indian wheat exports to Great Britain exceeded those of Russia and the USA, and the Punjab provided a major part of the Indian food grain trade. Exports from the Punjab brought cash and credit, thus making distant travel possible for Jat Sikh peasants. Independent emigrants from the Punjab were able to pay the fare to the Far East and then onwards to the Pacific states. The responsiveness of Punjabi villagers to opportunities in far lying countries — 'the Telia' (Australia) and 'Merika' (America) — was conditioned by the Punjab economy's integration into the international economy.

The colonial irrigation projects (known as the 'Canal Colonies') in the wastelands of western Punjab brought several hundred thousand Punjabi peasants from the over-populated districts of Amritsar, Jullundur, Gurdaspur, Hoshairpur and Ludhiana. New cities sprang up in the Canal Colonies, such as Lyallpur and Montgomery. The population of Lyallpur district increased from a mere 60,306 in 1891 to 2,157,000 in 1951. Large-scale migration took place from the crowded eastern districts to new and more fertile agricultural land between Jhelum and Sutlej. In terms of the shift in population across various districts of the Punjab, the Canal Colonies had a profound impact on demographic levels in the western Punjab. The districts of Lahore, Lyallpur, Multan, Montgomery, Jhang and Shahpur gained large populations from the eastern and central districts of Punjab.

The land policies of the colonial state in Punjab were geared towards protecting the rural peasantry, particularly the Canal Colonists, from the onslaught of urban financiers. This clear bias led to agitation by the urban elite — the first signs of discord appeared between a benevolent imperial authority and Punjabi rural society.

The second major impact of colonial rule on Punjabi society came from the complex circumstances leading to certain sections of the Punjabi population being classified as 'martial races' and fit for army recruitment. The crucial event was the 1857 mutiny. British rule faced a grave threat from a mutiny of Hindu and Muslim sepoys in the central and eastern provinces. Hurriedly raised Punjabi regiments fought loyally to defeat these sepoys and end the short reign of the Mughal emperor in Delhi. In the aftermath of the mutiny, a thorough reorganization of armies was undertaken and the East India Company's rule was replaced by a formal British takeover of India. Henceforth recruitment for British India armies was restricted to loyal peoples and provinces. Among the favoured Punjabi men, the Sikhs emerged as a particularly favoured 'martial race' fit to serve the empire.

Between 1858 and the onset of the First World War, the proportion of Punjabi men in the army increased steeply. The number of Sikh soldiers during the First World War increased to a record level of 150,000, a quarter of all armed personnel in India. As professional soldiers, they were deployed to the far corners of the British colonies — from Malaya in the Far East to the Mediterranean, to the British African colonies and protectorates in Africa and to Europe. Sikh soldiers who went abroad to fight for the empire were then inspired to settle away from sedentary rural life. Army service was usually short term and there-after they were the first to seek their fortunes abroad.

While the processes of economic development and army recruitment gave access to the outside world, the emigration from Punjab was not 'indentured' but 'free'. The Punjabi emigrants escaped the worst of the indentured system, particularly the hardships of sea voyages and the penalizing return conditions imposed on people from other provinces. The late entry of the Punjabis into the colonial emigration market also determined the destinations of a small number of those Punjabis who were enlisted by colonial agents.

Until the 1880s the Punjab was relatively untouched as far as indentured migration was concerned. The small numbers who did go were not the sort of recruits the colonial planters or farmers were looking for. The arrival of 'unfamiliar types' in the West Indies was duly noted and discouraged. The annual report for Trinidad (1902/3) mentioned that new migrants from Punjab and Rajasthan were unused to manual labour and classified them as 'undesirable' (Trinidad 1903). The reaction to Punjab migrants in the West Indies was also unfavourable. Its governor, Sir Everard Thurn, described the new arrivals as 'soldiers or something of that sort' and declared them unfit for labour (Tinker 1974: 59). Similarly, another administrator concluded that the valiant deeds of the Indian Army in North Africa had not helped the standing of the local Indians: soldiers belonged to 'martial races' and were willing to put up a fight for their rights.

Destinations

The Far East

A crucial element in Sikh emigration to the Far East was their recruitment into the police, other security forces and as junior personnel on the railways. These were the kinds of services in high demand in these colonies. The crucial link in initiating this demand was usually the personal influence of British officers who had served in the Punjab and United Provinces and had then gone to other colonies. A familiar example is that of a British police officer, C. V. Creagh, who had been transferred from Sind to Hong Kong as a deputy superintendent of police in 1865/6. He immediately recommended his trusted Sikh police from Punjab to be engaged as members of the colony's police. The first batch of 100 Sikhs arrived in Hong Kong in June 1867 and officials were so impressed that further recruitment was recommended. In the year 1871, there were 182 Sikhs and 126

Muslims from the Punjab in the colony's police force. In line with contemporary colonial thinking, Sikhs, Punjabi Muslims and Chinese were trained and raised in separate regiments under European officers. Each regiment or company had its own establishment staff of the same nationality. In 1939, Hong Kong's police force comprised 272 Europeans (including some white Russians), 774 Indians and 1140 Chinese. In 1952 the police force was completely Hong Kongized and Sikh personnel were expelled. Many Sikhs after completing ten-year periods of service were hired by private firms as security personnel or served at another port.

After Hong Kong, Malaya was the major desti-nation of independent Sikh migrants. Not until the opening years of the twentieth century did Malaya become a major importer of Indian labour. In 1900 there was a larger Indian population in British Guiana than in Malaya. But with the rubber boom, the demands of Malaya seemed insatiable. Madras sup-plied virtually all the labourers for the rubber estates. Before the war, a vast majority of south Indians were employed in rubber plantations. Sikhs were recruited into the mines, while some Punjabis went into mer-cantile and skilled labour categories. A number of Sikhs also served as security guards. Malaya was a major destination for a small number of Sikhs with police connections. First to enter Malaya were those recruited by Captain Speedy in 1873 to combat Chinese insurgency among the tin mines of Perak. Some of these pioneer recruits were subsequently drafted into government services, to form the nucleus of police and paramilitary forces of the state, follow-ing its passing into British control. The government following its increased demand started recruiting directly from Punjab. As the news spread of govern-ment jobs in Malaya, independent migrants started arriving there. Those rejected by security services would find themselves working in the private sector as caretakers, watchmen, bullock cart drivers, dairy keepers and mining labourers. Others drifted to neigh-bouring states of Thailand or Sumatra. Still others dreamed of America and Canada. Apart from police-men, some commercial immigrants came to Malaya. Some Sikh convicts also found their place in Malaya. The Malay states Guides and the Straits Settlements Sikh Contingent, two of the principal government bodies employing Sikhs, were disbanded in 1911 and 1926 respectively. The exact figure of Sikhs in Malaya is unknown, but it would be about 30,000. This compares with 10,000 in 1931 and 15,000 in 1947.

The first Sikhs in Australia arrived perhaps as early

as the close of the nineteenth century. This seemed to be a by-product of Punjabi recruitment to British armies and police. Those Sikhs who were stationed in Hong Kong and the Malay states in police and security duties were attracted to Australia. Some retired Sikh policemen from Hong Kong went to New Zealand, calling others to join them from home. For some Sikhs, New Zealand was the second step after entering Australia; others went from New Zealand to Fiji, lured perhaps by stories of sugar-cane fortunes.

New Zealand was a convenient route to Fiji for a small number of Punjabi migrants. Over 90 per cent of the Fijian Indian population is from the Gujarat, from the hinterlands of Barodas. In 1904 the first free immigrants arrived in Fiji from the Punjab via Noumea. In the decade before the First World War a small batch of Sikhs was recruited via an agent. Another avenue was for those who were policemen. These Sikhs were brought to Fiji from Shanghai and Hong Kong under contract without penal sanctions. Some of these decided to stay after their contract periods.

East Africa

The route to East Africa was also through army recruitment. A small number of Sikhs went to various colonies and protectorates of East Africa as soldiers. In 1895 the British government decided to establish a military base force known as the East African Rifles with headquarters in Mombasa. At the outset the force was composed of 300 Indians recruited from Punjab, 300 Swahilis and 100 Sudanese. Although during the next few years the East African Rifles participated in campaigns against Arab rebels and other insurgents, (Sikh troops with others were employed to quell the mutiny by Sudanese troops in October 1897), the contingent was not replaced at the expiration of the contract period in 1900. However, more Sikhs had arrived by then. In 1898, the Uganda Rifles and the East African Rifles were merged into the newly founded King's African Rifles for regular service in Nyasaland and Somaliland as well as Uganda and the East African Protectorate.

Sikhs were recruited from the Punjab for the development of the Uganda Railways project during the last years of the nineteenth century. Perhaps there is considerable truth in Grigg's statement that 'the railway is the beginning of all history in Kenya' (Hill 1949: 243). Most of the Indian labour on the railways was comprised of Punjabis, a majority of them Muslims with the rest being Sikhs and Hindus. For the first time Karachi became the embarkation post for Punjabi

emigrants. Among Sikhs who migrated to East Africa, most of them were artisans, belonging to the Ramgarhia class. As the railway line progressed, the number of imported labourers rose sharply – 3948 arrived in 1896, 6086 in 1897 and another 13,000 in 1898. Of these 16,312 were repatriated at the end of their contracts, 6484 were invalided and 2493 died. Only 6724 opted to remain in Kenya at the end of their contract in 1904; by then the railway line had reached Kisumu.

In Kenya the total number of Sikhs employed in the railways and security services during the period of railway construction (1895–1901) was nearly 3000. They built the first Sikh *gurdwara* at Kilindini in 1892. After the completion of the railways, the number of Sikhs declined sharply. In 1921, the census showed a Sikh population of 1619 out of 45,633 people of Indian origins. In the 1930s the Sikh population gradually increased again, both through families joining their men and through a fresh wave of migrants. In 1948 the Sikh population had gone up to 10,663, doubling to 21,169 in the next fourteen years. As Kenya gained freedom in 1963, the decline of the Asian population began rapidly. During 1962–69 it declined from 176,600 to 139,000 and by 1979 the numbers had been reduced to 78,600.

North America

Sikh migration to North America is also linked to military contacts. Queen Victoria's Diamond Jubilee in 1897 attracted Sikh soldiers for the parade. They toured Canada before returning. Five years later upon the coronation of Edward VII (1902) more than 1200 Indian troops went to London for the ceremony and included the 10th Jats, 15th Sikhs, and the 33rd, 20th and 1st Punjab infantries. Some of these troops had made their passage through Canada which left a deep imprint and subsequently initiated Sikh migration to Canada. Between 1904 and 1917 no more than 10,000 East Indians entered the USA.

After landing, either in Vancouver or San Francisco, the migrants rapidly moved southwards to southern California or settled in Washington, Oregon and British Columbia. In these latter areas, they found well-paid jobs in the lumber industries; some also worked on Pacific Railways, others became farm labourers. The rush years were between 1905 and 1908 when about 5000 Indians, mostly Sikhs, came to British Columbia. They were largely from Hong Kong, Singapore and other Far Eastern centres. By the year 1905, the Sikh presence in the Seattle–Victoria– Oregon areas was quite noticeable. Some of the

American papers dubbed their arrival as 'the tide of turbans' and others went further by describing it as 'the Hindu invasion'. The simmering racial hostility came to the surface in 1907 and 1908 when there was a temporary recession in the lumber industries and unemployed East Indians huddled together. Most of the Sikhs were called Hindus as distinct from North American Indians. This unemployment was blamed on the Hindus by white workers and anti-oriental feelings arose. In Canada, the racism broke into songs with the anthem:

> White Canada for ever
> To orient grasp and greed
> We'll surrender, no ever
> Our watchword the 'God save the King'
> White Canada for ever

The Canadian government acted quickly to implement hastily drafted regulations passed through Orders-in-Council under the Canadian Immigration Act. Entry into Canada was refused to persons who had not come from their country of origin by a 'continuous journey', and who could not produce a through ticket. In addition arrivals had to be in possession of $200, which replaced the small fee of $20. These deterrents were meant to dissuade Asian immigration, and the measures certainly produced desirable results. Only twenty-seven Hindus were able to enter between 1909 and 1913. The Canadian government also offered a plan to resettle Sikhs in Honduras. Tejā Singh, who became the first president of the Khalsa Diwan Society set up in 1908 among Vancouver Sikhs, rejected this offer. He also led a delegation to Ottawa for fair treatment to Sikhs.

However, such restrictive measures aimed at Asians of another British colony went against the spirit of 'free movement of peoples within the British empire'. Despite the intervention of the government of India against these measures, the Canadian authorities did little to ease Indians' entry. Sikhs stationed in the Malay states and other Far Eastern countries were to challenge the discrepancy between the stated ideals of the empire and its practical realities in a more dramatic way. Badly hit by these new measures of the British Columbian authorities, a determined effort was made to break through the web of the Canadian immigration laws in May 1914. Sikh businessman Gurdit Singh chartered a Japanese ship, *Komagata Maru*, and collected 376 passengers from Hong Kong and Shanghai fulfilling just about all the requirements of Canadian immigration laws. The ship arrived at Victoria harbour on 23 May 1914. The Canadian

Immigration Department after protracted negotiations prevented all but a few from landing. Despite strenuous legal battles, the local Sikhs could not force open the doors of Canada for their fellows. Eventually escorted by HMCS *Rainbow*, the *Komagata Maru* returned home. On landing at Calcutta Budge Budge port, they were met by police and, in resisting arrest, the Sikhs suffered severe casualties. The *Komagata Maru* voyage played a large part in the transformation of the Sikhs' cultural nationalism into a political expression of anger against British rule in the Punjab. The loyalty of proud ex-soldiers and policemen swung violently against the government and opened the Sikh soldiers to the nationalist propaganda.

Faced with strict immigration controls, with no possibility of calling for their families, many Sikhs responded positively to the exiled Indian leader's call for a return to India to wage a war against imperial rule. The newly formed organization, the Hindi Sabha, held several rallies in areas of Sikh settlement in California. With the generous offer of help from Sikh farmers, an office of the Gadr Party was established in San Francisco at 5 Wood Street, renamed Yugantar Ashram, where it started a weekly paper, *Gadr*. As the movement gained momentum, over 2000 Sikhs left the USA to fight for the liberation of India. The immediate impact of this return to the Punjab meant the Sikh populations of Canada and America were substantially reduced.

Between 1920 and 1947 Sikhs in Canada and the USA lived in small isolated communities. They could not own land or vote and their presence was irksome to ordinary Americans. In May 1913, the California Alien Land Act restricted the right to register land to American citizens only. In 1917 Sikhs were barred from entering the country and in 1923 they lost the right to become American citizens. The US Supreme Court delivered its verdict on a Sikh farmer's right to buy land, the famous 'Thind Case', when it ruled that Asian Indians were not 'free white persons' and therefore could not become American citizens.

Colonial rule ended in 1947 and for the Punjab this meant the partition of the province into two major regions, with the western districts becoming part of the new Muslim state of Pakistan. The eastern districts became part of the new Indian state. The tragic consequences of partition led to the migration of over six million Hindus and Sikhs and an equal number of Muslims crossing to the appropriate side of their future homelands. However, the tradition of migration started during the colonial era, combined with uncertainty and longstanding economic conditions in the

Punjab, prompted yet more emigration when the British economy needed labour. And later, in the 1970s, Canada and America relaxed their rules to allow more Punjabi settlers than previously. Of the overseas Sikh population, estimated to be about one million, over 75 per cent are settled in three countries, namely Britain, the USA and Canada (Tatla 1994).

For a community comprising less than 2 per cent of India's population, the ratio of overseas residents to the total Sikh population is strikingly high. This is especially so if we bear in mind that emigration has been restricted to a small tract of the Indian Punjab. Colonial emigration and recruitment into the armed forces gave a new vocabulary to the Punjabi language. Many folklore songs celebrated the 'emigrants' and asked about their wealth, while the experience of the armed forces introduced such names as Karnail, Jarnail and Major Singh, not to mention the young Sikh guerrillas of the post-1984 period who became the lieutenant-generals of the Khalistan Liberation Forces and split ranks over army nomenclature.

In large Sikh villages, retired army personnel would narrate their adventures to the young, or perhaps the two-storeyed buildings built with their overseas wages conveyed the worth of their adventures. The authorities also reserved special lands in the Canal Colonies for ex-army personnel. Young Punjabis of central Punjab could enlist into exclusive Sikh regiments and see the world.

References

Hill, M. F. (1949) *Permanent Way: The Story of Kenya and Uganda Railway*, Nairobi: East African Railways and Harbours

Tatla, Darshan Singh (1994) 'The Politics of Homeland: A Case Study of Ethnic Linkages and Political Mobilisation among Sikhs in Britain and North America', Ph.D. thesis, University of Warwick

Tinker, Hugh (1974) *A New System of Slavery: The Export of Indian Labour Overseas, 1830–1920*, London: Oxford University Press

Trinidad, Government of (1903) *Annual Report for 1902–3*, Trinidad: Government Printer

THE SETTLEMENT OF SOUTH ASIANS IN EAST AFRICA

MICHAEL TWADDLE

The settlement of South Asians in East Africa is sometimes regarded as a subject sufficiently researched. By implication, it is also sometimes considered of lesser importance than some other aspects of the subject (Mamdani 1993: 94). Yet, without further study of its origins, the consequences of South Asian settlement in East Africa are liable to be misinterpreted. Did South Asians migrate into East Africa with the main outlines of their communal groupings already established, or were important features of these socio-religious institutions shaped significantly by the course of South Asian settlement locally? If so, to what extent, and in what ways? To what degree, too, did internal divergences among East African Asians over matters of economic class or material interest change significantly during their years of settlement? Answers to all these questions require sensitivity to the number and manner in which persons of South Asian descent settled in Africa throughout these years as well as to their subsequent experiences there.

The first point to be made here is that, before the colonial partition of East Africa by European powers and the Egyptian and Ethiopian monarchies at the close of the nineteenth century, there was little communal crystallization of any sort in the East African interior between Arabs, South Asians and Turks. Numbers were too few, and differences in beliefs, customs and dress between these constituencies insufficiently articulate to others. Coastal city states like Lamu, Mombasa or Kilwa did have concentrations of both Arabs and South Asians, but as these cities were essentially creatures of Indian Ocean trade, their migratory tentacles tended to spread more densely across the sea than into the interior. When these tentacles started to extend into the interior with vigour, what A. M. Sheriff has described as 'some entirely Swahili-speaking communities in the older coastal centres' were joined by others whose relationships with Africans were to a far larger extent 'confined to the duka and the kitchen' (Sheriff 1973: 77).

This movement into the East African interior started to a significant extent only during the nineteenth century. First, it was stimulated by the severance of the Arab sultanate of Zanzibar from the rulership of Oman, and the development at Zanzibar of important South Asian financed ivory and slave trades. Then, from the close of the nineteenth century onwards, it continued by taking advantage of the linking of coast to interior by railway lines by incoming British and German colonial administrations, and by the slow but steady abolition of the earlier nineteenth-century slave trade (the ivory business would linger on in parts of East Africa for another generation), and the rapid expansion of African-grown crops like cotton and coffee and their sale overseas in aid (through taxation) of the new European colonialisms. None the less, the persons of South Asian descent who first sought fortune or sanctuary by moving into what are nowadays Uganda, Kenya and mainland Tanzania between the middle of the nineteenth century and the First World War did so as individual adventurers rather than as advance guards or representatives of socio-religious communities. Only subsequently would separate South Asian communities emerge strongly in the East African interior as social institutions in their own right. At least, that is the impression left by the first British travellers and colonial administrators in the interior during the nineteenth and early twentieth centuries and interviews with descendants of these adventurers more recently.

Richard Burton, for instance, reported the presence at King Suna's court in Buganda of one 'Isa bin Hosayn, a Baloch mercenary of H. H. Sayyid Said of Zanzibar. He had fled from his debtors, and had gradually wandered to Uganda, where the favour of the sovereign procured him wealth in ivory and a harem containing from 200 to 300 women.' Burton pointed out that this particular Baluchi immigrant 'was not permitted, nor probably did he desire, to quit the country,' but following the death of King Suna he had considered it wise to seek comfort and patronage in an East African kingdom other than Buganda (Burton 1860, ii: 193). By the time Ali Shakram, another Baluchi, opened a shop at Soroti in northern Uganda in 1913, many more Baluchi had entered and left Uganda for other parts of East Africa. But the dominant impression Ali Shakram conveyed in conversation towards the end of his life was still more that of the individual adventurer, or child of an adventurer, than of a Baluchi communalist. His father had 'had to leave Iran because of a family quarrel over looting and stealing of property by others. So he left and came to Zanzibar. You know that there were a lot of Baluchis at Zanzibar at that time acting as soldiers and that there are Baluchis in Pakistan today as well as Iran.' After working near the British fort at Kampala, his father had moved northwards and opened a small shop close to another British protectorate centre at Kaberamaido, 'to sell the usual things – cloth, cutlery'. Before moving there, Shakram had been educated up to P4 level at the CMS school in Mombasa, and this enabled him to work for another Baluchi trader who was illiterate in English when his father settled at Kaberamaido. Following his father's death in 1917, Ali Shakram worked in Kenya for a time before returning again to the retail trade in Uganda.

Communal connections with other Baluchis proved helpful, but not of overwhelming importance, in either Kenya or Uganda during the early twentieth century. Any Arab or South Asian wholesaler at Mombasa or Zanzibar, or in Kampala or at Jinja, would do business with a small shopkeeper like Ali Shakram, or his father, at Soroti or Kaberamaido. British protectorate officials also did not discriminate between Arabs, Africans and South Asians at this time. Insofar as there was any very prominent communal difference between traders at Kaberamaido or Soroti before the First World War, it was between Hindus and Muslims. Mosques in these places were attended by Arabs and South Asians alike, together with the few Africans ('mostly Basoga') who worked there for immigrant traders from the East African coast. Swahili was the main language of worship, 'though there were a few words in Arabic of course'. 'Did any Shias come?' 'The Shias then were extremely few,' Ali Shakram replied. Before the First World War most Muslim South Asian merchants at Kaberamaido and Soroti – and all Arab and African traders there – were Sunni Muslims like himself. Did Ali Shakram send money back to his relatives in Baluchistan? 'Not a cent!' he replied emphatically (Shakram 1965).

By the time British colonial rule ended in the 1960s, however, East African Asians were divided into a multiplicity of socio-religious groupings of which Baluchis formed one of the smaller communities. In many ways Baluchis were atypical of the generality of South Asian settlers in being Sunni Muslims, in being

unusually fluent speakers of the Swahili language, and in sharing with Africans living along the East African coast 'other characteristics of cultural assimilation such as dress, celebrations and dances' (Stroebel 1978: 28–9). But, as pointed out previously (Twaddle 1990: 154), this raises the critical question: which community *can* be considered typical of East African Asians at any time during the last 100 years?

Certainly not the Baluchis, for reasons just given. Baluchis were recruited during the nineteenth century as bodyguards for sultans of Zanzibar and were of roughly the same number as the Memons, another Sunni Muslim South Asian community. Baluchis and Memons both outnumbered Parsis residing locally (who were Zoroastrian in religious belief, but were themselves outnumbered by the start of the twentieth century by various Hindu trading castes operating along the East African coast such as the Banias, Bhatias and Lohanas). Along the coast, they were still further outnumbered by Shia Muslim sects like the Daudi Bohoras, the Ismaili Khojas and the Isthnaseris. Ismaili Khojas acknowledging the imamship of the Aga Khan had been the largest single South Asian community living in nineteenth-century Zanzibar (Gundara 1981). That preponderance continued until the First World War. Thereafter, Hindus, mostly moving into the East African interior as 'passenger migrants' and paying their own expenses for travel across the Indian Ocean, increasingly came to outnumber Muslim South Asians in the region as a whole. By the end of the European colonial era in the 1960s, Hindus accounted for around 70 per cent of all East African Asians.

Nonetheless, though losing out in comparative numbers to incoming Hindus (particularly to Patidars) for the remainder of the British colonial period, the Aga Khan's Ismailis retained the sociological initiative in several important respects. This was because, largely as a result of their imam's distinctive influence upon them, Ismailis were successfully persuaded to adapt to changing conditions more quickly and more completely than any other community of East African Asians. As the years passed, this made them even less typical of the generality of South Asian settlers in East Africa than the Baluchis, albeit with a paradoxical outcome. For through their establishment of special cemeteries, educational facilities and community care, Ismailis became veritable pacemakers for communal crystallization among other East African Asians too. Jains, Goans, Hindus of various kinds, Sikhs of at least three categories, and several other Islamic communities of both Shia and Sunni dispositions were all stimulated to establish separate burial grounds, schools and educational centres in response to pace-making activity in these spheres by followers of the Aga Khan (Morris 1968).

Population growth was also at first a stimulant to communal crystallization among East African Asians. This growth was both local and imported. Before the Second World War there was little opposition by British colonial administrators to continued immigration into East Africa from India. Only during and immediately after the Second World War was such immigration severely restricted – first, in 1944, under emergency regulations, then in 1948 by ordinance, allegedly because of the difficulties of providing decent housing for poorer immigrants from India. In fact, even before the war there had been the beginnings of restriction upon South Asian activity and movement into rural areas because of British colonial administrators' fears lest legitimate African entrepreneurial ambitions might be hampered unduly thereby. After the war this process intensified, with the result that South Asian settlement increasingly became concentrated in the larger cities.

Politically, the results of restricted immigration from the Indian subcontinent and the increased concentration within East Africa of South Asian settlers in towns were to strengthen communalism and to weaken local links with African anti-colonial activity.

Even without the restrictions upon further Indian immigration imposed during the 1940s, South Asian settlement would never have been as large in East Africa as in South Africa. In South Africa, South Asian settlement during the nineteenth and early twentieth centuries was much larger because of the far greater numbers of indentured labourers recruited to work on sugar plantations. Far fewer indentured labourers were recruited from the Punjab to build the railway from Mombasa to Lake Victoria, and of these only about 7000 stayed on after the railway was built. Most other South Asian immigrants came to East Africa as individuals looking for work or as friends or relatives of individuals recently settled. Personally almost always prepared to live more frugally than their European counterparts, they became players in an important international debate in the late 1910s and early 1920s, when 'the Indian question' became a contentious issue between nationalists in India, white settlers in Kenya and the government in Britain, because of the privileges then enjoyed by white but not brown settlers in East Africa. Both in those years, and immediately before immigration restrictions were imposed in Kenya, Tanganyika and Uganda during the 1940s, there was important South Asian involvement in basically African-inspired political activity. But this involvement was never as large nor as important as anti-colonial and anti-apartheid agitation by persons of South Asian descent in South Africa. The cessation of major South Asian immigration into East Africa during and after the 1940s also enabled communal leaders to assert authority over their respective socio-religious groupings much more strongly than might otherwise have been the case. Class-based politics decayed, and communalism blossomed among South Asian settlers in East Africa as never before.

References

Burton, R. F.(1860) *The Lake Regions of East Africa*, vol. II, London: Longman, Green, Longman & Roberts

Gundara, J. (1981) 'Fragment of Indian Society in Zanzibar: Conflict and Change in the 19th Century', *African Quarterly*, (21), 23–40

Mamdani, M. (1993) 'The Ugandan Asian Expulsion: Twenty Years After', *Economic and Political Weekly*, 16 January, 93–6

Morris, H. S. (1968) *The Indians in Uganda*, London: Weidenfeld

Shakram, A. (1965) Interview at Soroti, Uganda, 11 November

Sheriff, A. M. H. (1973) 'Indians in East Africa', *Tanzania Notes and Records*, (72), 75–80

Stroebel, M. (1978) *Muslim Women in Mombasa 1890–1975*, New Haven: Yale University Press

Twaddle, M. (1990) 'East African Asians through a Hundred Years', in C. Clarke, C. Peach and S. Vertovec (eds) *South Asians Overseas: Migration and Ethnicity*, Cambridge: Cambridge University Press, 149–63

PART FOUR

THE GREAT ATLANTIC MIGRATION
TO NORTH AMERICA

The Atlantic crossing by European migrants to the Americas is the stuff of legend. Hundreds of tons of wood pulp and thousands of miles of cinematographic film have been used to dramatize or record the reminiscences of those who made the crossing. Many of the immigrants – some 12 million people – were landed at Ellis Island in New York Harbour for immigration inspection. There they could see, in full sight, the nearby Statue of Liberty with its inspiring inscription by Emma Lazarus welcoming those of the world's 'huddled masses', who were 'yearning to be free'. With the Boston Tea Party, Lincoln's Gettysburg address and Washington's battles at Valley Forge, the immigrants' arrival into New York has become part of the founding mythology of the USA. The expressions 'The Land of the Free', 'The Golden Door' and 'From Rags to Riches' all stem from this powerful experience.

Like all myths there is an element of truth to these sentiments: the New World and the USA in particular did provide a great chance for those escaping the miserable conditions of nineteenth century Europe. However, we need to puncture the myth somewhat to gain some sense of its limits. Many destitute and sick people were turned back at Ellis Island as immigration legislation and practice became more selective. And, because the shipping companies had to pay for the costs of the return journey, they were increasingly reluctant to allow anyone to board in Europe who looked as if they might be rejected.[1] Not all who arrived had to go through the many humiliations of the inspection at Ellis Island: those in the cabins were landed straight onto the docks. This provides an illuminating demonstration that the USA did not escape the cloying constraints of the European class system. Moreover, as immigration historians and sociologists (for example, Portes and Rumbaut 1990: 29) have insisted, the Atlantic migration system has been overemphasized at the expense of Mexican migration to the south-west and Asian migration to California and the other Pacific states.

The bias in US immigration history is largely corrected in Part 8 of this volume, but mere equity is not the objectors' main point. What concerns them is that the whole of US history has been distorted through looking at it with a European lens. While this is true, it is important to remember that 'European' is a highly undifferentiated category and that many of the forms of discrimination that are now directed at Asian, Hispanic, African and Caribbean groups were once directed at subsets of European immigrants. Initially, there was a bias in favour of British immigrants for, as explained in Part 2, they had captured and substantially moulded the state's constitution and its principal institutions. Scots and Welsh were less desirable, but close enough to the English. As *Scally* shows, the Irish coming before 1845 were bilingual and often Protestant, thus making their acceptance in the USA easier. Their substantial numbers have led a number of Irish writers (for example O'Sullivan 1992) to minimize the impact of the potato famine on Irish emigration. Certainly, the famine only accelerated the Irish peasantry's long losing battle with subsistence farming. However, the numbers involved and the sight, in *Scally's* words, of 'emaciated near-corpses in filthy rags begging in the streets and dying in plain view', made the migrations of 1845–53 a new phenomenon for the USA. Here, for the first time in American eyes, was a white group as wretched and destitute as any African slave.

Although the numbers of migrants coming from Scandinavia were not so large as in the case of the Irish, as *Gjerde* shows, their per capita numbers put the Scandinavians just behind the Irish. Unlike the Irish, who tended to cluster in the urban areas, the first wave of Scandinavians journeyed from rural Europe to rural North America, mainly in the mid-western states and the prairie provinces of Canada. Those coming before the Civil War were particularly keen on acquiring cheap land, a bait that was similarly attractive to the Germans arriving from Germany and the Austro-Hungarian empire. As *Nugent* argues, their migration was essentially a conservative one, moving from the 'dwarf holdings' in their home areas to 100 acres or more in the Midwest, land being on a scale and at a price that permitted them to continue their preference for family farming. So concentrated was this migration that in 1980 in the states of Minnesota, Iowa, Missouri, the Dakotas, Kansas and Nebraska some 40 per cent of the population claimed German descent (Portes and Rumbaut 1990: 30–1).

For the most part, these farmer migrants were welcomed with open arms. They were seen as a civilizing influence. They were white, often respectable and, except for some German Catholics, were Protestant in denomination.[2] Moreover, they soon set about producing food on a scale that could feed hungry mouths in the rapidly urbanizing and industrializing cities of the north and north-east. There a new impulse was at work – mass factory production. A large consumer market had emerged in the USA, with new inventions and a new breed of capitalists with ideas, financial backing and aggression to match. Perhaps most important, two forms of power – steam power and labour power – were there for the taking. Indeed there was a direct connection between the two, for steam power was the condition of mass proletarian immigration across the Atlantic. Poles, Lithuanians, Ukrainians (covered by *Luciuk*), 'Russians' (a misnomer as *Morawska* explains), Latvians, Jews, Czechs, Slovaks and Hungarians poured into the USA in unremitting waves – perhaps about 20 million people from these groups before 1914. In Chicago a population of 4000 in 1870 rose to 1,700,000 in 1900 (Handlin 1951: 145).

No number could be too great for the industrial bosses. If the neophyte workers could not earn their keep, there were plenty more takers at the factory gate. To be one of those standing there was, often, all that mattered to those in the depressed regions of Europe. As *Morowska* notes, in 1900 un-skilled workers in US industries earned between $1.00 and $1.15 a day, seven to ten times more than the agricultural workers or artisans of eastern Europe. Henry Ford (cited Beynon 1984: 40) put it in his characteristically brutal way: 'In practically every case there is a required standard output below which a man is not expected to fall. ... Watchmen are paid for presence. Workmen are paid for work.' If the bosses were happy, the newspaper proprietors and eastern politicians were not so sure. Could the USA absorb all these unwashed masses with their strange languages and ways? African Americans who migrated from the south also looked on resentfully as they tried and failed to get factory employment. In 1891, a certain black dishwasher in Detroit (cited Thomas 1992: 14) expressed his disgust: 'First it was de Irish, den it was de Dutch and now it's the Polacks as grinds us down. I s'pose when dey [the Poles] gets like the Irish and stands up for a fair price, some odder strangers'll come over the sea 'nd jine de family and cut us down again.'

The East Europeans were superseded by an even more threatening group, the southern Europeans. The 'racial scientists' of the time were furious at the prospect of their being let in. The turn of the century was the high point of the American eugenics movement (Stephan 1987: 130–1). It campaigned vigorously for the intelligence testing of immigrants (the Jews came out badly) and for anti-immigration legislation. The restrictive legislation of 1924 was partly a result of their work. One bizarre theory that gained considerable credence at the time was that southern European women, with their supposed increased sexuality and fecundity, would induce a form of biological shock in the women of northern European origin such that their fertility would go into a steep nose dive. With their already large families and their new comparative advantage, southern Europeans would soon rule the roost, numerically and economically.

As *Baganha* and *Vecoli* show, the reality was rather less fanciful. Brazil was a more attractive destination for the Portuguese and those that came soon found a niche for their skills in market gardening and dairy production. The Italians were also part of a much more extensive, older and more complex migration system, involving high rates of emigration to many destinations, but equally high rates of return migration. A strong loyalty to homeland was also manifested by Greek migrants to the USA (not covered in this volume). As *Vecoli* demonstrates, the underdeveloped forms of capitalism that prevailed in Italy and its uneven nature bled the Italian countryside dry from the 1870s to the 1970s when finally an 'economic miracle' provided domestic alternatives to emigration.

Family farmers in the Midwest, industrial workers in the north-east and consumers in the burgeoning cities were the main growth poles in the extraordinarily rapid development of the USA as the world's leading industrial nation. As Handlin (1951: 66) reminds us, these poles were bonded together by a remarkable development of the transport system:

> With no machines, with only pick, shovel and sledge for tools, the boss and his gang contrived the numerous links that held the nation whole in these years. Out of their labors came first the chain of canals, and then an intricately meshed network of railroads – by 1910, more than 350,000 miles of them. And these tasks were hardly completed before bicycle riders and motorists began to call for and to get a paved highway system; 200,000 miles were already laid in 1910.

The great Atlantic migration from Europe to the USA has now been superseded in its volume and importance by Asian migrations across the Pacific (see later parts of this *Survey*), but it provided the essential human grist to the American mill just when the country was on the verge of becoming a 'great power'.

Notes

1. The practice of penalizing the carrier has recently been revived in Europe where a succession of Carriers' Liability Acts, starting in the UK, have specified that airline or shipping companies are fined for every person they carry without apparently *bona fide* documentation (see Part 14 of this *Survey*).
2. An excellent analysis of the contemporary patterns of discrimination against newcomers is found in Higham's (1965) book.

References

Beynon, Huw (1984) *Working for Ford*, Harmondsworth: Penguin

Handlin, Oscar (1951) *The Uprooted: The Epic Story of the Great Migrations that Made the American People*, Boston: Little, Brown

Higham, John (1965) *Strangers in the Land: Patterns of American Nativism, 1860–1925*, New York: Atheneum Publishers

O'Sullivan, Patrick (ed.) (1992) *The Irish World Wide: History, Heritage, Identity*, vol. I, *Patterns of Migration*, Leicester and London: Leicester University Press

Portes, Alejandro and Rubén G. Rumbaut (eds) (1990) *Immigrant America: A Portrait*, Berkeley: University of California Press

Stephan, Nancy (1987) *The Idea of Race in Science: Great Britain, 1800–1960*, Basingstoke: Macmillan

Thomas, Richard W. (1992) *Life for Us is What We Make It: Building Black Community in Detroit, 1915–1945*, Bloomington: Indiana University Press

THE IRISH AND THE 'FAMINE EXODUS' OF 1847

ROBERT SCALLY

At first sight, the exodus from Ireland in the nineteenth century hardly seems to require explanation. An impoverished and conquered island on the extreme periphery of Europe, Ireland had been the cul-de-sac of the westward European migrations for two millenia. By the nineteenth century, the country's population had become a roughly layered mixture of earlier migrants, settlers and conquerors who had come from the east, taking root in the island because they could go no further. Since the seventeenth century, the history of this immigration has been enshrined in the national memory as Ireland's calamity, a manifest destiny dictated by its geography and its powerful neighbour. But the westward impetus of these migrations is also preserved in the country's pagan myths and early Christian hagiography as a vision of salvation over the Atlantic horizon. Throughout the modern era, the west remained the direction in which hope and the future were sought. The opening of the Atlantic since the eighteenth century, it might be said, merely allowed the ancient flow to resume.

If the westward momentum stored in the island was released by maritime technology, the impulses that actually roused emigrants from their homes came from differing sources in each era and reached various classes and regions of the country selectively. The first major stimulus originated with the plantations of Ulster and Munster. In a great many ways, these were rehearsals for the later colonial leap across the Atlantic, driven by old regime adventurers and merchant entrepreneurs (Bottigheimer 1971; Calder 1981; Canny 1988; MacCarthy-Morrogh 1986). The plantation undertakers and their captains were out to plunder the wilderness, but the settlers themselves were most often *coloni-soldati*, people in need of land and willing to take and defend it by force. Many of these colonists, like the 'Scots Irish' of Ulster, had themselves been made landless not long before by the expansion of forces from the English core (Perceval-Maxwell 1973; Redford 1964). The movement of peoples that followed, first within the British Isles and then overseas, was a domino effect of that expansion. It contained mostly the weakest strata of Celtic and English societies, impoverished crofters and weavers, landless labourers and other dislodged remnants of the old regime facing the choice of poverty or emigration. Repeating the ancient pattern of migration, their movement displaced similarly vulnerable segments of the old Gaelic regime in Ireland, many of whom later accompanied or followed them into the American frontiers, emigrating from one colony to another and displacing still other native populations further west. These movements were impelled not by natural catastrophes either in Scotland or Ulster but by political economy and deprivation (Devine 1988). Similarly, when the Irish famine migration of 1845–53 is viewed as a part of this process, its historical causes are more easily found in the prolonged experience Ireland shared with these other colonial peoples than in sudden, inscrutable acts of god or nature like the potato blight.

The Atlantic migrations of the eighteenth century flowed mainly along routes and to destinations established by the extractive enterprises in tobacco, timber, furs, sugar and cotton. Whether travelling as free settlers, indentured servants or as slaves, the bulk of this movement was predominantly of migrant labour, carried westward in ships built and financed to export the products of their toil on the return voyages. This carrying trade itself demanded a massive expenditure of labour to man the ships and haul the goods on either side of the Atlantic, mobilizing seafaring hands from the coastal populations throughout the British Isles (Linebaugh and Rediker 1985). The industrialization of Britain and the eastern seaboard of North America in the nineteenth century set yet another wave of forces in motion which would peel away still deeper layers of marginal peoples from the hinterlands of the Irish Sea, prized from the land by poverty and drawn towards the new sources of wages. Other long-term factors, such as the intrusion of commerce into the countryside and fluctuations in the demand for labour in North America and for grains and meat in England, also helped to break the peasants' ties to the land. Once the first few links in the 'chain migration' were forged, the back-flow of remittances from earlier emigrants helped finance a competitive boom in the emigrant trade. Fares fell and conditions worsened for steerage passengers. But the human traffic rose rapidly each year before the famine, carrying mostly manual labourers to places like Lancashire and New York, the two main depots of the trade, at the height of their building booms. These motive forces behind the movement of people are at least partly measurable (Thomas 1954). Harder to gauge is the influence of information, fancy and myth about the outside world which leached into the countryside and the minds of potential emigrants.

Historians differ in deciphering this calculus of 'push and pull'. But some of the basic features of the nineteenth-century Irish migration are clear. Leaving aside the large internal movements within the British Isles and such categories of emigrants as political exiles or transported convicts, it is conventional to divide the migration into three phases, overlapping but each with distinct causes and characteristics. The pre-famine emigration of 1815 to 1845 was predominantly one of bilingual or English-speaking farmers, artisans and townsmen travelling in family groups (Adams 1932; Fitzpatrick 1984). They came from all regions of the country, but this phase drew most heavily from the north and east, where the influence of commerce and towns had penetrated most deeply. Because these districts also contained the greatest concentrations of Protestants, their proportion was higher in the pre-famine emigration than it was to be later (Cousens 1960). Emigrants of this description continued to leave during the rest of the century, but each year before the famine saw a rising number of poorer emigrants from the overwhelmingly Roman Catholic rural districts of Connaught and Munster, culminating in the massive exodus of 1845–53. This was made up mostly of small tenants and agricultural labourers fleeing the hunger, many of them in a state of extreme distress. Driven by recurrent food crises, the annual outflow of the next half-century was increasingly of younger emigrants travelling singly, now including large numbers of young women. Much the same pattern persists to the present day (Miller 1985).

These movements permanently reduced the population to about half of the 8.25 million it had been before the famine (Mokyr 1983). Huge quantities of data on the emigrants' numbers, ages, gender and regional origin have also been analysed and give a vividly clear picture of the objective details of the movement (Fitzpatrick 1984; Miller 1985; O'Grada 1975). But the emotional and cognitive experiences behind the migration are naturally less tidy than the statistics suggest. For example, the pre-famine phase is generally pictured as the most 'voluntary' of the three, a movement of those able to pay the relatively high fares which prevailed before the 1840s who were making a rational calculation about their individual futures should they emigrate or remain. For the post-famine emigrants, the decision to emigrate, especially to go alone, was similarly weighed on a scale of *prospects*, both personal and economic. For single women, the chances of marriage at home versus independence with or without marriage in America was probably the uppermost factor in this complex, life-altering decision. If it were freely made, such a choice was a modern decision, favouring individual expectations and desires over the bonds of kinship and tradition. At least to that degree, the voluntary emigrant can be said to have already broken mentally from the pre-capitalist old regime of fatalism and communal values (Miller 1992).

The famine emigration

Compared with the 30,000 to 100,000 per year who left during the two preceding decades, the outflow during the famine was a flood of nearly two million emigrants, to be followed in the following decade by nearly a million more (Fitzpatrick 1984; O'Grada 1975). In the succeeding generations, the departure of the young became an expectation of nearly every Irish family, a rite observed in the 'American wake' as a symbolic funeral for those never to be seen again. A great number of those who emigrated during the famine would undoubtedly have chosen to leave even without the potato blight. But almost every aspect of the poorer peasants' emigration during the hunger was coerced by one force or another: their hold on the land had been wrested loose by poverty and the law; evictions were made easier and mounted; congestion was growing among the poorest classes in the countryside and historically forced dependency on the potato blocked their access to the food chain when the blight struck.

It is the air of panic that has given the famine emigration its distinct character. The great majority consisted of a new sort of emigrant, one who had been seen boarding the emigrant ships before, but never in such numbers and such misery. And unlike the victims of any previous famine in Europe, these refugees were passing in their millions through the core of a great empire and the most dynamic centres of the world economy at the time, across the English-speaking rim of the north Atlantic (Coleman 1972; Scally 1994). The sights reported on entering the peasant cabins and seen on the famine roads, on the Liverpool docks, in the steerages and the North American quarantines, of emaciated near-corpses in filthy rags begging in the streets and dying in plain view, fixed the image of 'Paddy' in the outside world for years to come (Woodham-Smith 1962). The disgust that the details of this migration inspire and the odour of racism surrounding the emigrants' treatment also suggest to some that it should be seen as a special category of migration, a forced movement under ruthless duress and organized triage, bearing more resemblance to the slave trade or the trains of the holocaust than to the mostly merry Atlantic crossings of a later age (Gallagher 1982; Scally 1984).

While some of these calamitous features set the famine emigration aside, its social contours and timing correspond roughly to the increased movement of peoples in the rest of western Europe in the mid-nineteenth century (Erickson 1976). This is especially so if we conceive of 'the great famine' not only as the sudden destruction of the peasants' food supply but as the climax of a prolonged, losing struggle with subsistence. When that struggle began is undecided, but at whatever point the potato was established as the 'staff of life' in the diet of the Irish peasantry, the struggle was lost. By most accounts, that probably happened in the latter half of the eighteenth century (Connell 1950; Salaman 1987). The potato's demographic consequences alone seem to have guaranteed chronic poverty, if not certain disaster. With the introduction of the vulnerable 'lumper' variety, introduced to maximize the yield per acre and therefore increasing dependency on it, there would seem to remain very little chance of avoiding the catastrophe that came. There had also been a number of partial crop failures and localized hunger crises in the previous thirty years during which the numbers of emigrants steadily rose. In this light, what we see in the years 1845–53 is merely the deadliest moment of a forlorn process of increasing potato dependency, deepening poverty and the annual departure of those best able to leave. The famine emigration may then also be seen as a process, a learned response to history rather than a spasmodic reaction to nature, like fleeing before an avalanche.

Few of the famine emigrants understood the distant sources of their predicament, but most had long before contrived defences against the nearly annual threat of hunger and eviction that had faced them for generations. The nucleus of that defence was the 'townland' (or *baille*), the closest counterpart in Ireland to the villages of rural England and the continent. The more than 62,000 townlands of Ireland contained the bulk of the peasantry on the eve of the famine and it was from these communities that most of the famine emigrants emerged (Evans 1973; Scally 1994). Their appearance differed from the villages of Sussex or Picardy. They were mostly scattered settlements of one-storey cabins strung out beside the road with no discernible centre or geometry. Alexis de Tocqueville described one such townland in the 1830s as looking like 'a molehill upon which a passer-by had trod'. The Irish townland's poverty and isolation were manifested in the scarcity of the basic material signs of nineteenth-century European civilization; in general they lacked glass windows, dressed stone, chimneys or shops. The domestic possessions in townland cabins only rarely included such current amenities as mirrors, spectacles, combs, ceramic vessels, steel tools or manufactured shoes. This 'goods revolution' had also not yet reached many other peasant enclaves in Europe, but the complete absence of church steeples, market squares or public buildings of any kind in the townlands bespoke a distinct history which placed them unmistakably in the colonial world.

Other details of the emigrants' condition on the eve of their departure also attest to their material isolation. No word was more common than 'rags' in descriptions of their clothing, much of which came to them through country peddlars years after they had adorned respectable English men and women. Except for adult males, most were barefoot and bareheaded in all seasons. Even before the famine, dietary deficiencies and the conditions of daily life in the cabins, 'dripping soot from above and oozings from below', as a contemporary described them, also marked the bodies of the emigrants. As they flocked to the port towns and massed on the docks of Liverpool and New York, their physical condition, now emaciated by hunger and travel and beset by infectious disease (especially in the typhus year of 1847), produced a universal revulsion directed against both themselves and their landlords. Similar responses to such migrations occurred elsewhere, as in Paris after Napoleon and in Prussia at the end of the century, leaving lasting political effects and fixing the imagery of the 'alien' on the migrants (Chevalier 1958; Neal 1988; Pulzer 1964).

Accounts of the numbers who died of hunger and fever in Ireland, of the mortality aboard the 'coffin ships' and in the New World quarantines varied greatly in contemporary reports. But they can now be at least roughly fixed as follows: between 1 and 1.5 million 'excess deaths' in Ireland and about 5 per cent of the 1.5 million emigrants aboard the ships and in the quarantines (Mokyr 1983). The number succumbing at other stages en route or shortly after landing cannot be exactly fixed, but the total emigrant death toll between the cabin door and their resettlement in Britain, North America or the Antipodes was probably not less than 100,000 individuals. Less is known about the minds of the famine emigrants than about their bodies. The level of English literacy among the poorer classes was relatively high in Ulster and Leinster, where nearly half were able to read and/or write, but dropped off in the west, to about 39 per cent in Munster and 28 per cent in Connaught (Akenson 1970; Miller 1985). Even so, such census counting gives a poor picture of the mental life of the countryside, where a vivacious and pervasive oral tradition in Irish enriched daily intercourse in both languages. Many of those over fifteen years old at the time of the famine had learned their ABCs in the free National Schools which began to open in 1836. But private instruction had been flourishing in the countryside for generations in the form of the famous 'hedge schools', so named for their clandestine sites under the Penal Laws, and in the small fee-paying academies to be found in most provincial towns (Dowling 1935). Apart from their English letters and their numbers, it is uncertain how much practical knowledge was imparted to the children through the National School. Its curriculum was openly adversarial to the nativism and extreme individualism of the rival hedge schools, which it would eventually displace. It was a major factor in the demise of the Irish language but was also partly responsible for the advantage of English proficiency among the soon-to-be emigrants (Akenson 1970; Scally 1994).

New World settlement

It was once thought that more than 90 per cent of the famine emigrants settled in the big cities of North America, despite the abundance of cheap land and the fact that most of them had been land-hungry farmers before leaving. Various unsupported theories have been offered to explain this apparent anomaly, that they felt betrayed by the land, that they lacked the capital or the spirit to go far beyond the port cities, or that the lure of ready wages and food kept them near their first landings. More recently, their pattern of settlement has been made clearer and more nuanced. A large minority did settle in the big eastern cities, but many lived in urban peripheries, supporting themselves in a manner resembling their micro-economies at home of mixed wage labour and garden farming,

but without relying as heavily on the potato (Doyle 1991). An almost equal number settled in towns of middling size or smaller, many of which were only marginally industrialized or relegated the Irish to casual labour. What remained to most of the first-generation immigrants was irregular day labour, back-yard gardens and petty trading. For a great many, it was a round of daily life not radically different from that of the townland and one in which many traditional practices, including joint holdings, secret associations and kinship solidarity, were able to persist for decades as characteristic features of Irish enclaves in the New World.

The memory of the emigrant journey also became an intrinsic part of American Irish ethnic and political identity for at least a century following. Its most lasting image was the 'coffin ship', which was set beside the eviction scene in Ireland to visualize the famine in the emigrants' memory. This memory was both used and abused as a source of ethnic solidarity and political rhetoric and as an undying grievance against England. And by portraying emigration as a coerced, involuntary act, it also offered one means of dulling the guilt of the survivors by creating a 'cult of exile' that became and remains the foundation of American Irish nationalism (Miller 1985).

References

Adams, W. F. (1932) *Ireland and Irish Emigration to the New World from 1815 to the Famine*, New Haven: Yale University Press

Akenson, Donald (1970) *The Irish Education Experiment*, London: Routledge

Bottigheimer, Karl (1971) *English Money and Irish Land: The 'Adventurers' in the Cromwellian Settlement of Ireland*, Oxford: Oxford University Press

Calder, Angus (1981) *Revolutionary Empire*, New York: E. P. Dutton

Canny, Nicholas (1976) *The Elizabethan Conquest of Ireland: A Pattern Established, 1565–76*, London: Hassocks.

Chevalier, Louis (1958) *Les Classes labourieuses et Classes dangereuses à Paris pendant la Première Moitié du xxe Siècle*, Paris: Plon

Coleman, Terry (1972) *Passage to America: A History of Emigrants from Great Britain and Ireland*, London: Hutchinson

Connell, K. H. (1950) *The Population of Ireland, 1750–1845*, Oxford: Clarendon Press

Cousens, S. M. (1960) 'The Regional Pattern of Emigration during the Great Irish Famine', *Transactions of the Institute of British Geographers*, 28

Devine, T. M. (1988) *The Great Highland Famine: Hunger, Emigration and the Scottish Highlands in the 19th Century*, Edinburgh: Donald

Dowling, P. J. (1935) *The Hedge Schools of Ireland*, London: Longmans Green

Doyle, David (1991) 'The Irish and Urban Pioneers in the

United States, 1850–70', *Journal of American Ethnic History*, 10 (1 and 2), (Fall 1990, Winter 1991)

Erickson, Charlotte (1976) *American Industry and the European Immigrant, 1860–85*, Cambridge MA: Harvard University Press

Evans, E. Estyn (1973) *The Personality of Ireland: Habitat, Heritage and History*, Cambridge: Cambridge University Press

Fitzpatrick, David (1984) *Irish Emigration 1801–1921: Studies in Irish Economic and Social History no. 1*, Dublin: Economic and Social History Society of Ireland

Gallagher, Thomas (1982) *Paddy's Lament*, New York: Harcourt Brace

Linebaugh, Peter and Marcus Rediker (1990) 'The Many-Headed Hydra: Sailors, Slaves and the Atlantic Working Class in the Eighteenth Century', *The Journal of Historical Sociology*, 3 (3), September

MacCarthy-Morrogh, M. (1986) *The Munster Plantation: English Migration to Southern Ireland, 1583–1641*, Oxford: Oxford University Press

Miller, Kerby (1985) *Emigrants and Exiles: Ireland and the Irish Exodus to North America*, New York: Oxford University Press

— (1992) 'For Love and for Liberty: Emigration of Women to America between 1815 and 1939', paper delivered at Ireland House, New York University, November

Mokyr, Joel (1983) *Why Ireland Starved: A Quantitative and Analytical History of the Irish Economy, 1800–1850*, London: Allen and Unwin

Neal, Frank (1988) *Sectarian Violence: The Liverpool Experience, 1819–1914*, Manchester: Manchester University Press

O'Grada, Cormac (1975) 'A Note on Nineteenth-Century Emigration Statistics', *Population Studies*, (29)

Pulzer, P. (1964) *The Rise of Political Anti-Semitism in Germany and Austria*, New York: Wiley

Perceval-Maxwell, Michael (1973) *The Scottish Migration to Ulster in the Reign of James I*, London: Routledge

Redford, Arthur (1964) *Labour Migration in England, 1800–1850*, Manchester: Manchester University Press

Salaman, R. N. (1987) *The History and Social Influence of the Potato*, Cambridge: Cambridge University Press

Scally, Robert (1984) 'Liverpool Ships and Irish Emigrants in the Age of Sail', *Journal of Social History*, Summer

— (1994) *The End of Hidden Ireland: The Emigration of Ballykilcline*, New York: Oxford University Press

Thomas, Brinley (1954) *Migration and Economic Growth: a Study of Britain and the Atlantic*, Cambridge: Cambridge University Press

Woodham-Smith, Cecil (1962) *The Great Hunger*, London: Hamish Hamilton

THE SCANDINAVIAN MIGRANTS

JON GJERDE

In one sense, the emigration from Scandinavia to the Americas was yet another component of an expanding movement from and within the Scandinavian countries of Denmark, Finland, Iceland, Norway and Sweden, which commenced in the eighteenth century, long before the peasantry was generally aware of American opportunities. Internal migration, which had been common for centuries, quickened in the mid-eighteenth century. Within Norway, for example, peasants increasingly moved after 1750 to the cities, coastal regions and northern tracts, all of which were areas of perceived economic opportunity (Sogner 1979). Between 1626 and 1800 thousands migrated to other European locations, principally to the Netherlands. In seventeenth- and eighteenth-century Sweden, the migrational drift was also southward to European states and to growing Swedish cities (Norman and Runblom 1987). The migration in fact also reached the Americas when New Sweden, founded in 1638 in what became Delaware, included Finnish and Swedish settlers.

In another sense, however, emigration to the Americas in the nineteenth century was a distinct social phenomenon born from the changing Scandinavian world of that period. It irrevocably altered local Scandinavian societies and had important social consequences for the receiving regions in the Americas. Migration to the Americas began in 1825, when a ship departed from Stavanger, Norway. It soon spread to Sweden, where mass emigration began in the 1850s, and later to Denmark and Finland in the 1860s. In short, news of immense opportunities to work in and especially to own land in the USA and Canada, which filtered into the rural land-poor districts of Scandinavia in the nineteenth century, altered the calculus of migration. These fabulous prospects made emigration far more alluring than moving to the city or remaining at home. By the middle of the century, this form of emigration from many regions of Scandinavia had dwarfed the internal migration that had gone on before.

Immigrant destinations were disproportionately aimed at North America. Although scattered settlements were formed in Argentina, Australia and South Africa, well over 95 per cent of Scandinavian emigrants moved to the USA and, to a lesser degree, to Canada. During a century of migration between 1825 and 1930 (by which time US law had severely restricted free immigration), some 850,000 Norwegians, 1,200,000 Swedes and 300,000 Danes departed for the USA (derived from Thernstrom 1980: 1047–48). Over a quarter of a million Finns (274,000) obtained passports to travel abroad between 1893 and 1920 (Hoglund 1980: 364). About 15,000 Icelanders moved to the USA between 1870 and 1900 (Björnson 1980: 475). These numbers take on even greater meaning when set in the context of the Scandinavian population. Per capita migration in the nineteenth century from Norway, moreover, was second only to Ireland; that from Iceland was third; that from Sweden fourth (Gjerde 1985; Rice 1981). Roughly one-fifth to one-quarter of Swedes alive at the time of emigration (i.e. between 1845 and 1930) had at some point lived in the Americas (Rice 1981: 248). In sum, despite Scandinavian population growth and amid an urbanization that greatly enlarged Scandinavian towns and cities, the nineteenth-century emigration from the Scandinavian countries was an enormously important phenomenon to its society and economy.

Scandinavian immigration was informed by the cultural and economic forces transforming the region in the nineteenth century and by perceptions of opportunity in North America. Challenges to authority – to the state church, to the mercantilist economic order, to the former patterns of cooperative landowning – were in a sense expressed in migration. Early immigrants tended to be set apart from their neighbours and were typically more aware of new ideas and opportunities. The very first emigrants from Norway in 1825, for instance, consisted of religious dissidents, a group of Quakers and pietist Lutheran followers of Hans Nielsen Hauge (Blegen 1931; Semmingsen 1941). Likewise, the Janssonists – Swedish followers of pietist Erik Jansson – emigrated in their thousands and formed the Bishop Hill colony in Illinois in 1847. Scandinavians – especially Danes – were among the first Mormon settlers in Utah in 1846 (Norman and Runblom 1987). Detailed studies of the diffusion of emigration demonstrate that the first immigrants were relatively well-to-do, mainly literate peasants who were increasingly dissatisfied with the state church and the confines of opportunity at home (Ostergren 1988; Rice and Ostergren 1978).

If theological and political dissatisfactions were critical in informing the very earliest emigrants' decisions, a broad-based economic and demographic transformation that was altering Scandinavian society ultimately resulted in a widened emigrant stream. Most notably, population grew steadily from the mid-eighteenth century and into the nineteenth. Although population increased in the eighteenth century, it exploded in the nineteenth. Norwegian population grew, for example, at a rate of 0.7 per cent per annum between 1775 and 1795. Between 1815 and 1835, the comparable rate was 1.4. The average rate of growth between 1815 and 1865 in Norway was 1.30 per cent; in Sweden, it was 1.03; in Denmark, 1.01. Of the western European states, only the rates of Bremen and of England and Wales were higher than that of Norway during this period (Drake 1969). In sum, Norway, Sweden and Denmark, despite the stirrings of emigration, nonetheless were all about half again as large in 1850 as they had been in 1800 (Norman and Runblom 1987: 35–7).

The causes of the growth were varied. On the one hand, the easing of Malthus's positive checks of war and famine spurred population growth. There is certainly truth in the aphorism that 'peace, the potato, and smallpox inoculation' contributed to lower levels of mortality, especially among infants, in the decades around the turn of the nineteenth century. On the other hand, changing patterns of nuptiality also contributed to a growing population. Scandinavia, like much of western Europe, maintained a custom of marriage that demanded a livelihood upon which to base a marital union. Marriage age tended to be relatively high as a result (Coale and Watkins 1986; Hajnal 1965). Given the increased opportunities to marry afforded by new openings in society, however, ages at marriage began to fall in the nineteenth century. Population surged as a result, even though increasingly large segments of the society lived as landless farmers. The rural societies produced increasingly large harvests based on a widened array of crops, including the potato. A growing per capita caloric output – Martinius (1971: 604) argues that the agricultural output per worker increased 0.7 per cent per annum in Sweden between 1835 and 1870 – did not necessarily indicate a 'poorer' society. It did mean, however, that the structures of local society had been irrefutably altered.

Landlessness was increasingly common in societies that traditionally had large proportions of freeholding peasants by European standards. Both Norway and Sweden seemed less able to withstand the rural crises that periodically descended upon them, such as the virtual starvation of the 1860s (Beijbom 1980: 972). And although the marriage age fell, people were still less likely to marry in areas of Scandinavia than in other regions of Europe. One is struck by the correlations between regions with low values of I_m (an index of proportions married) on maps in Coale and Watkins (1986: 484ff.) with those of emigration intensity on maps found in Runblom and Norman (1976: 128ff.). It is not surprising that opportunities to own American land, which were beckoning Scandinavian peasants by the mid-nineteenth century, were often perceived as a godsend (Gjerde 1985).

In many ways, the migration patterns from Scandinavia were an extension of those which had already occurred in other regions of Europe. They paralleled, for example, the so-called provincial migration from the British Isles (Bailyn 1986). In Britain, a surge of emigration in the eighteenth century from the provinces (from Scotland, Ireland and northern England) reflected both the displacements resulting from change at home and the opportunities to reconfigure the old society in land-rich regions in the colonies. As with British provincial migration, the initial centre of migration from Scandinavia tended to be located in rather remote, yet rapidly growing, regions. In Norway, the most intense emigration came from the mountain and western fjord regions. Between 1855 and 1865, for example, the rate of emigration from Sogn was 1.7 per 100 per year; from Valdres, it was 1.6; and from Hallingdal 1.5 (Engen 1978; Gjerde 1985). In Sweden, the initial centre of emigration was the region of Småland, where the growing population had created landlessness and rural proletariatization. In Denmark, emigrants moved overwhelmingly from rural regions – especially the islands of Lolland-Falster and Bornholm (Hvidt 1975). In Finland, the areas of Vaasa and Oulu, among the least industrialized regions of the country, accounted for over three-fifths of the emigrants. The propensity of remote regions to be leaders in emigration was certainly partly due to the fact that cities and towns, in what has been termed the 'urban field of influence', siphoned off potential international emigrants from nearby outlying regions (de Geer 1977). Yet it is also true that despite long-standing traditions of internal migration, only when knowledge of the possibility of emigration diffused into remote

Norwegian peasant communities did out-migration rates explode (Gjerde 1991). Whereas 2000 residents of Vaasa left home for Helsinki between 1882 and 1902, for example, 103,000 departed for the USA. In short, American opportunities were fundamentally different from chances to move internally; they appealed to peasants from relatively remote locations who were less familiar with urban life and who hoped to retain conventional patterns of life thousands of miles from home.

Like the British provincial migration, moreover, the early Scandinavian destinations were principally located in land-rich areas in the Americas. Whereas colonial British emigrants settled on the broad arc of the American frontier, the early waves of Scandinavian migration were premised on landed futures in the USA where lost social worlds might be regained. By the mid-nineteenth century, immense tracts of land were available in the mid-western USA for purchase, either from the US government or from private firms and individuals. The principal locations of settlement were correlated with the primary areas of available land. Because they were among the first Scandinavians to emigrate, Norwegian immigrants predominated in Illinois, Wisconsin, Iowa, Minnesota and the Dakotas. Swedes, who tended to be later, were concentrated in Minnesota and the Dakotas. Nearly half the Finnish-born living in the USA resided in Minnesota and Michigan (Hoglund 1980: 365). Icelanders, later still, settled mainly on the prairie provinces of Canada.

Because this was a settler migration, its demographic features indicated the transplantation of communities. The emigrants moved principally in family groups; failing that, they moved as individuals with other families and were often embedded within a kinship network. Between 1841 and 1850, for example, more than two-thirds of those emigrating from Sweden were part of migrating families (Norman and Runblom 1987: 850). And since the early emigrants were mainly family members, their sex ratios were relatively even. In both Sweden and Norway, men comprised between 55 and 60 per cent of the emigrants in the early phases. Few, moreover, returned home. Rather, their residence was typically in settler communities, often in rural environments in which they would foster institutions such as the church and family and start up a newspaper in a new milieu. For decades they maintained their native tongue and religion, and tended to wed within their own ethnic group. It is not too much to suggest that the migration from Scandinavia to North America was

a 'radical attempt to conserve', i.e. to recreate former patterns of life in a distant milieu. Residents of remote Scandinavian locales were often more familiar with equally remote locations in the USA than they were with their own capital cities (Gjerde 1985; Semmingsen 1978).

As the emigration continued, however, two noteworthy and in some ways countervailing developments occurred. First, eastward flows of capital and information, in the form of letters and occasional visits from 'Americans' to their old home, fuelled additional westward migration. About two-fifths of emigrants leaving Oslo (Christiania) between 1872 and 1875 held prepaid tickets. From Sweden to Canada between 1883 and 1886, the figure approached 50 per cent (Hvidt 1975: 190–4). It often followed that those who were provided with the information and means to migrate engaged in 'chain migration': i.e. they relocated to places where friends and family lived. In so doing, they further enlarged the kinship communities that dotted the northern USA (Gjerde 1991).

On the other hand, as the century progressed so the character of Scandinavian immigration changed and by the final decades of the nineteenth century it had begun to mirror the 'industrial migration' in which immigrants from other European nations were enmeshed. These shifts were due to the changing character of transatlantic transportational networks and to altered opportunity structures in an industrializing North America. The closing of the American frontier betokened an end to fertile, easily available land, whereas American industrialization provided previously unavailable work opportunities. These changes in North America were complemented by modifications in Scandinavian society. As knowledge about opportunities in North America became increasingly widespread, it was weighed against the perceived opportunities within the nation's boundaries. As transport costs were reduced, many chose migration to America rather than movement internally. It was at this time that the frequency of emigration from Sweden and Denmark reached its zenith. Nearly 400,000 Swedish immigrants and almost 90,000 Danes entered the USA in the 1880s, a decade of particularly high emigration from the whole of northern Europe. Whereas the 1880s were also years of high emigration from Norway, the peak decade was actually between 1901 and 1910.

Given the shift in economic opportunities in the USA and Canada, later-arriving Scandinavian immigrants increasingly tended to move to urban locales.

PLATE 5: Southern Europe meets northern Europe on the roof of the detention centre at Ellis Island, New York. Bemused children celebrate the Fourth of July (the adoption of the Declaration of Independence).

To be sure, Scandinavian immigrants retained their distinctive proclivity to move to and live in rural places. As late as 1920, over half the Norwegian-born and nearly two-thirds of the second generation in the USA were rural dwellers (Qualey and Gjerde 1981: 230). Yet new destinations soon vied for the immigrants' attention. Norwegians began to move in large numbers to the Pacific north-west. Scandinavians in general began to choose urban residences. More so than the Norwegians, Swedish immigrants tended to move to cities. They clustered both in smaller industrial towns such as Jamestown (New York), Worcester (Massachusetts) and Rockford (Illinois), and in growing metropoli such as Chicago and the twin cities of Minneapolis and St Paul (Minnesota) (Norman 1974). In 1890, Swedes comprised the third largest national group in Chicago behind the Irish and Germans. Twenty years later, one-tenth of all Swedish immigrants and their children then alive in the USA lived in Chicago (Anderson and Blanck 1992: 1).

Symptomatic of industrial migration was the greater likelihood of return migration. Like emigration from other countries at this time, international migration was often premised on a return to the homeland. Between 1899 and 1924, for example, the quarter of a million Scandinavians who departed *from* the USA equalled 23.8 per cent of the immigration into the USA from Scandinavia. To be sure, this rate pales in comparison with 56.4 per cent for south Italy or 55.6 per cent for Slovaks, and it is lower than the total rate for immigration of 34.6 per cent (Thernstrom 1980:

1036), yet it indicates a new strategy practised especially by single males. Men comprised three-quarters of the returnees among the Swedish immigrants in the 1880s and two-thirds of them in the 1920s. Although in the main they moved from agricultural sectors, in America they tended to work in urban industrial occupations. When they returned to Scandinavia, they typically also returned to agriculture and often used the capital they had accrued in North America to finance new ventures in Scandinavia. One case study of the parish of Långasjö in Småland shows that 60 per cent of the return migrants from Canada purchased land in their home parish (Norman and Runblom 1987: 110).

It was during this industrial era that migration from Finland flourished. As from other Scandinavian countries, emigration from Finland was originally centred in rural areas. But since it grew during a period of improved transport and greater industrialization in the USA, Finnish migration had very much the same characteristics as industrial migration. The vast majority of immigrants were young and unmarried. Hoglund (1980: 365) notes that of the Finns who applied for passports between 1901 and 1920, three-quarters were unmarried and two-thirds were between the ages of 16 and 30. Secondly, they were more likely to work in industrial locations in the USA and were especially prominent in the mines of northern Minnesota and Michigan. Finally, the Finns, more so than other Scandinavians, were highly active in labour and socialist organizations in the USA. Inspired by their contacts with Russian radicalism, they introduced cooperative and socialist movements and led bitter strikes in the mining regions of Minnesota and Michigan in 1907 and 1913 respectively (Hoglund 1980; Norman and Runblom 1987: 234–41).

In sum, early Scandinavian migration to North America consisted of a movement from a region of Europe characterized by strict controls on nuptiality, rapid population growth, limited opportunities to own land and a fledgling urban industrial sector. The combination of these stimuli led to a massive migration to land-rich regions, especially in the USA and Canada. The Scandinavian migration was distinguished by its rural origins and by its tendency to move to rural destinations in North America. As the century of migration progressed, however, Scandinavian migration began to take on the characteristics of the industrial migration that typified the North American economy following the American Civil War.

References

Anderson, P. J. and D. Blanck (1992), Swedish-American Life in Chicago: Cultural and Urban Aspects of an Immigrant People, 1850–1930, Urbana: University of Illinois Press

Bailyn, B. (1986) Voyagers to the West, New York: Vintage

Beijbom, U. (1980) 'Swedes', in S. Thernstrom (ed.) Harvard Encyclopedia of American Ethnic Groups, Cambridge, MA: Harvard University Press, 971–81

Björnson, V. (1980) 'Icelanders', in S. Thernstrom (ed.) Harvard Encyclopedia of American Ethnic Groups, Cambridge, MA: Harvard University Press, 474–6

Blegen, T. C. (1931/1940) Norwegian Migration to America, Northfield, MN: Norwegian American Historical Association, 2 vols

Coale, A. J. and S. C. Watkins (1986) The Decline of Fertility in Europe, Princeton: Princeton University Press

De Geer, E. (1977) Migration och Influensfält: Studier av Emigration och Intern Migration i Finland och Sverige 1816–1972, Uppsala: Almqvist and Wiksell

Drake, M. (1969) Population and Society in Norway 1735–1865, Cambridge: Cambridge University Press

Engen, A. (ed.) (1978) Utvandringa: Det Store Oppbrotet, Oslo: Det Norske Samlaget

Gjerde, J. (1985) From Peasants to Farmers: The Migration from Balestrand, Norway to the Upper Middle West, New York: Cambridge University Press

(1991) 'Chain Migrations from the West Coast of Norway', in R. J. Vecoli and S. M. Sinke (eds) A Century of Migrations, 1830–1930, Urbana: University of Illinois Press, 158–81

Hajnal, J. (1965) 'European Marriage Patterns in Perspective', in D. V. Glass and D. E. C. Eversley (eds) Population in History: Essays in Historical Demography, London: Edward Arnold, 101–43

Hoglund, A. W. (1980) 'Finns', in S. Thernstrom (ed.) Harvard Encyclopedia of American Ethnic Groups, Cambridge, MA: Harvard University Press, 362–70

Hvidt, K. (1975) Flight to America: The Social Background of 300,000 Danish Emigrants, New York: Academic Press

Martinius, S. (1971) 'Jordbruk och Ekonomisk Tillväxt i Sverige, 1830–1870', Historisk Tidskrift, (34), 603–4

Norman, H. (1974) Från Bergslagen till Nordamerika: Studier i Migrationsmönster, Social Rörlighet och Demografisk Struktur med Utgångspunkt från Örebro Län 1851–1915, Uppsala: Acta Universitatus Upsaliensis

Norman, H. and H. Runblom (1987) Transatlantic Connections: Nordic Migration to the New World after 1880, Oslo: Universitetsforlaget

Ostergren, R. C. (1988) A Community Transplanted: The Trans-Atlantic Experience of a Swedish Immigrant Settlement in the Upper Middle West, 1835–1915, Madison: University of Wisconsin Press

Qualey, C. and J. Gjerde (1981) 'The Norwegians', in June Drenning Holmquist (ed.) They Chose Minnesota: A Survey of the State's Ethnic Groups, St Paul: Minnesota Historical Society Press, 220–47

Rice, J. (1981) 'The Swedes', in June Drenning Holmquist (ed.) They Chose Minnesota: A Survey of the State's Ethnic Groups, St Paul: Minnesota Historical Society Press, 248–76

Rice, J. and R. C. Ostergren (1978) 'The Decision to Emigrate: A Study in Diffusion', Geografiska Annaler, (60B), 1–15

Runblom, H. and H. Norman (eds) (1976) *From Sweden to America: A History of the Migration*, Minneapolis and Uppsala: University of Minnesota Press and Acta Universitatus Upsaliensis

Semmingsen, I. (1941/1950), *Veien Mot Vest: Utvandringen fra Norge til Amerika*, Oslo: Aschehoug, 3 vols

   (1978) *Norway to America: A History of the Migration*, Minneapolis: University of Minnesota Press

Sogner, S. (1979) *Folkevekst og flytting: En historisk-demografisk studie i 1700-årenes Øst-Norge*, Oslo: Universitetsforlaget

Thernstrom, S. (1980) *Harvard Encyclopedia of American Ethnic Groups*, Cambridge, MA: Harvard University Press

Vecoli, Rudolph J. and Suzanne M. Sinke (eds) (1991) *A Century of Migrations, 1830–1930*, Urbana: University of Illinois Press

UNBROKEN LINKS: PORTUGUESE EMIGRATION TO THE USA

MARÍA IOANNIS B. BAGANHA

Forty years ago old Silva come from the Azores. Went sheep-herdin' in the mountains for a couple of years, then blew into San Leandro. These five acres was the first land he leased. That was the biginnin'. Then he began leasin' by the hundreds of acres an' by the hundred-an-sixties. An' his sisters an' his uncles an' his aunts begun pourin' in from the Azores — they're all related there, you know; an' pretty soon San Leandro was a regular Porchugeeze settlement.

—Jack London, *The Valley of the Moon* (1913: 309)

The flow of Europeans across the Atlantic became essentially a free international labour movement after the independence of the American colonies, the ban on slave trade in the Atlantic and the progressive inscription of the freedom of movement in most European constitutions. In less than a century, 1850–1914, 36 to 40 million people are estimated to have departed from Europe overseas. The majority of the flow, roughly 70 per cent, went to the USA,[1] the bulk of the movement occurring after 1875.[2]

Although all western European countries contributed to this movement, neither the size nor the moment of the contribution are similar. In the Portuguese case, the country only became, relative to its demographic base, a high emigration area during the 1890s or, if we include clandestine departures, from the late 1870s.[3] But, while the preferred choice of destination for the majority of the departing Europeans was the USA, for the overwhelming majority of the Portuguese (at least 80 per cent) the preferred choice of destination was Brazil. In fact, the 175,000 Portuguese who between 1855 and 1914 entered the USA only represented 12–14 per cent of the Portuguese total migratory current overseas.

Population pressure and land fragmentation in rural Europe, the development of the New World, the spread of railroads and the progressive substitution of sailing boats by steamers are the most commonly listed determinants of transatlantic mass migration until the First World War.[4] These determinants may explain why the Portuguese were a part of this movement; they do not explain why so few Portuguese went to the USA or why so many went to Brazil. Scholarship on Portuguese emigration has not addressed this issue. Instead, it has accepted as a natural fact the choice of Brazil as the main area of destination of the Portuguese migratory flow. After all, it is usually recalled, political and cultural links existed between the two countries dating back to the sixteenth century.

Studies on the forces determining the direction of a migratory flow are relatively scarce, partially because the overwhelming majority of the research focus is on emigration to the USA. Still, as was perceptively noticed by J. D. Gould (1979: 605) and more recently by Dudley Baines (1985: 22), if the greater attraction of the USA may be attributed to some known advantages — namely being cheaper to reach, being more developed than the other receiving areas and, given its own size, being able to absorb relatively larger numbers of newcomers — this just leaves us with the problem of explaining why a part of the flow, over 30 per cent, took a different direction.

To address this question we need detailed information on migratory flows that took more than one direction, which is usually unavailable. In the Portuguese case, however, we do have the necessary evidence to contrast the main features of the migratory flow that went to the USA with those of the flow that went to Brazil in order to determine the main factors dictating the choice of direction.

This work has two purposes: to describe synthetically the main features of the Portuguese emigration to the USA, particularly after 1870, when this movement became a sustained and growing process; and to do so with the background objective of bringing to light the main factors dictating the choice of direction.

Finally, by contrasting some of the main features of the Portuguese emigration flow to the USA with those of the Portuguese flow to Brazil, I hope to prove that what channelled emigrants in either direction were the emigrants' personal characteristics and the characteristics of the receiving society's labour market, plus the existence or non-existence of channels of information and support to a given direction.

Table 4.1: *Portuguese-born residents in continental USA and Portuguese arrivals, 1850–1910*

Year	Portuguese residents	Date	Portuguese arrivals
1850	1,274	1840–1849	362
1860	5,477	1850–1859	4,225
1870	8,759	1860–1869	5,369
1880	15,650	1870–1879	14,265
1890	25,735	1880–1889	15,560
1900	40,431	1890–1899	26,376
1910	77,634	1900–1909	63,144

Source: Baganha (1990: 307).

Portuguese emigration to the USA

The first Portuguese migratory stream to the USA was induced by the needs of the American whaling and merchant fleets that, since the late eighteenth century, stopped at Faial harbour in search of supplies and crew members; it was strengthened by the establishment of American mercantile houses in that same Azorean island. After the American gold rush of the mid-nineteenth century, a new current was established, having as its final destination first the mining areas and, soon after, the rural and fishing areas of California. Information about the USA seems to have spread very slowly to the other Azorean islands, but from the 1870s onward all the islands were participating in a significant and growing flow. The migratory current increased until it was halted by the US anti-immigration legislation of the 1920s.[5]

As said, a sizeable permanent community in the USA only gained form after 1870. This fact can be confirmed by looking at the evolution of Portuguese-born residents in continental USA and Portuguese arrivals between 1850 and 1910.[6] This evolution is shown in Table 4.1.

Both the numbers of arrivals and the stock of the Portuguese resident in the USA is insignificant before 1870. But between that year and 1910, the Portuguese resident population grew at an impressive average growth rate of 5.6 per cent per year, mainly attributable to the snowballing number of arrivals. In 1910, the 78,000 Portuguese-born residents in continental USA represented a demographic base eight times larger than the base registered in 1870 and 61 times larger than that existent in 1850 (Baganha 1990: 307).

The Portuguese arriving in the USA at the turn of the century (from 1899 to 1910) were a very homogeneous group. More than 90 per cent of them came from the Azores, 68 per cent were illiterate, 88 per cent were unskilled, they were overwhelmingly single and between 16 and 25 years of age. Their financial resources, at entry, were also extremely low; 88 per cent declared themselves to be carrying less than thirty dollars, and 46 per cent of the incoming immigrants stated that their passage was paid for by someone other than themselves.

After arrival, the Portuguese immigrants were overwhelmingly concentrated in some very specific communities in the states of Massachusetts and California.[7] This tendency for new arrivals to flock into these two main areas of previous settlement became even greater from the 1870s onwards. In fact, while the Portuguese residents in these two states in 1870 accounted for 68 per cent of the total number of residents, by 1890 they represented 80 per cent, and by 1910 they corresponded to 83 per cent (Baganha 1990: 284–5).

In other words, after 1870 the Portuguese immigrant communities in the USA attained a sizeable base that was able to absorb increasing numbers of newcomers. That the flocking of new arrivals could be done to the main areas of previous settlement would obviously reduce the need for social interaction with English native speakers.

On this subject we may go further, since one of the noticeable characteristics of Portuguese immigrants in the USA is their very restricted need to interact outside their own ethnic group.[8] Here I review the main findings of a previous work on Portuguese communities in the USA based on the 1910 manuscript census of the USA (Baganha 1991a). The data contain a 10 per cent random sample of the households headed by Portuguese-born residents in the textile city of Taunton in Bristol county (Massachusetts) and all the households headed by Portuguese-born in Milpitas in the rural region of Santa Clara county (California) – overall 155 households, 61 for Taunton and 94 for Milpitas.

The Portuguese came initially to Massachusetts as crew members for the Bostonian whaling and merchant fleets, but by the 1880s they were profiting, like other 'new' immigrant groups, from the opening of low-skill job opportunities in the textile mills of the region. The occupations and the economic sectors of activity of the Portuguese male household heads in this city were quite restricted and clearly determined by the labour market of the receiving community. Of the Portuguese male heads in Taunton, 91 per cent were wage earners, and of those 79 per cent were industrial unskilled labourers.

During the mid-nineteenth century gold rush some of the Portuguese went to California, where they soon became farmers. But the available land, even at low prices, was not immediately affordable for the majority of Portuguese immigrants. Still, through a process of renting followed by buying, the Portuguese succeeded in establishing a niche for themselves in two branches of agriculture – market gardening and dairy production. The Portuguese in Milpitas were connected with market gardening. As in the previous case, the market economy of the receiving region determined their occupational structure; 95 per cent of the Portuguese household heads were connected with agricultural activities. Of these 95 per cent, 87 per cent were either employers or self-employed.

The mean size and type of Portuguese immigrant households in Milpitas were, relative to those in Taunton, larger and less dominated by nuclear families. The high proportion of households with employees and of extended family households indicates that the Portuguese immigrant households in Milpitas relied on both extended family members and wage-earners to satisfy their labour demands. The fact that all the employees in Portuguese households were themselves Portuguese, and that a substantial number of the extended family members were males who had arrived after the household head, indicates that Portuguese employers in Milpitas relied on kinship and informal migrant networks active at both ends of the trajectory (in this case the Azores and California) to supply their labour demands.[9] This practice, frequently referred to in immigrants' testimonies (Mayone Dias 1982), was so common among the Portuguese community in California that it was singled out in the Immigration Commissioners Reports of 1911 (Document 33, 1911: 490, 491).

In Taunton, the high proportion of households with boarders suggests that a significant share of Portuguese immigrant households in that city took in lodgers to supplement their incomes. Contemporary observers specifically refer to this household strategy among the Portuguese operatives in the cotton mills of New England (Lauck 1912: 712). Boarders in the Taunton sample were all first-generation Portuguese, indicating that the strategy to complement household earnings with boarders could be achieved within the Portuguese migrant network active in the region.

In sum, the Portuguese migrant network was active in both areas. In California, it offered readily available work in a setting where the spoken language was mainly Portuguese. Networking between California and the Azores seems to have been an effective 'informal' information system able to support a labour market based on both sides of the Atlantic. In Massachusetts, it offered logistical and cultural support, substantially reducing the costs of displacement for the new arrivals. Furthermore, economically, the Portuguese who went to California performed far better that those who chose or were directed to Massachusetts. In fact, the temporal pattern of ownership indicates that in Milpitas the Portuguese immigrants would in time attain some kind of property, while in Taunton only 25 per cent of each wave of newcomers could expect to become property owners.

Contrasting the USA with Brazil

Let us begin by considering some characteristics of Portuguese emigration to Brazil. The Brazilian Declaration of Independence in 1822 was followed by an anti-Portuguese sentiment that was vividly, and sometimes violently, expressed against the Portuguese community. These events restrained, at least for a while, potential migrants and even promoted a significant number of returns. After the mid-nineteenth century, nationalistic spirits had already calmed down and the flow to Brazil begun to regain strength. This new strength is said to have been eased by the existence of migratory channels opened up in the past, the existence of a large Portuguese community and by the use of a common language. It was pulled by the growing labour needs of the Brazilian economy and by the knowledge, in Portugal, of the existence of economic opportunities, particularly in retail trade. It was pushed by the existence of a surplus rural population which the slow economic growth of the country could not absorb, by land fragmentation which liberal reforms accelerated and by a long migratory tradition that led, particularly, the northern mainland and the islander peasantry to accept emigration as a natural strategy at a given phase of a male life cycle.

Taking into consideration the migrants' characteristics and their respective insertion in the Brazilian labour market, migration to Brazil may be divided into three groups.

The first group is composed of adolescents and young adults who went to join relatives or 'friends' to work in trade activities. This group departed almost exclusively from the northern regions of Portugal.[10] The second group is relatively older, and is formed by those that had some sort of property or skill, and could easily find a niche in the expanding Brazilian urban economy.[11] The third group is made up of those with no skills who enter the Brazilian unskilled labour market. According to Martins (1956: 231) and Evangelista (1971: 130), at the end of the nineteenth century the first group represented between 8 and 11 per cent of the total legal flow, while the second group accounted for a maximum of 10 per cent. Thus, the last group corresponded to close on 80 per cent of the flow.[12]

It seems reasonable to assume that, relative to the USA, the first two groups chose the destination that from the start maximized their skills or assets, since their transference was not blocked by the use of an unknown language and it was eased by the existence of a large Portuguese community. The choice does not seem as reasonable for the last group, not only because unskilled wages were higher in the USA, but also because insertion in this segment of the labour market did not necessarily require knowledge of the English language.

As we have seen, this is particularly true after 1870, when the Portuguese migratory flow to the USA became a sustained movement, backed by a growing Portuguese immigrant community. Although accurate and comparable figures are hard to come by, this group, which made up at least three-quarters of the Portuguese emigration to Brazil, seems, compared with migrants to the USA, to have performed economically quite poorly in the receiving area. After all, extremely high rates of mortality and subsidized returns from Brazil, either by indigence or extreme sickness, are repeatedly referred to in contemporary sources, but no such descriptions were ever made about the Portuguese immigrants in the USA.[13]

Why then did the unskilled emigrants not choose the USA rather than Brazil? Passport registers are perhaps the most useful sources for understanding the dynamics behind the choice of direction, for detailed information on the individual characteristics of the emigrants departing in each direction can be collected from them. We may observe the relative weight that the existence of information and channels of support play in the choice of direction, particularly if both directions are firmly established in the region's migratory streams.

In 1901, 709 Portuguese emigrants left from the Azorean island of Terceira overseas. More or less half of them went to Brazil and the other half to the USA. Based on their passport registers and using a logit-probit model, I tested whether their decision to emigrate to the USA or Brazil was a function of their personal characteristics (Baganha 1990).

My findings, for the topic being discussed, may be summarized as follows. Although losing ground relative to the USA, since departures to Brazil had been consistently decreasing since the 1880s,[14] Brazil's attraction increased with the migrant's age and skills and with the migrant's previous personal or familial migratory experience.

The probability of migrating to Brazil was consistently higher for migrants between 26 and 40 years of age than for migrants between 14 and 25 years of age, and was equally consistently higher for males with some skill or property than for labourers. The male migrant with the highest probability (a chance higher than 95 per cent) of coming to the USA from Terceira, in 1901, was an unmarried labourer between 14 and 25 years of age and without previous migratory experience. Conversely, the migrant most likely to emigrate to Brazil (98 per cent chance) was married, had a skill or property and had previous personal or familial migratory experience.

What these findings suggest is that network support was a particularly strong determinant in the early phases of the migrant's life cycle and more so if he was an unskilled labourer. This inference is also borne out by the migrants' life stories published by Mayone Dias (1982) and by the fact that a high percentage of emigrants had had their passages paid for by someone else.

Conclusion

In an area where half the migratory flow went to the USA and the other half to Brazil, factors like age, skills and property were found to be relevant in explaining the choice of direction. Furthermore, since information on Brazil and the USA was equally available to potential migrants from Terceira, it seems reasonable to assume that the choices of direction reflected the maximization of each emigrant's perceived chances of success in the receiving society. Thus we may conclude that migrants with some form of skill or property, as a rule older than the rest of the flow, and probably with less need to rely on established channels of support, enhanced their chances for betterment by going to Brazil. Young, unskilled migrants, who were unlikely to have the necessary means to leave on their own, relied on family support and on the migrant network active in the region to boost their chances of success in the receiving area. That network, in the Azores, directed them to the USA, where, in fact, the chances for upward economic mobility seem to have been greater than in Brazil.

We have seen that young unskilled migrants at the turn of the century made up at least three-quarters of the total migratory flow. Of these, roughly 90 per cent went to Brazil and only 10 per cent went to the USA. Since the latter were almost all departing from the Azores, the most likely reason for the overwhelming majority of young unskilled Portuguese emigrants having taken the 'wrong' direction is that neither information nor channels of support existed on the Portuguese mainland to direct them to the USA. This hypothesis is more in accordance with the existing historical evidence than the classic argument of political and cultural links with Brazil dating back to the sixteenth century.

This leads us to the conclusion that once a migratory flow is established, the dynamics of the migrant network active at both ends of the trajectory are the most powerful filters for determining the direction the movement takes. This is because they maximize the fit between the personal characteristics of the emigrant and the current demands of the labour market of the receiving area. Or, in other words, unbroken links are important in determining migratory movements, if not directly their size and fluctuations, at least their direction.

Notes

1. Between 1856 and 1915, the USA, Brazil, Canada and Argentina received 38 million aliens, 70 per cent of whom went to the USA (Ferenczi and Willcox 1929: 172).
2. American immigration sources registered the entry of 8,852,000 immigrants between 1820 and 1874, against 23,176,000 between 1875 and 1914 (Baganha 1990: 250–252).
3. I am using D. Baines's (1985: 10) threshold of an emigration rate of 4 per cent or more of a country's population in a decade to define a high emigration area. Portuguese yearly emigration rates by intercensal periods were: 4.2 for 1878 to 1890; 5.6 for 1891 to 1900; 6.9 for 1901 to 1911; and 7.1 for 1912 to 1920 (Baganha 1990: 217). On Portuguese sources on emigration see Serrão (1982) and Baganha (1990) and (1991b).

4. For a full list of factors influencing European overseas emigration see Qualey (1980: 36–38); for an appraisal of these factors see, for example, Gould (1979) and Baines (1985).
5. On Portuguese emigration to the USA see, for example, Baganha (1990), Bannick (1917), Morison (1961), Pap (1949), Trindade (1976) and Williams (1982).
6. This work only addresses Portuguese emigration to continental USA; the Portuguese stream to Hawaii is thus not referred to.
7. This tendency was specifically addressed by Williams in Higgs (1990: 145–57).
8. In fact the few surviving testimonies for this period, gathered by Mayone Dias (1982) among Portuguese immigrants in California, confirm what is being said. So do the scattered interviews published by Graves (1977) and Leder (1980), and the few biographical accounts of Andrade (1968), Oliver (1972) and Vieira (1963).
9. As many as 91 per cent. I am using the concept of migrant networks in a broad sense. The term here refers to both kin/community-based and impersonal structures of information and support. The term would encompass what Macdonald and Macdonald (1964) called chain-migration and impersonally organized migration, and what Tilly and Brown (1967) called 'auspices of kinship' and 'auspices of work'. The evidence on the Portuguese emigration of this period strongly suggests that kin/community migrant networks were more relevant than impersonal structures of information and support.
10. There is an extensive literature on this subject. See for example Brettell (1986) and Monteiro (1985).
11. Alencastro (1988: 43) mentions that in the 1872 census of Rio de Janeiro, three out of every four foreign craftsmen were Portuguese.
12. During the late nineteenth and early twentieth century the Portuguese were the largest foreign group connected with manual unskilled jobs in the urban industries like textiles and tobacco (Pescatelo 1970).
13. See, for example, Ministério dos Negócios Externos (1874 and 1885).
14. In 1887–89 departures to Brazil represented 27 per cent of all legal departures; in 1901–5 they accounted for 12 per cent; and in 1912–16 for a slim 5 per cent (Baganha 1990: 363–4).

References

Alencastro, Luís F. de (1988) 'Proletários e Escravos. Imigrantes Portuguese e Cativos Africanos no Rio de Janeiro, 1850–1872', *Novos Estudos*, CEBROP, 21, 30–55

Andrade, Laurinda C. (1968) *The Open Door*, New Bedford: Reynolds-De Walt

Baganha, Maria Ioannis B. (1990) *Portuguese Emigration to the United States*, New York: Garland Publishing

—— (1991a) 'Social Mobility in the Receiving Society: Portuguese Immigrants in the United States', *International Migration Review*, 25 (2), 277–302

—— (1991b) 'Uma Imagem desfocada: A Emigração portuguesa e as Fontes sobre a Emigração', *Análise Social*, 26, 112–13

Baines, Dudley (1985) *Migration in a Mature Economy*, Cambridge: Cambridge University Press

Bannick, Christian J. (1917) 'Portuguese Immigration to the United States: Its Distribution and Status', thesis, University of California

Brettell, Caroline B. (1986) *Men who Migrate, Women who Wait*, Princeton: Princeton University Press

Evangelista, J. (1971) *Um Século de População Portuguesa*, Lisboa: INE

Ferenczi, I. and W. Willcox (eds) (1929) *International Migrations*. Vol. I, Statistics, New York: National Bureau of Economic Research Inc.

Gould, J.D. (1979) 'European Inter-Continental Emigration 1815–1914: Patterns and Causes', *Journal of Economic European History*, 8 (3), 593–679

Graves, Alvin R. (1977) 'Immigrants in Agriculture: The Portuguese Californians, 1850–1970s', Ph.D. dissertation, University of California, Los Angeles

Higgs, David (ed.) (1990) *Portuguese Migration in Global Perspective*, Toronto: The Multicultural History Society of Ontario

Lauck, Jett W. (1912) 'The Cotton-Mill Operatives of New England', *The Atlantic Monthly*, CIX, 706–13

Leder, Hans H. (1980) *Cultural Persistence in a Portuguese-American Community*, New York: Arno Press

Macdonald, John and Leatrice Macdonald (1964) 'Chain Migration, Ethnic Neighborhood Formation and Social Networks', *The Milbank Memorial Fund Quarterly*, XLII (1), 82–97

Martins, Joaquim de Oliveira (1956) *Fomento Rural e Emigraçaõ e Comércio*, Porto: SEE

Mayone Dias, Eduardo (ed.) (1982) *Açorianos na California: Angra do Heroismo*, Lisbon: SREC

Ministério dos Negócios Externos (1874 and 1885) *Documentos Apresentados às Cortes*, Lisbon: Imprensa Nacional

Monteiro, Tania P. (1985) *Portugueses na Bahia na Segunda Metade do Séc. XIX: Emigração e Comércio*, Porto: SEE

Morison, Samuel (1961) *The Maritime History of Massachusetts 1783–1860*, Cambridge, MA: The Riverside Press

Oliver, Lawrence (1972) *Never Backward. The Autobiography of Lawrence Oliver: A Portuguese-American*, San Diego: Neyenesch Printers

Pap, Leo (1949) *Portuguese-American Speech*, New York: King's Crown Press

Pescatelo, Ann Marie (1970) 'Both Ends of the Journey: A Historical Study of Migration and Change in Brazil and Portugal, 1889–1914', unpublished Ph.D. dissertation, Los Angeles, University of California

Qualey, Carlton C. (1980) 'Immigration to the United States since 1815', *Les Migrations Internationales*, Paris, 32–8

Serrão, Joel (1982) *A Emigração Portugugesa*, Lisbon: Livros Horizonte

Tilly, Charles and C. Harold Brown (1967) 'On Uprooting, Kinship and the Auspices of Migration', *International Journal of Comparative Sociology*, 8 (2), 139–64

Trindade, Maria J. Lagos (1976) 'Portuguese Emigration from the Azores to the United States During the Nineteenth Century', *Studies in Honour of the Bicentennial of the American Independence*, Lisbon, 237–95

Vieira, João J. (1963) *Eu Falo Por Mim Mesmo. Autobiografia*, Porto: Livraria Escolar Progredior

Williams, Jerry (1982) *And Yet They Come*, New York: Center for Migration Studies

EAST EUROPEANS ON THE MOVE

EWA MORAWSKA

The region here called eastern Europe includes the territory of the turn-of-the-century Russian empire west of the Urals, together with Congress Poland (the fragment of Poland partitioned in 1795 under Russian rule) and the eastern province of the Austrian monarchy composed of the incorporated part of Poland called Galicia, including Bukovyna in its south-eastern corner. Peoples inhabiting this region who are the subject of this essay include, in order of the magnitude of their overseas migration, Jews, Poles, Lithuanians, Ukrainians and Carpatho-Rusyns (groups with kindred languages and shared religions, known then as Ruthenians or subsumed under the generic name of Russians), ethnic Russians and Byelorussians (during the time considered here, the latter had not yet differentiated themselves from the former), and Latvians.

Transatlantic migration of East Europeans started as a trickle in the 1870s and turned into a mass movement in the 1880s that continued to swell until the outbreak of the First World War in 1914. Whereas during the decade 1871–80 no more than 70,000 migrants from the eastern part of the European continent crossed the Atlantic, between 1881 and 1890 this number grew to more than a quarter of a million, and during the first decade of this century, to more than two million. (See Nugent in this volume on contemporaneous migration of peoples from the adjacent areas usually also considered as eastern Europe, i.e. Czechs, Slovaks and Hungarians). In all, more than four million people journeyed from eastern Europe to the Americas between 1880 and 1914. Nearly nine-tenths of this number migrated to North America, of whom about the same proportion went to the USA: approximately 1.8 million Jews; between 1.1 and 1.3 million Poles; about 300,000 Lithuanians and 250,000 Ukrainians/Rusyns (Ruthenians); 100,000–150,000 ethnic Russians (with Byelorussians); and 10,000–15,000 Latvians (Bobinska and Pilch 1975: 39–48, 84–101, 126–7; Ferenczi and Willcox 1929: I, 230–50, II, 507–29; *HEAEG* 1980: 182, 202, 580–1, 639, 668, 887, 998; Kuznets 1975: 39–51).

This contribution focuses primarily on migration to the USA, as it was the main destination of the trans-atlantic journeys of East Europeans (particular features of the migration to Canada are also noted). Travels to the USA, or simply America, as the migrants called it, were part of the intense multi-directional movement of East Europeans within their own region and towards central and western parts of the continent.[1]

Two major factors that simultaneously mobilized thousands of people to undertake the American journey can be distinguished. One of them operated at the macro-structural level and had two aspects: socio-economic and political. The socio-economic factor was related to the emerging system of exchange of capital, products and labour linking two sides of the Atlantic, facilitated by improved long-distance transport and communication (this multiple intercon-nectedness between Europe and America has been called the Atlantic world system). More specifically, it involved the socio-economic consequences of the progressive incorporation of eastern Europe, during the last four decades preceding the First World War, into the orbit of expanding modern capitalism on the one hand, and, on the other, of the rapid urbanization–industrialization of the USA (Hoerder 1985; Morawska 1989). The political factor conducive to mass migration involved the legal and civic status of members of particular classes and ethno-religious/national groups in eastern Europe, as well as the politics of migration in both the sending and the receiving societies.

The second mobilizing factor operated in the immediate or micro-environments of the migrants, and it was of socio-cultural nature. Of all the possible destinations that turn-of-the-century East Europeans could (and did) travel to, only America (the USA) had a 'great legend' of unmatched riches awaiting immigrants. Labour migration to other places was perceived as an opportunity for the family to make ends meet or at best gain a somewhat better livelihood. But going to America was viewed, in the opinion of W. Thomas and F. Znaniecki (1918–20), the authors of the classic study *The Polish Peasant in Europe and America*, as a project to alter radically the migrant's ordinary course of life, either by permanently settling overseas or after returning home. For members of oppressed national or religious minorities, such as Russian Jews, in addition to a promise of material affluence, America symbolized a paradise of civic and political freedom. In the remainder of this essay, we look at each of these two mobilizing factors somewhat more closely.

Macro-structural context of transatlantic migration

The eastern European and American parts of the Atlantic world system at the turn of the century can be viewed as the sending and the receiving sides of migration. The mechanisms linking them are the 'push' and 'pull' forces, respectively. Let us first consider the sending side, eastern Europe, and the macro-structural forces, socio-economic and political, that pushed people out of their places of residence and turned them into work-seeking migrants. Next, we shall examine the corresponding 'pull' forces on the side of the receiver, the USA, and note the differing circumstances in Canada.

It was only in the five decades preceding the First World War that eastern Europe began a long-term, uneven process of accelerated urban-industrial transformation and the accompanying social restructuring. The abolition of serfdom and the alienation of estates (in 1848 in the Austrian monarchy, including its Polish part, and in 1861/64 in the Russian empire/Congress Poland) produced cumulative long-term effects on the rural economy of eastern Europe. (By 1900 the majority of the Slavic, Lithuanian and Latvian population, the proportion ranging between 65 per cent and 80 per cent depending on the province, were still involved in farming, whereas the majority of Jews, with a similar regional variation, were occupied in rural and semi-rural petty trade and artisanry.) The main consequences of the enfranchisement of the peasantry were a rapid diminution of holdings as they were divided and redivided among peasants' progeny and the creation of a large mass of rural proletarians. On the one hand, the alienation of noble estates that traditionally employed Jewish lessees and land administrators, and, on the other, the growth of mass industrial production in the developing cities, caused the progressive disintegration of rural handicrafts and industries and, generally, the diminution of work traditionally performed by Jews in the *shtetls*, small towns in the countryside. This process produced, in turn, a commercial and proto-industrial Jewish proletariat (Berend and Ranki 1982; Joseph 1914: 43–99).

Combined with the unprecedented demographic growth of all groups in the region, this large-scale proletarianization of eastern European working classes both Christian and Jewish, sent millions of people in search of a livelihood. By the beginning of this century no less than one-quarter to one-third of the total adult male population of rural and semi-rural origins lived or worked in places different from those of their birth. Since the developing local urban industries, dependent to a large extent on western capital and lacking sufficient dynamism of their own, could absorb only a fraction of the 'superfluous' workforce generated by the socio-economic restructuring of the region, the majority had to seek employment farther away[2] (Balch 1910: 48, 132–40; Bodnar 1985: 9–11, 31–2, 43–5; Kuznets 1975: 68–82).

Political discrimination against particular ethnic/national groups by the institutions of the dominant society reinforced the 'push' effects of the economic and demographic factors. The situation of Russian Jews, particularly during three decades of harsh anti-Jewish legislation and popular outbursts, or pogroms, ushered in after the assassination of Tsar Alexander II in 1881, had been the most notorious case (that of Slovaks in the Hungarian monarchy could also serve as an example). The importance of the civic-political oppression in instigating emigration of a minority group's members is shown by a comparison of the contemporary rates of emigration to America by Russians and Galicians. (As Austrian subjects, the Galician Jews were included in the Emancipation Act of 1867, and although the Polish administrators of this province obstructed rather than facilitated the implementation of the constitutional laws regarding Jewish participation in public life and institutions, in Galicia there were no pogroms or anti-Semitic public hysteria comparable to those in Russia.) Whereas between 1899 and 1910, on average 74 of every 10,000 Jews in Austria emigrated to America, the proportion for Russian Jews during the same period was 125:10,000 (Joseph 1914: 56–80, 104, 112). An additional political factor that contributed to emigration of young Jewish and peasant men alike was military conscription, which drew disproportionately from the lower classes and, particularly in Russia, was popularly viewed as a symbol of oppressive rule by an alien power.

The oversupply of labour in eastern Europe coincided with a demand for it on the other side of the Atlantic, related to the restructuring of the rapidly expanding American economy that had shifted to heavy industry, construction and mass garment production. Each of these enterprises required large quantities of manual workers. With the decrease in the arrival of immigrants from western and central parts of Europe due to industrial development there, American employers were eager to draw labour from the underdeveloped and overpopulated eastern regions of the continent.

Contracting labour as a means of recruiting a foreign workforce by overseas agents of American employers was outlawed in 1885. But until the First World War the US government practised an open door immigration policy (open, we should specify, for people with white skins). This policy constituted an additional political factor encouraging mass immigration on the receiving side of the Atlantic world system and, to the extent that the policy was known in the villages and *shtetls* of eastern Europe, it was also a mobilizing element on the 'push' side. Indeed, during the last four decades preceding the outbreak of the First World War, about one-third of the increase in the American labour force came from immigration. By 1910, immigrants represented one-fifth of the US workforce: two-thirds of non-farm labourers and one-third of industrial operatives. As the nineteenth century came to a close, southern and eastern Europeans provided increasingly large proportions of immigrants to America: from 5 per cent in the decade 1870 to 1880, to 33 per cent between 1891 and 1900. By 1914, they made up close to 70 per cent of all arrivals (Balch 1910: 265, 460–1; Ferenczi and Willcox 1929: I, 418–39).

Much smaller in numbers, the migration of East Europeans to Canada differed from that to the USA in two important features, or, more precisely, the consequences thereof: the nature of the economic 'pull' and immigration policy on the receiving side. Regarding the former, rather than to secure labour for industrial production (of which it had little before the First World War), Canada's primary need was to populate the country's western territories and turn them into farmlands. The latter – and related – feature was the active involvement of the Canadian government, through its agencies in eastern Europe, in recruiting immigrants by offering free homesteads. And indeed, the majority of pre-First World War East European immigrants to Canada, most of them Galician and Bukovynian Ukrainians, settled on the prairies of Manitoba, Saskatchewan and Alberta (Heydenkorn 1975; Luciuk and Hryniuk 1991).

Micro-social environment of US migration

The configuration and pressure of macro-structural forces on the sending and the receiving sides of transatlantic migration set the general opportunity framework and delineated the principal directions of population flows, but it was at the level of their immediate surroundings that people defined purposes, made decisions and undertook actions. It was also at this level, through the circulation of letters and migrants themselves between eastern Europe and America, that the American legend was created and sustained, drawing, magnet-like, millions of people.

Transatlantic migration from eastern European *shtetls* and villages was not an individual but a collective undertaking from the time the idea became implanted in local minds, through organization of the journey, to establishing residence and procuring employment in America. The pioneer migrants were solicited by the recruitment agents of American employers and, after 1885, by the agents of steamship companies in Hamburg, Antwerp and Bremen, but after a seed-group of the *krajany* or *landslayt*, people from the same area, formed in America, the role of further mobilizers passed to the migrants and prospective migrants themselves.

An important element in this process was communication from the USA (over five million letters were sent in the seven years between 1900 and 1906) transmitting information about the 'incredible land' where within two weeks people made as much money as a peasant would earn working on a farm for the whole season from June until October. In fact, around the turn of the century, unskilled labourers in American industries earned $1.00 to $1.15 a day, or about seven to ten times more than agricultural workers and artisans in eastern Europe. To the recipients of this information the economic calculation was obvious: it meant, in local money, the unheard-of ability to afford a full hectare of land out of a single year's savings, or the price of a new brick house in nine. Photographs that accompanied letters from America were also impressive, showing successful emigrants in city attire. And, of course, there were remittances – staggering amounts of money in the perception of the local people – sent in money orders and letters, and savings brought by the returning migrants. For instance, in the five years between 1902 and 1906, money orders alone sent from the USA to Austria-Hungary and Russia amounted to $70 million. According to contemporary estimates, sums brought back during that time by the returnees added up to an even larger figure, and the investments in land and new buildings paid for by the savings of these *Amerikanci* made local people go 'wild with envy and desire'[3] (Balch 1910: 56, 144–5, 471–2; Kula et al. 1986; Morawska 1989: 255–66).

Most East European peasants travelling to the USA at the turn of the century went there as migrant labourers, not as permanent settlers. Their stay in America was intended to be temporary. Since the sojourn was not to exceed a few years, just enough to save enough money to elevate the family's socio-economic standing in the village, the majority of migrants were young, single men (the average proportion of women ranged between 33 per cent among Poles and about 15 per cent among Russians). In comparison, peasants heading to the Canadian prairies to homestead usually intended their migration as permanent resettlement and travelled with their entire families. Most of the Jews who left eastern Europe, especially Russia, not only for economic reasons, but also as political refugees, viewed their emigration as permanent; the proportion of females among them was therefore close (44 per cent) to that of men. Although a significant proportion of peasant migrants to the USA between 1880 and 1914 indeed returned home – 35 per cent to 45 per cent depending on the ethnic/national group, with men considerably more numerous than women – a majority eventually remained, extending their stay from one year to the next. Among Jews, the proportion of returnees was slightly over 20 per cent between 1880 and 1900, and then dropped to 7 per cent (Balch 1910: 144–5; Bodnar 1985: 53–4; Ferenczi and Willcox 1929: II, 484, 521; Gabaccia forthcoming; Sarna 1981: 256–69).

As the numbers of East Europeans in America increased, close-knit immigrant communities emerged and solidified. This development was facilitated by the immigrant groups' residential and occupational concentration in the areas where the expanding urban-industrial American economy needed them most. At the same time, by attracting more and more people from the old country through social networks of information and assistance, the growing East European colonies in America contributed, in turn, to increased concentration of immigrants in particular regions and cities and in specific industries. And so nearly 90 per cent of Slavs, Lithuanians and Latvians, and 97 per cent of Jews who came between 1880 and 1914 settled in urban areas. Between 70 per cent and 75 per cent of immigrants in the former groups made their homes in eight major urban-industrial centres in the eastern and mid-western parts of the USA (Philadelphia, Pittsburgh, New York, Chicago, Detroit, Cleveland and Boston), and about 10–15 per cent in smaller cities and towns of Pennsylvania, New Jersey and New England. Among East European Jews, about two-thirds settled in the north-eastern corridor from Boston to Baltimore (80 per cent of those in New York), and over one-quarter in the main urban centres of the Midwest. Employment figures (aggregate data for the USA) show similar high rates of concentration. Over nine-tenths of East European peasant immigrants in each group found jobs as common labourers in five industries: iron and steel production, coal mining, construction, slaughtering and packing meat, and textile and garment manufacturing. The majority, about two-thirds, of Jewish immigrants worked as skilled manual workers, mostly in garment and related industries, and 20–25 per cent were occupied in trade (*HEAEG* 1980: 202, 581–2, 792, 999; Kucas 1975: 28–58; Kuznets 1975: 102).

As social support networks for the prospective migrants in the old country, and for those already on their way to the USA, East European immigrant communities performed several functions. They were the source of news about current industrial conditions and advice regarding the job market, and thus they regulated to an extent the migratory flows from the old country. They also provided incoming migrants with the financial means for transportation: about two-thirds of the East Europeans arriving in US ports between 1908 and 1914 (by that time the arrivals included increasing numbers of women, either wives with children or prospective brides) declared that their passage was arranged by immigrants already in this country, and an even greater proportion were headed for destinations where they were awaited by kin or acquaintances from their home towns and villages.

Most newcomers relied on the assistance of relatives and friends in securing their first lodging. In a typical letter, Miriam Goldberg wrote from New York to her sister's niece in Lipno in Congress Poland: 'About Nella [a cousin], let her just come to America. ... Please give her my address. I shall meet her in Castle Garden and take her home with us until her husband will be able to make a living for the two of them' (Kula et al 1986: 240). Finally, it was through their group's support networks that new arrivals became incorporated into the US economy as workers. By assisting newcomers in finding employment, these group support networks functioned as micro-level social mediators or 'fitters' between the demands of the US economy and the migrants' human capital or individual characteristics and skills acquired in the old country: in the case of Jews, their proto-industrial and commercial experience; and in the case of the peasants, their physical strength and a stamina

PLATE 6: Orphaned Jewish children whose mothers were killed in a Russian massacre in 1908 posed in order of size on the roof of the detention centre at Ellis Island, New York.

sustained by a vision of a triumphant return home with enough savings to start a better life (Bodnar 1985: 57–84).

It can be argued that these complex networks of communication, travel, housing and employment assistance extending between the migrants' place of origin in eastern Europe and the USA provided an additional link in the Atlantic world system of interrelated parts.

Transatlantic migration after the First World War
The outbreak of the war in Europe in 1914 put an abrupt end to the surging mass migration to America. After the war ended, the transatlantic flow resumed, though on a diminished scale in comparison with the previous decade. Between 1919 and 1924 about a quarter of a million East Europeans came to the USA, of which Jews constituted over a half and Poles about a quarter. Post-war immigration was largely a family reunification movement: the (combined) average proportion of women, children and the elderly among the arriving immigrants exceeded the respective figures for young men. During the same period, Canada received approximately 50,000 East Europeans. On

the one hand, post-war redrawing of the political map of eastern Europe – specifically, the reunification of independent Poland and the creation of the independent nation states of Lithuania and Latvia – and on the other, the Communist revolution in Russia, attracted about 100,000–150,000 return immigrants from America (the most numerous, 65 per cent of this number, were Poles; 3–5 per cent were Jewish enthusiasts of the new order in Russia).

In 1924, the US Congress enacted the national quota system that sharply reduced immigration from eastern Europe, and the onset of the Great Depression on both sides of the Atlantic in 1929 further diminished inflows. They resumed on a larger scale after 1945, when, in the wake of the Second World War, several hundred thousand 'displaced persons' and war refugees arrived in North America (Ferenczi and Willcox 1919: I, 126–7, 473–97, 789; *HEAEG* 1980: 202, 639, 673, 791, 887, 998).

Notes
1. Intracontinental migration of eastern Europeans actually involved great numbers of people, in some cases exceeding the volume of travels to America. For example, between

350,000 and 400,000 Russian and Polish Jews resettled in the period discussed here in central and western Europe, and that does not count east–west migration within the German and Austrian empires. Seasonal labour migrations to Germany of Polish and Ukrainian/Rusyn inhabitants of Russian- and Austrian-dominated parts of Poland exceeded four to five times the number of transatlantic crossings made by these people. And, in the case of ethnic Russians, the bulk of long-distance migration was directed to Siberia and the Asiatic provinces of the Russian empire; the number of travellers to America constituted a mere one-thirtieth of that movement (Ferenczi and Willcox 1929: I, 227, 656, 774, 894; II, 512–20, 553–65; Morawska 1989: 246–55).

2. It should be emphasized, however, that rates of out-migration from one province or even locality fluctuated over time and varied from place to place, depending on local demographic and economic conditions.

3. Of course, not all migrant labourers managed to accumulate significant savings. An ethnographic study of American returnees to a Galician village reported 37 per cent of them as having brought back no savings at all, except for city clothing and various American gadgets for household use (Morawska 1989: 265). Such instances, however, even though not uncommon (and it is not unlikely that a considerable number among those who did not succeed in America had never returned to the old country, ashamed of their failure), apparently did not undermine the local people's belief in the Golden Land.

References

Balch, Emily (1910) *Our Slavic Fellow Citizens*, New York: Charities Publication Committee

Berend, Ivan and Gyorgi Ranki (1982) *The European Periphery and Industrialization 1780–1914*, New York: Cambridge University Press

Bobinska, Celina and Andrzej Pilch (eds) (1975) *Employment-Seeking Emigration of the Poles World-Wide XIX and XX C*, Cracow: Naktadem Uniwersytetu Jagiellonskiego

Bodnar, John (1985) *The Transplanted: A History of Immigrants in Urban America*, Bloomington: Indiana University Press

Ferenczi, Imre and Walter Willcox (1929) *International Migrations*, 2 vols, New York: National Bureau of Economic Research

Gabaccia, Donna (forthcoming*) From the Other Side: Women, Gender, and Immigrant Life in the United States, 1820–1990*, Bloomington: Indiana University Press

HEAEG (Harvard Encyclopedia of American Ethnic Groups) (1980) (ed.) S. Thernstrom, Cambridge, MA: Harvard University Press: Alisauskas, Arunas, 'Lithuanians', 665–76; 'Jews', 571–98; Greene, Victor, 'Poles', 787–803; Anderson, Edgar, 'Latvians', 638–42; Goren, Arthur and Paul Robert Magocsi, 'Russians', 885–94; *idem* 'Belorussians', 181–4; *idem* 'Carpatho-Rusyns', 200–10; *idem* 'Ukrainians', 997–1009

Heydenkorn, Benedict (ed.) (1975) *From Prairies to Cities: Papers on the Poles in Canada*, Toronto: Canadian–Polish Research Institute

Hoerder, Dirk (ed) (1985) *Labor Migration in the Atlantic Economies: The European and North American Working Classes During the Period of Industrialization*, Westport, CT: Greenwood Press

Joseph, Samuel (1914) *Jewish Immigration to the United States*, New York: Columbia University Press

Kucas, Antanas (1975) *Lithuanians in America*, Boston: Encyclopedia Lituanica

Kula, Witold, Nina Assorodobraj-Kula and Marcin Kula (1986) *Writing Home: Immigrants in Brazil and the United States* (translated and edited by J. Wtulich), Boulder, CO: East European Monographs

Kuznets, Simon (1975) 'Immigration of Russian Jews to the United States: Background and Structure', *Perspectives in American History*, (9), 35–126

Luciuk, Lubomyr and Stella Hryniuk (eds) (1991) *Canada's Ukrainians*, Toronto: University of Toronto Press

Morawska, Ewa (1989) 'Labor Migrations of Poles in the Atlantic World-Economy, 1880–1914', *Comparative Studies in Society and History*, 31 (2), 237–72

Sarna, Jonathan (1981) 'The Myth of No Return: Jewish Return Migration to Eastern Europe, 1881–1914', *American Jewish History*, 71 (3), 256–69

Thomas, William I. and Florian Znaniecki (1918–20) *The Polish Peasant in Europe and America*, 5 vols, Boston: Richard Badger

MIGRATION FROM THE GERMAN AND AUSTRO-HUNGARIAN EMPIRES TO NORTH AMERICA

WALTER NUGENT

Germany and Austria-Hungary, those bygone giants that bestrode central Europe in the decades before 1919, contributed significantly to the historic mass migration westward across the Atlantic – but in very different ways. In 1871, when the Prussian Chancellor Otto von Bismarck added Bavaria and other entities to form a united German empire, North America was already home to thousands of Germans, the first of whom arrived in 1683. German out-migration declined steeply after 1886. Austria-Hungary, on the other hand, donated few people until 1880, but from then until the 1920s, it sent a wide range of peoples, not only German-speaking Austrians but also Bohemians, Hungarians, Slovaks, Croats and others.[1] Germany provided more of a farm-family migration, Austria-Hungary more of a proletarian labour migration – though by no means all migrants fit these descriptions. The return migration rate, male and female ratios, and the probable initial intentions of migrants also distinguished the two groups. Differences aside, however, the two empires each contributed roughly similar numbers – over 4.5 million people – to the transatlantic flow, surpassed only by Britain, Ireland and Italy.

Migration to North America before 1815

Prior to the American Declaration of Independence in 1776, perhaps as many as 150,000 German-speakers (Benjamin Franklin's estimate) lived in Pennsylvania, with some thousands more in the easily reachable Great Valley of the Appalachians in western Virginia, in New York's Hudson Valley and in North Carolina's Piedmont. Although figures are disputed, German emigrants probably numbered between 60,000 and 80,000, with their numerous progeny making up a similar figure by the 1770s. Beginning in 1683, when Rhenish Mennonites led by Francis Daniel Pastorius arrived and founded Germantown just outside of Philadelphia, members of Anabaptist, radical Calvinist and other German Protestant sects migrated to south-eastern Pennsylvania and nearby northern Virginia (Jones 1992: 23–25). Conventional historiography and tradition stress their desire for religious

independence. But bad harvests and intermittent local warfare also motivated them, and the willingness of the Pennsylvania proprietors to distribute land and accommodate the sectarians guided the direction of their migration (Moltmann 1983: 15–16).

Economics rather than religion produced a surge of migration beginning in 1709 from the Palatinate and adjacent parts of Germany. Approximately 7000 arrived in Philadelphia in 1719 alone. Some came with enough means to establish independent farms; others, obliged to 'redeem' their passage, began their American lives as servants. The flow of redemptioners and others oscillated greatly. There were years in which hardly any Germans arrived, but in others, as many as 6000 or 7000 (1749–52 and 1757) came, even 22,000 in 1759. German princes raised about 30,000 troops to aid their comrade George III (Elector of Hannover as well as King of England) in trying to suppress the American independence struggle; of these, at least 5000 defected or were left behind by the retreating British, and made post-war homes in Pennsylvania and Virginia (Jones 1992: 55–6). By the 1780s, Germans could be found from Pennsylvania to the Cumberland Gap in extreme south-western Virginia, the place about to become the gateway to the trans-Appalachian west. From then until after 1815, migration of Germans or any other group slowed to the lowest levels in American history. Only after 1815, the end of the Napoleonic Wars, with its disruptions on the European continent and in Atlantic shipping, did German and other migration resume at appreciable levels.

Peasants into farmers, 1815–1871

Peace returned to the Atlantic region in 1815, providing a necessary precondition to transatlantic migration that would last without serious interruption until 1914. Changes in economic structures in both North America and Germany, though gradual, made migration increasingly possible. Chief among these were, in Europe, stiffer competition to home and cottage industry from factory production, the subdivision of family lands to the level of 'dwarf holdings',

Table 4.2: *International migration, 1820s–70s ('000s)*

	1820s	1830s	1840s	1850s	1860s	1870s
From Germany, all			183[1]	671	779	626
From Austria-Hungary, all			2[1]	31	40	111
Germany to USA (a)	7	152	435	952	787	718
Germany to USA (b)						556
Austria-Hungary to USA					8	73

Sources: For German and Austro-Hungarian out-migration, Mitchell (1976: 135) (series B8); for Austro-Hungarian out-migration, Ferenczi and Willcox (1929: 230–1). For migration from Germany to the USA: US figures (row a), US Bureau of the Census 1975 (*Historical Statistics of the United States*) I:105–6 (series C95); German figures (row b), Ferenczi and Willcox (1929: 336). For migration from Austria-Hungary (and after 1919, the successor states of Austria, Hungary, Czechoslovakia and Yugoslavia), to the USA, US *Historical Statistics* 1975: I:105–6 (series C97); to Canada, Ferenczi and Willcox (1929: 364–65). Migration from Germany to Canada from 1831 to 1924 (Canadian figures) was 223,376 (Ferenczi and Willcox 1929: 120); '1920s' means 1921–30. '1930s' means 1931–40, etc.
Note: [1]=1846–50

indicating to young Germans that home held a dismal future for them and, more positively, the creation of a railroad network and more regular passenger sailings (Mönckmeier 1912: 71–85). Bremen and Hamburg began catering to emigrants in the 1830s, beginning their epic histories as ports of embarkation (Walker 1964: 90–2). In the USA, a network of railroads and canals also came into being, while a series of generous federal laws together with the removal of Indians put the Ohio and Missouri valleys within practical reach of would-be farmers. Except for 1816–17, when an extremely cold summer brought famine and drove perhaps 20,000 Rhinelanders to the USA, not much German migration took place until the 1830s – officially only a few hundred a year, especially after 1819 when the long practice of redeeming one's ship passage by serving a period of indenture was outlawed by Washington. From the mid-1830s onward for a century, German migration to the USA never fell below 10,000 a year (see Table 4.2) and was usually much higher (US Bureau of the Census 1975 (1) 105–6).[2]

In 1834 nearly 18,000 arrived, many to settle west of St Louis, the majority on farms but some as artisans or entrepreneurs in towns and cities. The number of German immigrants rose to nearly 30,000 in 1840, 79,000 in 1850 and peaked at 503,000 in the three years 1852–54, and those figures probably understate the truth. A minority of the migrants, disproportionately vocal and visible, were political liberals facing reprisals from their efforts in the failed uprisings of 1848; some became 'Latin farmers', so-called because their Latin was more skilful than their farming.

The great majority, however, sought, in essence, to depart from unpromising and circumscribed peasant life in Germany and to become independent farmers of 100 acres or more in the American west. The potato blight that devastated Ireland in the late 1840s also did severe harm to the peasants of Württemberg, Baden, Hesse and the Rheinpfalz; and with local authorities often eager to assist the departure of people who might become public charges, the emigration spread. Yet motivations were psychological as well as economic (Walker 1964: 67–9). People feared immiseration for themselves or their children. They saw migration to the USA not as a radical move but as a way of preserving their farm-family lives; they would also escape rising taxes and conscription. They were, in the main, a rural lower middle class and as such they fitted very well into the mid-western context. Avoiding the already settled eastern seaboard and south (where land cost more and where slavery foreclosed labour demand), Germans followed a short distance behind the westward-moving frontier line. In the 1830s and 1840s, they went to Indiana, Illinois and Missouri; in the 1850s to Wisconsin, Iowa and Texas. Those already in America tempted family members and others with encouragement and passage money; migration chains multiplied.

The sources from within Germany began to shift eastward to include Thuringians, Saxons and others, as well as the usual southern and western Germans. About 50,000 went to the Canadian frontier, in Ontario, during the 1850s and 1860s – a much smaller flow than to the USA but a significant one in the Canadian population mosaic. Even during the American Civil War (1861–65) no fewer than 30,000 Germans arrived each year, unsettled by Germany's own wars with Denmark and Austria, its low wages

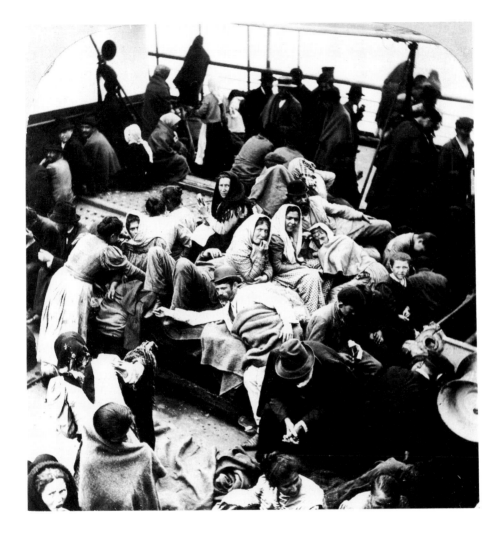

PLATE 7: Some of a group of 580 German emigrants on board ship destined for the USA in 1904.

Table 4.3: *International migration, 1880s–1940s ('000)*

	1880s	1890s	1900s	1910s	1920s	1930s	1940s
From Germany, all	1342	527	274	91	564	121	618
From Austria-Hungary, all	436	724	2342	788	229[1]		
Germany to USA (a)	1453	505	341	144	412	114	227
Germany to USA (b)	1237	479	255	64	>341		
Austria-Hungary to USA	354	593	1597	902	215	32	38
Austria-Hungary to Canada			121	79			

Sources: As for Table 4.2
Note: [1] = 1921–24.

and high food prices, and the continuing pressure on smallholding peasants. No longer traditionally agrarian, Germany was not yet fully industrial either. From 1866 to 1873, while Bismarck was unifying the imperial state and economy, over 800,000 Germans, many from Schleswig-Holstein and other northwestern areas, arrived in the USA.

The age of steam, 1871–1914
Steamships supplanted sailing vessels in the North Atlantic by 1871, providing faster, safer and more regular passenger traffic, as well as the means of transporting many hundreds of people instead of a few score on each voyage.[3] With the rail networks' expansion into eastern Europe and farther into the American west, steam-powered transport made possible 'proletarian mass migration' from Europe in the late nineteenth and early twentieth centuries.

Emigration from Germany to the USA continued in greater numbers than ever, peaking in 1882 (by the American entry figures) at 251,000. In many respects this mass migration continued the patterns of the preceding half-century, but in the 1880s both size and shape became quite different (see Table 4.3). Through the 1870s, farm families continued to leave southern, western, and central Germany for the Missouri Valley and the Great Plains. Agricultural depression in Germany in the early 1880s added many 'agrarians' from east of the Elbe, where large estates rather than smallholdings were the rule. Most of these 'agrarians' were wage-workers or on short contracts; with slender means compared with earlier German migrants, they moved to America as city-dwelling industrial workers, if in fact they left Germany at all (Mönckmeier 1912: 91–120). After German industry started generating thousands of jobs from the late 1880s onward, increasing numbers of migrants from provinces east

of the Elbe (especially West Prussia, Pomerania and Posen) went no further than Berlin, the Ruhr or other urban-industrial locations within Germany itself (Burgdörfer 1972: 184).

The eastward shift in the sources of German migration was paralleled by other shifts: from family groups to individuals, and from a fairly balanced sex ratio (around 55 per cent male) to a more male-skewed distribution. In the great surge of the early 1880s, workers outnumbered farmers for the first time, yet family members still made up more than half of the migrants. From the late 1880s on, a young working man, travelling alone, became the typical German emigrant. The Hamburg port statistics show that for 1880–84, farmers made up 34 per cent of migrants, workers (with or without a stated occupation) 44 per cent. But during 1885–89, farmers accounted for less than 16 per cent, workers for 59 per cent (Marschalck 1984: 47). And the numbers leaving for North America were falling; annual German migration to the USA never touched 100,000 after 1892, or 50,000 after 1894, except in two years after the Second World War. (These are gross figures; the net figures, after subtracting the repatriates who returned to Germany or Austria-Hungary, are considerably lower.) The German empire, its industry booming from the late 1880s onward, absorbed nearly all of its own people who might have emigrated earlier, and many more as well. Thus Germany became a net importer of people (20,000 a year in 1895–1900), and its population rose faster than that of any other country in Europe, from 36 million to 65 million between 1860 and 1910, despite losing several million to emigration.

In the USA, meanwhile, a distinctively German-American culture was flourishing. Cities large and small had their German-language newspapers. New York, Chicago, St Louis, Cincinnati, Milwaukee and other cities boasted 'Little Germanies' with their publications, churches, Turnvereins and other fraternal organizations, singing groups, saloons and orchestras. The German impact on the broader American culture ranged from Theodore Thomas's conducting of Beethoven, Brahms and Wagner, to the anarchist and socialist pronouncements of Johann Most and Friedrich Engels. Germans served in the Union army during the Civil War and actively took part in politics (Catholics as Democrats, Lutherans as Republicans, as a rule) thereafter. German-America, 'Das Deutschtum', came into being in the 1850s, flourished from the 1880s to 1914, and never recovered from the shock of war between the USA and Germany in 1917–18, followed by national prohibition of alcohol. German migrants still arrived in the USA at a fairly steady level of 30,000 to 40,000 between 1902 and 1914. That was a far cry, however, from earlier years, and nothing like the massive flows from other places, among which was Austria-Hungary.

With one major exception, migration to North America from the multi-ethnic Austro-Hungarian empire consisted modally of young men of marginal or landless peasant status seeking high American wages, much of which they planned to send or bring home. They resembled the east-Elbian Germans who migrated after 1885, when the peak of German migration was over.

The exception was the Bohemian (Czech) group. In most respects, language apart, they shared the characteristics of the south and south-west German land-seeking, family migration that predominated in the 1850s to 1870s. Males and females were fairly evenly balanced among Bohemian migrants. Overall, from 1820 to 1928, their sex ratio was 54 per cent male, 46 per cent female, a balance surpassed only by the Irish, who came to the USA in the nineteenth century in about equal numbers of males and females. Women were more prevalent among the Czechs than among the Germans, English and Scots, whose sex ratio was 58 to 42 per cent (Gabaccia 1989: Table 1). A balanced sex ratio usually meant that migrants travelled in family groups rather than as individuals, and as land-seekers rather than wage-seekers. So it was with the Czechs, subject as they were to much the same pressures as south-western Germans — uncertain harvests, diminishing markets for home industry, gradually less competitive grain prices, and the prospect of smallholdings subdivided beyond the point at which their children would have acceptable life chances. Learning of the rich and inexpensive farmland west of the Missouri River opening to settlement

in the 1870s, several thousand made their way to Nebraska, Kansas and Texas each year of that decade. They clustered in permeable enclaves and gradually mixed with German and English-speaking neighbours. Willa Cather's novel, *My Ántonia* (1918), lucidly describes Czech-American life in pioneer Nebraska.

For the most part, however, migrants from the Dual Monarchy came later, sought wages rather than land, travelled as individuals, were heavily male and repatriated often. In all of these qualities, they more resembled the mass Italian and Polish migration of 1880–1925, rather than the Irish, German or Scandinavian waves of 1845–80. Between 1899 and 1924, ethnic Austrians formed an important segment but were matched in numbers by Hungarians (Magyars) and Slovaks, with Croats and Slovenes chiefly next, followed by Ruthenians, and then Romanians and Serbs. Again, sex ratios differed from the Germans and Czechs: males outnumbered females among Austrians and Slovaks by 65 to 35 per cent, Hungarians by 68 to 32, Croats by 78 to 22 and Romanians by 82 to 18 per cent (Gabaccia 1989).

The social and economic consequences of these demographic imbalances were several and, although they were new and often frightening to the American receiving society, they were historically commonplace in much of Europe. Sex ratios as imbalanced as these indicate a reluctance to form families in the host society, strong family ties at home, and a slower rate of social and political assimilation. Austro-Hungarian emigrants very often planned at the outset to make only a short-term visit, whose rational purpose was to earn and accumulate capital to improve the lot of oneself and one's family *in the home country,* rather than to create, or recreate, a farm home in the new land.

Labour migration had been the lot and choice of many Europeans for hundreds of years. Railroads and steamships simply allowed them to select more distant targets. It cost more to go to New York than to Berlin, for example, but the payoff was greater; with steamships leaving Bremen and Hamburg two or three times a week, the crossing took only seven days or less. Thus the traditional practice of seasonal labour-seeking migration could be extended to the USA, chronically in need of workers.

Austria-Hungary thus surpassed Germany by 1895 in contributing its people to the USA and, in lesser numbers, Canada. In the 1890s, 724,000 people left the Dual Monarchy compared with 527,000 from Germany; in the pre-war years of 1901 to 1914, 3,073,000 from the Dual Monarchy, 353,000 from

Germany (to all countries) – a ratio of almost 9:1 (Ferenczi and Willcox 1929: 230–1). Rates of return migration are somewhat uncertain. But there is no doubt that groups differed enormously. Official American figures for outbound migrants in 1908 (the first year such figures were kept), compared with inbound migrants in 1907, show return rates for Czechs as 7.8 per cent, and Germans 15.5 per cent; but Hungarians 48.7 per cent, Slovaks 56.1 per cent, and Croatians and Slovenes 59.8 per cent.

Between 1876 and 1910, 83 per cent of migrants from Austria (whatever their ethnicity) went to the USA, 8 per cent to Canada and the rest to South America. An even larger proportion of Magyars and Slovaks went to the USA. Since Canada did not have an economy demanding large numbers of wage workers before the First World War, few went there. Canada did, however, still have a frontier of farm settlement. The great surge of people into the prairie provinces of Manitoba, Saskatchewan and Alberta did not get under way until the late 1890s, and continued until 1930. Through aggressive recruitment in Europe by government and railroads, migrants continued to flow into western Canada as land seekers well after the settlement frontier in the USA had halted. Many of these were Ukrainians, or Germans from Russia rather than Germany proper, but still the presence of Germans in the Canadian population rose from a quarter of a million to over 400,000 between 1881 and 1911, including a 30 per cent rise between 1901 and 1911.

Migration after 1914

The guns of August 1914 virtually ended the mass proletarian migration from Europe to North America. U-boats, conscription and labour demand at home reduced transatlantic migration to almost nothing during the war years. When they ended, and after the peace settlement terminated the German and Austro-Hungarian empires as political entities, migration resumed for about five years, from 1919 through 1924. The USA received (by official figures) about 300,000 more people from those areas.

In this five-year postscript to the pre-war migration, females outnumbered males, children and older people outnumbered young adults — indicating a whole-sale reuniting of families separated by the war, as well as a greater preference for permanent settlement in the USA than in an uncertain central Europe. The farm frontier still existed only in north-western Canada, and not for long. American labour demand levelled off, while European demand rose, reducing the

marginal benefit from migration. In 1924 the USA began restricting immigrants according to their national origins. The borders closed. After 1929 the economy slid into the Great Depression, and the USA for the first time experienced a net outflow of migrants during the 1930s. The one significant exception was the influx of several thousand refugees from German areas under Nazi control, an exodus of intellectuals, creative artists and scientists who, despite their dismally small numbers compared with those annihilated, greatly enriched the cultural life of the USA.

After 1945 a migration took place from central Europe of 'displaced persons' and others. That story is told elsewhere in this book.

Notes

1. This essay discusses German-speakers from the two empires, and non-German groups in Austria-Hungary, with the exception of Poles and Jews in either empire, who are considered elsewhere in this volume, as is migration after 1945.

2. Migration statistics of all countries are prone to errors and inconsistencies. For a brief discussion, see Nugent (1992: 29–30, 173 n.12.)

3. For a more extended treatment of German and Austro-Hungarian migration in this period, see Nugent (1992: Chapters 8 and 9).

References

Burgdörfer, Friedrich (1972) 'Die Wanderungen über die deutschen Reichsgrenzen im letzten Jahrhundert', *Allgemeines Statistisches Archiv* (Jena), reprinted in Wolfgang Köllmann and Peter Marschalck (eds), *Bevölkerungsgeschichte*, Cologne: Kiepenheuer & Witsch

Ferenczi, I. and W. F. Willcox (eds) (1929) *International Migrations*, New York: National Bureau of Economic Research

Gabaccia, Donna (1989) 'Female Migration and Immigrant Sex Ratios, 1820–1928', Unpublished paper

Jones, Maldwyn Allen (1992) *American Immigration*, Chicago: University of Chicago Press

Marschalck, Peter (1984) *Bevölkerungsgeschichte Deutschlands im 19 und 20 Jahrhundert*, Frankfurt: Suhrkamp

Mitchell, B. R. (1976) *European Historical Statistics*, New York: Columbia University Press

Moltmann, Günter (1983) 'The Pattern of German Emigration to the USA in the Nineteenth Century', in Frank Trommler and Joseph McVeigh (eds) *America and the Germans: An Assessment of a Three-Hundred-Year History*, Philadelphia: University of Pennsylvania Press

Mönckmeier, Wilhelm (1912) *Die deutsche Überseeauswanderung*, Jena: Verlag von Gustav Fischer

Nugent, W. (1992) *Crossings: The Great Transatlantic Migrations, 1870–1914*, Bloomington: Indiana University Press

US Bureau of the Census (1975) *Historical Statistics of the United States, from Colonial Times to 1970*, Washington: Government Printing Office

Walker, Mack (1964) *Germany and the Emigration, 1816–1885*, Cambridge: Harvard University Press

A CONTINUING PRESENCE: NORTH AMERICA'S UKRAINIANS

LUBOMYR Y. LUCIUK

After having been deleted from the maps of Europe for many centuries, Ukraine re-emerged as an internationally recognized state in December 1991. For several decades before that, however, there had been those in North America who described themselves as 'Ukrainian' for census purposes, asserting a national identity not always acknowledged as legitimate in their host societies. Over time these North Americans have come to be recognized as constituting one of the largest of the east European ethnic groups found in the New World. And, arguably, the organized Ukrainian constituency nestled within the much larger population of self-identified Ukrainians, has become one of the most politically active and, sometimes, even influential of the Slavic minorities in North America.

The importance of these North American Ukrainians is often said to derive from their numbers. Yet there has always been more than a modest amount of confusion among outside observers, and even among the immigrants themselves, about what precisely a Ukrainian might be. Often paternalistic and even racist attitudes intervened. Thus, in the late 1930s, one British analyst averred that Ukrainians were 'of artificial origin without any real claim to race distinction' and were 'in fact a collection of magnificent crossbred scallywags whose development was due more to political than ethnological causes'. Such ill-disposed notions about who the Ukrainians might be prejudiced official Anglo-American perspectives generally on the 'Ukrainian Question' in Europe, from the inter-war period to the recent past, and influenced the way in which Ukrainians were treated and numbered in the emigration. Suffice to note that describing oneself as a Ukrainian while living in North America has not always been a wise pairing of choices.

Certainly, census materials collected earlier in this century consistently under-reported the number of persons emigrating from Ukrainian lands in eastern Europe to North America. There was also considerable official confusion in appreciating, much less recording, the difference between the various Slavic immigrants' nationalities (i.e. their ethnic identity)

and their varying citizenships. This uncertainty was coupled with a widespread indifference about identifying precisely the national origins of the in-migrating masses. Very often a general regional categorization or quite imprecise nationality statistics were deemed sufficient for meeting the receiving country's requirements. Workers, farmers and miners were sought throughout central and eastern Europe from the late 1870s on, then brought to North America to open up the Canadian prairie frontier, labour in the mines and timber camps of the US north-east, and meet the expanding needs of industry for unskilled and semi-skilled labourers. Provided that an immigrant passed a basic medical examination, had sufficient resources to get established and was from an acceptable 'racial' group, he or she was admitted. As single, healthy young men were preferred, the sex and age profiles of the earliest Slavic immigrant populations were correspondingly distorted.

The authorities also did not pay much attention to whether an immigrant was a Ukrainian, a Slovak, a Russian or a Pole because before, during and for a long time after the end of the First World War, the nuances of nationality were considered less relevant than what was thought to be a self-evident truth, namely that these various immigrants would, by the second generation if not sooner, be reforged in the 'melting pot' of the New World, emerging as loyal Americans or British subjects. It was generally believed, and taught, that this was what these immigrants themselves wanted, which also explained why they had left their homelands.

These problems with official census figures, and host society attitudes, were often exacerbated by the low level of national consciousness of many immigrants themselves. At the turn of the century, and up until the early 1920s, perhaps beyond, most of those coming from Ukraine were confused about how best to describe themselves. Some did so by regional origin, calling themselves Galicians, Bukovynians or Carpatho-Rusyns, in reference to the three geographical regions of western Ukraine from which the majority emigrated. Others identified by religious affiliation. Western Ukraine's inhabitants were predominantly Uniate or Ukrainian Greek Catholic by confession. However, a significant minority, from Volhynia and Bukovyna especially, belonged to various Orthodox churches. And, later, independent Ukrainian Greek Orthodox churches were also formed in Canada and the USA. Many others simply allowed themselves to be identified with reference to the citizenship inscribed on the passports issued them by the states from which they emigrated, or fled. This meant that many Ukrainians were logged as 'Austro-Hungarians' or 'Russians' before the First World War, as 'Poles' or 'Nansen refugees' during the inter-war period and as 'Polish-Ukrainians', 'Soviet citizens' or 'stateless persons' in the aftermath of the Second World War. As a result it is doubtful whether anyone will ever be able to determine how many Ukrainians there were, or are, in North America.

Nevertheless, the numbers are said to matter. After the results of the 1981 Canada Census were released, for example, it was commonly asserted that Ukrainians formed the fifth largest ethnic group in Canada, preceded by the British, French, Germans and Italians. And, by 1991, over one million Canadians of Ukrainian heritage were being gleaned from the national census, representing approximately 2.6 per cent of the total Canadian population. In 1990, the US census reported 740,803 persons of Ukrainian 'ancestry', a small increase from the 1980 figure. Earlier, however, another student of the American-Ukrainian experience had suggested there were as many as 1.5 million Americans of Ukrainian descent. And one informed estimate records 650,000 additional Americans of Carpatho-Rusyn heritage, a group American Ukrainians have argued should be included with the Ukrainian total. In sum, it could be said that there are as many as 2.5 million persons in North America whose roots can be traced back to contemporary Ukraine. This represents a significant population when it is recalled that Ukrainians in Ukraine represent approximately 38 million of the 52 million citizens of that country, with nearly 11 million more Ukrainians in the other successor states of the former Soviet Union, among them just over 8 million in the Russian Federation. Another 760,000 Ukrainians live in the contiguous states of eastern Europe, particularly Poland, with 93,000 in western Europe, some 35,000 in Australia and New Zealand and possibly as many as 416,000 in South America, primarily in Brazil and Argentina. Therefore, of a world total of some 52 million Ukrainians approximately 14.6 million, or 28

per cent, are found in the diaspora. And of that global emigration approximately 17 per cent are North Americans.

How accurate such statistics may or may not be in terms of portraying the contemporary or future integrity of an organized Ukrainian minority in North America is an issue that will be returned to below. What is undeniable is that these North American Ukrainians have, especially in Canada in recent years, demonstrated an improved capability for securing considerable public funding from provincial, state and national governments for purposes which, however laudable, have essentially been of direct importance to their own particular group rather than having wider societal relevance. While the Ukrainians of North America are far from being unique in developing an ability to utilize general resources for their particular aims, they have been more remarkably successful than most other minorities, particularly in Canada. A wide variety of Ukrainian cultural, social and educational programmes receive some measure of public support. For example a research institute specializing in Ukrainian studies was established in 1976 at the University of Alberta, in Edmonton, and a chair of Ukrainian studies was endowed at the University of Toronto in 1980. Even multi-million dollar undertakings, like the publication of a five-volume, English-language *Encyclopedia of Ukraine*, have been made possible, in part, through the generosity of the Canadian public purse. Not surprisingly, Canada's Ukrainians are widely considered to be quite successful as an ethnic group, even if, among themselves, some would claim their numbers warrant an even greater 'share' of the modest resources Ottawa assigns to funding multiculturalism, a federal policy which was itself secured, in large part, by Ukrainian-Canadian lobbying in 1967.

Some segments within the 'community of communities' which North America's Ukrainians constitute have also become quite effective in articulating what their members perceive and publicly proclaim are the 'Ukrainian community's interests'. Uniting around causes deemed to require an especial commitment of resources and effort, these Canadians and Americans have established issue-oriented Ukrainian organizations which, whether ephemeral or more permanent, have taken on matters they deem urgent. Even if the causes they put forward are not always supported by others who are counted, officially, as being members of the Ukrainian population, some of these groups have nevertheless been quite successful at their self-appointed tasks. In part this is because

PLATE 8: Ukrainians detained in the Castle Mountain concentration camp,
near Banff, Alberta, during the First World War.

they have implied, rather disingenuously, that they actually represent a monolithic bloc of North American Ukrainians numbering in the millions. That myth has generally been accepted, or at least not challenged openly, by the wider society.

These new Ukrainian organizations have also tended to contest the authority of the more established and generally conservative bodies (for example, the Ukrainian Canadian Congress or the Ukrainian Congress Committee of America), which once affected to represent Ukrainian interests throughout North America or even those of Ukraine in the international arena (for example, the World Congress of Free Ukrainians). Thus, in Canada, groups like the Canadian Ukrainian Immigrant Aid Society, which began providing aid and counsel to Ukrainians in 1973, has since assisted in the sponsorship of over 7500 immigrants. A Civil Liberties Commission, active from 1985 to 1988, effectively countered what many

Ukrainians, especially those political refugees and displaced persons who came after the Second World War, rightly perceived as a Soviet-inspired disinformation campaign about the record of Ukrainian nationalism during that war, a controversial issue which arose during the hearings of a commission of inquiry on war criminals headed by Mr Justice Jules Deschênes. Meanwhile, other regionally based activists, largely indifferent to the 'war criminal' issue, which primarily engaged post-war Ukrainians settled in central Canada, struggled to develop a comprehensive blueprint for revitalizing what they believed was the community's traditional hearth in the Canadian west, doing so by forming groups like the Ukrainian Canadian Community Development Committee–Prairie Region. At present, a Ukrainian Canadian Civil Liberties Association continues to lobby the government of Canada in order to secure an acknowledgement and redress for the unwarranted and unjust internment of Ukrainian Canadians as 'enemy aliens' during the First World War. And in the USA there are bodies like the Washington Group, established in 1984 for the purpose of informing the public and government about issues of concern to Ukrainian Americans. All these kinds of issue-oriented groups, of which the aforementioned represent only a small sample, have further diversified what had previously already been described as an 'over-organized' Ukrainian population. Some have critiqued these developments as representing a 'fragmentation of the community' while others have welcomed the trend, asserting that this diversity is indicative of the Ukrainian group's continued vitality.

Most issue-oriented Ukrainian groups attempt to be active at the national or international levels. Concurrently, community-based groups remain very relevant, particularly in locally oriented cultural, social and religious endeavours (for example, there were eighty-eight Ukrainian folk dance ensembles, schools and clubs active in the province of Alberta in the early 1990s, servicing some 3700 students). Even so, it seems likely, if not inevitable, that it will be the issue-oriented groups which, within the next few decades, will assume the mantle of representing an organized Ukrainian presence in North America. Previously established organizations, several of which once numbered in the thousands of members, disposed of considerable real estate, published their own Ukrainian-language newspapers and supported national networks of women's, youth and veterans' affiliates (such as the Ukrainian National Federation, the Ukrainian Labour and Farmer Temple Association, the Ukrainian Self Reliance League, the Canadian League for the Liberation of Ukraine) may cling persistently to a mirage of relevance well into the next century, but the evidence suggests that organizations based on a particular political ideology or religious belief, period of immigration or regional background, have become almost irrelevant. Their place will be taken by groups that eschew the narrow partisan politics and regional and religious prejudices spawned in the homeland, and instead draw a voluntary membership from various generations, immigrations, religious confessions and political affiliations, as necessary and feasible. Almost by definition, these groups will be smaller, more professional and more transitory than the Ukrainian organizations of old.

This is partly happening because, as a consequence of several factors, the number of persons claiming to be single-origin Ukrainians has continued to decline throughout North America. For example, mortality will inevitably strip away that 14 per cent of Canada's Ukrainians who are today found in the 55+ age cohort. This will not only precipitate fundamental changes in the demographic characteristics of the overall Canadian Ukrainian population but it will have a major impact in those urban centres (for example, Toronto and Montreal) where this population is clustered. The effects of their passing will be especially noticeable with respect to language retention and the number of persons involved with the two traditional churches – the Ukrainian Catholic and the Ukrainian Orthodox. Historically, language use and mother tongue statistics have been regarded as important measures of the vitality of an ethno-cultural population and the traditional churches have served as a bar against assimilatory pressure by providing an important institutional structure around which group activities have coalesced. Today less than 50 per cent of those describing themselves as Ukrainians in Canada belong to either denomination, a situation paralleled in the USA. And, between 1961 and 1981, the number of Canadians who identified Ukrainian as a mother tongue fell sharply, a negative change of 19 per cent. As long as intermarriage rates remain high, levels of language retention will continue to decline. In the USA the number of persons who declared that they spoke Ukrainian at home decreased by 22 per cent between 1980 and 1990. Only 96,568, or approximately 13 per cent of the total American group claiming Ukrainian ancestry, speak Ukrainian. Ukrainian language use in North America seems fated to all but disappear.

The assimilation of almost all members of the second and subsequent generations, the progeny of the first wave of Ukrainian pioneer settlers and emigrants to North America, is continuing apace, the result of urbanization, intermarriage and upward social mobility. Today over 90 per cent of Ukrainian Canadians were born in Canada. The younger generations have essentially abandoned 'the virtual Canadian Ukraine' which once existed in the ethnic bloc settlements of the Canadian west. Even if most Canadians of Ukrainian heritage still live in the three prairie provinces of Manitoba, Saskatchewan and Alberta, they have gravitated to the larger cities of that region, like Edmonton, Winnipeg and Saskatoon, or moved to other metropolitan centres like Toronto or Vancouver. In Canada's larger cities, persons who might otherwise have remained part of a distinctly Ukrainian Canadian population are unlikely to find the same level of institutional completeness that once characterized the Ukrainian cultural landscape, built up over decades on the prairies. They probably will not remain particularly bound to a heritage, or be involved with issues considered particularly Ukrainian, although this does not necessarily mean they will abandon their cultural heritage entirely. A similar trend, already evident in the 1970s, has taken place in the USA, with the dispersal of American Ukrainians from the north-eastern states of New York, Pennsylvania, New Jersey, Illinois, Ohio and Michigan, where they had concentrated historically, to other states like Idaho, Tennessee, Arkansas, North Carolina, Oregon and New Mexico, where no significant numbers of American Ukrainians previously existed. With no established community to welcome them in these new locales, most of these internal migrants will gradually abandon whatever measure of affinity they may have had for their Ukrainian ancestry. It will simply have ceased to have much utility in their daily lives, or those of their children.

Finally, the lack of any significant immigration to North America from Ukraine from the 1950s to the present – a situation unlikely to change in the foreseeable future – has not allowed for any replenishment of the Ukrainian population. Those economic immigrants and refugees who did arrive in Canada or the USA during the late 1970s, 1980s and early 1990s settled primarily in cities like Toronto or New York, effecting conditions locally, sometimes even profoundly. But the small numbers involved will have no overall demographic relevance in terms of sustaining the Ukrainian presence in North America.

Most revealing about the nature of the transformations taking place within North America's Ukrainian population is how the number of single-origin Ukrainians compares with the number claiming a multiple-origin ancestry. In Canada, between 1981 and 1991, the number of single-origin Ukrainians *decreased* by 122,970 people, representing approximately 13 per cent of the total Ukrainian Canadian population. In the same period the number of Canadians of multiple origins who included a Ukrainian ancestor *increased* by 422,290, or approximately 35 per cent. A similar pattern was evident in the USA where, in 1990, less than 50 per cent of those reporting Ukrainian 'ancestry' were of single-origin. Increasingly, North Americans are asserting that their heritage is pluralistic rather than particularistic.

Linguistic capability or an affiliation with one of the traditional Ukrainian churches are certainly not essential in order to identify oneself as a Ukrainian in North American society, or to become involved in 'the community'. A critical mass of Canadians and Americans who identify themselves as having some Ukrainian heritage or ancestry already exists in North America. And that pool is likely to remain, even if there is no immigration from Ukraine in the near future to replenish it. Instead of being a hinterland population, however, whatever organized Ukrainian constituency continues to exist will increasingly be found in the cities of the North American heartland. Its members will persist in maintaining an abiding interest in the fate of their ancestral homeland, Ukraine, and continue to organize themselves around that basic value orientation. They will also attempt to mobilize others from within the larger pool of persons of Ukrainian descent, whenever they feel that might be required to meet exigencies dictated by domestic or international developments. Whether they will be successful in this, and to what degree, will be determined largely by how capable they prove to be in creating a belief among those other North Americans who share some Ukrainian ancestry that, collectively, the group's historical experience in the New World and in the 'old country' necessitates their remaining bound together. The impact of the existence of an internationally recognized state known as Ukraine still needs to be assessed.

Perhaps paradoxically therefore, it is probable that there will always be Ukrainians in North America. For as long as there are so many others – be they Franco-Manitobans, Jewish Americans, Afro-Americans, Acadians or native North Americans, to name but a few – who insist on organizing themselves around a shared sense of the past and the empowerment of group rights, as opposed to promoting a belief in the rights and responsibilities of individuals as equal citizens, there will always be a place, and perhaps even a need, for an organized Ukrainian presence in North America.

Two undeniable facts have been confronted. Ukraine exists again and persons describing themselves as Ukrainian have lived in North America for over 100 years. What the fate of Ukraine will be remains uncertain. But, given the emergent nature of ethnicity in North America, it is apparent that Ukrainians will continue to be found there regardless of the present, or future, geopolitical realities of Europe.

THE ITALIAN DIASPORA, 1876–1976

RUDOLPH J. VECOLI

A distinctive quality of Italy's emigration is that it persisted over such an extended period of time. Although beginning later than that of other west European countries, the exodus continued with considerable volume until the 1970s. Over the course of a century, some 26 million persons departed, giving Italy the dubious honour of having registered a larger number of emigrants than any other country. Migration statistics are notoriously imprecise and this is certainly true of the official Italian statistics which began to be collected systematically in 1876 (Rosoli 1978). Definitions of emigrant changed from time to time and, of course, the substantial clandestine emigration went unrecorded. Sums will, therefore, be rounded off to avoid the impression of a greater degree of exactitude than the sources warrant.

Italian migration was not a homogeneous phenomenon that can be analysed in terms of unitary causes, characteristics or itineraries. What was particular (but by no means unique) about the Italian diaspora was its variation over time in terms of types of migrations, modalities, volume, intensity, sources and destinations (Sori 1979). Since such characteristics varied significantly in various parts of Italy, this analysis will make reference to regions grouped into three geographical areas: the north (Piedmont, Liguria, Lombardy, Friuli (formerly Venezia Giulia) and Veneto); the centre (Tuscany, Emilia-Romagna, Latium, the Marches, Umbria); and the south or Mezzogiorno (Campania, Abruzzi-Molise, Apulia, Lucania (formerly Basilicata), Calabria, Sicily and Sardinia) (see Map 1). Contrary to common belief, of the total emigration, only some 40 per cent originated in the south, while 20 per cent departed from the centre and 40 per cent from the north. A rank ordering of regions by number of emigrants gives the place of honour to the Veneto (over 3 million), followed by Campania (more than 2.7 million), Sicily (2.5 million), Lombardy (2.3 million), Piedmont and Friuli (2.2 million each), and Calabria (2 million). Seven (out of a total of seventeen) regions accounted for some two-thirds of the total emigration (about 17 million).

Historians generally agree on the following periodization of Italian emigration. First, the classic period,

1876–1914, during which over half the total emigration took place; second, the period of low emigration, 1915–1945; and third, the period of renewed migration, 1946–1976, which accounted for 25 per cent of the total.[1] Of the 26 million emigrants between 1876 and 1976, some 52 per cent migrated to European countries (13.5 million), 44 per cent to the Americas (6 million to North America, 90 per cent of these to the USA, and 5 million to South America), 2 per cent to Africa and 1.5 per cent to Oceania, mainly Australia (Assante 1978; Rosoli 1978).

Another basic fact about the Italian emigration was the high rate of return migration; statistics are particularly imprecise or lacking for this phenomenon, but in the period 1905–76, more than 8.5 million remigrated (this figure does not include the high return migration from European countries prior to 1921). An estimate that at least half of all emigrants returned after shorter or longer sojourns abroad appears reasonable (Briani 1970; Cerase 1975).

A profile of the emigration in terms of age, gender and occupation reveals that three-quarters of the emigrants were male, 80 per cent of working age (between 15 and 45); 35 per cent had been engaged in agriculture; another 40 per cent were common labourers; and 25 per cent artisans (Martellone 1979). The number of persons in the professional and business categories was minuscule. Of course the mix of emigrants by gender, age and occupation changed over time and according to destination, but it is safe to conclude that the Italian emigration was above all proletarian and temporary.

The population of Italy was not sedentary prior to the late nineteenth century. There were considerable migrations during the *ancien régime*. Merchants, sailors, artists, musicians and artisans, particularly from Liguria and Tuscany, moved about freely at least from the twelfth century on, voyaging, sojourning, establishing permanent colonies, not only within the peninsula and the islands, but throughout the Mediterranean basin and indeed northern Europe (Pizzorusso and Sanfilippo 1990). While not a mass migration, neither was this limited to a tiny elite; these forerunners, seeking markets, custom and work,

Map 1: Regions of Italy showing key cities

established the itineraries, the mental maps and the permanent colonies for the many who were to follow.

Other centuries-old migration traditions functioned to link particular mountain villages – Braudel (1972: 51) called such communities 'a reservoir of men for other people's use' – in the Apennines with particular markets for specialized skills and wares throughout Italy and Europe (Castronovo 1986).

Stone cutters, masons, mosaicists, stucco workers and labourers left Alpine villages annually to build and ornament churches, fortifications, public buildings, dams and bridges in Austria-Hungary, Germany and Switzerland, and as far away as the Ottoman empire. Silk workers emigrated from Genoa to other Italian cities and to Lyon, where they established the silk industry of that city. Not as well regarded but equally economic migrants were the *girovaghi* (itinerants) who practised trades peculiar to their home towns: *figurinai* (statuette vendors), street musicians, tumblers, jugglers, pedlars, vendors, chimney sweeps and animal trainers from the hill towns of Lucca, Basilicata and Abruzzi who pursued their livelihoods on the streets of Paris, London and Vienna (Zucchi 1992).

Less dramatic, but involving greater numbers, were the seasonal migrations of agricultural workers from the mountain zones to work in the wheat fields of Apulia, the rice paddies of Lombardy, the olive groves of Sicily. Raised from childhood to a migratory existence, the earnings of these itinerants supplemented their families' meagre returns from subsistence agriculture. These temporary migrations were not disruptive or uprooting; rather they were essential to the economic survival of families and communities in such harsh environments. Specialized and seasonal migrations such as these continued well into the twentieth century, ending only with the ultimate abandonment of these mountain communities. While Italy was still a 'geographical expression', migration was already a way of life for many of its inhabitants. As the harp players from Viggiano sang: *L'arpa al collo – son viggianese – tutto il mondo e mio paese* (harp on my shoulder, from Viggiano I come. All the world is my home) (Foerster 1919: 102).

During the first period of Italian emigration history (1876–1915), 14 million (over 50 per cent of the total) emigrated within four decades (Rosoli 1978). Of these, 44 per cent headed for European destinations and 56 per cent for destinations outside Europe. During the years 1876–1900, of a total of 5.2 million emigrants some 50 per cent went to the Americas – Brazil, Argentina and the USA each received about 800,000 Italians during this quarter century. The first fifteen years of the twentieth century marked the high point of the emigration with almost 9 million emigrants, more than a third of the total for the entire century; of these 9 million, 60 per cent went abroad, almost all to the Americas. The USA now was the major attraction with some 3.5 million arrivals, while Argentina lagged behind with 1 million. The rate of repatriation during these years from both North and South America was in the range of 50 per cent.

While the magnitude of this emigration was unprecedented, it initially followed the traditional forms of migration, but with constantly engaging larger numbers and dispersal to more far flung destinations. The Napoleonic regime, by introducing administrative reforms and liberal ideas, had undermined surviving feudal rigidities and prepared the way for greater mobility. Meanwhile, compulsory military service and new public works projects requiring large numbers of workers stimulated internal movements among the regions of Italy. Improved systems of communication and transport – railroads, canals, steamship lines and newspapers – facilitated intra- and inter-continental migrations. The wandering trades, for example the *figurinai* of Barga, the organ players of Lucca and harp players from Viggiano, now appeared in St Petersburg, New York and Buenos Aires. Ligurians continued to be the pathbreakers in the initial phases of post-unification emigration; fruit pedlars from Chiavari, for example, pursued retail and wholesale commerce in the cities of North America. By the 1860s, thousands, including political exiles of the *Risorgimento*, but particularly enterprising merchants, artisans and sailors, made their way to Argentina, Brazil, Peru, Uruguay and the USA (Fondazione Giovanni Agnelli 1987).

If there was continuity, what distinguished this period of emigration (1876–1915) was a rising torrent which eventually broke out of the river beds of established itineraries of traditional migrations, carrying along with it vast numbers of settled *contadini* (peasants) and *artigiani* (artisans). This exodus was the result of certain fundamental changes taking place in Italian society and economy. Put simply, the expansion of capitalism, nurtured by the economic policies of the new kingdom of Italy, resulted in a sharply rising migration from the 1870s on (Sereni 1947). A late and immature form of capitalism which affected the various economic sectors and regions of Italy in different ways caused what Clough and Levi (1956) have termed 'uneven development'. Another underlying factor was the growth of Italy's population from

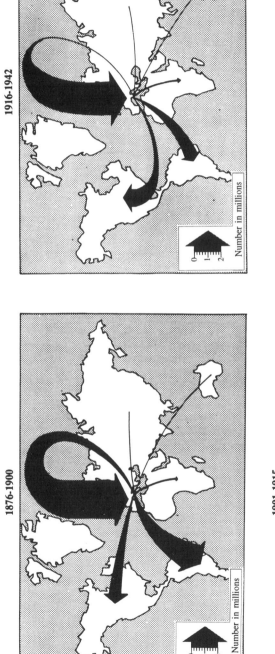

1876-1900

1901-1915

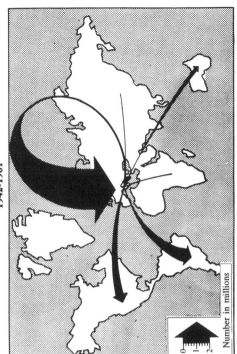

1916-1942

1942-1961

Number in millions

Number in millions

Number in millions

Number in millions

Source : Gianfausto Rosoli, (ed.) *Un secolo di emigrazione italiana : 1876 - 1976* (Rome: Centro Studi Emigrazione, 1978)

Map 2: Volumes and destinations of migration flows from Italy, by period

27.5 million in 1871 to 40.5 million in 1931, a 50 per cent increase despite the heavy emigration of those sixty years. Increased population generated demographic pressures on a too slowly modernizing economy. According to Ercole Sori's (1979) analysis, while capitalist innovations disrupted traditional forms of production and property relations, 'modernization' lagged behind. The industrial sector grew too slowly to absorb a growing underemployed agricultural proletariat, assailed by deep poverty, pellagra and malaria, and reduced to pauperism, vagabondage and brigandage. The agricultural crisis of the 1880s, precipitated by the fall in the price of grain on the world market due to burgeoning American and Ukrainian wheat production, spelled disaster for both the small landowner and the *bracciante* (agricultural labourer). Larger families, parcelization of landholdings, displacement of cottage industry by factory production and burdensome taxes all exacerbated the peasants' plight.

During the last decades of the nineteenth century, emigration took on marked regional characteristics. Relatively small numbers left from the central regions, while from the north, particularly from the Veneto, Friuli and Piedmont, the emigration took on vast proportions, continuing in part along its trans-Alpine paths, but significantly launching hundreds of thousands to South America, especially of *Veneti* to Brazil. Meanwhile, the Mezzogiorno, foremost the region of Campania, registered high rates of departures, for the most part to the USA.

The massive emigration to Brazil from northeastern Italy, from the Alpine and pre-Alpine zones and the Po Valley and river delta, which Emilio Franzina (1976) described as an expulsion, represented the stark face of this new emigration – a desperate flight from hunger. Seasonal migrations no longer sustained the fragile peasant economy; abrogation of communal rights to pasturage and woodlands, drainage of wetlands and the harsh terms of land contracts produced a rebelliousness expressed in banditry, peasant uprisings and emigration. Increasing numbers of men left for the mines and mills of Germany and France or for railroad construction in the Balkans, while women were employed as domestics and wet nurses in bourgeois families. Their purpose was to acquire land with their savings. However, the emigration to Brazil, which grew to great proportions in the 1880s, was composed of entire families recruited with promises of land from the Brazilian government.

A similar scenario was evolving simultaneously in the Mezzogiorno, particularly Campania, Calabria and Sicily, where economic deprivation and political reaction joined together to drive hundreds of thousands abroad, particularly to the USA (Barbagallo 1973). Unification had in various ways affected the southern regions adversely; worsening economic conditions and loss of political autonomy in the south resulted in a civil war between the army of the kingdom of Italy and the so-called brigands, a war which lasted many years and took many lives. By the 1870s, lower grain prices, starvation wages and high taxes had begun to expel small landowners and agricultural labourers, especially from the hill towns of Campania and Calabria; these were the pathfinders for the larger numbers who were to follow them to the cities of North America in the 1880s and 1890s (Capecelatro and Carlo 1973; Cerase 1975).

Sicily remained largely inert until the 1890s (Martellone 1979; Renda 1977). The island had not had the traditional forms of migration which characterized much of the mainland. The social and political tensions generated by the agricultural crisis exploded in the *fasci* uprisings of 1893 and 1894 (Renda 1977). Put down with draconian measures by the Crispi government, the repression inspired a massive exodus, termed a *silenziosa rivoluzione* by Gioacchino Volpe (1949: 228), of small proprietors, artisans and labourers. This resulted in a permanent emigration of families, with the Sicilians drawn predominantly to the higher wages of the USA. The Sicilian emigration, which had only amounted to a quarter of a million between 1876 and 1900, increased to well over a million in the first fifteen years of this century, assuming first place among the regions of Italy.

These population expulsions to overseas destinations around the turn of the century signified the emergence of a new phase of Italian emigration history. Despite the increasing attraction of the Americas, the movements to northern Europe, particularly France, Germany and Switzerland, continued to account for a significant component in the total Italian emigration; during the period 1901–15, the 3.5 million Italian emigrants within Europe equalled the number that chose to go to North America. The migrations to European cities, temporary and male in character, were largely composed of sojourning building craftsmen and *girovaghi*. But an expanding segment was absorbed into the industrial proletariat of the glass and textile factories and the steel mills and coal mines of France, Germany and Belgium (Bezza 1983).

Contemporary commentators characterized the European migrations as an asset because of their temporary, skilled and northern character, while the overseas migrations were denigrated as a national liability because they were thought to be a permanent exodus of untutored southern peasants (Manzotti 1969). The former was praised since it did not result in a loss of Italian blood and did honour to the Italian name; the latter was deplored since it deprived Italy of the labour of its children and brought disgrace to *la patria* because the *cafoni* (bumpkins) were organ grinders, rag pickers and strikebreakers. Such stereotypes reflecting regional and class prejudices had little validity. Increasingly, the overseas and the European migrations partook of the same character: temporary movements of rural males to industrial jobs. As has been noted, one of the striking characteristics of the overseas migration was its high rate of return migration, some 2 million during the decade 1905–15. The tone of the debates regarding overseas emigration became much more positive once the cornucopia of emigrant remittances commenced to pour its golden stream into the national coffers. In the years immediately prior to the First World War, remittances accounted for a full 25 per cent of Italy's balance of payments (Balletta 1972).

One of the factors shaping the peculiar contours of Italian emigration in the twentieth century had begun to manifest itself by the time of the First World War. Increasing mechanization, use of fertilizers, irrigation and crop rotation resulted in improved agricultural productivity in the north and central regions, making possible less onerous conditions for the peasantry who continued on the land. At the same time rapid growth in the industrial triangle of Genoa–Milan–Turin began to absorb surplus rural labour, first from the adjacent hinterland and then from more distant parts of the northern regions. While industrialization undermined a peasant economy based on proto-industrialism, many former agricultural workers now became factory hands. Rural–urban migration was accompanied by rural–rural migration as peasants moved from the highlands to the lowlands. These economic changes also produced a curious phenomenon, especially in the district around Biella in Piedmont, in which emigration and immigration occurred simultaneously as in-migrants from yet more marginal zones came in to take the places of those who were departing (Ramella 1991).

If this gradual modernization of the north and central regions did not in itself eliminate emigration, it did transform it from a desperate flight from hunger to a calculated decision based on differential wage standards in the international labour market. Events,

however, followed a different course in the Mezzogiorno. Gaetano Salvemini (1963) identified the emigration in the early 1900s as an integral component of *la questione meridionale* (the southern question). But it remained the Gordian knot that defied all efforts at solution by Italian economists and statesmen. Its essential character was the persisting economic diverence between the southern regions and the rest of Italy, a divergence expressed in lower levels of literacy and cultural development as well as higher rates of poverty. *La miseria* was thought to be the unalterable condition that drove the southern peasantry to emigrate *en masse*. But emigration itself was seen by some economists, such as Pasquale Villari (1909), as the solution to *la questione meridionale*: by reducing surplus population and thus improving agricultural wages and terms of agrarian contracts, it would provide incentives to the landowning class to invest in agricultural improvements. Such an optimistic forecast, however, was not borne out by subsequent developments.

Franceso Cerase (1975: 53–104) has argued persuasively that this chronic malaise of the Mezzogiorno has been due to what he calls its 'precarious economy'. The agriculture of the south was dependent on one or two crops and was dominated by large landowners who tolerated the existence of small marginal peasant properties. Small landowners eking out a marginal existence provided a reserve labour force for the large estates, keeping wages depressed. Meanwhile industrial activity remained at an artisanal level subordinate to agriculture. In sum, a dominant class of landowners with aristocratic pretensions defended its privileged position, investing its capital in land or government securities rather than agricultural improvements or industry. Southern agriculture remained wedded to archaic forms of land tenure, crops and techniques, resulting in low productivity and exploitation of the peasantry. In this backwardness lay the root cause of southern poverty and mass emigration.

Nor did mass emigration, characterized by a high rate of return migration and a large volume of remittances, serve as the redeeming force for the Mezzogiorno as some economists had predicted it would. Rather, again to cite Cerase (1975: 119), because of the obsessive 'myth of the small independent peasant property', land-hungry remigrants invested hard-earned savings in small parcels of often marginal land at inflated prices. Ironically emigration served to perpetuate the very archaic and abusive status quo which was its basic cause. After several generations of emigration, *la questione meridionale* remained unsolved; the economic discrepancy between the north and centre and the south actually increased over the course of the century. The progressive rationalization and mechanization of agriculture and industry which dampened the emigration from the north and centre did not take place in the south.

In the context of intensifying social upheavals in late nineteenth-century Italy, certain commentators saw emigration as an alternative to peasant revolt. Historians agree on interpreting the mass exodus as an expression of rebellion against oppression. Among Italian scholars, one school of thought has emphasized that, rather than a mindless flight from *miseria*, migration represented a conscious rejection by a segment of the peasantry of the new social order which condemned them to political and economic subordination. At the time conservatives and liberals alike viewed the increasing influence of socialism among workers and peasants with alarm and agreed that emigration provided an essential safety value for popular discontent. As Gioacchino Volpe (1949: 230) put it: 'The proletarians had found a new means to free themselves from the hard yoke of the *padroni* which did not take the form of the sterile revolt of preceding centuries or of brigandage.'

Cycles of protest, repression and emigration were in fact a recurring feature of Italian history in the late nineteenth and early twentieth centuries. From the 1870s on, popular uprisings followed by bloody governmental suppression triggered an exodus shortly thereafter; such it was with the peasant protests in the Po Valley in the 1880s, the Sicilian *fasci* of the 1890s and the socialist resistance to fascism in the 1920s (Del Carria 1970). The distinction between political emigrants and labour emigrants which had dominated earlier writings was first questioned by Ernesto Ragionieri (1962) in a ground-breaking article. Rather than being limited to a leadership elite, Ragionieri observed that emigrés fleeing from the *carabinieri* were often also peasants or workers seeking employment. In fact, the bulk of the *fuorusciti* (political exiles) were indistinguishable from the other emigrants. The larger theme to which Ragionieri (1962: 669) called attention was how mass emigration had given a character of 'proletarian internationalism to the Italian labour movement'. Through emigration Italian workers came into contact with and participated in more advanced labour movements in Europe and the Americas, resulting in the transfer of working-class ideologies and experiences (Bezza 1983).

A related historiographical debate has to do with the mentality of the emigrants in terms of their degree of class consciousness and militancy. Some thirty years ago, John S. MacDonald (1964) forwarded a provocative thesis that there was no direct correlation between intensity of emigration and degree of poverty. The prime indicator of the propensity for emigration was not *miseria* itself, but rather the pattern of landholding in a particular area and the social ethos resulting. To summarize, MacDonald found that in those areas where great estates prevailed, worked by large numbers of sharefarmers and *braccianti*, for example the wheat-growing areas of Apulia and Sicily, rates of emigration tended to be low, whereas in those areas where there was a fractionalization in the form of minute peasant holdings, for example Campania and Calabria, the rates were high. Forms of collective resistance (peasants' leagues, strikes) characterized the areas of large estates, while there was relatively little class-based protest where small peasant proprietorships prevailed. From this MacDonald concluded that a social ethos of solidarity characteristic of the landless proletariat led them to stay and engage in the class struggle; contrariwise, the small proprietors' individualistic (or familistic) ethos led them to seek a solution through emigration. While other studies have tended to corroborate the MacDonald thesis, it has been criticized for failing to take into account the sequel to failed revolts such as the Sicilian *fasci*. When popular uprisings were crushed, the will to fight appears to have been broken and an exodus ensued. In a study of Sicilian emigration, however, Donna R. Gabaccia (1988) has contended that militancy and migration were not mutually exclusive responses on the part of the peasantry, but rather could be contemporaneous and interrelated modes of resistance.

The second period of Italian emigration history (1915–45) – decades of war, migration restriction, fascism and economic depression – registered a sharp decline to less than 100,000 emigrants a year in the 1930s (Ciuffoletti and Degl'Innocenti 1978; Sori 1979). Of the total of some 4.5 million emigrants during this thirty-year interval, over a third went to France, the leading country of immigration in the inter-war years, while only a million headed for the USA and many fewer to South America. The great overseas exodus had come to an end, at least temporarily.

The First World War effectively blockaded migrations both within Europe and overseas. However, with peace came a rapid resumption of emigration, particularly to the USA. The enactment of immigration restriction measures by the USA (the law of 1924 established an annual quota for Italy of 3845), Argentina and Brazil reduced the overseas movement drastically. Rebuffed by such policies, Mussolini reversed his initially pro-emigration policy to one that proposed to direct Italy's surplus population to the new Roman empire. Despite strict controls on external migrations imposed in the late 1920s, a sizeable emigration to France took place, in part composed of anti-fascists, in part of small landowners and labourers seeking work, for example from Emilia-Romagna to Paris. However, in this instance, as in previous ones, it is not possible to divide emigrants into neat political and economic categories. Many of the anti-fascist refugees were artisans, factory workers and peasants of a leftist persuasion from the north and centre who were fleeing the fascists. In France, Belgium and to a lesser extent the USA, as Ragionieri (1962: 663) put it, the '*fuorusciti* were in large part workers who constituted an effective brake on the Fascist policy of controlling the Italian emigrants'.

In the third period of Italian emigration history, 1946–76, a strong resurgence of external migration encompassing some 7.5 million was paralleled by a massive internal migration (Rosoli 1978). The demographic and economic disequilibriums, summed up in *la questione meridionale*, which had bedevilled the country since unification, continued to defy solution. After almost a century, the sad scenes of departures, economic and social subordination and ethnic discrimination were being re-enacted by the grandchildren of the first emigrants. Based on reactivated chain migrations and the family reunification provision of American immigration policy, the USA maintained its position as the preferred overseas destination, but only slightly over Argentina, while new countries that had not figured prominently in the earlier periods – Canada, Australia and Venezuela – now attracted large numbers of Italians. Less than a third of the emigrants (some 2.5 million), however, embarked on transoceanic journeys and their number sharply declined after 1960. The proximity of high-paying employment in Europe, as well immigration barriers, caused overseas destinations to become less of a magnet for Italian labour.

During these three decades, over two-thirds of the emigrants headed for jobs in Switzerland, Germany, France and Benelux, in that order. Labour shortages created by the economic boom caused these countries to recruit workers in the Balkans, Turkey and Italy. But indicative of their status as *gasterarbeiter*, over 3.5 million of the 5 million Italians returned home from European countries. The recession of the 1970s brought the external migrations from Italy to an end; since 1973 there have been more repatriates than emigrants. In fact, as Italian migrants were discharged and sometimes paid bonuses to leave, a large scale return migration from the European countries took place, creating problems of absorption and readjustment (Agnoletti 1974).

The 'economic miracle' which transformed Italy into a leading economic power in the 1960s and 1970s provided alternatives at home to job-seeking migrants. As dynamic industrial growth expanded beyond the Genoa–Milan–Turin triangle throughout the north and centre, young people abandoned the countryside and the hill towns, resulting in a depopulation of rural Italy. Emigrants from the Mezzogiorno increasingly preferred northern Italy's industrial centres to other destinations. In 1967, per capita income in the north was twice as high as in the south. By the 1970s, Milan, Turin and other cities had entire districts populated by the *meridionali* (southerners), living under the most adverse conditions, working at jobs northerners disdained and subject to racial prejudice. The southerners became internal emigrants in their own country.

Although the recession of the 1970s also curbed internal migrations within Italy, the economic expansion of the north and centre appeared finally to have created a labour market adequate to absorb the bulk of the country's labour force. The southern question had not been solved, but contained, as the south continued to live largely on government subsidies from Rome and remittances. The stresses and strains of uneven economic development of the various portions of Italy remained a problem: witness the emergence of movements in the north for greater regional autonomy and even secession. But for the time being, one could say the epoch of the Italian diaspora had come to an end.

Note

1. For a comprehensive and critical review of the historiography of Italian migration, see Pizzorusso and Sanfilippo (1990) and Franzina (1989).

References

Agnolotti, Enzo E. (ed.) (1974) 'Emigrazione Cento Anni 26 Milioni', *Il Ponte*, 30 (11–12)

Assante, Franca (ed.) (1978) *Il Movimento migratorio italiano dall'unità nazionale ai giorni nostri* (2 vols.), Geneva: Librarie Droz

Balletta, Francesco (1972) *Il Banco di Napoli e le Rimesse degli Emigranti (1914–1925)*, Naples: Institut International d'Histoire de la Banque

Barbagallo, Francesco (1973) *Lavoro ed Esodo dal Sud, 1861–1971*, Naples: Guida editore

Bezza, Bruno (ed.) (1983) *Gli italiani fuori d'Italia. Gli italiani nei Movimenti operai dei Paesi d'adozione 1880–1940*, Milan: Franco Angeli editore

Braudel, Fernand (1972) *The Mediterranean and the Mediterranean World in the Age of Philip II*, vol. I, London: Collins

Briani, Vittorio (1970) *Il Lavoro italiano all'estero negli ultimi cento anni*, Rome: Italiani nel Mondo

Capecelatro, E. M. and A. Carlo (1973) *Contro la 'Questione meridionale': Studio sulle Origini dello Sviluppo capitalistico in Italia*, Rome: Giulio Savelli editore

Castronovo, Valerio (ed.) (1986) *L'emigrazione biellese fra Ottocento e Novecento*, Milan: Electra

Cerase, Francesco (1975) *Sotto il Domino dei Borghesi. Sottosviluppo ed Emigrazione nell'Italia meridionale, 1860–1910*, Assisi: Beniamino Carucci editore

Ciuffoletti, Zeffiro and Maurizio Degl'Innocenti (1978) *L'emigrazione nella Storia de'Italia 1868–1975*, 2 vols, Florence: Vallecchi editore

Clough, Shepard B. and Carlo Levi (1956) 'Economic Growth in Italy: An Analysis of the Uneven Development of North and South', *The Journal of Economic History*, 16 (3), 334–49

Del Carria, Renzo (1970) *Storia senza Rivoluzione Storia delle Classi subalterne italiane dal 1860 al 1950*, 2 vols, Milan: Edizioni Oriente

Foerster, Robert (1919) *The Italian Emigration of our Times*, Cambridge: Harvard University Press

Fondazione Giovanni Agnelli (1987) *Euro Americani*, 3 vols (vol. I *La Popolazione di Origine italiana negli Stati Uniti*; vol. II *La Popolazione di Origine italiana in Argentina*; vol. III *La Popolazione di Origine italiana in Brasile*), Turin: Fondazione Giovanni Agnelli

Franzina, Emilio (1976) *La grande Emigrazione. L'Esodo dei rurali dal Veneto durante il Secolo XIX*, Venice: Marsilio Editore

—— (1989) 'Emigrazione transoceanica e Ricerca storica in Italia: gli ultimi Dieci Anni (1978–1988)', *Altreitalie*, 1 (1), 6–56

Gabaccia, Donna R. (1988) *Militants and Migrants: Rural Sicilians become American Workers*, New Brunswick: Rutgers University Press

MacDonald, John S. (1964) 'Agricultural Organisation, Migration and Labour Militancy in Rural Italy', *Economic History Review*, 16, 61–75

Manzotti, Fernando (1969) *La Polemica sull'emigrazione nell'Italia unità (fino alla Prima Guerra Mondiale)*, Citta di Castello: Società Editrice Dante Alighieri

—— (1984) 'Italian Mass Emigration to the United States, 1876–1930: A Historical Survey', *Perspectives in American History*, 1, 378–423

Martellone, Anna Maria (1979) *I Siciliani fuori dalla Sicilia: l'emigrazione transoceanica fino al 1925*, Florence: Tipografia 'G. Capponi'

Pizzorusso, Giovanni and Matteo Sanfilippo (1990) 'Rassenga storiografica sui Fenomeni migratori a lungo raggio in Italia dal Basso medioevo al Seconda Dopoguerra', *Bolletino di Demografia Storica*, 13

Ragionieri, Ernesto (1962) 'Italiani all'estoro ed Emigrazione di lavoratori italiani: Un Tema di Storia del Movimento operaio', *Belfagor Rassegna di varia umanità*, 17 (6), 640–69

Ramella, Francesco (1991) 'Emigration from an Area of Intense Industrial Development: The Case of Northwestern Italy', in Rudolph J. Vecoli and Suzanne M. Sinke (eds) *A Century of European Migrations 1830–1930*, Urbana: University of Illinois Press, 261–74

Renda, Francesco (1977) *I Fasci siciliani, 1892–1894*, Turin: Editori Einaudi

Rosoli, Gianfausto et al (1978) *Un Secolo di Emigrazione italiana: 1876–1976*, Rome: Centro Studi Emigrazione

Salvemini, Gaetano (1963) *Movimento socialista e Questione meridionale*, Milan: Editori Feltrinelli

Sereni, Emilio (1947) *Il Capitalismo nelle Campagne (1860–1900)*, Turin: Editori Einaudi

Sori, Ercole (1979) *L'emigrazione italiana dall'unità alla Seconda Guerra Mondiale*, Bologna: Il Mulino

Villari, Pasquale (1909) *Scritti sull'emigrazione e sopra altri Argomenti vari*, Bologna: N. Zanichelli

Volpe, Gioacchino (1949) *Italia Moderna 1815–1915*, vol. I, Florence: G. C. Sansoni Editore

Zucchi, John (1992) *The Little Slaves of the Harp: Italian Child Street Musicians in Nineteenth-Century Paris, London and New York*, Montreal: McGill-Queen's University Press

PART FIVE

MIGRATION IN EUROPE, 1800–1950

Karl Marx was not alone in spotting that large-scale migration in Europe signified a momentous social transformation, though he was the first to draw from this process a general revolutionary theory. He dated the disintegration of the old order to the last third of the fifteenth century and the first few decades of the sixteenth. Then, peasant proprietorship collapsed and the glue that held early modern Europe together – the seigniories, monasteries and baronies – was dissolved. His language becomes quite extravagant in describing this period. This was the moment when 'great masses of men [were] suddenly and forcibly torn from their means of subsistence and hurled onto the labour-market' (Marx 1976: 876). Again, 'The process of forcible expropriation of the people received a new and terrible impulse from the Reformation. ... The dissolution of the monasteries, etc. hurled their inmates into the proletariat' (p. 881). Finally, quoting W. T. Thornton, Marx concludes that 'the English working class was precipitated without any transitional state from its golden age to its iron age' (p. 879).

With the collapse of the socialist experiments of the twentieth century it has now become *de rigueur* to ignore Marx's writings. However, where he is wrong he is gloriously wrong – in a way that permits counter-arguments to be made and new insights to develop. Because Marx saw the migratory process as sudden and violent, he inferred that a new, reactive and unwavering form of working-class consciousness would emanate in the towns and factories to challenge the emerging capitalist order. New research on Europe's migration history does not support the idea of a sudden transformation on the scale Marx posited. For example, *Moch*[1] has established that large-scale local and circular migration systems were still integrated into the agricultural calendar at the end of the eighteenth century. At that time there were seven, thriving, European rural–urban–rural migration systems, each involving 20,000 to 100,000 people. Moreover, the occupations of rural–urban migrants were by no means uniform. Serving girls, itinerant artisans, mercenaries, seasonal brick-makers, clergy, sailors, packmen, minstrels, hawkers, pedlars and actors were some of the more prominent categories of migrants who were not destined for the crucible of industrial employment (Lucassen 1987: 2–4). Another group of peoples, the gypsies, discussed in the *Survey* by *Lucassen* and *Willems*, also refused to knuckle under to the social transformation wrought by the industrial revolution. Nor, for that matter, did they accept the political demands of the emerging nation states.[2] Instead they used migration to retain an independent way of life. From the 1860s onwards, gypsy blacksmiths, coppersmiths and circus performers migrated in considerable numbers from eastern to western Europe and also to the USA. Gypsies exhibiting bears even travelled to New Zealand and Australia as early as the 1870s.

Reference to the migrating tradition and multiple destinations of the gypsies provoke the next – and decisive – refutation of Marx's analysis. Europeans were not all forced to the same wretched destinations in the squalid towns and cities of their own countries. Instead, their horizons were widened to include local, intra- and intercontinental possibilities. As *Bade* demonstrates, Germans founded nearly 3000 'mini' farming colonies in Russia, the Caucasus and Siberia, and further settlements in more familiar places like Hungary, Romania and present-day Poland. They also used 'the North Sea system' to transmigrate through Amsterdam to the East Indies and, later, from

German ports to the Americas. At the same time, there was considerable immigration from other countries *to* Germany, particularly for religious reasons – French Huguenots, Dutch Calvinists and Waldenser all found refuge there. By linking regional and transoceanic movements, migration scholars have been able to show that the 'final contradiction' between labour and capital that Marx foresaw could effectively be displaced to other countries or other continents. Migration, in short, was the crucial safety valve for dispossessed peasants and disgruntled workers.[3]

One of *Noiriel*'s contributions, that on the Italians and Poles in France, also shows how these two groups left their homes not only for the USA but for a buoyant neighbouring country. They arrived at the time (from 1881 onwards) that France's second wave of industrialization, based on coal, iron, metal-working and chemicals, commenced. As he suggests, industrialists were particularly receptive to foreign workers because the fertility rate in France had dropped just as her industrial production developed on a large scale. Though their labour was the predominant reason for the admission of Italians and Polies, the French have received migrants for political as well as for economic reasons. The constitution of 1793 contains a ringing declaration inviting those 'escaping tyranny' to find a haven in the territories of the French republic. Two groups who took up this invitation were 'white' Russians after 1917 and the Armenians following the atrocities committed by the Turkish troops in the First World War (Toynbee 1915). These groups are considered in *Noiriel*'s second contribution. There is no doubt that this revolutionary tradition influenced successive French governments to welcome refugee groups, but it is also unlikely that the French authorities were not cognizant of the demographic issues to which I have already alluded.

France is unusual among European countries in wanting to increase its population. The idea that France could never be a great country without a large population was indeed an *idée fixe* of political opinion from 1860 to the 1970s. To be sure, France was particularly unfortunate in having so many young men killed or maimed in the First World War (and a lesser, but also substantial number, in the Second). This sad loss favoured migrant groups coming *either* for political or economic reasons. However, there was a *quid pro quo* for the newcomers, which was linked to the French desire to sustain a language, culture and civilization of global proportions. This was the demand for 'assimilation' – a concept that was used without pejorative connotations in France until very recently. It was only when North African migrants refused to accept that their culture, language and religion were subordinate that mainstream French public opinion turned wholly against immigration.

The migrants and refugees considered by *Holmes* and *Kay* also generated debates about political and cultural acceptability on the one hand, and economic advantage on the other. As *Holmes* states, 'Jewish history is a history of migration.' The particular Jewish migration covered in this *Survey* was galvanized by the assassination of the Russian tsar in 1881. Between the 1880s and the First World War about 2.5 million Jews left eastern Europe for western Europe and the USA – the greatest post-biblical movement in their history (Marrus 1985: 27). They came from the Polish provinces of the Russian empire (the 'Pale of Settlement') from Austrian Galicia and Romania. Their sheer number, evident poverty and apparent devotion to a despised religion occasioned alarm, particularly in England, where the restrictive Aliens Act was passed in 1905, and in the USA, where similar restrictions were proposed. As Marrus (1985: 38) notes, popular anti-Semitism was compounded by a considerable degree of unease on the part of existing Jewish communities in Europe:

The 1880s saw the beginnings of a new wave of popular anti-Semitism ... which harped on the threat to European societies caused by all Jews, but particularly by unassimilated, Yiddish-speaking *Ost-juden*. Spokesmen for established Jewish communities in the West worried anxiously about how the presence of these outsiders might undermine their newly acquired social status, might cast aspersions on their own acculturation. Confronted with this reminder of their own pre-emancipation identity, many Westernized Jews felt discomfort, even distaste.

Half a century later and even after the horrors of the concentration camps had been exposed by Allied troops and journalists entering Germany in 1945, old prejudices ran deep. Throughout Europe, Jews were turned away. The British authorities, for example, recruited some 80,000–90,000 'displaced persons' from the camps in the British zones in Austria and Germany. Yet, they allowed only 3000 Jews to enter the UK. The Poles (who numbered 115,000 with their families) had fought for the Allies and were felt to deserve post-war sanctuary. The displaced persons were given a brand-new name, the European Voluntary Workers, though, as Kay and Miles (1992) have demonstrated, whether they were volunteers, labour migrants or refugees was far from certain.

The emptying of the displaced persons camps conformed to two political impulses and one more overriding economic imperative. The post-war refugee agencies and the UN were pressuring the occupying powers to solve the costly and embarrassing problem of leaving over one million people in the camps who refused to be repatriated to the east. The second political impulse was that many displaced persons were firmly anti-Soviet, a posture that now conformed to the west's position at the opening of the cold war. Finally, there was an economic imperative in that a number of European countries were desperately short of the labour needed to regenerate industrial production. As *Kay* suggests, despite these arguments, the destination countries began to operate a more explicit set of distinctions between 'desirable' and 'undesirable' immigrants. As we shall see later in the *Survey*, for the next thirty years European countries vacillated between recognizing the economic need for labour migrants and disliking the political and social consequences of their admission.

Notes

1. In this *Survey* and in her major book (Moch 1992).
2. Note on political correctness. It is now common to use the labels 'Rom', 'Roma' or 'Shinti', because of the derogatory connotation of 'gypsy'. However, I have followed our contributors' advice (see footnote 1 in *Lucassen* and *Willems*) in avoiding the newer appellations because of evidence that we are not describing one group with one origin. A number of reference books suggest that 'gypsy' is a corruption of 'Egyptian', another error, as there is no evidence that Egypt was the natal gypsy homeland. Given the number of unsatisfactory alternatives, 'gypsy' has the great virtue of being readily understood and is often self-attributed by 'gypsies' themselves.
3. The Irish provide another example of migration to a number of competing destinations (Canny 1985). Irish migration to the British mainland served to oversupply the labour market and, in some sectors at least, undermined the fledging labour movement. Marx and Engels were acutely aware of the effects of Irish migration – indeed how could they not be, for Engels employed many Irish workers in his Manchester factory. However, they were curiously blind to the same dynamic in other European countries and in the USA. Even more curious is that, despite some passing remarks, they did not see how profoundly transoceanic migration was bound to damage European labour and political organizations.

References

Canny, N. (1985) 'Migration and Opportunity: Britain, Ireland and the New World', *Irish Economic and Social History*, 12, 7–32
Kay, Diana and Robert Miles (1992) *Refugees or Migrant Workers? European Volunteer Workers in Britain, 1946–1951*, London: Routledge
Lucassen, Jan (1987) *Migrant Labour in Europe, 1600–1900: The Drift to the North Sea*, London: Croom Helm
Marrus, Michael R. (1985) *The Unwanted: European Refugees in the Twentieth* Century, New York: Oxford University Press
Marx, Karl (1976) *Capital: A Critique of Political Economy*, vol. I, Harmondsworth: Penguin (first published 1867)
Moch, Leslie Page (1992) *Moving Europeans: Migration in Western Europe since 1650*, Bloomington: Indiana University Press
Toynbee, Arnold (1915) *Armenian Massacres: The Murder of a Nation*, London: Hodder & Stoughton

MOVING EUROPEANS: HISTORICAL MIGRATION PRACTICES IN WESTERN EUROPE

LESLIE PAGE MOCH

The most noted migrations are the most spectacular: the movement of indentured workers in the tropical world, the transoceanic migrations of Europeans in the nineteenth century and contemporary movements into nations of the European Union. However, migration is also part of historical routines and practices. In the case of western Europe, migration was a long-standing and important facet of social life and the political economy. Expanding in the nineteenth and early twentieth centuries, mobility played significant and far-reaching roles in the two centuries before 1800.

Historical migrations reveal the key processes that have transformed Europe since 1650. They reflected changing agricultural practices and urban economies. At every geographic range – regional, national, international and transoceanic – the political economy shaped mobility. Transoceanic migrations were shaped not only by economic and demographic factors, but also by imperial and colonial practices. Likewise, migrations responded to and were shaped by the common stuff of historical narratives, such as wars and military invasion. More intimately, migration systems were rooted in extant demographic regimes and family formation systems. Human connections constituting migrant networks linked the individual migrant to global economic and political conditions.

Early modern Europe

In the seventeenth and eighteenth centuries, western Europeans moved out of their home parishes in rather routine *local migrations*.[1] Leaving home was a normal part of the life cycle for a sizeable proportion of young people. In rural areas they worked as farm servants – *valets de ferme*, servants in husbandry, *Gesinde* – while saving for their own land or dowry and training for agricultural life, moving to take a new position as often as once a year (Kussmaul 1981; Schofield 1970). Young apprentices and serving girls flocked to towns and cities (Clark 1979; Elliot 1981). For women especially, movement into another parish accompanied marriage and family formation. Even

inheritance practices encouraged the departure of some children, since systems of primogeniture excluded all but one sibling from running the family land, and systems of equal inheritance encouraged one sibling to manage the family land while the others departed or remained single (Darrow 1989).

In the primarily rural societies of western Europe, regional and international systems of *circular migration* marked the agricultural calendar. By the end of the eighteenth century, seven large systems of short-term circular migration, each involving 20,000 to 100,000 people per year, animated the continent, moving workers into East Anglia and London, the Paris basin, the North Sea coast, the Po Valley, central Italy, Castile, and the Mediterranean littoral of southern France.[2] Smaller regional systems activated the countryside in harvest seasons and brought rural people into towns and cities for winter work.

Migrants supplied pre-industrial cities as well as animating the countryside. Some moved to a regional capital in tight systems of *local migration*, others in *circular* systems that would return them home after a stint in the city, and still others in circuits of *career migration*, prompted by the national bureaucracy or mercantile employers. From London east to Danzig and Rostock south to Marseille, city records reflect the importance of migrants to urban populations (Bardet 1983; Clark 1979; Hochstadt 1983). Indeed, the total migration rate for pre-industrial cities is estimated at 0.10 (Hochstadt 1983: 208–9). Serving girls and unskilled workers from the surrounding countryside, regional elites, and merchants and bureaucrats operating in national and international circuits forged intimate ongoing ties with rural hinterlands and among cities (Bardet 1983; Poussou 1983).

In the seventeenth and eighteenth centuries, then, migration in western Europe was a complex phenomenon; it nonetheless systematically reflected economic circumstances, social organization, property holding status and the demographic characteristics of migrants themselves. Migration reflected and responded to regional and global economic circumstances. For example, in the eighteenth century, Bordeaux atypically doubled in size, largely through migration, because it was engaged in a booming transoceanic trade in sugar and wine. In that century, villages and small towns grew because a proto-industrial scenario was widespread: lowland manufacturing villages attracted newcomers and retained their own people; emigration from upland Swiss villages actually decreased as rural folk began to produce cotton cloth at home (Gutmann 1988; Head 1979; Levine 1977: 36–41; Poussou 1983). And although migration patterns reflected large-scale economic configurations, they simultaneously operated through human contacts at the most intimate level of the family and village society; people travelled where their compatriots had gone in local and circular migration streams, whether to work as a maidservant or to undertake trade across the Pyrenees (Poitrineau 1983). Migration proved selective: proletarian agricultural labourers and unskilled workers were most mobile, although journeymen artisans' travels constituted part of their training and some peasants also worked in seasonal migration streams to earn money for taxes and land. Sharecropper families relocated as a group. *Bürgerbucher* testify to the mobility of the urban propertied classes. Women moved to marry and, if poor, often moved to work before marriage. In short, stability was a privilege in this world, one most usually preserved for peasant men (Gaunt 1977; Hochstadt 1983; Todd 1975). In regions where rural industry proliferated in the eighteenth century, hybrid migration routines emerged: in Bedfordshire, girls began making pillow-lace before the age of ten, and continued into their teens or turned to the spinning of linen or knitting of jersey; their brothers left home to go into farm service. Likewise, while the women and children of smallholders along the Ems River in western Germany worked linen, their men trekked to Holland to cut hay (Lucassen 1987; Schofield 1970: 265–66).

Changing patterns in the nineteenth century

Between the end of the Napoleonic Wars in 1815 and the outbreak of the First World War in 1914, two trends underwrote dramatic shifts in migration patterns. First, an unprecedented surge of population outstripped the rate of growth that had begun in the 1750–1800 period, when the number of western Europeans had increased by 34 per cent. Between 1800 and 1850, the population increased by 42 per cent, then by another 76 per cent by 1914. During the nineteenth century, the number of inhabitants more than tripled in Denmark, Finland and Great Britain; it

more than doubled in Belgium, Holland, Germany and Austria-Hungary, and doubled in Italy; meanwhile France grew by only 55 per cent (Armengaud 1976: 29; Wrigley 1983). Second, rural economies suffered and urban economies grew. Crop failures, most notably the potato famine of the 'hungry forties' produced pernicious food shortages and undercut rural workers. The plagues on industrial crops such as the vine phylloxera (1863–99) and *pebrino* affecting silk worms after 1850 destroyed the livelihoods of country people (Moch 1983). The demise of rural industrial production – slow in some areas but ubiquitous – robbed rural textile and metal workers of the income that had maintained village life (Johnson forthcoming; Kamphoefner 1987: 16–38). Increases in the demand for temporary agricultural labourers undercut the demand for farm service that had supported young men and women year-round (Kussmaul 1981). Finally, the century closed with a long agricultural depression reducing agricultural prices. Thus the lives of rural Europeans, who remained in the great majority through the early 1800s, became demonstrably less secure. By contrast, urban economies expanded with the growth of mechanized industries demanding a centralized labour force and the expansion of the tertiary sector accompanying the explosive growth of the middle classes. The demand for urban manufacturing workers, construction labourers, shopkeepers and servants reached unprecedented heights.

These shifts in the population and economies of western Europe affected migration patterns in three ways, adding new itineraries to pre-existing patterns of local and circular movement. First, they eventually produced the urbanized and perhaps less mobile Europe of the late twentieth century, but in the years before a mature industrial economy provided adequate employment, they generated massive insecurity and temporary migration (Hochstadt 1981). Second, migration helped to generate large city growth and urbanization that transformed settlement patterns. Where there had been only 23 cities with populations of more than 100,000 in 1800, 125 stood a century later; likewise, while only 7 per cent of west Europeans lived in urban areas in 1750, by 1900 over half the population of England and Wales lived in towns of over 20,000 inhabitants, as did over a quarter of Belgians and Dutch, and one-fifth of Germans, French and Danes (Armengaud 1976: 32–33; de Vries 1984; Weber 1965). Increasingly, as health conditions improved, cities generated their own populations, but in France, Italy and Germany, where high urban mortality persisted, migration remained central to urbanization. Finally, people moved farther than before as regional migration systems became overlaid with international systems. Italians travelled not only to France, but to Buenos Aires, New York and San Francisco. Poles not only worked in Prussia, but in western Germany and the USA as well (Baily 1983; Morawska 1989). The same shifts that transformed migrations within western Europe developed the mass transoceanic migrations described in Part 4 of this Survey. In addition, these same patterns combined to move eastern Europeans into the west, as discussed below.

In the nineteenth century, new circular migration systems developed at the expense of long-standing local and circular patterns. Increased commercial agricultural production – of sugarbeets and potatoes as well as of grains – demanded teams of short-term workers rather than year-round farm servants. New machinery played a role: those who operated the widely used threshing machine performed in a few days one of the primary winter tasks of farm servants. The migrant agricultural labour force was an international one: Irish harvested English wheat; Belgians cut grain in northern France; Italians picked tomatoes in Provence. Similar teams of workers constructed the roads, railroad beds and tunnels of a new transport infrastructure, circulating in Britain, France, Germany and Switzerland.

The nineteenth century inaugurated an age of city building unprecedented since the Middle Ages as brick industrial cities such as Manchester, Verviers, Duisberg and Roubaix grew from villages and small towns. New and burgeoning cities engendered vast systems of construction workers, specialists like the German brickmakers of Lippe, French masons of the Limousin and Piedmontese navvies who travelled seasonally to ply their trade. Newcomers to these cities created a more international urban labour force that in previous centuries: the Irish worked in the mills of Lancashire; Belgians manned the looms of northern France; Dutch and Poles worked in the Ruhr Valley. Urban statistics reveal extremely high population turnover; for example, while the industrial city of Duisburg in the Ruhr Valley grew by 97,836 between 1848 and 1904, it temporarily hosted 719,903 individuals who moved to and from the city (Jackson 1982: 248). Urban total migration rates, which averaged under 0.10 in Germany at mid-century, peaked at about 0.20 just before the First World War (Hochstadt 1983: 209). The end product of this high mobility was urbanization, partly the result of *chain migration* that

brought people from small towns and villages to cities in Europe and across the oceans. With the growth of state functions, *career migration* also increased, relocating bureaucrats, schoolteachers and commercial employees.

Women's migration became more visible in the nineteenth century. While most female migration previously had been relatively localized marriage migration and pre-marital migration for service work, marriage markets expanded and the distance travelled by women workers extended as more women became urban servants and seamstresses (Moch 1983: 33–78). In addition, the textile cities of industrializing Europe attracted a highly visible female labour force. And in the fields, teams of seasonal farm workers included all-female groups: women harvested flowers and strawberries in Provence and, in Denmark and Germany, thousands of Polish women laboured in the sugarbeet and potato fields (Lucassen 1987: plate 20; Perkins 1981: 107–8). Even career migrants included women who took posts as rural schoolteachers towards the end of the century (Moch 1988). Finally, the transatlantic migrations to the USA from northwestern Europe included the highest proportion of women – over 40 per cent were female for the entire 1820–1929 period; most began as disproportionately male migration systems which became increasingly female after the turn of the twentieth century (Gabaccia 1994). The widespread emigration of single women from the countryside aroused concern about the viability of rural populations (Moch 1992: 171–2).

The long-standing migration traditions and changes forged during the nineteenth century applied throughout western Europe with an intensity and timing that varied by region. In Britain, the long-standing importance of London, early development of factory industry in the north and the demise of the peasantry triggered the earliest urbanization boom. Britain's demographic configuration – relatively early marriage, high birth rates and low death rates – underwrote its dynamic population increase and massive transoceanic migration, while its imperial history facilitated movement to colonial destinations (Baines 1985). In France, the history of strong provincial cities, the overwhelming importance of Paris, and urban growth in the industrial north and west made urbanization important; nonetheless, the persistence of its peasant population kept a greater proportion of people on the land. Relatively low birth rates and very slow population growth – and the paucity of transatlantic colonies after the eighteenth century – meant that the French did not develop strong practices of overseas migration (Ogden 1989). In western German territories, by contrast, rapid population growth generated early nineteenth-century emigration to North America and in the eastern regions, transatlantic migration swelled in the last decades of the century. The subsequent industrial and urban growth in the west drew German populations from the east and changed Germany from a labour-exporting to a labour-importing nation (Bade 1980). Italy's high birth rates spurred active and complex emigration practices late in the nineteenth century – from the agricultural south to North America, and from the north to South America and Europe. Indeed, Italians worked throughout the world as temporary migrants and contract labourers (Gould 1979; Rosoli 1985).

Overseas emigration was a subject of public debate after 1840, and European nations increasingly identified the foreigners in their midst; nonetheless, only Germany strictly regulated the entry of foreign labour (i.e. Poles). When hostilities broke out in 1914, international migration plummeted. The First World War marked the end of the free movement of labour; similarly it inaugurated a history of increasingly intrusive state attempts to document and control movement among nations (Herbert 1990; Noiriel 1988). Urbanization continued after the First World War and again after the deaths and displacements of the Second World War, generating increasing concern about the rural exodus, or *landflucht*. With the prosperity of the 1960s, western Europe demanded more unskilled and semiskilled workers than its educated indigenous populations were able to supply, especially since birth rates had dropped dramatically since the 1880s. These new workers recruited since 1960 to replace the moving Europeans of past centuries are the subjects of Part 9 of this Survey.

Notes

1. I adapt here the categorization of the social organization of migrations by distance from home and likelihood of return from Tilly's (1990) *local, circular, chain and career migrations*. For a general description of historical migrations in western Europe, see Moch (1992).
2. Systems of temporary migration were catalogued at a low point of activity by Napoleonic inquiries mounted in wartime, 1808–13; see Lucassen (1987: 1–17).

References

Armengaud, A. (1976) 'Population in Europe, 1700–1914', in C. Cipolla (ed.) *The Fontana Economic History of Europe*, vol. III, *The Industrial Revolution*, New York: Barnes and Noble, 22–76

Bade, K. (1980) 'German Emigration to the United States and Continental Immigration to Germany in the Late Nineteenth and Early Twentieth Centuries', *Central European History*, 13 (4), 348–77

Baily, S. (1983) 'The Adjustment of Italian Immigrants in Buenos Aires and New York, 1870–1914', *American Historical Review*, 88 (2), 281–305

Baines, D. (1985) *Migration in a Mature Economy: Emigration and Internal Migration in England and Wales, 1861–1900*, Cambridge: Cambridge University Press

Bardet, J.-P. (1983) *Rouen aux XVIIe et XVIIIe Siècles: Les Mutations d'un Espace social*, Paris: Société d'Edition d'Enseignement Supérieur

Clark, P. (1979) 'Migration in England during the Late Seventeenth and Early Eighteenth Centuries', *Past and Present*, (83), 57–90

Darrow, M. (1989) *Revolution in the House: Family, Class and Inheritance in Southern France, 1775–1825*, Princeton: Princeton University Press

de Vries, J. (1984) *European Urbanization, 1500–1800*, Cambridge, Massachusetts: Harvard University Press

Elliot, V. B. (1981) 'Single Women in the London Marriage Market: Age, Status and Mobility', in R. Outhwaite (ed.) *Marriage and Society*, London: Europa Publications, 81–100

Gabaccia, D. (1994) *From the Other Side: Women, Gender and Immigrants Life in the United States, 1820–1990*, Bloomington: Indiana University Press

Gaunt, D. (1977) 'Pre-Industrial Economy and Population Structure: The Elements of Variance in Early Modern Sweden', *Scandinavian Journal of History*, 2 (1), 183–219

Gould, J. D. (1979) 'European Inter-Continental Emigration, 1815–1914: Patterns and Causes', *Journal of European Economic History*, 8 (3), 593–679

Gutmann, M. (1988) *Toward the Modern Economy: Early Industry in Europe, 1500–1800*, New York: Knopf

Head, A.-L. (1979) 'Quelques Remarques sur l'Émigration des Régions préalpines', *Revue suisse d'Histoire*, 29 (1), 181–93

Herbert, U. (1990) *A History of Foreign Labor in Germany, 1880–1980*, Ann Arbor: University of Michigan Press

Hochstadt, S. (1981) 'Migration and Industrialization in Germany, 1815–1977', *Social Science History*, 5 (4), 445–68

—— (1983) 'Migration in Preindustrial Germany', *Central European History*, 16 (3), 195–224

Jackson, J. Jr (1982) 'Migration in Duisburg, 1867–1890: Occupational and Familial Contexts', *Journal of Urban History*, 8 (3), 235–70

Johnson, C. (forthcoming) *The Life and Death of Industrial Languedoc*, Oxford: Oxford University Press

Kamphoefner, W. (1987) *The Westfalians: From Germany to Missouri*, Princeton: Princeton University Press

Kussmaul, A. (1981) *Servants in Husbandry in Early Modern England*, Cambridge: Cambridge University Press

Levine, D. (1977) *Family Formation in an Age of Nascent Capitalism*, New York: Academic Press

Lucassen, J. (1987) *Migrant Labour in Europe, 1600–1900*, London: Croom Helm

Moch, L. P. (1983) *Paths to the City: Regional Migration in Nineteenth-Century France*, Beverly Hills: Sage Publications

—— (1988) 'Government Policy and Women's Experience: The Case of Teachers in France', *Feminist Studies*, 14 (2), 301–24

—— (1992) *Moving Europeans: Migration in Western Europe since 1650*, Bloomington: Indiana University Press

Morawska, E. (1989) 'Labor Migrations of Poles in the Atlantic Economy, 1880–1914', *Comparative Studies in Society and History*, 31 (2), 237–72

Noiriel, G. (1988) *Le Creuset français: Histoire de l'Immigration, XIXe–XXe Siècles*, Paris: Seuil

Ogden, P. E. (1989) 'International Migration in the Nineteenth and Twentieth Centuries' in P. E. Ogden and P. E. White (eds) *Migrants in Modern France: Population Mobility in the Later Nineteenth and Twentieth Centuries*, London: Unwin Hyman, 34–59

Perkins, J. A. (1981) 'The Agricultural Revolution in Germany, 1850–1914', *Journal of European Economic History*, 10 (1), 71–118

Poitrineau, A. (1983) *Remues d'Hommes: Essai sur les Migrations montagnardes en France, aux 17e–18e Siècles*, Paris: Aubier Montaigne

Poussou, J.-P. (1983) *Bordeaux et le Sud-ouest au XVIIIe Siècle*, Paris: Editions de l'Ecole des Hautes Etudes en Sciences Sociales

Rosoli, G. (1985) 'Italian Migration to European Countries from Political Unification to World War I', in D. Hoerder (ed.) *Labor Migration in the Atlantic Economies: The European and North American Working Classes during the Period of Industrialization*, Westport, CT: Greenwood Press, 95–116

Schofield, R. (1970) 'Age-Specific Mobility in an Eighteenth-Century Rural English Parish', *Annales de Démographie historique*, 261–74

Tilly, C. (1990) 'Transplanted Networks', in V. Yans-McLaughlin (ed.) *Immigration Reconsidered*, New York: Oxford University Press, 79–95

Todd, E. (1975) 'Mobilité géographique et Cycle de Vie en Artois et en Toscane au XVIIIe Siècle', *Annales: ESC*, 30 (4), 726–44

Weber, A. (1965) *The Growth of Cities in the Nineteenth Century*, reprint, Ithaca, New York: Cornell University Press

Wrigley, E. A. (1983) 'The Growth of Population in Eighteenth-Century England: A Conundrum Resolved', *Past and Present*, (98), 121–50

GERMANY: MIGRATIONS IN EUROPE UP TO THE END OF THE WEIMAR REPUBLIC

KLAUS J. BADE

In early modern history, Germany was a country of both immigration and emigration. From the sixteenth to the eighteenth century a great number of religious refugees – Dutch, Huguenots, Waldenser, residents of Salzburg – found refuge in Germany. At the same time there were substantial emigrations of Germans to eastern Europe and, to a lesser extent, North America, as well as labour migrations and emigrations to neighbouring European countries. In the nineteenth century transatlantic mass emigration became predominant; and in the late nineteenth century the long-term change from an emigration to an immigration country began (Bade 1987, 1992).

Emigration to eastern Europe

At the beginning of the emigrations, not German transatlantic movements to the west, but continental migrations to the east took place. In the middle of the twelfth century, the 'Siebenbürger Sachsen' immigrated to the kingdom of Hungary. Today the region of Transylvania (Siebenbürgen) belongs to Romania. They were given the term 'Saxons' by their Hungarian neighbours, but in reality the majority of them came from the Rhine and the Mosel. After the eighteenth century, other settlement groups from south-west and central Germany followed. In return for the attractive economic and cultural privileges they enjoyed, they were supposed to cultivate and secure the land (Dralle 1991).

Apart from present-day Romania, where their numbers have been decreasing over the past few years through resettlement in the Federal Republic, Germans in south-eastern and eastern European countries have for a long time lived in areas in which they have enjoyed special privileges. This was especially true of the tsarist Russian empire and later the Soviet Union. The Russian empire had been recruiting experts from the German states since the sixteenth century. Particularly military and administrative professionals, physicians, craftsmen and technicians made decisive contributions towards modernizing the economy, administration and military forces.

The history of the primarily rural German settlers, whose descendants still live in the CIS or who 'are migrating back' to Germany as repatriates (ethnic Germans) has been very different. Their history began in 1763 with Catherine II's manifesto, which was intended to recruit foreign settlers by offering numerous privileges. Between 1764 and 1767 about 27,000 settlers from German states migrated, mostly into the areas around the Volga, and between 1801 and 1825 a second strong influx followed. From 1763 to 1862 German settlers founded more than 3000 colonies, not only in the European part of the Russian empire, but also in the Caucasus and Siberia. At the end of the nineteenth century subsidiary colonies (secondary migration) by Russian Germans followed in Kazakhstan and central Asia.

The abolition of privileges in 1871 and increasing tensions between the Russian population and the German settlers, intensified by the pan-Slavonic movement, induced many Germans, above all Mennonites, to migrate to central Asia or abroad, especially to North America. But the majority of them remained. In 1897 the first census in the Russian empire registered about 1.8 million German-speaking persons, and in 1914 about 2.4 million lived in Russia. From 1924 to 1941 the 'Autonomous Socialist Soviet Republic of the Volga Germans' formed the focus of settlement, and was the centre of the Germans' cultural and political development. Due to forced collectivization, which began in 1928/9 and was disastrous for the German-Russian farmers, who mostly ran their farms very successfully under private ownership, the German Russian population decreased drastically. Only 1,427,000 Germans were counted in 1939. In 1941 the Soviet Union reacted to the German attack by disbanding the Volga republic and deporting nearly all German immigrants living in the western part of the Soviet Union to Siberia, central Asia and Kazakhstan (Bade 1990; Brandes 1992; Dietz and Hilkes 1992: 13 ff; Eisfeld 1992; Ferstl and Hetzel 1990; Malchow et al. 1990).

Migration via German ports

It was not until the 1830s that the continental stream

to the east was gradually overtaken by the secular stream of transatlantic mass emigration to the New World (see Nugent in this volume). By the time of the American Revolution, the flight from the Old World, for religious and ideological reasons or to satisfy economic and social aspirations, had led to about 225,000 German Americans. This number corresponded to 8–9 per cent of the total population of the British colonies. In Germany, remnants of religious or ideologically motivated group emigrations were still discernible in the first half of the nineteenth century. The secular transatlantic mass exodus, however, of which about 90 per cent went to the USA, was instigated mainly by socio-economic problems. They derived specifically from the lack of correspondence between population growth and employment opportunities during the crisis of the transition from an agrarian to an industrial economy. Emigration partly became the transatlantic export of the social question (Bade 1986).

Between the famine of 1816/17 and the beginning of the First World War in 1914, the transatlantic exodus brought about 5.5 million Germans to the USA. The high tide was in the five decades from 1846 to 1893, when the numbers often exceeded 100,000 emigrants a year in the 1850s and even more than 200,000 in the 1880s (Helbich et al. 1988; Kamphoefner 1987; Moltmann 1979; von Hippel 1984; Walker 1964). The picture of the three great emigration waves (1846–57, 1865–73 and 1880–93), though frequently applied in research, is nevertheless deceptive. It has also repeatedly led to erroneous attempts to regard particular factors and events as the supposed 'causes' of migration processes and patterns of migration behaviour. The idea that there was one single great 'emigration wave', starting with the increase of the transatlantic mass exodus in the 1840s and ending with the decline of the mass exodus at the beginning of the 1890s is much closer to historical reality. This wave had three climaxes and two phases of decline caused by events that took place between 1858 and 1864/5 (economic crisis, War of Secession 1861–65) and between 1873/4 and 1879 (economic crisis 1873–79) (Bade 1986: 264–70).

German colonial emigrations into the 'protectorates' of the short-lived German colonial empire (1884/5 to 1914–18) were relatively small. The visions of colonies presented in German publications in the late 1870s and early 1880s were part of a long tradition dating back to the emigration discussion of the 1840s and were influenced by British examples. They focused on the idea that colonies would offer an opportunity to divert emigration away from the USA. Emigration to the USA, considered with suspicion for economic reasons, was supposed to be replaced by a settlement migration into a German transatlantic empire. After the 'acquisition' of the most important German colonies in Africa and in the Pacific area, which were completely unsuitable for such plans, disillusionment rapidly set in. The similar dream of founding semi-colonial settlement areas by settling large numbers of Germans in South American states, especially Brazil and Argentina, also remained an imperial chimera (Bade 1975: 80–120, 190–200, 354–68).

There were no real emigration statistics in nineteenth century Germany, only fairly inadequate statistics on emigration derived from German (not foreign) ports. This makes it very difficult to trace movements into the various European countries via the 'dry' borders. Because of the predominance of the transatlantic and eastern European emigrations, we are far less informed about German emigrations into western European countries like England and France. There are great gaps in this area of research that still need to be filled (Grandjonc 1970, 1972, 1975; Panayi 1991, 1993).

From the early nineteenth century until the 1890s, transatlantic emigration reduced the population in Germany by about 5 million people. The tension between population growth and employment opportunities was further eased by immense economic growth in the highly industrialized empire during the decades before the First World War. Finally, at the time of the US economic crisis of 1893 ('panic of 1893') the secular transatlantic mass exodus of nineteenth-century Germany declined abruptly and shrank to a rivulet. In a sense, the transatlantic movement joined the streams of internal migrations from the rural areas into the expanding urban-industrial centres. Now the New World was situated in Germany itself (Köllmann 1974, 1976).

In nearly inverse proportion to the precipitous drop in German emigration, there was a massive rise in emigrations to the USA from eastern and southeastern Europe. However, although Germany was only touched in transit, this was extraordinarily important for the German shipping lines, whose agents, while not exactly creating 'emigration fever', clearly encouraged it. Since the decline in German overseas emigration in the early 1890s, the passages in steerage on the transatlantic liners were being filled by millions of east and south-east transit migrants.

With the immigration from southern Europe, this

'transit migration' (*Durchwanderung*) was part of the 'new immigration' to the USA. By the outbreak of the First World War, over 5 million emigrants from Russia (especially Poles and Jews) and Austria-Hungary had passed through German territory on their way to the ports. Most of them boarded a US-bound ship in Hamburg or Bremen. The transit migrants crossing Germany in special trains and special train departments were carefully shielded and strictly controlled. The strict Prussian-German 'transit migration control' (*Durchwandererkontrolle*) had the double purpose of keeping out epidemics and preventing illegal immigration from the east (Just 1988).

Of the approximately 2 million Jews who passed through the eastern borders between 1880 and 1914, roughly 78,000 remained in Germany, where they made up about 12 per cent of the Jewish population. Of the approximately 100,000 'East Jews' recruited in Poland during the First World War for the German war economy, who continued to flee into the empire from pogroms and acts of violence in Poland and the Ukraine until 1921, about 40 per cent emigrated again (Blank 1992; Maurer 1986; Wertheimer 1987).

Labour migration

German emigrations into European countries frequently overlapped with labour migrations of a very different kind and duration. These went to England, Holland and Belgium, as well as to France and Switzerland, and were closely integrated into various 'migration systems' which lasted in one form or another for centuries.

Under the North Sea Scheme, which covered the total coastal area of the North Sea, the maritime labour migrants aboard the Dutch and East Friesian herring and whale trawlers were called Greenland wanderers (*Grönlandfahrer*). Between the seventeenth and nineteenth centuries and under the same migration scheme, Lippe brickworkers (*Lippische Ziegler*) found employment mainly in the district around Groningen and in East Friesia, but later also moved to Scandinavia, Poland and Russia. The scheme was also used by Oldenburg stucco workers (*Oldenburger Stukkateure*), who mostly went to the Netherlands, but especially by gangs of lawn mowers (*Grasmäher*) and peat diggers (*Torfstecher*), known as Holland wanderers (*Hollandgänger*) (Bölsker-Schlicht 1987; Ebert and Vogtmeier 1980; Fleege-Althoff 1928). The latter were all seasonal migrants who, in agriculture and moor farming, sometimes faced the hardest labour conditions. Some of them came from the same villages in north Westphalia as the migrating traders,

known as *Tödden*. Labour migration, migrating trade or an interlinkage of both could, partly temporarily, partly permanently, immunize small peasants and rural proletarians against the increasing pull of transatlantic emigration from the same areas. Migrating trade could also result in emigration or permanent emigration if the labour migrants decided to settle in their distant markets (Oberpenning forthcoming; Reininghaus 1993; Rickelmann 1983).

Unlike the German temporary migrations under the 'North Sea Scheme', the German labour migrations to France and particularly to Paris created a sub-middle-class social milieu, which remained stable for some generations after the Restoration. This was quite different from the famous Paris colonies of the German furniture manufacturers of the eighteenth century and even more unlike the first courtly and later middle-class milieux. Lane sweepers (*Gassenkehrer*) from Hesse-Darmstadt, mill workers, construction workers employed on excavations, rag-and-bone men from Palatinate, and German and Alsatian maids lived in a kind of guest-worker milieu, with all the characteristics and problems of a temporary foreign subproletariat, namely low wages and bad labour and living conditions. They also served as 'buffers' in times of crisis, which could mark the end of their existence as labour migrants (Pabst 1992).

In the imperial German economy, the tension of supply and demand on the labour market turned into its very reverse at that time. The increasing labour shortage in agriculture and industry, in road and canal building turned the influx of foreign labour migrants to Germany into a mass movement. From 1880 to 1893 there were still about 1.8 million German emigrants. Then the shift from an emigration country to a labour-importing country began (Ferenczi 1930). On the eve of the First World War, official estimates already included 1.2 million foreign labour migrants in the empire. More than two-thirds migrated back and forth across the Prussian border (*Preußengänger*). Poles from Russian central Poland and Austrian Galicia made up the largest contingents in Prussia, followed by Italians and Ruthenians (Galicia) (Bade 1984; Del Fabbro 1993; Ferenczi 1930: 21).

In Prussia, a specifically political interest in controlling foreign labour migrants did not result from their volume, but from the national composition of the continental immigration. As a mass movement it was viewed with suspicion for reasons of internal security, but was nevertheless urgently desired for economic reasons and therefore not stopped at the borders. In view of the high percentage of Poles in the eastern

Prussian border districts, there was concern that the east would become 'Polonized' through immigration from the eastern foreign countries. Furthermore, the spectre of a 'Polonized west' emerged, which was imagined to happen when Polish migrant workers met 'Ruhr Poles' who had immigrated from the Prussian east into the district of the Ruhr and Emscher. In Prussia the spectre was quashed by the development of a restrictive system of controlling migration and foreigners.

Although it was only directed against foreign Poles, other migrant workers were included in its official field of observation. The 'Prussian policy of repulsion' (*Preußische Abwehrpolitik*) ensured that Polish migrant workers could be restricted to certain provinces and occupations and that their mass movement would remain an annual seasonal migration. This did not change until the First World War, when Russian-Polish migrant workers coming from a now 'hostile foreign country' were forbidden to return home and were forced to work in Germany. Without this foreign reserve army, which was considerably enlarged by prisoners of war, the 'home front' would have broken down very early (Bade 1980; Herbert 1986: 82–113).

In the Weimar Republic even in Prussia the admission of foreigners was no longer determined by the anti-Polish 'policy of repulsion', but by the economic reasoning of a labour market policy. The legislative and administrative basis of this was the creation and elaboration of a new system of labour administration, labour exchange and unemployment insurance, unknown in imperial Germany. According to the new 'obligatory approval' (*Genehmigungspflicht*), foreigners were only admitted if their employers could prove that there were no German workers available for the respective jobs. The employment of foreigners subsequently continued on a lower level and almost completely ceased at the time of the world economic crisis (Bade 1980).

Although full employment, with a growing labour shortage, had been reached in the Reich by 1938, foreign employment in national socialist Germany increased only slightly during the years between 1933 and 1938. The main reason for this was the introduction of restrictive foreign-exchange controls, which made it difficult to transfer wages. Foreign employment led to the enslavement of millions of foreign workers during the Second World War. These 'foreigners in employment' (*Ausländer-Einsatz*), comprising deportees (mainly from eastern Europe), prisoners of war and the inmates of concentration camps, were made to serve the national socialist war economy. In August 1944 the Reich employed a total of 7.8 million foreign civilian workers and prisoners of war and, in addition, about 1 million mostly foreign concentration camp prisoners. Nearly 30 per cent of all employed persons in Germany were foreigners. After the war, the surviving victims constituted the main contingent of the 10–12 million displaced persons (DPs) (Herbert 1985; Jacobmeyer 1985; Stepien 1989).

With the recruitment of the so-called 'guest workers' from European countries in the mid-1950s, labour market policy reverted to the traditions of the Weimar Republic. And Germany's transition from its historical status as a country of emigration to its present-day position as a country of immigration continued.

References

Bade, Klaus J. (1975) *Friedrich Fabri und der Imperialismus in der Bismarckzeit: Revolution–Depression–Expansion*, Freiburg: Atlantis

—— (1980) 'Politik und Ökonomie der Ausländerbeschäftigung im preußischen Osten 1885–1914: Die Internationalisierung des Arbeitsmarktes im "Rahmen der preußischen Abwehrpolitik"', in H.-J. Puhle and H.-U. Wehler (eds) *Preußen im Rückblick*, Göttingen: Vandenhoeck und Ruprecht, 273–99

—— (1984) '"Preußengänger" und "Abwehrpolitik": Ausländerbeschäftigung, Ausländerpolitik und Ausländerkontrolle auf dem Arbeitsmarkt in Preußen vor dem Ersten Weltkrieg', *Archiv für Sozialgeschichte*, 24, 91–283

—— (1986) 'Die deutsche überseeische Massenauswanderung im 19. und frühen 20. Jahrhundert: Bestimmungsfaktoren und Entwicklungsbedingungen', in K. J. Bade (ed.) *Auswanderer–Wanderarbeiter–Gastarbeiter: Bevölkerung, Arbeitsmarkt und Wanderung in Deutschland seit der Mitte des 19. Jahrhunderts*, 2 vols., 2nd edition, Ostfildern: Scripta Mercaturae, 259–99

—— (ed.) (1987) *Population, Labour and Migration in 19th and 20th Century Germany*, Oxford: Berg

—— (1990) 'Aussiedler: Rückwanderer über Generationen hinweg', in K. J. Bade (ed.) *Neue Heimat im Westen: Vertriebene, Flüchtlinge, Aussiedler*, Münster: Westfälischer Heimatbund, 128–49.

Blank, Inge (1992) '... nirgends eine Heimat, aber Gräber auf jedem Friedhof', in K. J. Bade (ed.) *Deutsche im Ausland – Fremde in Deutschland: Migration in Geschichte und Gegenwart*, München: C. H. Beck, 324–33

Bölsker-Schlicht, Franz (1987) *Die Hollandgängerei im Osnabrücker Land und im Emsland*, Sögel: Emsländische Landschaft

Brandes, Detlef (1992) 'Die Deutschen in Rußland und der Sowjetunion', in K. J. Bade (ed.) *Deutsche im Ausland – Fremde in Deutschland: Migration in Geschichte und Gegenwart*, München: C. H. Beck, 85–134

Del Fabbro, René (1993) 'Die Willkommenen Ausländer. Italienische Arbeitsmigranten im Deutschen Kaiserreich (1871–1918)', Ph.D., University of Florence

Dietz, Barbara and Peter Hilkes (1992) *Rußlanddeutsche: Unbekannte im Osten – Geschichte, Situation, Zukunftsperspektiven*, München: Olzog

Dralle, Lothar (1991) *Die Deutschen in Ostmittel- und Osteuropa.*

Ein Jahrtausend europäischer Geschichte, Darmstadt: Wissenschaftliche Buchgesellschaft

Ebert, Bettina and Michael Vogtmeier (1980) *Die Lippischen Wanderziegler*, Detmold: P. Meyer

Eisfeld, Alfred (ed.) (1992) *Die Rußlanddeutschen*, München: Langen-Müller

Ferenczi, Imre (1930) *Kontinentale Wanderungen und die Annäherung der Völker*, Jena: G. Fischer

Ferstl, Lothar and Harald Hetzel (1990) 'Wir sind immer die Fremden', *Aussiedler in Deutschland*, Bonn: Dietz

Fleege-Althoff, Fritz (1928) *Die lippischen Wanderarbeiter*, Detmold: Meyersche Hofbuchhandlung

Grandjonc, Jacques (1970) 'La Presse de L'Emigration Allemande en France (1795–1848) et en Europe (1830–1848)', *Archiv für Sozialgeschichte*, 10, 95–152

(1972) 'Etat sommaire des dépôts d'archives françaises sur le mouvement ouvrier et les émigré allemands de 1830 à 1851/2', *Archiv für Sozialgeschichte*, 12, 487–531

(1975) 'Eléments statistiques pour une étude de l'immigration étrangère en France de 1830 à 1851', *Archiv für Sozialgeschichte*, 15, 211–300

Helbich, Wolfgang et al. (eds) (1988) *Briefe aus Amerika: Deutsche Auswanderer schreiben aus der Neuen Welt, 1830–1930*, München: C. H. Beck

Herbert, Ulrich (1985) *Fremdarbeiter: Politik und Praxis des 'Ausländer-Einsatzes' in der Kriegswirtschaft des Dritten Reiches*, Berlin: Dietz

(1986) *Geschichte der Ausländerbeschäftigung in Deutschland 1880–1980: Saison-arbeiter-Zwangsarbeiter-Gastarbeiter*, Berlin: Dietz

Jacobmeyer, Wolfgang (1985) *Vom Zwangsarbeiter zum Heimatlosen Ausländer. Die Displaced Persons in Westdeutschland 1945–1951*, Göttingen: Vandenhoeck und Ruprecht

Just, Michael (1988) *Ost- und südosteuropäische Amerikawanderung 1881–1914: Transitprobleme in Deutschland und Aufnahme in den Vereinigten Staaten*, Stuttgart: Steiner

Kamphoefner, Walter D. (1987) *The Westfalians: From Germany to Missouri*, Princeton: Princeton University Press

Köllmann, Wolfgang (1974) *Bevölkerung in der industriellen Revolution. Studien zur Bevölkerungsgeschichte Deutschlands*, Göttingen: Vandenhoeck und Ruprecht

(1976) 'Bevölkerungsgeschichte 1800–1970', in H. Aubin and W. Zorn (eds) *Handbuch der deutschen Wirtschaft und Sozialgeschichte*, vol. II, Stuttgart: Klett, 9–50

Malchow, Barbara et al. (1990) *Die fremden Deutschen: Aussiedler in der Bundesrepublik*, Reinbek: Rowohlt

Maurer, Trude (1986) *Ostjuden in Deutschland 1918–1933*, Hamburg: Christians

Moltmann, Günter (ed.) (1979) *Aufbruch nach Amerika. Friedrich List und die Auswanderung aus Baden und Württemberg 1816/17. Dokumentation einer sozialen Bewegung*, Tübingen: Wunderlich

Oberpenning, Hannelore (forthcoming) 'Migration und Fernhandel: das "Tödden"-System im nördlichen Münsterland des 18. und 19. Jahrhunderts', Ph.D, University of Osnabrück/IMIS

Pabst, Wilfried (1992) 'Subproletariat auf Zeit: Deutsche "Gastarbeiter" im Paris des 19. Jahrhunderts', in K. J. Bade (ed.) *Neue Heimat im Westen: Vertriebene, Flüchtlinge, Aussiedler*, Münster: Westfälischer Heimatbund, 263–8

Panayi, Panikos (1991) *The Enemy in our Midst: Germans in Britain during the First World War*, Oxford: Berg

(1993) *Immigrants, Transmigrants, Refugees and Businessmen: Germans in Britain During the 19th Century, 1815–1914*, Oxford: Berg

Puhle, Hans-Jürgen and Hans-Ulrich Wehler (eds) (1980) *Preußen im Rückblick*, Göttingen: Vandenhoeck und Ruprecht

Reininghaus, Wilfried (ed.) (1993) *Wanderhandel in Europa*, Dortmund: Gesellschaft für Westfälische Wirtschaftsgeschichte

Rickelmann, Hubert (1983) *Die Tüötten in ihrem Handel und Wandel und die Wolle- und Leinenerzeugung im Tecklenburger Land*, Paderborn: Schöningh

Stepien, Stanislaus (1989) *Der alteingesessene Fremde. Ehemalige Zwangsarbeiter in Westdeutschland*, Frankfurt: Campus

Stürmer, Michael (ed.) (1980) *Die Weimarer Republik: Belagerte Civitas*, Königstein: Athenäum

von Hippel, Wolfgang (1984) *Auswanderung aus Südwestdeutschland. Studien zur württembergischen Auswanderung und Auswanderungspolitik im 18. und 19. Jahrhundert*, Stuttgart: Klett-Cotta

Walker, Mack (1964) *Germany and the Emigration, 1816–1885*, Cambridge, MS: Harvard University Press

Wertheimer, Jack (1987) *Unwelcome Strangers. East European Jews in Imperial Germany*, New York: Oxford University Press

WANDERERS OR MIGRANTS? GYPSIES FROM EASTERN TO WESTERN EUROPE, 1860–1940

LEO LUCASSEN AND WIM WILLEMS

'Gypsies'[1] are generally regarded as nomads and, therefore, as one of the most migration-prone people in the world. Strangely enough their (alleged) movements have never attracted the attention of scholars in the field of migration studies. An explanation could be that most studies focus on transnational migration and hence on the citizens of nations;[2] consequently gypsies were not treated as a separate category. Apart from this neglect of their migration patterns, it remains to be proven that gypsies are as inhibited from wandering around as has often been assumed. For the period covered by this volume we would like to illustrate this point with the case of the rather large Hungarian gypsy population at the end of the nineteenth century.

On 31 January 1893 a conscription was organized on behalf of the Ministry of Internal Affairs of the Hungarian kingdom. The idea behind it was to find a solution to the so-called problem of the wandering gypsies, who were considered an anachronism in a modern centralized state. Before they were turned into 'civilized' citizens more knowledge was needed, so the government argued. Looking at the results of the conscription one has to question the basic assumptions. Not only was the number of gypsies much higher than expected (274,940), but 90 per cent of them appeared to be sedentary already, and 7.5 per cent semi-sedentary. Only 8938 actually practised a 'travelling' way of life. Moreover, it is plausible that the number of sedentary and integrated gypsies was even higher, since the ones who 'passed' had become invisible.

The local authorities responsible for implementing the conscription were faced with the problem of who to consider as 'gypsies'. In practice it appeared that they could not use such objective criteria as language, way of life, physical characteristics or self-definition, since only 30 per cent of all these so-called 'gypsies' appeared to speak the gypsy language (Romanes) as their mother tongue, whereas another 20 per cent were merely familiar with it. More than half of the 300,000 or so people questioned spoke only Hungarian or Wallachian. Their professions also turned out to be

less deviant than was assumed. The 17,000 musicians (about 12 per cent), for example, were sedentary, had a good reputation and earned a decent living. The same held true for the coppersmiths (36 per cent). In fact the authorities simply labelled as 'gypsies' those people who were known as such to them or to the local population. How this categorization came about is one of the factors that still needs exploring. It is interesting, however, that gypsies were supposed to have racial features (as in the case of Jews), whereas the conscription paid no attention to this criterion, but nevertheless used it as a kind of popular notion.

The results of the Hungarian conscription show that for gypsies a sedentary existence was the rule. It is going one step further to state that a wandering life, or migration, was the exception. This is especially true of eastern Europe, but groups in western Europe (especially Spain) have also always displayed more modest migratory behaviour than is often thought. Most families in Germany, France, the Netherlands and Great Britain – if they moved at all – restricted their geographical mobility to certain regions. Only a few of them covered longer distances.

It is therefore important to keep in mind that the international migration of gypsy families from southeast Europe in the period from 1860 to 1940, on whom we will be focusing for the rest of this entry, was highly exceptional in relation to the large number of people in Europe who are labelled as 'gypsies'.

The traditional explanation

Among 'gypsy scholars' the time from about 1860 onwards is known as the period of massive gypsy migrations from eastern to western Europe. The basic assumptions are that we are dealing with great numbers and that this migration was caused by the abolition of slavery in the Romanian principalities of Moldavia and Wallachia, because of which for the first time in centuries gypsies were able to wander again. According to some authors, fewer than 200,000 gypsies took the opportunity to emigrate to the New World, especially to North and South America, but also to Australia and even India (the supposed

PLATE 9: Serbian gypsies arriving at Ellis Island, New York, c. 1904. Although the USA had an implicit policy of keeping gypsies out, this did not apparently hinder their immigration to any great extent.

homeland of gypsies).[3] The *Tiganii domnesti* (owned by the state or the nobility) would have profited especially from this new situation, because they already enjoyed some freedom of movement and had a tradition of craftmanship, for example kettle-mending.

This 'slavery hypothesis', however, is refuted by the scanty historical research in this field. We wish to refer especially to the history of 'gypsies' in the Netherlands, in which special attention is paid to the gypsy groups that left central Europe and the Balkans in the second half of the nineteenth century (Fraser 1992a; Lucassen 1990). Besides this, such studies also make clear how misleading it is to think of these various groups as 'one people' (Fraser 1992b).

Gypsy coppersmiths in the Netherlands and other western European countries

The gypsy coppersmiths who arrived in the Netherlands in 1868 had Hungarian passports, and the Dutch authorities have left us with numerous data concerning their places of birth. Most of them came from the

southern part of the kingdom of Hungary surrounding the city of Szegedin (Lucassen 1990: 65).

The idea that they came from Romania is therefore not affirmed, and the same holds true for similar groups of coppersmiths appearing in western Europe and Poland from 1861 onwards. They also had Hungarian passports and there is little proof that their homelands were the principalities that later formed the heart of the Romanian state.[4] It is possible, however, that these coppersmiths had left Moldavia and Wallachia as early as the eighteenth century and settled in Hungary (Vekerdi 1978: 10). This idea fits in with indications that these coppersmiths operated in Hungary from the beginning of the nineteenth century onwards (Mayerhofer 1987: 33), as well as with a report in a German newspaper of 1851, in which a Hungarian gypsy group of some 100 people was mentioned (*Intelligenzblatt der freien Stadt Frankfurt*, 22 April 1851).

The available information further makes it clear that we are dealing with small numbers. Although the average family group among these tinkers was quite big (forty men, women and children), and therefore attracted much attention from the authorities as well as from the public, the number of groups was small. In total probably only a few thousand left Hungary in the period following 1860. If we take a look at the extensive Dutch data between 1868 and 1924 (Table 5.1), we see that the peak of the migration was in the 1880s.

About 40 per cent of the total number of Hungarian coppersmiths who passed through the Netherlands in the years 1868–1924 came only in this one decade, with another 20 per cent in the 1890s. These figures are particularly interesting because they show a remarkable resemblance to the beginning of the overall emigration figures from south-east Europe in general and Hungary in particular (Nugent 1992: 83; Puskas 1991). It therefore seems more plausible that the migration of these Hungarian coppersmiths, many of whom only passed through Europe to earn money for the crossing, has to be regarded as part of a general migration pattern.

Not all these gypsies aimed at emigration to the Americas. Part of the original coppersmith group headed east and north, rather than west. They went to Poland and Russia and from there to Scandinavia, where they changed from smithing to horse dealing. At the beginning of the twentieth century a few hundred of the original group went to western Europe, not to embark for the Americas, but to stay. In France, Belgium and the Netherlands especially, a small number of families settled down and played an important role in the trade in cobs (Lucassen 1990: 130–3, 140–6).

The migration of the Bosnian bear leaders

A further argument to refute the slavery hypothesis is that the second important 'gypsy' group to migrate to the New World came from Bosnia and can by no means be linked to the Romanian principalities.

These Bosnians (from an area that was part of the Turkish empire until 1878), who formed small family groups and earned their money by exhibiting dancing bears or with small circuses, are known in the literature as *Ursari* (*urs* is the Romanian word for bear) or *Ludari*. The moment of their migration is almost simultaneous with that of the coppersmiths. The earliest record is from Germany, where the Bosnian bear leader Jovanovic and his family were noticed in 1867. In the Netherlands they first appeared in 1868, whereas in France the first recorded appearance is in 1872. It is remarkable that these Bosnians, with their rather exotic profession and outlook, at first only rarely

attracted the attention of the authorities. Only later were they also labelled as 'gypsies'. Their relative 'invisibility' can be explained by the fact that they travelled in smaller groups (mostly consisting of only one family) and had a less overt travelling way of life. Whereas the coppersmiths were known for their huge tents, the bear leaders chose to stay the night in the open field, with farmers or in lodges.

When we combine the Dutch data with the extensive information from German police records, and US immigration archives, we see that most of them came from the area around Banja Luka (Lucassen 1990: 84; Salo and Salo 1986; Winstedt 1955: 76–8).

Their migration pattern was similar to that of the coppersmiths. They travelled great distances and did not restrict themselves to Europe. Most did not linger on in western Europe but took the boat to Australia, New Zealand, but above all to North America. More than two visits by any one family rarely occurred. In the Netherlands one of the few who came more than once was Ottoman Kosta Georgjevic, born in Bosnia in 1823. He was first noticed in 1869 and then again eleven years later. The dispersion of the migrating groups is different, with the heart of the movements in the 1870s, against the 1880s for the coppersmiths, as can be seen on Table 5.2.

The destination of gypsy migrants

Having reached the North Sea coasts, most of the groups mentioned here headed for North America (including Canada), with the aim of settling down. One of the few studies in this field, using among other things sources deriving from the US Immigration Service, shows that their immigration was perfectly in tune with the general immigration from south and eastern Europe between 1880 and 1914, and the authors rightly state that: 'if there were any causes of immigration peculiar to gypsies, they did not play major roles in the decisions to immigrate' (Salo and Salo 1986: 90). Although the USA had an implicit policy of keeping gypsies out (derived from an *explicit* policy of barring paupers from 1882) this apparently did not hinder their immigration to any great extent. Many were not 'recognized' as such by the authorities, and what is more, the wealth of both the coppersmiths and the bear leaders seems to have been greater than that of the average immigrant. The coppersmiths especially were often well off. This fits in with the information we have on their short stay in western Europe. Time and again their wealth, a result of their craftmanship, was mentioned. To illustrate this we offer a quotation from a Warsaw paper dated

Table 5.1: *Number of Hungarian coppersmiths and their families passing through the Netherlands, 1868–1924*

Period	Number of groups	%	Number of people	%
1868–1870	4	4	89	7
1871–1880	21	23	240	17
1881–1890	43	46	553	40
1891–1900	14	15	310	22
1901–1910	10	11	170	12
1911–1920	–	–	–	–
1921–1930	1	1	35	2
Total	93	100	1397	100

Source: Lucassen (1990: pp. 324–8)

Table 5.2: *Number of Bosnian bear leaders and their families passing through the Netherlands, 1868–1924*

Period	Number of groups	%	Number of people	%
1868–1870	22	21	136	17
1871–1880	49	48	376	47
1881–1890	20	20	163	20
1891–1900	1	1	8	1
1901–1910	6	6	44	5
1911–1920	1	1	3	–
1921–1930	3	3	49	6
Total	102	100	779	100

Source: Lucassen (1990: pp. 328–33)

26 September 1863 (Ficowski c.1984: 32) describing a newly arrived group of coppersmiths from Hungary:

These are not however the usual tramps wandering about our villages and small towns, begging or stealing for their living, but travelling smiths. They are beautiful figures, well-built, with clear features and piercing eyes; these gypsies, some of whom wear Hungarian dress and others Banat-fashion in skirts. Their leader, who has a great staff bound in silver, like the marshal of the Seym or a doorkeeper at a great house, rules over the whole troop and deals on their behalf with outside authorities.

This is only one example, but there are many others in the period 1860–1914 that refute the stereotyped idea of gypsies as poor and parasitic. The bear leaders were less successful in amassing wealth, but they also made good living.

Notwithstanding the fact that they were hardly 'liable to become a public charge', as was stated in the Immigration Act to bar paupers, now and then gypsies were refused entry to the USA. This policy was aimed in the first place at steamship companies, because they were obliged to take back immigrants who were refused entrance to the USA. The restrictive policy began in the ports of disembarkation. The vicissitudes in 1886/7 of a large group of coppersmiths with Hungarian, Serbian and Greek passports provide a good example of the implications of this policy. They had more than enough money to pay the passage, but nevertheless the shipping company turned them down

(Marchbin 1934: 137). Thereupon they returned to Antwerp and tried their luck again with a Dutch shipping company in Rotterdam. After some hesitation they were accepted, but when this group, consisting of forty-two people, arrived in New York on 18 October 1886, they were denied entrance with the argument that 'nomads were not wanted'. Their leader, Giovanni Kalderas, tried in vain to appeal and five days later the entire group returned to the Netherlands (Lucassen 1990: 52). Other gypsies suffered the same fate, especially when they travelled in large family groups. However, this seems not to have been the rule, for although the rate of admission for gypsies was significantly lower than for the average immigrant, in the end (after appeal cases) some 75 per cent were allowed to enter the country (Salo and Salo 1986: 93). Moreover, many gypsies succeeded in bringing over relatives and made use of the common patterns of chain migration. Communication by letter and telegraph with relatives in Europe spread information about immigration policy and it seems plausible that many who came later decided to travel in small parties or alone to avoid being labelled as gypsies. Others steered a course for South and Central America and from there through Mexico to the USA, because entrance regulations there were more lenient. To some extent the same applied to Canada at the end of the nineteenth century (Marchbin 1934: 135).

Looking behind the label

This far we have given a brief survey of transnational migrations of various gypsy groups in the period c.1860–1930, in which we have challenged some traditional assumptions and explanations about the nature of their geographical mobility. A last point, however, remains to be addressed: why were these various groups brought together under the label 'gypsy' (as they still are)?

To start with, it is essential to keep in mind the fact that 'gypsy' is a term used by others to label certain people as such, although as a result of the labelling some of the groups concerned have adopted it. As far as we know the label was initially reserved for aliens who travelled with their families and followed itinerant trades. In the course of time it was also applied to all kind of itinerant groups, as well as to people who were supposed to descend from the 'original' gypsies. Furthermore, one has to realize that very little is known about how the different gypsy groups referred to themselves over time, and to what extent they have ever regarded themselves as belonging to a common ethnic group. There are no indications, for example,

that the Bosnian bear leaders and Hungarian coppersmiths, whose migration was discussed above, considered themselves in any way related. Even more disputable is the assumption that ties with groups living in western Europe had existed for centuries.

The idea that all gypsies belong to one and the same people is also refuted in the findings of a study of English gypsies undertaken in 1815 by the Quaker John Hoyland (1816). He belonged to a group of social philanthropists who wanted to improve the living conditions of the 'wandering heathens' in their country. As the Hungarian authorities were to do eighty years later, they sent questionnaires to all the magistrates in the counties of England.[5] Afterwards they checked their data with the leaders of different gypsy or traveller groups. The portrait deriving from these more or less empirical findings shows that the internal structure of this 'community' was based more on ideas than on reality. Most of the total number of 18,000 gypsies declared that they had no idea when their forefathers came to England, and appeared to be organized not as one community but in *different* groups. It is interesting that they did not feel they were related to other families or groups, let alone to gypsy communities in Europe. Therefore the idea of a shared past or solidarity with gypsy groups elsewhere in the world was absent. A closer look at the history of (formerly) itinerant groups and their migration patterns in relation to their professions, would probably correct a lot of the stereotyped ideas about gypsies as traditional wanderers.

Notes

1. In using the term 'gypsy' we do not follow the tradition of considering gypsies as 'a people', but define them as persons who have been labelled as such over the course of time, irrespective of the way they viewed themselves. The reason for this choice is mainly historical. In the past centuries the term 'gypsy' was first of all used by authorities (or other non-gypsies) to label groups with a certain way of life. To what extent this label corresponded with the self-definition of these groups is not known. Moreover, there is abundant proof that we are not dealing with *one* people, but with numerous distinct groups. This is also the reason why we write the term 'gypsy' with a small 'g' and do not use contemporary self-definitions such as Rom, Roma, Sinti and so on. For an elaboration of this viewpoint, see Lucassen (1994) and Willems (1995).
2. An important exception to this rule is the recent survey by Moch (1992).
3. Vossen (1983: 58) relies on Kenrick and Puxon (1972), but obviously has been a quick reader. Kenrick and Puxon do mention the number of 200,000, but only in relation to the total number of gypsy slaves set free, which does not automatically imply that they all emigrated. Apart from

Lucassen (1990), a comprehensive critique was offered by Fraser (1992a).

4. The same argument was elaborated by Fraser (1992a: 139), who used unpublished data on the birthplaces of gypsies who entered the USA after 1881.

5. Therefore not in other parts of Great Britain (p. 157), although Hoyland also obtained information from the sheriffs of Scotland (p. 170).

References

Ficowski, J. (c.1984) *The Gypsies in Poland: History and Customs*, Yugoslavia: Interpress

Fraser, Angus (1992a) 'The Rom migrations', *Journal of the Gypsy Lore Society*, 2 (2), 131–46

  (1992b) *The Gypsies*, Oxford: Basil Blackwell

Hoyland, J. (1816) *A Historical Survey of the Customs, Habits and Present State of the Gypsies; Designed to Develop the Origin of this Singular People, and to Promote the Amelioration of their Condition*, York: W. M. Alexander

Kenrick, Donald and Grattan Puxon (1972) *The Destiny of Europe's Gypsies*, London: Basic Books

Lucassen, Leo (1990) *En men noemde hen zigeuners. De geschiedenis van Kaldarasch, Ursari, Lowara en Sinti in Nederland: 1750–1944*, Amsterdam/The Hague: Stichting Beheer IISG/SDU-uitgeverij

  (1994) '"Zigeuner" in Deutschland 1870–1945: ein kritischer historiographischen Ansatz', *Zeitschrift für Sozialeschichte des 20. und 21. Jahrhunderts*, 9

Marchbin, Andrew A. (1934) 'Gypsy Immigration to Canada', *Journal of the Gypsy Lore Society*, XIII, 134–44

Mayerhofer, C. (1987) *Dorfzigeuner*, Vienna: Picus Verlag

Moch, Leslie Page (1992) *Moving Europeans. Migration in Western Europe since 1650*, Bloomington: Indiana University Press

Nugent, W. (1992) *Crossings. The Great Transatlantic Migrations, 1870–1914*, Bloomington: Indiana University Press

Puskas, Julianna (1991) 'Hungarian Overseas Migration: A Microanalysis', in R. Vecoli and S. M. Sinke (eds) *A Century of European Migrations 1830–1930*, Urbana: University of Illinois Press, 221–42

Salo, Matt T. and Sheila Salo (1986) 'Gypsy Immigration to the United States', in J. Grumet (ed.) Papers from the Sixth and Seventh Annual Meetings of the Gypsy Lore Society, North American Chapter, New York: Gypsy Lore Society, 85–96

Vekerdi, Jozsef (1978) 'L'histoire des tsiganes de Hongrie', *Etudes tsiganes*, (2), 7–10

Vossen, R. (1983) *Die Zigeuner*, Hamburg: Ullstein

Willems, Wim (1995) 'Op zoek naar de ware zigeuners (1783–1945)', doctoral thesis, Leiden University

Winstedt, E. O. (1955) 'Rudari in Germany', *Journal of the Gypsy Lore Society*, (34), 76–8

ITALIANS AND POLES IN FRANCE, 1880–1945

GÉRARD NOIRIEL

Table 5.3: *Principal immigrant communities established in France, 1881–1946*

Date	Belgians	Spanish	Italians	Poles*	Total
1881	482,265	73,781	240,733	–	1,001,090
1891	465,860	77,736	286,082	–	1,130,211
1901	323,390	80,485	330,465	–	1,037,778
1911	287,126	105,760	419,234	–	1,159,835
1921	384,986	264,980	450,960	46,766	1,532,000
1931	253,694	351,864	808,038	507,811	2,714,697
1946	153,299	302,201	450,764	423,470	1,743,619

*Poles were not included in census figures before Polish independence.
Source: Statistique Générale de la France (1881–1946).

As the statistics in Table 5.3 indicate, Italians and Poles account for almost half the total number of immigrants included in the censuses taken from 1931–46, and therefore form the two largest foreign communities which settled in France between these dates. The figures also demonstrate the scale and abruptness of this influx of immigrants which, in the case of the Italians, quadrupled in number over the fifty years between 1881 and 1931, and which, in the case of the Poles between 1921 and 1931, increased tenfold in as many years.

These two communities are particularly representative of the type of immigration brought about by the 'second wave of industrialization', based on the heavy industries of coal, iron, metallurgy and the chemical industry. This was a new phase, following on from the first wave of migration, which had been linked to the development of the textile industry and which was dominated by the arrival of immigrants from Belgium. Beginning in the 1960s, these two immigrant groups were themselves superseded by a further new wave of immigration, this time from the Iberian peninsula and the former French colonies of the Maghreb. This last wave followed the 'third industrial revolution', which was characterized by the widespread appearance of production lines in the car industry.

Unlike the Russians and Armenians, the Italians and Poles came to France principally for economic reasons. (There were, however, a small number of political refugees in both these communities: Italian anti-fascists who had fled Mussolini's dictatorship and, in the case of the Poles, a number of Jews who had fallen victim to anti-Semitic persecution.) The grave shortage in the labour force available to French industry between 1880 and 1930 provides an explanation for the mass immigration into France in those years. At the close of the eighteenth century, France had the largest population in Europe. Yet, by the end of the nineteenth century, due to a sharp drop in the birth rate across all social classes, it had only the fourth largest population. Another factor to be taken into account is the rigid stratification of the labour force. Even just after the Second World War in France, the proportion of the active population employed in working the land was still far higher than it had been in Britain in 1840! A vast number of smallholders clung onto their plots of land, therefore preventing an exodus from rural areas towards the industrial basins. Since universal suffrage had already been accorded to all citizens by 1848, the peasant population had become the largest electoral group. Given this situation, the government of the Third Republic would never have succeeded in taking authoritarian measures aimed to turn the people of the countryside into workers, such as those adopted by Bismarck in Germany. This explains why industrial development in France was only possible with the aid of mass immigration (Noiriel 1988).

In the years leading up to the First World War, the directors of the major industries and the larger land-owners, who were short of agricultural labourers, joined forces to form an association with the aim of recruiting miners in Italy and agricultural workers in Poland. The First World War cut the dwindling labour force still further. One and a half million French sol-diers were killed in combat and it is thought that a similar number were left with permanent injuries. In total, it is estimated that 10 per cent of the available industrial workforce before the war was subsequently lost, just at the time when France benefited from a period of exceptional economic dynamism in the 1920s, caused by the need to reconstruct the nation. In the space of a few years, several million immigrants had been recruited into industry and agriculture. France therefore became one of the foremost countries for accepting immigrants. By the end of the 1920s, the rising number of foreigners within its population was among the highest worldwide, even surpassing that of the USA, which had closed its doors to immigrants some years earlier. The Société Générale d'Immigration established by the directors of the heavy industries, including the committees for mines and ironworks, recruited workers throughout Europe, though principally in Poland and Italy due to existing political links which France had forged with these two countries. This phase of immigration was brought to an end by the crisis of the 1930s, at which time many foreigners were sent back to their countries. For those who remained, the period between 1930 and 1950 was a decisive one in terms of integration into French society.

Differences

Although the immigration of these two groups – Ital-ians and Poles – had many points in common, as dis-cussed above, they were also fundamentally different in several respects. As regards the Italians, the mass influx of the years 1880 to 1930 was just one in a whole cycle of migrations which had been in progress since antiquity (or, it could be said, since prehistory) and which only began to slow down in the 1960s (Milza 1993). The Italian immigration was therefore a key factor in the regeneration of the French popula-tion. It is now estimated that about 5 million French nationals are of Italian origin if their parentage is retraced over three generations. Since the time of the *ancien régime*, large numbers of navvies, musicians, pedlars and artisans had set out from Italy to ply their

trades in France. Close contact between French and Italians had been maintained for centuries in border regions, particularly in Provence. The fact that these ties were rooted in historical tradition was of great advantage to the Italians immigrating between 1880 and 1930. They were frequently able to make use of contacts through networks of migrants already in France and, in terms of their integration, they were greatly assisted by the small Italian communities which were by then well-established in France. How-ever, the demands of industry necessarily altered the migratory patterns of the previous centuries. While in the past migrants had had personal control over where they settled, the whole process was now in the hands of the country to which they migrated, and was sub-ject to the requirements of company managers and public authorities, and to new regulatory methods, such as employment contracts, passports and so on. In the nineteenth century, Italian immigration had been concentrated mainly in border regions, in the south-east of France. In about 1910, for instance, one in every five inhabitants of Marseille was Italian. In the twentieth century, however, Italian immigrants were dispersed throughout the industrial regions of France: the north, Lorraine, the valleys of the Alps and the Pyrenees, and the suburbs of Lyon and Paris. These immigrants came from every region of Italy: initially from the northern regions such as Piedmont and the Veneto, then from central Italy, in particular the Marche and Umbria, and finally, mainly after the Sec-ond World War, also from southern Italy.

The migratory patterns of the Poles differed from those of the Italians considerably. France had, of course, maintained close links with Poland since the *ancien régime*. Beginning in the eighteenth century, and continuing throughout the nineteenth, large num-bers of Polish patriots driven out by Russian, Prussian and Austrian armies had sought refuge in France. A similar situation occurred between 1880 and 1939 on a massive scale as Polish Jews poured into the coun-try. There is, however, little connection between this type of immigration, motivated by political grounds, and that of the 1920s, which was induced by the recruitment needs of industry. Differences in terms of religion, social background and location of settlement in France – most refugees chose to settle in the cities, particularly in Paris, while the immigrants who had been recruited for economic reasons were centred in the industrial zones in northern and eastern France – prevented those of Polish origin from establishing a community that brought them together effectively. What is most striking about the immigration of the

1920s is its massive scale and the abruptness and highly localized way in which it occurred. Whereas, for instance, there were only a few thousand Poles in France just after the First World War, by 1930 there were over 500,000. The Société Générale d'Immigration carried out a direct form of recruitment, bringing entire families into France, often together with their priests and teachers.[1] With the exception of some tens of thousands of agricultural workers who were dispersed throughout the villages of the Parisian basin, the majority of these immigrants were concentrated in the areas nearest the coalfields of the north and the Pas-de-Calais, which French miners had deserted *en masse* immediately after the war (Ponty 1990).

The above differences in the conditions of immigration are of far greater consequence than differences in ethnic origin in the attempt to explain the marked contrasts in the subsequent behaviour of the Italian and Polish communities who settled in France. The intense character of Polish community life and the tendency to cling to their traditions and native language (there were, for instance, two Polish daily newspapers, *Wiarno Polski* and *Narodowic*, in northern France for many years) were fostered by the nature of the recruitment process, which was at once collective and family-based. Although the Italian immigration was of greater significance in terms of numbers, it was more individual in character and took place over a longer period, thereby tending to produce a less close-knit community life. Both groups, nevertheless, went on to become integrated into French society in relatively similar ways (Girard and Stoetzel 1953).

Notes

1. By contrast, most of the Italian immigrants travelled to France by their own means: the men usually came first – in the hope of being able to return home as soon as possible – and eventually brought their wives and children to join them.

References

Girard, A. and J. Stoetzel (1953) *Français et Immigrés. L'attitude française, l'Adaptation des Italiens et des Polonais*, INED, Travaux et Documents, 19, Paris: PUF

Milza, P. (1993) *Voyage en Ritalie*, Paris: Plon

Noiriel, G. (1988) *Le Creuset français. Histoire de l'Immigration (19ème–20ème s.)* English translation: *The French Melting Pot*, University of Minnesota Press, 1995

Ponty, J. (1990) *Polonais méconnus. Histoire des Travailleurs immigrés dans l'entre-deux-guerres*, Paris: Publications de la Sorbonne

Statistique Générale de La France (1881–1946) *Recensements*, Paris: Imprimerie nationale

RUSSIANS AND ARMENIANS IN FRANCE

GÉRARD NOIRIEL

The Russians and Armenians who migrated to France between the end of the nineteenth century and the 1930s represent only a very small percentage of the total population of foreigners who have settled in France over the last century. On the eve of the First World War, when immigrants in the country already numbered over 1 million, there were still less than 50,000 Russians and Armenians (35,000 'Russian subjects' and 8000 'Turks' are listed in the census of 1911). By 1930, there were more than 3 million foreigners in France, of whom only 100,000 were Russians and Armenians. This perhaps accounts in part for the fact that to date there has been very little historical research about these communities; much of our knowledge about them comes down to us through autobiographical accounts (Bérbérova 1989; Verneuil 1985). Yet Russians and Armenians form one of the main groups of political refugees who have found a place in French society (Noiriel 1991). Since the end of the nineteenth century, their arrival has provoked a series of intense controversies.

The majority of the Russians who fled to France between 1880 and 1890 were Jews, victims of the pogroms which followed the assassination of Tsar Alexander II in 1881 (Green 1985). Their arrival in France coincided with the 'Dreyfus affair', a period in which anti-Semitism reached its height. The Russian Jews remained the target for nationalist propaganda until at least 1918. They were accused of introducing new diseases into France and of taking sides with Germany. In 1916, a commission of official inquiry, headed by the sociologist Emile Durkheim, made plain the inanity of such accusations (Elkarati 1990). The Armenians arrived in France *en masse* after the victory of the 'Young Turk' revolution in 1908, which marked the start of their persecution, orchestrated systematically by the new Turkish government. The fact that on the whole the French government retained a positive attitude towards them, despite the hostile nationalist movements of that period, was the result of the rallying of intellectuals. In particular, writers like Anatole France were engaged in the fight to ensure that France kept to the ideals of the French Revolution (the constitution of June 1793 had, in fact, been the first in the world to recognize the principle of the right of asylum).

In the period between the two world wars political controversy surrounding the refugees intensified. The number of Russians and Armenians seeking asylum in France rose sharply due to the massacres perpetrated by the Turkish army from 1915 onwards, and the resulting exodus of the surviving population on a massive scale. In Russia, the civil war and the Bolshevik victory forced millions of 'white Russians' to flee. Several tens of thousands of these refugees were granted asylum in France in the 1920s in order to boost France's diminished workforce.

Comparisons

Although official statistics dating from between the two wars frequently fail to distinguish between Russians and Armenians, these two communities were in fact markedly different, not only in terms of their socio-economic situation, but also in their cultural practices and the locations in which they settled. The Armenian refugees were mainly working class in origin; the majority of them came from villages in central Anatolia, with only a small number coming from the ports and larger towns of the Caucasus region (Hovanessian 1992). Most of them reached France via Marseille – which has always functioned as a 'turn-plate' for migrants arriving from all parts of the Mediterranean basin. While some of these refugees settled around the Mediterranean coast, many others headed inland. This accounts for the establishment of those small Armenian communities which may still be seen today in the moderate-sized towns along the Rhône Valley (like Valence and Vienne), in the area surrounding Lyon (Villeurbanne) and in the suburbs of Paris (Alfortville, Issy les Moulineaux). As regards their occupations, many Armenians found employment as labourers in the ports and the metallurgical industries, with a significant number also entering the silk industry. They represented the majority of unskilled personnel in many silk companies in 1930. A considerable number also broke out of the proletariat by establishing their own businesses, mainly in the smaller industries, such as clothing and leatherwork. In Paris, these trades traditionally took place in the insalubrious quarters of the Marais (fourth *arrondissement*) and the Sentier (ninth *arrondissement*). Georges Mauco (1932: 293) makes reference to this in his thesis: 'These peoples from central Europe and Asia Minor inhabit the poorest housing in the old part of Paris and often make do with hovels which double both as workshops and living quarters.'

The Russian émigrés represented a wider range of social backgrounds than the Armenians. While historians should avoid reiterating the myth – commonly heard in Paris in the 1920s – of the 'Russian prince' turned 'taxi driver', it is true that the French capital in that period was host to a significant proportion of the exiled Russian aristocracy as well as to a circle of Russian intellectuals, artists and writers, such as Stravinski, Chagall and Bounine. It ought not, however, be forgotten that the majority of Russian émigrés living in France comprised workers and self-employed artisans. Russian Jews who arrived before 1914 worked mainly in the clothing industry, particularly in the manufacture of caps. Those who had been privates in the 'white' armies defeated by the Bolsheviks took up employment, for the most part, in the car factories near Paris, especially those of Renault and Citroën (Le Guillou 1991). The diversity in social background represented by the Russian émigres is also indicated by the locations in which they came to settle. The majority settled in the region around Paris, with some small colonies being established in southern France, notably in Marseille and Nice. In Paris, Russians settled both in the '*beaux quartiers*' of the sixteenth *arrondissement*, and in the poorer *arrondissements*, such as the fifteenth, inhabited by most of the employees of Citroën. A similar situation is found in the suburbs, where Russians settled both in the bourgeois areas such as Neuilly and the working-class areas such as Boulogne and Billancourt.

With the crisis years of the 1930s, the refugees once more became the target of attacks by the nationalist right wing (Schor 1985). Although the main victims of such attacks were the German Jews and, to a lesser extent, the anti-Franco Spanish, the Russians and Armenians were by no means spared. A number of articles were published in the press and even some 'sociological' studies appeared (Dore and Gessain 1946) which claimed that the Russian and Armenian migrants could not become integrated into French society because their 'culture' differed too much from the French, and because they were inward-looking, living together in 'ghettos'. In reality this was by no means the case. Already by 1930, of all the foreign groups to settle in France, the highest percentage to apply for naturalization – 13 per cent – was found among the Russians. A monograph which looks at the Armenian population of Décines in the Rhône Valley indicates that the percentage of mixed marriages – 1.4 per cent between 1925 and 1929 – rose to 6.4 per cent in the 1930s, then to almost 52 per cent in the 1960s, finally reaching 75 per cent in 1970/1 (Bardakdjian 1973).

Russians and Armenians made a key contribution in the Resistance movement against the Vichy government and Nazi occupation during the Second World War: Manouchian and his fellow combatants were in fact among the first victims of the Gestapo. It has, however, been observed that it is predominantly the second generation that has attempted to become integrated, often at the expense of a 'denial' of their origins. This phenomenon is exemplified by the gallicized patronymics frequently used by intellectuals both of Russian origin, for instance the actor Robert Hossein and writer Henri Troyat, and of Armenian origin, for instance the singer Charles Aznavour and film-maker Henri Verneuil. Among the third generation – who reached adulthood in the 1970s – there appears to have been a marked desire to regain contact with their roots. The process evident in France may therefore be compared with that which was analysed by Oscar Handlin (1959) in the USA. This return to origins is most apparent among the Armenians. The year 1965, which marked the fiftieth anniversary of the genocide by the Turks, saw the beginnings of a movement which grew in following years, leading to the birth of the extremist party ASALA, who were responsible for numerous attacks against Turks, including eight deaths at Orly airport in 1983. Such violence has, however, been on the decline for several years now. The Armenian identity, which still thrives in France today, now finds its expression in a pacifist manner, through developing the life of its community and through its solidarity with the new Armenian state.

References

Bardakdjian, G. (1973) 'La communauté arménienne de Décines (1925–1971)', *Bulletin du Centre d'Histoire économique et sociale de l'Université de Lyon II*

Bérbérova, N. (1989) *C'est Moi qui Souligne*, Arles: Actes Sud

Dore, M. and R. Gessain (1946) 'Facteurs comparés d'Assimilation chez les Russes et les Arméniens', *Population, 1*

Elkarati, N. (1990) 'Emile Durkheim, défenseur des Réfugiés russes en France', *Genèses*, 2, 168–77

Green, N. (1985) *Les Travailleurs immigrés juifs à la belle Epoque*, Paris: Fayard

Handlin, O. (1959) *Immigration as a Factor of American History*, Englewood Cliffs, NJ: Prentice Hall

Hovanessian, M. (1992) *Le Lien communautaire. Trois Générations d'Arméniens*, Paris: Armand Colin

Le Guillou, O. (1991) *Eléments de Recherche sur l'Émigration russe en France. Les Russes de Boulogne-Billancourt en 1926*, Paris: Diplôme de Sciences Sociales, EHESS–ENS

Mauco, G. (1932) *Les Étrangers en France*, Paris: Armand Colin

Noiriel, G. (1991) *La Tyrannie du National. Le Droit d'Asile en Europe (1793–1993)*, Paris: Calmann-Lévy

Schor, R. (1985) *L'Opinion française et les Étrangers (1919–1939)*, Paris: Publications de la Sorbonne

Verneuil, H. (1985) *Mayrig*, Paris: Laffont, éd. de poche

JEWISH ECONOMIC AND REFUGEE MIGRATIONS, 1880–1950

COLIN HOLMES

Jewish history is a history of migration in which events originating in Europe between 1880 and 1950 assume particular importance (Wischnitzer 1948). That observation is especially underlined by developments in tsarist Russia and, later, in Nazi Germany and German-occupied Europe.

Jews in Russia

Any enquiry into Jewish migration in the late nineteenth century needs to begin in eastern Europe. Other countries had Jewish communities from which emigration occurred, from Germany to the USA, for example. However, the Jews in Russian Poland constituted the centre of world Jewry. In 1897, in the first national census of the tsar's empire, 5,189,401 Jews appeared in the returns in which they amounted to 4.13 per cent of the total population (Baron 1964: 76). At this time, unlike their co-religionists in western Europe, these Russian Polish Jews had not been emancipated. Restrictions stayed on their lives until 1917 (Baron 1964: 205–6).

The Russian state had secured a substantial increase in its Jewish population in the eighteenth century following the partitions of Poland, to the extent that 'each annexation of Polish territory brought into the expanding empire ever larger masses of Jews' (Baron 1964: 15). However, Jews were not perceived as an unmixed blessing by the Russian authorities and in the late eighteenth century the state began to confine them within the Pale of Settlement, a territory stretching from the Black Sea towards the Baltic (Zborowski and Herzog 1952). This area had assumed its definitive shape by 1834 (Frederic 1970: 23ff.). Simultaneously, the state pursued secular policies designed to break the spirit of the Jewish community. Furthermore, it encouraged the Christian church's efforts at conversion. Official policy relaxed slightly following the Crimean War (1854–56) and the 1863 Polish Revolt. In this atmosphere it was thought that concessions might be expedient. However, this climate soon changed. Following Alexander II's assassination in 1881 the Jews in Russian Poland faced a ceaseless wave of persecution and, in its swell, a growing but uncertain number of Jews migrated westward.

Persecution and migration

The migration was especially triggered by a number of specific developments. Violent attacks were launched on Jews following the tsar's assassination in 1881, in what a contemporary described as a 'savage orgy of official violence' (Frederic 1970: 128). The word 'pogrom', already heard, entered into common currency (Aronson 1990; Klier and Lambroza 1992). Then, in 1882, the May Laws placed additional restrictions upon movement and settlement. Some Jews previously permitted to reside beyond the Pale found that they were now obliged to live within it. Yet still the momentum of repression continued to whirl. In 1891, at Passover, the authorities expelled Jews from Moscow. In 1903 severe pogroms occurred at Kishineff. More hostility followed in 1904 and 1905 during the Russo-Japanese War and, in the latter case, in the shadow of the abortive revolution. Then, between 1911 and 1913 the world witnessed the spectacle of a great tsarist show trial, when Mendel Beilis stood accused of ritual murder (Rogger 1986: 40–55; Samuel 1967). Popular hostility fostered by the authorities underwrote this state opposition. As a result, Jews became special targets, although Harold Frederic (1970), a contemporary journalist, emphasized that other religious minorities in Russia also endured the lash of tsarist oppression.

These circumstances provided the necessary background to Jewish emigration. But other pressures contributed to the westward movement. The confinement within the Pale, coupled with the large families which characterized Orthodox Jewish households, acted as depressants on the wages of Jewish workers who, through a combination of such circumstances, were often in over-supply. Moreover, restrictions on employment opportunities compounded such problems. In short, economic pressures also stimulated Jewish emigration (Baron 1964: 1134).

Some Jews departed to other European countries

148

such as Germany (Wertheimer 1987) and France (Green 1985). Some others went to Britain (Gainer 1972; Garrard 1971; Gartner 1960). Outside Europe the USA acted as the strongest magnet, drawing large numbers of people from the *shtetlach* of eastern Europe to Ellis Island and the new world beyond (Higham 1963).

General observations

Between 1881 and 1917 Russian Jewry passed through a great crisis and the events of the time stimulated a number of specific Jewish responses (Frankel 1981). In particular, the emigration to Palestine, to western Europe and even further afield needs to be located within the turbulence of an epoch in which emigration continued despite the difficulties Jews frequently encountered. In Britain the growing arrival of Russian Polish Jews encouraged the state in 1905 to erect controls over alien immigration. Tensions also developed in France, Germany and the USA; in such circumstances public opposition towards these newcomers from eastern Europe enlisted some support from within established Jewish communities. In Britain, for example, Jewish grandees helped return fellow Jews to the darkness of Russian Poland, fearing that the immigration into Britain would stimulate anti-Semitism (Hochberg 1990: 153–99). Nevertheless, the westward migration led to permanent settlements and in countries such as the USA and Britain the communities created out of the immigration have secured a growing economic salience. However, circumstances in some other countries proved less favourable. The emigrants to France and Germany soon faced new terrors which many would not survive.

The impact of war and revolution

The First World War acted to restrict emigration from Russian Poland. Developments linked to the conflict also exercised a powerful influence on the later history of Jews and their subsequent migration. The October revolution in Russia become portrayed in some circles as a Jewish-controlled revolution and in extreme accounts became projected as an event that would lead towards Jewish world domination. This claim was to assume considerable historical significance. The message of a Red International gained more publicity from the events in 1919 in Hungary, where Bela Kun's communist government contained a number of Jews. The claim that revolutionaries born into Jewish backgrounds, though lapsed from any sense of Jewishness, were busily engaged in a Jewish

conspiracy strains one's sense of credulity. Even so, half truths can take hold and the belief persisted in a conspiracy beginning in Russia but spreading into other countries. Believers in this theory could turn for confirmation to their sacred text, *The Protocols of the Elders of Zion*, a confection whipped up by the tsarist secret police, the Okhrana (Cohn 1967). However, communist revolutionaries did not everywhere sweep all before them. With the collapse after 133 days of Bela Kun's government the so-called White Terror exacted a fearful revenge on Hungary's Jews and anti-Semitic legislation of 1920, 1938 and 1939, which restricted the civil rights of Jews and encouraged some westward migration (Braham 1981: 30, 125, 153). Similar restrictions in Poland also led some Jews to seek safety elsewhere (Gutman 1989; Heller 1977).

Not that it proved easy to find a refuge. Palestine absorbed some of the emigration, but entry remained controlled, as it did elsewhere. Following the First World War many countries erected immigration barriers. In Britain the 1919 Aliens Act placed strict controls on the entry and movement of aliens and the state assumed increased powers of deportation (Holmes 1988: 112–14). In the USA also tougher controls descended. The 1924 Johnson Reed Act 'erected a formidable wall' against immigration and further legislation in 1927 underlined that toughness (Higham 1963: 324). By now the fine sentiments of Emma Lazarus, engraved on the Statue of Liberty, had become badly tarnished.

Jewish problems in the Nazi epoch

By the 1930s the major focus in the history of Jewish migration had shifted towards central Europe and especially towards the territory controlled by the Nazis.

German Jews had long been assimilated by the time the Nazis came to power and by 1933 had evolved a distinctive German-Jewish identity (Frankel and Zipperstein 1992; Mosse and Paucker 1966; Sorkin 1987). However, in the Nazi epoch the community's development became savagely disrupted. The Nazi state began to organize the persecution of Jews as early as 1933. In 1935/6 the Nuremberg laws took such hostility a stage further. Then, following the *anschluss*, the union of Germany and Austria in 1938, and full German control of Czechoslovakia in 1939, Nazism's racial philosophies and policies become transplanted into the fertile soil of the greater Germany (Dawidowicz 1975).

Between 1933 and 1939 the National Socialists

permitted, indeed encouraged, Jewish emigration, although they gradually restricted the transfer of assets abroad (Fox 1984; Röder 1992: 345–53). Many Jews, however, confused and believing at first that Nazi anti-Semitism would blow itself out, revealed no marked enthusiasm to emigrate (Loewenstein 1966; Rosenstock 1956). However, following the *Kristallnacht* pogrom in 1938 when synagogues went up in flames and crowds smashed their way into Jewish property, some of this reluctance evaporated (Strauss 1980, 1981).

Emigration in such circumstances still encountered obstacles, including barriers which had to be negotiated outside Germany and German-controlled territory. As a result centres of refuge remained elusive. Between 1933 and 1939 Britain admitted only 56,000 refugees from the greater Germany, 50,000 of whom were Jewish (Wasserstein 1979: 7). In the early days of the Nazi epoch the British government pursued a particularly restrictive policy. Guarantees by Anglo-Jewry that such refugees would not become a public charge and an emphasis on re-emigration, particularly of young refugees to Palestine, secured some admissions but no significant swift liberalization of policy. However, in the deteriorating circumstances of 1938/9 some of the brakes were taken off the government's restrictive stance (London 1991, 1992; Sherman 1973). It was at this time, for instance, that the special children's transport brought some 10,000 unaccompanied children to Britain (Turner 1990). Even so, the absolute number of Jewish refugees remained stubbornly small and this niggardly British response cannot be regarded as unusual (Abella and Troper 1982). Between 1933 and 1939 an estimated 360,000–370,000 Jewish refugees left the greater Germany. Apart from the number who came to Britain, 57,000 departed to the USA. Furthermore, 53,000 made a new start in Palestine. France took in 40,000 refugees, counting Jews and non-Jews (Maga 1982; Thalmann 1979). Between 1933 and 1940, 25,000–33,000 refugees entered the Netherlands and by the time of the German occupation in 1940 an estimated 18,000 Jewish refugees remained in the country (Moore 1984: 80; 1986).

The refugees exercised a notable influence in countries such as Britain and the USA. Their economic and intellectual contributions have been well-recognized (Jackman and Borden 1983; Mosse et al. 1991). Germany's loss can be counted as another country's gain even if precise calculations relating to impact are difficult to calculate. Not that success was universal or indeed that success reveals everything we need to know. Some refugees never overcame the traumas of their transfer (Berghahn 1988: 128–38). Some of them, such as the young women who toiled as governesses, became deskilled and exploited (Kushner 1991). In any event, the limits of celebration centred on, say academics or businessmen, needs to be recognized. Like E. P. Thompson's poor stockingers and framework knitters of an earlier age, those refugees who toiled to less dramatic effect also have their place in history. Moreover, if we step outside Britain and the USA another dark shadow falls across our path. Many Jewish refugees who departed to countries such as France and Holland and subsequently failed to escape the Germans' clutches during the Second World War were to perish. Set against the important scientific achievements associated with wartime exiles in Britain and the USA the fate of those refugees who become camp statistics counts as stark testimony to the tragedy that unfolded in early twentieth-century Europe.

The Second World War and its aftermath

Following the outbreak of hostilities in September 1939 the Germans at first allowed the emigration of Jews through the agency of the Reich Central Bureau for Jewish Emigration, which in October 1939 came under the direction of Adolf Eichmann. However, 1941 witnessed a shift in policy. In August the emigration of Jews from German-occupied territory was forbidden. Then, on 23 October 1941, an order banned all further emigration from the Reich. Even before this date some Jews had been unable to emigrate. Those 'incarcerated in concentration camps, prisons or ghettos had little opportunity to escape' (Wasserstein 1979: 45). The majority of these people were destined eventually to end up in one of the death camps which the Germans began to construct in 1941 on occupied territory in Poland.

Those Jews who attempted to emigrate in order to escape from 'this season in hell' (Steiner 1971: 31–48) continued to find restrictions in potential places of refuge. The British government halted immigration from Germany and German-occupied territory immediately on the outbreak of war. As a result, the net increase in Jewish refugees during the war has been estimated at no more than 10,000. Britain, it should be emphasized, did not provide the only possible source of refuge. Some escapees entered the USA (Feingold 1970). Shanghai continued for a time to function as a refugee centre, just as it had before the war (Kranzler

1972/3). But, even on a worldwide perspective, the number of refugees who received sanctuary remained pitifully small (Wasserstein 1979).

Some of this clearest evidence of restriction shows up in the case of Palestine, which Britain had administered since 1922 on behalf of the League of Nations. Throughout the war the British government clung tenaciously to the tight entry provisions of the 1939 White Paper. Indeed, its policy proved even more restrictive. The White Paper envisaged the possible entry of 75,000 Jews to Palestine over a five-year period. In the event that quota was never fully met, Yet the British government persisted with a strict policy against illegal immigration (Lucas 1974: 194–202). In short: 'every practicable tactic was employed … to prevent significant numbers of Jews reaching Palestine' (Wasserstein 1979: 80). In such circumstances various agencies scoured the earth for suitable territory for refugees. But none of their schemes produced tangible results. It took considerable resilience, marked initiative and a fair slice of good fortune for Jewish refugees to secure a safe haven.

If the focus of attention is switched towards eastern Europe other important aspects of Jewish migration come into view. For a time Hungary pulled in refugees, notwithstanding its own tradition of anti-Semitism. But the key wartime developments in eastern Europe occurred in Poland and the Soviet Union (Kulischer 1948: 301–11; Marrus 1985: 241–52; Proudfoot 1957: 33–41).

One consequence of the Nazi-Soviet pact of August 1939 was the deportation of Poles from eastern Poland to Soviet labour camps. Some of these deportees were Jewish (Davies and Polonsky 1991; Pinchuk 1990). The subsequent enforced population transfer from the Baltic States, also undertaken by the Soviets following the Nazi-Soviet pact, likewise included some Jews. These traumatic deportations soon became overshadowed, however, by the events that followed the German invasion of the Soviet Union in June 1941.

This action brought in its train the extermination programme. In the USSR one possible escape route from the Germans lay in moving eastwards. Some movement of Jews occurred spontaneously: in other cases it reflected the *diktat* of the Soviet state. In the year following the German attack a report by Jewish agencies calculated that the Soviet Union contained between 200,000 and 350,000 Jewish refugees. A figure of between 50,000 and 150,000 has been offered for Jewish internees incarcerated in Soviet

camps during the war. The conditions endured by all these people defy decription (Marrus 1985: 247–8).

The post-war world

When the Second World War ended, a count of survivors in Displaced Person (DP) camps (Wyman 1989: Chapter 6) and other locations suggested that only a small fragment of Europe's Jews had survived. Jews from east and west who had fallen into German hands were likely to have perished. Moreover, hopes of a new beginning, free from anti-Semitism, soon became dashed by incidents such as the Kielce pogrom in Poland in 1946. Anti-Semitism in eastern Europe drove some Jews towards the Allied war zones in Germany, a base many refugees viewed as a staging post *en route* to Palestine.

By this time, in fact, the appeal of Palestine had undoubtedly increased. Nevertheless, official entry policy remained firmly in the hands of the British government and the early signs to would-be emigrants remained unfavourable. In such circumstances illegal immigration was organized by Zionist underground sources (Bauer 1970). Until the last days of the mandate, the British government, for its part, pursued a restrictive entry programme in accordance with the terms of the 1939 White Paper. It took the foundation of the state of Israel in 1948 and its open door policy on Jewish immigration, together with the admission of 40,000 Jewish DPs to North America and similar numbers to Latin America and Australia, to solve the Jewish refugee problem in Europe (Dinnerstein 1982; Isaac 1954: 220; Marrus 1985: 339).

The British government's cautious approach was additionally revealed by its responses towards the arrival of Jewish refugees in its war zones in Germany and Austria. Furthermore, 'Jews were consistently excluded from all [the] labour recruitment schemes' (Cesarani 1992: 77) that featured in post-war economic policy. Consequently, after 1945 only 2000 Jewish survivors of the Holocaust gained admission to Britain (Cesarani 1992: 80). By contrast, the British government recruited 90,000 European volunteer workers from DP camps in Europe; it also allowed 114,000 Polish ex-servicemen to remain in Britain and to be joined later by their dependants.

Epilogue

An uncertain number of Jews appeared among the 250,000 Hungarians who fled during or after the 1956 revolution. The unrest in Poland in 1968, when Jews become targets of state repression, also resulted in some migration, More recently still, Jews from the former USSR have departed in increasing numbers for Israel. Such movement underscores the continuity of migration as a force in Jewish history, in which history the events of 1880 to 1950 possess a central significance.

References

Abella, I. and H. Troper (1982) *None is Too Many: Canada and the Jews of Europe 1933–1948*, Toronto: Lester & Orpen Dennys

Aronson, I. M. (1990) *Troubled Waters, The Origins of the 1881 Anti-Jewish Pogroms in Russia*, Pittsburgh: University of Pittsburgh Press

Baron, S. W. (1964) *The Russian Jew under Tsars and Soviets*, New York: Macmillan

Bauer, Y. (1970) *Flight and Rescue: Brichah*, New York: Random House

Berghahn, M. (1988) *Continental Britons: German-Jewish Refugees from Nazi Germany*, Oxford: Berg

Braham, R. L. (1981) *The Politics of Genocide, vol I, The Holocaust in Hungary*, New York: Columbia University Press

Cesarani, D. (1992) *Justice Delayed: How Britain Became a Haven for Nazi War Criminals*, London: Heinemann

Cohn, N. (1967) *Warrant for Genocide: The Myth of the Jewish Conspiracy and the Protocols of the Elders of Zion*, London: Eyre and Spottiswoode

Davies, N. and A. Polonsky (eds) (1991) *Jews in Eastern Poland and the USSR 1939–46*, London: Macmillan

Dawidowicz, L. (1975) *The War against the Jews 1933–1945*, London: Weidenfeld & Nicolson

Dinnerstein, L. (1982) *America and the Survivors of the Holocaust*, New York: Columbia University Press

Feingold, H. (1970) *The Politics of Rescue: The Roosevelt Administration and the Holocaust, 1938–1945*, New Brunswick: Rutgers University Press

Fox, J. P. (1984) 'Nazi Germany and German Emigration to Great Britain', in G. Hirschfeld (ed.) *Exile in Great Britain: Refugees from Hitler's Germany*, Leamington Spa: Berg, 29–62

Frankel, J. (1981) *Prophecy and Politics: Socialism, Nationalism and the Russian Jews 1862–1917*, Cambridge: Cambridge University Press

Frankel, J. and S. Zipperstein (eds) (1992) *Assimilation and Community: The Jews in Nineteenth Century Europe*, Cambridge: Cambridge University Press

Frederic, H. (1970) *The New Exodus: A Study of Israel in Europe*, New York: Arno Press [1st edn. 1992]

Gainer, B. (1972) *The Alien Invasion: The Origins of the Aliens Act of 1905*, London: Heinemann

Garrard, J. A. (1971) *The English and Immigration. A Comparative Study of the Jewish Influx 1880–1910*, London: Oxford University Press

Gartner, L. (1960) *The Jewish Immigrant in England, 1870–1914*, Detroit: Wayne State University Press

Green, N. (1985) *The Pletzl of Paris: Jewish Immigrant Workers in the Belle Epoque*, New York: Holmes and Meier

Gutman, Y. (1989) 'Polish Anti-Semitism between the Wars: An Overview', in Y. Gutman et al. (eds) *The Jews of Poland between Two World Wars*, Hanover, NH: University of New England Press, 97–108

Heller, C. S. (1977) *On the Edge of Destruction: Jews of Poland between the Two World Wars*, New York: Columbia University Press

Higham, J. (1963) *Strangers in the Land: Patterns of American Nativism, 1860–1925*, New York: Atheneum

Hochberg, S. (1990) 'The Jewish Community and the Aliens Question in Great Britain 1881–1917', Ann Arbor: University Microfilms International.

Holmes, C. (1988) *John Bull's Island: Immigration and British Society 1871–1971*, London: Macmillan

Isaac, J. (1954) *British Post-War Migration*, Cambridge: Cambridge University Press

Jackman, J. C. and C. M. Borden (eds) (1983) *The Muses Flee Hitler: Cultural Transfer and Adaptation, 1930–1945*, Washington, DC: Smithsonian Institution Press

Klier, J. D. and S. Lambroza (eds) (1992) *Pogroms, Anti-Jewish Violence in Modern Russian History*, Cambridge: Cambridge University Press

Kranzler, D. (1972/3) 'The Jewish Refugee Community of Shanghai, 1938–1945', *Wiener Library Bulletin*, XXL, 28–37

Kulischer, E. (1948) *Europe on the Move: War and Population Changes, 1917–1947*, New York: Columbia University Press

Kushner, T. (1991) 'An Alien Occupation: Jewish Refugees and Domestic Service in Britain 1933–1948', in W. E. Mosse et al. (eds) *Entscheidungsjahr 1932: Zur Judenfrage in der Endphase der Weimarer Republik*, Tübingen: Mohr, 553–78

Loewenstein, K. (1966) 'Die innerjüdische Reaktion auf die Krise der deutschen Demokratie', in W. E. Mosse and A. Paucker (eds) *Entscheidungsjahr 1932: Zur Judenfrage in der Endphase der Weimarer Republik*, Tübingen: Mohr, 349–404

London, L. (1991) 'British Immigration Control Procedures and Jewish Refugees, 1933–1939', in W. E. Mosse et al. (eds.) *Entscheidungsjahr 1932: Zur Judenfrage in der Endphase der Weimarer Republik*, Tübingen: Mohr, 485–517

—— (1992) 'British Immigration Control Procedures and Jewish Refugees, 1933–42', Ph.D. thesis, University of London

Lucas, N. (1974) *The Modern History of Israel*, London: Weidenfeld & Nicolson

Maga, T. P. (1982) 'Closing the Door: The French Government and Refugee Policy 1933–1939', *French Historical Studies*, XII, 424–42

Marrus, M. (1985) *The Unwanted: European Refugees in the Twentieth Century*, New York: Oxford University Press

Moore, B. (1984) 'Jewish Refugees in the Netherlands', *Leo Baeck Institute Yearbook*, 29, 73–101

—— (1986) *Refugees from Nazi Germany in the Netherlands*, Dordrecht: Nijhoff

Mosse, W. E. and A. Paucker (eds) (1966) *Entscheidungsjahr 1932: Zur Judenfrage in der Endphase der Weimarer Republik*, Tübingen: Mohr

Mosse, W. E. et al. (1991) *Second Chance: Two Centuries of German-Speaking Jews in the United Kingdom*, Tübingen: Mohr

Pinchuk, B. C. (1990) *Shtetl Jews under Soviet Rule: Eastern Poland on the Eve of the Holocaust*, Oxford: Blackwell.

Proudfoot, M. J. (1957) *European Refugees, 1939–52: A Study in Forced Population Movement*, London: Faber

Röder, W. (1992) 'Die Emigration aus dem national sozialistischen Deutschland', in S. K. Bade (ed.) *Deutsche in Ausland: Fremde in Deutschland*, Munich: Verlag C. H. Beck, 345–53

Rogger, H. (1986) 'The Beilis Case: Anti-Semitism and Politics in the Reign of Nicholas II', in H. Rogger, *Jewish Policies and Right-Wing Politics in Imperial Russia*, London: Macmillan, 40–55

Rosenstock, W. (1956) 'Exodus 1933–39: A Survey of Jewish Emigration from Germany', *Leo Baeck Institute Yearbook*, 1, 380–405

Samuel, M. (1967) *Blood Accusation: The Strange History of the Beilis Case*, London: Weidenfeld & Nicolson

Sherman, A. J. (1973) *Island Refuge: Britain and Refugees from the Third Reich*, London: Elek

Sorkin, D. (1987) *The Transformation of German Jewry 1780–1840*, New York: Oxford University Press

Steiner, G. (1971) *In Bluebeard's Castle*, London: Faber

Strauss, H. A. (1980) 'Jewish Emigration from Germany-Nazi Policies and Jewish Responses (Part 1)', *Leo Baeck Institute Yearbook*, 25, 313–61

(1981) 'Jewish Emigration from Germany: Nazi Policies and Jewish Responses (Part 2)', *Leo Baeck Institute Yearbook*, 26, 343–409

Thalmann, R. (1979) 'L'Émigration du IIIe Reich dans la France de 1933 à 1939', *Le Monde Juif*, XCVI, 127–39

Turner, B. (1990) *And the Policeman Smiled ... 10,000 Children Escape from Nazi Europe*, London: Bloomsbury

Wasserstein, B. (1979) *Britain and the Jews of Europe 1939–1945*, Oxford: Oxford University Press

Wertheimer, J. (1987) *Unwelcome Strangers: East European Jews in Imperial Germany*, New York: Oxford University Press

Wischnitzer, M. (1948) *To Dwell in Safety. The Study of Jewish World Migration since 1800*, Philadelphia: Jewish Publishing Society of America

Wyman, D. (1989) *DP, Europe's Displaced Persons, 1945–1951*, Philadelphia: The Beach Institute Press

Zborowski, M. and E. Herzog (1952) *Life is with People: The Jewish Little Town of Eastern Europe*, New York: International Universities Press

THE RESETTLEMENT OF DISPLACED PERSONS IN EUROPE, 1946–1951

DIANA KAY[1]

Between 1946 and 1951 over one million displaced persons (DPs) were resettled in some forty-eight countries (Proudfoot 1957: 427). The term displaced person was initially restricted to those civilians (such as forced labourers) who had been displaced during the course of the war and who needed assistance to return to their country of origin (Jacobmeyer 1990: 286). In the course of the 1940s it was extended to encompass a larger group of civilians, some of whom fled their homelands in the east after the cessation of hostilities, on account of their rejection of communist regimes. In terms of national origins, Poles formed the largest group, but there were sizeable numbers from the Baltic states, Ukraine and Yugoslavia, and smaller numbers from Hungary, Romania, Czechoslovakia, Bulgaria and Byelorussia.

Allied policy in 1945 had been to congregate displaced persons in temporary assembly centres in Germany, Austria and Italy prior to their repatriation. However, by early 1946 it became clear that a sizeable proportion of displaced persons of eastern European backgrounds would not willingly return and after protracted discussion this population became the subject of an international resettlement programme (Holborn 1956). With respect to destination, the USA resettled the largest number (329,301), followed by Australia (182,159) and Canada (123,479). In Europe the largest resettlement schemes were those of the UK (86,346), France (38,445) and Belgium (22,477) (Proudfoot 1957: 427). In addition the state of Israel which was created in May 1948 independently financed and organized the resettlement of 132,000 Jewish DPs as the Arab–Israeli war made the UN reluctant to intervene in resettlement in this region (Marrus 1985: 345).

The resettlement of displaced persons is popularly represented as a 'success story' (Kismaric 1989: 183) and, judged in terms of numbers alone, the movement is impressive. However, close examination of the terms of the various resettlement schemes raises questions about the accuracy of their characterization as straightforward refugee movements inspired solely or mainly by humanitarian concerns. Displaced persons were not only categorized by receiving countries as 'victims of war' but also as 'surplus labour', as 'assimilable racial types' and as ideological weapons in the emerging anti-communist struggle. In other words, the resettlement of displaced persons was shaped by national assessments of their potential contribution to wider economic, political and demographic objectives.

The institutional framework

Immediately after the war displaced persons came under the formal responsibility of UNRRA (United Nations Relief and Rehabilitation Administration). Set up in 1943 as a temporary war-time relief organization, UNRRA's remit was limited to providing food, clothing and medical relief to those DPs not suspected of being Nazi collaborators or traitors prior to their repatriation. During the summer of 1945 some three million western Europeans displaced by the war and two million Soviet citizens were repatriated by UNRRA. By early 1946 it was clear that repatriation would not solve the entire DP question. Over a million eastern European DPs resisted return and remained in the DP camps in Germany and Austria. Resettlement to a third country was made possible by the formation of a United Nations special agency, the International Refugee Organization (IRO), which began operations in mid-1947 and provided both care and maintenance, and legal protection. To be eligible for IRO assistance, a DP had to present a valid case against repatriation to an IRO review board, to have entered the western zone before a certain date and be cleared of any voluntary collaboration with the Nazis. In practice, the criteria for eligibility became increasingly liberal with the passage of time (Salomon 1990: 166).

The IRO aimed to implement UN General Assembly resolutions which urged each individual member nation to give 'most favourable consideration to receiving its fair share of non-repatriables' (General Assembly resolution 54, 15 December 1946). The appeal was cast in voluntary terms – assigning fixed quotas of DPs to individual countries being regarded as an unacceptable infringement of sovereignty – so that national governments had some leeway to determine the nature and extent of their response. Although the IRO pressed for a broad family-based resettlement programme and for wide-ranging economic opportunities, national governments were more selective and circumscribed in their approach, as will be seen below.

Displaced persons as surplus labour

In determining the nature of their response to the UN appeal, some governments looked primarily to their own labour requirements. This was particularly true of the chronologically early resettlement programmes in western Europe. In the immediate post-war years, many west European economies experienced critical labour shortages in industries deemed essential for their economic recovery. International surveys of labour requirements in western Europe identified the displaced persons in Germany and Austria as one of the two main sources of surplus labour in Europe – the other being formed by unemployed Italians (Carey 1948; International Labour Review 1948: 756). Both the UK and Belgian governments had identified DPs in early 1946 as a solution to pressing domestic labour shortages (Caestecker 1992; Kay and Miles 1992). In these instances international obligations coincided fortuitously with national self-interests.

Defining displaced persons in terms of 'labour' had implications for the selection criteria adopted by recruiting governments and for the conditions under which DPs entered the country. Although the details of individual employment schemes varied (International Labour Review 1948: 434–51), the terms of the UK and Belgian schemes both demonstrate a concern with securing short-term contract labour rather than with offering refugee resettlement. In both cases eligibility was restricted to young, healthy and preferably single DPs. Both schemes defined dependants narrowly (in terms of spouse and dependant children) and both schemes directed DPs into priority employment (agriculture, mining, textiles and hospitals in the UK and mining in Belgium). Under the terms of the UK scheme, volunteers had to sign an 'undertaking' while still in the DP camps that they would accept the employment offered to them by the Ministry of Labour and National Service, and that they would not change that employment without official permission. In Belgium DPs had to sign a two-year contract to work in the mines. Both schemes reserved the right to return 'unsatisfactory recruits' within three months to camps in Germany or Austria

and both left the question of permanent residence or rights to citizenship vague (Caestecker 1992; Kay and Miles 1992: 57).

The employment controls on DPs not only eased specific shortages by tying DPs to 'essential' employment but they also eased labour market tensions by limiting the DPs' ability to compete openly with national labour. Both the UK and the Belgian schemes enshrined the principle that nationals should be privileged over aliens. Indeed it was the ability to control and direct DPs as aliens into priority economic sectors that constituted their main advantage as additional workers. The alternatives of extending controls over national workers or adjusting wage levels to attract workers into these sectors were politically and economically less feasible (although some war-time employment controls were retained in the early post-war years in the UK). In the case of the UK, the entry of displaced persons formed the subject of tripartite consultations between government, employers and trade unions. In addition employers and trade unions in those industries earmarked for recruitment negotiated more specific industrial agreements whose terms often restricted the DPs' access to skilled work and gave them inferior redundancy rights to national workers. However, entrenched fears of foreign labour being used to undercut British workers also led British trade unions to support the principle of equal pay for the DPs (Miles and Kay 1990).

The Australian, Canadian and US resettlement schemes differed in the extent to which they were labour-market driven. Canada operated both a labour quota scheme and a 'nominated close relatives scheme'. Under the former the Canadian government vetted requests for DP labour from employers, thereby exercising a degree of control over economic placement. Overall 60 per cent of the total resettled came to Canada via this scheme and were employed mainly as loggers, miners, farmers and domestics (Holborn 1956: 399). Under the 'nominated close relatives scheme' Canadian residents (often those of the same national origins as DPs such as the Ukrainians) nominated close relatives for acceptance.

Sponsorship was also a key characteristic of the US scheme under which a named sponsor (an individual or an organization) signed an 'assurance' which legally obliged them to provide housing and employment for a named DP thereby minimizing public expenditure and responsibility. However, there was some official concern to steer DPs in a certain economic direction, as seen in the provision reserving 30 per cent of visas for DPs engaged in agriculture before their immigration and willing to work in agriculture in the USA (Holborn 1956: 411).

Displaced persons and population concerns

Labour market considerations were only one strand underlying DP programmes. At the time of resettlement, many if not all receiving countries had a framework of immigration controls in place. National immigration policies varied in scope and impact but many explicitly or implicitly distinguished 'desirable' from 'undesirable' immigrants. This distinction was made on economic, political and also 'racial' grounds. Given that the political division of Europe made permanent settlement a likely outcome of any decision to resettle DPs, some receiving governments vetted the DP population not only with respect to 'muscle' but also to the implications for 'racial balance' or harmony. In effect, some receiving countries operated a racialized hierarchy of immigrants into which the DPs were inserted.

In the case of the UK the preferred source of foreign labour was west Europe 'whose traditions and social background were more nearly equal to our own' (Kay and Miles 1992: 47). Only when this was not forthcoming were DPs from eastern Europe considered. Furthermore Jewish DPs were 'routinely excluded' from recruitment (Cesarani 1992: 4–5) and a proposal to set up a similar official employment programme for British subjects from the Caribbean was rejected (Harris 1987). In this case non-Jewish displaced persons from eastern Europe, while not the government's first choice, were preferable to both Jews and 'black' labour from the Caribbean.

Considerations of 'racial homogeneity' also informed the Australian DP programme. Since 1901 Australia had pursued a restrictive and 'racialized' immigration policy, popularly known as the 'White Australia policy' (Huttenback 1976). This policy had the Asian population as its focus of exclusion and was racially biased in favour of 'Anglo-Saxon' immigration. After the Second World War, considerations of economic development and national defence led the Australian government to embark on a programme of mass immigration. By extending recruitment to east European DPs, the Australian government breached the former restriction on immigration to those of British 'stock'. However, racialized considerations still played a part as shown in the preference for north European Balts and for 'blue-eyed, blond DPs' (Holborn 1956: 394; Wyman 1989: 191).

In the USA existing immigration legislation (based on the national origins quota system of 1924)

intentionally discriminated against southern and eastern European immigration by pegging the number of visas available to any national group to their percentage of the American population in 1890 (Holborn 1956; Loescher and Scanlan 1986: 224). The entry of DPs to the USA involved special legislation in the form of the Displaced Persons Act of 1948 which authorized the entry of 200,000 DPs. However, specific provisions of the act built in certain racialized biases, notably against Jewish DPs. The provision which reserved 30 per cent of the available visas to those who had previously engaged in agriculture discriminated against the more urban Jewish DPs, as did that reserving 40 per cent of visas for those from areas 'de facto annexed by a foreign power,' a provision which favoured the Balts (Loescher and Scanlan 1986: 20).

DPs were not only ranked alongside other prospective immigrants but the different national groups among the DPs were also graded by the varying missions with DP programmes. As noted above, many programmes displayed a bias towards the Baltic DPs, who were popularly regarded as the elite of the DP camps. The UK scheme began with a recruitment scheme for hospital domestic workers which was restricted to Baltic women. These were officially regarded as a 'good and desirable element in our population' which would be 'rapidly assimilated' (Kay and Miles 1992: 50). In the USA Balts were characterized as 'genuine refugees' compared with Jewish DPs who were seen as seeking admission for employment purposes alone (Loescher and Scanlan 1986: 20).

Admitting DPs entailed some redrawing of the racialized boundaries of existing immigration policies. In particular anti-Semitism shaped and limited the response of resettlement programmes towards those who were the main victims of the Nazi holocaust and who arguably should have topped the humanitarian agenda. Compared with the main focus of exclusion (Asians in the case of Australia or 'blacks' in the case of Britain), the east European DPs were considered to be 'assimilable' and compatible with maintaining social order and 'racial' harmony.

Displaced persons and the cold war

A full understanding of DP resettlement cannot be gained by considering the local circumstances of receiving countries alone. The emerging cold war of the immediate post-war period helped to structure the response (Salomon 1990). Foreign policy considerations played a particularly significant part in the US

DP resettlement programme (Loescher and Scanlan 1986).

The fate of the DPs was debated extensively and with increasing rancour in the newly created United Nations (Penrose 1951). The home governments of the DPs insisted throughout on the repatriation of their nationals and rejected the principle that displaced persons should become the subject of an internationally assisted resettlement programme. Consequently, the USSR and other east European governments did not join the IRO, so that this became dominated by the West and notably by the USA, which contributed more than half the funds (Marrus 1985: 343). The Soviet Union and other east European governments repeatedly charged that the DPs were being forcibly held back from returning to their homelands and that the resettlement programmes were nothing more than schemes for the recruitment of cheap labour. Most emotively, the Soviet representative to the UN charged that resettlement was a continuation of the policy of transfer by violence begun by the Nazis (Kay and Miles 1992: 150–1).

The IRO had become operational in mid-1947 but it was not until a year later that the US government enacted special legislation to admit DPs. By this time relations between the USA and the USSR had deteriorated. Although there was considerable domestic pressure in the USA to admit DPs for humanitarian reasons (in the form of a widespread and effective citizens campaign), this was supplemented by foreign policy considerations of an anti-communist nature. In particular the concept of a 'haven' became more sharply ideologically defined to refer to the granting of protection to those fleeing communist regimes. The debate on DP legislation in the US Congress was infused with the rhetoric of the USA as the champion of freedom and democracy (Loescher and Scanlan 1986: 19).

The admittance of DPs provided the USA with an opportunity to further its anti-communist objectives. By voting with their feet and resisting repatriation the displaced persons could be seen within the wider ideological struggle between East and West as making a statement about the superiority of life in the West. In the UK a British member of parliament argued that 'their love of freedom' as demonstrated by their desire to remain in the West constituted 'the spirit and stuff of which we can make Britons' (Kay and Miles 1992: 54).

The growing anti-communist focus of US foreign policy was seen in the willingness of the USA to receive more recent (i.e. post-war) refugees from the east. The DP Amendment Act of 1950 extended eligibility for resettlement to those who had entered the western zones before 1 January 1949 (compared with the previous deadline of 22 December 1945). In addition, there was recognition of the more active role which anti-communist migrants could play in covert activities aimed at destabilizing communist regimes. In the British case, although domestic economic considerations played a major part in the setting up of the DP scheme known as 'Westward Ho!', there was subsequent consideration of the contribution which some DPs recruited by this programme could make to British military intelligence (Cesarani 1992: 160). In particular intelligence considerations may have played a part in the removal of an entire 14th Waffen–SS Galizien Division (some 8000 men) from Italy to Britain in May 1947 despite the officially acknowledged inadequacy of their screening for war crimes (Cesarani 1992: 161).

Contradictions and inconsistencies of resettlement schemes

In sum, the resettlement of displaced persons between 1946 and 1951 responded to a variety of conflicting motives. The early resettlement schemes in western Europe identified displaced persons as a labour surplus which could contribute to economic recovery. However, the emphasis some schemes (such as the British and the Belgian) placed on short-term contract labour could and did conflict with the realities of permanent settlement. Furthermore, the tension between the inferior labour market status assigned to DPs in the form of special employment controls and their status as refugees under the formal protection of the IRO was the focus of considerable discontent, not least among the displaced persons themselves who resisted the restrictions on their labour mobility. This level of disillusionment among some resettled DPs was exploited by the Soviet and east European governments who charged that displaced persons were being used as a form of forced labour by the West.

As the number of resettlement programmes expanded, and particularly after the opening of the US DP programme in mid-1948, the dissatisfaction of those placed in the earlier west European programmes increased. In the case of the UK, over a quarter of the original intake re-emigrated in the course of the 1950s, mainly to Canada or the USA (Kay and Miles 1992: 158). In Belgium the limited employment prospects of displaced persons and the poor living conditions caused widespread dissatisfaction. In protest, many displaced persons after the expiry of their two-year contracts in the mines took collective action and marched on Brussels. By the end of 1949 about a quarter of the total recruited had left Belgium and returned to Germany from where some found their way on to the Canadian or US schemes (Vernant 1953: 307).

A further contradictory consequence of the bias in favour of selecting young, healthy and single DPs was the formation of a 'hard core' of DPs who were left behind in the DP camps having been passed over or rejected by receiving countries. In mid-1949 nearly 175,000 DPs remained in camps because they were too old, too sick, had too many dependants or were too well-qualified to be eligible for resettlement (Marrus 1985: 345). For this group a solution had to found within western Germany. The Allied High Commissioners for Germany handed over part of their powers to the federal government on condition that DPs were granted acceptable rights. In April 1951 the Federal Republic of Germany passed the law of 'homeless foreigners' which granted DPs a legal status superior to the traditional rights of asylum but still inferior to that of the German refugees from the former East German provinces (Jacobmeyer 1990: 284).

Note

1. I am grateful to Dr Robert Miles for commenting on this contribution.

References

Caestecker, F. (1992) *Vluchtelingenbeleid in de Naoorlog-seperiode*, Brussels: VUB Press

Carey, J. P. Clark (1948) *The Role of Uprooted People in European Recovery*, Washington: National Economic Society Planning Association, Planning Pamphlet No. 64

Cesarani, D. (1992) *Justice Delayed*, London: Heinemann

Harris, C. (1987) 'British Capitalism, Migration and Relative Surplus Population: A Synopsis', *Migration*, (1), 47–90

Holborn, L. W. (1956) *The International Refugee Organization*, London: Oxford University Press

Huttenback, R. A. (1976) *Racism and Empire, White Settlers and Colored Immigrants in the British Self-Governing Colonies, 1830–1910*, New York: Cornell University Press

International Labour Review (1948) 'Manpower Requirements and Availabilities in Europe in 1948', *International Labour Review*, 58, 752–9

Jacobmeyer, W. (1990) 'The "Displaced Persons" in West Germany, 1945–1951', in G. Rystad (ed.) *The Uprooted: Forced Migration as an International Problem in the Post-War Era*, Lund: Lund University Press, 271–88

Kay, D. and R. Miles (1992) *Refugees or Migrant Workers? European Volunteer Workers in Britain 1946–1951*, London: Routledge

Kismaric, C. (1989) *Forced Out: The Agony of the Refugee in Our Time*, London: Penguin

Loescher G. and J. A. Scanlan (1986) *Calculated Kindness: Refugees and America's Half-Open Door, 1945 to the Present*, New York: The Free Press

Marrus, M. R. (1985) *Unwanted: European Refugees in the Twentieth Century*, New York: Oxford University Press

Miles, R. and D. Kay (1990) 'The TUC, Foreign Labour and the Labour Government 1945–51', *Immigrants and Minorities*, 9 (1), 85–108

Penrose, E. F. (1951) 'Negotiating on Refugees and DPs', in R. Dennett and J. E. Johnson (eds) *Negotiating with the Russians*, Boston: World and Peace Foundation, 139–68

Proudfoot, M. J. (1957) *European Refugees: 1939–52: A Study in Forced Population Movement*, London: Faber & Faber

Salomon, K. (1990) 'The Cold War Heritage: UNRRA and the IRO as Predecessors of UNHCR', in G. Rystad (ed.) *The Uprooted: Forced Migration as an International Problem in the Post-War Era*, Lund: Lund University Press, 157–78

Vernant, J. (1953) *The Refugee in the Post-War World*, London: Allen & Unwin

Wyman, M. (1989) *DP, Europe's Displaced Persons, 1945–1951*, Philadelphia: The Balch Institute Press

PART SIX

MIGRATION IN AFRICA

Was there ever a 'Merrie Africa', a Golden Age when Africans were perfectly integrated into their environments, when cattle lowed, well-fed children played and communities migrated only with the rhythm of the seasons? All societies have such mythological ages and in the USA the 'Afrocentric' political activists of recent years have certainly generated more than an average number of such quasi-fictional re-creations. Yet, one does not have to subscribe to an Afrocentric view of the world to accept that the intrusions by Arabs in East Africa and Europeans elsewhere on the continent disrupted the normal social life of African communities. True, there was a long history of violence, kidnapping, enslavement and, in Islamic areas, judicial support for domestic slavery. But the arrival of external social actors solidified the practice of slavery and accelerated the trade into new directions (Lovejoy 1981: 27–8). Many African communities reacted by getting as far away as possible from the slave-raiders and in so doing started the melancholy history of 'flight migration' with which the African continent continues to be plagued.

The displacement of peoples and their retreat into the interior was accelerated by the commencement of colonialism. The lesser colonial powers – Belgium, Portugal and Germany – were the most brutal in effecting their hegemony. Spurred by Stanley's discovery of forests of rubber in the Congo basin, King Leopold ordered Belgian army detachments to drive the Congolese into gathering rubber. Not for nothing was the crop called 'red rubber', for those who resisted were killed. One contemporary officer (cited Nzula et al. 1979: 23) lamented, 'We whites have to close our eyes to avoid the sight of horrifying corpses. ... We have to block our ears to silence the groans, sobbing and curses from every bush and inch of land'. General von Trotha, who carved out South West Africa for Imperial Germany, was apparently quite happy to look such horrors in the face. To those who had the impertinence to oppose German occupation of their land, he simply declaimed, 'The Herero nation must leave the country. If it does not do so, I shall compel it by force. Inside German territory every Herero tribesman, armed or unarmed, with or without cattle, will be shot' (cited SWAPO 1981: 12). Tens of thousands died from thirst and starvation as they fled; the remnants of the nation were dragooned into forced labour gangs to work for the German state.

The story of Portuguese Africa, covered by *Ishemo*, is but a variant of the Belgian and German cases. The Portuguese state seemed strangely compelled to provide legislative cover for its brazen policy of forced labour. As *Ishemo* notes, the basis for this was laid by a decree in 1875 which simply abolished the category of free labour (*liberto* status) in favour of compelled labour (*serviçal* status). Thanks to this ingenuous legal device, the state and its agents felt quite confident in raising levies for public works and in moving labour from one Portuguese colony to another. In this way, Angolans found themselves effectively used as slave labour in the notorious plantations of São Tomé and Príncipe. So shocked was the Quaker chocolate manufacturer, W. A. Cadbury, at the excesses on these islands that he published (1910) one of the first sustained critiques of the use of forced labour by the Portuguese.

The major consumers of labour supplied by the Portuguese were the mines of the Witwatersrand. The Anglo-Boer War (1899–1902) had virtually brought production to a halt just as the techniques for extraction at deep levels had evolved and the necessary risk capital had been invested. The mine owners were desperate for labour. Local Africans were reluctant to come forward because they initially profited from the market opened up for vegetables and meat. Their drive to independent and even prosperous peasant proprietorship was only halted by political means (Bundy 1979). Chinese workers were imported for a few years but sent home after a political row that rocked the government in Britain. A great part of the solution to the mine owners' dilemma was to be found in Portuguese East Africa.

Mozambique soon become a breeding ground for sleazy labour recruiters who rounded up groups of Africans, often at gunpoint, in order to sell them on for a contracted period to the various mining companies. Often, local chiefs were complicit in this arrangement and were paid to exert customary and more spontaneous forms of compulsion over the reluctant recruits. The Chamber of Mines was uncertain whether this source could be relied on. Wage rates fluctuated, transport and security arrangements were inadequate and officialdom was corrupted by dealing with the rival bids of the contractors. With some exasperation, the mine owners complained, 'at Delagoa Bay everything is done by bribery and everybody from the highest to the lowest takes a bribe' (Levy 1982: 66).

The contribution by *Crush* provides a comprehensive literature review of the ways of understanding how this system of labour circulation evolved to be the largest and most effectively organized in the world. As his own and his colleagues' earlier work (Crush et al. 1991) suggest, the system turned into an 'empire', with the mine owners' own agency, the Witwatersrand Native Labour Association, having to send its buses, trucks, ferries, trains and planes further and further into the interior in order to keep fresh supplies of labour arriving. *Crush* rightly notes that current scholars have begun to emphasize the functionality of the migrant labour system and to de-emphasize the elements of compulsion. Certainly no migrant labour system on that scale could have evolved without some voluntaristic and adaptive elements emerging, or without some part of the supplying societies benefiting from the relationship. However, one should not draw the exaggerated inference that the system was supply-led.

Jeeves deals with the control of migration in general by the apartheid state in the period 1948–89. He shows how the pass laws, the creation of the bantustans and the construction of townships on the edges of the big cities were all part of the government's counter-urbanization policy – which was driven in turn by its general fear of interracial mixing. In practice, the system was not viable. This was largely because the political demands of the white supremacists were in conflict with the labour demands of industry. By 1980, to fulfil the demand for labour, 800,000 workers resident in the 'homelands' were having to commute to the 'white areas' on a daily basis. At the same time, 600,000 pass law arrests were being made annually, thus criminalizing a good proportion of the labour force. With the collapse of apartheid, the homelands were reintegrated into the country and the pass laws were abolished. Undoubtedly, this was an immense step forward for the bulk of the African population whose free labour mobility had been restricted for centuries. However, it would be naive to think that the post-apartheid regime will not face severe difficulties. In the few years since the end of apartheid, squatter settlements have appeared (some on the scale of those around big Latin American cities), rural–urban migration has outstripped employment opportunities and there have been high levels of hostility by local Africans against the million or so displaced persons and economic migrants from other African countries.

Displacement is a common story in many African countries. As *Adepoju* shows, in addition to the normal, seasonal cross-border movements of people, post-independence Africa has triggered mass flows of two kinds. The first arose from what he calls 'the era of mass expulsions', when newly assertive nationalist politicians responded to populist demands to put nationals ahead of 'foreigners'. In situations where claims to citizenship and nationality were in any case poorly documented this often resulted in unjust attacks and roundups of peaceable, long-standing residents. The second form of mass migration resulted from political destabilization and civil war which have afflicted, *inter alia*, Ethiopia, Uganda, Sudan, Angola, Mozambique, Liberia and Somalia. It is difficult to see anything positive about these events, as so many people have been forced to abandon their livelihoods and flee for food and shelter. The only bright side is that most African countries bordering the refugee-generating areas have been conspicuously generous in their admission, recognition and settlement policies. Indeed it is morally instructive to see how open-hearted poor African governments and populations have been compared with their European and American counterparts (Zolberg et al. 1989: 258–82).

The three remaining contributions in this Part concern regional migration patterns, *Gould* covering East Africa, *MacMaster* covering North Africa and *Swindell* covering West Africa. In each case there is a tension between the changes consequent on political independence and the underlying continuities in labour migration derived from the pre-colonial and colonial periods. Whereas *Gould* argues that colonial patterns in Kenya were perpetuated into the post-colonial period, autarky in Tanzania and anarchy in Uganda severely disrupted old migratory flows. *MacMaster*'s account of French North Africa lays most stress on the rupture between the pre-colonial and colonial eras, the latter being marked by French settler migration, insistent demands for temporary and permanent African labour, then, finally, by a gruelling colonial war (1954–62) which precipitated a huge internal migration and the evacuation of many French. In the case of West Africa, as *Swindell* shows, the complexities arising from the normal antinomies of rural–urban, agricultural–industrial and colonial–post-colonial changes were compounded by the hugely uneven development arising from the Nigerian oil boom. Perhaps as many as two to three million non-Nigerians were attracted to the (relatively) high-wage low-cost economy – a movement that ultimately resulted in the Expulsion of Aliens Order in 1983.

African countries show very high rates of internal, regional and international migration, the last being constrained only by the high costs of transport and the fierce determination of European countries and the USA to protect their borders (see discussions in Parts 8 and 14). The high rates are partly because agricultural activities are often extensive, not intensive, but they are also part of the legacy of colonialism. Colonial settlers, mines and European farms and plantations imposed enormous labour demands on African pastoral economies, often threatening their very existence. As I have written elsewhere (Cohen 1985: 188), 'From the point of view of the colonial state, the ideal solution was one in which agricultural production remained sufficiently virile to produce an exportable primary product and to absorb returning migrants, but not so viable that it threatened the supply of cheap unskilled labour.' Such a balance was difficult to maintain anywhere. In apartheid South Africa the government sought to maintain it through brute force. Now, however, the destabilization of the countryside is endemic as civil wars, famine and external military interventions scorch the precious earth. As when Africans fled the slave-raiders and colonial butchers, migration is often not for economic opportunity, but for mere survival.

References

Bundy, Colin (1979) *The Rise and Fall of the South African Peasantry*, London: Heinemann Educational Books

Cadbury, W. A. (1910) *Labour in Portuguese West Africa*, London: Routledge

Cohen, Robin (1985) 'From Peasants to Workers in Africa', in P. C. W. Gutkind and I. Wallerstein (eds.) *Political Economy of Contemporary Africa*, Beverly Hills: Sage, 181–97

Crush, J. et al. (1991) *South Africa's Labor Empire: A History of Black Migrancy to the Gold Mines*, Boulder, CO: Westview Press

Levy, Norman (1982) *The Foundations of the South African Cheap Labour System*, London: Routledge and Kegan Paul

Lovejoy, Paul (1981) *The Ideology of Slavery in Africa*, Beverly Hills: Sage

Nzula, Albert et al. (1979) *Forced Labour in Colonial Africa*, London: Zed Press [first published in Russian in 1933]

SWAPO (1981) *To Be Born a Nation: The Liberation Struggle for Namibia*, London: Zed Press for the Department of Information and Publicity, South West African People's Organization of Namibia

Zolberg, Aristide et al. (1989) *Escape from Violence: Conflict and the Refugee Crisis in the Developing World*, New York: Oxford University Press

FORCED LABOUR AND MIGRATION IN PORTUGAL'S AFRICAN COLONIES

SHUBI L. ISHEMO

The principal feature of the exploitation of labour in the former Portuguese colonies was forced labour. The origins of this lay in the specific characteristics of the Portuguese capitalist formation and the mode of its penetration and accumulation in the colonies. The consequent social formation that this engendered in each colony explains why, in some post-colonial states, labour migration persists as a structural feature of the economy. Thus, throughout the history of Portuguese colonialism, forced labour constituted a form of labour migration and, invariably, labour migration was in effect an attempt to escape from forced labour.

This contribution is concerned with the significance of forced labour and labour migration in Mozambique, Angola, São Tomé and Príncipe, Guinea-Bissau and the Cape Verde islands during the period of Portuguese colonialism. All these colonies displayed similarities and variations. Until the mid-1850s, they were integral to the Portuguese and other European transatlantic slave trade. Mozambique, Angola and Guinea were important sources of slaves for that trade. São Tomé and Príncipe developed as a plantation economy and depended on slave labour from the mainland. Cape Verde developed as a colony of settlement with slaves drawn from the Upper Guinea coast. Both São Tomé and Príncipe, and Cape Verde served as transit points for the transatlantic slave trade. In Mozambique, especially in the Zambezi Valley and Mozambique Island, there were Portuguese settlements. These did not constitute the development of a colonial capitalist economy. Rather, they served as agents of merchant capital, extracting slaves and ivory for export.

Unlike the advanced capitalist powers, Portugal's abolition of the slave trade and slavery in the nineteenth century was not a consequence of a rapidly developing industrial economy. It was the result of diplomatic pressure from Britain. During the period of imperialist rivalry in Africa in the second half of the nineteenth century, Portugal's capitalist formation was backward and incapable of providing financial resources to valorize the economic resources of its colonies. Although two recent studies have sought to elevate Portugal to the status of an imperialist power (Clarence-Smith 1985; Pirio 1982), its economy remained subordinate to those of other European economies, particularly that of Britain. This explains why in colonies such as Mozambique, the role of non-Portuguese European capital was decisive. It also explains why the Portuguese state instituted extra-economic mechanisms as the principal vehicles for capital accumulation (Ishemo 1989; forthcoming).

The first colonial plantation economy was in São Tomé and Príncipe. In 1800 coffee was introduced, later to be followed by cocoa in 1822. Production was on small-scale landholdings dependent on slave labour acquired from the mainland (Hodges and Newitt 1988: 28–9). With the decline of the transatlantic slave trade, especially in the period 1855–75, coffee and cocoa production was increased. This was accompanied by an increased importation and exploitation of slave labour. Attempts were made to develop a plantation economy in southern Angola in the 1840s and 1850s with state-assisted immigration of Portuguese settlers. Here, the colonial state instituted a taxation regime on the African peasantry (Clarence-Smith 1979: 14–15).

Taxation was to constitute the principal weapon for the forced acquisition of labour in all Portuguese colonies. In Mozambique, particularly in the Zambezi Basin, Cape Verde, São Tomé and Príncipe and Angola, the creation of a new social category of *liberto* in 1854, 1858, 1859 and 1869 respectively, was a euphemism for the continuation of slavery. Indeed clandestine importation of Angolan slaves to the São Tomé cocoa and coffee plantations continued (Clarence-Smith 1979; Ishemo forthcoming; Meintel 1984: 70; Tenreiro 1961: 80). From Mozambique, the slave trade continued until the 1890s, cloaked as an indentured labour or *engagé* scheme, to the plantation economies of the French colony of Réunion. This was facilitated by an alliance between Portuguese landowners in Zambézia and French merchants, with the approval of the colonial state.

It was during the 1860s that it became official policy to institute indentured labour from other colonies for the developing plantation economy of São Tomé, with the Cape Verde islands as a principal source of this labour. The case of the Cape Verde islands merits special attention. Despite being the oldest Portuguese colony in Africa, Portugal never took measures to develop a viable economic base to sustain its population. Orchil extraction, small-scale cotton and indigo production, and the household cotton textile industry (dependent on labour extracted from slaves, free peasants and sharecroppers) had, by 1850, declined. This was compounded by the islands' vulnerability to drought, famine and epidemics. Between 1773 and 1776, 50 per cent of the population perished. In the periods 1830–33 and 1863–66, 35 and 40 per cent of the total population respectively died because of famine. The effect of this was twofold. First, some were enticed with promises of food only to be shipped off into slavery by English and French merchants. Second, the state took advantage of the famine to exploit the victims of famine in road construction. A lasting characteristic of the exploitation of famine victims was the colonial state's forcible exportation of Cape Verdian labour to São Tomé and Príncipe. Third, from the mid-nineteenth century, Cape Verdian emigration to the USA began. This was exclusively to New England, where they were treated as indentured servants (Cabral 1971; Matteos 1973; Meintel 1984: 26–48, 58–9).

It was from the 1870s that the foundation of later colonial labour policy was laid. In anticipation of the development of a plantation economy and hence a demand for supplies of labour, the Portuguese state passed a decree in 1875 abolishing *liberto* status and establishing the category of *serviçal* or contract labour. Central to the decree was the provision against 'vagrancy'. 'Vagrancy' came to mean every peasant not absorbed into the sphere of capitalist relations of production. The decree allowed the exploitation of child labour starting from the age of seven. In practice, however, the status of *serviçal* signified the continuation of slavery. Indeed, until 1911 the economies of Angola, São Tomé and Príncipe were characterized by slavery as the principal form of labour. It was highly significant that the decree extended the *serviçal* system by making provision for the transport of labour from one Portuguese colony to another and thus establishing the basis for the future transport of *serviçaes*, first from Mozambique (Zambézia and Nampula), Angola and Cape Verde, to the plantations of São Tomé and Príncipe, and secondly from Cape Verde to Angola. It is important to stress that the provisions of the 1875 labour code were not revoked

but formed the basis of later legislation in the 1890s, and the Salazar policies beginning in the late 1920s.

The use of extra-economic mechanisms to acquire labour for the development of a colonial capitalist economy were a central feature of the Portuguese colonial labour policy. Central to this policy was the imposition of taxation on the African peasantry. It was the decisively singular measure that transformed the African peasantry into forced sellers of labour power (Serra 1980: 49–50). The development of a plantation economy, *latifundia*, public works and a transport infrastructure, particularly in Mozambique and Angola, demanded an uninterrupted supply of cheap and abundant labour. The regulations of the early 1890s, which obliged peasants to pay tax in a combination of money, labour rent or rent in kind, were used by the non-Portuguese European concession companies and Portuguese *latifundistas* as the principal mechanism for capital accumulation. In turn, taxation disrupted the peasantry's production processes and laid the foundation for long-term material insecurity and conditions for frequent outbreaks of famine. Throughout the colonial period the levels of taxation far outstripped the level of wages. Taxation, therefore, was an instrument of forced labour. It created and reproduced conditions for labour migration and seasonal labour. Where and how this labour was exploited depended on the level of capitalist development. Let me briefly examine how this was manifested.

In Mozambique, the use of forced and migrant labour was related to the development of mining and agricultural capital in southern Africa. From the 1880s, southern Mozambican labour was recruited for the Transvaal gold mines. This was later extended to the centre and the north at the beginning of the twentieth century. Similarly, labour was recruited from the centre to the Southern Rhodesian mines and plantations. Protests from plantation companies in the centre and merchants in the south led to the Luso–South African agreement in 1913 to discontinue the export of labour from the north and the centre. Henceforth, contract labour for the Transvaal was restricted to southern Mozambique and labour for Southern Rhodesia was restricted to the central provinces of Tete, Zambézia, Manica and Sofala. Linked to the export of labour was the use of Mozambican ports and railways by South African and Rhodesian capital. The Portuguese state benefited from fees paid for every worker recruited, and deferred wages for workers paid in gold bullion by South Africa and sterling by Southern Rhodesia, but reimbursed in colonial *escudos* to returning workers after deducting tax. This arrangement continued, with periodic review, until independence in 1975 (First 1983; Katzenellenbogen 1982). Throughout the colonial period, Mozambique remained principally a rentier economy within the region dominated by the South African economy.

Between 1880 and 1910, cocoa production in São Tomé and Príncipe was intensified as a result of the concentration of land ownership in the hands of metropolitan Portuguese (backed by metropolitan financial) capital. During this period, Portuguese settlers in Angola took advantage of this and exported 131,446 *serviçaes* to São Tomé (Espirito Santo 1979). International condemnation of this slave traffic prompted plantation companies to turn to Mozambique, Cape Verde, Macau, Liberia, Ghana and Cameroon for labour. The first two became the principal sources. In Mozambique, a São Tomé plantation company leased *Prazo Lugela* in Zambézia and turned it into a labour reservoir. The colonial state also exported labour to São Tomé from Nampula and north-east Zambézia. By 1916, half the labour was from Zambézia and Nampula. Forced transportation of Mozambican labour to São Tomé continued until the early 1970s.

In the twentieth century two factors determined Cape Verdian emigration. First, the recurrent periods of acute drought and famine, which up to 1971 amounted to a total of twenty-one years and claimed 135,000 lives. Second, the colonial state, capital and *latifundia* were tied to planters in São Tomé. As Amilcar Cabral noted, they exploited famine 'on the one hand in order to strengthen their domination and on the other to gather cheap labour – in fact slave labour – which they exported to Angola and São Tomé' (Cabral 1971). It was during famine that the notorious 'vagrancy' laws were strictly applied. Between 1903 and 1970, about 80,000 people were forcibly transported to São Tomé.

By 1973, 75,000 Cape Verdians were employed in the USA, mainly in the cranberry bogs of New England (Matteos 1973; Meintel 1984: 65). Between 1926 and 1960, the economic nationalism of the fascist dictatorship encouraged a weak bourgeoisie to consolidate itself (in alliance with the landed classes) by centralizing and concentrating capital, and through a process of rapid industrialization, especially in textiles. The colonies would facilitate this process by producing cheap raw materials in exchange for manufactured products. Portugal would be able to compete on the world market. Based on the racist premise that Africans were 'lazy' and therefore had a 'moral'

obligation to work, the labour laws of 1928 compelled the peasantry to produce cash crops at very low prices. In central and northern Mozambique, peasants were forced to grow cotton and rice (Isaacman et al. 1980; Vail and White 1980: 272–82, 314–85); in Angola, cotton and tobacco; and in Guinea-Bissau, peanuts (Mendy 1987: 427–39). The repressive state apparatus guaranteed the accumulation of capital. Forced labour, forced cultivation of cash crops and migrant labour were central to this process. Faced with the anti-colonial struggles and protests from the ILO, Portugal abolished forced labour and forced cultivation of crops in 1961.

Between 1961 and 1973 Portuguese colonial capital faced a crisis because production of the principal commodities for export (like cotton and sugar) was declining. To rely on forced labour and forced cultivation of crops as the sole basis of accumulation was no longer feasible (Wuyts 1980). It was during this period that the Portuguese state embarked on restructuring capital. It encouraged the settlement of Portuguese migrants to engage in agricultural production, particularly cotton, coffee, fishing and cattle ranching. In the Angolan regions of Huila and Uige/Cuanza Norte land was expropriated for cattle ranching and coffee plantations respectively. Angolan fishermen were deprived of their living (MPLA 1972: 32–8). Labour shortages led to reactivation of forced recruitment and child labour. Reinforced by taxation and the disruption of their food production, peasants were forced to migrate.

Migration constituted an escape from forced labour. Historically, many Mozambicans migrated to Malawi, Zimbabwe, South Africa and Tanzania; Angolans to Namibia and Zaire; Guineans to Senegal, Guinea-Conakry and the Gambia; and Cape Verdeans to Senegal, Portugal, France, Holland and the USA. The famine of 1972 in the Cape Verde led to workers' strikes, particularly in the strategic Lisnave Wharf. Fearing an uprising, the state forcibly transported workers to Portugal. During the wars of national liberation (1960–75), thousands of Mozambicans, Angolans and Guineans sought refuge in the surrounding countries.

References

Cabral, Amilcar (1971) 'Cape Verde: The Oldest Portuguese Colony in Africa', *World Studies News* (Prague)

Clarence-Smith, W. G. (1979) *Slaves, Peasants and Capitalists in Southern Angola 1840–1926*, Cambridge: Cambridge University Press

(1985) *The Third Portuguese Empire, 1825–1975*, Manchester: Manchester University Press

Espirito Santo, C. (1979) *Contribuicao para a Historia de São Tomé e Principe*, Lisbon

First, R. (1983) *Black Gold: The Mozambican Miner, Proletariat and Peasant*, Sussex: Harvester Press

Hodges, T. and M. Newitt (1988) *São Tomé and Principe: From Plantation Colony to Microstate*, Boulder, CO: Westview Press

Isaacman, Adam et al. (1980) 'A resistencia popular a cultura forcada do algodao em Mocambique', *Noticias*, Maputo, 25 June

Ishemo, S. (1989) 'Forced Labour, Mussoco (Taxation), Famine and Migration in Lower Zambézia, Mozambique, 1870–1914', in A. Zegeye and S. Ishemo (eds) *Forced Labour and Migration: Patterns of Movement within Africa*, London: Hans Zell Publishers, 109–58

— (forthcoming) *The Lower Zambezi Basin in Mozambique, 1850–1920: A Study in Economy and Society*, Aldershot: Avebury

Katzenellenbogen, S. (1982) *South Africa and Southern Mozambique*, Manchester: Manchester University Press

Matteos, S. (1973) 'The Cape Verdeans and the PAIGC Struggle for National Liberation', *Ufahamu* (Winter)

Meintel, D. (1984) *Race, Culture and Portuguese Colonialism in Cabo Verde*, Syracuse: Maxwell School

Mendy, P. (1987) 'Portuguese Colonialism in Africa: The Tradition of Resistance in Guinea-Bissau', Ph.D. thesis, University of Birmingham

MPLA (1972) *Revolution in Angola*, London: Merlin Press

Pirio, G. (1982) 'Commerce, Industry and Empire: The Making of Modern Portuguese Colonialism in Angola and Mozambique, 1890–1914', Ph.D. dissertation, UCLA

Serra, C. (1980) 'O Colonialismo Colonial na Zambézia 1850–1930', *Estudos Moçambicanos*, (1), 33–52

Tenreiro, F. (1961) *A Ilha de São Tomé*, Lisbon: Junta de Investigaçoes do Ultramar 7

Vail, L. and L. White (1980) *Capitalism and Colonialism in Mozambique: A Study of Quelimane District*, London: Heinemann

Wuyts, M. (1980) 'Economia Política do Colonialismo em Moçambique', *Estudos Moçambicanos*, (1), 9–22

THE POLITICS OF INTERNATIONAL MIGRATION IN POST-COLONIAL AFRICA

ADERANTI ADEPOJU

Since independence, several African countries have experienced recurrent internal instability and ethnic or related conflicts resulting in population displacements. Indeed, contemporary migration in Africa (voluntary or forced, internal or international) is best understood in the context of the political and historical evolution of African societies, and of the current economic crises, ecological disasters and ongoing political events in the region. The combination of wars, civil unrest and the way both super powers (the former USSR and the USA) pursued their global interests in Africa generated both 'economic' migrants and refugees (including internally displaced persons).

This contribution focuses on the political experiences of post-independence sub-Saharan Africa and how these have triggered various movements and displacements of persons. Examples of massive expulsion of aliens in Ghana and Nigeria, refugee movements occasioned by the disintegration of Liberia, and conflicts in Somalia are reviewed.

The Organization of Africa Unity (OAU) introduced two important elements into the African migration scene: first, it broadened the definition of refugees to include internally displaced persons; second, it agreed on the inviolability of frontiers of member states inherited at independence, even when such arbitrary borders cut across homogeneous ethnic, linguistic and cultural groups.

It has been suggested that the siting of the OAU headquarters in Addis Ababa and Haile Salassie's strong personal influence and interest in the OAU's orientation, its doctrine of non-interference in the internal affairs of member states and the inviolability of existing boundaries were perhaps designed with Eritrea's situation in view (*West Africa*, April 1993). The other members were also mindful of potential seccessionist problems in their respective countries. As will become obvious below, some of these doctrines were put to the test in the case of Liberia and the long-running boundary disputes between Senegal and Mauritania, in Ethiopia, Somalia, Nigeria and Cameroon and a host of other cases.

Political independence and regulations governing inter-country movements

The attainment of independence in Africa, especially during the late 1950s and early 1960s, brought a new dimension to the significance of international boundaries. The new national governments, anxious to identify their own national territories as sovereign and independent states, adopted various measures to reduce the flow of immigrants as a whole, and limit entry to authorized immigrants who were admitted on the basis of their special skills (Addo 1982; Adepoju 1983b). These include the Employment of Visitors Act (1968) and Immigration Act (1966) in Botswana; the Immigration Act (1963) in Nigeria; an act of 1962 in Gabon to regulate the admission and stay of foreign nationals there; and the Immigration Quota System and issue of work permits in Sierra Leone designed to discourage the inflow of unskilled or unqualified persons into the country for the purpose of taking up employment. In Sudan, the Passport and Immigration Act (1960) and Manpower Act of 1974, the Immigration Act (1972) in Tanzania and the Immigration and Deportation Act in Zambia are similar examples (Adepoju 1983a; Ahooja-Patel 1974).

These laws and regulations governing the conditions for entry, residence and employment of non-nationals, the elaborate development of visa and passport regulations, customs and controls, and the need for 'foreign' workers to obtain work permits ushered in a period of restrictions on the free movement of persons across Africa; these were also aimed at preserving available employment opportunities for nationals in fulfilment of electoral promises. For once, also, the enactment of indigenization measures placed restrictions on the participation of aliens in major economic activities, and a distinction was made between legal and illegal aliens based on proof of nationality, passports, visa, residence and work permits which were hitherto irrelevant to the immigrants (Adepoju 1983a; ECA 1981).

It is often argued that national boundaries drawn by

colonialists paid little regard to the socio-cultural realities of the countries concerned. As a result, many ethnic groups found themselves split by international boundaries, especially the Yoruba (Nigeria/Benin), Ewe (Ghana/Togo), Kakwa (Uganda/Sudan/Zaire), the Somali ethnic stock (Kenya/Somalia/Djibouti/ Ethiopia), the Mende, Vais and Kroos (Liberia/Sierra Leone), the Makonde (Mozambique/Tanzania) and the Hausa-Fulani (Nigeria/Niger). Where ethnic groups live on both sides of national borders, as in the examples above, the people regard movements within their cultural realm as part of their normal life routine, but without travel documents they are seen as illegal 'international migrants', especially since their respective governments attained political independence. Such movements remain largely undocumented, for many such tribal people resent or ignore the boundaries they regard as a foreign imposition. At any rate, they cannot understand the meaning and relevance of international boundaries and other concepts like nationality, passports or visas (Adepoju 1983b). Indeed, the problem of how to classify 'aliens' or 'illegals' in countries with close ethnic and cultural ties is not easily resolved.

For one thing, the elaborate rules and regulations referred to above are hardly enforced or enforceable: the large porous borders, virtually uncontrolled and in fact unpoliceable by national governments, facilitate unretarded movement of 'illegal' immigrants along several bush paths. Even where control posts are mounted, the laxity and corrupt practices of immigration officials, who often collude with illegal immigrants to gain entry, considerably hinder effective implementation of these regulations. In any case, few nationals have easy access to national passports; others leave their countries illegally, thereby entering the host countries illegally (Adepoju 1988).

It was also widely held in political circles that a large-scale influx of 'undocumented' migrants could pose serious social, economic, political and even diplomatic problems for the receiving country and strain friendly relations with the sending countries. Ironically, such feelings gained ground even as attempts were made to forge a continental cohesion in a pan-Africanist strategy. In circumstances where 'undocumented' migrants are confined to a marginal existence, are involved in criminal activities, or where members of an opposition party flee into neighbouring countries and plot the otherthrow of their home government, relations between erstwhile good neighbours can be seriously strained. Togo and Ghana

(where the Ewe opposition groups in Togo are readily absorbed and, some say, assisted by the Ewes in Ghana) provide a good example.

The era of mass expulsions

Expulsions and deportation are common policy measures directed at illegal migrants in Africa as illustrated by the waves of expulsions of non-nationals from Sierra Leone (1968), the Côte d'Ivoire (1958, 1964), Ghana (1969), Chad (1979), Uganda (1972), Zambia (1971), Equatorial Guinea (1974), Zaire (1970, 1973), Kenya (1977, 1978–81), Senegal (1967, 1990), Cameroon (1967), Guinea (1968), Nigeria (1983, 1985) and Liberia (1983).

To illustrate with a few examples: In the late 1950s, the Côte d'Ivoire expelled more than a thousand migrants of Togo and Benin origin; Chad had also expelled illegal migrants from Benin. The mid-1960s was an era of mass expulsion by several countries: the Côte d'Ivoire expelled about 16,000 Beninoise; Senegal expelled Ghanaians from its borders; 800 Nigerians were expelled from Cameroon, Sierra Leone and Guinea while the Côte d'Ivoire expelled Ghanaian fishermen. In 1964, the Zaire government 'expelled' Rwandese refugees after they participated in the Mulelist uprisings in the country. In 1978, Burundi expelled 40,000–50,000 Zaireans, mostly Bembe refugees, from the 1964 Mulelist rebellion, and jobless migrant workers. In apparent retaliation Zaire quickly evicted Burundian Hutu refugees from the farms on which the UNHCR had earlier settled them in 1974 on the grounds that these were needed for the returnees (Zolberg et al. 1989).

Late in 1969, the enforcement of the Compliance Order in Ghana (which requested all aliens who did not possess a residence permit to obtain one within two weeks or leave the country) resulted in an estimated 500,000 expellees especially Nigerians, Nigeriens and Voltaïcs. In 1971, Zambia expelled all aliens – about 150,000 nationals of Zimbabwe, Botswana, Zaire, Tanzania and Somalia – without valid work permits. In December 1982, Sierra Leone expelled members of the Foulah community, and in September Ghana closed its Togo border. The expulsion of about 50,000 Asians from Uganda in 1972 is the most dramatic so far in East Africa. The collapse of the East African Community also triggered off the wave of expulsions of 'aliens'. Soon after (1979), Kenya expelled about 400 Community workers (Tanzanians and Ugandans) from Nairobi with their families (numbering about 2000 persons all together). Again in 1979, 2400 Ugandans who had no valid documentation were expelled from Kenya. These included refugees who fled from Uganda during Amin's regime. In late 1980 and early 1981, about 2000 Tanzanians working in the informal sector in Kenya were expelled. In October 1982, thousands of Banyarwanda were literally expelled from Uganda (Addo 1982; Adepoju 1983a, 1983b). The latter incident, like similar cases in Africa, finds its root causes in the post-independence politics of suppression (Winter 1983).

The expulsion of Guineans from Sierra Leone in December 1982 is explained in part by worsening economic conditions and rising unemployment (migrants competing for the unskilled jobs nationals scorn). Besides, immigrants relocate in the urban areas where problems of housing, jobs and transport are already endemic. The more than 500,000 aliens, mostly Nigerians, but also Togolese, Beninoise and Malians, expelled from Ghana in 1969 were accused of posing a threat to the economic survival of the country. The government, frightened by the existence of about 600,000 registered unemployed persons, hoped that the expulsion of aliens would relieve the situation. Officials also charged that the country's ailing balance of payment was worsened by the remittances of migrant labourers and traders, and by aliens engaged in smuggling minerals, especially diamonds (Adamako-Sarfoh 1974).

Aliens are usually scapegoats when governments are confronted with teething economic and political problems. The Nigerian situation illustrates this vividly. In 1981, described as the golden age of immigration into Nigeria by ECOWAS citizens, 90 per cent of the residence permits issued, reissued or replaced in that year were in fact for Ghanaians alone (Adepoju 1988). However, the economic situation had deteriorated so much that the military government (which had taken over power by the end of 1983) itself embarked on mass retrenchment of workers in the public sector on account of old age, low or declining productivity or inefficiency, among several other measures. The private sector was ordered to follow this line of action. As all sectors of the economy slumped, thousands lost their jobs. The pay restraint was reintroduced at a time when the cost of living rose sharply.

The government imposed an employment freeze and private sector employers retrenched their workers on a large scale. Anti-alien sentiments built up and on 18 January 1983, illegal aliens were given two weeks to leave the country. The precise number of aliens affected by the quit order may not be known. It is estimated that about 1.5 million were expelled: 700,000 Ghanaians, 180,000 Nigeriens, 120,000 Cameroonians, 150,000 Togolese and 5000 Beninoise are among the bigger groups (Adepoju 1983a, 1983b).

The expulsion of illegals from Nigeria in January 1983 and again in 1985 can better be understood within the context of the provisions of the Protocol on Free Movements and the prevailing economic situation and political climate in the country. The expulsion was targeted at immigrants who entered the country illegally – with no valid documents or visas – and particularly at those illegal immigrants with no skills and without viable jobs. Illegal immigrants who were in gainful employment were given the opportunity to regularize their stay in the country: their employers were required to apply for an expatriate quota to enable the aliens to obtain the necessary residence permits (Adepoju 1988).

It was widely speculated that the Nigerian government's quit order of January 1983 derived partly from a fear of the possible effects of large numbers of undocumented aliens on voting patterns, violence and civil disorder during the bitterly contested general election later that year (Adepoju 1983a). This is premised on the notion that the presence of large numbers of aliens, desperate for any means of livelihood, provides a ready reserve of recruits for public disorder and other subversive activities. Thus, in Ghana during Nkrumah's regime, the deportation of Mosi migrants of Upper Volta (now Burkina Faso) origin who expressed support for the opposition party was a measure to pre-empt potential subversion of the government (Peil 1974). The riots in Kano in northern Nigeria in 1980 and 1982, in which illegal immigrants from five West African countries were allegedly strongly involved, is an example of the security risk aliens sometimes constitute (Adepoju 1983a).

Where illegal immigration occurs on a large scale and the participation of such immigrants in economic activities is thought to compete with that of natives, as is the case of Nigerians in Ghana prior to their expulsion in 1969 and of Ghanaians in Nigeria prior to 1983, they become targets of hostility from the native population and are blamed for whatever economic, social and political problems arise in the country. Such expulsions are often justified on the argument that illegal aliens were aggravating the host country's economic conditions: in few cases were aliens expelled on the basis of the illegality of their status (Adepoju 1983b).

In most cases the justification for expelling aliens was the deteriorating economy of the host country;

however, this is often expressed politically in terms of the legality of the aliens' residence. Thus the political consideration merely translates into action on the economic crisis and has led governments concerned to pass laws to enforce registration of aliens who are often required to possess special identity cards (for example in the Côte d'Ivoire since 1991).

Totalitarian regimes and refugee flows

In the early to mid-1970s, the oppressions characteristic of the foreign dominated areas of Africa — Guinea Bissau, Rhodesia (now Zimbabwe), Angola, Namibia, Mozambique, South Africa — were a principal cause of refugees and internally displaced persons. Rather than stemming the wave of refugees, the attainment of independence in these countries in some cases exacerbated it, as in the prolonged civil wars in Angola and Mozambique (Adepoju 1982). The post-independence experiences of Liberia and Somalia are provided as case studies of refugee flows.

Political destabilization and civil strife in Ethiopia, Zaire, Togo, Uganda, Sudan, Angola, Mozambique and Liberia have severely eroded meagre developmental gains. Dictatorial regimes have degenerated into police states with severe abuse of human rights. Intellectuals, students and union leaders are invariably targets for harassment and intimidation (Adepoju 1991). Political instability in Ethiopia and the dictatorial regime in Uganda spurred massive emigration of highly skilled professionals. In Uganda, for example, more than half the high-level professional and technical personnel emigrated during Amin's prolonged iron rule (Adepoju 1991). The political fragility and instability of governments compounded the stressful socio-economic situation, which fuelled the exodus of high-level manpower.

Liberia

The history of Liberia, a settler state, has, since its inception in 1822, been 'filled with ironies, inequities, lofty ideals and base realities' (Rutz 1992). The first republic on the African continent since 1847, Liberia's settlement separates it from the rest of Africa in several respects. Unlike the situation in eastern and southern Africa, where the dominant settler groups were Europeans, 'the Liberian settler state was founded, controlled and dominated by a black elite' (Fahnbulleh Jr 1993). The nation that emerged was neither truly African nor western. The Americo-Liberian settlers exerted absolute control over the country's economic, political and social life. Though they initially constituted only 5 per cent of the country's population, they held themselves apart from the indigenous Africans 'whom they regarded as inferior and uncivilized' (Rutz 1992). Over the next century, the gulf between both groups widened.

With mistrust and suspicion ripe on both sides the basis for cooperation faltered. The narrow social base of the political elite was bent on maintaining domination and the mass of indigenous people were excluded from economic and political participation. As late as 1930, the League of Nations accused the Liberian government of 'promoting a form of slavery ... and ... making no effort to improve the lot of the indigenous population' (Rutz 1992).

As the deprived rural dwellers flooded the towns to participate in the modern economy, they became easy converts to mass movements demanding radical changes. The rice riot of 14 April 1979 was met by a massive show of force by the government. The tense political situation led to a military coup in 1980 whose plotters later allied with leaders of the mass movement. It was widely believed that the social injustices meted out to the marginalized indigenous population by the Americo-Liberians and the subsequent marginalization of the former in the scheme of things, coupled with corruption and mismanagement by the political elites, spelt the doom for the elite class.

The brutality that followed the military takeover culminated in a brazen dictatorship, the dismissal of the representatives of mass movements and a rigged election in 1985. Hence, by the time the National Patriotic Front of Liberia (NPFL) struck in December 1989, Liberians were psychologically prepared to use force against the dictator, Doe. The tyrannical and insensitive rule of Doe's regime led to the deaths of thousands of Liberians and the exile of many more. Today Liberia is a divided country.

Beginning in trickles in late 1989, Liberian refugees began to flee across the borders to neighbouring Guinea Conakry, Sierra Leone and Côte d'Ivoire. During the last week of December 1989 and early January 1990, 13,000 Liberian refugees entered Guinea Conakry; the number had swelled to 80,000 by mid-February 1990 and to 438,000 by end of the year. According to the USCR (1991), Guinea received the 'single largest new refugee influx in Africa during 1990'. Similarly, from 55,000 in late December 1989 and early January 1990, the Liberian refugees in the Côte d'Ivoire rose to 270,000 by December 1990. This influx coincided with 'increased social and political tensions in Côte d'Ivoire, a country that for years has been among the most prosperous and stable on the West African coast' (USCR 1991).

The initial stream of 20,000 Liberian refugees who entered Sierra Leone in May swelled to 125,000 between June and September 1990. The rebel incursion by the NFPL into Sierra Leone, initially apparently to revenge Sierra Leone's support to ECOMOG, led to the uprooting of 145,000 internally displaced persons while 169,000 refugees fled to Guinea (USCR 1992).

With more than 730,000 refugees, in 1990 Liberia is reputed to have produced the largest new outflow of refugees. Overall, by the end of 1991, there were more than 663,000 Liberian refugees in West African countries: 8000 in Ghana, 1000 in Nigeria, 397,000 in Guinea, 240,000 in Côte d'Ivoire, 7200 in Freetown and another 10,000 in other locations in Sierra Leone. Several thousand others were brutally murdered (USCR 1992). In addition, over 500,000 persons were displaced within the country. These have fled their home areas to Monrovia where security was relatively better. Thus 1,260,000 persons, or more than one half of the population of Liberia, were uprooted by the civil war. As the war gradually spilled over to Sierra Leone, thousands of Liberian refugees located there returned to Monrovia.

The inability to find a political solution to the crisis is evident in the series of breakdowns of ceasefire agreements, thereby generating even more refugees. In the meantime, the Sierra Leone-based ULIMO (United Liberation Movement for Democracy) entered the fratricidal war, further swelling the number of refugees and internally displaced persons.

Somalia

At independence in July 1960, the former British and Italian Somalilands merged to form a new nation which, by African standards, was relatively homogeneous: the Somali speak the same language, practise similar cultural traditions and have the same religion (Harsch 1993). A quarter of Somalia's population are settled farmers, but cultivation is confined to only 1.6 per cent of the total land area. Another half are nomadic pastoralists. However, the livestock and crop sectors are highly vulnerable: on average 'moderate droughts occur every three to four years and major ones every eight to ten years' (Harsch 1993). However, there were large concentrations of Somali speakers in neighbouring countries (Kenya, Djibouti and Ethiopia). Claims to these areas by Somalia, especially the Ogaden region in Ethiopia, led to the bitter war of 1977/8, which Ethiopia won. The Ogaden comprises about one-fifth of the Ethiopian territory 'ceded to Ethiopia in the late nineteenth

century by colonialists'. In the process several thousands were killed or rendered homeless (Gallagher and Martin 1992).

Despite the apparent ethnic homogeneity (i.e. by African standards) one does not need to scratch far beneath the surface to unveil the deep divisions between the clans, subclans and families that traditionally inhabit specific territories: the Dir, Isaaq and Darod in the north/north-west, Hawiye in the centre, Darod and Rahanwein/Dighel in south-west. Elders and chiefs of these clans wielded considerable authority and influence.

During the first decade of independence up to sixty political parties mushroomed, based largely on clan or subclan allegiances. The coup that brought Bare to power in 1969 put paid to these parties; he forced a single-party state based on socialist ideologies on the people and, in his obsession to recover the Somali-inhabited areas of the neighbouring countries, took advantage of cold war alignments (Harsch 1993).

The war of Ogaden (1977/8) triggered the first wave of refugees into Somalia. Estimates of refugees vary from 80,000 (UNHCR's figures) to 500,000 (government figures). By 1981, the refugee figure rapidly climbed to between 450,000 and 620,000. Another 450,000 refugees from the Ogaden relocated in Djibouti (Zolberg et al. 1989). The severe drought of 1980 displaced several thousand others.

Clan relations were severely strained by the resettlement of thousands of Ogadeni refugees from the Isaaq clan in Ethiopia and the unsuccessful coup to oust Bare in 1978. Bare moved to stifle dissent and vested political authority in his own clan and in those of his closest relatives. The Darod, Ogaden, Marchan, Dulbahante and other clans grew resentful and mobilized in opposition, despite the growing official intolerance of dissent (Harsch 1993). Several Somalis in exile formed the Somali National Movement in 1981, followed in 1988–90 by several other clan-based political factions or armed groups: the Somali Salvation Democratic Front among the Mijjerteyn subclan of the Darod; the Somali Democratic Movement of the Rahanwein-Dighil; and USC among the Hawiye. These developments set the stage for the fracticidal war into which Somalia plunged in later years and which completely devastated the country. At the time of the Addis Ababa meeting in January 1993, fourteen political movements participated.

The current Somali crisis is intricately rooted in a 'devasting combination of conflict, drought and political anarchy' (RPG 1992). After two decades of oppressive rule backed initially by the USSR and later by the USA, and years of civil conflict, Siad Bare was overthrown in January 1991. Several political parties based on clans and subclans emerged and took control of sections of the country: the political disintegration impacted severely on the social integration of traditional communities.

By the end of 1992 Somali refugees in Kenya were clustered around Mombasa (45,000), Liboi (45,000) Ifo, Dagabaley and Hagadera in the east (from 35,000 to 40,000 each), and Mandera (50,000) in the north (RPG 1992). It is believed by observers that Kenya's reluctance to accept Somali refugees rests on three concerns. The first is that Somali refugees have settled in 'some of the environmentally fragile parts of the country, causing concern about ecological damage' because these sites are poorly endowed with water. The second is that some of the locations near the border, especially Mandera, are politically sensitive. To reinforce this suspicion, successive Somali governments had earlier laid claim to this area as part of greater Somalia. As a result, Kenyan officials are afraid of a spillover of Somalia's clan rivalries into their country. To compound these problems are Kenya's own drought-affected zones – the worst in recent history. Apart from the more than 412,000 registered and 100,000 unregistered refugees (mostly from Somalia but some also from Sudan and Ethiopia) the drought also generated hundreds of internally displaced persons (RPG 1992).

Conclusion

Africa is home to the bulk of the world's refugees and internally displaced persons. The solutions to the refugee situation are to be found increasingly in the political rather than the economic sphere. The promotion and restoration of peace where war and armed conflicts prevail (Sudan, Somalia, Angola, Liberia) and where the process of democratization is fraught with disturbances and civil unrest (Togo, Zaire), as well as the promotion of economic and social justice and good governance, require the strongest resolve of African governments as much as pressure from the international community. Insofar as the refugee situation in Africa is as much traceable to abject poverty, political intolerance and tyranny as to ecological disasters and the like, assistance to Africa (home to more than two-fifths, some say one-half of the world's refugees and internally displaced persons)

is not only humanitarian but essential to world peace and development.

References

Adamako-Sarfoh, J. (1974) 'The Effects of the Expulsion of Migrant Workers on Ghana's Economy with particular reference to the Cocoa Industry', in S. Amin (ed.), *Modern Migrations in Western Africa*, London: Oxford University Press

Addo, N. O. (1982) 'Government Induced Transfers of Foreign Nationals', in J. I. Clarke and L. A. Kosinski (eds) *Distribution of Population in Africa*, Heinneman: London

Adepoju, A. (1982) 'The Refugee Situation in the Horn of Africa and Sudan', *Issue: Journal of Opinion*, 12 (1, 2)

—— (1983a) 'Illegals and Expulsion in Africa: The Nigerian Experience', *International Migration Review*, 18 (3)

—— (1983b) 'Undocumented Migration in Africa: Trends and Policies', *International Migration*, 21 (2)

—— (1988) 'Labour Migration and Employment of ECOWAS Nationals in Nigeria', in T. Fashoyin (ed.) *Labour and Development in Nigeria (Essays in Honour of Ukandi G. Damachi)*, Lagos: Landmark Publications Ltd

—— (1991) 'South–North Migration: The African Experience', *International Migration*, 29 (2)

Ahooja-Patel, K. (1974) 'Regulations Governing the Employment of Non-Nationals in West Africa', in S. Amin (ed.) *Modern Migrations in Western Africa*, London: Oxford University Press

ECA (1981) *International Migration: Population Trends and their Implications for Africa (African Population Studies Series No. 4)*, Addis Ababa: Economic Commission for Africa

Fahnbulleh Jr, H. B. (1993) 'Liberia's Struggle for Democracy', *West Africa*, 8–12 March, 15–21 March, 22–28 March

Gallagher, D. and S. F. Martin (1992) *The Many Faces of the Somali Crisis: Humanitarian Issues in Somalia, Kenya and Ethiopia*, Washington DC: Refugee Policy Group

Harsch, E. (1993) *Somalia: Restoring Hope (Africa Recovery Briefing Paper No.7)*, 15 January, New York: United Nations

Peil, M. (1974) 'Ghana's Aliens', *International Migration Review*, 88 (3)

RPG (1992) *Internally Displaced Persons in Africa: Assistance Challenges and Opportunities*, Washington DC: Refugee Policy Group

Rutz, H. A. (1992) *Uprooted Liberians: Casualities of a Brutal War*, Washington DC: US Committee for Refugees

UNHCR (1990) 'Refugees: Towards 1990', *Refugees and around the World*, 71, December, Geneva

USCR (1991) *World Refugee Survey: 1989 in Review*, Washington: US Committee for Refugees

—— (1992) *World Refugee Survey: 1992*, Washington: US Committee for Refugees

Winter, R. P. (1983) 'Refugees in Uganda and Rwanda: The Banyarwanda Tragedy', in USCR *World Refugee Survey 1983* (USCR 25th Anniversary Issue), Washington DC

Zolberg, A. R. et al. (1989) *Escape from Violence: Conflict and the Refugee Crisis in the Developing World*, Oxford: Oxford University Press

CHEAP GOLD: MINE LABOUR IN SOUTHERN AFRICA

JONATHAN CRUSH

Since the late nineteenth century, hundreds of thousands of young black migrants have crossed into South Africa to work on that country's gold and coal mines. Most were recruited through a far-flung network of rural offices whose influence reached deep into Angola on the west coast, and Tanzania on the east (Map 3). There they signed the legal contracts that whisked them southwards and guaranteed their return many months later. A centralized recruiting agency with two branches – the Witwatersrand Native Labour Association (WNLA) and the Native Recruiting Corporation (NRC) – manned these depots. The depots were also conduits for the repatriation of wages into the countryside, reducing the incentive of families to follow their breadwinners to town. The recruiting agencies operated an elaborate transport infrastructure of ferries, trucks, trains and, latterly, planes to move the migrants south. Caught in a web of legal and extra-legal controls on their movement, miners were forced to live in regimented, austere, single-sex barracks known as compounds or hostels. They were joined there by migrant workers recruited in a similar manner from within South Africa itself.

Mine life was brutal and dangerous. Between 1945 and 1984, over 50,000 miners died on the mines. Others – some 110,000 between 1972 and 1976 alone – were seriously injured or permanently disabled. The workforce was also regularly decimated by occupational disease such as tuberculosis and pneumonia (Baker 1989; Packard 1990). Wages were low and did not rise at all in real terms between 1910 and 1970.

What possessed men to work in such conditions and for so little apparent reward? Early answers to this question focused on the paltry benefits of migrancy. These were elevated to the status of 'bright lights' which appealed to workers in search of quick money or to warriors wishing to test their manhood (van Onselen 1975). Marxist critics focused instead on the deeply coercive character of this labour system (Innes 1984; Johnstone 1976; Lacey 1981; Levy 1982). Dispossessed of land, heavily taxed and deprived of alternative sources of income, rural workers had no choice. Without cheap labour there could be no cheap gold. Migrant labour was inexpensive, unskilled, disposable and subsidized by rural producers. When cheap labourers attempted to raise the price of participation through strike action or unionization, the state and the mining companies ruthlessly crushed all opposition (Moodie 1986).

More recent studies of labour migration in southern Africa have questioned this 'forced labour' model of unremitting repression (Crush et al. 1991; Dubow 1989; Duncan 1993; Greenberg 1987; James 1992a; Jeeves 1985; Lipton 1985). They argue that the model ignores conflict over the character of migrancy within the South African state, between different employers and their recruiters, and among the various supplier states. One reason that migrancy has persisted so long is the interests in the supplier areas that benefit from its perpetuation. The forced labour model also turns effects into causes. Migrant labour was cheap and exploitable, but this does not explain why the system came into being nor the tensions and instabilities that compromised its reliability (Crush 1992a). The model reduces black miners to the status of passive victims of corporate control and women to faceless subsidizers of cheap male labour in the rural reserves (Walker 1990). In fact, from the first, the individual and collective actions of miners and their dependants shaped the very character of the migrant labour system (Beinart 1982; Crush 1987; First 1983; Harries forthcoming; Moodie forthcoming).

Debating migrancy

At its inception mine migrancy was very much a part-time enterprise. Workers generally only went to the mines when they could not find other work. Some used the mines as a staging-post for more permanent urban employment. Others interspersed irregular periods of mine employment with equally irregular sojourns at home. Many died young. Those who did not retired early. Desertion was the only weapon that many workers had to protest against unacceptable conditions and they used it often. As a result, the mines' labour system became a labour empire. Like most empires, it endured because it could expand

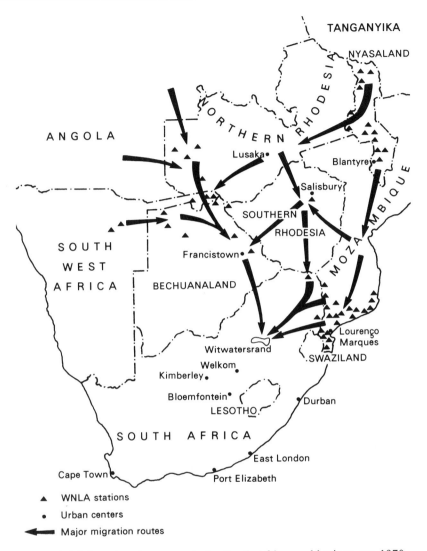

MAP 3: Major migration routes to the South African gold mines, pre-1970.

(Crush et al. 1991: 10–11). In their search for workers who had no other choices, who would work for the wages on offer, and who were inclined to work for longer periods and desert less, the mines rejected the promise of stabilized labour and expanded instead into ever-more remote regions (Jeeves 1986; Jeeves and Crush 1992). In the 1970s, when the mines' northern labour empire began to disintegrate, the mines ransacked new domestic sources in order to sustain the system (Crush et al. 1991: 101–50). Despite the shifts of the 1970s and 1980s, some 40 per cent of gold miners still come from outside South Africa. After 1987, when the low gold price precipitated mass

retrenchments in the mining industry (180,000 workers to mid-1993), South African workers were hardest hit.

By the early twentieth century, migrant labour to the South African gold mines had become a particularly enduring and entrenched way of life for many rural communities in the region. Whole areas came to depend on migrant remittances for their survival, rural social and family structures were deeply marked by the impress of migrancy, and many rituals and cultural practices had migrancy at their centre (Beinart 1982, 1987; Chirwa 1992; First 1983; Mayer 1980; Murray 1981). In the 1980s, with massive regional

PLATE 10: Miners destined for the South African gold mines with their tin trunks board a plane operated by the Witwatersrand Native Labour Association, the recruiting body of the mines.

unemployment, a mine job became a prized possession. The result is the 'career miner' who now works continuously or forfeits his job. This phenomenon – known variously as stabilization, commuter migrancy or inflexible migrancy – has exacted a heavy toll on miners' health and shut out a whole generation of new workseekers who could once count on a mine job, if nothing else (Crush et al. 1991: 151–76).

The entrenched character of migrancy makes it particularly difficult for policy-makers to envision concrete alternatives to the present system. Yet debate about the future of migrancy is almost as old as the system itself. In the late nineteenth and early twentieth centuries, the future of mine labour aroused great controversy in South Africa and Europe (Jeeves 1985; Richardson 1982). In the 1920s, the International Labour Organization took up the issue, a concern which persisted until well into the 1980s (Böhning 1981). Ironically, the ILO withdrew exactly when its

input was needed most. Within South Africa, the 1948 Fagan Commission debated the question of mine migrancy at great length, as did successive apartheid commissions – including Froneman in 1961, du Randt in 1975, Riekert in 1979 and Wiehahn in 1981 (Ashforth 1990). Outside South Africa, the frontline states placed the issue on their political agenda in the late 1970s and formed an ultimately ineffectual body to formulate a common policy (Crush 1991). All of these politicians, commissioners and advocates shared a common disregard for the voice of the workers themselves. Everyone claimed the right to speak on their behalf.

Since 1990, there has been renewed debate about the future of migrancy. Should it be abolished – and, if so, how and at what cost to the source regions? If migrancy continues, should it be 'internalized' since 200,000 fewer jobs for foreigners mean 200,000 more for unemployed South Africans? Should migrants be subject to the same draconian controls of the past and, if not, how best can these abuses be stopped? Should the hostels be dismantled and, if so, what should they be replaced with and who will pay for the alternatives?

How these highly politicized questions are resolved has very real implications for the miners and their dependants as well as their home communities. As in the past, all too little effort is expended on trying to ascertain what migrancy means for the migrant and his dependants, what they think about its abolition, and how they are responding to its erosion on the ground. Regardless of the policy-makers, migrant men and women are already reshaping the migrant labour system in important new ways (Moodie and Ndatshe 1992).

In 1986, the Anglo American Corporation (South Africa's largest and most powerful mining house) finally surveyed its workforce and triumphantly declared that over 50 per cent of the total mine workforce wished to remain migrant, as if this somehow justified the whole panoply of restrictions that make the migrant's lifestyle so unenviable (Crush and James 1991). When the National Union of Mineworkers (NUM) asked its membership virtually the same question and received almost the same answer, it quickly downplayed the results (James 1992b). Nonetheless, the ANC and NUM softened their hard-line on migrancy and pressed instead for a more humane and participatory system that recognizes the variable needs and aspirations of different groups of miners.

Though the mining houses are among the most reactionary employers in the country, they are cognizant of the last decade's relative shifts in power both within their industry and outside it (James 1992a). As the hostels were turned by workers into a site for organization and resistance, so mine managers began to consider moving workers into property which they owned (James 1990; Moodie, forthcoming).

When costs of sustaining the industry's elaborate recruiting apparatus began to outweigh the benefits, recruiting offices closed and whole regions were ousted from the system. When the rural poor trampled over the last vestiges of influx control and took up residence in the urban periphery, mine managers were alive to the advantages of employing labour closer to home (Crush and James 1991). As the social and health costs of virtually continuous hostel living began to mount, they started to consider rearranging the mine to accommodate family living.

Migrant labour is no longer as cheap as it was, but the alternatives still seem prohibitively expensive.

Anglo American instituted a much-publicized home ownership programme for black miners in 1987. There were fewer than 5000 buyers so, in 1992, the company shut it down (Laburn-Peart 1992). Given the alternatives, migrancy is still functional. Sacked and retrenched workers are quickly dispersed throughout the rural periphery making solidarity impossible. An ethnically divided workforce is still useful in the micro-politics of hostel governance. Mine owners still believe in an inherent connection between ethnicity and skill (Guy and Thabane 1988; James 1992a; Moodie 1992). Considerable effort is therefore devoted to ironing out the imperfections in the system. This is particularly evident in the application of computer technology to regulate the labour needs of the industry and to control workers on the mines (Crush 1992b). Managers foresee a more diversified workforce, but they expect (and want) migrancy to remain.

Migrants speak

The reshaping of the migrant labour system since 1970 has not, however, been the sole prerogative of management. In the 1980s, for the first time since the 1940s, the country's black miners had an institutional voice in the NUM. In the first five years of its existence, the NUM grew faster than any other union in the world and made dramatic gains in articulating the needs and aspirations of its membership (Crush 1989). Since the twin blow of the 1987 strike and massive (and continuing) retrenchments, the union's achievements have been less impressive. Many of the workers retrenched since 1987 have completely lost contact with the union (Seidman 1993). Not all workers are unionized (some 40 per cent remain outside the NUM fold) and the union, by its very nature, can only speak for its members in certain ways and on certain issues. British labour historian Vic Allen's (1992) official NUM-authorized history of black mineworkers is based on a limited range of documentary sources only. As a result, argues Wilmot James (1992c: 146), Allen lays a 'confining grid' over the rich cultural history of mineworker experience.

Recent attempts to break this grid and map the character of migrant culture mark a decisive shift in the historiography of South African mine labour away from the political economy perspectives that have dominated for the last two decades. Charles van Onselen's (1976) contrapuntal reading of colonial archives unveiled something of the rich culture of compound life as well as the travelling strategies of migrants *en route*. Van Onselen did not try to connect the culture of the compound with that of the country-side in any systematic way. Subsequent scholarship has begun to articulate these linkages (Beinart 1987; Bonner 1990; Breckenridge 1990; Delius 1989; Harries forthcoming; Leger 1992). In a major conceptual breakthrough, Dunbar Moodie (forthcoming) applies the concept of 'moral economy' to decode complex questions of mine sexuality, alcohol consumption, strike activity and violence.

Anthropological explorations of migrant culture have tended to work from the countryside towards the town. In Lesotho, the establishment of a viable rural homestead outside the migrant labour system is still the paradigm of a successful migrant career (Murray 1981; Shanafelt 1989). McAllister (1992) shows how, in the Transkei, distinctive ritual sanctions developed to establish, in the mind of the migrant, a rural-centric interpretation of migrancy. Among the Tshidi of the northern Cape, mineworkers represent their experience on the mines in a 'versatile and poetic language' of contrasting images of work. Only by 'unhitching the town from the countryside' could workers escape the domain of mine work and re-enter the more satisfying world of rural labour (Comaroff and Comaroff 1987: 204). In the Chopi areas of southern Mozambique, elaborate ritual performances – the *migodo* – mapped, in song, the experience of Portuguese colonial domination and labour migration to South Africa (Vail and White 1990: 112–54). The poetic-musical recitations of the Basotho miners present another form of articulating social identity. These performances aim to resolve the contradictions between village and mine as 'domains of experience' (Coplan 1986, 1987).

Social scientists have often managed to reduce the rich subterranean cultures of the migrant labour system into crude stereotypes that provide minimal insight into the consciousness of the migrant and the subjective experience of migrancy (Miles and Crush 1993). These discredited methodologies still appeal to policy-makers in search of a quick fix. The more painstaking, and necessary, task is to reconnect conceptually the town with the coutryside, as mapped in the consciousness of the miners themselves. Ultimately, when the material and symbolic links between the urban and the rural are severed in southern Africa, it will not be the result of any grand design but because the migrants themselves prefer it that way.

References

Allen, V. (1992) *The History of Black Mineworkers in South Africa*, Keighley: Moor Press

Ashforth, A. (1990) T*he Politics of Official Discourse in Twentieth-Century South Africa*, Oxford: Clarendon Press

Baker, J. (1989) 'The Silent Crisis: Black Labour, Disease and the Economics and Politics of Health on the South African Gold Mines', Ph.D. dissertation, Queen's University, Kingston

Beinart, W. (1982) *The Political Economy of Pondoland, 1860– 1930*, Cambridge: Cambridge University Press

—— (1987) 'Worker Consciousness, Ethnic Particularism and Nationalism: The Experiences of a South African Migrant, 1930–1960', in S. Marks and S. Trapido (eds) *The Politics of Race, Class and Nationalism in Twentieth-Century South Africa*, London: Longman, 286–309

Böhning, W. (ed.) (1981) *Black Migration to South Africa: A Selection of Policy-Oriented Research*, Geneva: International Labour Organization

Bonner, P. (1990) 'Desirable or Undesirable Basotho Women? Liquor, Prostitution and the Migration of Basotho Women to the Rand, 1920–1945', in C. Walker (ed.) *Women and Gender in Southern Africa to 1945*, London: James Currey, 221–51

Breckenridge, K. (1990) 'Migrancy, Crime and Faction Fighting: The Role of the Isitshozi in the Development of Ethnic Organisations in the Compounds', *Journal of Southern African Studies*, 16 (1), 55–78

Chirwa, W. (1992) '"Theba is Power": A Study of Labour Migration and the Malawian Fishing Industry', Ph.D. dissertation, Queen's University, Kingston

Comaroff, J. and J. Comaroff (1987) 'The Madman and the Migrant: Work and Labor in the Historical Consciousness of a South African People', *American Ethnologist*, 14, 191–209

Coplan, D. (1986) 'Performance, Self-Definition and Social Experience in the Oral Poetry of Sotho Migrant Mineworkers', *African Studies Review*, 29, 29–40

—— (1987) 'The Power of Oral Poetry: Narrative Songs of the Basotho Migrants', *Research in African Literatures*, 18, 1–35

Crush, J. (1987) *The Struggle for Swazi Labour, 1890–1920*, Montreal and Kingston: McGill-Queen's Press

—— (1989) 'Migrancy and Militance: The Case of the National Union of Mineworkers of South Africa', *African Affairs*, 88 (350), 5–24

—— (1991) 'The Chains of Migrancy and the Southern African Labour Commission', in C. Dixon and M. Heffernan (eds) *Colonialism and Development in the Contemporary World*, London: Mansell, 46–71

—— (1992a) 'Inflexible Migrancy: New Forms of Migrant Labour on the South African Gold Mines', *Labour, Capital and Society*, 25 (1), 46–71

—— (1992b) 'Power and Surveillance on the South African Gold Mines', *Journal of Southern African Studies*, 18 (1), 825–44

Crush, J. and W. James (1991) 'Depopulating the Compounds: Migrant Labour and Mine Housing in South Africa', *World Development*, 19 (4), 301–16

Crush, J. et al. (1991) *South Africa's Labor Empire: A History of Black Migrancy to the Gold Mines*, Boulder and Cape Town: Westview and David Philip

Delius, P. (1989) 'Sebatakgomo: Migrant Organization, the ANC and the Sekhukhuneland Revolt', *Journal of Southern African Studies*, 15 (3), 581–616

Dubow, S. (1989) *Racial Segregation and the Origins of Apartheid in South Africa*, Basingstoke: Macmillan

Duncan, D. (1993) *The Mills of God: The State and African Labour in South Africa, 1918–1948*, Johannesburg: University of Witwatersrand Press

First, R. (1983) *Black Gold: The Mozambican Miner, Proletarian and Peasant*, New York: St Martin's Press

Greenberg, S. (1987) *Legitimating the Illegitimate: States, Markets and Resistance in South Africa*, Berkeley: University of California Press

Guy, J. and Thabane, M. (1988) 'Technology, Ethnicity and Ideology: Basotho Miners and Shaft-Sinking on the South African Gold Mines', *Journal of Southern African Studies*, 14 (2), 257–78

Harries, P. (forthcoming) *Work, Culture and Identity: Migrant Workers in Mozambique and South Africa, 1860–1917*, New York: Heinemann

Innes, D. (1984) *Anglo American and the Rise of Modern South Africa*, Johannesburg: Ravan Press

James, W. (1990) 'Class Conflict, Mine Hostels and the Reproduction of a Labour Force in the 1980s', in R. Cohen et al. (eds.) *Repression and Resistance: Insider Accounts of Apartheid*, London: Hans Zell, 142–64

(1992a) *Our Precious Metal: African Labour in South Africa's Gold Industry, 1970–1990*, Cape Town, London and Bloomington: David Philip, James Currey and Indiana University Press

(1992b) 'Capital, African Labour and Housing at South Africa's Gold Mines', *Labour, Capital and Society*, 25 (1), 72–87

(1992c) 'Review of Allen (1992)', *Labour, Capital and Society*, 25 (1), 145–6

Jeeves, A. (1985) *Migrant Labour in South Africa's Mining Economy*, Montreal and Kingston: McGill-Queen's Press

(1986) 'Migrant Labour and South African Expansion, 1920–1950', *South African Historical Journal*, 18, 73–92

Jeeves, A. and J. Crush (1992) 'The Failure of Stabilization Experiments and the Entrenchment of Migrancy to the South African Gold Mines', *Labour, Capital and Society*, 25 (1), 18–45

Johnstone, R. (1976) *Class, Race and Gold: A Study of Class Relations and Racial Discrimination in South Africa*, London: Routledge & Kegan Paul

Laburn-Peart, K. (1992) 'Transforming Mine Housing in South Africa: The Anglo American Home Ownership Scheme', *Labour, Capital and Society*, 25 (1), 104–15

Lacey, M. (1981) *Working for Boroko: The Origins of a Coercive Labour System in South Africa*, Johannesburg: Ravan Press

Leger, J. (1992) '"Talking Rocks" – An Investigation of the Pit Sense of Rockfall Accidents Amongst Underground Gold Miners', Ph.D. dissertation, University of Witwatersrand

Levy, N. (1982) *The Foundations of the South African Cheap Labour System*, London: Routledge & Kegan Paul

Lipton, M. (1985) *Capitalism and Apartheid: South Africa 1910–1986*, Totowa, NJ: Wildwood House

Mayer, P. (ed.) (1980) *Black Villagers in an Industrial Society*, Cape Town: Oxford University Press

McAllister, P. (1992) 'Beer Drinking and Labour Migration in the Transkei: The Invention of a Ritual Tradition', in J. Crush and C. Ambler (eds), *Liquor and Labor in Southern Africa*, Athens and Pietermaritzburg: Ohio University Press and University of Natal Press, 252–68

Miles, M. and J. Crush (1993) 'Personal Narratives as Interactive Texts: Collecting and Interpreting Migrant Life-Histories', *Professional Geographer*, 45 (1), 95–129

Moodie, D. (1986) 'The Moral Economy of the Black Miners' Strike of 1946', *Journal of Southern African Studies*, 13 (1), 1–35

(1992) 'Ethnic Violence on the South African Gold Mines', *Journal of Southern African Studies*, 18 (3), 584–613

(forthcoming) *Going for Gold: Workers' Lives on the South African Gold Mines*, Berkeley: University of California Press

Moodie, D. and Ndatshe, V. (1992) 'Town Women and Country Wives: Migrant Labour, Family Politics and Housing Preferences at Vaal Reefs Mine', *Labour, Capital and Society*, 25 (1), 116–32

Murray, C. (1981) *Families Divided: The Impact of Migrant Labour in Lesotho*, Cambridge: Cambridge University Press

Packard, R. (1990) *White Plague, Black Labour: Tuberculosis and the Political Economy of Health and Disease in South Africa*, Berkeley: University of California Press

Richardson, P. (1982) *Chinese Mine Labour in the Transvaal*, London: Macmillan

Seidman, G. (1993) 'Shafted: The Social Impact of Downscaling on the Free State Goldfields', *South African Sociological Review*, 5 (2), 14–34

Shanafelt, R. (1989) 'Talking Peace, Living Conflict: The Mental and the Material on the Borders of Apartheid', Ph.D. dissertation, University of Florida

Vail, L. and L. White (1990) *Power and the Praise Poem: Southern African Voices in History*, London: James Currey

van Onselen, C. (1975) 'Black Workers in Central African Industry: A Critical Essay on the Historiography and Sociology of Rhodesia', *Journal of Southern African Studies*, 1 (2), 228–46

(1976) *Chibaro: African Mine Labour in Southern Rhodesia, 1900–1933*, London: Pluto Press

Walker, C. (1990) 'Gender and the Development of the Migrant Labour System c. 1850–1930', in C. Walker (ed.) *Women and Gender in Southern Africa to 1945*, London: James Currey, 168–96

MIGRANT LABOUR AND THE STATE
UNDER APARTHEID, 1948–1989

ALAN H. JEEVES

Migratory labour is a defining element of apartheid. It developed from two features of the South African racial order. First, whites broadly supported the notion of urban areas being zones of white privilege in which African residence was segregated and temporary. Enshrined in legislation from 1913, the idea of possessory segregation became the second basis for controlling the movement of Africans. The state divided the land into 'native reserves' (bantustans, homelands or national states) where Africans could own land, and reserved the remainder (more than 87 per cent of the total) for white ownership. As agriculture in the reserves first declined and then collapsed, making the inhabitants increasingly dependent on earnings remitted from labour in the white areas, the need to control the movement of Africans grew (Giliomee and Schlemmer 1985: 1–12).

Migrancy and the trauma of uprooting peasant societies in South Africa were not temporary phenomena in the transition from agrarian to industrial society, but became permanent features of the political economy. Oscillating migration developed first on the gold mines, as much from the preferences of the workers as from the needs of their employers or the demands of government (Crush et al. 1991: 4–5). By 1911 the Union government had entrenched it there with legislation, and it began to spread throughout the economy. In theory, contract workers shifted between temporary employment in town and their homes and families in the rural areas. For many, this description misrepresented both their own preferences and the length of time they spent in urban employment. Under apartheid, many Africans were defined as migrants only because they lacked the stringent legal qualifications for urban residence. Official policy kept them in that status through a variety of coercive means, including large-scale forced removals of millions of people from white to black areas (Platzky and Walker 1985).

National Party and development of 'influx control'
Beginning in 1923, twenty-five years before the onset of apartheid, the South African government legislated

first to permit and then to require municipalities to segregate African residential areas (Davenport 1971). Control of the movement of Africans began much earlier even than formal urban segregation. All the South African colonies and states had enacted pass laws during the course of the nineteenth century to regulate the movement of 'natives' to and within their territories. In 1937 and 1945, new legislation further restricted Africans' access to the cities as permanent residents and provided for the removal of those who did not meet stringent conditions (Davenport 1969; 95–109; Maylam 1989: 57–84).

After 1948, the National Party took more direct control over the supply and regulation of housing for Africans and, in the Group Areas Act (1950), extended urban segregation to all non-whites. It tightened the pass laws and, amid much resistance, extended them to women. A major innovation was the development of the labour bureaux system, which required all Africans to register as workseekers. Those without rights of permanent urban residence (styled Section 10 rights under the 1945 legislation, as amended) had to register in the homelands and return there at least annually to re-register.

From the 1960s, the government added another barrier to urbanization. It cleared the multiracial slums that had grown up around the major cities and replaced them with townships located farther away from city centres. In the early 1960s, the authorities stopped constructing black housing in white areas and shifted it to those homelands that adjoined major urban centres, while strictly enforcing the prohibitions against private construction and squatting in the white areas. Denied housing in established urban townships, black workers had to live in the homelands and commute to their work, often over long distances, on a daily or weekly basis. People were sometimes consigned to a homeland without being physically uprooted. The hapless residents of Kwa Mashu, a township near Durban, became commuter migrants at the stroke of a pen when the government transferred the township's administration to the KwaZulu homeland (Horrell 1978: 87). By 1980, there were 800,000 workers resident in homelands but working daily in a white area. In the management of migratory labour, the innovations of the 1950s and 1960s had less to do with new laws and regulations, and more with the growth of police control and the elaboration of the enforcement bureaucracy. The term 'influx control' included the whole edifice of law and administrative practice regulating African urban employment and controlling their movement (Horrell 1978: 171–95). As a description of policy, it is misleading, since the object was not merely to deny new workers rights of urban residence but also to remove to the homelands as many established residents as possible.

South Africa in southern Africa

The labour history of apartheid cannot be understood without reference to the regional labour market. In the 1950s it reached beyond southern Africa to tap the labour of Angola and Tanganyika (Tanzania). The survival of migratory labour required low-wage mine and farm employers to have access to workers from outside South Africa itself. These industries were uncompetitive for local workers who could earn higher wages in manufacturing. Increasingly, they found their labour farther afield, either by recruiting it in ever more distant areas, as the mines did, or by relying on clandestine immigrants, as many farmers did.

While the mines repatriated their migrants, control over farm workers was much less effective. Many of them fled the farms for the towns, and the farmers blamed city employers for enticing them away. A myth grew up among farmers that a huge surplus of 'idle natives' existed in the urban areas; they blamed the government for not returning them to the farms (Jeeves 1990: 105–44). Their fury partly explains the swing to the National Party in 1948. In office, D. F. Malan's government was no more able than its predecessors to eliminate foreign workers and not much more successful in keeping them on the farms.

Consistent with apartheid's demographic objectives, the Froneman Committee recommended in the early 1960s that foreign labour be dispensed with, even on the mines (Owen 1963). This proposal went nowhere. It would have intensified the scramble for labour in South Africa itself, pitting farm and mine employers against each other and forcing both to compete against higher industrial wages. To avoid a political uproar, the Verwoerd government quietly put aside Froneman's recommendations. The use of foreign workers on the mines increased steadily through the 1960s and early 1970s (Crush et al. 1991: 73).

However, on the farms, large-scale mechanization from the 1960s on sharply reduced the labour demands in that sector and led to the removal of millions of Africans from the white rural areas to the homelands. The resulting overcrowding and accelerating unemployment there greatly increased the pressure on influx control.

Black protests against urban-areas legislation, though ultimately unavailing, significantly slowed the enforcement of the restrictions on urban residence. In particular, their protests delayed the application of the law to women (Gerhart 1978: 212–56; Lodge 1983: 33–66, 139–52, 201–30; Walshe 1971: 401–3). Provoking the full weight of government repression, the anti-pass campaigns of the African National Congress and the Pan Africanist Congress were probably less effective than the informal, day-to-day struggles of individual Africans to evade the pass laws. The influx-control system dammed up in the impoverished homelands growing pools of unemployed and underemployed workers and their families. Increasingly desperate individuals found myriad ways to evade the regulations and the police and to make their way to the cities (Greenberg 1987: 48–55).

New perspectives

Recent research is revising our understanding of the development of migrant labour and influx control.[1] This new work stresses the limited capacity of the National Party before the 1960s to impose its labour control regulations and allocate labour effectively among competing employers. It now seems clear that apartheid cannot be understood as the product of a grand plan, something that sprang fully developed from the ideology of Verwoerd and his social engineers. Its development was more halting, more driven and altered by circumstances and competing political pressures than earlier writers recognized. An ideologue whose theories caused much pain and misery, Verwoerd undoubtedly was, but bureaucrats ran his system. While some shared his vision, others responded to their own sense of what was possible and desirable, and to a variety of contradictory political and other pressures.

So far as policy was driven by an over-arching vision, it appeared first in the report of the Sauer Commission (Sauer 1947). P. O. Sauer was appointed by the National Party before the 1948 election to give some policy substance and electoral packaging to the party's slogan, 'apartheid'. The most serious attempt to give meaning to the homeland idea and separate development came in 1955 with the Report of the

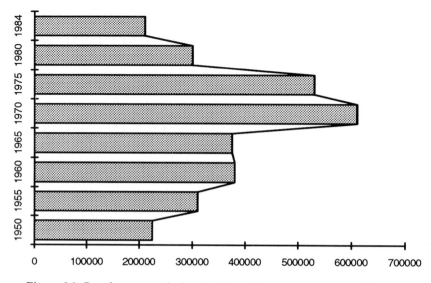

Figure 6.1: Pass law arrests in South Africa (five-year average), 1950–1984

Tomlinson Commission on the Socio-economic Development of the Bantu Areas. Tomlinson outlined the steps necessary to restore homeland economies from the effects of decades of neglect and misguided 'betterment planning'.

Recoiling from Tomlinson's expensive recommendations, the state shelved most of his agricultural rehabilitation programme. Administrative controls and the police, not the economic reconstruction advocated by Tomlinson, would keep Africans in the homelands. In maintaining grand apartheid (the homeland concept) through influx control, planners were constrained not only by lack of money but also by the demands of industrial employers, who increasingly found the migrant labour influx control delivered unsatisfactory results, and by the resistance of Africans, struggling to get to and remain in the cities. Furthermore, at least initially, there was no agreement in the National Party on precisely how growing black urbanization should be constrained (Posel 1991: 58–60).

Nevertheless, ideology was sufficiently powerful from the beginning to impose influx-control policies that hurt urban employers by reducing the number of suitable workers available. Even at its least oppressive, moreover, apartheid's influx control was much more centralized, intrusive and restrictive than that of earlier governments. Armed with a growing bureaucracy, a welter of new and reformulated regulations, an increasingly ruthless police force and, by 1958, commanding majority electoral support among whites, the

National Party set out in the 1960s to realize a more fully formulated version of grand apartheid (Greenberg 1987: 44–8; Posel 1991: 61–90).

Even during the most rigorous period of influx-control enforcement in the fifteen years after about 1960, however, the objective was less to impose a blanket prohibition on further urbanization and more to divide the labour force among each of the major employing sectors: mines, farms and manufacturing. Contrary to Verwoerdian fantasies that the African demographic tide would soon recede from the cities, the permanently urbanized black populations continued to grow. This was so despite rates of pass law arrests that exceeded 600,000 annually during the late 1960s (see Figure 6.1) and made statutory criminals of a large part of the black population (SAIRR 1975: 171).

The attempt to reinvent influx control

By the 1970s, pressures on influx control had intensified. Industrial employers had long wanted a more settled, skilled labour force than migrancy could provide; increasingly their associations called for the relaxation of the controls over urbanization. Black unions grew rapidly from the early 1970s. As union struggles led to higher wages, manufacturers responded with more pressure on the state to permit them to eliminate migrancy and to stabilize their workforce in family housing. 'Cheap' migrant labour no longer looked like much of a bargain for many of these employers (Hindson 1987a: 82–3). Amid

growing trade-union and township militancy following the Soweto upheaval in 1976, the government
began haltingly to reconsider its urban and labour-
control policies, and appointed Dr P. J. Riekert to
inquire (Riekert 1979).[2]

In a way that recalled the Report of the Commission
on Native Laws, which Smuts had appointed in 1946,
Riekert argued that permanent black urbanization was
a reality that the state had to recognize (Fagan 1948;
Riekert 1979). African workers who had qualified
under the existing stringent regulations for permanent
urban residence should be able to move freely to new
jobs provided that employment and housing were
available. Rather than rely on the old system of large-
scale pass-law arrests, Riekert proposed to make
urban living depend on jobs and housing. He wanted
to make both employers and workers responsible and
prescribed substantial fines for hiring undocumented
workers.

While easing the controls on established city
dwellers, the Riekert Commission accepted the central
aim of apartheid, to limit the size of the black urban
population. Thus, the report recommended intensified
influx control to keep rural dwellers out of the cities
except as migrants or commuters. Evidently, the
commission hoped to make allies of the privileged
'insiders' (those with jobs, housing and legal rights in
the city). Riekert believed that they would value the
protection that influx control gave them against the
competition of rural 'outsiders'. (Hindson 1987a:
83–7; 1987b) Few were won over in this way. Influx
control, even under Riekert's less oppressive reforms,
forced everyone to carry identification documents and
subjected all blacks in the city to intrusive bureaucratic supervision and harassment.

The commission called for major changes in the
administration of labour controls. It proposed to
dismantle the highly centralized labour allocation
system managed by the Department of Cooperation
and Development (earlier the Department of Bantu
Affairs and Development and the Department of
Plural Relations) and the regional Bantu Administration Boards set up in the early 1970s. Riekert
suggested making those functions less visible by
distributing them among other government departments (SAIRR 1979: 387–8). In line with this effort to
hide and deracialize the politically explosive control
of black labour, the state now labelled migrants as
immigrants from the 'independent' national states;
their hated reference books became passports and a
matter no longer for the labour-control bureaucrats but
for the Department of Foreign Affairs. Enforcement

was shuffled off to the national states, out of sight and
well away from Pretoria. By 1985, the Administration
Boards had been stripped of their responsibilities for
allocating labour and turned into Development Boards
under the Department of Constitutional Development
and Planning (Greenberg 1987: 87–9).

Conclusion

During the early 1980s, the state made several efforts
to carry out Riekert's reform of the influx-control
laws, all of which failed. Regulation of labour
migration in the now more refined form proposed by
Riekert proved no more workable than the old.
Rapidly rising population in the bantustans and the
deepening crisis of poverty and misery there increased
the pressures that were driving Africans out of the
countryside. High rates of unemployment which even
in the early 1980s reached 25–35 per cent of the black
labour force compounded the pressure. It was not
possible to seal the urban borders against homeland
refugees, as Riekert advocated. The growth of
commuter settlements in the homelands showed that
they were increasingly integrated in the national
economy. Also, as influx control faltered, squatter
settlements began to develop around all of the major
cities.

On 23 April 1986 the South African government
halted arrests under the pass laws. This decision
followed a remarkable finding of the State President's
Council that influx control had been administered 'in
a discriminatory fashion and had a severely detrimental effect on the quality of life of Africans'
(SAIRR 1986: I, 336). Subsequently the authorities
enacted the Abolition of Influx Control Act which
formally repealed the myriad regulations governing
the movement of Africans. The belated acknowledgement of a stark social reality for which the state
had been condemned for decades had all the signs of a
death-bed conversion. However, it was none the less
important. If one single step can be said to signal the
downfall of grand apartheid, the repeal of influx
control, coming three years before F. W. de Klerk
became state president and nearly four years before
the release of Mandela, was that step. Implicit in it is
the political and economic reintegration of the homelands that by 1994 had all but happened.

The repeal legislation simply acknowledged what
had become apparent on the ground. The enforcement
machinery could no longer hold a growing tide of
impoverished humanity in place in the bantustans. For
more than fifty years, however, influx control
impeded the stabilization in the cities of an African

working class. In other industrializing countries, migrancy was a phase marking the transition from rural to industrial society. Migrants eventually found permanent residence in the cities. Much evidence indicates that South Africa followed the same pattern, but an oppressive framework of laws and regulations kept nearly one-third of the economically active black population in the legal status of temporary migrants, a proportion that became much larger with the inclusion of the border commuters. The result was to blight the family life and economic prospects of millions of workers over many generations.

Notes

1. Crush et al. 1991; Drakakis-Smith (ed.) 1992; Smith (ed.) 1992; Giliomee and Schlemmer (eds) 1985; Greenberg 1987; Hindson 1987a; Lemon (ed.) 1991; Mayer (ed.) 1980; Maylam 1983; Platzky and Walker 1985; Posel 1991; Swilling et al. (eds) 1991; Tomlinson and Addleson (eds) 1987.

2. Riekert's was one of two major inquiries into labour matters that the government set up at about the same time. Professor Nic Wiehahn was appointed in 1977 to chair a Commission of Inquiry into Labour Legislation. By 1982, Wiehahn had produced six reports recommending sweeping changes concerning laws affecting African workers and their trade unions (Wiehahn 1982).

References

Bernstein, A. (1985) 'Influx Control in Urban South Africa: An International and Empirical View', in H. Giliomee and L. Schlemmer (eds) *Up Against the Fences: Poverty Passes and Privilege in South Africa*, New York: St Martin's Press, 85–103

Crush, J. et al. (1991) *South Africa's Labor Empire: A History of Black Migrancy to the Gold Mines*, Boulder, CO: Westview Press

Davenport, T. R. H. (1969) 'African Townsmen? South African Natives (Urban Areas) Legislation through the Years', *African Affairs*, 95–109

(1971) *The Beginnings of Urban Segregation in South Africa*, Grahamstown: Rhodes University, Institute for Social and Economic Research

Drakakis-Smith, D. (ed.) (1992) *Urban and Regional Change in Southen Africa*, London: Routledge

Fagan, H. O. (1948) *Report of the Commission Appointed to Enquire into the Operation of the Laws in Force in the Union Relating to Natives in or near Urban Areas; the Native Pass Laws; and the Employment in Mines and Industries of Migratory Labour, 1946–8* (Fagan Commission). UG 24

Gerhart, G. (1978) *Black Power in South Africa: The Evolution of an Ideology*, Berkeley: University of California Press

Giliomee, H. and L. Schlemmer (eds) (1985) *Up Against the Fences: Poverty Passes and Privilege in South Africa*, New York: St Martin's Press

Greenberg, S. (1987) *Legitimating the Illegitimate: State*

Markets and Resistance in South Africa, Berkeley: California University Press

Hindson, Doug (1987a) *Pass Controls and the Urban African Proletariat*, Johannesburg: Ravan Press

(1987b) 'Review Article: Reforming State Urban Policy in South Africa?', *Journal of Southern African Studies*, 14 (1), 160–6

Horrell, Muriel (ed.) (1978) *Laws Affecting Race Relations in South Africa, 1948–76*, Johannesburg: South African Institute of Race Relations (SAIRR)

Jeeves, Alan H. (1990) 'Migrant Labour in the Industrial Transformation of South Africa, 1920–60', in Z. A. Konczacki et al. (eds) *Studies in the Economic History of Southern Africa*, 2 vols, *Vol. II: South Africa, Lesotho and Swaziland*, London: Frank Cass

Lemon, A. (ed.) (1991) *Homes Apart: South Africa's Segregated Cities*, Bloomington: Indiana University Press

Lodge, Tom (1983) *Black Politics in South Africa since 1945*, London: Longman

Mayer, P. (ed.) (1980) *Black Villagers in an Industrial Society*, Cape Town: Oxford University Press

Maylam, Paul (1983) 'The "Black Belt": African squatters in Durban 1935–1950', *Canadian Journal of African Studies*, 17

(1989) 'The Rise and Decline of Urban Apartheid in South Africa', *African Affairs*, 89 (354), 57–84

Owen, K. (1963) 'Summary of Report by F. Platzky and C. Walker on Surplus People Project', Johannesburg, Surplus People Project

Platzky, F. and C. Walker (1985) *The Surplus People: Forced Removals in South Africa*, Johannesburg: Ravan Press

Posel, D. (1991) *The Making of Apartheid, 1948–61*, Oxford: The Clarendon Press

Riekert, P. J. (1979) *Report of the Commission of Inquiry into Labour Legislation*, Pretoria: RP 47–1979

SAIRR (1975), *A Survey of Race Relations in South Africa, 1974*, Johannesburg: SAIRR

(1979), *A Survey of Race Relations in South Africa, 1979*, Johannesburg: SAIRR

(1986), *A Survey of Race Relations in South Africa, 1986*, 2 vols, Johannesburg: SAIRR

Sauer, P. O. (1947) *Verslag van die Kleurvraagstuk Kommissie van die Herenigde Nasionale Party* (Sauer Commission)

Smith, D. M. (ed.) (1992) *The Apartheid City and Beyond: Urbanization and Social Change in South Africa*, London: Routledge

Swilling, M., R. Humphries and K. Shubane (eds) (1991) *Apartheid City in Transition*, Cape Town: Oxford University Press

Tomlinson, F. R. (1955) Commission for the Socio-Economic Development of the Bantu Areas, *Summary of the Report*, Pretoria: Government Printer

Tomlinson, R. and M. Addleson (eds) (1987) *Regional Restructuring under Apartheid: Urban and Regional Policies in Contemporary South Africa*, Johannesburg: Ravan Press

Walshe, P. (1971) *The Rise of African Nationalism in South Africa: The African National Congress, 1912–52*, Berkeley: University of California Press

Wiehahn, N. E. (1982) *The Complete Wiehahn Report*, Johannesburg: Lex Patria Publishers

REGIONAL LABOUR MIGRATION SYSTEMS IN EAST AFRICA: CONTINUITY AND CHANGE

W. T. S. GOULD

Since independence the three countries of East Africa – Kenya, Tanzania and Uganda, with a joint population estimated at 66 million in 1993 (25.0 million, 25.2 million and 16.9 million respectively) – have experienced considerable fragmentation of the regional labour migration system, which had been evolving through the colonial period towards an integrated structure. The three countries had different colonial histories. Kenya was a British colony with a settler economy. Tanzania was formed in 1964 with the union of Tanganyika, a German colony that after 1919 was mandated by the League of Nations to British authority, and Zanzibar, a British protectorate since 1873. Uganda was a British protectorate (1893–1963) and, like Tanzania, essentially had an African peasant farming economy. However, in all three there was a strong tendency towards common labour policies and free internal movement of labour. Most labour migration was to nearby destinations, and was therefore within each of the territories, largely to areas of settler farms, for example in the 'white highlands' of Kenya, or to areas of peasant cash crop production, for example in southern Uganda for coffee and cotton, the slopes of Mount Kilimanjaro in Tanzania for coffee, or Sukumaland to the south of Lake Victoria for cotton. Towns too, the administrative and commercial centres of the colonial economy, attracted migrants. They came largely from poor districts peripheral to these few so-called 'islands' of development, mostly to the nearest labour employment source, but there were substantial long-distance interterritorial migrations: for example, from western Kenya to Uganda by formal land settlers (Charsley 1968), as well as by labour migrants to urban destinations in Kampala and Jinja (Parkin 1969), and from the West Lake region round Bukoba in north-west Tanzania, also as rural and urban workers (Southall and Gutkind 1957). Furthermore, the East African system was not isolated from the rest of Africa, for it attracted 'foreign' workers in large numbers from Rwanda and Burundi to work in the rural economy in all three territories (Egero 1979), and there was a long history of labour recruitment in southern Tanganyika

for the mines of Zambia (then Northern Rhodesia) and South Africa (Gulliver 1957; Wilson 1977).

In all three territories the migrant labour systems were characterized by circular rather than permanent movement between source and destination, with a presumption of return to the home source area at the end of a formal contract or, less formally, after a period in wage employment. Walter Elkan's (1959) classic discussion of circular labour migration in East Africa (see Map 4) explores the rationality of the system as viewed by the colonial authorities and by the migrants themselves. In such a system the costs of reproduction of the labour force are borne in the rural source regions, while the benefits of the migrants' production accrue at the destinations areas. In spatial terms this necessitated the creation of a system of peripheral and poor labour reserves and a commercially dynamic core, the seat of capital formation. 'Reserves' were formally designated as such in Kenya, and were a critical instrument in the early organization of the space economy of the colony (Overton 1987; Zeleza 1989). As one Kenya settler wrote (Buxton 1927, quoted in Wrigley, 1965: 246): 'From the farmers' point of view, the ideal reserve is a recruiting ground for labour, a place from which the able-bodied go out to work, returning occasionally to rest and to beget the next generation of labourers.'

Reserves were merely implicit in economic policies in colonial Tanganyika and Uganda. The spatial and economic organization inherent in the system created a geography of widening social and economic disparities within, rather more than between, the colonial territories (Southall 1961).

Patterns of migration since independence

The characteristic pattern was of attraction to richer areas of new development, and out of poorer areas that were being actively deprived of their labour power. The constraints on movement that might have been intensified by territorial boundaries were largely irrelevant to the colonial authorities, as they were to the migrants themselves. However, with the coming of independence to Kenya in 1964, Tanganyika in

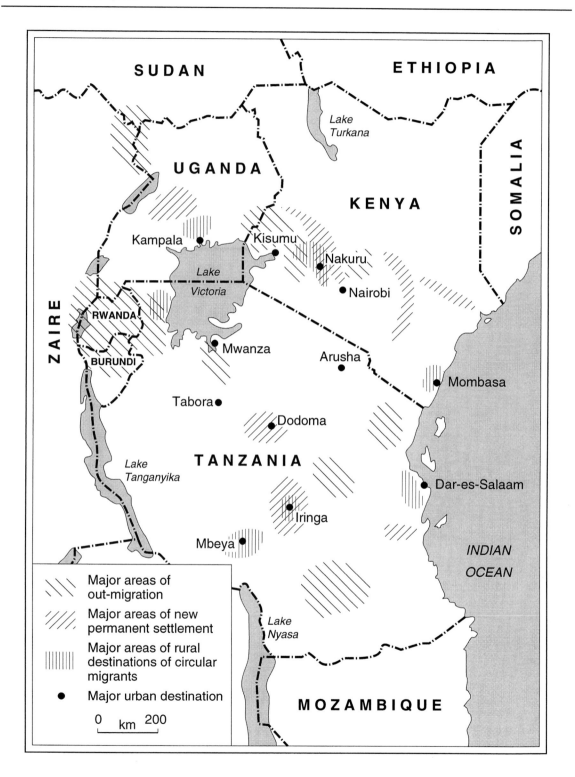

MAP 4: East Africa: major source and destination areas of migrants

1961, and Uganda and Zanzibar in 1963, there was a substantial change in the pattern of movement. For the first time international boundaries seemed to have some significance for migrants, even though these same essential processes of spatial differentiation within each country that were established in the colonial period have largely persisted since independence. This suggests a certain continuity in the labour migration system between the two periods. The traditional differentiation between internal and international migration is not helpful in this context, for both types of migration continue to be governed largely by similar processes of economic differentiation between source and destination (Prothero 1988).

With the coming of independence there was at first a continuity in patterns of development and structures of labour migration. The spatial patterns of economic development established in the colonial period, of a single national core (as in Uganda) or several minor and widely separated cores (as in Tanzania) surrounded by labour source areas, remained, even though governments sought to spread development out from these cores. The first national censuses since independence in Tanzania in 1967 (Claeson and Egero 1973), in Uganda in 1969 (Masser and Gould 1975) and in Kenya, 1969 (Gould 1992) all confirmed the continuity from the past in migration flows, with characteristic patterns of in-migration to the established areas of rural and urban development. Resettlement was not only in the settlement schemes in the Kenya highlands, with the resettlement of African farmers in high density and low density schemes on former European-owned land (Odingo, 1971), but also in 'frontier' movements to settle relatively empty areas in Uganda (Kabera 1985) and Tanzania (Moore 1979).

The first major breaks with the past came in Tanzania, associated with the Arusha Declaration, 1967, and the beginnings of the attempts to engineer a socialist transformation emphasizing rural development and villagization. The migration consequences were felt mostly at the local level with settlement redistribution and short-distance permanent migration to live in villages (Thomas 1985). There was a decline in rural labour migration to sisal estates, mostly near the coast, for these were broken up into cooperatives and peasant farms and ceased to be employers of labour (Lwoga 1985). However, despite the anti-urban thrust of policy, large urban areas, and particularly Dar es Salaam, continued to receive migrants in large and increasing numbers. As a result of administrative decentralization there was also a very rapid growth of

secondary centres, including the provincial capitals and Dodoma, which was designated national capital in 1973. There was also a rapid growth of migration to secondary towns in Kenya in this period (Obudho 1989). In Uganda the economic collapse of the 1970s and 1980s disrupted the established migration system, but the previously established pattern of development has reasserted itself with signs, however faltering, of economic recovery into the 1990s, with obvious implications for the re-establishment of a migration system which is not very different from that of thirty years before, with the exception that there are far fewer international migrants from Kenya, Rwanda or southern Sudan.

Changes in the patterns of labour migration since the colonial period have been most evident at the international level. Economic nationalism soon followed political independence, despite the pan-African rhetoric of the period, and the fledgling East African Community, with its common services such as Posts and Communications, Railways and Harbours, taxation, and East African Airways soon collapsed in the face of disputes over the distribution of costs and benefits between the three partner states. General Amin's crude economic nationalism in Uganda from 1971 extended not only to the expulsion of Asians but also, though much less publicized, to foreign African workers. Most Kenyans and Tanzanians as well as Rwandese and Burundians, Zaireois and Sudanese, especially those working in urban areas, returned to their country of origin during 1972. In a period of severe economic stress foreigners become the scapegoats for deteriorating wages and living conditions. In Kenya, too, by the 1970s and 1980s, as political relations with Uganda and Tanzania went from crisis to crisis, associated in part with the rival claims on the assets of the now defunct East African Community, there was also discrimination and public feeling against foreigners in general, widely pilloried as thieves, prostitutes or other social undesirables as well as taking jobs from the rising number of unemployed Kenyans.

Tanzania had stopped recruitment to the South African mines in 1962, and the Zambian mine recruitment had also substantially declined by the 1980s, so that potential migrants were obliged to turn to internal destinations within Tanzania. Also in southern Tanzania, many Mozambican refugees returned home in the years after that country's independence in 1975. The civil disruption in Uganda had generated, for the first time, refugee flows out of an East African country, into Sudan and Zaire, and also (though only for a short time) into Kenya and Tanzania. Uganda had become a net exporter of labour, no longer a destination for foreign workers. This was particularly evident in the case of Ugandan doctors, well-trained in the prestigious Makerere Medical School, who easily found well-paid positions in neighbouring countries, as throughout Africa (Gould 1988a). By the mid-1970s any thought of formal collaboration in and integration of the labour markets of these three closely related Commonwealth countries had disappeared under the weight of political and economic disagreements (Gould and Prothero 1981).

Processes of migration since independence

The complementarity between continuity and change in the patterns of movement has its roots in the broader tensions between continuity and change in the political economies of the three East African countries. Since independence they have each taken, whether deliberately or by default, very different paths to and strategies for development, and the regional and national labour migration systems reflect this broader context.

The most obvious contrast is between Kenya and Tanzania. In Kenya the characteristic feature of the development process has been its continuity from the colonial period in its external relationships – with the 'West' in political terms and with the IMF and the World Bank in economic terms – and in its internal relationships – it has come to epitomize the conditions of neo-colonialism (Leys 1974). This essential continuity in social and economic relations from the colonial period is shown by the largely unchanged spatial structure of the Kenyan economy some thirty years after independence (Obudho and Taylor 1979). There is a relatively prosperous core, to include Nairobi and surrounding areas, parts of Rift Valley Province, formerly the commercial farming area of the European highlands and parts of Central Province, once a labour reserve. Since the agricultural changes in the region associated with the Swynnerton Plan of the 1950s, many small farmers have become heavily involved in the commercial economy to their considerable benefit. These areas attract labour migrants from poor provinces, and particularly from Nyanza and Western Province, which account for over one-third of the population of the country, for they are both densely populated but have below national average incomes and overall levels of economic activity. Resettlement from these land-hungry and impoverished provinces into the highlands was an important valve for release of pressure on the land in the 1960s and 1970s, but by the mid-1970s almost all of the available highland land had been allocated, and resettlement activities (both organized and spontaneous) were being directed to the much less productive drier and lower lands on the highland margins (Dietz 1985).

Most labour migration, however, has continued to towns and to rural wage employment foci in estates, for example to the tea estates round Kericho (Oucho 1990), and most has continued to be circular in nature rather than permanent family migrations. Elkan (1976) updated his 1959 paper to argue that a proletariat had not been emerging in Nairobi since independence. Circular migration remains an objectively rational response and preferred option for most wage-earners, for it enables migrants to maintain household security in an uncertain modern sector labour market. Evidence from the rural end of the migration streams in Western and Nyanza Provinces has confirmed the persistence of circular migration in general terms (for example Hoddinot 1992; Moock 1973), and among specific groups, such as school leavers (Gould 1985). Rural poverty and the lack of opportunities for productive investment in agriculture in these areas (even if sufficient capital were to be available) sustain the conditions that are similar to those that prevailed earlier in the century in the colonial labour reserve, and migration seems to have had relatively little developmental impact.

Collier and Lal (1986), however, argue a very different case for the impact of migration on development in Central Province, also once a labour reserve, but since the 1950s a strong participant in the commercial economy. The province has easy access to the large and relatively prosperous Nairobi market, and also to the international market for its fruit, vegetables and dairy produce, as well as for the more traditional cash crops of tea and coffee. The substantial farm incomes have been supplemented by remittances of off-farm incomes from wage labour in Nairobi, and used for farm investments to stimulate further income growth. In these circumstances the interaction between town and country through the migration system has further confirmed the rationality of circular migration, for reasons that seem to be quite different from those suggested for the poorer provinces (Gould 1988b).

In Tanzania, by contrast, there has been a conscious attempt to restructure the economy since independence, and particularly since 1967, to move towards rural self-sufficiency in production and consumption. The success with which these have been achieved is a matter of very considerable dispute (see *inter alia* Bryceson 1990; Hyden 1980), but it has certainly had mixed effects on labour migration. In the first place, the changes created a national migration system from which contract emigration had been prevented, but into which migrants came from all regions of this large and sparsely populated country, as well as some foreign migrants, including refugees from Burundi (from the 1970s), Mozambique (from the 1960s), Rwanda (from the 1970s) and Uganda (during the 1970s). However, the presumption of the continued dominance of a migrant wage labour force was undermined by the restructuring of the rural economy to eliminate capitalist relations of production by emphasizing communal and family production units rather than estate production for export. This presumed that the traditional migrants, the young males and, to a lesser extent, women, would find work in their home areas, on their own family land or in the village communal land, thus significantly reducing the need for long-distance labour migration. Using evidence from the Iringa region, Lwoga (1985) argues that there has been a shift from long-distance migration to more seasonal and short-distance movement. The coastal sisal estates are now reorganized on a peasant farming basis, but developments in peasant tobacco farming in the Iringa region have created a seasonal demand for additional labour from relatively nearby areas of south-western Tanzania, traditionally a major source of long-distance migrants. Rural labour migration did not end; it merely adjusted to the new patterns of labour demand.

However, there was a strong element of continuity in rural–urban migration. The towns of Tanzania have grown rapidly in the years since independence. At first the largest growth in absolute and proportional terms was in the primate capital city, Dar es Salaam, but with the restructuring of the national space, with decentralization and job creation in smaller centres, migration to lower levels of the urban hierarchy became common (Kaluba 1982; Maro and Mlay 1979). As with the rural migrants, therefore, there was for many migrants a diversion to more local destinations, with associated shorter periods of absence and more frequent return where the migration remained circular. However, there is a strong presumption in a socialist state against circular migration, that permanent urban migration is a preferred option for some, though not necessarily many. Hazlewood et al. (1989) have shown how even in the colonial period there was a higher proportion of permanent urban residents in Dar es Salaam than there was in Nairobi,

though even in the 1980s most workers in Dar es Salaam still maintained regular contact with a rural home. Collier et al. (1986) were also able to argue on the basis of a national survey in 1980 that most urban dwellers remitted to support agricultural production in rural areas.

In the period of severe economic crisis that has characterized Tanzania since the early 1980s, a period of 'structural adjustment' measures to 'liberalize' the economy (rolling back the power of the state in economic affairs, retrenchment of civil servants, privatization of state enterprises), there has been a substantial growth in the informal economy, and migrants have been attracted to the capital and to other towns by new small business opportunities. Mbonile (1993) has shown how many migrants from Makete District, a former labour 'reserve' near the border with Malawi, have established businesses in Mbeya and Iringa, the nearest provincial headquarters and in other nearby towns. More significantly perhaps, he has shown how these migrants are no longer remitting cash for investment or consumption (in the form of housing or contributions to school buildings) to Makete, but instead are using their earnings to buy land and build houses in or near these towns. Also in Tanzania, Holm (1992) and Van Donge (1992) have similarly recorded declines in circulation in favour of permanent urban migration. In other recent studies, however, a permanent return of urban dwellers to take up farming in their rural areas has been recorded. Margaretha Von Troil (1992) records that in 1990 there was a lot of urban informal business and construction activity throughout Tanzania, but that where cash crop opportunities existed, as in her study area in Mtwara and Newala Districts in the south-east, the better prices available for these crops had persuaded some urban migrants to return to the land.

The contrasts between the essential continuity in migration in Kenya and the transformations in the migration system in Tanzania are clear. National migration systems reflect the wider political economies in which they operate, but even in Tanzania, a country that has gone further than most African states to move its economy away from the inherited colonial structures, the colonial legacy of the migrant labour system persists, and may be difficult to eliminate in a period of severe economic uncertainty that shows little sign of ending.

In the case of Uganda, the almost complete collapse of the economic system under the pressure of brutal dictatorship, 1971–79, and precarious political instability under the Obote and Museveni governments since then, has created a fragility in contemporary migration patterns. In the darkest days of economic collapse and the absence of any systematic rule of law, many urban dwellers returned to live in the relative physical safety and economic security of rural subsistence, in a country where the environment is sufficiently productive in most places to permit such a survival strategy. Urban populations probably fell, but when they recovered the migration system was probably more structured than hitherto along ethnic/ regional lines, with northerners, once a prominent proportion of the urban population, effectively excluded for fear of their own security and by informal discrimination in favour of southerners and westerners in public and private employment (Jamal 1991). The continuing uncertainty, however, helps to sustain a circulation system rather than permanent urban migration, even for the most educated and 'westernized'.

Conclusion

There is no longer anything that could be identified as a regional labour migration system in East Africa. There are in effect three independent systems, each with its own characteristics and controls, but all reflect the broader structures of the national political economy in which they operate. There is still relatively free movement across national borders, but within each country the need for work permits and formal identity papers, as well as the informal discrimination against foreigners at the factory or farm gate, effectively keeps most foreigners out of the national labour markets. This is particularly so at low skill levels, for local supplies of unskilled labour are always available. There are, however, some common features. In Kenya (Omogi 1992), in Tanzania (Bujra 1993) and in Uganda (Obbo 1991) there is a growing involvement of migrant women in the labour force. There are increasing, but differentiated pressures on rural environments that have their effect on migration. In some areas, the more ecologically benign, population pressure has led to intensification of the agricultural systems that have required more labour input and, thus, less out-migration; in other areas, generally drier, environmental deterioration has become a serious problem that encourages additional labour migration and often permanent out-migration to ensure household survival (Gould forthcoming).

There is much still to be discovered about the ways in which national and regional migration systems in Africa have responded to the changing economic and social environments in which they must operate. But the national migration system is not merely a passive response to these structural conditions. It is an integral part of them, directly affecting the pattern and strategies of development. The continuities and changes in migration in East Africa confirm the importance of the study of migration for an understanding of opportunities and constraints on its development.

References

Bryceson, D. F. (1990) *Food Insecurity and the Social Division of Labour in Tanzania, 1919–1985*, London: Macmillan

Bujra, J. (1993) 'Power and Empowerment: A Tale of Two Tanzanian Servants', *Review of African Political Economy*, (56), 68–78

Charsley, S. R. (1968) 'Population Growth and Development in North-East Bunyoro', *East African Geographical Review*, 6, 13–22

Claeson, C. F. and B. Egero (1973) 'Migration', in B. Egero and R. A. Henin (eds) *The Population of Tanzania: An Analysis of the 1967 Population Census, Volume 6*. Bureau of Resource Assessment and Land Use Planning, University of Dar es Salaam, 56–75

Collier, P. and D. Lal (1986) *Labour and Poverty in Kenya: 1900–1980*, Oxford: Oxford University Press

Collier, P. et al. (1986) *Labour and Poverty in Rural Tanzania*, Oxford: Oxford University Press

Dietz, T. (1985) 'Migration to and from Dry Areas in Kenya', *Tijdschrift voor Economishe en Sociale Geografie*, 77 (1), 18–26

Egero, B. (1979) *Colonization and Migration. A Summary of Border-Crossing Movements in Tanzania before 1969*, Uppsala: Scandinavian Institute of African Studies, Research Report 29

Elkan, W. (1959) 'Migrant Labour in Africa: An Economist's Approach', *American Economic Review*, 49 (2), 188–97

—— (1976) 'Is a Proletariat Emerging in Nairobi?', *Economic Development and Cultural Change*, 24 (4), 695–706

Gould, W. T. S. (1985) 'Migration and Development in Western Kenya, 1971–82: A Retrospective Study of School Leavers', *Africa*, 55 (3), 262–85

—— (1988a) 'Government Policies and International Migration of Skilled Workers in Sub-Saharan Africa', *Geoforum*, 19 (4), 433–5

—— (1988b) *Urban–Rural Return Migration in Western Province, Kenya*, Proceedings of the African Population Conference, Dakar, International Union for the Scientific Study of Population, Liège, 2 (4.1), 41–55

—— (1992) 'Population Mobility', in M. B. Gleave (ed.) *Tropical African Development: Geographical Perspectives*, London: Longman, 284–314

—— (forthcoming) 'Population Growth, Migration and Environmental Stability in Western Kenya: From Malthus to Boserup', in J. I. Clarke and B. Zaba (eds) *Environment and Population Change*, Liège: Ordina Editions for IUSSP

Gould, W. T. S. and R. M. Prothero (1981) 'Migration between Commonwealth Countries of Africa', in T. E. Smith (ed.) *Commonwealth Migration: Flows and Policies*, London: Macmillan, 170–200

Gulliver, P. M. (1957) 'Nyakusa Labour Migration', *Rhodes–Livingstone Journal*, (21), 32–63

Hazlewood, A. et al. (1989) *Education, Work and Pay in East Africa*, Oxford: Clarendon Press

Hoddinott. J. (1992) 'Rotten Kids or Manipulative Parents: Are Children Old Age Security in Western Kenya?', *Economic Development and Cultural Change*, 40 (3), 545–66

Holm, M. (1992) 'Survival Strategies of Migrants to Makambako: An Intermediate Town in Tanzania', in J. Baker and P. O. Pedersen (eds) *The Rural–Urban Interface in Africa*, Seminar Proceedings, no. 27, Uppsala: Scandinavian Institute of African Studies, 238–57

Hyden, G. (1980) *Beyond Ujamaa in Tanzania: Underdevelopment and an Uncaptured Peasantry*, London: Heinemann

Jamal, V. (1991) 'The Agrarian Context of the Ugandan Crisis', in H. B. Hansen and M. Twaddle (eds) *Changing Uganda. The Dilemmas of Structural Adjustment and Revolutionary Change*, London: James Currey, Kampala: Fountain Press, Athens, OH: Ohio University Press, 78–97

Kabera, J. B. (1985) 'Populating Uganda's Dry Lands', in J. I. Clarke et al. (eds) *Population and Development Projects in Africa*, Cambridge: Cambridge University Press, 112–22

Kaluba, S. M. (1982) 'Rural Settlement Policies in Tanzania', *Habitat International*, 16 (1/2), 15–29

Leys, C. (1974) *Underdevelopment in Kenya: The Political Economy of Neo-Colonialism*, London: Heinemann

Lwoga, C. F. M. (1985) 'Seasonal Labour Migration in Tanzania: The Case of Ludewa District', in G. Standing (ed.) *Labour Circulation and the Labour Process*, London: Croom Helm, 120–54

Maro, P. and W. F. I. Mlay (1979) 'Decentralization and the Organization of Space in Tanzania', *Africa*, 49 (3), 291–301

Masser, I. and W. T. S. Gould (1975) *Interregional Migration in Tropical Africa*, London: Institute of British Geographers, Special Publication, no. 8

Mbonile, M. (1993) 'Migration and Structural Change in Tanzania. The Case of Makete District', unpublished Ph.D. thesis, University of Liverpool

Moock, J. L. (1973) 'Pragmatism and the Primary School: The Case of a Non-Rural Village', *Africa*, 43 (3), 302–15

Moore, J. (1979) 'The Villagization Process and Rural Development in the Mwanza Region of Tanzania', *Geografiska Annaler B*, 13 (2), 65–80

Obbo, C. (1991) 'Women, Children and a "Living Wage"', in H. B. Hansen and M. Twaddle (eds) *Changing Uganda. The Dilemmas of Structural Adjustment and Revolutionary Change*, London: James Currey, Kampala: Fountain Press, Athens, Ohio: Ohio University Press, 98–112

Obudho, R. A. (1989) 'Urbanization and Urban Policy in East Africa', in K. Swindell et al. (eds) *Inequality and Development: Case Studies from the Third World*, London: Macmillan for the Commonwealth Foundation, 292–315

Obudho, R. A. and D. R. F. Taylor (eds) (1979) *The Spatial Structure of Development. A Study of Kenya*, Boulder, CO: Westview Press

Odingo, R. S. (1971) *The Kenya Highlands*, Nairobi: East African Publishing House

Omogi, M. S. (1992) 'Typology and Characteristics of Female Migrants in Nairobi, Kenya: A Case Study of Kariobangi', unpublished M.Phil. thesis, UN Regional Institute for Population Studies, University of Ghana

Oucho, J. O. (1990) 'Migrant Linkages in Africa', in Union for African Population Studies, *The Role of Migration in African Development: Issues and Policies for the '90s. Volume I: Commissioned Papers*, Dakar, 109–41

Overton, J. (1987) 'The Colonial State and Spatial Differentiation: Kenya, 1895–1920', *Journal of Historical Geography*, 13 (3), 267–82

Parkin, D. (1969) *Neighbours and Nationals in an African City Ward*, London: Routledge and Kegan Paul

Prothero, R. M. (1988) *International and Internal Migration: Some African Perspectives*, Proceedings of the African Population Conference, Dakar, Senegal, International Union for the Scientific Study of Population, vol. II (4.2), 31–7

Southall, A. W. (1961) 'Population Movements in East Africa', in K. M. Barbour and R. M. Prothero (eds) *Essays on African Population*, London: Routledge and Kegan Paul, 157–92

Southall, A. W. and P. C. W. Gutkind (1957) *Townsmen in the Making: Kampala and its Suburbs*, East African Studies, no. 9, Kampala: East African Institute for Social Research

Thomas, I. (1985) 'Development and Population Redistribution: Measuring Recent Population Redistribution in Tanzania', in J. I. Clarke et al. (eds) *Population and Development Projects in Africa*, Cambridge: Cambridge University Press, 141–52

Van Donge, J. K. (1992) 'Agricultural Decline in Tanzania: The Case of the Uluguru Mountains', *African Affairs*, 91 (1), 73–94

Von Troil, M. (1992) 'Looking for a Better Life in Town: The Case of Tanzania' in J. Baker and P. O. Pedersen (eds) *The Rural–Urban Interface in Africa*, Seminar Proceedings, no. 27, Uppsala: Scandinavian Institute of African Studies, 223–37

Wilson, M. (1977) *For Men and Elders: Change in Relations of Generations and of Men and Women among Nyakusa–Ngonde People, 1875–1971*, New York: African Publishing Company

Wrigley, E. A. (1965) 'Kenya: Patterns of Economic Life', in V. Harlow and E. M. Chilver (eds) *History of East Africa. Volume Two*, London: Oxford University Press, 209–64

Zeleza, T. (1989) 'Labour Migration, Coercion and Migration in Early Colonial Kenya', in A. Zegeye and S. Ishemo (eds) *Forced Labour and Migration: Patterns of Movement within Africa*, London: Hans Zell Publications, 159–79

LABOUR MIGRATION IN FRENCH NORTH AFRICA

NEIL MACMASTER

Prior to French colonial penetration of the Maghreb there had been ancient and extensive patterns of internal migration, of pilgrims and scholars, nomadic tribes, trans-Saharan traders, and seasonal labourers and peddlers. The French military occupation, the large-scale appropriation of land in the plains by settlers and capitalist enterprises, and the radical dislocation of traditional socio-economic structures, disrupted former patterns of migration and generated new movements of labour to serve the colonial economy. The depth of colonial penetration and dislocation was far more radical in Algeria, conquered from 1830 and exploited as a colony of European settlement, than in the cases of Tunisia and Morocco which became protectorates in 1883 and 1912.

During the period 1830 to *c*.1880 French policy in Algeria was to introduce as many settlers as possible through official colonization, but in reality the small French farmers faced enormous difficulties in working the land directly owing to isolation, poor communications, disease, drought and ignorance of farming techniques adapted to the harsh climatic conditions of North Africa. Despite the myth of the independent *colon* as a frontiersman, the settlers were, from the beginning, mainly dependent on Algerian labour (Bennoune 1988: 56–7).

In the period to *c*.1880 official colonization through a policy of *cantonnement* expelled the nomadic tribes from the plains. Relocated on rocky and infertile terrain on the periphery of the colonial settlement they were then re-employed as sharecroppers (*khammes*) to cultivate the lands they had previously owned. The heavy reliance on extracting rent in various forms perpetuated the low-yield, traditional farming techniques of the Arabs. However, from 1880 there was a dramatic modernization of the Algerian economy: ownership of land was concentrated in large estates at the expense of the small *colon*, investment increased and commercial exports grew dramatically. Europeans in Algeria increased their lands from 765,000 hectares in 1870 to 1,912,000 in 1900 and 3,028,000 in 1954. Vine cultivation, which was the motor of the colonial economy (40 per cent of exports by value in 1913), increased from 40,000 hectares in 1880 to 400,000 in

1940 and was ten times more labour intensive than cereals.

The development of capitalism in Tunisia and Morocco came later than in Algeria, but was far more rapid and intense. Europeans increased landholdings in Tunisia from 550,000 hectares in 1913 to 800,000 in 1950. There was an intensive development of commercial farming in Tunisia after 1900 (vines, wheat, citrus fruit, olives, market gardening) and in Morocco from *c*.1920. The same period saw the rapid growth of mining (iron ore, phosphates, lead, zinc), especially in Tunisia and Morocco. Large-scale construction projects – railways, roads, irrigation schemes, docks and urban building – also required large numbers of unskilled labourers.

In an initial phase of this expansion much use was made of more skilled migrant labour from European peasant societies, especially from Spain. However, Algerian wage rates were in general half those of Europeans and from 1880 native labour was substituted on an increasing scale for that of Europeans. By 1908 three-quarters of the wage bill on the vineyards in the rich Mitidja plain near Algiers went to natives.

The sources of colonial labour

The colonial economy was able to mobilize two quite distinct types of migrant labour – long-distance seasonal migration and a dispossessed semi-proletariat, of nomadic or peasant origin, which flocked to the colonial centres and settled permanently.

Seasonal migration

This was primarily from the sedentary and densely populated peasant societies of the interior – mainly mountainous zones (the Rif of northern Morocco, Kabylia, the Aurès, the Atlas), or from the Saharan south (the Mzab, the Souss of Morocco, and from Djerba and the Dahar of Tunisia). These societies had an ancient tradition of internal migration as seasonal labourers or petty traders towards the cities and plains of the northern littoral. Temporary migration from the island of Djerba and the Dahar of Tunisia or from Kabylia and the Mozabite towns of the Algerian Sahara was already established in the eighteenth

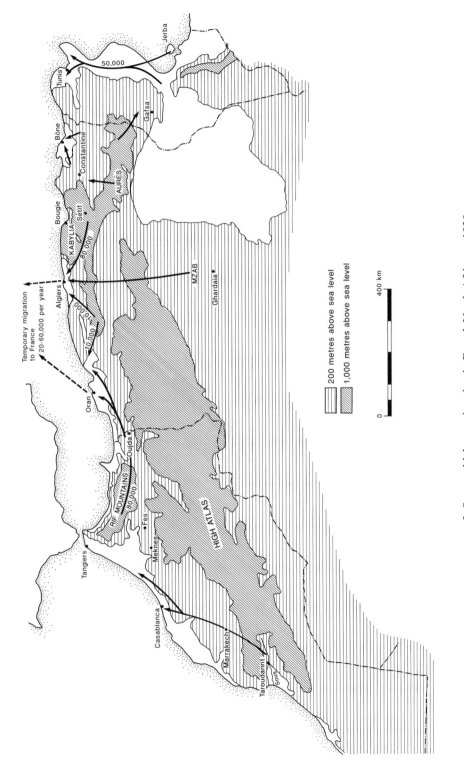

MAP 5: Seasonal labour migration in French North Africa, c. 1930

200 metres above sea level

1,000 metres above sea level

0   400 km

Temporary migration
to France
20–60,000 per year

50,000

Jerba

Tunis

Bône

Constantine

Gafsa

AURES

Bougie

KABYLIA

Sétif

80,000

Algiers

10,000

10,000

Oran

Oujda

MZAB

Ghardaïa

Tangiers

Rif MOUNTAINS
80,000

Fes

Meknes

Casablanca

HIGH ATLAS

Marrakech

Taroudannt

Sous

century (Simon 1979: 42–5). The French encouraged and redirected these traditional movements to provide seasonal labour for the colonial economy.

Most of the seasonal migration was from mountain zones of sedentary peasant peoples (mainly Berbers) where population pressure led to a search for external resources. This was a common pattern throughout the Mediterranean world (Braudel 1975: 24–53). Population density was as high as 100 to 200 people to the square kilometre in Kabylia and 30 in the Rif and among the Chleuh of Morocco compared with figures of 10 to 20 in the plains and 2 to 4 in the steppe zones bordering the Sahara. These were also zones that were hardly touched by colonial penetration and land expropriation since the settlers were not attracted to the inhospitable mountains, there was already a dense population that could not be easily displaced and land was usually held as a form of private property (*melk*) that was difficult to appropriate. Traditional social structures remained quite intact and cohesive, in contrast to the nomadic tribes of the plains which were systematically broken up.

These areas acted as labour reserves, based on strong, extended patriarchal family structures. Single young males were delegated by the group to seek external resources, while the farm and care of women was in the hands of male kin (Montagne 1953). Claude Meillassoux's theory of the 'domestic economy' fits the North African case well: the French colonial system to some extent protected the mountain tribes' subsistence base and in particular its reproductive capacity (Meillassoux 1981).

The single largest flow of seasonal migration was from Kabylia. During the 1860s and 1870s teams of Kabyle harvesters descended into the plains of the Mitidja, the Chélif, Bône and Oran and numbered about 15,000 to 20,000 men. By 1934 some 100,000 peasants travelled, often great distances of 100 to 200 kilometres, down from the hills onto the farms of the Algiers region. In some areas like Djidjelli and Mizrana between 40 and 100 per cent of men of working age were absent from the villages. The seasonal movement often took place during the 'dead' period of the agricultural cycle, before or after the harvest season. The complementarities of the climatic variations between mountain and plain enabled the Kabyles to gain wages as harvesters in the plains and then gradually to move homewards to work on the later ripening crops of the mountains. The failure of many small *colon* farmers and their movement to the cities; the replacement of higher-waged European migrant labour; and the increase in large estates

through land concentration meant an increasing reliance on native labour (Larnaude 1936; Mutin 1977: 30–53, 427–39).

After 1900 seasonal workers also began to migrate towards the mines, which were generally located in the interior, far from population centres. In the phosphate mine of Metaloui in Tunisia in 1907 a workforce of 2400 migrants lived in squalid encampments under a brutally policed regime. The diversity of migrant flows was shown by the presence of 1200 Kabyles, 400 Moroccans, 400 Tunisians and 400 from Tripolitania (Sammut 1977).

From both the Spanish and French zones of the Rif, the high mountains of northern Morocco, there was a considerable flow of seasonal labour into Algeria, especially to the vine region of Oran and the Mitidja where these workers often represented about 50 per cent of total annual labour input on estates. The migration of Moroccans across the border was already important in the 1860s but grew rapidly with the expansion of commercial agriculture. During the 1931 season, which lasted from about May to August, at least 80,000 Moroccans crossed the border and in 1949 it rose to 100,000 (Talha 1989: 59–62). After 1918 they increasingly replaced Kabyle seasonal labourers who began to emigrate to France where wages were higher.

Within the borders of Morocco there was a major flow of seasonal labour from the south, principally the Berber Chleuh of the High-Atlas and Anti-Atlas, towards the colonial towns and colonized zones of the north (Adam 1973; Ray 1938: 27–9). In Tunisia there was also an extensive seasonal migration of 50,000 to 60,000 men from the central steppe zone to the colonial estates of the Tell where they harvested cereals, grapes and olives (Simon 1979: 42).

Initially this pattern of seasonal migration appears to have reinforced the traditional structures of the mountain villages by bringing in external resources that were invested in the customary agricultural system. This pattern was also reinforced by settlers who preferred to tap distant reserves of labour, rather than have large native populations, including women and children, on or close to estates where they were perceived as a social cost and security risk.

Permanent labour migration

Colonization was a process which expropriated lands in the plains of the northern Maghreb, particularly those areas that were fertile, had good irrigation potential and modern infrastructures (roads, railway, telegraph). The native population that was dispossessed was frequently displaced onto the periphery of large estates, into scrublands, hilly and waterless areas, where they constituted a reserve of cheap labour which was close enough to be hired on a daily basis. This pattern operated in the Mitidja and the Chélif Valley of Algeria and the Haouz of Marrakesh (Mutin 1977: 427–32; Pascon 1986: 106–8, 157–61; Yacono 1955, vol. II: 312).

However, from about 1930 onwards a deepening economic and demographic crisis, which was particularly evident in Algeria, led to an accelerating and permanent family migration from the *bled* into the colonial towns. The roots of the crisis are complex, but in general had the characteristics of a classic Third World underdevelopment: agricultural production stagnated while population increased dramatically. Small peasants and sedentarized nomads, almost devoid of land, unable to find wage labour in the interior and facing chronic underemployment and conditions of near starvation, migrated towards the urban centres.

According to official estimates in 1951, 60 per cent of all rural families were living in extreme poverty. From 1930 there was a rapid growth of over-crowded inner-city slums, like the Kasbah of Algiers, and of squalid segregated shantytowns and so-called *villages nègres* on the outskirts of Constantine, Oran, Algiers, Casablanca and most other large and even medium-sized towns. By the 1950s one-third of the Algerian population of Algiers were living in *bidonvilles*. The native population of Tunis grew by 169 per cent or 180,000 people between 1936 and 1956, and equally dramatic growth rates were noted in Casablanca and Algiers — most of it due to migration rather than natural increase. In 1926 Algiers, like most Algerian towns, was a predominantly colonial city with 193,000 Europeans and 73,000 Algerians. By 1954 the balance had shifted dramatically owing to a flood of migrants and Algerians (293,000) outnumbered Europeans (277,000) (Descloitres 1961: 80).

Sétif provides a typical example of the processes at work. In the high plains surrounding the city, where dry-farming of cereals predominated, the Algerians were the victims of European land speculation, the consolidation of large estates and mechanization (the spread of tractors and harvesters from about 1930) which displaced labour. The rural poor flocked into the town (a 40 per cent increase 1936–48) and settled in inner-city slums and in peri-urban shantytowns. Some found work in agro-industries (flour milling, pasta workers, abattoirs) and construction, but in general there was an absence of work and most

migrants survived through an economy of makeshifts (hawking, prostitution, charity, public works) and through the aid of kin and fellow villagers. Rural–urban migration thus continued despite the lack of employment since the chances for survival were greater than in the desolate and desperate context of the *bled*, where peasants were reduced to a life of appalling hardship and periodically survived on wild plants (Prenant 1953).

Lack of employment opportunity in the towns was partly linked to the weak industrial development in the Maghreb since the colonial system favoured metropolitan interests and the export of raw and semi-processed materials for French manufacturing. Already in the 1930s the largest North African towns showed features of an unbalanced urban growth, with a huge mass of underemployed poor, which has become such a universal feature of Third World countries in the late twentieth century.

The colonial regulation of labour migration

Native labour did not migrate freely to serve the needs of the colonial economy but was controlled by a highly restrictive political/legal apparatus.

From 1880, with the rapid expansion of modern agriculture, the settler farmers — particularly on the large vineyard estates of Algeria — began to face a labour shortage. Some use was even made of prison and military labour, and there were projects to recruit 100,000 Sudanese and 50,000 Irish peasants. However, the main solution was found in a repressive body of laws known as the Native Code (*Code de l'indigénat*) instituted in June 1881, which regulated labour migration. Algerians were not allowed to move from their commune of origin without an official pass, nor could they emigrate to France. The code also enabled settler interests, represented in communal administrations, summarily to arrest, fine and terrorize local inhabitants and to haul them before special local courts manned by *colons* acting as magistrates.

The code was used to facilitate the flow of seasonal labour from the mountain tribes of Kabylia and elsewhere. In these zones travel permits were readily granted by officials who also saw the migration as a necessary safety valve for dense populations facing a Malthusian trap. Seasonal migration from Morocco across the border into Algeria was officially controlled until 1928 to protect the protectorate's nascent economy, but in practice a blind eye was turned to a huge 'illegal' movement that was not even stemmed at the height of the Rif War, despite anxieties about gun-running. French officials generally regarded internal labour migration from the dissident tribes of the *bled el Makhzen* of Morocco as a 'civilizing' process that would aid pacification.

In the colonized plains, on the other hand, mayors used the code to lock Algerians into the commune so that they could be exploited as a source of cheap labour. Travel permits were refused, sometimes to extort *backchich* payments, but also to drive down local wages or to extort various forms of *corvée* labour on settler farms and road construction.

The colonial exploitation of cheap labour in Algeria and Morocco was, however, increasingly threatened by emigration to France. Between 1905 and 1914 the Algerian government facilitated some Kabyle emigration to France and these workers were concentrated in Marseilles (docks, refineries), Paris (sugar refining, chemicals, transport) and the Nords (coal mining). But the major impetus towards emigration came during the First World War when 300,000 Algerians, 110,000 Tunisians and 76,000 Moroccans were recruited as both soldiers and workers. This represented an enormous percentage of the Maghrebin population, in Algeria one-third of all males of working age (Talha 1989: 70). The wartime experience of French life and industry triggered a large-scale post-war emigration, particularly of Algerians who were free to travel to France under a law of July 1914.

The conflict of interest between the colonial and metropolitan economies over access to Algerian labour was held in abeyance by the *union sacrée*. After 1918, however, an increasingly vociferous colonial lobby complained that emigration was creating a labour shortage, driving up wages and threatening the precarious viability of the colonial economy. It was often precisely people from zones like Kabylia, in which there was a tradition of internal migration to settler estates, who most readily made the transition to emigration to France where wages were higher.

Although the *colons* did face some problems of labour supply they greatly exaggerated their case and a number of measures guaranteed an ongoing supply of workers.

First, the decline in Kabyle seasonal migration was replaced by increased recruitment from mountain zones little affected by emigration – particularly the Rif. Second, a powerful colonial lobby, based mainly in Paris, persuaded the French government to introduce a complex body of administrative controls on emigration in 1924. In some types of agriculture –

most notably cereal farming – mechanization was increasingly used to replace native labour.

By the mid-1930s a population explosion in Algeria finally removed settler complaints about labour shortage. Indeed, a central concern in colonial discourse from *c.*1935 to the outbreak of revolution in 1954 was of a deepening Malthusian crisis and the threat presented by a huge mass of unemployed rural and urban Algerians. Projects for agrarian modernization and industrialization could not be implemented on a scale to mop up the rapid population increase. These pressures were far less severe in Tunisia and Morocco, partly because late colonization meant a less radical disintegration of pre-colonial society and because the balance between population and resources was fairly healthy.

Finally, in Algeria the war of 1954–62 triggered a huge internal migration. The French army's counter-insurgency policy involved the brutal *regroupement* and displacement of up to 3,525,000 people, or 50 per cent of the rural population (Sutton 1977). The experience of uprooting, the long-term abandonment of fields that had barely provided a subsistence, meant that with the coming of peace the great majority were not prepared to return to village life. The dramatic departure of almost the entire European population in the summer of 1962 created a vacuum in the urban centres and colonial estates. Like a dam bursting, the huge, impoverished populations of the *bled* that had been building up outside the perimeter of the colonized zones poured down into the plains (Bourdieu and Sayad 1964).

References

Adam, A. (1973) 'Berber Migrants in Casablanca', in E. Gellner and C. Micaud (eds) *Arabs and Berbers: From Tribe to Nation in North Africa*, London: Duckworth, 325–43

Bennoune, M. (1988) *The Making of Contemporary Algeria, 1830–1987*, Cambridge: Cambridge University Press

Bourdieu, P. and A. Sayad (1964) *Le Déracinement: La Crise de l'Agriculture traditionnelle en Algérie*, Paris: Minuit

Braudel, F. (1975) *The Mediterranean and the Mediterranean World in the Age of Philip II*, London: Fontana

Descloitres, J.-C. et al. (1961) *L'Algérie des Bidonvilles: Le Tiers Monde dans la Cité*, Paris: Mouton

Larnaude, M. (1936) 'Déplacement des travailleurs indigènes en Algérie', *Revue Africaine*, 360 (64), 207–15

Meillassoux, C. (1981) *Maidens, Meal and Money*, Cambridge: Cambridge University Press

Montagne, R. (1953) 'L'Immigration nord-africains en France: Son caractère familial et villageois', in *Hommages à L. Febvre*, Paris: A. Colin, vol. II, 365–71

Mutin, G. (1977) *La Mitidja: Décolonisation et Space géographique*, Paris: CNRS

Pascon, P. (1986) *Capitalism and Agriculture in the Haouz of Marrakesh*, London: Routledge

Prenant, A. (1953) 'Facteurs du Peuplement d'une Ville de l'Algérie intérieure: Sétif', *Annales de Géographie*, (334), 434–51

Ray, J. (1938) *Les Marocains en France*, Paris: Syrey

Sammut, C. (1977) 'La Situation du Prolétariat dans une Entreprise coloniale française en Tunisie', *Revue d'Histoire Maghrebine*, (9), 350–59

Simon, G. (1979) *L'Espace des Travailleurs tunisiens en France*, Poitiers

Sutton, K. (1977) 'Population Resettlement: Traumatic Upheavals and the Algerian Experience', *Journal of African Studies*, 15 (2), 279–300

Talha, L. (1989) *Le Salariat immigré dans la Crise*, Paris: CNRS

Yacono, X. (1955/6) *La Colonisation des Plaines du Chélif*, Algiers: E. Imbert, 2 vols

PEOPLE ON THE MOVE IN WEST AFRICA: FROM PRE-COLONIAL POLITIES TO POST-INDEPENDENCE STATES

KENNETH SWINDELL

Permanent migration, as well as seasonal and circulatory movements of population, have a long history in West Africa, and form an integral part of people's cultural and social lives and the production relations into which they enter. Migrations have emerged as a result of state formation, trading diasporas, ecological degradation, overpopulation, economic development and a rising tide of urbanization. At present, millions of West Africans are on the move each year, a majority of whom are searching for work in towns and countryside. Therefore labour migration has attracted a good deal of attention and theories basically rest on either behaviourist migrant-centred approaches, or structural analyses.[1]

This account attempts a historical overview of population mobility, and inclines towards structural explanations, but it recognizes that pre-colonial West Africa had its own political and economic imperatives. During the colonial period and afterwards, structural shifts in the world economy have been refracted through prisms of African society and culture to produce specific geographic and historic outcomes. In addition to migration being geared to international and regional forces, people also move as a result of contingencies and as part of the process of coping with their immediate conditions of existence – the seasonal search for pasture and fishing grounds, the response to drought, civil disturbance and warfare. Furthermore, over time migration flows have become institutionalized and taken on different cultural meanings, as well as creating social structures which facilitate and enable migration.

At a micro scale, population movements frequently take place within the context of extended and nuclear families. Many households as part of their survival or accumulation strategies straddle different economies, either permanently or seasonally (Stichter 1985; Swindell and Iliya 1992). The existence of straddling reminds us of the thinness of capitalist (and attempted socialist) transformations of West African societies and the coexistence of free and unfree forms of labour. Such partial transformations combined with a markedly seasonal agriculture result in an imperfect specialization of labour between agriculture and industry, which tends to generate labour circulation, as labour is constantly redistributed in order to make the economy work nationally and locally.

Given these circumstances, forms and patterns of migration are complex and not surprisingly the amount of census data on migration and population mobility in West Africa is strictly limited: much of what we know derives from specialized surveys conducted by a number of individual scholars and agencies.

Pre-colonial migrations

From the fourth century onwards the rise and fall of empires and petty kingdoms in the forests and savannahs precipitated shifts of population through conquest, colonization and enslavement. The great Sudanese empires of Ghana, Mali and Songhai were established either by invaders from North Africa, or by Sudanese who acquired the weapons of conquest via the trans-Saharan trade. Trade and religion also stimulated migration. The Hausa and the Mandinka were the most important of the trading peoples, and their economic presence throughout West Africa was underpinned by the establishment of migrant settlements, which in Hausa are called *zongos*, or *sabon garis* (Mabogunje 1972; Schildkraut 1978).

In the western Sudan the jihad of Umar Tal led to tens of thousands of Senegal valley residents (mostly Fulani) migrating some 400 miles to Karta where they joined the Umarian garrison at Nioro. When the French finally conquered the western Sudan in the 1890s half the Fulani population of Karta was forcibly returned to the Senegal valley (Hanson 1994).

States also developed in the forests, notably Oyo, Benin, Dahomey and Asante. The Yoruba kingdom of Oyo was at its height in the eighteenth century and expansion created colonies and petty tributary states. The founding and organization of the Asante state among the Akan owes something to migrants from the northern savannah states, while eventually the Akan migrated southwards, which subsequently led to the unification of several Akan states centred on Kumasi under the Asantahene (Fage 1988). Conditions in the pre-colonial states often led to mass movements of people who sought to escape from oppressive rulers, something which was facilitated by low population densities and the absence of formal political boundaries.[2]

The rise of the Sudanese empires and trade networks included the trade in slaves northwards across the Sahara, but it was during the late seventeenth and eighteenth centuries that there occurred a huge surge in forced migration, with the development of the Atlantic slave trade. Estimates suggest that from 1700 to 1809 approximately 4.5 million slaves were exported from West Africa. However, the Atlantic trade was contextually different: slaves became commodities in the world economy as West Africa became a labour reserve for New World plantations. On the African side the military expansion of states led to capture and enslavement of populations, while arguably the trade led to increased conflicts as rival states sought to control slave sales (Law 1986). Another factor in enslavement was periodic drought: in the great drought of 1738 slave exports in Senegambia rose, as people sold themselves into slavery as a last resort (Iliffe 1987).

The ending of the Atlantic trade in the early nineteenth century precipitated limited resettlement on the coast of former slaves, who were repatriated from the Americas or released from captured slave ships. Freetown in Sierra Leone, Bathurst in the Gambia and Monrovia in Liberia were towns and colonies set-up by Christian philanthropy. By 1860 some 100,000 liberated Africans were in Freetown and their rising numbers caused the British to send them to other locations, notably the Gambia which took 4000 between 1832 and 1843 (Webb 1994).

Commodity exports and labour migration

The Atlantic slave trade increased European influence along the coast but Europeans were still flies on the elephant's back. The ending of the trade led most importantly to the rise of legitimate commerce. From the 1830s onwards, European merchant capital filled the commercial void of the slave trade by developing the export of agricultural commodities, such as palm produce, groundnuts, cocoa, coffee, cotton and rubber.

Millions of rural households from the 1820s onwards were drawn into the world trading economy through agricultural exports, which led to the spread of European goods and currency followed by new forms of taxation. Commercial crop zones developed near the coast because of the moister climate and proximity to rivers. Here peasant farmers integrated the new crops into their existing cultivation systems, but as the export trade developed additional workers were needed to alleviate seasonal labour shortages during planting and harvesting, when massive inputs of labour were required. Towards the end of the nineteenth century colonial rule boosted the export trade and gradually the non-export zones, especially the Sudan-Sahel emerged as floating labour reserves where people could only access money for taxation and trade goods as migrant workers. Thus a pattern of seasonal circulation developed between the coast and the interior representing a new social and economic articulation of these regions.

Opinions vary about the positive and negative effects of seasonal labour circulation: arguably it keeps down wages, as the costs of reproducing the labour force are shifted towards the sending areas. Alternatively migration reduces food demands in the source areas and provides work in the dry season. But extended absences can adversely affect the household labour supply on food farms and there are real possibilities of a low level equilibrium developing between sending and receiving areas (Cleveland 1991).

One of the first migrant labour systems in West Africa was connected with the groundnut trade in Senegambia and the Casamance. Groundnuts were being exported in quantity by the 1850s and, according to reports from the Gambia, they were cultivated in part by Tillibunkas and Sera Woollies coming 500–600 miles from the interior (Swindell 1980).

The migrants (known as 'strange farmers' or *navetanes*) were involved in share contracts, which required them to give two or three days' work on the host's farm in return for which they received farms on which they could grow groundnuts. This system of labour renting was based on surplus land and a relative shortage of labour, especially as groundnuts are a wet season crop and are grown alongside the food staples. The migrant system was advantageous to local farmers who were relieved of cash payments, although they had to provide food for their workers.

At the turn of the century the British were concerned with abolition of domestic slavery, which gave further impetus to the migrant labour system. Owners were reducing their overheads by shedding slaves, whom they were obliged to feed and to pay taxes on as household members. Coupled with abolition and manumission ordinances, this released slaves who were now able seasonally to sell their labour to pay taxes and bridewealth. The effects of abolition, which had gathered momentum by 1910, produced a second wave of migrant workers who were a new class of poor farmers quite unlike the earlier pioneering migrants who evolved from the trading systems linking the Sudan and the coast (David 1981). As the twentieth century progressed the volume of migrants into Senegal reached 70,000 annually and into the Gambia in the 1970s there were still some 30,000 seasonal labourers drawn from within Senegambia, Mali and Guinea.

Migrant labour was crucial to the expansion of the agricultural export trade and once cocoa and coffee had been added to groundnuts and palm produce, the interior savannahs became the principal source of labour. Large numbers of seasonal workers headed for the Gold Coast, Ivory Coast and south-western Nigeria. The demand was for seasonal migrants because new cocoa farms are cleared and existing ones harvested during the dry season. In 1960 a survey estimated half a million men entered the Gold Coast and Ivory Coast each year, most of them from the densely populated Mossi area of Upper Volta, now Burkina Faso (Mabogunje 1972). Another survey in 1974/5 reconstructed 713,000 migrations which occurred during the period 1969–73 from the Mossi region, 205,000 of which were into the Ivory Coast (Coulibaby et al. 1980).[3] And in 1981 a World Bank survey confirmed the continuing importance of Burkina Faso as a supplier of migrant labour into the Ivory Coast, but migrants were staying away for longer periods (Zachariah and Conde 1981).

Another important southward migration stream originated in north-west Nigeria around Sokoto (Prothero 1959; Swindell 1984). This historic area was densely settled but economically marginalized under colonial rule, and became the source of some 200,000 seasonal migrants per annum. Migration among the Hausa areas became institutionalized and men constructed their migrations as Yawon Dande – 'the walk of the world' (Olofson 1976).

In the Gold Coast during the 1890s Africans who had made money out of palm oil trading began to acquire land for cocoa farms and pioneer farmers colononized sparsely settled areas in the western forests (Hill 1963). After 1900 the demand for labour increased as households could not clear new farms and maintain and harvest those coming into fruit. In the first instance labourers were hired as annual

contract workers; alternatively sharecroppers were employed on the basis of them receiving one-third of the crop. The system became widespread in the Gold Coast cocoa areas as well as among coffee farmers in the Ivory Coast.

In the Gold Coast, as the cocoa industry progressed so conditions of employment changed, reflecting the struggles between labour and capital (Van Hear 1982). After 1946 there was an increase in annual contracts, but as employers became increasingly devious over payment, so share contracts became preferred by experienced migrants. However, employers reacted by recruiting annual contract workers from northern Ghana. Share contracts were tightened by making workers tend hosts' food farms and pay a fee as a contribution to their maintenance, as employers became intent on extracting more surplus from their labour. At the same time casual day labour increased as labourers and employers found this a more flexible system and workers found they could bargain over daily rates and the length of the working day.

From the mid-1950s farm labour became scarcer. Commercial food farming was extended by the creation of state farms in the north. The state sector in general absorbed more labour, the timber industry expanded and there was a persistent drift of young men into the towns. In 1969 the supply of foreign labour was affected by the expulsion of aliens, while the price of cocoa began to plummet. The migrant stream into Ghana weakened, although it held in Ivory Coast which had become West Africa's leading coffee and cocoa producer. In the groundnut basin of Senegal, the Dakar labour market siphoned labour from the land while the Senegal Valley became a labour reserve for France, especially for construction workers (Adams 1981). In the older groundnut areas land became scarcer and share contracts declined as farmers turned to casual day and contracted gang labour, as farming became more capitalized through the use of ox-ploughs and weeder attachments.

The Nigerian oil boom

If by the 1970s long-distance movements of agricultural labour were beginning to sag, a new migration stream of impressive and possibly unique proportions appeared as Nigeria emerged as a world petroleum producer (Swindell 1990). Possibly between two and three million (mostly men) entered Nigeria between 1975 and 1983. Over one million came from Ghana (formerly a net receiver of labour), 500,000 from Niger, some 150,000 Chadians, 120,000 Cameroonians, 5000 Togolese and 5000 Beninoise. Most were illegal immigrants as they crossed uncontrolled borders, bribing border guards, while employers and officials did not bother to register unskilled workers. In 1979 ECOWAS issued a protocol concerning the free movement of goods, capital and people, which gave an additional boost to migration into Nigeria. Nigeria's attractions included cheap food and transport, relatively high wages, a wide range of consumer goods, often imported based on an overvalued naira. Employment opportunities were abundant as a result of a huge boom in public and private construction works. Many Nigerians left the land for towns and construction sites, but foreign workers suited a number of political and economic interests. Long-distance workers were easier to control, manage and manipulate and especially in the north posed no real threat to local ethnic and religious sensibilities. Workers came from everywhere, but it was Ghana which became the chief source: it had a cadre of skilled and professional workers, and by the mid-1970s it had a seriously flawed economy.

In 1979 the Nigerian economy was under strain; corruption in government was widespread, there was a sudden plunge into indebtedness as oil prices fell and interest rates rose, industry contracted and unemployment increased. Urban crime rates climbed, while in the north riots and deaths resulted from civilian and governmental confrontations with a charismatic Islamic sect (Lubeck 1985). These events led to the Expulsion of Aliens Order in January 1983. This was a sudden announcement, which caused confusion and recrimination, not least from the Ghanaians.

Migration and droughts

The droughts which affected the Sahel from 1968–74 and 1980–82 were responsible for a southward drift of population throughout the region. In times of difficulty people increasingly turn to resources outside their villages, which requires mobility over wider areas as the means of survival. Inevitably many looked towards the towns. In the 1970s the population of Nouakchott in Mauritania rose to over 200,000, which meant one-fifth of the country's total population was in the city. Further east the drought hit Niger, Chad and northern Nigeria, which caused a shift of population into the cities and southern regions of Nigeria, which were not only wetter, but part of an expanding oil economy. During the 1973/4 drought a survey of 631 north-eastern villages in Nigeria showed an increase of out-migration from 26 to 43 per cent and while Kano was the principal destination people were moving further south, to Zaria, Kaduna

and Lagos (Mortimer 1989). Of the movements into Kano city some 64 per cent came from Kano state and 22 per cent from Niger.

Evidence from north Kano state showed a relatively small amount of permanent redistribution of population; rather moves were short-term or seasonal ones. A detailed survey of five villages on the northern borders of Nigeria showed 47 per cent of household heads reported men absent in the 1973/4 dry season. And as the drought increased so women, children and the aged were taken along. Some men went as far as Lagos using Hausa *zongos*, where landlords employed them to sell goats, brought by lorry from the north. By 1980 these men were organizing the movement of goats from the north, as well as selling them in Lagos: thus innovation grew out of necessity.

Urbanization

Although seasonal movements of labour continue throughout West Africa, long-distance migration has become blunted by economic recession in host countries, rising population levels and increased resistance to foreign workers. However, since the 1950s urban migration has inexorably strengthened, associated with rural land shortages, better transport and new economic opportunities.

After independence townward migration accelerated and many urban areas were growing at 7 per cent per annum with strong inward flows of the young and economically active. At first these flows were dominated by males, but by the 1980s gender differences appear to have lessened (Vaa 1990).

Structural adjustment programmes have reduced employment, especially in construction work, which has radically altered casual circulatory migration between town and village (Gugler 1989). Many of the urban poor compete with their rural counterparts in the urban periphery, as both search for casual day labour on farms. Some workers have returned to the villages, while those who stay take longer finding a job and those who have one stick with it, which has led to increased bi-locality of households. But many men have been followed by their wives into the city, which has increased social costs, such that female (and child) employment are now crucial to the reproduction of the household. Although gender differences have lessened among migrants, the young still predominate, and a majority intend ultimately to return to their homes. In Lagos in 1978, 78 per cent of the population was under 30 years, while only 1.9 per cent was over 60 years, compared with a national average of 3.4 per cent (Peil 1991).

Apart from Nigeria and Ghana most West African states are dominated by their capital cities, where the limited job and educational opportunities are concentrated, as well as being the sites of political power, where a wide spectrum of interest groups vie for control of the state. Towns such as Freetown, Monrovia and Bamako expanded their populations by between 200 per cent and 400 per cent from the 1960s to the 1980s. In 1985 some 42 per cent of Bamako's population (710,000) was born elsewhere.

Refugees

Since independence rival interests have battled to control the state in West Africa, a battle sometimes shaped by ethnicity, sometimes orchestrated globally, which has led to political turmoil and waves of forced migration, both within and among countries.

In general West Africa has not seen the same levels of refugee activity as the Horn of Africa, or central and southern Africa, but there have been some serious incidents. In 1989 the Mauritanian–Senegal conflict led to the expulsion of Moors from Senegalese towns, while the Fulani on the Mauritanian bank of the Senegal River were pushed into Senegal (Santoir 1990). By July 1990 some 27,000 Fulani had been moved into the Senegalese district of Matam, while 20,000 Moorish shops were destroyed in Dakar. Observers have suggested this was not simply an inter-state or ethnic conflict, but rather a revival of the historic push southwards by Arab–Berbers of the Mahgreb, which had been suspended during the colonial period. The recent push was exacerbated by years of drought and the economic drain of fighting Polissario (the Sahrawi movement for independence) in former Spanish Sahara, which was divided between Mauritania and Morocco in 1974. In southern Senegal the Casamance region has been disrupted since the late 1980s as a separatist movement has developed, largely dominated by Jolas, who have been marginalized by both colonial and post-independence regimes.

Internal conflicts have also occurred in West Africa, notably in Nigeria where the civil war from 1967 to 1970 led to widespread disruption and dislocation. During the colonial period Igbos moved into the Islamic north as government workers, artisans and traders. After the assassination of northern political leaders by Igbo-led army officers, easterners became a target for reprisals leading to the September massacres of 1966, after which almost one million easterners fled southwards. The consequent civil war and the attempted secession of the east to form Biafra, was a product of differential development, exacerbated by

ethnic and religious factors, and not least because Nigeria's new oil wealth was located in the eastern region.

The most serious zone of contemporary conflict is in Liberia where something like 500,000 people (one-fifth of the total population) fled the country after the overthrow of the Doe regime in 1990, and the subsequent division of the country into warring factions. In addition to these refugees, an estimated one million people have been displaced within Liberia (Wells 1990). The war has also spilled over into eastern Sierra Leone, as one faction pursued another and tried to gain access to diamonds and timber to finance their forces. In the meantime, disaffected Sierra Leoneans have used the war to destabilize the former Momoh regime (overthrown 1992) and settle their own political scores. As a result some 200,000 Sierra Leoneans have been displaced in the eastern region.

Conclusion

Without widespread and reliable censuses, it is difficult to reach any firm conclusion about the present state of migration in West Africa. The indications are that long-distance international movements of labour have slackened, although given the conditions of existence in the interior migration is likely to continue. Internal population redistribution continues among farming communities, while environmental hazards cause temporary rather than permanent movements of people. West African towns still attract rural people, although there are contrary forces at work.

Political conflicts, although confined to specific locations, have produced some of the most recent and traumatic movements of people in West Africa. In the post-cold war world dominated by economic stringencies and a search for new regional identities, it would not be surprising if West African states find that the centre is less likely to hold, and things increasingly begin to fall apart. However, over a long period West African populations have shown a resilience to structural change and contingency, which has often been achieved through remarkable levels of mobility.

Acknowledgement

I would like to thank staff of Worcester College of Higher Education for their assistance in the preparation of this manuscript.

Notes

1. For examples of various theoretical and ideological positions on migration and population mobility, see the following: Amin (1974), Chapman and Prothero (1983), Cordell and Gregory (1987), Todaro (1985).

2. Migration to escape from social or political problems was common among the Yoruba, Edo and Fon. Asiwagu (1976) notes that the reign of Oba Ewuare of Benin in the mid-fifteenth century was so unpopular that it generated waves of protest migration, which ostensibly led to the foundation of many communities of closely related groups.
3. For an overview of Birkinabe migration see Cordell, Gregory and Piché (forthcoming).

References

Adams, A. (1981) 'The Senegal River Valley', in J. Heyer et al. (eds) *Rural Development in Tropical Africa*, London: Macmillan, 325–53

Amin, S. (1974) *Modern Migrations in Western Africa*, London: Oxford University Press

Asiwagu, A. I. (1976) 'Migrations as Revolution: The Example of the Ivory Coast and Upper Volta before 1945', *Journal of African History*, (17), 578

Chapman, M. and R. M. Prothero (1983) 'Themes in Circulation in the Third World', *International Migration Review*, 17 (4), 597–632

Cleveland, D. (1991) 'Migration in West Africa: A Savannah Village Perspective', *Africa*, 61 (2), 222–46

Cordell, D. and J. W. Gregory (eds) (1987) *African Population and Capitalism: Historical Perspectives*, Boulder, CO: Westview Press

Cordell, D., J. Gregory and V. Piché (forthcoming) *Hoe and Wage: A Social History of a Circular Migration System in West Africa*, Boulder: Westview

Coulibaby, S. et al. (1980) *Les Migrations Voltaiques*, vol. I, Ouagadougu: Centre Voltaique de la Recherche Scientifique

David, P. (1981) *Les Navetanes: Histoires des Migrants saisonniers de l'Arachide en Senegambie des Origines à nos Jours*, Dakar: Les Nouvelles Editions Africaines

Fage, J. D. (1988) *An Introduction to the History of Africa*, London: Unwin Hyman

Gugler, J. (1989) 'Women Stay on the Farm no More: Changing Patterns of Rural–Urban Migration in Sub-Saharan Africa', *Journal of Modern African Studies*, 27 (2), 347–52

Hanson, J. (1994) 'Islam, Migration and the Political Economy of Meaning: *Fergo Nioro* from the Senegal River Valley, 1862–1890', *Journal of African History*, 35 (1), 37–60

Hill, P. (1963) *The Migrant Cocoa Farmers of Southern Ghana*, Cambridge: Cambridge University Press

Iliffe, J. (1987) *The African Poor*, Cambridge: Cambridge University Press

Law, R. (1986) 'Dahomey and the Slave Trade', *Journal of African History*, 27 (2), 237–67

Lubeck, P. M. (1985) 'Islamic Protest under Semi-Industrial Capitalism', *Africa*, 55 (1), 369–89

Mabogunje, A. (1972) *Regional Mobility and Resource Development in West Africa*, Montreal: McGill–Queens University Press

Mortimer, M. J. (1989) *Adapting to Drought: Farmers, Famine and Desertification in West Africa*, Cambridge: Cambridge University Press

Olofson, H. (1976) 'Yawon Dande: A Hausa Category of Migration', *Africa*, 46 (1), 66–79

Peil, M. (1991) *Lagos, the City and its People*, London: Bellhaven

Prothero, R. Mansell (1959) *Migrant Labour from Sokoto Province*, Kaduna: Government Printer

Santoir, C. (1990) 'Les Peuls réfusés, les Peuls mauritaniens refugiés au Sengal', *Cahiers des Sciences Humaines*, 26 (4), 577–603

Schildkraut, E. (1978) *People of the Zongo: The Transformation of Ethnic Identities in Ghana*, Cambridge: Cambridge University Press

Stichter, S. (1985) *Migrant Labourers*, Cambridge: Cambridge University Press

Swindell, K. (1980) 'Navetanes, Tillibunkas and Strange Farmers: The Development of Migrant Groundnut Farming along the Gambia River', *Journal of African History*, 21 (1), 93–100

(1984) 'Farmers, Labourers and Traders: Dry Season Migration from Northwestern Nigeria, 1900–1933', *Africa*, 54 (1), 4–17

(1990) 'International Labour Migration in Nigeria, 1976–1986: Employment, Nationality and Ethnicity', *Migration*, (8), 135–6

Swindell, K. and M. A. Iliya (1992) 'Accumulation, Consolidation and Survival: Non-Farm Incomes and Agrarian Change in Northwest Nigeria', SSRC of America, Joint Committee on African Studies, Working Paper Series 6

Todaro, M. P. (1985) *Economic Development in the Third World*, 3rd edition, New York: Longman

Vaa, M. (1990) 'Paths to the City: Migrant Histories of Poor Women in Bamako', in J. Barker (ed.) *Small Town Africa*, Uppsala: Scandinavian Institute of African Studies, 172–81

Van Hear, N. (1982) 'Northern Labour and Development of Capitalist Agriculture in Ghana', Ph.D. thesis, University of Birmingham

Webb, P. (1994) 'Guests of the Crown: Convicts and Liberated Slaves on McCarthy Island, The Gambia', *Geographical Journal*, 160 (1), 136–42

Wells, R. (1990) 'The Lost of Liberia', *Africa Report*, 35 (5), 21–2

Zachariah, K. C. and J. Conde (1981) *Migration in West Africa: Demographic Aspects*, New York: Oxford University Press

PART SEVEN

LATIN AND CENTRAL AMERICAN MIGRATION

In one of the first novels in English, published in 1719, Daniel Defoe famously tells of the adventures of a footloose seaman, Robinson Crusoe. After suffering various misfortunes, including being himself enslaved for two years, Crusoe finds a modicum of success in 'the Brasils', where he begins 'to thrive and prosper very well upon [his] plantation'. He reminisces to his fellow planters about his two voyages to the Guineas and, in particular, about 'how easy it was to purchase upon the coast, for trifles, such as beads, toys, knives, scissors, hatchets, bits of glass and the like, not only gold dust, Guinea grains, elephants teeth, etc., but negroes, for the service of the Brasils, in great numbers'. Their eyes light up at the mention of the last commodity, for slaves were expensive and a monopsony was exercised by the kings of Spain and Portugal. His planter friends offer to fit out a ship if Crusoe will act as a supercargo to pick up slaves and return them, illegally, to Brazil. His greed gets the better of him and he accepts their offer, only to suffer the crowning mischance of a shipwreck and exile on a desert island.

Naturally this story can be dismissed as mere fiction, but economists have used the tale to anchor some of their most fundamental theories (Marx, for example, deployed it to illustrate his labour theory of value), while literary critics have concurred with Defoe's own remark that 'the Story, although allegorical, is also historical'. *Klein's* account of immigration to Brazil in this volume starts after the collapse of slavery in Brazil, but also captures some of the frantic atmosphere generated by the planters' insatiable desire for labour. With the liberated slave population getting as far away from the plantations as they could, the lucrative coffee bean crop could not be planted, cared for and harvested without massive injections of new immigrants. The solution was to be found in *colonato* contracts, which involved a combination of wage labour and sharecropping – the ideal mixture for an ambitious, if impoverished, Italian, Spanish or Portuguese farmer. Though many migrants from these countries were trapped by the system, many more found that with hard work and careful saving, independent proprietorship was possible after a few years in the coffee plantations (cf. Stolcke 1988). Attracted by the prospect of land, between 1880 and 1900 some 1.6 million European migrants were lured to Brazil.

The large influx of Europeans into Brazil was to be exceeded among the other South American countries only by Argentina. Absolute numbers raced ahead of Brazil from 1900 onwards. As *Adelman* recounts, nearly five million Europeans reached Argentina in the period between 1880 and 1930, making the country, in per capita terms, a far more popular destination than the USA. The key difference with the USA was that many coming to Argentina, particularly Italians, could be classified as 'sojourners' rather than immigrants.[1] In the 1920s nearly two-thirds of the migrants returned to their countries of origin. The third contribution in Part 7, predominantly concerned with European migration to the River Plate region, is by *Finch* on Uruguay, which is essentially a microcosm of its more populous and powerful neighbours. Again we find high rates of return migration (or transit migration to Argentina), the predominance of Italian and Spanish migrants and the overwhelming influence of immigrants in the political social and economic life of the country, particularly in its capital city, Montevideo.

While the story of transoceanic migration to Latin and Central America is essentially an Atlantic tale, it is vital not to overlook the important element of Pacific immigration. *Klein* draws attention to the large numbers of Japanese, many of them farm workers, who came to Brazil (over 14 per cent of those who landed in Santos between 1908 and 1936). The Japanese were also an important constituent element in the population of Peru, a country not separately covered in this *Survey*. This long association between Peru and Japan was dramatized by the election of the first Peruvian president of Japanese origin in 1990. As *Hu-DeHart* explains, part of the flow of Asian migrants to the Caribbean, and to South and Central America, was diverted from the USA after that country passed various anti-Asian immigration laws. Her own contribution focuses on the frequently overlooked Chinese indentured labourers travelling to Peru and Cuba and the free Chinese immigrants coming to Mexico during the presidency of Porfirio Díaz. The Chinese migrants demonstrated an extraordinary capacity to detect niche trading markets and occupations. This often ended in permanent settlement and prosperity, but occasionally resulted in resentment, hostility and expulsion – as, for example, tragically occurred in the case of the Chinese community in Mexico's Sonora state.

Two of the contributions in Part 7 focus on emigration. *Diaz* shows how the USA, then Venezuela, provided the point of convergence for the aspirations of Colombian university graduates, technicians and labour migrants. The oil-boom economy of Venezuela, in particular, was a powerful magnet for Colombians trapped by a failing economy and restricted access to political participation and social justice. In the case of Central America, covered by *Ferris*, the non-economic reasons for emigration were even more compelling than in Colombia. In the 1970s and 1980s, in both El Salvador and Guatemala, the political violence reached frightening, life-threatening proportions. Their civil wars followed the customary Central American fault line dividing a narrow, landowning political elite from a left-wing intelligentsia leading a coalition of impoverished workers and peasants. The ill-advised intervention of the USA on the side of the political right only served to compound the problem and draw in a consequent flow of defenders of and dissenters from the El Salvadorean and Guatemalan regimes as political refugees.

It is perhaps useful to remember that Latin America has historically found itself also a recipient, not just an exporter, of refugees and political exiles. The Portuguese court had to relocate in Brazil for a time, while Mexico played host to such diverse left-wing exiles as Leon Trotsky and his entourage, many Spanish Republicans and, later, US victims of the McCarthyite period. Sadly, as happened in Chile after the legitimate Allende government was violently overthrown in 1973, Latin America has also often been a producer of refugees. One was our contributor *Jaime Llambias-Wolff*, who sensitively depicts the fragilities and uncertainties of those who, finally, wish to return to their country of origin – and who remain psychologically caught between 'a beautiful nostalgia and a different reality'.

Note

1. The notion of a 'sojourner' has been most fully developed in the Chinese case, notably by Wang Gungwu (1991). The Italian case is addressed in Gabaccia (1992) who also shows how the Italian international labour movement was able to cross-cut countries of settlement among the Italian sojourners abroad.

References

Defoe, Daniel (1985) *The Life and Adventures of Robinson Crusoe*, Harmondsworth: Penguin [first published 1719]

Gabaccia, Donna (1992) 'Clase y Cultura: Los Migrantes Italianos de los Movimientos Obreros en el Mundo, 1874–1914', *Estudios Migratorios Latinamericanos*, 7 (22), 425–51

Stolcke, Verena (1988) *Coffee Planters, Workers and Wives: Class Conflict and Gender Relations on São Paulo Plantations, 1850–1980*, Basingstoke: Macmillan

Wang Gungwu (1991) *China and the Chinese Overseas*, Singapore: Times Academic Press

URUGUAYAN MIGRATION

HENRY FINCH

Although European migration to Uruguay is clearly part of a general movement of population to the River Plate region, there are particular characteristics of Uruguay's history and geography which make it a case apart. Uruguay emerged from Spanish colonial rule as an empty and remote province. Nationhood was not so much striven for as conferred upon it in 1828 by British diplomacy anxious to create a buffer state between Buenos Aires and the expansionism of the Portuguese empire in Brazil. This did not prevent Uruguay's two powerful neighbours from sponsoring and intervening in the civil wars which marked the first four decades of formal independence. Not until the advent of British capital in the 1860s did Uruguay begin to escape from Brazilian dominance, and in the 1870s the structure of a modern state finally took shape as Montevideo exerted central authority over the regional *caudillos* of the interior, and the modernization of the livestock export sector began.

Commercially, Montevideo enjoyed a dominant position in the trade of the River Plate basin, until the ports of Argentina and southern Brazil were improved at the end of the nineteenth century, and this was reflected in the size of the city relative to Uruguay's total population. In other respects Uruguay has consistently had marginal status in the region, largely as a result of its small size and less dynamic economic performance over the long run. The proximity of Buenos Aires and the fertile pampas region of Argentina, and the vast cattle ranches across an open land frontier in the Brazilian state of Rio Grande do Sur, have meant that Uruguay has been particularly open to emigration as well as immigration. The greater attractiveness of urban Argentina and the demand for labour on the wheat farms of the pampas persuaded many European immigrants who had landed in Montevideo to move onward. The outflow was swelled by Uruguayans, particularly from the interior, who migrated temporarily or permanently, especially in the 1890s. There were also reverse movements of Argentinians drawn to commercial activity in Montevideo, and of Brazilians acquiring land in the frontier departments in the north. The pattern of migration within the region became even

more complex when Buenos Aires was adopted as the principal destination of ocean steamships in the River Plate at the turn of the century, and a number of European immigrants arrived in Montevideo by river from Argentina. Given the deficiencies of the official statistics (there was no population census at all between 1908 and 1963), there is great uncertainty and disagreement about the scale of immigration to Uruguay. What is clear, however, is that Uruguay's regional marginality made it a provisional rather than a final destination for very many immigrants; and even in the late twentieth century native-born Uruguayans retain a predisposition to emigrate in search of greater economic opportunity.

At independence, Uruguay's population was a meagre 74,000, of whom perhaps 14,000 lived in Montevideo. By 1908, when total population was 1.04 million and Montevideo held 309,000, the demographic impact of immigration in Uruguay was already declining. Although immigrants continued to arrive in subsequent years the process of 'populating' Uruguay was effectively complete. About 17 per cent (and falling) of the total population was foreign-born in 1908, compared with over 25 per cent (and rising) in Argentina at the same period. Certainly for Uruguay this represented a reduction from previous levels. On the eve of the siege of Montevideo during the Guerra Grande, in 1843, 60 per cent of Montevideo's 31,000 residents were foreign-born, including members of the commercial elite from France and Britain. The effect of the war and siege, which ended in 1851, was especially discouraging to non-Uruguayans, who could move elsewhere. In 1860 the foreign-born proportion in the city was 48 per cent, a figure reproduced almost exactly in the Montevideo census of 1889. Nationally in 1860 the proportion was 35 per cent; those born in Spain, Italy and France (in that order) constituted the largest European populations, though Brazilians settled in the northern frontier region were the largest single non-native group. The surge of migrants in the second half of the 1880s, when the net inflow of Europeans averaged 8000 annually (Mourat 1969: 23), was dominated by Italians, such that by 1908 they represented 34 per cent of all immigrants. Spain had contributed 30 per cent, and the participation of those of Brazilian and French origin had declined to 15 per cent and 5 per cent respectively. Argentinians (10 per cent) were the majority of the remainder (Rial 1983: 75).

By 1908 the principal effects of the migration process had been felt. Arriving typically as young men from Mediterranean Europe, immigrants found little opportunity in the thinly-populated interior. The structure of landownership based on *latifundia* put access to land in the livestock sector beyond the reach of all but a tiny minority, and the pattern of extensive livestock production did not demand labour. On the contrary, from the 1870s the spread of wire fencing and the transfer to the state of the defence of property rights were destroying traditional functions and creating an impoverished native rural population. Arable agriculture, whose development by immigrant colonists was the dream of progressive politicians, was in reality little more attractive. Compared with Argentina the soils were thin, and land suitable for cereals, dairying, horticulture or viticulture was restricted to the southern and western departments (especially Canelones, Colonia and San José). Only 7 per cent of the interior population in 1908 was European, and although 30 per cent of those engaged in agriculture were immigrants, mostly from Spain and Italy, only a minority arrived with experience in farming. Their position as tenants or sharecroppers was unenviable (Barrán and Nahum 1978: 24–31).

Both their background and the environment they found on arrival dictated that immigrants stayed predominantly in Montevideo. In 1908 27 per cent of the city's population had been born in Europe (90 per cent of those in Italy or Spain); for the male population of working age the ratio was substantially higher, and very few of the population would not have had at least one grandparent born abroad. Migration to Uruguay was thus mainly urban in character, and the influence of migrants on the economic and social structure of the city was immense. Although after 1890 demand for labour slackened, the urban environment remained conducive to individual advancement. Broadly, immigrants contributed enterprise, skills and labour to the urban economy, whereas the native-born were predominant in government and clerical employment and the professions. The census of 1889 revealed that over 80 per cent of building workers, labourers, shoemakers, tailors (to choose occupations almost at random) were immigrants. A very few early immigrants acquired great wealth in industry, commerce or banking. Success on that scale was exceptional, but

the threshold of entry into small-scale distribution or workshop manufacturing was low enough to permit a disproportionate number of immigrants to establish themselves in these sectors. In 1925 a semi-official publication noted that success as entrepreneurs was largely the preserve of the foreign-born.

The attitude of government to immigration in the nineteenth century was generally positive but passive, and amounted to little more than short-term accommodation for new arrivals. But the weight of immigrants in Montevideo had a direct or indirect effect in promoting reform measures which eased their route upward. A liberal educational policy from the 1870s assisted the entry of the sons of immigrants into the dependent middle-class stratum which was largely closed to immigrants themselves, and the adoption and strengthening of a protectionist tariff in the last quarter of the century directly benefited the business ventures of immigrants producing for the domestic market. An alternative route for urban workers lay through collective organization, and the role of European immigrants from the 1890s onwards in trade unionism and the spread of socialist and anarcho-syndicalist doctrines was evident. Indeed, under President José Batlle y Ordóñez (1903–7, 1911–15) Montevideo became a haven for extremists and agitators expelled from Buenos Aires. It was Batlle's urban-oriented populist reformism, promoting the further diversification of the economy away from its livestock-product export base, which caused Uruguay to become known as 'South America's first welfare state'. This complex programme had as its main political aim the incorporation of the immigrant working class into Batlle's traditional non-class oriented Colorado party, and perhaps also the retention of a higher proportion of landed immigrants in Uruguay by increasing its attraction relative to Argentina.

Estimating the scale of net immigration to Uruguay is an even greater problem for the first half of the twentieth century than for the nineteenth. Official migration figures indicate net immigration of 101,000 for 1911–15, and 226,000 for 1916–30. However, the declared nationality of a high proportion of these arrivals was in fact Uruguayan, implying a net return of former emigrants which neither the general historical record nor population censuses in neighbouring countries can justify. Though the traditional version still has currency (Sánchez-Albornoz 1986: 130), sceptics reduced the figures to 14,000 (1910–14) and 89,000 (1915–29) by disregarding all arrivals by river (European or otherwise) (Barrán and Nahum 1979:

100–4; Pereira and Trajtenberg 1966: 76–113). In view of contemporary comment on the scale of European immigration in the years preceding the First World War, and the rapid growth of meat-freezing, construction and consumer goods industries in Montevideo at this time (and such effect as Batlle's policies may have had), a total of 40,000 for 1910–14 would be a plausible guess. Spaniards and Italians were once more the largest groups. Indeed they were to remain so, though the incomplete census of Montevideo taken in 1930 suggests that the predominance of Italians since the 1880s (though never as marked in Uruguay as in Argentina) had been reversed. It is likely that about a quarter of the 105,000 arrivals in the 1920s (Rodriguez Villamil and Sapriza 1982: 28) were from Spain, but the distinctive features of the decade were Jewish immigration, and the diversity of non-traditional origins in central and eastern Europe and the Near East.

During most of the twentieth century Uruguay was a net recipient of migrants and, because of its extremely small population in the first half-century after independence, the impact of immigration on the social, political and economic structures of Montevideo was very great. But Uruguay was also a country of emigrants, who were both Europeans who chose to move on and the native-born population, especially from the interior. As a result, from the 1890s onwards net immigration was modest in scale, perhaps only in the 1920s contributing more than 10 per cent of total population growth. After 1930 both immigration and emigration diminished somewhat; the traditional open-door policy was abandoned in 1936 (though the post-war decade saw a revived inflow), and wages and employment improved with the adoption of populist policies in the 1940s in support of import-substituting industrialization. By the late 1950s, however, Uruguay had entered a period of secular economic stagnation and growing social and political instability. In the late 1960s a significant emigration was underway, which by the time of the military coup in 1973 had assumed major proportions. Between 1963 and 1975 there was a net emigration of 0.17 million from a total 1963 population of 2.60 million (Aguiar 1982: 100). Argentina was, as in traditional emigration, the preferred destination of the majority, but the new Uruguayan emigrants, typically young educated urban males, settled also in Australia, the USA and Spain. Their emigration signified the loss of most of the net immigration in the twentieth century up to 1960, which the return of political exiles after 1985 did little to mitigate.

References

Aguiar, César A. (1982) *Uruguay: País de Emigración*, Montevideo: Ediciones de la Banda Oriental

Barrán, José Pedro and Benjamín Nahum (1978) *Historia Rural del Uruguay Moderno*, vol VII, *Agricultura, Crédito y Transporte Bajo Batlle 1905–1914*, Montevideo: Ediciones de la Banda Oriental

—— (1979) *Batlle, los Estancieros y el Imperio Británico*, Vol. I, *El Uruguay del Novecientos*, Montevideo: Ediciones de la Banda Oriental

Mourat, Oscar et al. (1969) *Cinco Perspectivas Históricas del Uruguay Moderno*, Montevideo: Fundación de Cultura Universitaria

Pereira, Juan José and R. Trajtenberg (1966) *Evolución de la Población Total y Activa en el Uruguay 1908–1957*, Montevideo: Universidad de la República, Instituto de Economía

Rial, Juan (1983) *Población y Desarrollo de un Pequeño País: Uruguay 1830–1930*, Montevideo: Centro de Informaciones y Estudios del Uruguay (CIESU)

Rodriguez Villamil, Silvia and Graciela Sapriza (1982) *La Inmigración europea en el Uruguay*, Montevideo: Ediciones de la Banda Oriental

Sánchez-Albornoz, Nicolás (1986) 'The Population of Latin America 1850–1930', in L. Bethell (ed.) *The Cambridge History of Latin America*, vol. IV, Cambridge: Cambridge University Press, 121–52

EUROPEAN AND ASIAN MIGRATION TO BRAZIL

HERBERT S. KLEIN

With the availability of an unlimited supply of African slaves in the first half of the nineteenth century the new imperial government of Brazil expressed only moderate interest in promoting foreign immigration (Klein 1987). Prior to the middle decades of the century, it supported European agricultural colonies primarily to guarantee the settlement of its southern frontiers. But with the successful closing of the Atlantic slave trade in 1850, it experimented with using European immigrant sharecroppers in the coffee fields. On the eve of the final abolition of slavery in the decade of the 1880s, came a third policy of subsidized immigration to provide free workers to replace the departing slaves in coffee. From then until the 1930s Brazil was a major recipient of European and Asian immigrant labour, again entering the international labour market in the immediate aftermath of the Second World War.

The agricultural colonization movement, which involved mostly German- and Italian-speaking European farmers, began in the 1820s and continued on a modest scale well into the twentieth century. It emphasized the establishment of a small propertied yeomanry and probably brought in conservatively between 100,000 to 200,000 immigrants by 1900 (Boni 1987–90; Oberacker 1967; Petrone 1982; Roche 1959; Willems 1946). The coffee sharecropping experiment of the 1840s and 1850s which involved some 10,000 Europeans failed because of the low savings potential involved and the coexistence of slave labour on the coffee *fazendas* (Buarque de Hollanda 1969; Dean 1976). Finally, with the approach of emancipation in the 1880s, the planter class – with government support – came up with a new immigrant labour regime known as the *colono* system, in which passage to the New World was fully paid for by the state and federal governments, and a complex wage and piece work payment system was arranged for the immigrant families who totally replaced slaves in coffee after 1888. The subsequent growth of coffee and the economy of the previously frontier region of São Paulo would finally spur a major flow of voluntary international migrants, who would outnumber the subsidized immigrants by the

first decade of the twentieth century. In total, from the founding of the independent Brazil in the 1820s until 1970, some 5.6 million foreign migrants arrived in this South American nation.

The post-1880 subsidized coffee labour migration brought the most intense migration. The free passage from Europe to the farm gate and the better compensation schemes proved immediately successful, and from 1889 to 1900 some 878,000 immigrants arrived in São Paulo alone, of which over three-quarters were subsidized. Fearing these immigrants might become temporary migrants, as occurred with the *golondrina* migration of European males to Argentina, the planters supported only a family migration. Subsidies for passage were offered only to families which contained at least one working age male (Dean 1976, Chapter 6; Holloway 1980, Chapter 3). It was this immigrant labour which permitted São Paulo to triple its coffee output in the decade after abolition, and there was a parallel growth in urban centres. This led to major increases in spontaneous European immigration to this frontier zone – most of whose cities were founded in the late nineteenth or early twentieth century. By the first decade of the twentieth century more non-subsidized European migrants arrived than did the subsidized farm workers.

Clearly immigrant workers were crucial in saving the desperate coffee industry which could not hold its liberated slave population. But was the work in the coffee fields of any advantage to the immigrant workers? An intense and bitter debate exists about the ability of the immigrant workers to profit from the system (Alvim 1986; Dean 1976; Holloway 1980; Klein 1991, 1992; Stolcke 1986). The *colonato* contract provided a fixed payment by the planter for the number of trees cared for by each worker, and a fixed price per weight of coffee harvested, plus salaries for any special day-labour performed. A family was contracted to maintain a minimum of 2000 to upwards of 15,000 trees, depending on the number of 'hoes' (i.e. able-bodied workers) that it could mobilize. The average family worked about 5000 trees. The income from the maintenance of trees accounted for between one-half and two-thirds of the total annual income of the free worker families (Holloway 1980: 75). Given the variation in productivity of trees, there was wide variation in the amount of coffee that workers could pick, and thus harvest income was much more variable than the wages paid for the care of trees. The immigrants were also granted lands to cultivate their own food crops and limited pasture rights to graze livestock, whose product was for their exclusive use or sale. All housing was provided free. By this new and complex system of piecework, annual wages, day labour, and free lands and housing, the planters hoped to hold down costs, guarantee labour stability, make labour as mobile as possible, and still make the work attractive to European immigrants by providing sufficient income that savings could be generated (Alvim 1986; Holloway 1980, Chapter 4; Stolcke 1986: 35ff.). Since wages varied even on a given *fazenda* depending on the age of the trees and the quality of the soil, it is difficult to measure the value of wages over time and place. It would seem that daily living costs absorbed about half of the gross profits of any family at the end of the year, and that total savings depended on a wide variety of factors from the health of the family to the number of able-bodied workers that it contained. The large number of strikes, complaints and surveys on local conditions under-taken by foreign consuls – which led for example to formal prohibitions of subsidized immigration to Brazil from Prussia, Italy and Spain – suggests that contracts were not always fulfilled (Alvim 1986: 102ff.). But recent systematic studies suggest that net savings for these *colono* workers were sufficient to make it a viable and attractive work arrangement. A typical family of two adults and two children could generate net savings in one year of 343$000 reis. With good land at a high 60$000 reis per hectare, it would mean the ability to purchase 5.7 hectares of prime land per annum, or some 28.6 hectares in five years (Alvim 1986: 93–5). Most likely, the majority found it necessary to sign on for more than one year in order to accumulate the desired income to purchase land, as well as seeds, supplies and implements to begin life as independent farm owners. But there is little doubt that savings and upward mobility were possible, that the overwhelming majority did not remain on the *fazendas* for more than a few years and that for many their goal of upward mobility was satisfied by their migration to Brazil.

The economic opportunities offered by coffee and the lack of competition from native-born workers – internal migration from north-eastern Brazil to the centre and south only began after 1920 (Graham and Buarque de Hollanda Filo 1984: 45ff.) – helps explain why immigrants went primarily to the states of the centre and south. São Paulo was overwhelmingly the dominant attraction, accounting for 70 per cent of all immigrants after 1880 (Merrick and Graham 1979: 92), though lesser streams of Europeans went to Rio de Janeiro, Espirito Santo, Paraná and the two southern provinces of Rio Grande do Sul and Santa Catarina. Minas Gerais, one of the three great coffee producing zones and the home of the largest slave population, had more than enough native-born pop-ulation to maintain its coffee fields without resorting to immigrant labour. Moreover, the high rates of natural increase of the native-born population guaranteed that the foreign-born migration stream would be a relatively small part of total population, though an important segment of the southern and south central regions. On the eve of the great migrations in the year of the first national census of 1872, foreign immigrants represented just 3.8 per cent of the national population, and but 3.5 per cent of the population of São Paulo. By 1900 they represented 7 per cent of the national population, but were now a very substantial 21 per cent of the population of the state of São Paulo – in 1920 the city of São Paulo still had 36 per cent of its population listed as foreign-born. In Paraná and Rio Grande do Sul they were 12 per cent of the total population, 10 per cent in Espirito Santo and 9 per cent in Santa Catarina. Although the growing poverty of Rio de Janeiro agriculture meant that ratio of foreign-born to locals was less than the national average, the city of Rio de Janeiro – like that of Sao Paulo – had between a quarter and a third of its residents listed as foreign-born in 1900 (EMASA 1983: vol. II, Tables 1–13, 1–14, 1–16; Merrick and Graham 1979: 94).

The mass migration dates from the year 1887 when the 50,000 per annum figure was reached. This doubled again in the next year and the 100,000 plus figure was the norm in most years that followed, with 1891 being the extraordinary year when 215,000 Europeans arrived, most of whom went to work in the coffee fields of São Paulo. In fact, between 1880 and 1900 1.6 million Europeans arrived in Brazil, over half of whom came from Italy and a quarter of whom came from Portugal, with Spaniards being the third group in importance. This volume guaranteed that in the 1890s Brazil was second in importance in the Americas only to the USA as a destination for European migrants. Argentina-bound immigration did not surpass that to Brazil until the first decade of the twentieth century. Nor did Brazil confine itself to

Table 7.1: *Characteristics of the principal immigrant groups arriving in the port of Santos, 1908–36*

	Italians	Portuguese	Spaniards	Japanese	Total
TOTAL POPULATION	202,749	275,257	209,282	176,775	1,222,282
No. of family groups	28,374	35,044	33,955	31,412	174,928
% alone	42	53	18	5	37
AGES:					
% over 12 years	78	81	68	70	77
% 7–12 years	8	7	12	11	8
% less than 7	14	12	20	19	15
SEX RATIO (MALE:FEMALE)	1.83	2.12	1.46	1.28	1.76
CIVIL STATUS:					
% married	42	43	37	42	39
% single	55	55	60	56	58
% widowed	3	2	3	2	2
ILLITERATES (%)*	32	52	65	10	34
OCCUPATIONS:					
% agriculturalist	50	48	79	99	59

Sources: São Paulo (1937), appendix unnumbered table, 'Movimento Immigratorio pelo porto de Santos: 1908 a 1936'; and Quadro A–16, p. 69.
Note: *This is % illiteracy among population seven years of age or older.

southern and eastern European migrants, being the first Latin American country to open its doors to Japanese migrants in 1908 just as the USA was closing its borders to these Asian migrants.

Given the crucial role of São Paulo as a destination, the state immigration statistical reports remain an important source for the nature of the foreign immigration in this period. As the only Brazilian government (state or federal) to provide detailed breakdowns of the arriving immigrants in terms of their age, education and occupation, the data for *paulista* bound immigrants between 1908 and 1936 is fundamental for describing the majority of this population (see Table 7.1).

Spaniards and Japanese migrants stand out in this migration as the most family oriented, the most sexually balanced and with the highest ratio of children, though clearly the weight of subsidization and the colonato contracts guaranteed that, overall, this Brazilian bound migration was the most highly family and child oriented transoceanic migration coming to America after 1880. Italians going to Brazil, for example, were more often married and brought more children than any other group of Italians going to the Americas (Klein 1989: 95–117). Spaniards and Japanese were also distinguished by being more categorized as farm workers, which may

explain why they later proved to be the most rural and interior town residents in all post-1900 Brazilian censuses. In turn, given the longevity and autonomy of the Portuguese migration – which nevertheless did not surpass the total of Italians until the 1960s – it is no surprise that the sexual and age division of the Portuguese immigrants differed from the rest. The Portuguese tended to arrive as single adult males, with few accompanying wives or children. They were also less likely to go to São Paulo or to work in coffee, though large numbers of them did so. It should be stressed, however, that overall in all state and national censuses, the foreign-born still had a higher ratio of males to females than native-born. This of course was due to the fact that voluntary migrants were more typical of general European immigrant trends – being more likely to be young single males.

Among all these migrants, even the Jews and the Japanese, there was also return and intra-American out-migration. In this the Italians and the Spaniards stand out as the most mobile. All studies have shown that any fall in coffee prices was immediately reflected in increasing rates of return migration and corresponding declines in arriving immigrants. Moreover, recent estimates from census returns and analysis of vital statistics by Ferreira Levy have revised upward the return migration rates first generated from the

Table 7.2: *Foreign ownership of coffee fazendas in São Paulo, 1934*

Origin	% of *fazenda*s	% of coffee trees	% of coffee production (in *arroba*s)	% of state population
Spaniards	9.1	7.4	7.5	2.5
Italians	24.2	21.5	21.4	4.7
Portuguese	6.3	6.0	5.5	2.7
Japanese	5.6	3.6	3.4	2.0
All foreign-born	47.5	42.2	41.2	14.5
Brazilians	52.3	57.4	58.4	85.5
TOTAL	100.0	100.0	100.0	100.0*
No.	82,305	1,480,433,324	80,625,015	6,433,327

Sources: São Paulo (1936a: 35); and for total state population in 1934, EMASA (1983: II,165 (tabela I–11); 171 (tabela I–21)).
*The 165 properties whose owners were unknown were excluded from this table.

same sources by Giorgio Mortara. She estimates an overall 36 per cent return rate, with the Spanish and Italians having the highest rates (Levy 1974: 62–7).

Acculturation and mobility

For those who made their life in Brazil, the question of their subsequent and often differing rates of social and economic mobility are difficult to document fully. The decline of mass migration in the 1920s, and the beginnings of the fundamental internal migrations from the north-east, meant that after 1940 there was little government interest in recording foreign immigrant activity. Also, unlike most other American states, the government did not distinguish second-generation children of immigrants, for these were simply considered Brazilians. This limits the ability to study both acculturation and mobility. What information exists is better for rural property ownership – a theme which concerned both the elite and the arriving immigrants – than on the participation of foreign nationals in commerce or industry. Given these constraints the following statistics are suggestive only of some general trends. Despite their initial poverty and educational disadvantages the fact that the majority of the recently arrived European and Asian immigrants were concentrated in the fastest growing and richest state of the nation meant that they did reasonably well in achieving early and important access to land. Though there is little doubt that coffee *fazendeiros* exploited the subsidized workers and that many families had negative experiences during their years of labour as *colonos*, there is also little question

that significant numbers of *colonos* succeeded in saving money and leaving the landless status. From census to census, their relative shares of ownership of coffee trees and total farm values increased, until immigrant farmers became serious competitors to the native-born *fazendeiros*. As early as 1905, immigrants held 22 per cent of the estates in the *planalto ocidental*, São Paulo's central coffee zone, though their lands were only worth half those of the native-born owners (Holloway 1980: 148, 150). At the national level, by 1920, when they accounted for only 5 per cent of the resident males, the foreign-born possessed 16 per cent of the farmland and now the average values of these were double those owned by native-born farmers (Brazil 1923: III, lxiii, 312–15).

During the expansion of the coffee industry in São Paulo in the early 1920s, foreign immigrants continued to do well. Even the impact of the Great Depression did not slow this expansion, for by 1932 foreign-born immigrants had increased their ownership share to 39 per cent of all coffee trees in the zone, with the Italians being the dominant immigrant group in coffee (Merrick and Graham 1979: 113). In a special state agricultural census of 1934, foreigners had increased their control of the state's 1.5 billion coffee trees to 42 per cent and they now dominated foodstuff production as well for the growing urban markets of the state (see Table 7.2). By 1940 the foreign-born in São Paulo had a very high state-wide participation – owning almost a third of all farms – and their average value per farm was almost 1.5 times greater than Brazilian-owned farms (Brazil 1941, III: 14–17).

Table 7.3: *Classification of industries in the state of São Paulo by nationality of owners, 1934 (values given in contos de réis)*

Origin	No. of factories	Capital	Workers	Motor force (HP)	Value of production
Brazilians	4,837	1997,907	149,898	188,808	1,692,425
Italians	2,181	126,984	20,586	16,639	215,452
Portuguese	460	38,232	5,215	5,478	61,821
Spaniards	275	10,172	2,040	1,087	23,518
Syrians	225	50,239	5,886	5,854	97,562
Germans	122	6,377	1,405	926	16,307
Japanese	62	1,449	405	197	2,924
Austrians	44	3,283	565	593	4,756
English	27	68,087	1,875	3,908	30,840
French	13	935	220	172	2,605
Americans	18	18,609	691	1,546	22,131
Canadians*	4	532,110	8,233	2,920	101,450
Others	307	57,315	5,881	3,743	74,909
Total	8,575	2,911,699	202,900	231,871	2,346,700

Sources: São Paulo (1936b, 28).

*The unusual nature of the Canadian participation is due to their ownership of the monopoly, 'São Paulo Tramway, Light & Power Company Ltd.'

Although the Japanese and the Spaniards in the state of São Paulo remained primarily in the rural areas and in agriculture, in contrast to all other immigrants, even they began to migrate to the cities. By the time of the state census of 1934, 50 per cent of the foreign-born lived in urban centres where they represented 20 per cent of the total population, compared with only 35 per cent of the native-born state population who lived in its cities (São Paulo 1939: 76–7). Though their mobility in the rural area was impressive, it was in the expanding urban sector where immigrants did best. They formed the basis for both the unskilled and skilled labour force and were often the first industrialists and merchants in these often newly established and/or recently expanding cities.

In 1911, for example, 82 per cent of São Paulo's 10,204 textile workers were foreign-born, and of the 2299 manual workers employed by the state in this same year, foreign-born represented 62 per cent of the work force. (São Paulo 1911–12a: I: 1–2, 74–5; São Paulo 1911–12b: I: 1–2, 120–1). The presence of foreign-born workers in the industries of the city of Rio de Janeiro were much less important – being of the order of 37 per cent in 1920 (Batalha 1986: I, 75). But by 1919 the state of São Paulo contained 32 per cent of Brazilian industries, and this concentration

would only increase in the coming years (Cano 1983: 192). This may explain why, of the some 760,000 male workers employed in all of Brazilian industry in 1920, 23 per cent were listed as foreign-born – though in the population as a whole they represented but 5 per cent of the whole (Brazil 1923, IV, 5ª, vol. I: xv).

Foreign immigrants also began doing well in ownership of industry and commerce. By the time of the state census of 1934, foreigners already owned 44 per cent of São Paulo's factories and shops (see Table 7.3). Their newer role was seen in the fact that they held only 31 per cent of total capital involved in these businesses, accounted for only 28 per cent of the value of total production, 26 per cent of the workers employed and just 20 per cent of the total motor power (São Paulo 1941: Tables 31, 35). But their relative importance kept increasing with each decade. In a detailed survey of São Paulo's industrial and commercial sector during the Second World War, foreign-born were to account for 42 per cent of the total capital invested in major factories with their share of these establishments being just 33 per cent of the total.

Finally, a survey of *paulista* industries in the 1970s showed that foreigners of up to the third generation represented 80 per cent of the directors of firms of

250 or more workers in the Greater São Paulo metropolitan region. Equally, among owners of companies with 100 or more workers in São Paulo first-, second- and third-generation foreign-born immigrants and their heirs controlled 73 per cent of these firms, with the Italians being the largest single ethnic group – even compared with Brazilians (Pereira 1974: 73, 78, 198–200 and Appendix Quadro 4).

All available materials point to the first-generation immigrant being endogamous and sharing few of the characteristics of the native-born population. Inter-marriage rates with native-born were low for all groups, though most extreme for the Japanese. Of the Japanese marrying between 1908 and 1962, only 3 per cent of the 38,729 males and 0.3 per cent of the 30,205 Japanese women chose non-Japanese partners. Even children of immigrants maintained this charac-teristic, with a 1958–62 survey reporting only 18 per cent of the male children of Japanese parents marrying out, and only 8 per cent of the second-generation women doing so (CRCJ 1964: 356). At the same time, immigrant women initially had higher birth rates than native-born women and they also had much lower ratios of illegitimate children. From analysis of the 1940 national census it was estimated that controlling for differing age structures between native and foreign-born still produced an extraordinary differ-ence of 540 children born per 100 potentially fertile native-born women over 15 years of age, compared with an overall immigrant rate of only 486 children per 100 fertile women (Levy 1974: 67). Of the half million births registered in the state of São Paulo from 1906 to 1910, immigrant women had an overall illegitimacy rate of 2.8 per cent, compared with 12.3 per cent for native Brazilian women (São Paulo 1906–1910). In crime, however, immigrant males in both Rio de Janeiro and São Paulo in the 1910s and 1920s tended to be more incarcerated than their ratio of the local populations would have warranted (Fausto 1984; Klein 1992). Finally, all immigrant communities developed complex local, regional and national welfare and social institutions to cater to their needs. The Portuguese and the Italians stand out in the importance of their hospitals, educational institutions and benevolent societies. Though even for these communities, the end of steady immigration after 1920 and the increasing intermarriage with other ethnic groups and native-born diluted their importance within Brazilian society by the 1960s (Klein 1991).

Post-war migration

Given the ongoing prosperity of Brazil in the 1930s and 1940s, and the crisis in post-Second World War Europe, it was inevitable that a new European and Asian migration would begin again in the l950s and 1960s. Although such countries as Canada and Venezuela were now the major recipients of these post-1945 European emigrants, Brazil also received a significant share of migrating Italians, Portuguese, Spaniards and even eastern Europeans. This migration was both voluntary and subsidized, the latter for the purpose of promoting the migration of skilled industrial workers. The Brazilian government in the 1950s embarked on a new era of industrial devel-opment under the government of Juscelino Kubitschek (1955–1961) by adopting a formal import subsidiz-ation programme and helped subsidize the migration of skilled European industrial workers.

During this period some 689,000 European and Asian immigrants entered the country. Almost a fifth of these Europeans were subsidized by the European based organization Intergovernmental Committee for Migrations which was founded in Geneva in 1951 by thirty-one governments of Europe and the rest of the world. From 1952 to 1970 the International Com-mittee of Migration sponsored the resettlement of 1.8 million Europeans. The major receiving country of importance was Australia, which alone absorbed some 600,000 workers. But Latin America was also a major area of reception, accounting for some 338,000 emi-grants. In total, Brazil received some 111,100 Euro-pean migrants in this 1952–70 period, second only to Argentina (35 per cent of the 338,000) and just ahead of Venezuela (which took 21 per cent) (Spain 1972: 205ff.).

But this emigration was relatively small and highly volatile, returning in large numbers to Europe when the latter economy itself took off in the late 1960s. These immigrants also shared more in common with comparative skilled and professional migrants going to Venezuela, Canada and Australia at this same time, than they did with the pre-war Spanish or Italian immigrant generations. Even the Portuguese, though they continued their traditional migrations to Brazil after that date, were now going in greater numbers to Canada, the USA, Africa, Australia and above all to western Europe.

By 1970, Brazil was no longer an attractive place for Asians and Europeans who now found their own economies expanding at a pace far outstripping those of this South American country. But Brazil was still attracting large numbers of poorer immigrants to its powerfully expanding economy – now ranked eighth largest in the world. But this time the migration was intra-continental as Spanish-speaking immigrants from Latin American became this sub-continent's new source of non-native labour.

References

Alvim, Zuleika M. F. (1986) *Brava gente! Os italianos em São Paulo, 1870–1920*, São Paulo: Brasiliense

Batalha, Claudio H. de Moraes (1986) 'Le syndicalisme "amarelo" a Rio de Janeiro (1906–1930)', Université de Paris-I, thèse de doctorat, 2 vols

Boni, Luis Alberto de (ed.) (1987–90) *A Presença italiana no Brasil*, 2 vols, Porto Alegre: Escola Superio de Teologia and Fondazione Giovanni Agnelli

Brazil (1908), *Boletim Commerativo da Exposição Nacional de 1908*, Rio de Janeiro, Directoria Gerai de Estatística

——— (1923), *Recenseamento do Brazil Realizado em 1 de Setembro de 1920*, Rio de Janeiro: Directoria Geral de Estatística

——— (1941) *Recenseamento Geral do Brasil (1º de Setembro de 1940)*, Rio de Janeiro: Directoria Geral de Estatística

Buarque de Hollanda, Sergio (1969) 'As Colônias de Parceria', in Sergio Buarque de Holanda (ed.) *História Geral da Civilizaçao Brasileira*, São Paulo: Difusão Européia do Livro, v, 245–60

Cano, Wilson (1983) *Raizes da Concentração Industrial em São Paulo*, 2nd ed., São Paulo: T. A. Queiroz

CRCJ (Comissão de Recenseamento da Colônia Japonesa) (1964) *The Japanese Immigrant in Brazil*, Tokyo: University of Tokyo Press

Dean, Warren (1976) *Rio Claro: A Brazilian Plantation System, 1820–1920*, Stanford: Stanford University Press

EMASA (1983) *Reconstituição da Memória estatística da Grande São Paulo*, 2 vols, São Paulo: Secretaria dos Negócios Metropilitanos, Empresa Metropolitana de Planejamento da Grande São Paulo

Fausto, Boris (1984) *Crime e Cotidiano, a Criminalidade em São Paulo (1880–1924)*, São Paulo: Brasiliense

Graham, Douglas H. and Sérgio Buarque de Hollanda Filho (1984) *Migrações internas no Brasil: 1872–1970*, São Paulo: Instituto de Pesquisas Econômicos

Holloway, Thomas H. (1980) *Immigrants on the Land: Coffee and Society in São Paulo, 1886–1934*, Chapel Hill: University of North Carolina Press

Klein, Herbert S. (1987) 'Demografia do Tráfico Atlântico de Escravos para o Brasil', *Estudos Econômicos* (São Paulo) 17 (2), 129–50

——— (1989) 'A Integração dos Imigrantes italianos no Brasil, na Argentina e nos Estados Unidos,' *Novos Estudos CEBRAP* (São Paulo), 25 (Outubro), 95–117

——— (1991) 'The Social and Economic Integration of Portuguese Immigrants in Brazil in the Late Nineteenth and Twentieth Centuries', *Journal of Latin American Studies*, 23 (2), 309–37

——— (1992) 'The Social and Economic Integration of Spanish Immigrants in Nineteenth and Twentieth Century Brazil', *Journal of Social History*, 25 (3), 505–30

Levy, Maria Stella Ferreira (1974) 'O Papel da Migração internacional na Evolução da População brasileira (1872 a 1972)', *Revista de Saúde Pública*, 8 (Supl), 49–90

Merrick, Thomas W. and Douglas H. Graham (1979) *Population and Economic Development in Brazil: 1800 to the Present*, Baltimore: Johns Hopkins University Press

Oberacker, Jr., Carlos H. (1967) 'A Colonização baseada no Regime da pequena Propriedade agrícola', in Sergio Buarque de Hollanda (ed.) *História geral da civilização brasileira*, São Paulo: Difusão Européia do Livro, 220–44

Pereira, Luis Carlos Bresser (1974) *Empresarios e administradores no Brasil*, São Paulo: Brasiliense

Petrone, Maria Thereza Schorer (1982) *O Imigrante e a pequena Propriedade*, São Paulo: Brasiliense

Roche, Jean (1959) *La Colonisation allemande et le Rio Grande do Sul*, Paris: Institut des Hautes Études de l'Amérique Latine

São Paulo (1906–1910) *Annuario estatístico de São Paulo*, São Paulo: Repartição de Estatística e Archivo do Estado

——— (1911–1912a), 'Condições do Trabalho na Industria textil do Estado de São Paulo', *Boletim do Departamento Estadual do Trabalho*, 1 (1-2), 35–80

——— (1911–1912b), 'Pessoal operario occupado pelo Estado de São Paulo', *Boletim do Departamento Estadual do Trabalho*, 1 (1–2), 109–24

——— (1936a), 'Recenseamento agricola-zootechnico realizado em 1934', Secretaria de Estado dos Negocios da Agricultura, Industria e Comércio

——— (1936b), 'Estatistica industrial do Estado de São Paulo, Anno de 1934', Secretaria da Agricultura, Indústria e Commercio, Directoria de Estatistica

——— (1937) Secretaria de Agricultura, Industria e Comérico, Directoria de Terras, Colonização e Immigração, *Boletim do DTCI*, 1 (1), Outubro

——— (1939) 'População urbana e rural do estado segundo as principais nacionalidades', *Boletim do Departamento Estadual de Estatística*, 1, Janeiro, 76–7

——— (1941), *Estatistica Industrial 1938 e 1939*, Directoria de Estatistica, Indústria e Comércio

Spain (1972) *Panoramica de la Emigración*, Valladolid: Ministerio de Trabajo, Instituto Español de Emigración

Stolcke, Verena (1986) *Cafeicultura, Homens, Mulheres e Capital*, São Paulo: Brasiliense

Willems, Emilio (1946) *A Acculturaçao dos Alemães no Brasil*, São Paulo: Companhia Editora Nacional

EUROPEAN MIGRATION TO ARGENTINA, 1880–1930

JEREMY ADELMAN

Argentina was the second largest recipient of European migrants (after the USA) during the 'great reshuffle' of peoples from 1880 to 1930. In per capita terms, it was by far the largest recipient. Migratory patterns percolated through every aspect of Argentine society and politics. And, of course, it left indelible marks on the republic's economy. So great was the effect in a country whose population grew from 2.5 million to 12 million in half a century, that it would be hard to distinguish migration from larger processes. For instance, by 1914, Latin America's largest city, Buenos Aires, once a backwater in the mid-nineteenth century, had a population of 2.5 million – 49 per cent were foreign born. For less important cities such as Rosario, the effects were even more pronounced.

This contribution is divided into four sections. The first explores the origins of Argentina's migrants, to show that the bulk came from southern European countries. The second analyses the flows of migrants over time, finding that international economic cycles account for much of the rising and declining numbers. The third looks at patterns of settlement within Argentina in both the rural and urban sectors. The fourth section connects migration to social and political movements led by Argentina's newcomers.

The migrants

We first need to establish the origins of Argentina's migrants. Table 7.4 summarizes second- and third-class passenger lists for arriving ships at Argentine ports. First-class passengers were only a tiny fraction and tended not to be 'migrants' as such.

Overall, long-run migratory trends from 1857 to 1924 reveal that 47.5 per cent came from Italy, 32.5 per cent from Spain, followed by 4.1 per cent from France and 3.1 per cent from Russia. With 80 per cent coming from Italy and Spain alone, migratory mechanisms drew from a narrow range of countries. It should be noted that we are still only dealing with in-migrants and not *net* migration – an issue to which I will return in the next section. Return migration in general does not affect the concentration pattern.

Given the importance of Italy and Spain, what can be said of the background of migrants? It was commonly believed that the bulk of Italian migrants to Argentina came from the south of Italy – perhaps an impression derived from US evidence. This is misleading. Over the course of the nineteenth century, Italian agriculture faced severe disruptions in the wake of modernization and demographic growth. With the *risorgimento* went rising rates of rural tenancy, worsening income distributions and declining artisanal activity.

Table 7.4: *National make-up of migrants to Argentina, 1880–1930*

Italian	2,326,059
Spanish	1,709,772
French	184,701
Russian	168,306
Ottoman empire	156,513
German	95,342
Austro-Hungarians	86,496
British	50,310
Total:	4,777,499

Source: República Argentina (1925: 4–5).

Emigration, even seasonal, operated as a 'safety valve'. The north was no less affected than the south. But southerners displayed a higher propensity to move to the USA compared with the Argentina. One calculation for 1876–1930 identifies 86 per cent of Italian migrants to the USA as coming from the south, while only 47 per cent of Italians going to Argentina originated in the south (Klein 1983: 309). In a word, more than half came from central or northern districts. This is important, for it meant that migrants to Argentina may have come from a relatively narrow cluster of countries, but the variety coming from Italian regions provided a broad spectrum of occupational, skill and rural–urban differences. Southern Italian migration during this period often evokes images of downtrodden lumpenproletarians. Whether or not this is true of southerners, it does not accurately portray the variety of backgrounds of almost half Argentina's newcomers.

What about Spaniards? Research has tended to let Italians overshadow Spaniards. One recent study, however, makes up for lost ground (Moya 1988). Several factors account for the exodus from Spain to Argentina. First was rising demographic pressure, especially in the countryside in the most heavily populated regions of the North Atlantic coast, the Mediterranean and Cantabria. Of greatest importance though was the poor province of Galicia, where some 40 per cent of all Spanish migrants to Argentina originated. Second, like Italy, Spain faced a veritable agrarian revolution, especially in Galicia and the Basque region. Rising tenancy rates undermined peasant autonomy, and drove rural dwellers to cities and abroad. Last, an industrial revolution swept older proto-industrial communities, especially the larger towns in Catalonia and the Basque region. More homogeneous than Italian migrants, Spaniards moving to Argentina were poor, rural and looking for a permanent place for resettlement.

The bulk of emigrants to Argentina were from southern Europe, but by no means did they all come from peasant backgrounds. The comparatively undifferentiated national background should not obscure the varieties of economic, social and regional experiences which migrants carried with them.

Migration flows

Two features dominate the pattern of migratory flows over time: the high rates of emigration (or as one author has suggested, remigration (Gould 1980), and wild swings in accordance with business cycles. Table 7.5 summarizes figures for annual migration to and from Argentina.

A very high percentage of migrants did not remain in Argentina permanently. We will return to this issue in greater detail when discussing the formation of the republic's labour market. It is worth noting that the high profile of Italians in the gross flow of migrants shaped the high propensity of migrants to Argentina to leave. Over the *longue durée* 1857–1930, more than 50 per cent of migrants leaving Argentina were Italians. Many Italians evidently did not treat Argentina as a place of permanent resettlement, but of temporary sojourn to earn a small fortune and bolster the livelihood of extended family networks in Italy. A related factor in this high remigration rate was Argentina's high proportion of seasonal migrants. A study of the timing of in- and out-migration (Adelman forthcoming) shows 'that the bulk of incomers timed

their arrival to coincide with the beginning of the harvest (when rural and urban wages were highest), and their departure with the end of the harvest.' Much of this high remigration reflects seasonal migration, especially from Italy to work on the harvests. These migrants earned the label '*golondrinas*' (swallows) to describe seasonal flows back and forth across the ocean.

Table 7.5: *Immigration to and emigration from Argentina, 1880–1929 ('000s)*

Year	Immigration	Emigration	Net
1880–84	281.5	75.2	206.3
1885–89	739.1	99.4	639.7
1890–94	400.7	295.9	104.8
1895–99	527.3	255.8	271.5
1900–04	601.4	356.2	245.2
1905–09	1362.9	589.0	773.9
1910–14	1552.7	893.9	658.8
1915–19	672.5	750.6	−78.1
1920–24	1316.9	832.5	484.4
1925–29	1705.7	1249.3	456.4

Source: Vázquez-Presedo (1976, vol. I, 15–16; vol. II, 30).

The other striking feature of migratory flows was their lock-step movement with business cycles. The periods can be broken down into several booms: the late 1880s, 1904–13 and 1919–24. In these years, not only did in-migration soar, but so did net migration rates. These were years of international economic prosperity, which induced Argentine export expansion, which in turn fuelled local economic activity. The crisis years of the early 1890s and the First World War saw both falling European–Argentine migration flows and negative net rates. The first crisis responded to the shocks of a local financial crisis; the second was clearly a more global phenomenon. Transatlantic shipping collapsed during the First World War. It remains to be seen whether European migration to Argentina follows the same inverse cycles as those described by Brinley Thomas for the North Atlantic (Fenoaltea 1988; Thomas 1973). What is undeniable is that Argentina's open economy was exposed to world trade and investment cycles, and these are closely correlated with migratory flows.

Settlement

Settlement patterns vary in the extreme. Background (village, skill, country), timing and actual landing place all affected residential patterns in multiform ways. What follows can only be a very aggregated description.

The first distinction to be drawn is between rural and urban settlement. While agrarian exports provided the motor for Argentina's economy, surprisingly little can be said of rural settlement – mainly due to inadequate primary research material. In general, Italians preferred the countryside to the city, while Spaniards opted for urban centres. Within the rural sector, however, a distinction must be made between seasonal migration to work on the harvest, semi-permanent migration to lease land with short-term contracts and permanent settlement. Overwhelmingly the largest numbers were seasonal. They seem to incorporate two groups: first, *golondrinas* fresh from Italy whose sojourn in the republic will last as long as the harvest (approximately five months from November to March as wheat ripens from the northern pampas to southern districts); and urban dwellers who remain in Argentina with permanent abodes in towns, but who work occasionally in the countryside. Statistical information furnished by the Immigration Department is of little use since it aggregates these seasonal migrants into generic categories of 'rural' dwellers.

Semi-permanent tenant farmers seem to have come largely from Italy. Their aim was to lease land from a large landowner for three to four years at a low rate, with a promise to leave the land sown with alfalfa or other forages for the landowner to then use for grazing. The farmer would then move on. With cooperative weather and good prices, this could prove lucrative for the tenant. Indeed, it was the hope of many that one or two contracts of this sort would earn a small fortune so that the farmer might return to the home country with enough money to afford a plot of land there.

In the main, this seems to have been a common expectation, especially of northern Italians driven off their plots but reluctant to leave their home districts permanently. Time, however, eroded the efficacy of this strategy. First, more migrants pursued this option after the turn of the century, in part inspired by earlier tales. Second, the stock of land allocated to arable agriculture stabilized around 1908 (though more land came available in the more remote pampean districts). Thus, a rising supply of tenants and dwindling demand for their services allowed landowners to push up rents, signalling the eclipse of this earlier model of migration, and provoking the first of a series of tenant revolts in the countryside in 1912 (Adelman 1989, forthcoming; Scarzanella 1983; Solberg 1989).

As for permanent rural migrants, timing was all important. Migrants who came earlier, when land was extremely cheap and credit was more abundant (especially in the 1880s), tended to take up direct ownership of land. During the first phase of agrarian expansion, prior to the 1890 financial collapse, most colonists came from northern Europe. Some came, as in the German and Swiss settlements of the 1850s and 1860s, to Santa Fe province, to become smallholding farmers. At the same time, in the province of Buenos Aires, Irish and Scottish immigrants, as well as others, came to work in the wool trade. By dint of effort and savings not a few managed to accumulate quite substantial holdings by the time land prices began to soar. After the financial collapse of 1890, access to land became more difficult, and the primary access to land was through leaseholds. The origin of most permanent rural dwelling migrants shifted now to the Mediterranean and especially Italy. Many of these farmers also managed to acquire their own plots, but rising land prices placed a ceiling on the number who made the leap, and ensured that fewer would make the fortunes of their predecessors. Increasingly, migration from Europe to the booming economy of the pampas adapted to rather than shaped the emerging pattern of landowning (Adelman forthcoming; Sabato 1985).

There is now a flourishing literature on urban settlement. Longstanding assimilationist models portrayed Argentine cities as Latin American melting pots – the operative term being *crisol de razas* – to describe the dilution of ethnic identity in favour of a synthesis, or new Argentine popular culture. Based on highly aggregated evidence earlier scholars pointed to high levels of upward social mobility, suburbanization into polyglot communities, and high degrees of exogamous marriage. Recent local studies have questioned all of these nostrums (Devoto 1991; Szuchman 1977). Instead, historians are finding ample evidence of surviving, indeed reinforced, ethnic identity – the term now being 'cultural pluralism'. First, high degrees of spatial mobility, the movement from downtown shantytowns to suburbs in pursuit of home ownership, did not disintegrate communities. This became more evident when historians focused less on national aggregates, but on communities, villages and extended kin networks, which reproduced themselves as populations fanned to urban outskirts. Moreover, many immigrants relied on mutual-aid societies for all types of social services. One of the oldest and largest of these, *Unione e benevolenza*, offered an extensive range of benefits and served as an important forum for the survival of the Italian language. Institutions such as these, once treated as stepping stones to assimilation, are treated more as important vehicles for adjustment and mediation with the host society (Baily 1982).

Immigrant associative patterns also say much about the emergence of a unique kind of ethnic leadership. Here again, timing seems to have been important. In the case of both Italian and Spanish immigrants, there was not as abrupt a shift from 'old' to 'new' immigrants (as American historians used to say), in which the latter simply followed pre-existing leaderships of native or other ethnic groups. Rather, Spanish and Italian leaders emerged at an early stage – many being propertied or skilled artisans with considerable influence over local social life. This reinforced the endurance of ethnic identity even if it created class fissures within each ethnic group (Baily 1983; Moya 1988).

Two general conclusions flow from recent research. First, Old World ties were important determinants of settlement patterns: people moved in village and language-based clusters to and within Argentina. Second, Argentina offered greater opportunities than did its main competitor, the USA. Easier access to land, newer industry and fluidity of leadership structures permitted a greater degree of ethnic opportunity. It would seem that, contrary to a longstanding conviction of historians and social scientists, migration and modernization did not necessarily imply homogenization.

Labour market and labour movement
Business cycles clearly influenced migratory flows, but what can be said of migratory effects on the local labour market over time? First, as has been said, Argentina's labour market became increasingly integrated into a transatlantic pattern of labour allocation. Structurally and seasonally, labour moved from labour abundant regions to areas where labour was expensive. Second, with time, the Argentine labour market became more saturated. As cities filled up and the stock of available arable land dwindled, so too did the opportunities for unfettered social mobility. This can be represented by two gauges: first, rural rents began to rise systematically after 1908; second, real urban wages rose until around 1910, when they stabilized, and then dropped in 1912. Wartime demand raised wages and rents in general, and the slump in 1920/1 took its toll on immigrant incomes. The rest of the 1920s seems to have been a decade of mixed performance, but few doubted that the golden age had begun to wane. With time, mass migration eliminated

the bounty the local labour market was supposed to afford newcomers.

Long-term trends and short-term disruptions stoked labour unrest. Immigrants took an important part in the early formation of the Argentine labour movement. Several channels gave expression to urban working-class opposition. The first were mutual-aid societies bearing a more plebeian stamp – usually gathering workers of a particular trade to contribute to a fund to support temporary unemployment, health care or burial services. The earliest, and perhaps most successful, was the organization representing typographers (Badoza 1992). While these sorts of organizations survived, they never broke beyond a narrow band of highly skilled artisanal groups (Falcón 1984). Next came anarchist groups. Here perhaps the direct influence of immigrant political culture was most evident as Italian and Spanish anarchists were overwhelmingly the leaders. While proclaiming themselves leaders of a universal movement, anarchism flourished only during the first generation of truly mass migration, especially between 1900 and 1910, during which Argentine cities, Buenos Aires and Rosario in particular, were rocked by waves of labour unrest.

Immigrant influence on the trade union movement, especially its mainstream syndicalist brand in the larger cities, is much more ambiguous. Two divergent forces ran against each other. Immigrants provided the rank and file and often the leadership of Argentina's most powerful unions in the ports and the railyards. In these sectors, workers provided the fulcrum of a robust movement against the power of managers (Adelman 1992; Goldberg 1979). Yet, at the same time, other important sectors, such as meat packing, were rent by inter-ethnic rivalries. Here plant managers manipulated communities against each other to undermine solidarity (Lobato 1992). There is no incontrovertible evidence to suggest whether immigration helped or hindered the emergence of a modern trade union movement. But since the labour movement never managed to gather more than a small share of the total labour force, most immigrants relied on other means for self-defence: through households, communities and individual mobility. Ethnicity and class were points of convergence and divergence in the constitution of a popular identity in Argentina.

This essay provides a brief survey of the main themes involving migration to Argentina. Immigration shaped all aspects of the republic's life. In general, it is safe to conclude that during the earlier phase of migration, newcomers found a more open and porous host society. By the eve of the First World War, this was less true. Increasingly, migrants fitted into pre-existing arrangements – arrangements which themselves bore the mark of earlier generations of migrants.

References

Adelman, J. (1989) 'Una cosecha por levantar: los socialistas y el campo antes de la primera guerra mundial', *Anuario del IEHS*, (4), 293–334

— (1992) 'The Political Economy of Labour in Argentina, 1870–1930', in J. Adelman (ed.) *Essays in Argentine Labour History, 1870–1930*, London: Macmillan, 1–34

— (forthcoming) *Frontier Development: Land, Labour and Capital on the Wheatlands of Argentina and Canada, 1890–1914*, Oxford: Oxford University Press

Badoza, S. (1992) 'Typographical Workers and their Mutualist Experience: The Case of the *Sociedad Tipográfica Bonaerense*, 1857–80', in J. Adelman (ed.) *Essays in Argentine Labour History, 1870–1930*, London: Macmillan, 72–90

Baily, S. (1982) 'Las Sociedades de Ayuda Mutua y el Desarrollo de una Comunidad Italiana en Buenos Aires', *Desarrollo Económico*, 21 (84), 485–514

— (1983) 'The Adjustment of Italian Immigrants in Buenos Aires and New York, 1870–1914', *American Historical Review*, 88 (2), 281–303

Devoto, F. (1991) 'Italian Emigrants and Argentine Society: Problems of Models and Sources', *Journal of European Economic History*, 20 (3), 629–43

Falcón, R. (1984) *Los orígenes del movimiento obrero (1857–1899)*, Buenos Aires: Centro Editor de América Latina

Fenoaltea, S. (1988) 'International Resource Flows and Construction Movements in the Atlantic Economy: The Kuznets Cycle in Italy, 1861–1913', *Journal of Economic History*, XLVIII (3), 611–34

Goldberg, H. (1979) 'Railroad Unionization in Argentina, 1912–1929: The Limitations of a Working-Class Alliance', unpublished Ph.D. thesis, Yale University

Gould, J. D. (1980) 'European Inter-Continental Emigration, The Road Home: Return-Migration from the USA', *Journal of European Economic History*, 9 (1), 50–111

Klein, H. (1983) 'The Integration of Italian Immigrants into the United States and Argentina: A Comparative Analysis', *American Historical Review*, 88 (2), 306–28

Lobato, M. (1992) 'Work and Conflict in the Meatpacking Industry, 1900–30', in J. Adelman (ed.) *Essays in Argentine Labour History, 1870–1930*, London: Macmillan, 112–41

Moya, J. (1988) 'Spaniards in Buenos Aires: Patterns of Immigration and Adaptation, 1852–1930', unpublished Ph.D. thesis, Rutgers University

República Argentina (1925) *Resumen Estadístico del movimiento migratorio en la República Argentina, 1857–1924*, Buenos Aires: Ministerio de Agricultura

Sabato, H. (1985) 'Trabajar para Vivir o Vivir para Trabajar: Empleo Ocasional y Escasez de Mano de Obra en Buenos Aires, Ciudad y Campaña, 1850–1880', in Nicolás Sánchez-Albornoz (ed.) *Población y mano de obra en América Latina*, Madrid: Alianza Editorial

Scarzanella, E. (1983) *Italiani d'Argentina: Storie di Contadini, Industriali e Missionari Italiani in Argentina, 1850–1912*, Venezia: Marsilio Editori

Solberg, C. (1989) *The Prairies and Pampas: Agrarian Policy in Canada and Argentina, 1880–1930*, Stanford: Stanford University Press

Szuchman, M. (1977) 'The Limits of the Melting Pot in Urban Argentina: Marriage and Integration in Cordoba, 1869–1909', *Hispanic American Historical Review*, 57 (1), 24–50

Thomas, B. (1973) *Migration and Economic Growth: A Study of Great Britain and the Atlantic Economy*, Cambridge: Cambridge University Press

Vázquez-Presedo, Vicente (1976) *Estadísticas Históricas Argentinas*, 2 vols, Buenos Aires: Ediciones Macchi

THE CHINESE OF PERU, CUBA AND MEXICO

EVELYN HU-DEHART

In 1990, Peruvians elected a son of Japanese immigrants as their president. Alberto Fujimori's election underscores the fact that not only Europeans, but Asians as well, have immigrated in significant numbers to Latin America and contributed in concrete ways to the social, cultural, economic and political development of various countries in this immense region. By the mid-twentieth century, every Latin American and Caribbean country had received some Asian immigrants. The vast majority came from China, Japan, India and, more recently, Korea.

When the conquistador Balboa became the first European to set eyes on the Pacific Ocean in 1513, Europe and Asia soon became connected through trade as Columbus and his patrons had intended. By the early seventeenth century, the presence of *chinos de manila* were noted in Mexico City, the result of the Manila galleon trade between Mexico and the Philippines. They might have constituted the earliest Asian community anywhere in the Americas, as suggested by a curious document dated 1635, a petition submitted by a group of frustrated Spanish barbers in Mexico City to the viceroy. They demanded the removal of all Chinese barbers from the centre of town to the outskirts, citing the long Chinese hours as constituting unfair business practice. Unfortunately, the paper trail ran cold, so we do not know the fate of this early Chinese colony.

It was not until the mid-nineteenth century that organized, large-scale Asian immigration to Latin America and the Caribbean took place, consisting almost exclusively of Chinese, Japanese and East Indians. Most of the Chinese went to Cuba, Peru, Mexico and parts of Central America; the Japanese settled largely in Peru and Brazil, with smaller numbers going to Bolivia and Mexico; and the East Indians were sent almost exclusively to the British West Indies. Whether forced or free, large-scale Asian migration to Latin America and the Caribbean was part of the international labour migration of the late nineteenth and early twentieth century in the wake of the worldwide development of capitalism and imperialism, and in direct response to the decline of African slavery.

After a period of labouring under harsh agricultural conditions on large estates – especially sugar plantations – most of the Asians made the transition to independent farming, shopkeeping or other commercial activities. The relative prosperity experienced by Asian communities in the early to mid-twentieth century resulted in anti-Asian violence and persecution in many Latin American and Caribbean countries, with the worst being the expulsion of the Chinese from northern Mexico during the Great Depression and the deportation and incarceration of Japanese Peruvians in US camps during the Second World War. Following the example of the USA, most Latin American countries seriously curtailed Asian immigration, although not necessarily to the point of outright exclusion. Since the Second World War, Asian migration to Latin America and the Caribbean has largely subsided, but in the 1980s and 1990s, a noticeable trickle of Koreans migrating to South America has been detected.

The rest of this contribution will focus on three Spanish-speaking countries with significant Chinese immigration: Peru, Cuba and Mexico. Together, they round out the story of the worldwide Chinese diaspora of the mid-nineteenth to the mid-twentieth century.

The Chinese in Peru and Cuba

From 1847 to 1874, as many as 225,000 Chinese 'coolies' under eight-year contracts, almost all male, were imported to Cuba and Peru, with 80 per cent or more destined for the plantations. In the case of Cuba, then still a Spanish colony, the Chinese worked alongside African slaves, the chief source of plantation labour, while in Peru, where slavery was abolished in 1854 shortly after independence from Spain, Chinese coolies supplanted black slaves. Scholars have argued whether *la trata amarilla* (the yellow trade) was a transition from slave to free labour, a substitution for slavery or a modified form of slavery. Not disputed is the indispensability of their labour to the maintenance of plantation-based economies of both societies from the middle to the end of the nineteenth century.

The first Chinese coolies in Peru were actually used to excavate guano off the coast. A product much valued by the British as natural fertilizer, guano-earning in Peru helped give rise to its coastal sugar and cotton plantations. Unable to entice the highland Indians down to the coast, Peruvian entrepreneurs imported over 90,000 Chinese coolies between 1848 and 1874 (given the high mortality on the long trip over, more than 100,000 were actually recruited and embarked in China). A small number were sent to an American railroad company in the highlands. Some 80 per cent eventually ended up on the coastal plantations. During the coolie period, sugar production in Peru shot up from 618 metric tons in 1860 to 56,102 metric tons in 1875. On most of the sugar plantations, Chinese coolies constituted the exclusive labour force (Stewart 1951).

In the 1870s, escaped coolies and free Chinese were among the pioneers who penetrated the Peruvian Amazon, cleared land for cultivation and colonization, and introduced rice, beans, sugar and other crops, as well as small-scale manufacturing. They helped build the Peruvian Amazon city of Iquitos, and served as intermediaries, translators and cultural brokers between other newcomers (mostly Europeans) and the native peoples. But in the official Peruvian version of the conquest of the Amazon, the Chinese trailblazers were written out. In the twentieth century, Chinese Peruvians became increasingly urbanized and quite diverse in their occupations, from owners of large agricultural estates to small shopkeepers, from poor labourers to wealthy retail merchants. In the capital city of Lima, their initial congregation around the central market district along the *Calle Capón* evolved into the *barrio chino* (Chinatown). At the end of the twentieth century, Chinese Peruvians remain a visible minority, their presence captured by the ubiquitous *chifas* or Chinese restaurants, a thoroughly Peruvian institution.

Of the approximately 125,000 Chinese coolies who arrived in Cuba, a small number were taken into domestic service, cigarette and other small manufacturing, and by the colonial government in large public works projects. The vast majority – 80 per cent – worked alongside African slaves on sugar plantations, where slavery was not abolished until the end of the nineteenth century (Helly 1979). As slave importation sharply declined, coolie importation concurrently rose: for example, in 1865, 145 African slaves and 12,391 Chinese coolies were imported.

The close physical proximity of these two groups of largely male workers spelled competition, resentment and conflict on a daily basis. And as men who were neither slave not free, neither black nor white, the presence of Chinese coolies was ultimately a disruptive force for the planters in that their presence and intermediary status in both labour and race helped break down the slave regime and the racialist ideology of Cuba's plantation society. For this reason, the powerful planters conspired to force the coolies to enter into continuous recontracting, thereby forestalling their transition to freedom. They also abruptly terminated a successful experiment with Chinese labour contracting in Cuba, because labour contracting edged perilously close to creating free labourers. No matter how miserable their condition, Chinese coolies were aware of their fundamental rights as contract labourers and able to articulate their desire to be free (Hu-DeHart 1993). Not surprisingly, therefore, from the 1860s to the end of the century, *chinos mambises* (freedom fighters) joined slaves, free blacks and whites to overthrow Spanish colonial rule and, by extension, bring an end to the plantation system. So valiant were the Chinese combatants that Cuba erected after independence a monument to their memory.

Like their compatriots in Peru, Chinese Cubans also became increasingly urbanized while pursuing various commercial activities. Chinese men formed unions with white and black Cuban women, producing hybrid families. The great Cuban artist Wilfredo Lam was the son of a Chinese father and an Afro-Cuban mother. In Havana, a *barrio chino* was also created along the *Calle Zanja*, which was originally outside the city walls. With the advent of the Cuban revolution in 1959, the largely petit bourgeois Chinese Cubans fled in large numbers to the USA, leaving only a remnant on the island.

The Chinese in Mexico

Free Chinese immigrants entered Mexico at exactly the same time that the USA enacted Chinese exclusion acts in the late nineteenth century and Mexico's most enduring dictator, Porfirio Díaz, took power. Among other things, Díaz promoted immigration, foreign investment and development, particularly along the border region between northern Mexico and the USA. Instead of assuming manual jobs in the mines and railroads, which were filled by Mexicans (mestizos and Indians), the Chinese entered new niches in the local economy, such as truck farming, small manufacturing and services ranging from canteens to laundries, boarding houses to tailoring (Hu-DeHart 1989). By the time of the Mexican revolution of 1910, all over the north, but especially in the state of Sonora across the border from Arizona (still only a territory),

Chinese immigrants had captured much of the retail trade. They prospered even during the tumultuous years of the revolution, in part by provisioning the various revolutionary armies.

In 1927, numbering over 24,000, the Chinese had become Mexico's largest non-Spanish immigrant community. They had settled in practically every state and territory. But their ubiquity and relative prosperity rendered them vulnerable to growing Mexican nationalism at a time of economic recession during the depression. Sporadic persecution over the course of decades culminated in 1929–30 with the massive expulsion of the large Chinese community of Sonora, after which their properties were expropriated and their businesses nationalized (i.e. turned over to private Mexican owners). Those who were not repatriated to China via the USA (which was still enforcing Chinese exclusion at the time) probably sought refuge in the interior of Mexico or across the gulf in the territory of Baja California Norte, which bordered the state of California.

At the time Baja California had its own Chinese community, which evolved under quite different conditions. Chinese workers had been brought to Baja at the beginning of the century by Chinese labour contractors to develop virgin land of the fertile Mexicali Valley, an extension of California's Imperial Valley. North American landowners and entrepreneurial Chinese in California formed partnerships to clear land for cotton cultivation in Mexicali, a successful venture that saw Chinese lessees and their Chinese contract workers raising 80 per cent of Mexicali's cotton crop by 1920. Although threatened many times, the Baja Chinese community escaped the dire fate of their Sonoran counterparts, and maintains to this day a vibrant commercial profile.

References

Helly, Denise (1979) *Idéologie et Ethnicité: Les Chinois Macao a Cuba, 1847–1886*, Montreal: Les Presses Universitaires de Montreal

Hu-DeHart, Evelyn (1989) 'Coolies, Shopkeepers, Pioneers: The Chinese of Mexico and Peru, 1849–1930' *Amerasia Journal*, 15 (2), 91–116

(1993) 'Chinese Coolie Labour in Cuba in the Nineteenth Century: Free Labour or Neoslavery?' *Slavery and Abolition*, 14 (1), 67–86

Stewart, Watt (1951) *Chinese Bondage in Peru: A History of the Chinese Coolie in Peru, 1849–1874*, Durham, NC: Duke University Press

THE MIGRATION OF LABOUR IN COLOMBIA

LUZ MARINA DÍAZ

International migrations of labour are inherent to the development of society throughout the world, and to the interrelationship between national economies and regional blocs with more or less relative development (Díaz and Gómez 1991).

From the economic point of view, the origin of the mobility of labour is both a precondition and a result of the relationships of interdependence between countries and regions at unequal stages of development. Specifically, the mechanisms that adjust markets, like increments in commerce and investment, have been unable to substitute or make unnecessary the mobility of labour between countries. Thus, sifting through whatever legal barriers are established to control migratory flows, the pressure of migrants grows and the volume of migration between countries and regions continues to expand (Lin Leam Lim 1993).

In the new situations of the restructuring of the international community – characterized by the globalization of economic processes, a simultaneous reconfiguration of regional blocs and an increase in vulnerability for less developed countries making them more dependent on the industrialized nations – migratory movements tend to expand, and this will continue to happen as long as differences in development between nations persist (EU, NAFTA, ECOWAS). Below, this process is briefly illustrated in the case of Colombian migration.

Since the middle of the twentieth century, Colombia has been first among Andean countries in terms of the international migration of labour and second in Latin America and the Caribbean, after Mexico, in terms of the population living abroad.

In effect, economic, social and demographic transformations in Colombia have been leading to high levels of international migration ever since the 1950s. 'Development within the country', that is, the application of an import-substitution development model with a captive domestic market and high tariffs as a strategy to generate economic development, induced a massive internal migration from rural to urban areas, principally targeted on Bogotá, Medellín, Cali and Barranquilla. In a thirty-year period, from 1950 to 1980, a predominantly rural country, with 38.9 per cent of its inhabitants living in cities, became a predominantly urban one, with 68 per cent of the population living in urban areas, according to the census information.

This dramatic internal migration was the basis for the growth of the cities. The expectation of industrial development encouraged this massive migration, but it was subsequently incapable of meeting the challenge of creating jobs, despite a growing demand for them. On the other hand, the introduction of technology to agriculture and the increase in rural violence also encouraged migration to the urban areas. At the beginning of the 1970s, the development model began to show signs of strain, as evidenced by the incapacity of cities to absorb the migrant population. Development thus remained unfinished and proved incapable of meeting the needs of a growing population. That is, social justice and political participation lagged behind economic development.

The difficulty of access to the benefits of economic development, the fluctuating instability of the job market, the growth of underemployment and the loss in the real value of salaries were factors which led growing sectors of the population to look beyond the national boundaries in their search for better incomes and services to improve their living standards.

During the 1970s, the USA operated as a powerful magnet for immigrants, especially university graduates and highly qualified technicians who were unable to earn enough in Colombia to belong fully to the consumer society. Colombians, especially those from urban areas, and with a high percentage of women among them, migrated for the most part to New York City and Miami.

A second wave of massive migration travelled to neighbouring Venezuela, especially during the years of that country's economic and financial boom, which was principally fuelled by oil exports. The increase in the price of oil on the international market and the nationalization of the production and marketing of oil produced a vast growth in the income of the Venezuelan state.

In 1977, the price of oil increased threefold and in

consequence large-scale investment plans using both public and private capital stimulated economic activity, especially industry and physical infrastructure, generating a growing demand for university graduates, technicians and unqualified labour, in excess of local supply (Gómez and Díaz 1983).

According to Venezuela's census of 1981, Colombians accounted for 45 per cent of the registered foreign population, though this percentage substantially underestimated the number of illegal residents in urban and rural areas, both stationary and permanently mobile ones.

The economically active population (EAP) of Colombian nationals legally registered in Venezuela according to the 1981 census was 5 per cent of the EAP and 40.6 per cent of the foreign-born EAP; 65 per cent of the Colombian EAP in Venezuela belonged to the formal labour force (Michelena and Betancourt 1983).

In terms of economic participation by economic sectors, for the 1976–80 period, 50 per cent were in the tertiary sector (services), 30 per cent in construction and 20 per cent in the primary economic sector (Ungar 1985).

Around the middle of the 1980s, the Venezuelan government initiated the Matrícula General de Extranjeros (MGE), the national register of foreigners, in order to quantify and legalize the clandestine population present in Venezuela for a minimum of two years and with previous work experience in that country. The MGE registered 266,795 persons, of whom 92.3 per cent were Colombian nationals.

However, there is little doubt that the illegal population was much greater than the registered one (Van Roy 1984: 542–3). The Venezuelan government had determined that definitive registration required a work contract and proof of permanent residence at a single territorial location during the two preceding years. Because of the difficulty in fulfilling these requirements in the case of the permanently mobile, temporary or seasonal populations working in harvesting, construction and services, or as independent and informal urban workers, the illegal population was substantially under-registered.

During the 1980s, called by some analysts Latin America's 'lost decade', the region experienced a deep crisis, simultaneously manifested on three fronts: an external debt crisis, a crisis in the profit levels of economic activity and finally a crisis in fiscal matters and public funding (Díaz and Gómez 1985). In Venezuela, this situation produced a real decrease in the purchasing power of salaries and an increase in

unemployment, both of which immediately affected the poorest sectors and Colombian workers, leading to more work in the informal sector, more poverty and generally worse living conditions for the working population. Subsequently, this situation deteriorated as a result of the economic measures taken by the Venezuelan government after the exchange crisis of 1983.

As a consequence of the situation, Colombian migration to Venezuela diminished substantially, because there was a notable reduction of the disparity in salaries and opportunities for work in the two countries that had stimulated the previous migration from Colombia to Venezuela. Colombia's migrants then redirected their sights to the USA and a number of European cities.

After the new US Immigration Law was presented to Congress in 1982 and in due course became the Simpson–Rodino Law in 1986, the debate on immigration from Latin America and the Caribbean intensified, and entry to the USA became more difficult for illegal immigrants. At the beginning of the 1980s, an estimated 673,000 Colombian immigrants had entered the USA (Russell 1993).

The structural adjustments that began to gain ground in Latin America in the 1980s to cushion the effects of the crisis are being consolidated during the present decade; they are basically directed to liberating market forces in the regulation of the economic system, imparting renewed flexibility to the relations between capital and labour, reducing the size of the state and its direct intervention in the economy and, finally, adopting a free-trade strategy in order to gain access to world markets.

Under present circumstances of increasing globalization of the world economy and the rise of regional industrial blocs – paradoxically affected by increased protectionism – developing nations are simultaneously more dependent on the First World and more isolated (Lin Leam Lim 1993).

Faced with this situation, countries like Colombia must make a great effort to become competitive in international markets, acquire labour-saving technology (despite present and future labour surpluses in many areas) and decrease the size of the state through attrition of its workers, to make it more efficient. These measures are having unfortunate effects in the short and medium terms for workers, reducing opportunities for finding work in the formal economy and access to the health, education and social security services exclusively offered by the public sector until now, and at present in the process of being privatized.

In sum, in Colombia the new development model is generating, and in the medium term will continue to generate, a decrease in living standards for important population sectors, with diminished real income and the growth of the informal sector.

This situation is creating conditions for a new migratory wave to the USA and Europe, where there are already signs of an increase in young Colombian nationals with scant qualifications surviving in informal activities.

These migrants' chances of securing proper housing, legal status and jobs, and of achieving satisfactory social, economic and cultural integration are becoming increasingly precarious due to the economic recession, the high level of unemployment and the xenophobia that are current in many parts of the world.

References

Díaz, Luz and Alcides Gómez (1985) 'Recesión Económica, Migración Laboral Internacional y sus Efectos en el Area Fronteriza Colombo–Venezolana', in *Internatonal Migration Project*, Washington and Geneva: Georgetown University/IWO

—— (1991) 'Las Migraciones Laborales de Colombia a Venezuela Durante las Dos Ultimas Décadas', in *Opciones Para la Integración, Papers of the First Andean Seminar on Migrations,* Ministerio del Trabajo, Caracas: OIM

Gómez, Alcides and Luz Díaz (1983) *La Moderna Esclavitud. Los Colombianos en Venezuela,* Bogotá: La Oveja Negra

Lin Leam Lim (1993) 'Growing Economic Interdependence and its Implications for International Migration', *Expert Group Meeting on Population Distribution and Migration,* Santa Cruz: UNFPA

Michelena, Alfredo and Norelis Betancourt (1983) *Características Económico-Laborales de los Inmigrantes Durante los Años Setenta,* Caracas: Universidad Lisandro Alvarado

Russell, Sharon Stanton (1993) 'Migration between Developing Countries in the African and Latin American Regions and its likely Future', *Expert Group Meeting on Population Distribution and Migration,* Santa Cruz: UNFPA

Ungar, Elizabeth (1985) 'Impacto de la Crisis Recesiva Venezolana sobre la Migración de Retorno a Colombia', *Hemispherical Migration Project,* Washington and Geneva: Georgetown University/IWO

Van Roy, Ralph (1984) 'La Población Clandestina en Venezuela: Resultados de la Matricula General de Extranjeros', *Migraciones Internacionales en las Américas,* II, Caracas: CEPAM

CENTRAL AMERICAN REFUGEES TO THE USA

ELIZABETH G. FERRIS

In the early 1980s a large number of Central American refugees began to cross the borders of the USA in search of safety from the violence sweeping their countries. They followed the well-established routes used by the tens of thousands of Central American economic migrants who had come to the USA in previous decades in search of employment and economic security.

Although there was a long tradition in the USA of immigration from Mexico and Central America, both legal and undocumented, and although the country had had twenty years of experience in dealing with Cuban and Haitian asylum-seekers, the arrival of the Central American refugees was a new phenomenon for the US government. They came from El Salvador and Guatemala (to escape the spreading violence there) and later from Honduras and Nicaragua, albeit in smaller numbers. But their arrival in the USA coincided with other major refugee emergencies – in Indochina, in Afghanistan and, with the arrival of some 140,000 Cubans known as *Marielitos*, in Florida. Their arrival also tested the US government's new refugee policy, the Refugee Act of 1980. The response of the US government to the Central American refugees was a product of these factors as well as of the government's foreign policy interests in Central America.

Reasons for flight

There is a long history of political violence in Guatemala. Amnesty International estimates that between 1966 and 1976, 20,000 Guatemalans were killed by death squads. But even this high level of violence was surpassed by the violence of the late 1970s and early 1980s. In response to growing popular support for Guatemalan opposition groups in the shadow of the successful Sandinista revolution, President Romero Lucas Garcia (1978–82) launched what Amnesty International has called a 'government programme of political murder'. Between 1981 and the end of 1982, the Guatemalan army forcibly uprooted over one million people in the indigenous highlands through the use of forced relocation, massacres and scorched earth policies. Displaced communities seeking to

return to their villages were directed to government-designed villages and carefully monitored. Between 1978 and 1983, when many Guatemalans were trying to escape from the massacres in the highlands by seeking refuge within the country, an estimated 250,000 to 350,000 Guatemalans were fleeing the country altogether, with some 200,000 going to Mexico. Many lived in the border regions, while many others eked out an existence on the outskirts of Mexico's major cities. Although some were documented by the government and eventually transferred to UNHCR-administered camps, most lived in the shadowy and vulnerable world of undocumented foreigners. The Mexican government estimated the number of undocumented Central Americans living in Mexico in the late 1980s as high as 385,000, of whom 250,000 were Salvadorians, 110,000 were Guatemalans living outside the camps and at least 25,000 were Hondurans and Nicaraguans. But like other Central American refugees, many Guatemalans continued their journey through Mexico to the USA in search of protection and economic survival. By the mid-1980s, the number of Guatemalans living in the USA was estimated at between 100,000 and 200,000, of whom approximately 60,000 to 80,000 lived in Los Angeles (Ruggles et al. 1985).

In El Salvador the violence erupting in the country in 1979 led the opposition to intensify the armed struggle and the government to begin a strategy of systematic bombing of areas suspected of harbouring guerrilla forces. At the same time, the death squads increased their activities, human rights violations rose dramatically, and torture and disappearance became a way of life. In 1979 about a thousand Salvadorians a month were killed by death squads. By 1985, casualties in the war reached 50,000. This widespread violence and fear displaced one million people – 20 per cent of El Salvador's population. About half remained within the country as internally displaced people, about 100,000 crossed into Honduras, of whom 20,000 ended up in government-controlled camps, and others sought security in more distant countries. By 1985, the number of Salvadorians in the USA was estimated at between 500,000 and 850,000, of whom 250,000–350,000 lived in Los Angeles (Ruggles et al. 1985).

While decrying the widespread violence in El Salvador, the US government supported the Salvadorian government, seeing it as a moderate alternative to communist rule. The victory of the Sandinistas in 1979 had increased the geo-political stakes of the Central American region and US foreign policy was to strengthen the ability of countries such as El Salvador and Guatemala to resist the leftist pressure. The arrival of large numbers of refugees from countries whose governments were supported by the USA was thus an embarrassment and a political liability for the US government. Their arrival also threatened the newly legislated Refugee Act of 1980.

US refugee policy

Since 1945, more than two million aliens have entered the USA outside the regular immigration channels – for example, displaced persons and refugees. These have included more than 800,000 Cubans, 700,000 Indo-Chinese and at least half a million central and eastern Europeans (Loescher and Scanlan 1986: 209).

The 1965 Immigration Act eliminated discrimination against Asians, mandated an end to the national origins quota system and placed a ceiling on visas for immigration from the western hemisphere. Refugee status was limited to those fleeing the communist-dominated countries of the Middle East and to 6 per cent of total visas. But provision was made for the attorney-general to allow entry for up to two years for people whose admission was deemed to be in the national interest. In 1979, the US president authorized 'extended voluntary departure' status for Nicaraguans in the USA immediately before and after the fall of Somoza. The move benefited about 20,000 people, but was not matched by similar initiatives for Salvadorians. In essence, before 1980 US refugee policy was largely based on resettlement, with people screened abroad and then admitted to the USA in accordance with their rank order on a waiting list.

The US Refugee Act of 1980 was an attempt to establish a baseline refugee quota with annual allocations to be determined by the president after consultation with Congress. The Refugee Act largely incorporated the UN definition of refugees and set up a full range of federal programmes to assist with resettlement. The act also provided for an asylum process, but the assumption was that most refugees would continue to come as resettlement cases. Only a few months after the passage of the act, the Mariel boat lift occurred in which over 120,000 Cubans arrived in Florida over a period of some five months. US President Carter moved to bypass the asylum procedures set up in the Refugee Act by reasserting the government's parole authority to admit the Cubans. At the same time, large numbers of Haitians were arriving by boat. Under political pressure, the US government granted them 'temporary entrant status' and quietly began a policy of interdicting Haitian boats thought likely to contain asylum-seekers. By 1980, the migration of Haitians, which had approached 12,000 per year, had slowed to a trickle.

It was in this context that the large number of Central American refugees began arriving in the USA. In 1979, there were 3000 applications for asylum in the USA. By 1981, the number was 40,000 and by 1983 it exceeded 140,000 (Meissner 1989: 130). These numbers overwhelmed the asylum system and tested the newly passed Refugee Act of 1980, in which it was assumed that the number of asylum applications would be small. Many of the asylum claims were filed by Central Americans, but all but a handful of their claims were rejected by the US government. Loescher and Scanlan (1986) note that 'the best available evidence indicates that in 1980, no Salvadorians were granted asylum, and that nearly 12,000 were deported.' In 1984, only 3 of 761 Guatemalan applicants (less than 0.5 per cent) and only 328 of 13,373 Salvadorians (less than 2.5 per cent) were granted asylum – compared with over 50 per cent approval rates for Bulgarians and Russians (Loescher and Scanlan 1986: 215).

Central American applicants for asylum were regarded as economic migrants, whose arrival in the USA had been motivated by poverty, rather than by political persecution as spelled out in the Refugee Act. The US asylum process includes participation by the State Department, which advises on the merits of the case. But, in pursuing its foreign policy goals in the region, the State Department has been reluctant to accept that applicants had a 'well-founded fear of persecution' by the very governments it was supporting.

While Central American refugees found little support from the asylum system, they did learn to use its appeal mechanisms and a variety of community and religious groups began to offer material and legal support. In 1980, 75 per cent of the Salvadorians arrested were returned to El Salvador. In 1981, 67 per cent were returned. By 1983, the percentage had fallen to 29 per cent. During the five-year period from 1980 to 1985, about 35,000 people were returned (Meissner 1989: 136).

The asylum provisions of the Refugee Act thus did not offer protection to most Central American refugees. Nor did the resettlement allocations established by the government. In 1982, only 579 of 3000 slots allocated for Latin Americans were actually filled and 577 of those slots went to Cubans.

Thus, for a decade or more, hundreds of thousands of Central American refugees have been living in the USA as undocumented foreigners with limited access to social services and vulnerable to exploitation by employers. Moreover, the restrictive admissions policy has ensured a relatively quiet population of refugees, for speaking out is very risky for undocumented refugees (Ferris 1987).

In response to their situation, church and community groups opened legal clinics and social service offices. In 1982, a Tucson Arizona congregation challenged the legality of the government's actions by declaring itself a public sanctuary for Central American refugees. The sanctuary movement grew to encompass some 300 public sanctuaries, in churches, synagogues, universities and community groups. In 1985, a group of sixteen sanctuary workers were indicted by the US government and, after a long court process, were given relatively mild sentences for conspiracy to abet illegal aliens.

By the mid-1980s, momentum was building to provide temporary protection for Central Americans who were afraid to return to their homelands because of the violence. The mechanism for this temporary protection existed in the form of 'extended voluntary departure', which had occasionally been used on behalf of national groups, such as Ugandans and Nicaraguans. As part of its 1990 Immigration Act, Congress established a 'temporary protected status' for individuals leaving their countries because of ongoing armed conflict, environmental disaster or other 'extraordinary and temporary conditions'. The act further designated nationals of El Salvador as eligible for 'temporary protected status' (TPS) and an estimated 180,000 took advantage of its provisions. Although TPS for Salvadorians expired in June 1992, the US government granted them 'deferred enforced departure' for another year – largely through fear that their return would disrupt the implementation of the Salvadorian peace process (Osuna and Hanson 1993: 42).

Although their status has only recently been regularized, the impact of Central American refugees on the USA has been considerable. On a social level, they have contributed to the growing Hispanic presence in particular states (such as California) and US cities (such as New York, Washington and Chicago). Politically, the administration exploited public fears of immigration to support its policies in the region. Thus, in June 1983, US president Ronald Reagan warned of a 'tidal wave of refugees swarming into our country if leftist movements in Central America are successful' (cited by Ferris 1987: 129).

They have also had a substantial economic impact on conditions in their countries of origin. In the case of Salvadorians, Segundo Montes (1989) estimates that Salvadorian refugees in the USA, although 30 per cent of them are unemployed, send an average of US $110 per month to relatives in El Salvador. Annually this represents about US $1.4 billion – a substantial contribution, overshadowing US foreign aid and efforts by international agencies to provide assistance to the country. Moreover, Segundo Montes estimates that the funds sent to relatives living in El Salvador provide 60 per cent of the income of those groups.

The future of the Central American refugees in the USA, like those dispersed throughout the region, depends on the establishment of peace and security in their home countries. Recent political changes in El Salvador have led some refugees to return, but many more are waiting to see what happens. Renewed violence in Guatemala makes it less likely that those refugees will return in the near future. And we know from other refugee cases that the longer refugees remain in exile, the less likely they are to return home.

References

Ferris, E. (1987) *The Central American Refugees*, New York: Praeger

Loescher, G. and J. A. Scanlan (1986) *Calculated Kindness: Refugees and America's Half-Open Door 1945–Present*, New York: Free Press

Meissner, D. M. (1989) 'Political Asylum, Sanctuary and Humanitarian Policy,' in Bruce Nichols and Gil Loescher (eds) *The Moral Nation*, Notre Dame: University of Notre Dame Press, 123–43

Montes, S. (1989) *Refugiados y Repatriados: El Salvador y Honduras*, San Salvador: Universidad Centroamericana José Simeon Canas

Osuna, J. P. and C. M. Hanson (1993) 'US Refugee Policy: Where We've Been, Where We're Going,' in *World Refugee Survey*, Washington: US Committee for Refugees, 40–8

Ruggles, H. et al. (1985) *Profile of the Central American Population in the United States*, New York: The Urban Institute

CHILE'S EXILES AND THEIR RETURN:
TWO FACES OF EXPATRIATION

JAIME LLAMBIAS-WOLFF

On 4 September 1970, a political event of major importance occurred in Chile: the presidential elections were won by a coalition of parties known as Popular Unity (*Unidad Popular*). This victory set a new precedent in Chilean political history. The head of this coalition of parties, Dr Salvador Allende, was called upon to form a new government as of November 1970. The objective of the new regime – to bring important transformations to the economic, political and social structures of the country – were soon to become an apparent threat to both national and foreign interests.

On 11 September 1973, a military coup took over power. Thousands of Chileans were confined to concentration camps. Political parties, as well as workers unions, were from then on prohibited. The senate and parliament were dissolved.

From that point onwards imprisonment, torture, repression and an absence of civil liberties became part of everyday life for Chileans. Under these circumstances another tragic event (less spectacular but replete with consequences) took place – exile.

Immediately after the coup the military regime introduced 'legal' procedures for imposing 'administrative exile' on anyone and under any circumstance. It also restricted entry to Chilean territory for anybody considered a threat to national security and for all those who had left the country for voluntary or involuntary reasons. All *de facto* procedures were 'legalized' by an unprecedented legal decree (December 1978) which stated that *all* laws and decrees dictated after the *coup d'état* that may be in opposition to the constitution automatically became constitutional.

The number of people who suffered exile has always been difficult to determine. However, if we add to the strictly political exiles the other exiles motivated by political unemployment, we can speak of about 200,000 persons. Also, if all those who left for economic reasons are included, hundreds of thousands of people are added to this emigration. Without doubt this has been the greatest emigration in Chilean history.

Consequences of exile

It is difficult to imagine quite how insecure an exile feels who, in both body and soul, undergoes the passage from one social reality to another. Some adapt with great difficulty to the new context, and suffer the sudden departure from their homeland as if it were a true trauma. Others live through it without major problems.[1]

After a certain euphoria born of the surprise and astonishment of the first moments lived in the host country, the exile begins a 'becoming conscious' phase, which permits him or her to understand that life will never again be the same.

The exiles deny being distressed and refuse to face their insecurity. They need to become conscious but do not seem to want to do so. Others feel guilt, thinking that the whole world is against them, that nobody tries to understand their predicament or even listen to their story.

In fact, the exiles gradually begin to feel marginal, and to find it difficult to establish contact and relate to others. Feelings of not going anywhere, of being constantly reminded of the same things, the same problems, the same people, are some of the symptoms of this stigmatized situation. Later, experiencing a sense of 'relative oblivion', the exiles slowly assume new responsibilities and redefine life in a calmer and more reliable fashion. They begin, however, to search for the guilty – the family, political leaders or the new country, refusing to search within themselves.

The considerable effort the exiles make to be accepted by others is the main characteristic of this stigmatized life. Only when they begin to comprehend their situation do they start to acquire the elements necessary to alleviate internal conflict and gradually get used to the new reality.

Then comes the time for important decisions, for making the radical changes that are needed to 'cut away' from the past. The Germans call this moment the '*Stunde null*' – the zero hour – when one's life seems like a column of smoke in the sky. Identity problems start to manifest themselves more and more. Life becomes artificial, depressing, filled with solitude, without perspective in time or space. Refusing to adapt, to know more, to learn, has now become a serious problem.

The exiles perceive their host community as foreign and hostile, as a place where other people's histories are being made, a world in which they are incapable of finding a place. They prefer to withdraw, to deprive themselves of fundamental links with the outside world, of the ties that are so important to their emotional stability.

In fact, the exiles have two choices – to let go and fall deep into the abyss, or to take on a new existence. Such a victory over adversity enables them to integrate socially and helps them to rediscover their own identities, this time accompanied by new visions that they themselves are able to accept.

However, whether for objective reasons or through nostalgia, the goal or dream of many Chileans is to return to their homeland. And, for all those willing to undertake this new step back to their old land, a new readaptation process begins. Returning is a highly complex business. It affects people in their daily lives with the additional stresses provoked by very practical concerns, such as housing, work, health, children and studies, as well as the more emotional aspects of social existence, such as social integration and acceptance, or the personal and family changes related to re-conquering their homeland.

The meaning of returning

It is not an exaggeration to say that, after 1973, Chileans could be found in almost any corner of the world. Knowing that close to 120 different countries received Chilean exiles, we can imagine the variety of cultures, experiences, values, costumes and languages that enriched the heritage of those going back home. The 'reintegration process' is of course mediated by all these different experiences.

In 1982 the military regime accepted the return of a limited number of people. Later, thanks to a political marketing operation by the dictatorship to regain public support for the 1989 referendum, exile came to an end. The military regime lost the referendum as well as the presidential election held the following year.

Returning means many things. In some cases it is a simple and rapid decision resulting in various practical procedures and activities that are necessary for the return trip home. In other cases, where there is an effort to minimize risks and to facilitate reintegration, the process is much longer. In many other cases the return process is only partial, when part of the family remains abroad. Many of the exiles had not only separated from their parents and grandparents, but also from their own children, who had grown up in another country with which they identified and in which they wished to stay.

Obviously, returning is not an easy process and the objective factors that influence this decision are many, including political developments, the experience of other returnees, family pressures, work expectations and overall prospects. But the objective factors are also accompanied by subjective elements, such as personal attitudes in relation to the idea of returning, images about the country, social expectations, the capacity to cope with a different society, reintegration to family life and building new social networks.

More than half of all registered returnees are between the ages of 30 and 49. Though they have fewer dependants than the average Chilean family, their numbers are not atypical of Chileans living in exile. Also, less than a third of the returned population, made up mainly of professionals and technicians, have jobs awaiting them on their arrival.

Three-quarters of the returnees seeking health care indicated that they had problems with their health. Only one-quarter owned a house, while almost half of them lived as guests with other members of their extended family. Also, 88 per cent of the Chileans returned permanently, with the remaining 12 per cent in transit. While one-quarter returned between 1986 and 1989, the great majority returned in 1990 and 1991. Finally, 42 per cent of returnees came from Latin America, 47 per cent from Europe and 6.5 per cent from Canada.

The readaptation process

Exile and return are two faces of the same dramatic and traumatic experience – expatriation. The contradictions faced during exile reappear in a different form when returning, when the distance enables the individual, personally and socially, to internalize the changes experienced. In other words, there is a loss of the images about the country, as well as of those things conquered during the period in exile.

Life therefore brings other ruptures to 'continuity' that reappear time and again. These contradictions, which may manifest themselves at different socio-psychological stages, can accelerate or postpone the social integration of the returnee. To every personal experience of exile there is a corresponding personal experience of return.

The 'first stage' of this process – the decision to return – is characterized by numerous known and unknown elements. Gathering information, minimizing risks and considering family implications are some of the aspects that influence the actual decision. Then, following the formal return, the returnees enter a so-called 'euphoric stage' in which they rediscover their own country: places, friends, language, images, food.

Later they begin to experience the changes that have occurred. People are different, communication is not the same, some customs become difficult to accept. This 'stage of the unexpected' is provoked by real and imaginary facts, by true changes in their country and by the perceptions of an individual who has become different after years of living overseas. Many exiles feel anger and have doubts and difficulties in adjusting. In other words, beautiful nostalgia has become a different reality. In some cases a 'depression' follows, in which the individual loses his or her self-esteem and dynamism. This carries the risk of reproducing the syndrome of the exile, of blaming others, of looking for other returnees with whom to share common experiences and of recreating a new social network of former exiles.

Those capable of accepting the limits of the new life will, however, develop the necessary strength to enter the next 'readaptation stage', i.e. seeing the future with realism, accepting the difficulties and enjoying the positive aspects of the return. This then leads to the 'reintegration stage', when the returnees feel themselves to be useful and rediscover the links between the past, the present and the future.

The capacity to go beyond the present, to be part of a society (and within the society) provides the individual with the necessary strength to face daily life with energy and hope. Teenagers, however, who may not remember their country of origin, experience a variety of personal difficulties. These range from a feeling of separation from their country, loneliness, the sense of being a stranger, and an incapacity to visualize a future or to identify conflicts. For teenagers this is not a return trip home.

Returnees need support in facing all the adverse situations associated with their new experience, for in building a new way of life they have to cope with the double emotional rupture of their involuntary departure and voluntary return. They need to rediscover their personal, social, physical and emotional space, to learn about their personal limitations within the new environment and to assume the paradox of readaptation to their own society, including all the subjective confusion that this implies. Furthermore, pressures to become as 'normal as everybody else' may provoke family, generational and professional conflicts and tensions that can only be reduced or resolved with time and understanding.

In summary, in an effort to feel like the 'others' and not like a 'stranger' in their own country, the returnees have no choice but to rediscover their personal and social identities. They must build a new daily life from a different starting point, one that is characterized by a break between the past and the present. In addition, they have to assume this reality with all the personal limitations inherent in their new situation, including the capacity to recover their new material (housing and employment), emotional (family, friends and neighbours) and social (social network) space.

The process of allowing the past and the present to converge in the future calls on important qualities and insights. Only then will the returnees recover their lost identity and feel they belong to the country in which they were born. Only then can exile be transformed into a positive experience that can enrich the future life of a repatriated individual.

Note
1. Data have been obtained from secondary sources (publications, working papers, institutional documents), official publications provided by governmental agencies and through informal interviews conducted with professionals assisting the returned population. This research was done 'in situ' in Santiago, Chile, during the months of May and June 1992.

PART EIGHT

MIGRATION TO NORTH AMERICA AFTER 1945

In his classic account of migration to the USA, Oscar Handlin (1951) depicts the tensions between the acceptance of the immigrant and the growth of restrictionist sentiment among recent arrivals. Americans, he says, 'cannot push away the heritage of having been all once strangers in the land'; nor can they 'forget the experience of having all been rootless, adrift'. However, the 'tiredness of the transient' produces a counter-reaction: 'The ideals of the nest, remembered even at the height of the flight, have triumphed. Men weary of a century or more of struggle, impatient of the constant newness, more eagerly than ever hunger for the security of belonging. Restriction becomes a part of their lives – and perhaps it must be so' (p. 306).

One can well imagine a less flattering description of the 'nesting', exclusionist attitudes Handlin describes. In his still widely cited account, John Higham (1955) considered such views as examples of 'American nativism'; others have used vaguer or cruder labels like 'nationalism', 'isolationism' or 'racism'. One can be more or less understanding, or more or less forgiving of those who pull the ladder up after their own ascent. However, it is clear that the contradiction between implicitly or explicitly encouraging new entrants, on the one hand, and excluding, deporting or repelling them, on the other, lies at the heart of the post-war immigration history of the USA.

Not far from that heart is the story of Mexican migration. As *Calavita* argues, the use of Mexican workers in US agriculture and services appeared to present a golden opportunity for employers profitably to relate immigration flows to economic demand. Mexicans, she says, 'provided a source of cheap labour whose stay in the USA could be terminated when demand had waned'. At a number of points in US history, including both world wars, this was precisely what happened. The system was institutionalized in 1942 in the Bracero Program, which regulated the flow of temporary 'stoop-back' labour to and from the field–factories of the south-west. But there was never a complete fit between economic logic, the rhythm of circulatory migration and US public opinion. The Bracero Program continued long after the war that occasioned its introduction had ended. In the 1950s when there was work to be had, public hostility to Mexicans resulted in the notorious deportation programme, Operation Wetback. The important 1986 act was an uneasy compromise between an amnesty for and repression of undocumented workers. Now, as *Cavalier* illustrates, a 'new nativism' has arisen in California, this time directed against illegal Mexicans gaining access to social security, health benefits or education. Again, no purely economic logic obtains, for whether undocumented Mexicans generate a fiscal surplus or create a drain on public spending remains a moot point.

The ebb and flow of migrants from Puerto Rico showed some similarities to the Mexican case for a number of decades. Though not, on the whole, destined for agricultural pursuits, up to the 1960s Puerto Ricans often started in the mainland as highly subordinate workers in sweatshops or in the provision of services. The differences with Mexico are, however, crucial. Since 1917, with the US occupation of the island, Puerto Ricans acquired the right to travel freely to the USA (even though Puerto Rico evolved a somewhat separated status as a 'free associated state' of the USA). In practice, free access to the US labour market meant little until the provision of cheap, regular air transport. Thereafter the flows of Puerto Ricans to and from the mainland were complex, massive and circulatory – following the ups and downs of different sectors of the island and mainland economies. As *Hernández Cruz* demonstrates, when assembly plants, tourism and construction boomed on the island, Puerto Ricans (sometimes derided as 'New Yoricans') returned 'home'. When, by contrast, skilled and professional opportunities opened out in the USA in the 1970s and 1980s, the island was relatively denuded of its brainpower.

While the US–Puerto Rican migration system was evolving, Puerto Rico itself became part of a set of regional migration currents (Marshall 1982; Pastor 1985), particularly from Haiti, the Dominican Republic and Cuba. The Anglophone Commonwealth Caribbean countries are covered in *Peach*'s contribution. As he shows, the rhythm and destinations of Caribbean emigrations were partly determined by immigration restrictions in the USA and Britain. For the first half this century, Anglophone Caribbean migrants were seen as part of the 'British' West Indies and counted within the relatively under-utilized British quota. In 1952, a restrictive immigration act in the USA reclassified the region and virtually halted inward migration. At the same time (and until about 1965 when a restrictive act in Britain produced the same effect), jobs were to be had for the asking in the UK. The flow to the USA started again in 1962 with the easing of entry laws. It is tempting to see the switch in destinations as merely a displacement effect of the restrictive legislation, but, as Peach himself has shown in his elegantly researched earlier work (1968), there was an uncanny correspondence between the rate of West Indian immigration and vacancies in the British labour market.

The liberalization of the US immigration laws in the early 1960s also provided a green light for Asian migration, hitherto constrained by anti-Asian legislation and hostility to the Japanese in the immediate aftermath of the Second World War. Even Japanese Americans born in the USA (two-thirds of whom had a median age of seventeen) were detained as security risks during the Second World War, one of the least edifying episodes in the USA's history. Although Asian women married to US servicemen, together with a variety of unskilled, semi-skilled and entrepreneurial migrants, entered the country after the Second World War, it was not until 1965 that 'hemispheric' quotas were removed and individual countries were assigned a generous number of entry visas. As *Liu* indicates, the result was dramatic. Middle-class and professional immigration was stimulated, while over the period 1965–93 over four million Asians entered, tripling the size of pre-1965 levels of post-war immigration and the size of the Asian-American population.

The sheer numbers and evident educational and economic success of the post-1965 Asian migrants triggered much envy and apprehension from the the white majority and from other minorities in the USA. WASP students at the University of California were constrained to demand an 'ethnic quota' for themselves in deference to the unremitting educational achievements of their Asian peers. The numbers of 'Asians', of course, concealed considerable ethnic diversity (Koreans, Chinese, Indians and Thais share little in common). Nor were all the Asians 'middle-class': considerable numbers of dispossessed Vietnamese, Cambodian and Laotian refugees were also admitted. Nonetheless, the increased awareness of 'Asians' as a total group signified a broad shift in the world's migration flows as a Pacific migration system came to rival the old, established Atlantic one.

A little blast from the Atlantic past was, however, visible in the form of black African migration to the USA, particularly from Nigeria and Ethiopia. Though the numbers are small, as *Bigman* demonstrates, the group is of great sociological interest. The first African diaspora was created by force; the 'second diaspora' is a largely voluntary and refugee phenomenon. Many of the Nigerians, whom a casual visitor to Washington will easily encounter (they have a niche as taxi drivers), started their lives in the USA as students. Either because they found themselves on the wrong side of the Nigerian civil war, or because their family or government sponsorship ran out (the oil boom in Nigeria was a mercurial affair), many Nigerians stayed on. The relationship of the new African migrants to the old African-American community is complex and often strained. Unlike the Haitians or Anglophone Caribbean blacks, who at least shared a common history of slavery and New World plantation employment, the migrants of the second diaspora have arrived directly from the continent. As a number of African Americans had adopted an ersatz African dress, hairstyle and set of beliefs, the encounter with 'the real thing' was sometimes painful and often mutually unintelligible.

The final contribution in this section comprises an extended analysis by *Richmond* and *Lam* of post-war migration to Canada. The significance of migration to the whole character of Canadian society can hardly be overestimated. Like Australia (and the turn-of-the-century USA), Canada is a 'migration country'. Over the fifty-year period, 1941–91, when European populations were stable or falling, the population of Canada nearly trebled, a demographic rise that vividly demonstrates the significance of immigrants and their descendants. In the immediate post-war period, the strong historical associations with Europe and the stress on family sponsorship tended to perpetuate the ethnically monochrome character of Canadian society. Though the seeds of change were there earlier, from the mid-1960s a fundamental transformation in policy occurred. Henceforth, immigrants were also to be admitted on a non-racial basis through a sophisticated 'points system' that matched labour force needs with immigrant skills. For the province of Ontario especially, which took over half the incoming migrants, the results were spectacular. The economy boomed. 'Ethnic' restaurants lined the main streets of Toronto, making the city a gourmet's delight. The authorities responded to the diverse influx with imaginative programmes to celebrate the country's multi-culturalism.

But behind the façade of goodwill, there were real problems. The 'points system' was only apparently open: publicly and behind the scenes there were fierce rows over the balance to be struck between family-sponsored, independent and refugee migration. In Vancouver, locals built up resentments against the 'yacht-people', as migrants from Hong Kong were labelled. And in Quebec, Francophone Canadians were either indifferent or hostile to the new immigrants. Many were in any case destined for the Anglophone areas, which tilted the balance even further against the Québecois, thus further fuelling their separatist sentiment. However, as Hawkins (1972: 220) argues of Quebec, some of the wounds derived from migration were self-inflicted. The Montreal city authorities provided only one-seventeenth of the budget for language training voted by their Toronto counter-parts and they allowed 90 per cent of the children of neither French nor British background to register in English-medium schools. Of concern to Canada as a whole is that there are considerable apprehensions about the possible effects of the North American Free Trade Agreement in the longer term. (At the moment the agreement does not cover migration.) Despite these doubts about the extent and nature of post-war migration flows, *Richmond* and *Lam* suggest that the Canadian authorities may rise to the challenge of a fair immigration policy, provide effective control of racist elements and equitably govern a country of considerable ethnic diversity.

References
Handlin, Oscar (1951) *The Uprooted: The Epic Story of the Great Migrations that Made the American People*, Boston: Little, Brown & Company
Hawkins, Freda (1972) *Canada and Immigration: Public Policy and Public Concern*, Montreal: McGill–Queen's University Press for the Institute of Public Administration of Canada
Higham, John (1955) *Strangers in the Land: Patterns of American Nativism, 1860–1925*, New Brunswick, NJ: Rutgers University Press
Marshall, Dawn I. (1982) 'Towards an Understanding of Caribbean Migration', in Mary Kritz (ed.) *US Immigration and Refugee Policy: Global and Domestic Issues*, Lexington: D. C. Heath
Pastor, Robert A. (ed.) (1985) *Migration and Development in the Caribbean: The Unexplored Connection*, Boulder, CO: Westview Press
Peach, Ceri (1968) *West Indian Migration to Britain: A Social Geography*, London: Oxford University Press

MEXICAN IMMIGRATION TO THE USA: THE CONTRADICTIONS OF BORDER CONTROL

KITTY CALAVITA

Alexander Hamilton told the US Congress in 1791 that immigration should be encouraged to increase the size of the labour force and ease the problem of the 'dearness of labor' (Hamilton 1791: 123). US policy makers ever since have recognized the key role of immigrants as an elastic supply of labour. An essentially open door immigration policy prevailed in the nineteenth and early twentieth centuries. Indeed, the first US immigration statute, *An Act to Encourage Immigration* (1864), was passed to increase immigration during the Civil War and keep labour costs down.

Employers in the late nineteenth century were pleased with the ever-increasing immigrant labour supply from Europe. Andrew Carnegie (1886: 34–5) called immigration 'a golden stream which flows into the country each year' and valued each adult immigrant at $1500. A business journal echoed Carnegie's appreciation for immigration: 'Men, like cows, are expensive to raise and a gift of either should be gladly received. And a man can be put to more valuable use than a cow' (*New York Journal of Commerce* 1892: 2). Laws prohibiting the immigration of those with contagious diseases and other 'undesirables' were passed, but they were carefully worded and implemented so as not to interrupt the 'golden stream'. By the turn of the century almost a million immigrants were entering the USA annually, mostly to work in the booming industrial centres of the east and midwest.

Mexican immigration increased substantially in the pre-First World War period, at a time when US policy makers and some employers were reconsidering the relative costs and benefits of the European source. In the early twentieth century, European immigrants increasingly formed the backbone of strikes, joined militant labour unions like the Industrial Workers of the World (IWW) and, more often than not, remained in the USA to become permanent members of society. Within this context, the Dillingham Commission on Immigration in 1911 pointed out the merits of the Mexican 'back door' (US Congress 1911: 690–1):

Because of their strong attachment to their native land

... and the possibility of their residence here being discontinued, few become citizens of the USA. The Mexican immigrants are providing a fairly adequate supply of labor. ... While they are not easily assimilated, this is of no very great importance as long as most of them return to their native land. In the case of the Mexican, he is less desirable as a citizen than as a laborer.

This contribution examines the nature of Mexican immigration to the USA over time, and the ambiguities and contradictions associated with efforts to control it. After a brief historical overview, I will focus particular attention on the Immigration Reform and Control Act of 1986 (IRCA) and its aftermath, as they bring into sharp relief the contradictions that have permeated US immigration policy since the nineteenth century and continue to plague policy makers in the 1990s.

Historical overview

Mexico has long been considered an ideal back-door source of cheap labour for US employers. In the late nineteenth century, Mexicans were central to expanding agricultural production in the American south-west, and constituted a large portion of the railroad workers on the Southern Pacific and Santa Fe railroads that transported the agricultural produce harvested by their compatriots (McWilliams 1968). In recognition of their role in the south-west economy, immigration restrictions often included specific exemptions for Mexicans. When the literacy test requirement was passed in 1917, for example, south-west growers convinced policy makers that the new provision should not apply to their Mexican workers. And, while quota restrictions were imposed on eastern hemisphere immigrants in the 1920s, no such quotas applied to Mexico until 1965.

These were not merely 'good neighbour' policies. Rather, the unique advantage of Mexican immigration was the flexibility derived from Mexico's proximity to the USA and the related ability to expand and contract the supply with the labour need, thereby mitigating the tensions associated with the more permanent European immigration. Congressional debates in the 1920s confirm the intention to use Mexican immigrants as a malleable supply of labour. Reisler (1976: 181) summarizes these debates: 'The Mexican, they pointed out, was a vulnerable alien living just a short distance from his homeland. ... He, unlike Puerto Ricans or Filipinos ... could easily be deported. No safer or more economical unskilled labor force was imaginable.'

Formal and informal policies during the 1920s and 1930s left little doubt about policy makers' willingness to capitalize on the vicinity of Mexico, the relative vulnerability of Mexican immigrants and the flexibility derived from both. For example, during the 1920s, in order to ensure the departure of Mexican agricultural workers at the end of the season, the Labor Department instructed employers to deposit 20 per cent of their pay with immigration officials, to be collected by workers as they exited the country (Calavita 1984: 136). The depression of the 1930s witnessed the massive repatriation of Mexicans, many of whom were in the USA legally and some of whom were US citizens.

When an agricultural labour shortage was proclaimed during the Second World War, the Bracero Program brought hundreds of thousands of Mexican workers to work in the fields of the south-west USA through bilateral agreements with the Mexican government. By the time of its termination in 1964, the Bracero Program had provided five million *bracero*s to US farms and ranches in a system that attempted to institutionalize the flexibility and temporary nature of the Mexican labour source. As one critic of the Bracero Program said bitterly, 'Like the sprinkling systems of mechanized irrigation, *bracero*s could be turned on and off' (Galarza 1977: 265).

A number of policies in effect during the *bracero* period contributed to the increase of illegal migration from Mexico that characterizes the contemporary movement. The agreement of 1949, for example, stipulated that 'illegal workers, when they are located in the USA, shall be given preference [for *bracero* status]' (quoted in Galarza 1964: 63). Illegal Mexican immigrants, or 'wetbacks' as they were called, were 'dried out' by the Border Patrol who took them to the Mexican border and brought them back as legal *bracero*s. Alternatively, the Border Patrol 'paroled' illegal immigrants directly to employers who took them on as *bracero*s (Calavita 1992). The President's Commission on Migratory Labor (1951) estimated that from 1947 to 1949, more than 142,000 illegal Mexican workers were legalized in these ways; during

the same period, only 74,600 *bracero*s were actually imported from Mexico (Samora 1971: 47–8).

The Immigration and Naturalization Service (INS) during this period encouraged illegal immigration from Mexico in other ways as well. The chief inspector at Tucson, Arizona, reported that he 'received orders ... each harvest to stop deporting illegal Mexican labor' (Kirstein 1977: 90). The INS district director in Los Angeles explained to the Labor Department that their policy was not to check farms and ranches for illegal workers during the harvest season (Calavita 1992: 33). In 1949, the Idaho State Employment Service told the President's Commission on Migratory Labor, 'The US Immigration and Naturalization Service recognizes the need for farm workers in Idaho and ... withholds its search and deportation until such times as there is not a shortage of farm workers' (quoted in the President's Commission on Migratory Labor 1951: 76). Congress too was 'splendidly indifferent' to the rising number of illegal immigrants, reducing the Border Patrol budget as undocumented immigration increased in the late 1940s and early 1950s (Hadley 1956: 334).

A key Congressional decision made employers immune to any risk involved in the employment of the undocumented. In 1952, Congress passed an act that made it illegal to 'harbor, transport, or conceal illegal entrants' (PL 283). However, an amendment to the provision, referred to as the Texas Proviso after the Texas growers to whom it was a concession, excluded employment *per se* from the category of 'harbouring'. The amendment was ostensibly introduced as a way to protect employers who were unaware of their workers' illegal immigrant status from prosecution under the harbouring clause. Despite assurances by Texas Proviso advocates that it did not provide a loophole for the knowing employment of illegal aliens, Congress rejected by a margin of 69 to 12 an amendment explicitly penalizing such knowing employment (see Calavita 1992: 66–70). The Texas Proviso was subsequently interpreted by the INS as a *carte blanche* for the employment of undocumented workers (see Greene 1972: 453–5).

Illegal immigration increased rapidly within this economic and legal context. From 1942 to 1952, when a total of 818,545 *bracero*s were imported from Mexico, the INS apprehended over two million undocumented workers, the vast majority of whom were Mexican (US Immigration and Naturalization Service 1959: 54). By 1953, the alarm was sounded that illegal immigration was depressing wages, displacing US workers and – in this period of cold war paranoia – jeopardizing the national security by providing an entrée to 'potential saboteurs and fifth columnists' (quoted in *Congressional Record* 1954: 2564). In response, 'Operation Wetback' was launched and hundreds of thousands of Mexicans were rounded up and deported (see Calavita 1992: 46–61). For the rest of the decade, the INS provided US growers with an ample supply of *braceros* as a substitute for the illegal workers of the past. By the time the Bracero Program ended in 1964, a relationship of symbiosis between Mexican immigrants and US employers had become well-entrenched, facilitated and nurtured by over fifty years of policy making. Almost five million Mexican workers had been brought to the USA as *braceros*; approximately five million illegal aliens were apprehended during the same period (Lopez 1981: 671).

Having set the stage for high levels of documented and undocumented immigration, US policies in the post-*bracero* period have perpetuated the pattern largely by default. Most important, budgetary decisions had the consequence of eliminating the counter-pressure to illegal migration. Between 1960 and 1970, the number of apprehended aliens rose from about 23,000 to 345,000, but the number of permanent INS positions remained constant at 6900 (Congressional Research Service 1980; US Immigration and Naturalization Service 1978: 19). By 1978, the number of annual apprehensions had risen to more than one million, while total INS personnel reached barely 10,000 (Congressional Research Service 1980: 76, 90). As the Congressional subcommittee that holds the purse strings of the INS put it in 1981, the agency 'has been chronically underfunded, under-manned and neglected' (quoted in Harwood 1983: 108).

Since the mid-nineteenth century, the appreciation of the economic role of immigrants to the USA has been accompanied by anti-immigrant nativism. Based on various combinations of racism, fears of tax increases, cultural and political protectionism, and organized labour's concerns over bargaining power, these anti-immigrant backlashes have intensified during economic downturns, perceived threats to national security and social transformations (Cornelius 1982; Espenshade and Calhoun 1993; Higham 1955).

The reaction against Mexican immigrants by the mid-twentieth century, while much like anti-immigrant responses of earlier periods, differed in certain respects. Most important, given the vicinity of Mexico and the undocumented status of many Mexican immigrants, they have been subject to abrupt policy changes at the administrative level in response to such backlashes. Mass expulsions and roundups of Mexicans during 'Operation Wetback' in 1954, for example, were reminiscent of the depression policies of the 1930s. This periodic tightening of the border with Mexico, which is often accomplished without recourse to statutory changes, is eminently compatible with the longstanding perception of Mexican migration as a flexible and temporary supply of labour.

In the past two decades, restrictionism is once again on the rise. As in the past, a vocal minority has blamed immigrants for virtually every social ill affecting US society, including crime, environmental deterioration and urban uprisings. And, as in the past, it is in large part because immigrants supply a cheap labour force (i.e. precisely that which employers and policy makers have appreciated) that they provide an easy target of backlash by wary taxpayers and domestic workers. The predominantly illegal nature of the contemporary flow enhances the reaction. As the fear spread in the early 1980s that the USA had 'lost control of its borders', immigration restrictionism and antagonism against those who personified this lack of control intensified.

The Immigration Reform and Control Act of 1986 (IRCA) fits well within this context. It can best be understood as an effort to respond simultaneously to the longstanding economic reality of undocumented immigration and to the political reality of increasing restrictionism. The following sections trace the roots of this legislation, examine its principal provisions and evaluate its impact.

The Immigration Reform and Control Act

IRCA contained three main provisions. The legalization clause allowed undocumented immigrants who had been in the USA in an illegal status since before 1 January 1982 to apply for legal residence. Employer sanctions made it illegal for an employer to hire undocumented workers. Finally, the Special Agricultural Workers' Program was a legalization plan for certain undocumented farmworkers. Despite the complex nature of IRCA and the importance of its legalization provisions, employer sanctions were its indisputable political centrepiece.

The possibility of a federal employer sanctions law was first seriously debated in 1971 when Representative Rodino's subcommittee on immigration held hearings on the topic of illegal immigration, a substantial portion of which dealt with the pros and cons of employer sanctions. By the time the Select Commission on Immigration and Refugee Policy (SCIRP) had recommended employer sanctions as the key to reform in 1981, this restrictionist approach was overwhelmingly supported by the majority of the US public (Gallup 1980).

One year after the SCIRP published its recommendations, the Simpson-Mazzoli Bill was reported out of the House and Senate Judiciary Committees. Both the House and Senate versions followed the commission's call for a federal employer sanctions law. The Senate passed its bill by 80 to 19 after only three days of floor debate. The bill foundered in the House, however, where civil rights advocates were concerned over the potential for abuse and discrimination against those who 'sound or look foreign'; growers' groups lobbied for additional provisions for foreign labour; and the US Chamber of Commerce vigorously opposed sanctions against employers. So controversial was the bill in the House that over 300 amendments were introduced in a successful effort to forestall a vote (Calavita 1989; Montwieler 1987).

A second Simpson-Mazzoli Bill passed the House and Senate in 1984, squeaking by the House 216–211, only to come apart in the conference committee. That year marked an important turning point for the reform effort. First, opposition to employer sanctions (most notably that of the Chamber of Commerce) began to subside, placated at least in part by the 'affirmative defence' clause which released employers from any obligation to check the authenticity of documents presented to them. Second, agricultural employers shifted their focus from opposition to employer sanctions to a campaign to secure alternative sources of foreign labour. As opposition to employer sanctions waned and growers' lobbying efforts for temporary worker programmes intensified, agricultural worker programmes began to outrank the employer sanctions component as the most controversial element of the reform. What had begun as a restrictive effort grounded in employer sanctions, had now come full circle to be mired in a debate over how best to *expand* the supply of foreign labour.

The following year, Senator Simpson reintroduced the bill that Congressional opponents called 'The Monster from the Blue Lagoon' because of its eerie ability to rise from the dead. By September this Senate version had already been passed, after an impressive show of strength by the Western Growers' Association. Arguing that employer sanctions would cut off an invaluable source of agricultural labour, Senator Wilson of California introduced an amendment to create a temporary farm labour programme. The amendment was defeated 50 to 48, only to be passed four days later after intensive grower lobbying. The Wilson amendment provided for a short-term guestworker programme in which 350,000 foreign workers annually would be given visas for a limited period to harvest perishable crops.

A number of key Democrats in the House vowed to kill any bill with such a *bracero*-like programme attached to it. By the end of the amendment process they had agreed to a complicated formula that provided temporary residence status and eventual eligibility for citizenship to those who had worked in agriculture for at least ninety days, and included a generous future replenishment clause, under the assumption that newly legalized workers might abandon farm labour. The compromise struck a delicate balance between civil rights advocates who argued against traditional guestworker programmes on the grounds that they provided employers with a captive workforce and hence invited abuse, and growers' representatives who were assured a plentiful and continual supply of foreign labour. On 14 October 1986, this rather unwieldy bill was finally endorsed by House and Senate conferees. As the president signed IRCA, he noted that the law was 'the product of one of the longest and most difficult legislative undertakings of recent memory' (quoted in Montwieler 1987: 18).

The most significant consequence of IRCA was the legalization of millions of undocumented immigrants who had for years lived and worked in the shadows. A total of 3 million immigrants applied to one of IRCA's two legalization programmes, far more than policy makers had expected. Approximately 1.7 million applicants filed for the general amnesty programme, with the approval rate at close to 98 per cent (Bean et al. 1989: 68); another 1.3 million applied for legalization through the Special Agricultural Workers' Program. The majority of these legalized immigrants came from Mexico, and five states – California, Texas, Illinois, New York and Florida – accounted for over 80 per cent of the applications (Baker 1990: 165).

But the political centrepiece of IRCA – employer sanctions – has had little concrete effect. Section 101 of IRCA makes it illegal to employ knowingly aliens not authorized to work in the USA. Further, the law requires that employers ask all new employees for documentation proving their identity and eligibility to work in the USA, that they fill out and sign an 'I–9' form for each new hire, listing the specific documents seen and their expiration dates, and that they keep this form on file. Penalties for violations of the 'knowing hire' provision range from $250 for the first offence to $10,000 for repeated offences. A 'pattern or practice' of violations may bring criminal penalties, including six months in prison. Fines for paperwork violations related to the I–9 form range from $100 to $1000 per violation (Calavita 1990).

Advocates for employer sanctions argued that once employers were thus precluded from hiring the undocumented, illegal immigration would decline. Border apprehension statistics at first seemed to validate advocates' claims about the law's deterrent potential. From 1986 to 1989, Border Patrol apprehensions along the US–Mexico border, where the overwhelming bulk of illegal aliens are apprehended, dropped from 1,615,854 to 854,939. However, a dramatic reversal of this decline began in the second quarter of 1989, and apprehensions have since approximated their pre-1986 levels (Brossy 1990: B3; Fix 1991). The most comprehensive study to date of the effect of employer sanctions on the volume of illegal border crossings (Crane et al. 1990) concludes that the initial reductions in apprehensions were a consequence of legalizing close to three million immigrants, many of whom had periodically crossed the border illegally prior to their change of status. The US Labor Department's study of the impact of employer sanctions similarly concludes that 'the drop in apprehensions in the immediate post-IRCA years may have been more of a pause than a change in behavior' (US Department of Labor 1991: 62). The Commission on Agricultural Workers, established by Congress to trace the effect of IRCA on agricultural conditions, reaches similar conclusions (US Commission on Agricultural Workers 1992), as do most academic studies (see, for example, Bean et al. 1989; Fix 1991).

In part, employer sanctions have had little deterrent effect because the provision is not rigorously enforced. In its first report to Congress on the impact of employer sanctions, the US General Accounting Office (GAO) noted that the INS expected to audit 20,000 employers in 1988 – one-third of 1 per cent of the approximately seven million employers in the USA (US General Accounting Office 1987: 27). INS records show that it fell short of even this goal (US Immigration and Naturalization Service 1988). Nor has the rate of inspection increased substantially in subsequent years. As one study put it, 'INS enforcement activity could not be characterized as hyperactive' (Fix and Hill 1990: 89).

The most potent ingredient affecting employers'

continued hiring of the undocumented, however, may be their perception of the protection accorded them by the I–9 form. A study of 100 employers in southern California (summarized in Calavita 1990) found almost universal compliance with this paperwork requirement. All but five of these employers systematically requested documentation and completed the required forms. Rather than seeing the paperwork requirement as burdensome, many of these employers viewed the I–9 form as an effective barrier between violation and prosecution. The director of human resources at a large plant who told the interviewer that 'evidently we have people who are illegal', pointed out that 'it [the I–9] would help protect us'.

The source of this paradox can be found in the legislative debates, during which compliance with the paperwork requirement came to stand in for compliance with the 'knowing hire' clause. In 1982, a 'good faith' clause was inserted in the Simpson-Mazzoli Bill. This clause stipulated that if employers check workers' documents, regardless of the validity of those documents, they will be assumed to have complied with the law. During the debate of the final Simpson-Rodino Bill in the Senate, Senator Alan Simpson reiterated the theme that had pervaded the lengthy proceedings. 'I can assure my colleagues', he said, 'that an innocent employer will be protected by following the verification procedures' (quoted in Montwieler 1987: 255).

By the time the Immigration Reform and Control Act was passed in 1986, this protection was spelled out carefully. It included a provision that the required document check, conducted in 'good faith' (Section 101), would constitute an 'affirmative defense that the person or entity has not violated [the "knowing hire" clause]'. Also important, it released employers from responsibility for detecting fraudulent documents, stating that 'a person or entity has complied with the [document check] requirement ... if the document reasonably appears on its face to be genuine'.

These protections were designed in part to minimize employer opposition to the law. As early as 1981, when the Senate subcommittee held hearings on 'The Knowing Employment of Illegal Aliens', the commissioner of the INS, Doris Meissner, stressed that 'implementation of the law is not designed to be and will not be anti employer' (US Congress 1981: 5). At the same hearing, Senator Simpson repeated, 'it [employer sanctions] must be the type of program which does not place an onerous burden upon the employer with respect to what he has to do to avoid a penalty' (US Congress 1981: 86). In 1985, the

Chamber of Commerce, convinced that employer sanctions would not pose an 'onerous burden', officially *endorsed* the measure.

Not surprisingly, the number of fines levied for violations of employer sanctions has been relatively low. An Urban Institute study of ten major cities covering all four INS regions found that in El Paso, where the most employer sanctions fines were served, only one fine was levied 'for every two months of agent service' (Fix and Hill 1990: 89). The rate in Chicago was one fine per two years of agent service. When fines are issued, they are relatively light, varying from $9459 in the northern region, to $2060 in the southern region. According to a US General Accounting Office study, these fines are usually further reduced by almost 60 per cent through negotiations (cited in Fix and Hill 1990: 86).

The Immigration Reform and Control Act of 1986 was hailed as landmark legislation that would 'regain control of the borders' and, as a prime example of pluralist compromise, offer something to everyone. This depiction of IRCA is wrong on both counts. While the mandate to regain control of the borders did provide the political motor of the reform effort, the only restrictive provision of the law (employer sanctions) was to remain a symbolic measure with little impact on immigration flows. At the same time, other provisions of IRCA, such as the Special Agricultural Worker Program, added to the stock of immigrant workers. Thus, not only did IRCA pull both ways at once, but ironically the consequence of this reform, which was fuelled by restrictionist fervour, was a continued increase in immigration, both documented and undocumented.

California and the new nativism

With the failure of IRCA and a lingering recession, illegal immigration has once again been pushed to the top of the political agenda, particularly in California where defence industry cutbacks and a collapse in the real estate market have contributed to a devastating economic downturn (Espenshade and Calhoun 1993). An assortment of Californian politicians, taxpayer associations and former INS officials have fuelled the backlash. Anxiety has been further heightened by several studies that purport to show that undocumented immigrants are a drain on taxpayers, costing vastly more in social services than they contribute in taxes (Rea and Parker 1992; Stewart et al. 1992).

These studies have been challenged on a variety of grounds, among the most important being that they overestimate the number of undocumented immi-grants in the state and underestimate their tax contribution. Several subsequent studies have concluded that the cost of immigration to the state of California is far lower than previously imagined and that at the national level there is a net fiscal gain (Bomemeier 1994: A1; Clark and Passel 1993; Edmonston and Passel 1992; Eisenstadt and Thorup 1994; Fix and Passel 1994: B7). The gain may be more significant than estimated even in these studies, since they generally do not include in their calculations the low cost of undocumented immigrant labour which subsidizes California agribusiness and other important industries (see, for example, Arax 1994: A3).

While the issue of the costs and benefits of immigration remains unresolved, an overwhelming majority of Californians support the enactment of new restrictionist measures and favour local politicians who use this issue as a political calling card (Decker 1994: A1; Gibbs 1994: 46–7; Klein 1993: Al). By early 1993, more than twenty restrictionist bills had been placed before the California legislature and several provisions, including one that bars the undocumented from receiving drivers' licences, have been passed (Bailey and Morain 1993: A3). Proposition 187, known as the Save Our State (SOS) initiative, is probably the most extreme of such restrictionist measures. The initiative, which was supported by a majority of Californian voters through a referendum in November 1994, would bar undocumented immigrant children from attending public schools (and require school administrators to request documentation from 'suspect' children), and would withhold from the undocumented all non-emergency medical care such as antenatal care and innoculations. Despite issues of its possible consti-tutionality[1] and inconsistency with federal statutes and regulations, as well as its potentially dangerous public health consequences, Proposition 187 easily passed. Most provisions of the proposition have been put on hold while numerous court challenges are processed (Decker 1994: Al; Gibbs 1994: 46–7; Nalik and Feldman 1994: A21).

Most recently, the US Commission on Immigration Reform – a bipartisan federal commission established by Congress in 1990 – released its recommendations. It proposed substantial cutbacks in the benefits extended to the undocumented, but stopped short of recommending exclusion of the undocumented from public schools. While the undocumented are already barred from receiving most forms of public assistance, the commission recommended withholding all the remaining forms of assistance except emergency medical care. A White House spokesperson said of the commission's report that it was 'very useful' and revealed that they were 'heading in the same direction' (Bomemeier and McDonnell 1994: A1, A25).

This latest round of restrictionism – focused primarily on the Mexican immigrant population – is much like that of earlier periods in that it is occurring at a time of economic insecurity and social trans-formation, and targets immigrants as the cause of the malaise. But this restrictionism has taken a new twist. While anti-immigrant fears in the past have largely focused on immigration as a cause of unemployment and wage depression – sometimes mixed with a substantial dose of racism and religious bigotry – today's restrictionists instead highlight immigrants' use of social services and its tax implications. Perhaps not surprisingly, at a time when California and the nation are mired in the worst fiscal crisis since the depression of the 1930s and the welfare state is undergoing unprecedented retrenchment, Mexican immigrants are now targeted as a cause of this fiscal and social crisis.

The near future is likely to witness continuing anti-immigrant rhetoric, and new restrictionist measures will undoubtedly be passed. While some of these measures will carry important symbolic messages, and some will no doubt have devastating impacts on the lives of immigrants in the USA, it is unlikely that they will have any substantial effect on the volume of undocumented immigration along the US–Mexico border. Triggered by powerful economic forces and nurtured by close to a century of formal and informal policies, Mexican immigration to the USA and the entrenched relationship between Mexican workers and US employers will not yield easily to legislative fiat.

Conclusion

A contradiction has permeated US immigration policy since the nineteenth century. While immigrants from Europe supplied an important source of cheap labour for the emerging industrial economy in the USA, at the same time the steady increases in the impover-ished immigrant population precipitated recurring restrictionist backlashes. Confined to the margins of the economy where they barely eked out a living, recent immigrants were singled out for their periodic dependence on charity and their disproportionate presence in gaols, hospitals and other caretaker institutions (US Congress 1911).

Mexican immigration in the early years seemed to offer an escape from this contradiction, providing a source of cheap labour whose stay in the USA could be terminated when the demand had waned. The chair of the House Committee on Immigration and Natural-ization, in debates surrounding the quota laws of the 1920s, questioned the director of the US Employment Service on the experience with Mexican labour during the First World War. He was particularly interested in the flexibility of the Mexican labour source, asking, 'You reserve the right to deport them when you get too many?' Another representative interjected, 'How did the thing work out? Were you able to deport them when the need had passed?' (US Congress 1919: 24–5).

The Bracero Program represented an attempt to institutionalize this temporary nature of Mexican labour migration. By the time of its termination in 1964, however, the labour programme had even more firmly entrenched the relationship between Mexican workers and US employers. Steady increases in undocumented Mexican immigration since the 1960s are indicative of this entrenched relationship. With this steady increase, and the entrance of Mexican workers into a wide range of non-agricultural sectors (such as the garment industry, restaurants and hotels, construction cleanup and landscaping), it has become apparent that this 'back-door' labour supply is less easily regulated than once thought. And the myriad contradictions associated with immigration – in particular the economic role of immigrants as cheap labour versus the political backlash their related poverty provokes – have resurfaced with a vengeance.

The Immigration Reform and Control Act of 1986 was a product of such contradictions in the political economy of immigration, as are current efforts at reform. The impact of these measures – which in California anyway are implicitly aimed at Mexicans – is likely to be primarily symbolic and political, while Mexican immigrants continue to provide the US economy with low-wage labour. This pronounced gap between the stated aims of immigration policies and their effects is not merely the result of the sheer difficulty of controlling immigration, nor incompe-tence on the part of Congress or the INS. More fun-damentally, it is related to the fact that the location of immigrants in the political economy is fraught with contradictions. As Swiss playwright Max Frisch once said of the guestworker system in Europe, 'We called for workers, and there came human beings' (quoted in Markovits and Kazarinov 1978: 373).

Note

1. In *Plyler v. Doe* (1982), the US Supreme Court declared that the Texas policy of allowing school districts to bar undocumented children from public schools a violation of the equal protection clause of the fourteenth amendment.

References

Arax, M. (1994) 'Raisin Farmers Hit by Shortage of Workers', *Los Angeles Times*, 27 September

Bailey, E. and D. Morain (1993) 'Anti-Immigration Bills Flood Legislature', *Los Angeles Times*, 3 May

Baker, S. G. (1990) *The Cautious Welcome: The Legalization Programs of the Immigration Reform and Control Act*, Santa Monica: The Rand Corporation

Bean, F. D., G. Vemez and C. B. Keely (1989) *Opening and Closing the Doors: Evaluating Immigration Reform and Control*, Lanham, MD: University Press of America

Bornemeier, J. (1994) 'US Study Fuels Debate on Illegal Immigrants' Impact', *Los Angeles Times*, 15 September

Bornemeier, J. and P. J. McDonnell (1994) 'US Panel Issues Sweeping Immigration Reform Plan', *Los Angeles Times*, 1 October

Brossy, J. (1990) 'Aliens Entering Without Papers Show Sharp Rise', *San Diego Tribune*, 12 March, B2–B3

Calavita, K. (1984) *US Immigration Law and the Control of Labour: 1820–1924*, London: Academic Press

(1989) 'The Contradictions of Immigration Lawmaking: The Immigration Reform and Control Act of 1986', *Law and Policy*, 11 (1), 17–47

(1990) 'Employer Sanctions Violations: Toward a Dialectical Model of White-Collar Crime', *Law and Society Review*, 24 (4), 1041–69

(1992) *Inside the State: The Bracero Program, Immigration and the INS*, New York: Routledge

Carnegie, A. (1886) *Triumphant Democracy: Or Fifty Years' March of the Republic*, New York: Charles Scribner & Sons

Clark, R. L. and J. S. Passel (1993) 'How Much Do Immigrants Pay in Taxes?', *Program for Research on Immigration Policy Paper PRIP–UI–26*, Washington DC: The Urban Institute Press

Congressional Record (1954) 83rd Congress, 2nd Session

Congressional Research Service (1980) *History of the Immigration and Naturalization Service. A Report prepared for the use of The Select Commission on Immigration and Refugee Policy*, Washington DC: US Government Printing Office

Cornelius, W. A. (1982) 'America in the Era of Limits: Nativist Reactions to the "New" Immigration', *Research Report Series, 3*, La Jolla: Center for US-Mexican Studies, University of California, San Diego

Crane, K. et al. (1990) *The Effect of Employer Sanctions on the Flow of Undocumented Immigrants to the United States*, Lanham, MD: University Press of America

Decker, C. (1994) 'Voters Back Service Cuts for Illegal Immigrants', *Los Angeles Times*, 29 May

Edmonston, B. and J. S. Passel (1992) 'Immigration and Immigrant Generations in Population Projections', *Population Studies Center, Policy Discussion Series, UI–PSC–10*, Washington DC: The Urban Institute

Eisenstadt, T. A. and C. L. Thorup (1994) 'Caring Capacity versus Carrying Capacity: Community Responses to Mexican Immigration in San Diego's North County', *Monograph Series, 39*, San Diego: Center for US-Mexican Studies, University of California, San Diego

Espenshade, T. J. and C. A. Calhoun (1993) 'An Analysis of Public Opinion toward Undocumented Immigration', *Population Research and Policy Review*, 12, 189–224

Fix, M. (1991) *The Paper Curtain: Employer Sanctions' Implementation, Impact and Reform*, Washington DC: The Urban Institute Press

Fix, M. and P. T. Hill (1990) *Enforcing Employer Sanctions: Challenges and Strategies*, Lanham, MD: University Press of America

Fix, M. and J. S. Passel (1994) 'Who's on the Dole? It's Not Illegal Immigrants', *Los Angeles Times*, 3 August

Galarza, E. (1964) *Merchants of Labor: The Mexican Bracero Story*, Santa Barbara: McNally & Loftin

(1977) *Farm Workers and Agri-business in California, 1947–1960*, Notre Dame: University of Notre Dame Press

Gallup, G. (1980) 'Most US Citizens Favor a Hard Line Toward Illegal Aliens', *San Diego Union*, 30 November, A22

Gibbs, N. (1994) 'Keep Out, You Tired, You Poor . . .', *Time*, 3 October

Greene, S. L. (1972) 'Public Agency Distortion of Congressional Will: Federal Policy Toward Non-Resident Alien Labor', *George Washington Law Review*, 40 (3), March, 440–63

Hadley, E. (1956) 'A Critical Analysis of the Wetback Problem', *Law and Contemporary Problems*, 21, 334–57

Hamilton, A. (1791) *Report on Manufacturing: American State Papers*, Finance I

Harwood, E. (1983) 'Can Immigration Law Be Enforced?', *The Public Interest*, 72 (Summer), 107–23

Higham, J. (1955) *Strangers in the Land: Patterns of American Nativism, 1860–1925*, New Brunswick, NJ: Rutgers University Press

Kirstein, P. N. (1977) 'Anglo Over Bracero: A History of the Mexican Workers in the United States from Roosevelt to Nixon', Ph.D. dissertation, Saint Louis University

Klein, D. (1993) 'Majority in State are Fed up with Illegal Immigration', *Los Angeles Times*, 19 September

Lopez, G. P. (1981) 'Undocumented Mexican Migration: In Search of a Just Immigration Law and Policy', *UCLA Law Review*, 28 (April), 615–714

Markovits, A. S. and S. Kazarinov (1978) 'Class Conflict, Capitalism and Social Democracy: The Case of Migrant Workers in the Federal Republic of Germany', *Comparative Politics*, 10 (2), 373–91

McWilliams, C. (1968) *North From Mexico*, New York: Greenwood Press

Montwieler, N. H. (1987) *The Immigration Reform Law of 1986*, Washington DC: Bureau of National Affairs

Nalik, J. and P. Feldman (1994) 'Santa Ana Schools Condemn Immigration Measure', *Los Angeles Times*, 24 September

New York Journal of Commerce (1892), 13 December, 2

President's Commission on Migratory Labor (1951) *Migratory Labor in American Agriculture. Report of the President's Commission on Migratory Labor*, Washington DC: US Government Printing Office

Rea, L. M. and R. A. Parker (1992) *A Fiscal Impact Analysis of Undocumented Immigrants Residing in San Diego County: Costs and Revenues of Significant State and Local Government Program*, Report by the Office of the California Auditor General, San Diego: Rea & Parker Incorporated

Reisler, M. (1976) *By the Sweat of Their Brow: Mexican Immigrant Labor in the United States, 1900–40*, Westport, CN: Greenwood Press

Samora, J. (1971) *Los Mojados: The Wetback Story*, Notre Dame: University of Indiana Press

Stewart, W. F. et al. (1992) *Impact of Undocumented Persons and Other Immigrants on Costs, Revenues and Services in Los Angeles County*, Report prepared for Los Angeles County Board of Supervisors, 6 November

US Commission on Agricultural Workers (1992) *The Final Report of the Commission on Agricultural Workers*, Washington DC: US Government Printing Office

US Congress (1911) Senate Immigration Commission, *Immigration Commission Report*, Senate Document No. 747

 (1919) House Committee on Immigration and Naturalization, *Prohibition of Immigration and the Problem of Immigration*, Hearing before the Committee on Immigration and Naturalization

 (1981) House Committee on the Judiciary, *Illegal Aliens*, Hearings before the Subcommittee on Immigration, Refugees, and International Law of the House Committee on the Judiciary

US Department of Labor (1991) Bureau of International Labor Affairs, *Employer Sanctions and US Labor Markets: Second Report*, Washington DC: US Government Printing Office

US General Accounting Office (1987) *Immigration Reform: Status of Implementing Employer Sanctions After One Year*, GAO/GGD–88–14. Washington DC: US Government Printing Office

US Immigration and Naturalization Service (1959) *Annual Report of the Immigration and Naturalization Service*, Washington DC: US Government Printing Office

 (1978) *Annual Report of the Immigration and Naturalization Service*, Washington DC: US Government Printing Office

 (1988) 'Employer Activity Report through October 31, 1988', unpublished internal report

ANGLOPHONE CARIBBEAN MIGRATION TO THE USA AND CANADA

CERI PEACH

Migration from the Anglo-Caribbean to North America, on one hand, and to Britain on the other has been counter-cyclical. During the nineteenth and first half of the twentieth centuries migration was aimed at North America but was small and slow. During the 1950s and early 1960s, there was a large upswing in migration to Britain and a decrease in the North American stream. From the 1960s onwards, there has been a strong stream flowing to North America, while the British stream has diminished and gone into reverse.

Immigration from the Anglo-Caribbean to the USA grew from a few hundred annually in the mid-nineteenth century to about 1000 by the end of the century (Ueda 1980: 1021). Migration was of two kinds: the temporary field workers who operated mainly in the southern states and the more permanent urban settlers. Many of the settlers were members of the brown middle classes who successfully sought advancement in the USA.

The imposition by the US government of national origin controls in the early 1920s had the paradoxical effect of assisting migrants from the British Caribbean, who were treated as part of the relatively unfilled British quota (Ueda 1980: 1022). From 1900 to 1930 between 80,000 and 90,000 Afro-Caribbeans entered the USA. Migration was by sea and the areas of greatest settlement were the north-eastern coastal cities, particularly New York, although pockets of settlement were found down the eastern seaboard to Florida. New York City in 1930 contained 65 per cent of immigrant blacks in the USA and the majority of these are thought to have come from the Caribbean (Ueda 1980: 1022). Between 1948 and 1952 about 20,000 Jamaicans, largely contract labourers, emigrated to the USA.

The favourable quota position of British Caribbean migrants was removed by the restrictive McCarran-Walter Immigration Act of 1952. Instead of using the unfilled British quota, British Caribbean territories were assigned their own small annual quota of 800. It was not until the liberal Hart-Celler Immigration Act of 1965 that migration increased. The period between the 1952 and 1965 acts coincided with the major migration of Afro-Caribbeans to Britain. Although Glass (1960: 7) and Ueda (1980: 1025) argue that the movement to Britain was partly a displacement of a frustrated North American movement, the ebbs and flows of the migration were closely tied to British economic cycles (Peach 1968, 1991). Bryce-Laporte (1992: 51) argues that US penetration of the Caribbean economies stimulated the need to migrate in the first place.

Nevertheless, the USA and Canada were the preferred destination of Anglo-Caribbean migrants (Thomas-Hope 1992: 85). Independence from Britain, liberalization of US and Canadian immigration laws and British restrictions in 1962, produced a new spurt in migration from the Anglo-Caribbean. The annual total of British West Indian arrivals in the USA grew from 5000 in 1962 to over 25,000 in 1970, levelling off at about 20,000 a year in the mid-1970s (Ueda 1980: 1025). In the 1980s the pace increased considerably. The annual average number of immigrants admitted to the USA from the Anglo-Caribbean from 1980 to 1988 inclusive was 74,000 (Jasso and Rosenzweig 1990: 44–5). By 1990, the number of persons living in the USA but born in the Anglo-Caribbean was 65 per cent higher than in 1980 and 666 per cent higher than in 1970.

The USA

In 1970 there were 78,000 first-generation and 52,000 second-generation Afro-Caribbeans living in the USA (Ueda 1980: 1020). In 1980, the Anglo-Caribbean born population was 315,000 and in 1990 it had reached 520,000. The Statistical Abstract of the USA (1992) gives those of Jamaican and West Indian ancestry in 1990 as 594,000. This suggests a lower second-generation figure than one would expect from Ueda's figures for 1970 or from a comparison with the second-generation Afro-Caribbean population in Britain, where the second generation is as numerous as the first. Assuming the same were true of the USA, the total number of former British West Indians living in the USA would be just over one million. However, it is clear that the West Indian population living in the USA has expanded rapidly since the 1970s and is now bigger than (possibly double) that living in Great Britain.

The bulk of the US Caribbean population comes from Jamaica – 63 per cent in 1980, 58 per cent in 1990. These percentages are close to those of Britain, where 65 per cent of the Caribbean-born population had come from Jamaica in 1961, 56 per cent in 1981 and 54 per cent in 1991 (Peach 1991: 13). The gradual reduction in the Jamaican percentage over time suggests that Jamaica is the pioneering island and that the smaller territories somewhat lagged behind, increasing their representation over time.

The shift in the movement to the USA and Canada instead of the UK was accompanied by greater selectivity. In 1977, 21 per cent of Jamaican migrants to the USA were in white-collar work (Thomas-Hope 1992: 61). Davison's (1962: 22) figures for Jamaican migrants to Britain in the 1950s suggest that white-collar workers were about 11 per cent of the working population, excluding dependants.

Lieberson and Waters's (1988) analysis of ethnicity in the US 1980 census regrettably combines Caribbean ethnicity with other groups. However, they show the Afro-Caribbean group of men born in the USA as having educational levels close to the national mean and above those of the US-born black population (12.6 years versus 12.0 for African Americans) with a similar pattern for Caribbean women and African-American women (Lieberson and Waters 1988: 107–8). US-born Caribbean men and women have higher representation in executive, administrative and managerial positions than African-American men and women (10 per cent versus 6 for men and 9 versus 5 for women). The same figures are true for American-Caribbean men in professional occupations when compared with black American men, but both Caribbean American women and black American women have the same higher representation in the professions: 13 per cent (Lieberson and Waters 1988: 156–7).

There was gender as well as occupational selectivity. A significantly higher proportion of women than men migrated to Canada, for example. In 1981 the ratio of Caribbean men per 100 women was 83 (Richmond 1989: 15). Lieberson and Waters (1988: 153) indicate that, once education and occupation were controlled for, Caribbean-American women received a fraction above what would be expected;

Caribbean American men received rather less than expected. Richmond, reporting on research by Ramcharan in the 1970s in Toronto, indicates that Caribbean women seem to have done better than men in getting jobs commensurate with their educational levels and in avoiding unemployment. Light-skinned women did best of all (Richmond 1989: 5).

Anglo-Caribbeans living in the USA present interesting contrasts with those in Great Britain. In the USA, although they constitute less than 4 per cent of the African-American population, Afro-Caribbeans have assumed economic, political and administrative leadership roles, not only in the African-American community, but in the wider society. British West Indians in the USA have been disproportionately concentrated in professional, white-collar and skilled occupations. They have achieved notable levels of leadership in politics, literature, home ownership and education, and have been active entrepreneurs (Ueda 1980: 1020). West Indian elite power in the African-American community goes back to the charismatic leadership of Marcus Garvey in the 1920s. General Colin Powell, the first black American to become chief of the armed forces, is a second-generation Jamaican American. Derek Walcott, the Nobel laureate for literature, lives in the USA; the novelist Paule Marshall is a second-generation Caribbean American. This is not to say that there have not been successful Caribbean writers in Britain, but in the British armed services there are very few Afro-Caribbean officers, let alone chiefs of staff. Afro-Caribbeans have provided an elite within the African-American population, whereas in British society, despite notable exceptions such as Bernie Grant MP, Diane Abbott MP and Bill Morris, general secretary of the Transport and General Workers, the largest British trade union, Afro-Caribbeans have been less prominent in leadership roles. Foner (1992: 108) cites work which suggests that West Indians in the 1930s formed one-third of the black professional class in New York City. In 1970, 8.6 per cent of American blacks and 15.4 per cent of West Indians in the New York metropolitan area were classed as professional, technical and kindred workers. The median family income for the former was $6881; for West Indians $8830 (Foner 1992: 109).

Foner (1992) states that there are two schools of thought to explain the superior position of British West Indians relative to African Americans in New York City. One argument is that the cultural advantages of being raised in a predominantly black Caribbean situation gave them more self confidence than African Americans born into a dominantly white society. The second school argues that, being marginal immigrants, they have been prepared to take the poorest jobs and to work their way up, and have manifested a typical immigrant drive to scrimp, save and succeed. Foner's comparison with the Caribbean position in London leads her to a third explanation. The greater degree of occupational selection of the Caribbean migration to the USA gave the immigrants to the USA a cultural advantage compared with both African Americans in the USA and with Caribbean migrants to Britain. These advantages persisted into the second generation. Second-generation West Indians had a higher socio-economic position than both African Americans and first-generation West Indians in New York in 1970 (Foner 1992: 116–17).

Canada

Very few Caribbean immigrants entered Canada before 1966; indeed the rules controlling immigration were relaxed in 1962, just as the British regulations were being imposed. Canadian immigration policy changed at this stage from one based on ethnic origin to one based on qualifications (Smith 1993). Immigration from the Caribbean reached a peak in the 1970s. The 1971 census showed 67,980 from the Caribbean in Canada, together with 38,080 from Guyana (Richmond 1989: 5).

The importance of Canada as a destination for persons from Jamaica, Barbados and St Vincent surpassed the UK by the late 1960s and Canada has remained the second most important destination since that time. Immigrants arriving in Canada from Jamaica ranged from 3000 to 11,000 per annum through the 1970s and from 3000 to 5500 through the 1980s; about 200 per annum came from St Vincent (Thomas-Hope 1992: 60).

The census of Canada asks a question about ethnicity, but its results are rather misleading in relation to the Caribbean population. The 1986 census put the number of Caribbean ethnicity at only 48,475. 'Caribbean ethnicity' includes settlers from the Hispanic and Francophone Caribbean, but the large majority of this number is thought to be from the Anglo-Caribbean. The ethnicity figure is misleading in two ways: first, it refers only to landed immigrants born in the Caribbean; second, about half the Jamaican-born (and other Anglo-Caribbean islands are much the same) gave 'British' as their ethnicity. It is clear, however, that the bulk of the immigrants were Afro-Caribbean. Less than 2 per cent gave Asian ethnic origins in the 1981 census, although this was the case for 18 per cent of

those originating in Trinidad and Tobago and 26 per cent of those from Guyana (Richmond 1989: 10).

Richmond (1989: 1), in a very detailed analysis of Caribbean immigrants in Canada, gives the total in 1981 as 211,295. The bulk of this group was from the Anglophone Caribbean: 85 per cent spoke English as their mother tongue (1989: 11). The Francophone percentage was 11, largely from Haiti. The Francophone Caribbeans were highly concentrated in French-speaking Quebec; there they constituted 56 per cent of the Caribbeans but in Ontario only 1 per cent. Over two-thirds of the Caribbean population was found in Ontario (67.6 per cent) while just over a fifth (21.8 per cent) were found in Quebec. Only 5 per cent of men and 4 per cent of Caribbean women in Canada were found outside a census metropolitan area (Richmond 1989: 11–12).

References

Bryce-Laporte, R. S. (1992) 'New York City and the New Caribbean Immigration', in C. R. Sutton and E. M. Chaney (eds) *Caribbean Life in New York City*, New York: Center for Migration Studies, 51–69

Davison, R. B. (1962) *West Indian Migrants*, London: Oxford University Press

Foner, N. (1992) 'West Indians in New York City and London', in C. R Sutton and E. M. Chaney (eds) *Caribbean Life in New York City*, New York: Center for Migration Studies, 108–120

Glass, R. assisted by H. Pollins (1960) *Newcomers: The West Indians in London*, London: Centre for Urban Studies and George Allen & Unwin

Jasso, G. and M. R. Rosenzweig (1990) *The New Chosen People: Immigrants in the United States*, New York, Russell Sage Foundation

Lieberson, S. and M. C. Waters (1988*) From Many Strands: Ethnic and Racial Groups in Contemporary America*, Committee for Research on the 1980 Census, New York: Russell Sage Foundation

Peach, C. (1968) *West Indian Migration to Britain: A Social Geography*, London: Oxford University Press

— (1991) *The Caribbean in Europe: Contrasting Patterns of Migration and Settlement in Britain, France and the Netherlands*, Research Paper 15, Coventry: Centre for Research in Ethnic Relations, University of Warwick

Richmond, A. H. (1989) *Caribbean Immigrants: A Demo-economic Analysis*, Ottawa: Ministry of Supply and Services

Smith, S. J. (1993) 'Immigration and Nation Building in Canada', in P. Jackson and J. Penrose (eds) *Social Constructions of Race, Place and Nation*, London: UCL Press

Thomas-Hope, E. M. (1992) *Explanation in Caribbean Migration*, Basingstoke: Macmillan for Warwick University Caribbean Studies

Ueda, R. (1980) 'West Indians', in S. Thernstrom and A. Orlov (eds) *Harvard Encyclopedia of American Ethnic Groups*, London: The Belknap Press of the Harvard University Press, 1020–7

MIGRATORY TRENDS IN PUERTO RICO: 1950 TO THE PRESENT

JUAN E. HERNÁNDEZ-CRUZ

The 1980 census shows the presence in the USA of 2,013,945 Puerto Ricans, of whom approximately 55 per cent (1,107,120) are first generation (born in Puerto Rico) and 45 per cent (906,825) second-generation, i.e. born in the USA of Puerto Rican parents. It is believed, however, that having been imprecisely calculated these data do not reliably reflect the Puerto Rican presence in the USA.[1] Besides, the continual circulation between the two poles of the Puerto Rico–US circuit makes a more precise count impossible. For this reason the figure of 2.5 million is generally accepted as more exact.

The bulk of this emigration came about in the early 1950s, with a net negative balance of 34,155 persons between exits and entries to Puerto Rico in some years, and an average of 46,086 for the decade. This movement coincides with the development of economic promotion on the island, in its first phase of establishing factories for light industries, with a view to providing jobs to absorb the high unemployment, product of the uprooting of the masses from their traditional mode of production, agriculture. It also coincides with the transition of the mode of production in the USA from monopolistic capital to competitive capital, when industry and government were still absorbing an abundance of unskilled workers (Rodríguez 1989).

Movement in the 1960s evidenced a considerable decrease in comparison with the previous decade, showing an average of 15,178 emigrants a year, with 1966 and 1967 having a higher exodus of 30,089 and 34,174 respectively. It is significant that in 1969 the net balance is positive (7047), with more arrivals than departures; that is, more returned to Puerto Rico than emigrated. This same pattern is repeated in 1972 with the impressive figure of 21,297, and later in 1976 with 5230.

During the 1960s the changeover to competitive capital was consolidated, and in New York it came about side by side with the increase in automation and the eventual shift of the location of factories to suburban areas and to other states. This was accompanied by changes in the workforce, requiring higher levels of skill (Rodríguez 1989). In Puerto Rico, meanwhile, new jobs were being generated as a result of the process of industrialization being in full swing, with the hotel and construction industries absorbing the greatest number of circulating workers.

The immediate effect of these changes on industry's pool of Boricua labourers in the USA was greater unemployment, sustained underemployment, or the circulation mentioned above: a return to Puerto Rico or migration to another state. From 1960 on, therefore, a movement away from the city can be noted which has continued to increase up to the present time. Fitzpatrick (1987) has pointed out that, of the Puerto Rican population living in the USA by 1950, 80 per cent were in the city of New York, decreasing to 70 per cent in 1970 and 43 per cent in 1980.

For 1971–79 we have a yearly average of 24,479 emigrants leaving Puerto Rico, but as has been noted previously, in 1971 and 1976 more returned than emigrated, 21,297 and 5230 respectively. It should be clarified that return emigration or circulation to Puerto Rico has always been constant, but it is from the 1970s that a prolonged and sustained pattern is seen. In the same way it should be understood that Puerto Rico has been the recipient of Cuban and Dominican immigrants in a constant stream since 1960.[2] As a result, the traditional theoretical perspective of viewing Puerto Rican migration within a Malthusian framework and the assimilation theory has been weakened. A new theoretical interpretation has thus received greater acceptance, that emigration arises mainly from the excess of workers in a specific production mode, as a result of economic and political transformations on the island.[3]

The decade of the 1980s does not differ much from the previous ones, revealing a yearly average of 38,184 emigrants, which constitutes the largest cohort of emigrants since the great exodus of the 1950s. Nevertheless, this emigration is different from previous ones in that it is towards other states or cities and involves a cohort of emigrants of a higher educational level. Among the states that most attract the new Puerto Rican emigrant of the 1980s are

Florida, Texas and Massachusetts, showing an increase from the previous decade (1970) of 236 per cent, 262 per cent and 227 per cent respectively. These data issue from a study by the Office of Puerto Rico in New York, in which it is inferred that it is the better educated and many professionals who move from New York and Puerto Rico to these states. The most outstanding cases are Florida and Texas, where a total of 28,166 and 6333 resided in 1970, which increased in 1980 to 94,775 and 22,938, respectively. Interviews conducted in Orlando, in central Florida (with thirty Puerto Rican immigrants), reported the reasons given by Puerto Ricans for moving there as 'looking for a warmer climate, and peace and quiet' (those who move from New Jersey, New York and Connecticut), and 'looking for a better quality of life, and peace and quiet' (those who arrive from Puerto Rico). However, during the course of the interviews the real reason came out, namely to find a job or a better job (*El Nuevo Día*, 20 May 1990). Although we do not have conclusive information as to how many of these new immigrants to central Florida are retired, the interviews mentioned and data coming out of real estate advertisements seem to indicate that this is an important segment.[4]

The median educational level of these new emigrants was 12.1 years of school completed, in comparison with 11.1 in the population in Puerto Rico in the same age bracket. Among the emigrants, 53.3 per cent had at least finished high school and 22 per cent had some college-level studies, in contrast with 45.6 and 21.4 per cent in those categories in the resident population. Furthermore, the percentage of the emigrants who had not completed any grade was 1.5 compared with 6.6 per cent among the total population in Puerto Rico (Planning Board 1986).

The purpose of emigration, nevertheless, is still the same as that of the exoduses of previous decades, to work. Of the emigrants aged sixteen years old or more, 64 per cent left the island with the idea of working (27.7) or looking for work (36.6), while 10.1 per cent were housewives, presumably with the intention of joining their husbands who had already emigrated.

When these data are seen in the context of the Puerto Rican community in the USA in parison with other Hispanics, the situation does not appear any better. Participation in the workforce in 1989 was 52.2 per cent for Puerto Ricans, compared with 62.3 per cent for other Hispanics, and 67.8 and 62.3 per cent respectively for Mexicans and Cubans. In the same way, the unemployment total was 9.1 per cent among Puerto Ricans, compared with 6.0 per cent for other Hispanics, and 8.5 and 6.1 per cent respectively for Mexicans and Cubans, while Puerto Rican men showed 12.1 per cent unemployment, compared with 6.7 per cent for other Hispanics, and 8.3 and 6.4 per cent respectively for Mexicans and Cubans. In terms of median income (for 1988) Puerto Ricans in the USA received $15,447, compared with $20,943 for other Hispanics, and $19,839 and $21,793 respectively for Mexicans and Cubans (Current Population Reports, 1990).

This situation is analysed by Rodríguez (1989) in the context of New York, and she considers that the economy of the city where there is still an important Puerto Rican section of the population has gradually evolved towards a post-industrial one based on services. This has had the effect of continuing to reduce the manufacturing sector and increasing structural unemployment among blue-collar workers. By that same year Puerto Ricans were still disproportionately employed in the manufacturing sector, 28 per cent, compared with 16 per cent and 13 per cent respectively of the white and black populations. These data contrast with the measures which have been taken in the case of the black population, from which the government has absorbed great numbers into public service. This is not the case with the Puerto Rican population, in spite of the fact that Puerto Ricans are also US citizens (Falcón 1985).

Rodríguez (1989) also maintains that a new pattern emerged in the 1980s which by its nature did not improve the position of the Puerto Ricans, namely the globalization of the economies of the world and of New York City. This is so because capital and workers moved within a world system and not so much within national boundaries, contributing to a convergence towards a world economy of cheaper transportation, advances in telecommunications and lowering of trade barriers. Development of the global economy, she says, causes more unskilled people worldwide to be drawn into this global system, resulting in a situation in which international migrants compete with local workers in almost all the developed countries, while at the same time jobs are moved to developing countries in search of cheap labour.

In New York, measuring the progress of the Dominican segment in the manufacturing sector, Ramona Hernández (1989) supported the above with data from a study by the Hispanic Research Center, maintaining that 72.4 per cent of Dominican women, compared with 6.3 per cent of the men, were connected with the peripheral industrial sector (secondary or lower), presumably in competition with Puerto Ricans. This leads Hernández to conclude that female Dominican labour turns out to be ideal for this type of industrial production, not only because of being little-valued socially, but also because Dominican women are politically powerless as immigrants (often without documents) in the country.

To summarize, conditions at both poles of the Puerto Rico–US circuit are what triggers the permanent and ceaseless traffic, almost impossible to evaluate because of the fragmentation and unreliability of available information. But even so, with the difficulties mentioned above, three significant tendencies are evident. First, a permanent movement of new emigrants to the USA; second, significant growth in the return movement to Puerto Rico, without regard to the generational status of the circulants;[5] and third, continual circulation from the traditional communities to new places, and return to the place of origin.

The information analysed above demonstrates that Puerto Rican workers in the USA form a movable force, or labour pool, with minimum participation in the ranks of the unskilled, domestic or clerical workers, generally in the declining and poorly paid sectors.

Immigrations: Cubans and Dominicans

Parallel to the emigrations of Puerto Ricans to the USA, immigratory currents have also emanated from different points: Cuba, Santo Domingo, Haiti, and other Caribbean and Central American countries. However, the most significant of these immigrations were those of the Cubans and Dominicans. Both movements coincided with political events in the respective countries: the Cuban revolution in 1959 and the assassination of dictator Rafael Leonidas Trujillo in 1961.

Vázquez Calzada (1979) estimates that by 1970, 29,000 Cubans were living in Puerto Rico, compared with 1070 in 1960. It has been estimated that they entered Puerto Rico at a rate of 3200 per year in the 1960s. It is felt that after 1973, when the great wave of 'Marielitos' came in, the Cuban population in Puerto Rico stabilized at approximately 30,000 persons (Duany 1991).

José del Castillo (1989) characterizes Dominican immigration to Puerto Rico as composed of two 'migratory movements or flows' in 'marked contrast': one occurred in the 1960s, essentially legal and middle class, and one happening in recent years, predominantly illegal and lower class or proletarian.

Census data confirm that the migratory group of the 1960s was composed of a strong middle-class representation, with high educational levels and high incomes. As time passed, this group became consolidated in Puerto Rican society, although an evaluative study has not yet been done of their process of adaptation.

The second migratory current of Dominicans is that which has been occurring in the last few years during which a great economic and social crisis is in evidence in the Dominican Republic. This current is characterized by the illegality of the immigrants, composed of the lower class or urban proletariat and some peasants. Among the different modalities of this illegal immigration, the one that crosses the Mona Channel separating the Dominican Republic from Puerto Rico is most prominent. It is accomplished by means of yawls, ketches and other light motorized vessels. This human exodus has caused the separation of Dominican families and the death of many of those unfortunates who risk their lives in this dangerous crossing.

The result of these migratory flows has been the legal admission of around 44,000 Dominicans at an annual rate of 2300, although in 1966 it rose to around 4000 immigrants. Newspaper reports speculate that if the undocumented ones were included in these estimates the amount would go up to around 60,000 Dominicans living on the island.[6]

The illegality of many of these immigrants and the constant circulation between the USA, the Dominican Republic and Puerto Rico make an exact estimate impossible, which leads one to believe that the figure of 60,000 Dominicans residing in the island may turn out to be a conservative estimate. The same is true of the naturalized Cubans who have free access to entrance into Puerto Rico and whose movements are not recorded in the figures of the US Immigration and Naturalization Service, which has jurisdiction in the island.

The pattern of settlement of these immigrants has been mainly in metropolitan areas, with preference toward San Juan – 87 per cent of the Cubans and 85 per cent of the Dominicans (Duany 1991; Hernández 1989), although the two groups occupy different social strata in the metropolitan area; the Cubans are concentrated in middle- and upper-class areas, and the Dominicans in peripheral and decadent urban areas.

Their incorporation into the working world also evidences the same contrast; while 70 per cent of Cuban workers were self-employed or worked for fellow countrymen (Cobas 1986), most of the

Dominicans were employed in blue-collar jobs or services in the secondary labour market (Duany 1991).

Conclusions

We may conclude that the above information illustrates Puerto Rico's importance as an intermediate component in Caribbean immigration, which supposedly, in the case of the Dominicans, has the USA as its ultimate goal. In this sense it demonstrates, with the new migratory movements of more highly-educated Puerto Ricans emigrating to non-traditional places, the semiperipheral position of Puerto Rico in relation to the capitalist system.

One little-studied but promising aspect in the analysis of these groups is the circulatory nature of their emigrations. In the case of Puerto Ricans who return to south-western Puerto Rico we have made studies, utilizing the life-history technique, which have allowed us to prove the circulatory nature of a labour pool which moves between states and towards the island in search of contact with capital.

The differences in the Puerto Ricans' migratory and circulating patterns is something which requires greater study, especially as it relates to the new segment of their emigration, characterized by a higher educational level than that of Puerto Rico's total population and a desire to better their lives qualitatively.

Recent studies (Muschkin 1991) also suggest that return emigration may mean acceleration of ageing in the Puerto Rican population, and may have an impact on the future growth of that population.

Finally, Puerto Rico's importance has been highlighted as an intermediate point in intra-Caribbean migration which supposedly has the USA as its goal (Hernández 1989). In addition, aside from the difficulties presented by Puerto Rico's not having the power to establish immigration and naturalization laws, these contemporary migratory patterns merit a rigorous analysis in order to arrive at some conclusions with regard to the amount of acculturation and social mobility achieved among Caribbean immigrants who use Puerto Rico as a springboard towards the USA.

Notes

1. The accuracy of US census estimates of the total Puerto Rican population between decades has been widely criticized. In response, the Bureau has explored an alternative method of estimating the population using components of change which contribute to the cumulative effects of births, deaths and emigration in the 1980 census. By means of this technique the Puerto Rican population in the USA has been estimated at 2,549,000 in 1988.
2. From 1966 to 1986, for example, 44,000 Dominicans entered the island legally, while an unknown number of illegals also arrived (Duany 1991).
3. The works following this perspective include: Centro de Estudios Puertorriqueños (1975); Centro de Estudios Puertorriqueños (1979); López and Petras (1974); Maldonado Denis (1976). Studies concerned with the experience of Puerto Ricans in the USA and interpretative documents stressing the assimilation perspective are: Chenault (1938); Fitzpatrick (1987); Glazer and Moynihan (1963); Mills, Senior and Goldsen (1950); Senior (1947); Senior and Watkins (1966).
4. The Planning Board, however, felt that in 1986 less than 1 per cent left Puerto Rico to retire.
5. Second-generation Puerto Ricans are also circulating to Puerto Rico in high proportions. This comes to light in reports in the daily press and in economic reports to the governor from 1972 to the present.
6. *El Nuevo Día*, 28 December 1985.

References

Centro de Estudios Puertorriqueños (1975) *Taller de Migración: Conferencia de Historiografía, Abril 1974* (Bilingual Publication), New York: Research Foundation of the City University of New York
―― (1979) *Labor Migration under Capitalism: The Puerto Rican Experience*, New York: Monthly Review Press
Chenault, L. R. (1938) *The Puerto Rican Migrant in New York City*, New York: Columbia University Press (reprinted 1970, New York: Russell & Russell)
Cobas, J. A. (1986) 'Puerto Rican Reactions to Cuban Immigrants: Insights from Trading Minority Interpretations', *Ethnic and Racial Studies*, 9 (4)
Current Population Reports, No. 444, May 1990
Del Castillo, J. (1989) 'La Inmigración Dominicana a Puerto Rico', in *Los Inmigrantes Indocumentados Dominicanos en Puerto Rico: Realidad y Mitos*, San Germán, Puerto Rico: Caribbean Institute and Study Center for Latin America
Duany, J. (1991) 'Caribbean Migration to Puerto Rico: A Comparison of Cubans and Dominicans', unpublished paper presented to the Conference on Current Trends in Caribbean Migration held in San Germán on 19 March, sponsored by CISCLA (Caribbean Institute and Study Center for Latin America)
El Nuevo Día, 28 December 1985; 20 May 1990
Falcón, A. (1985) 'Black and Latino Politics in New York City: Race and Ethnicity in a Changing Urban Context', *Report*, Institute of Puerto Rican Politics, New York
Fitzpatrick, J. P. (1987) *Puerto Rican Americans: The Meaning of Migration to the Mainland*, Englewood Cliffs, NJ: Prentice Hall
Glazer, N. and D. Moynihan (1963) *Beyond the Melting Pot*, Cambridge, MA: MIT and Harvard University Press
Hernández, R. (1989) 'Mercado de trabajo de los dominicanos en Nueva York', in *Los inmigrantes indocumentados dominicanos en Puerto Rico: Realidad y mitos*, San Germán, Puerto Rico: CISCLA
López, A. and J. Petras (1974) *Puerto Rico and the Puerto Ricans: Studies in History and Society*, New York: Schenckman Publishing Company
Maldonado Denis, M. (1976) *Puerto Rico y Estados Unidos:*

Emigración y colonialismo, México: Siglo XXI Editores S.A.

Mills, C. W., C. Senior and R. Goldsen (1950) *The Puerto Rican Journey*, New York: Harper

Muschkin, Clara (1991) 'Los Efectos de las Migraciones en el Envejecimiento y el Crecimiento de la Población en Puerto Rico, 1960–1980', Conference on Current Trends in Caribbean Migration held 19 March in San Germán, sponsored by CISCLA

Planning Board (1986) *Migration in Puerto Rico: Characteristics of the Migrant Population, 1983-84*, San Juan, Puerto Rico: Junta de Planificación de Puerto Rico

Rodríguez, Clara (1989) *Puerto Ricans: Born in the USA*, Boston, MA: Unwin Hyman

Senior, C. (1947) *Puerto Rican Emigration*, Río Piedras: Social Science Research Center, University of Puerto Rico

Senior, C. and Donald O. Watkins (1966) 'Toward a Balance Sheet of Puerto Rican Migration', *United States–Puerto Rican Commission on the Status of Puerto Rico*, August

Vázquez, Calzada (1979) 'Demographic Aspects of Migration', in Centro de Estudios Puertorriqueños, *Labor Migration under Capitalism: The Puerto Rican Experience*, New York: Monthly Review Press

A COMPARATIVE VIEW OF ASIAN
IMMIGRATION TO THE USA

JOHN M. LIU

After the hiatus of centuries from the first crossing of the Bering Strait, Asian migration to North America resumed as a trickle in the seventeenth and eighteenth centuries and is now a major tributary of legal immigration to the USA. Filipinos, who sailed on Spanish galleons between Manila and Mexico, were the first to arrive. Before the American Revolutionary War, some of these Filipinos migrated to and settled in the Mississippi river delta. The descendants of those settlers are now into their eighth generation.

Despite this early presence, only an estimated 1.3 million Asians entered between 1820, when the federal government began keeping admission statistics, and 1965, when Congress removed all racially based admission criteria from US immigration laws. This estimate includes the more than 100,000 Asians who went to Hawaii before it was fully incorporated as a US territory in 1900. Asians settling in both places represent less than 4 per cent of the total immigration to the USA during this period.

By contrast, in less than thirty years since 1965, immigration from Asia has risen phenomenally with the admission of more than four million Asians. Up until 1993, this constituted almost 25 per cent of all legal immigration. The distinctiveness of this postwar Asian immigration cannot be captured only by its rapid growth. It must also be seen in its contrast to immigration patterns prior to the Second World War.

Pre-1945 Asian immigration patterns to the USA

Asian immigrants entering before the Second World War came mostly between the 1850s and early 1930s. They emigrated principally from China (440,000), Japan (497,000), India (7000), Korea (8000) and the Philippines (180,000). The onset of their immigration arose with the ending of slavery and the economic development of the Pacific coast and Hawaii.[1]

Early in the nineteenth century, anti-slavery forces passed legislation in Great Britain, the USA, the Netherlands and Denmark that would eliminate the slave trade by the late 1850s. Termination of the slave trade, however, did not lessen the need for workers in plantations, where slavery had been the chief source of labour, or by budding railroad and mining interests in European colonies and the US frontier. In search of a cheap labour pool, western agricultural and industrial capitalists turned to Asia.

Labourers recruited by these interests remained mostly in Asia, but the 1848 discovery of gold in California and an emergent sugar industry in Hawaii led to a significant immigration of Chinese. These immigrants laid the basis for the subsequent arrival of Japanese, Koreans, Indians and Filipinos. Although coming from different societies, the Asians who immigrated before the Second World War shared many characteristics. These similarities can be attributed to the manner in which western capitalism penetrated Asia and to the racist practices that Asians encountered after their arrival in the USA.

Western nations established their direct presence in Asia by securing footholds in selected regions, usually port cities and capitals. The areas closest to the western sinecures experienced disruption of the native economy and social order as well as weakening of traditional political authority, all of which magnified existing domestic problems. Such intrusions directly or indirectly contributed to factors normally associated with forces pushing people to emigrate. For instance, British opium imports into southern China through Canton (Guangzhou) compounded the difficulties the Chinese were already experiencing with overpopulation, political ineptitude and natural disaster by physically incapacitating people from engaging or investing in economically productive pursuits.

Uneven capitalist expansion made Asian immigration highly regional. Over 90 per cent of the Chinese who migrated to the USA departed from eight rural districts surrounding Guangzhou. One of these eight districts, Taishan, sent between 40 and 50 per cent of the Chinese who went to the US mainland, while people from another of these eight districts, Zhongshan, comprised the majority of Chinese who settled in Hawaii. Similarly, eight prefectures in south-western Japan and Okinawa provided the bulk of Japanese immigration to the US mainland and

Hawaii. But within each prefecture, emigration was confined to a few districts. More than half the Koreans going to Hawaii were from the Seoul–Inchon–Suwon area, perhaps then the most westernized district of Korea. The vast majority of Asian Indians immigrating to the US were Sikhs who originated from five districts in the Punjab province, while Filipinos came mostly from four north-western provinces on the island of Luzon (Chan 1991: 3–23).

Given the dominance of British and US shipping interests in the Pacific in the mid-1850s, it was natural for most Asians who emigrated to settle in British and US controlled territory. Asians departing for the USA took advantage of the well-established shipping routes linking China, the Pacific coast and Hawaii that had developed with US entry into the China trade at the end of the eighteenth century. After arriving, Asians often persuaded others from their family or village to follow. A combination of factors, including the local custom to keep women at home, the risks of travelling abroad and the reluctance of employers to support families, i.e. pay for social reproduction, ensured predominantly male immigration to the USA. With the possible exception of Koreans, most Asian males were peasants (Cheng and Bonacich 1984).

Common origins and highly skewed gender ratios led Asians to establish distinct communities in the USA characterized by high ethnic solidarity and dominated by family-like organizations that provided emotional security, political representation, employment opportunities and recreational outlets. The formation of separate Asian communities was not wholly due to immigrant volition, but also to racial discrimination. Initially welcomed as important additions to US society, Asians soon encountered a barrage of local laws curtailing their civil and political rights, including anti-miscegenation laws prohibiting white women from marrying Asian men and alien land laws denying Asian immigrants the right to own land. When local agitation reached Congress it enacted legislation further restricting the fundamental rights of Asians.

One of the first laws was the Page Act (1875) requiring immigration officials to investigate whether each arriving Chinese woman was a prostitute. These humiliating investigations dissuaded many wives from joining their husbands. In 1882 Congress enacted the Chinese Exclusion Act prohibiting further immigration of Chinese labourers and making Chinese alien residents ineligible for naturalization. Subsequent judicial rulings extended both provisions to labourers' wives. Local anti-miscegenation laws, the Page Act and the 1882 law severely curtailed the

ability of all Asians, except Japanese, to form or reunite families. Future immigration legislation for other Asian groups incorporated the main features of the Chinese Exclusion Act of 1882 (Hing 1993).

Anti-Asian sentiment was still alive when the USA acquired the Philippines in 1900. Congress accordingly created a special status for Filipinos by classifying them as nationals who could travel freely to any US possession but could not become naturalized. To forestall subjecting its immigrants to similar legal restrictions, Japan voluntarily stopped labour emigration under the Gentlemen's Agreement of 1907/8 in exchange for the continued admission of women. Japan believed the USA would be more accepting of Japanese immigrants if they established families. Some 20,000 women entered under this exemption. This figure includes Korean women, who were treated as Japanese nationals after Japan's annexation of Korea in 1910. Enough women came to generate a second generation of Japanese, and to a more limited extent of Koreans. Ironically, successful Japanese family formation would play a major part in the near absence of immigration from Japan after 1945.

The Cable Act of 1922 further constrained family formation by rescinding the citizenship of female citizens who married 'aliens ineligible for naturalization'. That same year, the Supreme Court ruled in the *Ozawa* case that Japanese belonged in this category. Congress virtually ended all immigration from Asia by incorporating this clause into the 1924 Immigration Act. This law reaffirmed the denial of naturalization to Asian Indians, whose entry had been barred by the Immigration Act of 1917, after the Supreme Court ruled in the *Thind* decision that Indians were Asians. Congress did not exclude Filipinos until 1935.

The history of these discriminatory laws reveals the sequential nature of Asian immigration as each group of entering Asians compensated for the exclusion of a previous group. After the passage of the 1882 Chinese Exclusion Act and a similar law in Hawaii, the shortage of labourers led employers to seek out the Japanese. Koreans and Asian Indians came after the reduction in Japanese immigration imposed by the 1907/8 Gentleman's Agreement, while Filipinos became the sole source of Asian labour after the 1924 Immigration Act. Since one group replaced another, Asians mainly settled in the same areas and pursued the same occupations as their predecessors. Consequently, most Asian communities were clustered along the Pacific coast and Hawaii. This geographic concentration further contributed to the inability of white Americans to differentiate among the Asian groups and to apply similar discriminatory laws and stereotypes towards them. However, the proximity of Asian communities was a basis for an emergent pan-Asian identity among Asian immigrants, despite the enmities that existed among their countries of origin in Asia (Friday 1994). Changes occurring during and after the Second World War would dramatically alter the character of this pre-war immigration.

The Second World War and post-war transition

There was an escalation of pre-war anti-Asian sentiment with the 1942 incarceration of over 110,000 Japanese Americans, two-thirds US-born and with a median age of 17 (Daniels 1989). Revision of immigration laws regarding Asians seemed unlikely in this political environment. Yet, domestic and international forces were already chipping away at discriminatory laws and policies. Domestically, wartime exigencies required the hiring of non-whites in industries previously closed to them. More racial minority participation in industry and the military unleashed demands for greater equity, a process encouraged by the federal government. Asians originating from nations allied to the USA benefited from this reform movement. In 1943, Congress repealed the Chinese Exclusion Act. China received a token immigration quota and the right for Chinese alien residents to become naturalized citizens. Repeal of the Chinese Exclusion Act also served the international interests of the USA by countering Japan's propaganda condemning the mass incarceration of people of Japanese – but not those of German or Italian – ancestry.

Domestic and international pressures continued to erode discriminatory immigration walls after the war. Post-war economic growth allowed minorities to make political and economic gains that did not threaten whites. Employment and income advances translated into political improvements as racial minorities struggled for their civil rights. Organized labour, which had been an active proponent of Asian exclusion, now advocated more open immigration policies. The coalescence of these forces created a domestic socio-political context that complemented US actions at the international level. Decolonization, rising nationalism in Third World nations and communist expansion pushed the USA to broaden its legitimacy as leader of the 'free world' beyond possessing the most powerful military force. If the USA was to bolster its international image and leadership, then the abrogation of blatantly discriminatory immigration laws was necessary. With pressures for change emanating from both home and abroad,

Congress enacted legislation that paved the way for renewed large-scale immigration from Asia after 1965.

Congress's first steps were timid. In 1945 it passed the War Brides Act, which permitted the entry of women married to US servicemen. Some 6000 Chinese women entered under this law. The following year Congress gave India and the Philippines token immigration quotas and granted resident aliens naturalization rights. Additional revisions occurred with the Displaced Persons Act of 1948. This act opened the doors to refugees and would become one of the major means by which Asians gained entry during the cold war. Chinese fleeing the founding of the People's Republic of China were the main Asian beneficiaries of this and subsequent refugee legislation. Between 1949 and 1965 the USA accepted almost 25,000 Chinese refugees.

The 1948 act also recognized the growing importance of obtaining foreign professional and skilled labour by granting the first 30 per cent of visas to scientists and people with specialized technical skills. As the post-war economy increased in technical complexity it induced a shift in occupational needs towards university trained personnel possessing high technological skills. Creation of the occupational preference category opened a second channel for future Asian immigration (Ong et al. 1994: 46–54).

To consolidate some of these revisions, the USA overhauled its immigration legislation with the 1952 Immigration and Nationality Act (McCarran-Walter Act), which became the USA's basic immigration statute. The act created two general preference classifications – one for family members, the other for needed occupational workers – which have remained at the heart of US immigration policy. Under this law, highly skilled immigrants whose services were urgently needed, together with their families, received first preference and 50 per cent of the visas. The remaining visas went to parents and unmarried children of US citizens, the spouses and unmarried children of legal alien residents, and the siblings and married children of US citizens and their families. Spouses of US citizens were exempt from any quotas. This exemption proved to be crucial because of a continuing bias against Asian immigration.

Supporters of the 1952 law claimed it removed racially discriminatory criteria from admission policies by giving all nations an immigration quota. Nonetheless, racism was still integral to the law through its establishment of an Asia-Pacific triangle which included countries from India to Japan and to the Pacific islands north of Australia and New Zealand. Nations falling within this zone received an annual quota of generally 100 persons, with a ceiling of 2000 for the entire region. Moreover, any person at least one-half Asian by ancestry was charged against the zone's quota, even if that individual had been born outside the triangle. The determination of chargeability by blood rather than country of birth applied only to Asians. However, the exemption given to spouses of US citizens created a loophole for more than 70,000 Asian women to immigrate as the wives of US servicemen. Among these wives were 48,000 Japanese, 8000 Koreans and 16,000 Filipinos (Reimers 1992: 23). Most of these women were from working-class backgrounds. They provided a third source of future immigration with their entry serving as a basis for family related immigration and for the admission of semi- and unskilled immigrants after 1965.

Although highly skilled labour received the highest preference in the 1952 law, Asian professional and skilled workers did not use this provision because post-war reconstruction in Asia fully absorbed their labour. But the continued ability of Asian economies to absorb this labour diminished as the effects of US post-war aid to Asia materialized. Following the war, the USA funnelled most of its aid into reorganizing the educational infrastructure in selected Asian nations. It did so in the belief that teaching about democracy and modernization would immunize Asia both to the fascist tendencies of the past and the communist overtures of the future, as well as hasten Asia's entry into the ranks of the developed world. Many Asian nations readily accepted the US westernization message, particularly concerning the development of high-level talent.

US influence occurred in two areas: the revamping of educational institutions and curricula, and the training of educators in the home country or in the USA. With the Philippines and Korea the USA played a direct role in reconstructing the educational systems of both countries. In the cases of Taiwan, Hong Kong, Vietnam and India, the USA made its influence felt through the extensive use of exchange and joint educational programmes sponsored by private and public agencies such as the Asia Foundation and the Agency for International Development. By the mid-1950s, US colleges and universities enrolled more than 10,000 South and East Asian foreign students. As these foreign students returned to jobs and professorships in their home countries, they introduced western, primarily US, material and technology into their economic and educational systems.

By the beginning of the 1960s, the emphasis given to producing highly educated persons created a surfeit of professionals and other technical labour for many Asian economies. Japan was the major exception as its economy had experienced dynamic growth since the early 1950s when it served as the principal staging area for UN troops during the Korean War. The robustness of the Japanese economy provided full employment for its labour force, thus removing a critical structural incentive for Japanese to emigrate. Rapid restoration of the Japanese economy also enabled the USA to divert its foreign aid to Taiwan, South Korea, the Philippines and Vietnam.

US aid to these nations allowed their governments to stifle domestic dissent while pursuing an economic development policy that required substantial sacrifice from the populace. Land reform and state development transformed traditional class relations. Although class restructuring differed in each nation, a common outcome was the creation of a sizeable middle class that increasingly congregated in major metropoli. Rapid industrial growth in many East Asian nations during the 1960s intensified the urbanization process, creating overpopulation and environmental menaces. Amid economic growth, the foundation for later political discontent was also taking shape.

As part of this growing middle class, professionals played a major role in fashioning the emergent opposition. The inability to find employment adequate to their training caused increasing frustration. Their dissatisfaction created political conflict within the ruling class. Those professionals who did not become oppositional leaders sought a more liberal setting in which to mount their practices. US educational aid and support of totalitarian regimes created forces that encouraged professionals and skilled labour to emigrate, but did not offer a destination. Passage of the 1965 Immigration Act provided professionals and other middle-class members with an opportunity to immigrate to the USA (Ong et al. 1994: 74–9).

From 1965 to the present

The 1965 act abolished the Asia-Pacific triangle and allocated 20,000 visas annually to every nation. Hong Kong, as a British colony, received 200 visas per year. The act gave greater emphasis to family reunification by distributing 74 per cent of visas (80 per cent after 1980) to unmarried and married adult children as well as to siblings of US citizens, and to spouses and unmarried children of legal alien residents. Parents, spouses and minor-aged children of US citizens were exempted from any numerical limitations. Occupational immigrants received only 20 per cent of the visas. Although these changes to the 1952 act seem minor, they have given rise to an Asian immigration that is strikingly different from the pre-war migration in size, community formation and socio-economic composition.

From 1965 to 1992, over four million Asians immigrated, more than tripling pre-war levels. They came from a larger number of nations than did their predecessors, but only five groups accounted for about 80 per cent of Asian immigration: the Philippines (1,065,000), the three Chinese-speaking regions of mainland China, Taiwan and Hong Kong (914,000), Vietnam (718,000), Korea (682,000) and India (548,000). In the 1980s, Laos (266,000), Cambodia (216,000) and Thailand (69,000) also became significant contributors of immigrants. Rapid growth was possible because the admission of refugees and brides after the war and the presence of long-time Asian residents created enough sponsors to take full advantage of the family reunification preferences. Moreover, different Asian groups are immigrating simultaneously rather than sequentially as was the case before 1945. Post-1965 immigrants in turn extended the immigration chain by becoming sponsors themselves. Because the 1965 act favoured US citizens, it encouraged many Asians to naturalize. By the late 1970s, when the first of the post-1965 immigrants began naturalizing, more Asians started entering as exempted immigrants than under the family preferences, a pattern that has continued.

Another major source of new immigration has been the refugees from south-east Asia following the fall of Saigon in 1975 and the ensuing civil war in the region. Over a five-year period, the USA accepted more than 200,000 Vietnamese refugees with 168,000 in 1980 alone. To accommodate this influx, Congress passed the Refugee Act of 1980 which increased the annual limit for refugees to 50,000. This enabled another 400,000 refugees from Laos and Cambodia to gain admission during the 1980s.

Post-1965 immigration tripled the Asian-American population by 1990 and contributed to a tripling of the minority population in the USA between 1960 and 1990. Representing less than 1 per cent of the total population in 1970, Asian Americans constituted 3 per cent or about seven million people twenty years later (O'Hare 1992: 9). The growth is stunning considering the US population grew from 203 to 249 million people during this time.

Recent immigration has affected the population rank order among Asian-American groups. In 1970,

the rank order of Asian groups reflected the magnitude of their immigration before 1945. Japanese constituted 40 per cent of the population, followed by Chinese (29 per cent) and Filipinos (22 per cent). By 1990, the Chinese (24 per cent) and Filipinos (20 per cent) surpassed the Japanese (12 per cent), who were at parity with Asian Indians and Koreans (12 per cent each). The Vietnamese (9 per cent) closely followed. The decline in ranking for Japanese Americans is due to an annual immigration of only about 2000. Since many of the pre-war Japanese immigrants already had families, there were few additional members to sponsor in the post-war period. Japan's economic prosperity further dampened emigration. With low immigration and fertility rates below replacement, Japanese Americans are likely to fall into last place among the major groups in the next US census.

Post-1965 immigrants reinforced the residential patterns established before the war. Asian Americans continued to cluster in the western USA with 56 per cent living in the region compared with 21 per cent of the total US population in 1990. Nearly half the entire Asian-American population lived in just two western states, California (39 per cent) and Hawaii (9 per cent). Other major concentrations were found in New York (10 per cent), Texas, Illinois and New Jersey (each with 4 per cent). Residential concentration was even greater in the select number of metropolitan areas in which Asians resided. About 53 per cent lived in four consolidated metropolitan statistical areas: Los Angeles–Anaheim–Riverside, CA (20 per cent), San Francisco–Oakland–San José, CA (13 per cent), New York–Northern New Jersey–Long Island, NY–NJ–CT (12 per cent) and Honolulu, HI (8 per cent) (O'Hare and Felt 1991: 5–6).

Although different Asian-American groups tend to live in specific states and regions, the singular importance of California is evident in that the largest share of every major Asian group lives in the state. Between 39 and 52 per cent of all Chinese, Filipinos, Japanese, Vietnamese, Cambodians, Hmong and Laotians are Californians. Only 20 per cent of all Asian Indians and 30 per cent of Koreans live in the state. Even so, this still represents the largest single concentration for both groups. In San Francisco, nearly one-third of the population consists of Asian Americans, while the Asian population of Monterey Park in Los Angeles County is 58 per cent of the city's 60,000 people, earning that city the distinction of containing the first suburban Chinatown in the USA.

Despite this continued clustering, community formation differs greatly from the pre-war period. Many of the older settlements repopulated by the post-1965 immigrants no longer have the same ethnic cohesiveness. The shared regional origins and single status of earlier immigrants have been replaced by Asians coming from diverse areas within their home countries and by those who come as families. Many of the old immigrant organizations that provided *ersatz* family functions are no longer needed. Nor can these associations maintain their dominance with the growing intracultural diversity among Asian groups. This is evident in the proliferation of dialects. For instance, the majority of pre-war Filipinos spoke Ilocano while more recent immigrants speak Tagalog. Among the Chinese, Mandarin speakers and Cantonese speakers who no longer speak the Taishan dialect are the prevalent linguistic groups.

Intracultural diversity parallels major changes in the socio-economic composition of post-1965 communities. Pre-war communities possessed a relatively homogeneous class character because of the similarity in immigrant backgrounds and the limited range of available occupations. Community development since 1965 has grown in two directions. Older settlements such as urban Chinatowns have been rejuvenated by the influx of immigrants possessing limited skills and few English-speaking abilities. In contrast, the growth of new communities, such as Monterey Park, are due largely to the immigration of professionals and highly skilled people.

From 1965 to 1976, professional and technical kindred workers (PTKs) averaged 22 per cent of the total Asian immigration and 60 per cent of all PTK immigration. Filipinos comprised 32 per cent of the Asian PTKs, followed by Asian Indians (23 per cent), the three Chinese-speaking regions (15 per cent) and South Koreans (10 per cent). With the exception of India, this rank order reflects the extensiveness of political and economic ties between the USA and the Asian source nations after 1945 and the presence of a significant Asian population in the USA before the war. Since neither factor is present in the case of India, its position as the second largest contributor of Asian PTKs seems anomalous. A major reason for Asian Indian professionals to settle in the USA was the greater difficulty they encountered in immigrating to their principal destination before 1965 – the UK, which had imposed restrictions on PTK admissions from Commonwealth countries.

Asian PTKs who entered during this period tended to be doctors and nurses. This was true for two out of every three Asian Indian and Filipino PTKs, and three out every four Koreans. High-tech personnel, mainly

engineers and natural scientists, were prevalent only among Chinese PTKs. For Asian Indian, Filipino and Korean health professionals there was an additional variation. Doctors outnumbered nurses roughly 2:1 among Asian Indians while, for Filipinos and Koreans, the same ratio occurred but in favour of nurses. Part of the reason for the high percentage of Asian Indian physicians is that the USA, at the request of India, suspended administration of a screening test to Asian Indian medical graduates applying for internships and residencies in US hospitals. Health professionals came because of the huge demand for health services created by the implementation of Medicare and Medi-Cal in the mid-1960s, the growing popularity of private health plans and general economic prosperity. With US medical schools graduating only about 7000 physicians and 15,000 nurses annually, domestic sources could not meet the rising demand.

The percentage of Asian PTKs to total Asian immigration dropped to 7.5 per cent after 1976. Much of the drop was due simply to the tremendous increase in total Asian immigration from an annual average of 98,550 to more than 208,300. But there was a real drop in PTKs because of two legislative changes in 1976. The Eilberg Act stiffened admission criteria for health practitioners by requiring them to have job offers before immigrating. Previously, most doctors and nurses entered without having an employment offer because the US Labor Department had declared a shortage of health professionals. Congress also passed the Health Professions Educational Assistance Act, which declared that physicians and surgeons were no longer in short supply. These two acts immediately curtailed the immigration of doctors but did not stop the flow of nurses, particularly among Filipinos, and increased the percentage of high-tech personnel among PTKs from India and Korea (Liu 1992).

The steep decrease in PTK immigration underscored the US economy's continuing demand for highly educated personnel and contributed to a major revision in the 1990 Immigration Act. Major changes affecting PTK immigration included separating family unification and employment based preferences so that the availability of occupational visas was no longer dependent upon the number of people admitted as family immigrants. The act also doubled the number of visas for occupational immigrants and their families from 54,000 to 120,000, with 80,000 for highly educated workers. Members of professions with advanced degrees or aliens of exceptional ability received 40,000 visas, as did skilled and unskilled workers (with a cap of 10,000 for the latter). While skilled labour was the primary economic target of the act, the law eased the entry for capitalists by providing 10,000 visas to employment-creating investors. One group particularly sought after were Hong Kong residents seeking haven before the 1997 absorption of the colony by mainland China. For three years starting in 1991, Hong Kong received 10,000 visas, which increased to 20,000 after 1994.

Professional and high-tech immigration has bifurcated the socio-economic distribution of Asian America. The average median family income of Asian Americans ($39,000 in 1989) is higher than that of white families ($31,400), but their poverty rate is nearly twice that of non-Hispanic whites. This distribution corresponds to the two different chains of migration – one reflecting the entry of professionals and highly skilled immigrants, the other semi- or unskilled workers under the family reunification preferences. This dichotomy coincides with developments in the US economy where highly skilled workers command ever higher salaries, while employers hold back the wages of low-skilled workers, who captured only 3.6 per cent of the national income in 1993, the lowest since the mid-1960s.

Growing numbers, continuing residential concentration and socio-economic success for a significant portion of the Asian-American population has contributed to its greater visibility to the dominant white population. Not all this attention has been favourable as stagnant economic growth in the late 1970s and 1980s has renewed antagonism toward Asians and Hispanic Americans, the two largest immigrating groups since the mid-1960s. It is unlikely that the hostility toward Asians will ever again reach pre-war levels. Nonetheless, anti-immigrant sentiment still remains. This is particularly true in California, the major immigrant receiving state. Successful passage in 1994 of a state initiative that denies all illegal immigrants education and non-emergency social services has stimulated similar movements in other large immigrant states. It has also led the Republican majority in Congress to raise questions about whether all non-citizens, both legal and illegal alien residents, should be denied access to non-emergency social services.

Conversely, the same factors promoting visibility provide a basis to counterpose anti-immigrant sentiment. Numbers, residential concentration and socio-economic success provide Asian Americans with the political means to defend themselves (Espiritu 1992). Just as happened in the pre-war period, the rise in discriminatory actions by the dominant population has contributed to a growth in pan-Asian awareness. This overriding identity is based on the shared historical and contemporary experiences of immigrating to the USA and of the similar treatment received after arrival. How Asian immigration unfolds in the twenty-first century will depend in part on the political resourcefulness of pan-Asian coalitions and in part upon the importance of Asia to the USA's position within the global economy.

Note

1. Immigration data from US Immigration and Naturalization Service published statistics and microdata data sets for 1972–89. The figures represent gross immigration because the USA does not keep official emigration data. For pre-1945 Asian immigration, the absence of emigration data is especially significant. The estimated return rate, for instance, among the Chinese and Japanese range between 40 and 60 per cent. There is also double counting in the pre-1945 data because officials made no distinction between new and re-entering immigrants. Also, there are no estimates of how many Asians, particularly Chinese, entered the USA illegally from Canada or Mexico after the imposition of restrictive immigration laws. See for instance, Chan (1991) and Takaki (1989) whose works are standard references on Asian Americans.

References

Chan, Sucheng (1991) *Asian Americans: An Interpretative History*, Boston: Twayne Publishers

Cheng, L. and E. Bonacich (eds) (1984) *Labor Immigration under Capitalism: Asian American Labor before World War II*, Berkeley: University of California Press

Daniels, R. (1989) *Concentration Camps: North America Japanese in the United States and Canada during World War II*, Malabar, FL: Robert E. Krieger Publishing Company

Espiritu, Yen Le (1992) *Asian American Panethnicity: Bridging Institutions and Identities*, Philadelphia: Temple University Press

Friday, Chris (1994) *Organizing Asian American Labor: The Pacific Coast Canned-Salmon Industry, 1870–1942*, Philadelphia: Temple University Press

Hing, Bill Ong (1993) *Making and Remaking Asian America through Immigration Policy, 1850–1990*, Stanford: Stanford University Press

Liu, John M. (1992) 'The Contours of Asian Professional, Technical and Kindred Work Immigration, 1965–1988', *Sociological Perspectives*, 35 (4), 673–704

O'Hare, William P. (1992) 'America's Minorities: The Demographics of Diversity', *Population Bulletin*, 47 (4)

O'Hare, William P. and Judy C. Felt (1991) 'Asian Americans: America's Fastest Growing Minority Group', *Population Trends and Public Policy*, 19

Ong, P., E. Bonacich and L. Cheng (eds) (1994) *The New Asian Immigration in Los Angeles and Global Restructuring*, Philadelphia: Temple University Press

Reimers, D. M. (1992) *Still the Golden Door: The Third World Comes to America*, New York: Columbia University Press

Takaki, R. (1989) *Strangers from a Different Shore: A History of Asian Americans*, Boston: Little, Brown and Company

CONTEMPORARY MIGRATION FROM AFRICA TO THE USA

LAURA BIGMAN

During the 1970s and 1980s, African-born migrants became increasingly visible in the USA, particularly Nigerians and Ethiopians. While voluntary migration was not a new phenomenon, it took on nuances reflecting US–African relations, the international political economy and simply the fact that Africans from more places had friends or relatives who were or had been in the USA.

Numbers remained small both absolutely and in comparison with migrants from other parts of the world. However, US Immigration and Naturalization (INS) data show, for instance, the number of immigrant visas issued to Africans doubled every decade between 1940 and 1990, amounting to 36,179 in the fiscal year of 1991, about 2 per cent of the 1.8 million of all such visas in that year (INS 1992: 19, 32). The number of Africans who became US citizens trebled during the 1980s, reaching 10,230 for 1991 (INS 1992: 126). Moreover, in 1991, 196,000 Africans were admitted with non-immigrant status, 109,000 as tourists (INS 1992: 100), and nearly 5000 more entered as refugees or asylum seekers (INS 1992: 86). African migrants, including those admitted as refugees, tended to be from the more affluent, educated sectors of their own societies, in part because US law functioned as a net filtering in those most likely to assimilate to American society (Hawk 1988).

US immigration scholars virtually ignored the phenomenon because the numbers were small and because as 'others' in a Eurocentric society, Africans became part of the African-American community. Some African Americans of slave descent were uncomfortable with the notion that Africans would voluntarily choose to live in the USA and others perceived study of contemporary African migration as an attempt to divide the black community.

US–African relations and the historical context

In general, countries with larger populations sent more migrants – Nigeria, Egypt, Ethiopia, South Africa. In her seminal study, 'Africans and the 1965 US Immigration Law', however, Hawk (1988) analyses migration rates as a percentage of population, which reveals relations with the USA to be a major factor.

Relative to population size, Cape Verde and Liberia provided the largest contingents admitted on immigrant visas from the nineteenth century into the 1980s. Cape Verde had strong commercial links with the USA from the 1820s on. These were reinforced by islanders fleeing recurrent drought and famine who signed onto American whaling ships, later working in the cranberry bogs and textile mills of New England; in the 1980s, it was estimated that there were 300,000 Cape Verdeans living in the USA versus 390,000 in Cape Verde. Emigrant remittances enabled the independent republic to maintain a positive balance of payments despite an 8:1 import–export ratio. Liberia was founded by Americans who purchased land which by 1867 had been colonized by 20,000 African Americans; Americo–Liberians have run the government ever since, using the US dollar as official currency. US capital, led by Firestone Corporation, supervised financial interests after 1927.

In absolute terms, more African migrants into the 1990s were Egyptian, the number of those entering on immigrant visas burgeoning after US legislation in 1965. South Africans, a considerable proportion of whom were of European descent, made up a substantial contingent, not only of immigrants but of migrants granted temporary visas as skilled workers and as tourists. By the 1990s, Ethiopians and Nigerians entered the USA in larger numbers. Egypt, South Africa, Ethiopia and Nigeria were countries where the USA had strategic and business interests; English was an official language in all four. Moreover, as relatively urbanized and industrialized countries, their citizens were more likely to have skills that would enable them to meet INS preference categories and to survive in the USA.

After 1980, US legislation redefining 'refugees' enabled the US Black Caucus to secure slots for Ethiopians and Eritreans. But while Africa had the highest number of refugees of any continent (5.8 million in 1993), it had the lowest refugee ceiling

(7000 in the early 1990s), almost all of which went to Ethiopians and many of which went unfilled. Unlike Ethiopians who came to the USA as students in the 1950s and 1960s, the asylum seekers tended to be younger, less educated and arrived with the traumatic baggage of famine and civil war.

In 1986, the Immigration Control and Reform Act (ICRA) offered amnesty to aliens who had been in the USA since 1982 and had either entered illegally or failed to keep their visas in order. Within six years, nearly 45,000 Africans had applied, about 5000 of whom were Ghanaians and Nigerians who had entered the country illegally – a small testament to the numbers of Africans living in the USA, but not apparent from official data (INS 1992: 72).

Structural adjustment and the 'brain drain'

During the 1960s, more Africans from Anglophone West Africa as well as Ethiopia and southern Africa began coming to the USA to study. They were following in the footsteps of Kwame Nkrumah, first president of Ghana, and Nnamdi Azikiwe, first president of Nigeria, both of whom were US-educated. In turn, the students of the 1960s and 1970s paved the way for the migrants of the 1980s and 1990s, some of whom had previously acquired US degrees.

This was the period when most African countries gained political independence from European colonial powers, on the one hand, and when the USA saw itself competing with the Soviet Union for influence around the world, on the other. Africans from former British colonies who might automatically have opted for a British education found that it was sometimes easier or more desirable to enrol in a US college; and the USA, through various institutions, made this possible. Christian missionary organizations sponsored students from both Anglophone West Africa and Ethiopia. The African American Institute sponsored others, including some southern Africans for whom refugee status was not available prior to 1980.

Africans enrolled in colleges in small towns from southern Texas to northern Minnesota. In these environments, people knew nothing about African culture or history and considered the students objects of curiosity, even sending TV crews to capture 'African students eating'; almost every African who has lived in the USA has been asked whether Africans live in trees. Isolated by the ignorance of the community at large, students were warned by sponsors to stay away from the local African-American community. Other Africans matriculated at African-

American schools such as Howard University in Washington DC, taking on leadership of student organizations and contributing to the resurgence of pan-Africanism in the USA. Among the Ethiopians of this era were left-wing activists who organized Marxist study groups and African cultural presentations for the US left.

Although Egyptians were still the largest group, Nigerians arrived fleeing the Biafran civil war. Good times as well as bad times give rise to migration: Nigerian families who benefited from the oil boom of the early 1970s sent their children into the relatively open US university system. But the slump in oil prices followed by government austerity measures in 1986 caused Nigerian enrolment to fall off. Those already there, like Liberians and Sierra Leoneans whose countries became embroiled in civil war, could no longer rely on money either from their governments or their families. Not wanting to leave without their degrees and cautious about social conditions in Africa, former students took on full-time employment, aged, married and became part of American life.

According to the US Institute for International Education, during the 1985/6 academic year, there were 34,000 Africans studying in the USA; some 8000 new African students were admitted in 1991, the largest number then being from Kenya, followed by Egypt and Ethiopia (INS 1992: 100).

During the 1980s, social and economic conditions in Africa deteriorated. Compounding problems caused by the droughts of the 1970s and the wars of attrition dragged on through the 1980s. At the same time, thousands of civil servants had their jobs eliminated or real pay scaled back as African governments were obliged to implement International Monetary Fund (IMF) policies in order to reschedule overwhelming debt. Those who still had jobs often went months without pay. The economically strapped urban salariat posed a potential threat to which some regimes responded with political repression.

In response to this situation, Africans tried to migrate to the USA as well as other areas of the world where it was possible to find employment for hard currency, such as the Arab Gulf. Moreover, Africans already in the USA, most of whom had post-secondary education, decided to stay on and look for work. These included a number of university professors and medical doctors. Of 10,230 African-born citizens naturalized in 1991, 1384 were listed as having a 'professional speciality', but among Nigerians, for instance, the proportion of professionals and managers ran to nearly 30 per cent (INS 1992:

134–5). Hundreds classified as 'temporary workers' were employed by international organizations, such as the International Monetary Fund and the World Bank, or multinational corporations with headquarters in the USA. As foreign aid to Africa dropped off after 1989, the question raised in the 1970s of the 'reverse flow of technology' as a result of a 'brain drain' began to be raised in a new way by Africans (Apraku 1991). Some governments which had been calling on students and professionals to come home tried to encourage nationals to contribute through remittances or investment. Towards this end, in 1992 Nigeria officially recognized dual citizenship.

First-generation migrants and the myth of return

Like first-generation migrants the world over, Africans considered themselves temporary migrants who were planning to return home when they had completed their Ph.D.s, the rains fell, the government was ousted or the situation at home had stabilized. They saw permanent residence as tantamount to cultural betrayal; if nothing else, one's body had to be returned so that it could be buried with the ancestors. The ideology of return was particularly strong among political asylum seekers, such as the Eritrean refugees who donated a percentage of their salaries to the Eritrean Peoples Liberation Front (EPLF) which organized well-attended educational fund-raising events throughout the 1980s (Koehn 1991).

As both blacks and foreigners, despite educational achievements, Africans often found themselves in jobs that the native-born disdained. Lacking an American 'street sense', migrants working as taxi drivers and security guards were especially vulnerable to muggings. Women who had prior experience as nurses or midwives encountered stressful conditions exacerbated by the threat of contracting AIDS as low-paid medical para-professionals. Another risky occupation was that of drug trafficking for which some Nigerians were deported and others jailed. New Ethiopian migrants found a special niche as car park attendants and employees of 7–11 convenience stores, and in opening restaurants serving Ethiopian food, liquor stores and laundromats. Senegalese and Malians challenged Nigerian and Ghanaian importers

by street vending cloth, market jewellery and dolls at cut-rate prices. French-speaking migrants from North Africa as well as the Sahel worked as cooks, bakers and waiters or waitresses in restaurants, including chains with French names such as 'Au Bon Pain'. In an effort to exert more control over their lives, Africans who got residence permits and citizenship opened small businesses to serve the needs of their compatriots, such as ethnic clubs, restaurants and grocery stores, or to provide services, such as travel and estate agencies or accounting and law firms.

Like other migrants, Africans felt themselves to be 'part of two worlds' and tried to maintain that dual identity for themselves and their children by joining communal associations based on language or birthplace. Churches and mosques, which sometimes held language classes, were established; newspapers and magazines circulated, such as the Cape Verdean *Tchuba* or the Amhara *Negarit*. In 1992, forty-three Nigerian groups were represented at a meeting in Washington DC. In New York, Senegalese rented entire apartment buildings in which aspects of village life could be reproduced. In those urban areas where the largest numbers of migrants settled – New York, Washington DC, Atlanta, Dallas and Los Angeles – ethnic businesses, independence day celebrations and political demonstrations for democacy at home, in tandem with calls by Americans for 'multiculturalism' in US society, raised awareness of the African immigrant presence preserved in such immigrant accounts as Mark Mathabane's best-seller *Kaffir Boy in America*, Olaniyi Areke's movie *Disillusioned* about Nigerians in Washington, and decades of folk songs and poetry by Cape Verdeans.

References

Apraku, Kofi K. (1991) *African Emigrés in the United States: A Missing Link in Africa's Social and Economic Development*, London: Praeger

Hawk, Beverly Gale (1988) 'Africans and the 1965 US Immigration Law', Ph.D. dissertation, University of Wisconsin–Madison

Koehn, Peter H. (1991) *Refugees from Revolution, US Policy and Third World Migration*, Boulder CO: Westview

INS (1992) *1991 Statistical Yearbook of the Immigration and Naturalization Service*, Washington DC: US Department of Justice, Immigration and Naturalization Service

MIGRATION TO CANADA IN THE POST-WAR PERIOD

LAWRENCE LAM AND ANTHONY H. RICHMOND

Net migration to Canada in the post-war period accounted for a significant proportion of population growth, from 8.8 million in 1941 to 27 million in 1991, of which 16 per cent was born outside Canada. Although the UK remained the single most important source of immigrants through most of the post-war period, the proportion of immigrant arrivals from Britain fell steadily from 1970 onwards. In the period 1989–92, Hong Kong was the single largest source country, and the UK fell to eighth place. Other important countries of origin in 1992 were the Philippines, India, Sri Lanka and Poland. This contrasts notably with the period 1961–65, when no Asian country appeared in the top five countries of origin.

Canada admits immigrants in several different categories. These have varied over the years but the main classes are (i) the *independents*, selected for their occupational qualifications, together with their immediate dependents; (ii) close relatives who may be sponsored by Canadian residents under *family reunion* provisions, together with other assisted relatives who must meet some educational and occupational criteria; (iii) *refugees* and *designated classes* admitted for humanitarian reasons; and (iv) in recent years, a category of *business* immigrants (entrepreneurs and investors) has grown in importance.

The changing scale and composition of immigration in the last half-century reflects Canada's evolution, from a largely rural society whose wealth was derived from primary industries such as farming, fishing and mining, through a period of rapid urbanization and industrialization in the immediate post-war period, to the present post-industrial involvement in a continental trading system, a worldwide economy and a global communications system. The intended occupations of immigrants in recent decades reflect these developments, as professional, managerial, clerical and service occupations outnumbered those intending to enter agriculture or industry. For example, those in professional and managerial occupations increased from 5 per cent in 1950 to 25 per cent in 1990. However, not all immigrants are able to pursue their intended occupations immediately on arrival, due to language problems, non-recognition of qualifications, economic recession and structural changes (Richmond 1967, 1992).

Analysis of demographic trends is complicated by the special situation of the largely French-speaking province of Quebec. Until 1957, Quebec had very high fertility rates, which ensured that its rate of growth paralleled that of the rest of Canada with very little need for immigration. Subsequently, the Quebec birth rate fell dramatically and a rising tide of Quebec nationalism led to a net outward movement of Anglophone residents to other provinces. By 1968, Quebec had established its own provincial department of immigration and actively pursued a policy designed to encourage the immigration of French speakers and those from countries whose populations were believed to be 'Francophonizable', i.e. the Mediterranean region and Latin America (Hawkins 1988: 227–34). Although ultimately subject to federal approval, such immigrants constituted an increasing proportion of the total. However, once admitted they were not obliged to remain in Quebec and were free to move to other provinces.

Long-term trends in immigration are shown in Figure 8.1, indicating that 1956/7 was a high point in annual admissions. Canada also experienced emigration to the USA and other countries, and the remigration and return of those admitted for 'permanent' settlement. Remigration tends to be highest among those whose language and culture is closest to that of most Canadians, i.e. to the UK and the USA, although in recent years immigrants from Italy, the Caribbean and India have also shown high rates of return, up to 30 per cent of those arriving between 1981 and 1986 (Michalowski 1991; Richmond 1967: 229–52).

Reflecting the growing mobility of the world's population, increasing numbers of people have been admitted on a temporary basis, either as short- or long-term visitors, students, temporary workers or asylum applicants (Michalowski 1993). In the 1991 census, almost a quarter of a million people were

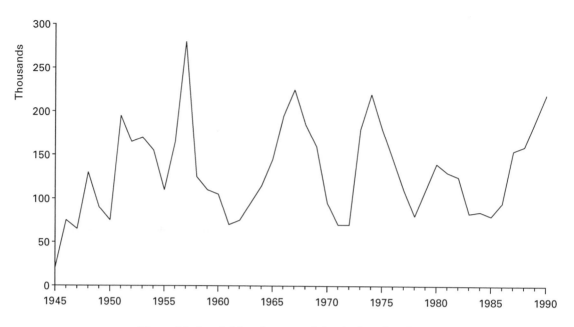

Figure 8.1: Landed immigrants arriving in Canada, 1945–90

enumerated as temporary residents. Temporary employment authorizations are used for agricultural workers during peak harvest seasons, domestic workers, sports, theatre and artistic employments, and to meet specific skill shortages. Since 1989, the free trade agreement with the USA has allowed cross-border movements of professional, managerial and business personnel, without restriction. A gradual movement from 50,000 long-term residents entering Canada in 1981 to in excess of 200,000 entering in 1990 is reported by Michalowski (1993).

The immediate post-war period, 1945–53

At the end of the Second World War, there were labour shortages in primary and secondary industries which were met by encouraging farmers from the Netherlands to emigrate, facilitating the immigration of Polish army veterans, selecting 'displaced persons' from European refugee camps and encouraging British immigrants to work in mines and manu-facturing industries (Petersen 1955; Richmond 1967; Sazewich 1991). In a statement to Parliament in 1947, Prime Minister Mackenzie-King made it clear that the government's policy, at that time, was to ensure the careful selection of permanent settlers who would be economically absorbed and that there was no intention to 'make any fundamental alteration in the character of the population, as a result of mass migration.' The

obverse of a strong preference for British and western European immigrants was discrimination against African, Asian and Caribbean migrants who, at that time, were subject to quotas and largely confined to those who already had close relatives in the country.

Until 1950, immigration was still controlled by legislation that dated back to 1931 and was adminis-tered by the Department of Mines and Resources. A Department of Citizenship and Immigration was created and a new consolidated Immigration Act came into force in 1953. This gave considerable power to the Minister of Immigration to draft regulations governing admission. A set of preferential categories was established which remained in force until 1962, when race or nationality ceased to be selection criteria, although the distribution of immigration offices abroad continued to favour those from Britain, Europe and the USA (Hawkins 1988). At the same time efforts were made to integrate settlement services and citizenship education with immigration selection and administration.

1954–71

The Soviet invasion of Hungary and the Suez crisis in 1956 caused a peak in the flow of Hungarian refugees and politically motivated British immigrants, although economic conditions at that time were not conducive to rapid absorption. Consequently, the numbers admitted in the following five years were significantly reduced. Italian immigrants, mainly sponsored by close relatives, moved into second place behind those from the UK, followed by Americans, some of whom saw Canada as a 'safe haven' for those unwilling to be drafted into the Vietnam war. The crisis in Czechoslovakia in 1968 also resulted in the admission of a number of refugees.

By 1966, there was a growing recognition of the need to relate immigration to labour force requirements. Following the publication of a 'white paper' on immigration policy in 1966, a new Department of Manpower and Immigration was created. The Citizenship Branch was moved to the Secretary of State's office where it tended to be subordinated to the concern with integrating the French-speaking population (in Quebec and other provinces) into a federal Canada, already threatened by growing separatist sentiments. Immigration was geared to economic needs through the adoption of a 'points system' of selection which gave considerable weight to education, occupational qualifications and a knowledge of English, French or both languages. The precise weight given to these factors has varied over the years. The current system also takes into account occupational shortages and demand. Family reunion continued to be given a high priority by churches and ethnic communities and, as a gesture to these bodies, assisted relatives received extra points when relatives were prepared to accept some financial responsibility, ensuring that the sponsored immigrant would not become a 'public charge'. As a result, the largest single group of immigrants admitted into Canada has continued to be in the family and other sponsored categories (Canada 1990a; Troper 1993).

One consequence of the increased emphasis on 'colour blind' selection by the points system, after 1967, was an increase in the admission of highly qualified professionals from Asia and the Caribbean. However, many of these well-educated immigrants found that there were barriers to the recognition of their qualifications by employers and professional licensing bodies (Cummings et al. 1989; Mata 1992; McDade 1988). Nevertheless, after five years or more, the majority of immigrants were achieving levels of income and occupational status comparable with, or above, those of average Canadians. The second generation, born and raised in Canada, was even more successful. This was partly because immigrants and their children were located in the economically prosperous and expanding metropolitan areas of the country. Older generations of Canadians (of British,

French and other origins) were disproportionately located in economically declining regions and industries.

A study of the impact of immigration up to 1961 showed the declining importance of those of British ethnic origin, a shift from Protestant to Catholic religion, the rapid urbanization of the foreign-born, the higher educational achievement of post-war immigrants and their greater labour-force participation rates, especially among women (Kalbach 1970). A decade later, census data revealed that these trends had continued (Richmond and Kalbach 1980). Comparison between the experience of immigrants in Quebec and the rest of Canada revealed that French Canadians were under-represented in managerial and professional employment at that time. Immigrants had filled many of the shortages in these fields. Further comparisons between first, second and third-plus generations by ethnic background confirmed that immigrants and their descendants were adapting well to the emerging post-industrial society of Canada (Richmond and Zubrzycki 1984).

1972–78

The 'points system' and other changes, such as elimination of racial and ethnic discrimination from Canadian immigration regulations and procedures (Troper 1993: 270), opened the door to a massive shift in immigration patterns. Third World countries became an increasingly important source of temporary and permanent workers admitted to Canada (Burstein 1991; Simmons 1990, 1993). The proportion of permanent immigrants from these countries increased from 8 per cent in the early 1960s to more than 50 per cent by the end of 1975 (Lanphier 1979). For a time visitors were permitted to apply for landed immigrant status after arrival and, if refused, could appeal. By May 1973, the backlog of cases before the Immigration Appeal Board exceeded 17,000 and the right to change status within Canada was revoked.

In 1973, a major public review of immigration policy was instituted and a four-volume report of the *Canadian Immigration and Populations Study* issued (CIPS 1974; Hawkins 1988: 375–7). The *Green Paper*, as the report was commonly known, reaffirmed the link between immigration and labour supply, but raised important questions concerning the effects of population growth, urban congestion and ethnic tensions. A subsequent parliamentary committee report adopted a more liberal and expansionist view.

Despite the controversy over the *Green Paper*, the

government went ahead with its own immigration agenda and a new Immigration Act was proclaimed in 1978. Its main objectives were:

- to facilitate the reunion of Canadian citizens and permanent residents with their close relatives from abroad;
- to foster the development of strong and viable economy and the prosperity of all regions in Canada; and
- to fulfil Canada's international legal obligations with respect to refugees and to uphold its humanitarian tradition with respect to the displaced and the persecuted.

Besides affirming universality and non-discrimination in its immigration policy, the act established three categories of immigrants, *viz* family class and assisted relatives, economic migrants and refugees. For the first time, the Minister of Immigration was mandated, in consultation with the provinces, to submit to Parliament a yearly target for the number of immigrants in the three categories. Other significant changes in the act were the adoption of the UN Convention definition of a 'refugee', and regulations which permitted Canadian citizens, or permanent residents, to sponsor refugees. This provision proved to be invaluable in resettling the Indo-Chinese refugees, after the fall of Saigon in 1975 (Adelman 1980, 1982; Hawkins 1988: 379; Neuwirth et al. 1985). However, it was the implementation of internal refugee status determination that forced subsequent changes in immigration regulations.

1979–90

The 'family class' remained an important component of immigration, constituting more than 50 per cent of the intake in the peak years 1983 and 1984. The number of 'kinship bonus points' available to assisted relatives was increased in July 1988 from ten to fifteen. The geographic sources of migration and consequent ethnic composition continued to shift away from traditional source countries (Britain, other European countries and the USA) to Asia, the Pacific, Central and South America, Africa and the Middle East. The impact of the shift from traditional to non-traditional sources resulted 'not so much from the magnitude of the flows but from their concentration in a small number of receiving communities since the majority of newcomers tend to settle in the major urban sectors' (Burstein 1991: 1), such as Toronto, Montreal and Vancouver.

Indo-Chinese refugees were admitted under a provision of the 1976 Immigration Act, which gave authority to the government to accept persons who were in 'refugee-like' situations, i.e. 'designated classes' who were in need of resettlement, even though they might not meet the strict definition of 'Convention refugee'. In two important respects, the admission of over 60,000 refugees from south-east Asia during 1979/80, marked the beginning of a new era in Canada's refugee policy (Dirks 1985; Hawkins 1988, 1991; Neuwirth et al. 1985; Simmons 1990, 1993; Simmons and Keohane 1992). First, it constituted the largest single group of refugees from developing countries to be resettled. Second, their resettlement was made possible by the active participation of the private sector. Combined government and private sponsorship programmes enabled Canada to absorb the highest number of 'boat people' per capita of any nation (Adelman 1982; Troper 1993).

While the majority of refugees were selected abroad for resettlement, an increasing number of asylum seekers arrived, by sea or air, and claimed refugee status after arrival. The number making such claims increased from 500 in 1977 to over 6000 in 1983. This led to a backlog of applications, which the refugee determination process, established under the 1978 Immigration Act, was incapable of handling expeditiously. By the end of 1989, the backlog had reached over 95,000 claims. The determination system was unable to handle such a heavy caseload (Burstein 1991: 32).

Pursuant to the Immigration Act of 1976, a refugee claimant was examined under oath, by a senior immigration official, and a transcript of the proceedings forwarded to the Refugee Status Advisory Committee. The transcript was reviewed and a recommendation as to acceptance or rejection made to the Minister of Immigration. There was no hearing at which a claimant could present his or her case. In 1985, the Supreme Court of Canada struck down this process in the case of *Harbajnir Singh v. the Minister of Employment and Immigration*. The court ruled that the *Canadian Charter of Rights and Freedoms* applied to all people inside Canada, even if their status had not yet been determined. Section 7 of the charter states that everybody has the right to life, liberty and security, and the right not to be deprived thereof except in accordance with the principles of fundamental justice. The court held that the procedures did not provide adequate opportunity for the claimant to state a case and that a full hearing should be provided.

This ruling delayed the determination process further. Increasing numbers of people sought asylum, including some economically motivated migrants. Rejecting the granting of a general amnesty as an appropriate measure on the grounds that it would encourage another flow of illegitimate claimants who would again clog the system and wait for the next amnesty, a case by case administrative procedure was adopted to clear the backlog, which was not completely removed until 1993. The overall acceptance rate of these applicants was 63 per cent. However, many who were refused had been in the country for several years. They went 'underground' and over 1100 warrants for arrest were issued (Refugee 1993: 5).

The refugee issue took a dramatic turn when two ships illegally stranded their respective refugee cargoes on the east coast in the dead of night (Troper 1993). These included 155 Tamils who arrived in Newfoundland from refugee camps in Germany, in 1986, and 174 Sikhs who landed in Nova Scotia in 1987. Fear that more boatloads of refugees might be on their way led the government to declare an emergency and Parliament was recalled in the summer of 1987. In addition to requiring transit visas for some nationals making stops in Canada *en route* to other countries, Bills C–55 and C–84, which dealt with with refugee status determination and introduced deterrent measures, were passed. These provided for substantially increased penalties for smugglers of illegal entrants and for transportation companies carrying undocumented persons, detention of those arriving without proper documentation until their identities could be established, and the removal of anyone posing a criminal or security threat. Individuals who had passed through another country deemed to be 'safe' and where a refugee claim could have been made, were to be denied the right to make such a claim in Canada. (This provision, the so-called 'safe third country' clause, was not enforced although it remains an option if bilateral agreements with the USA can be negotiated.)

Under the new legislation (Bill C–55), refugee determination became a two-phase process comprising an initial hearing to determine if the applicant had a credible basis for making a claim, and a second full hearing by the newly created Immigration and Refugee Board's Convention Refugee Determination Division. Credible basis decisions were based on the human rights record of the country allegedly responsible for the persecution. If the claim was deemed credible at the initial hearing, a work permit was issued, pending completion of the second stage. When claims were referred to the second level, a panel decided if the claimant met the definition of a Convention refugee. If the claim was recognized by one member of the two-person panel, the applicant could apply for landed immigrant status.

The number of claims rose from nearly 22,000 in 1989 to over 40,000 in 1992. The top source countries were Sri Lanka, Somalia, Iran, Lebanon, China, CIS (USSR), El Salvador and Guatemala. The overall acceptance rate declined from 70 per cent in 1990 to 57 per cent in 1992. The high rate of acceptance at the initial hearing (95 per cent), combined with government's inability to execute the 'safe third country' provision, created a new backlog (Richmond 1991: 157). Moreover, it was estimated that Canada's costs for asylum processing were in excess of $200 million (Adelman 1991: 9).

Another important change during this decade resulted from the government's deliberate policy encouragement of 'business immigrants' who brought with them capital for investment and others who planned to start businesses which would create employment. Including dependants, this group increased from 15,112 in 1988 to 18,126 by 1990. Hong Kong was the largest single source, accounting for 28 per cent of all business immigrants, followed by Korea, Taiwan and the USA (Burstein 1991: 15; Richmond 1991: 156; Wong 1991). However, there were abuses by those merely endeavouring to obtain entry to Canada without fulfilling their obligations (Cannon 1989; Fennel and DeMont 1989; Lai 1992; Malarek 1987; Nash 1987). This led the Minister of Employment and Immigration, in 1989, to initiate a monitoring programme designed to track entrepreneurs until they had complied with the terms and conditions of their acceptance (Canada 1992; Richmond 1991).

The number of temporary employment authorizations rose steadily in this period, from 83,912 in 1973 to 286,584 in 1989 (Burstein 1991). The authorizations are given for varying periods of less than a month up to one year with the possibility, in some cases, of renewal. 'Validated' authorizations are issued if there is no qualified Canadian worker available, while categories such as teachers, clergy and entertainers are 'exempt'. Two programmes (the Foreign Domestic Movement and the Caribbean and Mexican Seasonal Agricultural Worker Programmes) represented between 25 and 30 per cent of all validated employment authorizations. These workers generally come from poor Third World countries such as Jamaica and the Philippines. Furthermore, many experience discrimination and oppressive working conditions in the homes and institutions in which they are employed (Bakan 1987; Wong 1984).

1991–93

In 1990, the government presented a five-year immigration plan which was developed as a result of consultation with the provincial and municipal governments, special interest groups, individuals and organizations (Canada 1990b). It provided for an increase in immigration levels to 220,000 in 1991 and to 250,000 in each of the following four years, while claiming to maintain a balance between the family, refugee and independent categories. The retiree programme was discontinued after 1992.

Amendments were made to the Indo-Chinese designated class in August 1990, in accordance with the Comprehensive Plan of Action which was approved at a United Nations conference in Geneva in June 1989. This class applied only to Cambodians, Laotians and Vietnamese who entered countries of first asylum in south-east Asia before the established cut-off dates in 1989. The Political Prisoners and Oppressed Persons Designated Class applied only to El Salvador and Guatemala. The Self-Exiled Persons Designated Class was cancelled in 1990, because of changing conditions in eastern Europe and the USSR. Furthermore, following large-scale repatriation and decreased resettlement requirements (UNHCR identified only 42,000 refugees worldwide in need of third-country resettlement in 1993), fewer refugees (government-assisted or privately sponsored) were selected from abroad for resettlement in Canada.

A new Canada–Quebec Accord came into force on 1 April 1991. It maintains the federal government's exclusive control over fundamental immigration standards and objectives, including responsibility for admitting immigrants, granting permanent resident status, overseeing the control of aliens and providing citzenship services. However, the accord gives Quebec power in the selection of independent immigrants and refugees from abroad but not those determined in Canada. It grants Quebec new responsibilities for the integration of immigrants. Both parties agree to promote Quebec-bound immigration to a proportion equivalent to its share of the Canadian population. The federal government will provide $332 million in financial compensation to Quebec, over a four-year period, for providing services to immigrants that are comparable to those provided by the federal government. The compensation takes into account the additional expenditure that Quebec will incur because

only one-third of immigrants speak French upon their arrival, whereas one-half of immigrants entering the rest of Canada speak some English.

Reflecting the desire to increase the number and proportion of 'skilled workers', changes were made in the selection system in 1991 to make it more responsive to national and regional labour market needs. Qualified applicants would receive additional points and would be processed more quickly in occupations 'designated' as in short supply. In the selection of other skilled workers, whose occupations are listed as 'general' and who have relatively good employment prospects, more emphasis will be placed on arranged employment, education and language skills.

A new Immigration Act, Bill C–86, became law in January 1993. Previous amendments made through Bills C–55 and C–84 did not achieve what the government intended in terms of reducing asylum applicantions. There was a concern that Canada was losing control of its borders. These fears were fuelled by media reports suggesting that some refugee claimants were making multiple welfare claims, that criminals were making refugee claims, that a convicted terrorist had obtained refugee status and that organized smuggling of illegal aliens was taking place.

Bill C–86 gave the government the authority to set limits on the numbers of immigrants accepted in each category. Different classes of immigrants were assigned to three management streams. Applicants in Stream 1 include immediate family members of people already living in Canada (spouses, fiancé(e)s, dependent children, people found to be Convention refugees by the Immigration and Refugee Board, and investors who can contribute significantly to Canada's economic development). These applicants are processed on demand and there is no fixed limit to the total number of applications approved each year. Applicants in Stream 2 include parents and grandparents of Canadian residents, government-assisted and privately sponsored refugees, applicants who have pre-arranged employment, self-employed persons and live-in care givers. These are processed on a first-come first-served basis, with the total number in each category subject to limits set out in the annual immigration plan. Applications will no longer be accepted once there are enough cases in process to meet these goals. Applicants in Stream 3 include people applying as independents, those qualified in designated occupations and entrepreneurs with business experience. They are subject to the limits set out in the annual plan and are selected on competitive merit. Once the annual targets have been met, further applications are not accepted.

The most significant change under Bill C–86 is the legislative power given to the government to control and streamline the internal refugee determination process. In line with the Dublin Convention in Europe, it is intended to stop refugee claimants from 'asylum shopping', i.e. making multiple refugee claims in different countries. Bill C–86 empowers the government to fingerprint and photograph claimants. It may also make agreements with other countries whereby 'refugee claimants' can be sent back to so-called 'safe third countries'. This will reduce pressure on the refugee determination system and reduce the costs of social assistance, medical care and education provided to claimants pending their hearing. Bill C–86 eliminated the two-stage process and gives authority to the senior immigration officer at the port of entry to determine if the claim has a credible basis. If subsequently rejected, an appeal can be made but only in those cases identified by a trial division judge as involving a serious question of law (Canada 1992, 1993).

Bill C–86 also allows the government to increase efforts to intercept 'illegal migrants' overseas by providing training and technical assistance to airlines to help them identify passengers with fraudulent documents, and by increasing fines for airlines that 'do not undertake reasonable precautions' in screening passengers (unsuccessful claimants and other inadmissible passengers) they bring to Canada.

Conclusion

The effect of these massive and unprecedent legislative changes enacted between 1989 and 1993 remain to be seen. The Conservative government was defeated at the general election in October 1993. It was succeeded by the Liberal Party, which may have a different agenda (putting immigration and citizenship under one department and delaying the conclusion of the bilateral 'refugee sharing' agreement with the USA). Meanwhile, Canada is entering the 'post-industrial' age of a globalized, highly competitive, knowledge-based economy, and the need to develop a highly-skilled workforce is more important now than ever. Immigration will continue to play a vital role in developing such a workforce, but debates continue over how many immigrants should be accepted and the balance between categories. The debates may be further exacerbated by the Free Trade Agreement with the USA and the North American Free Trade Agreement (Martin 1993; Richmond 1991). It is

unclear whether the new government will make a significant humanitarian response to the global refugee problem. A major challenge for Canada (Angus Reid Group 1991; Decima Research 1993; Economic Council of Canada 1991) in the years ahead will be to enforce effective measures to deal with racism and to manage the ethnic diversity brought about by immigration.

References

Adelman, H. (1980) 'Changes in Policy', in H. Adelman (ed.) *The Indochinese Refugee Movement: The Canadian Experience*, Toronto: Operation Lifeline, 23–7

—— (1982) *Canada and the Indochinese Refugees*, Regina: L. A. Weigl Educational Associates Ltd

—— (1991) 'Refugee Determination: Bill C–55 Revisited', *Refuge*, 11 (2), December, 1–4, 8–18

Angus Reid Group (1991) *Multiculturalism and Canadians: National Attitude Study 1991*, Ottawa: Multiculturalism & Citizenship

Bakan, A. (1987) 'International Market for Female Labour and Individual De-Skilling: West Indian Women Workers in Toronto', *North–South: Canadian Journal of Latin American and Caribbean Studies*, (12)

Burstein, M. (1991) *Immigration in Canada: A Statistical Report for the Continuous Reporting System on Migration of the OECD*, Ottawa: Employment and Immigration Canada, Strategic Planning and Research Branch, Immigration Policy Group

Canada (1990a) *Immigrants in Canada: Selected Highlights*, Ottawa: Statistics Canada

—— (1990b) *Report on the Consultations on Immigration for 1991–1995*, Ottawa: Employment and Immigration Canada

—— (1992) *Managing Immigration: A Framework for the 1990s*, Ottawa: Employment and Immigration Canada

—— (1993) *The Management of Immigration*, Ottawa: Employment and Immigration Canada

Cannon, M. (1989) *China Tide: The Revealing Story of the Hong Kong Exodus to Canada*, Toronto: Harper & Collins

CIPS (1974) *Immigration Policy Perspective, the Immigration Programme, Immigration and Population Statistics, and Three Years in Canada*, Ottawa: Manpower and Immigration Canada.

Cummings, P. et al. (1989) *Access! Task Force on Access to Professionals and Trades in Ontario*, Toronto: Ontario Ministry of Citizenship

Decima Research (1993) *Canadian Attitudes Towards Race and Ethnic Relations in Canada*, Toronto: Canadian Council of Christians and Jews

Dirks, G. (1985) 'Canadian Refugee Policy: Humanitarian and Political Dimensions', in E. G. Ferris (ed.) *Refugee and World Politics*, New York: Praeger, 120–35

Economic Council of Canada (1991) *New Faces in the Crowd: Economic and Social Impacts of Immigration*, Ottawa: Ministry of Supply and Services

Fennel, T. and J. DeMont (1989) *Hong Kong Money: How Chinese Families and Fortunes are Changing Canadian Business*, Toronto: Key Porter

Hawkins, F. (1988) *Canada and Immigration: Public Policy and Public Concern* (2nd ed.), Kingston and Montreal: McGill–Queen's University Press

(1991) *Critical Years in Immigration: Canada and Australia Compared* (2nd ed.), Kingston and Montreal: McGill–Queen's University Press

Kalbach, W. E. (1970) *The Impact of Immigration on Canada's Population: 1961 Census Monograph*, Ottawa: Dominion Bureau of Statistics

Lai, D. Chuenyan (1992) 'Emigration to Canada: Its Dimensions and Impact on Hong Kong', in Jean Burnet et al. (eds) *Migration and the Transformation of Cultures*, Toronto: Multicultural History Society of Ontario, 241–52

Lanphier, C. M. (1979) *A Study of Third World Immigrants*, Ottawa: Economic Council of Canada

Malarek, V. (1987) *Haven's Gate: Canada's Immigration Fiasco*, Toronto: Macmillan of Canada

Martin, P. (1993) 'Trade and Migration: The Case of NAFTA', *Asian and Pacific Migration Journal*, 2 (3), 329–67

Mata, F. (1992) 'The Recognition of Foreign Degrees in Canada: Context, Developments and Issue Relevance, paper presented at the Conference on Migration, Human Rights and Economic Integration', Toronto: Centre for Refugee Studies, York University, 19–22 November

McDade, K. (1988) *Barriers to Recognition of the Credentials of Immigrants to Canada*, Ottawa: Institute for Research in Public Policy

Michalowski, M. (1991) 'Characteristics of Foreign-born Canadian Emigrants', *International Migration Review*, 25 (1), 28–59

(1993) 'Redefining the Concept of Immigration to Canada', *Canadian Population Studies*, 20 (1), 59–84

Nash, A. (1987) *The Economic Impact of the Entrepreneur Programme*, Ottawa: Institute for Research on Public Policy

Neuwirth, G. et al. (1985) *Southeast Asian Refugee Study: A Report on a Three Year Study on the Social and Economic Adaptation of Southeast Asian Refugees to Life in Canada, 1981–1983*, Ottawa: Carleton University

Petersen, W. (1955) *Planned Migration: The Social Determinants of the Dutch–Canadian Movement*, Berkeley: University of California Press

Refugee (1993) *Update*, Toronto: Jesuit Refugee Service Canada

Richmond, A. H. (1967) *Post-war Immigrants in Canada*, Toronto: University of Toronto Press

(1991) 'Foreign-Born Labour in Canada: Past Patterns, Emerging Trends, and Implications', *Regional Development Dialogue*, 12 (3), Autumn, 145–61, Nagoya, Japan: United Nations Centre for Regional Development

(1992) 'Immigration and Structural Change: The Canadian Experience 1971–86', *International Migration Review*, 26 (4), 1200–21

Richmond, A. H. and W. E. Kalbach (1980) *Factors in the Adjustment of Immigrants and their Descendants: 1971 Census Monograph*, Ottawa: Statistics Canada

Richmond A. H. and J. Zubrzycki (1984) *Immigrants in Canada and Australia, vol. II. Economic Adaptation*, Toronto: Institute for Behaviour Research, York University

Sazewich, V. (1991) *Racism and the Incorporation of Foreign Labour: Farm Labour Migration to Canada since 1945*, London: Routledge

Simmons, A. (1990) 'The Origin and Characteristics of "New Wave" Canadian Immigrants', in S. S. Halli, F. Trovato and L. Driedger (eds) *Ethnic Demography: Canadian Immigrant, Racial and Cultural Variations*, Ottawa: Carleton University Press, 141–60

(1993) 'Latin American Migration to Canada', *International Journal*, 40 (8), Spring, 282–309

Simmons, A. and K. Keohane (1992) 'Canadian Immigration Policy: State Strategies and the Quest for Legitimacy', *Canadian Review of Sociology and Anthropology*, (29), November, 421–52

Troper, H. (1993) 'Canada's Immigration Policy Since 1945', *International Journal*, XLVIII, Spring, 255–81

Wong, L. (1984) 'Canada's Guestworkers: Some Comparisons of Temporary Workers in Europe and North America', *International Migration Review*, (18), 185–9

(1991) 'Business Immigration to Canada: Social Impact and Racism', paper presented at Conference on Immigration, Racism and Multiculturalism: 1990 and Beyond, sponsored by the Social Research Unit, Department of Sociology, University of Saskatchewan, 22–23 March

PART NINE

LABOUR MIGRATION TO WESTERN EUROPE AFTER 1945

As we reach the end of the twentieth century, 'Fortress Europe' confronts immigrants and asylum-seekers trying to enter western European countries. It is difficult to recall that half a century ago governmental policies were very different. As the British, French, Russian and American tanks rolled into German-held Europe at the end of the Second World War, they confronted millions of displaced persons. Yet, despite the chaos of this period, the war-torn economies of western Europe needed labour and, within two to three years, all the displaced persons were settled.

One must not imagine that all were absorbed without difficulty. Within the British ruling class, for example, fine distinctions were drawn between those from the Baltic States who were seen as 'superior types' who would easily be assimilated and those from south-east Europe who were seen as 'alien Slavs' or 'simple peasant types' and were considered less malleable immigrants. And, despite the horrors witnessed by the British troops as the concentration camps emptied, the recruiters from the British Ministry of Labour only managed to find 3000 suitable Jewish immigrants (Cohen 1994: 75–6; Kay and Miles 1992: 124). So, in short, behind the need for labour there remained a deep-seated fear of the foreigner. As *Anwar* construes it, Britain sent out and received millions of ethnically similar migrants, yet the existence of an 'immigration problem' was only proclaimed once non-white Commonwealth labour migrants were attracted to the metropolis.

Although there are many similarities between all the post-war labour-importing European countries, *Ogden* rightly reminds us that the roots of large-scale immigration to France ran far deeper than in the case of Britain. Armenians, Russians, Poles and Italians were welcomed in the inter-war years. Unlike in Britain, there were long-held fears of demographic decline and a sense that if France was to retain its place as a major world power, immigrants had to be accepted and even nurtured. However, there was a logical price to this goodwill – the immigrants had to accept the rights and obligations of French citizenship, adopt the French language and assimilate to mainstream French life. This was a price that many Europeans, particularly in the pre-war period, were only too happy to pay, but the policy rapidly came unstuck as the neophyte labour recruits from North Africa insisted on retaining their cultural, linguistic and religious distinctiveness. 'Nationality' and 'citizenship' which once were fused became radically divorced and a powerful anti-immigration lobby developed.

In the case of post-war Switzerland, analysed by *Hoffman-Nowotny*, there was never a question of seeking to assimilate foreign workers. Instead the principle of 'rotation' was vigorously enforced in a desperate attempt to stop the acquisition of Swiss citizenship. The end result, as another Swiss academic lamented, was likely to be a strange, reverse colonial dystopia 'with the difference that the autochthonous would be the masters and the immigrants the servants' (Girod, cited in Castles and Kosack 1981: 383). As all good sociologists know, however carefully they are fabricated social policies are prone to unintended consequences. Good-quality labour became scarcer, employers were reluctant to part with experienced workers and the economy became geared to using more and more low-cost migrant workers. Despite the powerful and popular campaign against 'overforeign-ization', *Hoffman-Nowotny* suggests that the authorities have been unable successfully to control and regulate immigration to Switzerland. The ironic title of the contribution on Switzerland, namely 'a non-immigration immigration country', can be repeated, with variations, in the cases of two other countries covered here – the Netherlands and Sweden.

All three had politicians who recited the parrot-like slogan, 'We are not an immigration country!' All three sets of politicians were wrong. Long histories of immigration were often concealed by phenotypical similarity and an acceptance of the dominant culture and language by the newcomers. The crucial difference between pre-war and post-war immigration was that the latter was often more visible and therefore more politically sensitive. The Netherlands, like Britain and France, inherited obligations to colonial citizenries arising from the ending of the Dutch empire in the West and East Indies. Extensive repatriation from Surinam and Indonesia accompanied the decolonization process (see *Entzinger* in Part 10 of the *Survey*). In his contribution, however, *van Amersfoort* focuses on labour migrants from countries with which the Netherlands had no historical association. Turks and Moroccans were by far the most significant in the category of 'recruitment countries'. As *van Amersfoort* perceptively comments, the definition of the 'immigration problem' with respect to these communities kept shifting – from housing (when unmarried migrants predominated), to education (when families were constituted), to unemployment (as the second generation faces structural unemployment). Moreover, this last issue is not going to go away easily, as the demographic profile of the immigrant population shows a disproportionate number of very young Turks and Moroccans.

Hammar's contribution on Finnish–Swedish migration provides a useful contrast with the highly regulated labour markets of many of the west European states. The free movement allowed in the Nordic agreement of 1954 only confirmed what had already been custom and practice for generations. The Swedish-speaking minority in Finland often sought work in Sweden; many Finns were employed in the steel and car industries; Swedish migration to Finland was also considerable; there were high rates of return migration; and, unusually, there is strong evidence of early and contemporary independent female migration from Finland to Sweden.[1] The result is a complex set of cross-flows between the two countries and a high degree of cultural intermingling and intermarriage.

The expression 'a non-immigration country' can be applied with more accuracy to Italy and Greece (discussed by *Fakiolas*) and to Spain and Portugal (discussed by *Solé*). All four countries had very high rates of emigration. In Greece and Italy the roots of these emigrations can be traced to classical times, with the growth of trading diasporas. Both the Iberian countries exhibited high rates of emigration during their colonial periods. All four countries actively participated in the 'Great Atlantic Migration' (see Part 4) to North, Central and South America. Although it is true to assert that many migrants – particularly from Italy and Greece – returned periodically to their natal homes, or retired there, there is no doubt that the primary movement was outward not inward. So alarmed were the Greek authorities at this movement that they tried for a while to regulate and prevent the export of labour – a practice more normally associated with the Soviet Union and its satellites.

All four countries are now having to adjust to being immigrant countries. Pontian Greeks are returning 'home' from the Soviet Union while seasonal and illegal Albanian workers are common in both Italy and Greece. In addition to the East–West movement released by the collapse of the communist regimes, additional South–North flows are affecting all four countries from across the Mediterranean. Perhaps somewhat fancifully the Mediterranean Sea has been described as 'Europe's Rio Grande', implying that the level of unregulated migration from North Africa is akin to that of Mexican undocumented labour to the USA. This is certainly an exaggeration, but one which is a response to two political imperatives. First, the tendency towards free movement within the European Union (EU) means that the edges of 'Fortress Europe' have to be policed with particular tenacity (Fassman and Münz 1994: 3–35; Wrench and Solomos 1993). Second, in all European countries there has been a populist drive towards cultural and religious homogeneity. In deference to this sentiment, European politicians, particularly in France and the other Mediterranean EU countries, are particularly hostile to North African Muslim migration (Hargreaves and Leaman 1995; Cohen 1994: 177–9).

The two remaining contributions to Part 9 are concerned with source rather than destination countries. *Abadan-Unat* provides a comprehensive account of Turkish migration to Europe. The movement to Germany is, of course, well known, but perhaps not as clearly recognized was the significant spread to a number of other countries of the 2.5 million Turks in western Europe as a whole. Turks have become well-known butts of 'welfare chauvinism' and racial violence in Germany and, with the post-reunification emphasis on 'Germans first', their position has remained precarious despite their long residence. There are many ironies in their situation. Owing to Atatürk's fierce attack on Islamic ideas of theocracy and his drive to westernize the country, many Turks come from a secular or liberal Muslim background. However, the hostility toward them in Europe has led to the growth of a more introspective, more dogmatic brand of Islam. This leads to a greater sense of their alienness in western Europe and feeds the right-wing populist sentiments I alluded to earlier. Such imagery in turn delays Turkey's acceptance as a full member of the EU, the only circumstance that will finally resolve the difficult civic rights deficits that Turks in Europe experience.

Schierup furnishes an analysis of migration from the 'former Yugoslavia' (an inelegant term, but what else can one do with such a hotchpotch of micro-nationalisms that accompanied the end of communism there?). The period from after the Second World War to about 1990 mirrored Turkish migration, with Yugoslavs entering mainstream factory employment, often in considerable numbers. This period was notable as indicating how far Yugoslavia was from an orthodox Comecon country. Migration not only was encouraged, but was seen as essential to the generation of development funds. There is little use crying over spilt milk and even less bemoaning the fate of the form of participatory socialism that the Yugoslavs seemed intent on building as rotating migrants brought skills and capital to their home regions. Now most migration from the area is flight migration, as one group after another demands the 'ethnic cleansing' of its area. Of all the reasons for migration, this perhaps is the most demoralizing.

Note

1. In general, the issue of independent women's migration remains curiously under-researched, despite the long reach of feminist-inspired studies in so many other areas of social life (see, however, Buijs 1993; Phizacklea 1983; Simon and Brettall 1986). One reason why independent women have often remained hidden from migration history is that entry policies often insisted on 'family migration'. In several settings (Caribbean migrants to Britain, for example) it is clear that independent women migrating for independent reasons were passing themselves off as married in order to secure admission. *Campani* (see Part 15 of this *Survey*) suggests that women migrants are now more open about their motives and more numerous.

References

Buijs, Gina (ed.) (1993) *Migrant Women: Crossing Boundaries and Changing Identities*, Oxford: Berg
Castles, Stephen and Godula Kosack (1981) *Immigrant Workers and Class Structure in Western Europe*, London: Oxford University Press
Cohen, Robin (1994) *Frontiers of Identity: The British and the Others*, London: Longman
Fassman, Heinz and Rainer Münz (1994) *European Migration in the Late Twentieth Century: Historical Patterns, Actual Trends and Social Implications*, Aldershot: Edward Elgar for the International Institute for Applied Systems Analysis
Hargreaves, Alec G. and Jeremy Leaman (eds) (1995) *Racism, Ethnicity and Politics in Contemporary Europe*, Aldershot: Edward Elgar
Kay, Diana and Robert Miles (1992) *Refugees or Migrant Workers? European Volunteer Workers in Britain, 1946–1951*, London: Routledge
Phizacklea, Annie (ed.) (1983) *One Way Ticket? Migration and Female Labour*, London: Routledge
Simon, R. J. and C. B. Brettall (eds) (1986) *International Migration: The Female Experience*, Towtowa, NJ: Rowman & Allenheld
Wrench, John and John Solomos (eds) (1993) *Racism and Migration in Western Europe*, Oxford: Berg

'NEW COMMONWEALTH' MIGRATION TO THE UK

MUHAMMAD ANWAR

Over the centuries, the United Kingdom (UK) has received and absorbed large numbers of white people from other countries and many Britons went abroad to the colonies. But it is only in the last forty-five years that the UK has received in significant numbers from the former colonies workers and their dependants whose colour differs from that of the white indigenous population. They are largely from the New Commonwealth (NC) countries. In this entry we look at the process of migration, the numbers involved, reactions to immigration from the NC and the current settlement patterns of ethnic minorities.

The process of migration

Commonwealth citizens had free entry into the UK under the Commonwealth rules. In addition, with colonial links and the experience of the UK of several thousand soldiers and seamen from India and the West Indies during the Second World War, some of them decided to stay in the UK and others came back to work in the expanding industry after the war. The start of mass migration was the arrival of the *Empire Windrush* ship in June 1948. It came to Tilbury docks with 492 immigrants from Jamaica; most of these had been to the UK during the war, had returned to the West Indies and were unable to secure work. This was followed by SS *Orbita* and SS *Georgia*. After this the immigration progressed slowly by air and sea, and during the 1950s the number of immigrants from the West Indies increased, reaching an annual rate of 30,000 in 1955 and 1956. The Conservative government elected in 1951 encouraged both emigration and immigration, but some concern was expressed about the number of coloured[1] immigrants during that period. As pressure for immigration control grew, the Conservative Party changed its policy of free personal movement and migration for all Commonwealth citizens to a policy of immigration control and published a bill on 1 November 1961 to restrict immigration. However, as a consequence of the debate on immigration control, more and more West Indians immigrated to the UK to beat the impending ban. For example, between the beginning of 1961 and the middle of 1962, when the Commonwealth Immigrants

Act 1962 came into force, 98,000 persons migrated to the UK from the West Indies.

Immigration from India and Pakistan started later than from the West Indies, but also reached a very high level from 1960 onwards as people tried to enter the UK while there was still time (Rose et al 1969: 55–90). In the beginning the migration was not organized but later on turned into chain migration, with pioneer migrants encouraging and helping friends and relatives to follow them. The sponsorship and patronage of friends and relatives by those who were already in the UK resulted in a mass migration of people both from the West Indies and the Indian sub-continent. Mass migration in some cases resulted in the establishment of institutions, agents and organizations to facilitate the migration. This way even after the 1962 act, the introduction of the voucher system reinforced the sponsorship and patronage of friends and relatives because the migrants in the UK were in a position to obtain vouchers (Anwar 1979: 213–14). Later immigration legislation and debates on immigration forced the migrants to bring their dependants to the UK because of the fear of losing their right to entry.

In addition to the voluntary movement of people some institutional arrangements also helped the process of migration. These included the London Transport Executive loaning fares to the UK to several thousand Barbadians and the recruitment of workers in Trinidad and Jamaica in the mid-1960s. Many workers, particularly women, for the National Health Service were recruited. Two other reasons for migration of Indians and Pakistanis to the UK were the partition of India in 1947 when Pakistan was created and the construction of the Mangla Dam. In both cases large numbers of people were displaced and some looked for opportunities in the UK (Anwar 1979: 23–6).

Most New Commonwealth workers were economic migrants and they filled a gap for labour in the unskilled sectors and poorly paid jobs as a result of the reconstruction and expansion of British industry after the war. As they were granted access only to a limited range of occupations upon arrival they are

Table 9.1: *Immigration from the New Commonwealth,* * *1971–83: all acceptances for settlement ('000s)*

Year	Total accepted for settlement	Men	Women	Children
1971	44.3	10.9	16.7	16.7
1972	68.5	17.4	23.8	26.9
1973	30.3	5.3	13.5	11.5
1974	42.5	14.5	17.3	10.7
1975	53.3	16.6	21.4	15.2
1976	55.1	16.1	22.1	16.4
1977	44.1	10.7	19.6	13.8
1978	42.9	11.8	18.6	12.5
1979	37.2	9.9	16.5	10.8
1980	33.7	8.9	14.4	10.4
1981	31.4	7.4	13.3	10.7
1982	30.4	7.3	13.2	9.9
1983	27.5	6.3	13.0	8.1

*Includes Pakistan
Source: Home Office (1984)

concentrated in certain industrial sectors and this partly helps to explain their concentrations in certain towns, cities and regions.

The numbers involved

The immigration from the NC started slowly and peaked in 1961 and 1962. For example, in 1956 just under 47,000 people entered the UK while this number rose to 136,400 in 1961 and 94,900 for the first six months of 1962 up to the introduction of the 1962 act. Those who entered the UK before the 1962 act were predominantly economically active persons. The voucher system under the act gave the opportunity for those who were already here to arrange jobs for their relatives and friends but dependants of those already in the UK were allowed to come without vouchers. As a result the balance shifted between workers and dependants entering the UK. Between July 1962 and December 1968, only 77,966 voucher holders were admitted compared with 257,220 dependants. This meant a drastic decline in the number of immigrants coming as workers. The number of people arriving for settlement from all the NC countries between 1969 and 1977 was 318,521. Of these, 259,646 came as dependants and only 58,875 were male workers, thus continuing the decline in the number of immigrants entering as workers. This pattern of decline applied also to dependants and has continued. For example, the number of dependent

women and children has more than halved from about 50,000 in 1972 to about 21,100 in 1983. Table 9.1 shows the downward trend between 1971 and 1983.

On the other hand it is worth pointing out that between 1971 and 1983 more people left the UK than had entered it. Overall the net loss of migration during this period was almost half a million (465,000), mainly as a result of emigration to Australia, New Zealand, the USA and Canada. Overall acceptances, including removal of conditions of those already settled in the UK from the NC, in 1992 numbered 27,900 (52 per cent of all acceptances) (Home Office 1993). On the basis of these figures it is fair to conclude that large-scale immigration from the NC is now over and that the unification of divided families is the main source of immigration.

Political and public reactions

The arrival of the *Empire Windrush* in 1948 created some interest in the House of Commons in the form of MPs questioning relevant ministers, and the government set up an interdepartmental working party to look into the issue of non-white immigration. This working party and another interdepartmental committee in 1950 recommended ways and means of keeping colonial immigrants out of the UK. In its cabinet meetings the Labour government discussed the immigration of non-white immigrants in May and June 1950. It concluded that no decision should be taken; the numbers were too small and legislation to control immigration could be controversial (Cabinet Papers 1950). Between 1951 and 1955 the immigration issue was raised by MPs in the House of Commons; a few discussions took place in cabinet meetings and in November 1955 a Committee of Ministers was set up. No action was taken but the committee felt that non-white immigration was a problem and that it should be kept under review (Cabinet Papers 1956).

The turning point came with the race riots in Nottingham and Notting Hill in London in August and September 1958, which made the headlines in the national newspapers and broadcasting media; the issue of immigration control was discussed widely and became the subject of opinion polls. The Labour Party condemned the riots and issued a statement on racial discrimination, opposing both it and immigration control.

At the 1964 general election Labour accused the Conservatives of using immigration as an excuse for their poor performance in education and housing (Foot 1965: 147–75). In Smethwick Peter Griffiths of the Conservative Party, who ran an anti-immigration campaign, defeated Patrick Gordon Walker, Labour Shadow Foreign Secretary. It appeared that in some other areas anti-immigration candidates had also benefited. Griffiths was never repudiated by the Conservative Party leadership (Layton-Henry 1992: 78).

The Labour government passed the second Commonwealth Immigration Act in 1968 restricting the entry of Kenyan Asians with British passports. Enoch Powell MP, who was writing in newspapers and making speeches against large-scale NC immigration in 1967, made his 'river of blood' speech on 20 April 1968. Mr Heath, the Conservative leader, declared Powell's speech to be racialist in tone and dropped him from his shadow cabinet. However, this did not stop Powell getting some public support and making non-white immigrants a topic for his speeches in the following period. Mr Heath's government elected at the 1970 general election passed the Immigration Act 1971. Then came the expulsion of Asians from Uganda in 1972, when 27,000 entered the UK. There was intense media coverage of this development and Powell and his supporters used the opportunity to exploit public feelings about non-white immigrants. As a consequence the right-wing Monday Club started a 'Halt Immigration Now' campaign in 1972.

The issue of non-white immigration also led to the formation of several active anti-immigrant organizations. The first two to oppose immigration in 1960 were the Birmingham Immigration Control Association and Southall Residents Association. The National Front (NF) was founded in 1966 and started contesting elections, particularly in the 1970s, on an anti-immigrant platform. The NF received some votes for a period from right-wing supporters of other political parties and certainly received a lot of publicity. Later on it was totally rejected by the British public at the ballot box (Anwar 1986: 145). Another anti-immigrant organization was the British Campaign to Stop Immigration (BCSI), which contested the 1972 parliamentary by-election in Rochdale followed by local elections in Rochdale and Bradford.

In January 1978 Mrs Thatcher, leader of the Conservative Party, in an interview on the *World in Action* television programme, said that people were really afraid that the country might be rather swamped by people with different cultures (Granada TV, 30 January 1978). This interview brought the issue of non-white people in the UK once more onto the national public and political agenda. Events that helped focus on non-white people in the 1980s and early 1990s included the inner-city riots in the 1980s, the debate about Hong Kong British passport holders and other British dependent territories while the Nationality Act (1981) was going through Parliament, the British Nationality (Hong Kong) Bill in 1990, the Rushdie affair in 1989, and the issue of refugees and asylum seekers. All these issues received extensive media coverage. A more recent event is the victory of the British National Party (BNP) in a local council by-election on 16 September 1993 in Millwall in Tower Hamlets, London. This has highlighted racist attitudes and behaviour in the area and started a debate about the presence of ethnic minorities in the UK.

In sum, British public reactions to immigration from the NC have been harsh. Signs such as 'ALL BLACKS GO HOME' and 'SEND THEM BACK' were quite common. 'Paki-bashing' and other anti-immigrant activities conducted through leaflets, speeches and demonstrations were common. There is evidence of racism in the 1990s in the thousands of racial attacks and racial harassment cases (House of Commons 1990) and in the acts of racial discrimination many non-whites face every day (Anwar 1991).

From immigrants to ethnic minorities

In 1951 there were only 74,000 people of NC origin in the UK; this increased to 336,000 in 1961 and to 2.2 million in 1981. The 1991 British census for the first time included an ethnic question with nine categories.

Table 9.2: *Ethnic minorities in Britain, 1991 ('000s)*

Ethnic Group	GB	England	Wales	Scotland
White	51,873.8	44,144.3	2793.5	4935.9
Ethnic minorities	3,015.1	2,,910.9	41.6	62.6
Black Caribbean	500.0	495.7	3.3	0.9
Black African	212.4	206.9	2.7	2.8
Black other	178.4	172.3	3.5	2.6
Indian	840.3	823.8	6.4	10.1
Pakistani	476.6	449.6	5.7	21.2
Bangladeshi	162.8	157.9	3.8	1.1
Chinese	156.9	141.7	4.8	10.5
Other Asian	197.5	189.3	3.7	4.6
Other other	290.2	273.7	7.7	8.8
Total population	54,888.8	47,055.2	2835.1	4998.6

Source: Adapted from Owen (1992: 1)

The census shows that of a total population of 54.9 million, the ethnic minority population is just over 3 million (5.5 per cent), of which over half are British born. Almost half (49.1 per cent) are of South Asian origin and about 0.89 million (29.5 per cent) are black; the remaining 21.4 per cent of ethnic minorities are Chinese or from other parts of the NC. Table 9.2 shows details of all ethnic groups.

A large number of ethnic minorities live in a small number of local authority areas. Most of the ethnic minorities are to be found in the south-east (56.2 per cent) especially in the Greater London area (44.6 per cent), the Midlands (20.3 per cent), the north and the north-west (9.4 per cent), Yorkshire and Humberside (7.1 per cent) and the remainder (8 per cent) in East Anglia, the south-west, Wales and Scotland. Black Caribbeans are highly concentrated in the south-east (66.3 per cent), with almost 60 per cent in the Greater London area. Over half of those of Indian origin are also living in the south-east, as are 63.6 per cent of the Bangladeshis and 53.3 per cent of the Chinese, but only 29.9 per cent of the Pakistanis. Over 60 per cent of the total population of Pakistani origin live in the conurbations of the West Midlands (20.7 per cent), Yorkshire and Humberside (19.9 per cent), the north-west (16.2 per cent), and Scotland (4.4 per cent). Overall the settlement patterns of ethnic minorities were clearly determined by the availability of work in different areas.

The pattern of employment for ethnic minorities has changed little in the last four decades except that they are more likely than white people to be unemployed. Racial discrimination is seen as a contributory factor.

Ethnic minorities generally live in inner-city areas. They face the acute problems of the inner cities and these lead them to suffer an overall pattern of racial disadvantage and discrimination in housing and other services.

Conclusions

The debate about the 1962 act resulted in a greater increase of immigrants into the UK from the NC than had occurred before. For example, in the eighteen months before the act the net inflow was as much as it had been for the previous five years. Ongoing debates about the number of non-white immigrants and immigration controls have forced migrants to bring over their wives and children before losing the right to do so. The controls were primarily to prevent or slow down the entry of non-white people. Immigration acts since 1962 'have been largely directed at slowly removing the rights of colonial and Commonwealth citizens to full British citizenship' (Cohen 1987: 161).

There was and still is an argument that good community and race relations in the UK depend on strict immigration controls. Another argument is that the goodwill and tolerance of white people could not continue unless there were an end to non-white immigration. But the fact remains that political responses in the form of immigration legislation and strict control policies were reactions to racist attitudes in society and that a certain amount of discrimination has been taking place. In fact the UK has more immigration controls than any other EU country.

If the objective of the controls was to stem the net inflow this does not seem to stand examination, for almost every year since the war and certainly until 1983 more people have left the UK to settle abroad than have arrived to settle in the UK. It appears that the real objective was to control non-white immigration.

Ethnic minorities in the UK are to stay and are now an integral part of the population. Over half of them were born in the UK and are not 'immigrants' but native-born British, and most others have British nationality. They are disadvantaged, face ongoing hostility and experience widespread direct and indirect discrimination. It is ironic that after more than four decades of a significant presence in the country and after all the economic and other contributions they have made to society, non-white people are still seen as 'outsiders' and responsible for the higher unemployment, bad housing or lack of it, and the inadequate and poor quality schools. They are being used as scapegoats for the ills of society while they themselves are in fact the victims of these ills.

Note

1. The term 'coloured' was commonly used in early official documents and also by some researchers. But I prefer to use 'non-white' and 'ethnic minorities' for people whose origin in the NC, except where official and other sources are quoted with the original terms.

References

Anwar, M. (1979) *The Myth of Return*, London: Heinemann
 (1986) *Race and Politics*, London: Tavistock
 (1991) 'The Context of Leadership: Migration, Settlement and Racial Discrimination', in P. Werbner and M. Anwar (eds) *Black and Ethnic Leaderships*, London: Routledge, 1–14
Cabinet Papers (1950) *Coloured People From British Colonial Territories*, (50), 113, London: Public Records Office
 (1956) *Colonial Immigrants*, 129/81, London: Public Records Office
Cohen, R. (1987) *The New Helots*, Aldershot: Gower
Foot, P. (1965) *Immigration and Race in British Politics*, Harmondsworth: Penguin Books
Home Office (1984) *Control of Immigration Statistics United Kingdom 1983*, London: HMSO
 (1993) *Control of Immigration: Statistics 1992*, London: Home Office Statistical Bulletin
House of Commons (1990) *Racial Attacks and Harassment*, Report from the Home Affairs Committee, London: HMSO
Layton-Henry, Z. (1992) *The Politics of Immigration*, Oxford: Blackwell
Owen, D. (1992) *Ethnic Minorities in Great Britain: Settlement Patterns*, Coventry: Centre for Research in Ethnic Relations
Rose, E. J. B. et al. (1969) *Colour and Citizenship*, London: Oxford University Press

TURKISH MIGRATION TO EUROPE

NERMIN ABADAN-UNAT

Turkey is a latecomer in the history of out-migration. Legally, a free exit from Turkey for its citizens came about only with the adoption of the constitution of 1961, whereby leaving or entering the country became a fundamental right. By 1993, 3,076,434 Turkish citizens had taken up permanent residence in the various countries of five continents. In Europe their number had reached 2,536,783. The rapidity of this migration is impressive (see Table 9.3). Almost all initial out-migration took place at the invitation of the industrialized countries.

Phases of Turkish migration to Europe

Beginning in the late 1950s, Turkish migration to, and settlement in, European countries occurred in six major phases:

- recruitment through intermediaries (1956–61);
- migration on the basis of bilateral agreements (1961–72);
- recession and the employment of foreign workers and the legitimation of illegal ('tourist') migrants (1972–75);
- family reunification and the education of children (1975–78);
- introduction of visa, the increase in asylum requests and growing xenophobia (1978–85);
- spread of ethnic business, the role of ethnic/ religious associations and the demand for political rights (1986 onwards).

During the *first phase*, predominantly Turkish businessmen in Istanbul acted as intermediaries for 'nominated recruitment'. Individual workers had personal invitation letters, which included the necessary guarantee of employment as well as financial support and lodging during the duration of the recruitment. The recruits were skilled workers and they went mostly to the shipyard docks of Hamburg, Bremen and Kiel (Abadan-Unat 1976: 13). This phase ended with the guarante of free entry to Germany granted by the new constitution of 1961. Furthermore, German trade unions, anxious to prevent the competition of foreign cheap labour, urged the government to close down private recruitment agencies.

Table 9.3: *Turkish citizens living in Europe, April 1993*

	Total citizens	Total workers
Germany	1,854,945	762,775
Netherlands	248,656	83,400
France	240,000	99,000
Austria	150,000	55,749
Belgium	84,935	24,000
Denmark	37,000	12,773
UK	65,000	30,000
Norway	10,000	1,500
Sweden	50,000	10,000
Switzerland	73,024	36,815
Total	2,536,783	1,116,012

Source: Turkish Labour and Social Security Ministry (1993), 3T

These changes opened the path for a larger migratory wave in *the second phase*. The explosion of Turkish out-migration coincided also with the adoption of Turkey's first five-year development plan (1962–67). The architects of this first plan argued that, 'the export of excess, unskilled labor to western Europe represents one of the possibilities for alleviating unemployment' (Abadan-Unat 1976: 14). These planners assumed that the export of unskilled workers might facilitate the acquisition of new skills and thus contribute to the industrialization of the country. This perception and the growing needs of the West German labour market, particularly after the erection of the Berlin wall, led to a massive increase in emigration. While in 1960 only 2700 workers had left Turkey, the number rose to 27,500 in 1963 and reached 615,827 in 1973 (Abadan-Unat 1976: 7, Table 1).

During the second phase, the export of the labour force depended on the initiatives of the respective governments. Governmental bureaucracies on both sides assured the supply. This significant change occurred through the signature of a series of bilateral agreements. In 1961 Turkey signed its first bilateral agreement with West Germany, in 1964 with Austria, Belgium and the Netherlands, in 1965 with France, and in 1967 with Sweden. On the basis of these

Table 9.4: *Turkish citizens living in West Germany according to age and sex, 1991*

Age groups	Women	Men	Total
0–5	84,150	94,235	178,385
6–10	65,957	75,458	141,415
11–15	75,092	93,573	168,665
16–20	98,628	117,639	216,267
21–25	102,479	111,158	213,637
26–30	84,498	126,785	211,283
31–35	46,761	63,114	109,875
36–40	50,953	45,338	96,291
41–45	63,537	48,490	112,027
46–50	53,962	75,429	129,391
51–55	36,828	73,670	110,498
56–60	18,842	40,579	59,421
61–65	8,329	13,732	22,061
66 and over	4,945	5,425	10,370
Total	794,961	984,679	1,779,640

Source: *Bundes Statistik*, Amt, 31 December 1991.

agreements recruitment became a monopoly to be exercised only by the Turkish Employment Service and its counterparts in the host countries. All agreements contained terms and procedures for final selection of migrants, including a rigorous health examination, transportation costs and provisions for workers who desired or were compelled to return before their contracts expired. The major idea anchored in these agreements was the temporary nature of the employment expressed by the principle of 'rotation'. It was assumed that workers would go abroad for a single year and return to the home country. This article embedded in almost all work contracts was practically never implemented.

Although workers lived in male dormitories and had to endure separation from their families, they opted for a prolonged stay to accomplish their first priority: saving money in order to create a business for themselves upon their return. Thus the principle of rotation was not respected, both employers and workers opting for a prolongation of their stay.

The recession of 1966/7 did not provoke a massive return to the home country. During the *third phase* the host countries realized that foreign manpower was becoming 'permanent'. From this year on recession began, resulting in large-scale unemployment. Finally, from 1973, against the background of the oil crisis, official labour recruitment in all western European countries came to an abrupt stop. As a consequence, the host countries began to explore new policies for the implementation of 'full integration' of the non-returning, legally-admitted, foreign workers. A new influx of illegal workers was prevented by according the legitimation of illegal workers a priority. This was undertaken by offering amnesties and issuing official permits to 'pseudo tourists' if they first agreed to return to their home countries to wait for the granting of the necessary residence permit. Such amnesties were granted in Belgium (1966, 1974), Hessen and the Palatinate (1972), France (1973) and Holland (1978) (Hale 1978: 43).

The *fourth phase* is characterized by large-scale family reunification. West Germany's new child allowance policy made a distinction between the amount to be paid for children left behind and those living with their parents. This modification induced a very large increase in the number of dependent family members. Between 1974 and 1980 the number of Turkish children under the age of 16 living in West Germany increased by 129.8 per cent. In 1980, 40 per cent of the Turkish migrant population of West Germany, Switzerland, Sweden and Norway were under eighteen years of age (Abadan-Unat 1993: 314). These demographic changes were aggravated by ignorance of the host country's language, hardships in adapting to a different society and the difficulties of benefiting from an educational system full of complicated rules. Thus the prevailing pattern became reinforced segregation and the option of self-isolation within a network of relatives and friends. In West Germany three different models for the education of foreign workers' children added to this confusion. Some *Länder* segregated them in separate classes (the Bavarian model), Berlin opted for the total integration model in which the mother tongue was not taught, while Nordrhein-Westfalen chose a synthesis of both (Rist 1978: 201–2). Additional conflicts were aroused on the subject of Turkish teachers. Teachers appointed by the Turkish National Education Ministry offered classes in history and Turkish on a voluntary basis, but were unable to reach all the children in the area. Turkish teachers employed by the German, French and Dutch authorities helped children acquire the national language, though often not very well. These policies led to the syndrome of 'bilingual illiteracy', sharply criticized and partly modified in recent years.

The *fifth phase* is characterized by extensive associational activities, the introduction of visa requirements and increased requests for asylum. In the 1960s

Turkish workers' associations served as surrogate trade unions and supportive networks among Turks. Gradually these associations became involved in ideological controversies. Leftist and fanatically rightist, as well as religious, associations started recruiting members in large cities and became satellites of extremist political parties in the home country. Thus by 1973 the fascist-leaning National Action Party had established six sections in West Germany and had commandos called the Grey Wolves. These sections were banned in 1976. Similarly ultra-conservative religious associations not only supported the National Salvation Party at home, but also established private schools and Koran courses abroad in which ideological indoctrination was carried out (Abadan-Unat 1979: 23).

Accompanying these informal political activities, the ban on further recruitment in Europe led to an enormous increase in 'political refugees' requesting asylum. The hostility of German public opinion to the apparently uncontrollable rise of asylum seekers led to new policies. From 1980 on, applicants were compelled to take up residence in camps and were ineligible for work permits and social security entitlements. These new rules reduced requests for asylum in the 1980s, but due to the ongoing secessionist armed uprising in Turkey's south-east regions, a new increase was recorded in the 1990s. Relevant figures show 1548 asylum seekers in 1983, 14,873 in 1988 and 28,327 in 1992 (Turkish Ministry of Labour 1993: 13–14). During this phase, which began in West Germany, all European countries introduced a visa requirement for Turks. This measure reduced visiting between migrants and their families, and contributed to a growing tension between the host country and its immigrant workers. This phase was also marked by growing xenophobia due, in part, to rising unemployment. Latent anti-Semitism was transformed into open 'anti-Turkism'. The widely publicized former Jewish 'jokes' about Turks contained imagery ranging from ridicule to destruction: Turks were shown as ludicrously different in their food tastes, dress, names and even in their ability to develop survival techniques (Toelken 1985: 155). An openly racist climate of opinion received an additional boost through nationalistic manifestos like the Heidelberg Declaration signed by sixteen West German university professors, calling for a quick evacuation of all migrant workers in the interests of preserving the 'Christian Occidental values of Europe' (*Die Zeit*, 26 October 1982: 61).

The *sixth* and current phase is marked by the determination of a large number of workers to settle down in Europe, to acquire property and to establish businesses. At present more than 78,000 Turks living in West Germany are over the age of 55 and about 45,000 have bought houses or condominiums. Another 33,000 Turks have started private enterprises, securing an average of 125,000 new jobs. Their investment was about DM 7.8 billion in 1992 with a yearly turnover of about DM 28 billion. These enterprises are in close cooperation with the home country, 76 per cent dealing with imports from Turkey (Sen 1987: 19–20). Thus one may say that with the widening of ethnic communities and ethnic economic enterprises the presence of Turks creates new demands such as the granting of political rights, the extension of voting rights at local elections and the possibility of holding dual citizenship. All these new demands indicate that the politics of ethnicity has gained relevance. Parallel to these tendencies, physical violence and blatant racist attacks have also increased in importance and volume. The strong will to reside in Europe, where Turks have created highly visible centres of spatial concentration, has also contributed to a loss of sympathy with Turks. Open 'welfare chauvinism' in Europe has manifested itself particularly aggressively in western Germany. In 1992 extremist right-wing groups and individuals committed 2285 acts of violence, of which 90 per cent were of a xenophobic nature. During the same year seventeen persons (of whom seven were foreigners) became the fatal victims of such violence. In Mölln, Solingen, nine Turkish citizens fell victim to planned arson (Sen 1994: 3).

The sixth phase also reveals that the majority of Turkish workers are still struggling to consolidate their legal status. Although in 1991, 89.7 per cent of the officially employed 566,994 Turkish workers were in possession of a work permit, they were still deprived of the legal security provisions envisaged in the EU–Turkey Association Agreement. In this respect Turkish female workers are particularly affected. In the case of a death or divorce of a spouse, these women are unable to obtain a residence permit — which is normally granted only to the head of the family — and are thus obliged to leave Germany. Another extremely important issue for Turkish families is the educational provision for the second and third generations. Although an increasing number of Turkish students are now graduating from the Gymnasium (junior college) — 21,762 in 1990, 22,469 in 1991 — the great majority still go no further than the Hauptschule (Martin 1991: 78–9; Wilpert 1988).

There is also a significant increase at the level of higher education. In 1975 there were 4208 Turkish university students, but by 1990 this figure had increased to 12,816. However, the second and third generations, in spite of their excellent command of the language, do not believe they have equality of opportunity. Quite a number of them contemplate returning to Turkey in order to be able to use their occupational skills. Similar trends can be observed among the 16,000 Turkish university students in the Netherlands, France, Belgium, Denmark and Great Britain.

The impact of migration in Turkey

A major impact of migration has flowed from remittance incomes, which have helped bridge the gap in the balance of trade and provided precious foreign exchange. While in 1964 remittances were $45 million, they were more than $2 billion in 1980. During the 1960s and 1970s Turkish policy makers used remittances to maintain an overvalued exchange rate, encouraging imports but not foreign investment. In the 1980s Turkish policy changed. Remittances remained at peak annual levels of $2 billion partly because the Turkish government encouraged them with foreign currency accounts paying premium interest rates. Remittances increased income inequality in particular regions, while the benefits went predominantly to capital and finance centres like Istanbul and Izmir. Over the years special credit allocations were also used by the government to encourage investment. A special bilateral agreement signed between Turkey and West Germany in 1972 attempted to link credit allocation to definite return plans. However, this scheme did not work.

While the credit schemes yielded little, 'participatory investment projects' fared better. First launched in 1962 by the Ministry of Village Affairs, the Village Development Cooperatives (VDCs) were meant to generate employment and use migrants' savings productively. The VDCs also helped to establish priority ranking for their members to fill job vacancies abroad.

By 1966, there were 382 VDCs and in 1967 their number rose to 1349. After 1973, initiatives to establish new cooperatives came totally to an end. In retrospect the disguised purpose of the VDC programme (i.e filling job vacancies abroad) explains their failure. The cooperatives could have been of great benefit had they been properly conceived, developed and controlled.

A second major instrument for channelling the savings of Turkish workers towards employment generating investments was the Turkish Workers Companies (TWCs). The essential features of these are the following:

- TWCs are economic self-help initiatives of Turkish migrants who invest their savings in the form of shares to establish a firm in Turkey.
- The number of founding members is usually small; they are strongly dependent on other participants and local leaders.
- In their charters, TWCs exclude takeovers by large-scale investors.
- TWCs are primarily regionally oriented.
- On average they were intended to create about a hundred jobs, which were meant to facilitate the reintegration of returnees.
- TWCs were supported by governmental policies such as exemptions for imported machinery.

In 1982 there were about a hundred TWCs in the production stage, with a total employment of 10,972. Encouragement of foreign capital investment resulted in an increasing weakening and phasing out of TWCs after the 1980s. These companies only had a marginal impact on Turkish employment because of a high proportion of failures, the small scale of the TWCs, their vulnerability in competition and their irrelevance to Turkey's development priorities. TWCs suffered from inadequate management at the top, high debt ratios and shortages of working capital. Furthermore, one of the major causes of failure has been the strong motivation to choose sites less on the basis of rentability, adequate communication networks and transport facilities, and more for what could be defined as 'local patriotism'. Despite all their shortcomings, TWCs appear to be the most imaginative device for channelling savings into productive investment. The number of TWCs and the capital transferred are clearly admirable. By 1982, 104,773 shareholders living and working abroad had invested approximately $1.8 million to create 20,753 jobs. In addition to channelling savings into particular forms of investment, migrants also used savings for consumption and housing or land acquisition. Many returned migrants built houses for themselves and included an apartment or two to earn rental income.

A major effect of labour migration has been on the service sector. Relatively few migrants were employed in services before their departure (only 12 per cent by one estimate). However, remittances increased the size of the service sector for demand reasons. Migrants expanded the demand for transport, banking and communication services. Upon their return the majority used their savings to establish grocery stores, kiosks or restaurants. Turkish workers abroad stimulated business and tourist travel between EU countries and Turkey, which further enlarged the Turkish service economy.

What was the impact of migration on social mobility? Among the Turkish migrant population in host countries there has been some occupational mobility, specifically from agricultural occupations to industrial or tertiary occupations. However, most semi-skilled workers among the Turks in Europe did not experience upward mobility; Turkey actually lost a considerable amount of skilled labour and this loss has been accentuated by a parallel loss of 'brain drain' migrants. For example, a survey of the Turkish State Planning Organization from 1971 indicated that 47 per cent of the migrants had held skilled positions before their departure (Paine 1974: 80–2). There has also been noticeable downward mobility because of the large number of primary school teachers, accountants and the like who have opted for higher wages and a different lifestyle by leaving their white-collar jobs and becoming industrial workers. Once returned, particularly in the rural areas, despite their relatively passive attitude to work and their refusal to re-enter industrial work in Turkey, the majority of returnees accomplished a move upward on the social status scale. As *Alamanyali* (people from Germany, irrespective of the host country in which they actually lived), they represent a new rural and small town stratum.

How did migration effect sex roles and the position of women abroad and at home? Europe has registered an unexpectedly high number of female industrial workers. In West Germany alone, the number of Turkish female workers rose from 173 in 1960, to 177,143 in 1981 and 196,595 in 1992. This exodus of Turkish women both in terms of changing their place of residence and lifestyle produced fundamental changes. This had implications for the sharing of household tasks, decision taking and consumption patterns. It also reinforced a tendency towards spatial concentration. The consequent strong social control combined with increasing religious indoctrination also created restrictive patterns. Thus, out-migration produced a move to a more personal freedom in an economic sense, while socially speaking the female migrants were constrained to follow conservative community rules in terms of family life and the education of children. These contradictory tendencies

produced a substantial amount of marital strain and conflict (Abadan-Unat 1984: 145–6). Major generational differences are observable: first-generation women's aspirations were linked primarily to family goals – to promote their future social positions and the security of the family. For the second generation a set of work-related values exercised an important role. Nevertheless, for many young Turkish women marriage still remains the most important goal.

What about return projects? The dream to return has gradually given way to the postponement of return to a far, indefinite future or the abandonment of the idea of repatriation. In 1991, 83 per cent of the Turks living in West Germany indicated their unwillingness to return. The average number of definite returns at present ranges from 30,000 to 40,000 yearly. The major reasons for this unwillingness lie in a number of problems. The majority of first-generation migrants were unable to find satisfactory employment while they were still active, while the individual investment schemes undertaken did not yield the expected returns because of the way in which Turkey was developing its economic policies. The TWCs, about which people were so hopeful, practically disappeared from the scene after 1980. Also, the lack of reintegration measures affected the second generation, while the difficulties in establishing an equivalence scheme for school diplomas created major difficulties for the parents. Finally, though returnees from rural areas are unwilling to settle down in villages, they also face discrimination due to their relative wealth from their peers and neighbours in the cities (Abadan-Unat 1988: 56).

European countries such as the Netherlands and Denmark, where migrant workers are granted wider civic rights, such as the right to vote in local elections, display a more harmonious pattern of integration. However, in those countries that openly admit to being 'multicultural societies' and that recognize foreign workers as 'ethnic minorities', the one-sided interpretation of culture/religion creates new isolating islands and prevents the adjustment of the second and third generation. To conclude, Turks in Europe have opted to stay. They are confident that Turkey will one day join the EU. Meanwhile, their reception depends almost exclusively on the host societies' development of more democratic and flexible policies for their harmonious integration.

References

Abadan-Unat, N. (1976) *Turkish Workers in Europe, 1960–1975: A Socio-Economic Reappraisal*, Leiden: E. J. Brill

(1979) 'Die politischen Auswirkungen der türkischen Migration im In- und Ausland', *Orient*, 1, 17–33

(1984) 'International Labour Migration and its Effect upon Women's Occupational and Family Roles: A Turkish View', in Unesco, *Women on the Move*, Paris: Unesco, 133–59

(1993) 'Turkey: Late Entrant into Europe's Work Force', D. Kubat (ed.) *The Politics of Migration Policies*, New York: The Center for Migration Studies, 307–36

Hale, W. M. (1978) 'Country Case Study: The Republic of Turkey', University of Durham, International Migration Project, mimeograph

Martin, P. L. (1991) *The Unfinished Story: Turkish Labour Migration to Western Europe*, Geneva: ILO

Paine, S. (1974) *Exporting Workers – The Turkish Case*, Cambridge: Cambridge University Press

Rist, D. (1978) *Guestworkers in Germany: The Prospects for Pluralism*, New York: Praeger

Sen, F. (1987) *Turks in the FRG, Achievements, Problems, Expectations*, Geneva: ILO

(1994) *Auslaenderfeindlichkeit in Deutschland und die Auswirkungen auf die türkische Minderheit*, Turkish/German Psychiatry Congress, 16–22 April, Antalya

Toelken, B. (1985) '"Türken rein und Türken raus": Images of fear and agression in German Gastarbeiterwitze', in I. Basgoz and N. Furniss (eds) *Turkish Workers in Europe*, Bloomington: Indiana University Turkish Studies, 151–64

Turkish Labour and Social Security Ministry (1993) *1992 Report*, Ankara, 3T

Wilpert, C. (1988) *Entering the Working World: Following the Descendants of Europe's Immigrant Labour Force*, Aldershot: Gower Publishers

FORMER YUGOSLAVIA: LONG WAVES OF INTERNATIONAL MIGRATION

CARL-ULRIK SCHIERUP

The territory of former Yugoslavia has a history of more than a century of international migration. During the 1960s and 1970s Yugoslavia was one of the most important sending societies of the international migratory system upon which industrial development in north-western and central Europe depended. Today, forced migration from the region represents one of the world's most pressing problems of displaced populations.

Here, from a historical and contemporary perspective, I examine three long waves of international migration from the region. The subjects and periods covered are:

- international migration from the Yugoslavian region before the Second World War;
- labour migration from socialist Yugoslavia between 1945 and 1990; and
- the forced population displacements following ethno-national clashes in the post-cold war era and the break out of civil war in 1991.

Pre-Second World War migration

The large-scale transnational emigration which involved most countries of Europe throughout the nineteenth century also affected the territory of former Yugoslavia. Parallel to this, parts of the region (particularly Slovenia, but even to some degree Croatia) were integrated into the international migratory system, which developed in Europe: from the agrarian south and east to the rapidly industrializing regions of north, west and central Europe.

Migration from the Yugoslav lands, which (except for what is now central Serbia) were until 1914 under the rule of the Austro-Hungarian empire in the north and the Ottoman empire in the south, started generally (except for Dalmatia) later than in other parts of the European Mediterranean. This reflected the relatively late integration of the region into the money-commodity relations of the European and world economy. A continued strong presence of a rural subsistence economy made the peasantry less vulnerable to the market and to proletarianization. However, after the great European agricultural crisis during the 1890s, which hit the Balkan peasantry hard, and the first decade of the twentieth century, emigration grew into a mass exodus. In the Austro-Hungarian north, as in certain parts of the Ottoman south, emigration served as a security valve for rural poverty. Quantitative data from the period are scant. But according to various estimates between 300,000 and 500,000 left Croatia Slovenia alone (the greater part of today's republic of Croatia), which is estimated to represent between an eight and a fifth of the total population.

During the inter-war period, when the first Yugoslavian state was formed, the motivation for emigration, in what remained an economically backward and crisis-ridden periphery in Europe, was even greater than it had been in 1914, when the escalating transoceanic movement of labour was interrupted by the war. Emigration continued after the First World War, but the pre-war mass emigration to the USA was never repeated once new immigration laws came into force during the early 1920s. When Australia and Canada introduced similarly restrictive immigration policies, the main destinations for overseas migration from Yugoslavia became Brazil, Argentina and, to some degree, Canada. At the same time migration to western and central Europe also increased. Already from the beginning of the 1920s Yugoslav migrants had started to go to France, Belgium and Holland, where they mainly worked as miners. During the 1930s most migrants went to Germany, where the labour market was expanding because of the development of an armament economy.

During the period of most intensive emigration – between 1930 and 1938 – total emigration (from the whole of the Yugoslavian region) included 153,000 persons, while the total number of returnees was 96,000. Hence, inter-war emigration (in gross figures) was as a whole insignificant compared with the mass emigration of before 1914. It was, particularly, return migration which had an impact on the sending country. Migrants who returned home from overseas (the USA, Australia, New Zealand, South Africa or South America) used their, often considerable, savings

Table 9.5: *Changes in the number of migrants in Europe and from Yugoslavia in Europe, 1973–78 (end of year)*

	Total of migrants from European receiving countries (millions)			Migrants from Yugoslavia ('000s)		
	1973	1978	Difference 1978/73	1973	1978	Difference 1978/73
Workers	8.2	6.5	−1.7	860	695	−165
Supported	5.0	6.2	+1.2	250	385	+135
In total	12.8	12.3	−0.5	1,110	1,090	−20

Source: Estimates of the Centre for Migration Studies, Zagreb on the basis of a variety of Yugoslav and western European sources.

to buy up land in the villages or to invest as merchant and usury capital. In this way international migration acted to increase class differentiation in an economically backward, predominantly agrarian Yugoslavia during the inter-war years.[1]

Quest for return

The end of the Second World War marked the entry into a period of rapid socio-economic change, associated with the transformation of Yugoslavia into an industrial society. The second (socialist) Yugoslavia inherited a number of economic and social problems from the old society. Among these were high under- and unemployment and widespread poverty. Though the underemployed and poor in the countryside appeared to present a social, economic and political problem, they were to become the most important resource for economic development. The poor and semi-proletarianized peasant masses made up a huge pool of cheap labour, making it possible to undertake an initial industrial reconstruction and expansion in relative isolation from the world market. The socialist planners concentrated on the development of a self-sustained economic structure, thus attempting to avoid the kind of one-sided economic dependency on European great powers (France, Britain, Italy, Germany) which marked every aspect of life in the old Yugoslavia.

This labour-intensive industrialization process, which started immediately after the Second World War, triggered large scale intra- and interregional migration from agricultural towards urban/industrial areas.

During the 1960s a parallel process of international labour migration developed. It took the form of intra-industrial movements of labour between Yugoslav industrial centres and capitalist metropolises, as well

as a continued transfer of labour from Yugoslav agriculture towards the industrial centres of central and western Europe. In one decade (1964–73) the number of Yugoslav citizens in European and overseas countries had grown from a few thousand to almost 1.5 million. In 1973 one in ten migrant workers in western Europe was a Yugoslav. They belonged to many different population groups – Croats, Serbs, Macedonians, Albanians, Romanians, Turks, Slovenians and others. Germany, Austria, Sweden and France were the main receiving countries. But a considerable transoceanic migration also occurred. This came mainly from the local communities and regions from which the population had already started to emigrate before the Second World War.

During the first twenty years of its existence (1945–64) socialist Yugoslavia had – like other socialist countries in the Balkans, eastern Europe and the Soviet Union – been a closed country. The political decision to open up the borders of the Yugoslavian federation to emigration was associated with the launching of a radically liberal economic reform in 1965. This exposed the country to tight integration into the international division of labour on market economic terms. Internally market criteria were to determine the economic success and survival of individual enterprises and the prosperity of their employees would depend on their productivity.

It was envisaged that the reforms would cause a marked increase in unemployment (through the closure of enterprises and laying off of redundant workers) together with increased underemployment in the rural areas. Here, private farmers were exposed to increased structural pressure as a result of the sudden introduction of a free market.

Hence, international labour migration was seen as a social safety valve for increased structurally determined un- and underemployment. At the same time it was expected that emigration would be a short and generally positive interlude. A structurally transformed modern economy would rapidly overcome recession and prove capable of absorbing returning labour migrants as well as new generations entering the labour market. The bulk of the migrants would be unemployed manual workers and poor and underemployed petty farmers. Substantial migrant remittances in foreign hard currency would boost the economy of the migrants' regions of origin and the federation's economy as a whole.

None of these expectations proved to be valid. Emigration was initially to take off in metropolitan regions and came to involve an unexpectedly high number of skilled workers and highly educated persons. This gave international migration the character of a skill drain and a brain drain process, which was costly for the sending country. Some enterprises and regions were virtually emptied of important categories of their skilled labour force.

Other important migratory sites were the fertile agricultural areas from which many productive and comparatively well-off farmers went to work abroad. Migrants' remittances were predominantly put into unproductive activities and conspicuous consumption. This did not generate economic development, but rather tended to deepen structurally conditioned underdevelopment.

All this induced, from the beginning of the 1970s, Yugoslavian federal policy-making bodies to formulate a complex policy for organized return migration. This policy was to be implented in cooperation with the OECD and other international agencies with the intention of turning international migration into a 'factor of development'. It should, through systematic cooperation between central and local agencies in sending and receiving countries, stimulate training, organized return and productive reintegration in the country of origin of skilled workers. It should turn returning migrants' remittances into an economic booster through organized productive investment in industrial enterprises, in cooperative ventures, in local infrastructure, in modern small business and in a well-planned modernization of agriculture.

Yugoslavia was the sending country which, from the beginning of the 1970s, most extensively endeavoured to cooperate with the international agencies in order to make planned return and reintegration of migrant workers an element in 'a true partnership' between receiving and sending countries. This experiment, which – after the breakout of the 'oil crisis' and

the halt of immigration in various western European countries – was conceived as one important contribution to a 'more just international order', terminated, however, without any convincing measure of success.

The predominant integration policies of the receiving countries continued to favour a 'negative selection' of returnees. Skilled and highly educated people were generally induced to assimilate while various forms of pressure to speed up repatriation were mainly directed towards unskilled and disabled migrant workers.

In Yugoslavia, the liberal economic reforms of the 1960s did not, at the same time, lead to any leap ahead. They led, rather, to a disarticulation of the economy and contributed to a fragmentation of the federal political elite. This was, from the mid-1970s, followed by a major conservative backlash, which put any functioning market relationships out of operation. The political stage was to be dominated by localized political bureaucracies which build their power bases on informal relationships and traditionalist patron–client relationships focusing on ethnicity, kinship and locality. Yugoslavian research indicates a lack of motivation among local bureaucratic power elites to incorporate returning migrant workers into working life. The jobs of those already employed being defended by closed corporate working collectives and the widespread practice of recruiting new labour through networks of kinship, ethnicity and locality acted in the same direction. Criteria of professional qualification tended to be consistently overruled by criteria pertaining to primordial relationships. Similarly the development of any flexible arrangements for the reintegration of returnees in modern small business was blocked by excessive red tape and the obstruction of informal groups. Lack of reforms in agriculture inhibited the organized and productive reintegration of migrant farmers.

In this situation any organized policy for large-scale return and the productive reintegration of returning migrant workers soon came to a halt. Instead, a growing pressure for emigration built up within all parts of the federation. Given the conditions prevailing in Europe's main industrial countries, from the mid-1970s, emigration from former Yugoslavia took on mainly two forms. One was a continuous brain drain contributing substantually to an ongoing economic degradation of the Yugoslavian federation and its individual parts. The other was the constant circulation of a growing number of clandestine and seasonal migrants, the 'new helots' of western Europe's most marginal occupational ghettoes.[2]

Refugees, civil war and the post-cold war order

The present civil war in former Yugoslavia has caused the most extensive problem of refugees and displaced persons that Europe has experienced since the immediate aftermath of the Second World War. Of more than 4 million refugees, between 500,000 and 600,000 are currently residing in different European countries outside the region of former Yugoslavia, with Germany, Switzerland and Sweden (according to the UNHCR) as the main receiving countries. The rest represent 'internal refugees', of whom more than 2 million are to be counted within Bosnia and Herzegovina alone, about 700,000 in Croatia and as many on the territory of the rump of Yugoslavia (Serbia–Montenegro).

In a situation in which western Europe is itself marked by a deep crisis of political-economic restructuring, by social unrest and increasing inhospitality towards 'strangers', former Yugoslavia has become the most important testing ground for new models of 'containment' and 'internalization' marking, in general, the refugee regimes of the post-cold war global order. Emanating conceptions of 'temporary protection' in a number of European refugee-receiving countries have developed in conjunction with the Yugoslavian crisis and in particular with the challenges represented by the war in Bosnia and Herzegovina. The same is true for organized strategies to establish refugee centres in proxy areas (for Bosnian Muslims in Croatia, for example) or so-called 'safe havens' in the midst of the zones of armed struggle.

This new European refugee problem has developed in conjunction with so-called 'ethnic cleansing' in the service of current Serbian, Croatian, Muslim and Albanian ethno-nationalist policies on the Balkans. Ethnic cleansing is defined (by the United Nations) as the systematic elimination by the ethnic group exercising control over a given territory of members of other groups. In line with a series of other political upheavals after the Second World War giving rise to forced migrations, ethnic cleansing should be understood against the background of a specific combination of 'internal' and 'external' political-economic causes. Ethnic cleansing, brought about through alternating combinations of administrative, police and military violence, started to develop in former Yugoslavia during the 1980s, culminating during the early 1990s. The advent of the 1980s was marked by incapacitating debt traps and international super-austerity measures. This was, in Yugoslavia, to shape a situation of permanent economic, political and social crisis in which no penetrating domestic reforms or transformation of a staggering socialist system of government had a chance to solidify.

The long-term results were social disintegration, political chaos, maximalist ethno-nationalist movements and internal war. After 1991 armed violence itself came to act as an autonomous factor generating further economic disintegration, arid poverty and new sources of conflict. We experience a situation in which politically and economically motivated migration become increasingly difficult to distinguish. A growing number of people flee, not only because of outright ethnic cleansing, but because of politically induced mass impoverishment and existential insecurity. The contorted conditions of a permanent complex emergency have ensued which demand a profound scrutiny of the efforts, so far, to shape a new fair world order after the termination of the cold war.[3]

Notes

1   A more comprehensive account of the background to international migration from Yugoslavia between the two world wars is found in Schierup (1990: 23–54).
2   Schierup (1990) provides an exhaustive analysis of a number of aspects of international labour migration and migration policy with respect to socialist Yugoslavia.
3   A general background discussion on ethnic cleansing, economic and political development, and the current refugee problems in former Yugoslavia is given by Schierup (1994).

References

Schierup, Carl-Ulrik (1990) *Migration, Socialism and the International Division of Labour: The Case of Yugoslavia*, Aldershot: Avebury
    (1994) 'Eurobalkanism: Ethnic Cleansing and the Post Cold War Order', *Journal of Refugee Studies*

LABOUR MIGRATION TO FRANCE

PHILIP E. OGDEN

In a number of respects, France's experience of migration and demographic change over the last century has been distinctive. Never a country of mass emigration on the scale of its European neighbours in the nineteenth century, France was already a major importer of labour before the First World War. During the twentieth century, and particularly since 1945, France has continued to rely on migrant labour to fill many gaps in the labour force in both the public and private sectors. Migration has been central to economic growth. In addition, migration has taken place against a background of an unusual demographic evolution, with a generally slow population growth heightening political and public awareness of the perceived 'population problem'. While labour migration has by no means been fully under governmental control, state policy has nevertheless been crucial to determining the arrival of labour migrants and the way in which their integration has taken place. The 1980s and 1990s have been characterized by much concern about the immigration issue, with vigorous and controversial discussion not only about the control of migration but also about its cultural consequences and the relationship between nationality and citizenship. This contribution begins by looking at the historical background to immigration and then traces a number of themes of the post-war years.

Migration and recent French history

It is, indeed, important to emphasize that migration did not begin in 1945. While other European countries were certainly affected by migration movements in a variety of ways, France was distinctive in having a large migrant labour force much earlier than her neighbours. Tribalat (1991) has noted the long-term effects, estimating that of the current population resident in France some 14 million are of foreign nationality or have foreign ancestry no more than two generations back. Historians such as Noiriel (1986, 1988) and Lequin (1988) have begun to reconstruct this rather neglected aspect of French history, prompted by the intense recent political concern surrounding immigration, a concern which Schor

(1985) has noted has itself very strong historical roots. Figure 9.1 indicates that the numbers of foreign nationals living in France stood at over one million by 1881. Despite the beginnings of mass flows of migrants from the French countryside as peasant agriculture began its long decline, there was insufficient labour to meet the needs of a growing economy. France was not a major contributor to the great nineteenth century transatlantic emigrations (Ogden 1989). Rather, there had long been a tradition of artisan migration to Paris and other cities (on the Jews, for example, see Green 1985) and migrants from neighbouring European countries were increasingly being recruited for mining and manufacturing and also for certain parts of the agricultural system (especially seasonal labour in the south). In the years before the First World War this migration took on a new urgency, not least in response to a persistent decline in the birth rate. As Charles Gide, a prolific writer on population questions in the years before and after 1914, said 'when a people is no longer able – or willing – to produce its own offspring, its only chance of survival rests in adoption' (quoted in Pénin 1986: 148). Thus, Noiriel (1984) has traced the activities of the *Comité des Forges de l'Est*, for example, which from 1905 recruited labour for the mines and steel works of Longwy in northern France directly from Italy and later from Poland. Nationally, the number of Italians rose from 292,000 in 1896 to 419,000 in 1911. Cross (1983: 9–10) in his study of inter-war migration has suggested that as early as the 1880s immigration had created a dual labour market: 'a secondary sector dominated by foreign workers in such trades as construction, seasonal agriculture and in a variety of relatively arduous jobs; the primary sector dominated by French workers in more agreeable and better-paid occupations.'

These trends intensified in the inter-war years, the number of foreigners increasing to more than 2.7 million by 1931, accounting for over 6 per cent of the total population. There was a continuing shift in the pattern of recruitment from countries such as Germany, Belgium and Switzerland to Italy, Spain and

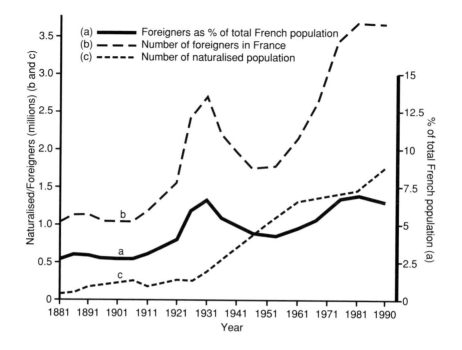

Figure 9.1: Evolution of foreign nationals in France, and as a proportion of the total population, 1881–1990

Poland. It was also at this time that the first migrants arrived from North Africa: 'a sub-proletariat among the foreign workers, hired in temporary jobs at the lowest levels of the occupational ladder' (Cross 1983: 216). State intervention began in earnest in the inter-war years, not least in response to continuing concern over the slow growth of the population (Spengler 1979). France became dependent on migrants in several economic sectors and as Cross (1983: 16) again has observed, foreign labour 'became a radically distinctive class in France.

Not merely were immigrants predominantly prop-ertyless and unskilled, but they were 'non-citizens', at least for the most part (some 517,000 were naturalized French by 1936). Nevertheless, economic recession in the 1930s took its toll, with a decline in the resident foreign population to 2.2 million by 1936. Repatri-ation was encouraged to an extent, entry restrictions were imposed and maximum quotas put on certain sectors of industry. Yet the total remained high, reflecting the by now structural character of immi-gration. As Schor (1985: 713) has indicated, oppo-sition to immigration also came to the fore during economic recession: 'the seriousness and duration of

the economic crisis, the multiplication of political crises, the arrival . . . of refugees . . . the fear of war . . . the apparent powerlessness of the public authorities . . . all these facts gave rise . . . to a growing xenophobia.'

Labour migration since 1945
These themes of a growing, if cyclical, dependence on immigration, an increasing involvement of the state and cycles of intense political concern about the immigration question have marked much of the post-war years too. Figure 9.1 illustrates the growth in the total foreign population and its relationship to the French population as a whole, while Figure 9.2 shows the evolution of selected nationalities since the war. Figure 9.3 demonstrates the cyclical pattern of arrivals of foreign workers between 1950 and 1990. The total foreign population increased from 1.7 million in 1946 to a peak of 3.7 million in 1982, with a slight fall to 3.6 million by the time of the most recent census in 1990. In addition, the numbers of those who had acquired French nationality increased from 853,000 in 1946 to 1.8 million by 1990.[1] Table 9.6 shows the origins of those resident in France at the later date.

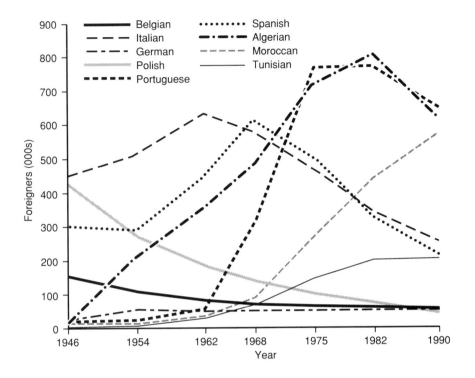

Figure 9.2: Evolution of the foreign population in France by nationality, 1946–90

These crude figures disguise a number of shifts both in the geographical origins of migrants, in their social and economic structure and in the attitude of successive governments to recruitment and control. Several fairly discrete phases mark the post-war years.

From 1945 to 1955: post-war reconstruction

Immediately after the war, immigration was identified by policy makers as vital to restore economic growth in the context of an assumed continuation of slow population growth. Objectives concerning migration became an integral part of successive National Plans (Weil 1991). Part of the aim was always to encourage permanent settlement of workers and families – 'to turn foreigners into French men and women' – in order to strengthen demographic structures.

Migration was to be selective on the basis of the supposed ease of assimilation: the Italians were

identified as the most appropriate candidates on the grounds of their cultural similarity and longstanding presence in France. The demographer Alfred Sauvy and his colleagues drew up careful estimates of the numbers required: the first plan proposed the recruitment of 1–1.5 million workers. Of great significance was the setting up of the Ministry for Population and the National Immigration Office (ONI) in 1946. The latter was given theoretical monopoly of recruitment and the government set up arrangements for labour supply with a number of potential emigrant countries (Sauvy 1946; Verbunt 1985). In the event, the policy was less easy to implement than had been hoped. Migrants from Italy proved more difficult to attract since they were drawn more readily to opportunities in, for example, Switzerland, West Germany or the USA. In addition, some labour shortages were met from a very rapid surge in migration from the French

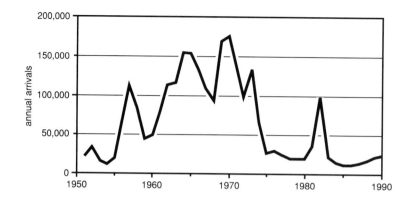

Figure 9.3: Annual arrivals of permanent foreign workers in France, 1950–90

countryside. By 1954, the foreign population had scarcely increased since the war and remained substantially lower than in the inter-war years. Despite governmental policy, there had been a small decline in the proportion of migrants from Europe and an increase in those from elsewhere, especially North Africa.

1955 to 1974: the apogee of labour recruitment

A second phase, from the late 1950s to the mid-1970s, saw the growth of large-scale immigration, the diversification of sources, the rise of worker rather than family migration and, above all, a degree of spontaneity which left much migration uncontrolled by government policy. The 1960s were a period of unprecedented economic growth. The recruitment of unskilled labour became central to the process of capital accumulation.

Thus, from 1954 to 1975 the total foreign population doubled and the role of foreign labour was at an all-time peak. Tapinos (1975) has suggested, however, that this period was itself marked by changing attitudes on the part of the government as well as by quite marked cyclical variations in immigrant arrivals. In the first decade, from the mid-1950s to the mid-1960s, it is fairly apparent that immigration 'policy' was determined almost entirely by French business and employers, that the ONI was ineffective and operated only retrospectively in 'regularizing' migrants after their arrival.

Thus, up to 80 per cent of migrants during the 1960s (Tapinos 1975: 66, 87) were given legal status

only *after* their arrival. This proved a crucial period for establishing the bases of the subsequent debate on immigration: 'just as immigration developed and as those countries which had been absent from traditional migrant flows played an increasing part, nothing was done to prepare public opinion for the integration of these new arrivals into French society. In addition, the deplorable conditions in which the entry and installation in France . . . took place had the effect of giving a very biased image to the supposed life-styles of this new population' (Tapinos 1975: 66). Thus, questions of secret and illegal entry, exploitative work at low salaries, work in the black market and life in the bidonville became the chief characteristics associated with immigrant labour.

From the mid-1960s to the mid-1970s, though, there was growing evidence of government concern, which itself reflected the emergent political significance of immigration. This was intimately concerned with a recognition that the variety of nationalities recruited was much greater than envisaged in the immediate post-war years, and increasingly drawn from outside Europe; and also that the assumption that much migration was of temporary labourers was not borne out by the facts. Free movement of labour was fully guaranteed within the European Common Market from 1968 and was seen by the government as a limiting factor in establishing full control on immigration. As far as Algeria was concerned, the free movement envisaged in the Evian agreements following independence gave way to attempts at migration control by the late 1960s. The growth in the numbers

Table 9.6: *Foreign population and naturalized population resident in France by nationality, 1990*

Nationality (present or former)	Foreigners	French by acquisition
Europe	**1,459,113**	**1,272,998**
Italian	252,759	
Spanish	216,047	1,020,468
Portuguese	649,714	
Yugoslav	52,453	30,537
Polish	47,127	160,399
Africa	**1,633,142**	**304,864**
Algerian	614,207	112,069
Moroccan	572,652	68,316
Tunisian	206,336	57,344
Other African	239,947	67,135
Asia	**424,668**	**154,059**
Cambodian, Vietnamese, Laotian	112,915	58,923
Turkish	197,712	14,773
Other	79,679	46,034
Total	**3,596,602**	**1,777,955**

Source: INSEE (1992: 16); Lebon (1992: 98)

from North Africa was, nevertheless, one of the defining features of this period. For all sources, the over-riding policy aim was to re-establish the control of the National Immigration Office (ONI) and to regulate if not reduce flows of migrants from diverse origins (Freeman 1989: 165–6).

This attempt to re-establish control should not, however, lead us to conclude that the state had been inactive in all spheres. While governments allowed unfettered spontaneous migration during the early 1960s, they were at the same time taking a very active role in organizing the migration of black workers of French nationality from the Caribbean and from Réunion (Condon and Ogden 1991). We should also mention here that the early 1960s saw the unprecedented immigration of large numbers of *pieds noirs*, French citizens forced to leave Algeria after independence, as well as a large number of *harkis*, Algerians who had sided with the French and who were eventually given full nationality rights. One of the side-effects of these flows was to boost the need for further immigrant labour for the construction trades, since the first group at least was relatively well off.

From 1974 to the present

A third phase began fully with the ban on the arrival of new foreign immigrant workers in 1974 consequent upon the oil crisis, economic depression and a general decline in demand for unskilled labour. The accompanying ban on family reunification was soon moderated (Blanchet 1985), but this general change in policy was of fundamental significance both to the character of immigration itself and to the ensuing political debate. Under the presidencies of both Giscard d'Estaing (1974–81) and of Mitterrand (1981–), immigration has remained a central political issue. The effect of the 1974 policy was soon felt. Between the censuses of 1975 and 1982, for example, the total foreign population grew but rather more slowly, and then stabilized up to 1990 (Table 9.7). There was a decline in the numbers of foreigners in employment. Above all, there was a rapid increase in family members, reinforcing the idea that temporary 'immigrants' were becoming permanent ethnic minorities. The continued rise in the proportion of foreigners from North Africa and Turkey was notable. For some nationalities the rise was indeed remarkable: a

Table 9.7: *Evolution of the foreign population in France by major national groups, 1975–90 (in '000s)*

	1975	1982	1990	Change 1982–90
All foreigners	3440	3680	3596	−84
Born in France	670	830	738	−92
Born outside France	2770	2850	2858	+8
Ratio of women to men	62	71	79	
EC foreigners	1870	1580	1312	−268
Born in France	340	310	213	−97
Born outside France	1530	1270	1099	−171
Ratio of women to men	82	84	88	
Non EC foreigners	1570	2100	2284	+184
Born in France	330	520	534	+14
Born outside France	1240	1580	1750	+170
Ratio of women to men	43	61	73	

Source: Labat (1991: 2); INSEE (1992: 28, 47)

60 per cent rise in the number of Moroccan nationals between 1975 and 1982, of whom 30 per cent were aged less than fifteen in 1982 (INSEE 1985: 56). Overall, the ratio of women to men in the foreign population grew from 62 per hundred in 1975 to 79 by 1990. As White (1986: 74) has maintained for north-west Europe as a whole, it was not so much that the oil crisis stopped migration (and controls on immigration in fact predated the crisis in some countries), but that it fundamentally altered its character. Lebon (1988) points to the decline of 43 per cent in the numbers of foreign workers in industry, between 1973 and 1985, 47 per cent in building and public works and a corresponding increase of 30 per cent in the service sector. Table 9.7 highlights the increasing feminization of the foreign labour force, especially in the non-European groups which had been so dominated by men in the 1960s. The results of the 1990 census reinforce the view that immigration both slowed and changed in character, and that migrant workers were being transformed into ethnic minorities as families formed and a second generation was born in France.

There have been a series of twists and turns in governmental policy since the mid-1970s (Costa-Lascoux 1989), although there has been little departure from the central decision to restrict arrivals of new workers, though its effectiveness has varied. Under Giscard d'Estaing, for example, a gradually harsher policy was adopted, including an unsuccessful attempt to encourage return migration through repatriation payments (Lebon 1979; Poinard 1979) and expulsion of certain categories of illegal aliens. In the case of Algeria, the two governments signed an agreement in September 1980 for the return of 35,000 Algerians per year: it was largely ineffective. One product of the Giscard years was, indeed, a substantial increase in the number of '*clandestins*' (Marie 1983) for which attempts at expulsion were a scant remedy. The persistence of illegal immigration draws attention to the disparity between state policy and the needs of employers for a flexible labour force. While neither president nor government suggested that the whole foreign population could in some sense be 'exported', and there was some attempt at dialogue over policy with immigrant groups, there was nevertheless a general equation of the problem of unemployment with immigration. This same equation has appeared at every election, not least the *Legislatives* in 1993. The various attempts at repatriation and expulsion, while numerically insignificant, did much to sour the political atmosphere. As Verbunt (1985: 146) indicates, this was a period when the distinction between 'good' and 'bad' immigrants, while not new, was at its most intense: 'demographic interests demanded the assimilation of some immigrants while social peace demanded the exclusion of others'. Europeans were the former; North Africans the latter.

From 1981, Mitterrand and the new socialist government tried to alter the tone of policy as well as its substance. Freeman (1989: 169) and Wihtol de Wenden (1984) give useful reviews, drawing attention to the halt placed on expulsions, the regularization of some 150,000 *clandestins*, shown clearly in Figure 9.3 (Tribalat 1983), and the emphasis on improving the lot of migrant workers, for example by giving immigrants broad rights of political association. While strong controls remained, the new government recognized the need to negotiate migration control, and particularly the reduction of illegal entries, with the countries of origin, and to try to foster in public opinion an acceptance of the inevitability of a large, permanent ethnic minority population. There was none the less, in the face of continuing economic recession, encouragement for migrant labourers to leave, with incentives being organized by government in negotiation with individual firms, some 3300 agreements being signed with the Office for International Migration (OMI) between 1984 and 1987 (Tribalat 1988: 183). It is worth noting that the OMI had replaced the ONI and the slight change in name was meant to represent the change of emphasis from recruiting labour to a broader-ranging remit to cover many aspects of the migration process.

A further significant element during the 1980s was France's relatively liberal attitude towards refugees, so that a further diversification of immigrant origins has taken place. In the French case, the demand for refugee status grew strongly in the late 1970s and 1980s in relation both to world events and to tighter immigration control (Tribalat 1988: 186). The sources are very varied, including south-east Asia, especially Vietnam and Cambodia (see Guillon and Léonetti 1986; Hommes et Migrations 1990a; Khòa 1990); Africa, especially Ghana, Zaire and Angola (Hommes et Migrations 1990b) and the ex-USSR and eastern Europe (Guillon 1989).

The consequence of policies during the 1980s has been a reduction both in the number of families arriving or being 'regularized' and in the arrival of new permanent workers. Above all, though, the degree of manoeuvre on policy towards immigrants and minorities has been greatly circumscribed by the Front National's ability to make vigorous political capital out of any policy smacking of 'liberality'. From the early 1980s, the Front secured a firm political base (Husbands 1991; Ogden 1987), campaigning on an overtly anti-immigrant ticket. For example, Mitterrand has from time to time expressed interest in the idea of giving certain foreign residents – in relation to period of residence in France, for example – the right to vote in municipal elections. On each occasion, he has been obliged to withdraw the idea. Millions of long-term residents, therefore, remain disenfranchised. The election of right-wing governments in 1986–88 and from 1993 brought about some further changes in policy, with both an increased vigilance of migration control and also a re-examination of the ways in which French nationality may be acquired.

Conclusions

This brief survey has highlighted a number of themes which are of great importance to modern French society. The post-war years have seen major immigrant flows, with major shifts in national origins away from Europe and a gradual tendency towards permanent settlement. The role of the state has been central to this evolution, successive governments and other state agencies (such as the nationalized industries and public services) actively engaged in migrant recruitment. Immigration has rarely been uncontroversial and the intensity of political discussion in the 1980s and 1990s led to a re-examination in some quarters of the concepts of 'nationality' and 'citizenship' (Silverman 1991), with the state suggesting that the acquisition of French nationality be made more difficult and migrant organizations insisting on a divorce between the two: 'the second generation is claiming a more participative citizenship, founded more on residence than on nationality and affiliation, within a multicultural society' (Wihtol de Wenden 1991: 330). Certainly, although migration is responsive to short-term economic fluctuations and government policy towards new arrivals has become tighter over the past two decades, migrants and their children remain at the heart of the French labour force in the 1990s, confirming a trend begun more than a century ago.

Note

1. Great care needs to be taken in the assumptions that are made when using official data. The most easily available data, in the population census for example, are those which relate to nationality. Yet the number of 'foreigners' provides only a partial and incomplete picture of the migration process. In addition to the 'naturalized' population mentioned in the text (and see Guillon 1988 and Massot 1985), the category of 'foreign' population needs to be used with care. Thus, in 1990, for example, almost 750,000 foreign nationals were born in France – the children of migrants. Over 2 million French nationals had been born abroad, migrating from, for example, the Overseas Departments and Territories (Réunion and the Caribbean islands) and from former French colonies. Of the 1.8 million naturalized population, 73 per cent had been born outside metropolitan France.

References

Blanchet, D. (1985) 'Intensité et Calendrier du Regroupement familial des Migrants: Un Essai de mesure à partir de Données agrégées', *Population*, 40 (2), 249–66

Condon, S. A. and P. E. Ogden (1991) 'Afro-Caribbean Migrants in France: Employment, State Policy and the Migration Process', *Transactions*, Institute of British Geographers, 16 (4), 440–57

Costa-Lascoux, J. (1989) *De l'Immigré au Citoyen*, Paris: La Documentation Française

Cross, G. S. (1983) *Immigrant Workers in Industrial France: The Making of a New Laboring Class*, Philadelphia: Temple University Press

Freeman, G. P. (1989) 'Immigrant Labour and Racial Conflict: The Role of the State', in P. E. Ogden and P. E. White (eds) *Migrants in Modern France. Population Mobility in the Later Nineteenth and Twentieth Centuries*, London: Unwin Hyman, 160–76

Green, N. (1985) *Les Travailleurs immigrés juifs à la Belle Epoque: Le 'Pletzl' de Paris*, Paris: Playard

Guillon, M. (1988) 'Les Français par Acquisition: Dossier documentaire', *Revue Européenne des Migrations Internationales*, 4 (3), 125–45

(1989) 'Réfugiés et Immigrés de l'Europe de l'Est', *Revue Européenne des Migrations Internationales*, 5 (3), 133–8

Guillon, M. and I.-J. Leonetti (1986) *Le Triangle de Choisy: Un Quartier chinois à Paris*, Paris: CIEMI/L'Harmattan

Hommes et Migrations (1990a) *Populations du Sud-est asiatique*, (1134), Paris

(1990b) *Les Africains noirs en France*, 1131, Paris

Husbands, C. (1991) 'The Support for the Front National: Analyses and Findings', *Ethnic and Racial Studies*, 14 (3), 382–416

INSEE (1985) *Recensement général de la Population de 1982: Les Étrangers*, Paris: INSEE

(1992) *Recensement de la Population de 1990. Nationalités. Résultats du Sondage au Quart*, Paris: INSEE

Khòa, Le Huu (1990) *Les jeunes Vietnamiens de la Deuxième Génération. La Semi-rupture du Quotidien*, Paris: CIEMI/L'Harmattan

Labat, J.-C. (1991) 'La Population étrangère. Recensement de la Population de 1990', *INSEE Première*, 150

Lebon, A. (1979) 'L'Aide au Retour des Travailleurs étrangers', *Economie et Statistique*, (113), 37–46

(1988) 'L'Emploi étranger à la Fin de 1985', *Revue Européenne des Migrations Internationales*, 4 (1–2), 85–105

(1992) *Aspects de l'Immigration et de la Présence étrangère en France 1991/2*, Paris: Ministère de Affaires Sociales et de l'Intégration

Lequin, Y. (ed.) (1988) *La Mosaïque France. Histoire des Étrangers et de l'Immigration,* Paris: Larousse

Marie, C.-V. (1983) 'L'Immigration clandestine en France', *Hommes et Migrations, Documents*, 1059, 4–21

Massot, J. (1985) 'Français par le Sang, Français par la Loi, Français par le Choix', *Revue Européenne des Migrations Internationales,* 1 (2), 9–19

Noiriel, G. (1984) *Longwy: Immigrés et Prolétaires, 1880–1980*, Paris: Presses Universitaires de France

(1986) 'L'Immigration en France: Une Histoire en Friche', *Annales, Economies, Sociétés, Civilisations*, 41 (4), 751–69

(1988) *Le Creuset français. Histoire de l'Immigration XIX–XX Siècles*, Paris: Seuil

Ogden, P. E. (1987) 'Immigration, Cities and the Geography of the National Front in France', in G. Glebe and J. O'Loughlin (eds) *Foreign Minorities in Continental European Cities*, Wiesbaden: Steiner Verlag, 163–83

(1989) 'International Migration in the Nineteenth and Twentieth Centuries', in P. E. Ogden and P. E. White (eds) *Migrants in Modern France. Population Mobility in the later Nineteenth and Twentieth Centuries*, London: Unwin Hyman, 34–59

Pénin, M. (1986) 'Les Questions de Population au tournant du Siècle à travers L'Oeuvre de Charles Gide (1847–1932)', *Histoire, Economie et Société*, 5, 137–58

Poinard, M. (1979) 'Le Million des Immigrés', *Revue Géographique des Pyrénées et du Sud–Ouest*, 50, 511–39

Sauvy, A. (1946) 'Evaluation des besoins de l'immigration française', *Population*, 1 (1), 91–8

Schor, R. (1985) *L'Opinion française et les étrangers en France, 1919–1939*, Paris: Publications de la Sorbonne

Silverman, M. (1991) 'Citizenship and the Nation-State', *Ethnic and Racial Studies*, 14 (3), 333–49

Spengler, J. J. (1979) *France Faces Depopulation: Postlude Edition, 1936–76*, Durham, North Carolina: Duke University Press

Tapinos, G. (1975) *L'Immigration étrangère en France, 1945–1973*, Paris: INED/Presses Universitaires de France

Tribalat, M. (1983) 'Chronique de l'Immigration', *Population*, 38 (1), 137–59

(1988) 'Chronique de l'Immigration', *Population*, 43 (1), 181–206

(1991) *Cent Ans d'Immigration. Etrangers d'hier, Français d'aujourd'hui,* Paris: INED/Presses Universitaires de France

Verbunt, G. (1985) 'France', in T. Hammar (ed.) *European Immigration Policy: A Comparative Perspective*, Cambridge: Cambridge University Press, 127–64

Weil, P. (1991) *La France et ses Etrangers. L'Aventure d'une Politique d'Immigration 1938–1991*, Paris: Calmann-Lévy

White, P. E. (1986) 'International Migration in the 1970s: Revolution or Evolution?', in A. M. Findlay and P. E. White (eds) *West European Population Change*, London: Croom Helm, 50–80

Wihtol de Wenden, C. (1984) 'The Evolution of French Immigration Policy after May 1981', *International Migration*, (22), 199–213

(1991) 'Immigration Policy and the Issue of Nationality', *Ethnic and Racial Studies*, 14 (3), 319–32

LABOUR MIGRATION TO SWEDEN:
THE FINNISH CASE

TOMAS HAMMAR

Among many pairs of migration countries, Finland and Sweden may be close to an ideal type. For centuries, migration between these two countries has gone in both directions, though mainly from Finland to Sweden. These two neighbouring countries have a long common history. They were in fact up to 1809 united in one state. Finnish and Swedish are two very different languages, but in both countries minorities speak the other country's language. The geographical distance between the two is short and travel across the Baltic Sea has for centuries been easy and inexpensive. On both sides, the information about the other country has been rich and easily accessible, not least thanks to earlier migrants. Chain migration has been a traditional form of recruitment of new migrant workers.

In 1954, a Nordic agreement about free circulation of labour gave citizens of four Nordic countries full access to a common labour market. During the following twenty years, Sweden registered a considerable net immigration from the three other Nordic countries, and first of all immigration from Finland grew heavily up to a peak in 1969/70. As a consequence of this large migration, Sweden and Finland, in several public sectors and on all administrative levels, developed a system of close cooperation both in formulation and in implementation of migration policy.

This large emigration of about 415,000 Finnish citizens from 1946 to 1977 must primarily be explained by rapid industrialization of Finland, a significant internal rural–urban migration, and by major differences in job opportunities, as well as in wages and working conditions between Finland and Sweden. Return migration to Finland, considerable during the whole period, was from 1981 larger than or about as large as emigration from Finland to Sweden. The previous economic imbalances had been reduced, overcome or even changed to the advantage of Finland. Also in this respect the Finnish–Swedish migration pair may be of general interest in any discussion about migration pressure and future flows of migration.

Early migration from Finland to Sweden

Finnish belongs to the Finnish-Urgic language family, like the Sami languages. Swedish, on the other hand, is an Indo-European and Germanic language. Before recorded history Finnish immigrants from the east arrived in the Baltic region, while Scandinavians came from the south. The distance between the two languages is tremendous, but the Baltic Sea has made the travel distance short and brought people together rather than separated them from each other.

For many centuries up to 1809 Finland had been a province of or duchy within the Swedish state. Administration and legislation was the same in Finland as in Sweden. The only university was the Swedish Academy in Åbo/Turku. Many traditions from this Swedish period were kept going during the nineteenth century when Finland was made a grand duchy of the Russian tsar, but a Finnish national movement, growing in strength in the middle of the century, resisted Russianization attempts and soon demanded national independence, which was won in 1917. Since then the state of Finland is officially bilingual and of its 5 million people about 300,000 or 6 per cent are Swedish-speaking.

Medieval documents show that migration from Finland to Sweden has been continuous and strong, including all social strata: servants, merchants, farmhands, warriors, clergy and nobility. The main entrance port for this migration was Stockholm, and numerous Finnish-born migrants have been registered in the parish books of the Finnish church in this city. At the end of the sixteenth century, some 10,000 Finnish colonizers settled in Sweden, invited to introduce their methods of clearing new land by burning and beating. Finally, in the very north, a Finnish-speaking population of about 20,000 remained on the Swedish side of the border, which was drawn in a peace treaty with Russia after the war in 1808/9. Together with the Sami, also in the north, the Jews and the gypsies, these Tornedal-Finns constitute the four small Aboriginal and autochtonous minority populations in Sweden. After the civil war in Finland in 1918, Sweden received a few thousand political refugees. During the Second World War, Swedish families gave shelter to 65,000 children, escaping the warfare in Finland. Finally, in 1944, a civilian population of more than 50,000 small farmers and their families escaped from Finnish Lapland into Sweden. However, most of these groups of political refugees or war refugees soon returned.

Labour migration after 1945

Some Finnish labour immigration had taken place in the inter-war period, and already at that time the Swedish authorities were giving priority to Nordic citizens. From 1943 Finnish citizens were again allowed to work in Sweden without work permits. But a new era began in 1954 with the Nordic agreement on a common labour market. From this time Nordic citizens were free to take employment in Finland, Norway, Denmark and Sweden. And even though Iceland was not yet formally included, citizens of Iceland still enjoyed priority status. In 1982 when the Nordic labour market agreement was revised and renewed, Iceland joined this free labour market. During the first twenty years Sweden was the main receiving country within this zone of free circulation; and the only flow of migration of any real significance was emigration from Finland to Sweden.

After 1945, Finland experienced a period of quick industrialization, and of both internal rural–urban migration and sizeable international emigration. In the period 1946–70 about 400,000 left the country, of which 81 per cent went to Sweden. A considerable housing shortage in the south of Finland and a relatively large wage differential between the countries were among the push factors, but the employment situation in Sweden decided the timing and the size of the flows. The peak years were 1969 and 1970 when net migration to Sweden amounted to about 40,000 per year. In 1972 Sweden stopped its recruitment of non-Nordic labour and in 1973 a Finnish-Swedish agreement was made to the effect that labour should be recruited through the public employment service and not by employment campaigns organized directly by the companies. Even if only Nordic workers were now available, labour migration from Finland stayed at a low level and from 1981 declined even further.

From around 1970, Swedish-Finnish political and administrative cooperation in the field of migration policy was accelerated. Concerned by the growing loss of population and income, the Finnish government started a major research programme and appointed a commission on emigration to prepare a policy programme, including proposals for Finland's support to its emigrants in Sweden. For example, in 1972 in a speech in Stockholm, President Urho Kekkonen demanded that Finnish citizens be given voting rights in local elections in Sweden, a demand which was granted three years later. A series of bilateral commissions and more or less permanent study groups were assigned the tasks of discussing the position of Finnish workers in Sweden, for example their working conditions, cultural life, social activities and schooling, in a joint interest to promote the integration of Finnish immigrants in Sweden.

The flows

From 1946 to 1960 migration increased slowly to about 10,000 per year, lower some years and higher again when job vacancies were again available in Sweden. Between 1953 and 1956, immigration increased (see Figure 9.4), but less than might have been expected given the introduction of the Nordic labour market agreement in 1954. The labour market had been sufficiently free before that date, and the size of the flows was caused less by regulations than by the Swedish demand for labour.

The curves also show that return migration has followed immigration as a shadow, increasing or decreasing one or two years after a change in immigration. For example, after the peak years of 1969 and 1970, return migration in 1971 for the first time exceeded immigration, i.e. Sweden registered a net (re-)emigration to Finland, repeated in a similar way ten years later. During the 1980s emigration from Finland fell to a sort of equilibrium level. Although the Nordic countries still formed a free circulation area and large recent migrations had removed many of the social barriers to further flows within this region, economic incentives to migrate had been weakened. The previous one-way migration came to an end and was replaced by a balanced two-way traffic.

The economic background to these changes should, however, be mentioned. With the encouragement of the Finnish authorities, in the 1970s, instead of employing Finnish labour in Sweden some Swedish textile industries started production in Finland. But the wage differences that made this export of capital profitable began to fall and within a short period of time capital started to flow in the other direction, from Finland to Sweden. In the 1980s, Finnish industries began to invest in Sweden and bought several Swedish companies. Even some Finnish banks entered the Swedish financial market. Consequently, a new kind of Finnish immigrant appeared in Sweden, namely the economic and administrative professionals.

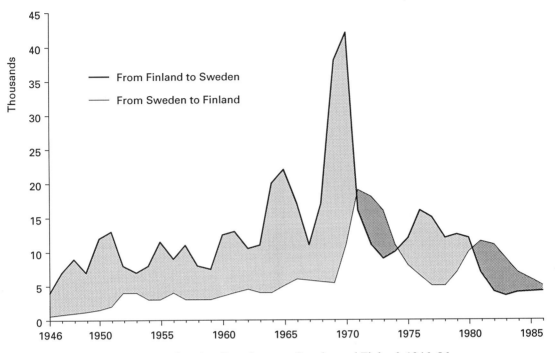

Figure 9.4: Migration flows between Sweden and Finland, 1946–86

Who were the migrants?

As in most large migration flows, more than two-thirds were young people between fifteen and thirty-four years of age. But unusually, young women predominated both at the beginning of the period and again in the 1980s, and throughout represented at least half of the migrant population. Also, a higher proportion of women than men has tended to stay on in Sweden, and many have married or formed partnerships with Swedish men. The educational background of emigrants to Sweden is the same as that of corresponding age groups in Finland. No accurate data exist, but several surveys indicate that around 25 per cent, or one in four emigrants, was unemployed, underemployed or outside the labour force when they left Finland. On the other hand, three out of four had left a job in Finland to seek employment in Sweden.

More than two-thirds of Finnish workers found employment in Swedish industries, whereas only about 30 per cent of them had previous industrial experience in Finland. Particularly during the 1950s, many migrants had worked as farm and wood labourers in northern Finland, a region of unemployment and out-migration. A few Finnish intellectuals had always worked in Sweden, and this group grew somewhat in importance during this migration period, but it was still relatively small compared with the main flows of workers. The result has been a social imbalance in the composition of the Finnish community in Sweden, and this seriously impedes the ethnic mobilization of the Swedish-Finnish minority.

Swedish-speaking Finns were highly over represented during the 1950s, and their propensity to emigrate to Sweden has remained high. As mentioned previously, they comprise some 6 per cent of the population in Finland, but they constitute about 20 per cent of Finnish immigrants in Sweden. In other words, the mother tongue of one in five Finns in Sweden is Swedish. Since Finland's Swedish-speaking population tends to live in certain regions in the north-east (around the city of Vasa), in the south, and particularly on the island of Åland, these are also regions of large out-migration. This over-representation needs little explanation. While Finnish speakers encounter considerable language difficulties in Sweden, Swedish speakers obviously do not. Several of them would, however, has encountered great difficulties had they chosen to migrate to the Finnish-speaking regions of Finland. In searching for a job, Sweden offered them better opportunities than Finland.

Furthermore, Swedish-speaking Finns do not suffer from the minority complex characteristic of some of the Finnish speakers, who regard a Swede as big brother and Sweden as the dominant centre. On the other hand, even if Swedish-speaking Finns have easy access to Sweden, thanks to their Swedishness, they may sometimes feel that Swedes look down on them and do not fully accept them as the Swedes they in fact are. Historical relations between Finland and Sweden are thus psychologically important to Finnish immigrants in their encounter with Sweden and the Swedes.

Integration into Sweden

Finnish migrants have settled in the major cities and industrial centres of middle Sweden and in the very north, in the mining and steel industry areas. The highest level of Finnish immigration is into Stockholm, where ferries to the very centre of the city arrive daily. Göteborg, the second city, has recruited many Finns to Volvo (cars) and SKF (ball-bearings), and quite a few have also settled in the southern industrial city of Malmö. A high concentration of Finns is found in Bergslagen (the old iron-ore mining district some 200 km north-west of Stockholm), but also in several industrial cities like Västerås (ASEA), Södertälje (Saab) and Eskilstuna.

In comparison with other immigrant nationalities, relatively few Finns live in the suburban areas in which immigrants are mainly concentrated, though some of those who arrived during the peak years around 1970 are still there. Over time many Finns have experienced upward social mobility, both with regard to their jobs and to the area in which they live. Their housing careers often incorporate moves from the first industrial barracks, to an inexpensive apartment, to a cooperative apartment and then on to a privately owned family house. In this sense, as apartment or house owners, many Finnish immigrants have become well-integrated settlers. Others have been less successful, however, and some have remained in the modest apartment they first obtained. Many others have of course returned to Finland.

Finns in Sweden have also improved their status in their working careers, though this is less pronounced. In 1970, no less than 70 per cent were employed in the production sector, and many performed hard physical work, often under difficult conditions (with respect to heat, noise and high accident risks). Since then the total number of persons employed in Swedish industry has fallen drastically, from over 30 per cent in 1970 to under 20 per cent in 1993, and this drop has also affected Finnish workers. Nevertheless, the proportion of Finns in the production industries is still almost twice as high, or about 40 per cent. At the same time the rate of unemployment, for many years approximately double that of the Swedes, has started to rise even further.

A Finnish minority in Sweden?

Migration is not regulated within the Nordic labour market. Migrants can move without control or permits. Therefore, the size and direction of the flows are less the result of political decisions than of individual decisions based on economic (or perhaps just as often non-economic) considerations. Individual migrants are free to travel and to apply for a job. Because the system lends itself to a certain amount of trial and error, we can expect less long-term planning for permanent settlement and more return migration, or even repeated migration, i.e. a sort of commuting between Finland and Sweden.

On arrival, most Finnish migrants, like other immigrants, intend to stay for only a short period. In fact many postpone a planned return once or twice before finally realizing, after a number of years, that they have in fact already settled. This prolonged period of indecision, which is typical of Finnish migrants in Sweden, delays their integration and diminishes their incentive to learn the language and to plan for the future. Finns in Sweden often travel to Finland and many of them own summer houses there in which they spend their vacations. Both migration and return migration decisions are less final for them than for migrants from more distant countries, who have fewer opportunities to realize their return dreams.

Many very short migrations have never been counted, for only those migrants who intend to take up residence in Sweden for a whole year are registered as immigrants. Our statistics only cover those who are so registered and these show that variations in the return rate are related to variations in the labour market situations in both countries. Disregarding these fluctuations, the return rate from 1968 to 1985 (see Figure 9.4) averaged about 20–25 per cent after two years of staying in Sweden and about 40–50 per cent after five years. But, as I mentioned, after a few years many return migrants went to Sweden again for the second time (20–30 per cent during 1968–85).

The population of persons born in Finland increased from 100,000 in 1960 to 250,000 in 1970 and then decreased again to 220,000 in 1990. If we add the 100,000 sons and daughters of Finnish immigrants (or of one immigrant and one Swede), at least numerically, there seems to be a reasonable chance of this Finnish community becoming an important 'immigrant minority'. Several increasingly active claims to this effect have been made by representatives of the approximately 100,000 organized Finns in Sweden, but the prospects of this happening are, however, rather slight.

By 1975 Sweden had already adopted a pluralistic policy and was even granting voting rights in local elections to foreign citizens who had been legally resident in the country for three years. Over a hundred Finnish-born politicians are elected to local assemblies and a few are MPs. Finnish is the language of instruction in many schools and is taught to Finnish children in others. In 1992, the first wholly Finnish publicly financed elementary schools were opened in some municipalities. The new Sami Parliament and recognition of the Sami people as an original minority, have kindled new hopes that Swedish Finns will be given similar recognition.

Finns are spread all over Sweden and everywhere assimilation is rapid and strong. Intermarriage is legion and the Finnish language is only actively transferred to the second generation when both parents are Finnish-speaking. Swedish-speaking Finns in Sweden, about 25 per cent of those born in Finland, are not organized in the National Federation of Finnish Associations, but in separate associations, which are less interested in promoting a Finnish minority status. In the 1990s, immigration and refugee policy have become restrictive, and Sweden is unlikely to extend minority rights to any of the immigrant communities. Should this happen, however, the Finnish community in Sweden would be the first to receive it.

SWITZERLAND: A NON-IMMIGRATION IMMIGRATION COUNTRY

HANS-JOACHIM HOFFMANN-NOWOTNY

Switzerland, a self-declared non-immigration country, nevertheless has both a history of immigration of more than a hundred years and a considerable share of aliens (on 31 December 1992 it was 17.6 per cent of its permanent inhabitants). And it has also a history of immigration-related conflicts between the different subsystems of Swiss society and, consequently, a history of how the political system coped with problems created by immigration of guest-workers for a long time mainly determined by the needs of the economy. Most recently, however, the focus of attention and debate has shifted from questions related to labour migration to problems created by an increasing number of asylum-seekers and illegal immigrants.

Emigration country to immigration country

For several hundred years Switzerland had been distinctly emigration-orientated. The transition from an emigration to an immigration country came about with the process of industrialization, which took off in Switzerland in the period between 1850 and 1875, even though it was only later, in the second half of the 1880s, that Switzerland became a true immigration country, with a net migration surplus.

Within the first wave of immigration which lasted until 1914 we can distinguish two periods, separated by the economic crisis of 1878–1885.

The foreign workforce during the first period consisted mainly of immigrants from the adjacent areas of Germany, France and Austria. These immigrants were generally more highly qualified than the majority of the indigenous labourers released from agricultural work. By contrast, the second period, which correlated with the drop in emigration from Switzerland, was characterized by a rapid growth in the proportion of mainly poorly-qualified Italian immigrants. The foreign population increased steadily and reached a peak in 1914 when foreigners constituted 15.4 per cent of the total population. The rapidly increasing number of foreigners gave rise to fears on several levels. The expression *Überfremdung* (over-foreignization) first came into use at this time.

Immigration regulations and policies

Throughout the entire period from the establishment of the modern Swiss federation in 1848 until the First World War, the political and legal regulation of the migration process was characterized by classic economic liberalism, which saw the free flow of goods, capital and labour as fundamental to economic development. The right of free immigration and emigration was taken for granted. The only evident difference remaining between foreigners and Swiss was the exclusion of the former from political rights (as was the case in other countries as well). Proposals for controlling foreign penetration, in contrast with the situation today, provided almost exclusively for the promotion of naturalization. Before 1876 there were no restrictions at all, and even after that date anyone who had been in the country for two years or longer could apply for citizenship.

The policy of integration via naturalization did, however, fail. The relative failure of the naturalization policy was at the time interpreted as reluctance on the part of the Swiss to accept new citizens. This reluctance was due to economic rather than nationalistic motives. Other reasons for the failure of the naturalization policy were the bureaucratic and economic costs that candidates were subject to and, finally, the lack of interest on the part of foreigners themselves.

After 1900 the introduction of *jus soli* was demanded in order to increase naturalization and reduce the number of foreigners. Under this law all children born in Switzerland of foreign parents would no longer have the option but would receive Swiss citizenship automatically (so-called compulsory naturalization). The preliminary work to introduce the *jus soli* was practically concluded by 1914; a bill could have been submitted to the federal parliament if work had not been interrupted by the outbreak of the war.

The decisive factor in assuring a high degree of continuity in the *laissez-faire* regulation of immigration before the First World War was the lack of any single interpretation of the concept of over-foreignization:

- The Swiss labour movement focused its fears on the Italian immigrants, who were seen as preordained wage-cutters and strike-breakers, who would undermine any labour dispute and thus perpetuate the exploitation of the workers.
- Conservative elements associated 'over-foreignization' mainly with politically active qualified German workers and craftsmen, who were suspected of revolutionary activities.
- The liberal bourgeoisie and the French-speaking Swiss saw the danger of 'over-foreignization' in the cultural hegemony of high status Germans and a Prussian-dominated German Reich.

In view of this state of affairs there seemed to be no need for the government to change or to question the liberal migration policy which was in the interest of the economic system and its leading actors.

The inter-war period

Wartime mobilization and the deepening economic and social crisis which followed the First World War, made foreigners appear as (at least potentially) dangerous elements, and decreased the demand for foreign labour dramatically, consequently nipping the liberal immigration policy and the integrationist approach in the bud. Increasingly isolationist policies came to be adopted: entrance visas were introduced, the internal registration and monitoring of immigrants by the Alien Police was extended, and an extremely restrictive practice was adopted with regard to the granting of residence and work permits.

Consequently, there was a dramatic drop in the foreign population of Switzerland: between 1914 and 1941 the number of foreigners living in Switzerland fell from some 600,000 in 1914 to 223,000 in 1941, or from 15.4 per cent to 5.2 per cent of the total resident population.

Restrictive measures were first introduced by the federal government under emergency law. In 1934 a comprehensive new federal law on 'Foreigners Rights of Residence and Domicile' was introduced which has more or less remained in force to this day.

The main features of the new legislation were as follows.

First and foremost, permits of abode and work permits were now linked; permits of abode are only issued if employment is secured, and are withdrawn if the immigrants lose their jobs.

Second, three different classes of aliens were defined: seasonal workers (holding a work permit and a permit of stay for a maximum of nine months per

year), immigrants with annually renewable work permits (and permits of abode), and immigrants with permits of permanent residence (granted after an immigrant had lived in Switzerland for a minimum of ten years).

The problem of over-foreignization was explicitly mentioned and dealt with by issuing a directive to the authorities to take into consideration the 'economic *and* cultural interests' and the 'degree of over-foreignization' of the nation when deciding whether or not to grant permits.

This body of legislation reflected the consensus that had evolved in the meantime on how to deal with the question of immigration and solve the problem of 'over-foreignization', without foregoing the army of immigrant industrial 'reservists' who, it was intended, could be called upon as the economic situation demanded. The risk of 'over-foreignization' was felt to depend, not on the sheer number of foreigners in the country, but on the length of their stay, and the solution to this problem was the introduction of the 'principle of rotation', i.e. immigrants should come to Switzerland, work there for a limited span of time, return to their home countries and be replaced by new immigrants.

If we compare this approach to the problem of over-foreignization with that favoured until 1914, we find a complete reversal of policy towards foreigners. Before the First World War integration was seen as the solution to the problem of over-foreignization. Now, however, there was to be a rapid turnover of foreigners.

The second wave of immigration

After the Second World War, Switzerland's economy experienced the greatest boom in its history which created a correspondingly high demand for foreign labour, and the authorities were willing to respond to this demand by opening the borders for an unrestricted immigration.

In accordance with the principle of rotation, unmarried and already qualified applicants were given preference as far as possible. There was an uninterrupted period of growth lasting until 1974 (the year of the oil crisis), with the foreign population of Switzerland doubling during the 1950s, and again during the 1960s, the large majority of whom were Italians. In 1974 the total foreign population of Switzerland reached its first peak, both in absolute terms (1,064,526) and in relation to the total population (16.7 per cent). And that 1974 was also the turning-point in the ethnic composition of immigrants can be identified with a good degree of precision: it occurred during the acute recession of the mid-1970s, when the number of Italians fell by 71,613 from 554,925 in 1974 to 483,812 in 1976, and after the economic recovery Yugoslavs, Portuguese and Turks took the traditional place of Italian immigrants. The proportion of Yugoslavs in the foreign population increased from 3.4 per cent in 1975 to 14.5 per cent in 1991 – or, in absolute numbers, from 34,347 to 172,657 over the same period. In 1980 the Portuguese made up 1.2 per cent (10,863) of the foreigners, which increased to 8.5 per cent (101,582) in 1991. The Turkish presence increased from 2.6 per cent in 1975 to 5.9 per cent in 1991. In absolute terms, the number of Turks roughly tripled from 26,093 in 1975 to 70,501 in 1991.

For nearly a hundred years immigrants from neighbouring Germany, France, Italy and Austria constituted the overwhelming majority of foreigners in Switzerland (97.3 per cent in 1860; 95.3 per cent in 1910; 87.0 per cent in 1960). Within 30 years their share has gone down to just 46.0 per cent (1991).

Unintended consequences of immigration

During the 1950s there was little or no opposition to the purely demand-orientated recruitment policy. Immigrants occupied low-income and low-status positions; thanks to the illusion of 'going back home' associated with the principle of rotation and the extremely restrictive official practice with regard to the admission of foreign workers' families, immigrants were not a significant burden on the nation's infrastructure; and, not least because they were denied any form of social insurance, they were cheap. Nor was the question of over-foreignization a problem: the principle of rotation seemed to have forestalled any possible xenophobic reactions. Nevertheless, even though this perpetual mobility of 'alien policy' fitted in so well with the general growth-based euphoria of the 1950s and gave such a miraculous boost to the workforce upon which Swiss economic prosperity depended, it still had its unexpected drawbacks.

In the first place, the development differential between Switzerland and Italy, the main source of migrant labour, diminished and Switzerland itself began to face competition from other industrialized nations striving to offer more attractive conditions of residence and employment; thus, foreign labour became scarcer, so that higher wages had to be paid and a lower general level of qualifications had to be accepted.

At the same time the principle of rotation was increasingly called into question. Employers were largely opposed to it, and were reluctant to part with foreign workers who, after 'learning by doing', could now be considered qualified. It became clear that a less restrictive policy would have to be adopted towards the question of long-stay foreign workers, and thus towards the admission of their families.

Next, the purely demand-induced recruitment of foreign labour proved not to cushion cyclical instability, but actually to cause it. With the increased and diversified supply of jobs in a booming economy, the demand for cheap labour grew continually, to the point where the entire economy rested on a foundation of foreign workers and, with the rapid growth of demand, construction and export activity, tended to overheat and lead to inflation. This cheap basic workforce created investment capital, and investment in turn created jobs which called for more immigration.

Largely as a result of the unprecedented expansion of the production workforce occasioned by these factors, investment directed towards increased productivity tended to be neglected. Now, however, as the cost-benefit ratio of foreign labour deteriorated, the advantage gained by low wage levels was gradually lost, and Switzerland's outdated industrial infrastructure became more and more of a burden.

The doubling of the foreign population between 1950 and 1960 and the weakening of the principle of rotation together destroyed the illusion that the foreign population was a passive and flexible entity which could be manoeuvred at will to regulate the growth of the economy. The question of over-foreignization again began to emerge as a major political issue. The broad consensus which had been established in the 1930s with regard to immigration and the prevention of over-foreignization broke down.

Fighting over-foreignization

The political apparatus was challenged at the beginning of the 1960s when public opinion rose against further uncontrolled immigration. The government and the federal parliament eventually came under strong pressure. In 1965 the Democratic Party of the canton of Zurich launched the first constitutional popular initiative[1] against over-foreignization; it demanded an amendment to the federal constitution stating that the total number of foreigners with a permit of abode and a permit of permanent residence should not be allowed to exceed 10 per cent of the total population of Switzerland.

As a reaction to this grassroots movement the government introduced emergency measures aimed at reducing immigration. The initiative of the Democratic Party was withdrawn in 1968; that is, it did not come to a vote because the initiators declared themselves satisfied with the measures already taken by the authorities.

When it later became obvious that the number of foreigners continued to increase despite these measures, a second initiative was launched by the 'National Action against the Over-Foreignization of the People and the Fatherland' *(Nationale Aktion gegen die Überfremdung von Volk und Heimat)*. This initiative demanded that foreigners should not be allowed to exceed 10 per cent of the Swiss population in any canton, with the exception of Geneva. The plebiscite took place in June 1970 and the initiative was defeated by a narrow majority (54 per cent against versus 46 per cent in favour). If this initiative had been accepted by the voters it would have been necessary, at that time, to reduce the number of foreigners by 44 per cent.

This threat made such an impression that vigorous and effective political action became imperative, and the global ceiling was introduced. Without stating any numbers the global ceiling proposed that a balanced relationship be sought between the size of the Swiss and the foreign populations. As an instrument to help achieve the global ceiling a quota system for permits of abode was introduced in 1970: not more than 10,000 work permits should be issued per year.[2]

The introduction of the global ceiling eased the social tensions. But finally, it was only the recession of 1975/6 that reduced the number of foreigners for some time and thus took the edge off the grassroots movement – at least temporarily.

When the number and share of immigrants continued to increase again after the recession was over a whole series of further initiatives was launched, demanding more or less drastic reductions in the number of foreigners in Switzerland. Though none of this series of initiatives was ever passed, the narrow margin of defeat for the 1970 initiative made it quite clear that the Swiss government had to hold strictly to the (ultimately unsuccessful) policy of the global ceiling. The message of the results of this series of constitutional initiatives is a quite simple one: a large majority of the Swiss do not want the foreign labour force to be repatriated, but an even larger majority wants it to remain in low status and in a legally inferior position.

It is quite clear from this discussion that immigration policy in Switzerland has for the past twenty-five years been primarily a reaction to the grassroots movement.

Because the quota system policy had the character of a compromise between the demands of the economic system and racist circles, this policy mitigated social tension induced by immigration, indicated for example by the outcome of the over-foreignization initiatives after 1970. Since the middle of the 1980s, however, the intended stabilization policy has definitely lost its grip as can be shown by the recent increase in the share of foreigners to 17.6 per cent in 1992 – which has happened although a serious economic recession has been hitting Switzerland since the beginning of the 1990s.

From labour migration to asylum migration

Despite the mentioned increase in the foreign population, grassroots pressure has, since the middle of the 1980s, not been aroused primarily by fear of over-foreignization by regular immigrants. Rather, a migratory movement stands in the foreground now which lies beyond any controlling instruments of Swiss policy on foreigners: the stream of applicants for asylum, which has been increasing since the early 1980s (see Table 9.8). In pronounced contrast with the prominent position this issue takes in polarized public debate, this migration at present has only little influence on the growth of the permanent foreign resident population. This is the case in spite of the marked increase in the number of applicants for asylum (3,010 in 1980, 9,703 in 1985, 35,425 in 1990 and 41,629 in 1991)[3] because, at the same time, the share of those granted asylum, and thus the number of foreigners recognized as refugees and included in the permanent foreign resident population, has fallen well below 5 per cent. In 1992 the number of applications for asylum decreased to 18,000. It seems, however, that this is mainly due to the fact that nearly 100,000 Yugoslavs were allowed into Switzerland on humanitarian grounds.

By applying for asylum it is possible to circumvent immigration restrictions. The lengthiness of asylum procedures makes it possible for the applicant to stay in Switzerland in most cases for several years (with a work permit after the first three months of stay in Switzerland) and to earn an income, even if the final decision on asylum is then negative. But even if the application for asylum is refused, it is possible to obtain a provisional residence permit: refused asylum seekers may be allowed to remain in Switzerland on a temporary basis due to conditions in their home countries (in most cases, armed conflict), but also on a permanent basis as hardship cases when the length of asylum procedures has led to extensive integration of

Table 9.8: *Applications for asylum in Switzerland, 1991 (excluding special programmes)*

Country	Number	%	Country	Number	%
Yugoslavia	14,205	34.2	Bangladesh	593	1.4
Sri Lanka	7,349	17.7	Nigeria	515	1.2
Turkey	4,324	10.4	Ethiopia	394	0.9
Romania	2,682	6.4	Afghanistan	233	0.6
Zaire	1,426	3.4	Iran	222	0.5
Lebanon	1,352	3.3	Bulgaria	217	0.5
Pakistan	1,339	3.2	Syria	179	0.4
Somalia	910	2.2	Iraq	160	0.4
India	886	2.1	Vietnam	86	0.2
Ghana	852	2.1	Poland	60	0.1
Angola	796	1.9	Others	2,849	6.9
Totals	36,121	86.9		5,508	13.1
Grand total	41,629				100.0

the applicant in Swiss life, and repatriation would be unreasonable. Thus, of a hundred applicants for asylum who have entered the country more than fifty may legally remain in Switzerland. Of those finally required to leave the country, only an estimated two-thirds actually do so.

When stabilization policy fails

The most recent data on the development of the foreign population in Switzerland show that the stabilization policy adopted in 1970 finally failed because the classical instruments of controlling immigration do not function any more. Immigration has become a self-dynamic system and has more or less gone out of control of both the economic and the political system. This is due to unintended consequences of political decisions as well as to developments beyond the influence of a single nation state.

The obvious failure of the traditional instruments to control immigration, especially the circumvention of immigration regulations by foreigners via application for asylum which has led to an increasingly stronger politicization of public debate on the asylum issue, now resulted in an official proposal to combine what were separate policies on immigration and asylum into a coordinated policy on migration. The aim of this consolidation would be to control the number of foreigners by defining the net migration of the permanent foreign resident population (holders of permits of abode, holders of permanent residence

permits, international functionaries, recognized refugees) in relation to the size of the temporary resident foreign population (seasonal workers, persons residing for short periods, border commuters, applicants for asylum). It seems, however, that for the time being the political machinery is paralysed by all kinds of cross pressures, and that it will take some time before a coherent migration policy can be defined and agreed upon by the economic system on the one hand and by the grassroots movement on the other, so that it can be implemented by the Swiss authorities. But it remains doubtful whether any single national policy – or any policy at all – is conceivable which might successfully control and regulate immigration. It seems, however, that finally Switzerland is on its way to accepting that it has become an immigration country.

Notes

1. The constitutional initiative and the referendum are the two most notable characteristics of the plebiscitary element in Swiss democracy. The referendum gives the Swiss people the opportunity to react immediately to the outcome of parliamentary decision making. If 50,000 voters can be mobilized to sign a petition regarding a law already passed by parliament, then the federal government is obliged to submit that law to a popular vote. Because of the possibility that parliamentary decision making may afterwards be submitted to a popular vote, it is attempted to obtain the consensus of all interested groups concerned with a particular bill as early as possible. The referendum can force the rejection of laws already accepted by parliament, but it cannot be used to force parliament directly to pass a certain

law. This can be accomplished indirectly, however, through the constitutional initiative, which can be used to change or amend the constitution. If 100,000 voters endorse a proposed constitutional amendment the government must submit the initiative to a popular vote. If the initiative receives a majority, the government and parliament must thereafter act in accordance with the new constitutional article(s). Initiatives that are rejected by only small majorities, such as the over-foreignization initiative of 1970, usually force the Federal Council to change its policy; in fact, this is how the change in immigration policy came about. It is thus correct to state that the plebiscitary element of the Swiss political system has proved a very important precondition for past and present immigration policy.

2. However, since the quota for permits of abode is very small in relation to the total number of resident foreigners, this instrument does not provide immigration regulation much scope.

3. If one relates the number of applications for asylum to the population of European countries Switzerland is ahead by far: in 1991 there were 690 applications per 100,000 inhabitants. In Austria, Germany, France and Italy the corresponding figures are 346, 332, 88 and 47.

FROM WORKERS TO IMMIGRANTS: TURKS AND MOROCCANS IN THE NETHERLANDS, 1965–1992

HANS VAN AMERSFOORT

After the Second World War the Netherlands had a serious population problem. The country had suffered severely from the war; it had a relatively high fertility rate and a high level of unemployment. The government thought it necessary to stimulate emigration to countries like Canada and Australia.

In these circumstances the Dutch refused to consider the possibility that the Netherlands was, to a certain extent, also an immigration country. The term immigrant exists in Dutch but is never used for people settling in the Netherlands. Even when the net migration, which had indeed been negative during the first post-war years, became consistently positive in the 1960s, the Dutch did not consider the Netherlands to be an immigration country. However, there is no doubt that the Netherlands has now become an immigration country and will remain so in the foreseeable future (de Beer and Sprangers 1993; van Amersfoort 1993).

The migration surplus is the net result of various migration flows from a variety of types of immigrants. This makes the migration process difficult to describe. Statistics are often based on different and inconsistently used criteria, like country of birth, nationality, country from where the migrant arrived and 'type of migrant'. It has to be pointed out right away that the 'types of migrants' in these classifications are defined from the point of view of the receiving country. When we speak of 'labour migration' or 'family-reunification migrants', we indicate the residence title, but the names suggest that we know the motives of the migrants. In fact our statistics do not tell us anything about the motives for migration. These motives can at best be deduced from certain (demographic) characteristics.

When I use the label 'labour migrants' I do not pretend to know their motivation, but only describe migrants who enter the Netherlands with a work permit that enables them to enter the Dutch labour market (legally). This excludes Dutch nationals, for instance from the Antilles, and EU nationals, who do not need such a permit, but includes, for instance, Americans and Japanese.

Because I do not intend to analyse the internationalization of the labour market, as it manifests itself in more or less reciprocal migration flows between countries of the developed world, I will concentrate on 'classical labour migration', that is to say on the migration of poorly skilled labour from less developed regions to more developed areas.

The migration of Turks and Moroccans to the Netherlands is a good example of this kind of migration. The Turkish and Moroccan population in the Netherlands consists almost entirely of former 'guest-workers' and their descendants.

At first sight this kind of migration is easy to explain and control. When there is a need for labour 'the sluices are opened', to use a popular Dutch metaphor, and when there is no longer any need for labour they are closed again. The state acts as a regulator in the interest of capital accumulation by issuing work permits when labour is needed and by exporting unemployment when the business cycle goes down. This, in a nutshell, is the neo-Marxist wisdom of the 1970s. Some migrations, for instance from Surinam to the Netherlands, could never be described within this frame of reference. But with regard to the labour migration from Turkey and other Mediterranean countries this approach seemed for a time appropriate (Marshall-Goldschwartz 1973).

Unfortunately the reality proved to be more complicated. Once the migration flows had come into being they developed much further than the governments had ever intended. After the oil crisis of 1973/4 the recruitment of labour stopped, but the migrants did not return home and brought over their families instead. To date 215,000 Turkish and 170,000 Moroccan nationals reside in the Netherlands.

In this contribution I describe how these migrations have developed and why the measures taken to control the migration could not prevent the workers becoming immigrants.

The recruitment of labour

western Europe's economy recovered much more rapidly from the world war than expected. Even in the

PLATE 11: A Moroccan grocery shop in Groningen, the Netherlands.

Netherlands, with its relatively high natural growth, some sectors soon found it difficult to find enough hands to do the jobs. First, Italians were recruited by employers in the coal mines and the textile industry. But after 1960 other Mediterranean workers were hired. In many cases work permits were acquired in the Netherlands by migrants who had come on their own initiative, following the example of friends and relations. This led to various difficulties, for instance, breaches of safety regulations and conditions in lodging houses that were considered unacceptable in a modern welfare state.

The state intervened and formulated rules for the recruitment of labour. The regulations were made at a state level giving the governments of both the sending and the recruiting societies a certain measure of control over where labour could be recruited and under what conditions. Such 'recruitment agreements' were made with Italy (1960), Spain (1961), Portugal (1963), Turkey (1964) and Greece (1966). In 1966/7 the Dutch economy suffered from a recession and the need for foreign labour seemed to be over. But the economy recovered quickly again and already in 1969 (with Morocco) and 1970 (with Yugoslavia and Tunisia) new agreements were made. The peak years both for the import of labour and regulation by the government were between 1969 and 1972. The main instrument of government control was the work permit, which could now only be acquired in the home country and no longer in the Netherlands, at least not once someone had entered the country as a 'tourist' (Penninx 1979: 98–107).

After the oil crisis of 1973 new work permits were issued only in exceptional circumstances. The labour-intensive industries moved to countries with lower wages or went through a process of technological rejuvenation that made them dependent on a much smaller but more highly skilled labour force. When the paradoxical situation developed in which recruited workers became unemployed, the import of labour came to a sudden halt.

Table 9.9: *Citizens from 'recruitment countries' legally residing in the Netherlands, 1965 and 1992*

Country	1965	1992
Greece	3,042	5,235
Yugoslavia	1,034	15,148
Portugal	1,521	8,659
Spain	21,025	16,945
Turkey	8,822	214,830
Morocco	4,502	163,697
Tunisia	–	2,576
Cape Verde	–	2,757

Sources: Penninx (1979: 95); Muus (1992: 28).
Note: Italians are not included because recruited workers and their descendants form only a small part of the Italian population in the Netherlands.

Yet when we look at the figures presented in Table 9.7 we have to conclude that the end of the labour import did not mean the end of immigration. Only in the case of the Spaniards has the number decreased since 1965; they have indeed partly returned home. All other nationalities involved, and in particular the Turks and Moroccans, are more numerous than in the days of labour recruitment. The measures taken by the Dutch government to discourage immigration and to stimulate return migration have had no effect, just as similar measures in France met with only very partial success at best (van Amersfoort and Penninx 1993; Verbunt 1984).

Turks and Moroccans in the Netherlands
Muus and Penninx point out that an important background variable in Turkish and Moroccan migration to western Europe is the long-term lack of opportunity in the labour markets of Turkey and Morocco. Both countries suffer from heavy population pressure, political tensions, violence and economic crises, all conditions that create a permanent 'push factor' (Muus and Penninx 1991: 34–46).

When we look at the development of migrations, however, we observe that this 'push factor' provides only a partial explanation for the course of the migration process. The dynamics of migration flows are

increasingly being determined by decisions taken by migrants already residing in the Netherlands. A shift from labour migration (only adult men) to family unifying migration (wives and children) has resulted in the formation of settled immigrant communities. This is not to say that all immigrants look upon their stay as permanent. Many of them still harbour a wish to return home one day, but the majority will never return once their families have settled and their children (and eventually their grandchildren) have grown up. The return rate of Turks and Moroccans from western Europe has always been very low. Moreover, a substantial proportion of the returnees remigrate to the Netherlands (De Beer et al. 1991).

The settlement of families induced after some time a new type of immigration. If we look at the ages of male Turkish and Moroccan migrants, we see a remarkable development in the age category 15–29 years after 1984. We see in that period the migration of this particular age category gaining momentum again. There is a similar development for women in the 15–24 age group.

Once a community settles, its children grow up and in time reach marriageable age. So long as the number of eligible partners in the country of settlement remains small, and the cultural distance to the host country substantial, marriages will generally be contracted with partners from the homeland. This was particularly true of the Turks and Moroccans, for their marriages are traditionally arranged by the fathers. The great difference in prosperity between the Netherlands on the one hand and Turkey and Morocco on the other, made young people in the Netherlands very attractive marriage partners. Ancient custom and secular economic reasoning soon joined forces. In Turkey bride prices as high as 20,000 guilders (an enormous sum by Turkish standards) have been observed for 'brides from Holland' (Böcker 1992). The custom of patrilocality was immediately disregarded for these marriages. Marriage with a partner residing in the Netherlands is practically the only way of getting a residence permit for Turks or Moroccans who do not classify as 'dependants'. However, there are indications that, at least among the Turks, this kind of marriage migration has passed its peak. Young Turks reaching marriageable age have increasingly been socialized in the Netherlands and, especially among teenage girls, there is mounting resistance to an arranged marriage with a complete stranger. This may lead to an increase in endogamous marriages within the Turkish immigrant communities in western Europe and/or to an increase in mixed marriages.

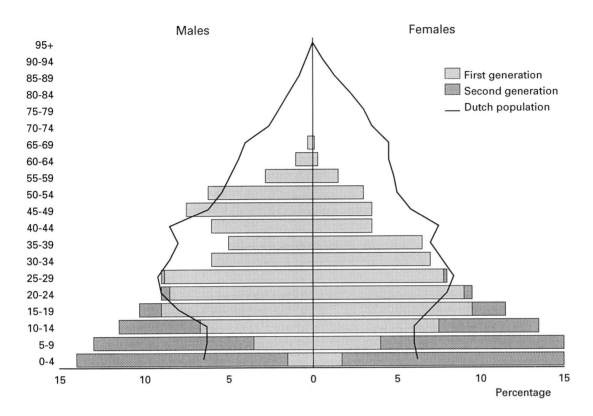

Figure 9.5: Age structure of the population with a Moroccan background in the Netherlands, 1 January 1990

Though the number of the latter is still small, it is rapidly increasing (Muus 1992: 20).

If unable to qualify as either a family member or marriage partner, the last legal option open to those who wish to migrate to the Netherlands is to apply for refugee status. There is a small, though from year to year erratic, number of immigrants in this category among the Turks (15 per cent of the entries in 1985, but only 5 per cent in 1989). So far this category hardly exists among the Moroccans.

Although the Turks have always been a step ahead of the Moroccans, Turkish and Moroccan migration to the Netherlands has gone through similar stages. The Turks came earlier, they started to bring over their families earlier and gave rise to the phenomenon of marriage migration earlier. The dynamics of this migration process not only caused an increase in the numbers of Turks and Moroccans in the Netherlands, but also changed the characteristics of the immigrant populations.

At each stage of the migration process there is a shift in what is considered to be the main problem with regard to the immigrants. In the first stage housing was seen as the most serious problem. When family reunification brought over complete families with children of all ages, the integration of these children into Dutch schools became a major issue. Now it is the high unemployment of especially the young Turks and Moroccans that causes most concern.

There will be further changes in the coming years. Figure 9.5 shows that the structure of the Moroccan population is exceptionally young. The Turkish population shows a similar profile. This means that even when migration slows down in the coming years (as expected) and fertility rates decline (as observed among married women under thirty) these populations will still grow substantially and will in the meantime develop a more balanced demographic structure. There will also be changes in social characteristics. Children born in the Netherlands are now already dominating the youngest age cohorts. Whatever their problems in the Dutch school system, these children will not have the same problems as the immigrant children of the past twenty years. It will also become more difficult to define Turks and Moroccans in the Netherlands. Nationality will become less satisfactory as a criterion in descriptions of Turks or Moroccans as an 'ethnic group'. By the year 2000, 15,000–20,000 persons of Turkish and 30,000–40,000 persons of Moroccan descent will have acquired Dutch citizenship.

Why control failed

The recruitment of labour during a relatively short period (1964–73) has led to substantive immigration, contrary to the wishes of the Dutch government. Why did the Dutch (like the Germans, French and others) fail to control these migration flows? Van Amersfoort and Penninx (1993) give a detailed analysis of the measures taken to control the migration and of the reasons for their limited success. Basically there are two categories of obstacles to effective migration control.

The first is the practical difficulty of implementing the regulations effectively. To enter the country Turks and Moroccans need a passport and nowadays even a visa. Though this might appear to be an efficient first check against 'unwanted immigrants', in reality it offers only a symbolic measure of control. It is virtually impossible to control everybody who passes a Dutch border. This would require an 'iron curtain' and would greatly hamper the daily flow of businessmen and tourists. Moreover, it is untrue that most 'illegals' enter the country illegally. They enter legally (for instance as tourists) and become illegal residents after some time. Who can tell if somebody entering as a tourist is in reality looking for a job? In theory this is of course not allowed. In reality illegal residents go unnoticed as long as they do not in one way or another attract the attention of the police or other bureaucrats. And even in such cases police officers often prove to have more important worries than coping with a worker who works in the Dutch bulb fields for a season without a work permit. In short, the construct of legality (entrance, residence and work) is much vaguer in reality than it seems on paper.

The second category of obstacles is created by the contradictory principles of the welfare state. The modern state is not a single unit acting with a one-dimensional purpose. Even direct organs of the state, such as the various ministries and courts of justice, have different priorities and responsibilities. In addition, the courts in the Netherlands have articulated the rights of immigrants in such a way that their position

is strengthened by their length of residence. A temporary residence permit can only be given for the first five years, after which an immigrant is entitled to a permanent residence permit. This gives them almost the same rights as citizenship, for instance the right to bring over a marriage partner. Dutch law and Dutch courts have been somewhat more generous than their western European counterparts. (In Germany an immigrant has to wait eight years and in Switzerland even ten years before a permanent residence permit is acquired.) However, these differences are not fundamental. All West European states experience the same kinds of impediments to effective migration control. This explains why we are seeing the same movement from workers to immigrants in all West European states. The case of the Turks and Moroccans in the Netherlands is only an exceptionally clear example of this development.

References

Böcker, Anita (1992) 'Gevestigde migranten als bruggehoofden en grenswachters: kettingmigratie over juridisch gesloten grenzen', *Migrantenstudies*, 8 (4), 61–78

De Beer, J., H. Kuijper and R. Noordam (1991) 'Gezinsherenigende, gezinsvormende en retourmigratie van Turken en Marokkanen', *Maandstatistiek van de Bevolking CBS*, 39 (1), 38–49

De Beer, J. and A. Sprangers (1993) 'Het effect van de buitenlandse migratie op de omvang en de samenstelling van de bevolking', in H. van Amersfoort (ed.) *Migratie, Bevolkingsontwikkeling en Politiek*, Amsterdam: Instituut voor Sociale Geografie, Universiteit van Amsterdam, 11–25

Marshall-Goldschwartz, A. (1973) *The Import of Labour: The Case of the Netherlands*, Rotterdam: Rotterdam University Press

Muus, Philip J. (1992) *Migration, Minorities and Policy in the Netherlands. Report on Behalf of the Continuous Reporting System on Migration (SOPEMI) of the OECD*, Amsterdam: Institute for Social Geography, University of Amsterdam

Muus, Philip J. and R. Penninx (1991) *Immigratie van Turken en Marokkanen in Nederland*, Den Haag: Ministerie van Binnenlandse Zaken

Penninx, R. (1979) *Etnische Minderheden. Rapport no.17 van de Wetenschappelijke Raad voor het Regeringsbeleid*, Den Haag: Staatsuitgeverij

Van Amersfoort, Hans (1993a) 'International Migration and Population in the Netherlands', *Tijdschrift voor Economische en Sociale Geografie*, 84 (1), 65–74

Van Amersfoort, Hans and Rinus Penninx (1993) 'Migratie-ontwikkeling en Migratiebeheersing', in H. van Amersfoort (ed.) *Migratie, Bevolkingsontwikkeling en Politiek*, Amsterdam: Instituut voor Sociale Geografie, Universiteit van Amsterdam, 57–84

Verbunt, Gilles (1984) 'France', in Tomas Hammar (ed.) *European Immigration Policy*, Cambridge: Cambridge University Press, 127–65

ITALY AND GREECE: FROM EMIGRANTS TO IMMIGRANTS

ROSSETTOS FAKIOLAS

Despite a long tradition of extensive emigration (until the late 1960s) and high levels of unemployment (about 9 per cent of the labour force), Italy and Greece, which are both at the intermediate stage of economic development, employ thousands of immigrants from the Third World and the former socialist countries in low-status jobs, so far without any major labour market conflict or serious trade union objection. The majority work without permits or social insurance and at about half the market rate of pay, thus raising questions about the economic rationale and social justification for rigid labour market regulations concerning high minimum wages, strict dismissal procedures and 'generous' welfare benefits. Large unrecorded employment leads to abuses against the immigrants and fuels further underground economic activity (in both countries about 30 per cent of the total).

Italy (with a population of 57 million and a per capita income in terms of purchasing power at about 80 per cent of the EU average) and Greece (with a population of 10.4 million earning about 65 per cent of the EU average) have faced a dramatic decline in birth rates – by approximately one-third since the early 1980s – leading to an actual population decline. They have also suffered long periods of undemocratic government (Italy from 1924 to 1945 and Greece from 1936 to 1944 and again from 1967 to 1974). Greece has no recent 'imperial' past but its 1946–49 civil war caused, among other things, the expatriation of about 65,000 political refugees to the socialist countries, of which over three-quarters are now back in Greece.

Internal political stability under democracy and early post-war economic development enabled Italy to become a founder EEC member (under the Treaty of Paris in 1952 and the Treaty of Rome in 1957). Greece joined in 1981, but the free movement of its dependent labour took effect only from 1987, although net repatriation had already started in 1974. The average 6 per cent annual growth rate of both economies between 1950 and 1973 – among the highest in the world – increased incomes fivefold and

transformed Italy from a backward country into the world's fifth largest economic power. However, since then it has dropped to 1.5 per cent.

The wide discrepancies between an industrialized north and an underdeveloped south, characteristic of Italy, do not exist in Greece. Neither do the two countries have similar administrative structures. Italy is a regional state with autonomous French- and German-speaking minorities in the Alps. However, though Greece also contains minorities – there are over 100,000 Muslims in Thrace in the north, other Muslims (the Pomacs), many gypsies who move around offering useful seasonal work in agriculture and an unspecified number of Slavs – it is highly centralized.

From emigration to immigration

There was a net emigration from Italy of about four million between 1945 and 1970 and from Greece of nearly one million between 1945 and 1973. About half of these emigrated to northern Europe, with the overwhelming majority of the rest going to the USA, Canada and Australia. Approximately ten million people have emigrated from these two countries since the mid-nineteenth century. However, about half of those who emigrated to other European countries since the early 1970s have repatriated and now only a few thousand (mainly invited family members) emigrate overseas annually, reflecting both the considerable difference in the type of emigration between the two areas and the almost complete drying up of overseas emigration.

Until the early 1980s working immigrants, largely of Italian and Greek origin, amounted to about 1 per cent of the labour force and were registered. There are now six to ten times more (mainly unregistered) immigrants from the Third World in Italy, and from Poland and Albania in Greece. Many are not easily categorized. Some Italian and French nationals commute daily to work in France and Italy respectively; the EU defines residency in another member country as 'free movement of people within a Community of Citizens'; many 'northerners' live in the south as 'working tourists or pensioners'; some Third World businesses have 'provisionally' transferred offices and employees to Italy and Greece for security reasons. Are these then all immigrants?

Furthermore, about 50,000 former Soviet citizens of Greek origin have settled and become naturalized in Greece (mostly in the last five years). In 1992 they left Pontos, where they had lived for centuries before it became part of the Soviet Union, and about half a million more still want to emigrate. Some, though they have Greek names, do not speak Greek and a few have never even visited Greece. Like the German *Aussiedler* or the former Soviet Jews settling in Israel, they are not strictly immigrants, returnees or repatriates.

Official statistics on legally employed foreigners in Greece show that numbers have remained more or less constant over the last three decades, at between 28,000 and 34,000, of whom about a third are of Greek origin. One in five work in domestic and other services (especially the thousands of young women from the Philippines) and a few thousand are employed in industry and the navy. Their actual number is thought to be between 300,000 and 450,000, or 8–11 per cent of the labour force of 3.9 million. Many of the 800,000 Albanians deported in 1991–94 have returned and more are still coming across the extensive border separating the two countries. The coast guards tend to arrest only a few of the Third World 'boat people'. OECD statistics recorded 773,000 employed foreigners in Italy in 1990 (0.4 per cent of the labour force), up from 400,000 in 1985. However, the widespread measures to 'legalize', deport or prevent them from disembarking suggest a much larger number.

Italy and Greece assist political refugees and asylum-seekers and allow some of them to work legally. But as with all other immigrants, only a few hundred in Italy and few dozen in Greece become naturalized each year. 'This is not an immigration country' declare the authorities.

Pull and push factors for migration

With notable exceptions (the USA, Canada, Australia and Ireland) migration is linked to capital flows and foreign trade. At the early stages of economic growth most countries 'export' unskilled labour and raw materials and 'import' experts, capital and technology. With rapid growth emigration and eventually capital imports decline and exports of industrial goods increase. With further growth fewer people emigrate and 'exports' consist mainly of capital, high-tech commodities, advanced producer services and quali-

fied persons; local people avoid low-status jobs, thus inducing foreign labour to enter.

Post-war emigration from Italy and Greece resulted mainly from high manifest and latent unemployment brought about by the rapid population growth (about 1.5 per cent annually) and the increased productivity of agricultural labour, employing about half the labour force in Greece and one-third in Italy. It was also due to wages abroad being between three and six times higher than those at home. By inviting about 30 million foreigners, the receiving countries once more indicated the limited advantages of substituting capital for labour. With rapid growth in Italy and Greece emigration declined and eventually turned into net repatriation, even before unemployment rose in Europe after 1973 (ESF 1982; Fakiolas and Voss 1989).

The first economic immigrants to Italy and Greece arrived in the early 1980s from Poland and later from other socialist countries. The economic reforms in eastern Europe in the 1980s turned high latent unemployment into open unemployment when firms moved away from their 'traditional' policy under Marxist socialism of keeping people on the payroll irrespective of advancing mechanization and/or slack demand for the product. Political liberalization allowed the unemployed and low-paid to seek work abroad (Hellenic Foundation 1992). Large-scale immigration from the Third World started when the more 'familiar' receiving countries (the ex-colonial European powers) imposed immigration restrictions, followed ten years later by dramatic economic, political and demographic developments in the neighbouring Arab countries.

The main pull factor for immigration has been the demand for flexible labour, strong throughout the year but especially so in the summer because of the high seasonality in the major productive branches of agriculture, construction and tourism. Despite rapid mechanization many production processes remain labour intensive (from picking most kinds of fruit and vegetables to catering, cleaning and house repairs), whereas active welfare policies secure an income for most unemployed people and the institutional framework discourages labour mobility and part-time employment. High minimum wages and restrictions on dismissals, coupled with high social insurance costs, tend to discourage further new hirings. Under such circumstances shortages of unskilled labour induce neither higher capital intensity nor labour upgrading and the use of new techniques. In fact such shortages may well hinder rapid growth.

Policy dilemmas

For Italy and Greece, the gateways to other European countries, immigration is a 'rapid-growth business' involving increasing regulation by the police. Its many positive effects are, however, offset by the difficulties of formulating and implementing rational policies. It is also an issue over which governments are being forced to collaborate, as evidenced for example by the numerous high-level consultations about Albanian migration and the issuing of 30,000 permits to Albanians for seasonal work in Greece, discussions about illegal immigration between Greece and Turkey in September 1993 and a large ministerial meeting on migration in Athens in November 1993. However, such initiatives do not necessarily yield the required solutions.

While the economic immigrants remit some foreign exchange back home, they tend to consume local goods and, being mainly young and without family obligations, make very little use of the heavily subsidized social infrastructure (housing, schools and hospitals). However, because much of their employment is illegal, they boost the underground economy and contribute little to the ailing social insurance system (despite repeated reforms, the 1992 accumulated deficit in Greece was US$5 billion). Furthermore, living in a social environment where about one in six compatriots is an emigrant or has spent more than one year abroad, Italians and Greeks see millions of economic immigrants trying to share their material prosperity. Nonetheless, this is largely offset by official tolerance for illegal immigrants and there is mounting pressure to give them more opportunities to integrate.

Thanks to trade union indifference and social harmony, the authorities have so far avoided the economic and administrative costs of imposing strict controls. With high unemployment, however, the dangers of large-scale immigration (whether legal or illegal) should not be underestimated. Witness, for example, the violence against immigrants in Germany, the growing social unrest in southern France and the revival of nationalism and religious fundamentalism, which have been occurring despite moves to create multi-state administrative and political bodies and a pronounced trend towards economic globalization. The Albanians, however, who are increasingly being blamed for the rise in criminality, are not creating the problem. They have lived in the Balkans for over twenty-five centuries, thousands of Greeks speak Albanian, and there is a sizeable Greek minority in Albania with its roots in antiquity. Having been under the same state administration for many years, Albania and Italy also have close links. If peace settles in the area and political progress continues in Albania, increased cross-border labour mobility will be highly beneficial to all, in much the same way as Finnish emigration had been to the other Scandinavian countries forty years earlier.

It appears then that the most serious immigration problems will arise from the growing unemployment in the neighbouring Arab world. But this is not a problem for Italy and Greece alone.

References

ESF (1982) *Cultural Identity and Structural Marginalization of Migrant Workers*, Strasbourg: European Science Foundation

Fakiolas, R. and W. Voss (1989) *Wanderungsbewegungen aus und nach Griechenland seit 1973*, ISOLPLAN, Saarbruecken-Lauderdale: Verlag Breitenbach

Hellenic Foundation for Denfence and Foreign Policy (1992) *The Southern European Yearbook 1991*, Athens: Eliander

OECD (various years) *Economic Surveys* (Italy, Greece)

PORTUGAL AND SPAIN: FROM EXPORTERS TO IMPORTERS OF LABOUR

CARLOTA SOLÉ

The 'Carnation Revolution' and the return of democracy to Portugal are at the root of Portugal's present immigratory phenomenon. In Spain, the traditional flow of emigration to the USA and Europe dried up in 1975. The development of the domestic economy and the international situation gradually reversed the migratory process and, in the first five years of the 1980s, Spain became a receiving country. By the end of the decade, and following the passage of the *Ley de Extranjeria* in 1985, legal immigrants in Spain numbered approximately half a million and came from Europe, Latin America, Africa and Asia (CIDE 1992: 18; IOE 1989). In addition, there were an estimated 250,000 or more illegal immigrants and foreigners whose papers were not in order (Izquierdo 1992: 191).

The 1974 events in Portugal and the consequent start of the decolonization process provoked three different reverses in the migratory flows characteristic of the years of the Salazar dictatorship:

- the return of the emigratory flows whose destinations shifted in the 1960s from North America (the USA and Canada) and Latin America to industrialized Europe;
- the beginning of inflows from Third World countries with historic colonial and linguistic ties with Portugal; and
- the return of emigrants repatriated from the former colonies (Esteves 1991).

The immigrants coming from the ex-colonies signified the arrival of a young and qualified population – African students – as well as a population of non-qualified workers – mainly from Cape Verde – who came to Portugal to fill the gaps in the labour market left by Portuguese workers who had moved to Europe. This Cape Verdian population was to become the main immigrant community in the country: the largest proportion of immigrants to Portugal are Cape Verdians; their working and living conditions are the most precarious and they also account for the highest proportion of underachievers in school.

The first methodological problem we encounter when analysing the phenomenon is the ambivalent concept of the term 'immigrant'. The following factors must be kept firmly in mind: Portugal has no tradition of immigrants; figures on immigration are unreliable (there are only two sources: figures furnished by the *Serviço de Estrangeiros* and data from the 1981 census); the ambiguous sense of 'national' (many people from the former colonies consider themselves foreign but actually have Portuguese passports); and the massive proportion of the population whose situation is irregular. In Spain, the most reliable figures come from the Ministry of the Interior, the *Dirección General de Migraciones*, the 1981 census, population surveys and statistical estimates of the number of illegal immigrants. The semantic confusion that reigns among Spanish jurists and sociologists over terms such as 'first- and second-generation immigrants', 'ethnic minorities' and 'cultural communities' is gradually being resolved. The distinction between legal and illegal immigrants has been clear since the *Ley de Extranjeria* was enacted in 1985.

Composition of the immigration flows

The second factor that determined Portugal's role as a receiver of immigrants dates back to 1981, when the foreign population experienced an important growth: from 0.33 per cent of the total population in 1960 to 1.24 per cent in 1981 (Rocha-Trinidade 1992). The bulk of the legal immigrants comes from PALOP (*Paises Africanos de Língua Oficial Portuguesa*) countries: Cape Verde, Angola, Mozambique, Guinea-Bissau, São Tomé and Principe, and from the European Union, which account for 40 per cent and 27 per cent of the total of legal immigrants respectively (CGTP 1991).

Legal immigrants break down in numerical order as follows: Cape Verde ranks first with 29,532 legal immigrants in Portugal, followed by Brazil 12,064, Angola 5596, Guinea-Bissau 4630, Venezuela 4509, Mozambique 3297, São Tomé and Principe 2171, Pakistan 732, India 640, and China 1346. In 1992 the main nationalities for legal residents were: Cape Verdian (31,129), Brazilian (14,007), British (9264), Spanish (7740), North American (7490) and Angolan (6568). When figures for 1990, 1991 and 1992 are compared the increase in the number of Cape Verdian and Brazilians is greater than the increases registered by the other nationalities (Departamento de Fronteiras 1993).

The main countries of origin are those with a special link with Portugal because of their colonial background: PALOP countries, Brazil, Timor (annexed to Indonesia in 1975) and India (Indians and also Pakistanis who had first emigrated to Mozambique). In 1961 India annexed Goa, Damão, Diu, Padrá and Nagar Aveli, and Macao (a former Portuguese possession in China). Although the flow of immigrants from India and China is small, it has begun to increase over the past few years.

According to statistics furnished by the Spanish *Dirección General de la Policía* and published by CIDE in 1992, 125,858 of Spain's legal immigrants (43.1 per cent of the total) are from EU countries, 7000 are from eastern Europe (1.3 per cent) and 39,513 are from other European countries (7.2 per cent). Exactly 23,473 legal immigrants (4.3 per cent of the total) are from North America, while 103,729 (18.9 per cent) are from Latin America. African immigration accounts for 15.6 per cent of the total (66,193 legal immigrants from North Africa and 19,210 from other parts of the continent). Asian immigrants number 51,594 (9.4 per cent of the total), but only a very few of these are from the Far East.

Immigration to Spain from North Africa and the other African and Asian countries, traditionally lower than immigration from Europe, has increased over the past ten years. Immigration from Africa increased fivefold between 1980 and 1992, with Morocco accounting for 60 per cent of the increase. Other African immigrants come from Senegambia, Guinea, Nigeria, Cape Verde and elsewhere. Asian immigrants come from Pakistan, India, China and particularly the Philippines.

Unlike European immigrants, the majority of immigrants from the so-called Third World come to Spain for economic reasons, which explains the way in which foreign immigrants are distributed throughout the country. While European immigrants concentrate in Madrid, Barcelona and the resort areas (the Balearic and Canary Islands, Malaga and Alicante), African and Asian immigrants settle in the parts of Spain where economic activity is greatest: Catalonia, the greater Madrid area, Andalusia and Valencia.

Among the foreigners who have immigrated to Spain for economic reasons are a relatively large number of illegal aliens, most of whom are located in the provinces of Barcelona, Madrid, Gerona, Lerida, Malaga and Alicante. Judging from the number of applications for combined residence and work permits, 30 per cent of the economic immigrants are located in Catalonia, followed by Andalusia, the greater Madrid area, and the resorts in the Balearic and Canary Islands (Izquierdo 1992: 181). Portuguese gypsies are an exception to this rule, tending to settle in the provinces bordering on their native country and in the north of Spain, and generally working at seasonal jobs in agriculture.

Illegal immigration is more common among women than men. In some cases this is due to families attempting to reunite and, in others, to the demand for workers in certain 'female' occupations (like domestic service, nursing and cleaning) (Solé 1993: 21). Illegal immigration is far higher among women than men from the Dominican Republic and the Philippines, as well as Chinese, Cape Verdians and Guineans, even though, on the whole, male immigrants outnumber their female counterparts (CIDE 1992: 2).

The start of the migratory process

The survey directed by the Cámara de Lisboa (1991) reveals the following reasons for emigrating: economic and work (61 per cent work and 15 per cent to join their families) for the most numerous communities, i.e. natives of Cape Verde, São Tomé, Guinea and India. The Indians also mentioned political reasons: 31 per cent of them referred to the situation in Mozambique in terms of war and independence (CIDE 1992: 12).

In addition to the north–south structural imbalance, PALOP countries have had to contend with many other pressures. Portugal's African colonies began securing their independence in 1974, following the end of colonial occupation and the demise of the Salazar dictatorship. Though similar to the decolonization process in African countries after the Second World War, independence came much later to the Portuguese colonies than to the rest of the African countries. Since the 1960s Angola and Mozambique have been living with the hardships of violent civil wars, which have destroyed their societies and economies. Although Guinea-Bissau and São Tomé and Principe are not presently at war, they have as yet been unable to achieve economic viability. Countries like Cape Verde and Guinea-Bissau have been listed among the world's ten poorest countries. Although

PLATE 12: Returning from Africa at the end of the Portuguese empire

the five aforementioned countries were long ruled by authoritarian governments, São Tomé and Cape Verde have managed to embark on a transition to democracy without too much trouble (Marques da Costa and Nátalia 1992).

In Cape Verde, the anachronistic distribution of land, consecutive droughts (the country's already limited natural resources are beset with ecological problems), the population explosion, widespread uncertainty about the future, the government's stance on migration, the desire of students to make contacts abroad, the migratory tradition (forced or spontane-

ous) and the blend of an 'adventurous Portuguese past' and 'African strength' have combined to give the country one of the Third World's most emigratory populations.

Cape Verdian emigration may be triggered by political factors and a population explosion, but economic factors are always present, making people dissatisfied with the social, economic and political situation. Economic dissatisfaction stems from the high rate of unemployment in the subsistence sectors of the economy (farming and fishing). In a situation like this, emigration is a sort of decompression for individuals and families – improving the socio-economic level of the family – and for their society, which benefits from the remittances emigrants send home from abroad.

The largest number of Cape Verdian emigrants come from Santiago, the most densely populated island, followed by S. Vicente, Sta. Antão e Fogo and S. Nicolau (de França 1992). The migration pattern is based on a family strategy, which involves gradual reunification (the first to emigrate is the father, followed by the eldest son). Meanwhile the wife takes over from the husband in working the farm or selling fish in order to earn some money to add to her husband's remittances for their children's needs.

Male emigrants from Cape Verde are generally labourers and farmers, while female emigrants are either statistically non-active or work in service jobs (Direcção Geral do Planeamento 1988, quoting Andrade). Remittances from abroad attract other Cape Verdians, who then migrate with the help of 'call letters' and travel expenses advanced by the first emigrant (de França 1992). Electrical equipment is the preferred form of remittance because of Portuguese currency devaluations. Money is usually sent home with other Cape Verdians who act as couriers.

Emigrants generally enter the country on tourist or business visas. Once in Portugal they can seek asylum. Cape Verdians tend to travel by plane. Tickets are paid for by the godfather system: the richest people in the villages become money lenders (Andrade 1993). Angolans, Zaireans and Guineans arrive via clandestine African networks. They work illegally for half the minimum wage, receive no welfare benefits and live in poor housing. After six months to a year in Portgual they are often sent on to Germany or France, where similar living conditions await them.

Many Zaireans went first to Luanda (Angola) and then to Portugal. They are the descendants of people who went to Zaire in the 1960s when the armed struggle broke out in Angola and they still hold Angolan passports. The Cape Verdians have used clandestine channels, usually either going to Dakar or escaping aboard foreign ships anchored in Cape Verde (Direcção Geral do Planeamento 1988). Cape Verdian emigration to Dakar has also been a springboard for emigration to other African countries and to Europe (mainly France). Their 'umbilical' relationship with Portugal (in many cases the official language of their native country is Portuguese or they have relatives or friends already living in Portugal) explains why many Cape Verdians and Angolans choose Portugal as their destination.

The destinations of the Cape Verdian diaspora have been (in order of the largest Cape Verdian communities abroad in 1988) America (USA, Argentina, Brazil 250,000), Africa (Angola 35,000–40,000, Senegal 22,000–25,000, São Tomé and Principe 8000, Guinea-Bissau 2000, which demonstrates the rotation between Cape Verde, Angola and São Tomé) and Europe (Portugal 50,000, the Netherlands 10,000, Italy 8000–10,000, France 7000–9000, Spain 5000–8000 and Luxembourg 3000) (Direcção Geral do Planeamento 1988: 99).

Brazilian economic migrants choose the USA as their first destination – Vianna (1993) estimates a Brazilian colony of between 30,000 and 40,000 people – whereas those who choose Portugal do so because of family links, job transfers, and educational and professional goals.

The foreigners who immigrated to Spain from Africa and Asia during the 1980s were relatively young: most of them were between twenty-two and forty years of age and had little education beyond primary school, which some of them had not even finished. The proportion of immigrants who have completed primary school is highest among African and Asian males under the age of thirty-two, who are almost always bachelors or at least unaccompanied by their families. Differences in educational background are particularly notable among the Moroccans: while as many as 30 per cent say they have never been to school, a sizeable number claim to have a secondary or higher education. The Asians are somewhere in the middle.

Nevertheless, foreign immigrants are familiar with several languages and have varying levels of proficiency, not only in languages of their countries of origin but European languages as well. All the Africans can at least read and write Arabic and also speak other local languages such as Mandinga, Olof or Sarankole. The Moroccans appear to have less of a command of Arabic than the Africans (57 per cent speak it and 40 per cent write it), and all of them speak Berber. Though many of the young single Africans speak English as well as the languages of their native countries, few of them have much knowledge of Spanish (Solé and Herrera 1991).

Africans decide to emigrate to Europe after having attempted to secure better living conditions in their own countries. Some of them decide to go straight to Spain, but most of them simply want to cross the country in order to get to the heart of Europe. Fairly soon after their arrival in Spain they usually decide to settle in Catalonia, Madrid or Andalusia.

Foreigners usually immigrate to Spain for economic reasons. They tend to emigrate more from cities in which there are few opportunities for securing permanent employment than from villages and their goal is to find a permanent job and to earn better wages. They are not people who were unemployed in their native countries. Most of the Africans worked in the construction industry while most of the Moroccans were employed in wholesale or retail trade. This explains why they had sufficient means (savings, property, jewellery) to pay the costs of emigration. Even so, most of them do not manage to obtain all the papers they need to enter Spain legally. Those who decide to leave their countries when jobs are scarce tend to be younger, single men. This is particularly true of the Asians and Africans. Only a very few Moroccans decide to emigrate in order to look for better paid jobs.

The Africans, and to a lesser extent the Moroccans and Asians, know absolutely nothing about Spain before boarding the ship or, in a few cases, the aeroplane that will bring them to this gateway to Europe.

In only a few cases does chain emigration take place. Most of them therefore settle in boarding houses (particularly single African men) when they first arrive. Very few stay in the houses of relatives, friends or acquaintances. The Asians help one another with housing and other matters more than their Moroccan and African counterparts. Entering Spain is a risky business for all foreign immigrants. All the Asians and half the Africans and Moroccans interviewed in 1987 (Solé and Herrera 1991) admitted that they had entered the country 'without all the papers', with younger, single men taking greater risks than their older or married counterparts.

From 1980 to 1985 it was relatively easy for immigrants to find a first job in Spain, albeit temporary and seasonal, through some relative or other intermediary. It was more difficult to obtain the work and residence permits that would entitle them to remain in the country. Although all the immigrants interviewed say they now have these permits, more than half of them said they had acquired them through an intermediary (this was particularly true in the case of the Africans) rather than directly from the government and that they had cost between 10,000 and 40,000 pesetas. Generally speaking, young, single Africans relied more on intermediaries to find them their first steady, though temporary, jobs, than did Asians and Moroccans who were generally helped by some relative, friend or acquaintance.

References

Andrade, Arnaldo (1993) Vice-President of the Capeverdian Association, Lisbon. Interviewed in May

Câmara de Lisboa (1991) *Minorias étnicas pobres em Lisboa*, Lisbon: Centro de Reflexão Cristã

CGTP (Confederação Geral dos Trabalhadores Portugueses) (1991) *Coloquio sobre os Trabalhadores Migrantes em Portugal. Documento base*, October, Lisbon: CGTP

CIDE (Centro Nacional de Investigación, Documentación y Evaluación) (1992) *Censo de Inmigrantes Extranjeros Residentes Legales en España 1992 Dossier*, Madrid: CIDE

De França, Luís et al. (1992) *A Comunidade Cabo Verdiana em Portugal*, Lisbon: Instituto de Estudos para o Desenvolvimento.

Departamento de Fronteiras (1993) *Estrangeires residentes en T. M. por Nacionalidades até 31 de Dezembre de 1991*, Lisbon: Departamento de Fronteiras

Direcção Geral do Planeamento (1988). 'Integração das Variáveis Demográficas na Planificação', *Documentos do Primeiro Seminario Nacional*, Praia, Capo Verde, 19–20 December

Esteves, Maria do Céu et al. (1991) *Portugal, Pais de Imigração*, Lisbon: Instituto de Estudos para o Desenvolvimento

IOE (1989) 'España, Frontera sur de Europa', *Documentación Social*, Madrid, 77, 101–11

Izquierdo, Antonio (1992) *La inmigración en España 1980–1990*, Madrid: Ministerio de Trabajo

Marques da Costa, Fernando and Falé Nátalia (1992) *Guia Politico dos PALOP*, Lisbon: Fundação de Relaçoes

Rocha-Trinidade, Maria Beatriz (1992) 'Portugal: O Novo Enquadramento das Políticas Migratórias', paper presented to conference on Migration Trends in the 1990s: Old Themes, New Issues, Lisbon, 6–8 April

Solé, Carlota (1993) 'Realitat social de les Minories etniques', *Barcelona Societat*, 1, Barcelona

Solé, Carlota and Encarna Herrera (1991) *Los Trabajadores extranjeros en Cataluña*, Madrid: Centro de Investigaciones Sociológicas

Vianna, Carlos Henrique (1993) Vice-President of the Casa do Brasil, Lisbon. Interviewed in May

PART TEN

REPATRIATES AND COLONIAL AUXILIARIES

The reason why the notion of a 'repatriate' seems distant to native English-speakers is that the relevant experience has been unusual in British and American history. However, repatriation has occasioned deep political traumas in other countries. Let me provide some examples. In 1960, the Belgians scrambled out of the Congo amidst scenes of chaos and destruction. Tearful nuns and frightened settlers fled on hastily improvised flights back to Brussels. The following year the UN secretary-general, Dag Hammarskjöld, was tragically killed in an air crash as he tried to intervene in the Congo crisis. The French in Indochina and later in Algeria had to evacuate many French nationals as their own imperial missions came to an end in those countries. Again, these events were of great political moment, as the French army lurched to the right in protest against what it saw as a betrayal by mendacious, weak politicians. The creation of the Fifth Republic in 1958 by de Gaulle was a direct result of the failures in Indochina and Algeria and the repatriation that followed.

In terms of the numbers of repatriates in relation to the natal population, the return of the Portuguese from their African empire is the most startling case. *Rocha-Trindade* numbers the *retornados* (as the repatriates were called) at 800,000 – a massive influx compared to the ten million locals. The Portuguese had had a dry run in the 1960s when they were forced to evacuate Goa, but nothing prepared them for the scale and speed (it all happened over the period 1974–9) of the African evacuation. It is a great testimony to the open-heartedness of the Portuguese people and the strength of their fledgling democratic institutions that the absorption of the repatriates took place with remarkable success. (It is also worth drawing attention to the negative inference that whereas Portugal, with its modest standard of living, had little difficulty accepting one newcomer for every 12 inhabitants, wealthier European countries refuse to consider for admission a minute fraction of this ratio as refugees or asylum-seekers. Clearly the blood of a common ethnicity runs thicker than the water of a common humanity.)

The Dutch in Indonesia had a somewhat similar experience to the Portuguese in Africa, although over two decades earlier. In the period 1950–58, nearly 300,000 were forced to 'return' to the Netherlands after the violent struggle for independence in Indonesia. I put the notion of 'return' in inverted commas because many of the Dutch were born in the East Indies and, as *Entzinger* remarks, two-thirds were of mixed racial origin. Again, as in the Portuguese case, it is remarkable how quickly this group, this time mainly Eurasian, entered the mainstream of Dutch life. *Entzinger* indeed suggests that the process of assimilation was almost too swift, with some of the colonial repatriates experiencing a sense of lost identity. The Dutch also absorbed a special group of 'colonial auxiliaries', the Amboinese or South Moluccans, who had served in the Dutch colonial army and were left awash when the triumphant Indonesians refused to recognize their claims for independence. Finally, 'Creoles' (Afro-Surinamese) and Indo-Surinamese were repatriated in significant numbers to the Netherlands from the former Dutch West Indies.

There is undoubtedly a great ambiguity surrounding the exact definition and rights to be accorded to descendants of colonial settlers of mixed race, to allies of the colonists and to groups that had been shipped to far parts of the world to aid mercantilism and the plantation economies established by the colonial powers. What is clear is that, on the whole, the Dutch faced up to their colonial responsibilities while, by contrast, successive British governments writhed and wriggled on the end-of-empire hook. Nowhere is this better illustrated than in the example of the East African Asians. Perhaps because of the lack of a repatriate experience in the UK, the character of this group has been ill-understood in Britain. In many respects they closely resembled the colonial auxiliaries recognized by the Dutch. However, the leader of the chauvinist pack could see no such obligation. Enoch Powell (cited Goulbourne 1991: 117) claimed that 'When the East African countries became independent there was no suggestion, let alone undertaking, in Parliament or outside, that those inhabitants who remained citizens of the United Kingdom and Colonies would have a right of entry into this country.' 'Suggestions' there clearly were, both by colonial secretaries and by visiting colonial officials; certainly most East African Asians thought they had been given cast-iron assurances that they could either opt for local citizenship or use their UK passports to enter Britain. Finally, the Heath government recognized its obligations to UK passport holders and, amidst much public protest, admitted many Ugandan Asians over the period 1972–3. And what was all the fuss about? As *Robinson* (1993 and this *Survey*) argues, East African Asians, despite the gloomy prognostications at the time, have settled well. Compared with their white-British and Indian-British counterparts, they have better formal qualifications, are over-represented in self-employment, have better housing and experience greater social mobility.

The cases we have considered so far have had colonial settings, and this context also informs the case of the Tamils in independent Sri Lanka, 337,066 of whom had been repatriated to India by January 1986. As *Kanapathipillai*, notes, the use of the expression 'repatriation' is controversial locally, for it seems to concede too much to the claims of the Sri Lankan government. Unlike in East Africa, the British colonial government had managed to wriggle off the hook completely, leaving it to the Indian and Sri Lankan governments to determine the citizenship of the Tamils, most of whom had been brought to Ceylon as plantation workers during the colonial period. After much wrangling, a Solomon-like judgement was reached, with the Sri Lankans agreeing to recognize 375,000 Tamils and their 'natural increase' for citizenship. India, on the other hand, agreed to admit 525,000 and their descendants.

There was considerable arm-twisting in Sri Lanka to persuade local Tamils to accept repatriation to India, but nothing compared to the forced repatriation of Soviet citizens at the end of the Second World War. The Soviet citizens included released prisoners of war, forced labourers, concentration camp survivors, those who opposed communism in Russia and those who had always refused to accept it as the Communist Party bullied and cajoled the many national minorities in the Soviet Union. As *Sword* demonstrates, the story of the forced repatriation was not an edifying one as far as the Allied forces were concerned, with millions being summarily sent back to a country they despised.

Forced repatriation is to be strongly distinguished from the sponsored, voluntary repatriation described by *Koehn* in the case of African returnees. This is an extremely important precedent as the policy of voluntary repatriation has been accepted by the United Nations High Commission for Refugees and by a number of powerful Western governments as the only way that the vast and accelerating number of refugees (see later Parts of the *Survey*) can be resettled. It is a depressing but realistic thought that such are the numbers involved and such the level of xenophobia in the countries of refuge, that the long-term settlement of most refugees in destination countries now looks like a pipe dream.

References

Goulbourne, Harry (1991) *Ethnicity and Nationalism in Post-imperial Britain*, Cambridge: Cambridge University Press
Robinson, Vaughan (1993) 'Marching into the Middle Classes? The Long-term Resettlement of East African Asians in the UK', *Journal of Refugee Studies*, 6 (3), 230–47

THE REPATRIATION OF SOVIET CITIZENS AT THE END OF THE SECOND WORLD WAR

KEITH SWORD

In the course of the Second World War, huge population movements took place on the European continent. It has been estimated that in the years 1939–45 some 30 million people were displaced, and that by 1945 some 7 million non-Germans were living in Germany and Austria. (Proudfoot 1957: 169). The surviving civilian and military personnel became, as displaced persons (or DPs), the responsibility of the Allied governments once the continent began to be liberated from German control. They included released prisoners of war, forced labourers and concentration camp survivors, but also collaborators and civilian refugees who had fled to the West to evade coming under Soviet control. In the early days the brunt of the DP problem fell upon the military, its efforts co-ordinated by the Supreme Headquarters Allied Expeditionary Force (SHAEF). Only in the course of 1945 was the United Nations Relief and Rehabilitation Administration (UNRRA) able to take over responsibility.

Soviet citizens figured prominently among the displaced, the two most numerous categories being civilian forced labourers, seized during the Wehrmacht's successful drive against the Soviet Union in 1941/2, and prisoners of war or deserters from Red Army formations. In the period from 1941 to 1945 a staggering 5,245,882 Soviet troops were taken prisoner by the Germans. However, the brutal exploitation of Red Army prisoners as slave labour led to astronomic rates of mortality. Only 2,000,735 of these prisoners were subsequently returned to the Soviet Union, leaving a figure of more than 3 million missing presumed dead (Erickson 1993).

Western politicians and officials became aware that large numbers of Soviet citizens might resist repatriation. In the course of the war, the Soviet government had appeared indifferent to the fate of its captured or abducted citizens. The Soviet leadership had steadfastly refused to sign the 1929 Geneva Convention on the treatment of prisoners of war and initially seemed reluctant to acknowledge that its troops had in fact been captured in significant numbers. The struggle against the Nazis took on the trappings of a holy war

and official expectations were that Red Army soldiers would choose death rather than surrender. A Soviet decree of 1942 had openly stated that any soldier captured alive by the enemy was a traitor, and warned that the families of captured officers faced severe punishment (Dallin and Nicolaevsky 1948: 282).

Large numbers of the Soviet prisoners and refugees were opposed to the political regime in the homeland. These included Russian patriots, who desired to free their motherland from the grip of the communists, but also members of the Soviet Union's numerous national minorities – such as Georgians, Azerbaidjanis, Ukrainians, Kalmuks and Ossetians. Many of these national groups had been conquered by the Bolsheviks in the 1920s but had never fully reconciled themselves to communist rule.

For a combination of reasons, therefore – illtreatment by the Germans, abandonment by their own authorities and genuine hatred of the Soviet system – some Red Army soldiers were only too ready to enlist in German-led formations. More than a quarter of a million soldiers from the Red Army crossed over to join the struggle against the Soviet regime. Indeed, some of the non-Russian nationalities from the USSR were better represented in the ranks of the German army than in the Soviet forces. Relatively few were used in a front-line combat role, most being directed to labour units or to anti-partisan duties. By the end of the war these '*Osttruppen*' were scattered in various theatres from Norway to the Mediterranean (Elliott 1982: 17).

Soviet personnel had been falling into Allied hands in Italy and North Africa before the Normandy landings, but their numbers increased markedly after D-Day (6 June 1944). Although the British government had sent a request to the Soviet government in May 1944 enquiring what it should do with liberated Soviet citizens, there was no immediate reply from Moscow. Not until 23 August 1944 did the Soviet government request the return of all released prisoners 'at the earliest opportunity' (Tolstoy 1974: 78). On 17 October 1944, during talks in Moscow, the British foreign secretary, Anthony Eden, agreed with his

Soviet counterpart that Soviet citizens who came into British custody would be repatriated, whether or not they wished to return. Some weeks later the Americans expressed similar intentions, adding the proviso that only 'those claiming Soviet citizenship' would be returned.

These understandings with the Soviet government were formalized during the 'Big Power' conference in the Crimea (February 1945), where an agreement was signed which provided for reciprocal treatment and return of each state's liberated POWs (Tolstoy 1974: 121). This agreement became the benchmark by which subsequent policy was justified, but it did not refer to the use of force to effect repatriation. On the other hand it made no reference either to prisoners' rights or the provisions of the Geneva Convention. Significantly, these agreements were not made public until long after the war.

Following the Normandy landings, both the British and the Americans removed some thousands of Soviet *Osttruppen* captured during the Allied advance, from the European theatre. The first repatriation transports of those who had been shipped to the USA left from west coast ports at the end of December 1944. Transports also began from holding camps in Britain, once the prisoners had been screened. Between 1944 and 1946 more than 32,000 POWs of Soviet origin were despatched to the USSR from British shores. These were for the most part men who had served in the '*Todt*' labour battalions and the '*Ostlegionen*' – but the parties included large numbers of women and children. Cases of resistance, including suicide, were encountered in both Britain and the USA, but in neither case did these halt the repatriation process.

Thus repatriation of Eastern bloc citizens began before the war in Europe had formally ended. Indeed repatriation measures were set in motion so rapidly that many DPs, freshly released from German captivity, had little time even to contemplate other options. By far the largest repatriation movement took place from the western zones of Germany and Austria, where refugees and DPs were segregated according to national origins and placed in assembly centres, most of which were under military guard. Soviet repatriation missions crossed into the western zones to liaise with their Allied counterparts. Consistent with the terms of the Yalta Agreement, such missions operated in the Mediterranean theatre, in Britain, France, Norway – wherever in fact Soviet repatriates were being held.

In the first phase of the repatriation programme – from March to September 1945 – more than ten million people were repatriated. This figure included two million Soviet citizens. Some three million Soviet citizens also returned from the eastern (Soviet-occupied) zones of Germany and Austria. At its height the number being moved from the western zones reached 50,000 souls per day (Proudfoot 1957: 211). In a number of cases where resistance to repatriation was encountered, Allied troops used force.

Those who resisted repatriation included the Russian Liberation Army under General Andrei Vlasov which fell into American hands, and many of the 40,000 Cossacks who came under British military control in southern Austria in the spring of 1945. Both forces had been under German orders and protection. But the Cossack groups included not only large numbers of women, children and elderly, they also embraced pre-war *émigrés* – men who had left Russia following the collapse of resistance to Bolshevik rule and had never been Soviet citizens. These did not therefore qualify for repatriation under the terms agreed with Moscow. Nevertheless, according to Tolstoy (1974: 188 ff.) all were handed over to the Soviet authorities following a shameful process of deception by British officers and the use of violent measures against the most recalcitrant elements (Bethell 1986).

A second phase of repatriation from the western zones began at the end of 1945 and lasted until the repatriation movement ceased in 1948. New guidelines adopted by the Americans excluded the use of force against Soviet civilians, but compulsion was still employed against those captured in German uniforms, deserters from the Soviet armed forces or those charged with having 'voluntarily rendered aid and comfort to the enemy' (Elliott 1982: 111). On 17 January 1946, at the former German concentration camp of Dachau, American troops attempted to load Russians onto a train bound for the Soviet zone.

> The scene inside was one of human carnage. The crazed men were attempting to take their own lives by any means. Guards cut down some trying to hang themselves from the rafters; two others disembowelled themselves; another man forced his head through a window and ran his throat over the glass fragments; others begged to be shot. . . . Thirty-one men tried to take their own lives. Eleven succeeded; nine by hanging and two by knife wounds. Camp authorities managed to entrain the remaining 368.
>
> (Quoted in Elliott 1982: 93)

Faced with horrifying scenes such as this many Allied soldiers and their officers began to question their orders or chose to ignore them, turning a blind eye to escapees from the detention camps. Why did western politicians and diplomats agree to the policy of forced repatriation of Soviet citizens?

Historians have pointed to two main reasons. On the one hand, it was known that the Soviets would be liberating Allied POW camps in eastern Germany and Poland; in September 1944 it was estimated that two-thirds of British and Commonwealth prisoners held by the Germans would be liberated by the Red Army. Western governments wanted to ensure the safe return of their own personnel and were reluctant to face accusations that they were 'obstructing' the return of Soviet prisoners. A more general reason was the desire to convince the Soviet leadership of the West's good faith, hopeful that it would co-operate in the post-war settlement. Thus, the principles of asylum enshrined in international law collided with responsibilities and undertakings made to a dubious wartime ally. The fact remains though that the politics of ingratiation had little effect. They did not stop the onset of the cold war.

Certain groups were excluded from the repatriation measures. There was never any question of forcibly repatriating people who came from territories first occupied by the Soviets during 1939/40 (eastern Poland, the Baltic states, north Bukovina, Bessarabia). Although Moscow claimed the inhabitants of these and other territories annexed in the course of hostilities as 'Soviet citizens', such claims were denied. The western Allies' definition of Soviet citizenship was based upon the situation on 1 September 1939. They did not accede to the Soviets' attempts to accord citizenship retrospectively. Thousands of former Soviet citizens, particularly Ukrainians, made use of this loophole by claiming to originate from eastern Poland (Boshyk 1988: 204). What happened to those who returned?

The Red Army soldiers of all ranks who returned were systematically humiliated by their NKVD (People's Commissariat for Internal Affairs) guardians. Their lengthy interrogations centred on why and how they had fallen into German captivity and were frequently accompanied by beatings and accusations of collaboration. Executions, which took place randomly at first, were later infrequent. Generally only those who served the Germans at a senior level were shot. Members of pro-German formations were usually sentenced to between fifteen and twenty-five years in a corrective labour camp. Some of the civilians, including the elderly and women, were allowed to return home, but they were stigmatized with the entry 'socially dangerous element' in their NKVD file and were generally treated as second-class citizens (Dallin and Nicolaevsky 1948: 283; Elliott 1982: 190 ff).

References

Bethell, N. (1986) *The Last Secret*, London: Corgi

Boshyk, Y. (1988) 'Repatriation and Resistance: Ukrainian Refugees and Displaced Persons in Occupied Germany and Austria, 1945–1948', in A. C. Bramwell (ed.) *Refugees in the Age of Total War*, London: Unwin Hyman

Dallin, D. J. and B. I. Nicolaevsky (1948) *Forced Labour in Soviet Russia*, London: Hollis and Carter

Elliott, M. R. (1982) *Pawns of Yalta: Soviet Refugees and America's Role in their Repatriation*, Urbana: University of Illinois Press

Erickson, J. (1993) 'Review of Volumes by Hoffman and Streit', *English Historical Review*, 426, January, 153–4

Proudfoot, M. J. (1957) *European Refugees, 1939–1952: A Study in Forced Population Movement*, London: Faber

Tolstoy, N. (1974) *Victims of Yalta*, London: André Deutsch

THE REPATRIATION OF INDIAN TAMIL PLANTATION WORKERS FROM SRI LANKA TO INDIA

VALLI KANAPATHIPILLAI

The definition of the term repatriation is 'to restore or return to native land' (*Oxford Dictionary* 1990). Repatriation has been documented for colonial Sri Lanka. But the scale of repatriation in the post-colonial period increased massively. By 30 January 1986, 337,066 persons were repatriated to India.

In the context of the situation that arose among the plantation workers in the post-colonial period, applying the term repatriation as defined above is controversial. This is because, although they were still immigrant and temporary in the eyes of the general population, they had in fact been settled in Sri Lanka for over a century.

By 1968, when the actual repatriation started, very few if any could claim to have been born outside Sri Lanka. Since it is used officially and has come to form part of common parlance, the term 'repatriation' will continue to be used in this contribution to describe this phenomenon.

Overview of historical background

Plantations were established in Ceylon by the British in the nineteenth century, and formed an integral element of colonial expansion. As commonly observed in plantation sectors, labour formed an essential component of the system since plantation crops require labour-intensive methods of production.

Because of a shortage of labour from among the indigenous population to work the plantations during the colonial period, migrant labour was drawn from the labouring poor in the south Indian region of Tamil Nadu. This resulted in a constant movement of labour between the two countries, which lasted until 1939 when a ban was imposed on further migration. Following the ban those remaining behind settled in Sri Lanka, forming part of the permanent population of the country. Particularly since family employment was practised on the estates, the plantation workforce took on the characteristics of a 'captive' labour force. Each family was housed in what was called a 'line room', with men, women and children being employed on the tea and rubber estates. Women in fact formed 50 per cent of the labour force in the plantation sector; they were the producers and reproducers of labour.

Beckford (1983) has described plantations as 'total institutions' regulating all aspects of the lives of those who worked within them. This description can be applied to the plantations in Sri Lanka, as the plantation labourers of Indian Tamil origin were separated from the rest of the population in the country. This was by virtue of the particular system of production on the plantations as well as because of their distinct characteristics of language, religion and caste, which visibly distinguished them and, in effect, alienated them from the other ethnic groups in the country. This in turn had a bearing on their political, social and economic position in the country.

According to Sri Lanka's 1981 census, the Indian Tamil population on the island formed 5.5 per cent of the total population, the majority residing in the estate regions. They formed the third largest minority on the island, next to the Sri Lankan Tamils and Muslims.

Citizenship acts of 1948 and 1949

Following independence in 1948, the government of Sri Lanka attempted to redefine the country's citizenship, and thereby its nationhood, by passing two acts in Parliament in 1948 and 1949 respectively. The first, the Citizenship Act No. 18 of 1948, set out the guiding rules and criteria for acquiring general citizenship in Sri Lanka. The second act, the Indian and Pakistani Residents (Citizenship) Act of 1949, allowed for persons of Indian and Pakistani origin to obtain citizenship by registration under certain conditions.

The provisions of the two acts disqualified the majority of Indian Tamil workers from receiving citizenship.[1] By restricting the franchise to those who had citizenship, a third act, the Parliamentary Elections Amendment Act No. 48 of 1949, effectively disenfranchised the Indian Tamil plantation workers.

The acts of 1948 and 1949 were viewed unfavourably both by the representatives of the Tamils of Indian origin in Sri Lanka and by the government of India. Trade union and other representatives of the Indian Tamils, including the left-wing parties in Sri Lanka, protested and demanded that these laws be changed and that they too be admitted into the fold of Sri Lanka's polity.

In the ensuing years, the governments of Sri Lanka and India had many discussions and negotiations on the political status of the Indian Tamils resident in the country. The government of Sri Lanka held these people to be Indian nationals and only those who received Ceylonese citizenship would be considered legitimate nationals of the country. India disagreed on this stand on the grounds that only those registered in accordance with Article 8 of the Constitution of India were Indian nationals; all other Indians resident in Sri Lanka were legitimately citizens of Sri Lanka as it was in that country that they had been permanently settled for several generations.

While the political status of the Indian Tamil population had been an issue for almost four decades, the magnitude of the problem came to a head when, in 1962, on completion of registering citizens under the 1948 and 1949 citizenship acts, it was found that only 134,187 persons qualified for Sri Lankan citizenship out of an estimated 829,619 applicants. In 1962 Sri Lanka therefore had to face the problem of having almost a million people categorized as 'stateless', which meant they had neither political rights nor economic bargaining power.

The repatriation agreements

In October 1964, an agreement was drawn up between the governments of India and Sri Lanka to repatriate significant numbers of Tamil plantation labour from Sri Lanka to India. Government estimates indicated that there were some 975,000 persons of Indian origin without citizenship (this figure excluded Indian illicit immigrants and Indian passport holders), and it was decided that over half a million of them (525,000 persons and their natural increase) would be granted Indian citizenship and be sent to India over a period of fifteen years. Another 300,000 persons (and their natural increase) would be granted Ceylonese citizenship and given the right to permanent residence on the island.

The remaining 150,000 persons remained 'stateless' and their future was decided by a subsequent agreement between the two countries in 1974. By this, each country pledged to grant citizenship to 75,000 persons

(and their natural increase) and this process was to be phased over a period of another two years. As the 1964 agreement was dated 30 October 1964, and the total time allocated for the process was 17 years (15 + 2), the final date for the application for citizenship was 30 October 1981.

The granting of citizenship to the 75,000 would commence after the 300,000 persons of Indian origin (under the 1964 agreement) had been given citizenship. And the granting of citizenship would be on a fixed ratio to those repatriated to India. This meant that roughly 20,000 among the stateless would be registered as citizens of Sri Lanka, while around 35,000 would be repatriated to India annually.

According to the agreements of 1964 and 1974, Sri Lanka was to take a total of 375,000 persons and their natural increase as citizens, while India was to take about 525,000 and their natural increase.

Implementation of the agreements

The government of Sri Lanka and the Indian High Commission in Colombo called for applications for citizenship from among the Indian Tamil population on the 24 April 1968. Applications had to be in by 30 April 1970, by which time it was found that an estimated 400,000 persons requested Indian citizenship as against the stipulated number of 525,000 in the agreement, while 625,000 persons had applied for Sri Lankan citizenship, although the agreement provided for only 300,000. By 1981, at the end of the fifteen-year time limit, it was found that about 94,000 of the people whose applications for Sri Lankan citizenship had been rejected did not wish to take the alternative option of returning to India. They thereby continued to remain as stateless persons in Sri Lanka.

The prime ministers of the two countries would undoubtedly have thought of the 1964 agreement as a breakthrough in solving what they considered an 'Indo-Lanka' problem. It naturally followed, therefore, that both sides would want to implement the agreement speedily, both to minimize the number deemed 'stateless' by the enactment of the two acts of Parliament, and to remove what had been a bone of contention between the two countries for decades. However, speedy implementation was not achieved; in fact the whole process was delayed.

The extent to which the implementation was delayed can be seen by observing the facts. For a start, the whole process of implementation on Sri Lanka's part did not begin until four years after the 1964 agreement had been signed.

To quote Urmila Phadnis and Kumar Lalit (1975):

Table 10.1: *Tamil repatriation from Sri Lanka to India under the 1964 agreement*

	Registered as Indian citizens	Repatriated to India	Granted SL citizenship
30 Oct. 1964 to June 1974	70,879	13,733	8,519
July 1970 to end of Dec. 1973	115,062	92,690	52,294
Jan. to Dec.1974	89,514	35,141	52,294

Source: Phadnis and Kumar (1975).

An index of the progress in the implementation of the (1964) Pact is found in the grant of its citizenship by Sri Lanka to 60,813 and by India to 185,941 persons in the period November 1964–December 1973. This is not an impressive figure. However, Sri Lanka did achieve a feat in 1974 by sending more than the stipulated number in the Pact. According to the provisions of the 1964 Pact, by December 1974, both countries should have given citizenship to about 700,000 'Stateless' along with the natural increase. However, the number of these registered as Indian and Ceylon citizens was 362,431, thus failing to meet the arrangement by half.

The data are provided in Table 10.1:

The political climate and events in Sri Lanka could have been partly responsible for the delay. For instance, the agreement was signed in October 1964, but before it could be implemented the Sri Lanka Freedom Party (SLFP) government led by Mrs Bandaranaike was defeated in the March 1965 election, and Dudley Senanayake's United National Party (UNP) formed a coalition government.

The change of government delayed the enactment of the enabling legislation for implementation, namely the Indo-Ceylon Agreement (Implementation) Act of 1967.

The bill for this legislation was introduced in the House of Representatives on 6 December 1966, and became law on 5 June 1967. It was only on 24 April 1968, four years after the signing of the agreement, that the Indian and Sri Lankan governments could call for applications for either Sri Lankan or Indian citizenship.

The introduction of this bill was also delayed by different interpretations of the agreement by the two main parties, the UNP and the SLFP. The UNP's position on implementing the agreement has to be seen in the light of the coalition it had formed with the Tamil parties. The Tamil Congress, the Federal Party and the Ceylon Worker's Congress (CWC)[2] had opposed the 1964 agreement. Therefore, when these parties formed part of his national government, Prime Minister Dudley Senanayake needed their support, and so had to accommodate their views and demands. The pact had to be implemented through the introduction of enabling legislation piloted by a government operating in an altered political climate.

For instance, the actual ratio by which each country would grant citizenship to the stateless became a point of controversy. The UNP government introduced the enabling legislation, establishing a ratio of 4:7, that is for every four persons to be granted Sri Lankan citizenship, seven would be granted Indian citizenship and not be linked to actual repatriation as laid down in the original agreements. This change, however, became a point of controversy between the UNP and the SLFP and in each successive government formed by these two parties, new legislation was introduced, which gave different interpretations to this as well as other aspects of the act. This also contributed towards delaying implementation of the agreements.

The period of UNP rule (1965–70) was spent on enacting the enabling legislation, calling for applications for citizenship in 1968 and processing applications.

Having formed a coalition with the parties on the left, the SLFP then formed the United Front, which governed the country from 1970 to 1977. Although this government was committed to faring better than the UNP by speedily implementing the agreement, actual implementation was slow, apart from the year 1974 when 35,304 persons were repatriated to India — slightly more than the number stipulated for repatriation in a year.

Apart from the delays caused by political changes in the country, there were those caused by long and tedious administrative and bureaucratic procedures. There were also financial reasons for the delays. Prime Minister Dudley Senanayake used the non-availability of foreign exchange as a reason for curtailing the numbers to be repatriated. According to the terms of the pact, Sri Lanka agreed to allow each repatriated family to remit up to Rs 4000 in savings and assets. However, when the Indo-Ceylon Agreement (Implementation) Bill was being debated in Parliament, Prime Minister Dudley Senanayake pointed out that this would mean that Sri Lanka would lose about 500 million rupees if a total of 125,000 families were repatriated. Therefore he declared that the numbers to be repatriated would be conditional on the availability of foreign exchange. Senanayake was also unwilling to restrict repatriation to fifteen years, for if repatriation took place at the agreed rate within that period, Sri Lanka would lose a considerable amount of foreign exchange and face severe economic hardship. Another financially induced delay came from employers holding back the estate population's financial dues, in some instances even refusing to transfer their assets and thereby causing undue delays in implementing the agreements.

While ethnic violence in Sri Lanka in the post-1977 period caused anxiety and made estate workers of Indian origin reluctant to continue to live in Sri Lanka, the problems besetting the Indian government's rehabilitation programmes also caused confusion in the minds of the Indian workers about going back to India. As a result, even seventeen years after the expiry of the agreements in 1982, the problems of the people of Indian origin have only been partly resolved.

Recent developments

In 1977 a UNP government came into power taking over from the SLFP-led United Front government. The new government had a different set of political objectives and this had an effect on the issue of repatriation.

Three significant issues affected the implementation of the agreements of 1964 and 1974. One was the inclusion of Thondaman, the leader of the CWC, in the UNP cabinet, where he wielded considerable power. His influence came from the support he derived from the electoral significance of the plantation workers. By the 1980s, those given Sri Lankan citizenship under the 1964 and 1974 agreements had become a significant voting bloc in the central electoral districts, which was also why the UNP government under J. R. Jayawardene acted favourably on behalf of the plantation workers.

The second issue to influence the decisions taken by the Jayawardene government was renewed recognition of the importance of the plantation sector to the country's economy. The government had introduced a liberalized economic system in which emphasis was placed on exports from the country. Tea plantations still provided a significant percentage of the country's earnings. As tea production is labour intensive, there was a heavy demand for skilled labour on the

plantations, which the government could ill afford to repatriate. Therefore, those who should have repatriated were encouraged to stay and work on the plantations until their retirement.

The third issue to affect repatriation in the time of the UNP government, both under J. R. Jayawardene and Premadasa,[3] was the ethnic and civil war in the country. The plantation areas were badly affected by the ethnic riots of 1977, 1981 and 1983. The violence they experienced during these riots probably encouraged repatriates to leave for India rather than stay in Sri Lanka. The ethnic and civil war, which had engulfed the north and east of the country since the riots of 1983, led to the closing of the ferry from Talaimannar,[4] which meant that those still to be repatriated could not be sent back.

These various factors obviously influenced the government's decision to implement the Grant of Citizenship to Stateless Persons Act No. 5 of 1986, by which the government of Sri Lanka pledged to grant citizenship to the 94,000 stateless persons and their natural increase residing in Sri Lanka, in addition to the 375,000 and their natural increase who were to be given Sri Lankan citizenship. These persons were to be registered as citizens within eighteen months. However, registration was not completed within this time because of bureaucratic delays. Therefore, mainly due to pressure from the CWC and other trade unions representing the plantation workers of Indian origin, the government passed the Grant of Citizenship to Stateless Persons (Special Provisions) Act of 1988, by which all those who were stateless were granted Sri Lankan citizenship. They need apply for a citizenship certificate only if they wished to; it was not a requirement.

Implementation on the Indian side remains incomplete. About 506,000 persons were to be granted Indian citizenship, but by 31 August 1989 it had been granted to only 421,973 persons and their natural increase. Also, of those recognized as Indian citizens only 337,464 and their natural increase have left for India. India has yet to register as Indian citizens 84,027 persons, whose applications for Indian citizenship are pending in the Indian High Commission. India has still to make arrangements to accept the repatriation of 84,509 persons and their natural increase who have been registered as Indian citizens.

Notes
1. The act of 1948 did not provide for the gaining of citizenship by virtue of a person's birth in the country. Citizenship was

linked to a person's family ties going back at least two generations. Most Indian immigrants found it difficult to prove that their father, paternal grandfather or great grandfather had been born in Sri Lanka, as Section 4 (i) a and b of the act required, particularly since the registration of births was only introduced in Sri Lanka in 1895.

2. A leading trade union cum political party, which has represented the plantation workers for the past fifty-two years.

3. J. R. Jayawardene, president (1978–88), R. Premadasa, president (1988–93).

4. Talaimannar is a small port in the north-west of Sri Lanka.

References

Beckford, G. L. (1983) *Persistent Poverty: Underdevelopment in Plantation Economies of the Third World*, London: Zed Press

Census of Population and Housing. General Report (1981), vol. III, Department of Census and Statistics, Ministry of Plan Implementation

Oxford Dictionary (1990), Oxford: Oxford University Press

Phadnis, Urmila and Kumar Lalit (1975) 'The Sirimavo-Shastri Pact of 1964: Problems of Implementation', *Indian Quarterly*, 31 (3)

THE MIGRATION OF EAST
AFRICAN ASIANS TO THE UK

VAUGHAN ROBINSON

Mamdani (1993) has argued that the expulsion of Asians from Uganda in 1972 should not be seen as the historic event it is often portrayed as in the western media and academic literature. He points out that in many ways it was unexceptional. Indian trading minorities have been expelled from countries such as Iraq and Burma without attracting significant international interest or concern, and other groups such as the Jaluos and Rwandese were expelled from Uganda in much larger numbers but also failed to become objects of great interest. In fact, he suggests that the prominence accorded the Ugandan Asians stems from one main factor, namely their deportation into the heart of western metropolitan nations, rather than their displacement into adjacent African states.

While Mamdani is correct to indicate that the expulsion of East African Asians was not a unique event, his argument understates the significance of the migration. In the 1960s in countries such as the UK, Australia and Canada, the concept of a refugee was still firmly rooted in the circumstances of post-war Europe and embodied in definitions such as that of the 1951 UN Convention. Refugees were widely thought of as white Europeans displaced within that continent by war or the dislocation which followed it. They were not 'visible' minorities, and they were assimilable. Moreover, refugee crises were still often seen as local phenomena which could be resolved by short distance displacement in which there was little contact between the southern and northern hemispheres. In addition, Britain was still reacting to the recent influx of black migrant labour and had succeeded in controlling this through restrictive and selective immigration legislation. For countries such as Britain, the East African Asian crisis represented a new, and unwelcome, departure which required new attitudes, new legislation and new policies. The East African crisis involved a relatively large number of acute refugees who were not white, many of whom still held British citizenship and who needed to be resettled immediately. Britain thus had to resolve both the immediate problem of resettling the Ugandan Asians in the face of public hostility to further

'coloured' immigration (Kohler 1973), and the longer term problem of preventing the recurrence of a similar crisis. The immediate problem was resolved through international cooperation with other Commonwealth countries that saw Ugandan Asians being accepted by India, Canada and Australia, and an officially funded and organized British programme of reception and resettlement within the UK. The longer term issues were initially addressed in 1968 and 1971 with further changes in immigration and citizenship laws, and ultimately through the more restrictive and selective refugee admission regime of the 1980s. The Ugandan crisis thus established several precedents which still guide refugee policy today within the UK: namely, the need to make it appear that non-white refugees are treated in a similar fashion to non-white labour migrants; the idea of 'burden sharing' in which the UK accepts a quota of refugees only if others agree to do the same; and the policy of putting in place limited duration and specific centrally planned reception and resettlement programmes for quota refugees within the UK.

Historical context

As was the case in other British colonies, the Indians in East Africa were a middleman minority. From the earliest days of their settlement in the thirteenth century (Delf 1963), the Indians were traders and storekeepers who survived by acting as intermediaries between local African producers and European exporters. Even the arrival of 32,000 Punjabi Sikhs and Muslims to build the East Africa Railway failed to break the patterns established by the Gujurati Hindus, who prospered under British colonial rule to the extent that they controlled 90 per cent of the trade of Uganda in the period prior to the Second World War (Delf 1963). In the post-war period, the Asian communities diversified and sought to gain occupational mobility through education (Tinker 1977). They were the first to establish schools in Uganda; by 1962 they had achieved considerable success in entering the professions and the Civil Service, and they had strengthened their position in clerical employment. Economic success was not, however, matched by social acceptance, for black Africans widely regarded the East African Asians as an exploitative and exclusive privileged minority. This perception was not challenged by events after independence. Some Asians, particularly those in Kenya, began to transfer their wealth out of Africa; others made plans to leave the continent, and many failed to give up their British citizenship in favour of the citizenship of the newly independent states (less than one-third in Uganda according to Swinerton et al. 1975).

Independence brought about an intensification of Africanization policies, first begun in Uganda by the colonial administration in 1952. Although there is some argument about whether a minority of Asians colluded with Africanization in the 1960s and used it as a way of strengthening their economic position, there is little doubt that it succeeded in undermining the livelihoods and rights of many more. Asians were excluded from public employment, limitations were placed on their ability to own businesses in large swathes of the country, they were restricted to trading in specified commodities, and non-citizens were prevented from going to university.

Flight

The exodus of Ugandan Asians can be divided into three main phases beginning with the anticipatory refugees who left prior to the formal expulsion (Robinson 1986). Over 24,000 Asians left Uganda between 1969 and 1971, largely to come to the UK, but also to enter Canada and the USA. Initially, migrants were eldest sons sent to acquire housing and to investigate the opportunities offered by both the labour market and the educational system. As Africanization policies began to threaten the livelihood of more Asians, the migration shifted into a second phase – that of whole households. These were often of an intermediate economic status. Few contained the elderly, who preferred to await the outcome of developments in Uganda or apply for entry to India.

The events that led up to the expulsion of the Ugandan Asians on 4 August 1972 and that ushered in the third stage in the migration have been well documented elsewhere (see Marett 1989), including the claims and counterclaims of Africans and Asians. Indecision and uncertainty are often hallmarks of refugee episodes and this was certainly true of several aspects of the Ugandan Asian expulsion. Initially President Amin announced the expulsion only of those Asians who had not acquired Ugandan citizen-

ship. The Final Edict of 9 August appeared to exclude a further group of people defined by occupation – those in the professions, bank managers and agricultural technicians. Finally, on 20 August Amin changed his mind again and expelled all Asians, regardless of nationality or occupation. On 22 August the president declared that proceeds from the enforced sale of Asian property and businesses (estimated as worth between £100 million and £150 million) would be given to the expellees, but when details later became available it was clear that the departing Asians were being forced to sell to a government agency and not on the open market; and at the end of August it was announced that, in any case, the expellees would be allowed to take only £50 per head out of the country.

While the initial reaction of the Asians might have been one of complacent disbelief, the string of edicts and pronouncements from within Uganda and the great gravity with which the situation was being treated by the media and governments outside Uganda soon impressed upon them the seriousness of their plight. Although Amin had given the Asians only ninety days to vacate the country, by mid-September just 4000 of the 80,000 thought to be under threat (a figure later revised down to 42,000) had come forward to begin the departure procedure, and several of the special emergency flights to the UK had had to be cancelled for lack of passengers. Later in September several factors combined to increase the pace of the exodus. On the 22nd, the Ugandan Security Forces were given orders to ensure that those Asians who had been cleared for departure were ejected immediately from the country. India began to transport its citizens in closed trains across the border into Kenya, for processing there. The airlift to Britain got under way once it had become clear that the British government would underwrite the cost, albeit still charging the refugees the equivalent of £100 per adult fare. Malawi offered to accept Asians who would be allowed to join relatives there. The Canadian government had announced arrangements for flying 6000 of the 11,000 Asians who had applied for settlement out of Kampala, the USA announced that it would be taking two quotas, one sponsored by government, the other by the American Council of Churches, and Australia, Argentina, Bolivia, Brazil and Sweden had also come forward with places. India, too, reiterated its offer of temporary resettlement for British passport holders.

By the expiry of Amin's ninety-day deadline, all but 2000 Asians had left Uganda and, of those remaining, less than 500 were Ugandan citizens. Britain had accepted nearly 29,000 for immediate resettlement (Uganda Resettlement Board 1974), Canada took 8000 (Swinerton et al. 1975), the USA accepted 3000 (Marett 1989), India agreed to host 15,000 on the proviso that they would retain the right to enter the UK as vouchers became available (Swinerton et al. 1975), Malawi resettled 1000 and Australia and New Zealand had taken 600.

Because of the speed of the exodus, few records were kept of the characteristics of the East African Asians on arrival in their new countries of abode. A subsequent national survey of ethnic minorities in the UK (Smith 1977) undertaken in 1974 found the East African Asian population to have migrated to the UK later in life (29 per cent aged thirty-five years or more) than their subcontinental counterparts, to be more likely to be resident in an extended family and to have an imbalance of fifty-six males to every forty-four females. Some 62 per cent were Hindus, 19 per cent Sikhs and 15 per cent Muslims. Swinerton et al (1975) provide more detail for a smaller sample of eighty-seven Ugandan Asian households interviewed in two London boroughs. They found 69 per cent of males to have previously held a managerial position with commercial companies, a further 22 per cent to have been 'white collar workers', 5 per cent professionals and only 4 per cent to have previously had skilled manual employment; 80 per cent could speak English and 39 per cent were educated to, or beyond, A-level standard.

Resettlement policy

While Britain did have experience of the planned resettlement of groups of acute refugees (the Hungarians) and less urgent quota refugees such as the Poles (Peach et al. 1988) it did not have experience of resettling black refugees. In addition, at the time of the Ugandan Asian crisis, 'coloured' immigration was still a highly charged and politicized issue. The extreme right-wing group, the National Front, was becoming more active on a blatantly anti-immigrant platform and was threatening to take votes from the Conservative Party. Enoch Powell was continuing to argue the costs and disbenefits of further black immigration, and public opinion was against further significant black/Asian immigration (Robinson 1987). Even the Labour Party had legitimized racial discrimination by rushing through the 1968 Commonwealth Immigrants Act, which was designed to slow Asian migration from East Africa.

Once news of the expulsion of the Ugandan Asians

reached the UK there was a highly publicized public response. Early in September, workers from London docks and the meat market marched on the Home Office carrying placards bearing messages such as 'STOP IMMIGRATION' and 'BRITAIN FOR THE BRITISH'. Leicester City Council placed an advertisement in the *Ugandan Argus* advising Asians not to come to the city. Two respected national newspapers took an uncompromising stance against resettlement of the refugees in the UK. Enoch Powell commented that the Ugandan Asians were the 'thin end of a very thick wedge'. And a variety of local councils of both main political persuasions argued publicly that they were unable to accept any Ugandan Asians for resettlement: Ealing argued that it would be 'physically impossible' for it to accept more immigrants and Birmingham said its schools were at 'saturation point' as a result of newly arrived immigrant families. Even the new towns, which had been advertising that they had vacant housing, made it clear that they would be unwilling to offer resettlement places to Ugandan Asians.

There is little doubt that subsequent government policy towards the resettlement of the Ugandan Asians within the UK was shaped by such outspoken and well-reported hostility. As Bristow (1976) noted, the government had to design a programme that would provide immediate help for the refugees but not so much help that it alienated its own supporters. Its chosen solution was to distance itself from the practicalities of resettlement through the creation of an intermediary, the Uganda Resettlement Board (URB). Since this body would have the task of receiving and resettling refugees, it would therefore also be this body that would receive any resulting criticism. In a similar vein, the government refused to force local authorities to offer accommodation and instead only requested it. Thus if local authorities chose to rehouse Ugandan Asians, it would be they who had to answer to their local electorate, not central government. And lastly, although the government was, in other respects, willing to pursue a *laissez-faire* policy it determined to be interventionist when it came to the matter of where within Britain Ugandan Asians should be allowed to settle. Ghettoization was not to be allowed (Robinson 1992).

Newly arrived Ugandan Asians were initially housed in 'transit camps', but once it became clear that many had no accommodation or employment to go to in the UK, these were increasingly labelled resettlement centres. The centres were funded and coordinated by the URB but they were staffed by

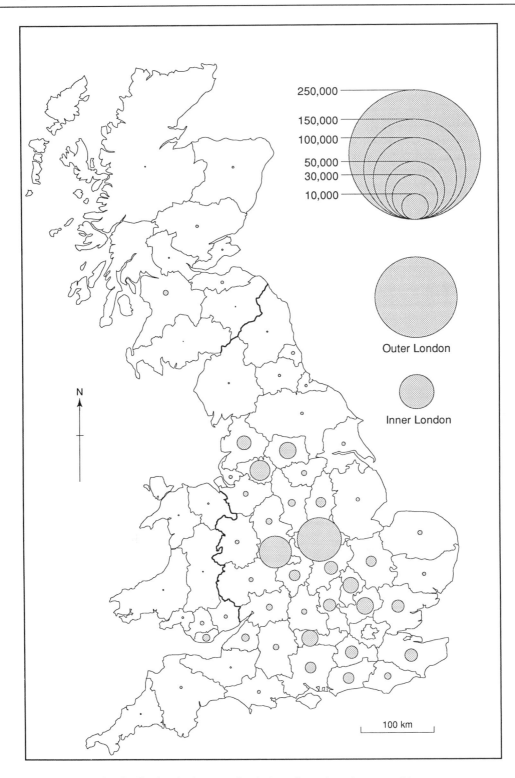

Map 6: Distribution in the UK of 'ethnic Indians' born in East Africa, 1991

workers belonging to charities such as the Red Cross and Women's Royal Voluntary Service, with later assistance from URB resettlement officers. When it became clear that many Ugandan Asians had lost everything in the exodus and were not in a position to resettle themselves rapidly, sixteen camps were eventually opened. At the peak, the camps accommodated 13,000 refugees.

A major restriction on the ability of the URB to achieve its goals was the level of funding allocated to it. The government adopted a dual funding policy. It increased the Rate Support Grant made directly to local authorities by some £2 million in 1973/4 in order to assist them with the costs of additional staff employed under the provisions of the 1966 Local Government Act. It also funded the URB directly. This was eventually given £6.1 million, of which nearly £5 million was spent on the resettlement camps, with only £610,000 being passed on to the local authorities that would have to service the needs of the Ugandan Asians in the medium and long term. Funding was thus heavily skewed towards reception at the expense of resettlement.

In line with its views on responsible citizenship, the Conservative government also encouraged the involvement of volunteer workers in the programme, largely under the aegis of the Coordinating Committee for the Welfare of Evacuees from Uganda. There was undoubtedly friction between the different charities with their contrasting methods and philosophies, as there was also between the charities and the URB. One commentator even argued that 'the British Government reacted tardily and chaotically to a crisis which the knowledgeable had been predicting for some time. What they should have done, instead of relying on nostalgic wartime faith in muddling through, is to have recruited professional staff, professional social workers and to have paid them professional salaries to do the job' (Hamilton-Preston 1973: 72).

Given the public apprehension about the geographical pattern of resettlement and the potential political consequences of this, the government opted for a public policy of dispersal. This was operationalized through the designation of 'red' areas in which refugees were to be discouraged from resettling, and 'green' areas to which refugees were to be directed. Swinerton et al. (1975) list the four main criteria for designating areas green and red: these were pressure on housing, schools, social services and employment. If a city had difficulties with two or more of these, then it became a red area. Others have, however,

suggested that the presence of a large existing Asian community was the main criterion for defining areas as red (Dines 1973). In practice, the zoning of the country was somewhat academic since refugees could only be resettled where housing had been offered, and families could not be compelled to move to areas against their wishes. Many Ugandan Asians had relatives or friends already settled in the UK who were in a position either to help with accommodation or employment. As a result, some 23 per cent of the refugees who passed through the hands of the URB made their own arrangements for accommodation without entering a camp: most of these went straight to red areas. In addition a further 39 per cent ultimately found their own accommodation despite a period of residence in a resettlement camp: again this would probably have been in red areas. Bristow (1976) thus argues that, despite the public utterances about dispersal, only 38 per cent of the Ugandan Asians were actually found accommodation in green areas. He accounts for the discrepancy between the government's stated policy of dispersal and the actuality of concentration as follows: 'the political reality which restricted settlement location mainly to red areas was that allocation of council housing to Asian refugees could be expected to be unpopular. For this reason, the government did not make it obligatory for local authorities to allocate housing, and, for the same reason, many did not do so' (Bristow 1976: 276). The net geographical impact was to ensure that the East African Asians were more concentrated within the UK than either Indians or Pakistanis, with particular concentrations being found in London and Leicester (Robinson 1986).

A longitudinal perspective

There was a good deal of interest in the immediate fate of the Ugandan Asians after resettlement. A number of pieces of research assessed their status within the UK. Their assessment was decidedly pessimistic. McCart (1973) noted that 25 per cent of household heads in Wandsworth were still unemployed, 75 per cent were housed unsatisfactorily and three-quarters were living below the poverty line. Dines (1973) commented on the social isolation of those who had been dispersed. And Kumar (1973) described how almost all the Ugandan Asian businessmen in Manchester were still looking for work and how those few refugees who had found work had experienced considerable loss of status.

As is often the case with refugee migrations (Robinson 1990), the immediate public and academic interest in the Ugandan Asians soon waned and as a result there has been little longitudinal analysis of the progress of the group over the medium term. However, Robinson (1993) has undertaken such a piece of work using national data-sets measuring standard indicators of socio-economic status for the whole East African Asian minority in the UK. He noted the absence of qualitative inputs to the analysis and underlined the significance of these when considering the well-being of refugee groups. His findings were that, despite the powerful forces of racial exclusionism at work in every facet of life in Britain, the national profile of the group had changed considerably between the early 1970s and the mid-1980s despite the deepest recession the country had seen since the 1930s. East African Asians had acquired better formal qualifications than their Indian or white British counterparts, were over-represented in self employment, had transformed their socio-economic profile more rapidly than either of the other two groups, were found in better accommodation than were Indians, and had achieved all of this without the secondary migration which was such a feature of the subsequent Vietnamese arrivals.

Conclusion

The migration of East African, and more particularly Ugandan, Asians to the UK has a significance beyond the numbers involved. Although a small migration in world terms, it was the first time that a sizeable number of non-white acute refugees had claimed asylum in the UK. The ensuing shock to the national psyche resulted in dramatic changes to Britain's immigration policy, refugee admission policy and refugee resettlement policy. Immigration and nationality laws were revised to prevent a repetition of the migration. A new resettlement policy was also devised, specifically to appease the majority white electorate and to assuage any fears they had of incipient ghettoization. And the East African Asians might also be seen as one of the catalysts behind the changing refugee admission regime within the UK in the 1980s, which now places much greater emphasis upon local resettlement rather than long-distance international migration.

References

Bristow, M. (1976) 'Britain's Response to the Ugandan Asian Crisis: Government Myths Versus Political and Resettlement Realities', *New Community*, 5 (3), 265–79

Delf, G. (1963) *Asians in East Africa*, London: Oxford University Press

Dines, M. (1973) 'Ugandan Asians: One Year Later', *New Community*, 2 (4), 380–3

Hamilton–Preston, J. (1973) 'Camp on John Bull island', *Nova*, April, 68–72

Kohler, D. (1973) 'Public Opinion and the Ugandan Asians', *New Community*, 2 (2), 194–7

Kumar, S. (1973) 'Ugandan Asians One Year Later: Manchester Report', *New Community*, 2 (4), 386–8

Mamdani, M. (1993) 'The Ugandan Asian Expulsion: Twenty Years After', *Economic and Political Weekly*, 16 January, 93–6

Marett, V. (1989) *Immigrants Settling in the City*, London: Leicester University Press

McCart, M. (1973) 'Ugandan Asians One Year Later: Wandsworth. Unsettled Ugandan Refugees', *New Community*, 2 (4), 383–6

Peach, C., V. Robinson, J. Maxted and J. Chance (1988) 'Immigration and Ethnicity', in A. Halsey (ed.) *British Social Trends since 1900*, Basingstoke: Macmillan, 561–616

Robinson, V. (1986) *Transients, Settlers and Refugees: Asians in Britain*, Oxford: Clarendon Press

(1987) 'Regional Variations in Attitudes towards Race', in P. Jackson (ed.) *Race and Racism*, London: Allen & Unwin, 160–88

(1990) 'Into the Next Millenium: An Agenda for Refugee Studies', *Journal of Refugee Studies*, 3 (1), 3–15

(1992) 'British Policy towards the Settlement Patterns of Ethnic Groups: An Empirical Evaluation of the Vietnamese Programme 1979–89', in V. Robinson (ed.) *The International Refugee Crisis: British and Canadian Responses*, Basingstoke: Macmillan, 319–55

(1993) 'Marching into the Middle Classes? The Long-Term Resettlement of East African Asians in the UK', *Journal of Refugee Studies*, 6 (3), 230–47

Smith, D. (1977) *Racial Disadvantage in Britain*, Harmondsworth: Penguin

Swinerton, N., W. Kuepper and L. Lackey (1975) *Ugandan Asians in Great Britain*, London: Croom Helm

Tinker, H. (1977) *The Banyan Tree: Overseas Emigrants from India, Pakistan and Bangladesh*, Oxford: Oxford University Press

Uganda Resettlement Board (1974) *Final Report*, London: HMSO

THE REPATRIATION OF PORTUGUESE FROM AFRICA

MARIA BEATRIZ ROCHA-TRINDADE

During April 1974 a change of political regime took place in Portugal. The two main causes for this were, first, the existence of a dictatorship almost half a century old that was becoming unbearable due to internal and external pressures in favour of democracy and, second, a widespread feeling of discontentment on the part of the Portuguese armed forces, which had been fighting an ongoing war for more than a decade against liberation movements in the African colonies. Simultaneously, the success of 'The Carnation Revolution' encouraged the rapid resolution of the two above mentioned problems. The democratization process was therefore directly associated with the decolonization one.

Despite some inherent difficulties, the democratization process was basically positive and safe. The same cannot be said for decolonization. This was accomplished too rapidly and created some extremely serious problems, which have led, for example, to the invasion and illegal occupation of Timor by Indonesia, and to the continuing civil wars being fought in Angola and Mozambique.

Decolonization also caused the massive exodus of hundreds of thousands of Portuguese people residing in the colonies, particularly after independence in October 1975, little more than a year after the sudden political changes in Portugal.

Generally referred to as *retornado*s (returnees), according to official counts their total number exceeded half a million, but can probably be estimated at about 800,000. Bearing in mind that Portugal's population at the time was approximately ten million, this was the most serious mass repatriation to have taken place in the post-war era, both numerically and in terms of the great speed at which it occurred (1974 to 1979).

This study draws on some relevant publications (Cunha 1977; Dias and Laranjo 1976; Leandro 1984; Pires et al. 1987) as well as on qualitative information collected from government institutions and other agencies directly involved with the settlement and integration of the *retornado*s. I provide a summary of the main characteristics of the complex social phenomenon of the repatriation of the Portuguese from Africa.

Main causes

Through their structural impact on Portuguese demography, Portuguese migratory movements to and from the African colonies manifested characteristics similar to those of international emigration.

People went to Africa mainly for economic reasons, especially if living conditions in the colonies were better than those at home. Some eventually returned, others stayed on indefinitely, particularly in Angola and Mozambique (in 1973, according to an estimate by Cónim and Carrilho (1989), the former had 324,000 residents of European origin and the latter 190,000).

Oddly enough, the colonial war, which had been waging in the overseas territories since 1961, contributed to an increase in emigration to Africa. Along with its war effort the government embarked on a significant programme of economic and social development, making considerable investments in the infrastructure, agriculture, industry and education. Thus, there were more new settlers going out to the colonies during the war years than there were families returning to Portugal.

The programme the military initiated for the 1974 revolution expressed an intent to put an end to the hostilities, to negotiate peace with the local liberation movements and to prepare for the independence of the territories.

With Portuguese sovereignty now under threat, there was a steady increase in the number of families returning to Portugal. Many, however, chose to remain in the colonies and to chance their luck with the new *status quo*. This applied particularly to those who had been born in Africa and considered it their homeland.

The situation remained stationary for a year, leaving those who wished to return enough time to make all the necessary arrangements.

Therefore one may consider that at this initial stage the return to Portugal was accomplished without too much trouble. However, the situation started to change as independence approached and was totally reversed after the Portuguese troops left Africa and the transference of sovereignty took place. The signs of intolerance appeared as the residents of European origin lost their rights along with those natives accused of collaborating with the colonial regime.

Nationalization, and the confiscation and occupation of private property were followed by intimidation and psychological and physical pressure, which spread panic among the population.

As the situation became more serious so did the pressures on regular air and sea transport. The Portuguese provisional government started an air bridge and began to organize the return of the *retornado*s. This was the biggest and fastest logistics operation ever carried out and it brought a new orientation and operation style to already existing government structures.

Post-arrival settlement: institutional framework

In 1974, as a decade earlier when Portugal lost its sovereignty over the *Estado da Índia* centred in Goa, the Grupo de Apoio aos Desalojados do Ultramar/ Ministério da Coordenação Interterritorial (Support Group for the Homeless from Overseas/Ministry of Interterritorial Coordination) was created, as it was expected that the decolonization process, which was just starting, would lead to the return of an indefinite number of overseas residents.

The objective of this support group was to receive and help integrate the Portuguese who had returned from Africa. However, given the large numbers of people returning and the increasing signs of alarm being reported, the government was forced to create a new more powerful and more flexible structure with which to face the emergency situation that might arise at any moment. To operate this new entity more efficiently, the Instituto de Apoio ao Retorno de Nacionais (Institute for the Support of the Repatriation of Nationals), simply known as IARN, was placed directly under the Presidência do Conselho de Ministros (Ministerial Cabinet Presidency).

IARN received 275,600 *retornado*s from Angola between June and November 1975. Of these 175,000 arrived via an air bridge and the remainder arrived in Portugal by their own means.

Due to the large number of *retornado*s it handled, IARN's institutional dependence had to be altered. The Secretaria de Estado dos Retornados (Secretariat of State for Returnees) was created in October 1975 to reinforce IARN's operational capacity. But this

solution was short lived. When the first constitutional government took office following the 1976 elections, the Secretaria de Estado dos Retornados ceased to exist and the Alto Comissariado para os Retornados (High Commission for Returnees) took its place – a change more of designation than of policy, for the new post of high commissioner was equivalent to that of a secretary of state.

Both IARN and the para-governmental entity that controlled it were disbanded in 1979 when the process of return was considered accomplished.

Looking back it is interesting to analyse the set of objectives and areas of intervention of IARN as well as to understand the type of solutions that made such a task possible.

Among the expressed objectives a few should be stressed. These included supporting, guiding and aiding citizens and their families who had returned to Portugal; providing them with work and credit; preparing identification and civil registration files; applying for social security and legal aid; helping them obtain professional and academic certification; and, finally, trying to obtain from the new African countries indemnity for property losses and for breaches of work agreements. This last objective was unrealistic and was thus never accomplished.

Realities of repatriation

The above objectives, expressed at a very early stage in the process, were a far cry from the reality IARN had to face.

During the most acute phase of the exodus of the Portuguese from Africa and after a long wait for transport thousands of people arrived in Portugal destitute. They had no identification, no money, and some of them had absolutely nothing but their clothes. A few fortunate ones managed to send their baggage by sea, but only many months afterwards did they succeed in retrieving it. Some, who were afraid of being prevented from leaving, left without their families, with no notice or time to plan. Many children travelled alone under the care of other passengers, while their relatives waited at airports for days or even weeks on end hoping for a seat on some other plane. According to witnesses directly involved in the sheltering process, the *retornado*s felt desperate and outraged at having lost their lifelong, hard-earned possessions.

IARN's legal commitment to 'support and guide' was translated into the Herculean daily task of receiving thousands of exhausted passengers, providing them with a place to rest, feeding them, obtaining their identification, supplying them with basic goods, finding them temporary shelter and transferring them to locations where permanent lodgings were more easily found. Parallel to this immediate action it was necessary to create job opportunities for those already settled or help them establish their own businesses.

IARN transformed large vacant public and private buildings (for instance old convents, sanatoriums, schools or army quarters) into hotels of temporary residence. If a *retornado* had family in Portugal whose whereabouts were known, immediate transport and financial support were provided for his or her daily subsistence during the period of settlement. This measure proved to be rather effective, for it both appealed to family solidarity and avoided the need to create a gigantic refugee camp.

Concomitant with this strategic orientation, the main principles characterizing IARN's performance were completely alien to those of the Portuguese public administration. IARN reduced bureaucracy to a minimum, encouraged the creativity and individual initiative of all its employees and agents, and emphasized flexibility. Otherwise insurmountable administrative situations (such as not having vital identification documents, civil status information, academic qualifications or property titles) were overcome by unorthodox means, such as using witnesses' declarations and affidavits. The state played an important role in financing accommodation for months or even years, providing for daily subsistence needs, opening lines of credit for house building, and establishing incentives to promote entrepreneurial activities and businesses.

National solidarity was manifested mainly in terms of bilateral relations between host families and families of *retornado*s. Internationally the support provided in emergency clothing, food and medicine was substantial as well as the creation of exceptional quotas for the admittance and settlement of the *retornado*s abroad.

Finally, an important factor in the integration of *retornado*s into Portuguese society was the network of interpersonal relations that they were able to establish and maintain among themselves which have lasted to this day. This network was instrumental in creating 'lobbies' in the labour and housing markets whereby those who were already settled attempted to influence decisions about job opportunities and housing facilities for other African *retornado*s.

Critical discussion
The numbers
It was already mentioned above that there was a discrepancy in the estimates regarding the total number of *retornado*s resulting from the following factors:

- all *retornado*s who applied for IARN services were counted; the others, who for some reason or other did not use its services, were not officially accounted for;
- in many other cases *retornado*s who came at a later date were also not counted, for they arrived during a more stable period and, being able to transfer assets and funds, did not require the services provided by IARN;
- there were also cases in which re-emigration to other countries was achieved so rapidly that they stayed in Lisbon only temporarily. In still other situations the outflow of *retornado*s to other host countries occurred directly – like the exodus of residents from Mozambique to South Africa, from Angola to Zaire and from Guinea to Senegal.

Even the most reliable estimates obtained directly and exhaustively through the 1981 census fail to account for those who had already settled in countries other than Portugal.

Settlement difficulties
In such a large and complex operation occurring in a situation of great instability it is difficult to avoid errors and omissions. Luggage was lost and never found or recovered by its owners; unscrupulous hosts exploited employers and the state by charging for services that were never delivered; and support schemes and subsidies were sometimes allocated to those who least needed them.

Many *retornado*s blamed the Portuguese state for their situation. They accused the government of having abandoned them and of having sacrificed their interests in Africa for a rushed and ill-conceived decolonization process.

On the other hand, the international community was never properly acknowledged for the generous support it provided. Over US$30 million was given in direct aid to the repatriation and settlement programmes. Also noteworthy was the aid provided by the Council of Europe, the USA, the FAO and the Nordic countries (Leandro 1984: 378).

Support for the returnee population was implemented through various government programmes that aimed to facilitate the integration of the *retornado*s. Economic aid was channelled into providing credit for housing programmes and creating job opportunities. It is also important to mention the contribution of non-

PLATE 13 (above): The docks at Lisbon. Portuguese repatriates from Africa look for their crates.
PLATE 14 (below): A reception centre for repatriates, Portugal.

governmental organizations such as Caritas, the União de Caridade Portuguesa (Portuguese Union of Charity).

Positive outcomes

Whether through the aid and support programmes to assist in the settlement and integration of the *retornado*s or through sheer determination, hard work and dedication, it is generally recognized that the *retornado*s' integration into Portuguese society was a success.

There are external manifestations of their prosperous presence all over Portugal. Coffee shops, hotels, restaurants, factories, workshops, commercial agencies, transport enterprises and other services have designations that evoke their owners' African experience.

In addition, the public administration and services as well as the municipal agencies employ significant numbers of *retornado*s who served in or had ties with the overseas administration.

Particularly interesting has been the integration of instructors, young professors and administrative staff from African universities who have accelerated the creation of new metropolitan universities.

There is a general consensus among the Portuguese population that the success attained by the majority of *retornado*s is the result of individual capabilities and skills acquired in the overseas context. Prolonged residence in 'frontier territories', where there is a need to create and develop individual initiative, generates leadership qualities and self-reliance.

A distaste for bureaucracy, an informal relationship with the power structure and a high level of sociability, which may be understood as a result of isolation, have characterized the social outlook of the *retornado*.

This psychological make-up may partly explain the success of their integration both at the level of social participation in mainstream Portuguese society, and at an individual level in terms of professional and economic achievement.

References

Cónim, C. and M. Carrilho (1989) *Situação Demográfica e Perspectivas de Evolução. Portugal, 1960–2000*, Lisboa: Instituto de Estudos para o Desenvolvimento, 182 (16)

Cunha, S. (1977) *O Ultramar: A Nação e o '25 de Abril'*, Coimbra: Atlântida, 363

Dias, M. and A. Laranjo (1976) 'Report. African Returnees' Assistance Programme in View of the Emergency Situation', *Final Report and Evaluation of Project 76/01. Resettlement of Refugees*, Lisbon: Catholic Relief Services

Leandro, J. Marques (1984) 'Retorno de Desalojados e Retorno de Emigrantes', *Emigração e Retorno na Região Centro*, 354–78

Pires, R. M. et al. (1987) *Os Retornados: Um Estudo Sociográfico*, Lisboa: Instituto de Estudos para o Desenvolvimento, 228 (14)

EAST AND WEST INDIAN MIGRATION
TO THE NETHERLANDS

HAN ENTZINGER

The geographical position of the Netherlands explains why the Dutch have a long tradition as seafarers and merchants that goes well beyond the limits of Europe. Since the late sixteenth century, seafaring, trading and colonizing have been going hand in hand. The remnants of Dutch colonization can still be seen in places as different as New York, Brazil, Ghana, South Africa, Sri Lanka and even Japan. Sooner or later, however, the Dutch had to abandon these territories. The special cultural and linguistic links persisted only with South Africa, even though these were frozen for several decades because of the apartheid regime.

By the dawn of the twentieth century, when the European powers had divided most of the world outside Europe among themselves, the Netherlands had preserved three of her colonies: the Netherlands East Indies (now Indonesia), Surinam (or Netherlands Guyana) and Curaçao, the main island of what later became the Netherlands Antilles. Because the Netherlands East Indies was by far the largest and richest of these three, it was obvious that this colony had a stronger appeal than the others to Dutch people wishing to settle overseas.

Dutch colonial policy differed from the policies of both Britain and France. In Britain a sharp distinction was drawn between colonies for European settlers (in particular Canada, Australia, New Zealand and South Africa) and colonies that mainly served economic and geopolitical purposes. Most of the latter type had a significant or even a very large indigenous population. In these colonies much of the existing social and political fabric was kept intact. An elite from the mother country, mainly officers, administrators and some merchants, was superimposed on the existing structures. These elites were relatively small: a vast country like India never had more than a few tens of thousands of British colonizers.

French colonial policy was quite different. The French never used their colonies for settlement– with Algeria being an obvious exception – but they were much keener than Britain to export their political and cultural values. The political and educational systems of the French colonies were modelled after the French

example, and the local elites were educated in the mother country on a much larger scale than under the British system.

Dutch colonial policy, in particular towards the Netherlands East Indies, combined elements of both British and French models, while adding its own touch (De Jong 1984; Van Doorn 1994; Wesseling 1988). The British system of 'indirect rule' prevailed, but the number of settlers was much larger. Between 1880 and 1940 the 'European' population grew from 60,000 to 300,000. Three factors contributed to this steep rise: continuing immigration, the high birth rate among the settler population, but most of all the large number of mixed marriages and other liaisons with members of the local population. Most spouses (usually the wives) and children born of these marriages were given the legal status of European settlers. It is estimated that in the late 1940s roughly two-thirds of the 'Europeans' in the archipelago were of mixed racial origin (Ellemers and Vaillant 1985: 16). Yet these 'Eurasians' were considered to be Dutch; they held Dutch passports, received a Dutch education and many of them occupied key positions in the colonial administration. In this respect, there are certain similarities with the French model, though only very few actually received their education in the mother country in Europe.

'Repatriation' from Indonesia

In 1945 Indonesia declared itself independent; this independence was recognized by the Netherlands in 1949 after a bloody (and for the Dutch unsuccessful) military intervention. The events of those years provoked such strong hostility between the Indonesians and their former colonizers that in the following period practically everyone of European descent felt obliged to leave the country. In late 1957 any remaining Dutch people were asked to leave and all Dutch property was nationalized. Many of the 'Europeans' who left Indonesia had never thought of themselves as colonizers who had come to defend the interests of the mother country. Their ancestors might have come as settlers, but that was some generations before. In racial terms, many were of mixed origins; some were even exclusively Indonesian or Chinese (Willems and Lucassen 1994). Where should they go?

In the late 1940s it was not at all obvious that the roughly 300,000 'Europeans' living in the East Indies would be allowed to settle in the Netherlands. The country was recovering from the damaging effects of the Second World War and was in a phase of rapid population growth. This, in combination with the high population density and the need to restructure Dutch agriculture, incited several hundreds of thousands of Dutch people to emigrate, in particular to Canada and Australia. Under such circumstances, it was doubtful whether 300,000 people from the former colony would be accepted by the people of the Netherlands. A major reason for the western half of the island of New Guinea being excluded from the transfer of sovereignty in 1949 was so that it could serve as a safe haven for those who wished to leave. Indeed, several tens of thousands went to this territory, which until then had been almost forgotten. Others wishing to go left for one of the 'traditional' immigration countries, in particular the USA. Between 25,000 and 30,000 settled in California, where they are still regarded as a community.

The vast majority of 'Europeans' in Indonesia, however, had no option but to leave for the Netherlands, as the Dutch authorities gradually began to recognize. In that all 'Europeans' in Indonesia were entitled to full Netherlands citizenship, it was difficult to deny them access to the country of which they held a passport. The so-called repatriation process – the bulk of the '*re*patriates' were going to the Netherlands for the first time in their lives – stretched out over a rather long period. Most of the 300,000 came between 1950 and 1958. The process came to an end in 1963 when Netherlands New Guinea was transferred to Indonesia.

Once the Dutch had accepted that repatriation was unavoidable, an effort was made to integrate the new arrivals into Dutch society as quickly as possible. Of enormous help, of course, was the fact that most repatriates spoke Dutch, often as a mother tongue, and had been educated in a school system that was almost the same as that of the mother country. Also, most of the repatriates themselves were highly motivated to integrate, if not 'assimilate' – the term was used quite frequently in those days – in the understanding that there was no chance of returning (Ex 1966; Van Amersfoort 1982).

Housing was a major part of the integration policy for the repatriates from Indonesia. In the 1950s there was a housing shortage in the Netherlands. Upon arrival, most repatriates were housed in temporary accommodation – pensions, hotels or private homes. It was a deliberate policy to spread the newcomers all over the country, since this was thought to speed up their assimilation. Subsequently, 5 per cent of all newly built houses were put at their disposal. Given their relatively high skill level and strong motivation to integrate, most repatriates were quickly able to find employment, though often at a lower level than in Indonesia. The newly created Ministry of Social Work coordinated their reception; social workers played an active role in promoting assimilation.

After some initial hesitation, the Dutch population soon began to accept the repatriates as their neighbours, colleagues and fellow citizens. In fact, the integration of the repatriates from Indonesia is often presented as a role model. Indeed, there have been no noticeable tensions or processes of social marginalization among this group. The intermarriage rate, often used as an indicator of integration, is extremely high. In 1990 – three to four decades after the peak repatriation years – 200,000 people living in the Netherlands had been born in Indonesia (the other 100,000 repatriates had died in the intermediate period). The second generation – the first born in the Netherlands – included 70,000 people whose parents had both been born in Indonesia and no less than 200,000 with one parent born in that country and the other in the Netherlands (Prins 1991: 33).

Of course, the other side of this 'assimilation coin' is that nowadays little is left of Indonesian habits and culture in the Netherlands, with Indonesian food (*rijsttafel*) being a notable exception. Many repatriates, especially as they grow older, feel that the 'assimilation' process may have forced them to abandon too much of their identity. They feel this particularly acutely when they compare their own experiences with those of immigrants who have settled in the Netherlands in later years and who have been allowed to preserve their cultural identities to a much greater extent.

The Moluccans: the long chase of a shadow
Indonesia's independence not only resulted in the migration of about 300,000 settlers and their offspring from that country to the Netherlands, it also led to the arrival of a much smaller group with a very different background. These were the Amboinese or Moluccans. In colonial times the Dutch had granted preferential status to certain smaller ethnic groups within the vast Indonesian archipelago. This was a popular

measure among colonial powers, though many younger states are still feeling its effects in the form of inter-ethnic tensions. In the Netherlands East Indies, the Amboinese – from the island of Ambon in the (South) Moluccas in the eastern part of the country – were recruited to serve in the lower ranks of the army. During the negotiations for independence the Dutch claimed a special autonomous status for the Moluccas, but the Indonesians did not keep their word. Then, in 1951, a group of South Moluccans declared the independence of their territory, thus placing those soldiers of Moluccan origin still serving in the colonial army in an impossible position. By order of a Dutch court these 4000 military men plus their 8500 family members were transferred to the Netherlands, where they were 'to await their eventual return' (Bartels 1989).

Upon arrival in the Netherlands the Moluccans were demobilized – to their own surprise and anger – and housed in camps, segregated from Dutch society. Initially they were not allowed to take up employment: the state would take care of them. The rationale behind this policy of non-integration was that it would underline the temporary character of their stay in the Netherlands and enable them to preserve their own group identity. Thus, the approach to the Moluccans was the complete opposite to that of the 'repatriates'. Gradually, however, it became clear that the Moluccans' quick return was not to be expected. From around 1960 they had to move into more permanent housing, concentrated in a number of neighbourhoods especially built for them, mainly in rural areas (Entzinger 1982).

For many years the Dutch authorities left the rapidly growing Moluccan community in this situation of temporality, without any clear perspectives. It is generally assumed that this was the main motivation behind a series of terrorist acts committed by Moluccan youngsters in the mid-1970s. These included two train hijackings, which were widely covered in the world press. Only after these acts did it become clear to all involved that a return was not to be expected. The Dutch authorities took these acts as a signal that more effort was needed to promote integration, not only of the Moluccans, but also of other recent immigrant groups both of colonial and non-colonial origins. In the early 1980s the government launched a 'minorities policy' aimed at fuller integration as well as at promoting respect for the cultural identities of all these groups (Entzinger 1994).

At present, more than forty years after the Moluccans were shipped to the Netherlands, their number has risen to around 40,000, and a third generation is emerging. On the whole, this third generation seems better integrated educationally and occupationally than the first and second (Veenman 1990). To most of its members the dream of returning to a free Republic of the South Moluccas has lost its appeal.

Surinam: independent but tightly linked

After Indonesia's independence the Dutch gradually began to take a wider interest in their territories in the West Indies – Surinam and the Netherlands Antilles. In those days, the two territories combined contained less than 1 per cent of Indonesia's population of 60 million. Surinam had a typical plantation economy, whereas Curaçao and Aruba, the main islands of the Antilles, had important oil refineries. The populations of both countries contain a variety of ethnic communities derived from all over the world: the outcomes of slavery and labour migration. Neither of the two has an old settler community originating from the Netherlands.

In 1954, in an attempt to enlighten colonial policy after the loss of the East Indies, the Netherlands, Surinam and the Antilles drew up the Statute of the Kingdom of the Netherlands, under which the three countries became equal partners. This resulted in all the inhabitants of both West Indian territories obtaining full Netherlands citizenship, thereby permitting them to take up residence in the 'mother country' without any restrictions. (Paradoxically, the reverse is not the case: the 'European Dutch' have no entitlement to free settlement in the Caribbean parts of the kingdom.)

In the 1950s and 1960s there was little traffic between the European and overseas parts of the kingdom: only the local elite obtained their higher education in Europe (Oostindie and Maduro 1986). The smallness of the countries imposes limitations on their educational infrastructures. At present, the two plus Aruba (which split away from the Antilles in 1986 to continue as an autonomous state) have only 650,000 inhabitants – 400,000 in Surinam and 250,000 on the islands. Gradually, in the late 1960s, the flow from Surinam to the Netherlands started to increase. As more people began to discover the advantages of free settlement in the Netherlands, an exodus seemed imminent. In an attempt to stop this trend, Surinam was given independence in 1975, but economically and culturally (and thus also politically) it continued to depend heavily on the Netherlands.

After a lull during the first years of independence, emigration from Surinam again gained momentum

PLATE 15: West Indian street carnival in Amsterdam. Here the white Carnival Queen is married to a Surinamer.

around 1980, when the military took over the country (Van Amersfoort and Surie 1987). At present, the number of people of Surinamese origin living in the Netherlands is estimated at 260,000, while 400,000 Surinamese live in Surinam. Many Surinamese families are rooted in both countries, which explains why commuter migration is quite common.

When immigration from Surinam began to increase in the early 1970s, the Dutch government decided on a policy similar to the one for the repatriates from Indonesia twenty years earlier. Again, housing and social work were important elements, and again an attempt was made to spread the newcomers evenly throughout the country. Major differences, however, were the non-compulsory character of the reception policy for the Surinamese, the lack of job opportunities, especially in rural areas, and the fact that neither the authorities nor the migrants them-selves were convinced of the permanent character of their stay in the Netherlands. It was generally understood that many Surinamese had taken an unconsidered decision, and that they would eventually return. In reality, however, this proved to be the exception rather than the rule.

The reception and integration policy for the Surinamese in the 1970s was far less successful than its counterpart had been for those who came from Indonesia in the 1950s. Contrary to the government's intentions, substantial numbers of Surinamese people concentrated in the larger cities: many Creole Surinamese settled in Amsterdam, whereas The Hague became popular among the Surinamese of South Asian origin – 57 per cent of all Surinamese in the Netherlands live in Amsterdam, Rotterdam, The Hague or Utrecht, as against 13 per cent of the population as a whole (Muus 1991: 29). The housing situation of the Surinamese is satisfactory, but registered unemployment is high, although not as high as among migrants of Turkish or Moroccan origin. There are indications that the second generation is doing better, especially at school (Entzinger et al. 1994; Penninx et al. 1993). It should be kept in mind that – just like the 'Europeans' in the East Indies – the Surinamese have been familiar with the Dutch language and school system since colonial days, even though identification with the mother country was less strong in Surinam than among the elite in the former Netherlands East Indies.

The Dutch Caribbean islands

Today, the Netherlands Antilles and Aruba are the only remaining parts of the Kingdom of the Netherlands. This is likely to continue for some time, for both countries strongly favour the present situation over independence. Culturally and economically the six islands in the Caribbean are less oriented towards the Netherlands than is Surinam, even since the latter's independence. The islands also have strong links with neighbouring Latin American states and with the USA. Nevertheless, about 100,000 islanders now live in the Netherlands. Some have gone there to receive an education, others because they have no economic prospects in the Antilles (Cross and Entzinger 1988).

For this mixture of reasons, the social situation of Antilleans in the Netherlands is very heterogeneous. Their level of education is roughly the same as for the Dutch, but unemployment is higher, particularly at the lower skill levels. There are also deep concerns about delinquent behaviour among certain groups of youngsters of Antillean origin.

Current migration between the Dutch Caribbean and the Netherlands is typically of a commuter nature. The incidence of return is high: Aruba even has an immigration surplus, explained by the expanding tourist industry. Curaçao's migration balance, by contrast, has been negative for a long time, but here too there is substantial back-and-forth migration. During the peak season three or four Jumbo flights per day make the trip from the islands to Amsterdam and back, thus tightening the links between people on either side in a way that was inconceivable when Jan van Riebeeck set foot on the Cape, or even when Soekarno proclaimed Indonesia's independence.

References

Bartels, D.(1989) *Moluccans in Exile*, Leiden: COMT

Cross, M. and H. Entzinger (eds) (1988) *Lost Illusions. Caribbean Minorities in Britain and the Netherlands*, London: Routledge

De Jong, L. (1984) *Het Koninkrijk der Nederlanden in de Tweede Wereldoorlog. Deel 11a: Nederlands–Indië I*, The Hague: Staatsuitgeverij

Ellemers, J. E. and R. E. F. Vaillant (1985) *Indische Nederlanders en gerepatrieerden*, Muiderberg: Coutinho

Entzinger, Han (1982) 'Government Housing Policies for the Moluccan Minority in the Netherlands', in John Rex and John Solomos (eds) *Migrant Workers in Metropolitan Cities*, Strasbourg: European Science Foundation, 205–24

—— (1994) 'A Future for the Dutch "Ethnic Minorities" Model?', in B. Lewis and D. Schnapper (eds), *Muslims in Europe*, London: Pinter, 19–38

Entzinger, H., J. Siegers and F. Tazelaar (eds) (1994) *Immigrant Ethnic Minorities in the Dutch Labour Market*, Amsterdam: Thesis

Ex, J. (1966) *Adjustment after Migration*, The Hague: Nijhoff

Muus, Philip (1991) *Migration Minorities and Policy in the Netherlands (SOPEMI–Netherlands–1991)*, Amsterdam: University of Amsterdam, Department of Geography

Oostindie, Gert and Emy Maduro (1986) *In het land van de overheerser. Antillianen en Surinamers in Netherland 1634/1667–1954*, Dordrecht: Foris

Penninx, R., J. Schoorl and C. Van Praag (1993) *The Impact of International Migration on Receiving Countries. The Case of the Netherlands*, Amsterdam: Swets and Zeitlinger

Prins, C. J. M. (1991) 'Partial Enumeration by Nationality and Country of Birth, from Municipal Population Registers, 1 January 1990', *Maandstatistiek Bevolking*, (1), 18–37

Van Amersfoort, Hans (1982) *Immigration and the Formation of Minority Groups. The Dutch Experience 1945–1975*, Cambridge: University Press

Van Amersfoort, Hans and Boudewijn Surie (1987) 'Reluctant Hosts: Immigration into Dutch Society 1970–1985', *Ethnic and Racial Studies* 10 (2), 169–85

Van Doorn, J. A. A. (1994) *De laatste eeuw van Indië. Ontwikkeling en ondergang van een koloniaal project*, Amsterdam: Bert Bakker

Veenman, J. (1990) *De arbeidsmarktpositie van allochtonen in Nederland, in het bijzonder van Molukkers*, Groningen: Wolters Noordhoff

Wesseling, H. L. (1988) *Indië verloren, rampspoed geboren*, Amsterdam: Bert Bakker

Willems, Wim and Leo Lucassen (1994) *Het onbekende vaderland. De repatriëring van Indische Nederlanders (1946–1964)*, The Hague: Sdu

REPATRIATION OF AFRICAN EXILES: THE DECISION TO RETURN

PETER KOEHN

We have lived that moment of the scattering of the people –
   Immigrant, Migrant, Emigrant, Exile,
    Where do the birds gather?
That in other nations, other lives, other places has become:

The gathering of last warriors on lost frontiers,
The gathering of lost refugees on lasting border-camps,
The gathering of the indentured on the sidewalks of strange cities,
The gathering of émigrés on the margins of foreign cultures.
   Immigrate, Migrate, Emigrate, Exile,
    Where do the birds fly?

In the half-life, half-light of alien tongues,
In the uncanny fluency of the other's language,
We relive the past in rituals of revival,
Unravelling memories in slow time; gathering the present.
   Immigrant, Migrant, Emigrant, Exile,
    After the last sky, Where do the birds fly?

(Migrations by Abena P. A. Busia)

Dr Sadako Ogata, United Nations High Commissioner for Refugees, has proclaimed the 1990s as the 'decade of repatriation'. This entry explores the decision to return, focusing on Ethiopia and Eritrea. The discussion aims to inform the wider context of return migration to the African continent. The importance of repatriation is underlined by estimates that in some cases, including Ethiopia, Sudan and Uganda, more than half the country's skilled professionals are estimated to be living outside their homeland (*Chronicle of Higher Education*, 9 June 1993: A33).

For nearly everyone involved in assisting refugees, as well as for most exiles, secure voluntary repatriation is unquestionably the 'preferred solution' to the tragic condition of external dislocation (Cuénod 1989: 242; Hendrie 1991: 200; UNECA 1991: 25). Nevertheless, the return of refugees to their homeland is an uncommon event in international politics. Most African cases of mass repatriation have involved peoples dislocated as a result of anti-colonial struggles that eventually succeeded in evicting foreign subjugators (Mazur 1988: 57; Mwase 1990: 113–20; UNECA 1991: 26, 28–9).[1]

Refugee repatriation in Africa

The number of refugees from revolutions and other post-colonial political conflicts estimated to return to their homeland through formal UNHCR repatriation programmes or spontaneous repatriation generally remains small in comparison with the total exile population. In 1992, returnee estimates (*World Refugee Survey* 1993: 53) for Africa were: Angola (45,000), Burundi (38,000), Chad (4400), Ethiopia (23,000), Liberia (50,000), Mauritania (5000), Mozambique (40,000), Sierra Leone (1600), Somalia (100,000) and Uganda (2700). Most returning refugees came from neighbouring countries of asylum, where many others are poised to go back.[2]

Ethiopia

In May 1991, Mengistu Haile Mariam's regime collapsed and the autocratic ruler fled from Ethiopia. The Ethiopian People's Revolutionary Democratic Front (EPRDF) seized control of Addis Ababa and the Eritrean People's Liberation Front (EPLF) captured Asmara. The leaders of the EPRDF moved to establish a provisional government based on ethnic diversity and promised to allow a UN-sponsored referendum in 1993 on independence for Eritrea.

About 375,000 refugees returned to Ethiopia in 1991, fleeing conflict in Somalia (*Refugees* 1992: 10). Small numbers of Ethiopians residing in Kenya repatriated spontaneously in 1992 and a UNHCR-organized programme began in December 1992 (*World Refugee Survey* 1993: 64). Although reliable figures are not available, only a tiny fraction of the 425,000 projected returnees to Ethiopia actually repatriated in 1992 (*Refugees* 1992: 10).

Eritrea

An estimated one million Eritreans are living outside Eritrea (*Africa Recovery* 1993: 36). In 1992, roughly 50,000 Eritreans repatriated from Sudan without international assistance after years of exile. Perhaps half this group later returned to Sudan because of difficult conditions in Eritrea. Another 530,000 Eritreans remained in Sudan – 280,000 in camps. Eritrean authorities reported that a quarter of the refugees in Sudan had left Ethiopia more than ten years previously and that 52 per cent were below fifteen years of age (*World Refugee Survey* 1993: 62; also see Mekuria Bulcha 1988). Funding disagreements between the Eritrean government and UNHCR stalled repatriation throughout 1992. Eritrean officials rejected UNHCR's proposed $69 million two-year repatriation plan and insisted on a $200 million programme involving the provision of schools, clinics and other services needed to ensure the reintegration of refugees in a country lacking virtually all infrastructure after decades of war. Once an organized programme is agreed upon and in place, 'UNHCR expects 250,000 Eritreans will choose to repatriate' (*Refugees* 1992: 10; *World Refugee Survey* 1993: 62).

Exile repatriation from industrialized countries

The repatriation of official refugees and other political exiles living in the industrialized world occurs even less frequently than return from neighbouring countries of first asylum. The next part of this contribution, which sheds light on what key considerations affect repatriation decision making, examines the findings of a study I undertook in the mid-1980s on exiles from Ethiopia and Eritrea living in the Washington DC metropolitan area.

Important repatriation considerations

Under what circumstances are exiles living in industrialized countries likely to go back to their home country? After assessing the importance of various factors in terms of personal decision making, respondents in the Washington DC study identified their overriding, or most important, and second most important considerations. An open-ended explanation supplemented responses to the standardized questions.

The Washington DC exiles had little difficulty distinguishing between relevant and irrelevant factors in terms of their personal repatriation decision making. The most frequently cited considerations of what would provoke serious contemplation of voluntary repatriation all involved changes in homeland conditions. One factor, political change resulting in a new homeland regime, stands out from all others in terms of the proportion of household heads who identified it as a consideration that would play an important part in their decision about returning permanently to the country of origin (see Table 8.6 in Koehn 1991).[3]

While it is conceivable that some refugees might be 'propelled' to return home by negative forces associated with the place of exile, the Washington DC findings indicate that key push forces are not operative among most of the US-based exiles who participated in the study. For instance, 90 per cent of the respondents did not view economic deprivation in the USA as an important consideration affecting repatriation calculations.

Most decisive repatriation considerations

When asked to identify the two most important considerations, the respondents' choices confirmed that a change of regime was the most crucial repatriation factor. Nearly two-thirds of the Ethiopians interviewed and about one-third of the Eritreans identified political change resulting in a new regime they did not oppose as the one development that would most decisively affect their decision to return to live in their home country. 'If only the present regime is overthrown for the better', are the words used by one Ethiopian interviewee asked to describe the conditions under which he would return to his sending country. Another exile referred to the need to eliminate 'fear of one's own government'. According to this respondent, 'there can be no guarantees when the protector is the abuser'.

By 1993, less than 25,000 Ethiopians had returned permanently from Europe and North America (Yohannes Gebresellassie 1992; *New York Times*, 13 May 1993). In the case of Ethiopian refugees, the most decisive consideration is likely to have become the individual migrant's evaluation of the post-Mengistu regime. In interviews following Mengistu's flight from Ethiopia, Helene Moussa (1993: 247) found that Ethiopian women exiles in Toronto had a 'wait and see attitude' to return because of uncertainty over the 'Provisional Government's policy of self-determination of different nationalities'.

In the Washington DC study, more than half the Eritreans (54 per cent) viewed realization of the goals of a nationality movement as most decisive in their deliberations. With the arrival of independence in 1993, therefore, the principal barrier to repatriation no longer existed for most Eritreans.

The only other conditions frequently ranked among the two foremost considerations affecting repatriation decision making were: (1) the opportunity to help people, use one's education and practise one's profession in the homeland – one-third of the Ethiopian exiles and 16 per cent of the Eritreans (Maigenet Shifferaw and Getachew Metaferia 1988: 32); and (2) an end to armed conflict and improved personal security – about 20 per cent in both cases (Moussa 1993: 247, 252).

Return from industrialized countries
Refugees wishing to go home are most likely to return to the sending country if their perception of the homeland situation is congruent with certain self-imposed preconditions. The relevant preconditions among political exiles living in industrialized countries usually involve changes in the homeland. The findings of the Washington DC study reveal that fundamental political transformation in the homeland is *the* most critical concern of those willing to consider repatriation. Such transformations include replacement of the existing regime with a new political system acceptable to the individual exile and/or the success of a national liberation struggle. Research among exiles living in Washington DC and Toronto also suggests that one other development is likely to be decisive among a substantial proportion of those willing to entertain the prospect of returning to their homeland. This is a (perceived) opportunity to provide a service to the homeland by helping one's people, using one's educational attainments and/or practising one's profession.

African refugees in industrialized countries often remain ambivalent about their current status (Moussa 1993: 247–8). The hope and urge to return home remains strong – especially among the earliest arrivals. Many are torn between the desire to help their compatriots in the homeland and to be near family members on the one hand, and the fear of personal danger and committed opposition to a post-revolution regime on the other. For some exiles,

economic and social adaptation and stability, and/or responsibility for children raised exclusively in the receiving society, will override the strong desire to return. In addition, there are long-term individual, family and national political and economic advantages that result from retaining networks in the north. This understanding has motivated EPLF leaders to select candidates for repatriation from the USA by balancing the need for contacts with transcultural compatriots living in the north against pressing demands at home for returnees who possess skills that are in short supply.

While material comforts and cherished freedoms may be available in western countries, it is often difficult for refugees to find satisfaction and sound mental health in the new land (Hung 1985: 204; Takaki 1989: 455). In the context of a desperately poor home country, such as Ethiopia or Eritrea, the contrast between personal lifestyle abroad and the condition of those at home is especially acute. This situation compounds the agony of exile.

Ensuring successful voluntary repatriation
As we approach the midway point in the decade of repatriation, the return of refugees continues to take place in circumstances that are far from ideal. The protection and safety of returnees is often not assured. Moreover, 'most refugees repatriating in this post-Cold War era are doing so with relatively little help, largely left to fend for themselves in their war-ravaged homelands' (Ruiz 1993: 20). The Organization of African Unity has appealed to the governments of countries of origin to encourage and facilitate repatriation by:

- redressing the situations that motivated refugees to leave their country;

- assuring refugees that they would be welcomed back to resume normal and useful lives without fear of persecution or punishment for having left their country;

- assisting refugees wishing to return as a result of these assurances to resume normal lives in their countries of origin; and

- granting a general amnesty to those whose fear of persecution for political reasons needs to be allayed and assuring them of a general welcome and reintegration into their own society, with full rights and privileges restored.

(UNECA 1991: 25–6)

Home country protections

To ensure successful voluntary repatriation, the guiding principle must be *the interest of the refugee* (Goodwin-Gill 1989: 283). In addition to regime change and the realization of nationality-movement objectives, the safe and durable return of exile populations requires guarantees that returnees of diverse political persuasion, nationality and organizational affiliation no longer will be persecuted or subjected to life-threatening violence in their homeland. To ascertain that such protections are in place, 'UNHCR should take the lead in investigating, first-hand, the conditions in the refugees' home areas' (Ruiz 1993: 24–5). Determining that the requisite protections exist is also facilitated through advance fact-finding missions by representatives of various refugee factions (Goodwin-Gill 1989: 264, 284).

Next, the fundamental human rights of the returning population need to be guaranteed. Negotiations with authorities in the country of origin can play a vital role in securing formal human-rights guarantees following regime change (Gordenker 1987: 127; Ruiz 1993: 21). In the light of the intensity of their political commitments, firm assurances of free political expression and association are likely to be instrumental in the successful repatriation of former exiles. Returnees must be individually identified, accepted and available for follow-up contacts.

Finally, UNHCR and independent NGOs must be granted unhindered, long-term access to returnees in order to ensure that they are not mistreated,[4] that their rights to political participation are protected, and that rehabilitation efforts and objectives are not subverted – in short, 'to monitor fulfilment of such guarantees as may have encouraged them to repatriate' (Bach 1989: 314; Goodwin-Gill 1988: 163–4; Helton 1992: 40).

The experience of the initial group of returnees is likely to exert the most profound influence on those who are seriously entertaining repatriation. Exiles communicate on a regular and rapid basis with people in the homeland. The first returnees will report back favourably if they encounter (1) a new regime that respects the democratic process, diversity and human rights, (2) individual and family security and prospects of peaceful relations continuing in the future, and (3) a warm reception and ease of economic integration and social adaptation. In short, 'if states want their people to return, they must create conditions which are conducive' to repatriation (Harrell-Bond 1989: 61).[5]

Returnee reintegration

Although voluntary repatriation is the 'optimal desired durable solution of refugee problems in African countries' (UNECA 1991: 26), it is accompanied by its own set of problems. Many contemporary African refugees have lived in exile for a decade or longer. A long period of exile makes homeland reintegration particularly difficult (Koehn 1991: 386). In some cases, serious conflicts arise over land formerly possessed by refugees before flight. On the other hand, the receiving country stands to benefit from the transfer of skills acquired by refugees during exile (UNECA 1991: 27).

The successful and sustainable reintegration of returnees depends upon effective rehabilitation and development measures.[6] Even prior to repatriation, the refugee- and development-assistance communities need to devote attention to the preparation and training of refugees for participation upon return in the development of their homeland.[7] As Hiram Ruiz (1993: 28) points out, 'it is irresponsible to encourage refugees to repatriate without ensuring that adequate relief and rehabilitation assistance will be made available to them in their home country.' Donor policies designed to facilitate repatriation would promote development projects that incorporate a major role for exiles (including short-term opportunities for those who continue to reside abroad) so that they might use their skills, knowledge, capital and energy for the benefit of the homeland population (Koehn 1991: 385). Donor support must include (re)training for returning refugees who are out of touch with homeland conditions, have never lived in their parents' country, and/or have become dependent upon international aid and are no longer self-reliant. One vehicle for promoting the application within African countries of useful skills, along with the acquisition of relevant and sustainable development experience, would be through the establishment of an 'international refugee corps' (Koehn 1994: 106–7).

Sustainable repatriation also requires that donors provide extended assistance for communities that receive large numbers of returnees (see interview with Sadako Ogata, *Refugees* 1991: 35; Cuénod 1989: 243). Attention to the reconstruction of villages, towns and cities devastated by years of armed conflict, and external support for permanent employment opportunities for returnees will lay the foundation for local self-sufficiency (see Ruiz 1993: 27). Reconstitution of an appropriate educational system at all levels presents one particularly urgent challenge.

To ensure successful voluntary repatriation, UNHCR must expand and enhance its recovery-assistance role in the original sending country (see Cuénod 1989: 243; Ruiz 1993: 28–9 for existing restrictions on UNHCR participation). A useful vehicle for this purpose is the cross-mandate operation. This inter-agency approach is embodied in the *1992 Tripartite Agreement Between the Governments of Sudan and Ethiopia and UNHCR*. In part, the agreement provides that (pp. 4, 6):

> The UNHCR shall provide assistance to the returnees comprising transport, relief and rehabilitation as well as community-based and cross-mandated assistance to upgrade/reinforce the absorptive capacity of the respective areas of reintegration in terms of water supply, roads, health services, education, etc.
>
> The reintegration assistance will be undertaken through a cross-mandated approach involving UNDP, WFP, UNICEF, FAO, WHO, ILO etc. with the UNHCR playing the lead role and shall to the extent possible focus on the upgrading and/or establishment of vital infrastructural inputs.

The cross-mandate approach, which already had been applied with positive results in the Ogaden and southern Ethiopia, includes a food for recovery programme, provisions for providing community-based assistance to newly arriving refugees, drought victims, locally displaced persons and returnees 'without discrimination' (*Memorandum of Understanding on the Implementation of the Cross-Mandate Concept,* p. 2), and options whereby NGOs can participate through individual agreements (interview by the author with Mandefro Tegegn, Director, Administration for Refugee/Returnee Affairs, Government of Ethiopia, Addis Ababa, 18 November 1992). When coupled with a commitment to involve the clients in vital project-planning, and executing and evaluating roles (Mazur 1988: 59), the cross-mandate approach promises to address the basic reintegration needs of returning exiles in Africa.

Notes

1. In other types of repatriation situations, Ugandans returned to their homeland after the fall of Idi Amin (Gordenker 1987: 127) and thousands of refugees crossed back into Ethiopia from Somalia in 1988 (Gersony 1989: 45, 55). The 1987 Tigrayan repatriation ranks as one of the largest in Africa (Hendrie 1991: 201).
2. For a detailed, country by country breakdown of refugee populations in African countries and repatriation prospects as of late 1992, see *World Refugee Survey* (1993: 56–77).

For global refugee repatriation estimates for the period 1975–93, see Table 1 in Stein (1993).
3. Regime change also proved to be the decisive factor affecting repatriation decision making among most of the refugees from Ethiopia in Sudan questioned by Cultural Survival interviewers (Clay and Holcomb 1985: 150, 162). Among all African émigrés living in the USA, Kofi Apraku (1991: xiv) argues, there is eagerness to return provided that economic and political reforms occur that allow for personal freedoms, civil liberties, and political and economic pluralism in the homeland. Unfortunately, this argument is weakly substantiated by the author.
4. In this regard, there is a need to develop 'practical and effective methods of monitoring the security of those returning' (Goodwin-Gill 1989: 285).
5. A political system built on principles of equity, decentralization (Abdul Mohammed 1991: 73–6), respect for diversity, popular participation and the public accountability of officials is likely to be conducive to the repatriation of skilled refugees.
6. See Hendrie (1991: 214) on the inability of aid personnel during the 1985 Tigrayan repatriation 'to shift their conceptual framework from relief assistance to refugees in a camp context to recovery assistance to poor farmers returning to cultivate their land'. In contrast, the Eritrean Relief Association, an indigenous organization with strong support from the exile community, introduced self-help projects across rural Eritrea aimed at re-establishing the economic and ecological conditions required to facilitate the eventual repatriation of refugees on a self-reliant basis (Sorenson 1991).
7. It is interesting in this connection that all the Ethiopian and Eritrean women interviewed by Moussa (1993: 252) who had not yet completed their education 'insisted that they would not return until they had a skill or profession that would make them useful for their country'.

References

Abdul Mohammed (1991) 'Beyond the Conflict: Peace and Cooperation in the Horn', *Voices From Africa*, 3 (March), 73–6

Africa Recovery (1993) 7 (7), June

Apraku, Kofi K. (1991) *African Émigrés in the United States: A Missing Link in Africa's Social and Economic Development*, New York: Praeger

Bach, Robert L. (1989) 'Third Country Resettlement', in G. Loescher and L. Monahan (eds), *Refugees and International Relations*, Oxford: Oxford University Press, 313–31

Busia, Abena P. A. (1990) *Testimonies of Exile*, Trenton: Africa World Press

Chronicle of Higher Education (1993) 9 June

Clay, J. W. and B. K. Holcomb (1985) *Politics and the Ethiopian Famine, 1984–1985,* Cambridge: Cultural Survival

Cuénod, J. (1989) 'Refugees: Development or Relief?', in G. Loescher and L. Monahan (eds), *Refugees and International Relations*, Oxford: Oxford University Press, 219–53

Gersony, Robert. (1989) 'Why Somalis Flee: Conflict in Northern Somalia', *Cultural Survival*, 13 (4), 45–58

Goodwin-Gill, Guy S. (1988) 'Refugees: The Functions and Limits of the Existing Protection System', in A. Nash (ed.) *Human Rights and the Protection of Refugees Under International Law*, Halifax: Institute for Research on Public Policy, 149–82

—— (1989) 'Voluntary Repatriation: Legal and Policy Issues', in

G. Loescher and L. Monahan (eds) *Refugees and International Relations*, Oxford: Oxford University Press, 255–85

Gordenker, Leon (1987) *Refugees in International Politics*, New York: Columbia University Press

Harrell-Bond, Barbara E. (1989) 'Repatriation: Under What Conditions is it the Most Desirable Solution for Refugees? An Agenda for Research', *African Studies Review*, 32 (1), 41–69

Helton, Arthur C. (1992) 'Repatriation or Refoulement', *Refugees*, 90, September, 38–40

Hendrie, Barbara (1991) 'The Politics of Repatriation: The Tigrayan Refugee Repatriation 1985–1987', *Journal of Refugee Studies*, 4 (2), 200–18

Hung, Nguyen Manh (1985) 'Vietnamese' in D. Haines (ed.) *Refugees in the United States: A Reference Handbook*, Westport: Greenwood Press, 195–208

Koehn, Peter (1991) *Refugees From Revolution: US Policy and Third-World Migration*, Boulder: Westview Press

—— (1994) 'Refugee Settlement and Repatriation in Africa: Development Prospects and Constraints', in H. Adelman and J. Sorenson (eds) *African Refugees: Development Aid and Repatriation*, Boulder: Westview Press, 97–116

Maigenet Shifferraw and Getachew Metaferia (1988) 'Trained Manpower Exodus from Ethiopia to the United States and Adjustment Issues in the United States', paper presented at the 31st Annual Meeting of the African Studies Association, Chicago

Mazur, Robert E. (1988) 'Refugees in Africa: The Role of Sociological Analysis and Praxis', *Current Sociology*, 36 (2), 43–60

Mekuria Bulcha (1988) *Flight and Integration: Causes of Mass Exodus From Ethiopia and Problems of Integration in the Sudan*, Uppsala: Scandinavian Institute of African Studies

Moussa, Helene (1993) *Storm and Sanctuary: The Journey of Ethiopian and Eritrean Women Refugees*, Dundas: Artemis Enterprises

Mwase, Ngila R. L. (1990) 'The Repatriation, Rehabilitation and Resettlement of Namibian Refugees at Independence', *Community Development Journal*, 25 (2), April, 113–20

New York Times (1993) 13 May

Refugees (1991) 84, April

Refugees (1992) 88, January

Ruiz, Hiram A. (1993) 'Repatriation: Tackling Protection and Assistance Concerns', *World Refugee Survey 1993*, Washington, DC: US Committee for Refugees

Sorenson, John (1991) 'The Eritrean Relief Association: The Response of an Indigenous Organization to the Refugee Crisis in the Horn of Africa', paper presented at the 20th Annual Meeting of the Canadian Association of African Studies, Toronto, May

Stein, Barry N. (1993) 'Repatriation During Conflict', *Round Table Consultation on Voluntary Repatriation*, Geneva: United Nations High Commissioner for Refugees, Division of International Protection

Takaki, Ronald (1989) *Strangers from a Different Shore: A History of Asian Americans*, Boston: Little, Brown & Company

UNECA (1991) *Guidelines on the Methods of Evaluating the Socio-Economic and Demographic Consequences of Refugees in African Countries*, Addis Ababa: United Nations Economic Commission for Africa

World Refugee Survey (1993)

Yohannes Gebresellassie (1992) 'Reflections on a Trip to Ethiopia', *Centre for Refugee Studies Newsletter*, York University, September

PART ELEVEN

MIGRATION IN ASIA AND OCEANIA

The formation of new nations often has dramatic consequences for migration flows. As we approach the end of the twentieth century we can anticipate the creation of an additional 140 new nation states since the founding of the United Nations in 1945. Many recognized states, as Zolberg et al. (1989: 233) have maintained, have been created through constitutional, peaceful means. However, where things go wrong, they often go terribly wrong (Zolberg 1983). The negative case normally arises when the three cognate processes of decolonization, the implosion of empire and the demands for self-determination do not entirely match. Beyond that generalization there are a host of particularities which cannot all be specified in detail here. Often a weakened empire still has sufficient resilience to negotiate an ordered withdrawal. (This happened, for example, in many countries of the British Commonwealth and in French West Africa and Equatorial Africa.) Sometimes the process of implosion has gone too far – the circumstance that confronted the Soviet Union after 1989. Those pressing for decolonization or statehood can adopt a range of peaceful or violent means in pursuit of their objective. In a number of cases there is a complicating factor arising from the presence of a significant numbers of settlers from the former metropolis. (Where the movement for self-determination is strong or violent, this can result in the repatriation of the settlers, as explained in Part 10.) Again, dominant and subordinate minorities may not agree about the shape of the new state or which national, religious or ethnic groups form a legitimate part of it.

It is this last circumstance that informs two of the contributions in this section of the *Survey*. The first considered is the separation of India and Pakistan covered by *Kiernan*. When Winston Churchill proclaimed at the end of the Second World War that Britain had not fought so bitterly only to give up its empire, this was recognized as a vainglorious, empty boast even at the time. Mountbatten, who was sent as governor to India by the more pragmatic Attlee, well knew that he was there to negotiate India's independence. The main difficulty was that the Hindu and Muslim parts of the raj had radically different views of the future. Separation was inevitable, but extremely costly in human terms. Kiernan estimates that there were anything from half a million to a million deaths in massacres and murders. Eight million Hindus fled from Pakistan to India, the same number of Muslims from India to Pakistan. Those who have seen newsreels of the time could not but be moved by the scale of human tragedy. As far as the eye could see – or at least the shaky camera could record – thin lines of refugees silently walked past each other in opposite directions. To the outsider, they looked identical in dress and appearance.

Fortunately, the decolonization process was somewhat more peaceful and less momentous in the case of present-day Singapore and Malaysia. Nonetheless, at the end of empire, as *Kwen Fee* records, Malaya contained three minority groups – Indians, brought as plantation workers to the rubber estates; Chinese, who were farmers, miners and traders; and Indonesians who spontaneously entered the farming districts and whose numbers were probably under-recorded. The principal antagonism was between the Malays and the Chinese – the former in the majority with a fierce adherence to the land, the latter dominating commerce and skilled occupations. Though the principal Chinese political leader, Lee Kuan Yew, genuinely tried to make a multicultural identity work, after the outbreak of Sino-Malay riots, Singapore separated from Malaysia in 1965. Again, this separation had largely benign consequences, with both Singapore and now increasingly Malaysia being able to create extraordinarily successful economies.

One of the problems of segmenting states at the moment of decolonization is that there is often a process of multiplying sub-units as regions and minorities begin also to demand separate territorial recognition. One can perhaps have greater sympathy with the demands for independence by those in East Pakistan, for, despite their bond of sympathy with their co-religionists in West Pakistan, a joint state cut off by the broadest stretch of India was hardly practical. Unlike in Singapore and Malaysia, however, the economic result was not beneficial. Bangladesh remains one of the poorest countries in the world, hopelessly dependent on crops with poor world prices and subject to frequent devastation by flooding and cyclones. The result, as *Islam* describes, is that the export of migrants and the return of their remittances 'have been acclaimed as the major factors in keeping the Bangladeshi economy afloat in recent years'.

Nation-building also tended towards ethnic homogeneity in the case of Vietnam. This followed a prolonged and bloody war of national liberation, first against the French, then against the USA. What is rarely appreciated in discussions of the boat people, who emerged as refugees from Vietnam, is that many of them were ethnic Chinese fleeing ethnic discrimination. *Chan Kwok Bun* notes, for example, that in the peak year (1979) of arrivals of Vietnamese in Hong Kong some 73 per cent were ethnic Chinese. This does not of course mean that we do not need to account for the remaining 27 per cent who were repelled by the political repression and economic incompetence of the country's post-independence rulers. A different reading of the same data would point to the devastation caused by years of American saturation bombing and the continuing US trade ban and diplomatic war. However the facts are interpreted, the Chinese minority and other Vietnamese felt they had to resort to desperate measures to escape post-liberation Vietnam. But, as *Chan Kwok Bun* shows, neither their desperation nor their co-ethnicity cut much ice with the hard-headed folk of Hong Kong, who felt they had enough on board already.

Economics rather than politics was the main impelling factor in the case of Nepal, discussed by *Seddon* in this volume. As in Bangladesh, a high population density combined with poverty has forced many Nepalese to seek work abroad. The vent for surplus for the hill people in the forest zones has now disappeared with increasing land scarcity, so men confront the unpalatable alternatives of service in the British army – which is cutting back its Gurkha regiments – or unskilled employment in India. Nepalese women who had previously been household-based are having to take up the slack to preserve the household's income, many of them entering the sex industry in other parts of Asia.

The remaining contributions in this Part fall into two categories – migration to Australia (covered by *Collins* and *Bottomley*) and illegal migration (considered by *Loiskandl* and *Hugo*). As *Collins* notes, the end of the Vietnam war was the catalyst that restarted Asian migration to Australia. 'Restarted', as it is instructive to remember that Asian migration to Australia has longer roots than many who advocated a 'white Australia' policy for so many years conceded. The major shift from European to Asian immigration only occurred in the 1980s and it did so for several reasons. First, the Asia-Pacific region as a whole is highly differentiated in terms of material prosperity, with some of the world's poorest and richest nations living side-by-side. Migrants are the bridge that connects the two zones, and Australia, like other rich countries in the region, found itself a target destination for migrants from the poorer countries. Second, Australia was complicit in the US war effort in Vietnam and had to bear some of the migration consequences when that conflict finally ended. Third, after Britain made its fateful commitment to the European Community, Australia had to face the geopolitical reality that it was an Asian, not a European power. The result has been a historical volte face in immigration policy, with great emphasis being placed on the economic benefit particular classes of migrants can bring rather than their ethnic, regional or racial background. Though *Collins* suggests that Asians face considerable discrimination in Australia, the formal immigration policy remains a remarkable transformation of the old 'whites only' entry requirement.

As *Bottomley*'s contribution reminds us, the stress on the shift from European to Asian immigrants to Australia can lead to an undifferentiated view of each category. Just as Asian immigrants are diverse in their origins, so too is it important not to overlook the non-British European population. In the 1991 Australian census, migrants from Greece, Italy, Malta, Spain and Portugal numbered over 500,000, a number which trebles if we include their descendants. Her analysis of this group is overwhelmingly positive, showing how they have contributed to Australia's cultural diversity and to a new 'hybridity' by not burying their heads in the sand so far that they isolated themselves in ethnic enclaves and ghettos.

Illegal workers have little alternative but to keep their heads down. As *Hugo* and *Loiskandl* agree, whatever the difficulties of measuring and documenting illegal migration in Asia, there is no doubt that it has massively increased over the last fifteen years. *Hugo* attributes this to a number of interrelated factors, some of which are: the increased flow of passenger traffic in general; increased awareness of other countries; the widening gap in economic fortune between Asian countries; rising levels of education; poor detection and border controls; and the rise of an 'immigration industry'. This is a wholly convincing list of factors among which I want to isolate only two for special emphasis. First, the reference to an 'immigration industry' is important, especially in Asia. I have already alluded to the crucial roles that emigration and remittance income play in Bangladesh. However, there are a number of other countries (for example the Philippines and Thailand) which officially sanction and actively promote the export of labour. It is not hard to see why. In addition to remittances the export of labour can reduce home unemployment and lower consequent social tension. Having seen governments promote emigration, it is hardly surprising that the private sector responded in like manner. Lawyers, travel agents, employment bureaux and 'fixers' of all kinds provide services to those who wish to emigrate permanently or sojourn abroad. Second, networks having been created, chain, family, kin and neighbourhood migration proceeds apace, sometimes after the economic logic of the original migration has disappeared This is a point also made by *Hugo*, but the central role of networks is reinforced in a powerful and comprehensive synthesis of much of the existing literature on the causes of migration (Massey 1994).

The issues raised by illegal immigration are graphically illustrated in the case of Japan. The strong Japanese sense of national identity and the proclamations of the need to maintain homogeneity are commonly observed by visitors. As *Loiskandl* avers, this is something of a myth when we recall the indigenous Ainu population and the long-established Korean and Chinese minorities. Nonetheless, the myth strongly informed immigration policy. As the economy overheated and a precipitate demand for unskilled labour grew, the government frantically encouraged ethnic Japanese in China and South America to return. The economy soon outstripped these relatively minor labour pools and Japan, kicking and screaming and often with a good dose of dissimulation by government officials, has had to accept implicitly the presence of both legal and illegal foreign workers.

References

Massey, Douglas (1994) 'An Evaluation of International Migration Theory: The North American Case', *Population and Development Review*, 20, 699–752

Zolberg, Aristide (1983) 'The Formation of New States as a Refugee-Generating Process', *Annals of the American Academy of Social and Political Sciences*, 467, May, 24–38

Zolberg Aristide, et al. (1989) *Escape from Violence: Conflict and the Refugee Crisis in the Developing World*, New York: Oxford University Press

THE SEPARATION OF INDIA AND PAKISTAN

VICTOR KIERNAN

The Second World War made inevitable not only Indian independence but also a partition of India between the mainly Hindu and the mainly Muslim areas. A new country was breaking away, made up of two wings, West Pakistan in the north-west, and a much weaker East Pakistan (now Bangladesh) in eastern Bengal. Partition was accompanied by one of the twentieth century's most terrible explosions. In the north murders and massacres, worst in the warlike and now divided Punjab, may have resulted in anything between half a million and a million deaths. Approximately 8 million refugees fled from Pakistan, and about the same number from India, in each case roughly 5.5 million from or to West Pakistan (Alavi 1966: 161; Menon 1957: 431). The main flood of late 1947 across the East Pakistan border was followed by minor but troublesome ones in subsequent years; in the north-west some 400,000 Hindus may have quitted the province of Sind – none were left elsewhere in West Pakistan.

For both new governments the task of coping with the massive immigrations of 1947 was of 'truly Himalayan proportions' (Menon 1957: 432). A complication that further embittered relations between them was the 'evacuee property' left behind by refugees. Agreements were made for its reciprocal use in providing compensation for losses, but they worked badly. For one thing, those leaving Pakistan belonged largely to the better-off classes, and left behind vastly more property than those from India; on balance the Muslims of undivided India had been much the poorer community. As the Indian premier Nehru said, a full settlement would have required Pakistan to pay to India a sum far beyond its means; though he perceived also that there were 'some forces at play in Pakistan' which had no desire for good relations, as well as 'some influential persons' who had got hold of valuable refugee properties and had no wish to relinquish them (Nehru 1985: 3.461).

Not until 1953 did Nehru's government feel able to embark on an interim scheme of compensation payments, followed by a final one in 1955. On both sides it was proving very difficult to identify and take charge of abandoned lands and buildings, while claims on them were equally hard to verify. Much recrimination arose over land assignments in India; influential claimants came off best (Rai 1965: 163). On the Pakistani side a promising start was made in the province most deeply affected, the western Punjab, where much fertile irrigated land in the 'Canal Colonies' had belonged to Hindus and Sikhs. Mian Iftikharudin, provincial minister for refugees and rehabilitation, and one of the very few progressive landlords, allotted the 'evacuee land', on a provisional basis, to all incomers who wanted it, in plots of one acre for each family member. This swelled the ranks of the small farmers; it did not satisfy the more ambitious applicants who were ready to assert that in India they had possessed whole estates. Proof of their former wealth was seldom produced, but a well-placed bribe could be just as convincing. In 1954 a landlord ministry reversed the allotment by giving successful claimants up to 500 acres of irrigated or 1000 of unirrigated land. To make room for them many smallholders were evicted, and reduced to sharecroppers or hired labourers (Tariq Ali 1970: 41; fuller information kindly supplied by Hamza Alavi). Later on Ayub Khan, as head of a military regime that could disclaim responsibility for what had happened, truthfully declared that it had 'opened the floodgates to dishonesty and immorality' (Ayub Khan 1967: 93–4).

Muslims in the eastern or Indian Punjab not engaged in farming had been very largely craftsmen of many kinds, potters for instance, and their disappearance left 'a tremendous gap', to remedy which vocational training centres were set up (Rai 1965: 133–4, 141). By and large, however, India was neither impoverished nor enriched, in any great degree, by human losses or gains. It was by far the bigger and more advanced country, and was amply furnished with business and professional people. To retarded Pakistan, where such functions had been very largely left to Hindus, replacements from over the border were now a vital need. It could be met because Muslims who had lived in provinces with Hindu majorities, like the UP (United Provinces, now Uttar Pradesh) and Bombay, were on average more urban, more up to date, than people in the solidly Muslim, mainly agrarian regions that now formed Pakistan.

In particular, the mercantile coastal fringe of western India, centring on Bombay, had nurtured commercial communities or sects of Muslims, like the Bohras and Khojas, and the Gujerati-speaking Memons of Bombay. A great many of their members were prepared to take the short road to Karachi. They might fear for their future prospects in India; still more, in Pakistan they could hope to rule the roost, free from the too-powerful competition of Hindu capital. They took the title of 'Muhajirs', Muslims emulating the *hijrah* (hegira) of those who in the infancy of Islam followed the Prophet in his exodus from Mecca to Medina; at the same time they were shrewd men of affairs, scenting opportunity. They flocked into every province of West Pakistan, principally into nearby Sind, and formed the nucleus of a bourgeoisie or capitalist class that the country would otherwise have lacked.

These newcomers were welcomed far more warmly by the ruling interests than by ordinary folk, in whose eyes they were a privileged class as alien as their predecessors, the wealthy Hindus and Sikhs. This was felt most keenly in Sind, an exceptionally backward and feudal region. In its chief city Karachi, for a while Pakistan's capital and always its boom-town, before long four-fifths of the inhabitants were strangers. In every sphere Sindhis were being degraded into inferiors in their own land (Malik 1977: 294–5). A running fight was breaking out, and making Karachi one of the world's most strife-torn cities. Language played a prominent part. Urdu, or Persianized Hindi, was being made the official language of Pakistan, though it was not the vernacular of any section of the country. It was the mother-tongue of immigrants from the Ganges valley, and of many from further west; it threatened to displace Sindhi, an insecure national language only of late evolved out of local dialects (Gankovsky 1971: 195).

Nationalist leaders have often come from frontier-lands or further away. Jinnah, the founder of Pakistan, was a rich lawyer from Bombay, Liyaqat Ali, his lieutenant and successor, a rich landowner from the UP; their staunchest adherents were their fellow immigrants. After Liyaqat Ali's assassination in October 1951 power was taken over by an oligarchy of bigger landlords, chiefly those of the Punjab; they had control of the army, which most of the time has been the country's real government. Unpopular and vulnerable, the Muhajirs had to rely on the patronage of the government and civil service, and to make sure

of it by liberal bribery and corruption, a prominent feature of Pakistan's history throughout. It has been argued that their disappointment at the loss of their political ascendancy, and their imperfect integration in the national life, have been among the causes of Pakistan's failure to achieve a constitutional pattern of politics (Wright 1974). It may be added that muddles and delays in the rehabilitation programme were among the army's pretexts for seizing power.

Meanwhile the landlords, though remaining feudal enough in some of their habits, were undergoing a commercializing process. They were stepping into the shoes of Hindu moneylenders and traders. They supplied credit to peasants in need – which would often lead to small farms being taken over – and marketed rural produce, or operated cotton-ginning and rice-husking mills, mostly in Sind and previously run by Hindus.

Twenty-seven 'satellite towns and colonies' were planned at the outset, many of them round Karachi, with two others in the east wing (Government 1957: 241). As S. J. Burki writes, 'The early decision-makers in Pakistan came from among the refugees', and hence were sensitive to refugee needs, though chiefly to those of urban settlers (Burki 1977: 149–50). Encouragement of small industries was left in the main to provincial administrations, but the central government set up a Directorate of Cottage and Small Scale Industries, along with a Refugee Rehabilitation Finance Corporation. Manufactures were essential if the country was to be viable, and their large-scale growth was stimulated by subsidies and tariffs. Textiles led the way. A mushroom growth of trade, industry and banking followed highly monopolistic lines; there was soon talk of the 'twenty families' at the pinnacle. In 1968 they were estimated to control two-thirds of all industrial capital (Nations 1975: 255), and a high proportion had come from India.

The working class was at first meagre. A third of it had been Hindu, but this was more than made up for, above all in Karachi, by the arrival of Muslim workers from India and impoverished areas of the north-western Punjab and the north-west frontier. Ethnic differences could easily be exploited by employers aided by a repressive government and arbitrary police. Attempts at self-protection were further hindered by the enforced disappearance of the communists, mostly Hindu or Sikh, who had taken the lead in setting up trade unions and peasant organizations.

East Pakistan had a different destiny. This half of Bengal had been largely owned by Hindu landlords, while Calcutta, in the western area, was the centre of commercial and professional life. In 1950 anti-Hindu rioting in Dacca, the East Pakistan capital, led to acute tension with India, and war was only narrowly averted. What was happening was a continued squeezing out of the Hindu landholding and money-lending classes, and the outcome here was more favourable than in West Pakistan to the Muslim peasantry, because there was much less of a strong Muslim landed class to snap up the gains. There emerged 'a rural social structure dominated by a mass of peasant smallholders', most of them owning less than five acres (Nations 1975: 256), but also dominated by poverty as these acres were divided and subdivided.

Refugees from East Pakistan differed markedly from those leaving West Pakistan in their ability to adapt themselves to new situations. Often in history the trauma of exile has given a sharper definition to 'national character', or collective temperament moulded by historical experience. In the Bengali case this had fostered a sort of inertia or passivity which hampered any energetic response. Escapers from the east might be seen for years hanging about the railway stations where they arrived, and could seldom be induced to move further than Calcutta. In its streets a shanty-town life sprang up: families 'lived with the stray cattle, like the stray cattle, drinking gutter-water, eating garbage, sleeping on the curb' (Zinkin 1962: 25).

What industry East Pakistan had was nearly all owned by outsiders, and its profits were siphoned off to Karachi. Workers too were flocking in, most of them Muslims from Bihar who were preferred by employers as more reliable, in other words less inclined to complain (Feldman 1975: 42). Hence the riots against them, with hundreds of deaths, in the Dacca jute mills in 1953. It was another grievance against them that instead of wanting to be assimilated the Biharis kept to themselves, and went on speaking Urdu: a sore point, as in Sind, because the central government was seeking, very absurdly, to impose Urdu on Bengal as well. A final crisis broke out in 1971, with fresh multitudes of Hindus forced out of the country, and Indian intervention leading to defeat for Pakistan and independence for Bangladesh, where the Biharis were a hated minority.

In the ten years from partition a total of nearly 8.9 million 'displaced persons' entered India, 4.7 million of them from West Pakistan (Government of India 1958: 152). Their settlement put a severe strain on Indian resources. On the other hand the challenge was a stimulus to the fledgling government, and the efforts of many of the refugees themselves to find a footing made a contribution to the country's productive energy. No doubt they, as well as the Muslims who left India, carried with them to their new homes a rancour against their old ones that inflamed the chronic and costly hostility between the two countries.

The 1951 census showed 8,229,699 individuals as having been born in what was now Pakistan. There were 3.4 million in west Bengal and Assam, originating from East Pakistan. From West Pakistan, apart from substantial numbers in Rajasthan and Bombay, the great majority were to be found in a broad band of northern territory, the Punjab, with 2.4 million, and Delhi and UP each with nearly half a million. In all cases there was a predictable surplus of males over females, totalling some 800,000; women had suffered disproportionately in 1947. Rehabilitation was undertaken at first by a 'Central Emergency Committee'; soon a ministry was created, mainly to deal with urban problems, and each state concerned set one up, mainly for rural relief. Prime Minister Nehru's circular letters to the chief ministers of the states show how much urgency the question had for him. 'Relief and rehabilitation. These words', he wrote in September 1950, 'have become our daily and hourly companions during the last three years' (Nehru 1985: 2.180). It was part of general policy to build up small as well as large-scale industry, and this could have a big place in schemes for providing employment for displaced persons. A National Small Industries Corporation was one of the bodies set up. Nehru's letter of 15 August 1949 stressed the asset that cottage industry could be; an officer had been sent to Japan, and had come back 'with a multitude of ideas' (Nehru 1985: 1.439–40).

In December 1950 a conference of Ministers of Rehabilitation was held, and Nehru paid tribute to their work, but added that there was still much to be done, and – characteristically – that they must always 'remember the human aspect of this problem' (Nehru 1985: 2.290). Seven years later there were still women, children, old people, in need of care or training. In the north and west nineteen new townships had been founded. Delhi was sprouting a whole crop of suburbs or colonies on its northern fringes, where small-scale manufacturers were flourishing. All this can be regarded as part of the prologue to the impressive industrial advance that India has made. On the eastern side especially there was still great need of housing, and of improvements to no fewer than 137 'squatters' colonies' (Government of India 1958: 154).

In 1947, 4.4 million persons quitted the eastern Punjab, while 3.8 million entered it, most of them from the western areas of the old province (Rai 1965: 117–18). Some of these entrants moved on, seeking opportunity further afield. Not many of them, especially among the Sikhs, the most sturdily independent, sank to the level of landless labourers. Irrigation was being expanded, and the Punjab held its place as one of India's granaries. 'Displaced persons' showed praiseworthy energy, as Rai says, but the ordeal that called this out also accentuated an always self-assertive Punjabi spirit, and made them 'more aggressive, ruthless and careless about moral values of life'. Those among whom they settled often turned hostile, resenting their 'cut-throat competition' (Rai 1965: 144, 110). Sikhs were welcomed by fellow Sikhs, and reinforced the inward-turning mood of a community that had borne much of the brunt of the 1947 horrors. Uneasy relations between them and their Hindu neighbours led to separation in 1966, with a new, mostly Hindu state of Haryana, southward towards Delhi, and the Punjab left with a 60 per cent majority of Sikhs.

But not many years later not much less than a quarter of all Sikhs were living elsewhere, mostly in Delhi or in urban areas of adjacent provinces. Army service in the British empire had fanned a roving Punjabi instinct. But the Sikh dispersal has been only part of a wider phenomenon; and mobility within both India and Pakistan, hastened by the upheaval of 1947, has been spilling over into emigration world-wide.

References

Alavi, Hamza (1966) 'The Army and the Bureaucracy in Pakistan', *International Socialist Service*, March–April

Ayub Khan, M. (1967) *Friends not Masters: A Political Autobiography*, London: Oxford University Press

Burki, S. J. (1977) 'Economic Decision-making in Pakistan', in L. Ziring et al. (eds) *Pakistan: The Long View*, Durham, NC: Duke University Press

Feldman, H. (1975) *The End and the Beginning: Pakistan 1969–1971*, London: Oxford University Press

Gankovsky, Y. V. (1971) *The Peoples of Pakistan*, Moscow: Nauka Publishing House

Government of India (1958) *India: A Reference Annual 1958*, Delhi: Ministry of Information

Government of Pakistan (1957) *Ten Years of Pakistan*, Karachi: Pakistan Publications

Malik, Hafeez (1977) 'Nationalism and the Quest for Ideology in Pakistan', in L. Ziring et al. (eds) *Pakistan: The Long View*, Durham, NC: Duke University Press

Menon, V. P. (1957) *The Transfer of Power in India*, London: Longman

Nations, R. (1975) 'The Economic Structure of Pakistan and Bangladesh', in R. Blackburn (ed.) *Explosion in a Subcontinent*, Harmondsworth: Penguin

Nehru, Jawaharlal (1985) *Letters to Chief Ministers 1947–1964*, edited by G. Parthasarathi, Delhi: Government of India

Rai, S. N. (1965) *Partition of the Punjab*, London: Asia Publishing House

Tariq Ali (1970) *Pakistan: Military Rule or People's Power*, London: Jonathan Cape

Wright, T. P. (1974) 'Indian Muslim Refugees in the Politics of Pakistan', *Journal of Commonwealth and Comparative Politics*, July

Zinkin, Taya (1962) *Reporting India*, London: Chatto and Windus

BANGLADESHI MIGRATION: AN IMPACT STUDY

MUINUL ISLAM

The migration of labour overseas has become the most burning manpower issue in Bangladesh. The gradual acceleration of the migration flow in the late 1970s brought it to the forefront of the country's economic considerations in the 1980s. The export of manpower and the resultant inflow of remittances have largely been acclaimed as the crucial factors in keeping the Bangladeshi economy afloat in recent years.

Apart from the two major traditional destinations of Bangladeshi migrants, the Middle East and the UK, the following receiving countries have also recently become popular: the USA, Canada, Japan, Germany, South Korea, Singapore, Malaysia, France, Sweden, Taiwan, Brunei, Italy, Pakistan and India. Hugh Tinker correctly realized a long time ago that it was futile to try to estimate how many Bangladeshi migrants there were – 'this "numbers game", as it is called, is never very productive' (Tinker 1977: 10). In that an increasing proportion of these migrants have been adopting informal, illegal or even clandestine channels of emigration, such estimates become mere conjectures, or wild guesses. However, from official estimates for the period 1977–90, the countries in the Middle East can be ranked according to their popularity as destinations as follows: Saudi Arabia (37.6 per cent), United Arab Emirates (13.78 per cent), Oman (12.08 per cent), Kuwait (10.92 per cent), Iraq (8.11 per cent), Qatar (7.97 per cent), Libya (3.95 per cent), Bahrain (3.92 per cent) and others (1.67 per cent) (Mahmood 1991: 10).[1]

Despite heroic efforts to estimate the annual flow of remittances into Bangladesh (Mahmood 1991: 27–53), we remain in the dark on this issue, for the widespread use of informal channels has turned this too into another guessing game. The officially quoted figure of approximately $800 million for the years 1991/2 and 1992/3 is believed to be a gross underestimation, but there is no way of ascertaining the probable range of the underestimation.[2]

A Bangladeshi government agency (the Bureau of Manpower, Employment and Training) quotes the following figures on the skill composition of Bangladeshi migrants for the year 1990: professionals and semi-professionals – 5.78 per cent; skilled workers – 34.38 per cent; semi-skilled workers – 20.04 per cent; and unskilled workers – 39.8 per cent.[3] Notwithstanding countrywide variations in skill categories, the above distribution seems to be convincing because the two major destinations give credence to the picture. The proportion of unskilled workers has, however, been gradually shrinking in recent years. This is accounted for by the changing demands of the receiving countries.

Most of these overseas migrants come from two regions of Bangladesh – Sylhet and Chittagong. Though other regions are fast catching up, migrants from Chittagong still dominate the migration flow to the Middle East and over 90 per cent of Bangladeshi immigrants in Britain have come from Sylhet. Other destinations show no such systematic regional bias. Patterns of comparatively recent migration flows differ from those of the two earlier ones. Recruiting agents and individual migrants now play a more crucial role, whereas earlier flows depended far more on pioneer migrants and on prospective employers in the receiving countries.

The first migrants to settle in the UK were some seamen from Sylhet who, lured by the employment opportunities in labour-short Britain, abandoned their ships in British ports immediately after the Second World War. These pioneer settlers are believed to have formed the core of Bangladeshi migrants in Britain (Adams 1987). Alam (1988) believes that the real impetus came when the British immigration authorities introduced employment vouchers in the late 1950s and early 1960s and that, despite the gradual tightening of British immigration laws starting in 1962, the flow was able to gain momentum through the strong chain of family and kinship structures. With early immigrants having obtained British citizenship, family immigration still keeps the flow going despite Britain's recent discriminatory attitude towards Bangladeshi immigrants. Besides family reunion, numerous legal manipulations and illegal practices now flourish to circumvent the legal restrictions. False declarations about family members, forged passports or visas, and remaining illegally after temporary visits have become fairly familiar tricks.

PLATE 16: Rohingya refugees arrive in Bangladesh from Burma, April 1992. The tiny sailing boats that brought them are just visible in the background. Bangladesh is one of the poorest and most densely populated countries in the world, with high levels of emigration. This did not inhibit immigration from the war-torn areas of Burma.

Travel agencies and manpower recruiting agents proliferate throughout Bangladesh to make arrangements for the smuggling of migrants. Bureaucratic rent-seeking at both ends of the chain, the complicity of some airline crews and loopholes in policing mechanisms help keep the flow of illegal migration going.

The story of Bangladeshi migration to the Middle East is quite different:

Beginning in the early 1960s, small numbers of people, mostly from the district of Chittagong, started to migrate to oil-rich Middle East countries and sheikhdoms like Bahrain, Kuwait, Qatar and Saudi Arabia. (A number of these migrants were earlier pushed back from Burma.) Until the late 1960s, the number of such migrants from Bangladesh was not very significant. The 1973 oil-boom opened the floodgate to foreign workers in the oil-rich countries, but Bangladesh followed a somewhat restrictive manpower export policy till the end of 1975. In 1976, Bangladesh joined the race to secure a share of the cake of the Middle-East labour market. By that time the market was almost captured by the western countries, on the one hand (for highly paid jobs), and by India, Pakistan, the Philippines, Korea, Taiwan, Sri Lanka and other non-oil Arab countries, on the other. Nevertheless, the flow from Bangladesh increased each year from 1976 to 1982. Then it tapered off, though remaining at a substantial level even today.

(Islam et al. 1987: 11–12)

Despite a large return flow from Kuwait and Iraq as a result of the 1990/1 Gulf War, two parallel flows — one legal and the other illegal — continue to most of the Middle East countries through the efforts of migrant workers, recruiting agents, travel agencies and manpower smuggling rackets.

There are some qualitative differences between these two major flows. Migrants to the UK are increasingly likely to be seen as semi-permanent or permanently settled immigrants, whereas migrants to the Middle East are regarded as transient workers and are thus unlikely to take their families with them.

Table 11.1: *Importance of overseas remittances for the Bangladesh economy*

Remittances as percentages of:	1980/1	1987/8
Gross domestic product	3.16	4.76
Gross domestic savings	136.11	83.81
Export earning	53.96	55.75
Import payments	16.62	25.06
Balance of trade deficit	23.02	45.51
Government tax revenue	34.78	53.28
Government non-tax revenue	110.43	273.52
Total government current revenue	26.45	22.53
Annual development programme	26.16	50.85

Source: Mahmood (1991: 112).

Their legal status in each of the two destinations also differs and this has important ramifications for behaviour.

I focus on the impacts of overseas migration on the economy and society of Bangladesh at both the macro and micro level.

Impact on the economy

The Central Bank of Bangladesh officially estimated overseas remittances to Bangladesh during the period 1977 to 1990 at $6.4 billion, which is believed to be a gross underestimation. The government's estimates for the year 1993/4 claim that annual remittances during the previous financial year exceeded $800 million. The ever increasing use of informal channels for sending remittances in cash and kind has made it impossible even to guess the range of the underestimation. But official figures suggest that, from the late 1970s onwards, the flow of remittances has been growing fast (with the exception of the years 1984 and 1985), which has made the present flow more than 35 times larger than the flow in 1977 – it has moved from Tk. 866 million in 1977 to about Tk. 31 billion in 1992. The following are the major trends of remittances:

- Annual remittances from the UK have stagnated in recent years, whereas from the Middle East they have been increasing fast. Other destinations are also gaining in relative importance.

- The *hundi* system,[4] the main informal channel of sending remittances, has been gaining ground over formal channels and is believed to be providing a crucial source of finance for the fast growing illegal international trade in Bangladesh.

- The accompanied and unaccompanied baggage of homecoming migrants continues to be a major informal channel through which overseas savings are brought into the country. Here, a rent-seeking system has been institutionalized to circumvent official rules and regulations and to evade tariffs and taxes. The composition of goods brought in changes from time to time, but this remains an attractive system for obtaining a premium exchange rate for foreign currencies.

- The import trade has introduced a wage earners' scheme (WES) in an attempt to attract foreign currency that would otherwise have been diverted into illegal channels. This scheme is also regarded as a blanket arrangement for attracting black-market money originating in Bangladesh for international trade. More than a third of Bangladesh's import payments are financed through this scheme. It is significant that the value of actual imports under the WES surpasses the total amount of officially reported remittances every year.

To illustrate the importance of overseas remittances for the Bangladeshi economy, Mahmood (1991) has compiled a table showing remittances as percentages of macro parameters such as gross domestic product, gross domestic savings, export earnings, import payments, government tax revenues and the government's annual development programme. Some of these figures are reproduced in Table 11.1 for the selected years of 1980/1 and 1987/8.

They demonstrate the crucial part remittances play in the macro-economic viability of the country in that these earnings ease both the savings–investment and balance-of-payments gaps afflicting the economy.

Manpower export has already become the country's single largest foreign-exchange earner. Remittances have been providing investment funds for housing and construction, agriculture, small-scale manufacturing and transport, as well as for the economic and social infrastructure. Manpower export provides some relief from acute unemployment, both rural and urban. It encourages the development of vocational and technical skills among both returned and intending migrants; it has also led to the rapid development of travel agencies, hotels, catering, transport and communication services, improved educational facilities in the rural areas, jewellery shops, modern shopping centres and department stores.

As regards negative impacts at the macro level, one can mention the inflation generated by money pouring in. Especially in the absence of large-scale productive investment of overseas earnings, a substantial proportion of the funds is spent on purchasing land, jewellery, consumer durables and food, and on social and religious ceremonies. These consumption-oriented uses of the remittance money do not add significantly to the productive capacity of the economy. Another negative impact is related to the economic and social rehabilitation of returned migrants within the context of increasing unemployment in the country and their changed expectations and attitudes about what constitutes a suitable job and an appropriate wage or income.

Socio-economic impact on sending communities

The overseas migration flow has affected some parts of Bangladesh disproportionately because of the mass migration of mainly rural labour from them. These areas are mostly located in the two pioneering regions – Sylhet and Chittagong. Survey research in these migration-special rural communities has brought out some interesting findings, which are broadly categorized under the following subheadings:

- impact on agrarian production relations;
- effects on migrant expenditure behaviour;
- effects on the employment pattern;
- impact on infrastructure development;
- effects on demand and supply patterns; and
- social effects.

Impact on agrarian production relations
Islam (1988: 24–6) notes the following major changes in the predominantly rural and agrarian sending communities of Sylhet and Chittagong:

- Land purchase has attracted the major share of migrants' home investment. The resultant buying spree has caused an accelerated concentration of landownership in the migrant households at the expense of non-migrant households of the same communities. This has accelerated the landlessness process among non-migrant households. Both homestead land and cultivable land attract migrant attention. Both groups of migrants show more than 50 per cent gain in landownership during their migration periods. This has resulted in a hyper-inflation of land prices for both cultivable and homestead land. Cultivable land prices are three to four times higher in the study areas than in the respective control areas. Homestead land prices in the study areas are almost double those of the control areas.

- Migrant households have made gains in land-ownership, but very few of their members report agriculture as their primary occupation. This may imply that real peasants are gradually being pushed out of land ownership and that a new non-cultivator, 'pseudo-rentier' landowning class is emerging.

- Land tenancy on migrant-owned farms is characterized by an unusually large proportion of sharecropping and leasehold arrangements. A relative dearth of family labour, coupled with a growing sense of rural elitism (cultivation has become distasteful to the members of nouveau riche migrant households), serve as compelling reasons for this high incidence of sharecropping and leaseholding.

- The cultivable holdings of migrant households comprise a number of plots, large and small, attained through purchase. These plots are fragmented and geographically widely scattered. This implies that the larger migrant landholdings are formed mainly by adding plots to land owned, rather than by consolidating the size of adjoining plots.

- The effect on cropping intensity is mixed, but crop diversification has suffered. The adoption rate of high-yielding varieties (HYV) of rice has had a boost from migration in Chittagong, but has not changed much in Sylhet. Vegetables and rabi crop cultivation have been adversely affected.

- Chittagong study areas have shown a marked improvement in the use of modern inputs, with the adoption rate of HYV Boro cultivation among migrant household farms (more than three-quarters of all acreage) being much higher than the national average. The Sylhet study areas are, however, disappointing on this count. Absentee landownership may be the key reason for this failure.

- Out-migration of adult male labour has turned the study areas into labour-scarce communities, with agricultural labour being hit the hardest. The huge boost in construction, trade, commerce, services, transport and migration-related activities has been acting as a strong pull factor to draw labour out of agriculture into non-agricultural and tertiary activities. Migrant labour from other districts has poured in to fill the vacuum.

- Remittances have generally eased the agricultural credit situation in the sending communities and there are cases of migrant households replacing traditional moneylenders. Input sharing arrangements have improved.

- Migration has also helped agricultural marketing. Post-harvest operations have improved; better storage facilities have been built; roads have improved; modern transport systems have been introduced; market places have been built or improved; links with urban centres have been made easier and less costly; and banking facilities have become more generally available.

- Agricultural wages in the study areas are 50 per cent higher than they are in the control area. The cost of crop production has gone up because of this wage-boost, whereas agricultural prices have remained comparable to national ones. Thus, in that crop production has become cost-inefficient, this has particularly harmed farms operated by non-migrant peasant households. They are increasingly joining the swelling rank of landless people.

Effects on expenditure

A World Bank study (Ali et al. 1981) estimated that rural migrant households on average spent 45 per cent of remittances on consumption and that urban households spent 41 per cent. Mahmood (1991: 59–60), however, describes the following use pattern:

- house building and development (19 per cent);
- purchase of land (15–25 per cent);
- machinery and equipment, vehicles and consumer durables (4.69 per cent);
- fixed deposit (9.11 per cent);
- business (4.04 per cent);
- education of children (1.88 per cent);
- repayment of loans (4.39 per cent);
- donations to relatives (2.07 per cent);
- weddings (8.86 per cent); and
- medical treatment (3.34 per cent).

This accounts for about 73 per cent of the remittances, leaving about 27 per cent for other consumption purposes. Islam et al. (1987) add the following features of expenditure behaviour of migrant households:

- 'The consumption-pattern of migrant households has become markedly import-biased' (1987: 87).

- 'Remittance receiving households spend relatively more on social ceremonies and religious rituals' (1987: 90).

- 'Migrant households spend a significant amount on expensive health care services' (1987: 91).

- 'Migrant households have grown the habit of using hired domestic help, house tutors, religious teachers, etc.' (1987: 93).

- 'As trade and commerce, new construction, purchase of land and gold, consumer durables, etc. have been the principal attractions of the migrant households, traditional cottage industries have been adversely affected by the change in consumption habit' (1987: 189).

Effects on the employment pattern

There is a noticeable change in the patterns of employment in migration-special communities. Though migrant households have increased their land ownership, a large proportion of their adult members have abandoned agriculture as a profession, and have moved into trade and services. Migrant labourers from outside the localities have poured in to take up jobs as agricultural workers. Non-agricultural employment opportunities have increased in construction, transport, trade and commerce and other service activities.

Unemployment among returned migrants has become fairly widespread. It has afflicted unskilled migrants the most. Returned migrants seem to prefer self-employment because of the changed perception about what constitutes 'suitable jobs' for them.

Small-scale manufacturing – bakeries, furniture makers, sawmills, brick manufacturers, rice mills, flour mills, jewellery shops – has received noticeable boosts in the sending communities. Rickshaws, auto-rickshaws, buses, minibuses, mechanized boats and trucks have also attracted remittance money.

Impact on infrastructure development

There have been noticeable developments and improvements in the economic and social infra-structures of the migration-special communities. Such changes are evident in:

- improved roads and market places;
- modern shopping facilities;
- electrification and telecommunication facilities;
- banking;
- kindergartens and institutions of religious education;
- youth clubs and recreation facilities;
- secondary schools and colleges;
- tubewells and better sanitation facilities;
- pharmacies, health centres and private clinics;
- marriage halls;
- mosques and religious shrines.

Effects on demand and supply pattern

The inflow of remittances has generated a localized hyper-inflation of prices and wages in the sending communities. Prices of consumer items like fish, meat, clothes, bread, vegetables and sweetmeat, and the cost of the services of, for example, doctors, tailors, laundries, barbers, photographers, travel agents and decorators are comparatively higher in these communities because of increased demand. Fares are higher for transport vehicles like rickshaws or auto-rickshaws. There has been a tremendous boost in the price of land for both agriculture and housing in these areas. Wages are higher for masons, carpenters, agricultural workers, construction workers, electricians and daily labourers.

The inflow of remittances has diversified the demand and supply pattern for goods and services to reflect the changed lifestyles of migrant households. A section of the migrants also resorts to conspicuous consumption of luxury goods and imported electronic gadgets.

Social effects

The following social effects seem to be significant:

- Migration has increased the practice of late marriage among males, but has led to a reduction of age at first marriage for females. It has also increased the incidence of polygamy among the male migrants.
- There is a sharp reduction in the infant mortality rate in migration-special areas.
- Migrants tend to have larger families than non-migrants.
- The secondary school 'drop-out' rate among males has increased dramatically, but female education seems to have got a boost.
- Marriages have become very expensive because of lavish ceremonies and the widespread practice of providing a dowry.
- Pseudo-religious ceremonies have increased significantly. Community feasts have become a common phenomenon in these areas.
- Litigations have increased dramatically.
- Migrants have emerged as attractive suitors for marriages.
- Liquor, gambling, robbery, hijacking, drug addiction and gangsterism have increased noticeably.
- There is a noticeable shift in the village power structure in favour of migrants or members of migrant households because of their vastly improved economic and social status and financial strength.
- Migrant households tend to move to the urban centres once a threshold of economic prosperity is reached.

Conclusion

I have tried here to identify some of the major impacts of overseas migration at both the macro and micro levels. These are described in the form of tendencies or trends, which may have both positive and negative consequences for the economy and society. Though it is popularly believed that overseas migration is a major blessing for densely populated poor countries like Bangladesh because of the ever-increasing flow of remittances it brings, some of its outcomes may not augur well for the country in the long run. One should also think about the human side of the story.

The sweat and toil of Bangladeshi migrants working in the Middle East have earned them the derogatory appellation of *miskins* (beggars) in the lands of their dreams, but their hard-earned money has not yet found productive avenues for investment in their homeland. This sadly implies that in most cases the affluence temporarily achieved during the tenure of migration may not be sustained for long in the event of a permanent return. In the UK, most of their brethren live in underclass ghettos in the inner cities and have become hapless victims of racism and discrimination. In other words, circumstances at both ends of their journey are making their prospects of a permanent return to Bangladesh increasingly remote.

These groups are harassed and ruthlessly exploited by unscrupulous and corrupt customs, police and immigration officials in their own country, as well as by the notorious *Adam Beparis* (manpower exporting agents). They often fall victim to robbers, cheats and local ruffians. They are frequently blamed by their neighbours for their eccentricities, reckless and ostentatious consumerism, obsession for land, outlandish spending sprees and idiosyncratic excesses, but the society seems to be quite oblivious of the painful struggles and horrendous travel experiences of these oft-ridiculed *Dubaiwalas* or *Londoni Sahibs*.

Compared with its competitors, Bangladesh continues to send abroad relatively unskilled, untrained and almost illiterate migrant workers, but still wastes government revenues and public savings on unproductive items like defence, internal security and civil administration. Essential nation-building activities such as providing education, training, health care, poverty alleviation and rural development continue to be neglected in the prioritization of public investment needs. The authorities are well aware that an increasing proportion of remittances are being diverted into smuggling or facilitating the flight of capital, but public policies do not reflect any noticeable concern for that. Rather, government policies seem to be deliberately designed to encourage such diversions.

I conclude with a clarion call to put man before money. Remittances are flowing in, but the men who are toiling for the money should hold the centrepiece of any policy regarding migration. In the end, that should augment the flow of both man and money.

Notes

1. The rankings of Kuwait and Iraq have been affected by the Gulf War, which are not reflected in the rankings given here. The total number of Bangladeshi migrants to the Middle East countries during the period 1977–90 has been quoted as 811,318 persons, which, I suspect, could be grossly underestimated.

2. More disturbing is the fact that various data sources quote widely divergent figures. *The Statistical Yearbook of Bangladesh* (published by the Bangladesh Bureau of Statistics), *Monthly Statistical Bulletin* (published by the Bangladesh Bureau of Statistics), *Economic Survey of Bangladesh* (published by the Ministry of Finance), *The World Bank Report* and others give different estimates of remittances for the same accounting periods.

3. *Professionals and semi-professionals*: Doctors, engineers, accountants, computer experts, administrators, teachers, nurses, foremen.
   Skilled workers: Masons, drivers, plumbers, mechanics, welders, cooks, electricians.
   Semi-skilled workers: Rod binders, mason helpers, mechanic helpers, cook helpers.

4. In the *hundi* system, organized gangs or individuals collect remittances in foreign currencies from overseas migrants and pay a premium rate to recipients at home. A parallel foreign-exchange market helps this process. This informal system often works more efficiently and provides security and secrecy to the remitters. A demand for *hundi* funds may arise through a need for foreign travel, medical treatment, foreign education, capital flight, accumulation of assets in overseas lands, smuggling or repatriation of savings of foreign nationals working in Bangladesh.

References

Adams, C. (1987) *Across Seven Seas and Thirteen Rivers*, London: THAP Books

Alam, F. (1988) *Salience of Homeland: Societal Polarization within the Bangladeshi Population in Britain*, Coventry: Centre for Research in Ethnic Relations, University of Warwick

Ali, S. A. et al. (1981) *Labour Migration from Bangladesh to the Middle East*, Washington: World Bank Staff Working Paper No. 454

Islam, M. (1988) 'Overseas Migration from Rural Bangladesh: Effects on some Agrarian Relations in the Sending Communities', *Migration*, 88 (3), 5–28

Islam, M. et al. (1987) *Overseas Migration from Rural Bangladesh: A Micro Study*, Chittagong: Rural Economics Programme, University of Chittagong

Mahmood, R. A. (1991) *Employment of Bangladeshis Abroad and Use of Their Remittances*, Dhaka: Planning Commission, Government of Bangladesh (mimeo)

Tinker, H. (1977) *The Banyan Tree: Overseas Migrants from India, Pakistan and Bangladesh*, Oxford: Oxford University Press.

MIGRATION: NEPAL AND INDIA

DAVID SEDDON

Throughout the eighteenth century, Nepal was relatively sparsely populated. Major efforts were made by its rulers to promote the settlement and reclamation of wasteland through land grants and sponsored immigration from Tibet, Sikkim and India, and to introduce systems of compulsory labour for the development of infrastructure through 'public works'. These efforts, together with the changes in farming systems that resulted from the introduction of new crops and new agricultural technologies, were generally successful, and there are indications of population growth and increased competition for land in many parts of Nepal in the early part of the nineteenth century. Substantial emigration from Nepal to India took place – partly as a result of increasing taxation and rising rents, partly as a result of the subsequent indebtedness to local moneylenders, and partly as a result of new employment opportunities in the armies of the British East India Company and the native government of the Punjab – during the first half of the nineteenth century.

This emigration appears to have involved small producers from the hill regions in particular. There, population pressure was growing rapidly, despite the undoubted intensification of agriculture. As Regmi (1971: 197–8) observes, 'people who left Nepal to settle in India did so primarily because they were unable to maintain themselves at the customary level of subsistence.' In the forested and sparsely populated plains (the *terai*), by contrast, the reclamation of wasteland continued, and immigration from India was encouraged, both to increase agricultural production and to raise taxes and land revenues. During the nineteenth century, Indian *zamindar*s were enabled to take land in the Nepalese *terai* and induce tenants to work it. Gaige (1975: 26) reports that 'the mid-western *terai* was settled largely in this manner between the 1890s and the 1930s.' The major effect of immigration into the Nepalese *terai*, and of state policies to encourage land reclamation, was an increase in agricultural output (particularly of rice) and in the export of agricultural commodities. If significant changes in agricultural technology and practices were undoubtedly taking place throughout Nepal during the second half of the nineteenth century, it was in the *terai* that a virtual 'agricultural revolution' took place. In the sixty years between 1831 and 1891, it has been estimated that trade between Nepal and India increased tenfold, with Nepal moving progressively from a trade deficit to a surplus, largely based on the export of rice and other agricultural products from the *terai*. At the end of the nineteenth century, rice from the *terai* accounted for nearly 40 per cent of Nepal's exports to India.

Already by the latter part of the nineteenth century, the differentiation (which was to become so striking during the twentieth century) between the hill regions – where the growth in agricultural production failed to keep pace with population growth and where emigration soon became a common alternative to declining yields and deteriorating living standards – and the plains (or *terai*) – where increasing population density was associated with increasing agricultural productivity and output – was becoming established (Seddon 1987: 1–38).

But if the plains exported agricultural produce, the hill regions came increasingly to export manpower. From the beginning of the nineteenth century a significant number of hill men were recruited into the army of the British East India Company; even before the war between Nepal and the Company in 1815 the latter was able to recruit four irregular corps of Nepalese troops – a total of some 5000 men – to take part in the invasion of their own country. Population pressure in the hills was to lead to an ever increasing extent over the next century or more to mercenary employment abroad. In 1857/8, Nepalese troops were sent by the ruling prime minister, Jang Bahadur Rana, to help the British put down the Sepoy rising (or Indian Mutiny), and from that time onwards, the recruitment of hill men from Nepal into the British 'Gurkhas' became an established tradition. Over 50,000 recruits offered themselves as soldiers for Gurkha regiments in the First World War, and when 11,000 were discharged at the end of the war only one-third returned to Nepal. The 'Gurkha' regiments of the British army continued to recruit throughout the 1920s and 1930s, and many hill men from Nepal fought and died for the Allies during the Second World War. After partition and Indian independence, recruitment to the Indian army began to grow and large numbers of hill men joined specially created 'Gurkha' regiments. At the same time, the British army still took 'Gurkhas' and posted them to the various outposts of empire on active service: in the Far East, the Middle East and even in Europe. 'Gurkhas' even participated in the brief war in the Falklands. During the 1980s, 'defence cuts' led to a drastic reduction in the manpower of 'Gurkha' regiments and a drop in recruitment, but by then only a very small proportion of those working abroad were employed by the British army in any case.

By no means all of those leaving Nepal for employment abroad went into the army, however. A significant number left to find land and/or employment in the highland areas of northern India, in Assam, for example, where they came to constitute a substantial minority community, or in Bhutan or Sikkim. Others left to seek employment in Indian cities. Already by 1901, the Indian census indicated that there were 200,000 Nepali speakers settled in India, most of them in Darjeeling and Jalpaiguri districts of west Bengal, in Sikkim and in Assam. By the early 1930s about one Nepalese-born person in twenty was living in India. Most of these had come from the hills. In 1961, over one million people speaking Nepali and hill languages were enumerated in India.

But if international migration between Nepal and India was clearly of major significance throughout the latter part of the nineteenth century and first half of the twentieth, many of those leaving the Nepalese hills in search of land or work moved south into the Nepalese *terai*. The forests of the *terai*, however, were malaria infested and often protected for logging by the Nepalese nobility; although immigration from India had been taking place for over a century, it was really only with the elimination of malaria in the 1950s and increasing control of private exploitation of the forests that migration from the Nepalese hills into the *terai* began to acquire dramatic dimensions. With population pressure in the hills still growing, the *terai* afforded an obvious 'safety valve', and the 1960s saw a massive wave of emigration from the hills into the *terai*. During the 1960s, while the population of the hills and mountains increased at around 1–2 per cent a year, that of the *terai* increased by between 3 and 5 per cent annually. This was the result, however, not only of immigration from the Nepalese hills but also of a continuing influx from the more densely populated Indian districts to the south. At this time,

the density of population in the eastern Indian border districts was two to three times greater than in the Nepalese eastern *terai*, while in the west, the Indian districts were three to four times more densely populated. (Map 7 of population density in the border districts of the Nepalese and Indian plains at the beginning of the 1960s reveals the enormous discrepancy between the two sides of the border.)

This process of immigration into the Nepalese *terai* from both the north and the south continued into the 1970s. As Gaige (1975: 23) remarks, 'it must be remembered that the *terai* culture is simultaneously being merged into that of the north Indian plains as a result of migration from Uttar Pradesh and Bihar.' As the pressure on land in the *terai* increased, and the numbers of immigrants from the Nepalese hills and adjacent Indian states grew, so too did the social tensions and conflicts, significantly sharpening divisions and enmities of caste, ethnicity and – particularly – nationality. In Nepal, the Citizenship Act of 1952 declared as a citizen anyone born in Nepal, anyone permanently settled in Nepal with at least one parent born in Nepal, or any woman married to a citizen. It also stated that anyone who had resided in Nepal for at least five years could acquire citizenship. But the 1962 constitution was more restrictive and introduced much stricter requirements for naturalization. The 1952 edition of the Legal Code allowed foreigners to settle on land, pay taxes on it and become landowners; the 1964 Lands Act made citizenship a prerequisite for landownership. These changes were, undoubtedly, the government's response to the perceived threat of massive immigration into Nepal from India. The result was increasing tension in the Nepalese *terai*, particularly between 'indigenous Nepalese' and 'Indian immigrants'; public disturbances in several *terai* districts between 1966 and 1969 were at least partly the result of tensions created by the government's citizenship and land tenure policies. During the 1960s, the issues of citizenship and nationality were politically 'hot', both at the local and at the national level. Curiously, according to official statistics, the foreign-born population resident in Nepal did not increase between 1961 and 1971.

The number of Nepalese officially resident abroad, by contrast, increased during the 1960s from 328,000 to 361,000, although these figures certainly grossly underestimate the number of Nepalese living abroad, and do not include those involved in 'temporary' migration – undoubtedly a very substantial number. Several experts have suggested that Nepal as a whole experienced net immigration during the 1960s and

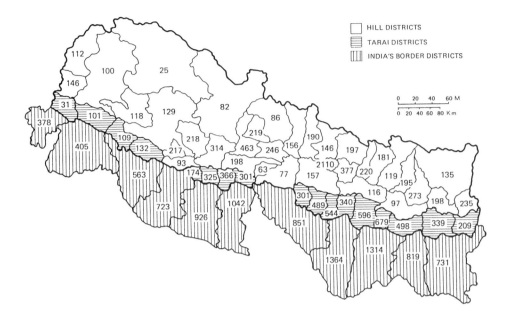

HILL DISTRICTS
TARAI DISTRICTS
INDIA'S BORDER DISTRICTS

Sources: *Census of Nepal* (1961, vol. II, 1–4); *Census of India* (1961, vol. I, part 2-A(i), 74–5, 86–8). Base map: Survey of India, (1959, 3rd edn, 1 (2), 534, 400).

Map 7: Population density in districts of Nepal and India's border districts, 1961

1970s, largely as a result of immigration from India into the *terai*, but it is impossible to confirm this. What is certain, however, is that immigration from India into the Nepalese *terai* continued to take place on an appreciable scale. The annual compound rate of population growth in the *terai* between 1971 and 1981 was more than two and a half times that for the rest of Nepal. To those actually settling in the *terai* must also be added those who emigrate on a temporary or seasonal basis from Indian states to work in agriculture, construction or other sectors in the Nepalese *terai*. The World Bank (1991: 46) has noted that 'the labour market in the *terai* is affected by substantial inflows of Indian labour' attracted by somewhat higher wages for casual labour and competing with locals seeking work.

During the 1970s and 1980s, as population pressure continued to grow in the hills, and the 'safety valve' afforded by the *terai* in earlier decades became in effect no longer available as population densities increased and land and employment opportunities became scarcer, the impetus to emigrate abroad has grown correspondingly. At the same time, employment opportunities abroad have tended to decline.

Long-term temporary migrants (over six months) still go overwhelmingly to India, where they work in the cities as watchmen, or in Assam and the border areas as construction workers, porters at coal depots or in forestry (according to the World Bank 1991: 45). Some stay for two years and do bring back some savings, albeit generally very small amounts; others return without savings, or fail to return. It seems as though it has become increasingly difficult over the past decade to find employment. As one recent study of migration in Nepal (Ghimire 1992: 182) has observed:

Employment in Indian cities as manual workers and recruitment in the British and Indian armies as 'mercenary' soldiers have been important sources of employment for a large section of the rural population. But recent evidence suggests that these prospects are also getting slimmer. A rising population and the growing unemployment in India are such that the Nepalese migrants, who in general are uneducated and unskilled, are faced with an increasing level of competition for employment there. Furthermore, recent political violence against 'foreigners' (including the second-generation) in Assam and anti-Hindu campains by Sikhs in Punjab and other neighbouring states have discouraged the Nepalese poor from migrating into India.

Recruitment of men from Nepal into the Indian army has undoubtedly declined, while the numbers of Nepalese 'Gurkhas' in the British army has declined drastically over the past twenty-five years (down from 10,000 in 1966 to 4500 by the end of the 1980s) and is likely to be reduced still further after the handover of Hong Kong (where half of them are currently based) in 1997, with no further recruitment at all.

But if opportunities for male employment abroad are evidently becoming more restricted, there is evidence of a significant increase over the last decade or so in female emigration. Nepalese women working in casual employment, and particularly in jobs associated with the sex industry, in India – and even further afield (notably in Thailand) – have grown in numbers very considerably. The numbers involved are not known, but one source suggests that 'Bombay alone may have about 45,000 Nepali prostitutes' (Dixit 1990: 27). Although such estimates probably err on the high side, there is growing concern in Nepal at the implications of this new pattern of labour migration, both as regards the social and moral dimension, and as regards the potential for a spread of venereal diseases and, particularly, AIDS, into Nepal. Male emigrants, especially soldiers, have always been a source of sexually transmitted diseases; today the chances of their returning from employment abroad with HIV are appreciable. Despite the increasing difficulty of finding employment abroad, the total of short- and long-term Nepalese foreign migrants must still be somewhere between 500,000 and one million. The risk of their contributing to the spread of HIV and AIDS into Nepal is high.

References

Dixit, Shanta B. (1990) 'Hear no AIDS, See no AIDS, Speak no AIDS', *Himal*, September–October, 26–30

Gaige, F. H. (1975) *Regionalism and National Unity in Nepal*, Berkeley: University of California Press

Ghimire, K. (1992) *Forest or Farm? The Politics of Poverty and Land Hunger in Nepal*, Delhi: Oxford University Press

Regmi, M. C. (1971) *A Study of Nepali Economic History, 1768–1845*, New Delhi: Manjusri Publishing House

Seddon, D. (1987) *Nepal – A State of Poverty* (2nd edition with additional chapter, 1993), New Delhi: Vikas Press

World Bank (1991) *Nepal: Poverty and Incomes*, Washington, DC: World Bank

ILLEGAL MIGRANT WORKERS IN JAPAN

HELMUT LOISKANDL

There are heated debates in Japan over the influx of foreign workers. While each government is united in its insistence that Japan is not and never should become an immigration country, and industrial circles produce economic arguments to support a partial lifting of the bans, the public is treated to a veritable wave of books, articles and documentaries on the topic. The issue of whether foreign workers should or should not be allowed to work in Japan is often compared in importance to the arrival of Commodore Perry in 1853, which raised the question of whether to keep the country closed (*sakokku*) or to open it up (*kaikokku*). There are remarkable similarities between the two situations and, not surprisingly, some of the same arguments are being used.

The perceived uniqueness of Japan is, and was in the last century, one of the main arguments in support of *sakokku* (closing the country). Even using examples like the emperor system, the specific modes of Japanese community organizations and the special Japanese world view (Yano 1988: 46–9), this uniqueness is assumed to be based on ethnic and cultural homogeneity. The notion of Japanese society as a big kinship group is a widely accepted myth and social cohesion and order are seen as consequences of it. Nishio (1988) points to cohesion problems in multi-ethnic countries as a warning; other writers expect a significant rise in crime should immigration restrictions be lifted.

On the other hand, the proponents of *kaikokku*, the opening of Japan to foreign workers, argue mainly on the basis of economic benefits and humanitarian considerations. It would make Japan a better member of the international community and meet its obligations as a wealthy country and one of the leading economic powers (Miyajima 1989). By comparing Japan with Germany (Goto 1990; Tezuka 1990) or France (Miyajima 1989), the advocates of openness basically agree with the opponents that the economic benefits would come at a social cost. The difference in conclusions is a result of a different perspective on costs and benefits.

Attitudes among the Japanese public reflect this discussion. Two surveys by the Mainichi newspaper group, one in December 1988 and the other in January 1990, had the public almost evenly split on the issue. The first survey reported 45 per cent 'for' and 48 per cent 'against', while the second one had 51 per cent 'for' and 44 per cent 'against'. The increase in acceptance seemed to be correlated with a growing realization that the Japanese themselves did not really wish to do dirty, dangerous jobs. Still, almost half the respondents expressed the attitudes of what has recently been labelled a 'fortress Europe' mentality – a preference for homogeneity, which outside observers often regard as close to inherent racism, for the majority of the illegals deported from Japan are also relatively dark-skinned.

Homogeneity and boundary maintenance

While the Japanese myth of origins stresses the identity of people and country and the unadulterated cultural tradition, a critical historical analysis would understand the present relative homogeneity of Japan more as the result of successful assimilation and consolidation.

Linguists argue that the Japanese language almost certainly originated somewhere in the Central Asian highlands; anthropologists point to the different racial elements visible in Japan's population and to cultural traits of everyday life, which clearly can be traced to China, Southeast Asia and the Pacific area; historians identify periods of intense contact with China and Korea. Northern Japan, with its native Ezo population, only became part of the Kyoto-centred political system a thousand years ago (Ameno 1990), Hokkaido and the native Ainu population less than two hundred years ago. As a modern nation state Japan continued and even intensified its policy of assimilating the Ainu population, and almost succeeded in making the Ainu disappear like the Ezo before them. But there was a counter tendency to the politics of integration. Social closures developed on a non-ethnic and non-racial basis; as a consequence Japan now has between one and two million outcasts, the

Table 11.2: *Registered aliens in Japan by nationality, 1960–89*

Nationality	1960	1970	1980	1985	1989
Total aliens	650,566	708,458	782,910	850,612	984,455
Asia	629,410	672,280	734,476	789,729	891,299
Bangladesh	—	—	260	684	2,205
China	45,535	51,481	52,896	74,924	137,499
India	783	1,266	1,944	2,546	2,926
Indonesia	420	1,036	1,448	1,704	2,781
Korea	581,257	614,202	664,536	683,313	681,838
Malaysia	71	451	744	1,761	4,039
Philipines	390	932	5,547	12,261	38,925
Thailand	266	721	1,276	2,642	5,542
Vietnam	57	557	2,742	4,126	6,316
Other Asia	631	1,634	3,083	5,768	9,228
Europe	6,766	11,548	15,552	19,151	23,123
Americans	13,223	22,182	27,462	35,847	62,085
Other	1,167	2,448	5,420	5,885	7,948
Total population ('000)	94,096	104,331	116,807	120,837	122,982
Aliens as percentage of total	0.69	0.68	0.67	0.70	0.80

Source: Japan, Management and Coordination Agency, Statistics Bureau. *Japan Statistical Yearbook 1990*, Tokyo (1990: 45).

burakumin (De Vos and Wakatsumatsu 1967; Loiskandl and Yawata 1984). One could agree, however, that Japanese politics over the last millennium has been geared towards achieving cultural and ethnic homogeneity, using as its tool assimilation in the areas incorporated and exclusion of foreign migration. That is even true of the period between 1921 and 1931, when there was a net immigration of over 400,000 Koreans to Japan, or for the whole period from 1915 to 1940, when the Korean population in Japan proper grew from 4000 to over one million (Skeldon 1991: 47).

One has to keep in mind that Korea as well as parts of China had become incorporated in the Japanese empire; it was the internal migration of this period that created the basis for the two leading ethnic minorities in contemporary Japan – the Koreans, with 681,838 registered aliens in 1989, and the Chinese, with 137,499 in the same year. These Chinese and Koreans (often second- and third-generation) became foreigners in 1945 when Japan was reduced to its present size and only a tiny percentage ever took out Japanese citizenship (Huguet 1992: 258).

Up to now Japan has tried to preserve its supposed homogeneity by strict controls on population movements. The number of foreigners admitted as residents has been kept small by any comparison, and the admission process is rather selective. Only very few legal residents eventually qualify for permanent residence. In June 1990 a new immigration law came into effect which actually increased existing controls. This was at least partly the result of developments in Europe, where it was thought that the acceptance of temporary labour had created permanent migrant and ethnic communities. The new law led to an immediate crackdown on illegal foreign workers, with over 25,000 expelled in a relatively short period. True to the expressed goal of homogeneity, existing labour shortages have recently been addressed by stepping up efforts to have vacancies filled by ethnic Japanese from China (the so-called 'war orphans') and second- and third-generation ethnic Japanese from South America. In the last half of 1990 alone it has been estimated that between 30,000 and 50,000 Latin Americans of Japanese descent went to Japan under contract to work (Skeldon 1991: 49). Ironically this move turned out to be more beneficial to multiculturalism than to homogeneity, for these people of Japanese descent are no longer culturally Japanese.

The regional perspective

For the above reasons, there is relatively little

Table 11.3: *Japan: aliens apprehended for illegal employment, by nationality and sex, 1982–89*

	1982	1984	1985	1986	1987	1988	1989
Total	1,889	4,783	5,629	8,131	11,307	14,314	16,608
	(1,705)	(4,433)	(4,942)	(5,945)	(7,018)	(5,385)	(4,817)
Philippines	405	2,983	3,927	6,297	8,027	5,386	3,740
	(396)	(2,887)	(3,578)	(4,797)	(5,774)	(3,698)	(2,451)
Thailand	412	1,132	1,073	990	1,067	1,388	1,144
	(387)	(1,078)	(953)	(826)	(777)	(1,019)	(775)
Pakistan	7	3	36	196	905	2,497	3,170
	(0)	(0)	(0)	(0)	(0)	(2)	(2)
China	775	466	427	356	494	502	588
	(691)	(330)	(301)	(195)	(284)	(272)	(272)
Bangladesh			1	58	438	2,947	2,277
		(01)	(0)	(1)	(8)	(2)	
Korea	132	61	76	119	208	1,033	3,129
	(97)	(27)	(41)	(50)	(99)	(264)	(920)
Others	154	138	89	115	168	566	2,560
	(134)	(111)	(69)	(77)	(83)	(127)	(395)

Source: Morita (1990: 6). Figures in parentheses indicate females.

labour migration to Japan, be it legal or illegal. Skeldon (1991: 47) estimates there are between 100,000 and 300,000 illegal foreign workers in Japan. Japanese newspapers in 1993 usually accepted the higher figure. As Nagayama (1992: 631) points out, most illegal migrant workers enter Japan legally, under the provisions of the Immigration Control Act, and then work illegally. While the control of immigration at the ports of entrance is rather strict, control policies on people inside the country are relatively lax. Once foreigners have entered legally as tourists, they can work with relative ease. Others, who are in the country legally but prohibited from joining the labour force, such as the growing number of foreign students, are also tempted by the strong yen to work illegally. Only a small percentage of the illegal labour force in Japan has entered illegally. To quote Nagayama (1992: 631): 'Although there are cases where immigration officers take bribes to allow foreign nationals who would otherwise not pass immigration control to enter Japan, such cases are extremely rare.' But for a long time there has been a problem with stowaways, first from Korea, but increasingly also from China. The Japanese crime syndicate, Yakuza, is reportedly involved in many of these cases of organized illegal entry and also seems to be quite active in the forged travel documents industry.

In 1990 the various categories of legal residence were revised. The first now comprises diplomats, officials, professors, artists, people involved in religious activities and journalists. Residence is granted for three years, except for diplomats and their families who can stay for the period of their mission. The second category includes investors, business managers and people involved in legal and accounting services; they can reside in the county for up to three years initially. This category also includes medical researchers, instructors, engineers, specialists in humanities and international services, intra-company transferees, skilled workers and entertainers. They are admitted for one year initially. Large numbers of women enter Japan legally each year as 'entertainers'. There were about 71,000 of them in 1988 alone, up from 20,580 in 1980, arriving mainly from the Philippines and Thailand (Skeldon 1991: 48). They are one of the main sources of female overstayers; many of them find illegal employment as prostitutes in the shady world of the 'water trade'. The third category probably provides the main opening for potential illegals, as it includes temporary visitors such as tourists. They can stay for a maximum of 90 days. A one-year residency is allowed for people involved in non-income oriented cultural or artistic activities, or for students of Japanese culture. The fourth category, with an initial maximum stay of one year, includes college students, pre-college students and trainees. They also provide a fair share of illegals, as the officially allowed hours of work per week (twenty-six) can not be effectively controlled, and some students enrol but never show up for class. The fifth category allows the Ministry of Justice to admit foreigners not identified in the other categories to a period of stay ranging from six months to three years. On the whole, these categories limit the activities of foreigners to a narrow range of professional and skilled labour, making only nominal concessions to unskilled labour by introducing the concept of trainees. Trainees, however, are restricted in wage level and fringe benefits, and are not protected by industrial security provisions.

Despite these openly discriminatory and restrictive policies, international migration to Japan and the number of migrant workers in Japan have increased significantly over the past ten years.

These phenomena have to be understood against a regional background. The push-pull factors can be easily understood if we look at population figures like Pakistan's growth rate of 3.2 per cent against Japan's 0.6 per cent. Even more cogent are the economic figures. Per capita GNP varies from over US $21,000 in Japan to less than $200 in Bangladesh; the average monthly income from $22 in Bangladesh, $39 in Burma and $41 in Sri Lanka to about $3000 in Japan. Quite a few national economies in Asia, such as Bangladesh, Pakistan or the Philippines, are rather limited in their capacity to generate rewarding employment opportunities. On the other hand, the economies of countries like Hong Kong, Singapore, South Korea, Taiwan and Japan are characterized by relatively low labour force growth rates and high rates of growth of productive jobs in both industry and services; job projections actually exceed the capacity of these countries to fill them from internal sources (Stahl and Appleyard 1992: 419). In the case of Japan, the country's economic growth in combination with a very slowly growing labour force has led to widespread labour shortages. In 1992 it was reported that job vacancies exceeded job seekers by 35 per cent. While it is assumed that some of the demand was satisfied by the legal foreign resident population of 984,000 persons, the work available in Japan is attracting widespread regional interest. Over a twelve-month period in 1990/1, the immigration authorities turned back 13,934 foreigners for

attempted illegal entry. The largest group among them were South Koreans, followed by Malaysians, Thais, Iranians and Taiwanese. Over the same period, the authorities indicted 36,264 foreigners for staying illegally and for activities not allowed to them. Of the persons indicted, 29,883 were found to have worked illegally and were deported.

Illegal migrant workers

Japan has modern civil and labour laws, and legal workers enjoy adequate protection. This does not extend to illegal migrant workers. As their work has not been approved officially, they face formidable legal, social and economic hurdles. It might be useful to look at some of them.

Problems with labour mediators

Illegal migrant workers in Japan face certain structural barriers. First, the labour placement agents are often associated with organized crime. According to a 1990 police white paper, 'labour mediators' illegally send large numbers of migrant workers into Japan and pocket huge sums of money in charges and commissions. When entering Japan, foreign migrant workers are often forced to live in substandard accommodation run by the labour mediators, and they have to accept the work arranged for them by these same people. A police survey of people later deported showed that about 80 per cent had had their entrance to Japan and/or work organized by labour mediators. As the Japanese press constantly points out, these labour placement agencies are heavily involved in issuing false passports or visas, giving misleading information on work in Japan, and on the underworld control associated with these activities. In 1990, the police arrested 160 persons for violation of the Labourer Dispatch Law, but attempts to identify and regulate the existence and functions of clandestine labour placement agencies have a long way to go.

Problems with the workplace

The Japanese refer to the jobs open to illegal workers as the 3K-range (*kitsui, kitanai* and *kikken*), translated into English as 3D-jobs: difficult, dirty and dangerous. Subcontractors in the construction industry, in restaurants and snack bars, in the transport industry and in stockyards look for illegal foreigners to fill job vacancies, for the Japanese are growing reluctant to accept work that involves heavy physical labour and a harsh working environment. The subcontracting system means that orders to subcontractors from parent firms have to be completed at a lower cost than those of the parent companies. Thus, these small enterprises have to employ labour at the lowest cost possible, resulting not only in low pay but also in poor working conditions. Sometimes these jobs are opened to legal foreign 'trainees'. A report of a 'typical' case in the construction industry in the *Asahi Evening News* (24 July 1991) claimed that workers entering for construction training begin with a three-month Japanese language training course, followed by fifteen months of work on construction sites at a monthly wage of $438. While this might sound tempting to people from poor Asian countries, for the Japanese it is below the poverty level. Special workplace problems for female illegal workers are introduced by the nature of their main occupation, which is as 'hostess', stripper or prostitute (about 70 per cent of deported female illegal workers are listed in this category). As most of these workplaces are Yakuza-controlled, it is very difficult for the women employed there to move away.

Problems with the law and with unions

Illegal migrant workers are not protected by the civil and labour laws that cover legal workers. They can be treated solely as commodities to generate profits, as the employment contracts of illegal migrant workers bear out. To quote Nagayama (1992: 634): 'Since employers make contact with them irregularly, even if their labour contract is legal, they can not be treated as official workers protected by labour laws and the social security system. Thus, employers utilize illegal migrant workers as buffer in the industrial/business cycle, where they can dismiss them without any financial loss.' Their insecurity of tenure means they are not covered by health insurance and cannot go to court if an employer decides not to pay the wages agreed upon, for they would then face deportation.

And illegal migrant workers are ignored by the Japanese trade unions as union membership only extends to legal permanent workers. As an iron rule labour organizations do not negotiate improvements for non-members in any country and Japanese trade unions also do not extend their labour agreements to other workers who are seen as competitors in the same labour market, or worse, as intruders endangering the benefits gained. These feelings seem to be widespread among union members – a situation not unfamiliar to students of migrant labour in Europe. But regardless of feelings, the Japanese labour movement's historical administrative and juridical policies rarely allow labour agreements to extend across industries or workers.

The problem of illegal migrant workers in Japan, which should be seen against the background of uneven development in Asia, will remain urgent because concern for human rights is no longer a solely national issue. Also, migration to Japan as such cannot be understood in isolation, and its resultant social problems have to be analysed at an international level.

References
Ameno, Yoshihiku (1990) *Nihonron no Shiza: Retto no Shakai to Kokka*, Tokyo: Shogakan
De Vos, G. and H. Wakatsumatsu (1967) *Japan's Invisible Race*, Berkeley: University of California Press
Goto, Junichi (1990) *Gaikokkujin Rodo no Keizaigakku*, Tokyo: Toyo keizai Shinposha
Huguet, Jerrold W. (1992) 'The Future of International Migration within Asia', *Asian and Pacific Migration Journal*, 1 (2), 250–77
Loiskandl, H. and Y. Yawata (1984) 'Race and Ethnic Relations in Japan', in H. Loiskandl (ed.) *Australia and her Neighbours – Ethnic Relations and the Nation State*, Occasional Papers in Anthropology, University of Queensland, Brisbane
Miyajima, Takashi (1989) *Gaikokkujin Rodosha Mukaeire no Ronri*, Tokyo: Akashi Shoten
Morita, Kiriro, (1990) 'Japan and the Problem of Foreign Workers', paper presented at Cross-National Labour Migration Conference, UN Centre for Regional Development, Nagoya
Nagayama, Toshikazu (1992) Clandestine Migrant Workers in Japan, *Asian and Pacific Migration Journal*, 1 (3–4), 417–76
Nishio, Kanui (1988) *Senyaku-teki Sakokuron*, Tokyo: Kosaido Shuppan
Skeldon, Ronald (1991) 'International Migration within and from the East and Southeast Asian Region: A Review Essay', *Asian and Pacific Migration Journal*, 1 (1), 19–63
Stahl, C. W. and R. T. Appleyard (1992) 'International Manpower Flows in Asia: An Overview', *Asian and Pacific Migration Journal*, 1 (3–4), 417–76
Tezuka, Kazuaki (1990) *Rodoryoku-ido no Jidai*, Tokyo: Chuokoron-sha
Yano, Toru (1988) *Nihon no Kokusaika O Kangaeru*, Tokyo: Nikkan kogyo Shinbunsha

ASIAN MIGRATION TO AUSTRALIA

JOCK COLLINS

Asian immigration has been the most controversial chapter in Australia's remarkable immigration history. Asians were the first visitors to call on Australian shores in the seventeenth century, establishing contact with Australia's Aboriginal people (Choo 1993). Chinese and other Asians featured prominently in the immigration wave following the gold rush in eastern Australia in the middle of the nineteenth century, when legislation to restrict Chinese immigration was introduced. The 'white Australia policy' – as the 1901 Immigration Restriction Act was popularly called – was the bedrock of the new Australian nation at federation in 1901, blocking entry for Asian and other 'coloured' people to Australia until the 1960s (Markus 1979; Price 1974).

The end of the Vietnam war in 1975 was a catalyst for the return to large-scale Asian migration to Australia for the first time in nearly a hundred years. Between 1975 and the early 1980s, 150,000 Vietnamese people arrived (Chetty 1993: 16). By the 1980s Asians were arriving in Australia in increasing numbers so that by 1983/4 Asia replaced the UK and Europe as Australia's main source of migrants, with Asians the fastest growing overseas-born population group in Australia in the past decade (Khoo et al. 1993: 1). In 1990/1 eight out of the top ten source countries of Australia's migrants were Asian (Inglis 1992: 25). Increasing Asian immigration has corresponded with changes that have given Australia's immigration programme a sharper economic focus and produced the 'new migration' with emphasis on education, qualifications and capital (Inglis et al. 1992: 224). In 1991/2, nearly half the settlers from Asian countries were professionals, managers or administrators (BIPR 1993a: 28).

By 1991 there were 687,850 Asian-born Australians, who comprised 4.3 per cent of the total Australian population (HREOC 1993: 161–2), excluding West Asians.[1] Of this number, 2.2 per cent or 377,751 were born in Southeast Asia (Brunei, Cambodia, Indonesia, Laos, Malaysia, Burma, the Philippines, Singapore, Thailand and Vietnam). Another 1.2 per cent or 199,288 were born in Northeast Asia (China, Hong Kong, Japan, North Korea, South Korea, Macau, Mongolia and Taiwan). The remaining 0.7 per cent or 110,811 were born in South Asia (Afghanistan, Bhutan, India, Maldives, Nepal, Pakistan and Sri Lanka). In 1992/3, Hong Kong was Australia's largest source of Asian immigrants, followed closely by Vietnam, the Philippines, India, China, Sri Lanka, Malaysia, Taiwan and Indonesia (BIR 1993a: 1).

Moreover, increasing numbers of Asians enter Australia as temporary migrant workers, students or tourists (Sloan and Kennedy 1992). Asians comprise more than half Australia's long-term overseas visitors and 38 per cent of Australia's short-term visitor or tourist arrivals, up from less than 10 per cent in 1966 (Kee Pookong et al. 1993: 10–12). Hong Kong, Malaysia and Singapore are the main sources of Australia's full fee-paying overseas tertiary students who generate an income of $500 million per year (BIPR 1993b).

Asians in Australian society

The Asian population in Australia has undergone a diversity of experiences between and within birthplace groups, though racism is a shared Asian experience. Factors relating to social class, ethnicity and gender shape migrants' lives in Australia (Collins 1991) just as they do those of non-migrants. Whatever patterns emerge as differences in socio-economic position before emigrating to Australia, time of arrival and category of entry influence the experiences of Asians in Australia. Half Australia's Asian-born population has arrived in Australia since the late 1980s (Khoo et al. 1993: 4). Migrants from Indochina (Vietnam, Cambodia and Laos) generally arrived as refugees or family migrants in the 1970s and early 1980s, while many of those born in Southeast Asian countries continue to arrive under family migrant categories. Those from Northeast Asia are more recent migrants and tend to arrive under skilled/ professional or business categories (Khoo et al. 1993: 1). Most persons born in Taiwan, Korea, Japan and Hong Kong have arrived since 1986, as have more than half of the Chinese Hong Kong-born Filipinos, Thais, Afghans and Bangladeshis. Many migrants born in Vietnam,

India, Burma, Cambodia, Laos and Singapore arrived in Australia before 1981.

Northeast Asians and South Asians have a high proportion of workers in the 'managers and administrators' and 'professional and para professional' occupations compared with the Indochinese. In 1991, 30 per cent of Japanese and Taiwanese-born men were managers or administrators compared with 16 per cent of the Australian-born. Those born in Hong Kong, Korea and Malaysia tend to cluster in the finance and business sectors of the economy, while the Chinese, Japanese and Thai-born are concentrated in the personal and recreational services, including the restaurant and tourist industries. In contrast, Indochinese men and women are concentrated in low-skilled jobs in the struggling manufacturing industry (Khoo et al. 1993: 9), with Vietnamese women over-represented at eight to twelve times the rate of Australian-born women in the declining clothing industry (Castles et al. 1991: 82–5).

Asians and other immigrants have borne the greatest burden of unemployment since the 1990s' economic recession: when the rate of unemployment among Australian-born males in 1991 was 11.48 per cent, the Vietnamese-born had unemployment rates of 35.9 per cent and the Lebanese-born 33.7 per cent (ABS 1991). Other Asian birthplace groups with higher rates of unemployment than the average include Taiwan (27.5 per cent), Indonesia (17.0 per cent), the Philippines (16.6 per cent), Korea (14.5 per cent), China (14.9 per cent) and Hong Kong (13.5 per cent). However, those born in South Asia had, on average, a rate of unemployment of 9.4 per cent, lower than the national average (HREOC 1993: 165–6). High Indochinese unemployment is linked to their occupational concentration in the declining Australian manufacturing sector, which has been hit by a combination of national and international economic restructuring, reduced levels of protection and an economic recession (Castles 1992: 56–8; Viviani et al. 1993). Unemployment rates of Asian-born women exceed those of Asian men for the first ten years of settlement (Khoo et al. 1993: 8).

The English language ability of Asian immigrants has often been linked to their success in the Australian labour market. Over 85 per cent of migrants recently arrived in Australia from Malaysia, Singapore, India, Sri Lanka and the Philippines are proficient in English or speak it a home. On the other hand, less that one-quarter of the recently arrived migrants born in Vietnam, Cambodia and Laos spoke English well or very well (Khoo et al. 1993: 14). Recent data on main languages spoken at home reveal that Cantonese is spoken by 165,000 and Vietnamese by over 110,000. Just under 60,000 people speak Filipino languages or Mandarin at home, while over 20,000 people speak Indonesia Malay, Japanese, Hindi and Korean as their main language at home. Many other languages are spoken at home in smaller numbers, including Chinese, Khmer, Tamil, Singhalese, Thai, Urdu, Burmese, Bengali and Tetum (BIR 1993b: 2).

One route to Australia for wealthy Asians is via the 'business migrant' category. More than half the applications under the Business Migration Programme during the period 1987/8 to 1991/2 were from Hong Kong and Taiwan, with Malaysia, Indonesia and South Korea also prominent (DIEA 1993: 2). The contribution of Asian migrants to the Australian small business sector is disproportionately large. Many migrants, particularly those from Asia, are over-represented as self-employed and employers (Castles et al. 1991). In 1991, when 7.15 per cent of the Australian-born males were employers, 11 per cent of those born in Korea and Taiwan were employers. While 7 per cent of the Australian-born were self-employed, many Asian birthplace groups had a significantly greater presence among the self-employed, including Korea (20 per cent) and Taiwan (17 per cent). Other Asian birthplace groups, such as the Vietnamese, Malayans, Chinese, Japanese, Indian and Sri Lankan-born, had significantly lower rates in small business than the Australian-born (Lever Tracy et al. 1991).

Rates of citizenship for migrants born in Asian countries vary from a low of 20.5 per cent for those born in Japan to 77.7 per cent for those born in Cambodia. Those migrants who have left countries such as Cambodia, Vietnam or the Philippines have high rates – over 70 per cent – of citizenship, while other Asian countries such as Korea, Taiwan and China still have citizenship rates that encompass more than one-half of immigrants (BIR 1993b: 2). Rates of in-marriage also vary considerably between Asian birthplace groups, with those born in Vietnam, China, Turkey and Lebanon having high levels of in-marriage, while Malayan-born and Filipina-born women were found to have unusually low degrees of in-marriage (Hugo 1990: 74).

Many Filipina women arrive in Australia as 'mail order brides' whose experiences in Australia have attracted concern from the Australian and Filipino governments as well as women's groups (DIEA 1992). At the same time, other Filipina women reject the stereotype of 'prostitute' and the 'passive but sexually available connotations routinely accompanying "Asian" women' (Coupe and Jakubowicz 1992: 67). Many women from Indochina and Southeast Asia are to be found in low-paid, unregulated 'outwork' following the demise of large sections of the clothing and textiles industries (Alcorso 1991; CWWCL 1986). Many of these women would have been refugees who had experienced severe trauma prior to arrival in Australia.

Racism and Asian migrants in Australia today

Racism also shapes the lives of Asians in Australia. One of the most recent and detailed surveys of racism in contemporary Australian society concluded that while racist violence on the basis of ethnicity was viewed as nowhere near the level that it is in many other countries, racist violence against migrants nevertheless 'exists at a level that causes concern and it could increase in intensity and extent unless firmly addressed now' (HREOC 1991: 219). Asians featured prominently among those groups with experience of racial violence, particularly those from the Middle East who reported escalating racism during the Gulf conflict (CDAAA 1992). Racial discrimination is also experienced by many migrants, including Asians, in the Australian workforce (Foster et al. 1991).

Asian migrants were the centre of two major national debates in Australia in the 1980s. The 1984 debate emerged after prominent Melbourne historian, Geoffrey Blainey, publicly opposed the Asian 'influx' that he claimed was against the interest and wishes of the Australian people and had destroyed 'the Australian way of life'. Asian immigration caused unemployment for the Australian-born, and was 'a sure recipe for social tension' in the 'frontline' suburbs where they settled, Blainey (1984) argued. Economists rejected the links between Asian immigration and unemployment, while studies showed that areas of high Asian immigration showed the greatest tolerance to Asians (Collins 1984). Blainey received little support from business, government, trade unions, churches or other major institutions, while the public support for far-right parties in Australia is minimal (Markus and Ricklefs 1985).

In 1988, Australia's bicentennial year, the leader of the conservative Federal Opposition, John Howard, attempted to gain political capital for the national election by committing his government to reduce Asian immigration and abandon multiculturalism. Howard attempted to mine the vein of anti-Asian sentiment in Australia, but was rejected by his party before the election. In the final analysis, this stance was dysfunctional: widespread reportage and criticism of Howard's stance by the Asian media contradicted with corporate interests to improve economic relations with Australia's Asian neighbours. Howard's move also threatened to disaffect many Asians who tend to be conservative voters (Collins 1988; 1991: 302–6).

The wheels of Australian immigration history have turned full circle. For most of its history Australia attempted to exclude Asians from Australian life, but in the last decade Asia and Asians have played a greater role in Australian society than at any time in its history. Today widespread consensus puts Australia's future economic success as dependent on economic integration – formally or informally – with the dynamic Asian region (Garnaut 1990). But Australia's anti-Asian history is a fetter to such developments, with anti-Asian racism one factor complicating Australia's new relationship with Asia and Asians.

Note

1. There are different definitions of what constitutes 'Asia'. The Australian Bureau of Statistics defines Asia to include the countries Egypt, Iran, Iraq, Israel, Jordan, Kuwait, Lebanon, Saudi Arabia, Syria and Turkey. The Department of Immigration and Ethnic Affairs defines these countries as the 'Middle East', not part of Asia. As Castles (1992: 70) points out, the historical origins of this relate to the 1960s when the Immigration Department wanted to widen recruitment to include the Middle East as 'honorary whites'.

References

ABS (Australian Bureau of Statistics) (1991) Census Data, Table BPLP12

Alcorso, C. (1991) *NES Background Immigrant Women in the Workforce*, Wollongong: Centre for Multicultural Studies

BIPR (Bureau of Immigration and Population Research) (1993a) 'Asia Pacific Migration to Australia', *BIPR Bulletin*, 10, November

—— (1993b) 'DEET Figures Show Major Economic Importance of Overseas Full-fee Paying Students', *BIPR Bulletin*, 10, November

BIR (Bureau of Immigration Research) (1993a) *Asia-Pacific Migration to Australia: Statistical Information Sheet No. 1*, September

—— (1993b) *Asia-Pacific Migration to Australia: Statistical Information Sheet No. 2*, September

Blainey, G. (1984) *All For Australia*, North Ryde: Methuen

Castles, Stephen (1992) 'The "New" Migration and Australian Immigration Policy', in C. Inglis et al. (eds) *Asians in Australia: The Dynamics of Migration and Settlement*, Sydney: Allen & Unwin, 45–72

Castles, Stephen et al. (1991) *The Global Milkbar and the Local Sweatshop: Ethnic Small Business and the Economic Restructuring of Sydney*, Wollongong, Centre for Multicultural Studies, University of Wollongong for the Office of Multicultural Affairs

CDAAA (Committee on Discrimination Against Arab Australians) (1992) *Racism, Arab and Muslim Australians and the War against Iraq*, 2, November 1990–July 1991, June

Chetty, S. (1993) 'Refugee Flows in Asia: How they Affect Australia', *BIPR Bulletin*, 10, November

Choo, Christine (1993) 'The Impact of Asian-Aboriginal Australian Contacts in Northern Australia', paper to the Conference on Asia-Pacific Migration Affecting Australia, Darwin, 14–17 September

Collins, Jock (1984) 'Why Blainey is Wrong', *Australian Society*, 3 (9), September

(1988) 'The Bicentennial Immigration Debate and the Politics of Prejudice', *Migration Action*, 10 (3)

(1991) *Migrant Hands in a Distant Land: Australia's Post-war Immigration*, Sydney: Pluto Press

Coupe, B. and A. Jakubowicz (1992) *Nextdoor Neighbours: A Report for the Office of Multicultural Affairs on Ethnic Group Discussions of the Australia Media*, Canberra: Australian Government Publishing Service

CWWCL (Centre for Working Women's Co-operative Limited) (1986) *Women Outworkers: A Report Documenting Sweated Labour in the 1980s*, Melbourne: Footscray

DIEA (Department of Immigration and Ethnic Affairs) (1992) *A Bride for all Reasons: Report on a Pilot Survey of Filipino Brides*, Melbourne: DIEA and Philippine Consulate General

(1993) *Migration of Business People to Australia: A Discussion Paper*, October

Foster, Lois et al. (1991) *Discrimination Against Immigrant Workers in Australia*, Canberra: Australian Government Publishing Service

Garnaut, Ross (1990), *Australia and the Northeast Asian Ascendancy*, Canberrra: Australian Government Publishing Service

HREOC (Human Rights and Equal Opportunity Commission) (1991) *Racist Violence: Report of the National Inquiry into Racist Violence in Australia*, Canberra: Australian Government Publishing Service

(1993) *State of the Nation: A Report on People of Non-English Speaking Backgrounds*, Canberra: Australian Government Publishing Service

Hugo, G. (1990) 'Demographic and Spatial Aspects of Immigration', in M. Wooden et al. (eds) *Australian Immigration: A Survey of the Issues*, Australian Government Publishing Service, 24–109

Inglis, C. (1992) 'An Overview of Australian Migration Policy and Flows', paper to the Conference on Immigration and Refugee Policy: The Australian and Canadian Experiences, York University, Toronto, Canada, 2–5 May

Inglis, C. et al. (eds) (1992) *Asians in Australia: The Dynamics of Migration and Settlement*, Sydney: Allen & Unwin

Kee Pookong et al. (1993) 'People Movements Between Australia and Asian-Pacific National: Trends, Issues and Prospects', paper to the Conference on Asia-Pacific Migration Affecting Australia, Darwin, 14–17 September

Khoo Siew-Ean et al. (1993) 'Asian Immigrant Settlement and Adjustment in Australia', paper to the Conference on Asia-Pacific Migration Affecting Australia, Darwin, 14–17 September

Lever Tracy, C. et al. (1991) *Asian Entrepreneurs in Australia: Ethnic Small Business in the Chinese and Indian Communities in Brisbane and Sydney*, Canberra: Australian Government Publishing Service

Markus, A. (1979) *Fear and Hatred: Purifying Australia and California 1850–1901*, Sydney: Hale & Iremonger

Markus A. and M. C. Ricklefs (eds) (1985) *Surrender Australia? Essays in the Study and Uses of History: Geoffrey Blainey and Asian Immigration*, Sydney: Allen & Unwin

Price, C. (1974) *The Great White Walls are Built: Restrictive Immigration to North America and Australasia 1836–1888*, Canberra: Australian National University Press

Sloan, J. and S. Kennedy (1992), *Temporary Movements of People to and from Australia*, Canberra: Australian Government Publishing Service

Viviani, N. et al. (1993) *Indochinese in Australia: The Issues of Unemployment and Residential Concentration*, Canberra: Australian Government Publishing Service

THE VIETNAMESE BOAT PEOPLE IN HONG KONG

CHAN KWOK BUN

Three background factors need to be borne in mind when attempting to reconstruct and analyse Hong Kong's experience with the Vietnamese boat people over two decades. First, with a population of 5.8 million, of whom 98 per cent are Chinese, Hong Kong has a total land area of 1074 square kilometres, three-quarters of which is hillside or barren islands. Compared with 26 per square kilometre in the USA and 230 in the UK, Hong Kong's population density, at 5390 persons per square kilometre, is one of the highest in the world. Second, illegal immigration from China has been an important part of the history of Hong Kong, as well as a major factor in its population growth. For the year 1992, a daily average of 97 illegal immigrants had been intercepted while attempting to make their way into Hong Kong. All such illegal immigrants from China are immediately repatriated, regardless of whether they have close family links in Hong Kong. Third, with the impending 'take over' of Hong Kong by the Beijing regime in 1997, many Hong Kong people themselves are looking for an 'escape route' to other countries – some in vain. In the eyes of these people, rightly or wrongly, the chances for the Vietnamese to leave Hong Kong are higher than theirs since the Vietnamese are still on the agenda of international discussion and deliberations (Chan and Lam 1991: 11).

Inflows and outflows of Vietnamese

The first batch of 3743 Vietnamese boat people arrived in Hong Kong on board a Danish container ship, *Clara Maersk*, in May 1975. Open centres, where freedom of movement and work outside are permitted, were immediately set up to house the 11,544 Vietnamese who landed in Hong Kong in that year – until their resettlement overseas. Less than 1200 arrived in small boats as 1976 and 1977 passed by. The number went up to 6609 in 1978 when reports came to Hong Kong suggesting that the Vietnamese government was to expel the politically and economically 'unassimilable' – allegedly a large segment of the country's ethnic Chinese population. As Davis (1988: 151) writes:

Ethnic Chinese, already reduced to the status of second-class citizens through dismissals from jobs, suppression of businesses and the confiscation of their property, were being presented with the direst of options: removals as labourers to 'new economic zones' in areas of the countryside least capable of sustaining life, or escape by raising enough gold or hard currency to buy permission to leave.

The year 1979 saw a peak influx of 68,748 Vietnamese arriving in Hong Kong. Their status as refugees at the time was in general seldom questioned. In that year, only 27 per cent of arrivals were Vietnamese; the rest were ethnic Chinese. During the first five-year period since 1975, Hong Kong coped with over 80,000 arrivals from Vietnam, as in the words of Rita Fan (1990: 149), an outspoken member of the Executive and Legislative Councils of Hong Kong, 'cheerfully and uncomplainingly' while 'public sympathy lay overwhelmingly with the people fleeing their own country, who were clearly refugees'. Over 6700 and 8470 Vietnamese arrived in small boats or through ship rescue vessels in 1980 and 1981 respectively.

On 2 July 1982 a 'humane deterrence' policy was implemented by the Hong Kong government whereby new arrivals are indefinitely detained, until resettlement overseas, in closed centres operated by the Correctional Services Department that routinely runs Hong Kong's many prisons. The closed centre policy, in restricting physical movement within the centre while dampening hope of resettlement elsewhere, though 'humanely never turning away anyone seeking asylum', was meant to be a deterrence to stem continuing arrivals. Total arrivals dipped slightly to 7836 for the year 1982 and ranged between 1112 and 3651 from 1983 to 1987. In response to the 1979 crisis, over 64,000 Vietnamese were resettled in the subsequent three years. The rate then dropped to an average of about 3000 per year through the 1980s.

The USA, Canada, the UK and Australia continue to be the main countries of resettlement, having taken in, respectively, 55.5 per cent, 18 per cent, 11.5 per cent and 5.5 per cent of the 115,710 Vietnamese from

Hong Kong between 1975 and 1988. From 1979 to 1980, the period of peak arrivals, 37,468 departures were recorded; the numbers quickly fell to 17,818 in 1981, then 9242 in 1982; and dropped to an all-time low of 2875 in 1988 – a phenomenon attributed to the international community suffering from what is dubbed 'compassion fatigue'.

The screening procedure

In the first five months of 1988, the rate of arrivals from Vietnam jumped abruptly to over 5000, and totalled 18,449 by the end of the year. There were instances of more than 1000 arrivals on a single day. In Hong Kong, questions were beginning to be asked about whether these Vietnamese were in fact 'genuine' refugees. With the falling rate of resettlement and the pressure of increased arrivals, the Hong Kong government, on 16 June 1988, instituted a policy whereby all incoming Vietnamese are placed in detention centres and treated as illegal immigrants unless they are classified, after a screening procedure, as refugees under the 1951 UN Convention. Those determined to be 'refugees' would be housed in refugee camps pending resettlement in the Pillar Point Vietnamese Refugee Centre managed by the Hong Kong Housing Services on behalf of the UNHCR. Those determined as 'non-refugees', or illegal immigrants, are to stay in the detention centres pending repatriation to Vietnam.

Refugees in open centres are free to move about and are allowed to take up employment. The Pillar Point Centre is equipped with basic facilities such as dormitories, dining halls, communal bathrooms, toilets, washing areas and open space for outdoor activities. Also available are medical and dental services, as well as classroom and workshop facilities for language and skill training programmes. At the nine detention centres in the territory, the detainees are subjected to security measures and are not allowed to leave the centres except for special purpose trips such as educational excursions for the children or for hospital treatment. Under the auspices of the UNHCR, voluntary organizations continue to provide basic social services.

The manifest purpose of the screening policy and procedure is to determine who among the Vietnamese boat people merit the status of a refugee and are thus entitled to protection and resettlement, and who are not and are thus subject to detention and eventual repatriation. As pointed out by Tsamenyi (1983: 356–7), the 1951 Geneva Convention Relating to the Status of Refugees defines a refugee as any person who must satisfy the following criteria: (1) he must be outside the country of his nationality or the country of his habitual residence if he is a stateless person; (2) he must be outside the country owing to a well-founded fear of persecution for reasons of race, religion, nationality, membership of a particular social group or political opinion; (3) the persecution for the above-mentioned reasons must be attributable to political events; and (4) the person concerned must be unable or unwilling to avail himself of the protection of the country of his nationality or must be unwilling or unable to return to it if he is stateless. Central to such a definition of who is a refugee is an interpretation of what constitutes 'political events'. It is often extremely difficult to distinguish between events that are political and those that are not. As Tsamenyi (1983: 361) argues: 'After all, practically all government actions may be considered political. Thus any persecution at the hands of a government or tolerated by a government may be considered political. When a government initiates strictly controlled economic measures and enforces drastic changes in the working and living conditions of some sections of the community, through directing some people to new occupations and re-education camps, these should be interpreted as political events.' To Tsamenyi (1983: 360), 'there must be a rupture of normalcy of relations between him and his state, which rupture must derive from events which are political in nature.' In a similar vein, Johnson (1980: 84) concludes: 'So far as the "boat people" are concerned, it may well be argued that a person must have a well-founded fear of being persecuted if he is willing to part with a substantial amount of property for the privilege of being allowed to undertake a hazardous journey across the ocean in a small boat.'

In a more recent fieldwork report, Hitchcox (1991: 18), in analysing the motivations of Vietnamese asylum seekers, reiterates that their judgements on deciding to leave Vietnam are based on

> reasons ranging from escape after years of re-education at one end of the spectrum to avoidance of criminal charges at the other. In between lie the numerous cases of those who have experienced a mélange of political oppression, discrimination (capable of being just as injurious and life threatening as persecution), and economic persecution, all factors being closely interrelated, as one would predict under a one-party system.

The logic, rationality and empirical evidence of these observations notwithstanding, screening procedures have been completed for 47,389 people of whom 5515 have been 'screened in' as refugees and 41,874 have been 'screened out' as non-refugees or illegal immigrants – representing a rate of 11.6 per cent positive first instance decisions. At the appeal stage, in 766 cases involving 2006 persons, the first stance position was overturned and in 15,067 cases involving 31,966 persons, it was upheld. This represents a 5.9 per cent rate of positive decisions on review. Taken together, i.e. screening and appeal stage positive decisions, the rate at present is 15.9 per cent. This overall 'screened in' rate, six years after the refugee status determination procedure was first implemented, comes rather close to Hong Kong officials' predictions *before* screening that only 15 per cent of the Vietnamese asylum seekers were 'genuine' political refugees (Fan 1990: 150). This 'alarming consistency' has prompted Wolf (1990: 161), senior consultant to the Refugees International, to argue that 'this is not mere coincidence; for the prophecy was self-fulfilling'. The International Council of Voluntary Agencies maintains that the screening procedure is 'deliberately distorted to meet predetermined governmental objectives' (Wolf 1990: 171).

Citing reports of Amnesty International and the Lawyers Committee for Human Rights (1989), Wolf (1990: 163) has identified the following flaws in the screening procedure: lack of adequate legal advice and assistance; denial of the right to have counsel present during the screening interview; biased and incompetent immigration officers; incompetent and poorly trained interpreters; failure to provide an accurate interview record; failure to inform asylum seekers adequately of the reasons for the denial of their claims; and appeals conducted in closed sessions by a panel composed mainly of lay persons. To these flaws, Wolf (1990: 163) adds failure to make provisions for the submission of written representations prior to the initial interview and failure to permit asylum seekers to bring notes to the interview. Hitchcox's (1991: 86) report points to her Vietnamese respondents' 'gloomy expectations regarding the screening interview'. No one interviewed by Hitchcox (1991: 86) 'admitted receiving any preparation or counselling for the (screening) interview and there was little faith in the ability of the immigration officials to understand the background from which they had come'.

The Hong Kong government (Fan 1990: 150) and the UNHCR continue to dismiss criticisms that the screening procedure is flawed, inhumane and unjust by asserting that adequate legal counselling personnel

had been provided for during the appeal stage (Yau 1992: 117). Wolf (1990: 163, 171) articulates best the sentiment of academics and international human rights groups (Le 1990) when he asserts that the latent (and real) purpose of the Hong Kong screening programme is to 'screen out', to detain and repatriate, and to solve the refugee problem by discouraging the flow while the manifest purpose (largely for public consumption) is to 'screen in', to identify which of the boat people are genuine refugees and are thus entitled to protection and resettlement – 'a more subtle and insidious form of inhumanity than forcible pushbacks, but inhumanity none the less'.

Repatriation to Vietnam

To facilitate the return of Vietnamese 'non-refugees' to Vietnam, the UNHCR implemented the Voluntary Repatriation Programme. Between March 1989 and April 1993, 27,830 Vietnamese have returned to Vietnam under the scheme. Another 23 were repatriated to Vietnam on 1 December 1990 under UNHCR's 'non-objectors' scheme. On 29 October 1991, a Statement of Understanding signed by the United Kingdom, Hong Kong and Vietnam confirms acceptance by Vietnam of all 'non-refugees' in the Hong Kong camps, who include the 'double-backers' (those who had returned to Vietnam under the voluntary scheme and then found their way back to Hong Kong again for further UNHCR financial assistance) and all new asylum seekers promptly screened out on arrival. On 12 May 1992, Vietnam and Hong Kong worked out details of an orderly repatriation programme. All non-refugees who return home will receive safety guarantees from Vietnam as well as reintegration assistance from the UNHCR which is charged with the responsibility of monitoring their treatment upon their return. All returnees will be eligible for assistance under a European Community Programme whose aim is to provide job creation opportunities, start-up loans for business, vocational training courses, and other forms of community assistance, both for returnees and for local residents.

In July 1992, the Hong Kong government contributed HK$10 million towards current international efforts in the poorer migrant producing areas in Vietnam to assist Vietnamese returnees' reintegration. Including estimates for 1994 and 1995, the Hong Kong government's total expenditure since 1975 on the care and maintenance of Vietnamese boat people is HK$6638 million, which compares rather favourably with the British government's

HK$849 million and the UNHCR's HK$1253 million.

So far, 1085 illegal immigrants (75 'double backers' and accompanied family members), 48 new arrivals and 962 non-refugees from the detention centres have been returned under the October 1991 agreement. As at October 1994, the total population of Vietnamese migrants in Hong Kong consisted of 1715 refugees (including 987 who arrived after 15 June 1988 but were 'screened in'), and 24,084 post-15 June 1988 migrants (174 persons awaiting screening and 23,912 already 'screened out' as non-refugees). The number of Vietnamese arrivals dropped from 20,179 during 1991 to 12 and 94 in 1992 and 1993 respectively. A total of 11,793 Vietnamese were repatriated to Vietnam in 1991 and 1992, at a rate of above 1000 per month, representing a 167 per cent increase over the previous year. As at 1 October 1994, altogether 42,898 people had returned to Vietnam under the UNHCR repatriation scheme. All this has prompted a Hong Kong observer of Vietnamese boat people (Yau 1992: 111, 113–15) to hail the period from July 1991 to June 1992 as a 'year of breakthrough'.

From humanitarianism to hostility and restriction
Over the past twenty long years of experience with the Vietnamese boat people, Hong Kong has gone through a number of twists and turns. In the first five years since 1975, Hong Kong responded with humanitarian concern and sympathy to the plight of tens of thousands of Vietnamese taking sudden flight in unseaworthy boats. This humanitarian stance was construed amidst unprecedented world media attention on perhaps the gravest tragedy of this century. It was also a natural enough stance during a period when the western world was actively pursuing various refugee resettlement programmes.

As the major resettlement countries began to suffer from 'compassion fatigue' while themselves pre-occupied with their own domestic racial and political problems in relation to internal policies towards Asian and other third-world immigrants, Hong Kong began to feel the strain of the ever-present excess of inflows of Vietnamese. The duration of stay of Vietnamese in Hong Kong continues to increase, thus multiplying the number of 'long-stayers' in the camps. Hong Kong's stance towards the Vietnamese migrants thus evolved into an interim state of deep ambivalence and such other attendant emotions as political helplessness and impotence (Sutter 1990: 158–9) arising from lack of policy-devising powers,

and a sense of betrayal and abandonment by the British and Chinese governments (Chan and Lam 1991), while a need was increasingly felt to devise step-by-step policies of deterrence of varying degrees of severity.

The closed camp policy in 1982 did not achieve the expected deterrent effect, though it resulted in various socio-psychological effects of institution-alization in closed camps: deprivation of personal privacy, stress, hunger strikes, suicides, murders, rapes, bouts of interpersonal and group violence among camp residents as well as between camp guards and camp residents, and criminalization. These adverse conditions of camp life have drawn severe criticisms from the international community (Chan and Loveridge 1987; Davis 1988; Hitchcox 1990, 1990; Knudsen 1983, 1988, 1992; Oxfam 1987; Refugee Action 1986; Thomas 1988). Journalists describe these camps as prisons, and camp life, 'in the iron cage', behind the barbed wire, as a life of waiting, doing time and yet more waiting.

In the meantime, Hong Kong experienced immense frustration in its dealings with the British government, for the latter had repeatedly refused to increase its own refugee intake, while insisting that Hong Kong not abdicate its role as country of first asylum. Feeling sensitive about their political powerlessness in their dealings with Britain and China (with the 1997 handover just around the corner), the stance taken by the Hong Kong citizens and mass media towards the Vietnamese degenerated into outright hostility. The June 1988 screening policy came out at a time when public anti-Vietnamese sentiment in Hong Kong was at its height. Few public current affair topics occupied the attention of the average Hong Kong resident as much as the Vietnamese problem. Local feature-length Cantonese films were shown to portray the adverse impact of the criminal activities of Vietnamese gangs (in and out of camps and detention centres) on public morality and social cohesion. The Vietnamese were held responsible for 10 per cent of all crimes committed yearly in Hong Kong (Chan 1990: 101). Press editorials and newspaper as well as television stories tended to sensationalize the trafficking and usage of illicit drugs, the fights between North and South Vietnamese (using handmade weapons and firearms smuggled into the camps) and extortionism. The territory's radio stations set up phone-ins and talk shows for the public expression of anger and hostility towards the Vietnamese. All this culminated in the forced repatriation of fifty-one boat people from a detention centre: on 12 December 1989, at 3.00 a.m., under the cover of darkness, they were literally 'taken from their beds, bundled into caged trucks', transported to the airport by eight security units (200 heavily armed riot policemen) and placed on a specially chartered flight to Hanoi. Supported by its people, this move of the Hong Kong government immediately drew criticism from the international community (Chan and Lam 1991: 2–3; Muntarbhorn 1992: 66). The forced repatriation scheme came to an involuntary halt.

Between now and 1997, what will happen to the 'screened out' Vietnamese migrants being detained and languishing in Hong Kong's many detention centres? What will happen to those who have been 'screened in' as refugees and are thus entitled to legal protection and resettlement, which seems increasingly unlikely? With the voluntary repatriation programmes presently well in place, the international community has thus far failed to reach a formal consensus on forcible repatriation. Attempts to articulate and formulate an intermediate mechanism between forced and voluntary repatriation will continue, while Hanoi, eager to expedite the economic rebuilding of Vietnam and to normalize relations with the West and with the Southeast Asian region, has shown increased flexibility on alternative forms of repatriation of non-refugees under the UNHCR's monitoring of returnees, international guarantees, as well as substantive European reintegration assistance.

On 3 and 4 February 1992, 24 Vietnamese boat people were killed and 114 injured in a fire at Sek Kong detention centre. The tragedy, precipitated by a quarrel over alcohol debts, was the worst disaster in the twenty years of Hong Kong's experience with the Vietnamese (Yau 1992: 119–20). Violence and injury is an expected outgrowth of stressful and over-crowded conditions of camp life where detainees have for years suffered extreme deprivations and degradation, and have over time lost their sense of normality.

Restrictionism, control and deterrence in the global treatment of migrants, forced or voluntary, will become more comprehensible when seen within the framework of a political theory of the nation states which, among other things, have taken upon themselves the tasks of political and geographic boundary maintenance; protection and enhancement of self-interests of the state and its citizens; and formation and maintenance of national identity through a sustained but distorted definition of otherness as embodied in migrants having crossed

such boundaries, legally or illegally. One may venture to argue that such sentiments of restrictionism and hostility towards migrants are being increasingly internationalized through a transnational diffusion of attitudes, rhetoric, rationalizations and justifications (Chan 1990: 2; Chan et al. 1995). For that matter, Hong Kong's attempts to self-justify its increasingly austere policies towards the Vietnamese over the past twenty years must be seen within the larger context of similar rationalizations of equally austere policies towards the Indochinese asylum seekers on the part of other countries of first asylum.

The Vietnamese boat people phenomenon reminds one of Arendt's (1973) insightful analysis of the relationship between state building and victim groups. As a state chooses to forge an identity on the basis of race, religion, nationality or ideology, it produces target minorities and victim groups – the process of forming a new state is often itself a refugee generating process (Tarzi 1991: 442; Zolberg 1983). Paraphrasing Arendt (1973: 268), those whom the persecutor has singled out as scum of the new state will actually be received and treated as scum of everywhere, anywhere. Having decided, with strong and compelling reasons, to take flight from Vietnam, and now sojourning in a country of first asylum that does not want them, has determined them as non-refugees and will subject them to repatriation, the Vietnamese migrants have become stateless; they carve out their provisional, minimal existence within the 'cracks' of nation states, while, in the meantime, helplessly watching themselves being classified, labelled, stigmatized, reclassified and relabelled. The agony of the Arendtian condition of statelessness persists. For the states, this 'curse bears the germs of a deadly sickness' (Arendt 1973: 290). For the Vietnamese boat people, this curse bears testimony to the nation states of this century which, in the face of their self-interests and the various attendant dilemmas, could not help themselves.

References

Arendt, H. (1973) *The Origins of Totalitarianism*, 5th edition, New York: Harcourt Brace Jovanovich

Chan Kwok Bun (1990) 'Hong Kong's Response to the Vietnamese Refugees: A Study in Humanitarianism, Ambivalence and Hostility', *Southeast Asian Journal of Social Science*, Special Issue on 'Indochinese Refugees 15 Years Later' edited by Chan Kwok Bun, 18 (1), 94–110

Chan Kwok Bun and L. Lam (1991) 'Vietnamese Boat People in Hong Kong: A Study in Hostility and Distrust', unpublished manuscript, Singapore: Department of Sociology, National University of Singapore, 17 pp.

Chan Kwok Bun and D. Loveridge (1987) 'Refugees "in Transit": Vietnamese in a Refugee Camp in Hong Kong', *International Migration Review*, (21), Fall, 749–59

Chan Kwok Bun et al. (1995) 'Asian Transmigration: Themes, Issues and Debates', in J. H. Ong, Chan Kwok Bun and S. B. Chew (eds) *Crossing Borders: Transmigration in the Asia Pacific*, Singapore: Prentice Hall, 3–32

Davis, L. (1988) 'Hong Kong and the Indochinese Refugees', in Chantavanich and E. B. Reynolds (edS) *Indochinese Refugees: Asylum and Resettlement*, Bangkok: Institute of Asian Studies, Chulalongkorn University, 150–69

Fan, R. (1990) 'Hong Kong and the Vietnamese Boat People: A Hong Kong Perspective', *International Journal of Refugee Law Special Issue*, September, 144–60

Hitchcox, L. (1990) *Vietnamese Refugees in Southeast Asian Camps*, Houndmills: Macmillan

(1991) 'Preliminary Notes on the Circumstances of Vietnamese Asylum Seekers in Hong Kong', Research Report, Oxford: Institute of Anthropology and St Antony's College, University of Oxford, 103 pp.

Johnson, D. H. N. (1980), 'Refugees, Departures and Illegal Migrants', *University of Sydney Law Journal*, (9)

Knudsen, J. C. (1983) 'Boat People in Transit: Vietnamese in Refugee Camps in the Philippines, Hong Kong and Japan', *Bergen Occasional Papers in Social Anthropology*, No. 31, Bergen: University of Bergen, Norway

(1988) *Vietnamese Survivors: Processes Involved in Refugee Coping and Adaptation*, Bergen: University of Bergen, Norway

(1992) *Chicken Wings: Refugee Stories from a Concrete Hell*, Bergen: Magnat Forlag

Lawyers Committee for Human Rights (1989) 'Humane Deterrence: The Treatment of Boat People in Hong Kong', New York: Lawyers Committee for Human Rights, 66 pp.

Le, X. K. (1990) 'Forced Repatriation of Asylum Seekers: The Case of Hong Kong', *International Journal of Refugee Law*, Special Issue, September, 137–43

Muntarbhorn, V. (1992) *The Status of Refugees in Asia*, Oxford: Clarendon Press

Oxfam (1987) *Vietnamese Refugees in Hong Kong: The Way Forward, Hong Kong*, Oxford: Oxfam, 23 pp.

Refugee Action (1986) *Refugees From Vietnam in Hong Kong*, Derby, UK: Refugee Action

Sutter, V. O. (1990), *The Indochinese Refugee Dilemma*, Baton Rouge: Louisiana State University Press

Tarzi, S. M. (1991) 'The Nation-State, Victim Groups and Refugees', *Ethnic and Racial Studies*, 14 (4), October, 441–52

Thomas, Martin (1988) *Vietnamese Boat People in Hong Kong: A Report for the Parliamentary Liberal Party*, London: Parliamentary Liberal Party, 22 pp.

Tsamenyi, B. M. (1983) ' "The Boat People": Are they Refugees?', *Human Rights Quarterly*, 349–73

Wolf, D. (1990) 'A Subtle Form of Inhumanity: Screening of the Boat People in Hong Kong', *International Journal of Refugee Law*, Special Issue, September, 161–71

Yau, S. H. B. (1992) 'Vietnamese Boat People', *The Other Hong Kong Report 1992*, Hong Kong Chinese University Press, 111–25

Zolberg, A. (1983) 'The Formation of New States as a Refugee Generating Process', *The Annals*, (467), 24–38

SOUTHERN EUROPEAN MIGRATION TO AUSTRALIA: DIASPORIC NETWORKS AND CULTURAL TRANSFORMATIONS

GILLIAN BOTTOMLEY

As T. S. Eliot (1935) wisely reminded us in his poetic echo of Herakleitos, time present, past and future are each contained within the others. This fluid and interactive notion of time is particularly pertinent to the process of migration, where different times and places continue to influence the historical present. Within the limits of space available, this contribution will sketch some of the parameters of the historically, socially, culturally and geographically based networks that continue to develop between and beyond Australia and southern Europe as a consequence of migration. These diasporic networks have time depths and global coverage that can make country-specific studies appear rather limited, but, from the perspective of comparative sociology, they also provide insights into countries of immigration because those countries can be seen as particular examples of a range of possibilities. In other words, studies of migratory networks cast a new light on the receiving countries as well as on the experiences of those who migrate. I have developed this comparative and interactive perspective elsewhere, with reference to several immigrant-receiving countries (Bottomley 1992). Here, Australia will be the major focus of attention, as a specific site of immigration from Greece, Italy, Malta, Spain and Portugal.

Despite debates about precedence and hegemony, all non-Aboriginal Australians are of relatively recent immigrant origin. The celebration of two hundred years of European settlement in 1988, for example, coincided with the thousandth anniversary of the Greek city of Thessaloniki. In the same year – to extend the comparison – the city of Melbourne had a larger Greek-born population than any Greek city other than Athens and Thessaloniki – an indication of the magnitude of Greek emigration to Australia within one generation.

Although Australia has been largely populated by immigration, this process markedly increased in pace and diversification after the Second World War. In 1947, the Australian government established a Depart-ment of Immigration to oversee a comprehensive programme of planned migration, which transformed the population during the second half of the twentieth century. At the census taken in that year, less than 10 per cent of the predominantly Anglophone population of 7,666,358 were born overseas, and 60 per cent of those came from Britain. Within forty years the population had grown to 15,602,156; 22 per cent were overseas born and less than one-third of immigrants were British. According to the 1986 census, 14 per cent of the population daily used a language other than English and 5 per cent of the total population were of non-European descent (Jupp 1991). In the census of 1991, settlers from Greece, Italy, Malta, Spain and Portugal accounted for more than half a million people. If one includes second- and third-generation descendants of immigrants, this figure rises to one and a half million.

Patterns of settlement and survival

The classic reference work on southern European migration was written by a demographer and social historian, Charles Price. His scholarly and elegant work *Southern Europeans in Australia* (1963) covered the geographical, social and political background as well as the migration and settlement experiences of settlers from 'the Mediterranean islands, the Iberian, Italian and Balkan peninsulas and the continental zones connecting these peninsulas' (Price 1963: 3). Price noted, and it is worth repeating, that the term 'southern European' and the various national labels included within it, conceal a great diversity of populations and inevitably falsify the complexities of migration streams. For example, the Greek-speaking population includes people from Egypt, Romania, Asia Minor, Cyprus and other parts of the Greek diaspora, with quite specific and different historical, social and cultural experiences, which also require specific analyses. In the case of people described as Italian, such differences may also be inflected by the kind of regionally-based linguistic, economic and socio-political distinctions delineated by Gramsci (1971) in his essay, 'The Southern Question'. Bearing these limitations in mind, I shall continue to use national designations, while attempting to recognize regional, political and economic differences.

Table 11.4: *Settlers in Australia from southern Europe, 1891–1947*

	1891	1921	1947
Italians	3,900	7,250	33,700
Greeks	600	4,600	12,500
Maltese	–	10	1,400
Spanish (Basques and Catalans), Portuguese, southern French	1,000	1,700	1,500

Source: Price (1963: 11).

The earliest Italian migrants to Australia were Catholic missionaries, who worked with Spanish priests among the Aboriginal population during the 1840s. The gold rush of the 1850s drew larger numbers, including Raffaello Carboni, who joined and described the famous Eureka Stockade rebellion of 1854 (Carboni 1855). Few Greek and Spanish migrants appear in records from the first half of the nineteenth century, but the Greek population of Sydney was large enough in 1898 to establish a Greek Orthodox community and church, together with a school in which the children of immigrants could learn some of the rudiments of Greek language and history. Maltese emigration was encouraged by the British as part of their imperial strategy, and a group of seventy men were sent to the sugar plantations of northern Queensland in 1833 in an unsuccessful experiment in contract labour (York 1988).

In general, southern European immigration was minimal until the late nineteenth century, as Table 11.4 indicates:

By 1947, figures demonstrate a marked increase in absolute numbers, but also in the proportion of southern Europeans in the total immigrant intake. In comparative terms, their migration was much more significant in Australia than in the USA, where northern Europeans predominated (Price 1963: 10).

Immigrants from southern Europe have always encountered xenophobia in Australia, in various forms that have included official descriptions of them as 'undesirable', 'cheap black labour' and 'semi-white', unofficial designations as 'dagoes' and 'wogs' and

outright racist attacks. In 1934, 'anti-dago' riots broke out in the goldfields of Western Australia, when British-Australian miners looted southern European shops and burned Italian, Greek and Slav hotels, clubs and houses. The miners claimed that migrants had undercut their wages – a frequent and partly factual claim that fails to explain the extent of anti-immigrant feeling. In practice, southern European workers readily joined and became influential members of trade unions. Many were also non-competitive with British Australians in that they became owners of properties or businesses. Moreover, large numbers returned to their countries of origin in times of economic hardship, as in the late 1920s and, more recently, since the mid-1970s. One aspect of diasporic networks is their function as communication channels, providing information about relative advantage and disadvantage. Most southern European immigrants had access to news from kin in other countries, and often had the added comparative perspective of people who came from countries with long traditions of emigration and who had lived in or near major ports such as Naples, Genoa, Piraeus and Barcelona.

Another significant characteristic of migration from southern Europe is that it flourished despite a relative lack of governmental assistance. The mass migration programme favoured British immigrants, then through a descending hierarchy of those deemed most similar to the British – mostly northern Europeans – through to southerners and non-Europeans. During the periods of heavy European immigration, in the 1950s and 1960s, only about one-quarter of southern Europeans were assisted immigrants compared with three-quarters or more of those from the north. The southern European pattern of self help had several consequences. One is what Price called 'chain migration', whereby immigrants assisted kin and friends to follow their example, notably depleting the population of islands such as Kythera, Ithaca and Lipari. Another was that southern Europeans faced additional economic hardship, as they struggled to pay back loans and to support other emigrants. These shared struggles increased the emphasis on solidarity among kin or among those who came from the same village or region. What are often interpreted as cultural tendencies to communality have also been essential survival strategies.

Not surprisingly, immigrants tended to settle in areas where familiar institutions, such as churches and food shops, had already been established and where it was possible to continue to speak one's mother tongue. Despite – or perhaps because of – their rural

PLATE 17: Proud Greek-Australian proprietors outside their refreshment rooms
in Singleton, New South Wales, 1911.

origins, few southern Europeans moved into the countryside, especially in the post-1947 period when employment became dominated by industry. Nevertheless, some fruit and wine producing areas have sizeable populations of Italian, Greek and Maltese speakers. The prosperous New South Wales country town of Griffith was the site of an early experiment in bilingual broadcasting, when the 'father of multiculturalism', Al Grassby, who later became Minister for Immigration, introduced bilingual radio programmes in 1952 (Huber 1977). Another aspect of the generally urban settlement pattern is that a number of southern Europeans became what Price called 'metropolitan farmers', developing large market gardens and orchards on the outskirts of cities. These were overtaken by urban growth, hence transformed into valuable real estate. Macquarie University, for example, stands on the site of market gardens established by Italian immigrants, many of whom still live in the area in rather stereotypical 'success villas' of palatial proportions, surrounded by flowers and the occasional domestic vegetable garden.

One of a number of specific patterns of settlement was that of Greeks, mainly from the island of Kythera,

who established café-milkbars in New South Wales and in some Victorian and Queensland country towns. These families have gained almost mythic status as providers of sustenance for travellers and locals, and might even have invented the 'typically Australian' meal, the mixed grill. Interestingly, many of the people who established these restaurants returned to live in cities, closer to Greek churches, clubs and coffee-houses, once they had supported their offspring through a professional education. This kind of trajectory contradicts a simple notion that immigrants assimilate over time by becoming more like the 'natives'. To some extent, people could relax and enjoy their cultural capital, once they had fulfilled their primary family obligations (Bottomley 1979).

Whether in country or city, southern Europeans preferred to be self-employed. At the 1947 census, half of Italian-born males were in this category. Greeks were even more concentrated, with 72 per cent working in the catering industry, mostly as business proprietors. By comparison, barely one-quarter of Australian-born males were either self-employed or employers (Collins 1992: 75). Many of these businesses were, and are, run by families working

PLATE 18: Victoria Street, Darlinghurst, 1993, showing Italian cafés and influence.

long hours in unpropitious circumstances, but some have been highly successful enterprises, and the catering and construction industries are particular enclaves of southern European/Australian million-aires. There is, however, a marked divide between pre-war and post-war settlers, mainly defined by occupation. By 1971, for example, almost 60 per cent of Greek-born workers were labourers and operatives, and Italian-born men were heavily employed in manufacturing and construction. Similarly, southern European women were concentrated in manufacturing during the 1960s and 1970s.

More recently, the decline in both manufacturing and southern European immigration has combined with a shift in employment patterns and higher representation in employer and self-employed categories, especially among Greek and Italian-born men (i.e. some 25 per cent compared with 16 per cent of Australian-born men, according to 1986 figures). The Maltese, Spanish and Portuguese have remained mostly wage labourers (Jones 1991, Table A.12). More Greek and Italian-born women than Australian-born women were classed as employers and self-employed in the 1986 census, but a relatively higher proportion are not in the labour force, indicating another change from their high level of participation in the 1960s and 1970s. Despite these movements, southern Europeans are under-represented in pro-fessional occupations, although this changes in the second generation. Second- and third-generation Greeks, both men and women, have a particularly high proportion of professionals in the 25–54 age bracket (Jones 1991, Tables B.18, B.19, C.18, C.19).

Culture and communality

With notable exceptions, southern European settle-ment in Australia remains predominantly urban. Almost 98 per cent of first-generation Greeks, Portuguese and Spanish, and some 93 per cent of Italians and Maltese, are urban dwellers. As a result, Australian cities are obviously heterogeneous, and some urban areas show a predominantly southern European influence. One example in Melbourne is around Lygon Street, Carlton, where elegant food and clothing shops, as well as numerous restaurants and cafés, are Italian-owned and act as a social focus for young Italo-Australians and for a wider range of people delighted by a lifestyle that differs markedly from the Anglo-Irish pub and pie. Largely as a result of the diversity of the immigrant intake, Australian cities have become treasure troves for both gourmets and gourmands, with a vast range of restaurants, cafés, and food and wine shops. Italians and Greeks pioneered the reconstruction of the Australian diet at every level, and maintain a certain dominance despite the more recent increase in South Asian migration. Spanish, Portuguese and Maltese migrants have a much lower profile, the former being perhaps swamped by the larger population of Spanish-speaking Latin Americans. In the case of Italians and Greeks, cultural input at this level has been transformative.

Despite relative concentrations of people of one nationality, Australia has not developed immigrant ghettoes. In practice, residential concentrations are not the homogeneous 'communities' of common parlance, but are usually the site of contradictory tendencies. On the one hand, proximity can enhance an awareness of differences rather than similarities between members of the same national grouping. For example, there is some rivalry and limited social interaction between Italians from the Veneto compared with those from Calabria who have settled in Griffith, as well as in the 'Italian' suburb of Leichhardt in Sydney (Huber 1977). Robert Pascoe (1992: 94) notes that 'Italy's stubborn regionalism is everywhere evident in immigrant neighbourhoods.' At the same time, a sense of 'community' can be generated in the sharing of churches, newspapers and shopping areas, and by economic and political cooperation at the local level. Pascoe also analyses the significance of locally based Italian festivals (1992: 95) which 'sacralise the urban environment – often in contest with the host culture'. Melbourne, in particular, has taken over the *fiesta* as a prototypical, and increasingly hybrid mode of celebration. Other, more clearly 'ethnic' rituals such as Orthodox Easter, have also become increasingly popular with non-Orthodox Australians.

Official multicultural policies of the last twenty years have also encouraged contradictory tendencies. One is the development of a remarkable hybridity, most clearly seen in the arts, but also apparent in everyday life, and in the increasingly mixed ancestral backgrounds of the population. In 1988, the 'pure Anglo-Celtic element' constituted 48 per cent of the population, but the mixed and fastest-growing section was 37 per cent (Price 1993: 8). The other tendency has arisen from the definition of multiculturalism as a form of pluralism, where ethnicity takes precedence over other social characteristics. This model contains a notion of ethnic 'communities' as homogeneous and clearly delineated entities represented by (mostly male and middle-class) 'community leaders': a definition being increasingly challenged, either by direct opposition or by the obvious erosion of these politically defined boundaries.

Increasing unemployment and decreasing social welfare provisions have nourished conditions for resurgent racism, but Asian and Muslim migrants, and Australian Aborigines, are the major butts of racist action, undertaken both by Anglo-Australians and by people of non-Anglo origin. The positive aspects of hybridity require infrastructural support to erode continuing sector inequalities, and it is not clear that the policy of multiculturalism, despite its unquestioned successes, is adequate for such a task.

From another perspective, some of the most impressive reflections of the heterogeneity of the Australian population can be seen in creative work. In literature, music, performance and plastic arts, imaginations and energies have been nourished by a multilingual and internationalist population whose experience of crossing borders, challenging pre-conceptions, coping with the pains of separation, fragmentation and hostility, as well as the resources of rich cultural understandings, have resulted in highly sophisticated and imaginative forms of artistic representation. In these endeavours, as in other aspects of Australian life, southern Europeans and their offspring have effectively moved from the margins to the centre.

Note

I am indebted to the photographer Effy Alexakis for the illustrations accompanying this text. Effy, an Australian of Greek parentage, is working on an ever-growing photographic project representing immigration experiences, return migration and diasporic imagery.

References

Bottomley, G. (1979) *After the Odyssey: A Study of Greek Australians*, Brisbane: University of Queensland Press

(1992) *From Another Place: Migration and the Politics of Culture*, Melbourne: Cambridge University Press

Carboni, R. (1855) *The Eureka Stockade*, Melbourne: J. P. Atkinson

Collins, J. (1992) 'Cappucino Capitalism: Italian Immigrants and Australian Business', in S. Castles et al. (eds) *Australia's Italians*, Sydney: Allen & Unwin

Eliot, T. S. (1935) 'Burnt Norton', in *Collected Poems, 1909–1962*, London: Faber & Faber

Gramsci, A. (1971) 'The Southern Question', in Q. Hoare and G. Nowell Smith (editors and translators) *Prison Notebooks*, New York: International Publishers

Huber, R. (1977) *From Pasta to Pavlova*, Brisbane: University of Queensland Press

Jones, F. L. (1991) *Ancestry Groups in Australia: A Descriptive Overview*, Canberra: Office of Multicultural Affairs

Jupp, J. (1991) *Immigration*, Melbourne: University of Melbourne Press

Pascoe, R. (1992) 'Place and Community: The Construction of Italo-Australian Space', in Castles et al. (eds) *Australia's Italians*, Sydney: Allen & Unwin

Price, C. (1963) *Southern Europeans in Australia*, Melbourne: Oxford University Press

— (1993) 'Ethnic Intermixture in Australia', *People and Place*, 1 (1), 6–8

York, B. (1988) 'Early Maltese Immigration' and 'Maltese Settlement in Sydney', in J. Jupp (ed.) *The Australian People: An Encyclopaedia of the Nation, its People and their Origins*, Sydney: Angus & Robertson

MIGRATION AND THE FORMATION OF MALAYSIA AND SINGAPORE

LIAN KWEN FEE

When the idea of the nation state emerged as the basis of a modern political community in Malaya as a consequence of decolonization after the Second World War, migrants previously viewed as necessary labour in the colonial state became potential citizens. This produced changes in the jurisdiction and membership status of not only migrants but also indigenes, the experience of which was traumatic for both as they struggled to reconcile their ethnic past with a community in search of a political identity – or what is commonly referred to as nation-building.

As the term implies, nation-building is essentially a synthetic process engineered by intellectual minorities. States that were a direct consequence of colonization were imposed on peoples whose leaders, on independence, were left the infrastructure of a state but not the unifying nationality. In ethnically heterogeneous societies like Malaya, when independence was transferred to the hands of local leaders in less than a decade, the task of nation-building became urgent.

Nation-state formation facilitates the process of ethnicization. Ethnic identities become the basis of political group formation in an open and competitive political system. The politicization of ethnic identities is made acute when ethnic distinctions are reinforced by the difference between immigrant and indigenous statuses – as in the case of the distinction between non-Malay (Chinese/Indian) and Malay respectively in Malaya. In the struggle to articulate a Malayan nationality such statuses were politicized.

Concomitant with the building of nationhood and the formation of the modern state is the development of citizenship. If states actively seek the allegiance of individuals and require of them certain obligations, individuals too expect them to ensure access to political participation and economic opportunities. The requirements for citizenship status then become a point of contention between ethnic communities as they compete for political control in newly independent states. While citizenship is usually viewed as having a formal and legal status, conceptions of nationality are less clear. While it may appear that nationality implies citizenship and vice versa, one can be a citizen without having a sense of nationality. Hence nationality and citizenship issues should be kept analytically separate.

State-formation, nation-building and citizenship development may take on separate trajectories and should be understood as such. The presence of immigrants in Malaya, the product of colonial labour policy, posed a daunting problem to a nation state in formation. What follows is an attempt to weave the phenomenon of migration in Malaya into these trajectories, which eventually led to the formation of Malaysia and the separation of Singapore as an independent state.

Migration and the emergence of plural society

The understanding of migration in Malaya should begin with the migrants' perception of their intention to uproot themselves, and this has much to do with the culture of migration. Within the Malay world the experience of migration is expressed in the term *merantau* (Wang 1985: 44). To *merantau*, Wang Gungwu writes, is to leave one's home or village temporarily, for a long time or forever – to work hard, seek knowledge, skills or experience which will contribute to the security and happiness of oneself, relatives or the village. There is no compulsion to return. In contrast the Chinese/Indian conception is best encapsulated in the word 'sojourn', which means to dwell temporarily in a place, the eventual intention being to return home. It is understandable that the concept of *merantau* does not include the idea of ultimately returning home. Most Malay migration occurred within the regional confines of the Malay archipelago, the 'home' of the Malay population.

The main flood of Chinese migration did not begin until well into the second half of the nineteenth century when the world demand for tin grew. By 1911 more than half the total Chinese population in the Federated Malay States lived in the tin-mining districts of Kinta and Kuala Lumpur, while the rest were concentrated in and around the ports of Singapore, Penang and Malacca (Smith 1964: 175).

While the Chinese dominated immigration to Malaya at the close of the nineteenth century the first two decades of the twentieth century saw the massive influx of Indian labour as a consequence of the large-scale development of European-owned rubber estates in the west coast states. Unlike the Chinese, whose occupations were more varied (they were involved in mining, rice trade and milling, and the cultivation of commercial crops such as sugar, pepper and gambier), the Indians were primarily employed in the rubber plantations.

A major consequence of migration was the evolution of a 'plural society', within which political developments in Malaya in the first half of this century may be viewed. In 1911, less than 24 per cent of the Chinese population of the Straits Settlements were local-born; the corresponding figure for the Federated Malay States was just over 8 per cent (Smith 1964: 174). The number of Straits-born Indians was very low. By the mid-1920s the Chinese population showed clear signs of being a permanently settled community as more females and the families of immigrants arrived, and as the proportion of local-born increased. In contrast, the Indians continued to be a transient community for two reasons (Smith 1964: 176). First, it was easier, quicker and less expensive for Indians to return to their homeland than for the Chinese. Second, political conditions in India and China encouraged the Indians to return but deterred the Chinese. The depression in the 1930s drove more Indians back to India than Chinese to China. Independence in India in 1947 precipitated another exodus of Indians from Malaya (Smith 1964: 182). The communist victory in the civil war in China in 1949 effectively closed the option for those Chinese, particularly the China-born, to return.

One important development to accompany the changing demographic composition of the Chinese population in Malaya in the period under review was the proliferation of private Chinese schools, sponsored by surname, district or dialect associations, business guilds and wealthy individuals (Murray 1971: 61). Dialects were initially used as the medium of instruction, reinforcing intra-ethnic identities within the Chinese population. The supply of teachers and textbooks came from China. After the 1911 revolution Chinese education in Malaya reflected the sweeping tide of Chinese nationalism, and after 1920 the medium of instruction shifted to Mandarin (Murray 1971: 62). By the mid-twentieth century the sojourner status of the Chinese had given way to a permanent community in Malaya, intent on articulating an ethnic

identity in 'Malayan' terms. The Indians, for reasons already referred to, took longer to come to terms with their political identity in Malaya.

Migration literature on Malaya mainly refers to the Chinese and Indians. With few exceptions Indonesian migration to the Malay peninsula has escaped the attention of scholars. One such exception is the work of Bahrin (1967: 273) who noted that the periods of maximum Indonesian arrivals coincided with the expansion of smallholdings and government-initiated rice cultivation programmes, to which they were most attracted.

Bahrin (1967: 285) also states, on the basis of census reports, that between 1911 and 1957 the Indonesian population never exceeded 15 per cent of the total Malaysian population in Malaya, the only exception being Johore. He concludes that the Indonesian presence was not as great as assumed in the past and their numbers were small relative to the other communities.

However, a note of caution must be sounded. It is notoriously difficult to track the extent of Indonesian immigration even to this day because, given the geographical character of the Indonesian islands in relation to Malaya, the points of arrival were unlikely to coincide with the major ports of disembarkation where statistics were recorded. Official records therefore under-report the Indonesian presence. Because these migrants identified with regional origins such as Javanese, Banjarese, Boyanese and Sumatrans rather than 'Indonesian', they were unlikely to have any impact on political developments in Malaya except within some notion of a Malay identity *vis-à-vis* the Chinese and Indians.

Indonesian migrants, who viewed their leaving home as *merantau* rather than sojourn, were more likely to settle permanently than their Chinese or Indian counterparts for the comparable period. However, this did not prevent attempts at articulating a Malay identity in the peninsula in terms of a 'Greater Indonesia', as will be seen later.

Official estimates of the Federated Malay States in 1935 put the Malay population at 36 per cent of the total (Emerson 1964: 182–3). Rubber and tin, the two major sources of economic production in the Federated Malay States, were controlled by non-Malay interests – estate production in rubber by Europeans and the tin industry by the Chinese. While there were a large number of Malay rubber smallholders, their individual acreages were small compared with those of the Chinese and Indians. The relation between the Malays and the immigrant communities was reversed in the Unfederated Malay States. The number of Malays was almost double that of the non-Malays; the former constituted 66 per cent of the population in 1941 (Lau 1991: 15). The Chinese were a distinct majority in the Straits Settlements. They constituted more than 70 per cent of the population in Singapore in the 1930s (Emerson 1964: 282–3). In the 1931 census 38 per cent of the Chinese in the Settlements were recorded as Malaya-born.

Taken as a whole, Malays were the dominant ethnic group with close to 54 per cent of the population in British Malaya in 1911 (Lau 1991: 15). They were outnumbered by 1931 and formed only 41 per cent of the population in 1941. The Indians remained constant at 14 per cent in this period. The Chinese grew from 34 per cent in 1911 to 43 per cent by 1941, outnumbering the Malays. 'The presence of an economically preponderant and majority non-Malay community by the early 1930s', Lau (1991) comments, 'ensured that, while Malay rights could not be neglected, those of the Chinese and Indians equally could not be ignored.'

In search of nationality

British control over Malaya was effectively established by the 1910s. However, the colonial administration was fragmented into three – the most organized Straits Settlements, the Federated Malay States and the loosely administered Unfederated Malay States. It was inevitable that the administration of the three constituencies had to be rationalized to reduce government expenditure. The drive towards centralization and the establishment of a cohesive state began after the First World War, but it was not until the end of the Second World War that the British government put in place a concrete plan to incorporate the Federated Malay States, Unfederated Malay States, Penang and Malacca into a unitary state called the Malayan Union. Committed to a policy of decolonization Britain viewed the proposed union as a prelude to nurturing a common Malayan nationality – from a plural society to an integrated community.

A liberal citizenship policy would have granted citizen status to anyone born in the union including Singapore or who had resided in either territory for a minimum period (Andaya and Andaya 1982: 255). Singapore was excluded from the Malayan Union partly because the British feared that Malay support would not be forthcoming if the island's predominantly Chinese population qualified to be citizens (Andaya and Andaya 1982: 254). It, however, left the door open for Singapore to be part of the mainland at

a future date by making it eligible for its inhabitants to be given Malayan Union citizenship. Another significant provision of the Malayan Union was the transfer of the sovereignty of the Malay rulers to the British Crown, a major departure from colonial policy in pre-war Malaya (Turnbull 1989: 229).

Malay objections to the union were swift and widespread, in contrast to the lukewarm support given by the non-Malays who stood to gain most from the proposals. The opposition was led by the English-educated Malay administrative elite, which had close connections with the Malay rulers. The United Malays' National Organization, which dominated the government after independence, was formed to represent Malays and fight the British plan. The British, surprised by the hostility, entered into negotiations with the Malays. They revoked the union and replaced it with the Federation of Malaya Agreement in 1948, which laid the blueprint for self-government in 1957. The agreement reverted to the pre-war policy of recognizing Malaya as primarily a Malay country (Ratnam 1967: 77).

The sovereignty of the Malay rulers was restored and the special position of the Malays was preserved (Stockwell 1979: 92). Qualification for citizenship was made more restrictive for non-Malays, which included a longer period of residence and knowledge of the Malay or English language. Furthermore, birth and residence in Singapore were no longer regarded as grounds for citizenship on the mainland (Ratnam 1967: 79). A 'Malay' was automatically a citizen, and was constitutionally defined as a person who habitually spoke the Malay language, professed the Muslim religion and followed Malay custom (Ratnam 1967: 78). The emphasis in such a definition was on cultural attributes and would have applied to migrants from Indonesia but excluded those Chinese and Indians who were born in Malaya (Ratnam 1967: 79).

The effect was to create two types of citizenship. The citizenship provisions in the independence constitution distinguished between indigenes and immigrants – they favoured the former who were later officially described as *bumiputra* (prince of the soil) to further enhance the distinction. For this reason the practice of citizenship worked against the nurturance of a common nationality. Out of the crisis of the Malayan Union was born a Malay *ethnie* (otherwise referred to as *bangsa Melayu),* the French term which combined cultural differences with a sense of historical community (Smith 1986: 21–2). Malay ethnic identity was subsequently institutionalized in the constitution and the government.

In a belated attempt to head off the pro-Malay federation proposals, a loose coalition comprising the Malayan Democratic Union (MDU), the Communist Party of Malaya, the Malay Nationalist Party, a group of Malay intellectuals with sympathies for a greater Indonesia and several Chinese business interests was organized to oppose the revised scheme (Yeo 1973b: 34). What is noteworthy about this development is that it was essentially Singapore-based, the initiative taken by middle-class left-wing intellectuals who were anti-colonial and committed to fighting for a united and independent Malaya, which included Singapore (Yeo 1973a: 89). The MDU, for example, was largely spearheaded by this group. They also expounded a non-partisan Malayan political identity transcending ethnic loyalties. The joint coalition collapsed mainly because of its failure to win widespread Chinese support, especially the powerful business interests (Yeo and Lau 1991: 122). The majority of the China-born were indifferent to the federation proposals probably because they could still entertain the option of returning to China until the communist victory in 1949.

The exclusion of Singapore from the Malayan Union scheme, subsequently underlined in the Federation Agreement, conditioned political development on the island and left the question of merger hanging in the political agendas of the two territories for the next fifteen years. During this period the Malays on the mainland, the crisis of the union still fresh in their minds, viewed with suspicion any proposal to include Singapore's predominantly Chinese population in a unification plan. In 1954 the People's Action Party was founded by a group of university and English-educated graduates, which included Lee Kuan Yew and the two Malayan-born Goh Keng Swee and Toh Chin Chye. This influential group believed that the time had come to organize and foster a broad-based Malayan nationalist movement, sentiments which echoed its forerunner – the MDU, which transcended narrow communal loyalties; and to fight for an independent Malaya which included Singapore (Yeo and Lau 1991: 128). To this end the People's Action Party assiduously cultivated a Malayan outlook, accepting Malay as the national language and supporting Malay education, to demonstrate its commitment to Malaya.

The proportion of Singapore Chinese who were Malayan-born grew from 60 per cent in 1947 to 73 per cent in 1957 (Smith 1964: 177). Despite the fact that the majority of Chinese were local-born, most of them were educated in private schools, the curriculum

of which espoused a Chinese nationalism that had grown out of decades of resentment against the humiliation inflicted by the Western powers and Japan on China, and the impotence of the Manchu rulers. In the aftermath of the communist victory in China in 1949, the Chinese in both the mainland and Singapore were forced to come to terms, emotionally and politically, with their identity in Malaya.

From 1948 when the Federation Agreement was signed until Malayan independence in 1957, the two major protagonists, the Malays and the Chinese, were involved in protracted negotiations with each other and the British over the final touches of the independence constitution. The Malayan Chinese Association, founded by mainly English-educated and Straits-born Chinese in the mainland, conceded Malay political dominance in exchange for a more liberal citizenship policy that would make it possible for more Chinese to qualify as citizens. The Chinese-educated were unwilling to accept that Malaya was *Tanah Melayu* (Malay land), and that the Malay language and culture were the foundation of the new state. Led by teachers in Chinese schools, they argued that acquisition of citizenship in the new federation meant that the Chinese as a *community* should be treated as equal to the Malay community, and that the Chinese language and culture should be given the same recognition as the Malay language and culture. The new state was to be a 'plural society' in Furnivall's (1956) sense.

In Singapore the People's Action Party, led by Lee Kuan Yew, was locked in a battle with the communists to win the support of the Chinese-educated, from whom it drew its electoral strength. It found itself treading the fine line between appeasing the demands of the Chinese-educated and dampening the Chinese character of the island in order to persuade Tunku, the leader of the United Malays' National Organization, to accept Singapore into a British-initiated expanded federation of Malaysia, which also included the north Borneo states. Tunku finally relented, primarily because he was convinced that left-wing influence in the island could only be checked by Singapore's inclusion.

Malaysia was formed in 1963 but Singapore's stay was short-lived. The People's Action Party became increasingly strident in championing the cause of multiracialism, expressed in the political rhetoric of a 'Malaysian Malaysia', on the mainland. When expounded by the prime minister of Singapore most Malays regarded it as an insidious plan by which they gradually lose their privileges and power to the more industrious Chinese (Leifer 1965: 70). The rhetoric, however, struck a chord with non-Malays on the mainland, who saw it as an effective counter against the rise of Malay nationalist feelings in a state still grappling with its national identity. Singapore separated from Malaysia in 1965, after years of acrimony and turbulence, punctuated by Sino-Malay riots, and became an independent state.

Conclusion

Until the Second World War the colonial administration of Malaya was decentralized in three constituents – the Straits Settlements, where the non-Malay migrant population was predominant, the Unfederated Malay States, where Malay indigenes were the majority, and the Federated Malay States, with a balanced ratio of migrant to indigenes. The attempt to incorporate them into a union was the culmination of partly the inevitable process of state-formation and centralization, and partly the British commitment to disengage itself from the peninsula. The result was the creation of a state without a nation. Critical to the development of an independent political community was the question of its membership and citizenship. The Malayan Union adopted a liberal citizenship policy, which accorded equal status to both migrants and indigenes. However, the Federation Agreement, which revoked the union scheme in the face of Malay opposition, favoured an exclusivist citizenship policy, which privileged indigenes. The politics of citizenship, which preceded independence in 1957, contributed to the emergence of a Malay *ethnie* and a Chinese *ethnie*. For this reason the evolvement of citizenship was divisive and failed to cultivate a unifying nationality. The inclusion of Singapore's predominantly Chinese population in an expanded Malaysia provided migrants with the opportunity to forge a political identity that challenged the rise of Malay *ethnie* on the mainland. The separation of the island from Malaysia was the culmination of a series of pendulum swings, which oscillated from migrant to indigenous priorities. The existence of the two states, whose histories are so intimately woven by their colonial origins, is a final testament to the irreconcilability of migrant and indigenous aspirations.

References

Andaya, B. W. and L. Y. Andaya (1982) *A History of Malaysia*, London: Macmillan

Bahrin, Shamsul (1967) 'The Growth and Distribution of the Indonesian Population in Malaya', *Bijdragen*, (123), 267–86

Emerson, R (1964) *Malaysia: A Study in Direct and Indirect Rule*, Kuala Lumpur: University of Malaya Press

Furnivall, J. S. (1956) *Colonial Policy and Practice*, New York: New York University Press

Lau, A (1991) *The Malayan Union Controversy 1942–1948*, Singapore: Oxford University Press

Leifer, Michael (1965) 'Singapore in Malaysia: The Politics of Federation', *Journal of Southeast Asian History*, 6 (2), 54–70

Murray, D. P. (1971) 'Multilanguage Education and Bilingual-ism: The Formation of Social Brokers in Singapore', PhD dissertation, Stanford University

Ratnam, K. J. (1967) *Communalism and the Political Process in Malaya*, Singapore: University of Malaya Press

Smith, A. D. (1986) *The Ethnic Origins of Nations*, Oxford: Basil Blackwell

Smith, T. E. (1964) 'Immigration and Permanent Settlement of Chinese and Indians in Malaya', in C. D. Cowan (ed.) *The Economic Development of Southeast Asia*, London: George Allen & Unwin, 174–85

Stockwell, A. J. (1979) *British Policy and Malay Politics during the Malayan Union Experiment, 1942–1948*, The Malaysian Branch of the Royal Asiatic Society, Monograph 8

Turnbull, C. M. (1989) *A History of Malaysia, Singapore and Brunei*, Sydney: Allen & Unwin

Wang Gungwu (1985) 'Migration Patterns in History: Malaysia and the Region', *Journal of the Malaysian Branch of the Royal Asiatic Society*, (58), 43–57

Yeo, K. W. (1973a) *Political Development in Singapore 1945–55*, Singapore: Singapore University Press

(1973b) 'The Anti-Federation Movement in Malaya, 1946–48', *Journal of Southeast Asian Studies*, 1 (4), 31–51

Yeo, K. W. and A. Lau (1991) 'From Colonialism to Independence, 1945–1965', in E. Chew and E. Lee (eds) *A History of Singapore*, Singapore: Oxford University Press, 117–53

ILLEGAL INTERNATIONAL MIGRATION IN ASIA

GRAEME HUGO

The last decade has seen a huge increase in the scale of illegal migration both within Asia and from Asia to North America, Europe and, to a lesser extent, Australia. A number of factors have contributed to this development, including the following:

- The greatly increased flow of information to Asian countries of opportunities at potential destinations. This has been facilitated by increased short-term movement of tourists, students and business people to those destinations, and the strengthening of mass media linkages and influences.

- Increasing numbers of friends and family already established (both legally and illegally) in destination countries to provide 'anchors' for potential illegals.

- Increasingly stark contrasts in the labour supply and demand situation in countries, whereby in some nations rapid economic growth and expanding employment demand has come at a time when fertility declines of two decades ago have meant local labour forces are static or shrinking, while in others labour surpluses have been inflated by rapid population growth and slow growth of employment demand.

- With rising levels of education in rapidly developing Asian countries the aspirations of local workers have risen considerably and they are unwilling to take on the so-called '3D' jobs — dangerous, difficult and dirty. Accordingly, demand for unskilled labour in some niches of the economy is being maintained even where there are significant levels of unemployment.

- The development of what can be called an 'immigration industry' involving a diverse group of recruiters, lawyers, agents, organizers, travel agents and intermediaries of various kinds comprising networks linking origin and destination countries. These groups have become crucial gatekeepers in encouraging and facilitating illegal (as well as legal) migration.

- In some cases the great increase in illegal immigration in the Asian region is being implicitly supported if not encouraged by governments at origin and destination through poor policing and little investment in detection of illegals.

- On the other hand, increasingly tight legislation and control of legal family-based immigration in traditional immigration countries and closing of loopholes in immigration regulations has 'forced' potential legal migrants into adopting illegal strategies.

- The development of an 'emigration fever' in some countries (for example Sri Lanka, the Philippines, Pakistan and Bangladesh) where economic and political pressures for emigration are increasing.

- The overall change throughout Asia whereby international migration is increasingly being considered within the calculus of choice of a wider range of socio-economic, gender and ethnic groups in their attempts to improve their life chances.

All these elements have come together to encourage illegal migration of various kinds out of Asian countries. Moreover these migrants are constantly expanding and strengthening social networks between their origin countries and destination areas. These networks inject a self perpetuating dynamism into illegal flows which lead to movement continuing long after original economic reasons for the flow have been superseded or rendered redundant.

Quantification of the scale and composition of illegal migration is by definition not possible since such migrants usually do not pass through border surveillance systems and attempt to avoid being counted in censuses, surveys and other official data collection activities, since a major premium is placed on avoidance of detection by the host government. Moreover, knowledge of the causes and consequences of this movement is limited because field work is also difficult among this group through lack of sampling frames, suspicion and difficulties of detection. Hence, in the summary of contemporary Asian illegal migrations which follows, numbers quoted must be considered as being approximate in the extreme. Nevertheless, the fact that such movement cannot be precisely quantified should not deter recognition of this crucially important phenomenon for the social, economic and demographic situation in origin and destination areas.

Illegal flows involving Asian migrants can be divided into the following types.

- Movements to countries outside the Asian region.
- Movements to Japan and the newly industrializing countries (NICs) or 'economic tigers' of South Korea, Taiwan, Hong Kong and Singapore.
- Movements to other countries in the Asian region.

First, regarding movements outside of the Asian region most attention has been focused recently on the influx of illegal Chinese migrants into the USA, which was estimated in the early 1990s to be occurring at around 100,000 per annum (Mooney and Zyla 1993). A US Senate committee report indicates that a smuggling ring, which organizes this movement, operates 17 to 20 refitted cargo ships and the business is worth $3 billion annually. One official estimate within China is that three-quarters of a million Chinese have emigrated illegally in recent years – 200,000 having settled elsewhere in Asia, 200,000 in the USA, 150,000 in Russia and 100,000 in Europe (*Far Eastern Economic Review*, 31 March 1994: 13). There are also less substantial but nevertheless significant flows from other Asian countries, especially from South Asia.

California is a major destination of such movement and one estimate of the total number of illegals from all areas in the state is above two million (Berthelsen 1993). Of the three million applicants for legalization in the USA under the 1986 law, 147,317 people from Asia have been included, with the largest numbers from the Philippines, Pakistan and India (Papademetriou 1991: 29).

Canada is also experiencing a significant illegal migration from Asia and, although no estimates of numbers are available, the increasing significance of the movement is reflected in enhanced official attempts to intercept these flows. 'Each year tens of millions of people enter Canada as visitors or as migrants. Increasing numbers of people try to bypass regular immigration procedures, often aided by increasingly significant "migrant" smugglers and document forgers. Foreign criminals also try to take advantage of our relatively open borders, and our generous legal system, in order to enter or remain in Canada' (Employment and Immigration Canada 1992: 18). In 1991, 11,520 people were detected with fraudulent travel documents attempting to enter Canada and this must be regarded as only the visible tip of the iceberg of illegal migration into Canada.

In the remaining 'traditional' immigration nation, Australia, it has long been assumed that illegal migration has been of minor significance because of the absence of a common land border with any other nation. Nevertheless, there are strong indications that illegal migration is increasing in significance and Australia is one of the few countries in which it is possible to gain relatively accurate estimates of these flows. This is because all persons arriving and departing complete a card which allows matching and detection of 'overstayers'. The stock of detected overstayers in 1992 was 81,500 and the significance of this can be appreciated by the fact that the net gain by legal migration to Australia for 1992/3 was 35,100. The most common Asian country of origin among the overstayers was China (9.8 per cent), but Indonesia, Fiji, Japan, the Philippines, Malaysia, Thailand, Korea, Tonga, Sri Lanka and Pakistan accounted for another 36.5 per cent (Shu and Khoo 1993: 44).

In the early l990s it was estimated that there were between two and three million illegal migrants in the European Community nations (Ardittis 1990: 461). The estimate of current illegal inflows are around one million persons per year (Fraser 1993: 81). While east Europeans and Africans are very important in this flow it is clear that Asians are also an important component. The flow of illegal migrants from Asia to Europe via Russia has become of major significance. *The Moscow News* (Ivanov 1993) reported that 'organizing the flow of illegal immigrants is becoming a lucrative well organized business. ... It is run by a huge syndicate involving up to 5000 people in Southeast Asia and Iraq as well as individual officials within the Russian emigration authorities.'

Some of the largest flows of illegal migrants in Asia are directed towards Japan and the so-called 'economic tigers' – Taiwan, South Korea, Hong Kong and Singapore. Indeed these flows have grown such that a columnist in a regional newspaper (*Bangkok Post*, 14 March 1993) designated 1992 the 'Year of the Illegal Migrant'. Ivanov (1993: 23) says that 'the number of illegals in Japan and the Newly Industrializing Countries of East Asia has skyrocketed in the last decade going from less than 200,000 in 1980 to as many as 2–3 million today, with most of these illegal workers being supplied by their less well-off neighbours.' In these nations, rapidly expanding economies have created labour shortages, especially in unskilled and semi-skilled areas. In Japan, for example, a government report of 1991 projected shortfalls of labour of 5.2 million workers by 1996 and 9.1 million in 2010 (Isberto 1993). Despite strong government barriers to immigration and policies to encourage Japanese investors to locate in labour surplus nations in Asia, there has been a significant influx of legal as well as illegal workers into Japan in recent years so that in 1992 there were 1.22 million foreign workers in Japan (*Asahi Evening News*, 2 April 1993). Sassen (1993: 83–4) shows that the former include professions, unskilled company trainees, students, 'entertainers' and descendants of Japanese people born abroad. Official estimates of the number of overstayers in Japan approached 300,000 by the end of 1992, most of them Asian (*Japan Times*, 25 February 1993). This was an increase of 35.3 per cent over 1992. The largest numbers were Thais (53,219), South Koreans (37,491), Malaysians (34,529), Filipinos (34,296), Chinese (29,091), Bangladeshis (8161), Pakistanis (8056) and Taiwanese (7283). Many work in low-skill occupations with the majority of male illegal migrants apprehended being in the construction (47 per cent) and industrial (40 per cent) areas (Spencer 1992: 758). On the other hand, many female illegal migrants work 'as bar hostesses, with others involved as prostitutes and strippers in the ironically named "morals industry". Women are also employed in industrial and commercial positions as domestic servants and waitresses' (Spencer 1992: 757). The tendency for the greater proportion of female illegal migrants to work in areas other than the hostess area has increased in recent years. Moreover, as the scale of illegal migration has increased the proportion of females has been reduced. Nevertheless, the vulnerability of female illegal migrants in Japan to all kinds of exploitation is a major and increasing problem. One aid group for Asian women in Japan puts the number of illegal women workers at 300,000. Sakamaki (1994: 38) explains that many of these women

enter Japan with a fake passport and are employed in the entertainment industry by Japanese yakuza or gangsters. ... The number of foreign women employed in the Japanese sex trade has been rising, say analysts, because Japanese men have grown more cautious in seeking sex abroad for fear of contracting Aids. Instead, the yakuza have been importing Asian women, mainly Filipinos and Thais, to work in Japan.

The demand for labour in Japan appears not to have been significantly dampened by the depression of the early 1990s. The Tokyo Chamber of Commerce has lobbied for an immediate open quota of 600,000 jobs

for foreigners (Prasai 1993: 23). However, opinion in Japan about the desirability of immigration of foreign workers remains divided. Almost half of all local governments in Japan bar foreign nationals from taking jobs in their offices (*Mainini Daily News*, 15 April 1993). In 1990 adjustments were made to the Immigration Control and Refugee Recognition Act to expand the number of categories for which skilled workers would be accepted in Japan on a temporary basis, but on the other hand they sought to restrict the inflow of unskilled and semi-skilled workers and imposed sanctions on those employing and contracting illegal workers. However, the law does little to control the activities of the contractors and criminal gangs in procuring illegal workers (Morita 1992). Nevertheless, the demand for labour is still in evidence and there has been if anything an acceleration of illegal worker migration to Japan (Nagayama 1992). A crucial question relates to the extent to which illegal migrants intend to settle permanently in Japan. One study of Filipinos (Ballescas 1993: 45) found that most

could not give a definite answer regarding their intended length of residence. ... Despite unequal pay and benefits compared with Japanese workers as well as problems such as loneliness and alienation within Japanese society, the respondents wanted to stay in Japan until they could fulfil their plans to set up their own business to uplift and secure the condition of their family or to be able to buy their own house and lot upon their return to the Philippines.

Although South Korea is one of the major sources of illegal migrants to Japan it also is experiencing an influx of illegal migrant workers from elsewhere in Asia. Estimates of the numbers of illegals range between 70,000 and 100,000 with an increasing trend evident in recent years (Isberto 1993: 93). As with Japan, demand for unskilled workers is being created by a rapidly expanding economy in a context where low fertility for two decades has resulted in slow growth of the local workforce. 'South Korean immigration laws ban foreigners from working in the country except for those under technical training and a few specialized occupations. Faced with rising wages and growing labour shortages, the government tried in 1991 to devise means for importing labour. But Seoul backed off when trade unions raised a howl. As a result "irregular migration" has been increasing' (Isberto 1993: 93). Filipinos are the largest group numbering between 25,000 and 30,000, but there are also substantial numbers from Pakistan, Sri Lanka, Bangladesh and Nepal (*Philippine Daily Register*, 25

May 1993). Monthly wages, even in the most exploitative situation in South Korea, still approximate the annual GNP per capita in the migrants' home countries. Some 90 per cent of illegals in Korea work in manufacturing where substantial labour shortages are being reported. For example, in 1991 an association of small and medium-sized enterprises claimed they were short of 360,000 workers (Isberto 1993). Similarly, Baum (1990: 16) reports that 'the lure of Taiwan's economic miracle and the exaggerated promises of overseas Chinese labour recruiters in Southeast Asia have drawn foreigners to the island in the expectation of high wages, comfortable living standards and plentiful jobs'. Official estimates of the number of illegals is 41,000 but 'social agencies' of the Roman Catholic Church of Taiwan, however, estimate that there are at least 200,000 illegal foreign workers on the island — mainly from the Philippines, Malaysia, Thailand and Indonesia. Some come from as far away as India, Pakistan and Africa and many have migrated from Sri Lanka since civil war erupted there.' More recently, there has been an increase in illegal movement across the Taiwan Straits from China, especially Fujian province. One mid-1993 estimate put the numbers at around 36,000 with 500 being arrested and deported each month (Baum 1993: 24). This has become a significant issue in the delicate negotiations between the two nations carried out by 'Taipei's Taiwan Straits Exchange Foundation and Peking's Association for Relations Across the Taiwan Straits' (Baum 1994: 14). Most illegal migrants in Taiwan are male and work in low-skilled occupations. The government has responded to labour shortages in specific industries and projects by concluding temporary worker agreements with the Philippines in an attempt to reduce illegal migration (Tsay 1992: 654). Planners and entrepreneurs tend to favour the legalization of foreign workers to maintain Taiwan's international competitiveness, but labour leaders are opposed to the use of imported labour (Selya 1992).

Illegal migration to Hong Kong from China has been important since the early 1960s (Wu and Inglis 1992: 603). Initially the migrants were treated sympathetically, but in the early 1970s vigorous attempts to track down illegal migrants from China were initiated. Nevertheless, Hong Kong Immigration Department estimates of illegal migration from China between the 1970s and 1990 amount to 614,214 (Wu and Inglis 1992: 605). There is an annual quota on legal migrants from China of 27,500 and while Hong Kong was 'quite successful in the 1980s in controlling

the number of illegal immigrants from China ... this will be subject to increasing pressures as the number of those who consider they have a "legitimate" reason to be in Hong Kong increases' (Wu and Inglis 1992: 605). Another major stream of migrants to Hong Kong has been the 'boat people' from Vietnam. In 1988, amid accusations that significant numbers of these boat people were not genuine refugees, the Hong Kong government reclassified them as illegal migrants and subjected them to detention and possible repatriation. Between 1975 and 1990, 190,785 Vietnamese boat people arrived in Hong Kong and 141,139 subsequently left, most of them to third countries of settlement, although repatriations became more significant after the 1988 reclassification of boat people as illegal migrants. In recent years illegal migrations from other Southeast Asian countries have increased. Some enter the colony legally to work as domestic workers but then illegally seek other work once they are in Hong Kong (*South China Morning Post*, 10 January 1993). China represents a vast reservoir of potential illegal migrant workers not only to Hong Kong but globally, with a labour surplus in rural areas alone of some 130 million people (*South China Morning Post*, 10 July 1993).

Singapore, the other NIC, has a substantial legal foreign workforce and tight immigration policy with draconian penalties. Despite this 'Tiny Singapore has anywhere between 200,000–300,000 undocumented workers, the bulk of them are Malaysians from over the border. Some 60,000 of Singapore's undocumented workers came from the Philippines, Sri Lanka and Thailand and are known to be in Singapore mostly as maids and construction workers' (Prasai 1993: 23). A government crackdown in 1989 saw the Thai government negotiate a two-week amnesty for its citizens without proper documentation and some 10,000 came forward. Sullivan, Gunasekaran and Siengthai (1992) conducted a survey of a sample of this group and found most were male, in their late teens or early twenties, worked in unskilled jobs especially in construction and came to Singapore through the activities of recruiters (37 per cent) or family-based social networks (47 per cent).

It is not only in the five economic tigers of Asia that illegal migration has assumed significant proportions. Thailand, an important source of illegal migrants in the countries already considered, is itself now a significant target of illegal immigrants. Official estimates in 1993 indicated that the stock of illegal immigrants may exceed 200,000 and comprise two major streams. The first are Indians, Pakistanis and

Sri Lankans who are predominantly people overstaying visitor visas, while the second are Laotians, Chinese, Burmese and Cambodians who slip across land borders (*Bangkok Post*, 14 April 1993). Thailand is now a 'near NIC' with a rapidly growing economy and low levels of fertility. Accordingly labour shortages are emerging in some areas. For example in the fishing industry 'some 40 per cent of crewmen on fishing boats, about 70,000 people, are Burmese, Mon or Karen. They are employed not because of their cheap labour, but because there is a shortage of labourers who like to work at sea' (*Bangkok Post*, 15 September 1993). It is estimated in an official report that more than 300,000 Burmese are illegally working in Thailand, 'mainly involved in farming, mining, charcoal production and construction. They are popular with employers who pay them less than the national minimum wage' (Tasker 1993: 27). Between 1975 and September 1993, 757,531 displaced people arrived from Indochina. Most have been resettled in third countries or repatriated but significant numbers are working illegally in Thailand. Chinese are moving into Thailand 'as a transit point to get fake passports and visas with the help of well organized gangs' (Trisophan 1993) to resettle in third countries such as Australia or the USA (Lintner 1993). However, there are reports of some 5000 girls from Yunan province being sold into prostitution in Thailand (Gooi 1993: 36). The largest flow of illegal migrants, involving perhaps one million workers, involves Indonesians moving to Malaysia (Hugo 1993). There are two major streams, one from Java and Sumatra to peninsular Malaysia, and the other from east Indonesia and Sulawesi to Sabah and, to a lesser extent, Sarawak. Most work in low-paid unskilled occupations in the plantation, agricultural and construction sectors of the fast growing Malaysian economy, although increasingly they are found working in urban-based occupations. The movement is complicated because of the common ethnic background of the migrants and the Malay majority of the Malaysian resident population. In addition, there are around 30,000 illegal Thai workers in Malaysia (*Bangkok Post*, 1 July 1993) as well as some 100,000 illegal Filipinos in Sabah.

It is clear that the strict immigration laws in place in countries throughout the world will come under increased pressure from illegal migrants from Asia in the 1990s. The ILO is recommending to governments in Asian countries with distinct labour shortages that they legalize worker movements (Tasker 1993: 19)

and there are some signs that this is beginning to occur. Certainly illegal status tends to expose international workers to greater risk of exploitation and the newspapers of the region have been replete over the last decade with stories of exploitation of both legal and illegal overseas workers in destination countries. One of the more disturbing elements in this type of movement is the emergence of people-smuggling on a large scale. Asian countries rank poorly in terms of ratifying International Labour Organization conventions (Isberto 1993) so that illegal migrants are very exposed to exploitation. This especially applies to females. The need to protect such workers is considerable. Labour surplus nations in Asia are increasingly becoming reliant upon remittances from migrant workers, both legal and illegal. Currently for example it is estimated that the Philippines exports some 700,000 legal migrant workers and 300,000 illegally and their remittances (US$1.76 billion annually), which are the major single source of export earnings (*Far Eastern Economic Review*, 4 November 1993: 54). Illegal migration in Asia is increasing in significance with each year, and it must be given more attention by policy makers and researchers to address the rights of the people involved and maximize the benefits for both origin and destination countries.

References

Ardittis, S. (1990) 'Labour Migration and the Single European Market: A Synthetic and Prospective Note', *International Sociology*, 5 (4), 461–74

Ballescas, R. P. (1993) 'Undocumented Filipino Workers in Japan', *Asian Migrant*, 6 (2), 41–5

Baum, J. (1990) 'The Work Ethics', *Far Eastern Economic Review*, 13 September, 16–17

—— (1993) 'Human Wave', *Far Eastern Economic Review*, 5 August, 31

—— (1994) 'Chinese Gambit', *Far Eastern Economic Review*, 6 January, 14

Berthelsen, J. (1993) 'Politics of Exclusion', *Far Eastern Economic Review*, 18 November, 27–8

Employment and Immigration Canada (1992) *Managing Immigration: A Framework for the 1990s*, Employment and Immigration Canada, Quebec

Fraser, M. (1993) 'France Gets Tough. Target: Illegal Migrants', *The Gazette* (Montreal), 22 August, 131

Gooi, K. (1993) 'Cry of the Innocents', *Far Eastern Economic Review*, 9 September, 36–7

Hugo, G. J. (1993) 'Indonesian Labour Migration to Malaysia: Trends and Policy Implications', *Southeast Asian Journal of Social Science*, 21 (1), 36–70

Isberto, R. (1993) 'Illegal Aliens Fill Labour Shortages in Rich Asian Countries', *Bangkok Post*, 5 September

Ivanov, A. (1993) 'Russia Serving as a Conduit to the West', *Bangkok Post*, 13 September

Lintner, B. (1993) 'Rocks and a Hard Place', *Far Eastern Economic Review*, 9 September, 26–7

Mooney, P. and M. Zyla (1993) 'Braving the Seas and More', *Far Eastern Economic Review*, 8 April, 17–18

Morita, K. (1992) 'Japan and the Problem of Foreign Workers', Research Institute for the Japanese Economy, Faculty of Economics, University of Tokyo-Hongo

Nagayama, T. (1992) 'Clandestine Migrant Workers in Japan', *Asian and Pacific Migration Journal*, 1 (3–4), 623–36

Papademetriou, D. G. (1991) 'International Migration in North America: Issues, Policies, Implications', paper prepared for the joint UN Economic Commission for Europe/UNFPA meetings in Geneva, 16–19 July

Prasai, S. B. (1993) 'Asia's Labour Pains', *Far Eastern Economic Review*, 29 April, 23

Sakamaki, S. (1994) 'Stateless Children', *Far Eastern Economic Review*, 20 January, 38

Sassen, S. (1993) 'Economic Internationalization: The New Migration in Japan and the United States', *International Migration*, 31 (1), 73–102

Selya, R. M. (1992) 'Illegal Migration in Taiwan: A Preliminary Overview', *International Migration Review*, 26 (3), 787–805

Shu, J. and S. E. Khoo (1993) *Australia's Population Trends and Prospects 1992*, AGPS, Canberra

Spencer, S. (1992) 'Illegal Migrant Labourers in Japan', *International Migration Review*, 26 (3), 754–86

Sullivan, G. et al. (1992 'Labour Migration and Policy Formation in a Newly Industrialized Country: A Case Study of Illegal Thai Workers in Singapore', *ASEAN Economic Bulletin*, 9 (1), 66–84

Tasker, R. (1993) 'Last Refugee', *Far Eastern Economic Review*, 16 December, 27

Trisophan, T. (1993) 'PM Orders Arrest of Illegals', *Bangkok Post*, 14 April

Tsay, C. (1992) 'Clandestine Labour Migration to Taiwan', *Asian and Pacific Migration Journal*, 1 (3–4), 637–56

Wu, C. and C. Inglis (1992) 'Illegal Immigration to Hong Kong', *Asian and Pacific Migration Journal*, 1 (3–4), 601–22

PART TWELVE

MIGRATION IN THE MIDDLE EAST

There are two radically different interpretations of the migration of Jews to Palestine in the late nineteenth and the twentieth century. The conventional Zionist view looks to the biblical connection of the Jews with the area and depicts the migration as a return, a homecoming after centuries of exile. Of course there is some force in this view. Zionists argued that the plight of the Jewish minorities abroad could not be overcome without a territorialization of their identity, i.e. without a state of their own. However, when a chunk of Uganda was offered by the British government in a bout of misplaced[1] generosity, the Zionists turned it down. Not any territory would do; it had to be one with symbolic and historic significance. Migration to Palestine was described by the Zionists as an *Aliyah* ('going up'), a spiritual journey, no doubt fraught with many perils, but nonetheless infinitely superior to life in 'Babylon', the godless half-world of the diaspora.[2]

The second interpretation of Zionist migration has been pioneered by a group of 'revisionist' Israeli historians, including *Shafir*, who have laid much more emphasis on the resemblance of this stream of Jewish migration to European colonization and settlement. *Shafir* also makes a good case. Migration to Palestine was a minority taste – only a tiny minority of the two million Jews leaving eastern Europe between 1882 and 1914 selected Israel. Zionists aimed at creating a settler-immigrant community that was dominant. Their settlements displaced local Arabs, while a good number of the newcomers were not averse to using Arab labour in agricultural and unskilled settings. More particularly viniculture, on the North African plantation model, was introduced by a member of the Rothschild family to support the failing settlers. In short, *Shafir* concludes, 'As a settlement movement, Zionist nationalism may be seen fruitfully as a part of European overseas expansion and the creation of European "white settler" societies'.

Whatever reservations we may wish to make about his comparison (where, for a start, is the metropolitan country in the analysis?), it is highly suggestive in analytical terms. It provides, for example, one possible explanation for the flight of some 780,000 homeless Palestinians from the lands controlled by the newly independent Israel. This dramatic event and its consequences are graphically described in the contributions by *Lippman Abu-Lughod* and *Adelman*. If we assume that the Zionist settlers were essentially like white-settler colonies, then the displacement of Palestinians is akin to the displacement or annihilation of the Inuit in Canada, Native Americans in the USA, Maoris in New Zealand, Aborigines in Australia or the San and Khoi-khoi in South Africa. In effect, violence, brutality and the occupation of the land held by the local people were all to be expected from the colonists.

I said this was one possible explanation for the creation of the Palestinian refugees who, as *Adelman* notes, in 1992 numbered 5,400,000 (including descendants). However suggestive, the colonial analogy does not quite go far enough. Another reason for the displacement of the Palestinians lies in the mechanism of state formation described in Part 11. Many nations at the moment of their birth, or in periods of nation-building fervour, tend towards ethnic homogeneity. It happened thus in the First World War when 1.75 million Armenians were forcibly deported from Turkey to Syria, 600,000 dying on the journey (Toynbee 1915). It happened with the separation of India and Pakistan in 1948, as we saw in the previous section of this *Survey*. It is happening with a vengeance in the last part of the twentieth century in former Yugoslavia and the former southern states of the Soviet Union. This, of course, is not to condone the excess of Israeli violence in 1948 and again in 1967 and 1982, all of which showed a reprehensible disregard on the part of the Israeli government of the rights of others.

One of the areas where Palestinians found temporary (or in many cases permanent) havens was in the Gulf states where they were often prominent in the educational sector and in the civil service. With the fivefold bonanza of state revenues occasioned by the oil boom of the early 1970s, the Gulf states engaged in a massive expansion of their infrastructures and social services. Palestinians were welcome and, as *Abella* shows, so too were 3.5 million Asian migrant workers and workers from other Middle Eastern states who were imported as construction workers and to sustain the many retail outlets and services provided for the Gulf citizenries. This edifice of citizens standing on the shoulders of foreign subjects was suddenly rocked by the outbreak of the Gulf War. With the help of the international community, 450,000 Asian workers in the danger zones were repatriated – probably the largest evacuation of civilians in a short space of time since the Second World War. The unexpected return of their workers to Bangladesh, Pakistan, the Philippines, Sri Lanka and Thailand was to cause serious problems, as workers dissipated their hard-earned savings to finance long periods of unemployment (Amjad 1989: 19).

Asians were not the only migrants affected. Some 750,000 Yemenis were quietly sent back to their country from Saudi Arabia when their government backed Saddam Hussein. Similarly, as *Van Hear* describes, the Palestinians in Kuwait fell victim to charges of political disloyalty after some were seen welcoming the Iraqi invasion and Yasser Arafat declared his qualified support for Saddam Hussein. Most of the deported Palestinians found themselves in the first instance in Jordan, the country of refuge for so many others. Many were repatriated elsewhere, but Jordan had to accommodate 300,000 Palestinians who held nominal Jordanian citizenship by virtue of having once been residents of the West Bank. Most countries could be expected to experience difficulties if they added 10 per cent to their populations and Jordan was no exception. However, *Van Hear*'s analysis strikes a remarkably upbeat note. The refugees and returnees brought skills and capital with them. Their arrival seems to have triggered a 'surprise economic boom', a circumstance that gained Jordan the no doubt alluring label of a 'Singapore in the desert'. Clearly refugees can sometimes be good news.

Notes

1. 'Misplaced', among other reasons, because the Ugandans were not consulted.
2. Babylon was the place of first exile, to which King Nebuchadnezzar dragged off the Jewish leader, Zedikiah, and his followers. Thereafter the word 'Babylon' came to designate the assumed folk experience of displacement, estrangement and loneliness. This meaning was later also adopted by Africans in the American diaspora. Whether 'Babylon' was quite so bad as it was cracked up to be is questioned in Cohen (1995).

References

Amjad, Rashid (ed.) (1989) *To the Gulf and Back: Studies on the Economic Impact of Asian Labour Migration*, New Delhi: United Nations Development Programme and the International Labour Organization
Cohen, Robin (1995) 'Rethinking "Babylon": Iconoclastic Conceptions of the Diaspora Experience', *New Community*, 21 (1), 5–18
Toynbee, Arnold (1915) *Armenian Massacres: The Murder of a Nation*, London: Hodder and Stoughton

ZIONIST IMMIGRATION AND COLONIZATION IN PALESTINE UNTIL 1948

GERSHON SHAFIR

In this entry I will briefly present (a) the causes of Zionist immigration to Palestine from its beginnings in 1882 to the establishment of the state of Israel in 1948; (b) examine the institutional frameworks of immigration and colonization, and the relations among different waves and groups of settler-immigrants and between the Jewish immigrants and the native-born Palestinian Arab population; and finally (c) offer some reflections on the relationship between Zionist immigration and colonization and the Israeli–Palestinian conflict.

Causes of Zionist immigration to Palestine

During the last decades of the nineteenth century, the belated arrival of modernization undermined the traditional Jewish middleman role in the manorial economy of the Russian Pale of Settlement and central Europe and plunged Jews into an existential crisis. Though prior to the First World War a significant portion of the Jewish population was able to use its commercial skills and urban traditions to attain remarkably rapid social mobility, and frequently assimilate culturally, the majority was made redundant or displaced. Rapid demographic expansion fuelled the immiserization of the Jewish masses. At the same time, fear of competition led to waves of pogroms in southern Russia, quashing Jewish hopes of emancipation and/or assimilation. In the inter-war years, the defeat in the First World War, the inter-war economic crises and additional immigration from the east, radically reversed Jewish social advances and led to various forms of discrimination, which were justi-fied by modern nationalist and/or racist ideologies.

In response to this climactic sequence of changes, eastern European Jews, in a remarkable outburst of creativity, experimented with a variety of alternatives: hopes of emancipation and facts of assimilation, universal and Jewish socialism, cultural nationalism and autonomism, and retreat behind the walls of a revivalist and fundamentalist orthodoxy. Finally, masses of Jews chose to emigrate from eastern Europe to western Europe, the New World and, those who were the proponents of Zionism, to Palestine. The anterior wave of large-scale migration took the expelled Jews of Reconquista Spain in 1492 eastward to the less developed parts of Europe and the Mediterranean where their advanced skills were in demand. Now Jews were moving in the opposite direction. The first wave of modern pogroms made 1882 into a turning point in Jewish history, marking it as the commencement of Jewish migration and, *inter alia*, of Zionism. Zionist immigration to Palestine differed from other, including Jewish, migrations, in its political aims.

At the outset, Zionism was a variety of eastern European romantic nationalism, that is, an ethnic movement in search of a state. Unlike other eastern European nationalist movements, Zionism needed to seek out a territory for immigration and colonization. In an epochal debate in the Sixth Congress of the World Zionist Organization (an organization which was established in 1897 by Theodor Herzl, an assimilated Viennese journalist), a tentative British offer to settle in Uganda was rejected and, with the support of the representatives of the secular but more traditional eastern European Zionists, Palestine was affirmed as the 'old-new-land' of Zionist colonization. While this decision was nourished by the sacredness accorded Eretz Israel (Land of Israel) in antiquity and classical Judaism, an instrumental focus on territory was a departure from the classical rabbinical lore which, under the experience of diaspora life, subscribed to even by the great medieval sage Maimonides, ignored or spiritualized the doctrine of the Holy Land.

Indeed the step towards Zionism was neither self-evident nor widespread. Before 1933, only a small minority chose Zionism – the Jewish national move-ment aiming at the acquisition of territorial rights and political sovereignty in Palestine. Territorial national-ism – so different from and alien to the religious and ethnic Jewish way of life – was, as it were, imposed on Jews as a last resort. Between 1882 and 1914, of more than two million Jewish emigrants only a little less than 3 per cent chose Palestine. Only the barring of the gates of the USA by the Johnson–Lodge Act started orienting Jewish migrants to the shores of Palestine. Even during the peaks of pre-1948 immigration to Palestine, in 1925 and 1935 respectively, only 30 per cent of Jewish overseas migrants chose Palestine as their destination.

The minority choice became, however, with the Great Depression and Hitler's assumption of power, the only viable refuge. Between 1933 and 1936, close to 200,000 Jewish refugees arrived in Palestine. Palestinian Arabs, fearful of displacement by such large numbers, revolted in 1936 and forced the closure of the gates of Palestine too. In the poignant words of the Zionist leader, Chaim Weizmann, before the British Royal Commission (the Peel Commission) in 1937, the plight of European Jews consisted in the division of the world into places where they could not stay, could not live and could not enter. A year later, the abysmal failure of the Evian Conference, convened by President Roosevelt to assist German and Austrian Jewish refugees, but not allowed to discuss immigration to Palestine, confirmed Weizmann's judgment.

At the conclusion of the Second World War the same cruel dilemma facing the Jewish refugees, but in much smaller numbers, reappeared. The United Nations Relief and Rehabilitation Administration (UNRRA) was put in charge of temporarily housing and subsequently repatriating people driven from their homes by the Nazis and the vicissitudes of war. While successfully repatriating the overwhelming majority of these 'displaced persons', it could not apply the same solution to the 200,000 and more Jewish displaced persons. Many of the estimated 50,000 concentration-camp survivors and other refugee Jews, who initially returned to their countries of birth, upon finding their families, communities and homes destroyed, began trekking back to the displaced persons' camps in the American zone in Germany. This movement received an enormous impetus after the 4 July 1946 armed pogrom – the largest in the post-Nazi era – in Kielce, Poland, in which forty-two Jews were murdered. The British authorities refused to allow fleeing Jews into their zone, or to let those in temporary camps enter Palestine. The destination of these displaced persons who, in a UNRRA poll, overwhelmingly expressed a desire to settle in Palestine, became a pivotal international issue. In spite of international pressure, the British, conscious of Arab opposition, allowed only a trickle into Palestine. In response, Zionist bodies organized a series of risky overcrowded boat rides, which smuggled about 40,000 Jews into Palestine. But the

realization of the enormity of the crimes committed against Jews, the pressure of Jewish refugees in the American zone and the anti-colonial climate of the post-Second World War era, led to the return of the mandate to the United Nations which, on 29 November 1947, voted for the partition of Palestine between Jewish and Palestinian-Arab states. The first act of the provisional Israeli government was the abolition of immigration restrictions on Jews.

Immigration and colonization

The 1881–89 census (it took the Ottomans a long time to count their subjects) of the three Ottoman *sanjaks* that made up Palestine put its population at 426,566. About 24,000 were Jews, inhabitants of the four holy cities – Jerusalem, Hebron, Tiberias and Safed. This community was roughly 5 per cent of Palestine's population and about 0.3 per cent of world Jewry. It was made up of some Sephardic Jews (hailing from North Africa and the Middle East) and the rest were religiously motivated *ashkenazi* Jewish (European provenance) immigrants who arrived with the improvement of security conditions in the second half of the nineteenth century.

The change in the character of Jewish immigration, from religious to nationalist, led the well-informed Ottoman authorities to forbid Jewish immigration and land purchase as early as 1882. They were, however, unable to enforce these restrictions against many of the immigrants who, as foreign individuals, were protected by the European powers under the capitulation system. A dramatic change in the legal status of immigration occurred with the international recognition given to Zionist aspiration by the Balfour Declaration on 2 November 1917 and its subsequent incorporation into a mandate of the League of Nations. In the declaration the British government committed itself to view 'with favour the establishment in Palestine of a national home for the Jewish people' without, however, prejudicing 'the civil and religious rights of existing non-Jewish communities in Palestine'. The declaration obviously contradicted itself and the British, seeking to balance their commitments to Jewish nationalist and Palestinian communal and individual interests, swung widely in their policies. In response to Arab violence in 1921, 1929, 1936 and 1939 they restricted Jewish immigration, but in response to Zionist protests, with the exception of the crucial years between the beginning of the Arab Revolt and the end of the mandate, relented.

The rate of Jewish immigration to Palestine

Table 12.1: *Jewish immigration waves and Jewish population in Palestine, 1882–1948*

Immigration wave	Years	Number of immigrants	Natural increase	Population at beginning of period
First Aliya	1882–1903	20–30,000		
Second Aliya	1904–1914	35–40,000		
Third Aliya	1919–1923	29,500	6,500	56,000
Fourth Aliya	1924–1927	57,125	26,013	92,000
Fifth Aliya	1932–1938	195,175	42,413	175,138
Second World War	1939–1945	89,440	61,667	412,722
Post-World War	1946–1948	55,309	30,495	563,829
14 May 1948				649,633

Sources: David Gurevitch, Ahron Gertz and Roberto Bacchi (1944) *The Jewish Population of Palestine*, Jerusalem, Department of Statistics of the Jewish Agency for Palestine, 4–5; and M. Sicron (1957) *Immigration to Israel:1948–1952*, vol. II, Jerusalem, Israel Central Bureau of Statistics, , Statistical Supplement, Tables A2 and A3.

fluctuated widely and the wave-like character of Zionist immigrations left its imprint on the character of the emerging Jewish society – the *yishuv* (literally settlement, the pre-independence Jewish community of Palestine). (See dates and numbers of immigrants in each wave in Table 12.1.)

The first *aliya* (wave of immigration, pilgrimage), inspired by the eastern European *Hibbat Zion* (Lovers of Zion) network, set up in the coastal and inland valley smallholding villages (*moshavot*, colonies) of mostly rain-fed field crops in imitation of their Arab neighbours. The inexperienced immigrants soon discovered that they could not attain their accustomed urban European standard of living, paltry as it was. They, and the whole immigration effort, were rescued by a member of the Rothschild family from Paris who introduced them to plantation type agriculture, mostly vineyards. The new agriculture was based on cheap seasonal native labour, in imitation of French settler agriculture in North Africa, and limited the employment available to Jews.

The turbulent years of the second *aliya* are credited with creating the institutions that led to, and shaped, the state of Israel. To attain employment, the new immigrants sought to 'conquer labour', i.e. to displace the lower-paid Arab workers who had made it impossible for them to attain a 'European standard of living' in the plantations of the first *aliya*. They failed, however, to sway the owners. Alternatively, to overcome this uneven competition, the workers' organizations allied themselves with the World Zionist Organization, which in the meantime had been established in Vienna, and a subsidized economic sector, settling and employing only Jews, was formed. The pivotal institutions of its vertically and horizontally integrated cooperative community were the *Histadrut* (General Trade Union of the Hebrew Workers in Palestine) and the World Zionist Organization's land purchasing agency – the Jewish National Fund. Whereas the former ensured exclusive Jewish employment, the latter reserved the land purchased by it for Jewish renters. The *kibbutz*, a cooperative farm of Jewish workers on land that could not be sold or rented to Arabs, became the prototypical tool of Zionist colonization. The *Histadrut*–Jewish National Fund alliance incorporated pioneering (the redemptive activities of physical labour, agricultural settlement and military service) into the core values of the new *yishuv* and assured the political predominance of Labour Zionism in Israeli society.

The third *aliya* was in many ways a continuation of its predecessor, though, under the influence of the Russian Revolution, with clearer socialist ideals. The new immigrants, however, faced new conditions: the placement of Palestine under a British mandatory authority in the wake of the dismemberment of the Ottoman empire radically improved the conditions of immigration. A network of national *Hehalutz* (pioneer) bodies, under the authority of the World Zionist Organization, trained potential immigrants in manual labour, farming, the ideals of Labour Zionism and Hebrew before their immigration. The 1920 London Conference of the World Zionist Organization set up *Keren Hayesod* (the Foundation Fund) to channel worldwide Jewish contributions to defray the costs of immigration and settlement. Finally, the mandatory authorities, in accord with the conditions of their mandate, established a labour schedule, drawn up every six months, to regulate the number of immigration certifications issued to different classes of Jewish immigrants. The main classes were persons of independent means, professionals, small tradesmen and artisans with capital, and, finally, workers with definite prospects of employment. While the Zionist bodies accepted that immigration should be based on the economic absorptive capacity of Palestine, the size of the largest category of immigrants – workers without means, the Achilles heel of Zionist colonization – remained a bone of contention between the World Zionist Organization and the British.

Labour Zionism gradually established its hegemony in the *yishuv*. Around its core of 'virtuous' immigrant-settlers, who actively participated in the labour movement's colonizing and military bodies, there formed a periphery of the other immigrants. The latter's contribution to Zionism was seen as indirect: by immigrating to Palestine, they helped bring closer the day when Jews would form a majority in Palestine. Among these were the middle-class immigrants, who after 1924 outnumbered Labour Zionist immigrants, but also the small numbers of *mizrachi* (Jews from the Middle East and North Africa) immigrants. As a result of differential access to Zionist institutions an 'ethnic gap' in occupational distribution and educational attainment opened up between *ashkenazi* (European immigrants) and *mizrachi* Jews.

With the imposition of restrictions by the Soviet authorities on *Hehalutz*, and the closing of the gates of the USA, the fourth *aliya* brought to Palestine mostly middle-class Jews threatened or ruined by economic crisis and anti-Jewish policies in Poland. But now the 1926/7 economic depression in Palestine led to the re-emigration of about 23,000 Jews. During the fifth *aliya* the flight of middle-class Jews expanded to include German Jews and other stateless Jews and, for the first time, assumed massive proportions. The immigrants of these two waves were involved in the establishment of many new commercial and industrial enterprises and cultural institutions.

The restrictions that resulted from the response to the Arab Revolt and the conditions of the Second World War slowed immigration to around 90,000 immigrants, of whom about one-third arrived illegally between 1939 and 1945. Among the little over 55,000 immigrants who arrived between 1946 and May 1948, the number of legal and illegal immigrants was about the same. During the entire mandatory period close to half a million Jews, one-third of Jewish overseas migrants, arrived in Palestine, and about 60,000 re-

emigrated. 87 per cent of the immigrants were from Europe, 10 per cent from Asia and 3 per cent from the rest of the world. In May 1948 the population of Palestine consisted of 649,633 Jews in contrast to over 1.269 million Arabs.

Colonization and the Israeli-Palestinian conflict

As a settlement movement, Zionist nationalism may be seen fruitfully as a part of European overseas expansion and the creation of European 'white settler' societies. Israel is not completely different from some of the other European overseas societies that were shaped in the process of settlement and sustained conflict with the already existing societies they were displacing. Like other 'pure settlement colonies' with their own immigrant labouring class (in contrast with colonies inspired by military aims and with limited white populations), Zionist bodies aimed at creating a relatively homogeneous settler-immigrant population that would become the majority in the new land. A typical expression of the pivotal place of demography and immigration in the Israeli-Palestinian conflict is Ben-Gurion's conclusion that: 'the real, [that is] the political, opposition, between us and the Arabs is that we both want to be the majority.' As a late instance of colonization, undertaken by members of a dispersed minority without a colonial metropolis, Zionist immigrants faced more severe impediments than most other colonial ventures.

Whereas in most of North America and Australia, and in large areas of South Africa, the indigenous peoples were at a hunting-gathering stage, only a small section of the Palestinian population was tribal and nomadic; and it was in the process of expanding its own area of residence and cultivation from the hilly regions of Palestine to the costal zone and the inland valleys.

Jewish planters, in contrast to their counterparts on most other colonial frontiers, had no access to slaves or indentured workers and relied on seasonal unskilled wage labour. Whereas colonial companies and great powers encouraged immigration into their colonies, not until the onset of the British mandate was Jewish immigration facilitated into Palestine, and even then only for a limited period. Whereas land was 'free' in many colonies, Palestinian land was not easy to come by.

Land had to be purchased and the need to lay out money for land created a 'low frontiery' (Jews purchased about 20 per cent of the cultivable land and slightly over 6 per cent of Palestine's total land area by 1948). Thid, at the same time, brought in its wake a process of primitive accumulation that, until the military territorial land accumulation during the 1948/9 War of Independence, remained less violent than most other colonizations.

The question, of course, is how did Zionists manage to accomplish as much as they did under such adverse conditions and within such a limited time span? The answer seems to be that Zionism required a variety of external resources, both great power support and massive financial subsidies, as well as a willingness to adjust its demands to the realities, first of limited Jewish immigration and later of the destruction of the largest pool of its potential immigrants – the very people Zionism was created to attend to and sustain.

Two such accommodations stand out. The first was the recognition of the impossibility of turning Palestine into a settlement colony, and especially of a 'pure settlement' type, through the workings of the free market. The separatist methods adopted by the *Histadrut* and the Jewish National Fund were generated with the purpose of creating extra-market mechanisms that would render unnecessary the uneven competition between the immigrants and lower-paid Arab workers in the market. Second, the mainstream of the labour movement was willing to limit Zionist territorial aspirations and accept partition plans that tailored the boundaries of a Jewish state to Jewish demographic and economic potentials. In a nutshell, in place of a maximalist 'territorial' design, which early on characterized all Zionists and later remained the policy of the Revisionists (the progenitors of the Likud), the major rival of Labour Zionism, a 'demographic' policy was adopted. At the same time, until recently Zionist accomplishments remained partial and limited, i.e. none of the solutions offered by Zionist institutions of colonization disposed totally of the weaknesses caused by the limited demographic potential.

References

Gurevitch, David, Ahron Gertz and Roberto Bacchi (1944) *Settlement and the Demographic Changes of the Eretz Israeli Population*, Jerusalem: The Statistical Department of the Jewish Agency for Eretz Israel

Sicron, Moshe (1957) *Immigration to Israel, 1948–1953*, Jerusalem: Falk Project for Economic Research in Israel

THE DISPLACEMENT OF THE PALESTINIANS

JANET LIPPMAN ABU-LUGHOD

The customary categories employed in migration analyses are inadequate to describe the case of the Palestinians. This is true for several reasons. First, the disappearance of the country to which Palestinians belong and the transformation of the political, physical, demographic and social environment to which they hold allegiance, have caused Palestinians to experience 'exile', whether they remain on their own soil or have migrated (Abu-Lughod 1988). Second, the migration of Palestinians has been forced, whether directly in connection with wars, or indirectly in response to the denial of their economic and political rights and opportunities. And third, unlike other migrations (voluntary or forced), the return of most migrants has been prevented by political acts of the 'successor' state, Israel. In contrast, then, to the more common circular movement of migrants, the migration of Palestinians has been in only one direction – out.

There may now be some 6 million persons[1] in the world who trace their descent from the 1.4 million Arabs who lived in Palestine when that country was dismembered in 1948 and who now identify themselves as Palestinians, even though they may never have lived there. Few Palestinians think of themselves as 'migrants', although most of them currently reside outside the borders of a country that now has no juridical existence.[2] And even those who are physically present within the former borders feel themselves 'exiled', politically if not socially.

The process of their successive displacement has been relentless over the past forty-five years. The steady trend of attrition has been periodically intensified during periods of upheaval associated with regional wars. The first phase of their displacement occurred in the 1948 struggle between Palestinians and Israelis – a struggle Zionists refer to as their 'War of Independence', and Palestinians simply call 'The Catastrophe'.

When Britain announced that it was terminating its mandate over Palestine, the United Nations, then dominated by Western powers, recommended partitioning the country between its Jewish and Arab inhabitants. At that time, Arabs constituted two-thirds of the population whereas most of the Jews had arrived only since the 1930s.[3] Arab protests and Jewish violence precipitated a 'civil war' in which the newly declared state of Israel emerged victorious, expanding its *de facto* frontiers well beyond those recommended in the partition plan and causing the flight of some 780,000 Arabs from the territory it then controlled.[4] In addition, another 120,000 persons were later classified as refugees because they had lost their lands and sustenance, although not their homes.[5]

Most of the refugees remained on Palestinian soil, however, crowded, along with the original inhabitants, into the as yet unconquered 'West Bank' (of the Jordan River) and the 'Gaza Strip'. In 1949, Jordan extended citizenship to residents of the West Bank as well as to the more than 100,000 refugees who had crossed the river to the East Bank. Meanwhile, Egypt 'administered', without conferring citizenship on, more than 200,000 residents of the Gaza Strip, of whom some 60 per cent were officially refugees. The rest of the displaced population found refuge in camps set up in the adjacent countries of Syria and Lebanon.

By 1952 the air of battle had cleared and statistics could be collected by Israel, Jordan, Syria and Egypt.[6] Using these separate figures, it is possible to calculate the effects of the 1948 war on the forced migration of Palestinians. Table 12.2 shows that 76 per cent of the estimated 1.6 million (since population had grown through natural increase in the interim) remained in former mandatory Palestine, albeit under a variety of different circumstances. According to Israeli figures, about 180,000 or 11 per cent lived 'behind the Green Line' (i.e. in *de facto* Israel, as specified in the ceasefire signed at Rhodes after the war), although a significant proportion of these had been forcibly removed from their original places of residence and could therefore be considered 'internal refugees'. Some 742,300, according to a Jordanian Census of Housing conducted in 1952, lived on the so-called West Bank, of whom about 40 per cent had moved there from their lands that had been occupied by Israel. And about 300,000 lived in the Gaza Strip, of whom perhaps 200,000 were refugees from other parts of Palestine. Of the 24 per cent who had settled

Table 12.2: *Distribution of Arabs of Palestinian birth or descent, 1948–92 (in percentages)**

Residence	1948	1952	1961	pre-1967	post-1967	1970	June 1982	1992
PALESTINE	**100**	**76**	**65**	**63**	**50**	**46**	**41**	**40**
Israel		11	11	12	15**	15**	12	12
West Bank		47	37	34	22	20	18	16
Gaza		18	17	18	13	11	10	12
OUTSIDE PALESTINE		**24**	**35**	**37**	**50**	**54**	**59**	**60**
East Bank		9	17	18	27	30	24	28
Leb./Syria		12	13	13	13	13	14	11
Other***		0	5	6	10	11	21	21
Millions	**1.4**	**1.6**	**2.2**	**2.65**	**2.7**	**3.0**	**4.5**	**6.0**

Notes:

*   The dates are end of calendar years, except for the pre-and post-war dates (June and December) of 1967, the post-1982 Lebanese invasion, and the very approximate figures for post-Iraq invasion of Kuwait and subsequent expulsions.

**   Includes the Arab population of East Jerusalem.

*** This includes all other Arab countries, as well as Europe, Canada, the United States and South America. The constant percentage conceals significant changes. In the 1970s and 1980s, the major destinations of migrants were the oil countries of the Gulf. This ended with the economic retrenchment in the oil countries and the expulsion of Palestinians from Kuwait during and after the Iraqi invasion. The increase in the proportion of population in Jordan in 1992 reflects their repatriation. There has been a recent increase in migration to non-Arab countries.

Sources:

The figures in this table have been derived by the author by complex methods of demographic estimation. The multiple sources and methods used to reach the estimates for 1948 through 1967 are explained in Abu-Lughod (1971); detailed estimates of the subsequent dispersal of Palestinians up through 1980, including sources and methods, appear in Abu-Lughod (1980). In general, wherever official country-by-country counts and censuses were available, these were adopted. The total population of Palestinians was estimated by projecting from surrogate measures of fertility and mortality derived from partial known populations (Kossaifi 1976). After aggregating official enumerations, the remainders (very few cases) were estimated from non-official sources. Consistency tests were run for intercensal estimates. Estimates for 1982 (after the invasion of Lebanon) and for 1992 (after the Iraqi invasion of Kuwait) are less accurate, being of necessity 'guesstimates' based on political documents and estimates of the magnitude of the forced emigrations.

outside Palestine (primarily in refugee camps), 9 per cent lived east of the River Jordan, 7 per cent in Lebanon and 5 per cent in Syria. Less than 2 per cent had relocated to Egypt, Iraq or non-adjacent countries.

Between 1952 and 1961,[7] despite modest dispersal, some 65 per cent of the estimated two million Palestinians still remained on Palestinian soil, by virtue of a complex compound of choices and constraints. Residents of Gaza, who lacked any internationally recognized citizenship, were most entrapped, and their number had increased to almost 370,000, chiefly from natural increase. The Arab population within Israel's 'green line' had risen to 247,000, again primarily from natural increase, although some of the increase was due to repatriation under the family-reunification programme or the belated enumeration of those whom the Israelis bizarrely termed 'the absent present'.[8] Over 800,000

still resided on the West Bank, although their numbers were being gradually depleted by an out-migration pushed by economic hardship and facilitated by their Jordanian passports.

Some resettled on the East Bank. However, because the Jordanian government did not distinguish between 'original' Jordanians and Palestinians who had been extended Jordanian citizenship, our estimate of about 380,000 Palestinians living on the East Bank by 1961 is only approximate. The numbers in Lebanon increased a bit more than natural increase, whereas the percentage in Syria remained constant at 5 per cent. But changes in opportunities were already beginning to occur, as the oil states of the Arab Gulf region (especially Kuwait and Saudi Arabia) began to admit skilled immigrants as guest workers. Despite this, little change in the overall distribution of Palestinians occurred until the outbreak of war in June 1967. The

PLATE 19: The grim mass housing of Gaza, home for many Palestinians.

table demonstrates the dramatic impact this war had on further dispersal.

This crisis precipitated a second 'shaking loose' of Palestinians. While the war created no officially recognized set of new refugees, the population movements it induced, both in the short and long terms, certainly cannot be said to be part of a normal process of migration. The fact that Israel occupied all of the residual areas of Palestine (the West Bank and Gaza) and continues to hold them and their residents as conquered territories and people, has had lasting effects on the context within which subsequent migrations would occur.

In 1967, when Israel enumerated the population under its occupation, it counted some 350,000–400,000 *fewer* Palestinians in the territories than had

been resident just before the war. Some of those 'missing' had been temporarily abroad for work, but the sizeable number of Jordanian students who entered East Bank schools in the fall of 1967 and had to have their records transferred from the West Bank (confirmed by Jordanian records of school transfers) suggests a very large and real displacement. Many of those displaced were refugees for the second time.

Since 1967, politically motivated expulsions and economically driven out-migrations, especially from the West Bank, have continued. High rates of natural increase, however, have helped to maintain the population on the West Bank, despite emigration, and have caused enormous increases in population in the already overcrowded Gaza Strip.

Where did the emigrants go? At first, most resettled

in the East Bank of Jordan, where economic conditions deteriorated further in the wake of the loss of
territory and an influx in refugees. However, the oil-
rich countries of the Gulf eventually began to serve as
a magnet for populations experiencing severe economic deprivation, both in Jordan and under Israeli
occupation. The number of Palestinians working
abroad, particularly in Kuwait, the United Arab
Emirates and Saudi Arabia, increased dramatically,[9]
especially after 1973 when Egypt's attempt to dislodge Israelis from the territories occupied in 1967
failed. Deprived of hope for an early end to the occupation, Palestinians sought temporary relief. Many
males took employment outside, sending remittances
to their wives and children who remained at home, a
fact clearly evident from the imbalanced sex ratios –
especially on the West Bank where the absence of
males of a productive age is particularly marked.

Nor were conditions better for those Palestinians no
longer on Palestinian soil. Two subsequent crises led
to their further uprooting. Israel's invasion of
Lebanon in June 1982 precipitated a drop of about
100,000 in the population that had earlier sought
refuge in Lebanon. And, in the wake of the Iraqi
invasion of Kuwait, there was a massive expulsion of
perhaps 70–80 per cent of the 450,000 Palestinians
who had been living and working there. Many of
those with Jordanian citizenship returned to the East
Bank of Jordan, even those whose normal place of
residence had been the West Bank. Others eventually
emigrated to Europe, South America, Canada and the
United States, in search of livelihoods and refuge.

Table 12.2 presents estimates of the changing
distribution of persons of Palestinian origin and
descent over the past forty-five years, demonstrating
the effects of successive wars, expulsions and economically motivated migrations brought on by political
events and existential circumstances. These figures
poignantly demonstrate the unique situation of a
'nation' seeking a restoration of its country.

Notes

1. Because the initial displacement of Palestinians occurred
    some forty-five years ago, and most of the population now
    lives within the borders of other states, it is virtually
    impossible to determine this total with any degree of
    accuracy. Furthermore, since there is no government nor,
    indeed, any official country called Palestine in today's
    panoply of nations which could collect official statistics, we
    have had to estimate. The figures in this contribution use, as

a base, my detailed monograph produced in 1980, which
employed a careful country-by-country methodology of
demographic estimation (see Abu-Lughod 1980).

2. Only the approximately 650,000–700,000 Palestinians
    living in the Gaza Strip have the right to documents that
    specify them as Palestinians, although these are not recog-
    nized internationally.

3. The last official census of Palestine, conducted in 1931,
    enumerated only 17 per cent of the population as Jews, and
    of these, almost 60 per cent had been born outside Palestine.
    According to the last population estimates made by the
    British administration in 1946, Jews still constituted only 31
    per cent of the total population.

4. This total was reached by carefully estimating the number
    of Arabs who *would have been residing* in Israeli-held
    territory in November, had there been no war, minus the
    number who actually were counted in the Israeli Defence
    'census' of that month. The difference yields a displacement
    of 770,000 to 780,000. Detailed figures are presented in
    Table 3 (Abu-Lughod 1971: 160), which also explains the
    methodology.

5. UNRWA placed the number of refugees, as of the Armistice
    Agreement of November 1949, at 900,000, which is
    consistent with our estimates.

6. Lebanon never conducted a census; therefore, the estimates
    from that country are based on UNRWA registrations.

7. The year 1961 has been selected as a bench mark because
    both Israel and Jordan conducted official censuses in that
    year.

8. These were individuals who had been missed by the Israeli
    Defence Census, although they had never left the territory.
    Their political rights were abrogated, although eventually
    their presence was acknowledged.

9   At the peak, almost three-quarters of a million Palestinians
    were living in those burgeoning countries (Birks and
    Sinclair 1979), but without citizenship, political rights or
    even secure tenure.

References

Abu-Lughod, Janet (1971) 'The Demographic Transformation
of Palestine', in Ibrahim Abu-Lughod (ed.) *The
Transformation of Palestine*, Evanston, IL: Northwestern
University Press, 2nd edition 1987, 139–63. Pagination is
from second edition

(1980) *Demographic Characteristics of the Palestinian
Population*, annex I to the Palestine Open University
Feasibility Study (Paris: UNESCO, June 1980 mimeo-
graph). An Arabic translation of this document is available

(1988) 'Palestinians: Exiles at Home and Abroad', *Current
Sociology*, special issue on refugees, 51–9

Birks, J. S. and C. A. Sinclair. (1979) 'International Labour
Migration in the Arab Middle East', *Third World Quarterly*,
April, 87–99

Kossaifi, G. (1976) 'Contribution à l'Étude démographique de la
population palestinienne', thèse de doctorat de 3ème cycle
de démographie, 2 vols, Paris: Université de Paris I

Said, Edward et al. (1983) *A Profile of the Palestinian People*,
Chicago, II: Palestine Human Rights Campaign, esp. 11–18,
where I have updated the earlier estimates

THE PALESTINIAN DIASPORA

HOWARD ADELMAN

In the clash between Arabs and Jews, Palestinian nationalism and Zionism, and Arabs and Arabs, the Palestinians have been forced to flee time after time. The Palestinian Arab diaspora began in 1948. It was reinforced by subsequent waves of out-migration. Whether or not many or most Arabs in Palestine were the descendants of migrants and peasants originating from other lands who arrived in a sparsely populated Palestine during the nineteenth century (Peters 1984: 196) is irrelevant to their being Palestinian. So is the claim that Jews constituted the majority of the population in Safed and Tiberias and the largest plurality in Jerusalem by the middle of the last century. The fact is that when the Anglo Committee of Inquiry undertook its survey of Palestine in 1946, the 1944 Arab population was set at 1,179,000. At the time of the UN vote for the partition of Palestine on 29 November 1947 (Resolution No. 181 II), there were over 1,300,000 Arabs living in Palestine; they constituted the clear majority of the population and almost half the population of the territory allocated for the Jewish state by the UN partition resolution.

After the 1948 war, the proportion of Arab Palestinians in the Jewish state that emerged from the war was less than 15 per cent. In 1993, Palestinian Arabs were a minority in the entire land of the 1947 former British Mandate of Palestine. Palestinians were scattered throughout the Middle East and the world. During the decade and a half leading up to the full outbreak of war in 1948, British policy may have enhanced the movement of Arabs and inhibited the movement of Jews into Palestine, but subsequent events reversed that pattern dramatically. This article traces the pattern of that out-migration over forty-five years from 1948 to 1992.

An overview

By 1992, the world population of Palestinians had more than quadrupled to 5,400,000. Within historic Palestine, the population had almost doubled through reproduction. But over half the Palestinians (almost 3,000,000) lived outside of what had been the British Mandate of Palestine in 1948. And of the population within that territory (2,460,000), over a quarter

(220,000 in the West Bank and 435,000 in Gaza) would be classified as refugees using UNHCR criteria. An additional almost 12 per cent were stateless in Gaza. Even the 35 per cent (880,000) who were indigenous to the West Bank and had been citizens of Jordan since Jordan annexed the West Bank following the 1948 war had their citizenship cancelled by Jordanian decree on 20 August 1988, though they remain eligible for temporary two-year passports from the Jordanian government. The only Palestinians in the former mandate territory with citizenship were, ironically, members of the Jewish state, Israel. Almost 30 per cent of the Palestinian world population were Jordanian citizens.

Definitions

The United Nations High Commission for Refugees (UNHCR) defines a refugee (Goodwin-Gill 1983: 5–6) as

> any person who is outside the country of his nationality ... because he has or had a well-founded fear of persecution by reason of his race, religion, nationality, membership of a particular social group or political opinion and is unable or, because of such fear, is unwilling to avail himself of the protection of the government of the country of his nationality.

By contrast, the United Nations Relief and Works Agency for Palestine Refugees in the Middle East (UNRWA) defines a Palestine refugee as

> a person whose normal residence was in Palestine for a minimum of two years preceding the conflict in 1948 and who, as a result of this conflict, lost both his home and means of livelihood and took refuge in 1948 in one of the countries where UNRWA provides relief. Refugees within this definition and the direct descendants of such refugees are eligible for Agency assistance if they are: registered with UNRWA; living in the area of UNRWA operations; and in need.

In the UNRWA definition, Palestine refugees originally included about 30,000 Jews who had fled areas occupied by the Jordanian army but it is now used exclusively in referring to Palestinian refugees. However, the UNHCR definition has become the

Table 12.3: *A profile of the Palestinians, 1991*

	Refugees	Indigenous lacking protection of a state	Citizens or landed immigrants	Migrant workers	Palestinian population	Total population
Canada			15,000		15,000	26,000,000
Egypt	44,200				44,200	54,200,000
Gaza Strip	435,000	296,000			721,000	721,000
Iraq	24,000				24,000	18,900,000
Israel			640,000		640,000	4,882,000[1]
Jordan	50,000		1,520,000		1,570,000	3,100,000
Kuwait				50,000	50,000[2]	800,000[3]
Lebanon	293,900		45,000		338,900	3,350,000
Libya				24,000	24,000	4,600,000
Qatar				33,500	33,500	450,000
Saudi Arabia				156,600	156,600	15,500,000
Syria	301,000				301,000	12,500,000
United Arab Emirates				50,000	50,000	1,800,000
USA			210,000		210,000	253,000,000
West Bank and East Jerusalem	220,000	880,000			1,100,000	1,100,000
Rest of world			80,000	41,300	121,300	
Total	1,368,100	1,166,000	2,510,000	355,460	5,399,500	

1. The Palestinians in East Jerusalem are included with the West Bank total and not with the Israeli total given that Palestinians in East Jerusalem are overwhelming not citizens of Israel.
2. In 1990, the estimated Palestinian population in Kuwait was 360,000.
3. This was the population of Kuwait in 1990 before the outbreak of the Gulf War.

world standard, whereas the definition of Palestine refugees is particular to that group. The base reference for the UNHCR definition is the country of nationality, which is a political reference, whereas in the case of Palestinians, the reference is geographical; the Palestinian refugees need only to have resided in Palestine for two years prior to 1948.

Further, whereas under the universal definition, a refugee need only be outside his country of nationality, Palestinian refugees are only counted in countries of the Middle East where UNRWA operates. The major difference, however, is that UNHCR refugees are defined in terms of the denial of rights in relationship to loss of protection of the country of nationality so that the person who fled did so out of fear of persecution, while Palestinian refugees are defined by needs, that is, whether they lost their home and means of livelihood. Thus, if a UNHCR refugee receives citizenship and, hence, the protection of another state, that individual ceases to be a refugee. In the case of the Palestinians, the fact that so many became citizens of Jordan did not end their refugee status because the status was assigned relative to their original position in 1948 and their current geographical location, and not whether they subsequently obtained citizenship *or* were forced to flee or were exiled after 1948. Further, since UNRWA openly acknowledges the inaccuracy of its own figures as a result of double counting, or failure to eliminate persons who died, we have not used the UNRWA definition but divide the Palestinian population according to whether they are refugees according to the UNHCR definition, indigenous stateless persons or citizens.

Palestinians in the West Bank, Gaza and Jordan
The shift in population of the Palestinians in the West Bank illustrates the change in status of the Palestinians over time. By the end of 1948, there were about 260,000 refugees in the West Bank and about

460,000 indigenous Palestinians without citizenship in a state. With the annexation of the West Bank by Jordan in 1951, both groups were made citizens. Since the major development of Jordan proceeded on the east bank of the river, the population of the West Bank stayed relatively constant as about 450,000 Palestinians migrated to what is now Jordan, to the Gulf states and elsewhere. With the capture of the West Bank by Israel in 1967, the population of the West Bank can be divided into three groups. First, 225,000–235,000 fled, largely to the East Bank of the Jordan. Second, the UNRWA-registered refugees, who had always retained their refugee status, became real refugees again, except that they had Jordanian citizenship and were within their homeland. But they lacked the protection of a state. The third group, the indigenous populations who had never fled, now also lacked the protection of a state, but were not UNRWA-registered refugees.

Under the Israeli occupation, the outflow of Palestinians continued. In spite of the high birth rate, by 1992 the total population of the West Bank had only increased by about 25 per cent. Further, since Jordan had effectively removed the Jordanian citizenship of all West Bankers in 1988 (the passports were only renewed as a form of travel document), all residents of the West Bank (approximately 1,100,000) lacked both the protection of a state of which they were members and citizenship in any state.

The situation in Gaza was dramatically different and much worse than the West Bank. First, in 1948, the ratio of refugees to the indigenous population was much higher. There were slightly over twice as many UNRWA-registered refugees in comparison with the 80,000 indigenous population. Second, Gazans, indigenous or refugees, never received any form of citizenship. Third, the movement out of Gaza has been much smaller than that from the West Bank, in spite of the much more depressed situation there. During the Egyptian occupation from 1948–67, relatively few Palestinians managed to leave the Gaza strip, so that, with the high birth rate, the Gazan population had almost doubled to 431,000: 265,000 refugees and 156,000 indigenous people without citizenship.

Over 70,000, however, fled with the occupation by Israel in 1967. Another group, almost 145,000, managed to migrate or were expelled by 1992. So the Gazan population, despite a very high birth rate, consisted of about 720,000 people, approximately half of whom were indigenous and the balance UNRWA registered refugees. Jordan, itself, in 1948 had only a

population of about 88,000 Palestinian refugees. They were soon given full citizenship and would have been delisted as refugees under UNHCR criteria. In contrast to both the West Bank and Gaza, the net outflow of Palestinians from Jordan after 1948 has been virtually nil. But there have been large numbers of arrivals – 300,000 odd migrating from the West Bank between 1948 and 1967. Further, there was a large influx in 1967 with the Israeli capture of the West Bank (over 160,000) and following the defeat of the Iraqi occupation of Kuwait in 1991 (almost 400,000). With the restoration of Kuwaiti rule, over a very short period, most of the almost 400,000 Palestinians in Kuwait were forced out by the Kuwaiti authorities because some Palestinians had visibly and openly welcomed the Iraqi forced seizure of Kuwait. There was also one acute large outflow during this period, largely to Lebanon, when King Hussein of Jordan in Black September of 1970 crushed the Palestinians who were viewed as setting up a state within the state to provide a base from which to attack Israel. With the high birth rate and continual movements into Jordan, by 1993 the Palestinian population of Jordan was over 1.5 million.

Lebanon and Syria

In 1948, Lebanon received about 84,000 Palestinian refugees and Syria almost 70,000. Unlike Jordan, Syria did not give any Palestinians citizenship although they were allowed to live as freely as any Syrian citizen in an authoritarian state. Lebanon granted 30,000 Palestinians, primarily Christians, Lebanese citizenship after they came to Lebanon in 1948. Following the Six Day War in 1967, Lebanon received an additional 25,000 refugees and Syria another 3,000. Lebanon also was the major recipient of the Palestinians expelled by Jordan following Black September in 1970. Further, Lebanon went through a fifteen-year civil war in which Palestinians played a significant role. As a result of the civil war as well as the aftermath, large numbers of Palestinians left or were expelled from Lebanon following the Israeli invasion of Lebanon in 1982. As a result, the Palestinian population was about 300,000 in Syria and almost 340,000 in Lebanon in 1993.

Israel

In contrast to both Lebanon and Syria, all Palestinians in Israel were granted citizenship. By 1967, the 165,000 indigenous Palestinians had become over 300,000 Israeli citizens which, again because of a relatively high birth rate, had doubled to about

600,000 in 1993. In spite of the many complaints about the second-class status of those Palestinians, there has been a relatively small out-migration from Israel. Nevertheless, particularly following the occupation of the West Bank and Gaza, and greatly exacerbated by both the *intifada* and their relatively second-class social and economic status in Israel, Israeli Palestinian citizens have felt torn between their Palestinian nationality and their Israeli citizenship.

Conclusion

The movement of the Palestinian population has been largely the result of forced or volunteer flight from situations of conflict with significant (1967 and 1982) and (1948) very large outflows. Economic opportunities in the Gulf states and abroad provided the other major incentive for movement of Palestinians. Except where the Palestinians were given full and equal opportunities in Jordan, and an influx of Palestinians went to Jordan, the nature of the state (democratic but primarily Jewish in Israel, relatively anarchic in Lebanon and authoritarian in Syria) in which they lived seemed to make little difference to overall net migration. Thus, the populations of those areas remained relatively constant, taking into account natural increases as a result of a high birth rate of 3.0–3.4.

Presumably, the peace accords between the PLO and Israel signed in September 1993 will make some difference to these Israeli Palestinians. It will certainly affect the lives of the rest of the Palestinian population. For those not formally called refugees under the UNRWA definition – those displaced in 1967 and the late-stayers whose permits expired – Article XII of the agreement explicitly provides for the 'the admission of persons displaced from the West Bank and Gaza Strip in 1967' back into the West Bank and Gaza. On the other hand, the accord states that the original group of refugees will be dealt with 'no later than the beginning of the third year of the interim agreement'. For the first time in almost half a century, one can anticipate the real possibility of an end to the Palestinian refugee problem.

References and Bibliography

Abu-Lughod, Janet (1971) 'The Demographic Transformation of Palestine' in Ibrahim Abu-Lughod (ed.) *The Transformation of Palestine*, Evanston: Northwestern University Press

— (1980) 'Demographic Circumstances' in Edward Said et al. (eds) *A Profile of the Palestinian People*, Chicago: Palestine Human Rights Campaign

Adelman, Howard (1983) 'Palestinian Refugees', *World Refugee Survey*, New York: US Committee for Refugees

— (1985) 'Palestinian Refugees and the Peace Process', in Paul Marantz and Janice Stein (eds) *Peace-Making in the Middle East*, London: Croom Helm

Adelman, Howard et al (eds) (1992) *Palestinian Refugee and Demographic Report*, prepared for the Middle East Peace Negotiations Working Group on Refugees, Toronto: Department of External Affairs for the Government of Canada

Badran, Nabil A. (1969) *Education and Modernization in Palestine, 1918–1948*, Part I, Palestine Monograph No. 63, Beirut: Palestine Liberation Organization Research Centre

Benvenisti, Meron and Shlomo Khayat (1988) *The West Bank And Gaza Atlas*, Jerusalem, distributed by *The Jerusalem Post*

Cainkar, Louise (Director of the Palestine Human Rights Information Center), unpublished statistics, April 1992

Gabbay, Rony E. (1959) *A Political Study of the Arab–Jewish Conflict: The Arab Refugee Problem*, Paris: Librairie Minard

Goodwin-Gill, Guy (1983) *The Refugee in International Law*, Oxford: Clarendon Press

Hagopian, E. and A. B. Zahlan (1974) 'Palestine's Arab Population: The Demography of the Palestinians', *Journal of Palestine Studies*, 1 (4)

Lukacs, Y. (ed.) (1984) *The Israel–Palestinian Conflict*, Cambridge: Cambridge University Press

Morris, B. (1987) *The Birth of the Palestinian Refugee Problem, 1947–1949*, Cambridge: Cambridge University Press

Peters, Joan (1984) *From Time Immemorial: The Origins of the Arab–Jewish Conflict Over Palestine*, New York: Harper & Row

UNRWA. (1986) *UNRWA, Past, Present and Future: A Briefing Document*, Vienna: UNRWA

Whitaker's Almanac (1991) London: Whitaker's Unlimited

ASIAN MIGRANT AND CONTRACT WORKERS IN THE MIDDLE EAST

MANOLO I. ABELLA

One of the unexpected outcomes of the oil boom in the early 1970s was the migration of millions of Asian workers to the oil-rich states of the Middle East and North Africa. While Indian divers have always been recruited for seasonal work in the pearling industry of the Trucial coast, the flow of Asian labour to the region became significant only after OPEC's decision to implement a five-fold increase in oil prices had caused a global redirection of income flows towards this previously isolated part of the world. Since then, millions of South Asians and orientals from as far away as Indonesia and the Republic of Korea have found their way to the region to take on better-paid jobs than they could get at home. At the peak of construction activities in 1983, about 3.5 million Asian workers were employed in the region, far outnumbering the non-national Arabs, who have likewise been drawn to the Gulf by the economic boom.

The early origins of the migration system

There were small but thriving Indian communities in the area long before oil was discovered in the region. Sindhi and Gujarati merchants, bringing textiles and gold from India and East Africa to various places up and down the Arabian peninsula, have been involved in the region's trade for centuries. And, with their Arab partners, they dominated the commercial and financial life of the small settlements along the coast (Weiner 1982). In the nineteenth century there was also a notable presence of Indian civil servants in areas under British control. The discovery of oil started a new migration stream from the subcontinent, for British and US oil companies needed skilled and semi-skilled artisans and clerical workers whom they could not find locally. According to Birks, Seccombe and Sinclair (1988), many Indians were in the employ of companies under British management even before the Second World War, and were disproportionately represented in workforces over which the British had relatively strong control, as in Kuwait and Qatar. Their numbers grew with the growth of oil exports, but the total Asian workforce did not exceed 100,000 until after 1970.

Migration after the discovery of oil in the Gulf

The discovery of oil had a momentous impact on the economies of the region, but the real boost came after oil prices escalated in the autumn of 1973. The combined oil export revenues of the Arab members of OPEC rose from $181,800 million in 1971–75 to $617,600 million in 1976–80. With this virtual explosion in oil revenues the Arab oil-producing states were able to embark on an unprecedented scale of development spending, unmatched in other developing nations. Total investments in the Gulf Cooperation Council states (Saudi Arabia, Kuwait, Oman, Qatar, United Arab Emirates and Bahrain) rose nine and a half times between the first and second half of the 1970s. In Saudi Arabia alone the growth of capital formation averaged an incredible 27.8 per cent a year during the whole of the 1970s (Sherbiny 1985).

It became evident from the very beginning that a shortage of labour would be a serious impediment to the realization of the grand development plans that these states, with their enormous revenues from oil, wanted to undertake. The GCC states had a combined national workforce of only 1.36 million, and Libya had only about half a million. Only Iran and Iraq had sizeable national workforces of 9.5 million and 2.9 million respectively. Also, with the bulk of these populations engaged in traditional occupations, very few people had the skills appropriate for modern industry. For a variety of reasons there was very little elasticity in the supply of labour. Extremely low rates of participation by women, longer periods spent in school as educational opportunities became available, and a phenomenon of early retirement have contributed to very low rates of participation (22 per cent in 1975) in the labour force.

Population quickly swelled as employment expanded and attracted immigration from neighbouring areas. In the early stages of the oil industry's development the migration was mainly limited to those from within the Arab Gulf region, such as the Nejdis and Hasawis who went to Bahrain, and to a few thousand Indians who went to Iran for the construction of the refineries in Abadan. As more and more labour was needed, the sources expanded to include Yemen, Egypt, Sudan, Jordan and Pakistan. The population of the Trucial coast was estimated at about 179,000 in 1968, but by 1975 a census showed a population exceeding 655,000 (Lenczowski 1981). The combined populations of Saudi Arabia and Kuwait (less than 3.3 million in 1960) almost doubled within ten years to 6.5 million. The small quiet towns along the coast gradually became urban centres with large expatriate communities, whose skills were needed for the oil industry, and for the trade, commerce and services the expanding population in turn generated, and for the governments of these states that needed quickly to acquire the capability to plan and oversee ambitious infrastructure development programmes. At the beginning of the 1970s there were around 65,000 Asians living in Bahrain, Kuwait and Qatar consisting almost entirely of people from the Indian subcontinent. There were probably more in the Trucial sheikdoms now comprising the United Arab Emirates, but no data exist to confirm it. By the end of the decade the Asian population had risen nine times, while the total population had grown by less than 73 per cent.

Asian penetration of Gulf labour markets

The shift to Asian sources of labour is a curious aspect of the migration system that evolved in the region as a consequence of these developments. During the period 1970–75 the GCC states received about three-quarters of a million expatriate workers, many of whom were on one- to two-year work contracts. According to Birks and Sinclair (1980), by 1975 the non-national workforce in the GCC states was already some 1.4 million strong, consisting of about 1.1 million other Arabs and about 368,000 South Asians. The whole Asian workforce represented roughly 20 per cent of the total non-national workforce in the region, but it was not evenly spread. In Oman, the UAE, Qatar and Bahrain, Asians already formed the dominant expatriate group of foreign workers in 1975, but in Kuwait they were a minority.

The non-national workforce climbed to 2.2 million in 1980 and to 5.1 million in 1985. During that period the share of Asians rose from about 30 per cent to over 63 per cent. Only a few thousand Asians had by that time found their way to Libya and Iraq, but in Saudi Arabia they numbered over 2 million. Of the total Asian workforce of 3.2 million in 1985, slightly over a million were from the Far East. Most of them were employed in Saudi Arabia, whose economy dwarfed those of the neighbouring states and where

employment was growing at close to 14 per cent a year during the first half of the 1980s.

Table 12.4: *Estimated mid-year stock of Asian workers in the Middle East, 1975–90*

GCC States	1975	1985	1990
UAE	163,500	472,700	450,000
Oman	58,700	285,400	
Saudi Arabia	38,000	2,094,700	1,554,900
Qatar	34,000	50,200	
Kuwait	33,610	273,900	400,000
Bahrain	16,604	81,600	
Iraq	10,000	87,000	
Libya	5,500		

Sources: Birks and Sinclair (1980) for 1975; Birks, Seccombe and Sinclair (1988) for 1985; for 1990 the author's estimates based on reports from countries of origin.

The first Asian workers to arrive in the Middle East consisted mainly of construction workers from the subcontinent with skills ranging from professional engineers to managers, accountants, foremen, carpenters, masons, heavy equipment operators, mechanics, cooks and ordinary labourers. The profile of the Pakistanis in the Middle East illustrates this configuration of the Asian workforce in the region. Some 42.5 per cent of the Pakistani workers were unskilled labourers, 40.6 per cent were skilled, 6 per cent were sales workers, 4.3 per cent were professionals, 2.2 per cent were service workers and 1.5 per cent were clerical workers (Gunatilleke 1986). Probably close to three-quarters of these people were recruited for construction jobs when they were first brought in, but some progressively found their way to more stable jobs in the services sector.

Unlike their Arab counterparts, governments in the Asian countries of origin were prepared to get involved directly and indirectly with the recruitment and placement of their workers in foreign countries. In the early 1970s the South Korean and Philippine governments, for example, actively 'marketed' their manpower skills abroad and entered into labour-supply agreements with other governments and private organizations. They likewise encouraged their construction companies to go abroad and engage in international contracting, an area in which they saw some comparative advantage and long-term gains. All the Asian countries allowed private agencies to undertake recruitment and subsequently had to

establish elaborate administrative systems and procedures for overseeing or regulating their activities
because of rampant abuses and malpractices.

Table 12.5: *Annual flows of migrant labour from Asia
to the Middle East*

Year	A	B	C	D
1975	93,100	97.3	2.0	0.7
1976	152,500	71.6	24.5	3.9
1977	311,000	66.9	26.4	6.7
1978	359,500	55.1	36.3	8.6
1979	424,000	45.5	42.7	11.8
1980	526,700	34.8	54.1	11.1
1981	688,400	31.8	52.0	16.2
1982	968,700	37.3	49.1	13.6
1983	986,800	34.8	53.8	11.4
1984	843,000	34.6	53.2	12.2
1985	793,000	30.6	55.1	14.3
1986	683,500	24.5	58.1	17.4
1987	740,200	25.4	57.7	16.9
1988	809,200	30.5	53.7	15.8
1989	795,900	27.2	50.7	22.1
1990	737,774	34.3	40.0	25.7
1991	933,800	36.0	42.0	22.0

A = Asia total; B = Pakistan and India (%); C = Southeast and
East Asia (%); D = Bangladesh and Sri Lanka (%).
Source: ILO (Bangkok) estimates based on official reports of
Asian countries of origin.

From the economic standpoint there were certainly
advantages in hiring more Asians than Arabs. The
Asian contractors were reliable, their workers
accepted lower wages and they did not require the
same social support services as the Arabs, who were
more likely to settle and bring their families. But
observers agree that political rather than economic
considerations were decisive in the shift (Nagi 1986).
Because their own populations were so tiny, the Gulf
states were concerned that a further build-up of any
single group of foreign nationals could easily result in
their native population being outnumbered. Fear of
over-dependence on any one group of foreign workers
prompted the governments of the Gulf states to opt for
a policy of diversifying and rotating supply sources
(Keely 1990; Weiner 1982). A related but probably
more serious concern, however, was that the
uncontrolled inflow of some non-national Arab
communities would sooner or later pose a serious risk
to the security of the existing political order. Not only
had the Egyptians and Yemenis overthrown their own
monarchial systems, but the Palestinians were likely

to drag the oil-rich states further into their protracted
struggle to regain their homeland. There was also
some anxiety that they might influence Gulf nationals
towards accepting the idea of 'Pan-Arabism', which
was evidently incompatible with the self-interest of
the ruling groups in the Gulf. The latter clearly saw
that Pan-Arabism would erode their hold on power
and force them to share their oil wealth with their
poor Arab cousins.

The 1980s saw an eastward shift in the composition
of Asian nationalities migrating to the Gulf. While the
initial flows consisted almost wholly of Indians and
Pakistanis, their share of the growing flows dropped
very considerably over the years, first in favour of the
orientals, and later in favour of the Bangladeshis and
Sri Lankans. The penetration of the Middle East
labour markets by the Filipinos, Koreans and Thais
during the boom in construction is due partly to the
skills they displayed in winning and executing
contracts, and partly to the unwritten policy of the
employing states to diversify their sources. Oriental
companies were less expensive than US or European
ones and were adept at seeking out local partners.
They recruited and deployed the workers, housed and
fed them in self-contained work camps, provided for
their needs for medical and recreational services, and
arranged their orderly repatriation after completion of
their projects. Unlike the non-national Arabs or some
of the Indians and Pakistanis, the workers from East
and Southeast Asia had no links with the local
community and were quite happy to live apart in
'enclaves' built by their companies.

The growth of Asian labour migration to the Middle
East continued well into the 1980s until the collapse
of oil prices in 1985 prompted cutbacks in infrastructure investments throughout the region. As much
as a third of all expatriate workers in the Gulf were
engaged in construction work and the cancellation or
postponement of many projects led to years of decline
in the volume of flows of Asian workers to the region.
Between 1983, the peak year, and 1986 the annual
volume of contract labour migration to the Middle
East from Asia dropped by almost a third, from
986,800 to 683,500 workers. The fall would have
been more severe if not for the growth in employment
in the service sector (from hotels to personal services),
which absorbed ever increasing numbers of workers,
especially women, from Sri Lanka, Bangladesh,
Indonesia and the Philippines.

Role of state policies

State policies (of the countries of both employment

and of origin) have played a role in shaping migration patterns and processes in the region, though it is easy to overstate their importance (Abella 1991). In the countries of employment they reflected the delicate balance that had to be maintained between the objectives of fostering economic growth on the one hand and not jeopardizing security or their cultural identity on the other. What emerged was a 'guest-worker' policy characterized by diversification of supply sources, tight security, restrictions on mobility and short duration of permissible stay. To exercise greater control over foreign workers their 'importation' was allowed only under sponsorship by so-called *khafeel*s; work permits were limited to one to two years and did not allow the worker to change employers; a residence visa was granted only on the strength of a work permit and was coterminus with it; in Saudi Arabia travel within the country was restricted.

The migration regime that emerged out of these policies had the effect in some countries of effectively disenfranchising the workers of many of their basic rights. Upon entry into the countries of employment their travel documents are surrendered to the sponsor or *khafeel*, who must give his clearance before the worker is allowed to leave the country. Since workers cannot change employers they are totally at the mercy of the *khafeel* who in places such as Saudi Arabia can at any time have them deported or imprisoned. But the establishment of the *khafeel* or sponsorship system (a form of franchise to import foreign labour granted to loyal subjects) has had the unexpected effect of increasing the dependence on foreign labour. The *khafeel*s profited handsomely from the importation of foreign workers, especially since most of them pay money for the chance to get a work permit and a better paying job in one of the oil-rich countries.

In the Middle East only Iran and Iraq have agreed to enter into bilateral labour agreements with the governments of the Asian countries of origin. Because of their weak bargaining position *vis-à-vis* the employing countries the Asian governments have concentrated on the establishment of minimum conditions for work contracts which they tried to enforce, albeit with little success, through the licensing and supervision of recruitment companies and hiring agents. In the Philippines, recruitment agents are deemed by law to be liable for any claims of the workers judged to be valid by designated authorities. To give teeth to this legal provision, all recruitment agents are required to deposit security bonds with the government before they are granted a licence to operate.

Asian governments generally refrained from adopting policies that restricted emigration. Even the socialist states of Vietnam and China adopted policies to promote the employment of their nationals abroad, although they maintained strict controls on the exit of individuals. Some countries have restrictions or prohibitions on the emigration of certain categories of labour, for example Pakistan and India, which ban the recruitment of female domestic helpers below a certain age (35 years and 30 years respectively), and the Philippines, Thailand and Bangladesh, which ban the placement of female domestic helpers in certain countries because of the strong local reaction to reports of physical and sexual abuses their women migrants suffered.

Remittances of migrant workers

Despite the deterioration of the conditions of their migrant workforces in the Gulf, the policies of the Asian states of origin have generally supported further migration. This is largely due to the huge flows of remittances that their nationals have been sending home to their families and the impact these have had on their economies. Between 1978 and 1987 Pakistan received over $22 billion in remittances through official banking channels, and these do not include monies sent home through informal channels and in other forms such as durable consumer products. India received even more during the period. These remittances paid for half of Pakistan's total imports, a third of Bangladesh's and almost a fifth of India's. Remittances also boosted external resources at a time when their terms of trade had been gravely eroded by the oil price increases and no doubt contributed to reducing the need for external borrowing to finance development. In Pakistan the large inflows of remittances enabled the country to take steps to liberalize trade policy with a view to building a more competitive industrial structure (Amjad 1989).

Because of the huge impact of remittances on their balance of payments and potentially on investments and growth, the Asian governments adopted various measures to encourage migrants to remit more of their incomes home. Prior to the liberalization of foreign exchange markets, which took place recently in a number of countries, governments experimented with special privileges to migrants to open foreign currency accounts, higher interest rates on foreign currency time deposits, dual exchange rates, allowing migrants' remttances to be exchanged in special auction markets and tax privileges for the import of capital equipment.

PLATE 20: An Indian printer at work in Kuwait.

Changing patterns of labour migration to the Gulf
The migration system linking the Gulf labour markets to Asia (to which the oil bonanza gave rise) survived the collapse of oil prices in 1985. After a few years of markedly reduced flows to the Gulf region (and increased return flows to Asia) there was a strong revival, which was only briefly interrupted by the Gulf crisis. This revival was characterized by a change in the composition of the flows: from a few occupations needed in construction to a wider variety in services and manufacturing, from migration organized by corporations to migration of individuals recruited by households for domestic service, and from traditional sources in South and Southeast Asia to Bangladesh and Sri Lanka. These trends suggest that, despite attempts by the states to 'indigenize' or nationalize their labour markets, the dependence on foreign labour has in fact deepened over the years and also widened to include more economic sectors and more occupations within each sector.

Iraq's invasion of Kuwait in 1990 and its repercussions throughout the Gulf region revealed the extensiveness of the migration system that evolved over the previous two decades. At the height of the crisis there were fears in the Asian region that most if not all of the 3.5 million Asian workers in the entire Gulf region would at some stage need to be repatriated. Fortunately the conflict was contained, but an estimated 450,000 Asian workers and their families actually left Kuwait and Iraq, most of them evacuated through an unprecedented airlift operation organized by their governments with the assistance of a number of international organizations.

The crisis appears to have important long-term consequences on the migration system. The total number of Asian workers migrating to the Middle East region in 1992 was 18 per cent higher than the total for the pre-crisis year of 1989. Some of the increase is likely to be temporary as it arises from Kuwait's requirements for reconstruction, but there are definite indications that the upsurge is related to security concerns of the Gulf states. Because their government backed Saddam Hussain, over 750,000 Yemenis residing and working in Saudi Arabia were quietly sent home by the Saudi government during the crisis and only a few have since been allowed to re-enter the kingdom. Egyptians and friendlier Arabs, as well as Pakistanis, Indians and workers from Southeast Asia appear to be progressively taking over their places in the labour market. A similar shift appears to be taking place in the other Gulf states, which used to employ large numbers of Palestinians and Jordanians, particularly in the civil service and educational sector.

None of the factors that have played a role in shaping the migration of labour from Asia to the Middle East suggest that there will be major changes in the foreseeable future. Present high rates of fertility will ensure faster growth of the national labour force in the coming decades, but this is no guarantee that nationals will eventually take over the jobs currently being performed by cheap migrant labour from Asia. In many ways dependence on foreign labour has become a structural feature of these economies, for their own national workforces have participated very little in any productive activities other than oil extraction. Because the income from oil exports has been sufficient to support comprehensive welfare state systems and maintain the citizens in relative affluence and security, there is little incentive for people to seek employment in the private economy, where jobs are less secure and where (because policies are presently geared towards bringing in foreign labour), wages and salaries have remained low and even deteriorated. The rotational system of migration of temporary foreign labour, especially from Asia, has apparently worked well in balancing the economic and political interests of these states and there has been surprisingly little political opposition to its maintenance. Indeed it was observed that during an earlier economic slump in Kuwait there was considerable 'hoarding' of labour. While the wage differentials that once drew many Asian workers to that region have narrowed considerably over the past decade, due to declining wages, the enlargement of the labour pool to include the least developed countries in Asia would ensure that labour supplies would not be short. Barring major political changes, it is therefore likely that this migration system will survive for many years to come.

References

Abella, M. (1991) 'International Migration in the Middle East: Patterns and Implications for Sending Countries', paper for Informal Expert Group Meeting on International Migration, United Nations Commission for Europe, Geneva

Amjad, Rashid (1989) *To The Gulf and Back*, International Labour Organization, New Delhi: ARTEP

Birks, J. S. and C. A. Sinclair (1980) *International Migration and Development in the Arab Region*, Geneva: International Labour Office

Birks, J. S., J. Seccombe and C. A. Sinclair (1988) 'Labour Migration in the Arab Gulf States: Patterns, Trends and Prospects', *International Migration*, 26 (3)

Gunatilleke, Godfrey (1986) *Migration of Asian Workers to the Arab World*, Tokyo: United Nations University

Keely, Charles (1990) *Asian Worker Migration to the Middle East*, New York: The Population Council (Center for Policy Studies Working Paper 52)

Lenczowski, George (1981) *The Middle East in World Affairs*, Ithaca: Cornell University Press

Nagi, M. H. (1986) 'Determinants of Current Trends in Labor Migration and the Future Outlook', in F. Arnold and N. M. Shah (eds) *Asian Labor Migration: Pipeline to the Middle East*, Boulder, CO: Westview Special Studies in International Migration

Sherbiny, Naiem (1985) *Labour and Capital Flows in the Arab World: Critical View*, The Industrial Bank of Kuwait KSC Series No. 16, February

Weiner, Myron (1982) 'Migration and Development in the Gulf', *Population and Development Review*, 8 (1)

DISPLACED PEOPLE AFTER THE GULF CRISIS

NICHOLAS VAN HEAR

Up to five million people were uprooted in the Middle East in the wake of the Gulf crisis of 1990/1, one of the largest mass displacements in recent times. The crisis recast the complex patterns of migration and displacement in a region long used to population upheaval, as previous contributions in this section have shown. After outlining the dimensions of the uprooting that the Gulf crisis set in motion, this contribution turns to some of its longer term consequences in the Middle East.

Five main waves of forced migration took place (Van Hear 1993). First, in the wake of the invasion of Kuwait by Iraq in August 1990, Arab and Asian migrant workers and their families resident in Iraq and Kuwait fled into Jordan and other neighbouring countries, an involuntary movement that was closely followed by the mass expulsion of expatriate Yemenis from Saudi Arabia. These two migrations may have involved two million people. Between the outbreak of the war in January 1991 and the ceasefire, a second, smaller wave of displacement took place, as about 65,000 people left the war zone, although the numbers displaced within Iraq may have been much larger. The third period began with the uprisings and their suppression in northern and southern Iraq, which precipitated the mass flight of up to two million Iraqi Kurds and Shias towards Turkey and Iran. Meanwhile large numbers of people were stranded or rendered *de facto* refugees in southern Iraq, Kuwait and Saudi Arabia in the aftermath of the armed conflict. A fourth period was under way by May 1991 – the mass return of refugees from Turkey and Iran. Two months later, most of those who had fled for Turkey and Iran had returned within Iraq's borders, although many remained internally displaced during the political and military stalemate that subsequently prevailed. From mid 1991 a fifth wave of displacement gathered pace with the resumed exodus of Iraqis from Iraq and of Jordanians and Palestinians from Kuwait following the restoration of the emirate's regime; the exodus of Palestinians continued in substantial numbers until late 1992.

Besides Iraq and Kuwait, the mass displacement involved several hundred thousand nationals of Egypt, Yemen and Jordan, more than 100,000 nationals of India and Pakistan, and more than 10,000 nationals of at least nine other Middle Eastern and Asian countries. As well as refugees who crossed international boundaries as they left their homelands, large numbers of migrant workers, professionals and business people were expelled or obliged to leave their countries of work and residence; others were unable to return to their countries of habitual residence; large numbers of people were internally displaced; and smaller though substantial numbers were rendered stateless, or made the transition from prisoners-of-war to refugees. The fallout of this mass displacement continued well after the initial period of uprooting. The remainder of this contribution examines the enduring consequences of this displacement for two countries in the Middle East that received large numbers of displaced people in the wake of the Gulf crisis: Jordan and Yemen.

The character of Jordan's returnee population

Most of the third-country migrants who arrived in Jordan from Kuwait and Iraq were repatriated within weeks to their homelands in other parts of the Middle East (principally Egypt) and in South and Southeast Asia. Jordan was nevertheless obliged to accommodate in the longer term some 300,000 of its own nationals. Most were of Palestinian origin, holding Jordanian nationality by virtue of having been residents of the West Bank. The majority left in the first wave of exodus identified above, fleeing the chaos of the Iraqi occupation and later for fear of impending war. A smaller though substantial wave left after the defeat and ejection from Kuwait of the Iraqi forces, first as a result of persecution by Kuwaiti militia groups avenging alleged collaboration with the Iraqis, and later as a result of harassment and insecurity fostered by the Kuwaiti authorities, part of the restored regime's attempts to reduce the emirate's dependence on foreigners. Palestinians and Jordanians were also obliged to leave Saudi Arabia and other states in the region.

The Palestinian community forced to leave Kuwait was long-settled there, its presence dating from the

PLATE 21: Egyptian migrant workers in Jordan.

uprooting of 1948/9 and subsequent upheavals (see Brand 1988 and Ghabra 1987 for accounts of Palestinian migration to Kuwait). While attachment to the homeland remained active and strong – evidenced not least by the frequency of visits and the volume of remittances – the Palestinian population had increasingly constituted a semi-permanent community in Kuwait, with an increasing proportion born and brought up there and knowing no other home.

A majority of those who arrived in Jordan between 1990 and 1992 had never lived there before, making the widely used term 'returnee' problematical when applied to them (Hashemite Kingdom of Jordan 1992a; Van Hear 1995). While this did not necessarily mean that they had no kin to call upon for help in Jordan, it presented real difficulties of integration for many so-called 'returnees'. Their long residence abroad also meant that there was a high proportion of dependants among the returnees. One estimate suggested that the ratio of economically active persons as against dependants was about one to four among Jordanians and Palestinians in Kuwait before the invasion (ILO 1991).

The returnees to Jordan were typically characterized, not least by many Jordanians, as a wealthy class of middlemen and professionals. Many in the Palestinian community indeed conformed to the notion of a 'middleman' or 'auxiliary' minority (Bonacich 1973; Tinker 1977), akin perhaps to some communities of South Asians abroad or of the overseas Chinese. The returnees certainly did include many who had run businesses, and those who had held professional, technical, managerial and administrative positions in Kuwait. But the returnees also included less well-off former labourers, drivers, clerks, artisans and other semi-skilled workers in the emirate.

While the characterization of the returnees as a wealthy class obscured the diversity of wealth among them, even those who had not accumulated wealth on any substantial scale had led relatively comfortable lives in Kuwait and other Gulf states. A majority of returnees now found themselves impoverished, relatively or absolutely in Jordan (Van Hear 1995). Their circumstances much depended on the recovery of assets from the countries they were obliged to leave. While almost all households were obliged to leave behind some of their assets and property, or to sell their assets at a loss, many were also able to bring or later to recover substantial assets, including employment-related entitlements, savings and capital. However, in many cases these assets were rapidly depleted on living expenses. While some of the wealthier returnees re-established themselves in their businesses or professions, Jordan's labour market provided little respite for the majority who remained unemployed. Of those who had found regular means of livelihood, most were self-employed, often in businesses more suited to the affluence of the Gulf than the Jordanian market.

Living costs were partly offset for some returnee households by the ownership of housing or access to the homes of extended families. Nevertheless more than half of returnee households were obliged to resort to the highly priced rental sector. Family and kin networks were important for initial support and for finding accommodation; but such support had its limits, could lead to hardship and tension within households, and diminished as a source of supplementing livelihood as time went on. Other sporadic sources of income included borrowing, charity and recourse to returnee self-help organizations. In a telling reversal of roles, remittances from relatives abroad became an important source of income for many returnee households.

Thus, as might be expected following the massive uprooting, returnees experienced general 'downward mobility' (Van Hear 1995). But former socio-economic status in Kuwait or elsewhere in the Gulf was not a safe guide to such status after arrival in Jordan. While the poor and wealthiest strata were largely maintained, there appeared to be considerable dissolution of intermediate levels. Thus a good proportion of skilled workers and artisans found some employment in Jordan and owned their homes. Conversely, many professionals and business people could not find employment; while some owned their homes, many were obliged to rent expensive private accommodation. Many of those who had run businesses with Kuwaiti majority partners or guarantors were unable to recover their assets and added to the impoverished middle class after their arrival in Jordan.

The impact on Jordan of the mass return

The mass migration from Kuwait and the Gulf added up to 10 per cent to Jordan's population, pushing it to around 3.8 million. This appeared yet another blow to an already beleaguered economy, for recession in the 1980s had culminated in a currency crisis in 1988/9, forcing the government into a range of austerity measures overseen by the International Monetary Fund and the World Bank. The returnees seemed to add a further enduring burden (Central Bank of Jordan 1990, 1991; UNICEF 1992).

Demand on educational, health and other social services greatly increased following the mass arrival. Of the pressures put on Jordan's resources, the impact on water supply may turn out to be critical. Although estimates vary greatly, unemployment increased immediately after the mass return, thereafter declining marginally from perhaps 25 per cent at the beginning of 1992 to 20 per cent by that year's end (Hashemite Kingdom of Jordan 1991b; UNICEF 1992). Poverty among returnees matched rather than exceeded national levels (Hashemite Kingdom of Jordan 1991a); but returnee impoverishment contributed to increasing the overall spread of poverty in Jordan, not least because those formerly reliant on remittances from Kuwait not only saw those remittances disappear, but also had to support returning relatives as well as themselves.

While the immediate consequences of the mass arrival were indeed negative and disruptive, some longer term potential benefits to the national economy had become apparent within a couple of years. First, the mass arrival meant that large numbers of well-educated, professional and skilled people entered Jordan's labour market, which was likely ultimately to be beneficial even if they could not find employment in the short term. Second, the return led to a large inflow of capital into Jordan, although in future years remittances (at about $600 million in the late 1980s) would be greatly reduced. Estimates of the inflow of funds ranged between $1.5 billion and $3 billion (Central Bank of Jordan 1991, 1992). To put this figure into perspective, this was just under half of Jordan's current foreign debt of $6.5 billion. Evidence of this capital inflow was most obvious in construction activity, particularly in the capital Amman; in greatly increased bank deposits; and in heavy investment in the stock market, whose annual volume of trade more than doubled between 1990 and 1992 (Van Hear 1995).

However, substantial returnee investment in viable, productive ventures was slow to be realized. Many small-scale shops and businesses were set up with capital brought back, but few returnees reported much success with these, often because they were not familiar with market conditions in Jordan. Industrial activity increased substantially in Jordan in the early 1990s (Central Bank of Jordan 1992), but with a few exceptions, participation of returnees in large-scale industrial ventures was slight. The returnees' contribution to industrial development, as to other forms of economic activity, came rather in the form of making capital available for others to invest. There was probably more returnee involvement in agriculture. Nationally, agricultural production and the area brought under cultivation increased markedly between 1989 and 1992 (Hashemite Kingdom of Jordan 1992b), some of the credit for which may be attributed to returnees.

The aggregate effect of these developments was a 'surprise economic boom' (Edge 1993; Edge and Dougherty 1992). GDP grew by 11 per cent in 1992, with 6 per cent growth projected for 1993 and 5 per cent subsequently; given the exceptional population increase from 1990 to 1992, per capita GDP growth was of course lower, but it was still substantial. The relative importance of the returnees' contribution and of the government's structural adjustment programme was a matter of debate. Government officials stressed the stability of the currency, lower inflation and reduction of the budget deficit, which they attributed to the adjustment programme; this had created the conditions for returnees and others to invest in Jordan, they claimed. On the other hand, wealthy returnees were strong advocates of the benefits they had brought, both in terms of expertise and capital. Such claims were supported by some outside commentators. Based on economic conditions generated by structural adjustment and by the influx of returnee skills and capital, Jordan was described by one business analyst as a potential 'Singapore in the desert' (Morland 1993). The realization of such a vision obviously depended on many factors, not least developments in the regional political arena, but its very articulation represented a great shift from the gloomy prognosis that accompanied the arrival of the returnees during the crisis of 1990/1.

The character of the Yemeni returnee population
The Republic of Yemen was obliged to accommodate some 800,000 of its nationals forced to leave Saudi Arabia, Kuwait and other states of the region during the crisis (Republic of Yemen 1991; Van Hear 1993, 1994). The majority returned from Saudi Arabia,

whose authorities sought to put pressure on the Yemeni government for its apparent support for Iraq, and at the same time to get rid of part of the kingdom's surplus labour force. The mass exodus was precipitated by the extension to Yemenis of regulations governing work and running businesses from which they were hitherto exempt, coupled with a campaign of harassment and the fostering of insecurity among the Yemeni expatriate population. The mass repatriation put great pressure on the fledgling state formed just months before, from the unification of the Yemen Arab Republic ('North Yemen') and the People's Democratic Republic of Yemen ('South Yemen') in May 1990 (Edge 1992).

The mass return to Yemen comprised both short-term migrants away intermittently for up to ten years, and long-established expatriates settled for several decades (Van Hear 1994). The latter were of two types: a 'middleman minority' of traders, merchants and those engaged in services, and a lumpen minority who made a living in the informal sector. Their emergence in part reflected changes in the Saudi economy as demand for wage labour contracted and many Yemenis set up their own businesses in the service sector. The experience of mass return varied considerably from region to region in Yemen (Republic of Yemen 1991; Van Hear 1994). Four broad divisions might be made: the experience of returnees to the Tihama, the plain running down the west coast of the country; of those who returned to the highlands in the interior; of those who returned to the Hadramawt, in the east of former south Yemen; and of returnees to Aden and its hinterland in the south of the country.

The Tihama
Just under half the returnees settled in the Tihama plain. Most of these had been away for long periods – many for 20, 30 or 40 years – and they included some third-generation returnee children. Many had effectively made their lives in Saudi Arabia and did not intend to come back to Yemen, links with which they had all but severed. They were the least able to reintegrate into Yemeni society and populated shanty settlements in and around the Red Sea port of Hodeidah and other main towns. Their conditions of life and employment prospects were generally very poor (Stevenson 1993; Van Hear 1994).

The highlands
Just over one-third of the returnees returned to Yemen's highlands, including the capital Sana'a. Migrants from the highlands had tended to stay in

Saudi Arabia for shorter periods than had those from the Tihama; they had remitted money and they had made at least occasional visits home, thus keeping up their links with the home community. Thus, most were able to find some accommodation on their return and some means of livelihood, albeit with difficulty. Self-employment in retailing, services, transport and agriculture figured among the occupations of those who had found some means of livelihood back in Yemen (Stevenson 1993; Van Hear 1994).

The Hadramawt

Just under one-eighth of the returnees returned to the Hadramawt region in the former People's Democratic Republic of Yemen. These tended to be wealthier than other returnees, had maintained links with the homeland and invested substantially in property and construction. The Hadramis' centuries-old tradition of residence abroad made their position somewhat different from that of other Yemeni migrants; they constituted a diaspora of merchants, traders and bankers, not only in Saudi Arabia and elsewhere in the Arab world, but also in East Africa, and South and Southeast Asia (Serjeant 1988).

Aden and its hinterland

Aden and the surrounding area received about 5 per cent of the returnee total. As a port Aden had always attracted a conglomerate of migrants and nationalities, and so received its share of returnees in 1990/1; many lived in very poor conditions in shanty settlements with little prospect of employment. The position here was complicated by the accommodation of people fleeing the conflict in Somalia, who included substantial numbers of Yemeni origin, in addition to the returnees from Saudi Arabia and Kuwait.

Concurrent and subsequent migratory movements rendered this broad, fourfold regional pattern more complex. By no means all returnees made for their region of origin, but many gravitated to major towns in other regions instead. Thus many Tihamis were found in Sana'a and particularly in Aden, where they have formed new shanty settlements; conversely some people from the highlands went to Hodeidah to settle. There also appeared to be a drift of returnees, particularly Tihamis, to Hadramawt to work in construction financed by Hadrami returnees.

The impact of the mass return on Yemen

Yemen is classed as a poor country, with GDP per capita of $520 in 1991 (World Bank 1992, 1993). Life

expectancy at birth in 1990 was fifty-two years, only 39 per cent of the adult population were literate, only 35 per cent of the population had access to health services and only 46 per cent had access to safe drinking water (UNDP 1992).

Already among the worst in the region, many of these indicators of human well-being were exacerbated by the demographic impact of the mass return. Assuming that the estimate of 800,000 returnees was accurate (see Birks and Sinclair 1990 and Findlay 1987 on the difficulties of estimating the volume of Yemeni migration), Yemen would have absorbed a 7 per cent increase to its population within three months in 1990. Taking into account natural increase, the new republic's estimated population rose from 11.3 million as of mid-1990 to 12.5 million in mid-1991 (World Bank 1992, 1993). Since many of the returnees were of working age, perhaps 15 per cent was added to the workforce, estimated at about 2.5 million in mid-1990, before the mass return (ODI 1991; Republic of Yemen 1992c).

One of the main damaging impacts on Yemen's economy of the mass return was held to be loss of remittances, for long a major source of foreign exchange for both North and South Yemen (Edge 1992). Although remittances were already on the decline after peaking at up to $1.7 billion for both Yemens in 1983 (Birks and Sinclair 1990; Edge 1992), the earnings of Yemeni workers abroad still accounted for much of Yemen's official foreign receipts (Edge 1992), as well as a large volume that did not pass through official channels.

However, to term these remittances 'lost' as a result of the events of 1990 is a little misleading (Van Hear 1994). The mass return appears to have had a dramatic positive effect on Yemen's current account balance, which has habitually recorded a heavy deficit. This turnaround was almost wholly due to a near threefold increase in private transfers by returnees, to the equivalent of about $1.3 billion in 1990. As substantial amounts were also remitted through unofficial channels, it is not unreasonable to suppose that total transfers were substantially greater than the officially recorded figure. In addition, goods and equipment said to be worth $374 million at current official rates of exchange were brought back by returnees (Republic of Yemen 1991). The impact on the current account balance was temporary, since annual remittances of between $400 million and $500 million were not forthcoming in subsequent years. On the other hand, since the equivalent of three years' worth of remittances was received in a single year, the subsequent shortfall was in a sense already accounted for. Moreover, since it was unlikely that all of this large sum would be used for consumption, a substantial amount could have been available for investment. The longer term impact of this injection of capital may therefore not be negligible.

This potential was very slow to be realized. The impact of returnee investment was limited regionally and sectorally. Some returnees, particularly in the Hadramawt, invested their capital accumulated or recovered from abroad in construction. Returnees had a considerable impact on agriculture in certain areas, where they took up farm loans and expanded cultivation (Van Hear 1994). But their impact on agriculture nationally was much less clear. In the first year after the mass return, the area of land under cultivation and gross agricultural output actually declined sharply. Although both the area under cultivation and total output revived markedly between 1991 and 1992, this may have been due as much to better rains as to input of significantly greater labour by returnee farmers (Republic of Yemen 1992a, 1992b).

More than two years after the mass arrival, investment and employment creation by returnees had not made significant inroads into the greatly increased unemployment the mass return had precipitated (Van Hear 1994). A large proportion of returnees remained unemployed, contributing to an unemployment rate nationally of about 40 per cent early in 1993, in great contrast to the labour scarcity in Yemen generated by emigration in the 1970s and 1980s.

Conclusion

The Gulf crisis set in motion profound shifts in the pattern of displacement in a region with a turbulent history of forced migration. The consequences of the large-scale, involuntary repatriations to Jordan and Yemen were among the most enduring of these mass displacements.

For substantial proportions of both migrant populations, their length of stay abroad threw into doubt the utility of the terms 'return' or 'repatriation', and had implications for attempts to integrate them. This was particularly the case for many of the Palestinians, many of whom had moved directly to Kuwait at the creation of Israel or after the 1967 war, and for many of whom Jordan was therefore not 'home'. It was also true for many of the Yemenis long resident abroad who had brought up their families abroad and lost any meaningful social and economic ties with Yemen.

The view held by many Jordanians of the returnees from Kuwait was that the Palestinian community formed a wealthy mercantile, professional, managerial or administrative class in Kuwait that could fend for itself in Jordan with minimal assistance. Much of the Palestinian community indeed conformed to the profile of a 'middleman' or 'auxiliary' minority with large numbers engaged in the professions, in managerial or administrative posts, in trade and in services. However, there was a significant minority of skilled and semi-skilled manual or office workers, and of labourers. While relatively comfortably-off in Kuwait, almost all returnees suffered a decline in their living standards after their arrival in Jordan. The returnee population thus comprised dispossessed capitalists, disgruntled professionals and under-employed technicians, as well as additions to Jordan's impoverished underclass.

The Yemenis abroad included long-established residents as well as classic short-term labour migrants. Yemenis long resident in Saudi Arabia, Kuwait and other states included wealthy merchants and bankers, those engaged in middle-level services and retailing, and a lumpen population eking out a living in the lower reaches of the informal sector. The expatriates' experience after the involuntary mass return depended largely on links they had maintained while abroad through remittances and visits home, but all suffered a decline in the standard of living they were accustomed to in Saudi Arabia or elsewhere in the affluent Gulf.

Macro-economic indicators suggest that a strong economic turnaround accompanied the arrival of 300,000 Jordanians from Kuwait and the Gulf. These positive macro-economic signs coexisted with individual trauma and tragedy, unemployment and spreading poverty. Even the economic benefits were ambivalent. For understandable reasons (among them insecurity resulting from the recent trauma of uprooting and the prospect of a political settlement in the Occupied Territories), after investing in building, returnees with capital generally tried to keep their investments liquid, rather than setting up businesses that created employment directly. Nevertheless, it was still possible to turn to Jordan's advantage the third major population influx that the country had had to accommodate since 1948.

Evidence of the positive impact of the mass return was less convincing for Yemen than for Jordan. There was a large influx of capital, which though smaller than that to Jordan was still substantial and may eventually have some comparable effects. Returnee investment was seen in parts of the country and the economy, but for most of the minority of returnees who were able to find work, conditions were uninspiring, and the prospects were grim for those with no alternative but to scratch out a living in shanty settlements. Nevertheless, as in Jordan, there was still potential to turn the massive population return to Yemen's advantage, suggesting that the enduring consequences of such sudden, large-scale, involuntary repatriations need not necessarily be negative.

Note

This contribution is based on research funded by the UK Economic and Social Research Council (research award R000 23 3831), and draws on Van Hear 1994 and 1995.

References

Birks, J. and C. Sinclair (1990) 'The Crisis in Yemeni Return Migration from Saudi Arabia in 1990: Background, Nature and Consequences', World Bank Human Resources Sector Study Team, draft working paper, Durham, December

Bonacich, E. (1973) 'A Theory of Middleman Minorities', *American Sociological Review*, 38

Brand, L. (1988) *Palestinians in the Arab World: Institution Building and the Search for State*, New York: Columbia University Press

Central Bank of Jordan, (1990, 1991) *Annual Report 1990, 1991*, Amman: Central Bank of Jordan

(1992) *Monthly Statistical Bulletin*, Amman: Central Bank of Jordan, December

Edge, S. (1992) 'Yemen: Arabian Enigma', *Middle East Economic Digest*, 7, EMAP Business Information, London

(1993) 'Special Report: Jordan', *Middle East Economic Digest*, 28 May

Edge, S. and P. Dougherty (1992) 'Jordan Returns to the Fold', *Middle East Economic Digest*, 2 October

Findlay, A. (1987) *The Role of International Labour Migration in the Transformation of an Economy: The Case of the Yemen Arab Republic*, International Migration for Employment Working Paper, Geneva: International Labour Organization

Ghabra, S. (1987) *Palestinians in Kuwait: The Family and Politics of Survival*, Boulder, CO: Westview Press

Hashemite Kingdom of Jordan (1991a) *The Socio-Economic Characteristics of Jordanian Returnees*, Amman: National Centre for Educational Research and Development

(1991b) *Ministry of Labour Annual Report 1991*, Amman: Ministry of Labour

(1992a) *Returnees, 10 August 1991 to 30 November 1992*, Amman: Department of Statistics

(1992b) *Annual Agricultural Statistics, 1992*, Amman: Department of Statistics

ILO (International Labour Office) (1991) 'Migrant Workers Affected by the Gulf Crisis', Report of the Director-General, Third Supplementary Report, GB.249/15/7, Geneva: ILO

Morland, M (1993) *Emerging Markets: Egypt, Jordan, Morocco, Syria, Tunisia: The Stockmarkets of Mediterranean Arabia*, London: Lehman Brothers

ODI (Overseas Development Institute) (1991) *The Impact of the Gulf Crisis on Developing Countries*, ODI briefing paper, London: ODI

Republic of Yemen (1991) *Expatriates: Final Statistics of the Returnees since 2 August 1990*, Sana'a: Ministry of Planning and Economic Development, Central Statistical Organization

(1992a) *Agricultural Statistics Year Book 1991*, Sana'a: Ministry of Agriculture

(1992b) 'Summary of Provisional Agricultural Statistics 1991–1992', Sana'a: Ministry of Agriculture

(1992c) *Statistical Yearbook 1991*, Central Statistical Organization: Sana'a

Serjeant, R. (1988) 'The Hadrami Network', in D. Lombard and J. Aubin (eds), *Marchands et Hommes d'affaires asiatiques dans l'Ocean Indien et la Mer de Chine, 13e–20e Siècles*, Paris: Editions de l'Ecole des Hautes Etudes en Sciences Sociales

Stevenson, T. (1993) 'Yemeni Workers Come Home: Reabsorbing One Million Migrants', *Middle East Report*, March–April

Tinker, H. (1977) *The Banyan Tree: Overseas Emigrants from India, Pakistan and Bangladesh*, London: Oxford University Press

UNDP (United Nations Development Programme) (1992) *Human Development Report 1992*, Oxford: Oxford University Press

UNICEF (United Nations Children's Fund) (1992) *The Hashemite Kingdom of Jordan: Unicef Annual Report 1992*, Amman: UNICEF

Van Hear, N. (1993) 'Mass Flight in the Middle East: Involuntary Migration and the Gulf Conflict, 1990–91', in R. Black and V. Robinson (eds) *Geography and Refugees: Patterns and Processes of Change*, London: Belhaven

(1994) 'The Socio-Economic Impact of the Involuntary Mass Return to Yemen in 1990', *Journal of Refugee Studies*, 17 (1)

(1995) 'The Impact of Involuntary Mass "Return" to Jordan in the Wake of the Gulf Crisis', *International Migration Review*, 29 (2)

World Bank (1992, 1993) *World Development Report 1992, 1993*, Oxford: Oxford University Press

PART THIRTEEN

REFUGEES FROM POLITICAL CONFLICT

Throughout this *Survey* I have been cognizant of the incidence of refugee migration, and of the sudden displacement of people during periods of war and state formation. By the last quarter of the twentieth century refugee migration has become the most visible and the most sensitive form of world migration. The numbers too are startling – getting on, by UN 1995 estimates, for 20 million people. Of course one has to be very careful about evaluating such a figure. Displaced people, victims of civil wars and those fleeing natural disasters ('ecological refugees') are often included – certainly a good proportion of the total would not conform to the definitions of a (political) refugee laid down in the 1951 Geneva Convention. On the other hand, it is arguable that the Convention was drafted with post-war European conditions in mind and that it is in any case being selectively and too narrowly applied by governments anxious to limit the asylum claims even of genuine refugees.

Many of the most dramatic refugee flows have occurred in Africa, the pathetic victims looking sadly at the television cameras that beam their images onto our television screens. It is all too easy to jump to the conclusion that Africa is simply a benighted place, struck by random famines and oppressed by endemic and inevitable 'tribal' conflicts. What, so the thought runs, can possibly be done other than to place a few coins in a collection box for the world's victims? Perhaps the beginnings of an alternative solution lie in an alternative understanding of the problem. *Wilson*'s contribution on southern Africa provides plenty of clues. He shows, principally, how local political and military struggles in Angola, Namibia, Mozambique and Zimbabwe were set within wider regional and international conflicts. This is not to argue that Africans were mere puppets, but that conflicts of interests were fanned and exacerbated by outside interests.

The South African government was fighting a long war of position as it tried to blunt the force of African nationalism in the surrounding countries. Like the apartheid regime, and sometimes in collusion with it, the US government needed surrogates to fight its war against communism. For their part the Soviets and their Cuban allies propped up increasingly implausible quasi-Marxist governments in Angola and Mozambique. Arms and logistical support poured in. The results in human terms were calamitous. Civilian populations were driven into the protected villages or refugee camps so that they could no longer serve as the 'sea' within which the rebel 'fish' swam (to use Mao Zedung's suggestive analogy). Meanwhile the rebel forces tried to achieve 'ungovernability' by killing local officials and destroying services and infrastructure. People were cut off from their lands, for they could no longer get electricity or water, fertilizers or credit. The crops failed and the streams of refugees began.

With the exception of the South African interest, many of the same dynamics were at work in the Horn of Africa, considered by *Zegeye*. As he puts it, 'Most refugees are fleeing from areas of conflict rather than from environmental problems. However, the increasing mobility of people in search of food and water is adding to these numbers.' Of course this is a difficult calculation and one *Zegeye* makes more precise in the case of the Sudan where, he maintains, three million people were displaced by drought and desertification in 1984/5 compared with four million displaced by civil war and intertribal conflict. Together, the displaced people constituted over one-third of the entire population. Some of the most important, and ill-understood, arguments lie in the subtle links between environmental and political problems. In a landscape blighted by desertification and erosion, traditional certainties and ways of life are questioned. Older and wiser hands are cast aside in desperation as a battle for survival ensues. A group of pastoralists may, in *Zegeye*'s example, be tempted to cross a border area to find grazing, only to trigger a violent response. When these competitions over scarce resources are set within a religious context (as southern Sudanese Christians clash with Muslim northerners), or a political context (as nationalists slug it out with federalists), natural enmity is given the additional fervour of conviction. The cattle die, the crops fail and the streams of refugees begin.

The story of the West's efforts to aid refugees shows considerable resistance to any consistent or principled stand. While most Western countries signed the Geneva Convention in 1951, in practice their acceptance of refugees has followed one or more of four main criteria. Have the refugees any use value? Can something be gained politically, particularly in terms of foreign policy? Is there a labour shortage or demographic decline such that all kinds of migrants are welcomed? Is there a significant co-religious or co-ethnic group lobbying for the admission of a particular group of refugees? (Cf. Cohen 1994: 69–72; Joly 1993.) In the case of the USA, as the Zuckers' earlier work (1987) has illustrated, the shifts in American foreign policy are an important determinant of whether particular cohorts of refugees are welcomed or spurned. So it proves in the cases *Zucker* and *Zucker* examine in this *Survey*, namely Cuba and Haiti. Like the authors, many readers would have some difficulty in distinguishing the respective merits of 'a communist dictatorship' and 'a right-wing kleptocracy' in deciding whether refugees left legitimately. In the period of the Cold War, no such difficulty taxed the minds of the US authorities. The Cuban *émigrés* were legitimate refugees and should be welcomed;the Haitian boat people were economic migrants and should be sent back. With the end of the Cold War, these ideological certainties have now evaporated. Some of the counter-logics – which have always been there – are now asserting themselves. To be sure there is a politically powerful Cuban lobby (much more powerful than its Haitian equivalent) demanding that the USA permits the dissenters from Castro's regime to leave. But the political and social cost of earlier welcomes was high: for example, open-door policies towards Cubans severely undermined Carter's presidency, and the State of Florida became, for a while, virtually ungovernable. The end of the Duvalier regimes and the advent of a successor military regime in Haiti also posed a dilemma for US policy-makers. The tide of Haitians trying to leave finally convinced President Clinton that he had to restore the elected, but socialist-inclined, Aristide to power – if for no other reason than that it might help to stem the demands for admission by Haitian asylum-seekers.

In the case of Indochinese refugees, to the context of the Cold War must be added the story of France's doomed attempt to decolonize without bloodshed. *Mignot*'s contribution considers the exodus of Indochinese from Laos, Cambodia and Vietnam. Many of the refugees were to end up in France or the USA. It is a crude but effective riposte to the xenophobes of each destination country to respond: 'They are here, because we were there.' In 1975, the USA's attempt to stop the 'domino' falling in South Vietnam collapsed in a heap around the American embassy in Saigon. Lifting off the roof of the embassy were giant helicopters stuffed with the USA's allies. Soon 130,000 were evacuated to the US base in Guam and thence to the USA. France's historic role in the area also gave her a special responsibility, while settlement there was particularly attractive to Francophone refugees. To be sure, other countries – Canada, the rest of Europe and Oceania – became involved, but the principal destination countries remained the USA and France. As *Mignot* notes, the resettlement programmes established by the destination countries were neither uniform nor by any means wholly successful. Indeed so dramatic was the downward mobility of many of the Indochinese, that the first generation is regarded as 'sacrificed', with all hope of integration, acceptance and mobility resting with the next generation.

Unlike most of the rich countries, many poor nations have shown remarkable generosity in offering aid and succour to refugees from neighbouring countries. This was true too of Pakistan, which housed some 3.5 million Afghan refugees in the post-1978 period when the pro-communist regime took control of Afghanistan. The anti-communist convictions of the Pakistani government together with strong sentiments of Islamic religious solidarity helped, of course, to persuade the government that this hospitality was necessary and justified. *Cammack* concentrates her examination of the Afghan refugees in Pakistan on the 26 per cent of women who lived in the refugee camps. She shows how the opportunity to enskill these women and to deploy them in the rehabilitation of the post-communist regime in Afghanistan was lost. Traditionalists wanted to confine the women to *purdah*; there was a strong resistance to them being educated on the grounds that dangerous ideas were precisely what led to the communist seizure of power. Western aid agencies often reinforced conservative ideas by showing too little sensitivity to deeply held religious convictions.

Suhrke presents an important analysis of Islamic ideas on asylum, trying precisely to compare and reconcile Western and Islamic traditions. This is crucial, if for no other reason than that Muslims make up some two-thirds of refugees worldwide, with current conflicts in the Caucasus, Central Asia and the Balkans likely to contribute further to that proportion. The story of the *hijra* – Muhammad's flight to Medina – is interpreted to mean that Muslims have an *obligation* to leave a land of oppression in order to find liberation in a true Muslim country. Equally, as the Pakistanis showed in the Afghan case, it is a sacred duty to offer aid and support. The story of the *hijra* stresses *voluntary* flight yet the realities on the ground often suggest involuntary displacements of Muslims, a phenomenon that is more difficult to integrate into the theological tradition. Slowly, however, the powerful and wealthy Islamic states are not only recognizing their obligations to the Islamic world, but also beginning to cooperate more fully with the United Nations High Commission for Refugees on an international basis. *Suhrke* reminds us that this movement was aided by the alliance between Saudi Arabia and the USA during the Gulf War, but, sadly, it was also thrown into reverse in Bosnia, where the West was seen as letting down the Muslims, even though their cause was manifestly just. The world's refugees potentially have much to gain by careful efforts to reconcile the Western and Muslim traditions.

References

Cohen, Robin (1994) *Frontiers of Identity: The British and the Others*, London: Longman

Joly, Danièle (1993) 'Political Decisions on Refugees', Paper to an International Seminar on Emerging Trends and Major Issues in Migration and Ethnic Relations in Western and Eastern Europe organized by UNESCO and the Centre for Research in Ethnic Relations, University of Warwick, Coventry, 5–8 November

Zucker, N. L. and N. F. Zucker (1987) *The Guarded Gate: The Reality of American Refugee Policy*, San Diego: Harcourt, Brace and Jovanovich

REFUGEES, DISPLACED PEOPLE AND RETURNEES IN SOUTHERN AFRICA

K. B. WILSON[1]

Much of the recent history of southern Africa revolves around migration, which became a major force both integrating the region, and reflecting its integration and uneven incorporation into a changing world order. Southern Africa witnessed for the best part of a century the world's largest and most coercive regional labour migration network and the largest forced displacement of rural populations off prime agricultural land expropriated by settlers in modern times (for example, Katjavivi 1988; Palmer 1977; Ranger 1985). Tens of thousands of people were also evicted from game reserves and national parks (Marks 1986), and from the sites of major dams on the Zambezi (Colson 1971) and other river systems. The twentieth century also saw huge rural–rural migration both within and between the countries of the region in search of economic opportunity and less harassment; indeed hundreds of thousands of people moved across the arbitrarily defined borders from the Portuguese colonies into British Central Africa to escape forced labour and related injustices.

Southern Africa's recent decades of conflict have since generated some of the world's highest per capita levels of refugees and internal displacement. The long history of mobility across a highly differentiated political-economic system critically influenced the experience and strategies of these refugees, for whether in flight, initial survival or in integration, they were able to utilize their longstanding cross-border social and economic networks to great effect. Indeed, so dynamic were the identities of the communities of labour migrants in neighbouring states that it was they who laid much of the foundation for political activism and provided many of the recruits and funding for the refugee guerrilla armies discussed below. Furthermore, some of the populations seeking repatriation at the end of conflicts are people who have been away from their homelands for decades. These include the descendants of Herero who fled Namibia for Botswana in 1904/5 on suppression of a rebellion against German rule and who have been seeking to return since 1954. In 1989, a Herero chief, who was president of the Democratic Turnhalle

Alliance, caused controversy by trying to woo 40,000 of them from Botswana to counter SWAPO returnees, but they were deemed no longer to be refugees by the UNHCR, the Botswana government and the Namibian authorities (Matlou 1992: 70).

This contribution will concentrate as much on processes as on numbers and locations. This is partly of necessity: there have simply been too many complex movements with poor documentation and little research coverage. To obtain accurate numbers is particularly problematic (Kibreab 1991). Most refugees made great efforts to avoid detection and thus control. Liberation movements, governments and agencies had institutional interests in misrepresenting the figures; and, whenever aid distribution was underway, fraud and confusion were normal, given a breakdown of trust between donors and recipients (Harrell-Bond et al. 1992).

To structure the contribution a broad functional periodization has been followed. First, refugees and the anti-colonial wars are examined, with a focus on the militarized refugee camp. This is followed by a discussion of flight in the post-independence civil wars, with a focus on how refugee movements come to identify with guerrilla and counter-insurgency tactics. Third, the challenges to return and peaceful reintegration are addressed.

Refugees and the anti-colonial wars

The first round of refugees in southern Africa's history was associated with its anti-colonial wars in Angola, Mozambique, Namibia and Zimbabwe. Refugees from these conflicts were both combatants and political cadres who chose to leave their homes with the aim of joining the armed struggle, and also civilians who left because of the violence of counter-insurgency operations in the war zones. In practice these two groups were often integrated, not least because the liberation movements sought to use civilians to secure aid from humanitarian agencies. Most such refugees lived in rural camps, many experiencing serious health and other welfare and livelihood problems. Agricultural settlement schemes

Table 13.1: *Size and locations of major liberation struggle refugee populations in southern Africa*

Country of origin	Years of struggle	Liberation movement/s	Peak refugee years	Country of asylum	Aproximate population	Year of return
Angola	1961–74	MPLA/FNLA		Zaire	400,000	1974–75
		UNITA	1966–74	Zambia	25,000	few return
Namibia	1966–89	SWAPO	1980s	Angola	74,000	1989–90
				Others	7,400	1989–90
Mozambique	1964–74	FRELIMO	1968–74	Tanzania	100,000	1974–75
				Malawi	25,000	1974–75
				Zambia	15,000	1974–75
Zimbabwe	1972–79	ZANU/ZANLA	1975–79	Mozambique	150,000	1979–80
		ZAPU/ZIPRA	1974–79	Zambia	43,000	1979–80

Sources: I have used official sources for populations adjusted as far as possible to account for known distortions. 'Liberation movements' refer only to those who controlled the administration of camps with large refugee populations. Other movements lacked necessary political support from host countries. Botswana and Malawi also hosted refugees affiliated to liberation movements, but due to their lack of *de facto* independence from their white neighbours they did not allow overt politico-military organization. Botswana was unusual in that at least in the 1980s it allowed refugees in the camps to choose whether or not to affiliate to the different political organizations present.

for Mozambicans in Tanzania (Feldman 1971) and Angolans in Zambia (Wilson 1986), were rather unsuccessful largely due to technocratic planning and inadequate resources (Refugee Policy Group 1986). In some areas, notably along Angola's border with Zambia, there was substantial self-settlement by refugees who sought to maintain their independence (Hansen 1979).

The 'refugee camp' became in this context a quasi-military base run by a liberation movement.[2] These political movements maximized refugee organization and participation, avoiding many of the abuses of domination by paternalistic Western aid agencies, but in the context of war and political infighting they were usually highly authoritarian. Abuses of power and a scant regard for human rights were the norm, often reflecting personal struggles for wealth and power. International opposition to the white minority regimes meant humanitarian agencies largely ignored this and made little effort to ensure that aid reached beneficiaries. Political dissidence was not tolerated, and there was a stream of deserters and defectors. In the context of pressures for unified opposition to colonial regimes, host countries used political leverage and even the security services to back favoured leaders. Tanzania's President Nyerere, for example, stifled all opposition to Frelimo's first president, Mondlane (de Brito 1991), and in much the same way Frelimo later secured Mugabe's control of ZANLA in Mozambique, and the MPLA maintained control of SWAPO (and ANC) camps in Angola.

Many countries and/or agencies refused to assist refugees who did not accept membership of recognized liberation movements. While much was achieved in the struggle against white domination, this state of affairs ultimately weakened the liberation movements, facilitated rather than prevented penetration by enemy security services, and created a foundation for poor human rights and political records after independence.

Host countries paid dearly for providing the liberation movements with a springboard and for supporting sanctions against the illegal white regimes they were seeking to dislodge (Gasarasi 1988). The armies of Rhodesia and South Africa in particular regularly raided such camps, by both air and ground attack forces, usually killing local people as well as refugees, and often damaging infrastructure (Martin and Johnson 1981). Southern Angola – the rear base for Namibia's SWAPO – was devastated by a series of South African invasions and its support for UNITA. In Mozambique, Rhodesia and South Africa supported the proxy force, Renamo, as a political lever to prevent the Mozambique government assisting Zimbabwe's ZANLA and the South African ANC. In 1984 Mozambique signed the Nkomati Accord, which officially ended ANC military-base activity in exchange for an ostensible reduction in South African support for Renamo (Vines 1991a). Zambia also paid heavily economically for supporting most of the region's nationalist guerrilla groupings, but was sufficiently large and distant not to give in.

Botswana (Matlou 1992), Swaziland and Lesotho, on the other hand, were obliged to capitulate from time to time to their economically and militarily powerful neighbour.

The independence of the Portuguese colonies in 1975 and of Zimbabwe in 1980 saw large-scale repatriation movements. The UNHCR initially sought a high profile role, having completed in 1972/3 its first major African assignment in repatriation in the southern Sudan (Reid 1991). However, in each case the vast majority of refugees who returned actually self-repatriated. The political activists tended to move much earlier than the planning process had intended, with the intention of securing politico-military control (Angola/Mozambique) or electoral success (Zimbabwe) in the home country (Maranya 1994), while civilian refugees were generally better placed to make their own return movements than the agencies who tried to assist them. Most of the refugees who chose not to return belonged to groups that failed to win power and/or lived outside the camps and had hence integrated into the local economy and society. Repatriation to Namibia in 1989/90 differed markedly from previous return movements in the region because of the comparatively small numbers, the high international profile and the unusually long distances involved. This facilitated a massive UNHCR operation centred around chartered flights, in which SWAPO, governments and other agencies successfully organized people's transport, despite continuous logistical problems and inefficiency (Mwase 1990; Preston et al. 1993). The mobilization of local government, churches and (in Zimbabwe) of local non-governmental organizations played a key role in securing economic and social reintegration of returnees in the short term. In the longer term their welfare was dependent on national political and economic performance. In southern Africa (as elsewhere) returnees tended to continue to show high geographical and socio-economic mobility in both positive and negative directions. The demobilization of ex-fighters proved particularly problematic. In Zimbabwe, for example, despite substantial programmes, most ex-combatants were still unemployed after ten years and were facing ongoing integration difficulties. One of the greatest demobilization challenges in Namibia concerns the fate of the so-called 'Bushmen' trackers and soldiers the South Africans used against SWAPO, many of whom are now subject to an agricultural settlement programme.

Flight and the post-independence wars

Three southern African states (Angola, Mozambique and Zimbabwe) returned to armed conflict after independence. Movements that had failed to secure political power gathered strength from covert military aid under cold war and South African destabilization agendas (Johnson and Martin 1986) and took advantage of largely regionally based popular opposition to the new governments. The resulting wars were fought over civilian populations and, except in Zimbabwe, generated much higher rates of displacement both within and beyond the countries than had the liberation struggles. These wars were also qualitatively different from earlier conflicts in that the provision of relief became part and parcel of the conflicts (Keen and Wilson 1994). Though the white regimes of colonial southern Africa used defensive villagization as a tool for controlling guerrilla access to civilians (Coelho 1993; Weinrich 1977) and, in Operation Turkey, Rhodesians attempted to destroy farmers' crops to starve guerrillas of food, these techniques were usually implemented in a cumbersome fashion with poor intelligence and were mostly counter-productive. Because colonial forces faced guerrillas with substantial rear bases, controlling the economy and population of the war zones was a poor defensive tool: they instead focused on seeking to penetrate and destroy nationalist operations and to obtain military intelligence through torture and blackmail to enable counter-attacks.

Civilian experience of post-independence conflicts was generally harsher and followed a regular pattern established in the Horn of Africa, the Middle East, Central America and South Asia. The strategy is for government forces to drive civilian populations into submission and/or dependence on relief provided by their units (or by international agencies) so that they can no longer willingly or unwillingly feed, support or hide the rebel forces. Governments achieve this by displacing them and/or destroying their crops, terrorizing them into abandoning their homes and cutting their market access. Meanwhile the rebel forces seek to destroy the government, not militarily, but by wrecking the national economy and by achieving ungovernability by murdering local officials and smashing state social services. The rebels also seek to terrorize and starve out populations in government-held zones and garrisons by cutting commercial and relief supply routes and ambushing

Table 13.2: *Refugees and displaced people in post-independence conflicts in southern Africa*

Country of origin	Years of conflict	Areas of origin	Refugees or internally displaced	Numbers involved	Main location of populations
Angola	1975–91	East	Refugees	103,000	Zambia
	1975–80s	North	Refugees	310,000	Zaire
	1975–78 and				
	1990s	Cabinda	Refugees	150,000	Zaire/Congo
	1975–91	National	International	1,500,000	Cities + towns
Mozambique	1984–92	North	Refugees	100,000	Tanzania
		North	Refugees	1,200,000	Malawi
		North	Refugees	30,000	Zambia
		Centre	Refugees	200,000	Zimbabwe
		South	Refugees	75,000	Swaziland
		South	Refugees	250,000	South Africa
		National	International	4,500,000	Cities + towns
Zimbabwe	1983–88	West	Refugees	1,300	Botswana
		West	Internal	30,000	Bulawayo

Sources: UNHCR and government figures have been adjusted by known distortions (such as numbers of people living outside of official assistance programmes). Note that numbers change continually: figures reflect peak levels. Dates of 'years of conflict' refer to the periods when large amounts of displacement occurred.

people straying beyond the defended camps. Bizarre and sometimes ritual mutilations are used especially by rebel forces to attempt to frighten civilians into submission and to terrify enemy units (Wilson 1992c). Drought is cynically used by both sides as another opportunity to gain physical control of people, and to destroy the enemy's war economy and logistics.

Despite numerous international legal agreements and norms, the civilians affected by these wars received almost no protection (Africa Watch 1989, 1992). Aid agencies and international human rights organizations, which, for geopolitical reasons were usually in sympathy with government rather than rebel forces, did little to protect displaced people from their governments. Even where they did protest, they were often ignored by the governments responsible. Meanwhile, rebel forces allowed next to no effective access to the few international humanitarian agencies that were prepared to work with them and were impervious to international condemnation. Thus, during the 1980s, rural people in western Zimbabwe (Werbner 1991) and in most of Angola and Mozambique found themselves sandwiched between rebels and government and facing the deliberate destruction of their livelihoods. They also risked land mines and other indiscriminate violence, arbitrary

arrest, torture and mutilation, systematic rape, forced military conscription and, in the case of Mozambique's Renamo, virtual enslavement on bases (Brennan 1987; Gersony 1988; Wilson and Nunes 1994). Given such circumstances people had strong motivations to escape beyond the war zones, though to be found fleeing could be dangerous. Renamo became notorious for killing the relatives of anyone who fled its areas. Nevertheless, particularly in Mozambique, where there were few front lines and almost no part of the country was spared, the displacement of millions of rural people resulted in huge relief camps around the garrison towns, sprawling peri-urban settlement around the cities and large refugee movements to neighbouring countries. By 1993 the Cabindan enclave of Angola had more refugees in the diaspora than in its own territory, where only 100,000 remained (Vines, personal communication).

By the late 1980s some two million southern African victims of post-independence civil wars had taken up the opportunity of asylum. However, host countries varied in their receptivity to these influxes, particularly where refugees were followed by cross-border attacks. Zimbabwe, for example, which suffered from a particularly brutal Renamo campaign of murder and destruction, sought to impose stringent security. It rounded up most Mozambican refugees into camps and, during the late 1980s, reputedly forcibly repatriated those it could not handle. Most of the other states in the region also emphasized encampment, although in all the countries thousands of refugees – sometimes even most of them – managed to avoid being brought into the settlements or camps run by aid agencies and governments. These self-settled refugee populations were often regarded positively by local populations, who protected them and assisted them in obtaining legal documentation. In Botswana one group of Angolans was even granted citizenship on the basis of its political commitment to the ruling party candidate (Zetterqvist 1990).

South Africa maintained its shameful record by establishing an electrified fence to hamper Mozambican flight into the country and by deporting any Mozambicans found without papers as 'illegal work seekers' (Le Scour 1989; Morrison 1991a; Vines 1991b). Only in two of the nearby 'homelands' did the quasi-independent governments grant asylum. Accounts of virtual and even actual slavery of Mozambicans on white farms and in the black townships abound, as does evidence of the security forces forcibly recruiting Mozambican asylum seekers for military service. Even during 1993, while the UNHCR was desperately trying to negotiate an agreement to work in the country on behalf of Mozambicans and to secure an orderly and assisted repatriation, the security services stepped up their forced deportation in August, apparently without cabinet approval. As anticipated, presssure to deport 'aliens' perceived as competing for economic opportunities only increased after the achievement of black majority rule.

Other asylum countries were not immune to political pressures from neighbouring governments, or from their domestic constituencies. Botswana came under enormous pressure after the Unity Agreement in Zimbabwe to repatriate the remaining Zimbabwean refugees; the Malawi government reported continually in the last years of the war in Mozambique that it could no longer host its staggering burden of a million refugees, although this also reflected an attempt by it to put pressure on the donors with whom it was negotiating over the cutoff of developmental assistance on the grounds of its human rights record.

Massive professional and bureaucratic expansion transformed international assistance for refugees in the 1980s. Given its technical and professional advances, criticism of this 'aid regime' has shifted from its ineffectiveness to its destructive impact on national government capacity and its failure to relate to refugees' own initiatives and to environmental and gender issues. Huge programmes of food distribution were undertaken by the World Food Programme, other donors and local partner agencies. And, despite supply failures, inadequate quantities and sometimes inappropriate composition, food distribution became the assistance programmes' most effective plank (Wilson 1992a; Wilson et al. 1989;), yielding more benefit than the income-generating social development schemes of large donor allocations made through NGOs (Zetter et al. 1993). Research findings consistently showed that the greatest contribution to the refugees' livelihood, sense of community and social integration with local people came from their own initiatives (Wilson 1992a, 1992b). Opportunities for aid agencies to launch development rather than relief-focused assistance programmes were largely missed, with this approach being either ignored or interpreted as licence for yet more poor agricultural settlement schemes (Black et al. 1990). Only rudimentary attempts were made by aid agencies to ensure benefits to local people alongside refugees. Increasing attention to psycho-social issues by agencies did not yet mean that such basic issues as death and burial were adequately addressed (Harrell-Bond and Wilson 1990), and the new environmental sensitivity was also not as yet often translated into programmes that addressed the real issues in natural resource management (Wilson 1992a). Most programmes of assistance showed little awareness of their gender impacts: it was only the extraordinary initiative of women that enabled them to keep going or even to improve their standing through the processes of displacement and exile (Chingono 1994; Nunes 1992; Spring 1982; Wilson 1992a). Displacement has tended to transform and widen women's social worlds and responsibilities more than those of men; what people have experienced in camps and cities in and out of the country will have a strong socio-economic impact on the affected regions for many years after peace (Chingono 1994; Wilson 1991).

Returnees and the challenges of peace

The implosion of South Africa's violent hegemony, the end of the cold war and the desperate desire of ordinary people for peace, brought a welcome end through negotiation first to the conflict in Angola (where the protagonists were highly dependent on external aid) and then to Mozambique. UN-brokered transitions have, however, yet to prove effective. In Angola, where the legacies of war in terms of infra-structural destruction, economic dislocation, copious weaponry and land mines made the task of peace-building and recovery quite formidable (Africa Watch 1993a; Green 1992; Morrison 1991b), a weak and poorly structured UN-brokered transition collapsed after the defeat of the UNITA rebels at the polls. Unprecedented levels of fighting then erupted in the struggle to control key strategic locations, economic resources (diamonds, oil, food producing regions) and populations (Vines 1993). In a war previously marked by the comparative stability of its front lines, civilians have suffered considerable displacement, privation and mortality. This is due essentially to the rapid and unpredictable spread of the war and to the changes in fortune of the protagonists. New refugee influxes occurred into Zaire and Zambia and these included people who had repatriated after the peace agreement. Namibia has also started hosting Angolans. Meanwhile, at the time of writing the UN operation in Mozambique appears to be working in a more favourable environment and claims to have learnt its lessons from Angola. However, it appears that success to date in Mozambique is largely because an inefficient UN, an inactive Frelimo government, and a still cautious and rather confused Renamo leadership have been unable to contain popular Mozambican initiatives on the ground for peace and reconciliation. The main challenge for the UN in Mozambique is whether it can obtain and implement an agreement on demobilization and the creation of a new national army. It also remains to be seen how elections will be organized and conducted, and whether an electoral system really can be translated into an effective system of distributing and managing political power in the longer term.

Peace in Mozambique raises issues of repatriation of refugees and return movements of internally displaced persons, as of how returning home is linked to issues of de-mining and reconstruction. Ignoring its experience to date the UNHCR continued for several years with a formal repatriation planning exercise for Mozambique, under which it would transport all refugees to transit camps and then on to their home areas (Wilson and Nunes 1994). Only once peace had come and donors had demonstrated their lack of confidence in the UNHCR programme did the agency realize its logistical impossibility and the need to direct available resources not to transport (most refugees were within walking distance of their homes) but to reconstructing the infrastructure and to supporting livelihoods during the transition (Wilson 1993). Exaggerated fears about the extent of mines, and then a failure to deal with them in the locations where they were a serious problem, further incapacitated formal programmes (Africa Watch 1993b). In the event, at the time of writing (1993) most Mozambicans were successfully organizing their own repatriation movements with minimal assistance, and often in the face of official hostility. Their future hangs on the deeper transformations of the Mozambican political economy. Could this now massively indebted and aid-dependent nation deliver a viable economic and service environment to its peasants? Would the re-emergent merchant and land-acquiring local and international elite give the peasantry their space?

Notes

1. With thanks to Julia Powles for bibliographic assistance, and to Terence Ranger for a cautionary remark.
2. There are virtually no academic studies of such camps: my sources include Pepetela (1983), the press and interviews with Zimbabweans, Mozambicans, and Namibians (both civilians and soldiers) who have lived in such camps.

References

Africa Watch (1989) *Angola: Violations of the Laws of War by Both Sides*, New York: Human Rights Watch
— (1992) *Conspicuous Destruction: War, Famine and the Reform Process in Mozambique*, New York: Human Rights Watch
— (1993a) *Land Mines in Angola*, New York: Human Rights Watch
— (1993b) *Land Mines in Mozambique*, New York: Human Rights Watch
Black, R. et al. (1990) *Ukwimi Refugee Settlement: Livelihood and Settlement Planning for Mozambicans in Zambia*, London and Oxford: King's College and Refugee Studies Programme
Brennan, T. O. (1987) *Uprooted Angolans: From Crisis to Catastrophe*, Washington: United States' Committee for Refugees
Brito, L. de (1991) 'Le Frelimo et la Construction de l'Etat National au Mocambique', Ph.D. thesis, Université de Paris VIII-Vincennes
Chingono, M. (1994) 'War, Social Change and Development in Mozambique: Catastrophe or Creation of a New Society?', Ph.D. thesis, University of Cambridge
Coelho, J.-P. Constantino Borges (1993) 'Protected Villages and Communal Villages in the Mozambican Province of Tete (1968–1982): A History of State Resettlement Policies, Development and War', Ph.D. thesis, University of Bradford
Colson, E. F. (1971) *The Social Consequences of Resettlement: The Impact of the Kariba Resettlement on the Gwembe Tonga*, Manchester: Manchester University Press
Feldman, D. (1971) 'The Economic Viability of Refugee Settlements in Southern Tanzania', Ph.D. thesis, University of East Anglia

Gasarasi, C. P. (1988) 'The Effect of Africa's Exiles/ Refugees upon Inter-African State Relations: Conflict and Cooperation, 1958–1988', Ph.D. thesis, Tulane University

Gersony, R. (1988) *Summary of Mozambican Refugee Accounts of Principally Conflict-Related Experience in Mozambique*, Washington: Report to Ambassador J. Moore and Dr C. A. Crocker, Bureau for Refugee Programs, State Department

Green, R. H. (1992) 'The Four Horsemen Ride Together: Scorched Fields of War in Southern Africa', Refugee Studies Programme, Queen Elizabeth House Seminar, 11 November, 43 pp and 18 pp annex, unpublished

Hansen, A. (1979) 'Once the Running Stops: Assimilation of Angolan Refugees into Zambian Border Villages', *Disasters*, 3 (4), 369–74

Harrell-Bond, B. E. and K. B. Wilson (1990) 'Dealing with Dying: Anthropological Reflections on the Need for Assistance by African Refugee Programmes for Bereavement and Burial', *Journal of Refugee Studies*, 3 (3), 228–43

Harrell-Bond, B. E. et al. (1992) 'Counting the Refugees: Gifts, Givers, Patrons and Clients', *Journal of Refugee Studies*, 5 (3/4), 205–25

Johnson, P. and D. Martin (1986) *Destructive Engagement: Southern Africa at War*, Harare: Zimbabwe Publishing House

Katjavivi, P. (1988) *A History of Resistance in Namibia*, London: James Currey/OAU Inter-African Cultural Fund

Keen, D. and K. B. Wilson (1994) 'Engaging with Violence: A Reassessment of Relief in Wartime', in J. Macrae and A. Zwi (eds) *Wars of Hunger*, London: Zed Books

Kibreab, G. (1991) *The State of the Art Review of Refugee Studies in Africa*, Uppsala: Uppsala Papers in Economic History, Research Report, No. 26

Le Scour, J. P. (1989) *The Snake of Fire*, 11-page memorandum on the electric fence between Mozambique and South Africa, Johannesburg: South African Bishops Conference, Bureau for Refugees

Maranya, S. T. (1994) 'The Desire to Return: Effects of Experiences in Exile on Refugees Repatriating to Zimbabwe in the Early 1980s', in T. Allen and H. Morsink (eds) *When Refugees Go Home*, London: James Currey

Marks, S. (1986) *The Imperial Lion*, Boulder, CO: Westview Press

Martin, D. and P. Johnson (1981) *The Struggle for Zimbabwe*, London: Faber & Faber

Matlou, P. (1992) 'Refugee Policy in Botswana (1958–1989): The Interaction between State Security, Refugee Agency Interests and Refugee Needs', Ph.D., University of Essex

Morrison, J. S. (1991a) *UNHCR Enters South Africa: A Constrained Mandate*, 16-page issue brief, Washington: US Committee for Refugees

(1991b) *The Long Road Home: Angola's Post-War Inheritance*, Washington: US Committee for Refugees

Mwase, N. (1990) 'The Repatriation, Rehabilitation and Resettlement of Namibian Refugees at Independence', *Community Development Journal*, 25 (2), 113–20

Nunes, J. (1992) *Peasants and Survival: The Social Consequences of Displacement*, Maputo: Swedish International Development Authority

Palmer, R. H. (1977) *Land and Racial Domination in Rhodesia*, London: Heinemann

Pepetela, Artur Carlos Mauricio Pestana dos Santos (1983) *Mayombe* (translated by Michael Wolfers), Harare: Zimbabwe Publishing House

Preston, R. et al. (1993) *The Integration of Returned Exiles, Former Combatants and other War-Affected Namibians*, Windhoek: Namibian Institute for Social and Economic Research

Ranger, T. O. (1985) *Peasant Consciousness and Guerrilla War in Zimbabwe*, London: James Currey

Refugee Policy Group (1986) *Older Refugee Settlements in Africa*, Washington: Refugee Policy Group

Reid, A. (1991) 'Political Studies in the Voluntary Repatriation of Refugees', Ph.D. thesis, Deakin University

Spring, A. (1982) 'Women and Men as Refugees: Differential Assimilation of Angolan Refugees in Zambia', in A. Hansen and A. Oliver-Smith (eds) *Involuntary Migration and Resettlement: The Problems and Prospects of Dislocated People*, Boulder, CO: Westview Press

Vines, A. (1991a) *Renamo: Terrorism in Mozambique*, London: James Currey

(1991b) 'Mozambique: Slaves and the Snake of Fire', *Anti-Slavery Reporter*, 13 (7), 41–5

(1993) *One Hand Tied: Angola and the United Nations*, London: CIIR Briefing Paper

Weinrich, A. K. H. (1977) 'Strategic Resettlement in Rhodesia', *Journal of Southern African Studies*, 2, 207–29

Werbner, R. (1991) *Tears of the Dead: The Social Biography of an African Family*, Edinburgh: Edinburgh University Press for the International African Institute

Wilson, K. B. (1986) 'The Integration of Angolan Refugees in Western and North Western Zambia', unpublished paper, Oxford Refugee Studies Programme

(1991) *Conceiving of the Future amongst Mozambican Refugees in Ukwimi Refugee Settlement in Zambia*, Oxford: Refugee Studies Programme

(1992a) *A State of the Art Review of Research on Internally Displaced Refugees and Returnees from and in Mozambique*, Studies in Emergencies and Disaster Relief, No. 1, Stockholm: Swedish International Development Authority

(1992b) 'Enhancing Refugees own Food Acquisition Strategies', *Journal of Refugee Studies*, 5 (3/4), 226–46

(1992c) 'Cults of Violence and Counter-Violence in Mozambique', *Journal of Southern African Studies*, 18 (3), 527–82

(1993) *Assisting Repatriation: Recent Lessons from Self-Repatriation in Mozambique*, Helsinki: Finnish Refugee Council

Wilson, K. B. and J. Nunes (1994) 'Repatriation to Mozambique: Refugee Initiative and Agency Planning', in T. Allen and H. Morsink (eds) *When Refugees Go Home*, London: James Currey

Wilson, K. B. et al. (1989) *Food Provisioning amongst Mozambican Refugees in Malawi: A Study of Aid, Livelihood and Development*, Rome: World Food Programme

Zetter, R. et al. (1993) *Aid, Non-Governmental Agencies and Refugee Livelihood: Recommendations for a Way Forward. A Report on Mozambican Refugees in Malawi and Zimbabwe, Report for Governments and Agencies*, Oxford: Refugee Studies Programme (University of Oxford), School of Social Work (University of Zimbabwe) and University of Malawi

Zetterqvist, J. (1990) *Refugees in Botswana in the Light of International Law*, Uppsala: Scandinavian Institute of African Studies

HUNGER, WAR AND FLIGHT: THE HORN OF AFRICA

ABEBE ZEGEYE

There has been a change in character in the movements of people from the Horn. They are now driven not only by the fear of armed conflict, but by the spectre of hunger that hovers over an increasing number of periodically drought-stricken countries. Refugees are among the most food-insecure groups in the Horn of Africa, yet Ethiopia has moved from being the source of many refugees in the early 1980s to being one of the largest recipients of refugees — 0.75 million in 1989. The Harshen and Harisheik shelters were filled with Somali refugees fleeing the armed conflict in north-west Somalia. The western Ethiopian shelters of Itang, Fugnido, Domma and Assosa contained Sudanese refugees escaping the secessionist war in southern Sudan. The Somali refugee population in the Horn is estimated at 600,000. Two million Sudanese have been displaced by environmental degradation and at least 1.33 by the war. The number of refugees in Sudan itself has increased from 420,000 in 1979 to 1,063,000 in 1989. They come from Ethiopia, Chad and Zaire. Under conditions of severe civil strife food production and security are adversely affected, and a major part of the total population of the Horn now faces problems of food insecurity.

Four million Sudanese have been displaced by drought and war and the country is home to a further 0.75 million refugees from Eritrea, Ethiopia, Uganda, Chad and Zaire. The number of people displaced by civil war in Somalia runs into hundreds of thousands, and includes over 800,000 refugees from Ethiopia (UNHCR Factsheet 1990). Ethiopia is home to 380,000 refugees from Sudan and 333,000 from Somalia. Djibouti has the largest percentage of refugees, predominantly northern Somalis, in proportion to the native population.

Most refugees are fleeing from areas of conflict rather than from environmental problems. However, the increasing mobility of people in search of food and water is adding to these numbers. Many abandoning the countryside, which no longer feeds them, are migrating to the urban areas, swelling the number of people living in poor and unsanitary conditions in the cities of the Horn.

Displacement has a ripple effect. The arrival of large numbers of displaced people can introduce new stresses into competition for what are already inadequate natural resources for the local population. This causes tension between refugees and local people and leads to conflict, more degradation and further conflict. In many rural areas this tension is a daily occurrence. Displacement is a form of psychological and physical violence; it disrupts social and cultural traditions and destroys family networks. The effect on women and children whose lives are often more circumscribed by cultural traditions has been especially severe.

Displacement in the Sudan

Drought and desertification are major causes of the migration of Sudanese from different parts of the country to urban centres. In 1984/5 the number displaced by drought was nearly 3 million, in addition to over 4 million people displaced from southern regions because of civil war and intertribal disputes in Kordofan and Darfur. This puts the total number of displaced people in the country at nearly 7 million, out of a total population of 22 million.

Drastic changes have been taking place in the social fabric of rural communities in the Horn of Africa. Most affected are nomadic pastoralists and traditional rain-fed farmers. Large-scale deterioration in their income base, together with little off-farm employment, has resulted in many moving to other areas and to the cities. This has affected over 80 per cent of the rural population of Darfur, Kordofan and parts of the north-central and eastern regions. Due partly to the effects of serious environmental degradation there is a tendency for large-scale movement from rural to urban centres. Consequently there has been a decrease in the rural growth of population in Sudan relative to urban population growth. In the eastern region from 1973 to 1983 the urban population increased by 64 per cent, the rural sedentary by 45 per cent and rural nomadic by 34 per cent.

Desertification and erosion have completely changed the nomadic pastoralists' traditional migration patterns and have affected the sedentary agricultural population's patterns of movement. In normal years traditional farmers often left their farms at the end of the harvest (December–January) and returned from off-farm engagements in April and May to prepare for the wet season. This type of migration was voluntary, seasonal and, in normal years, involved between 13 and 29 per cent of adult males. Now large-scale migrations involving whole families are evident, particularly during droughts.

Movements are taking different directions, but because of the overall lack of rural employment opportunities many are moving to nearby towns and major cities. Of the displaced population of north Kordofan, 49 per cent have moved to Khartoum and other big cities, with their numbers swelling the ranks of the marginal urban poor. And, mainly as a result of poverty and unhealthy urban living conditions, these people are becoming increasingly food insecure. Among the permanently displaced the ratio of children to women to men is 3:2:1. The women are shouldering most of the burden; not only do they have to take care of the children, but many also have to support their families economically in the absence of husbands through migration in search of work, conscription or war. Most of the displaced settle near Khartoum and other towns, either in camps or in shantytowns.

Hillat Shook is a settlement of 20,000 displaced people from west and south Sudan lying to the south of Khartoum. Disease is rife and tribal traditions and custom have broken down under economic pressures. Widows who would have been taken care of by their husband's relatives have no one to care for them. They are forced to work with no one to look after the children; the children are compelled to work selling water, cigarettes and fruit in the streets. Half the vagrant children in Khartoum are displaced people and women are in very vulnerable positions. Men no longer able to fulfil traditional tribal obligations have deserted them, and in the Muslim north economic activity by women is discouraged.

In Sudan, over 10,000 people have been displaced by tribal warfare in Darfur, in the areas of Jebel Marra, Zalingie, Um Kedada, Um Haraz and Mellit. Between 1976 and 1980 pastoralists from northern Darfur were displaced to the south by drought and their search for water. In 1980 conflict broke out between Rezeigat nomads and Fur farmers when the Fur farmers tried to stop the nomads moving south. Many have moved to shanties in the towns for safety. Darfur has been severely damaged by desertification. There is no longer any grazing land and pastoralists

have lost over half their cattle in the fighting. Because of the state of civil insecurity around Mellit, the Fur have been forced to depend on relief or become labourers in towns.

For many years, the Sudanese government denied there was war in Darfur between Arab tribes and Fur farmers. In 1989 conflict reached a peak and the regional governor declared officially that there was racial conflict in the region. Arab tribes in Jebel Marra attacked a police station and killed twenty policemen who were trying to protect Fur villagers. The governor of Darfur declared the region a military operation zone and asked the army to intervene. The defence minister and then prime minister, Sadiq el Mahdi, visited the area and accused Chad of arming the Fur and fuelling the conflict. This angered Chad and soldiers were sent to the border.

In June 1989, the government launched a military operation in the area inhabited by northern Rezeigat tribes in Jebel Marra. In three villages, 3000 automatic weapons, 140,000 unused hand grenades, and 50,000 rounds of unused ammunition were found. In modern times Sudan is exceeded only by Lebanon in the formation of private armies or militias. The government is institutionalizing the burgeoning tribal militias in Darfur in pursuit of a policy to accommodate unsettled Arab groups in productive areas. The groups are given arms, ostensibly to defend themselves against the southern Sudanese rebels, but in practice the Arabs use their guns to defend themselves against farmers. They also fight among themselves over grazing and water holes. Nothing can deter any one tribe, whether farmer or pastoralist, from using the new arms to settle old scores. This use of firearms adds a new dimension of instability to the traditional conflicts between farmers and nomads, not only in the Sudan but also in other countries in the Horn.

The agricultural and industrial sectors are on the point of collapse having been starved of funds diverted to the military. Poverty in the south has increased. Because of the terrible damage inflicted on people, environment and infrastructure the Dinka and Nuer have lost several million heads of cattle and 75 per cent of them have been displaced from their homes along the River Nile.

Conflict over resources in border areas

Disintegration or weakening of traditional communities can have many causes, war being the most dramatic. But environmental changes of a permanent or temporary nature, which destroy a community's economic viability, can have the same effect. The communal social structures and traditions built up over generations on a particular way of life in a particular region disintegrate. Individuals lose their role in society and may become socially alienated as well as materially destitute. Traditional social regulatory mechanisms, sanctions, moral codes and authority patterns that normally prevent antisocial behaviour become ineffective.

The traditional way of life of the Lahawin tribe in east Sudan is becoming impossible as a result of attacks from bandits (*faloul*) along the border between Sudan and Ethiopia. In this case, displacement resulting from the war was the principal cause of the alienation of the outlaws, but the simultaneous dearth of natural resources, because of the drought, made it less likely than it might otherwise have been for the dislocated people to settle and become independent. The *faloul* are desperate and fighting for survival. Their numbers are growing as the border areas are caught up in wars out of reach of the law.

Drought is forcing the Lahawin to take their herds to border areas where they become vulnerable to attack. Along the border between Sudan and Ethiopia, relationships between the various groups are tangled, tense and often violent. There are the pastoralists affected by drought who cross the border to compete for resources with other nomadic and local groups; Eritrean and Tigrayan liberation movements fighting against the Ethiopian government and needing access from Sudan to the territory they control in Ethiopia; and refugees from these long-running wars as well as from drought and famine. Some border areas that were firmly under the control of the Ethiopian government are now in the hands of the liberation movements; others are disputed but years of war, lack of strong governmental control and drought have created a region characterized by social breakdown, lawlessness and violence. Groups of dislocated and uprooted people live by robbery and the gun, attacking and robbing traders. After decades of war arms are plentiful.

Splinter groups within the liberation movements, such as the Eritrean Liberation Front (ELF) defeated in 1977 and driven into Sudan by the dominant EPLF, are referred to as *faloul*. The ELF was caught along the border in a period of severe drought with no financial, political or military support. Thousands of fighters left Eritrea for Sudan, abandoning their weapons on the way. Others became *shifta* (looters). Others included old supporters of feudal landlords fighting the EPRP, with no political objectives as

such. The Ethiopian government has not sought to subdue them because they pose no threat to the government and have fought the TPLF. All prey on the pastoralists.

The land on the Sudanese side of the border has been hit by drought. The Lahawin, who for centuries have been pastoralists, are now forced to seek a sedentary way of life in order to survive. The drought has decimated their animal stocks while vast areas of traditional grazing lands have been appropriated for mechanized farms. Refugees were given other parts of their grazing land for settlement and then denuded the surrounding areas of the trees and shrubs that the Lahawin need for fuel and building materials. Along the border with Ethiopia they are threatened by bandits. The Lahawin asked the government for land on which to settle. Accordingly, they were allocated an area near Wad el Hijay in Maharegat. When they started to build they were stopped by local police, whom they attacked. In eastern Sudan, Tigrayan refugees, who are not allowed to carry arms, are subject to attack by Arabs and are vulnerable to violence when they look for work.

Civil war in Somalia

This is another war in which the government used existing tension and communal rivalry to try to secure itself in power. Although environmental issues are not the primary cause of this war they are certainly part of the complex of tensions which made possible the escalation of rivalry into war. It was into a tradition of tribal competition over access to resources that the government of Siad Barre brought its policy of favouring one tribe at the expense of others, resulting in the outbreak of war.

Territorial intrusions and subsequent wars have increased with the deterioration of the ecological conditions of the country, while modern forms of government have proved ineffective in dealing with the way of life of the Somali nomad. There has been a process of unequal development of resources and the siting of development projects to favour Siad Barre's Mareehaan clan (part of the Darood clan family). The Issaq tribe of the north, seen as the strongest and wealthiest clan, has been systematically undermined. More than 70 per cent of high military and civil service posts were held by members of the Darood family. In 1977 an influx of Ethiopian refugees (predominantly Ogadenis of the Darood family clan) were settled in northern Issaq settlements. This was seen by the Issaqs as a calculated policy to replace them, especially when the government recruited refugees into the army and created paramilitary groups among them. The Issaqs founded an opposition movement, the Somali National Movement (SNM), in London in 1981 and sent a mission to Ethiopia establishing their headquarters there. With the backing of Ethiopia the SNM began border operations against the military garrisons of the Somali army.

In 1987 Barre offered the Ethiopian government a peace treaty in which Somalia gave up its territorial claims on the Ogaden region in return for depriving the SNM of its Ethiopian bases. Ethiopia agreed and the SNM decided to attack northern Somalia and establish a base there. It captured Burao, strategically the most important town in northern Somalia. By mid-1988 Somalia was involved in one of the worst civil wars in Africa involving the government and five armed but disunited opposition groups, including the United Somali Congress (Hawiye), SNM (Isaaq) and Somali Patriotric Movement (Ogadenis). More than a million people have fled to Ethiopia and Kenya and other parts of the world. Tens of thousands of civilians have also been displaced internally and many killed. The fighting culminated in the fall of Siad Barre in January 1991 and his flight to Kenya. There is a continuing state of civil unrest throughout the country, with large-scale malnutrition, primarily in the heavily disrupted urban areas. NGOs and the UNHCR at one stage withdrew totally from the country and there is a profusion of arms. Hargeisa and four other towns, as well as numerous villages and settlements, mostly in northern Somalia, have been reduced to rubble. At a conservative estimate, between 50,000 and 60,000 civilians have been killed by government forces in the streets.

This fighting has affected refugees from the earlier fighting in the Ogaden war. Well-established refugee camps in western Somalia, close to the border with Ethiopia, have been abandoned because the UNHCR has ceased to be able to operate. Ethiopian refugees from the Ogaden war have abandoned camps on the banks of the Shebelle River near Beled Wayne and have fled back up-river to Ethiopia. On the Juba River, the Halba refugee camp has also emptied as refugees attempt now to cross into Kenya. The UNHCR representative in Nairobi states that 5000 non-Somali refugees have entered Kenya and 10,000 have gone into Ethiopia. A UNHCR Geneva representative stated in February 1991 that refugees along the border with Ethiopia had not received any food aid since the organization withdrew in December 1990. The number of Somali refugees in Djibouti also rose during the 1980s to reach 30,000.

Resettlement in Ethiopia

In Ethiopia the government of Mengistu Haile Mariam resettled people in an attempt to relieve the pressure on overcultivated and exhausted lands in the north of the country. The history of famine in Ethiopia goes back centuries. The first historically documented famine occurred in the thirteenth century and Ethiopia has been struck by cyclical famine ever since. The recent severe famines in 1974/5, 1984/5 and 1990/1 have occurred primarily as a result of droughts. The droughts were so disastrous because they affected agricultural areas already suffering from serious environmental degradation and reduced productivity.

Wollo, Tigray and the highlands of Eritrea were most affected by the series of famines and droughts. These regions have experienced a long period of human settlement and over-utilization of the land. Moreover, population growth (averaging approximately 3 per cent per year) began to place an unbearable burden on the already denuded highlands. Increased cutting of trees for fuel and building were leaving hillsides bare and prey to heavy seasonal rainfall which washed away the soil in torrents.

The 1974 famine caused suffering and death to millions of Ethiopians. It was known as the hidden famine because the government of Emperor Haile Selassie deliberately concealed information in order to avoid damaging world opinion about developments in Ethiopia. The famine was secretly filmed and resulted in further discrediting the crumbling monarchy. The new revolutionary regime, the Dergue, under President Mengistu Haile Mariam, had to deal with the problems of drought and famine as a matter of urgency. Moving farmers away from the overcrowded hillsides of the famine-affected area to less densely populated areas further south was seen as a lasting solution, improving land use and food production.

Famine in 1984/5 in North Wollo, Tigray and Eritrea added further impetus. These areas were at war with the government in Addis Ababa, with Eritrean rebels fighting for independence and the Tigrayans for a more democratic government. Critics alleged a political motivation to resettlement. The 1984/5 famine affected almost ten million people. A serious reduction in rainfall over large parts of Ethiopia in 1984 led to a shortfall of about 20 per cent in agricultural production, a loss of about one million tons, mainly cereals and pulses. The RRC Cooperative Service Department orginally resettled 14,000 families. With the famine a further 500,000 to two million people were resettled in the three south-western regions of Wollega, Illubabor and Kaffa.

However, the operation was carried out in haste and without adequate assessment of conditions in the resettlement camps. Diseases, such as malaria, and tsetse flies, absent in the highlands, were rife and settlers had little resistance to them. The clay soils were easily compacted and farmers who were used to working independently were expected to join cooperatives. Some local people, such as the Ketto in Wollega, were hostile; local crops such as sorghum and maize had been little used in the highlands. The communal system undermined enthusiasm for farming. The very heavy soil needed lots of hoeing and ploughing but oxen could not be used because of their vulnerability to disease. Waterborne diseases, such as malaria, yellow fever, river blindness, trypanosomiasis and jigger fly infestation were common.

Environmental degradation and conflict in Eritrea

Eritrea has a population of an estimated four million, of whom one million are refugees, and an area of 124,320 square kilometres. Its 1000-kilometre coast stretches from Ras Kasar in the north to Bab el Mandab at the southern tip of the Red Sea. Eritrea is a microcosm of peoples and cultures of Hamitic, Cushitic and Nilotic origin. It is made up of nine ethnic groups, Islamic and Christian, who speak nine different languages. Some 70 per cent live in the countryside. The physical environment in Eritrea consists of arid and semi-arid coastal plains, central plateau highlands, northern massif and western lowlands or Sudan plains. The vegetation is as varied as the physical environment and offers diverse natural resources for the population. The environment consists of montane, coastal, riparian, savannah and desert scrub. The ecological and physical diversity offers agricultural opportunities for growing different crops, vegetables and fruits as well as rearing a variety of livestock species.

Over the past thirty years there has been severe degradation of the environment and the displacement of over half the civilian population. Degradation due to overgrazing and high population density (both human and livestock) in the highland regions of Eritrea and their peripheries was already in an advanced stage well before the war. FAO literature in the early 1960s clearly reinforces this view. Firewood and construction materials were also becoming in short supply but not as desperately as today. The survival strategy among Eritrean peasants then was to migrate and use grazing agricultural land in less populated areas around the green belt known as Bahri, and the western lowlands particularly the Gash and

Setit areas. There is now open conflict over grazing and water resources between ethnic groups in these areas.

The war situation itself has displaced an estimated half a million people within Eritrea and has led to higher population concentrations in the Gash and Setit areas. At present, communities representing seven of the nine ethnic groups are found in the Gash and Setit areas. There is always a potential for inter-ethnic conflict in the area but the cessation of hostility between Ethiopia and Eritrea could reduce some of the tension. After independence many of the settlers are likely to return to their traditional home base. Others may not if such areas are too degraded to support any form of livelihood. Tensions over agricultural grazing and water resources are likely to continue in future.

Security hamlets

In the late 1960s, the Ethiopian government introduced the idea of security hamlets. What began as a small project in western Eritrea became a national security project throughout the country, involving the large-scale rounding up of traditionally scattered villagers to government designated areas. Many villages were then destroyed. The environmentally negative implications of these hamlets are numerous. A curfew in these hamlets from 6.00 p.m. to 6.00 a.m. inhibits free movement, and working time is reduced. Peasants could not return to traditional grazing and farmland. With 5000 to 6000 households, these huge concentrations of people and livestock, and intense competition for grazing, firewood and water make the areas around the security hamlets the most degraded locations in Eritrea. The defending army around the security hamlets also requires water and shelter. They burn straw and dried dung, once valuable sources of fodder and fertilizer. Living in concentrated security hamlets, as opposed to the more scattered traditional pattern of settlement, effectively diminishes the ability of rural society to be economically self-sufficient.

The state of fear and insecurity caused by the state of emergency, coupled with high livestock taxation by the government, pushed pastoralists in particular to divert their livestock trade to eastern Sudan and sell more cheaply there. Eritrean refugees also provided cheap labour in Sudan. Traditionally, agropastoralist farmers in the Hamsien plateau took advantage of winter rains (November–February) to move with their livestock to the eastern escarpment of 140 kilometres east to the east. They would harvest in February and return in time for planting for the summer rains in

May. In 1985, these farmers were moved to new security villages and restricted to a ten-kilometre radius of movement.

In the western lowlands, cattle raisers traditionally migrate to wet and dry season camps within 40 to 100 kilometres of each other. During the long dry season (December–April) in western Eritrea, non-milking cattle are traditionally taken south for grazing deep into Gondar Province and south-east Sudan. Since 1978, the wet season camp and territory have been under the control of the EPLF and the dry season camps under that of Ethiopian troops. The war situation, involving air strikes, meant many were unable to continue in their pastoralist activities and they fled to refugee camps in Sudan leaving their cattle behind.

Conclusion

It is clear from the above that the effects of war are inextricably linked with migration as a result of large numbers of population being displaced. In an area such as the Horn of Africa, where nomadism has been an important part of the economy, the effect has been all the more deleterious. It is impossible to separate these population movements from their adverse effect on the environment, which was often already precarious. Even if military activity in the Horn of Africa ceased tomorrow, it would be difficult to re-establish the conditions necessary to meet the needs of the population. But whatever policies are implemented, they should be derived from the local communities, whose knowledge of the problems is likely to be far greater than that of outside experts.

US ADMISSION POLICIES TOWARDS CUBAN AND HAITIAN MIGRANTS

NAOMI FLINK ZUCKER AND NORMAN L. ZUCKER

The Caribbean has consistently exported a larger percentage of its people than any other area of the world (*New York Times*, 6 May 1992: 1). From most of these countries, the exodus has been impelled by poverty and drawn by opportunity. But in two of the Caribbean nations, Cuba and Haiti, the poverty is intensified by repression – in Cuba by a communist dictatorship, in Haiti by a right-wing kleptocracy. While many from the Caribbean migrate to the USA, the USA has singled out Cubans and Haitians for diametrically opposite treatment. Cubans who quit their island are assisted in coming to the USA, are called political refugees and given asylum, while Haitians who leave their island are labelled economic migrants, interdicted at sea and returned to Haiti.

The special attention given to Cubans and Haitians is rooted in a mixture of US foreign and domestic policy concerns. The unwavering anti-communism that for decades dominated America's foreign policy also dominated its refugee policy. Thus, when in 1959 right-wing dictator Fulgencio Batista fell and Fidel Castro came to power, US foreign policy decreed that fleeing Cubans be welcomed as refugees from communism. Cubans who escaped from Castro's Cuba were said to have 'voted with their feet'. By coming to the USA, they condemned Cuban communism and validated American democracy. Since 1959 nearly one million Cubans have been resettled in the USA, the overwhelming majority of them having been given a pro forma grant of political asylum.

Just forty miles to the south-east of Cuba, across the Windward Passage, lies Haiti. For the brutal dictators 'Papa Doc' Duvalier and his son Jean-Claude, Haiti's strategic location was a bargaining chip. They offered undeviating support of the USA (in the OAS Haiti voted to expel Cuba and to impose sanctions on it), and permitted the US military to use Haitian ports and, during the Cuban missile crisis, airfields (Zucker and Zucker 1987: 180). For nearly thirty years, US policy dictated that if the Duvalier stranglehold were loosened, the political disorder that followed would have led to a communist takeover.

But US refugee policy is not determined by foreign policy alone; rather it is governed by a troika of interests: foreign policy, the costs of resettlement and domestic pressures. If foreign policy argued for the admission of refugees, or at least of refugees fleeing communism, the spectre of resettlement costs argued against the admission of large numbers of refugees. Here the third interest – domestic pressure groups – became decisive (Zucker and Zucker 1989). Although Cubans emigrated to the USA in greater numbers than the Haitians, and might have provoked the USA to close the floodgates against them, the community of Cuban exiles exercised considerable political power. Thus domestic pressure weighed in on the side of foreign policy and admission. Domestically, the Haitians, unlike the Cubans, were neither politically nor economically powerful and carried no weight against the fear of numbers.

The Soviet Union has now collapsed, and with it the foreign-policy component of US refugee policy. US refugee policy can no longer maintain its staunch anti-communism. Moreover, the fall of communism greatly increased political instability and, with it, the numbers of migrants. Fear of numbers has now become paramount. In the future, Cubans, as well as Haitians, may be turned away.

Cuban migration to Florida began as early as the 1830s, and by the end of the nineteenth century a permanent Cuban community was in existence (Masud-Piloto 1988: 8–11). After Cuba's independence, small groups of Cubans escaping domestic political turbulence fled to the USA. It was not, however, until 1959, when Castro seized power, that the largest migration of Cubans to the USA began, a migration that still continues.

The ebb and flow of Cubans to the USA was conditioned by cold war events – the Bay of Pigs and the Cuban missile crisis – and by Castro's caprice. From the early days of the Castro revolution until the diplomatic break in relations in January 1961, Cubans flowed directly to the mainland, the beneficiaries of an extraordinarily liberal non-immigrant visa policy in Havana and a pro forma grant of political asylum in the USA. By November 1960, 1700 Cuban refugees were pouring into Florida each week (Zucker and Zucker 1987: 33).

In 1961, the USA severed relations with Cuba, and thereafter Cubans were admitted as refugees. The following year the USA imposed a full trade embargo on Cuba, cutting off the commercial flights that had been bringing Cubans to the USA. For the next three years, Cubans who wished to come to the USA had to leave without exit visas and travel first to a third country. Migration continued, but at a sharply reduced rate.

Suddenly, in 1965, Cuban President Fidel Castro, faced with mounting popular unrest, opened the port of Camarioca as a safety valve. All who wished to leave could do so. Responding to the challenge, US President Lyndon Johnson expansively proclaimed that all Cubans 'who seek refuge here will find it'.

Cuban-American exiles hastily assembled a flotilla of boats which began ferrying Cubans to Florida. When the sea journey proved dangerous, it was quickly replaced by an American airlift. By the time the airlift ended in 1973, over 3000 flights, costing over $1 billion, had brought out 260,561 Cubans (RPU 1992: 13).

The Camarioca exodus resulted in the passage of the Cuban Adjustment Act of 1966, which specifically allows Cubans arriving in the USA to become permanent residents. The Cuban Adjustment Act remains in force today, allowing Cubans – whether they come as undocumented boat people or as tourists who overstay their visas – to acquire permanent residency.

Some two years before Castro seized power in Cuba, François Duvalier had assumed power in Haiti. Unlike Castro, who had revolutionary reformist goals, Duvalier's primary goal was to establish absolute personal power. Duvalier, who had himself declared president-for-life, maintained power through his army and his personal militia. Duvalier tightened his hold, beginning in the early 1960s, forcing an exodus of professionals and business people. At his death, in 1971, he was succeeded by his son, Jean-Claude.

Haitians first sought political asylum in the USA in 1972. In December of that year twelve political prisoners bribed their way out of one of Jean-Claude Duvalier's infamous gaols and, with their families, sailed to the Florida coast. The Immigration and Naturalization Service denied their request for asylum, ruling that the Haitians were economic migrants and had nothing to fear from the Haitian government (*New York Times*, 13 December 1972: 4; *New York Times*, 23 August, 1973: 36). The government policy had been established: the Haitians did not have a well-founded fear of persecution.

By 1979 many Haitian boats were drifting onto the shores of southern Florida. To prevent the Haitians from receiving asylum, and also to deter further departures from Haiti, the INS instituted a Haitian Programme under which Haitian asylum seekers were to be detained, denied due process and deported. A class action suit was brought on their behalf, and Judge James Lawrence King (see Zucker and Zucker 1987: 198) ruled that:

This Program, in its planning and executing, is offensive to every notion of constitutional due process and equal protection. The Haitians whose claims for asylum were rejected during the Program shall not be deported until they are given a fair chance to present their claims for political asylum.

Although the court had ruled against the government, the government was unwilling to acquiesce, and, until 1991 when the asylum system was reformed, similar programmes were repeatedly put into effect.

By 1979, the admission of refugees had become an area of contention between the executive and the legislature. At issue were not only admission numbers, but, just as importantly, legislative prerogative. Congress was unhappy with the president's use of parole power to admit large numbers of Cubans and Southeast Asians. From 1959 to 1980, more than 750,000 Cubans had been paroled in (Zucker and Zucker 1987: 61). To remedy the situation, in March 1980, the Refugee Act was passed.

In the Refugee Act, Congress restricted the attorney-general's parole power and established a flexible numerical ceiling based on executive–legislative consultation. Most importantly, the act adopted the refugee definition of the United Nations Convention and Protocol, removing the previous geographical and ideological anti-communist bias from refugee admissions and asylum decisions. Almost as an afterthought, the act also statutorily established the principle of asylum; it was wrongly assumed that few people would apply for asylum (Zucker and Zucker 1987: 52; 1991; 1992).

The Refugee Act of 1980 had scarcely been launched when it was all but submerged in the backwash of the Mariel boat lift, a boat lift that in less than six months brought to the USA some 125,000 Cubans and 15,000 Haitians. By the time the Refugee Act was passed, there was a policy presumption that *all* Cubans were refugees and were to be given specific entitlements. A large and powerful community of Cuban exiles was now established in the USA, a community bent towards the eventual overthrow of Fidel Castro and the more immediate evacuation of their countrymen. When Castro opened the port of Mariel, the Cuban Americans were ready with a fleet of boats to evacuate their compatriots. Within a week, over 2000 Cubans had been brought to the USA, and there were reports that more than a thousand vessels were waiting at the port of Mariel to take on émigrés (*Washington Post*, 27 April 1980: 1).

There was an election in 1980 and, campaigning against President Jimmy Carter, was cold warrior Ronald Reagan, who declaimed that if no other country was willing to take in the Cuban refugees, the USA should take them all (*Dallas Times Herald*, 10 April 1980: 1). Carter met the challenge and declared that the USA would receive the Cubans 'with an open heart and open arms', and, further, that he would ask Congress for the monies to meet their needs (*Washington Post*, 6 May 1980: 1). No such words greeted the Haitians who, within a few weeks, had joined the refugee stream. Rather, during congressional hearings on the Mariel crisis, Thomas O. Enders (1981: 3), assistant secretary of state for inter-American affairs, described the Haitians as having come by choice from a country whose 'friendly government is interested in enforcing its laws and ... wishes to cooperate with the USA in bringing illegal migration under control'.

When the flow of boat people had finally been staunched, the administration was inclined to give refugee status to the Cubans, but not to the Haitians. Congress, on the other hand, cognizant that many of the Mariel boat people, both Cuban and Haitian, would not have qualified as refugees, created a new status for the Mariel arrivals: special entrant, a status that did not permit either Cubans or Haitians to apply for permanent residency, the first step towards citizenship.

The equality of mistreatment, however, would be short-lived. In 1984, the Justice Department ruled that, under the Cuban Adjustment Act of 1966, all Cubans arriving in the USA — whether boat people or tourists on expired visas — were entitled to permanent residency. The Haitians were denied that status until 1986, when the Immigration Reform and Control Act granted a general amnesty.

By the fall of 1980, the haemorrhage of Cuban boat people had slowed to a trickle. But Haitians persisted in their flight. The US government now entered into discussions with the 'friendly government' of Haiti and, in September 1981, an agreement was reached under which the US coast guard would interdict at sea Haitians attempting to leave their country.

Any Haitian who asked for political asylum was to be questioned by a representative of the Immigration Service; if he was found not to have a credible claim, he would be returned to Haiti and the Haitian government notified. From the time the agreement went into effect in 1981 until the ousting of President Aristide in 1991, 21,600 Haitians were interdicted and questioned; only 28 Haitians were brought to the USA to pursue their asylum claims (Johnson 1992).

The Haitian numbers are of interest in another respect. According to the presidential proclamation that announced the Haitian interdiction agreement, undocumented arrivals by sea 'severely strained the law enforcement resources of the INS' and 'threatened the welfare and safety of communities' in the USA. Government figures from that time, however, show that only 2 per cent of the undocumented entrants to the USA were Haitians (Petition 1990: 8).

While US refugee policy remained entrenched in its staunch anti-communism, monolithic European communism was disintegrating. By the end of summer 1991, Mikhail Gorbachev had been replaced by Boris Yeltsin, who pledged to initiate a new era. The Soviet Union was remaking itself. The threat of communism – once the strongest pillar of US refugee policy – had cracked. There was no urgency now to admit those fleeing communist oppression. The State Department, caught in a time warp, nonetheless continued to favour a policy of anti-communist refugee admissions. In the fiscal year 1992, the four leading refugee-source countries were the Soviet Union (60,866), Vietnam (43,941), Laos (7272) and Cuba (3845) (Refugee Resettlement Program 1993: 6).

Since the State Department is slow to change, it may be some time before its policies conform to altered reality. In the meantime, the two remaining pillars of refugee policy – concern for costs and domestic pressures – are assuming increased importance. A weak US economy is, inevitably, giving rise to xenophobia, and pressure is mounting both to restrict the numbers of those admitted and to reduce the costs of assisting them.

Nowhere does the heightened fear of large numbers of asylum seekers show itself more than in the most recent chapter of US policy towards the Haitians. The years since the ousting of Jean-Claude Duvalier from Haiti had been chaotic and violent for the island, and the refugee flows continued unabated. Finally, in 1991, Haiti held its first democratic elections, and Jean-Bertrand Aristide was elected president. For the first time in decades Haitians were hopeful and emigration slowed. Then suddenly and, ironically, just two months after the dissolution of the Soviet Union, Aristide himself was overthrown in a violent army coup. A reign of terror followed. For one month, Haitians held still, but then, in October 1991, they began to leave the island. On 28 October the first boatload of 19 arrived in the USA. By 25 November, 4530 Haitians had been apprehended by American authorities; of those, 3600 had been interdicted and were being held on US vessels (*Refugee Reports*, 29 November 1991: 1).

In Haiti there was wholesale slaughter of civilians by the army; an economic embargo of the country was causing widespread starvation. The numbers of Haitian asylum seekers surged. When the US ships could hold no more, a few hundred were received by Venezuela and Honduras. For the rest, a detention camp was opened on Guantanamo Naval Base, in Cuba. A procedure was established whereby all interdicted Haitians were brought to Guantanamo, where their asylum claims were screened. If a Haitian was found to have a 'credible' fear, he or she was then brought to the USA for a full asylum hearing.

The procedure on Guantanamo was unprecedented in US practice. No group had ever before been subjected to pre-screening. Even more importantly, the Haitians were not being questioned, as previously, by ill-prepared and often hostile Immigration Service personnel; rather, the interviews were conducted by a newly trained and impartial corps of asylum officers. Although the approval rate fluctuated widely, overall, nearly one-third of the Haitians on Guantanamo were being admitted to the USA as asylum seekers.

The State Department and the Bush White House were alarmed by the spectre of another election-year Mariel, a Haitian Mariel. There were only two ways to prevent such a nightmare. The first option was to work more forcefully for the restoration of democracy in Haiti. That course of action was rejected because, it is widely believed, President Bush did not want to disrupt American business operations in Haiti. At the same time, he could not risk incurring the wrath of the Cuban Americans in Florida, who both supported the Republican party and opposed involvement in Haiti, as well as Haitian immigration (*New York Times*, 19 May 1992: 7).

With American intervention in Haiti not a viable option for Bush, he chose a second option. On 25 May 1992, President Bush issued what has come to be called the Kennebunkport Order. Thenceforth, the coast guard would interdict Haitians and return them to Haiti. There would be no screening for possible asylum claims. Instead, Haitians with a 'well-founded

fear of persecution' were told that they could now appear at the US embassy in Port au Prince and apply for refugee status.

This was the first instance of peacetime admission of refugees from a non-communist country. Refugee-processing in Haiti, however, soon assumed both a dangerous and a desultory character. It was dangerous for the Haitians, who first had to present themselves to Haitian security officials at the embassy (Lutheran Immigration and Refugee Service, 15 June 1992). It was the embassy itself that was desultory. In the first eleven months of refugee processing in 1991, they received nearly 5000 applications for refugee status; 154 cases were approved, but by the end of 1992, only 61 cases, 136 people, had been admitted to the USA (*Refugee Reports*, 29 January 1993: 4).

Presidential candidate Bill Clinton opposed the Kennebunkport Order in his campaign, but once elected, he reversed his position and, in a joint statement with President Bush, announced that he would continue the policy.

The Kennebunkport Order and its perpetuation by President Clinton represent an ominous shift in American refugee policy and a dangerous precedent for other refugee-receiving countries. Although, as a signatory to the UN Protocol, the USA is bound not to return any individual to a country where he has a 'well-founded fear of persecution', in both policy and practice the USA now does just that. The policy was challenged in a legal suit that reached the Supreme Court. The court, in an astounding decision, found that the prohibitions of the Refugee Act against refoulment apply 'only to aliens who reside in or have arrived at the border of the USA'. Associate Justice Harry Blackmun, the sole dissenter (*Refugee Reports*, 30 June 1993: 1–2), found it 'extraordinary ... that the Executive, in disregard of the law, would take to the seas to intercept fleeing refugees and force them back to their persecutors – and that the Court would strain to sanction that conduct'.

There had been many earlier suits brought against the actions of the US government towards asylum seekers; all of those suits confronted the issue of fairness. What distinguished this suit was that it concerned not so much fairness, as right – the right to a*sk for* asylum. In this case the highest court in the USA has decided that refugees who flee their country do not have that right.

It is probably only a matter of time before the right of asylum is further eroded. At present, it appears to be an unchanging policy that the door of asylum will open for Cubans and remain shut to Haitians. But there are foreshadowings of change. Within Cuba, an ageing Castro, no longer the beneficiary of Soviet largess, and facing an economy in ruins, is moderating his policies. He has welcomed mixed ventures with Western countries, for the first time allowed Cubans legally to spend foreign currencies, invited Cuban Americans to visit, lowered age restrictions on exit visas, expressed a willingness to negotiate reparations for confiscated American properties, and announced he would welcome US participation in a half-built Soviet nuclear power plant (*New York Times*, 8 August 1993: 4; *New York Times*, 16 June 1993: 10).

And while Castro may have domestic problems, he no longer fears a US-sponsored invasion. In May 1993, nine members of Alpha 66, who had planned to incite a revolution, were arrested. The State Department, in a radical departure, announced it does 'not support, condone or encourage any such illegal activities' and would prosecute those caught organizing attacks against Havana (*New York Times*, 27 June 1993: 16).

Within the USA, the Cubans are no longer a monolithic pressure group. The powerful Cuban-American National Foundation is being challenged by rival exile groups. The foundation, furthermore, has less influence with the current Clinton Democratic administration than it had with former Republican administrations. Funding for a foundation pet project, TV Marti, was killed by the House of Representatives' Appropriations Committee (*New York Times*, 10 July 1993: 7). And there is growing support for the United Nations' resolution calling on the USA to end the Cuban embargo.

It is inevitable that Castro's regime will end. How it will end, and how the State Department and the US Cuban community will respond is not yet clear. What is clear, however, is that Washington, in the words of Robert S. Gelbard, deputy assistant secretary of state for inter-American affairs, 'does not want a large number of Cuba's ten million citizens arriving in flotillas on Florida's shores' (*New York Times*, 30 July 1993: 3).

In the first seven months after the Cuban government lowered the age restrictions on exit permits, the USA interests section in Havana issued 32,000 non-immigrant visas. By the end of July 1991, with a backlog of 28,000, the processing of new applications was suspended (*Refugee Reports*, 31 July 1991: 11). The fear of numbers, of another Mariel flood tide, has impelled Washington to discuss with Havana the normalizing of immigration and

deportation procedures. And Washington, which formerly gave asylum to every Cuban pilot who defected, is now – to the dismay of the Cuban exile community – cooperating with Havana to bring air-piracy criminal charges against a pilot who flew a Cuban aircraft and its passengers to the USA (*New York Times*, 6 August 1992: 12).

That same fear of numbers, of another Mariel, is likely in the future strongly to influence a great deal of US refugee policy. If refugees no longer serve the government's foreign policy goals, even if there are strong domestic pressure groups urging their admission, there will be less inclination to welcome them. In a post-Castro era, large numbers of Cubans will probably be turned away, just as Haitians are now.

References

Enders, Thomas O. (1981) *United States as a Country of Mass First Asylum*, US Congress, Senate, Committee on the Judiciary, Subcommittee on Immigration and Refugee Policy, hearing, 97th Congress, first session, Washington, DC: US Government Printing Office, 31 July

Johnson, Harold J. (1992) *Refugees: US Processing of Haitian Asylum Seekers*, United States General Accounting Office GAO/T–NSIAD–92–25

Lutheran Immigration and Refugee Service (1992) 'Action Alert', New York

Masud-Piloto, Felix Roberto (1988) *With Open Arms: Cuban Migration to the United States*, Totowa: Rowman & Littlefield

Petition to the Inter-American Commission on Human Rights of the Organization of American States, submitted on Behalf of Organizational Petitioners, Haitian Centre for Human Rights et al. against the Government of the United States of America, 1990

Refugee Reports (1991, 1993) US Committee for Refugees, Washington, DC

Refugee Resettlement Program (1993) Report to Congress, US Department of Health and Human Services, Office of Refugee Resettlement, 31 January

RPU (Refugee Programs Update) (1992) State of Florida, Department of Health and Rehabilative Services, September

Washington Post, 1980

Zucker, N. L. and N. F. Zucker (1987) *The Guarded Gate: The Reality of American Refugee Policy*, San Diego: Harcourt Brace Jovanovich

—— (1989) 'The Uneasy Troika in US Refugee Policy: Foreign Policy, Pressure Groups and Resettlement Costs', *Journal of Refugee Studies*, 3 (2), 359–72

—— (1991) 'The 1980 Refugee Act: A 1990 Perspective', in H. Adelman (ed.) *Refugee Policy: Canada and the United States*, Toronto: York Lanes Press, 224–52

—— (1992) 'From Immigration to Refugee Redefinition: A History of Refugee and Asylud Asylum Policy in the United States,' in G. Loescher (ed.) *Refugees and the Asylum Dilemma in the West*, University Park: Pennsylvania State University Press, 54–70

REFUGEES FROM CAMBODIA, LAOS AND VIETNAM, 1975–1993

MICHEL MIGNOT

The exodus of refugees from Vietnam, Laos and Cambodia should be viewed within the context of an unsuccessful decolonization by the French after the Second World War and in terms of the confrontation between the Western and communist blocs brought about by US attempts to fight the spread of communism. While the French were defeated by the Vietnamese army in Dien Bien Phu in 1954, the USA lost its influence over the region with the succesive falls of pro-Western governments in Laos, Cambodia and Vietnam in March and April 1975.

Thus began the great exodus of Indochinese refugees, for which France and the USA were recognized as being largely responsible. The first refugees from Laos reached the Thai border in February and March 1975. The Cambodians followed after 17 April, when Phnom Penh collapsed. On 30 April 1975, the USA organized a large helicopter airlift from Saigon of the regime's most politically prominent personalities. About 130,000 gathered in Guam Island to be taken to temporary camps in California under the control of the US army. According to the UNHCR, at the end of 1992 there were approximately 1,435,000 refugees from the region – 835,000 from Vietnam, 360,000 from Laos and 240,000 from Cambodia. The peak period was between 1979 and 1981 when international organizations registered 193,000, 245,000 and 205,000 arrivals respectively per year in the other countries of the region. Since then the numbers have steadily decreased. Though there were 110,000 in 1982, in 1992 there were no more than 4500, of which 2350 came from Vietnam, 1850 from Cambodia and 320 from Laos.

Apart from the historical and political contexts, it is important to understand how seriously the refugee problem has loomed in world opinion: here the media has played a major role. The conflict itself was widely reported during the war, as were its consequences throughout the largest refugee flows, which lasted from 1975 to 1982/3. Innumerable articles describing the refugee situation were published in every country's local and national press. I refer, for instance, to articles in the press in Darwin (northern Australia) about boat people arriving by sea, in the local French press about their conditions of reception, and in the Canadian press about the same subject. Innumerable TV programmes commented on humanitarian issues in the refugee camps. Concerned interest groups were therefore well informed and took initiatives through national and local associations to solve humanitarian problems at home and abroad. The governments themselves relayed the message by ordering official reports, such as the *Reports to the [US] Congress* from 1975, or *Les Réfugiés originaires de l'Asie du Sud-Est* ordered by the French government in 1979, or the British Home Office's 1982 *Report of the Joint Committee for Refugees from Vietnam*. This already considerable and ever-growing knowledge of the refugee situation encouraged all parties concerned to organize the resettlement process as efficiently as possible. Organization based on information was the key to the resettlement countries' relative success. This attempt at organization can be found in every aspect of the refugee process – the exodus, the periods of transit and the resettlement.

The exodus

The first step was to develop the infrastructures necessary for receiving refugees in neighbouring countries (with the agreement of their governments) and the international community responded rapidly to the UNHCR's various appeals to do so. The refugee camps into which arrivals were received covered an extensive area. The countries concerned were Thailand (mainly for refugees from Laos and Cambodia) and Malaysia, Indonesia, the Philippines, Macao and Hong Kong (for refugees from Vietnam). Other refugees landed on the coasts of Japan and Australia and others still went to faraway countries like Argentina, Brazil, Greece, the Ivory Coast and Turkey.

The importance of the exodus and its economic and political consequences in the region forced the international community to act jointly, as if in a linked chain. On one end were the countries of origin; on the other were the countries able to offer settlement; and between these were the so-called countries of 'first asylum'. These were mainly third-world countries that invoked their economic weakness and the possible political damage to their relations with Vietnam. On different occasions, mainly in 1979, Malaysia and Indonesia threatened to return the boat people to the sea if the international community did not increase its offers of resettlement. The main event that showed a will to organize a chain of support was the international conference held in Geneva in July 1979. It was a period of extreme urgency. Since the autumn of 1978, boat people from Vietnam had reached the coast of Malaysia, Indonesia, Singapore and Hong Kong. For example, the *Southern Cross* arrived in Singapore in September 1978 with 800 refugees on board, the *Hai Hong* docked in Indonesia's Anambas Islands in November 1978 with 2500 refugees, while the *Huey Fong* landed in Hong Kong in January 1979 with more than 3300 boat people. The number of boat people reaching the countries of first asylum increased dramatically in May and June 1979. Some 26,000 were registered in April, 51,000 in May and 54,000 in June. The Vietnamese authorities were accused of encouraging this large exodus and of making a profit from it. The countries of first asylum accused the resettlement countries of not offering enough departures for the refugees. The refugee camps were overcrowded with problems of security and hygiene. The boat people were often victims of atrocities carried out by pirates on the China Sea. Apart from raising funds to solve the humanitarian problems inside the refugee camps and increasing offers of departure to the resettlement countries, the Geneva Conference worked on the beginning of the chain, i.e. the refugees' countries of origin, to try to reduce their exodus and to make conditions of exit safer. An agreement was finally reached between the UNHCR and the Vietnamese authorities, called the Orderly Departure Programme, the purpose of which was to permit the Vietnamese to join their families in resettlement countries directly from Vietnam. Despite the administrative red tape imposed by the Vietnamese, an organized exodus from Vietnam began to parallel the clandestine one. At the end of 1992, 439,000 Vietnamese and 14,200 Cambodians left Vietnam under the Orderly Departure Programme. This represented 24 per cent of the total.

The transit period

This was the period of selection by the resettlement countries. Most countries involved (the USA, Canada, Australia, France and Germany) established annual or monthly quotas. Others responded to the appeals launched by the UNHCR on different occasions. This was the case of the UK and Sweden. Selection was based on a number of criteria linked to foreign or home policies.

The main criteria were juridical, former attachment to the resettlement countries, family reunion and professional skills. In order to be eligible for selection, the persons concerned had to be declared 'refugees' by the UNHCR or to be considered of equivalent status in the national legislations concerned. People with relatives in resettlement countries or who worked directly or indirectly for those countries' companies had preference. This applied mainly to the USA and France, who previously had influence in the region. As to family reunion, a debate was initiated as to whether the nuclear family (father, mother and children) or the extended family, base of the social organization in Southeast Asia, was salient. Australia liberalized its legislation in 1981 to permit brothers and sisters to join their families. By contrast, France only gave credence to the nuclear family. Again, the refugees' professional skills, their age and their knowledge of English or French were of great importance.

Selection sometimes had a political character. For example, the UK selected almost only those refugees who had arrived in Hong Kong. Australia chose refugees mainly from Malaysia 'in order to offset diplomatic pressure from the Malaysian government, reinforced by the fear of further boat arrivals in Australia' (Viviani 1984: 116). France's refugees came mainly from Thailand to avoid a large immigration of refugees solely of Chinese origin. Canada and the USA based their choice on their policy of sponsorship. Official delegations and private organizations tried to reconcile the refugee families' situation with the wishes expressed by their future sponsors in the respective countries. The refugees' selection was as diverse as the number of countries engaged in the movement of international solidarity.

The list of ressettlement countries is very impressive. The dispersion of the Indochinese refugees all around the world was something new in the refugee history. In the past, the refugees' resettlement was concentrated in one zone, Africa for example. Of the refugees over the last ten years, few fled to other continents. Again, refugee flight was normally oriented towards only a few directions. For example, the Russian refugees resettled almost only in western Europe and North America.

In December 1979, the list contained twenty-nine countries. The main resettlement areas were North America with Canada (181,000 at the end of 1992) and the USA (1,102,500), western Europe (229,000) where France's share was nearly 52 per cent followed by Germany (13.5 per cent) and the UK (10.5 per cent), and finally, Oceania (184,400) with Australia (171,900) in first position and New Zealand (12,500) in second position. All together these countries represented 95 per cent of the total. Most of the western European countries were involved: Sweden, Denmark, Finland, Norway, Iceland, Spain, Italy, Greece, Austria, Switzerland and Luxembourg all admitted Vietnamese. The secondary resettlement areas were Asia (especially Hong Kong, Japan, Malaysia, the Philippines, Singapore and Taiwan), the Middle East (Israel), Africa (Ivory Coast, Senegal) and South America (Argentina). In all they received about 77,000 people.

Despite this impressive list, there were still 140,000 refugees in the camps on 31 December 1992. Of these, 60,000 were in Thailand, 45,000 in Hong Kong, 15,000 in Indonesia, 10,000 in Malaysia and 5500 in the Philippines. Very few of this group are likely ever to be resettled in a third country. Instead many are being returned home under the Voluntary Repatriation Programme conducted by the UNHCR. At the end of 1992, 36,400 went back to Vietnam, 18,400 to Cambodia and 12,300 to Laos.

The resettlement

The major resettlement countries were Australia, Canada, France and the USA to which can be added Germany, Sweden and the UK. The volume of the Indochinese refugees' movement forced all these countries to be innovative in their reception and their social policies.

With respect to reception, two strategies were developed. The first, the *étatist*, involved the government assuming the social and financial responsibilities of the reception, even if it delegated its power to private organizations. In this case, the refugees were received in specific centres for a temporary period, called immigration centres in Australia or *foyers d'immigrés* in France. The UK, Germany and Sweden also adopted this option. The second strategy was *private* in that the population was invited to play the same social and financial role as the state. In this case, families, groups of families or private associations took care of the refugees. This was called 'sponsorship'. The USA was the most fervent proponent of this strategy. The case of Canada was a little different,

as it practised both strategies simultaneously. The first strategy was used to disperse the refugees. In 1985, they were assigned to the provinces as follows: Ontario 37 per cent, Alberta 20 per cent, Quebec 18 per cent, Columbia 14 per cent, Manitoba 6 per cent and Saskachewan 5 per cent. However, within each province sponsorship was used.

In 1988 the highest concentrations of Indochinese refugees in the USA were in California, Texas, Washington, New York, Illinois, Massachussetts, Pennsylvania, Virginia and Minnesota. In France, 12 of the 21 regions took 60 per cent of the refugees. In the UK (in 1982) 25 per cent of the refugees were in London, 10 per cent in the West Midlands, 8 per cent in Yorkshire/Humberside, 7 per cent in the north-west and Scotland, 6 per cent in Merseyside and 5 per cent in the north-east. Australia had a somewhat different policy. The government dispersed the refugees only in the metropolitan areas: Sydney, Melbourne, Brisbane, Canberra and Adelaide. This policy of dispersion was corrected in subsequent years by spontaneous secondary migrations. This was due mainly to the refugees' aspirations to be concentrated so as to allow the organization of their communities.

Today, more than half the Indochinese refugees in the USA live in California, and in the UK in London. Secondary migrations in Canada took place from declining to more developed economic zones, and from small towns to big cities, where chances of employment and the capacity for organization inside the refugee community were higher. Sponsored refugees are twice as likely to remigrate as those received by the government authorities. In France in the 1980s, Paris and its suburbs were the first poles of attraction. Other popular regions were the Rhône Alps and Provence. According to US surveys (Forbes 1984), secondary migrations are not always definitive. About one-quarter of migrations fail, with the migrants returning to the regions from which they have come.

The degree of the integration of the refugees into the resettlement countries depended on services offered by the societies. These services were distributed in a certain sequence depending on the strategies of reception and the social organization. The normal sequence was learning the language, medical care, employment, housing and contact with the population. The refugees' integration also depended on economic circumstances in the resettlement countries, on the refugees' level of education, their professional skills and on specific economic initiatives taken by the resettlement countries in their favour to avoid unemployment as far as possible.

At the end of the 1970s and during the 1980s, the industrial countries suffered a serious recession. The extreme case was that of the UK, where there were few jobs for the refugees from 1979 to 1985. 'In 1982, at the depths of a recession', remarked Bach and Seguin (1985: 3, 4) in the USA, 'one out of four refugees actively seeking work could not find a job.'

Some US surveys (Bach and Seguin 1985; Forbes 1984; Haines 1989) insisted that the refugees' educational backgrounds explain the differences in labour force participation between the successive waves of Vietnamese refugees. Dunning (1989: 64), for example, reported that 'the proportion of time spent in the American labour force increased by 3 percentage points for each additional year of education completed in Vietnam, independently of the effects of other background characteristics'. Scholars in all the resettlement countries noted from 1975 to 1985 a significant degradation of the refugees' educational level and professional skills. They saw more and more arrivals of people who were illiterate in their own languages. A longitudinal survey conducted in San Diego, CA (Rumbaut 1989) indicated that the percentage of illiterate people increased from 2.6 in 1975 to 34.9 for the period 1980–3. Females were more illiterate than males. Hmong were the least educated (73.4 per cent illiterate), followed by the Khmer (34.1 per cent), those of Chinese origin (18.4 per cent) and the Vietnamese (1.2 per cent).

I want also to consider four aspects of economic adaptation. First, the resettlement countries noted significant levels of downward occupational mobility between the country of origin and the receiving society. As Haines (1989: 39) reported, 'For Cambodians and Vietnamese, the percentage in professional and managerial occupations in the United States was about half of what it had been in [the] country of origin; for Laotians, it was about a fourth.' In Australia, the majority found semi-skilled or operative jobs. This included 94 per cent of the Khmers, 80 per cent of the Laotians and 72 per cent of the Vietnamese (Keys Young 1980). In France, manual workers come first (47 per cent) followed by employers (11.5 per cent), trades people and crafts people (1 per cent). White-collar workers constituted only 0.6 per cent (Hassoun 1983; Mignot 1984).

Second, economic adaptation varied with ethnicity. The reasons mainly related to the educational and professional backgrounds of the Vietnamese. On the USA, Kim (1989: 96) avers that: 'The Lao and

Vietnamese refugees show a more positive situation than the Hmong and the Cambodian refugees.' According to him 46.8 per cent of the Vietnamese, 52.2 per cent of Lao, 69.7 per cent of Hmong and 72.3 per cent of the Cambodians had incomes below $700 a month. This was also true of Australia where the Cambodians were perceived to be 'less educated, have lower job skills ... and less facility with English prior to arrival' (Keys Young 1980: 82). Fass (1991: 11) found the same applied to the Hmong in Wisconsin: 'Adults were illiterate in their language; they had little prior vocational skill ... and negligible exposure to Western society.'

The third aspect is directly linked to unemployment. Unemployment rates vary not only with ethnicity but also between the resettlement countries. The country with the worst situation was certainly the UK, partly because of its policy not to make special employment provision for the refugees. Jones's study (1982) revealed an unemployment rate of 73.3 per cent (67.4 among males and 80.4 among females). Equivalent figures were from 26 to 32 per cent in Australia at the beginning of the 1980s, and 11.5 per cent in Lyon (France) in 1980. Ethnically speaking, the Hmong were the most unfavoured refugees. Their unemployment rate was from 80 to 85 per cent in 1982–84 compared with 10 to 30 per cent for the other Indochinese refugees in the USA.

Fourth, economic adaptation varies with social groups (women, young and elderly people) because of difficulties of access to the labour force and cultural changes within the family group. Viviani (1984: 194–5) speaks about 'alienation, physical violence and drinking' among the young Vietnamese in Australia because the older ones 'are too old for school ..., have gaps in their education from Vietnam' and also because 'there is very little future for them'. A Wilder Foundation (1990: 3) survey conducted in Minnesota reported that one out of ten families had a child 'with a chronic and severe physical or mental health problem or disability that interferes with their daily activity'. The change of cultural values introduced by the immigration to Western countries deeply modified the family hierarchy. Women's access to the work force and the Western pattern of family relationships had important effects on relations between husband and wife, youth and elderly people, of whom Viviani (1984: 195) says some are 'devastated by the move to Australia while some blossom'.

One no longer counts the programmes developed by

governments or organizations to overcome the respective difficulties of the different social groups. Nevertheless, I would like to say a few words here about those that were set up for the Hmong and, more particularly, the agricultural programmes. In France, some attempts were made to resettle the Hmong in forest areas. Conducted without prior experience, they generally failed and the Hmongs migrated to the towns where conditions of life were better (Hassoun 1983). In Minnesota two agricultural programmes were conducted. One failed because of financial problems. The second failed, too, because of problems of organization. The programme also suffered from pressures imposed on the federal government by some grocers who created unfair competition. The budget was cut. Having been initiated into the US agricultural system, some Hmong families are still engaged in agricultural activities, but as a second job and usually for their own subsistence (Mignot 1993).

The future

For refugees still in camps in Southeast Asia, it appears they have no future other than to return to their country of origin. This applied to the 200,000 Cambodians who left Thailand at the beginning of 1993. The UNHCR is also deeply implicated in the return of Vietnamese refugees in Hong Kong to Vietnam. Some eighteen years after the events in question, offers of resettlement are few and far between.

The future of the resettled refugees is in the hands of the next generations. The first wave is generally considered as 'sacrificed'. It does not appear that they have any likelihood of return, except, perhaps, for elderly people who would like to die if possible on their ancestors' land. The different ethnic groups are going to constitute minority groups inside the receiving societies. In all the destination countries the degree of integration with the native populations remains low.

References

Bach, R. L. and R. C. Seguin (1985) 'Labour Force Participation of Southeast Asian Refugees in the United States', *International Migration Review*, 22 (2), 381–404

Dunning, B. B. (1989) 'Vietnamese in America: The Adaptation of the 1975–1979 Arrivals', in David Haines (ed.), *Refugees as Immigrants: Cambodians, Laotians and Vietnamese in America*, Totowa, NJ: Rowman & Littlefield, 55–85

Fass, Simon M. (1991) *The Hmong in Wisconsin, On the Road to Self-Sufficiency*, Milwaukee: The Wisconsin Policy Research Institute, Report 4 (2), April

Forbes, S. S. (1984) *Residency Patterns and Secondary Migration of Refugees: A State of the Information Paper*, Washington, DC: Refugee Policy Group

Haines, David W. (ed.) (1989) *Refugees as Immigrants: Cambodians, Laotians and Vietnamese in America*, Totowa, NJ: Rowman & Littlefield

Hassoun, J. P. (1983) *Hmong Réfugiés: Trajectoires ethno-sociales*, Paris: EHESS

Jones, Peter R. (1982) *Vietnamese Refugees*, Home Office: Research and Planning Unit, Paper 13

Keys Young, M. S. J. (1980) *Attitudes toward Refugees and Migrants in Host Community in Sydney and Melbourne*, Surrey Hills: M. S. J. Keys Young

Kim, Young Yun (1989) 'Personal, Social and Economic Adaptation: 1975–1979 Arrivals in Illinois', in David Haines (ed.) *Refugees as Immigrants: Cambodians, Laotians and Vietnamese in America*, Totowa, NJ: Rowman & Littlefield, 86–104

Mignot, M. (1984) *Les Réfugiés de la Péninsule indochinoise en France: Un Centre d'Hébergement, une Commune, une Région*, Vienna: Wilhelm Braumüller

(1993) 'Secondary Migrations of Southeast Asian Refugees: State Policies and Community Gathering', in Paul James Rutledge (ed.) *In Search of Tradition and Adaptation: Vietnamese Refugees around the World*, St Louis: University of Missouri Press

Rumbaut, Rubén G. (1989) 'Portraits, Patterns and Predictors of the Refugee Adaptation Process: Result and Reflection from the IHARP Panel Study', in David Haines (ed.) *Refugees as Immigrants: Cambodians, Laotians and Vietnamese in America*, Totowa, NJ: Rowman & Littlefield, 138–67

Viviani, Nancy (1984) *The Long Journey: Vietnamese Migration and Settlement in Australia*, Carlton: Melbourne University Press

Wilder Foundation (1990) *St Paul PHA Family Survey*, St Paul, MN: Public Housing Agency, June

REFUGEES AND ASYLUM IN THE MUSLIM WORLD

ASTRI SUHRKE

By the opening of the 1990s, about two-thirds of the world's estimated 18 million refugees were Muslims or refugees in Muslim states. The trend was expected to continue, with upheavals in Central Asia, the Caucasus and the Balkans contributing their part. This situation has generated growing interest in the subject of Islamic concepts of refugee and asylum. What are the formal concepts and how do they relate to the practice of states? Is there a case for closer ties between the Islamic world and the international refugee regime anchored in the United Nations? This essay will approach these questions by examining Islamic concepts of refugee and asylum, and the main historical events that have shaped them.[1]

Formal concepts

While Western traditions of refugee and asylum in part have religious origins, the equivalent Muslim concepts are central to the genesis of Islam itself (Masud 1990; Meier 1991). The flight of the Prophet Muhammad and his followers from hostile Mecca to friendly Medina in AD 622 came to be known as the *hijra* – the migration. Medina's welcome enabled the Prophet to regroup and successfully lead a holy war (*jihad*) against Mecca. From this point onwards, Islam developed as a global religion. The flight and battle which made this possible became the defining elements of Islamic thought regarding refugees. A generic Arabic term for migration, *hijra* came to signify movement from a land of infidelity or oppression to the land of Islam, from *dar al-harb* to *dar al-Islam*. The process could involve a *jihad* and triumphant return to the liberated land of Islam, or an expansion of the frontiers of *dar al-Islam* by establishing a new Muslim community, or yet a third alternative of settling in an existing Muslim state.

The model for receiving refugees – i.e. granting asylum – likewise was determined by the Prophet's experience when he reached Medina and was warmly welcomed. Formalized in the fourth *surah* of the Koran, the obligations of the receiving society (*ansar*, i.e. host) are derived from the characteristic nature of the migration itself: 'He who emigrates in the path of God will find frequent refuge and abundance.'

While Western concepts of refugee emphasize the involuntary nature of the movement, and contemporary international law defines a 'refugee' with respect to the nature of abuse feared or inflicted, the Islamic tradition clearly differs. In its classic sense, flight is a sacred duty to be undertaken by Muslims who live in non-Muslim societies regardless of the kind of oppression to which they might be subjected. The obligation is premised on the indivisibility between state and society, which holds that a Muslim society cannot exist in a non-Muslim state. The notion of 'persecution', which figures so prominently in Western jurisprudence governing refugee status, thus becomes secondary, as does the common sociological distinction between voluntary (migration) and involuntary (refugee) movements. *Hijra* is simply a duty.

Time and a changing world modified the classic concepts. Yet the evolution of Islamic doctrines continued to centre on obligations to exit (in contrast to the Western focus on conditions of entry). The preoccupation reflected the stagnation and eventual retrenchment of secular Muslim power in the late medieval period and again from the eighteenth century onwards.

As Christian states started to conquer Muslim lands, the question of flight was posed more often and in stark term: must Muslims flee from land that once had been, but now had ceased to be *dar al-Islam*? The dominant theological interpretation in the late medieval period upheld the obligation to perform *hijra*, but conditions permitting exceptions were later enumerated by Islamic scholars, and some – mainly the Sufi – interpreted *hijra* as a spiritual withdrawal from a hostile society rather than a physical movement.

The refugee in history

In practice, the *hijra* command was rarely followed, and all but one took place in the context of immediate violence. When Granada fell in AD 1492, many Muslims did indeed leave the Iberian peninsula as called for by Islamic doctrine, but persecution and eventual expulsion left them little choice. Centuries later, when millions of Muslims in the Middle East and Africa came under European colonial rule, only one major case of *hijra* is recorded. Thousands of Algerians left their homes from Libya in protest against French colonialism, but also to escape repression after the failed Abdulqadir revolt (1832–47).

Other population movements commonly referred to as *hijra* in the nineteenth and early twentieth centuries occurred as the Ottoman empire was pushed back, as were millions of Muslims who mostly fled to the interior regions of the Ottoman realm (Karpat 1985). When the Russians conquered Crimea and most of the Caucasus, Muslims were pushed out to make room for Christian Slav settlers. From all sides, the Muslims were pressured: 'The destruction of native social and political institutions, the implementation of a land policy intended to favour Russian ownership and its attendant serf agriculture, and concern that most Muslim natives posed security problems for the state, all combined to produce pressure on [them] ... to leave' (Fisher 1987: 356). Russian officials spoke of the 'cleansing' of Crimea already in 1837 (Fisher 1987: 359). Later, the Tartars were deemed doubly undesirable by virtue of their suspected collaboration with the Ottoman forces during the Crimean War (1853–6). In the Caucasus the Russians needed three years and some 100,000 soldiers to subdue an armed rebellion led by the Sufi Naqshbandi order. Large-scale out-migration of the defeated Muslims followed.

As the line of conflict between the Christian and Muslim worlds shifted southward, the exodus reached massive proportions. At its height (1855–66), between 700,000 and 900,000 Muslims moved from the Crimea and the Caucasus towards the inner regions of the Ottoman empire. Moving on their own without assistance from humanitarian organizations, which only later developed to aid refugees, the migrants suffered severe deprivations and thousands died on the way from smallpox, dysentery, fever or exhaustion.

The other main migration into the Ottoman realm in this period was the *hijra* from the Balkans after the Turco-Russian war (1877–8) and the Balkan wars of 1912–13. The wars further decimated the Ottoman empire, breaking off chunks that were reconstituted as independent states. The Muslims were fragmented by new state boundaries and transformed into minorities in various non-Muslim states. Immediately they were 'encouraged or forced to emigrate' (Karpat 1990: 132).

Russian penetration of the independent Muslim *khanate*s on the Ottoman periphery in Central Asia also provoked armed resistance and flight – a pattern continued for almost a decade after the Bolshevik revolution of 1917. Most fled to neighbouring Muslim territory – Afghanistan and the nominally Chinese ruled part of Turkestan – from where the resistance continued (Olcott 1981). Emphasizing the religious nature of their refugee condition, some referred to themselves as *muhajir*, i.e. one that performs the *hijra* (Shalinsky 1982/3: 75).

The principal *hijra* that was initiated as a protest rather than an escape took place in India after the First World War. Calling for self-determination for Indian Muslims and simultaneously the recognition of the Ottoman sultan as the head of the entire Islamic world, some 20,000–30,000 Muslims proclaimed a *hijra* and *jihad*, and marched to neighbouring Afghanistan to seek support for the war. The quixotic march ended in defeat as hundreds died of exhaustion on the way and the survivors failed to get support or recognition either in Afghanistan, Turkey or the Middle East (Holt et al. 1980; Smith 1958; Yapp 1992).

By the early twentieth century, foreign rule, failed rebellions and ultimate displacement of Muslim peoples had come to define the reality of the refugee experience in the Islamic world. The original concept of *hijra* as a sacred duty leading to the victorious expansion, or restoration, of the Islamic realm had been overtaken by historical events. Moreover, millions of Muslims continued to live in secular states under colonial rule, or as minorities in Christian, Hindu or Buddhist societies. Few had any realistic alternative. Unlike in medieval times and in the Ottoman period – when Muslims could freely settle anywhere in the realm – an emerging world of nation states with formal border controls increasingly posed barriers to migration also in the Muslim world.

While the option of settling freely anywhere in *dar al-Islam* narrowed, a reverse movement simultaneously became more attractive. Increasingly Muslims sought to migrate to non-Muslim countries for educational and economic advancement. Scholars posed new questions to redefine *hijra*. From where does one not need to migrate? To where can one migrate? (Masud 1990).

The image of the Muslim refugee as someone forcefully displaced by non-Muslim powers was reinforced during the second half of the twentieth century as three prominent refugee populations appeared – the Palestinians, the Afghans and the Bosnian Muslims. The Palestinians clearly were subjected to expulsion during the partition of Palestine and its aftermath (Morris 1987), as were the Bosnian

Muslims forty years later when the former Yugoslavia dissolved into war. The Afghan case was more a matter of escaping the violence of war brought on by a local revolution (1978) and Soviet intervention, but there was also the element of withdrawal from enemy-ruled territory to regroup and fight on. The liberation struggle called for in the classic linking of *jihad* to *hijra* was launched. To emphasize the point, many Afghan refugees referred to themselves as both *muhajir* and *mujahedin* (i.e. the noun for participants in both activities) (Shahrani 1992). The Palestinians tenaciously fought displacement by making the 'right of return' – however defined – central to their political and military struggle and, by some factions, defined in classic Islamic terms. In the former Yugoslavia, the culturally European Muslims of Bosnia rarely depicted their refugee condition in Islamic terms, at least not during the first two years of the war. Until the war, their religious identity had limited saliency compared with language and kinship identities (Hammel 1993).

Asylum

While Islamic theories of asylum are not highly developed, the core is clear. To provide asylum is a precondition for *hijra* and thus a sacred duty. But also others – non-Muslims and Muslims who flee from Muslims – have a right to protection according to the Koran: in effect, all who 'emigrate in the path of God' (the Koran, *surah* 4.100). For Muslims, the right is also derived from their common membership in the Islamic community (*umma*).

By this standard, the asylum policy of the principal receiving entity for many centuries – the Ottoman empire – was exemplary. In the late medieval period, both Muslims and Jews expelled from Spain were welcome, and the door remained open for Muslims and non-Muslims alike. Only towards the end of the nineteenth century did the sultan emphasize the religious element by declaring the empire open to all Muslims who would come to settle – a shift shaped by the intensified conflict with Russia and the European powers.

The population movement from the periphery to the centre of the Ottoman empire has been estimated at between five and seven million in the period between 1860 and 1914. Demand for manpower in thinly populated regions helped sustain the liberal immigration policy. New settlers were given tax and other incentives, as well as assistance upon arrival. The influx also led the Ottomans to codify admissions practice. The first civil refugee code in the Muslim

world, the law of 1857, probably made no distinction between migrants and refugees, but used the term *muhacir* – equivalent to the Arabic *muhajir* – to denote all subjects (Shaw and Kural 1977).

By the mid-twentieth century nation states had replaced empires, demographic conditions had changed, and the successor Muslim states brought entirely different perspectives to asylum and immigration issues. Apart from the Gulf states, most were poor countries with a large labour surplus. While most governments recognized in principle their Islamic duty to provide asylum, practice was clearly influenced by economic and political constraints. As in most countries, refugee policy was a multidimensional and often multi-purpose process. Iran, for example, gave extremely liberal asylum to Afghan refugees, but variously opened and closed its borders to Kurdish refugees in the 1970s. Pakistan had welcomed over three million Afghan refugees as long as the war in Afghanistan was internationalized (1979–89), but closed its borders in 1993 when it feared that international aid to refugees would cease.

More generally, a dual tension is apparent in the asylum policy of Muslim states. The tension between humanitarian ideals and political realism is a universal phenomenon shared by all reasonable governments. Particular to Muslim states is the form this tension takes, shaped on the one hand by traditional principles of asylum – which are broad and generous, derived from Islamic canons as well as pre-Islamic tradition in many areas – and the demands on the modern state to ration benefits to 'non-members'. Asylum, as Khadija Elmadmad points out in her study of Afro-Arab states, has passed from the traditional stage as an act of protection generally accorded by individuals and leaders to anyone seeking it, to the modern stage where asylum has become exclusively a state function to be precisely defined. Since few Muslim states have civil laws to regulate modern asylum, practice tends to be random or restrictive, and, some fear, could be influenced by the restrictive European example (Elmadmad 1993).

International cooperation

The predominant image of Muslim refugees as victims of advancing non-Muslim power had by the second half of the twentieth century clearly given way to more varied movements. Many were the result of conflict in or between Muslim states. Protracted warfare in the Horn of Africa produced several million refugees, revolution in Iran and the subsequent war with Iraq led to massive outflows, as did the Gulf War of 1990/1. Civil war in Central Asia caused large displacements in the early 1990s. Two decades earlier, the break-up of Pakistan had generated perhaps nine million refugees.

Recognizing the need for international cooperation to deal with the complexities of forced migration, African Muslim states and most Afro-Arab states signed the refugee convention of the Organization of African Unity (1969) as well as the UN Convention on Refugees, or its 1967 Protocol. The Arab world, however, was weakly tied to the international refugee regime. Except for Tunisia, Algeria and Morocco, no Arab state had signed the 1951 Convention or the 1967 Protocol. For years, rich Arab Gulf states gave only symbolic financial contributions to the United Nations High Commission for Refugees (UNHCR). Change did not come until the refugee crisis during the Gulf War and the close political cooperation between Saudi Arabia and the West during that conflict. The Saudi-initiated Organization of the Islamic Conference subsequently signed agreements with UNHCR to promote cooperation in all matters concerning refugee assistance in the Muslim world. In a related development, efforts were underway in the early 1990s to establish cooperation among Arab League states for the protection and support of refugees (Elmadmad 1991).

Notes

1. This contribution draws on an earlier study by Suhrke and Aarbakke (1993).

References

Elmadmad, Khadija (1991) 'An Arab Convention on Forced Migration: Desirability and Possibilities', *International Journal of Refugee Law*, 3 (3), 461–81

—— (1993) 'L'Asile dans les Pays afro-arabes avec une Référance spéciale au Soudan', thesis, Casablanca University, Faculty of Law

Fisher, Alan (1987) 'Emigration of Muslims from the Russian Empire in the Years after the Crimean War', *Jahrbücher für Geschichte Oseuropas*, 1, 356–71

Hammel, E. A. (1993) 'Demography and the Origins of the Yugoslav Civil War', *Anthropology Today*, 9 (1), 4–9

Holt, P. M. et al. (1980) *The Cambridge History of Islam*, vol. IIA, Cambridge: Cambridge University Press

Karpat, Kemal (1985) *Ottoman Population 1830–1914*, Madison: University of Wisconsin Press

—— (1990) 'The *Hijra* from Russia and the Balkans: The Process of Self-definition in the Ottoman State', in Dale F. Eickelman and James Piscatori (eds) *Muslim Travellers: Pilgrimage, Migration and the Religious Imagination*, New York: Routledge, 131–52

Masud, Muhammad Khalid (1990) 'The Obligation to Migrate: The Doctrine of *Hijra* in Islamic Law', in Dale F. Eickelman and James Piscatori (eds) *Muslim Travellers: Pilgrimage, Migration and the Religious Imagination*, New York: Routledge, 29–49

Meier, Fritz (1991) 'Über die umstrittende Pflicht des Muslims, bei nichtmuslimischer Besetzung seines Landes auszuwandern', *Der Islam*, 68 (1), 65–86

Morris, Benny (1987) *The Birth of the Palestinian Refugee Problem 1947–49*, Cambridge: Cambridge University Press

Olcott, Martha (1981) 'The Basmachi or Freemen's Revolt in Turkestan, 1918–24', *Soviet Studies*, 33 (July), 352–69

Shahrani, Nazif M. (1992) 'Afghanistan's *Muhajirin* (Muslim "Refugee-Warriors") in Pakistan', paper prepared for the UNU/WIDER Workshop, Bergen (Norway), 11–13 June

Shalinsky, Audrey (1982/3) 'Islam and Ethnicity: The Northern Afghanistan Perspective', *Central Asian Survey*, 1 (2–3), 71–83

Shaw, Stanford J. and Ezel Kural (1977) *History of the Ottoman Empire and Modern Turkey*, vol. II, Cambridge: Cambridge University Press

Smith, W. (1958) *Modern Islam in India*, Oxford: Clarrendon Press

Suhrke, Astri and Vemund Aarbakke (1993) *Refugees in the Muslim World: Concepts, Law and Practice*, Bergen: Chr. Michelsen Institute, Report prepared for the Norwegian Refugee Council

Yapp, M. E. (1992) ' "That Great Mass of Unmixed Mahomedanism": Reflections on the Historical Links between the Middle East and Asia', *British Journal of Middle Eastern Studies*, 19 (1), 16–30

DEVELOPMENT AND FORCED MIGRATION: THE CASE OF AFGHAN REFUGEE WOMEN IN PAKISTAN

DIANA CAMMACK

Forced migration is as old as war, but it need not be as destructive if the period in exile is used by the refugees and international community to develop the human resources and institutions needed to reconstruct the society. Among a handful of refugee communities in the 1980s this was done, but in most places, such as in Pakistan where over 3.5 million Afghans took refuge, the chance to foster real development, especially among women, was largely missed.

Modernization and war

Even before a decade of war laid waste to Afghanistan it was a poor country. It was poised on the bottom rung of the world indicators of per capita income, life expectancy, literacy, infant and maternal mortality, and the rural population especially was malnourished, rarely immunized, had few clinics and little clean water. In spite of its backwardness, it was a country of proud people, whose social traditions and mores were complex and whose long history was a grand tale of resistance. More importantly for the women of Afghanistan, though, it was a country in the process of modernizing.

Islam, while not overly prohibitive in Afghanistan and the traditions of tribal society that vested a family's honour in the protection men afforded their females, combined to assure that rural women rarely left their villages (though they could move around them with few restrictions), that their social relations were prescribed, and that their productive lives were restricted to domestic and farm chores and to home-based craft production.

As in other parts of the world, it was among the elite in the capital that the transformation of Afghan society began. A first attempt at reform was made at court in the 1920s, but was generally unacceptable until 1959. Then followed for nearly two decades, until the Saur revolution of April 1978, a gradual liberalizing trend, where a number of women's rights were realized. For instance, legal measures were enacted that gave women more power to choose and divorce partners, while 'brideprice' and child marriage were theoretically abolished. The 1964 constitution enfranchised women when it outlawed discrimination and by 1977 the 20 member Constitutional Advisory Committee included 2 women and the nearly 400-member Loya Jirga, a dozen (Dupree 1991).

Moreover, female educational opportunities began to expand. The first girls' school opened in Kabul in the 1920s, and by the mid-1970s, at least 10 per cent of the pupils in the country were girls. Of course, most of these girls lived in the urban areas, where mobility, education and employment were already seen as normal for women. Yet men in the towns did encourage their kinsmen in the villages to send their daughters to school, and this was increasingly done. Nevertheless, by the time the war started, the illiteracy rate for females remained upwards of 95 per cent — not very different from the 92 per cent or so for men nationwide.

By 1978 women were also well-ensconced in the paid workforce, where they were entering new professions. Where before women in paid employment worked mostly as nurses and midwives, in the 1960s and 1970s more women became technicians, teachers, administrators, doctors, and industrial and office workers. In other words, as Afghanistan was integrated into the world economy and as the domestic economy industrialized and differentiated, women gained access to education and the workplace, while traditional restrictions on their mobility, political rights and social behaviour relaxed.

It would be erroneous, though, to assume that these social and economic transformations had taken root in the hinterland. Indeed, the same forces that for centuries reinforced tribal and regional isolationism and kept integrative political and economic forces at bay ensured that rural women were largely confined to their farms and villages; in youthful, polygynous and arranged marriages; illiterate, malnourished and weakened by frequent pregnancies. On the eve of the war, the division between town and country remained in place and conflicting views about a woman's role in Afghan society were only one of the many rural–urban contrasts.

461

The Saur revolution of April 1978 brought the Afghan communists to power. The following year the Soviet army entered from the north to bolster the factionalized and beleaguered leftist cause. These two events – and the imposition of revolutionary reforms on the countryside – brought an end to any hope of gradually transforming Afghan society, or a woman's place within it.

The vanguard Afghan communists who came to power in 1978 aimed to revolutionize what they considered a backward and oppressive feudal regime. To do so meant imposing central government control over the relatively autonomous and factionalized countryside, a move that generated as much opposition as their reforms. Moreover, the harsh and uncompromising way the reforms were implemented by urban cadres caused additional resentment in the villages, as did the introduction of a mass rural literacy campaign. In principle, the communists' reforms seem quite ordinary, considering the overwhelming need to modernize and integrate the impoverished political economy. The three decrees giving the most offence were those enacted to break the cycle of peasant indebtedness to landlords, 'remove unjust patriarchal and feudalistic relations' between husband and wife, and abolish 'feudal and pre-feudal relations' by redistributing land (Hyman 1992: 87–8).

This attack on rural institutions and the elite, and on a mixture of religious and tribal mores became identified in the minds of the peasantry with outsiders' attempts to alter the rightful position of women, the corrupting secularism of westernized Kabul, central government interference in tribal affairs, and with mass education. The Soviet invasion provided an additional dimension: an attack on the Afghans' right of national self-determination.

Relief and the failure of development
By 1979 the countryside was in rebellion, and refugees were leaving for Pakistan and Iran. Where there had been 1400 refugees in Pakistan in 1975, by the time the Soviets invaded there were some 400,000. During the following two years almost 100,000 a month crossed the border into Pakistan and by mid-1981 their number had climbed to over 2 million. Thereafter the exodus slowed, yet by 1988 Pakistan hosted at least 3.5 million, nearly three-quarters of whom lived in the North-West Frontier Province including the tribal agencies, and the rest in Baluchistan and the Punjab. Just over half of them were children, and an estimated 26 per cent were women.

By and large the Afghans settled in refugee villages (some 350 of them by the mid-1980s), where they were initially provided with tents – though they soon built mud *katcha* houses enclosed by high 'purdah walls' – with food, water, clothing, bedding, medical care and sometimes cash. Here, as in all refugee crises, stabilizing the situation to prevent famine, exposure and disease was the initial priority of the government and the United Nations High Commission for Refugees (UNHCR). Only from the mid-1980s did their thoughts turn to Afghan self-reliance and development.

While the horrific statistics on Afghan underdevelopment and destitution demanded that wide-ranging training, educational and income-generating programmes be introduced, especially for women, relatively few development projects were in fact designed or implemented. There were a number of important and complicated reasons for this, reasons that must be addressed in the future if development assistance is to be provided to impoverished Muslim refugee women elsewhere.

First, it was difficult for the aid community even to reach the women, for the vast majority were subject to *purdah*, or seclusion, which was traditional to Afghanistan. In fact, Afghan women in the refugee villages of Pakistan were much more restricted in their movements and social intercourse than they had been at home, partly because it is common for refugees anywhere to assert their traditions as a psychological reaction to displacement and as a means of combating social disorder and disintegrating ideals and institutions.

Purdah was also reinforced because extended families who previously lived in isolated villages in Afghanistan were mixed together with others in the Pakistan camps, so that women could no longer move freely among their relatives' homes. The fact that an Afghan male's honour depended in part on how well he protected his womenfolk put additional pressure on women in exile to remain behind their walls, out of sight of strangers, including aid workers.

Unable to see or meet with women, relief officials therefore found it nearly impossible even to count them, let alone survey their immediate relief or long-term development needs or to register their requests for help.

Second, a fearsome form of Islam was used increasingly in the 1980s by various members of the Afghan elite in exile – from the displaced village mullahs to well-armed Islamist politicians and their youthful disciples – to shape public opinion and

PLATE 22: Afghan women refugees weaving carpets in Surkhab, Baluchistan, 1982.

behaviour. Also important in this regard was the fact that the Afghans had taken refuge in Pakistan at a time when Islamic zealotry was on the rise there too. Consequently the belief was nourished that the coup and invasion were the result of the acceptance by the Kabul elite of secular ideas and Western behaviour and that the communists would be defeated only through the adoption of strict Islamic values. The moral high ground was thus captured by the most ardent Islamist exiles – those strengthened by the relief programme, and financed and armed by the Pakistan government and, ironically as it turned out, by the Western powers. And any Afghan opponent, from moderate democrats to royalists and traditional elites, as well as any aid agency, staff member or programme, could effectively be undermined by labelling them 'un-Islamic'.

This had a profound impact on middle-class refugee women, for any seen moving about, employed or being trained by the NGOs, or studying in Western-supported schools, could be branded un-Islamic, and they, their fathers and brothers, threatened. For peasant women in the camps, the stigma attached to education and training – where schools were seen as both un-Islamic and as 'breeding grounds for [the] communistic ideas' that led to war (Dupree 1988:

855) – and to Western institutions generally, reinforced the traditional prohibition against leaving the house and mixing with foreigners, and absolutely with men. Taken together, these retarded the growth of relief and development programmes to help the women.

For instance, women were rarely allowed to be seen by male doctors, even in emergencies; nor could they be visited by male health visitors unless they were close relatives. Naturally, this impaired their health and their understanding of disease and its prevention long after male refugees, who were far more likely to consult and be trained by foreign medical personnel.

It goes without saying that Afghan women were not in control of the local distribution of food (as has been advocated generally to foster equity in provisioning); nor were they even allowed to participate in the public disbursement of other forms of aid. This meant that some categories of women and children were especially vulnerable to under-supply, particularly when for one reason or another they were without close male relatives and had to rely instead upon distant kin or Islamic concepts of charity in the increasingly impoverished Afghan community.

One of the most notable discrepancies in the assistance programme was in education. As noted previously, less than 10 per cent of the population could read before the war, but by 1987 as many as 60 per cent of school-age Afghan boys in the Pakistan camps could claim to be literate – a remarkable achievement indeed. At the same time, though, only 6 per cent of girls aged 6–11 years and 3 per cent of girls aged 12–17 were literate. This reflected the amount of time girls spent in school in Pakistan[1] (Christensen and Scott 1988: 27–30) and ultimately, the relatively little emphasis placed upon, and the amount of funds allocated to girls' education by donors.

In the mid-1980s, income generation and skills training programmes were initiated by the refugee regime, openly to foster self-sufficiency (an illusory goal) but equally to promote self-esteem and mental health in villages where life was increasingly becoming 'a life of dependency' (Boesen 1983: 2). Though traditional restrictions on mobility and outside employment remained, many Afghan women, when surveyed over the years, expressed their eagerness to participate in income generating and training programmes, partly out of boredom, but more often to enable them to earn a wage. Nevertheless, in the 1980s the vast majority of, though certainly not all, programmes were started for men. (Connor 1989; Meijer and Weeda 1990; Sinclair 1991).

The reason for this has been identified by a number of people, including the Women's Commission for Refugee Women and Children (1990: 5):

> Members of the donor community state that they fund programs for the community at large [and] ... do not see the need to target the special needs of women. Although donors envision equitable distribution of program benefits, religion and traditional constraints ... inhibit women and girls from receiving or participating in services and programs.

Others have been less diplomatic: policy makers in the Afghan programme were 'male-oriented' and viewed women 'as a dependent group, and not [as] individuals with their own needs and resources'. Aware of difficulties in designing and implementing women's programmes 'due to the socio-cultural set-up', S. Zia Al-Jalaly has emphasized that the paucity of projects was also due to the 'absence of policy orientation towards women' (Al-Jalaly n.d.).

Development in exile: lessons learned

How might the aid community combat a similar combination of tradition, hostility and paralysing cultural sensitivity in the future? First, at the broadest level it must accept that women's rights are human rights and are not culturally determined. Further, it must acknowledge that it has an explicit duty to protect these rights during programme design and implementation.

Second, policy planners must appreciate that flight and refuge are radically transforming experiences: it is impossible for people to return home as they left, without being influenced in some way by their exile. Indeed, refugees are introduced to modern technology, infrastructure, techniques, hygiene, sanitation, health care, education and training, and will be forever changed by them. This being the case, members of the aid community must decide which forces of change they want to foster and devise their programmes accordingly. After all, relief work (after the first emergency phase) is really development work in exile, and individuals and agencies should not idealize any traditional society (or a woman's role in it) to the point of refusing to work for its transformation.

At the field level this means that 'agencies should be prepared to give women the opportunity to take risks themselves', as Safia Halim argued about Afghans, and at the same time 'be more imaginative in considering how to establish programmes targeted to women' (Women in Development 1992: 8). This does not mean that women's projects should be appended separately to the aid programme, but should be 'mainstreamed' or integrated into programme planning and delivery, as women's programme specialists suggest (UNHCR 1990, 1991, 1992a, 1992b). Indeed, the Afghan experience demonstrated that 'women's roles and women's issues must be clearly defined and incorporated into policies, plans and institutional changes at all levels in order to increase women's productivity and improve their health and educational status' (Christensen and Haffenden 1989).

A number of recommendations emerge from the various successful programmes run for Afghan women by agencies. When working in a strict Muslim culture where *purdah* is rigidly enforced, it is essential that women aid workers be used in the field rather than men. Further, the refugee patriarchy must be consulted, at least initially, to facilitate access to women. Only rarely and with care should programmes endeavour to bring ordinary women out of their homes, but should be based in a house that is accessible to as many women as possible. In certain unusual cases meeting at a central location to run projects, secluded from men, might be permissible.

For health and education projects mobile clinics are more accessible to secluded women, as are small classes for girls and women in an extended family. Logistically it may be easier to train and employ middle-class women in an urban environment, but changes in the political and religious climate should be monitored carefully for their safety.

Most income-generating projects for women in Pakistan were home-based and concentrated on handicrafts – producing quilts and school uniforms, embroidered clothes and accessories, for instance. Yet there are a number of reasons why female handicraft production is unsustainable and why domestic production can intensify already exploitative household conditions (Connor 1989; Kassam 1991; UNHCR 1990). Therefore, agencies in similar situations in the future should also look for other ways to help women earn money – such as cultivating tree seedlings, market gardening, and poultry and egg production – as was done in Pakistan.

With the capture of Kabul by the *mujahedeen*, the refugees' dreams of repatriation took shape. But very little in the nature of the continuing war, of the new Afghan administration (*Guardian*, 1992; Islamic State of Afghanistan, 1992), of the ongoing aid programme in Pakistan,[2] or of Afghanistan's plan for reconstruction (Dupree 1989) give cause to hope that the needs and resources of Afghan women are now going to be 'mainstreamed' or that their human rights are going to be protected. Consequently, the lament of one Afghan woman refugee remains ringing in our ears: 'We have been left out of programs, education and skill building. We have lost everything and are returning to Afghanistan with empty hands and nothing to offer.' (Symposium of the Women's Commission for Refugee Women and Children 1992).

That should be our incentive to do better next time.

Notes

1. In a survey of nearly 3000 households in 58 villages, it was discovered that about 51 per cent of boys aged 5 to 17 years were in school, compared with 4 per cent of girls ages 5 to 11 and 1.4 per cent of girls ages 12 to 17.
2. It should be stated though, that ACBAR, the coordinating body of non-governmental organizations working with Afghans in Peshawar, acknowledged in the early 1990s that 'after years of extreme caution, the assistance community is moving towards the recognition that women's needs must be addressed more effectively' (ACBAR 1992: 29).

References

ACBAR (Agency Coordinating Body for Afghan Relief) (1992) 'Overview of NGO Assistance: Afghan Programmes, 1990–1991', Peshawar, Pakistan, March

Al-Jalaly, S. Zia (n.d.) 'Carpet Weaving Afghan Refugee Women: A Study of their Living and Working Conditions in the Camps in Pakistan', (n.p.) File FA/FP 85.2: Refugee Studies Programme, University of Oxford

Boesen, Inger W. (1983) 'From Autonomy to Dependency: Aspects of the "Dependency Syndrome" among Afghan Refugees', paper delivered at Bureau International d'Afghanistan Conference, Geneva, 4–6 November

Christensen, Hanne and Fay Haffenden (1989) 'Afghan Women and Planning: Report from the Workshop, 21–23 August 1989', New York: UNICEF, September

Christensen, Hanne and Wolf Scott (1988) 'Survey of the Social and Economic Conditions of Afghan Refugees in Pakistan', Geneva: UNRISD

Connor, Kerry M. (1989) 'Development Potential for Aid Projects Targeting Afghan Women', Swedish Committee for Afghanistan, November

Dupree, Nancy Hatch (1988) 'Demographic Reporting on Afghan Refugees in Pakistan', *Modern Asian Studies*, 22 (4)

(1989) 'Seclusion or Service: Will Women Have a Role in the Future of Afghanistan?', The Afghanistan Forum *Occasional Paper*, 29, December

1991) 'Constitutional Requirements for Afghan Women', *WUFA* (Writers Union of Free Afghanistan), 6 (2), March–April, 54–5

Guardian (1992) 'Afghan TV pulls plug on women', 29 July, UK

Hyman, Anthony (1992) *Afghanistan under Soviet Domination, 1964–91*, Basingstoke: Macmillan

Islamic State of Afghanistan (1992), Draft 'Protocol Agreement' [between the government and aid agencies], 2 June

Kassam, Sabrina (1991) 'A Report Submitted to OXFAM, Pakistan, Based on Fieldwork in Quetta from 10 March to 3 April 1991', Report No. 2, OXFAM, July

Meijer, Marijke and Mieke Weeda (1990) 'Travel Report: Pakistan', Dutch Interchurch Aid, November

Sinclair, Margaret (1991) 'Income-Generation Programmes for Vulnerable Groups: Some Experiences from Afghan Refugee Assistance Projects in Pakistan', UNHCR/Radda Barnen, 22 April

Symposium of the Women's Commission for Refugee Women and Children (1992) 'Going Home: The Prospect of Repatriation for Refugee Women and Children', 8 June, Washington, DC

UNHCR (1990) 'Note on Refugee Women and International Protection', EC/SCP/59, 28 August

(1991) 'Progress Report on the Implementation of the UNHCR Policy on Refugee Women', EC/SC.2/47, 17 July

(1992a) 'Progress Report on Implementation of the UNHCR Guidelines on the Protection of Refugee Women', EC/SCP/74, 22 July

(1992b) 'Progress Report on Implementation of the UNHCR Policy on Refugee Women', EC/SC.2/55, 26 August

Women in Development (1992) 'Women in Development: Report of a Seminar Held on 25th April 1992', *ARIN Newsletter* (Afghan Refugee Information Network), 38, November

Women's Commission for Refugee Women and Children (1990) 'Afghan Refugee Women: Needs and Resources for Development and Reconstruction', Delegation to Pakistan, May–June

PART FOURTEEN

MIGRANTS AND ASYLUM-SEEKERS
IN CONTEMPORARY EUROPE

'Europe' has always been less than the sum of its constituent parts. It is a curious regional description not least because no-one is quite sure where it begins or ends. The name 'Europa' first appeared in classical times when a Phoenician princess of that name was ravaged by the Greek god, Zeus. The classical use, oddly, then reverted to denoting Greece itself, first to distinguish the mainland from the islands, later to describe the full reach of Greek culture and civilization.[1] By about 300 BC a *koiné*, or common Greek language, had emerged around the eastern Mediterranean. The Mediterranean basin was to provide the crucible for subsequent civilizations – the Roman, Judaeo-Christian and Islamic cultures intimately linking what we would nowadays call the Middle East, the Maghreb and southern Europe. I am aware how crudely the statement just made summarizes a very complex history, but the principal inference I want to draw is that 'Europe' could not be distinguished from 'the Mediterranean' until perhaps the end of the fifteenth century (Pirenne 1939; Braudel 1972/3).

The reference to 'the end of the fifteenth century' alludes to a crucial date – the capture of Granada from the Moors in 1492. (Ten years later Queen Isabella expelled all Muslims.) 'Europe' now became the zone of Christendom, particularly Western Christendom. The idea of a Christian, Western Europe was at the heart of the European ideology some five centuries later. The southern line was soon drawn around white and Christian Europe and explicitly sought to detach the continent from any African or Muslim connection. As *Dummett* and *Joly*'s contributions show, the EC and later European Union (EU) countries soon set about defining the remaining outer perimeters of 'Europe'. Within these perimeters free movement, as much as free trade, was to be encouraged. However, determined efforts would be made to police the outer edge of the European Union. An overbureaucratized, Brussels-led construction of the notion of 'Europe' soon began to show cracks and holes:

- Despite the official encouragement to internal free movement, the 1993 figures showed that only 1.4 per cent of the total EU population were EU nationals living in a country other than their own. By contrast many illegal and legal professionals and labour migrants were working in EU countries from 'third countries' with historic, colonial or economic links with particular members of the EU.
- A few members of the EU, particularly Britain, remained resistant to dropping 'internal' border controls between the EU countries on the grounds that they could not then distinguish EU from non-EU nationals.
- The eastern border of the EU and of Europe as a whole remained unclear. In one way or another all the remaining contributions to Part 10 are concerned with migration along the uncertain eastern edge of Europe.[2]

The contribution by *Basok* and *Benifand* describes the patterns of emigration by Soviet Jews, an outflow that commenced twenty years before the disintegration of the Soviet Union, but markedly accelerated when the breakup occurred. It was always an assured stick with which to beat the Soviets that they restricted emigration – an act that did indeed expose the lack of consent given to the communist system. To those who were explicit political dissenters must be added those who were victims of the periodic waves of anti-Semitism. Others had more positive reasons for emigration, including joining their families abroad or being able to realize their Zionist or religious beliefs. When the lid on emigration finally was lifted in 1989/90 the principal deterrents to emigration were, ironically, the restrictions on entry to the Western countries.

Two other contributions are concerned with migration flows largely in the former Soviet Union. *Ushkalov* and *Polyakov* point out that migration, particularly forced migration, was at the core of the whole Soviet experiment, forming part of the 'state policy of political and ethnic repression' and 'the development of virgin territory by so-called "special settlers"'. Under the 'nationality policy' two million people were evicted from their historical homelands in Russia to Kazakhstan and the central Asian republics. Even more, 2.5 million *kulaks* (rich peasants), were sent to collective farms in northern Russia, Siberia and the Urals. Volga Germans and Crimean Tartars were deported *en masse* because of their assumed loyalty to Nazi Germany. Another massive movement, often left unconsidered by migration scholars, was the evacuation of no less than twenty-five million Russians from the path of the advancing Nazi troops, many of whom failed to return home after the Germans were pushed back.

Karlsson picks up the story at the moment of the Soviet disintegration in 1989. In that year, some twenty-five million Russians were living in non-Russian Soviet republics. It is perhaps a general rule that when empires (which are, by definition, multi-ethnic entities) collapse there is a reassertion of what *Karlsson* calls 'ethno-territoriality'. He makes a suggestive distinction between the Stalinist era when the state was sufficiently powerful to force migration flows in the direction determined by the political bosses and the post-Gorbachev era when unrestrained refugee and voluntary migration forced the politicians to recognize the realities being made on the ground. As each nationalist and ethnic assertion of power took place, so there were pressures, either subtle or more overt, to ensure a high degree of ethnic homogeneity in the emerging states. Officially, Russia recognizes two million Russian refugees from the former non-Russian republics of the Soviet Union. In reality, the figure is much higher as soldiers and settlers from the outlying areas of the old empire begin to drift back. Many of the returnees provide grist to the populist mill being worked by Vladimir Zhirinovskii, a highly controversial and probably dangerous politician who openly talks of re-establishing 'the Russian boot' from the Baltic to the Black Sea.

I alluded earlier to the extensive colonization, often forced colonization, of Siberia by people of Russian, normally European, origin. The movement started as early as 1850 when the first Russian port in the Far East, Nikolaevskna-Amur, was built. Successive waves of peasants, industrial workers, Cossacks, soldiers and sailors were poured into the area, particularly after the Sino-Soviet dispute. At the height of that conflict there were no less than 1.5 million troops deployed along the Soviet border. Today, the long hard haul to Europeanize Siberia looks like it might be going into reverse. This dramatic development has not, as yet, been studied by specialist migration scholars, but it has received notice in a short but notable article by Medvedev (1995) in the educational press. Medvedev reports that after 1990, once the economic reforms had begun, the highly subsidized army presence could not be supported. About one million people, troops as well as hundreds of thousands of civilians supporting the troops, began to pour back to the Russian heartland. Industrial production fell by 50 per cent, agricultural production by 30 per cent. By contrast, traders, workers and farmers from China have entered the south of Russia's eastern border district in very considerable numbers – the lowest estimate being 300,000, the highest two million. It is almost certain that this very rapid switch in population in only three years will be the prelude to a long-term Sinicization of the area, with unpredictable political consequences. Watch this space!

The movement of populations from east to west is hardly a new phenomenon, as *Fassman* and *Münz* note. When we take into account the thirty million people leaving the European continent between 1850 and 1920 and the many intra-continental movements from east to west, it might be possible to venture a bold hypothesis: migrants in Europe 'naturally' flow from east to west; politicians seek to halt or reverse the flow. This hypothesis fits well with the forced migration to Siberia in the Soviet period and the reverse flow after *perestroika*. It fits well too with the data provided by *Fassman* and *Münz* for the post-war period. In the five-year period 1945–50, some twenty million Europeans moved in the westerly direction, the only major reverse flow being accounted for by the forcible repatriation of Soviet and east European citizens by the Allied authorities after the Second World War. It is a useful historical corrective to current political fears that total East–West migration from 1950 to 1992/3 is somewhat less than in the 1945–50 period, namely just over fourteen million. It is, however, worth qualifying the data in three respects. First, for the purposes of their calculations, *Fassman* and *Münz* use the iron curtain as the dividing line between East and West. If we look just across that curtain to Hungary, Bulgaria and the Czech Republic we can see very considerable evidence of immigration from further east and south. Second, some of the potential emigration from the Soviet Union has been bottled up, despite the relaxation of travel controls. Poverty, the slow bureaucracy in processing passports, and a 'wait and see' attitude by many Russian people have constrained what must surely be a further outflow. Third, although fourteen million over twenty-two years is a lot less than twenty million over five years, the character of that migration has changed. It is now more ethnically diverse, and includes many refugees and a significant number of illegals – elements all highly threatening for western European politicians and public opinion.

Whether western European fears of East–West migration will ultimately turn out to be realistic or exaggerated is still perhaps a moot point. The movement for the protection of the existing states of Fortress Europe against migration is accompanied by a countervailing movement slowly to add more and more states along Europe's eastern frontier to the western European core. Finland, Austria and Sweden are hardly likely be difficult mouthfuls to swallow, but the prospect of Hungary, Turkey and a number of others who seek associated or full status with the EU is more troubling, not least because of the issue of East–West migration. What is hardly a gleam in the eye of the visionaries is the idea of absorbing all the European countries up to the Urals. Jean Monnet, the guru of European integration, is often quoted as saying, 'If I should start it all over again, I would start with culture.' Instead, of course, integration started with the European Coal and Steel Community, a materialist and instrumental base which is still at the heart of the EU. While we still have a narrow and confused vision of Europe, the politicians will continue to raise their drawbridges in an ever more frantic attempt to stop East–West and South–North migration.

Notes

1. Or, perhaps, feminists could argue 'not so oddly', as Zeus had possessed, brutalized and conquered the representative of an earlier civilization.
2. I've treated Russia here as part of Europe though in truth this claim is somewhat ambiguous. Although Russia was Christianized, it received its Christianity via Byzantium, not Rome. Moreover, it never went through the Renaissance, the Reformation and the Enlightenment, all of which may be held to be central experiences of European civilization. On the other hand, now that the Cold War is over, the Urals do seem a more natural dividing line than the artificial 'iron curtain' fabricated by Winston Churchill. Moreover, the ideology that attempted to cement the very diverse elements of the Soviet Union, namely Marxism, was a very European product – even if the Soviets gave to it some distinctive local elements.

References

Braudel, Fernand (1972/3) *The Mediterranean and the Mediterranean World in the Age of Philip II* (vol. I, 1972; vol. II, 1973), London: Collins
Medvedev, Zhores A. (1995) 'Sino-Russian Borders', *The Times Higher Educational Supplement*, 13 January, 13–14
Pirenne, Henri (1939) *Mohammed and Charlemagne*, London: Unwin

EUROPEAN EAST–WEST MIGRATION, 1945–1992

HEINZ FASSMANN AND RAINER MÜNZ

Since the middle of the nineteenth century migration has led to an East–West shift of Europe's population. Between 1850 and 1920 more than 30 million people left the continent for North and South America. During the same period several hundred thousand Polish and Ukrainian workers migrated to the emerging centres of the coal, iron and steel industries in France (Lorraine), Germany (the Ruhr, Upper Silesia) and even England (the Midlands). Large numbers of ethnic Italians moved to France, Switzerland and western Austria. The growing cities of continental Europe also attracted large numbers of Slav immigrants from the Czech lands, from Galicia and from the Prussian parts of Poland. Several hundred thousand eastern European Jews fled from the rising tide of anti-Semitism, pogroms and economic misery in Ukraine, Galicia and the Baltics, and established themselves as large ethno-religious minorities in the booming metropolitan areas of the late nineteenth and early twentieth centuries: Berlin, Vienna, Paris and cities like Lwow, Warsaw and Prague.

Second World War, Yalta and Potsdam (1945–50)

The second phase of East–West mass migration was directly related to the Second World War and its consequences for post-war Europe. At a rough estimate, which takes into account only the main migration flows, some 15.4 million people had to leave their former home countries. Some 4.7 million displaced persons and POWs were repatriated (partly against their will) from Germany to eastern Europe and the USSR. The total number – including 'internal' migration flows – would probably be as high as 30 million people.

During the collapse of the Nazi regime and in the second half of the 1940s more than 12 million ethnic Germans (estimate for 1945–50) either fled or were displaced from the eastern parts of the former Reich and territories formerly occupied by the German Wehrmacht (Poland, the Baltics, Bohemia, Moravia, Slovenia, Serbia, Ukraine) or ruled during the Second World War by allied fascist and authoritarian regimes (Slovakia, Croatia and Hungary). Another 2 million lost their lives as a result of this ethnic cleansing.

In Poland the expulsion of 7 million ethnic Germans and former German citizens – 3.5 million from territories that belonged to Poland during the inter-war period, and another 3.5 million from German territories administered since 1945 by Poland and later annexed to this country (Stola 1992) – was accepted or even encouraged by the Allies. But of these 7 million, more than 1 million remained in the country. Catholics in particular and people living in mixed marriages were allowed to stay (Urban 1993). Another one million people had already left the area just before the end of the Second World War, bringing the number of German emigrants (1945–50) to 7 million (see Table 14.1).

The same procedure was applied by Czechoslovakia. In 1945–47 its government ordered almost all 3.2 million ethnic Germans to leave the country and organized their expulsion (Stola 1992). During the same period the Hungarian authorities expelled 225,000 of the 400,000 ethnic Germans living there. In Yugoslavia the detention and expulsion of some 360,000 ethnic Germans and former German citizens was arranged by local authorities or resulted from collective measures against this ethnic minority which was suspected of having collaborated with the Nazis (Kosinski 1982; Wehler 1980).

During the same period, some 4.7 of the 10.5 million displaced persons, POWs, forced labourers and survivors of the concentration camps living in Germany and Austria in 1945 returned to their central and eastern European countries of origin. Many displaced persons from the Soviet Union were forced to return against their will. Only in late 1946 did the Western Allies stop forced repatriation to what then became the communist part of Europe.

Between 1945 and 1950 almost 65 per cent of these German refugees and expatriates were resettled in the western part of Germany, then occupied by the Western Allies, and some 32 per cent in the eastern part of Germany, then controlled by the Soviet army (Bade 1992a, 1992b). Smaller numbers (530,000 or 3 per cent) stayed in Austria (Stanek 1985).

The new international boundaries drawn at Yalta and Potsdam and the ethnic cleansing approved by the

Table 14.1: *European East–West migration, 1945–50 (partly estimates)*

Country of origin	Country of destination	Number
Poland (incl. former German territories)	East and West Germany (mainly)	7,000,000
(former) Czechoslovakia (today Czech Republic, Slovakia)	East and West Germany and Austria	3,200,000
(parts of former) Soviet Union (today Russia, Belorussia, Ukraine, Baltics)	East and West Germany (mainly)	1,500,000
(former) Yugoslavia (today Bosnia, Croatia, Macedonia, Montenegro, Serbia, Slovenia)	East and West Germany and Austria	360,000
Hungary	East and West Germany and Austria	225,000
(parts of former) Yugoslavia (today Croatia, Montenegro, Slovenia)	Italy	200,000
Slovakia, Romania, (former) Yugoslavia	Hungary	315,000
Hungary	Slovakia	73,000
(parts of former) Soviet Union (today Russia)	Finland	400,000
(parts of former) Soviet Union (today Belorussia, Lithuania, Ukraine)	Poland	1,496,000
Poland	(parts of former) Soviet Union (today Belorussia, Lithuania, Ukraine)	518,000
(former) Czechoslovakia	(parts of former) Soviet Union (today Ukraine)	50,000
(parts of former) Soviet Union (today Ukraine)	(former) Czechoslovakia	42,000
SUBTOTAL		15,400,000
Germany, Austria (DPs, POWs)	Poland, (former) Czechoslovakia, (former) Yugoslavia, (former) Soviet Union	4,700,000
TOTAL		20,100,000

Note: Country of origin and country of destination are defined by the boundaries of 1946/50. People who fled or were forced to leave but died before reaching the country of destination are not included. Some migratory flows of the period 1945–50 (for example, the displacement of ethnic Germans, Estonians, Latvians, Lithuanians within the former Soviet Union) are by definition not part of the 'East–West migration'.

Source: Bade (1992a, 1992b); Chesnais (1992); Dövényi andVukovich (1994); Heršak (1983); Kosinski (1982); Stanek (1985); Stola (1992) ; Urban (1993); Wehler (1980).

Allies also affected other nationalities. Some 1,496,000 ethnic Poles and Polish Jews had to leave their traditional settlement areas, formerly in eastern Poland but now part of Lithuania, Belorussia and Ukraine (Kersten 1968). They were settled in east and west Prussia and Silesia, in the same areas from which the German population had been expelled (Urban 1993). Under similar circumstances 115,000 Czechs and Slovaks (from Hungary and Carpatho-Ukraine) were resettled in northern and southern Bohemia, southern Moravia and central Slovakia. About 50,000 Ukrainians had to leave Czechoslovakia, while 518,000 Ukrainians, Belorussians and Lithunians had to leave Poland and were resettled east of the Soviet–Polish border established in 1945.

Some 200,000 ethnic Italians were forced to leave Istria and Dalmatia (Heršak 1983), while 315,000 members of the Hungarian minorities in southern Slovakia, Transylvania (Romania) and the Voyvodina (Serbia) were transferred to Hungary or 'exchanged' by order of their respective governments (Dövényi and Vukovich 1994).

East–West migration also took place in northern Europe. From 1941 to 1946, 400,000 Carelians fled to Finland because of the cession of their territory to the Soviet Union. In the same period some 14,000

Latvian, Lithuanian and Estonian refugees went to Scandinavia in order to escape the Nazi occupation and the Red Army.

From 1950 to 1992/3

The cold war and the iron curtain significantly reduced European East–West migration, but did not bring the flow to a complete halt. For a long time this third phase of European East–West migration (starting in 1950) was characterized by distinct 'waves' of migration directly linked to political events or even to political bargaining between the countries involved.

Between 1950 and 1992 the documented number of European East–West migrants (see Table 14.2) was about 14 million people. The overall number must have been higher because for regular 'migrants' flow data are not always available. The data for asylum-seekers are annual flows concentrating on peak years. Information on labour migrants and their family members comes from data on the stock of foreign population in major receiving countries. The number of new and irregular labour migrants is partly based on estimates.

Typology of European East–West migration

'Ethnic' migration

More than 75 per cent of all European East–West migrants of the period 1950–93 can be classified as 'ethnic' migrants. But it is clear that this classification is not always precise. Many of the 'ethnic' migrants were taking the opportunity to leave their home country for economic or political reasons. The 'ethnic' factor also shows that East–West migration was and remains a subject of bilateral agreements. In many cases it is less a question of economic disparities than of political negotiations and relations between sending and receiving countries.

The large majority of East–West migrants belonging to ethnic or religious minorities were and are backed either by a Western nation or a well-organized lobby. The two most obvious cases are those of Jewish and ethnic German emigrants. Because of the constitution of the Federal Republic of Germany, migrants of German origin enjoy privileged treatment. Therefore, between 1950 and 1993 some 3 million ethnic Germans have immigrated to their 'mother' country, most of them from Poland (51.4 per cent), Romania (17.5 per cent) and the USSR/CIS (24.6 per cent) (Leciejewski 1990; Ronge 1993). Migration between the two German states, closely

linked to the history of the cold war, also fits into this pattern. Between 1949 and 1990 some 5.3 million GDR citizens migrated to the Federal Republic, another 0.5 million migrated from the FRG to the GDR (Rudolph 1994). Since 1991 this particular type of East–West migration has become part of Germany's internal migration. Migration between East and West Germany peaked during the years 1989–92: 1.2 million people moved from East to West Germany, 230,000 (re-)migrated to the eastern part of Germany (Grundmann 1994; Hullen and Schulz 1994; Münz and Ulrich 1994; Rudolph 1994).

Between 1950 and 1991 some 1.5 million people left the USSR, 700,000 in 1990 and 1991 (Chesnais 1991; Sabatello 1994; Shevtsova 1992; Vishnevsky and Zayonchkovskaya 1994). Almost all of them belonged to an ethnic or religious minority. More than 50 per cent were Soviet Jews who went to the USA or Israel – 80 per cent of all Jewish migrants chose Israel as their country of destination and about 20 per cent the USA. In Israel they enjoy a privileged position. Like Jewish immigrants from other countries they get immediate citizenship and are eligible for a range of measures and benefits to further their integration. A third (37 per cent) of the Soviet emigrants belonged to the group of ethnic Germans who left for the Federal Republic of Germany. The rest were Armenians (7 per cent), Greeks (2 per cent) and members of small Protestant churches (1.5 per cent) (Chesnais 1992; Heitmann 1987).

Much less attention has been paid to the mass migration of other eastern European minorities such as ethnic Turks, Muslim Slavs (Pomaks, Bosniaks) and ethnic Hungarians. The migration of these groups, however, follows similar patterns (Bobeva 1994; Centar za demografska istrazivanja 1971; Dövényi and Vukovich 1994; Vasileva 1992).

Refugees and asylum-seekers

About 10 per cent of all European East–West migrants can be classified as political refugees and asylum-seekers. In most cases the migration streams were linked to political crises and conflicts in the countries of origin. The best-known examples since 1950 were the following:

- 1956–57: Some 194,000 Hungarians left their native country just before the Kádár regime, with the military support of Soviet troops, re-established the iron curtain between Hungary and Austria (Dövényi and Vukovich 1994).

Table 14.2: *European East–West migration, 1950–92/3 (partly estimates)*

Country of origin	Destination	Number	Period	Type of migration
				ethnic
GDR	FRG	5,275,000	1950–90/2	ethnic Germans (*Uebersiedler*)
Poland	FRG	1,430,000	1950–92	ethnic Germans (*Aussiedler*)
USSR/CIS	FRG	746,000	1950–92	ethnic Germans (*Aussiedler*)
Romania	FRG	402,000	1950–92	ethnic Germans (*Aussiedler*)
Czechoslovakia	FRG	105,000	1950–92	ethnic Germans (*Aussiedler*)
Yugoslavia	FRG	90,000	1950–92	ethnic Germans (*Aussiedler*)
Bulgaria	Turkey	630,000	1950–92	ethnic Turks and Slav Muslims
Yugoslavia	Turkey	300,000	1950–66	ethnic Turks and Slav Muslims
USSR/CIS	Israel, USA	750,000	1950–92	Jews
USSR/CIS	Greece, France, USA	170,000	1950–92	Armenians, ethnic Greeks, Pentecostals
Romania	Israel, USA	500,000	1960–92	Jews
Romania	western Europe (mainly FRG)	240,000	1991–93	mainly gypsies
Yugoslavia, Romania	Hungary	124,000	1988–93	mainly ethnic Hungarians
				political refugees
Yugoslavia	FRG	355,000	1991–3	'sudden wave' of refugees
Yugoslavia	rest of W. Europe	330,000	1991–3	'sudden wave' of refugees
Poland	FRG, Austria and others	250,000	1980/1	'sudden wave' of refugees
Hungary	Austria, USA, UK, Yugoslavia, Canada	194,000	1956	'sudden wave' of refugees
Czechoslovakia	FRG, Austria, USA, Canada, Australia	162,000	1968/9	'sudden wave' of refugees
				regular labour migration
Yugoslavia	FRG	755,000	1991	labour migrants/family members
Yugoslavia	Austria	281,000	1992	labour migrants/family members
Yugoslavia	Switzerland	171,000	1991	labour migrants/family members
Yugoslavia	France	52,000	1990	labour migrants/family members
Yugoslavia	Sweden	41,000	1991	labour migrants/family members
Yugoslavia	Italy	35,000	1991	labour migrants/family members
				new, irregular labour migration
Albania	Greece, Italy	350,000	1993	Albanians, some ethnic Greeks
Poland	Germany, Austria, Scandinavia, Greece	300,000	1993	Poles
Czech Republic, Slovakia, Hungary	Germany, Austria	100,000	1993	Czechs, Slovaks, Hungarians
Total (1)		14,160,000		

Note: This sum includes data on migration flows and on stock of foreign population.

Source: All data on Albania: Misja (1993); on Bulgaria: Bobeva (1994), Vasileva (1992); on German 'Uebersiedler' and 'Aussiedler': German sources (Bundesverwaltungsamt in Cologne, BIB Wiesbaden, Statistisches Bundesamt), see also Grundmann (1994), Münz and Ulrich (1993), Ronge (1993), Rudolph (1994); on Hungary: Dövényi and Vukovich (1994); on ethnic emigration from former Yugoslavia: Centar za demografska istraživanja (1971); on refugees from former Yugoslavia: UNHCR Information Notes on Former Yugoslavia 11 (1993); on refugees from Poland and former Czechoslovakia: Fassmann and Münz (1993); on USSR/CIS: Chesnais (1992), Heitman (1987), Shevtsova (1992), Vishnevsky and Zayonchkovskaya (1994. All data are cumulated flow-data except those covering labour migrants and their family members which are stock-data. Data about foreign population in western European countries are from OECD/SOPEMI (1994), Table B1 (France, FRG, Italy, Sweden, Switzerland), data on Austria from the Austrian Central Statistical Office.

- 1968–69: About 160,000 Czechs fled their country during the 'Prague spring' and shortly after its suppression by the Warsaw Pact (Chesnais 1992; Fassmann and Münz 1992).
- 1980–81: A huge wave of Polish refugees arrived in western Europe (estimate: 250,000) trying to escape the imposition of martial law and political persecution of the Solidariry movement (Chesnais 1992; Fassmann and Münz 1992).
- 1990–91: Tens of thousands of Albanians applied for asylum in Greece, Italy and Malta. Most of them were repatriated by force (Misja 1993).
- 1991–93: Some 700,000 people fled to western Europe from repression in Serbia and from war and ethnic cleansing in Croatia and Bosnia-Herzegovina following the collapse of Yugoslavia. For that reason, this flow could also be regarded as ethnic migration.

The migration 'waves' caused by major crises in communist rule in eastern Europe usually received wide international media coverage. In line with the logic of the cold war, these emigrants were seen by the West as political refugees, whatever their individual motives. This contrasts with the perception of those who have left eastern Europe and the Balkans in periods of war and political crises since 1989.

Labour migration

So far the proportion of East–West migrants coming to the West for largely economic reasons has been relatively small. Less than 15 per cent can be classified as (regular or irregular) labour migrants or as dependent family members of labour migrants. This was a result of the political and economic split between eastern and western Europe. East–West trade remained on a low level and there was scarcely any mobility of capital and labour. The sole exception was Yugoslavia. Since the late 1960s Yugoslavia was the only communist country whose citizens had the right to emigrate. About half a million Yugoslav workers, followed by an unknown number of dependants, were recruited by the Federal Republic of Germany and Austria. Between the mid-1970s and mid–1980s this number decreased as a result of the economic recession and some restrictive measures. Thereafter remigration to Yugoslavia set in (Malacic 1994). The period from 1989 to 1990 marked a turning point for which there were several reasons. First, following German reunification, there was a short but unforeseen boom in the West German and Austrian economies bringing new foreign labour (including

many ex-Yugoslavs) to these countries. Then came the wars in Croatia and Bosnia and the ethnic conflicts in Kosovo and Voyvodina which were accompanied by economic collapse and widespread poverty in most parts of former Yugoslavia, bringing new migrants from this area to western Europe (Malacic 1994; Morokvasic 1993; UNHCR Information Notes on Former Yugoslavia 11/1993; UN/ECE International Migration Bulletin 3/1993).

New and partly irregular labour migration also took place between Poland and some Western countries (Germany, Austria, Greece), and between Albania and Greece (see Fassmann and Münz 1994; Misja 1993; Morokvasic and de Tinguy 1993; Rudolph 1994).

The 'geography' of migration

European East–West migration includes the migration from east-central and eastern Europe, the former Soviet Union and the Balkans to western Europe, overseas countries and some countries belonging geopolitically to the West (for example, Turkey). During the analysed period (1950–92) the largest part of East–West migration took place within Europe (including Turkey). The flows to Israel and overseas were considerably smaller. The main countries of origin and destination are shown in Table 14.3.

Until 1949 the dominant migration flows in Europe were East–West (see Table 14.1). After 1950 the cold war reduced this pattern to a flow (of considerable size until 1961) between the two Germanies. All in all after the mid-1950s, migration from the south to the north became more important (see Table 14.4). This was the case both within Europe and for immigration from several countries of the 'Third World' to western Europe. But until 1970 the number of emigrants from Europe was higher then the number of immigrants from Turkey, Asia, Africa and the Caribbean. Only after 1970 the net balance shows that Europe as a whole had become a continent of immigration. At that time immigration started to play a role in most countries of southern Europe as well. After a short period of little international mobility in the early 1980s the course of migration changed again: East–West migration increased dramatically. After the fall of the iron curtain Poland, the former Soviet Union/CIS, the collapsing GDR and parts of the Balkans again became main sending areas.

Countries of origin

The main countries of origin within the framework of European East–West migration were the former GDR, Poland, former Yugoslavia, the former USSR and

Table 14.3: *European East–West migration: main countries of origin and destination, 1950–93*

Country of origin	Number of emigrants[a]	%	Country of destination	Number of migrants[a]	%
GDR	5,275,000	37.3	FRG	9,640,000	68.1
Yugoslavia	2,435,000	17.2	Israel[b]	1,150,000	8.1
Poland	1,980,000	14.0	Turkey[b]	930,000	6.6
USSR/CIS	1,670,000	11.8	USA[c]	700,000	4.8
Others	2,800,000	19.7	Others	1,740,000	12.3
Total[d]	14,160,000	100.0	Total[d]	14,160,000	100.0

Notes: [a] The number of migrants is calculated as the sum of all major migration waves listed in Table 14.2. In most cases these figures differ from the official number of emigrants given by the countries of origin. But only in the case of Romania and Poland the differences are significant (Korcelli 1994; Trebici 1990). [b] Israel and Turkey are receiving countries but also major sending countries. According to our geopolitical definition only European immigrants to these two countries are part of the East–West migration but not emigrants from these countries. [c] In the census of 1990 more than 1 million people living in the USA as first-generation immigrants declared a birth place in eastern Europe (including the USSR). Some of them immigrated before 1950, others first emigrated to Israel or another third country. The data in Table 14.3 only show the country of origin and the first country of settlement after emigration from eastern Europe. [d] This sum includes both data on migration flows and on stock of foreign population.

Table 14.4: *European migration balance by groups of countries, 1950–90*

Region	1950–1960	1960–1970	1970–1980	1980–1990	1950–1990
East*	− 2.7	− 1.0	− 1.0	− 2.6	− 7.3
USSR	− 0.0	− 0.0	− 0.7	− 0.7	− 1.0
North	− 0.5	− 0.3	+ 0.1	+ 0.2	−0.5
South	− 3.5	− 3.8	+ 0.5	+ 1.6	− 5.2
West	+ 3.7	+ 4.9	+ 3.0	+ 4.3	+15.9
Total Europe	− 3.0	− 0.2	+ 2.3	+ 2.8	− 1.9

Note: *The former USSR is not included in this group.
Source: Chesnais (1993), own calculations.

other countries, mainly Bulgaria and Romania (see Table 14.3).

Former GDR

During the twelve years between the establishment of the two German states (1949) and the erection of the Berlin wall some 3.8 million East German citizens emigrated to the FRG while 400,000 West Germans decided to settle in the GDR. During the existence of the wall 810,000 people managed to leave the GDR. Most of them were either retired persons (free to travel abroad) or part of the 300,000 cases, including political prisoners, negotiated individually between the two German governments. Between 1950 and

1992 some 37 per cent of the total European East–West migration originated in the former GDR.

For West Germany this migration from the GDR was a strong argument in support of the market economy and democratic system. It was often claimed that emigrants were 'voting with their feet'. The erection of the Berlin wall was, after all, an attempt by the GDR to stop having to find a political solution to the problem by preventing emigration as such. After 1961 the continuing East–West migration became a financial matter. Both German states granted citizenship to migrants from the other side. The FRG even offered financial compensation for the release and emigration of 30,000 prisoners and other GDR citizens.

In 1989 the mass emigration of some 181,000 people before the fall of the Berlin wall and of another 218,000 thereafter largely contributed to the collapse of communist rule in East Germany and to German reunification. In 1990 another 395,000 East Germans moved to West Germany. Since 3 October 1990 this flow has become an internal migration of unified Germany. Since that year internal East–West migration within Germany has reduced its pace while the number of people moving (or returning) to the eastern part of Germany is growing (Grundmann 1994; Hullen and Schulz 1994; Münz and Ulrich 1994).

Poland
Between 1950 and 1992 about 14 per cent of all European East–West migrants were from Poland. Unlike from elsewhere origin Polish emigration was ethnically heterogeneous (Korcelli 1994). The largest group of migrants were ethnic Germans and others who could claim West German cititzenship. The so-called resettlers (*Aussiedler*) came to West Germany in several waves: 1956–67 (216,000), 1976–82 (about 242,000) and since 1987 (753,000 between 1987 and 1990). Until 1990 this migration was actively supported or even promoted by West German governments and was seen as a return favour for Western economic aid to Poland (Bade 1992b; Urban 1993).

At the end of the 1960s, in reaction to the anti-Semitic campaign led by the state itself, a large proportion of Jewish Polish citizens went to western Europe, Israel and the USA. This exodus would not have occurred without the strong practical support of Poland's ruling elite, the USA and Israel.

In 1980/1, however, the emigration of about 250,000 Poles fleeing from the imposition of martial law to the West – especially to Austria and Germany – was spontaneous. They were much less warmly received there than were the Czech and Slovak refugees in 1968. Perhaps this was because the Red Army did not intervene in Poland. In the following years about half the Polish emigrants of 1980/1 returned to their home country (Fassmann and Münz 1992).

From 1986 on, when it became possible again to leave Poland and to emigrate, a larger number of Poles of non-German origin tried to gain a foothold in the West. Between 1950 and 1990/1 about 2.1 million people emigrated from Poland, more than 1 million of them in the second half of the 1980s. Since then, however, about 60 per cent of the non-ethnic German immigrants to the West have returned to Poland (Korcelli 1994). Since the late 1980s Poland has become a country of origin of new and partly irregular flows of labour migration. A growing number of Poles have started to look for job opportunities in Germany, Austria, Scandinavia and even Greece.

Former Yugoslavia
In the 1950s and early 1960s emigration from Yugoslavia primarily involved two groups: first, Muslims of Turkish origin and Muslims of Slavic origin from Bosnia and Sandjak; second, political opponents of the Tito regime. The overwhelming majority of the first group went to Turkey while the second group headed for western Europe and overseas (Kosinski 1982). Data are only available for the first group. During the 1950s some 300,000 ethnic Turks left Bosnia, Macedonia and other south-eastern parts of Yugoslavia for Turkey (Centar za demografska istravivania 1971).

The wars in Croatia (1991/2) and Bosnia-Herzegovina (1992/3) and the repression of ethnic minorities in Voyvodina (Croats, Hungarians), Serbia and Kosovo (Albanians, other Muslims) led to the largest wave of migration since 1945/6. Between 1991 and 1993 more than 5 million citizens of former Yugoslavia became refugees or displaced persons. Only 700,000 of them went to western Europe, of whom 355,000 went to Germany, 80,000 to Switzerland, 74,000 to Sweden, 70,000 to Austria and 70,000 to France. Most were not recognized as political refugees but tolerated as *de facto* refugees. In 1993 most Western countries closed their borders to the victims of war and ethnic cleansing from that part of the Balkans. Thus 4.3 million refugees and displaced persons are still living in the states that emerged from the break-up of Yugoslavia. In mid-1993 there were more than 690,000 of them in the parts of Croatia controlled by the Zagreb government and another 110,000 in the rest of this country controlled by Serbian militia, 565,000 in Serbia, 82,000 in Montenegro, 45,000 in Slovenia, 27,000 in Macedonia and 2.74 million in Bosnia-Herzegovina (UNHCR 1993).

With 2.4 million emigrants and displaced persons living abroad, former Yugoslavia is a major sending area of East–West migration (17 per cent). But as a consequence of war and ethnic cleansing a much larger group of people is living as homeless victims of war, as ethnic refugees or as displaced persons on the territory of former Yugoslavia (4.3 million). Because of the political situation in the Balkans, the substantial and growing economic gap with western Europe and the prevailing ethnic conflicts, the successor states of former Yugoslavia are likely to remain countries with a considerable emigration potential.

Former USSR/CIS

Between 1950 and 1992 about 12 per cent of all European East–West migrants came from the Soviet Union. In the 1950s and 1960s it was almost impossible to emigrate from the USSR. Thereafter the USA and some Western European countries brought political pressure to bear in order to ease the restrictive Soviet emigration policy.

In 1973 the US Congress made this a precondition for the removal of trade barriers. In 1976 in the CSCE Treaty the USA and western Europe forced the eastern side to recognize the principle of freedom of travel and emigration. As a consequence, during the 1970s (1973–80) some 340,000 people were in fact able to leave the Soviet Union. Following a brief revival of the cold war (Afghanistan, SDI) a second large wave of emigration took place from 1987 onwards under Gorbachev. In all some 1.5 million people emigrated from the USSR between 1950 and 1991 (Heitman 1987; Shevtsova 1992; Vishnevsky and Zayonchkovskaya 1994).

By far the largest migration is not oriented towards the West but has taken place since 1991 between the former Soviet republics which have become sovereign states (now CIS member countries and the Baltic states). In the majority of cases ethnic Russians (25 million living outside Russia) are returning from the periphery of the former Soviet empire to Russia (Oswald 1993; Vishnevsky and Zayonchkovskaya 1994). The withdrawal of the Red Army including soldiers' family dependants from central and eastern Europe also led to substantial emigration.

Other migration is taking place in the CIS, for example between Armenia and Azerbaijan (mainly as a result of the war in Nagorny Karabach), and between Central Asia and Ukraine (for example Crimean Tartars returning to their former homeland).

Other East–West migrants

Another 2.8 million East–West migrants mainly came from Romania and Bulgaria, but to a smaller extent also from Albania, former Czechoslovakia and Hungary.

Bulgaria

Between 1950 and 1952 some 155,000 ethnic Turks were allowed to leave Bulgaria. Another wave of 43,000 followed in the years between 1969 and 1976 under the provision of the 1968 agreement between Bulgaria and Turkey, which granted the right of emigration to a total of 95,000 Bulgarian citizens (Bobeva 1994). The most recent wave began during the collapse of the communist regime in Sofia. In the years 1982–92 some 350,000 ethnic Turks and Slavic Muslims (Pomaks) fled from collective oppression, enforced Bulgarianization and economic problems. Most of them made their way to Turkey before the Turkish government closed the border with neighbouring Bulgaria. Of these people, 150,000 are reported to have remigrated to Bulgaria (Bobeva 1994; Vasileva 1992). The closing of the Turkish border has led to higher numbers of Bulgarian citizens trying to apply for asylum in western Europe.

Romania

In 1945/6, in contrast to Yugoslavia, Hungary, Czechoslovakia and Poland, the Romanian regime had not collectively expelled ethnic Germans living in this country. Nevertheless, from the 1970s the Federal Republic of Germany sought to organize ethnic German emigration at the base of bilateral agreements with the Romanian authorities.

Between 1970 and 1989 some 230,000 Romanians of German origin took advantage of this opportunity to emigrate. In return the FRG gave generous financial support to the Ceausescu regime. Following a final large-scale migration wave organized in 1991, and involving almost 200,000 people, there are hardly more than 120,000 ethnic Germans left in Romania. Most of them are either not able or not willing to emigrate (Leciejewski 1990; Ronge 1993). Between 1960 and 1992 Romania lost almost all its Jewish population. During this period some 500,000 Jews emigrated to Israel and the USA.

Since 1987 about 60,000 members of the Hungarian minority have managed to leave the country legally. Most of them, however, went to Hungary (Dövényi and Vukovich 1994). This is also a form of selective East–West migration. Between 1990 and 1993 a further 240,000 Romanian citizens applied for asylum in western Europe. A majority of them were of Gipsy origin. In spite of their obvious discrimination and casual pogroms many of them were turned back to Romania which in the view of most Western governments now qualifies as a 'safe country'.

Albania

Between 1991 and 1993 between 300,000 and 400,000 Albanians left their country. Most of them are now living as irregular migrants in Greece, others as refugees in Italy. After forty years, during which this country has been more or less sealed off from the rest of Europe, almost 10 per cent of Albania's population has emigrated (Misja 1993).

Countries of Destination

Germany

Within the framework of European East–West migration Germany was and remains the main country of destination. Between 1950 and 1992 some 68 per cent of all East–West migrants moved to Germany (see Table 14.3). Most immigrants were either ethnic Germans or labour migrants and family dependants. No other European country has played a comparable role in this process.[1]

Israel

The second most significant receiving country is Israel. From 1950 to 1992 it became the destination of 8 per cent of all East–West migrants. The number of immigrants becomes even more significant when compared with Israel's present-day population of about 5 million. Since 1950 Jewish immigrants of east European origin have mainly come from the former Soviet Union and the CIS, but also from Poland and Romania (Basok and Brym 1992; Sabatello 1994). Within the framework of international migration Israel is also a major sending country.

Turkey

The third most significant receiving country for European East–West migrants (7 per cent) is Turkey (Bobeva 1994; Centar za demografska istrazivania 1971; Kosinski 1982; Vasileva 1992). For Bulgarians of Turkish origin, Bosnians and other Muslim minorities Turkey plays a similar role as Germany has for ethnic Germans and Israel for Jewish emigrants. This migration to Turkey would not have been possible without the vigorous support of Turkish authorities and Muslim organizations. Since the mid-1960s Turkey has also become a major sending country. Today some 2.3 million Turkish citizens are living in western Europe, 80 per cent of them in Germany (Fassmann and Münz 1992). But according to our geopolitical definition, this flow is not categorized as East–West migration.

USA

In the past the USA was the preferred destination of European migrants. In the census of 1970 more than 1.6 million people living in the USA as first-generation immigrants declared a birthplace in eastern Europe (including the USSR). Many of them had come to the USA before 1950. In 1990 the number of first-generation immigrants with a birthplace in eastern Europe (including the USSR) had dropped to just over one million (OECD/SOPEMI 1994, Table C1). In contrast to the first half of the twentieth century not all immigrants from eastern Europe came directly to the USA. Many first emigrated to Israel or another third country. Between 1950 and 1992, however, the USA admitted about 700,000 east Europeans, including persons categorized as political refugees but also 'regular' immigrants from this area (i.e. 5 per cent of all European East–West migrants).

Austria

Another receiving country is Austria, to which since 1950 more than 500,000 people from eastern Europe have migrated. Those who stayed on either came as refugees or as labour migrants and their dependants (Fassmann and Münz 1992). In relation to its population (1994: 8 million) Austria has absorbed a high proportion of East–West migrants.

Future aspects

Since the Second World War the overwhelming majority of all European East–West migrants has stemmed from ethnic or religious groups with an ethnic 'mother country', or at least a 'foothold' or a strong lobby in the West. In contrast, eastern Europe's quantitatively and politically dominant nationalities (with the exception of the Germans from the former GDR and to a certain extent also with the exception of the Poles) hardly ever came to the West in large numbers. This is linked to the fact that until 1989/90 European East–West migration relied to a large extent on bilateral agreements between eastern and western European countries, while spontaneous waves of migrants remained the exception. But since the fall of the iron curtain an increasing number of immigrants has been arriving with neither the support nor the consent of any Western country. The increased international migration is part and parcel of a 'new normality'. It comprises ethnic minorities, economic refugees and new labour migrants.

Between 1989 and 1993 more than 5 million Europeans left their own countries, including 1.8 million war refugees from Bosnia, Croatia and Serbia. Another 3.2 million displaced persons are still living within the Bosnian and Croatian borders. There are also many new labour migrants from east-central

Europe, whose number can only be roughly estimated. Most of them are arriving at the labour markets of western European metropoli without having been recruited bilaterally. There has been no comparable wave of migration on this continent since 1945/6. This is why the euphoria in the West at the end of the cold war and of divisions in Europe has disappeared. Western Europe has reacted to the new wave of immigration with a mixture of fear, rejection and massive administrative measures including the deployment of specialized police and military along the borders, at ports and airports. And yet mass migration is neither a new phenomenon in Europe nor does it represent the historical exception. Spatial mobility has been a characteristic of Western societies ever since the beginning of the industrial revolution.

In our view all scenarios predicting the imminent exodus of 5–25 million people from eastern Europe and the former Soviet Union/CIS to the West are exaggerations of the expected flows. Even if such a migration potential exists, it is highly unlikely that western Europe would accept such a flow of immigrants. But we have to take into account that the main factors promoting migration in recent years will probably not change in the foreseeable future. In parts of Europe there is no end in sight to ethnic conflicts and 'cleansing', to the conflicts over territory and resources and to political violence against minorities. In the southern and south-eastern perimeter of Europe economic progress is unable to keep pace with demographic growth. Although the eastern half of Europe is not over-populated, the number of economically and socially marginalized citizens is growing, together with that of ambitious, highly-qualified people who see no future for themselves and their children in their own country. The number of these potential emigrants will grow unless economic and political changes bring lasting improvements to people's living conditions. This does not, however, automatically mean more immigration to western Europe. For since the beginning of the 1990s the countries of western Europe have tightened their immigration and residence laws, imposed very limited immigration quotas and established a *cordon sanitaire* between them, the CIS countries and the Balkans. Thus all countries having common borders with western Europe are considered as 'safe countries' and are increasingly confronted with immigration themselves (Dövényi and Vukovich 1994; Korcelli 1994; Novak 1993).

Nevertheless, the economic gap between western Europe and its immediate neighbours will continue to promote some degree of migration, although all the rich industrial nations are currently trying to insulate themselves. The border which separates western Europe from its eastern neighbours and the countries south of the Mediterranean will never be completely controllable as was the frontier between the FRG and the GDR until 1989. Comparative evidence for this comes from the border between the USA and Mexico. Armed border guards, fences and a rigid asylum policy are neither the only nor the best solutions to the migration pressure on western Europe. For mere insulation is no substitute for a considered migration policy. And it solves none of the problems which today are forcing people to leave their home countries in eastern Europe and elsewhere.

Note
1. 'To talk of European East–West migration under these circumstances and at this time means, for the most part, to talk about Germany' (Ronge 1993: 17).

References
Bade, Klaus J. (ed.) (1992a) *Ausländer, Aussiedler, Asyl in der Bundesrepublik Deutschland,* Hannover: Niedersächsische Landeszentrale für Politische Bildung
—— (ed.) (1992b) *Deutsche im Ausland – Fremde in Deutschland. Migration in Geschichte und Gegenwart,* Munich: C. H. Beck
Basok, Tania and R. J. Brym (eds) (1992) *Soviet–Jewish Emigration and Resettlement in the 1990s,* Toronto: York University Press
Bobeva, Daniela (1994) 'Emigration from and Immigration to Bulgaria: Past, Present and Future', in H. Fassmann and R. Münz (eds), *European Migration in the Late 20th Century,* Aldershot: Edward Elgar, 221–38
Centar za demografska istrazivanja (1971) *Migracije stanovni stava Jugoslavije,* Belgrade: Institut drustvenih nauka
Chesnais, Jean-Claude (1991) *The USSR Emigration – Past, Present and Future,* Paris: OECD
—— (1992) 'Introduction', *People on the Move: New Migration Flows in Europe,* Strasbourg: Council of Europe, 11–40
—— (1993) 'The New Migratory Deal in Europe', in Bundesinstitut für Bevölkerungsforschung (ed.) *Materialien zur Bevölkerungswissenschaft,* 79 Wiesbaden: BIB, 87–100
Dövényi, Zoltán and Gabriella Vukovich (1994) 'Hungary and the International Migration', in H. Fassmann and R. Münz (eds) *European Migration in the Late 20th Century,* Aldershot: Edward Elgar, 187–206
Fassmann, Heinz and Rainer Münz (1992) *Einwanderungsland Österreich? Gastarbeiter – Flüchtlinge – Immigranten,* Vienna: J. & V.-Dachs
—— (eds) (1994) *European Migration in the Late 20th Century,* Aldershot: Edward Elgar
Grundmann, Siegfried (1994) 'Wanderungen', in Klaus Freitag et al. (eds) *Regionale Bevölkerungsentwicklung in den neuen Bundesländern,* Berlin: GSFP, 81–122
Heitman, Sidney (1987) *The Third Soviet Emigration: Jewish, German and Armenian Emigration from the USSR since World War II,* Cologne: Berichte des Bundesinstitutes für ostwissenschaftliche und internationale Studien

Heršak, E. (1983) 'Migracijska razmjena izmedju Italije i Jugoslavije', *Migracije,*1, 131–9, Zagreb: Centar za istrazivanje migracije

Hullen, Gerd and Reiner Schulz (1994) 'Bericht 1993 zur demographischen Lage in Deutschland', *Zeitschrift für Bevölkerungswissenschaft,* 1, 3–70

Kersten, K. (1968) 'International Migration in Poland after World War II', *Acta Poloniae Historica,* 19, 49–68

Korcelli, Piotr (1994) 'Emigration from Poland after 1945', in H. Fassmann and R. Münz (eds) *European Migration in the Late 20th Century,* Aldershot: Edward Elgar, 171–86

Kosinski, Lezek A. (1982) 'International Migration of Yugoslavia During and Immediately After World War II', *East European Quarterly,* 2, 183–99

Leciejewski, Klaus (1990) 'Zur wirtschaftlichen Eingliederung der Aussiedler', Aus Politik und zeitgesdrichte (Das Parlament), B3, 52–62

Malacic, Janez (1994) 'International Economic Migration in Former Yugoslavia since 1960', in H. Fassmann and R. Münz (eds), *European Migration in the Late 20th Century,* Aldershot: Edward Elgar, 207–20

Misja, Vladimir (1993) 'Des Aspects de la Migration internationale en Albanie', paper presented at the Workshop on Causes and Consequences of Emigration from Central and Eastern European Countries, Geneva: UN/ECE

Morokvasic, Mirjana (1993) *Flucht und Vertreibung im ehemaligen Jugoslawien,* Demographie aktuell 2, Berlin: Humboldt University

Morokvasic, M. and A. de Tinguy (1993) 'Between East and West: A New Migratory Space', in R. Hedwig and M. Morokvasic (eds) *Bridging States and Markets. International Migration in the Early 1990s,* Berlin: Sigma, 245–63

Münz, R. and R. Ulrich (1993) 'Migration und Ausländerbeschäftigung in Deutschland', *Stadtbauwelt,* 118, 1270–3

(1994) *Was wird aus den Neuen Bundesländern?,* Demographie aktuell 3, Berlin: Humboldt University

Novak, Fadela (1993) *Refugees from the East in the Czech and Slovak Republics,* Prague: Organizace pro pomoc oprchlikum

OECD/SOPEMI (1994) *Trends in International Migration, Continuous Reporting System on Migration, Annual Report 1993,* Paris: OECD

Oswald, Ingrid (1993) *Nationalitätenkonflikte im östlichen Teil Europas,* Berlin: Landeszentrale für politische Bildungsarbeit

Ronge, Volker (1993) 'Ost–West Wanderung nach Deutschland', *Aus Politik und Zeitgeschichte, (Das Parlament)* B7, 16–28

Rudolph, Hedwig (1994) 'Dynamics of Immigration in a Non-Immigrant Country: Germany', in H. Fassmann and R. Münz (eds), *European Migration in the Late 20th Century,* Aldershot: Edward Elgar, 113–26

Sabatello, Eitan (1994) 'Migrants from the USSR to Israel in the 1990s', in H. Fassmann and R. Münz (eds), *European Migration in the Late 20th Century,* Aldershot: Edward Elgar, 261–74

Shevtsova, Lilia (1992) 'Post-Soviet Emigration Today and Tomorrow', *International Migration Review,* 2, 241–57

Stanek, Eduard (1985) *Verfolgt – verjagt – vertrieben. Flüchtlinge in Österreich 1945–84,* Vienna: Europa-Verlag

Stola, Dariusz (1992) 'Forced Migrations in Central European History', *International Migration Review,* 2, 332–41

Trebici, Vladimir (1990) 'Sa Vorbim despre Dinamism demografic', *Tribuna Economia,* 8, 22–23

UNHCR (1993) *Information Notes on Former Yugoslavia,* 11

UN/ECE (1993) *International Migration Bulletin,* 3

Urban, Thomas (1993) *Deutsche in Polen – Geschichte und Gegenwart einer Minderheit,* Munich: Beck

Vasileva, Darina (1992) 'Bulgarian Turkish Emigration and Return', *International Migration Review,* 2, 342–51

Vishnevsky, Anatoli and Zhanna Zayonchkovskaya (1994) 'Emigration from the Former USSR: The Fourth Wave', in H. Fassmann and R. Münz (eds) *European Migration in the Late 20th Century,* Aldershot: Edward Elgar, 239–60

Wehler, Hans Ulrich (1980) *Nationalitätenpolitik in Jugoslawien. Die deutsche Minderheit 1918–1978,* Göttingen: Vandenhoek & Ruprecht

INTERNAL MOVEMENT IN THE
EUROPEAN COMMUNITY

ANN DUMMETT

The European Economic Community established by the Treaty of Rome in 1957 was intended, from the beginning, to be an area within which workers could move freely from and to any part of Community territory, and Articles 48 to 58 of the treaty provided that employees, the self-employed, companies and persons establishing businesses or agencies should enjoy freedom of movement without any discrimination on grounds of nationality between the nationals of member states. Exceptions were closely limited: persons could be denied movement only on grounds of national security, public health and public policy, all of which were to be defined in Community law and not by the national authorities of member states.

The purpose was to establish a single economic area and a single labour market: Community legislation progressively defined people's rights specifically, and subsequent amendments to the treaty in the Single European Act (1986) and the Treaty on European Union (1992) extended the original plan so that now any EC national, whether economically active or not, may move freely within the territory of what is now called the European Union and reside in any part of it indefinitely. These developments derive from political as well as economic aims: both can be found in the original treaty, whose preamble expressed determination 'to lay the foundations of an ever closer union among the peoples of Europe' as well as resolution 'to ensure the economic and social progress of their countries by common action to eliminate the barriers which divide Europe'.

But unprecedented economic growth in some EC countries in the 1950s and 1960s sucked in labour from outside the EC, and there were soon more migrants from outside EC territory than cross-border migrants within it. Even before the recent recession, there were unemployed EC nationals within member countries while non-EC migrants (third-country nationals) were arriving to work. Employers often preferred them for their cheapness, while they were attracted by what for them were high wages.

There is a misfit between the laws on internal migration in the EC and the laws on entry from outside it: the first is determined by Community law, overriding national laws, and the second has been left to member states' governments, acting individually, though since the mid-1980s procedures for intergovernmental cooperation have been established and have been formally endorsed in the Maastricht Treaty.

In considering internal migration between EC countries one must use data with caution. The EC did not begin in a vacuum: long-established patterns of emigration and immigration were already laid down, for example, large-scale movement of Italians to France between the wars. One must also take into account the different dates at which countries joined the EC. The original six (France, Belgium, Netherlands, Luxembourg, Germany and Italy) were members from 1957 to 1973. Britain, Ireland and Denmark joined in 1973, Greece in 1981, and Spain and Portugal in 1986. In 1990 18 million East German citizens automatically became EC nationals on the reunification of Germany.

Thus, stock statistics for resident EC foreigners in EC countries are not an accurate indicator of internal movement in the EC. They show the present position, which needs a great deal of interpretation. Moreover, different countries compile their figures differently, and there are often gaps where one wants to make comparisons. Percentages of population must be related to changes in total population, particularly in Germany.

Free movement itself poses problems in estimating movement. Within the EC generally, people often move for a short time to another country and move back again, or on to a different country. Frontier workers, living in one country and working in another a couple of miles away are a common phenomenon. These categories cannot be accurately counted, though economically they are highly important.

Movement between EC countries is not exclusively a movement of EC nationals. Under Community law, an EC national has the right to be joined in any EC country other than his or her own by a spouse, dependent children under 21, and dependent parents and grandparents *of any nationality*. (On subsequently returning to his or her own country, the person may bring these dependants there.) It has been proposed by the Economic and Social Committee of the EC, by some members of the European Parliament, and most recently in a Commission Green Paper on Social Policy that all legally resident third-country nationals, after a period of residence, should be entitled to move within the EC for work. A single labour market does not, after all, make sense if a significant part of the labour force is not free to move.

Another group of third-country nationals which moves consists of non-EC employees of multinational companies, other business people (notably Americans and Japanese), journalists and other professionals whose work requires travel and short or long stays in different countries. An unknown quantity is the internal movement between EC states of illegal entrants from outside. Probably the number is negligible.

The main movement we are here concerned with is internal movement by EC nationals. An EC national is a person whom the government of an EC country has designated one of its nationals for EC purposes. In most countries, this designation coincides with the definition of nationality used for all other purposes. There is some uncertainty, however, about the inhabitants of dependent territories of member states, for example Dutch nationals from the Caribbean. Originally their position was to be defined by general agreement: no such formal agreement has taken place.

French people from overseas departments are, however, not dependent-territory citizens but full French citizens, and therefore any of them in an EC country other than France will be counted as an item in internal movement rather than in migration from outside. Similarly, for a British citizen who has lived most of his or her life in South Africa and who moves, say, to Germany to live and work. The British definition of British nationality for EC purposes includes British citizens, certain persons connected with Gibraltar (which is part of EC territory), and a small group of people of UK descent whose families lived for generations past in British India. Other categories of British national are excluded. Thus a Hong Kong restaurateur is a third-country national, while a Macau restaurateur (who is a full Portuguese citizen) is an EC national.

All the considerations listed above show how difficult it is to analyse the movement of EC nationals between member states. Sociological categories (particularly ethnic or racial ones), economic categories and legal definitions by nationality do not come anywhere near matching each other.

According to Eurostat, the official EU statistics service (Rapid Report 1993, no. 6) the EC had a population of 344 million on 1 January 1991. Of these, 334 million (97 per cent) were citizens of member states. (Undocumented residents are not included in the first figure: one can probably add, unofficially, about 2 million to the total by including them.)

EC nationals living in their own states accounted for 95.8 per cent of the officially estimated total population, and 1.4 per cent of the total were EC nationals residing in states other than their own.

By far the largest national group to have migrated in the EC consists of Italians, well over 1 million of them having moved elsewhere in EC territory. About three-quarters of a million Portuguese come next, followed by Ireland (over half a million), Spain (half a million), the UK (over 400,000) and Greece (about 400,000). However, there has recently been considerable return migration to Italy, Portugal, Spain and Greece (Haskey 1992: 37–47).

If we look at these emigrants from another point of view, that is as proportions of the nationals of their home countries, and consider how high a percentage of each country's population has emigrated, we find that Ireland heads the list: in 1991 13.5 per cent of all Irish citizens were living in the EC but outside Ireland; 8.1 per cent of Portuguese outside Portugal; 4.9 per cent of Luxembourgers outside Luxembourg; 3.8 per cent of Greeks outside Greece; and 2 per cent of Italians outside Italy. Next in order come Dutch, Spanish, Belgians, Danes, British, French and finally Germans, of whom only 0.4 per cent have emigrated (Rapid Report 1993, no 12).

The proportion of females to males among EC nationals outside their own countries varies considerably between receiving countries. For every 100 males in the category, there are 130 female EC migrants in Italy, 122 in the UK, 116 in Greece, 100 in Ireland, 99 in Luxembourg, 91 in Portugal, 88 in France, 85 in Belgium, 79 in the Netherlands, 77 in Germany and 69 in Denmark (Rapid Report, 1993, no. 6. No figures are available for Spain). This disparity between males and females is more marked than among either resident nationals or non-EC immigrants. In age structure EC and non-EC migrants are both younger on average than resident nationals, but EC migrants are less markedly younger than the host population.

Movement within the EC may have increased slightly in the last few years, after having remained more or less stable throughout the 1980s. From 1990 to 1991, the number of EC nationals from other countries rose by about 100,000 in Germany, remained stable or rose by less than 1 per cent in all the other countries except the UK, and fell by nearly 100,000 in the UK. However, most of those who left the UK were Irish, while in Germany children born on the territory to foreign nationals are foreigners, not German, by birth: births could account for part of the German increase. It is too soon to say whether the coming of the single market is making any difference to movement.

Eurostat's Rapid Report 1993, no. 12, records immigration flows for selected EC countries in 1991 and points out that a large part of migration flows consists of return migration by nationals. The proportion of other EC citizens per country does not differ greatly between emigration and immigration. 'For example, 35 per cent of total immigrants in Belgium are Other EC, and 35 per cent of total emigrants in Belgium are also Other EC.' Internal EC migrants often go to a country that is physically close to home. Three-quarters of Portuguese emigrants are in France; Luxembourgers go to Belgium, Germany and France; most Irish go to the UK.

However, there is considerable variation within this picture. The following figures, rounded to two decimal places, are from Rapid Report 1993, no. 6.

Germany

Total population 79.75 million. Other EC: 1.44 million. Germany is far the largest EC country by population since reunification, which added 16 million German citizens to its total. With the strongest economy in Europe it has attracted more immigrants from all sources than any other EC country, and its liberal regime on asylum (amended in 1993) has also added significantly to population. Registers in 1993 showed more than 6.5 million foreign nationals living in Germany (Schröder and Horstkotte 1993).

Most available data were compiled before reunification, but figures for EC nationals are scarcely affected, since virtually none were in the east. On 1 January 1991 Germany had nearly 1.5 million residents from other EC countries, including 552,400 Italians, 320,000 Greeks, 135,500 Spaniards and 96,500 British citizens. Among these, many are long-term residents, notably Italians and Greeks who were already migrating steadily in the 1960s and 1970s.

The German authorities have favoured immigration as a means to spur economic growth.

Belgium

Total population: 9.99 million. Other EC: 0.55 million. The foreign population on 1 January 1991 was about 904,000 or 9 per cent of the total population. EC nationals accounted for 60 per cent of the foreigners. (OECD 1992). This seems at first easily accounted for by Brussels' position as headquarters of many EC institutions: not only do other EC nationals come to work for those institutions but business people, lawyers and providers of services have arrived in force. However, the bulk of EC residents is composed of Italian, French, Spanish, Portuguese and others who have arrived over a long period as workers, many of them in southern Belgium.

Luxembourg

Total population: 3.84 million. Other EC: 1.02 million. Foreigners form over 41.9 per cent of the labour force. Over 94 per cent of foreign workers are EC nationals: 27 per cent Portuguese, 24 per cent French, 17 per cent Belgian. Over the last twenty years, Italian entry has declined while Portuguese has risen rapidly. Most work is in construction and services (OECD 1992). Luxembourg, like Belgium, is host to important EC institutions.

Netherlands

Total population: 15.01 million. Other EC: 1.69 million. In 1991 there were over 44,000 Germans, 39,000 British people, just over 17,000 Spaniards and just under 17,000 Italians residing in the Netherlands. According to the OECD report (1992), there was a slight increase in British and German entry in 1990.

France

Total population 56.65 million. Other EC: 1.31 million. The proportion of EC nationals entering France is declining, from over 50 per cent for work purposes from the mid-1980s to less than 35 per cent in 1990, while entry from central and eastern Europe has risen.

The largest EC immigrant group was Portuguese, at 650,000. Next in order came 253,000 Italians, 216,000 Spaniards, and something over 50,000 each of Belgians, Germans and British. Figures for other countries are very low.

Denmark

Total population: 5.15 million. Other EC: 0.028 million. Next to Luxembourg, the smallest EC country, Denmark has the lowest number of other EC residents. The only sizeable groups are British (10,200) and Germans (8400). The German group is partly accounted for by the links between Schleswig-Holstein, with a largely ethnic Danish population holding German citizenship, and Denmark.

A few of the British residents are of Indian ethnic origin, including people who have been naturalized as British and used their freedom-of-movement rights to go and work in the jewellery industry in Copenhagen. (This group is mentioned only as an example of the important point that acquiring any EC nationality provides a gateway to internal migration.)

Spain

Total population: 38.99 million. Other EC: 0.27 million. Spain's foreign population more than doubled between 1980 and 1990, from about 200,000 to 415,000 officially registered residents. Of these, 60 per cent are EC nationals (OECD 1992). The period coincides with rapid growth in the Spanish economy, particularly since Spain joined the EC. The largest group of EC foreigners is British (86,100). Next come Germans (49,700), Portuguese (37,600) and French (32,500). Other groups are smaller, but more Danes have moved to Spain (13,300) than to any other EC country except Germany. Eurostat estimates that about 37,000 EC nationals have work permits. A large proportion of EC foreigners is in Spain for leisure, with second homes or for retirement from the chilly north.

Portugal

Total population: 9.86 million. Other EC: 0.29 million. Traditionally a country of emigration, Portugal has recently had emigrants coming back from working abroad, at a rate of about 25,000 a year (OECD 1992). Some studies show that in the past ten years 400,000 have returned from other EC countries. Foreign immigrants account for only 1 per cent of total population, with nearly half coming from Portuguese-speaking African countries, a quarter from Brazil and the USA, and just over a quarter from the rest of the EC, mainly from the UK (8500), Spain (7500), Germany (4800) and France (3200).

The returning Portuguese have responded to an improving economy and a fall in unemployment.

Italy

Total population: 57.8 million. Other EC: 0.15 million. Italy achieved spectacular economic growth in the 1970s and early 1980s. Since the mid-1980s, GDP has been low and unemployment high compared with rates in other OECD countries. Italians continue to emigrate, but many return: the net outflow in 1989 was only 6000. There are marked regional differences: Italian emigration has always been mainly from the south, which gained little from the boom years, and from which there is still net emigration.

The only substantial numbers of EC residents are German (42,100), British (26,800), French (24,400) and Greek (21,000). The entire EC total is very small compared with immigration from Africa, the USA, Asia, and central and eastern Europe.

Greece

Total population: 10.12 million. Other EC: 0.845 million. According to the Greek Ministry of Labour, there were 14,500 EC nationals in Greece in June 1991 with work permits. However, it is uncertain whether this figure reflects reality: since Greece became part of the EC, records of EC arrivals have been deficient (OECD 1992). As in Italy and Spain, there is a good deal of unofficial employment. Greek emigration to other EC countries has fallen recently. The largest body of EC residents listed by Eurostat is British (18,600), with Germans next at 13,000.

United Kingdom

Total population: 56.7 million. Other EC: 0.782 million. By far the largest group of EC residents is Irish (510,000). Next come Italians (86,000), Germans (42,000), French (38,000) and Spanish (29,000).

Like Italy the UK has many migrants from central and eastern Europe and from other continents: EC nationals (Irish excepted) are a small proportion of the migrant population. British emigration to other EC countries has, however, been increasing, particularly among young people.

Ireland

Total population: 3.52 million. Other EC: 0.068 million. The largest EC group is British (58,200). As with Irish in Britain, the number represents a longstanding connection between the two countries. Ireland is the only country of net emigration in the EC and although its economy has benefited from EC membership, employment prospects are poor and many young people continue to emigrate while very few EC nationals except from Britain have moved there. Germans (3300) come next after British.

EC membership has provided an opportunity for the Irish to migrate beyond Britain, and there are 10,300 of them in Germany and 3400 in the Netherlands.

General conclusions

The lack of adequate and comparable data makes any conclusion rash, particularly as the economic future is uncertain and economic factors play a large part in migratory patterns. It is clear, moreover, that with such wide differences between EC countries as even this summary shows, any generalizations about movement of EC nationals within the EC risk being meaningless.

Since 1 January 1993 five EFTA countries (Finland, Austria, Sweden, Norway and Iceland) have joined with the EC in a European Economic Area within which there is freedom of movement for workers as under EC legislation within the Community. Finland, Austria and Sweden joined the EC on 1 January 1995. New EU members, EFTA country nationals exercising their rights to free movement and some east European countries anxious to become full members of the EU, will complicate even further the task of those analysing movement. As the EC grows figures will need constant readjustment and reinterpretation.

References

Haskey, John(1992) 'The Immigrant Populations of the Different Countries of Europe: Their Size and Origins', *Population Trends*, (69), 37–47

OECD (1992) *Sopemi: Trends in International Migration*, Paris: Organization for Economic Cooperation and Development

Rapid Report (1993) 'Population and Social Conditions', Luxembourg: Eurostat, nos 6 and 12

Schröder, Karstem and Herman Horstkotte (1993) 'Foreigners in Germany', *Social Report for Visitors' Information*, Bonn: Inter Nationes

MIGRATION AND SOVIET DISINTEGRATION

KLAS-GÖRAN KARLSSON

During the Stalinist period, a far-reaching political, administrative and ideological apparatus determined the nature, orientation and scope of Soviet migration. Migration was often characterized by direct force, as during the deportations of substantial groups of freeholding peasants, so-called *kulak*s. Newly released documents from the archives of the Ministry of the Interior reveal that in 1930/1, 1.8 million individuals were expelled from the agricultural areas in Ukraine and Russia to labour camps in Russia's Arctic zone, Siberia and central Asia (Zemskov 1991: 3).

Recently opened archives also shed light on the large-scale deportations of entire peoples, i.e. Volga Germans and Crimean Tartars, which Stalin ordered before and during the Second World War as a preventive measure, or as punishment for alleged cooperation with the Nazi enemy. The sources furthermore suggest that forced population transfers were viewed as an integrated element of the planned economy system. When the systematic deportations were eventually interrupted and access to a forced labour force thus halted, the entire Soviet economy was negatively affected (Khlebnyuk 1992: 13).

Stalin's methods of regulating internal migration included the reintroduction of the tsarist system of domestic passports and work permits – *propiska*. This was in effect throughout the Soviet era, and entailed that migration proceeded according to conditions dictated by the ministries, large Soviet industry and the defence forces. Until the final days of the Soviet state, free individual migration required access to contacts, special privileges or substantial bribing resources.

Ideological aspects also determined the conditions for migration, which were classified under the collective heading of Soviet patriotism in the ideological handbooks. Migration was here depicted as a mutually advantageous exchange of labour, which was boundless, free of conflict and productive. Uniform levels of development and eternal ties of friendships among peoples – *druzhba narodov* – were said to facilitate the transfers.

A contradiction lay in the fact that despite these ideal images, migration was in fact surrounded by extensive administrative and legal restrictions. This duality was particularly prominent in the question of emigration: although Soviet ideology maintained that voluntary emigration from the highly developed socialist Soviet state was illogical, the state nevertheless passed legislation and set up border controls which prevented Soviet citizens from emigrating. Furthermore, a massive propaganda campaign against emigration was introduced.

With Mikhail Gorbachev's policy of openness, outspoken journalists and social scientists began to call attention to the growing discrepancy between ideology and the realities of Soviet migration. The organizers of migration were criticized for having failed to take into account the existence of regional differences within the Soviet state, the influence of cultural factors on the tendency to migrate and the migrants' chances of adapting to a new environment. Actual problems were ventilated in an ever more open manner. Certain areas in central Russia outside the fertile black earth zones had been depopulated, resulting in serious production problems within agriculture. In central Asia, the problem was just the opposite: an insufficient will to migrate coupled with a high birth rate had led to population strain and rising unemployment (Rybakovski and Tarasova 1989: 73–79).

The Soviet urbanization process and urban environment became the focus of a series of critical studies. Ethno-sociological studies revealed that the uniform and rapidly growing industrial cities were not the problem-free organisms as maintained by Soviet ideology, but rather accumulations of individuals with tangible material, social and cultural problems (Shkaratan 1986).

Popular rural authors reinforced the bleak picture of individual alienation in modern industrial cities and the hankering after a lost and older Russian rural life. In the cultural debate it was claimed that the limited possibilities for out-migration had driven the Soviet peoples to travel internally, within their own history, oriented towards a better, non-Soviet future (Tolstaya 1990: 93–5).

Gorbachev's *perestroika* was partly aimed at

increasing the population's physical and psychological mobility, to be achieved by political, economic and cultural stimuli rather than by the force of central decrees. The reform supporter Aleksandr Yakovlev (1990: 18) described mobility not just as an economic necessity, but also as a way of counteracting some of the negative aspects of the stagnant Brezhnev years, such as favouring local interests and the widespread black market in both labour and goods. Towards the end of *perestroika* there was a hope that new migration patterns would develop harmoniously out of the reigning spirit of reform.

Migration as a catalyst

Gorbachev's reform programme created expectations of rapid economic progress, as well as the conditions for the political mobilization of this platform. However, the discrepancies between expectations and the increasingly bleak reality allowed for mobilization around the ethnic factor, particularly among the critical intelligentsia in the big cities. The rise of ethnic awareness was of decisive significance to the collapse of the Soviet Union.

The link between ethnicity and migration lies in the concept of territoriality, the actual or perceived connection of an ethnic group to a given territory as a central part of its origin. Political mobilization on ethnic grounds is often accompanied by allegations of the territory in question being threatened, either by ecological deterioration or demographic change. The last-named threat can be met in two ways: either by the out-migration of the foreign ethnic element, or by the in-migration of representatives of the given ethnic group. The final aim is generally presented as the re-establishment of a 'natural' and 'original' ethno-territorial order.

Ethno-territoriality was in fact the constitutional principle behind the Soviet Union itself, and had been since its birth in 1922. Each major ethnic group within the framework of the union was to be administered by and to draw political weight from its given autonomous territory. This Leninist principle was, however, seriously disrupted in the early 1990s by labour migration and forced population transfers.

In the late Soviet period, the explosive potential of the ethnic element was reinforced through four different, relatively distinct migration patterns. First, in certain areas increased labour migrations reduced the ethno-territorial population. The group's apprehension over becoming a minority in its own ethno-territory and over being subject to increased ethnic competition and discrimination was most tangible in Latvia and Estonia, where the birth rate of the ethno-territorial population was notably low. In the Baltic republics, the popular fronts were at the forefront of ethnic mobilization and inspired other Soviet peoples to resist the Soviet state. Here, fears of a disadvantageous ethno-demographic development were strengthened by the fact that the bulk of the migrants were Russians, who were perceived as being close to the central Soviet power.

Second, migration coupled with a high birth rate led to a concentration of the ethno-territorial population; ethnic homogeneity thus increased in other areas, particularly in central Asia and Transcaucasia. Migration had a dual orientation – people returned to their own ethno-territories and non-territorial groups, particularly ethnic Russians, moved out. This process, which was speeded up by ethnic conflict in the final Soviet years, laid the foundations for political mobilization on ethno-territorial grounds against both the Russian-dominated Soviet state and neighbours of a different ethnic affiliation.

Third, ethnic consciousness was stimulated by the Crimean Tartars and Soviet Germans who had once been punished by Stalin, and who now launched a struggle for repatriation. Sections of this population returned to and made historical claims on the areas from which they had been forced during the war years, and this resulted in new ethnic tensions and migration flows. Broad layers of Soviet society were thus made aware of the fact that ethnic affiliation in Soviet society was intimately linked with phenomena such as discrimination, persecution and deportation.

Fourth, the liberalization of emigration laws led to ever larger groups moving out of the Soviet Union. Emigrants consisted mainly of Jews, Soviet Germans, Armenians and Greeks, who in increasing numbers turned back to their non-Soviet home countries or to countries housing large diaspora populations. In accordance with Armstrong's theory of 'mobilized diaspora' (1992: 231–6), these emigrants can be described as highly skilled groups, whose prominence during the Soviet modernization period had been increasingly disturbing to other ethnic groups. The emigration of these ethnically demarcated groups was accompanied by rising media interest in the causes and effects of this emigration, which contributed to the fact that the ethnic dimension was highlighted still further.

Migration steers politics

From the above discussion on migration patterns, it appears that the late and post-Soviet periods have been marked by a different link between politics and migration than that which prevailed during the Stalinist era: migration has been a determining factor for a vacillating policy dependent on the ethnic factor. In contrast to the realities of Stalinism, the power of the state in today's successor countries is weak and fragile; the state's ability to initiate and direct social change is limited. Migration streams have become increasingly irregular and forced and, accordingly, are less and less likely to result from conscious calculations. Large refugee flows have been triggered and serve to create both economic and political conflicts between regions and newly established states.

The new migration is not, however, linked exclusively to ethnic conflicts. Natural and environmental disasters, such as the Armenian earthquake in 1988, the reactor breakdown at Chernobyl in 1986 and the accelerating desiccation of the Aral Sea, have all resulted in enduring migration flows. It is symptomatic that these transfers have also shaped or served to intensify ethnic conflicts; Armenians have, for example, criticized both the Russian-dominated Soviet power and the prime Azerbaijan enemy for having shown a lack of interest and having actively obstructed migration and reconstruction following the earthquake.

Consequently, ethno-territoriality has put its mark on migration in an ever more obvious manner. In autonomous states and republics experiencing armed ethnic conflict, the minorities involved have in fact become refugees[1] because, through direct violence or the threat of violence and persecution, they have been forced to abandon their homes. This was particularly true in the Caucasus, where population transfers involving hundreds of thousands of individuals have taken place because of the conflict between Armenia and Azerbaijan over the Nagorno-Karabakh area and because of tensions in Georgia between Georgians and minority groups such as the Abkhazians and Ossetians. The flight of masses of people to their own ethno-territories has created increasingly homogeneous ethnic territories throughout Transcaucasia. Open conflicts in Moldova, Uzbekistan and Tadzhikistan have also triggered refugee flows. Due to faulty administration and border controls, as well as distorted information from the various parties in the conflict, it is difficult to find reliable estimates on the total number of refugees.

In areas where ethnic tensions have remained at the verbal level, new legislation with narrow, historically founded regulations concerning citizens and property rights have laid the grounds for similar migration patterns within groups who perceive themselves as systematically wronged. Due to their sheer numbers and their historical association with the Soviet power, the ethnic Russians have been severely affected. In 1989, 25 million Russians lived in the non-Russian Soviet republics. In the past few years, however, substantial and long-established Russian groups have moved away from the central Asian republics. Furthermore, opinion polls among Russians in the Baltics and central Asia indicate that due to fears of persecution and discrimination, many wish to migrate to Russia (Kotov 1992: 40). Similarly, ethnic Russians in Russia have in increasing numbers exited the non-Russian autonomous areas, particularly in the northern Caucasus and Siberia.

Post-Soviet migration problems

Forced migrations have created a difficult situation for the migrants, and the problem is reinforced by the absence of relevant refugee legislation as well as by bureaucratic inflexibility. For the recipient countries unused to handling refugees, the influx of migrants has aggravated already severe economic conditions, promising continued political instability and social tension. The Russian republic has been particularly affected and had (up to June 1993) received about two million registered refugees. In Russia, the politician of discontent, Vladimir Zhirinovski (1992: 35), has painted threatening images of a future marked by the invasion of hundreds of thousands of Russian refugees, and aggressive demands for an authoritarian single-party regime which could re-erect the Russian-dominated empire throughout the former Soviet territory.

For the power holders in the out-migration areas, an ethnically homogeneous territory might initially appear politically and culturally attractive, but could cause serious economic problems in the long run. This is especially true of the underdeveloped central Asian republics, which are highly dependent on the Russian population for their technical/industrial labour force.

Still greater technical/economic problems are created by the rapidly escalating migration from the former Soviet republics to the West. In 1991 over 1.2 million individuals emigrated from the dissolving Soviet state, primarily Soviet Jews and Germans. A significant portion of these were well-educated intellectuals, and their exit has left the former Soviet Union and its economically strained successor states with a significant brain drain.

It is difficult to speculate on the manner in which

the recipient countries are affected by this ethnically delimited migration. However, one form of migrant from the former Soviet Union to the West can be identified as a problem. Geographical mobility can be expected to be particularly high among the underworld Mafia types, who are now in a strong social position as a result of the general state of collapse and their stable anchor in certain ethnic groups and in the older state and party apparatus. With the loss of profitable markets for narcotics, prostitution and arms in the former Soviet Union, it is likely that these groups will attempt to penetrate neighbouring states. Crime syndicates from Russia, Ukraine and the Baltics are already posing a problem for the authorities in Poland and eastern Germany. A new and lucrative market for the illegal smuggling of human beings has also been created. Many refugees from countries outside the USSR make intermediate stopovers in Moscow where they are forced to pay dearly for assistance in reaching their final destinations in the West.

Note

1. In Russian legal prose, a distinction is made between refugees and forced migrants. Refugees are individuals who flee from their homeland through fear of persecution, but who plan to return after the situation has normalized; they are not entitled to Russian citizenship. A forced migrant, on the other hand, is an ethnic Russian or individual belonging to another ethno-territorial group within Russia and, according to the 1992 law, has a right to Russian citizenship. However, in this contribution, the term refugee is employed for both categories.

References

Armstrong, J. (1992) 'The Ethnic Scene in the Soviet Union', in R. Denber (ed.) *The Soviet Nationality Reader*, Boulder, CO: Westview Press, 227–56

Khlebnyuk, O. (1992) 'Prinuditelnyi trud v ekonomike SSSR. 1929–1941 gody', *Svobodnaya mysl*, 13, 73–84

Kotov, V. (1992) 'Etnodemograficheskaya situatsiya v RSFSR v 60–80-e gody', *Otechestvennaya istoriya*, 5, 32–41

Rybakovskii, L. and N. Tarasova (1989) 'Sovremennye problemy migratsii naseleniya SSSR', *Istoriya SSSR*, 2, 68–81

Shkaratan, O. (1986) *Etnosotsialnye problemy goroda*, Moscow: Nauka

Tolstaya, T. (1990) 'The Lisbon Conference on Literature', *Cross Current: A Yearbook on Central European Culture*, 9, 75–124

Yakovlev, A. (1990) *Realizm – zemlja perestroiki*, Moscow: Izd. Politicheskoi Literatury

Zemskov, V. (1991) 'Kulatskaya ssylka' v 30-e gody', *Sotsiologicheskie issledovaniya*, 10, 3–21

Zhirinovski, V. (1992) 'Mezhnatsionalnye protivorechiya v Rossii: Strategiya partii i obshchestvennykh dvizhenii', *Sotsiologicheskie issledovaniya*, 11, 34–6

MIGRATIONS IN SOCIALIST AND
POST-SOCIALIST RUSSIA

ALEXEI POLYAKOV AND IGOR USHKALOV

During practically the whole period of socialist development, Russia had the specific political status of being one of the republics of the USSR. This explains the need to adopt an individual approach to studying the migrations of that period. We would like to define two categories of migration – near (inter-republican within the USSR) and distant.

In addition, the migrations should be placed within the categories of 'voluntary', 'forced' and 'violent'. The first are caused by the individual motivations of the migrants themselves and are regulated exclusively by indirect state instruments. The second are migrations of persons leaving their residences as a result of occupations, military conflicts, natural calamities or through fear of becoming victims of political or ethnic persecution. The third are organized mass involuntary displacements of populations during periods of political or ethnic repression.

It is necessary to emphasize that studying external migrations in Russia during the socialist period is complicated by a number of objective factors such as the numerous changes of frontiers, the non-comparability of the results of some population censuses, the absence or inaccessibility of many data concerning forced or violent migrations and the casualties of repression and wars.

This is why it is expedient to examine general migration tendencies before looking at some of the more characteristic events in the development of near and distant migrations in Russia.

First, for a long time Russia was the donor territory for both near and distant migrations. This tendency was marked by the practical absence of any substantial flows of immigrants from foreign countries and by a number of important 'waves' of emigration, as well as by the role of Russia as the major migrating nation of the USSR. As a result of this tendency the concentration of Russians in their own ethnic territory changes appreciably. From 1926 to 1979 the proportion of Russians living in other parts of the USSR grew from 6.7 per cent to 17.4 per cent (*Russie Etnosociologicheskie* 1992).

Second, the increase of Russian migration into the rest of the USSR was greatest during the period of rapid urbanization. Before the Second World War urbanization basically affected the European part of the USSR; after the war it spread to the other regions. And the Russians, being the most mobile sector of the population, rushed to the rapidly growing cities of other republics. This process was also enhanced by the relatively low standard of living in the rural regions of central Russia. In the 1960s the total increase of the Russian population outside Russia was 2.4 times higher than its natural increase (*Migracija naselenija* 1992).

Third, in the 1970s a new pattern of migration began in Russia characterized by an increase in ethnic emigration abroad (first of Jews, then Germans) and by a new tendency for Russians to return to their own ethnic territory, initially from the republics of the Caucasus and central Asia. The above mentioned tendencies also developed in the 1980s, reaching their height after the collapse of the USSR.

Fourth, as a predominantly social and economic phenomenon, migrations during the socialist period were subject to the immense impact of the prevailing ideological doctrine and of the country's political regime. This resulted in the long and practically total isolation of Russia, as part of the Soviet Union, from the rest of the world. Such hostility arose through the failure to observe the basic human right to free movement on the one hand, and the mass violent migrations (practically unique in world history) during the period of political and ethnic repression, on the other. During the Stalinist period alone more than ten million people were subjected to violent migrations, including five million who were made to leave the territorial borders of Russia.

The near migrations

Because of the absence of reliable and comparative statistical data on inter-republican migrations within the former USSR, the migration balance of Russia can only partly be reconstructed from various historical facts and material.

Up to the mid-1950s the most distinctive feature of

the near migrations was the large proportion of violent migrations in all territorial population movements. These violent migrations formed part of the state policy of political and ethnic repression aimed, in particular, at the development of virgin territory by the so-called 'special settlers'.

The largest migration flows of this kind came from other republics to Russian territory (most of the concentration camps and forced labour camps of the state security system were located in Siberia and the northern region) and from Russia to Kazakhstan and central Asia, where Russians deported from the Crimea and the northern Caucasus were settled.

Substantial waves of migration were associated with the implementation of 'forced industrialization' (the new industrial centres of the Urals, Siberia and Kazakhstan required considerable labour resources), with collectivization in the second half of the 1920s and the 1930s, as well as with the ethnic purges during the latter years of the Second World War.

During the period of collectivization about 2.5 million *kulaks* (relatively rich peasants) were removed to specially organized settlements; most of them (about 80 per cent) were located in the north of Russia, the Urals and Siberia (Zemskov 1991). Taking account of the fact that the percentage of Russians in the total peasant population of the USSR was considerably lower, it can be assumed that, within the category of 'violent migrations', Russia showed a positive migration balance, while Ukraine, Belorussia and a number of other non-Russian territories suffered losses.

The main cause of forced migration in the 1930s was mass starvation, which broke out in the rural districts of the main grain regions of the USSR (Ukraine, the northern Caucasus and the Volga region) and led to the migrations of hundreds of thousands of people who were trying to save their lives by moving to more favourable places.

The violent migrations of this period led to a very specific phenomenon, namely the appearance of industrial cities and settlements in the previously unsettled polar regions on the Kolsky peninsula, in Siberia and in Kamchatka. The first people in these settlements were basically exiles and convicts.

On the whole, the migration flows of that period were characterized by their orientation towards the eastern regions of Russia (Siberia, the Urals and the Far East) and towards the so-called 'national outskirts' of the USSR, the economic and cultural development of which was proclaimed as a priority in Soviet government policy. The largest forced migration flow consisted of the evacuation of the population of the European part of the USSR as a result of the threat of occupation at the beginning of the Second World War to Siberia, the Urals, Kazakhstan and, to a lesser degree, central Asia. The total number of evacuees was 25 million and many of them remained where they had been sent when the war was over (*Russkie Etnosociologicheskie* 1992).

In the mid-1940s Russia also sustained substantial migration losses associated with the mass violent movement of some national groups at the end of the war on the grounds that they were imputed to have 'cooperated with the German occupants'.

Most of the ethnic purges affected national groups living on Russian territory – Germans, Crimean Tartars, Chechens, Ingushes and Kalmyks – who were moved to Kazakhstan and the central Asian republics. According to the state's own figures, in 1948 some 1,806,000 deportees were registered, including 774,000 in Kazakhstan, 125,000 in Kirgizia and 167,000 in Uzbekistan.

Over two million people were evicted from their historical homelands in Russia, including approximately one million Germans, 666,000 Chechens and Ingushes, 220,000 Crimean Tatars and 90,000 Kalmyks (Pushkareva 1992). The lands previously inhabited by these people were settled by populations from central Russia and this migration was actively stimulated by the state. These violent migrations paved the way for the nationality policy of the USSR, which caused a considerable amount of conflict during the period of *perestroika* and the collapse of the USSR, and greatly encouraged the emigration of Soviet Germans to their ethnic motherland.

The increased migration of Russians to other USSR republics in the immediate post-war period can be explained by the following factors. First, Russians were the most mobile national group within the USSR. The index of migration mobility (i.e. the proportion of the total population of a particular national group settled in certain places for less than two years) was higher for Russians than for practically any other large group of people. Second, in the post-war period the process of rapid urbanization took place in the other republics (having been completed in Russia before the war), which explains why numerous flows of Russian migrants rushed to the rapidly growing cities of the provinces of the USSR. In the 1960s, the height of the 'urbanization boom', the numbers of Russians outside Russia increased by 5.2 million persons or 31 per cent (*Migracija naselenija* 1992). The most intensive outflow of Russians was to

Table 14.5: *The balance of inter-republican migration in the USSR, 1961–90* ('000s)

	1961–70	1971–80	1981–90
Russia	−1114	+673	+1773
Ukraine	+530	+199	+253
Belorussia	−160	−84	−22
Kazakhstan	+414	−562	−900
Moldavia	+68	−58	−72
Lithuania	+49	+68	+90
Latvia	+144	+104	+73
Estonia	+93	+60	+44
Georgia	−94	−162	−93
Armenia	+144	+85	−309
Azerbaijan	−69	−96	−393
Uzbekistan	+414	+150	−743
Tadjikistan	+120	+3	−158
Turkmenija	+10	−9	−82

Source: National statistics

the republics of central Asia and Kazakhstan, where the rural population was not mobile, had no experience of industrial work and was reluctant to move even to its own national cities. As a result of this low mobility of the local population, the rapidly growing labour market relied on the mass influx of migrants from the European part of the USSR, particularly from Russia. Because the intensive growth of the Russian population in the Baltic republics was combined with a low growth of the national population in this region, the cities were not developed at the expense of the local population. Third, most of the one million migrants who moved to Kazakhstan in the 1950s to cultivate virgin lands were Russians (*Russkie Etnosociologicheskie* 1992).

In the 1970s Russians gradually began to lose their historical role as 'the nation of migrants'. During their settlement new centrifugal processes led Russians to concentrate on Russian territory. At the same time Russia became the centre of gravity for other national groups within the USSR. In the 1980s, as a result of migration, the Ukrainian population on Russian territory increased by 11.3 per cent and the Azerbaijanian, Armenian, Georgian and Uzbek populations increased by several times (Topilin 1992).

The distant migrations

A number of distinctive periods can be identified during Russia's exchange of migrants with foreign states. The first lasted until the mid-1920s when, because of the civil war, no strict frontier controls had

been established and the 'iron curtain' had not yet been dropped around Russia. During this relatively short period about 1.5 million persons left the country to escape communist repression, chaos, starvation and war. The large majority of the emigrants of that period belonged to the upper social groups – the nobility, prosperous entrepreneurs, merchants, regular servicemen and intellectuals. The main centres of the Russian foreign diaspora, formed by the emigrants from this first wave, were Paris, Prague, Berlin and various other European cities. Smaller numbers went to the USA, China and several Latin American countries.

During the same period Russia accepted a few groups of emigrants from different countries of the world who sought to create progressive agricultural communes in the 'new' Russia and were officially supported by the communist regime. Immigration to Russia in this period also included groups of revolutionary-minded migrants from neighbouring countries such as China, Latvia and Hungary.

This period was followed by one of practically complete isolation – up to the 1970s – broken only by the Second World War, which generated the mass violent movement of hundreds of thousands of Russians to Germany. Nevertheless, it is necessary to identify certain characteristic migration 'events' in this period:

- the violent deportation of and withdrawal of citizenship from intellectuals opposed to the regime in the late 1920s;

- the search for political sanctuary in Russia as a result of the development of fascism in Europe in the 1930s. During this period about 30,000 Czechs immigrated to Russia;

- deportations of populations from territories adjoining the USSR (western Ukraine, Moldavia and the Baltic republics) to Siberia. From the Baltic region alone over 100,000 people were deported and settled in Russia (*Otechestvennaja istorija* 1992). Ukrainian nationalists opposed to the Soviet regime were forcibly relocated on the same scale up until the beginning of the 1950s;

- after the end of the war not everyone displaced from Russia and released by the Allied countries in Europe returned to their motherland. Between 1947 and 1951 about 150,000 Russian and Ukrainian displaced persons were settled in different countries of the world – 74,400 in the USA, 25,200 in Australia and 23,200 in Canada (Pushkareva 1992).

Table 14.6: *Emigration from the USSR after the Second World War, 1948–90 ('000s)*

	48–70	71–80	81–86	87–90
Emigrants including	59.6	347.1	42.9	834.2
Jews	25.2	248.9	16.9	n/a
Germans	22.4	64.2	19.6	n/a

Source: Sydney Heitman (1989) and national statistics

At the end of the 1960s special international and political conditions arose that predetermined a more liberal attitude on the part of the official authorities towards emigration from the country and gave impetus to a long and mass 'wave' of emigration, mainly of an ethnic character.

One of the conditions that forced the communist authorities to abandon their traditional antipathy to voluntary emigration and to make concessions was the pressure of world public opinion, i.e. the insistence of the USA, Germany and Israel on the right to emigrate from the USSR, coupled with the consolidation of the human rights movement within the country.

The distinctive feature of ethnic emigration from Russia is its territorial concentration. At the end of the 1980s 40 per cent of emigrants from Russia were resident in the agglomerations of Moscow and Leningrad (*Migracija naselenija* 1992). Another peculiarity of the so-called 'third emigration wave' from Russia was the noticeable change of the geographical orientation of the emigration. This was due essentially to the rapid decrease in the proportion of Jews emigrating to Israel as opposed to other destinations, from practically 100 per cent to only 10–12 per cent by the end of the 1980s.

The specific period in the development of distant migration was determined by the conclusion of agreements with other Warsaw Pact countries conerning mutual labour migration and the use of foreign workers in the construction of numerous projects in the USSR (mainly in Russia). From the mid-1970s thousands of workers from Bulgaria and Cuba were employed in cutting timber, while others from Poland, Czechoslovakia and Hungary were used in the construction of gas and oil pipelines. In 1981 an agreement with Vietnam was concluded in which the USSR committed itself to helping Vietnam train skilled personnel for its enterprises. In the 1980s, 13,500 Poles and 5300 Romanians (Ioncev 1992). In 1990 a special agreement was concluded between the USSR and China to regulate labour migration from China to Siberia and the Far East. According to this agreement family migration was prohibited and contracts were limited to one year. At the same time, beginning at the end of the 1980s and especially after the collapse of the Warsaw Pact, the structure of labour migration began to change, with an increase in the proportion of Turkish, German and Yugoslavian workers employed in Russia's construction industry.

Table 14.7: *Emigration from various Soviet republics, 1987–89*

	1987	1988	1989
USSR as a whole including	39.1	108.2	235.0
Russia	9.7	20.7	47.5
Ukraine	6.6	17.7	50.0
Kazakhstan	7.1	23.5	52.9
Armenia	5.9	15.8	12.2

Source: National statistics

Migrations in post-socialist Russia

Migration in Russia in the post-socialist period is characterized by the development and intensification of earlier tendencies (such as an increase in ethnic emigration and the return migrations of Russians to Russia) and the appearance of new migration patterns. Among the latter are mass refugee flows from areas of military and ethnic conflict, and from ecological catastrophes within the former USSR, the gradual development of labour emigration, and the formation of transit migration routes through Russia of refugees from Asia and Africa seeking sanctuary in Europe.

The main characteristic of migrations between Russia and the republics of the former USSR is the relative increase of Russians compared with refugees and migrants from the Caucasus, central Asia and the Baltic countries. In 1992 Russia's share of migrants increased by 1.4 times and reached 200,000 persons (*Statisticheskij press-bulleten* 1993).

In many respects the emigration of Russians from central Asia has assumed the features of 'flight migration', which is brought about by the increase in ethnic and military conflict and the consequent exclusion of migrants from the labour market through the granting of privileges to the native population.

Besides, ousting populations from these territories is aggravated by the continuing demographic 'explosion' in the region, which has created a population size in the region that does not correspond to its economic and labour potential.

Various national contradictions (which are essentially ethnic or cultural in the Baltic countries and economic in central Asia) are delaying the potential return of Russians to Russia. According to the results of a survey, more than 50 per cent of the Russians in the Baltic region wish to return, as do the majority (up to 80 per cent) in central Asia (*Migracija naselenija* 1992).

Thus, Russia should be ready to accept a huge influx of compatriots returning home. Besides, in the near future the migration of central Asians back to their territories is also likely to increase given that a zero increase in the economically active population has been forecast for the European part of the country from the year 2005.

Another phenomenon, nowadays becoming increasingly important, is 'internal Russian emigration', i.e. emigration from the so-called autonomous regions (there are twenty of them) to the territory of native Russia: first of all from the Muslim republics of the Volga region (Tatarstan, Bashkortostan), from the northern Caucasus (Chechnya, Degestan, Ingoushstan) and from certain Siberian autonomous regions. The reasons for this emigration are discrimination, tension in the sphere of social relations and labour-market competition.

For all this, it is necessary to mention that the size of the native population in some Russian autonomous regions is not large. Bashkirs make up only 22 per cent of the population in Bashkortostan, Buryats only 24 per cent in Buryatia and Yakuts only 33 per cent in Yakutia. In the autonomous regions of northern and eastern Siberia the relative sizes of the native populations are even lower (*Argumenty I fakty* 1991).

The tendency to grant a special status to the native population also exists in Russia. According to various population surveys carried out by the Centre of Sociology of the Russian Academy of Management, together with the Institute of Complex Social Studies, only 36 per cent of the population believe that Russia should accept citizens from all the other republics of the former USSR irrespective of their nationality; 51 per cent believe only Russians by birth should be accepted; 11 per cent are against accepting any migrants or refugees at all; and 2 per cent did not answer the question.

The socio-economic crisis, the deteriorating situation in the labour market and increasing ethnic tensions have led to a surge of migration, both external and internal.

Internal migratory flows consist mostly of refugees and other involuntary migrants. After the collapse of the USSR about 25.3 million ethnic Russians found themselves in fourteen newly independent states. Three-quarters of these live in more or less politically stable regions – Ukraine, Belarus and Kazakhstan.

Most repatriates to Russia are expected to come (and are already coming) from central Asia, where the number of prospective migrants is estimated at 3.5 million. The Federal Migration Administration registered 600,000 migrants from central Asia to Russia in 1991 and 1,270,000 in 1992 (*Izvestija* 1993). The refugee problem is bound to become ever more important in the years to come, for many experts anticipate more ethnic tension and further disintegration of the former Soviet Union in the future (*Emigracija* 1993).

According to projections, the total immigration to Russia in 1993 amounts to approximately two million people (*Radikal* 1992). There is also mounting migration within Russia, with more ethnic Russians moving from autonomous republics (mostly Muslim ones) to the native Russian areas.

Important refugee flows are also triggered by ecological disasters – nuclear accidents in Chernobyl, the Urals and Siberia, a dangerous situation near the nuclear testing grounds in Semipalatinsk (north Kazakhstan) and an environmental crisis in the Aral sea area. Ecologists have identified seventeen disaster areas in the former USSR, and the number of migrants from these areas is steadily growing and may reach several hundred thousand annually. Over the next few years there may also be an outflow of 'economic' refugees from the northern areas of Russia and from the regions most seriously affected by unemployment.

Acute as the refugee problem in Russia is no consistent effort has yet been made to resolve it in an organized way.

All these factors intensify the trend towards emigration. Sociological polls have indicated that 1.5 million people in Russia are actually seeking jobs abroad, while another 5 million are considering this possibility (*Radikal* 1992). From 1993 potential emigration became a reality since the new 'Law on Entry and Exit' removed most domestic controls over emigration.

Reviewing various forecasts of east-west migration (Layard et al. 1992; Salt 1993) and using our own calculations based on the analysis of the international labour market and ethnic emigration trends, we expect about 3 to 4 million Russian citizens to leave Russia for the West before the end of the century (among them 1.5 million labour migrants).[1]

Analysing the labour markets of the labour-importing countries and assessing potential migratory flows from Russia, we expect that the biggest share of all labour migrants (up to 30 per cent) will go to the central and eastern European countries, for they require no entry visas and are close to Russia not only geographically, but also linguistically and technologically. About 10 per cent of all migrants are expected to go to the Middle East and the Persian Gulf area, 25 per cent to the USA and Canada, 25 per cent to western Europe, and 10 per cent to other regions, especially Latin America.

A special problem affecting both Russia and the international community, particularly western Europe, is that of 'transit refugees' coming from Africa and Asia and entering western Europe via Russia. Several factors have made this possible: the easy availability of Russian entry visas (often obtained illegally), the absence of clear borders in the former USSR (especially in central Asia, Azerbaijan and Moldova), corrupt officials, and the lack of legislation in Russia on immigration and refugees (unlike other countries Russia has no immigration quotas). It is also important that no visas are required to travel from Russia and other former Soviet states to eastern European countries, and from there it is easy to proceed to western Europe.

The scale of this 'transit immigration' is already quite great. The Federal Migration Administration of Russia estimated the number of transit refugees in 1993 at more than 150,000, including about 50,000 from Afganistan, 40,000 from Iraq, 25,000 from India and tens of thousands from some African countries.

These trends, taken together, lead to the conclusion that Russia will become a major migratory pole in the future, substantially increasing the growing globalization of migration movements in the world.

Note

1. According to official data at the beginning of 1993 there were about 60,000 legal and 100,000 illegal labour migrants from Russia in the West. By 1992 the annual emigration outflow had reached the level of 90,000–100,000.

References

Argumenty i fakty (1991) 13
Bugaj, N. F. (1990) 'Pravda o deportacii chechenskogo i ingushskogo narodov', *Voprosy istorii*, 7
Emigracija (1993) 2, 3
Heitman, Sydney (1989) *Soviet Emigration since Gorbachev*, Cologne
Ioncev, V. A. (1992) *Mirovye migracii*, Moscow: Znanie Publishers
Izvestija (1993) 1
  (1993) 19, 7
Layard, R., O. Blauchard and R. Dornbusch (1992) 'East-West Migration', *Alternatives*, London
Migracija naselenija (1992) Institut socialnoeconomicheskich problem naselenija, Moscow
Otechestvennaja istorija (1992), 4
Pushkareva, N. L. (1992) 'Puti formirovanija russkoi diaspory posle 1945 goda', *Etnograficheskoe obozrenie*, 6
Radikal (1992) 47
Russkie Etnosociologicheskie ocherki (1992), Moscow: Nauka Publishers
Salt, J. (1993) 'The Future of International Labour Migration', *International Migration Review*, 100
Statisticheskij press-bulleten (1993) 1
Topilin, V. A. (1992) 'Vlijanie migracii na etnosocialnuu structuru', *Sociologicheskie issledovaniya*, 7
Zemskov, V. N. (1991) 'Kulackaja ssylka v 30-e gody', *Sociologicheskie issledovanija*, 10

WHOSE PROTECTION? EUROPEAN HARMONIZATION ON ASYLUM POLICY

DANIÈLE JOLY

The permanence and salience of asylum issues in international relations and domestic policies, has become evident to all concerned, as well as the importance of refugees for security and stability.

The Europeanization of these issues came to the fore in the 1990s as crises leading to refugee flows broke out in Europe, which has now become a region of origin, transit and reception for refugees, while refugees continue to arrive from non-European countries of origin.

From uncoordinated liberalism to harmonized restrictionism

In the early 1970s European states were implementing a fairly open policy with regard to asylum seekers. However, this resulted from general circumstances producing lax immigration controls. Until recently there was little coordination among European countries about their asylum policy and vast discrepancies in procedures existed between one state and another. The 1951 UN Convention had gradually been ratified by European states; sixteen ratified it before 1960 (Jaeger 1992) and they then proceeded to ratify the 1967 Protocol. Nevertheless, in many cases there was no special mechanism to deal with asylum applications. These were introduced through the 1970s into the 1980s. Refugees from eastern Europe were almost automatically recognized within the cold war context. The 1967 Protocol had been recently adopted which made it possible to grant refugee status to non-European asylum-seekers as well. Moreover, until the mid-1970s European countries were still welcoming foreign labour to meet the needs of stable economies. As a consequence many refugees from the Third World entered Europe either as immigrant workers or as students as was then made possible by loose immigration controls (Blaschke 1989). In those years it was non-governmental bodies such as the Council of Europe and the UNHCR which were crying out for some form of European coordination to correct discrepancies.

In the mid-1980s the whole matter of European policy on asylum began to change. The trend started to revert in several ways: formerly liberal policies became increasingly restrictive and a process of convergence replaced the separate policy making that had obtained until then. The question of asylum, which had remained pretty uncontroversial, also became more and more debated.

The current paradigm: restrictions, convergence, secrecy

In the 1980s restrictive measures tended to be implemented at first in specific countries and subsequently were taken up in several other European countries without any formal coordination. This resulted from a combination of factors, including the economic recession, the tightening up of immigration policies and the migration flows of asylum-seekers demonstrating an upsurge in the numbers arriving in Europe. There were some 13,000 asylum applications in Europe in 1972 and by 1980 the numbers had risen to 158,500 (Joly 1990). In 1990 there were 425,100 and in 1991, 550,625 (*France Terre d'Asile* 1992). As they began to arrive in greater numbers, Europe and its governments woke up to the fact that refugee movements were a structural mass phenomenon and that they were no longer being confined to the regions of the world from which they had originated (i.e. Asia, Africa and Latin America). This is confirmed by current events in eastern Europe. The economic and ideological bases for these views are complex and include the recession, unemployment, 'national' and 'European' nationalisms.

EU policy as a model

EU states are at the core of coordinating initiatives on the question of asylum (Joly and Cohen 1989). This was prompted by the plan for a united Europe without internal borders as enshrined in the Single European Act which became effective in January 1993. Some of the EU countries seemed to fear that the absence of borders would enhance the already existing imbalance in the distribution of asylum-seekers, who tended to congregate in the more 'prosperous' northern countries. In the years 1988–90, about 80 per cent of all asylum applications lodged in the European Community were submitted to two countries: Germany (60 per cent) and France (20 per cent) (Commission of the European Communities 1992). Southern countries such as Italy, Greece, Portugal and Spain were perceived as transit countries from which asylum-seekers travelled on. This concern contributed to the creation of the Schengen Group, launched in 1985 by the Benelux countries, Germany and France. These countries signed the Schengen Agreement in June 1990 and were subsequently joined by Italy, Spain and Portugal. The Ad Hoc Immigration Group, including all twelve members of the EU, prepared two conventions – the Dublin convention signed in 1990, determining the state responsible for examining applications for asylum, and the convention on controls at EU external borders, which is still to be signed. All the discussions in preparation of these agreements and conventions were held behind closed doors, thus preventing any public debate on these issues. Restrictions entail further restrictions, for asylum-seekers are being diverted elsewhere in Europe and this is provoking a fear in other countries that they will bear the brunt of refugee reception. The EU thus becomes a model for other European countries.

The above agreement and conventions will be implemented as soon as they have been ratified by the countries concerned. EU efforts at harmonization are continuing and are playing a leading role in European thinking about asylum and about how it influences (and acts as a pole for) non EU countries, even those with traditionally liberal policies on asylum. Coordinating efforts are now being stepped up both within and outside the EU, with former EFTA countries and with eastern European countries. The Maastricht Treaty has placed asylum firmly within its remit (11 October 1991). The Ad Hoc Immigration Group (of the twelve countries) is busy formalizing the adoption of new restrictive concepts and measures leading to recommendations and resolutions are gaining sway in international discussions, for example, the notion of safe countries, internal flight alternatives and an accelerated procedure. Convergence of policies towards further restrictions continues to be the order of the day, and these are discussed in secrecy.

What has happened is that the seat of policy formulation on asylum has shifted from human rights/humanitarian fora to governments and inter-governmental fora. And what used to be one key concern over asylum issues, namely the protection of refugees, has now become the 'protection' of the receiving countries' borders.

Governments are grappling with the fact that they do not have control over refugees on their borders, for they are bound by international conventions such as the 1951 Geneva Convention: in principle numbers are only limited by the merit of each case. The main contestable datum is therefore the definition of what constitutes a meritable case. Currently, only applicants who satisfy the narrowest interpretation of the Geneva Convention definition, i.e. those with a well-founded fear of persecution on grounds of race, religion, political opinion or belonging to a particular social group, will be considered. Applicants who would be entitled to protection under other international instruments, such as the European Convention on Human Rights and Fundamental Freedoms, are not even mentioned in the Schengen and Dublin texts. All other asylum-seekers, such as most of the three million Yugoslavs who are victims of civil wars but fail to suffer individual persecution, are thus not recognized as existing and are excluded from their remit. In governmental phraseology and throughout the media these are called 'bogus' refugees. Merit is defined according to the letter of the Geneva Convention and not according to the social reality of today's refugees (Joly 1990). And yet several European countries grant some form of status and residence to such 'humanitarian' refugees who are occasionally referred to in the subsequent resolutions, including temporary protection for refugees from former Yugoslavia. Moreover, inconsistencies can be revealed in the policies and concepts put forward by EU harmonization. EU texts emphasize the treatment of refugees as individuals, since individual persecution has to be demonstrated to qualify for refugee status. However, at the same time the notion of the treatment of refugees as groups is being reintroduced by the concept of safe countries, which excludes applicants for asylum from consideration if they are nationals of countries appearing in the safe countries list. The paradigm running throughout these coordination efforts and giving rise to them is essentially restrictive: it is dictated by an overriding concern to reduce the numbers of asylum-seekers in Europe. The historical duality between the treatment of refugees as individuals and/or as groups (Melander 1987) is being instrumentalized by governments to serve specific policies of restrictions, thus leading to inconsistencies and incoherence in the rationalization of these policies.

Governments claim that all these restrictive measures are aimed at illegal immigrants and not at refugees. In the best of cases the whole process demonstrates failure to distinguish the former from the latter. It appears, however, that refugees eventually bear the brunt of these measures: for instance the combination of visas and carrier sanctions makes it hardest for genuine refugees to reach Europe and apply for asylum, condemning them to remain in their country of origin often in the face of persecution and even torture.

In almost every European country there have been consistent attempts to discredit and deprive refugees of their dignity in the eyes of the majority population. They are increasingly portrayed as people who *are* a problem rather than people who *have* a problem. Sometimes extreme political parties lead the call to limit, to refuse or to deport asylum-seekers, attempting to whip up a hysterical outcry against an easy political target; sometimes governments themselves take the lead, frequently for cynical political gain, a call echoed and amplified by sections of the media.

Politician and media

The media generally exacerbate the situation. Restrictive measures and declarations in turn enhance hostility and prejudice against foreigners and refugees, and these hostile attitudes appear to be given some justification when political leaders confirm them, or fail to condemn them.

Thus the circle continues, spinning into greater hatred and prejudice. The backlash from governments has been matched and, in some cases, superseded by that of the public. In several European countries refugees and asylum-seekers have been the victims of violent physical attacks.

A continuous array of protests and criticisms have arisen from NGOs, the European Parliament and the Council of Europe. In the 1990s, a number of campaigns and initiatives are endeavouring to defend the right of asylum and to protect refugees in western Europe. The issue has gained greater prominence among NGOs, the churches, the legal profession and, to a lesser extent, among trade unions.

The organized sectors of civil society are challenging restrictions on asylum policies and holding up human rights. Against Charles Pasqua's statement 'La démocratie s'arrête ou commence la raison D'Etat', Gérard Soulier answers 'le respect du droit d'asile [est] preuve et garant du droit democratique' (Soulier 1987).

Beyond restrictionism and secrecy

In the post-Schengen and post-Dublin period EU states seem to be considering a comprehensive and long-term strategy aimed at reducing immigration through cooperation and the harmonization of policies. The first and main leg of this strategy relates to controls and restrictions at entry and prior to arrival through a tight and complete body of measures. Second, immigration over and above asylum is not completely ruled out, but harmonization is envisaged for selected and controlled cases – humanitarian aims and employment (Ad Hoc Group on Immigration 1991). A third area of policy includes the treatment given to asylum-seekers and reception facilities as well as the possibility of obtaining a de facto status. Fourth, additional long-term measures are mentioned, which relate not so much to limiting entry as to preventing departure from countries of origin. In the report to the Maastricht Summit these are encompassed under an analysis of the causes of immigration pressure followed by cooperation towards the removal of these pressures (European Council 1992). The Edinburgh meeting reiterated and elaborated on the principles guiding this cooperation. These include working towards the preservation and restoration of peace (as well as respect for human rights) in order to reduce flights into asylum, but also encouraging and helping displaced people to 'stay in the nearest safe area to their home'. General aid and economic cooperation leading to social and economic development are also mentioned.

It remains to be seen whether these measures will be made concrete or stay in the shape of '*voeux pieux*'. Will there be more 'openness and transparency'?

A noticeable change occurred after the signature of the Schengen and Dublin conventions. The outcry caused both by the substance of these conventions and the secrecy surrounding their preparation seems to have hit home among the governmental circles concerned. Note was taken of the considerable (and critical) attention attracted by the discussions having been held behind closed doors: 'the impression remains that there is insufficient transparency' (Ad Hoc Group on Immigration 1991). Its main preoccupation stems from the fact that the chances of success of this harmonization process will be influenced by society's perception of it (ibid.).

The Treaty on Political Union

The institutional framework for dealing with asylum policies in EU countries is likely to change in the future, how much and how fast is still to be seen. The greater measure of openness and consultation with the

Commission, and to a lesser extent with the European Parliament, follows from the Treaty on Political Union. A 'communitarization' of asylum issues is likely to take place away from intergovernmental agreements. Indeed asylum issues occupy a privileged position, for the separate declaration on asylum contained in the treaty stipulates that questions related to asylum policies will be a priority for a transfer to Community matters. However, it is still difficult to surmise what impact this situation will have on asylum and refugees in the EU.

The EU and eastern Europe

At the very beginning of the 1990s a major upheaval altered the map of Europe and had a profound impact on asylum issues, namely the dismantling of communist regimes and the end of the cold war. On the one hand it produced the lifting of exit controls in eastern European countries. On the other hand the crises and conflicts which ensued entailed a mass refugee movement from former Yugoslavia and the threat of further population movements from other parts. This has prompted a variety of initiatives.

Control and restrictions are the prevalent trend. One measure designed to control entry has been to impose visa requirements on nationals of eastern European countries, in particular when they are producing or likely to produce movements of population. Another initiative has been to prepare readmission agreements with 'frontline' eastern European countries bordering western Europe, thus creating a 'sanitary belt'. To deal with countries of origin some limited aspects of policies addressing the causes of population movements are also implemented at Community level.

Crisis in former Yugoslavia

As far as former Yugoslavia is concerned, most of the more specific decisions have been taken under pressure from the UNHCR. However, the level of coordinated response and burden-sharing for the admission of refugees from that region has remained disproportionately low and slow relative to the amplitude of the crisis and the magnitude of horrors.

At a meeting in London on 30 November 1992, the EU states adopted a resolution on people displaced by the conflict in former Yugoslavia (European Council 1992). In Copenhagen on 1 June 1993, the EU states adopted a resolution setting out certain guidelines on the admission of particularly vulnerable groups of persons from former Yugoslavia (European Council 1993). By then there were three million refugees from former Yugoslavia, of whom the vast majority had

remained within ex-Yugoslav territory, i.e. more than two million, while 650,000 were outside the territory of former Yugoslavia.

The crisis in former Yugoslavia has brought about a new arsenal of concepts and practices among Western countries' asylum policies, which will certainly set the tone for ulterior policies aimed at reducing the number of refugees received in western Europe.

Internalization

The notion of internalizing refugees means maintaining them within their area of origin in Bosnia-Herzegovina (Suhrke 1993); 'safe havens' were created to be guaranteed by and under the supervision of the UN, although it initially had not favoured this option.

Containment

If internalization was not possible EU states promoted containment, i.e. a narrow interpretation of regionalization whereby refugees should remain within the territory of former Yugoslavia (ECRE 1993a).

Temporary protection

Finally the main concept adopted and implemented is that of temporary protection. Temporary protection has entered the European scene *à l'Européenne*, i.e. with the sole prospect of returning as soon as the situation permits. This concept was the answer to the crisis in former Yugoslavia when admissions could no longer be avoided. But it has come to stay.

Conference on Security and Cooperation in Europe

The EU states have taken the lead in establishing exclusion and control zones. Former EFTA states are taking the hint and frontline eastern European states are drawn into agreements to further this strategy. However, one has to ask how far back exclusion and control zones can be pushed. It seems difficult to envisage any country agreeing to be the last-post settlement for all asylum-seekers. Therefore, it is likely that a consortium of the more vulnerable countries will call for more equitable burden-sharing. There are two possible fora for such a route.

One is the Council of Europe, which made reports and recommendations on these issues even before governments took much interest in a European view, and has also been integrating more and more European states. The Council of Europe included twenty-six members in 1992, four of which were eastern European states. The other forum is the Conference on Security and Cooperation in Europe

(CSCE), which augmented its interest in refugee issues at each of its meetings, for the developing situation demonstrated the salience of refugees for general security and stability.

The theme of migration and refugees is destined to occupy a key position in CSCE discussions as they relate so closely to both human rights and security concerns. The CSCE has the unique advantage of bringing together so many western and eastern European states at a time when refugee issues are exacerbated in Europe. It is a flexible mechanism with a tradition of openness; it has in the past relied on publicizing its debates widely for a maximum impact through public support (Lawyers Committee for Human Rights 1991). It has also given a specific place to NGOs and the UNHCR. This is evidenced by the incorporation of NGOs' submissions to the Helsinki document, albeit not in their entirety (Rudge 1991). The fact that the CSCE comprises countries of reception, transit and origin (ECRE 1993b) gives it more balanced orientation than that of, for instance, EU states and offers 'a particularly appropriate platform for a comprehensive approach to the search of durable solutions' (NGOs 1993). The CSCE Human Dimension Seminar on Migration including Refugees and Displaced Persons in Warsaw in April 1993 seems to have revealed three groups of countries. The EU states received strong criticism from other states. The former EFTA/Nordic states in part have a more open view on refugees and asylum, for example the Swedish government which submitted a proposal on temporary protection. Central and eastern European states are concerned about bearing the brunt of the refugee crisis in Europe. The Hungarian delegation for instance calls for more burden-sharing (Komoroczki 1993).

The CSCE had been posited in 1991 as the one organization with the potential to deal with asylum and refugee issues (Joly et al. 1992). This has been confirmed by the Warsaw human dimension seminar examined above. But it is only a first step concretized into mere statements. The role of the CSCE is not yet clear when it comes to practice and implementation.

Conclusion

The main trend in Europe, particularly in western Europe is still that of increased restrictions on asylum. EU states have kept their lead and march on with an accelerated process of harmonization of their policies. These are taking the shape of a coherent and watertight body of policies. Former EFTA states are following in the wake and will soon accede to the

relevant conventions. Moreover, readmission agreements with frontline eastern European countries establish a *cordon sanitaire* preventing entry into western states. From being the protection of refugees the main priority has now become the 'protection' of borders.

However, the greatest source of pressure brought to bear against western states' restrictive policies comes from eastern European countries, as they are potential countries of origin, transit and settlement for asylum-seekers. They might not be placated forever into readmission agreements by development programmes. And they are deeply concerned about potential influxes of population. Their views are best conveyed when they are gathered in a forum that puts EU states in the minority such as in the CSCE, where they also receive a certain measure of support from some former EFTA countries.

Finally, the central role of the UNHCR has been evidenced throughout the crisis in former Yugoslavia alongside NGO contributions which were at the forefront of promoting human rights and the rights of refugees.

References

Ad Hoc Group on Immigration (1991) *Report from the Ministers Responsible for Immigration to the European Council Meetings in Maastricht on Immigration and Asylum Policy*, Brussels, 3 December (WG1 9301 SN 4038/91)

Blaschke, Jochen (1989) 'Refugees and Turkish Migrants in West Berlin', in D. Joly and R. Cohen (eds) *Reluctant Hosts: Europe and its Refugees*, Aldershot: Avebury, 96–104

Commission of the European Communities (1992) 'Background Report: Immigration and Asylum', 10 March, ISEC B6 92

ECRE (European Consultation on Refugees and Exiles) (1993a) 'Temporary Protection Note', ad hoc meeting of ECRE agencies, Schiphol, 12 February

(1993b) Report of ECRE bi-annual general meeting, Berlin, 23, 24, 25 April

European Council (1992) *Conclusions of the Presidency*, European Council on Edinburgh

(1993) *General Secretariat of the Council Brussels*, 2 June 1993. Press release subject, Meeting of Ministers with responsibility for immigration, Copenhagen, 1 and 2 June

France Terre d'Asile (1992) Statistical leaflet, Paris: FTDA, June

Jaeger, Gilbert (1992) 'Comparative Asylum and Refugee Jurisprudence and Practice in Europe and North America', in Jacqueline Bhabha and Geoffrey Coll (eds) *Asylum Law and Practice in Europe and North America*, Washington: Federal Publications Inc., 1–8

Joly, D. and R. Cohen, (eds) (1989) *Reluctant Hosts: Europe and its Refugees*, Aldershot: Gower

Joly, D. with Clive Nettleton (1990) *Refugees in Europe*, London: Minority Rights Group

Joly, D. with Clive Nettleton and Hugh Poulton (1992) *Refugees: Asylum in Europe?*, London: MRG

Komoroczki, Istvan (1993) 'Opening Statement', head of

Hungarian delegation, MFA, CSCE Human Dimension

Seminar on Migration Including Refugees and Displaced Persons, Warsaw, 20–23 April

Lawyers Committee for Human Rights Europe (1991) 'Report on US Foreign Policy and Human Rights', topic II, Conference on Security and Cooperation in Europe, 1 September, Washington, DC: Patlon, Boggs and Blow

Melander, Goran (1987) *The Two Refugee Definitions*, Lund: Raoul Wallenberg Institute of Human Rights and Humanitarian Law, Report No. 4

NGOs (1993) 'NGOs Statement to Closing Plenary', CSCE Human Dimension Seminar on Migration, Including Refugees and Displaced Persons', Warsaw, 20–23 April

Rudge, Philip (1991) Letter from Philip Rudge, dated 24 September to Mr Pankin, His Excellency the Foreign Minister, Union of Soviet Socialist Republics, Moscow

Soulier, Gérard (1987) 'Le Respect du Droit d'Asile, Preuve et Garant du Droit démocratique', *France Terre d'Asile*, La Lettre d'information, Lettre No. 65, June.

Suhrke, Astri (1993) 'Safeguarding the Right to Asylum', International Conference on Population and Development 1994, Expert Group Meeting on Population Distribution and Migration, Santa Cruz, Bolivia, 18–22 January

SOVIET JEWISH EMIGRATION

TANYA BASOK AND ALEXANDER BENIFAND

Soviet Jewish emigration flows have fluctuated since the out-migration of Soviet Jews began in 1968. Until recently the emigration rate of Soviet Jews was kept in check by the Soviet authorities' reluctance to open the gates widely for all Jews to leave. At that time, western governments persistently insisted on the Soviet state recognizing the universal right to the freedom of movement. Eventually, most restrictions on Soviet Jewish emigration were lifted. Ironically, at that time western states started erecting walls to restrict the inflow. Unfortunately, it is in recent years that the rise of ultra-nationalism and anti-Semitism has put the life of Soviet Jews in real danger. At the time when Soviet Jews need protection the most, the Western countries have decided to curtail their admission levels for the former USSR. These two factors, Soviet emigration policies and western immigration quotas, are important in explaining fluctuations in Soviet Jewish emigration flows. But the explanation would be incomplete if we did not examine the internal conditions experienced by Soviet Jews and influencing their decision to leave the country.

Emigration flows

The history of Soviet Jewish emigration from 1968 to the present can be broken into four periods. The first period, from 1968 until 1973, was characterized by an ever-increasing outflow of Jews bound for Israel (see Table 14.8). Most of them were coming from the Soviet 'periphery' where Soviet Jews had maintained a strong Jewish identity and Zionist sentiments, making Israel an attractive point of destination. Between October 1968 and 1970, only 4235 Jews left. But already in 1970 considerably more Jews were emigrating to Israel. During the second period, from 1974 to 1979, both the destination and the origin of emigrants changed. Those leaving the Soviet Union started directing their steps to the USA and other Western countries, such as Canada, Australia and New Zealand. To facilitate this process, the Hebrew Immigrant Aid Society (HIAS) and the American Joint Distribution Committee (Joint) set up transitory camps in Vienna and Rome. By that time, even the

Table 14.8: *Soviet Jewish emigration, 1968–92*

Year	Volume	Year	Volume
1968	229	1981	9,447
1969	2,979	1982	2,688
1970	1,027	1983	1,314
1971	13,022	1984	896
1972	31,681	1985	1,140
1973	34,733	1986	914
1974	20,628	1987	8,143
1975	13,221	1988	19,365
1976	14,261	1989	72,500
1977	16,736	1990	201,300
1978	28,865	1991	197,000
1979	51,333	1992	152,100
1980	21,471		

Sources: 1968–84, Scherer (1985); 1985–88, Heitman (1989); 1989–92, Heitman (1993).

most assimilated Jews living in large urban centres in Russia and Ukraine became swept by the emigration wave. These migrants were interested in getting out of the Soviet Union but not in living in Israel. The first few years of this period were characterized by a drop in the levels of emigration. The number of Soviet Jewish immigrants started rising in 1978, reaching its peak by 1979. From then until 1987 there was a slump in Soviet Jewish emigration. Fewer emigrants left in the eight-year period from 1980 to 1987 than in the preceding year. But in the four years that followed, the emigration level increased almost twenty-five times. Then it started declining again (see Table 14.8). In the first five months of 1993, only 40,000 people left the Soviet Union (Hiatt 1993). In the early 1990s there was a sharp reversal of the earlier tendency of Soviet Jews to migrate to the West. In 1990, 90 per cent of all immigrants went to Israel. Since then the proportion of those destined for Israel has gone down, but has nevertheless remained significantly high: 74 per cent in 1991 and 44 per cent in 1992. In the first five months of 1993, half the Jewish emigrants leaving the former Soviet Union ended up in Israel (Hiatt 1993).

Internal conditions

The factors motivating Soviet Jews to leave their country include:

- anti-Semitism,
- disagreement with the political system,
- economic concerns,
- family reunification, and
- ethnic-religious reasons.

Anti-Semitism, both popular and at the level of state policies of employment and admission to educational institutions, has always been the most significant factor influencing the decision of Soviet Jews to emigrate (Benifand and Basok 1992; Feinstein 1981; Frankel and Jacobs 1981; Gilison 1981; Gitelman 1976; Glickman 1991; Levkov 1989; Simon and Simon 1985). As the intensity of anti-Semitism varied in the last twenty-five years so did the emigration flows.

The Soviet emigration in 1968 can, in part, be attributed to the rise in anti-Semitism in the USSR provoked by significant international events – principally the 1967 Arab–Israeli War and the unleashing of officially-sponsored anti-Semitism in Poland (Salitan 1992: 30). The trend continued into the 1970s. The regime became the sponsor of a strident anti-Semitic propaganda campaign masked as 'anti-Zionism' (Gilison 1989: 10–11). The Jewish emigration stirred a kind of anti-Jewish backlash, making the lives of those staying behind more difficult and forcing even more Jews to conclude that they and their children had no future in the Soviet Union, thereby prompting them to emigrate (Gilison 1989: 13).

In the early 1980s there was a temporary and short-lived retreat from overt and aggressive official anti-Semitism. In 1981, the Soviet regime, in its desire to discourage Jews from emigrating, announced a new policy towards Jews at the 26th Congress. Jews were now permitted to develop some rudiments of their culture; the mass media stopped putting out anti-Semitic propaganda and official educational and occupational discrimination was discontinued. Of course this new policy did not eliminate popular anti-Jewish prejudice and discrimination. Nor did it prevent the renewed prominence of officially inspired anti-Semitism during Israel's invasion of Lebanon in 1982 and 1983 (Friedgut 1989: 10–11).

Gorbachev's policy of *glasnost* created an atmosphere conducive to the development of cultural and religious self-expression and Jews were allowed to open Hebrew classes, synagogues, *yeshiva*s, cultural clubs and research centres. These positive developments, along with other exhilarating changes that the first years of *glasnost* and *perestroika* brought, gave hope to Soviet Jews. However, their optimism was short-lived because, along with improvements in Jewish cultural and religious life, an unprecedented growth of ultra-nationalist organizations unleashed open and aggressive grass-roots anti-Semitism, which alarmed many Soviet Jews. At the end of 1989 rumours of possible pogroms against Jews were widely circulating and announcements of possible dates and places of pogroms were made on radio and television. Although these rumours never materialized, they created panic and propelled even those Jews who had not yet considered emigration to request Israeli invitations for permanent settlement (*vyzovs*). The atmosphere of ethnic tension in which Jews are often blamed for the communist past and for the ills of today, has continued into the 1990s. But the fear that such a situation provokes in Jews has subsided because no mass-scale anti-Jewish violence has taken place. The attacks on Jews expressed in newspapers and on radio and television have become so common that they are often ignored by many, including Jews. They do not seem to go beyond mere words. And if they are just words, then throughout their lifetime, many Soviet Jews have developed immunity to them. However, as many Soviet Jews realize, current political developments in Russia suggest that mass violence against Jews will remain a strong possibility (Basok and Benifand 1993).

The significance of other factors prompting Soviet Jews to emigrate has also fluctuated. Most of those who emigrated in the 1970s and 1980s were dissatisfied with the political system (Feinstein 1981; Frankel and Jacobs 1981; Gitelman 1976; Levkov 1989). Political instability in the late 1980s and early 1990s, the rise of nationalism in many regions and former republics, and the government's failure to save the country from economic collapse, curb ethnic violence or control rising crime have also alerted many Soviet Jews into thinking of fleeing (Benifand and Basok 1992). In addition, family reunification has played an important role in the decision to emigrate (Simon and Simon 1985; Gitelman 1976; Levkov 1989). Not surprisingly, family reunification was less significant for the early arrivals than it was for those who followed them (Glickman 1991).

Although less important than the first two factors, better economic opportunities have also provided an incentive for Soviet Jews, subject to discrimination at work and in access to educational facilities, to leave (Frankel and Jacobs 1981; Gilison 1981; Markus and Schwartz 1984). This was not always the case. Thus, difficulties experienced by Soviet immigrants during the 1974–76 economic recession in the USA dissuaded their friends and relatives remaining in the Soviet Union from emigrating (Birman 1979: 55). At that time, unemployment and inflation in the USA and other Western countries seemed particularly discouraging, especially compared with the stable economy and almost universal employment in the Soviet Union. In the late 1980s and 1990s, the recession in the West began to look less gloomy than the hyperinflation, growing unemployment and scarcity of basic food staples in the former Soviet Union. At that time many Soviet Jews decided to leave for economic reasons (Benifand and Basok 1992).

Zionist sentiments played an important role in the early Jewish emigration of the late 1960s and early 1970s. Most of the people coming from the Soviet 'periphery' ended up in Israel. Among those who immigrated to the USA or other Western countries, ethnic factors (for example, the desire to practise Jewish religion and culture freely) did not play a significant role (Markus and Schwartz 1984; Zaslavsky and Brym 1983: 49). Even though in the late 1980s there was a rise in ethnic consciousness among Soviet Jews and Zionist ideas became more popular in the Soviet Union, ethnic factors continued to play a less significant role in their decision to emigrate (Benifand and Basok 1992).

Finally, in the late 1980s and early 1990s the growing crime rate and the environmental pollution and catastrophes became significantly alarming to prompt Jews to leave the country (Benifand 1992).

Soviet emigration policy

While the Soviet authorities have always regarded emigration with scorn, at times their policy was more relaxed. In the 1970s the authorities permitted a number of Jews to leave while still maintaining a restrictive emigration policy. Soviet Jews who desired to leave the country were harassed at every level of the bureaucracy. A variety of intimidating tactics, including threats, house searches, disruption of postal and telephone services, public denunciations in the work place, interrogations, short-term detention, military call-ups, incarcerations in psychiatric hospitals and 'show' trials, often followed by prison, labour camps or exile, were used in an effort to curb the growing movement (Salitan 1992: 36). For a short

time, from August 1972 to the beginning of 1973, an 'education surtax', or a compensation for education, was required from all applicants as a precondition for an exit visa. Permission to leave was denied to people in possession of 'state secrets'. Although this practice was in compliance with the international conventions on migration (for example Articles 12–13 of the 1966 International Covenant on Civil and Political Rights), this clause was misused by Soviet authorities who withheld permission to emigrate for indefinite periods, even in cases where there was no exposure to state secrets (Salitan 1992: 55–6).

In late 1979 Soviet emigration policy suddenly changed course. To prevent Jews emigrating *en masse*, interaction with Jews outside the Soviet Union was strictly prohibited. From 1980 to 1987 very few Soviet Jewish applicants were successful in getting their requests for exit visas approved. In the 1980s a new regulation was introduced requiring invitations from Israel to be sent by first-degree relatives (i.e. parents, children and siblings). Other mechanisms used to block the emigration movement included reducing the working hours of the Office of Visas and Registration in many cities (Alexander 1981: 8).

Democratization of Soviet society under Gorbachev also brought changes to its emigration policy and, in 1987, long-term *refuseniks* (those denied exit visas) were invited to reapply. Very little was done to deter emigration in the post-1986 period (Salitan 1992: 66). Some of the new ease in emigrating reflected compliance with agreements on freedom of movement reached at the November 1988–January 1989 meeting in Vienna of the Conference on Security and Cooperation in Europe (Salitan 1992: 66–7).

The 'state secret' clause was still used to deny exit visas to some applicants. The condition that invitations from only direct relatives were valid became entrenched in law. However, these restrictive measures did not impede the emigration of thousands of Soviet Jews.

Another important policy change was a decree of the Council of Ministers dated 28 August 1986, which removed the restriction on destination of the emigrant and thus enabled relatives from any country to send *vyzovs* to their family members (Friedgut 1989: 18). This policy change made it possible for those who wished to settle in the USA or other Western countries to apply for a visa to these countries directly from the Soviet Union. Consequently, in October 1989, the 'Vienna–Rome pipeline' was closed.

Western scholars vary in their explanation of changes in Soviet emigration policy. Some (for instance, Freedman 1989b and Goldman 1989) believe they reflect changing superpower relations and pressure from other Western countries. Others regard these factors as of only secondary importance, with domestic pressures and concerns being of primary significance (Brym 1988; Salitan 1992; Scherer 1985; Zaslavsky and Brym 1983).

Those emphasizing the role of external factors present the following arguments. The Kremlin's policy on emigration was a bargaining chip in political and trade negotiations with the USA and a reflection of the state of *détente*. Emigration decreased in 1974 after the passage by the US Congress of the Jackson-Vanik and Stevenson amendments, which refused the most-favoured-nation status to countries that denied their citizens the right to emigrate. The sharp increase in emigration levels in 1979 was caused by the legislation in the summer of that year superseding the Stevenson amendment, by the rumours that the waiver to the Jackson-Vanik amendment would be invoked in 1979, and to the signing of the SALT II Treaty in June. With the deterioration in US-Soviet relations as a result of the December 1979 Soviet invasion of Afghanistan, the presumed complicity of the Soviet Union in the imposition of martial law in Poland and the shooting down of a South Korean passenger jet by a Soviet fighter-plane in 1983, emigration dropped sharply. Finally, the increase in emigration in 1987 was a response to the thaw in US–Soviet relations initiated by Gorbachev and to agreements on freedom of movement reached at the Vienna meeting (November 1986–January 1989) of the Conference on Security and Cooperation in Europe (Freedman 1989a; Goldman 1989; see also discussion in Salitan 1992: 66–98).

There are others who argue that the Soviet authorities manipulated the emigration issue to gain concessions from the West while, in fact, responding to domestic concerns, such as pressures coming from the pro-emigration and dissident movements and labour supply and demand. The post-Stalinist political 'thaw' allowed for the re-emergence of the Zionist movement. At the same time, Jews participating in the dissident movement had realized by the late 1960s that democratic reform was impossible in the country and that emigration was the only possible solution for Jews. Emigration activists were becoming more daring, resorting to such tactics as demonstrations, hunger strikes, press conferences with foreign journalists, petitions, letters of protest, telegrams and declarations to Soviet and international bodies, *sumizdat* writings and official complaints made personally to authorities

responsible for emigration (Salitan 1992: 34; Zaslavsky and Brym 1983: 37–48). The initial decision to allow Jewish emigration was an attempt to curtail the emigration potential by permitting Jewish leadership and relatively small groups of Zionist-oriented Jews to leave (Salitan 1992: 86). Furthermore, in the 1970s, there was an oversupply of highly educated workers, many of whom were Jews. This explains why the Soviet authorities were so eager to part with their Jewish population (Brym 1988). The policy change in the early 1980s was a response to the general growth in repression in the country and to the re-emergence of labour shortages (Brym 1988; Salitan 1992: 96–7). Finally the 1987 policy turnaround was motivated by the decision to get rid of a large group of *refuseniks*, viewed by Gorbachev as a political liability, and as part of the general trend towards domestic liberalization (Salitan 1992: 98–101).

Immigration and resettlement policies

While Soviet emigration from the USSR was restricted, the USA and other Western countries generously accepted those Jewish immigrants who managed to get an exit visa. Until 1988 the US government admitted virtually all Soviet applicants coming through the Vienna–Rome 'pipeline' as refugees on the basis of 'presumptive eligibility', and no proof of a well-founded fear of persecution, as defined by the United Nations definition of a refugee, was required (Beyer 1992). Similarly in Canada, Soviet Jews were brought in as refugees under relaxed criteria (Basok 1992).

As the number of Soviet Jews (and other Soviet *émigrés*) started increasing dramatically in 1989, Western countries grew more concerned. In the USA the flood of Jewish immigrants came at a time of high budget deficits, increasing illegal immigration from Latin America and a growing 'compassion fatigue' with refugees. This led to a re-evaluation of the generous policy towards Soviet emigrants (Heitman 1989: 22). Two policy changes were introduced. In 1988 the US attorney-general decided to start direct processing of immigration applications in Moscow. In 1989 the 'Lautenberg Amendment' was introduced and it defined several categories of Soviets as targets of persecution, including Jews, Evangelicals and active participants in the Ukrainian Catholic Church and the Ukrainian Autocephalous Orthodox Church. However, these selection criteria apply only to those Soviet applicants with close family or other ties to the USA (Beyer 1992). In Canada important policy changes took place in 1990 when the special programme for Soviet and eastern European refugees was cancelled. Since then, those interested in immigrating to Canada have been able to apply to the Canadian consulate in Moscow as economic immigrants or under family reunification (Basok 1992). At the same time, it has become extremely difficult for Soviet Jews to obtain visitors' visas which they could use to apply for asylum while already in the USA or Canada.

In sum, Soviet Jewish emigration flows have fluctuated over the last twenty-five years in response to three factors – internal conditions experienced by Soviet Jews, Soviet emigration policy and Western immigration intakes. Now that Jews are most threatened by anti-Semitism in the former Soviet Union and the Soviet authorities are presenting the fewest obstacles to their departure, Western governments have introduced lower immigration quotas and have erected other obstacles to prevent Soviet Jews from arriving in their countries. Thus, the Soviet Jewish emigration flow is still kept in check.

References

Alexander, Z. (1981) 'Jewish Emigration from the USSR in 1980', *Soviet Jewish Affairs*, 11 (2), 3–21

Basok, T. (1992) 'Soviet Immigration to Canada: The End of the Refugee Program?', in T. Basok and R. J. Brym (eds) *Soviet Jewish Emigration and Resettlement in the 1990s*, Toronto: York Lanes Press, 141–57

Basok, T. and A. Benifand (1993) *Anti-Jewish Violence in Russia: Its Roots and Consequences*, Toronto: York Lanes Press

Benifand, A. (1992) 'Jewish Emigration from the USSR in the 1990s', in T. Basok and R. J. Brym (eds) *Soviet Jewish Emigration and Resettlement in the 1990s*, Toronto: York Lanes Press, 35–52

Benifand, A. and T. Basok (1992) 'Growing Anti-Semitism in Russia and the Refugee Movement', unpublished paper presented at Global Migration and Development Conference, Berlin, March

Beyer, G. A. (1992) 'The Evolving United States Response to Soviet Jewish Emigration', in T. Basok and R. J. Brym (eds) *Soviet Jewish Emigration and Resettlement in the 1990s*, Toronto: York Lanes Press, 105–39

Birman, I. (1979) 'Jewish Emigration from the USSR: Some Observations', *Soviet Jewish Affairs*, 9 (2), 46–63

Brym, R. J. (1988) 'Soviet Jewish Emigration: A Statistical Test of Two Theories', *Soviet Jewish Affairs*, 18 (3), 15–23

Feinstein, S. C. (1981) 'Soviet Jewish Immigrants in Minneapolis and St Paul: Attitudes and Reactions to Life in America', in D. N. Jacobs and E. Frankel Paul (eds) *Studies of the Third Wave: Recent Migration of Soviet Jews to the United States*, Boulder, CO: Westview Press, 57–76

Frankel Paul, E. and D. N. Jacobs (1981) 'The New Soviet Migration in Cincinnati', in D. N. Jacobs and E. Frankel Paul (eds) *Studies of the Third Wave: Recent Migration of Soviet Jews to the United States*, Boulder, CO: Westview Press, 77–114

Freedman, R. O. (ed.) (1989a) *Soviet Jewry in the 1980s. The Politics of Antisemitism and Emigration and the Dynamics of Resettlement*, Durham, NC: Duke University Press

(1989b) 'Soviet Jewry as a Factor in Soviet–Israeli Relations', in R. O. Freedman (ed.) *Soviet Jewry in the 1980s. The Politics of Antisemitism and Emigration and the Dynamics of Resettlement*, Durham, NC: Duke University Press, 61–96

Friedgut, T. (1989) 'Passing Eclipse: The Exodus Movement in the 1980s', in R. O. Freedman (ed.) *Soviet Jewry in the 1980s. The Politics of Antisemitism and Emigration and the Dynamics of Resettlement*, Durham, NC: Duke University Press, 3–25

Gilison, J. M. (1981) 'The Resettlement of Soviet Jewish Emigres: Results of a Survey in Baltimore', in D. N. Jacobs and E. Frankel Paul (eds) *Studies of the Third Wave: Recent Migration of Soviet Jews to the United States*, Boulder, CO: Westview Press, 29–56

(1989) 'Soviet Jewish Emigration, 1971–80: An Overview', in R. O. Freedman (ed.) *Soviet Jewry in the 1980s. The Politics of Antisemitism and Emigration and the Dynamics of Resettlement*, Durham, NC: Duke University Press, 3–16

Gitelman, Z. (1976) 'Demographic, Cultural, and Attitudinal Characteristics of Soviet Jews: Implications for the Integration of Soviet Immigrants', in J. M. Gilison (ed.) *The Soviet Jewish Emigre. Proceedings of the National Symposium on the Integration of Soviet Jews in the American Jewish Community*, Baltimore: Baltimore Hebrew College

Glickman, Y. (1991) 'Soviet Jewish Immigrants in Canada: Threat to Jewish Corporate Survival or Promise of Ethnic Renewal?', unpublished paper presented at the conference organized by the University of Toronto and the USSR Academy of Science, Moscow, 9–10 December

Goldman, M. I. (1989) 'Soviet-American Trade and Soviet Jewish Emigration: Should a Policy Change be Made by the American Jewish Community?', in R. O. Freedman (ed.) *Soviet Jewry in the 1980s. The Politics of Antisemitism and Emigration and the Dynamics of Resettlement*, Durham, NC: Duke University Press, 148–61

Heitman, S. (1989) 'Soviet Emigration Under Gorbachev', *Soviet Jewish Affairs*, 19 (2), 15–24

(1993) 'Jewish Emigration from the Former USSR in 1992', unpublished paper

Hiatt, F. (1993) 'Mountain Jews Leaving Russia, Biblical Ways Behind', *Washington Post*, 26 July

Levkov, I. I. (1989) 'Adaptation and Acculturation in the United States: A Preliminary Analysis', in R. Freedman (ed.) *Soviet Jewry in the 1980s. The Politics of Antisemitism and Emigration and the Dynamics of Resettlement*, Durham, NC: Duke University Press, 109–42

Markus, R. L. and D. Schwartz (1984) 'Soviet Jewish Emigres in Toronto: Ethnic Self-Identity and Issues of Integration', *Canadian Ethnic Studies*, 16 (2), 71–88

Salitan, L. P. (1992) *Politics and Nationality in Contemporary Soviet Jewish Emigration, 1968–89*, New York: St Martin's Press

Scherer, J. L. (1985) 'Soviet Emigration Policy: Internal Determinants', *Soviet Jewish Affairs*, 15 (2), 37–44

Simon, R. and J. L. Simon (1985), 'Social and Economic Adjustment,' in R. Simon (ed.) *New Lives: The Adjustment of Soviet Jewish Immigrants in the United States and Israel*, Lexington, MA: Lexington Books

Zaslavsky, V. and R. J. Brym (1983), *Soviet Jewish Emigration and Soviet Nationality Policy*, London and Basingstoke: Macmillan Press

PART FIFTEEN

EMERGING TRENDS

The purpose of Part 15 is threefold: first, to draw attention to new forms and patterns of world migration; second, to cover aspects of migration that gained only passing expression in the previous Parts of the *Survey*; and, finally, to assess the significance of global migration flows from ethical and political standpoints.

Often, of course, new forms of migration turn out to be older forms in fresh disguise. Thus it is with contract-labour migration, which *Castles* succinctly defines as 'temporary international movements of workers, which are organized and regulated by governments, employers or both'. As he notes, such migration has plenty of precedents – from the Asian indentured labour described in Part 2, the 'foreign Poles' who were recruited for industrial work in nineteenth-century Germany, the mine workers in South Africa and the Bracero Program in the USA, to the western European 'guest-worker' system. The intention of the employers and the government was twofold: to avoid any long-term commitment to the contracted migrants (thus allowing hiring and firing to match the economic cycles) and to inhibit settlement (thus reducing social costs and lessening the chance of resentment by the local workforce). These two desiderata still remain for many firms and governments. Source countries are now mainly in Asia (a region that provided nearly 12 million contract workers worldwide in the period 1969–89), though, as *Castles* shows, the Middle East has now declined in importance as a destination area in the wake of the Gulf War and the growth of demand in the emerging hothouse economies of Asia itself.

Contract labour of a very different sort is described by *Findlay* in his contribution on 'skilled transients'. As our author says, the phenomenon is rarely noticed and its volume has to be inferred from large aggregate data such as passenger surveys and population censuses. If we take Britain alone, 1.5 million British citizens emigrated in the 1980–90 decade, but 64 per cent of returning citizens had been away for three years or less. Not only were Britons leaving for contract work abroad; skilled and managerial personnel were entering Britain in significant numbers. How do we understand this phenomenon? When considering transients entering rich countries, what we are observing is largely a change in demand similar to that experienced by the indigenous labour force, as industrial employment shrinks and white-collar and information-related employment soars. At another level we are witnessing the increasing integration of the world economy as large multinationals post their workers abroad. The 'skilled transients' often remain invisible, probably for two reasons. First, the collective phenomenon is concealed by a host of individual decisions and arrangements between employer, employee, host and sending governments. Second, because the transients rarely make housing, health, educational or welfare claims on the destination governments (because these issues are covered contractually) their presence is unlikely to cause political objections.

Political passions are, however, aroused to a fierce pitch in the case of illegal workers, discussed by *Miller*. We have already covered, in earlier sections, illegal workers in Asia (with a specialist contribution on Japan) and undocumented Mexicans in the USA. However, this contribution provides a global picture of a global issue. One way to situate the phenomenon of worldwide illegal migration is to accept that it will ultimately be impossible to separate the free flow of people from

507

the free flow of capital, goods and ideas. Changes in the technology and prevalence of mass transport and in the awareness of it have uncovered fresh destinations so that, in addition to the well-trodden routes to North America, western Europe and Australia, the oil-rich states of the Middle East and the economic hothouses of East Asia have increasingly been brought into the world migration area. In 1994, fifty-one million travellers went through the turnstiles at London Heathrow airport alone, one-third of whom were in transit, connecting with flights to other destinations. Governments, of course, seek to regulate and control this movement, often with increasingly harsh immigration legislation and internal police measures designed to pick up illegal entrants. They have by no means lost the battle, but the sheer scale of movement is slowly beginning to tire the mightiest Leviathan.

I have suggested that the global flows of migrants are shifting away from old routes. *Skeldon* dramatizes this suggestion with a remarkable comment. From 4 May 1984 there were, according to his source, more aircraft above the Pacific than there were above the Atlantic. If this trend is confirmed, we will have reached a historical turning-point when the Atlantic system, on which generations of migration scholars have lavished their attentions, will be seen as of declining significance. The main supply countries, as may be expected, are the two giants, China and India, the main international destination the USA. However, that by no means tells the whole story – there are many other points of emigration and the Asia-Pacific area itself (excluding the west coast of the USA) has experienced considerable immigration. One important dimension of contemporary transpacific migration, which contrasts with the bulk of the transatlantic flow, is the practice of 'bilocality'. In this mode, the family is split, with the children (and sometimes the mother) being located at a destination country to secure residency, education and citizenship. The breadwinner, by contrast, might remain in Asia and vary his (it is normally a male) residence according to economic fortunes, political factors or the stage reached in work or family life.

I mentioned at the beginning of the section that the second function of Part 15 was to provide an opportunity for the further development of themes that were neglected or only lightly touched upon elsewhere in the *Survey*. This applies particularly to the next three contributions. The first, by *Chan Kwok Bun* and *Ong Jin Hui* considers the issue of 'ethnic entrepreneurship', a theme that has been uncomfortably poised between studies of race and ethnic relations, on the one hand, and the occupational and social mobility of immigrants, on the other. There is, of course, no need artificially to separate the two sub-fields, as the opportunities for entrepreneurship may crucially depend on the pattern of inter-ethnic interaction which may in turn be conditioned by the type, timing and numbers of immigrants from the particular group considered. There is an old sociological question that our contributors pose – does the very fact of immigration as a social process itself confer a sociological advantage? This question can be immediately spotted as a variation of Weber's famous hypothesis of 'the elective affinity' between Protestantism and capitalism. With a century's more observation of many successful non-Protestant entrepreneurs, we can pose the issue of whether Weber mistook the Protestant trees for the migrant wood. From this classical hypothesis, our contributors range far and wide in a comprehensive exposition and critique of the literature – particularly the contemporary US literature – on ethnic entrepreneurship.

Gugler, on the urbanization of the globe, is left to discharge the task of plugging an enormous gap created by my (sadly necessary) decision to focus the *Survey* as a whole on international migration. As is well known, the bulk of all migration is internal rural–urban migration, as villages empty and towns and cities are filled, often almost to breaking-point. With rare exceptions (apartheid South Africa and the Soviet Union being two), there have never been large-scale, systematic attempts to try to stop this rural–urban movement. *Gugler* makes the fair point that the level of urbanization is not that different from the equivalent historical levels in European settings. Rather, it is the rate of urbanization combined with lower mortality and increased birth rates that caused such intolerable burdens in many cities in poor countries. Some of the features that other authors have highlighted in international migrations are also visible to *Gugler* – the increasing prominence of women, the use of kin, family and friends to buttress the migration decision (not so much a new feature as a renewed emphasis in the literature), the phenomenon of bi-locality as migrants try to straddle the urban and rural world and the difficult social relations that arise in the new destinations.

The emerging significance of independent women migrants in internal settings is particularly stressed by *Gugler,* who records that women may now be dominant in rural–urban flows in Latin America, the Philippines, Thailand and Ethiopia. When we turn to the international setting, *Campani* also finds that migrating women are increasingly emerging as independent social actors. It is possible (as indeed *Gugler* suggested) that patriarchal domination in source areas is diminishing as old value systems erode and as the gender division of labour changes. That alone would account for much of the flow of women migrants. But *Campani* also emphasizes key shifts in demand. As service employment replaces industrial employment, as the formal economy gives way to the informal economy, new opportunities for women are created. Particular niches – in the entertainment and sex industries, in restaurants, bars and clubs, in nursing and domestic labour – also favour women, who are increasingly entering such occupations regionally and internationally.

With the increased volume and political sensitivity of world migration, the study of the phenomenon can no longer be confined to historians, geographers, sociologists and demographers, who have overwhelmingly dominated the field. Two particular fields have been added here to end this *Survey* – moral philosophy and international relations. In the former, *Bauböck* provides a succinct account of the central moral dilemma. On the one hand, states have always arrogated to themselves the right to control and police their borders. Indeed, that function is at the origin of the nation state and still provides a central meaning to the idea of the nation state, particularly since so many other functions have been reduced or lost to the maw of globalization. The authorities base their moral legitimacy to regulate immigration (though rarely emigration) on the grounds that they are protecting the interests, perhaps the rights, of their citizens and taxpayers. On the other hand, there is clearly a contrary right, which derives from humankind's common ownership of the earth and therefore (as Kant opined) a 'world citizen's right to free movement'. This dilemma is resolved by *Bauböck* in careful stages that need the reader's own attention.

The field of international relations too is now vitally concerned with the question of international migration. The more cynical among us may care to observe that as the threat of 'World Communism' disappeared after 1989, so other items seemed, almost mysteriously, to appear on the agenda papers of those institutions (like the North Atlantic Treaty Organization) concerned with world security. Now the key threats are 'Islam', 'Drugs' and 'International Migration' (sometimes in combination). Are such organizations simply trying to stay in business? Does the world system of states only function through a kind of free-floating anxiety that fixes on different objects as old foes appear as increasingly unlikely hazards? *Loescher* provides some reassurance that these surmises are somewhat too wild. There is indeed a legitimate concern that large-scale, sudden outflows of refugees and displaced persons can overwhelm weak state structures, particularly in Africa, Asia and central Europe. The forms of intervention that exist, namely humanitarian aid from agencies like the United Nations High Commission for Refugees, may now simply be inadequate to cope with the scale and ramifications of forced migration flows. Though certainly compromising the principle of state sovereignty, it may be that forms of preventive diplomacy and multilateral armed intervention may be necessary to stabilize the world disorder. It is a sobering note on which to end this *Survey*.

CONTRACT LABOUR MIGRATION

STEPHEN CASTLES

Contract labour migration may be defined as temporary international movements of workers, which are organized and regulated by governments, employers or both. Such movements have been significant since the late nineteenth century, and grew in volume considerably after 1945. Areas of destination for contract labour migrants have included most western European countries, the USA and, more recently, oil-producing countries and newly industrializing countries in Asia, Africa and Latin America. Contract labour migration is limited in duration. The period may be an agricultural season, the time it takes to carry out a construction project or a specified number of months or years.

Contract labour migration may be organized by the governments of sending or receiving countries, by employers, by special agencies – or by combinations of these. However, some participation by the government of the receiving country is necessary – otherwise the movement would be seen as a spontaneous or illegal one. Often contract labour migration is regulated by bilateral agreements between sending and receiving countries, or by multilateral agreements to which several states are party. The recruitment agreements or employment contracts may specify wage levels, duration of employment, working conditions and labour market rights of the workers. The agreements may also lay down obligations for the employers or public authorities to provide housing, family allowances, health care and social insurance. The recruitment agreements, together with laws and regulations of the receiving country, also define the legal status of the contract migrant with regard to residence and family reunion, as well as social, civil and political rights. Generally, the situation of the temporary workers is a highly restricted one which denies them many of the rights of citizens or permanent residents.

Historical antecedents

Contract labour migration may be seen as one form of 'unfree labour' (Cohen 1987) through which a group of workers is controlled by a regime that limits their rights compared with other workers. It is related to other forms of labour mobilization with coercive elements, such as recruitment of indentured workers from England for the early American colonies, and the large-scale use of indentured workers from India and China in the British and Dutch colonial empires in the nineteenth and early twentieth centuries. The South African mine labour system is a colonial type of contract labour migration that still exists today.

Contract migrant labour was important in European industrialization. In the late nineteenth century, workers of Polish ethnicity (but with German citizenship) moved west to provide labour for the new industries of the Ruhr. The eastern German *Junkers* (landlords) replaced them with 'foreign Poles'. Fearing that a Polish influx might weaken German control of the eastern provinces, the Prussian government introduced a rigid control system. 'Foreign Poles' were recruited as seasonal workers only, were not allowed to bring in dependants and had to leave German territory for several months each year. At first they were allowed to work in agriculture only, but were later permitted to take industrial jobs in Silesia and Thuringia, but not in the Ruhr. The migrant workers had to accept contracts laying down rates of pay and conditions inferior to German workers. Special police sections were established to deal with indiscipline through imprisonment or deportation. Such measures were deliberately used as a method to keep wages low and to create a split labour market (Dohse 1981: 33–83).

In France too, contract labour was recruited by farmers' associations and mines before 1914. During the First World War, recruitment systems were set up to bring in workers from southern Europe, North Africa and Indochina. After 1918, when war losses led to serious labour shortages, a sophisticated contract labour system was established. Labour agreements were concluded with Poland, Italy and Czechoslovakia. Recruitment was organized by the *Société générale d'Immigration* (SGI), a private body set up by farm and mining interests. Foreign workers were controlled through a system of identity cards and work contracts, and channelled into manual jobs in farming, construction and heavy industry. About 567,000 workers were recruited by the SGI in the

1920s. However, greater numbers – about 1.5 million – came spontaneously. In the Great Depression of the 1930s, many migrant workers were sacked and deported (Cross 1983).

The German and French experiences showed the value for employers of a contract labour force. It created a pool of cheap labour, which could be easily exploited and controlled, and deported if no longer required. The Nazis made extensive use of foreign labour – both forced and voluntary – to fuel their war machine. Dohse (1981) argues that the need for labour was one reason for the attack on Poland. By 1944, there were 7.5 million foreign workers in the Reich, of whom 1.8 million were prisoners of war. The Nazis took exploitation of rightless migrants to an extreme which can only be compared with slavery, yet its legal core – the sharp distinction between the status of national and foreigner – was to be found in both earlier and later contract labour systems.

The US Bracero Program

Although the USA is seen as a country of permanent immigration, use has been made of contract labour, especially for agriculture. Labour shortages in the First World War led to the admission of 76,802 Mexican workers, and smaller numbers from the Bahamas and Canada. In the Second World War, the US government created a Mexican labour programme (known as the Bracero Program, from the Spanish word for day-labourer). This was renewed during the Korean War and continued due to pressure from farmers until 1964. The *braceros* were mainly employed in the agribusiness of the south-western states, though some found industrial jobs in other regions. At the height of the programme in the mid-1950s, nearly half a million Mexican workers per year were involved. The regulations laid down wage protection, medical care, transportation, housing and other benefits, but little was done to enforce them. Braceros generally had poor pay and conditions, and this had negative effects on the situation of US workers – often themselves members of ethnic minorities, such as Chicanos and Afro-Americans (Briggs 1986: 996–99; Cohen 1987: 45–55).

The Bracero Program was stopped in 1964, but created migratory patterns which led to large-scale illegal movements, often resulting in settlement. Undocumented workers from Mexico, other Latin American countries and the Caribbean became an important and enduring part of the US labour supply. Border control and periodic crackdowns – such as 'Operation Wetback' in 1954, in which over one million illegal immigrants were apprehended – did little to stop the movements. The US government refused to penalize the employers, who had a strong interest in Mexican labour. The 1986 Immigration Reform and Control Act provided an amnesty for undocumented workers, with over three million applying. It also set up a Replenishment Agricultural Workers Program, to bring in legal contract workers, if a shortage of labour should develop. However, illegal migration continued.

Western European 'guest-worker' systems

In the post-war economic boom, virtually all western European countries made use of contract labour migrants, although in some cases this played a smaller part than entries from former colonies. Early examples were the British European Voluntary Worker scheme and the Belgium *contingenten-systeem,* which recruited workers from refugee camps (in the British case) and from Italy (in both cases), particularly for heavy industry. France established an *Office National d'Immigration* (ONI) in 1945 to organize recruitment of foreign workers from southern Europe. This included up to 150,000 temporary agricultural workers per year, and larger numbers for manufacturing and construction. However, the government soon lost control of movements, so that by the late 1960s over 80 per cent were coming illegally, with ONI regularizing their situation once they had found work.

Switzerland too followed a policy of large-scale labour import from 1945 to 1974. Workers were recruited abroad by employers, while admission and residence were controlled by the government. The basis principle was 'rotation': workers were to stay only a few years, and were forbidden to change jobs or bring in their families. By the the early 1970s foreign workers made up nearly one-third of the labour force. The need to attract and retain workers, together with diplomatic pressure from Italy, led to relaxations on family reunion and permanent stay, leading to settlement.

The key case for understanding the 'guest-worker system' was the highly developed state recruitment apparatus established by the Federal Republic of Germany (FRG). Starting in the late 1950s, the Federal Labour Office (*Bundesanstalt für Arbeit* – BfA) set up recruitment offices in the Mediterranean countries. Employers requiring foreign labour paid a fee to the BfA, which selected workers, checking their skills, health and police records. Employers had to provide initial accommodation. Recruitment, working conditions and social security were regulated by bilateral agreements between the FRG and the sending countries: first Italy, then Greece, Turkey, Morocco, Portugal, Tunisia and Yugoslavia. The number of foreign workers in the FRG rose from 95,000 in 1956 to 1.3 million in 1966 and 2.6 million in 1973. Foreign women played a major part, especially in the later years: their labour was in high demand in industries like textiles, clothing and electrical goods.

German policies conceived migrant workers as temporary labour units, which could be recruited, utilized and sent away again as employers required. To enter and remain in the FRG, a migrant needed a residence permit and a labour permit. These were granted for limited periods, and were often valid only for specific jobs and areas. A worker could be deprived of his or her permit for a variety of reasons, leading to deportation. Entry of dependants was discouraged, but it proved impossible to prevent family reunion and settlement. Some migrants were able to get employers to request their spouses as workers. Competition with other labour-importing countries for workers led to relaxation of restrictions on entry of dependants in the 1960s. Families became established and children were born. Foreign labour was beginning to lose its mobility, and social costs (for housing, education, health care) could no longer be avoided. When the federal government stopped labour recruitment in November 1973, the motivation was not only the looming 'oil crisis', but also the belated realization that permanent immigration was taking place.

The case of the FRG shows both the principles and the contradictions of contract labour systems. These include the belief in temporary sojourn, the restriction of labour market and civil rights, the recruitment of single workers, the inability to prevent family reunion, the gradual move towards longer stay, and the inexorable pressures for settlement. Contract worker migration to western Europe was virtually stopped after 1974. However, the now-established migratory chains continued through entries of family members, illegal workers and asylum seekers, while the former migrant workers were transformed into new ethnic minorities (Castles et al. 1984).

Labour migration to oil countries
The rapid increases in oil revenues after 1973 encouraged oil-producing countries to embark on ambitious programmes of construction and industrialization. The Arab oil countries hired expatriate experts in Europe, the USA and in other Middle East

countries. Low-skilled workers came from Arab countries, such as Egypt, Yemen and Jordan, as well as from Asian countries, particularly India, Pakistan, Bangladesh, Sri Lanka, the Philippines and South Korea. The total number of foreign workers in the six Gulf Cooperation Council states (Bahrain, Kuwait, Oman, Qatar, Saudi Arabia and the United Arab Emirates) rose from 685,000 in 1970 to 2.7 million in 1980, when they made up 70 per cent of the total labour force (Birks et al. 1986: 801). Libya recruited workers in Egypt, Tunisia and other parts of Africa. Non-Arab oil state like Venezuela and Nigeria also employed large numbers of migrant workers, though most came spontaneously rather than through contract labour systems.

The distinguishing feature of labour recruitment to the Arab oil countries was the high degree of regulation, designed to prevent settlement. Arrangements varied: most Arab workers came spontaneously, but were subject to strict control once in the country. As time went on, the Gulf monarchies became worried about threats to labour discipline and public order allegedly posed by Arab workers, especially Palestinians and Yemenis. They therefore increased reruitment from South and Southeast Asia. The movements were organized by the governments of both sending and receiving countries, as well as employers and special recruiting agencies. The Philippine government established an Overseas Employment Administration to encourage migration and to safeguard workers' conditions. In some cases, workers were recruited by international construction firms which were undertaking major projects in the oil states. Korean building companies made a successful business of providing their own labour – a practice enouraged by strict government control. By contrast, most workers from South Asia were recruited through private agents based in the countries concerned. This gave rise to a lucrative 'migration industry', which increased the impetus to move abroad, even when governments wanted to restrict migration (Abella 1992: 150–2).

Between 1969 and 1989, nearly 12 million Asians are estimated to have worked in other countries, mainly the Middle East. At first the great majority were men, but the proportion of women migrating as domestic servants, nurses or office workers increased over time. Worker rights were highly restricted: migrants were not allowed to settle nor bring in dependants, and lacked civil or political rights. They were generally segregated in barracks. They could be deported for misconduct, and were often forced to work very long hours. Women domestic workers were subjected to exploitation and sexual abuse. The big attraction for workers was the wages: often ten times as much as could be earned at home. However, wage levels declined during the 1980s as labour demand fell, and competition between labour-sending nations increased. Many migrant workers were exploited by agents and other intermediaries, who took large fees (up to 25 per cent of their first year's pay). Agents sometimes failed to keep their promises concerning employment, transportation, wages and working conditions.

The governments of labour-sending countries saw the migrations as vital to their development programmes, partly because they hoped they would reduce unemployment and provide training and industrial experience, but mainly because of the worker remittances. Billions of dollars were sent home by workers, making a vital contribution to the balance of payments of countries with severe trade deficits, such as Pakistan and India.

The vulnerability of contract workers was demonstrated in the mid-1980s, when oil prices fell and labour demand declined. There were mass expulsions from Nigeria in 1983 and 1985 and from Libya in 1985. The 1990/1 Gulf crisis led to even greater disruption: some migrants were killed or injured, and many more endured hardship when forced to flee the area. An estimated five million people were displaced, resulting in enormous loss of remittances and income for countries from Southeast Asia to North Africa. After the crisis, many workers did return to Kuwait and other Gulf countries, but at the same time new patterns of labour migration were becoming evident within Asia.

Labour migration in Asia

In recent years rapid economic growth and declining fertility have led to considerable demand for migrant labour in some Asian countries, including Japan, Hong Kong, Taiwan, Singapore and oil-rich Brunei. South Korea and Thailand are on the verge of making the transition from labour export to import.

Japan has been experiencing severe labour shortages in recent years. In the 1980s, increasing numbers of women were admitted mainly from Pakistan, the Philippines, Bangladesh and Korea to work as waitresses and entertainers. They were followed by male compatriots, who worked – generally illegally – as factory or construction workers. The Japanese government is reluctant to introduce a contract labour system, due to fears of overpopulation and concern to preserve ethnic homogeneity. In 1990, revisions to the Immigration and Refugee Recognition Law introduced severe penalties for illegal foreign workers and their employers. However, various arrangements tantamount to a 'backdoor' contract labour system were permitted. These included recruitment of unskilled foreigners of Japanese origin (the so-called 'Japanese Brazilians'), employment of 'trainees' from developing countries in industry, and admission of foreigners who register as students of Japanese language schools and are allowed to work twenty hours a week. Once Japan comes out of the recession of the early 1990s an official contract labour scheme seems probable.

Singapore is heavily dependent on unskilled workers from Malaysia, Thailand, Indonesia and the Philippines: about 160,000 foreign workers make up 11 per cent of the labour force. They are strictly controlled. The government imposes a foreign worker levy (S$300 in 1990) to equalize the costs of foreign and domestic workers. Unskilled workers have to rotate every few years and are not permitted to settle or to bring in their families. Unskilled workers are forbidden to marry Singaporeans and women have to undergo regular pregnancy tests. In 1989 there was an amnesty for illegal workers, after which a mandatory punishment of three months jail and three strokes of the cane were introduced. On the other hand, Singapore is eager to attract skilled and professional workers, particularly those of Chinese ethnicity from Hong Kong. They are encouraged to settle and are quickly granted permanent residence status (Skeldon 1992: 44–6).

Fast-growing countries like Korea and Thailand are sending fewer workers abroad, as job opportunities open up locally. In 1983, 225,000 Korean workers were abroad, of whom 42 per cent were construction workers. By 1989 only 76,000 were abroad, of whom 10 per cent were construction workers. Korea is considering recruiting unskilled workers from China (Martin 1991: 188). In Thailand, Burmese and Cambodians work on the farms of the north-east, many of which belong to migrants who are in the Middle East. Brunei has about 40,000 foreign workers, over 40 per cent of the labour force. Hong Kong has shortages of both skilled and unskilled workers. Some unskilled workers are recruited legally from China. There are also foreign workers from the Philippines and South Asia, and even from Nigeria. In all these cases, the number of illegals considerably exceeds the legal contract workers. Taiwan is one of the world's most densely populated countries, yet economic growth has led to labour shortfalls. There are thought to be up to 300,000 illegal workers, and the government has now decided to admit foreign workers on one-year visas.

Conclusions and perspectives

Contract labour migration is often portrayed as a highly organized system of labour recruitment to meet temporary needs, such as rapid economic growth, industrialization, special construction projects or reconstruction after a war. The workers are supposedly brought to the receiving country for a specific period, do not seek social integration, send their savings home and are repatriated when the job is completed. The reality is usually different. Many receiving countries have used contract workers to meet long-term labour needs. Length of stay has increased, both because employers still needed the workers and because the migrants did not wish to return. The US Bracero Program and the European 'guest-worker' systems demonstrate how contract labour systems can establish migratory flows, which continue in new forms even when receiving governments try to stop them. The result is permanent settlement and formation of ethnic minorities. Such groups tend to be disadvantaged and socially isolated, because of their legal status as non-settlers without citizenship rights. Hostile reactions from local populations are exacerbated by the fact that governments have portrayed the movements as temporary ones, which would not lead to settlement.

Many contract labour systems have been poorly organized, workers have been employed under exploitative conditions, and their special status has denied them recourse to normal legal or political remedies. Trade unions in receiving countries have been faced with the dilemma of opposing contract labour because it might damage the conditions of local workers, or trying to organize the migrants to prevent abuse. The borderlines between contract labour migration, individual temporary labour migration and illegal movements are often fluid. This is especially evident in the case of contemporary labour movements in Asia. Governments may tacitly accept illegal movements because it is politically inopportune to set up a contract labour system; this applies as much to Japan today as it did to the USA after the abolition of the Bracero Program in 1964.

In the past, contract labour migration concerned predominantly low-skilled workers going to a limited number of destinations. Today, contract labour

arrangements are to be found in many parts of the world, and their scope and range is increasing. This brief survey has described only a few important cases. Other examples include the recruitment by Nigeria of skilled personnel such as teachers from the Philippines. Australia's Northern Territory Trade Development Zone encouraged the entry of Chinese workers who produced goods for offshore countries at wage rates far below official levels, until local trade unions intervened. Many highly-skilled workers, such as managers, financial experts and technicians migrate on temporary employment contracts. It is hard to draw a precise line between the privileged 'professional transients' moving within international labour markets and the vulnerable low-skilled migrants.

These shifts, and the slippage between contract labour migration and other forms of migration, indicate that the phenomenon cannot be usefully analysed in isolation. Contract labour migration is just one aspect of the increasing global mobility of people, which in turn is closely linked to growing movements of capital, commodities and ideas (Castles and Miller 1993). With rapid improvements in transport and communication, and the growth of migration networks, old distinctions between labour migration, settler migration and movements of asylum-seekers are breaking down. Movements can no longer be clearly separated into permanent or temporary, and migration chains are becoming two-way streets.

References

Abella, M. (1992) 'The Troublesome Gulf: Research on Migration to the Middle East', *Asian and Pacific Migration Journal*, 1 (1), 145–67

Birks J. S. et al. (1986) 'Migrant Workers in the Arab Gulf: The Impact of Declining Oil Revenues', *International Migration Review*, 20 (4), 799–814

Briggs, V. M. Jr (1986) 'The "Albatross" of Immigration Reform: Temporary Worker Policy in the United States', *International Migration Review*, 20 (4), 995–1019

Castles, S. and M. J. Miller (1993) *The Age of Migration: International Population Movements in the Modern World*, London: Macmillan Education

Castles, S. et al. (1984) *Here for Good: Western Europe's New Ethnic Minorities*, London: Pluto Press

Cohen, R. (1987) *The New Helots: Migrants in the International Division of Labour*, Aldershot: Avebury

Cross, G. S. (1983) *Immigrant Workers in Industrial France: The Making of a New Laboring Class*, Philadelphia: Temple University Press

Dohse, K. (1981) *Ausländische Arbeiter und bürgerliche Staat*, Konistein/Taunus: Hain

Martin, P. L. (1991) 'Labor Migration in Asia: Conference Report', *International Migration Review*, 25 (1), 176–93

Skeldon, R. (1992) 'International Migration Within and From the East and Southeast Asian Region: A Review Essay', *Asian and Pacific Migration Journal*, 1 (1), 19–63

SKILLED TRANSIENTS: THE INVISIBLE PHENOMENON?

ALLAN M. FINDLAY

In most advanced economies there is a significant level of international migration which goes unnoticed. It is not noticed because it poses no threat in terms of perceived social and economic burdens for the sender and host societies, as well as often being invisible in terms of ethnicity. These invisible migration streams are made up of highly skilled persons moving internationally on relatively short-term assignments before returning to their place of origin or transferring to another international location. It is the purpose of this chapter to review this 'skilled transient' phenomenon and to consider its growing significance as a feature of population circulation in the global economy.

This contribution commences by considering the scale and characteristics of this type of migration.[1] This is followed by consideration of the processes responsible for initiating and sustaining the circulation of skilled transients within the changing world order. This leads to the issue of whether those participating in international skill exchanges, either through intra-company transfers or through other channels, are acting purely as pawns in a complex global labour market requiring an ever increasing mobility among certain skill groups, or are themselves opportunists exploiting the lucrative packages offered to staff willing to undertake foreign assignments.

From settlers to skilled transients

Many countries in western Europe have a long history of settler emigration. For example, Britain is estimated to have lost seven million people by emigration between 1851 and the end of the nineteenth century. Although Baines (1991) and others have shown that significant numbers of migrants subsequently returned home for a variety of reasons, most emigrants from Britain may be considered to be settler migrants since they left with the purpose of settling permanently in other countries and in particular in the countries of the Old Commonwealth and the USA. Different destination patterns, but similar underlying settler emigration processes, could be traced for many other West European countries.

Table 15.1: *International migration of British citizens, 1979–90 ('000s)*

	79–81	82–84	85–88	89–90
Inflows	205	287	329	299
Outflow	440	412	370	400
Inflow:outflow	1:2.2	1:1.4	1:1.1	1:1.3

Source: OPCS (1991)

It would be wrong to think that the exodus of British citizens is something of the past, but the character and purpose of movement have changed dramatically. According to the British International Passenger Survey almost 1.5 million British citizens emigrated from the UK between 1980 and 1990, but as Table 15.1 shows this outflow must be set against a substantial inflow of British citizens. The sizeable inflows do not reflect an increase in a 'return of failure' or any other traditional form of return movement (King 1986). They indicate a rise of circulatory movements of British citizens going to live or work abroad for short time periods of two or three years before returning to the UK. For example, 64 per cent of British citizens entering the UK in 1991 were persons who had been abroad for three years or less. Similar trends towards an increase in transient migration have been reported for many of the more advanced nations in the world economy (Ford 1992; Salt and Findlay 1989).

In the first half of the 1980s there was a clear rise in the proportion of immigrants to the UK who were re-entrants (i.e. people returning to the UK who had previously resided there). Associated with this trend towards increased transient migration was an identifiable shift towards an increased proportion of professional or managerial immigrants. Among actively employed migrants in the re-entrant flow, professional and managerial staff rose from 56 per cent of the total in 1980 to 73 per cent by 1985. Among all immigrants (i.e not just re-entrants) the number defined as belonging to the professional and

515

Table 15.2: *Professional and managerial immigration to the UK under the work permit scheme, 1984–90*

Year	1984	1985	1986	1987	1988	1989	1990
Professional and managerial staff	6,957	7,515	8,103	8,170	10,789	13,156	15,356
Professional and managerial staff as % of all work permits	85.9	85.3	85.3	84.0	84.8	83.0	80.8

managerial occupations more than doubled during the 1980s. Given this trend it would seem that Appleyard's (1985) term 'skilled transient' serves as a useful descriptor of a very significant part of British immigration in the 1980s. Similar trends were also evident among non-British citizens coming into the country under the fixed-term work permit scheme. As Table 15.2 shows between 80 and 90 per cent of all work permits issued by the UK to non-EU citizens were given to professional or managerial staff.

Not only were professional and managerial employees the dominant group among skilled transients entering the UK in the 1980s, but there was also an increased demand in the UK for this kind of labour. A work permit is only issued by the British Department of Employment if it considers that no suitable resident labour exists to fill a particular post. Employers of immigrants under the work permit scheme must guarantee that the job is being made available at wage levels and under conditions that are no less favourable than would be offered to a British employee. Despite these controls, which quite rightly seek to protect the domestic labour market, the number of work permits issued continued to rise during the late 1980s and early 1990s. This was despite rising domestic unemployment. This paradoxical situation reflected a growing demand for the very specific types of skills offered by skilled transients. Employers using the scheme appear to have favoured particular types of skills such as experience of work in large companies in other parts of the world economy and especially experience of working for their own company in other parts of its international operations. To quote from Ford (1992: 31): 'Large organizations require individuals able to offer more general management skills across many different divisions or locations. Often these skills are more specific to the organization than they are to any one task or responsibility.'

Before considering the processes responsible for generating skilled transient flows in more detail, it is valuable to identify three more general characteristics evident from the study of secondary data sets

concerning skilled international migration. The first of these is the scale of the process, second the time dimension of these movements and third the spatial selectivity of the transfers.

The figures included in Table 15.2 suggest quite a limited scale of movement, albeit relating to a rising trend. It should be remembered, however, first that the statistics relate only to immigration to the UK of non-EU citizens and second that Table 15.2 excludes the dependants of immigrants. Researchers looking at skilled transient migration to other parts of the globe note a rising and ever more significant role for this type of movement.

'Highly skilled workers are a major element in current European migrations, their relatively small numbers belying their economic importance. ... It is difficult to see anything but a general increase in the migration of high level skills as all modern economies engage in brain exchanges' (Salt 1993: 15). Salt notes, for example, the 40 per cent growth which has taken place in the 1980s in the numbers of foreign scientists, managers and administrators in the Netherlands compared with a 10 per cent growth in other immigrant employment. Between 1984 and 1990 Britain's stock of immigrants from other EU countries rose by 29 per cent to 889,000. Although Labour Force Survey information on this immigrant group is limited, the 1990 survey shows that EU immigrants (excluding the Irish) are more likely to belong to professional and managerial occupations than the British-born population (Findlay 1992: 23). The numerical significance of skilled transients can be better assessed when one compares Home Office statistics for the level of immigration of work permit holders and their dependants with data for other kinds of immigration. In 1992 the scale of transient migration associated with the work permit scheme lay at 51,100 persons, roughly similar with the level of overall settler immigration (52,600) permitted under current immigration legislation.

Turning to the time dimension of skilled transient migration, it is interesting to note that significant differences exist in the length of expatriate postings.

This varies both in terms of the destination region and company culture involved. Research among large companies involved in inward investment to Hong Kong found that typically Japanese companies sent expatriate staff for four to five years, while American companies deployed expatriates for only one or two years. Variations in the duration of foreign postings also seem to be changing over time. The British work permit scheme indicates a switch to shorter expatriate postings over time by companies bringing staff into the UK. From a situation of near parity in 1989/90, short-term permit issues (less than twelve months) rose by 1992 to account for two and half times the number of longer-term permits.

The geographical pattern of skilled transient flows is the final dimension of this phenomenon which is worthy of consideration before turning to more detailed discussion of the underlying processes. A register of expatriate labour use, established by the US Employment Relocation Council to monitor the staffing policies of major US companies, indicates a very widespread global presence of US expatriates (Salt and Findlay 1989). Within the general pattern of a global spread of small pools of expatriates there exist identifiable regional concentrations. For example, western Europe had more than three times as many US expatriates as any other world region. Beaverstock (1992) has suggested that within western Europe, the USA and Japan there exists a small set of global cities which are the particular focus for highly skilled business migrants.

Patterns of migrant origin show an even stronger concentration than patterns of destination. In 1990, for example, the USA and Japan accounted for 45 per cent of all long-term work permits and first permissions given by the UK. A similar pattern exists for skilled migration to Australia. Setting aside the regional labour market effect of links between Australia and New Zealand, the USA, Japan and the UK emerge as the lead sender countries (Ford 1992).

In this section I have sought to establish a picture of skilled transient migration. The fragmentary evidence available for this small but ever increasing category of movements suggests that it consists of highly skilled persons moving for short time periods (perhaps of increasingly short duration) between core countries of the global economy such as the USA, Japan and those of western Europe. Although the pattern of interaction is a global one, the intensity of interaction is greatest between these core regions. Because of the temporal and socio-professional composition of these migration flows it is not surprising that in many respects it has gone almost unnoticed. In the remainder of this contribution I argue that the significance of these 'invisible' migrants should not be under-emphasized, and that they provide a good example of a migrant group providing key economic benefits both to employers and to host societies.

International skill exchanges through intra-company transfers

Many mechanisms account for the increased circulation of highly skilled persons around the globe. Gould (1988) has suggested a typology of such flows including the international movement of people for training, the self-generated flow of professional expatriates towards locations offering them lucrative returns for their skills, and the transfer by large companies of skilled staff from one country to another within their internal company labour markets. Findlay (1990) has suggested that the last of these categories constitutes a distinctive migration channel which is powered by economic trends towards the globalization of production. By contrast professional expatriates moving outside the organizational framework of large international companies may have their movements 'channelled' by other gatekeepers such as international recruitment agents. Garrick (1991) has sought to extend this channels framework and has identified from a survey of Scottish skilled emigration the existence of several other significant migration channels. The importance of the channels concept lies in the suggestion that explanation of international skill transfers lies at levels other than the motives and abilities of the individual migrant and that the hierarchically organized global system of production has produced new influences which have actively structured the character of skill exchanges between countries. A number of migration channels are now discussed in greater detail.

By far the greatest attention in skilled migration research has been devoted to the role of large companies in influencing migration patterns through facilitating intra-company transfers. The global shift of investment by large employers to locations where production is possible at lower wage levels than in the older industrial economies has 'necessitated the transfer of an increasing number of managerial and technical staff to supervise operations resulting from foreign investments' (Findlay and Gould 1989: 4). Salt (1988) has argued that these transfers have been achieved to a considerable extent by firms organizing the international transfer of their staff within their labour markets. It is not simply that large companies

Table 15.3: *Expatriates working for companies involving overseas investment in Hong Kong by job nature and migration channel, 1991*

Job type	MIGRATION CHANNEL			
	Intra-company transfer	Other expatriate labour	Imported labour scheme	Immigrants as % of all employees
Operatives	322	258	602	2.6
Technicians	119	24	41	3.0
Research and development*	224	74	16	7.8
Managerial	573	222	125	14.9
Other	52	41	91	1.0
Total	1209	638	875	3.6

Source : Adapted from Hong Kong Government Industry Department (1992: 98).
*Research and development category includes operation staff

need particular specialist skills at a range of international locations and can achieve this by moving staff from country to country (this type of skill demand could arguably be met less expensively by hiring local skilled labour). What the internationalization of business activities seems to have produced is the need for large companies to have mobile managerial staff, who not only know their job, but who also know their company. For the individual migrant international moves such as these become attractive through inducements offered by the employer including career advancement and lucrative expatriate employment packages that may include free or subsidized housing and foreign posting allowances.

There is much evidence to support this linkage between the emergence of skilled transient flows, particularly between the older industrial economies and the newly industrializing countries, and the conception of a 'new international division of labour' as defined by Fröbel et al. (1980). It is in these terms, for example, that Salt and Findlay (1989) explain the increased level of skill flows from developed to developing countries as well as the complex pattern of expatriate usage by American companies referred to above. Salt (1992: 11) notes that more than four out of ten work permits issued by the UK in 1990 related to intra-company transfers, and that this was part of a sustained upward trend.

Beaverstock (1992) has developed these ideas relative to the role of world cities (Sassen 1991) as critical nodes in the ownership, locational organization and internationalization of capital (Dunning 1988; Thrift 1987). Highly skilled professional and managerial skills, it was argued, were directed towards world cities such as London, New York,

Tokyo, Paris and Hong Kong because these had become key locations where corporate capital was concentrated. This geographically uneven international division of highly skilled labour was interpreted as being due to at least two interlocking forces – the uneven spatial organization of structures (Sassen 1988) and the uniqueness of specific geographical labour markets in terms of their structure and combinations of labour quality (Smith 1989). While not conducting the role of internal labour markets within large companies in facilitating intra-company transfers between world cities, Beaverstock (1992: 17) adds that 'the attractiveness of working and living in a world city … is strengthened by the possibility of higher wages and by the cultural facilities and amenities offered by them'. This is an interesting comment, hinting as it does at the idea that highly skilled persons may be strongly attracted to certain types of global location and may seek to move to these locations independently of whether they can transfer within a formal migration channel, such as that provided by the internal labour market of a large company.

Table 15.3 provides an empirical lens through which the importance of intra-company transfers can be compared with other channels of international skilled migration. It provides occupational and migration channel data for expatriates working for companies in Hong Kong which involve an element of foreign investment. The data were collected by the Hong Kong Government Industry Department in 1992 in relation to 536 inward investment companies. It shows first of all that the largest single migration channel by which these expatriates entered Hong Kong was through intra-company transfers. It also shows that use of expatriates by job type varied substantially with expatriates making up almost 15 per cent of the managerial staff of these companies, but only 3 per cent of technical and operative staff.

The data presented in Table 15.3 can be taken as partial evidence of the operation of internal labour markets and intra-company transfers as the mechanisms responsible for significant levels of skilled transient movement. Equally it is important to note from Table 15.3 that even within the internal labour markets of large companies such as those responsible for inward investment in Hong Kong (the archetypal environment in which one would expect intra-company transfers to be a powerful explanatory element of the skill exchange system) one can find significant numbers of expatriates who have moved internationally by other means. This leads to the useful question as to why the proposed explanatory mechanism (intra-company transfers) is not more powerful. Two possible categories of answer immediately emerge. First, one could search for other structural devices such as other channels which could offer an explanation of the phenomenon. Second, one could suggest that the framework itself is flawed and that the actions of skilled transients should not be interpreted as mere responses to external structures, but reflect intentional and meaningful behaviour negotiated by individuals relative to their changing position in a complex international labour market. Only the former option can be explored within the scope of this chapter.

A diversity of migration channels

That skill transfers take place through many channels and not only through intra-company transfers is clear. Table 15.3, for example, shows the existence of a migration channel in Hong Kong referred to as 'the imported labour scheme'. Under the scheme companies apply to the government for permission to introduce, for a limited time period, a quota of migrant labour (mainly from China) to carry out specific tasks for their company. The migrants have a range of skill levels, but are significantly less skilled than the Hong Kong workforce, largely filling jobs which Hong Kong workers would not accept because of the low wages and the much more lucrative and higher status work opportunities available to them. The scheme operates in the context of Hong Kong's labour market with its minimal levels of domestic unemployment, high labour turnover and potentially inflationary wage situation. Unlike the former guest-worker system in western Europe the scheme enforces

the return of migrants after the contract is completed, with firms eager to comply with the official regulations in fear of being disqualified from future participation in the system. This category of migration, like the intra-company transfer channel, places explanation of the process primarily in the sphere of the external structural constraints on the system. Other structurally imposed migration channels identified by researchers include international recruitment agencies (Gould 1987) and international linkages between professional institutions (Garrick 1991).

Pursuing the view that a fuller understanding of skilled transience can best be achieved by analysis of a wider set of migration channels, one can readily find evidence of a diversity of channels accounting for the range of mobility types identified by Gould (1988) For example, the international movement of people for training has both increased and changed over time in relation to the emergence of new international training programmes. Within the EU this trend is evident in the complex network of inter-institutional linkages established between European universities to facilitate the temporary transfer of both students and staff (Table 15.4). In 1992 EU-sponsored schemes allowed no less than 86,000 students to study in other European countries, while less than a decade earlier in the absence of the structures for exchange only a few hundred students circulated at undergraduate level between the states of the EU. It is interesting to note that this mushrooming of international mobility is widely welcomed by both the states and the individuals involved. This may seem ironic in view of the growing concern in western Europe in the 1990s about the social tensions created by immigration. It would appear that temporary mobility of skills is not perceived to pose a threat to host societies. Invisibility seems almost to have become a prerequisite for migrant acceptability.

There is not scope here to consider in greater detail the diversity of migration channels which might exist or which could emerge to support 'invisible' skill exchanges between countries. It is important, however, to present briefly a critique of this perspective of international skill exchanges. The starting point for such a critique might well be Lipietz's (1993) identification of the concept of the new international division of labour as a part of a new orthodoxy. Lipietz (1993) is not concerned in his argument with skilled international labour, but his case is important for those concerned with international skill transfers. Studies of the evolution of

Table 15.4: *Skill mobility in Europe in relation to university educational exchange programmes, 1992/3**

State	Coordinating institutions	Students sent	Students received	Teachers reviewed
Belgium	194	5,029	4,871	359
Denmark	57	2,236	2,028	196
Germany	274	13,058	12,399	708
Greece	54	2,207	1,791	261
Spain	195	9,619	9,384	591
France	345	16,360	16,939	870
Ireland	41	2,299	2,592	193
Italy	207	7,309	6,739	565
Luxembourg	1	8	5	1
Netherlands	165	6063	5,774	415
Portugal	50	2,559	2,131	305
UK	473	16,688	19,060	998
Austria	32	822	750	47
Finland	9	374	292	53
Sweden	24	1,417	1,287	64
Norway	6	400	375	16
Switzerland	8	347	376	32
Total	2,135	86,811	86,815	5,443

*Compiled by the author from Tables 2, 3 and 6 of the Erasmus Bureau Annual Report (1992/3). Total students sent and received differ slightly due to minor flows of students to two other participating countries.

production systems show that, while the organized capitalist system implied by the international division of labour continues to operate in a powerful fashion, new forms of flexible specialization have also emerged. These have been based on the spatial form of industrial districts rather than the hierarchical pattern of the large international firm with its headquarters, regional offices and branch plants. If such an evolution of production forms has taken place then it would imply that a continued growth of skill transfers within the hierarchically structured internal labour markets of large firms is not inevitable. Not only might expatriation as a form of skill transfer be affected on the one hand by other forms of mobility such as increased business travel and greater use of telecommunications, but it equally could be influenced by new forms and scales of skill mobility related to the dynamics of flexible forms of accumulation.

These ideas can be developed with reference to the Hong Kong case study introduced above. For example, there is no necessary reason for foreign direct investment in Hong Kong and in its hinterland to continue to expand in the same fashion as in the past. Within Hong Kong there is ample evidence of endogenous industrial development. There are many examples of locally developed industrial districts of the kind identified by Lipietz as representative of the modes of flexible accumulation. The evolving relation between these districts and the global production systems of large foreign firms operating in Hong Kong is hard to summarize. For many of the small indigenous industries the key relation with global companies is one of subcontracting. Although in Lipietz's terms this would imply the old hierarchy (of the international division of labour) 'making a return in force under the market pretence of subcontracting' (Lipietz 1993: 14), from the perspective of migration analysis it represents something new. In place of intra-company labour market links, subcontracting requires extra-company skill transfers, but do these linkages take the form of long- or short-term skill transfers? Do they involve as with internal labour market moves the exchange of technical expertise or merely the transfer of marketing information? Only future research can answer fully these questions which seek to relate the changing geography of skilled migration to changes in the mode of production.

Not all commentators would interpret the current crises as transitory, but would ascribe the changes to a fundamental shift to a new production regime involving complex networks of high technology contractors and suppliers (Sunley 1992). Nor would all commentators interpret subcontracting as inevitably reflecting the desire by large firms to sustain smooth internal production systems by subcontracting out cynical effects. Lawson (1992) notes that specialization subcontracting occurs because of the minimum efficient scale limitations in the parent firm, which make it more efficient to use technologies designed and operated by subcontractors. The employees of the subcontractor maintain considerable control over their work because of the high skill levels involved and find it easy to transfer their skills from one firm to another. In global cities clusters of small technically advanced subcontracting firms may exist with high levels of staff mobility between them. In a survey of the Hong Kong electronics sector Findlay et al. (1994) found high levels of employee mobility between firms to be the most frequently cited problem identified by employers. From the perspective of skilled international migration the relevance of this point is twofold. First there are certain exceedingly scarce technical skills which permit the relatively free international movement of those with these skills. This movement need not be channelled through the international labour markets of large firms and may in part account for the large numbers of expatriates listed in Table 15.3 who had not moved through intra-company transfers. Second, global cities with clusters of technically specialized subcontracting firms may prove increasingly attractive to persons possessing certain skills. This is not only because lucrative job opportunities may be available, but also because people working in these sectors may wish to sustain their professional skill advantage by locating close to foci around the globe where new technologies are being developed.

Although these interesting developments are listed here, it is important not to exaggerate their significance. Sayer (1989) notes that the hierarchical systems of mass production and the more localized systems of flexible accumulation are not alternatives. From the perspective of the analysis of skilled international migration two points of importance emerge. First, trends in international skill transfers cannot be adequately explained only in terms of models of skill mobility within the internal labour markets of large hierarchically organized firms. Second, the power of individual migrants to position themselves advantageously within the evolving world economy should not be underestimated, especially if they hold key professional, managerial or technical skills.

Conclusion

Skilled transient migration is now a major feature of global migration systems. In this contribution I have argued that the lack of attention given to this category of migration arises largely from its invisible nature. Despite this it is of major economic and political significance. The fact that most states welcome skilled transients in an era when other forms of migration engender such hostility is in itself interesting, and attests the economic benefits if not economic necessity perceived to be attached to this form of highly skilled migration. This in turn raises the important question of whether other more visible migration streams might not also share some of the positive characteristics of skilled transient flows, and whether migration policies have not become unduly blinkered to these productive dimensions of international migration.

The full significance of skilled transient flows will not be fully appreciated until a fuller explanatory framework is achieved. Although a major part of highly skilled international flows takes place through the internal labour markets of large companies, it has been shown that this is only one of many channels of movement. Not only is a wider analysis needed of the diversity of migration channels which have emerged in recent years, and of the ways in which skill mobility is altering in relation to new productive regimes, but there is also the need to recognize the diversity of skilled transients themselves, and to give greater emphasis to the intentionality of their migration actions.

Note

1. I would like to acknowledge the considerable influence on my thinking of many friends and colleagues. In particular joint research projects concerning skilled migration shared with Mark Boyle, John Jowett, Eva Lelievre, Lin Li, Ronan Paddison and Ron Skeldon have been highly significant in moulding my ideas.

References

Appleyard, R. (1985) 'Processes and Determinants of International Migration', paper presented to the IUSSP seminar on Emerging Issues in International Migration, Belagio, May

Baines, D. (1991) *Emigration from Europe, 1815–1930*, London: Macmillan

Beaverstock, J. (1992) *A New International Division of Professional and Managerial Labour*, Department of Geography, University of Loughborough Occasional Paper 17

Dunning, J. H. (1988) *Explaining International Production*, London: Hyman

Findlay, A. (1990) 'A Migration Channels Approach to the Study of High Level Manpower Movements', *International Migration*, 28, 15–24

(1992) 'The Economic Impact of Immigration to the United Kingdom', *Applied Population Research Unit Discussion Paper,* University of Glasgow, 92 (5)

Findlay, A. and W. Gould (1989) 'Skilled International Migration: A Research Agenda', *Area,* 21, 3–11

Findlay, A. et al. (1994) 'Expatriates in the Hong Kong Electronics Industry', *Applied Population Research Unit Discussion Paper,* University of Glasgow, 94 (1)

Ford, R. (1992) 'Migration and Stress among Corporate Employees', Ph.D., University College, London University

Fröbel, F. et al. (1980) *The New International Division of Labour,* Cambridge: Cambridge University Press

Garrick, L. (1991) 'A Channels Framework for the Study of Skilled International Migration', Ph.D., Glasgow University

Gould, W. (1987) 'Recruitment Agencies and British International Migration', *Area,* 19, 374–6

(1988) 'Skilled International Migration', *Geoforum,* 19, 381–6

Hong Kong Government Industry Department (1992) *1992 Survey of Overseas Investment in Hong Kong's Manufacturing Industries,* Hong Kong: HKGID

King, R. (ed.) (1986) *Return Migration and Regional Economic Problems,* London: Croom Helm

Lawson, V. (1992) 'Industrial Subcontracting and Employment Forms in Latin America', *Progress in Human Geography,* 16, 1–23

Lipietz, A. (1993) 'The Local and the Global', *Transactions, Institute of British Geographers,* 18, 8–18

OPCS (1991) *International Migration,* 18 (Series MN), London: OPCS

Salt, J. (1988) 'Highly Skilled Migrants, Careers and International Labour Markets', *Geoforum,* 19, 387–99

(1992) 'UK Sopemi Report 1992', mimeo paper

(1993) *Migration and Population Change in Europe,* Geneva: UNIDR

Salt, J. and A. Findlay (1989) 'International Migration of Highly Skilled Manpower', in R. Appleyard (ed.) *The Impact of International Migration on Developing Countries,* Paris: Organization for Economic Cooperation and Development, 159–81

Sassen, S. (1988) *The Mobility of Labour and Capital,* Cambridge: Cambridge University Press

(1991) *The Global City,* Princeton: Princeton University Press

Sayer, A. (1989) 'Postfordism in Question', *International Journal of Urban and Regional Research,* 13, 666–95

Smith, N. (1989) 'Uneven Development and Location Theory', in R. Peet and N. Thrift (eds) *New Models in Geography,* London: Unwin Hyman, 142–63

Sunley, P. (1992) 'An Uncertain Future', *Progress in Human Geography,* 16, 58–70

Thrift, N. (1987) 'The Fixers: The Urban Geography of International Commercial Capital', in J. Henderson and M. Castells (eds) *Global Restructuring and Territorial Development,* London: Sage, 219–47

THE MANY FACES OF IMMIGRANT ENTREPRENEURSHIP

CHAN KWOK BUN AND ONG JIN HUI

The literature on ethnic or immigrant entrepreneurship[1], an increasingly popular sub-field in race and ethnic relations, grew out of a larger concern with economic achievement and mobility of immigrants and racial minorities in advanced industrial societies. Among others, two observations emanating from analyses of such genre were noted: first, the confinement of immigrants and minorities to the secondary labour market – and their subjection to what economists call 'super-exploitation' (Hill 1980); second, the disproportionate representation of foreign-born persons among the self-employed relative to the native, white population. In the former observation, immigrants, on the basis of ethnicity, suffer from blocked opportunity, or, simply, a racial disadvantage. In the latter case, the somewhat contrary suggestion is that migration and immigration as social processes bestow on immigrants as groups a sociological advantage in the form of an internal ethnic cohesiveness and collectivism, which appears to be conducive to doing business. These two observations of course are not unrelated to each other. Faced with a disadvantage, immigrants as a sociological group turn it into an advantage; blocked opportunity ironically opens up alternative opportunities. Precluded from entry into the mainstream capitalist economy, immigrants respond by creating their own capitalism (Portes 1981: 297). The greater the disadvantage, the greater the frustration, the greater the motive and incentive for change (Light 1984: 198).

Right from the beginning, with Light's classic *Ethnic Enterprise in America* (1972), an upbeat and enthusiastic atmosphere has infused the literature on immigrant entrepreneurship. An edited volume, *Ethnic Communities in Business*, by Ward and Jenkins (1984), retains a similar spirit. The publication of *Ethnic Entrepreneurs: Immigrant Business in Industrial Societies* in 1990 by Waldinger et al., arguably the most wide-ranging single-volume treatment of the subject to date by a study group of diverse interests and persuasions, saw in its index fifty ethnic groups – Asians, Cubans, Greeks, Jewish included. It is indeed one of the most active subjects in the twin fields of

race and ethnic relations and of international migration. In fact, substantively and theoretically speaking, the analysis of ethnic entrepreneurship marries the two fields.

Fusion of structure and culture

Sociological attempts to theorize about immigrant entrepreneurship have given rise to a rich conceptual language and vocabulary. One can classify these attempts at theorization into two approaches: cultural and structural. The cultural approach focuses its attention on the 'supply side' of entrepreneurship, or ethnic resources internal and indigenous to the group or community concerned. Imported or transplanted culture in terms of values and beliefs are being retrieved, invoked, produced and reproduced to start and to maintain ethnic business. Ethnicity as culture is useful and beneficial for immigrants intent on pursuing an entrepreneurial pathway to economic achievement and mobility. Stressing how ethnicity as resources is being 'put to use', researchers following the cultural approach emphasize the 'ethnic advantage' enjoyed by immigrants in terms of ready access to start-up capital available at rotating credit associations within an ethnic community; incessant supply of cheap, dependable, loyal family or co-ethnic labour; support and assistance from immigrant institutions in matters relating to information about business type, size and location; and specific norms and values prevailing in an ethnic community that infuse employer–employee relations. Ethnic resources thus include those distinct cultural and group characteristics that predispose and direct members of an ethnic group towards entrepreneurial activities in the host society. It is obvious to students of sociology that the transplanted culture thesis is essentially a variant of Weber's (1958) Protestant ethic hypothesis of capitalistic growth – which is not without its critics.

A structural explanation of the development and growth of ethnic entrepreneurship focuses on the contextual or *external* forces of society, the constraints *and* opportunities, the 'supply side' of entrepreneurship. Explanations of such genre attribute the emergence of ethnic enterprise to immigrants as middleman minority (Bonacich 1973; Loewen 1971) filling in a status gap created by dominant and subordinate groups who desire little interaction between themselves but cannot do without it. Li (1976, 1979) locates the structural determinants in the institutional racism that has historically restricted many opportunities for the Chinese in the core economy in the USA and Canada. To such a condition of blocked mobility, the Chinese responded by seeking and exploiting other possibilities in the opportunity structure – which are under the *total context* of social, economic and political forces within which the immigrants operate while engaging in entrepreneurial pursuits. Integral to the opportunity structure are market conditions and government policies pertaining to immigration intake, taxes and ethnic business development. For any business to start, there must be a demand for the goods and services it offers. Among the businesses that first developed among the immigrants were purveyors of culinary and cultural products. The immigrants have special social adjustment needs, tastes and preferences that cannot be met by the non-ethnic sector, thus the rise of businesses to fill an ethnic niche, itself a structural condition the immigrant businessmen are eager to exploit.

Another niche consists of markets that are underserved or abandoned by the majority business groups, thus leaving behind vacancies for the ethnic businessman to fill. A variant of the structural explanation, the ecological succession thesis (Aldrich 1975; Aldrich 1980; Aldrich and McEvoy 1984; Aldrich and Reiss 1976; Aldrich et al 1985b), drawing upon writings of Park (1936) and Burgess (1928), argues that openings for ethnic business emerge when the older, more established native business group in a residential area no longer reproduces itself fast enough given a naturally high rate of failure in small businesses – thus creating vacancies for nascent immigrant entrepreneurs in a process of succession, of one ethnic group after another replacing its predecessor. Immigrant groups, one after another, move into markets abandoned by local, native small businessmen and strive to generate whatever marginal profit there is left.

In such markets, economies of scale are relatively low; ethnic business people can maximize efficiency and profit by engaging in a strategy of self-exploitation: longer, unsocial hours, year-long and personalized service and lower prices. Also, barriers of entry into such markets are generally low – the

setting up of small businesses, say, a grocery store or a hand laundry, requires little start-up capital, small labour size, very little technical know-know or training. Yet another niche in the general opportunity structure arises as a result of a demand among the majority population for exotic, ethnic goods and services – the immigrants thus seize the opportunity to market ethnic commodities and gradually begin to control a protected, captive market (Aldrich et al. 1985a).

An outgrowth of a desire to integrate or fuse culture with structure, ethnic resources with opportunity structure, 'supply' with 'demand' – or, to emphasize the historical, transactional dialectics of the two 'seemingly' contrasting types of determinants of ethnic entrepreneurship – the *interactive* explanation, based on a series of industry case studies in New York (Waldinger 1984, 1985) and several ethnic group studies (Mars and Ward 1984; Ward 1983), argues that 'ethnic businesses proliferate in industries where there is a congruence between the demand of the economic environment and informal resources of the ethnic population' (Waldinger et al. 1985: 591).

In this approach, the demand for business and the supply of skills and resources *interact* to produce ethnic entrepreneurship. The explanation is formulated to move beyond the culture vs. structure debate, 'to recognize the artificiality of an either/or framework on whether culture or structure dictates the trajectory of socio-economic attainment' (Nee and Wong 1985: 284). When viewed processually and historically, supply and demand, culture and structure are in a continuous dialectical exchange (Boissevain and Grotenbreg 1986), thus nullifying any attempt at a sharp division between them. History articulates the dialectical interplay of culture and structure. The market for entrepreneurship having a demand and a supply side (Smelser 1976: 126), Light (1977: 475) concluded from his comparative study of the blacks and Chinese in the vice industry in 1880–1940 that illegal enterprise, itself a type of entrepreneurial activity, albeit illegal, is best viewed as a *synthesis* of illicit goods and services that the public wants to buy (demand) *and* what and how much disadvantaged ethnics intend to offer (supply). As he (Light 1977: 475) puts it, 'demand does not, therefore, explain supply because provider culture, social organization and demography intervene'. It is a more nuanced view that acknowledges that structure provides the context for opportunity, yet also insists that culture in terms of group characteristics defines the manner in which supply is provided.

The fusion of explanations in terms of culture and structure is of course not new. It is anticipated by Yancey (1976) who, in his formulation of the concept 'emergent ethnicity', argues that ethnicity is 'manufactured' in the host society rather than imported or transplanted wholesale from overseas. While immigrants do bring along an 'orthodox' culture with them that shapes their initial orientations and behaviours, it is the structural conditions in the local context that significantly bear on their long-term cultural and economic patterns (Hirschman 1982: 479), albeit necessarily mediated and intervened by culture and personality. In a long course, culture is rarely transplanted as is, but rather reproduced *and* produced, deconstructed *and* constructed, in exploitation of structural advantages as well as in adaptation to structural constraints.

The distinction between cultural and situational variables by Turner and Bonacich (1980: 145, 148) parallels Light's (1980: 34–6) distinction between reactive and orthodox cultural contexts of entrepreneurship. The often-observed and much-discussed internal solidarity of many immigrant groups – the so-called cornerstone of ethnic enterprise (Hraba 1979: 374) – is a reactive solidarity, a collective response to new contextual requirements. As Light (1984: 200) puts it, 'Immigrants belong to a primary group which did not exist as such in their country of origin … a reactive solidarity which required alien status to *liberate*' (emphasis added). Emergent or reactive immigrant culture is culture adapted; it is 'culture fused with structure' *par excellence*.

A model that represents a most recent attempt to capture the interactive, adaptive and emergent character of immigrant entrepreneurship is formulated by Waldinger et al. (1990). Placed at the centre of the model are various ethnic strategies which emerge from the interaction of two factors, opportunity structure and ethnic group culture – ethnic entrepreneurs adapt to the constraints in the social structure and, building on their group characteristics, attempt to carve out their own niche. Implicit in such a model is a view of migration as an emancipatory process, a positive act (Chan 1992: 130–1; Chan and Chiang 1994: 344; Park 1950: 147, 169; Wickramagamage 1992) – it opens up potential opportunities for social mobility, for growth and development of the immigrants as individuals and as a group. The immigrants attempt to grapple with history and social structure. Embedded in the migrant's experience and everyday life is a vast reservoir of resources and opportunities to be exploited, thus the

triumph of immigrant entrepreneurship, often in full view of *and* in spite of all odds. Research on immigrant entrepreneurship, among other things, shows how ethnicity can be and indeed has been put to use by some, if not by all. The migrant (as individual and as group member) engages in what Giddens (1976) calls a 'dialectic of control' with history and social structure. By this, Giddens includes the ability of the weak to turn their weaknesses back against the powerful, the compact majority. What is emerging is thus a conception of the immigrant entrepreneur himself[2] and with others of his kind, relentlessly improvising, innovating and strategizing in the context of a shifting balance of the dialectic of control between history, personality, ethnicity, race, gender, class and social structure. Integral to such a conception is the view that ethnic strategies are changing, dynamic and emergent – but, most important of all, *social* and *collectivistic* in nature (Waldinger et al. 1990: 131–56).

Two sides of ethnic entrepreneurship

While there has been this theoretical debate on the relative explanatory power of culture or structure in accounting for the rise and development of ethnic entrepreneurship, a corresponding empirical debate in the literature has emerged as to whether *the reality* is one of ethnic advantage (culture) or contextual disadvantage (structure). Has culture in fact overcome structure, ethnicity over constraint? In seeking an answer to the question of whether minority business development is in fact the much-heralded pathway to economic achievement and social mobility, academic opinion, according to Aldrich et al. (1984: 190) in an essay that deserves wider, deeper reading, 'seems torn between two opposing views', 'two apparently irreconcilable images', somewhat in an 'intellectual schizophrenia'.

One image is that of ethnic advantage in terms of internal solidarity, that of immigrants possessing a remarkable capacity for entrepreneurial achievement and, in turn, upward mobility; ethnic businesses provide group members with 'the means for escaping minority status and gaining entry into the bourgeoisie' (Aldrich et al. 1984: 191). It is a success story played again and again, many times over, in many an advanced industrial society, be it England, the USA or Canada. Another starkly contrasting image is one of racial disadvantage, of racial exclusion, of external and structural exclusion rather than internal and ethnic inclusion, whereby a virtual racial monopoly by the native whites of the mainstream economy continues to present barriers the immigrant entrepreneurs *appear* to have overcome but, in reality, have not. While engaging in what they call 'an exercise in deglamorization', Aldrich et al. (1984: 209) conclude that Asian business activity in Britain 'represents a truce with racial inequality rather than a victory over it'. Disguised by a surface gloss of ethnic self-determination (Jones 1979), the facade of Asian business success is little but a story of an exceptional minority within a minority, merely 'exchanging the role of marginal worker for that of marginal proprietor' (Aldrich et al. 1984: 209), marginal, dependent and vulnerable nevertheless, proprietor or no proprietor.

There are at least two contributions emanating from this 'deglamorization exercise'. One is a much-delayed need to focus one's analytical attention on the *real* structural and structured barriers faced by ethnic enterprise, granted the initial journalistic and academic euphoria over its rise and success. The other contribution revolves around what Bonacich calls the *cost* of immigrant entrepreneurship (Bonacich 1988: 425–36) or what she most recently calls the 'other side of ethnic entrepreneurship' (1993: 685–93). Besides the writings of Aldrich and his associates, Morokvasic and Bonacich are the two other critics of the workings of immigrant entrepreneurship in relation to the system of advanced industrial capitalism. Both being women sociologists, they are perhaps particularly sensitive to issues of social inequality and oppression of female labour. In her study of the involvement of immigrants in the Parisian garment industry, Morokvasic (1987) serves the timely reminder that for those not gainfully or advantageously employed, self-employment is merely a means of survival, a disguised unemployment. Relations between the minority entrepreneur and his compatriot workers are often based on fear, dependency and 'expected' employee loyalty – all of which lend themselves to oppression and exploitation (Bonacich 1993: 691; 1988: 431), especially of women labour, as one of the few ways for immigrant entrepreneurs to accumulate capital (Morokvasic 1987: 453). Besides, native garment capitalists are more than eager to exploit the ambiguity and precariousness of the minority entrepreneur's status as an intermediary: they transfer their production risks and labour oppression to them (Bonacich 1993: 689). These intermediaries are intimately bound to the native capitalists 'not as their competitors, indeed, but as their dependants' – the minority entrepreneurs 'behave as if they had left the proletariat but have to

accept a dependent status, *vis-à-vis* the *true garment capitalists*' (emphasis added) (Morokvasic 1987: 460). In the end, it is the minority labour that must absorb much of the brunt of their intermediary employers' precariousness and instability. Morokvasic insists on calling the migrant labourer, not the immigrant entrepreneur, the cornerstone of the survival and revival of garment industry in the metropolises of the advanced, industrial states – be it Paris, New York, Toronto or London.

Bonacich adds to her exposé of 'the other side' of immigrant entrepreneurship by arguing that minority self-employment rarely decreases, but rather increases inequality at the nation state, as well as world, level. Yet a continued euphoria about the promise of immigrant entrepreneurship, to Bonacich, is itself lending ideological support to free enterprise capitalism. By holding the few successful immigrant entrepreneurs up as models, as folkloric heroes, it holds the failures themselves responsible for their plight – in a deep sense, it blames the victims, yet also hiding or, worse still, denying racism and its role in perpetuating social inequality. The cost of immigrant entrepreneurship also lies in its perhaps 'unintended consequence' of the white establishment creating intergroup conflict along ethnic lines, of 'pitting them against each other in a "divide and rule" strategy', adds Bonacich, perhaps a bit over-emphatically (Bonacich 1988: 433; 1993: 691).

Bonacich is not oblivious to other personal problems and dilemmas faced by the immigrant entrepreneurs either. She draws attention to the life of hard work and poor health immigrants must endure: the long arduous hours of self-exploitation create family problems and cause marital breakdowns in the Korean community of the USA (Bonacich 1988: 431). Self-exploitation is a critical ethnic strategy for personal survival precisely because one can hardly do without it (Aldrich et al. 1981: 183–6).

Perhaps one of the most visible indicators of structural disadvantage faced by the Asian enterprise in Britain is lack of markets and their low rewards – in the long term, with the ratio of customers to entrepreneurs diminishing, immigrant business, as a result of internal competition among co-ethnics, may not be able to escape from its own 'demographic inevitability', a probable cause of its eventual demise (Aldrich et al. 1984: 206). Internal competition among co-ethnics within an enclave economy happens when there is an excess of similar types of business cashing in on a similar ethnic niche and competing for a limited pool of customers. Internal competition is thus often structurally built into the very configuration of ethnic enterprise when immigrants follow each other's 'commercial footsteps' too closely – a cause of saturation and fierce competition. Ethnic enterprise thus often finds itself caught in an unending vicious circle of cost cutting and operating long unsocial hours – competitive behaviour soon feeds on itself. So, ironically, one may argue that the more institutionally complete an ethnic community is, the stronger the centripetal and the weaker the centrifugal forces, the stronger the propensity of internal competition would be. While family ties, kin networks and ethnic institutions are enabling because of the myriad of ethnic resources embedded in them, they can also be limiting, possibly leading to 'ghettoization of ethnic business' and, worse still, business failures or bankruptcies (Chan 1992: 128).

So, as observed by Aldrich et al. (1981: 188), Asian business may have given its owners the autonomy and independence they desire. But, paradoxically, this protection from competition with the white economy is itself the root cause of their disadvantage. Economic isolationism breeds cultural and self segregation. Continued dependence on segregated, ethnic markets will make it unlikely for Asian self-employment to serve as a pathway towards achieving socio-economic parity with the whites in Britain.

New-wave ethnic entrepreneurs: future research

The debate on ethnic entrepreneurship operates at two different levels. On the ideological level, it is between the claim among 'pro-capitalists'[3] of ethnic entrepreneurship providing opportunities for apprenticeship in small business and upward mobility, and their critics' accusation of labour exploitation and maintenance of social inequality. On the conceptual, theoretical level, the quarrel takes the familiar form of arguing which has priority of influence: culture, structure or fusion of the two. Such a theoretical debate of course necessarily locates itself in the larger philosophical concern in the sociology of knowledge with the human agency social structure or individual society dialectics, which often, though not necessarily, splits the observers into two camps: the 'optimists' or idealists with their belief in the *promise* of action and structuration attempts of the human agency, individual and culture; and the 'pessimists' or realists, who accentuate social *limits* and structural constraints. We thus have two contrasting images of ethnic entrepreneurship: one of *human* emancipation and possibility, the other of *social* entrapment and impossibility. Waldinger (1992: 13), a long-time

student of ethnic entrepreneurship, most recently reached a compromising, rather level-headed, conclusion: 'My own sense is that immigrant business, like everything else, is *a mixed bag, with positive and negative features*' (emphases added).

Of course, the problem at hand runs deeper than what the mere empirical surface of the immigration–ethnic enterprise correlation would suggest. For one, the character of the incoming immigrants in the advanced industrial states, as well as the processes of international migration, has changed. Some observers have noted the ascendancy of the 'new middle class' among Chinese immigrants in Canada (Chan 1992; Li 1983: 13), the so-called new overseas Chinese (Skeldon 1994). Another (Ma Mung 1993: 6) has observed the propensity of Chinese entrepreneurs in Paris towards trade expansion and diversification and creation of 'upstream enterprises' that involve trade with an *outside* community formerly monopolized by non-Chinese businessmen. In articulating their business networks and economic arrangements within a larger global 'diaspora economy' and by appropriating 'spatial resources' in a transnational space, Chinese entrepreneurship in Paris has taken on an international, extraterritorial character. The otherwise amorphous structure of such a diaspora economy, however, is given substance by the many localities or poles as networks, be they in New York, Bangkok, Jakarta, Shanghai, Hong Kong, London or Toronto.

Such a global economic system thus has its own internal as well as external principles of social organization; the potentials of growth can be staggering. The observed gradual shift from a reliance on ethnic to class resources among the Koreans in Chicago (Yoon 1991), the Chinese in Canada (Chan 1992), or the Iranians and Israelis (Waldinger 1992), suggests the critical importance of the evolving *external* elements of an immigrant economy. As Waldinger (1992: 12) puts it, 'recourse to outsiders, it turns out, is one of the fruits of entrepreneurial success'.

Our foregoing review of the literature on ethnic entrepreneurs provides an understanding of a significant form of adaptation by various ethnic or immigrant groups. Despite differences in the economic milieu presented by the host societies, common patterns of coping exist. However, most of the processes of adaptation studied have been at the level of small immigrant businesses – which are reflected in the structural and cultural models we have articulated. In many ways, these same processes can still be found among recent migrants from, for example, Indochina. But increasingly one must ask if they are representative of the new migratory developments taking place.

In countries such as Canada and Australia and in the less visible migrant stopping-off points like Singapore, Malaysia and other Southeast Asian countries, policies of attracting high-end ethnic entrepreneurs (or economic investors or business immigrants, as variously called) have become the vogue. The basis for host country migrant transactions is the commitment to invest in the host country in exchange for a passport and permanent residency or citizenship. The consequence of such selective immigration policies is that the new migrants and entrepreneurs are from a very different social category compared with those of the earlier waves (Chan 1992; Smart 1995).

The phenomenon of the new middle-class migrants (some are distinctinctly in the highest socio-economic stratum) deserves a more than cursory look because they add a new face to the ethnic enterprise. In fact, they become the potential big employers in the host society – the very reason for them being pursued in the first instance. In the previous wave, the migrants were employed by the host. Confining themselves to living within an ethnic enclave, they were unlikely to intrude immediately and forcefully into the stratificational structures of the host societies. However, there are now locations such as Vancouver or Toronto, Canada, where the new middle-class immigrants and entrepreneurs have become a significant element and cannot be ignored. No longer ghettoized socially or economically, the integration of these new entrepreneurs into the host community occurs on multiple levels. In some cases, the integration with the 'older' migrant communities has not been without problems. Vancouver has provided examples (albeit in journalistic reports) of the newly arrived, financially well-endowed, migrants making inroads into the economy as well as imposing new patterns of consumption and lifestyle on the established community. Their sociological impact is thus not just on the settled middle-class segment of the dominant host community – an impact now wider in scope than before – but also on the ethnic community with which the new migrant is culturally similar but economically different. The consequences of a *flexibility* of migration rules and procedures for economic gains to be made by a region or country is still not well understood. Research into such areas is necessary if we are to move forward in this field. In many ways,

the future frame of reference for the study of these new entrepreneurs is likely to be found as much in the theories of social stratification as in race and ethnic relations, adaptation and migration.

However, we hasten to note that, despite their economic advantage, these new middle-class entrepreneurs still exhibit some of the predilections of the early migrants – especially in the willingness to move further on or even to return to their home country. The notion of temporary migration or migratory transiency is back in force in the latest wave – they are not unlike the earliest waves of migrants who saw themselves as sojourners, temporarily rooted to make some money but always anticipating a return. The current wave is open to the exploration of a third, or fourth, country's advantages and opportunities because they have the wherewithal to be mobile and to seek out relative economic advantage. The ease of international transference of their largely portable assets and resources makes the concept of a multinational migrant an intriguing new sociological phenomenon. The new migrants are likely to shift bases more readily than those who have entered seeking permanent residency. It is this latter category of permanent settlers that the existing literature on ethnic entrepreneurship focuses on, certainly not the former one.

Migrant entrepreneurship has now taken on a new 'exploitative' face. In the earliest wave, coolies and migrants were exploited. In the second wave, the advantage of the host society was exploited by those seeking to establish themselves permanently. In the third, newest wave, the attraction of a host society may be a function of the availability of opportunities for entrepreneurship. The fact that there are those who have migrated to Canada and Australia and who are now seeking to return to their origins such as Taiwan, Hong Kong or Singapore, or to move on to another location based on business rather than social or cultural needs, forces a rethink of the 'classical' factors of migration. The pull of a social space and the intent to integrate fully into the structure of the society within the limits of the existing constraints are now not the only factors – there are many more. These are new realities in the migrant equation which must be factored into a future, broader explanatory model.

There is thus a disjuncture between the emergent empirical reality and what is offered in the existing literature on ethnic entrepreneurship. The fact that the literature is still focused on the small business is itself a problem of the sociology of knowledge. Traditionally, it is the manual workers or small businessmen who get 'interrogated' by sociologists, not the bigger, more global players. Faced with a sociologist's interrogation, ability to safeguard one's secrets, one's commercial information, one's self interests, is apparently a function of differential possession of personal and social resources. This has obvious methodological implications for the sociology of business, large and small. By and large, the viability of government policies on business immigrants and economic investors' programmes remains understudied. Data on enterprises of high finance, ethnic or not ethnic, are much less likely to be available, especially those involving multimillion-dollar investments. Sociologists continue to have difficulty in tracking down the flows of capital across political boundaries. Also, at this level of financial commitment, governmental policies on migration become more of an economic development programme than a basis for encouraging human resettlement. The end result is that migration becomes a stratified, two-tiered phenomenon, one which needs to be considered in the development of new explanatory models of ethnic entrepreneurship in particular and migration in general.

Interestingly, the modern equivalent of the 'gold mountain' is still a component in the imagination of such new-wave migrants though they now are expected to put in more than their predecessors. Those who now enter a country at the upper level of the two-tier system also expect to utilize their financial resources to achieve their business objectives. However, in the process, they will fulfil the dream of the development of a 'gold mountain' *for* the host society. The irony of the turnabout probably escapes them as they pursue dreams not very different from those of coolies. Ironically, when Canadian immigration officials are coming to Hong Kong or Taiwan to woo 'big time' economic investors, the high-end immigrant entrepreneurs, one wonders where the modern-day 'gold mountain' is, in the East or the West?

The literature on ethnic entrepreneurship is limited in yet other ways. The focus on small-scale ethnic enterprises is problematic in terms of the kinds of comparisons that may be made with processes occurring in other culturally and politically different societies. Most past research has been focused on those who have migrated to established societies where the host is dominant politically, economically, culturally and demographically. The difference between an ethnic minority entrepreneur in such a dominant-host setting and his peer in a, for example,

colonial setting, is vast. Also different is the current context of the ethnic minority entrepreneurs in the post-independence context of countries in Southeast Asia. And, where they are the majority, as in Singapore, the model of economic development is sociologically and politically different from the other examples – as well as the whole gamut of variations in between (Chan and Chiang 1994). These entrepreneural developments and the differences in socio-economic patterns need to be recognized. It would leave a theoretical lacuna if research is focused only on the adaptations of migrants in host-dominant economies. Even if studied as special cases, greater sense may be made of these processes in host-dominant countries *when compared with* those found in other contexts.

The dialect-based networking in Singapore and Southeast Asia presents yet another form of adaptation that should be noted. The new forms of networking, although economically quite different from those possible under the old dialect-, village-, region-based networking, nevertheless show some distinct characteristics. There are now well-endowed Asian conglomerates that function across international borders but which operate on principles not unlike those reminiscent of village organization. The small group approach to Asian businesses may be adopted when they are compared with businesses in other cultures or societies. This will allow us to ascertain empirically if reliance on family, kinship and clan ties in business transactions is a uniquely Asian characteristic or not.

Indeed, one of the most pressing questions confronting research in the ethnic enterprise concerns itself with the hows and whys of *observed variations* in entrepreneurial type, size and performance in different immigrant groups and in different societal contexts, *over the long haul*. While still in its infancy stage, the field is perhaps too young to throw up enough empirical examples or historical experiences for a more nuanced, comparative, cross-cultural, as well as longitudinal analysis. The notion of a fusion between culture and structure, hope and anguish, is a mature, sophisticated one though one is best reminded that the impetus for casting a sociological eye on the entrepreneur owes its origin to a scholarly as well as lay fascination with (though not proper understanding of) the miracles an enterprising individual can produce. This drive and free spirit of the entrepreneur, intriguing and elusive as it is, is best borne in mind while one is implicated in the debate on culture or structure, agency or constraint, freedom or entrapment. Like many other things in life, ethnic entrepreneurship indeed has many faces, each revealing a partial truth.

Notes

1. In this contribution we make no distinction between ethnic entrepreneurship and immigrant entrepreneurship, and use the two terms interchangeably. We are aware of the conventional view in the field of race and ethnic relations that suggests a processual progression from the immigrant to the ethnic status.
2. Here we use 'he' and 'himself' in reference to the immigrant entrepreneur partly because such a person, rightly or wrongly, has hitherto been most probably a male. We acknowledge the recent appearance of women as ethnic entrepreneurs.
3. In her 'dialogue' with Waldinger et al. (1990), Bonacich (1993: 686) calls their work, *Ethnic Entrepreneurs: Immigrant Business in Industrial Societies*, a 'pro-capitalist' book.

References

Aldrich, Howard (1975) 'Ecological Succession in Racially Changing Neighbourhoods: A Review of the Literature', *Urban Affairs Quarterly*, 10 (3), 327–48
    (1980) 'Asian Shopkeepers as Middleman Minority: A Study of Small Business in Wandsworth', in A. Evans and D. Eversley (eds) *The Inner City: Employment and Industry*, London: Heineman, 389–408
Aldrich, Howard and D. McEvoy (1984) 'Residential Succession and Inter-ethnic Competition for Business Sites', paper presented at Annual Meeting of American Sociological Association
Aldrich, Howard and Albert J. Reiss (1976) 'Continuities in the Study of Ecological Succession: Changes in the Race Composition of Neighbourhoods and their Businesses', *American Journal of Sociology*, 81 (4), 846–66
Aldrich, Howard et al. (1981) 'Business Development and Self-segregation: Asian Enterprise in Three British Cities', in C. Peach, V. Robinson and S. Smith (eds), *Ethnic Segregation in Cities*, London: Croom Helm, 170–90
    (1984) 'Ethnic Advantage and Minority Business Development', in R. Ward and R. Jenkins (eds) *Ethnic Communities in Business*, Cambridge: Cambridge University Press, 189–210
    (1985a) 'Minority Business Development in Industrial Society', *European Studies Newsletter*, 14 (4), 4–8
    (1985b) 'Ethnic Residential Concentration and the Protected Market Hypothesis', *Social Forces*, 63 (4), 996–1009
Boissevain, Jeremy and Hanneke Grotenbreg (1986) 'Culture, Structure and Ethnic Enterprise: The Surinamese of Amsterdam', *Ethnic and Racial Studies*, 9 (1), 1–23
Bonacich, Edna (1973) 'A Theory of Middleman Minorities', *American Sociological Review*, 38 (5 October), 583–94
    (1988) 'The Costs of Immigrant Entrepreneurship', in I. Light and E. Bonacich, *Immigrant Entrepreneurs*, Berkeley: University of California Press, 425–36
    (1993) 'The Other Side of Ethnic Entrepreneurship: A Dialogue with Waldinger, Aldrich, Ward and Associates', *International Migration Review*, 27 (3), 685–92
Burgess, Edna (1928) 'Residential Segregation in American Cities', *Annals of the American Academy of Political and Social Science*, 140, 105–15

Chan Kwok Bun (1992) 'Ethnic Resources, Opportunity Structure and Coping Strategies: Chinese Businesses in Canada', *Revue Européene des Migrations Internationales*, 8 (3), 117–37
Chan Kwok Bun and Claire Chiang (1994) *Stepping Out: The Making of Chinese Entrepreneurs*, Singapore: Prentice Hall
Giddens, A. (1976) *New Rules of Sociological Method*, New York: Basic Books
Hill, R. C. (1980) 'Race, Class and the State: The Metropolitan Enclave System in the United States', *Insurgent Sociologist*, 10, 45–9
Hirschman, Charles (1982) 'Immigrants and Minorities: Old Questions for New Directions in Research', *International Migration Review*, 16 (2), 474–90
Hraba, J. (1979) *American Ethnicity*, Ithaca: F. E. Peacock
Jones, Trevor P. (1979) 'The Third World Within: Asians in Britain', paper presented to Institute of British Geographers' Annual Conference, Manchester
Li, Peter S. (1976) 'Ethnic Business Among Chinese in the US', *Journal of Ethnic Studies*, 4, 9–41
    (1979) 'A Historical Approach to Ethnic Stratification: The Case of the Chinese in Canada, 1858–1930', *Canadian Review of Sociology and Anthropology*, 16, 320–32
    (1983) 'Minority Business and Ethnic Neighbourhood: Some Observations on Chinese-owned Firms in Vancouver', paper presented at Annual Meeting of Canadian Sociology and Anthropology Association, 1–3 June, University of British Columbia, Vancouver, 24 pp
Light, Ivan (1972) *Ethnic Enterprise in America*, Berkeley: University of California Press
    (1977) 'The Ethnic Vice Industry, 1880–1944', *American Sociological Review*, 42 (3), June, 464–79
    (1980) 'Asian Enterprise in America', in S. Cummings (ed.) *Self-Help in Urban America*, New York: Kennikat Press, 33–57
    (1984) 'Immigrant and Ethnic Enterprise in North America', *Ethnic and Racial Studies*, 7 (2), April, 195–216
Loewen, James W. (1971) *The Mississippi Chinese: Between Black and White*, Cambridge: Harvard University Press
Ma Mung, Emmanuel (1993) 'Economic Arrangement and Spatial Resources: Elements of a Diaspora Economy', paper presented at International Conference on Overseas Chinese, sponsored by Ethnic Studies Department, University of California in Berkeley, 26–29 November, San Francisco, 24 pp
Mars, G. and Robin Ward (1984) 'Ethnic Business Development in Britain: Opportunities and Resources', in R. Ward and R. Jenkins (eds), *Ethnic Communities in Business*, Cambridge: Cambridge University Press, 1–19
Morokvasic, Mirjana (1987) 'Immigrants in the Parisian Garment Industry', *Work, Employment and Society*, 1 (4), 441–62
Nee, Victor and Herbert Y. Wong (1985) 'Asian American Economic Achievement: The Strength of the Family Bond', *Sociological Perspectives*, 28 (3), July, 281–306
Park, Robert (1936) 'Succession: An Ecological Concept', *American Sociological Review*, 1, 171–9
    (1950) *Race and Culture: Essays on the Sociology of Contemporary Man*, New York: Free Press
Portes, Alejandro (1981) 'Modes of Structural Incorporation and Present Theories of Labour Immigration', in M. M. Kritz, C. B. Keeley and S. M. Tomasi (eds) *Global Trends in Migration*, Centre for Migration Studies, New York: Staten Island, 279–97

Skeldon, Ronald (1994) 'Hong Kong in an International Migration System', in R. Skeldon (ed.) *Reluctant Exiles? Migration from Hong Kong and the New Overseas Chinese*, New York: M. E. Sharpe, 21–51

Smart, Josephine (1995) 'The Changing Pressure in International Migration: A Case Study of Hong Kong Immigration to Canada Before 1997', in J. H. Ong, K. B. Chan and S. B. Chew (eds) *Crossing Borders: Transmigration in the Asia Pacific*, Singapore: Prentice Hall

Smelser, N. J. (1976) *The Sociology of Economic Life*, Englewood Cliffs: Prentice Hall

Turner, J. H. and E. Bonacich (1980) 'Toward a Composite Theory of Middleman Minorities', *Ethnicity*, 7, 144–58

Waldinger, Roger (1984) 'Immigrant Enterprise in the New York Garment Industry', *Social Problems*, 32 (1), 60–71

—— (1985) 'Immigration and Industrial Change: A Case Study of the New York Apparel Industry', in M. Tienda and G. Borjas (eds) *Hispanic Workers in the United States Economy*, New York: Academic Press, 323–49

—— (1992) 'The Ethnic Enclave Debate Revisited', unpublished manuscript, 13 pp

Waldinger, Roger et al. (1985) 'Ethnic Business and Occupational Mobility in Advanced Societies', *Sociology*, 19 (4), 586–97

—— (1990) *Ethnic Entrepreneurs: Immigrant Business in Industrial Societies*, Newbury Park: Sage

Ward, Robin (1983) 'Ethnic Communities and Ethnic Business', *New Community*, 11, 1–9

Ward, Robin and R. Jenkins (eds) (1984) *Ethnic Communities in Business: Strategies for Economic Survival*, Cambridge: Cambridge University Press

Weber, M. (1958) *The Protestant Ethic and the Spirit of Capitalism*, translated by Talcott Parsons, New York: Scribner

Wickramagamage, Carmen (1992) 'Relocation as Positive Act: The Immigrant Experience in Bharat Mukherjee's Novels', *Diaspora*, (1), 171–200

Yancey, William L. et al. (1976) 'Emergent Ethnicity: A Review and Reformulation', *American Sociological Review*, 41, 391–403

Yoon, In-Jin (1991) 'The Changing Significance of Ethnic and Class Resources in Immigrant Businesses: The Case of Korean Immigrant Businesses in Chicago', *International Migration Review*, 25 (2), 303–32

THE EMERGENCE OF TRANS-PACIFIC MIGRATION

RONALD SKELDON

The 4 May 1984 may become one of those apocryphal dates in recent global history. From that night on, there supposedly have been more commercial aircraft crossing the Pacific Ocean than crossing the Atlantic (Winchester 1991: 21–4). The daily tide of human interaction shifted from a North America–Europe axis to a North America–Asia axis giving definite substance to the otherwise nebulous concept of a Pacific basin community. Part of this increasing trans-Pacific population mobility is the migration of Asian peoples to the traditional European settler societies of Canada, the USA, and Australia and New Zealand.

The migration of Asians to these settler societies is, of course, not new. From the middle of the last century, tens of thousands of people moved from China and Japan, in particular, to North America and Australasia. During the peak years of Chinese migration from 1876 to 1890, an estimated 200,000 were taken to the west coast ports of North America (Tsai 1986: 8). They moved to seek their fortunes in the gold-fields of California or Victoria but also found jobs as labourers on railway construction camps and in fishing and agricultural sectors in California and Australia. In addition, many tens of thousands moved to Central and South America to work as virtual slaves on sugar plantations in Cuba and mining guano for fertilizer in Peru. Most of the Chinese were unskilled, young, unaccompanied males. The vast majority intended to return to their homes after saving enough money after a few years away; they went overseas as sojourners. The fact that many died overseas or became trapped through indebtedness or some other reason does not deny the essential circular nature of the system. This circulation of Chinese sojourners has been seen as a contrast to the migration of settler Europeans, but it is important not to draw too sharp a contrast between settler Europeans and sojourner Chinese and Asians. Many of the Europeans too intended to, and did, return (Chan 1990). For example, in the early twentieth century, 40 to 50 per cent of Italians returned home and, of the English and Welsh who left between 1861 and 1913, close to 40 per cent returned (Baines 1991: 39), compared with about 33 per cent of the Chinese (Chan 1990: 38).

The critical difference between Chinese and European nineteenth-century migration was that the Chinese were moving into a country governed by institutions established by the Europeans. This was to lead to institutionalized prejudice towards the Asian. With the arrival of increasing numbers of Chinese, tension arose between non-Chinese and Chinese; the European legislators at the various destinations, responding to public pressure, moved to limit the numbers of Asian migrants, particularly Chinese. The path towards the adoption of restrictive legislation on Asian immigration was long and complicated, beginning in the late 1850s in South Australia and New South Wales but not seriously affecting the migration until the 1880s (Price 1974). New Zealand effectively began to close its doors from 1881, Canada from 1885, the USA from 1888 and the Australian colonies from 1888–9. Although there was new legislation and changes were made to existing legislation, the immigration policies of these countries were essentially based upon race until after the Second World War, and it was not really until the 1960s that these discriminatory policies were finally swept away. Hence it is to the late 1960s and early 1970s that we look to the emergence of the new Asian migration across the Pacific.

In the period from the mid-1950s through the mid-1960s, Asian countries accounted for about 8 per cent of migrants to the USA and 5 per cent or less of migrants to Canada, Australia and New Zealand (Kritz 1987: 33). Europeans still dominated the settler intake at that time. By the early 1990s, about 43 per cent of the annual immigrant intake into Canada and the USA and 49 per cent of settlers to Australia were from Asia. European sources accounted for only about one-fifth of migrants to Canada, less than one-third of settlers to Australia and only about one in seven of immigrants to the USA. In terms of absolute numbers, Asians accounted for some 256,000 migrants to the USA in 1990, 91,000 to Canada and 56,000 to Australia.

The principal areas of origin vary depending upon the destination country. The main Asian sources of the largest flow, that to the USA, are the Philippines,

Thailand, India, China, South Korea, Hong Kong and Taiwan. In the case of Canada, since 1987 Hong Kong has been the principal source, not just of migration from Asia but for all immigration. In 1992, almost 39,000 people, or over 15 per cent of landed immigrants in that year, came from Hong Kong. Although no other Asian source even approaches half of this number, the Philippines, India and China were nevertheless significant sources of immigrants to Canada. Hong Kong is the second most important source of settler migrants to Australia, after the UK, again accounting for about 15 per cent of the settler intake in 1991–2. The other major Asian source countries are Vietnam, the Philippines, India and, until recently, Malaysia.

As we might expect, the two demographic giants of China (population 1,134 million in 1992) and India (population 850 million in 1992) figure prominently in all the flows. However, the explanation for the development of the trans-Pacific flows cannot be attributed to size alone. In the case of the USA, the main source areas include those areas where the Americans have had their greatest political, military and economic involvement in Asia: the Philippines, Taiwan, Vietnam and South Korea. The trade and political linkages are reinforced by human flows; one in nine American servicemen based in South Korea, for example, is estimated to return home with a Korean wife (Kuznets 1987). These linkages are forged down to the local level, with those particular small areas where American bases were located being among the principal sending areas in the source countries (Carino et al. 1990). When we look at the trans-Pacific flows as a whole, it is also clear that Chinese or Chinese-influenced culture areas play a dominant role: China, Taiwan, Hong Kong and South Korea. In fact, the position of the Chinese is underrepresented if we consider only these areas. Large numbers of Vietnamese taken in as refugees by western countries in the late 1970s were ethnic Chinese, as are large but unknown numbers of those leaving Thailand, Malaysia and probably the Philippines, as well as Singapore. As will become clearer below, it is the movement of the Chinese peoples which is ultimately likely to make the greatest impact on the destination societies over the long term.

The flows include a great variety of types of migrant. Some older or unskilled migrants have entered under family reunification schemes, which still dominate the annual intake into the USA, for example, accounting for almost two-thirds of the preference system. It is well known, however, that highly educated, skilled or professional people, or those with access to considerable financial resources, figure prominently among the Asian migrants. For example, in the flow out of Hong Kong in the early 1990s, over two-thirds of emigrants of working age were identified as 'managers and administrators, professionals and associate professionals'. Some 16.7 per cent of the emigrants had a degree or a postgraduate qualification. Skilled migrants are not just to be found among the Chinese or the Koreans (Park et al. 1990) but also among the Indians who 'may still be the best educated of all immigrants [to the USA]' (Bhardwaj and Rao 1990: 200). This is not to say that the majority of the Asian migrants fall into this category – there are large numbers of poor and unskilled among their numbers, particularly from countries such as Vietnam – but that the minority who do are likely to have a significant impact on origin and destination areas. Migrants from Hong Kong and Taiwan have dominated the various business immigration programmes of Canada, Australia and New Zealand. They accounted for 54 per cent of the business migrants to Canada in 1991, for example, with a net worth of almost C$5500 million (Wong 1992).

It is not possible, however, to argue that a net transfer of skills and wealth across the Pacific acts to the detriment of the areas of origin. The migration from Hong Kong, Taiwan and South Korea has been from some of the fastest growing economies in the world and it is difficult to imagine them growing even faster if the migrants had remained at home. Many migrants return to their home country with greater skills, with some 20 to 30 per cent of professionals in South Korea, for example, having been trained abroad, mainly in the USA, but also in Japan (Kuznets 1987). There is thus a two-way flow of population and ideas across the Pacific. There is also a curious new form of spatially extended family that is evolving which is a product of the Asian migration in the context of modern communications. The existence of this pattern shows that the figures on the number of immigrants need to be treated with some caution as they reveal nothing about circulation or about return movements.

The Hong Kong and Taiwanese migrants, in particular, appear to engage in what have become known as the 'astronaut' and 'parachute kids' syndromes. The former involves leaving wife and children in a house purchased at the destination country, while the husband returns to the place of origin to continue his business or professional activities. The latter involves establishing the children, usually teenagers, in a house in a destination country, while the parents continue their activities in the place of origin. This bilocality achieves several objectives. It allows people to have access to citizenship through the spouse, or the children once they become of age, although the main breadwinner remains outside the destination country most of the time. More significantly, it represents a risk-minimization strategy which allows people access to markets in areas that may be at very different stages of the international business cycle or of political development. People are then in a position to organize their migration: if there is a recession in North America and growth in Asia, they are likely to flow to Asia; but if there is political risk or an economic slowdown in Asia, then they can move the other way within the widespread family networks established.

Until recently, there was little more than anecdotal evidence to suggest that this type of flow was occurring, and we still know relatively little about its volume and extent. It must be assumed that it is limited to a wealthy minority of migrants who can afford to commute regularly across the Pacific. Data from the most recent censuses of Australia and New Zealand have revealed that this pattern of bilocality may be extensive. The age–sex structure of the Hong Kong-born or those whose last place of permanent residence was Hong Kong revealed marked female bias in the 25–39 years age cohorts – the wives 'left' at destinations – and much higher proportions of young people than would be expected given prevailing family structures in the places of origin (Ho and Farmer 1994; Kee and Skeldon 1994). A survey taken by the University of California, Los Angeles, has suggested that there are 40,000 'parachute kids' aged 8 to 18 years in the USA, mostly from Taiwan (*International Herald Tribune*, 25 June 1993).

Data from Australia also suggest that up to 30 per cent of the Hong Kong-born settlers who arrived in Australia between 1 January 1990 and 30 June 1991 had returned to Hong Kong by the time of the census in early August 1991 (Kee and Skeldon 1994). This Australian case may be more extreme than Canada, and certainly than the USA, but significant return migration probably exists from these destinations too. The existence of such commuting and return migration raises interesting political as well as social and economic issues: questions of national allegiance and cultural identity, for example, within these trans-Pacific networks. Canadian and Australian authorities hope to make Canadians or Australians out of immigrants and settlers, yet these transnational migration networks presuppose no simple national loyalties among their rootless populations. We may be seeing the emergence of powerful and influential groups without clear national identities.

The numbers of settlers or immigrants referred to above represent but one part of the trans-Pacific population movement. Students are not included among their number. Although many students stay on at their destination after completing their studies, many also return home, taking the knowledge they have acquired. In the early to mid-1960s, only about 5 per cent of students from Taiwan studying in the USA returned home, but more recent evidence suggests that the rate of return has increased substantially (see Skeldon 1992). Asian countries accounted for over half of the almost 420,000 students in the USA in 1991/2, with China, Japan, Taiwan, India and South Korea sending the largest numbers of students. If we look back over thirty years to 1960, we find that there were only a relatively small number of foreign students in the USA at that time, just over 31,000, although the roots of today's substantial numbers were already in place, with China (including Taiwan and Hong Kong) second after Canada as the major source of students, and India, Iran, South Korea, Japan and the Philippines all figuring prominently among the top ten source countries (IIE 1992). In many cases, the students pioneered the trans-Pacific pathways; today, the dramatic increase in their numbers attests to the important role of the USA, and of Canada and Australia, in the education of peoples around the Pacific. There were over 70,000 foreign students in Canada in 1989, 54 per cent of whom were from Asian countries, and some 52,500 in Australia, 86 per cent of whom were from Asian countries.

In addition to settlers and students, large numbers of other migrants are moving back and forth across the Pacific on a short- or medium-term basis. There are the skilled migrants and business executives sent by their companies to carry out specific contracts in particular areas. We still know little about these movers as few countries keep detailed statistics. South Korea is one of the few in Asia that does; there, travel for business increased from annual numbers of 20,000 to 30,000 in the mid-1970s to over 400,000 in 1990. The most important destination was Japan, which accounted for just over half of the moves, but the second most important destination was the USA, with 12 per cent of these business moves (Korea 1991: 66–7). It has been estimated that there were over 103,000 skilled 'transients' from Taiwan overseas in 1990, the majority in the USA, but also in Japan and elsewhere in the region (Skeldon 1992: 43). As Asian multi-national corporations increase in number, so too will the volume of this type of movement which, together with the astronauts discussed earlier, contributes so much to the increase in airline traffic highlighted in the opening paragraph of this chapter.

The last type of short-term mobility is associated with tourism. Tourist arrivals grew faster in the Asia-Pacific region during the 1980s than anywhere else in the world. This partly reflects the new affluence of Asians themselves, but it also reflects the increasing importance of Asia as a destination for Americans and Australasians, as well as Europeans. Annual inter-national tourist arrivals increased from around 20 million in 1980 to 46.5 million in 1990 for the East Asian and Pacific region (Harrison 1992: 4). Japan is now a major source of tourists not only to Southeast Asia but also to the USA, particularly Hawaii.

The new Asian migrant, whether settler or transient, tends to be highly educated and skilled, quite different from the old labour migrants of the nineteenth cen-tury. Whereas the latter were primarily young males, women are participating as much as men in the new trans-Pacific flows, particularly of settlers. The migration flow from South Korea to the USA is female-dominant, and much of the migration out of the Philippines is of young women as nurses, domes-tic servants and entertainers, for example. There are, however, continuities with the 'old' pattern of over-seas Chinese migration in the present illegal move-ment out of China to the USA. It is estimated that the volume of this illegal movement has increased from a few thousand in the mid- to late 1980s to perhaps 100,000 in 1992. The boats, often Taiwanese coastal freighters or traders, carrying between 200 and 500 immigrants across the Pacific have caught much international media attention, particularly since the grounding of the *Golden Venture* on a New Jersey beach and the death of several migrants as they strug-gled to reach the shore. The majority, however, still almost certainly travel much of the way by aeroplane, using the networks of overseas Chinese communities in Latin America and the Caribbean to provide documentation and onward air or land passage into the USA. As in the nineteenth century, most of the ille-gals are young men, many, if not most, are advanced the US$30,000 required for the trip and thus become essentially bonded labour. The majority hope to return to China after making money in the USA and so the sojourner system persists to the present day.

One of the matters of most concern to authorities dealing with the increasing trans-Pacific illegal migration is the influence of organized Asian crime. Much of the money advanced to prospective migrants and the logistics of the passage are arranged through triads in Hong Kong or Taiwan, or tongs in the Chinese communities in America. The smuggling of people is a business worth some US$3000 million a year. Many of those transported are hardworking labourers, mainly from Fujian province in southern China, but small numbers of hardened criminals among them are joining the gangs in New York and San Francisco. Allied with the international drug trade, this migration is seeing the establishment and reinforcement of trans-Pacific and global criminal networks controlled by Asian groups. This is likely to have a profound effect on destination societies and any future new world order (Skeldon 1994).

When the movements out of Asia began in the 1960s, fertility in all Asian countries except Japan was high, and population growth rates in countries such as South Korea and Taiwan were generally in excess of 2.5 per cent per annum. It is too simplistic to associate emigration with rapid population growth and, since the 1960s, fertility has come down throughout most of the East Asian and Southeast Asian region. Although there is no apparent correlation between fertility decline and the pattern of emigration, the sustained low levels of fertility have resulted in the slow growth of the labour forces throughout much of the region. The boom economies of South Korea, Taiwan, Hong Kong, Singapore, Malaysia and Japan are all in labour-deficit. All tightly control immigration and have responded to the labour shortages by moving labour-intensive industrialization offshore to areas where there is labour. For example, the numbers employed in manufacturing in Hong Kong declined from over 900,000 in the mid-1980s to about 600,000 in 1992 as industrialists moved their operations into southern China. These areas have also responded by importing contract labour to fill positions at all skill levels: from the dirty, dangerous and demanding jobs at the bottom end of the spectrum, which the local population are becoming increasingly reluctant to undertake as their education levels and aspirations rise, to the highly skilled specialisms for which there are no local sources of supply. Thus, a series of regional flows of contract labour migration have been set in motion and, in a faint echo, as yet, of what has occurred in southern Europe, there has been a turnaround from countries of mass emigration towards countries of increasing immigration. This applies to South Korea, Taiwan and Japan in particular. The Philippines, with its English-speaking and skilled labour force, is a major source of supply of labour to many destinations in the East Asian region, although increasing numbers of South Asians are also being found in Taiwan, South Korea and Japan. As in the migration to North America, illegal or undocumented flows are increasing. The majority land legally but overstay their visas and, in Japan, it is estimated that there are some 320,000 illegal workers (Spencer 1992), the majority from the Philippines, Pakistan, Bangladesh and South Korea. In countries which traditionally have seen their societies as homogeneous, the future impact of these movements is likely to be great indeed. For an insightful account of what it means for an Asian to be 'underground' in Japan, see Ventura (1992).

Over the last twenty-five years we have seen a major shift in the global systems of international migration. From a system dominated by movement out of Europe across the Atlantic and to Australasia, there has been a shift to trans-Pacific movement out of Asian countries to the traditional destinations for European settlement. These trans-Pacific flows of the twenty-first century could easily come to rival the trans-Atlantic flows of the late nineteenth and early twentieth centuries. Among Asian migrants, it is the Chinese, with their high levels of education, entrepreneurial skills and financial resources, who are likely to make the biggest impact on the destination societies. Asian Americans are emerging as well-supported local and regional political leaders, as we saw in the contest for mayor of Los Angeles early in 1992. As China develops too, we can expect increasing involvement of its people in international flows, both legally and illegally. With fertility below replacement levels throughout western Europe and the developed countries of North America and Australasia, it is international migration that will be the major demographic force for change in the next century. There is already a struggle to attract the best and the brightest among the migrants by destination countries, and this will intensify as other countries join the search for labour as a consequence of their low fertility. The global networks of human interaction established as the result of these international movements are an important factor in accentuating the interdependent nature of the world community. Nowhere is this more important than in the most dynamic growth areas of the Pacific rim.

References

Baines, D. (1991) *Emigration from Europe 1815–1930*, London: Macmillan

Bhardwaj, S. M. and N. M. Rao (1990) 'Asian Indians in the United States: A Geographic Appraisal', in C. Clarke, C. Peach and S. Vertovec (eds) *South Asians Overseas: Migration and Ethnicity*, Cambridge: Cambridge University Press, 197–217

Carino, B. V. et al. (1990) 'The New Filipino Immigrants to the United States: Increasing Diversity and Change', *Papers of the East–West Population Institute*, No. 115, Honolulu, Hawaii

Chan, Sucheng (1990) 'European and Asian Immigration into the United States in Comparative Perspective, 1820s to 1920s', in V. Yans-McLaughlin (ed.) *Immigration Reconsidered: History, Sociology, and Politics*, New York: Oxford University Press, 37–75

Harrison, D. (1992) 'International Tourism and the Less Developed Countries: The Background', in D. Harrison (ed.) *Tourism and the Less Developed Countries*, London: Belhaven, 1–18

Ho, E. and R. Farmer (1994) 'The Hong Kong Chinese in Auckland', in R. Skeldon (ed.) *Reluctant Exiles? Migration from Hong Kong and the New Overseas Chinese*, New York: M. E. Sharpe/Hong Kong: Hong Kong University Press, 215–32

IIE (1992) *Open Doors: Report on International Educational Exchange*, New York: Institute of International Education

Kee, Pookong and R. Skeldon (1994) 'The Migration and Settlement of Hong Kong Chinese in Australia', in R. Skeldon (ed.) *Reluctant Exiles? Migration from Hong Kong and the New Overseas Chinese*, New York: M. E. Sharpe/Hong Kong: Hong Kong University Press, 183–96

Korea (1991) *Korea Statistical Yearbook 1991*, Republic of Korea: National Statistical Office

Kritz, M. M. (1987) 'The Global Picture of Contemporary Immigration Patterns', in J. T. Fawcett and B. V. Carino (eds) *Pacific Bridges: The New Immigration from Asia and the Pacific Islands*, Staten Island, New York: Center for Migration Studies, 29–51

Kuznets, P. W. (1987) 'Koreans in America: Recent Migration from South Korea to the United States', in S. Klein (ed.) *The Economics of Mass Migration in the Twentieth Century*, New York: Paragon, 41–69

Park, I. N. et al. (1990) 'Korean Immigrants and US Immigration Policy: A Predeparture Perspective', *Papers of the East–West Population Institute*, No. 114, Honolulu, Hawaii

Price, C. A. (1974) *The Great White Walls Are Built: Restrictive Immigration to North America and Australasia 1836–1888*, Canberra: Australian National University Press

Skeldon, R. (1992) 'International Migration within and from the East and Southeast Asian Region: A Review Essay', *Asian and Pacific Migration Journal*, 1 (1), 19–63

—— (1994) 'East Asian Migration and the New World Order', in W. Gould and A. Findlay (eds) *Population Migration and the Changing World Order*, London: Belhaven

Spencer, S. A. (1992) 'Illegal Migrant Laborers in Japan', *International Migration Review*, 26 (3), 754–86

Tsai, Shih-shan H. (1986) *The Chinese Experience in America*, Bloomington: Indiana University Press

Ventura, R. (1992) *Underground in Japan*, London: Cape

Winchester, S. (1991) *The Pacific*, London: Hutchinson

Wong, L. L. (1992) 'Chinese Business Immigration to Canada', paper presented at the International Conference on Overseas Chinese, San Francisco, 26–29 November

ILLEGAL MIGRATION

MARK J. MILLER

When the more industrially advanced states of the North Atlantic began to regulate international migration in the second half of the nineteenth century, their qualitative and quantitative restrictions on entry created the possibility for unauthorized entry, residency and employment by aliens. Usage of terms like illegal immigration, illegal aliens, clandestine or irregular migrants often is imprecise and emotive. The bulk of illegal immigrants in many countries entered legally, say with a student or visitor's visa, but then violated the terms of their entry by overstaying. This pattern prevails, for instance, in Australia where, due to its remoteness, relatively few aliens succeed in penetrating the country illegally, although some unauthorized landings on the northern coast have occurred. As all aliens are required to obtain visas to enter, Australian authorities generate quite accurate estimates of their illegal alien residents by matching authorized entries against recorded departures of aliens.

In other lands, such as the USA, Spain or Italy, unauthorized entry and subsequent illegal residency and employment is more prevalent, although it does not necessarily constitute the predominant mode of infringement upon immigration laws. Every night along the 2000-mile-long border between the USA and Mexico, thousands of aliens attempt to enter illegally. Many are caught and returned to Mexico. But many others succeed. Most are Mexican citizens, but other Latin Americans and increasingly people from around the world go to northern Mexico to seek to evade US immigration restrictions.

The magnitude of such illegal entry to the USA is very difficult to measure. Estimates are made on the basis of individual aliens apprehended at various borders and demographers have made calculations on the basis of census data comparisons, using residual and other techniques. An August 1993 General Accounting Office report estimated the illegal alien population in the USA in 1990 at 3.4 million, with a 5.5 million figure representing a maximum estimate. The truth of the matter is that no one knows with any precision just how many aliens illegally reside in the USA. But this has not prevented politicians and academics from making widely diverging estimates. It is not only in the USA that prudence has succumbed to the siren of quantifying the uncountable. Estimates of illegal alien populations in France are bandied about, particularly during electoral periods, often with the aim of discrediting one party or another.

Estimates of illegal alien populations, hence, should always be treated with caution. Particular care should be taken not to confuse illegal alien employment with illegal employment in general. French enforcement statistics reveal, for instance, that only about one-third of detected illegal employment involves illegally employed aliens. Most illegal employment arises from French citizens working 'off the books'. Nevertheless, illegal or clandestine employment is frequently equated with illegal alien employment. One sure indication of the growing saliency of illegal migration worldwide by the late twentieth century was precisely the perceived need to come up with reliable information on the scope of the phenomenon. Such a need was not apparent at the turn of the century or even as late as 1950.

It is also possible for aliens to be legal residents of a country but to be illegally employed. In many western European countries, asylum applicants, students, tourists and family members of alien residents are subject to employment restrictions. Nonetheless, they take up employment and thereby violate the law, sometimes unwittingly. By the 1990s, most asylum applicants in Germany and France were barred from employment for periods up to five years. The aim was to discourage aliens from circumventing restrictions on alien employment via asylum provisions. Yet, many apparently succeeded in finding employment despite the restrictions.

A generic term like illegal migration thus covers a variety of situations. Its connotation is often quite negative, although not necessarily so. Many illegal migrants consciously violate immigration laws. But, in other situations, illegal immigrants are produced overnight by changes in politics and policies or by the complexities of maintaining legal residency. For example, millions of West Africans emigrated to Nigeria during the 1970s and early 1980s believing that their entry, stay and employment was authorized under the West African regional integration pact known by the acronym ECOWAS. Plummeting oil prices, an economic downturn and a change in government led to a reinterpretation of their status. Many formerly tolerated alien residents became illegal aliens subject to deportation. Millions of aliens fled or were repatriated as a result.

Similarly, in various parts of the Arab world, legally resident alien populations have lost their legal status overnight. This happened to a number of Yemenis who were ordered out of Saudi Arabia during the Gulf crisis of 1990/1. Also, hundreds of thousands of Palestinians were shamelessly evicted from Kuwait after the defeat of Iraq. When US, French, Italian and British troops were dispatched to Beirut, following the Israeli invasion in 1982, they rounded up and delivered to a still unknown fate thousands of 'illegal aliens'. Likewise, the mercurial state of relations between Libya and its neighbours resulted in a sudden change of status and subsequent expulsion for tens of thousands of Tunisian and Egyptian workers.

Some of the estimated 25 million Russians living outside the borders of the post-USSR Russian Federation risk becoming illegal migrants if they decline to become citizens of a Soviet successor state or otherwise cannot adjust their status to altered political circumstances. In many cases, designation of ethnically distinctive population groups as illegal immigrants is motivated by historical resentments and/or national security considerations. Populations branded as illegal immigrants figured prominently in regional and bilateral tensions in the immediate post-cold war period. It became increasingly clear that international migration, inclusive of millions of illegal migrants worldwide, had become a major cause and effect of the new international disorder. Governments of Western democracies began to consult feverishly to grope for ways to prevent feared mass, unwanted migrations. This forced a long overdue reckoning with the determinants of illegal migration.

The history of illegal migration sheds a great deal of light on the factors, processes and relationships that result in foreigners violating immigration laws. As in all history, interpretation of illegal immigration is shaped by divergent perspectives and interests. Many in advanced industrial societies are wont to interpret illegal immigration as driven by forces from without — overpopulation, economic misery, political turmoil and the like — while many in the developing world are prone to view illegal immigration as a response to

forces within advanced industrial states. From this viewpoint, illegal migrants are impelled by shortfalls of labour, the lure of high wages, or by indigenous populations simply shunning certain types of labour.

Rarely, however, does it suffice to account for illegal migration in such bald terms. A great deal of illegal immigration occurs between developing countries and fits poorly into a south to north schema. Indeed, two of the most striking points to be made about late twentieth century illegal migration are its globalization, with transportation and communication advances facilitating migration that was scarcely possible several decades earlier, and its decoupling from historically set patterns. While immigration history still explains why more Algerians are illegally present in France than in Germany and more Turks are presumably illegally present in Germany than in France, what is increasingly striking is the diversity of origins of illegal populations. They come from around the world and not just from countries that traditionally have supplied large numbers of migrants to another. It is important to note too that considerable numbers of illegal immigrants in the most economically advanced countries originate from other economically advanced countries. Recent French and Italian legalizations, for instance, have permitted substantial numbers of Americans to accede to legal status. A 1993 study of illegal immigrants in New York City determined that Italians comprised the single largest group of illegal migrants living there.

Policies permitting aliens to legalize their status became commonplace in the 1970s and 1980s. Some countries had long practised legalization. France routinely legalized aliens from 1946 to 1970. As late as 1968, more than 80 per cent of migrants admitted to residency technically arrived outside of established procedures. Such diverse countries as Argentina, Venezuela, Malaysia, Sweden, the UK, the Netherlands and Australia authorized legalizations. These policies have shed considerable new light on illegal migration, although even here caution is the byword. Some of the major limitations on knowledge about illegal migration derived from legalizations stem from the nature of the legalization policies. They typically were limited to certain classes of illegal residents and their efficacy hinged on publicity as well as a perception that the amnesty offered was genuine and generous. It is generally thought, though sharply disputed in the case of the French legalization of 1981/2, that major legalization efforts failed to legalize all illegal alien residents, thereby casting a shadow over the representativeness of research findings based on the sampling of legalizing aliens. Despite limitations such as this, the results of studies done on legalizing aliens have provided a sound understanding of the key patterns and characteristics of illegal alien populations.

Illegal migrants are typically disproportionally young and concentrated in certain geographical areas, particularly major urban centres. Most work and are clustered in specific industries. Construction, labour-intensive agriculture, hotel and restaurant employment, the garment industry, gardening and domestic services often attract significant numbers of unauthorized foreign workers Physically difficult, risky, servile or 'dirty' work is common as are low wages and long or irregular hours. However, many illegal alien workers are paid at or above minimal wage rates and many pay into social security systems and, where available, health insurance schemes. Caution is required in interpreting findings because it is possible, indeed probable, that many of the most exploited illegal foreign workers do not figure in studies of legalized aliens. Their employers, who are themselves often of the same national origin, were less prone to cooperate with legalization policies. Legalization policies were usually accompanied by a period of grace for employers to encourage their cooperation over the duration of the legalization period. At the end of the period, employers of illegal aliens were subject to reinforced civil and even criminal penalties. In the US case, longstanding employers of illegal aliens were specifically exempted from punishment by what was known as the Texas Proviso to the 1952 immigration law. The exemption suggested *de facto* toleration of illegal migration, which only ended in 1986.

The single largest legalization effort occurred in the USA between 1987 and 1989. About three million aliens were accorded legal status and eventually residency under the terms of several specific legalization opportunities. Mexicans proved to be the major beneficiaries, with roughly three-quarters of successful applicants having come from Mexico. Other major legalization efforts in the 1980s and early 1990s included a series of Italian policies which confirmed the substantial presence of Senegalese and Moroccans in Italy, the French programme which legalized some 130,000–140,000 aliens including significant numbers of North Africans, and the Spanish programmes which resulted in tens of thousands of Moroccans acceding to legal status.

Despite legalization policies, the imposition and reinforcement of sanctions against employers of illegal aliens and a host of other measures adopted by governments to prevent unauthorized alien entry, residency and employment, the phenomenon looms as a major challenge to governments in the twenty-first century. The expectation is that there is likely to be more rather than less illegal migration in the future. By the 1990s, fear of uncontrollable mass migration, particularly from the former Warsaw bloc states, had already fuelled xenophobic reactions in western Europe.

Yet, the spectre of mass, uncontrollable migrations from the former Soviet bloc appears exaggerated. Many of the millions of emigrants who succeeded in leaving the area after 1989 were ethnic minorities welcomed as citizens elsewhere. To get out, most people would have to obtain a visa or emigrate illegally. Due to the isolation of the area from the rest of the world from 1945 to 1989, there did not appear to be the networks in place to facilitate mass illegal migration from the East. And most aspiring migrants found it difficult to obtain a visa. Moreover, western democracies were taking steps to ensure that states like Poland, Hungary and the Czech Republic functioned as an immigration *cordon sanitaire* or buffer to unwanted migration from the East.

For all the permeability of states in the late twentieth century, they still could exercise considerable, if imperfect, control over entry. For all their shortcomings, measures like employer sanctions, border controls and visa policies most probably considerably discouraged illegal migration. In all likelihood, only a minority of those aspiring to emigrate outside of legal procedures succeeded in establishing viable residency abroad. While their numbers were substantial and fated to expand, there was little reason to expect sovereign states to be overwhelmed or submerged by uncontrollable hordes of aliens. In the worst scenario, and governments increasingly thought of illegal immigration in terms of bad, worse and calamitous scenarios, huge influxes of aliens would be countered with extraordinary steps, including the use of the military, as witnessed in Austria, Italy and Spain in the late 1980s and early 1990s. In post-cold war rethinking of national security policies, prevention of illegal migration and unwanted migration assumed a novel significance on policymakers' agendas.

Measures like regional socio-economic and, in some instances, political integration, trade liberalization and increased humanitarian and development assistance to less developed regions held out some prospect of attenuating illegal migration over the long run. However, as evidenced by the US debate over ratification of the North American Free Trade Agreement (NAFTA) signed in 1992, such measures paradoxically could increase illegal migration over the short to medium term. NAFTA, for instance, was touted by its proponents as a way of diminishing illegal migration to the USA from Mexico. But the short- to medium-term expectation was for NAFTA and other Mexican economic liberalization policies to increase illegal migration from Mexico as subsidies to the traditional *ejido* agricultural sector, which employed about one-fifth of the Mexican workforce, were phased out. It was unclear whether the employment-creating investment fostered by NAFTA could keep pace with the anticipated exodus of Mexican workers and their families from a traditional agricultural sector doomed by its inability to compete with US agriculture.

The NAFTA debate indicated that there were no short-term 'silver bullets' or single-stroke solutions to the complex issues of illegal migration. The track record of humanitarian and development assistance as a means of attenuating illegal migration was not encouraging. And the protracted negotiations during the Uruguay round of GATT underscored the very real poltical constraints on trade liberalization. The only certainty seemed to be that illegal migration reflected global inequalities and disorder. These appeared to be growing rather than decreasing. Illegal migration also could not be satisfactorily stemmed unilaterally. Bilateral, regional and global approaches were required to address a phenomenon forged by growing interdependency, globalization of the economy and inextricably linked to a thickening web of transnational relations. By the late twentieth century, it had become abundantly clear that international migration, including millions of illegal migrants, had become the world's most humanly intensive transnational phenomenon and that people in addition to states would shape the future of global politics.

THE URBANIZATION OF THE GLOBE

JOSEF GUGLER

Most migration in the world is distinguished from international migration by one significant detail: it does not cross international borders. Guards on those borders have succeeded in keeping international migration at a level that is insignificant compared with internal migration. Most of that internal migration is rural–rural, but here I shall focus on rural–urban migration. Past such migrations have nearly depleted the countryside in industrialized countries, and they are now effecting the urban transition in Latin America, Asia and Africa as well. A few years ago two-thirds of the population of these regions lived in rural areas; in little more than a generation two-thirds will be urban residents. We are witnessing one of the profound human transformations: the urbanization of the globe.

Like international migration, most internal migration reflects the spatial distribution and redistribution of economic opportunities. In most poor countries the differences between urban and rural standards of living are substantial: dramatic testimony is provided by infant and child mortality rates that are higher in rural than in urban areas, frequently by a large margin, in all but a few countries (Gilbert and Gugler 1992: 66–7). Lipton's *Why Poor People Stay Poor* (1977) has prompted considerable debate as to the extent to which public policy in less developed countries is guided by an urban bias that concentrates resources on the urban sector and hence exaggerates its attraction for migrants (Varshney 1993).

A related debate concerns the proposition that less developed countries suffer from 'over urbanization'. In sharp contrast to the urbanization experience of the north, most of the labour force in the cities of the south is found in government administration, commerce, workshop production and repairs, and domestic work, rather than industry. Unemployment and underemployment are widespread. In addition, it may be argued that there is substantial mis-employment: large numbers of people are employed in a wasteful manner, contributing little to social welfare because their labour is so cheap relative to the incomes of the elite and the middle class (Gugler 1995).

Whatever the advantages of urban over rural conditions, various sectors of the urban population are constantly threatened by new arrivals from the countryside competing for jobs and seeking to share in urban resources. The exceptions are the city states where the increases in the standard of living were never diluted by large masses of immigrants from rural areas: Singapore seceded from the Federation of Malaysia in 1965, and Hong Kong is separated from its hinterland by a colonial border until 1997.

Urban privilege relative to rural areas might be protected by restrictions on rural–urban migration. But few governments have established controls on internal migration. The policing that is taken for granted on international borders is rarely acceptable within countries. The notable exceptions were, until a few years ago, totalitarian regimes such as the Soviet Union and China, as well as the South African police state.

The south is urbanizing rapidly, but not any more rapidly than the north did at an earlier time. The increase in the proportion of the population living in urban areas in the south was similar between 1950 and 1975 to the rate that characterized the urban transition in Europe seventy-five years earlier. The rate of urban growth, however, is without precedent. This 'urban explosion' is due to the combination of rapid urbanization and the high rates of natural population growth, in both rural and urban areas, characteristic of most of the south since the Second World War. High natural population growth rather than rapid urbanization is the new phenomenon in world history (Preston 1988).

Three developments have reoriented migration studies in the south in recent years: an interest in the gender dimension of migration; an appreciation of the social embeddedness of migration; and a recognition that a great deal of rural–urban migration is temporary.

Gender in migration

Recently there has been considerable interest in women in migration, but little research has as yet been published. To date, most books and articles purporting to deal with the migration of people in fact focus on the migration of men. An additional problem is that the migration research that does include women in its purview usually treats them as the dependants of migrating men. There is every indication that this will change dramatically within the next few years.

Distinct gender patterns characterize rural–urban migration in different countries. Men dominate in net migration in South Asia and in many Middle Eastern and African countries, but in Latin America, the Philippines, Thailand and Ethiopia there is a preponderance of women. Many of these women come to town to work, at least initially, as domestics. Gender selectivity in net rural–urban migration is reflected in urban sex ratios: women outnumber men in the urban populations of every Latin American country, whereas men outnumber women by a substantial margin in the cities of every country in South Asia.

These regional contrasts may be explained in terms of women being more or less tied down in rural society. In most peasant societies women marry early and bear many children and, unlike their husbands, are most unlikely to migrate on their own. In contrast, where women remain unmarried for some years beyond puberty, they are potentially mobile. Such independent women are usually faced with limited rural opportunities and are attracted by cities that offer better opportunities in terms of work as well as (re-)marriage.

The preponderance of women in the urban population is a recent phenomenon in some countries. In a number of other countries the preponderance of men in the urban population has declined abruptly over the last few decades (Gugler and Ludwar-Ene 1994). On one hand, fewer men working in the city leave their wives and children in the village. On the other, more women migrate on their own.

These trends may be seen in terms of a decline of patriarchy. In most societies patriarchs controlled daughters, arranged their marriages, controlled wives, and put pressure on separated, divorced and widowed women to remarry. Their control has been weakened by several modern developments: birth control, education, women gaining access to work outside the home. Later marriage, reduced fertility and greater independence are modifying cultural definitions of women's roles as wives and mothers, and set them free to move. Substantial numbers of never married, separated, divorced and widowed women seize the opportunities the city offers them – and transform the gender composition of net rural–urban migration.

The social context of migration

For about two decades a political economy approach emphasized the structural determinants of migration and dismissed an earlier focus on the individual migrant as irrelevant. Of late there has been renewed interest in the micro-level, but rather than focusing on the individual migrant there is now a recognition of the role of family, kin and friends. Migration is seen to be embedded in social relations: the option to migrate is informed by the experience of others, the decision to migrate is taken in a family context, and the migratory move is assisted by relatives and friends.

The social embeddedness of migration is highlighted where the rural–urban migration of individuals is part of the strategy of a family or kin group to ensure the viability of the rural household. Watson's (1958) classic study, pointedly entitled *Tribal Cohesion in a Money Economy*, described how the Mambwe people of present-day Zambia had made a success of deploying their labour in both subsistence farming and urban employment. Village life flourished despite a high rate of labour migration. More recently, Arizpe (1981) has shown how peasant families in Mexico have their members take turns in migrating to supplement household production. And Parry (1979) reports from the Kangra District in India that the remittances of migrants provide the material base for the perpetuation of rural social structure.

The family character of the migration decision is obvious where young women are sent out to supplement the family income from their urban wages. Trager (1988) describes such a strategy in the Philippines. Young (1982) relates what she terms the 'expulsion' of young daughters from rural Oaxaca, Mexico, to the requirements of their parental households. These accounts problematize the notion that the migration of single women reflects an expansion of the opportunities open to them.

Frequently, of course, it is the male heads of young families who migrate, and they often take family decisions largely on their own. More generally, as we conceptualize the family deploying its members across the rural and urban arena, we have to keep in mind that male household heads usually dominate migration decisions. In addition to the urban bias that affects migration decisions, we have to recognize the male bias in the formulation of migration strategies.

Temporary migration

The new emphasis on the social relations surrounding

PLATE 23: Village life among the Chakma in the Chittagong Hills, Bandarban, Bangladesh, 1990. Will such villages disappear? Or will a 'dual-system' strategy allow the continuance of village life, with villagers commuting to the towns and cities?

the individual migrant is related to a third development in migration studies, the growing awareness that a good deal of rural–urban migration in the south continues to be temporary. Indeed, at least four migration strategies need to be distinguished:

- circular migration of men;
- long-term migration of men separated from their families;
- family migration to urban areas followed by return migration to the community of origin; and
- permanent urban settlement.

Circular migration is a function of the recruitment of men at low wages. It was common in tropical Africa in colonial days when the authorities and commercial interests typically pursued a cheap labour policy. In parts of British colonial Africa, as well as on some Pacific islands, a pattern of circular migration was aimed at for political reasons as well, and policies were adopted to that purpose.

South Africa presented, until a few years ago, the extreme case of temporary migration imposed by law on a large part of the urban labour force for over a century. Pass controls were used to promote organized recruitment, enforce contracts of limited duration and prevent permanent settlement of workers in the mining districts. This 'cheap labour power system' benefited the mines and other sectors employing migrant labour: the costs of the reproduction of labour power were borne by the rural sector. However, Hindson (1987) has shown that agricultural production in the South African 'reserves' declined sharply not only in per capita but even in absolute terms in the late 1950s. By 1970 agricultural production as a proportion of subsistence requirements was negligible. The system had collapsed: the cost of reproduction of the urban labour force could no longer be displaced onto the rural sector. Pass controls continued, however, to serve the interests of *apartheid*: not only was urban surplus labour resettled in the 'bantustans', but a large proportion of the urban labour force continued to be recruited on temporary contracts while their dependants were forced to live in the 'bantustans'.

In China stringent controls on rural–urban migration kept permanent migration extremely low while meeting the labour requirements of the urban economy through contract labour. Blecher (1988) describes the temporary recruitment of workers from rural areas to work in urban jobs in Shulu, a county in Hebei Province. In 1978 contract workers constituted over half the workforce in county-level industry. In the 1980s Shanghai was reported to have 1.8 million temporary migrants, Beijing and Guangzhou more than 1 million each (Goldstein 1990).

Circular migration has become very much the exception. Virtually all the regimes that were prepared to impose it are gone. And from the perspective of migrants it is a strategy that has little to recommend it since urban unemployment has become the rule. The search for a job may take months, and the outcome is aleatory. The migrant who has secured regular employment now has good reason to hold onto it. Long-term migration replaces circular migration. Dandekar (1995) provides a historical perspective on migration from the Maharashtra Deccan to Bombay. Since the late nineteenth century men pursued a circular migration strategy, coming to the city for the six months of the year following the wet season when agricultural tasks were few. But by 1942 temporary jobs had become much more difficult to obtain, and men began to remain on the job in Bombay for the whole year.

Many such long-term migrants leave their wives and children behind in the village – we may speak of a dual-household pattern. Short visits to the family replace the extended stays that characterize circular migration. Instead of an economic cost to the employer – a labour force characterized by high turnover and absenteeism – there is now an increased social liability for the worker: long separations strain relationships with wife, children, extended family and village community. A good deal of interest has been shown in the argument that the temporary migration of men shifts the costs of reproducing labour power to the rural sector. There is renewed interest in the contribution urban workers make to the viability of rural households. But the consequences of the dual-household pattern for the family – the hardship and emotional stress it involves, the incidence of desertion – have received virtually no attention

The dual household is subject to the vagaries of the marital relationship, in particular the single migrant's involvements in the urban setting. Two threats to the connection have always been important but have become even more so in recent years. The sufferings caused by the transmission of sexually transmitted diseases have become excruciating with the spread of the AIDS epidemic. And the neglect or even outright abandonment of rural households threatens the very survival of growing numbers of households that have become heavily dependent on urban–rural transfers.

Settling down in town with a family is usually for the long term, perhaps for a working life. However, it does not necessarily signify a permanent move. In south-eastern Nigeria a pattern of temporary family migration has continued for a generation (Gugler 1988). It may be characterized as life in a 'dual system'. Such a migration strategy entails a continuing commitment to a rural collectivity. Migrant families settle in the city for the long term, perhaps for a working life, but all the while they remain involved in their community of origin: they visit, they (more or less enthusiastically) welcome visitors, they let themselves be persuaded to contribute to development efforts, they build a house, they plan to retire and want to be buried 'at home'.

The 'dual-system' strategy is sustained by kinship groups that control rural resources, in particular access to the ancestral lands. The village assures a refuge in a political economy that fails to provide economic security to much of the urban population and that often threatens an uncertain political future. For many urban dwellers, the solidarity of rural kin provides their only social security, meagre but reliable. Often they look forward to coming 'home'.

Improvements in transport have dramatically reduced the time and resources required to bridge distances in many countries. Migrants maintaining a 'dual-household' or 'dual-system' pattern can visit family, kin and village more frequently. Patterns of weekly or even daily commuting are becoming more common. Hugo (1995) reports that the daytime population of Indonesian cities outnumbers the resident population by a large margin.

The south is in the midst of the urban transition. But we need to be aware that in many countries large numbers of urban dwellers are not permanent residents but temporary sojourners who remain deeply involved in a rural community.

Migrant identities in urban conflict

Most migrants move to a city where they can expect to be assisted by relatives or friends. This pattern of initial urban association encourages people from the same village, region or ethnic group to form residential clusters. But even when residentially dispersed, people of common origin frequently become integrated into a social network of 'home people'. Links among home people are reinforced where they maintain ties to a common home.

Larger ethnic networks are established as migrants reach beyond the limited pool of kin and home people and draw on schoolmates and affines. These ethnic networks tend to be delineated by the regional recruitment of schools, by patterns of endogamy and by common language. Thus urban dwellers tend to identify themselves and others in ethnic terms in many countries. To refer to this pattern as 'tribalism' is problematic. The term 'tribe' acquired pejorative connotations in the imperialist era, and the concept of 'tribalism' is quite misleading. Ethnic identities in the urban setting bear a rather tenuous relationship to traditional societies and their culture.

Ethnic identities are fashioned in the confrontations of the urban arena, even while they draw on regional distinctions, cultural differences, and language. They are articulated in the competition over jobs and housing and often structure alignments in political conflict. Internal migration, like international migration, brings people together who speak different languages – and who all too often disagree with what they hear of other tongues.

References

Arizpe, L. (1981) 'Relay Migration and the Survival of the Peasant Household', in J. Balan (ed.) *Why People Move: Comparative Perspectives on the Dynamics of Internal Migration*, Paris: UNESCO Press, 187–210

Blecher, M. (1988), 'Rural Contract Labour in Urban Chinese Industry: Migration Control, Urban–Rural Balance, and Class Relations', in J. Gugler (ed.) *The Urbanization of the Third World*, Oxford: Oxford University Press, 109–23

Dandekar, H. (1995), 'Changing Migration Strategies in Deccan Maharashtra, India, 1885–1990', in J. Gugler (ed.) *Cities in Asia, Africa and Latin America: Multiple Perspectives*, Oxford: Oxford University Press

Gilbert, A. and J. Gugler (1992), *Cities, Poverty and Development: Urbanization in the Third World*, Oxford: Oxford University Press

Goldstein, S. (1990) 'Urbanization in China, 1982–87: Effects of Migration and Reclassification', *Population and Development Review*, 16, 673–701

Gugler, J. (ed.) (1988) *The Urbanization of the Third World*, Oxford: Oxford University Press

—— (ed.) (1995) *The Urban Transformation of Asia, Africa and Latin America: Regional Trajectories*, Oxford: Oxford University Press

Gugler, J. and G. Ludwar-Ene (1994) 'Gender and Migration in Africa South of the Sahara', in J. Baker and T. A. Aina (eds) *Migration in Africa*, Uppsala: Scandinavian Institute of African Studies

Hindson, D. (1987) *Pass Controls and the Urban African Proletariat in South Africa*, Johannesburg: Ravan Press

Hugo, G. (1995), 'Urbanization in Indonesia: City and Countryside Linked', in J. Gugler (ed.) *The Urban Transformation of Asia, Africa and Latin America: Regional Trajectories*, Oxford: Oxford University Press

Lipton, M. (1977) *Why Poor People Stay Poor: Urban Bias in World Development*, London: Maurice Temple Smith

Parry, J. P. (1979) *Caste and Kinship in Kangra*, London: Routledge & Kegan Paul

Preston, S. H. (1988) 'Urban Growth in Developing Countries: A Demographic Reappraisal', in J. Gugler (ed.) *The Urbanization of the Third World*, Oxford: Oxford University Press, 11–31; revised from *Population and Development Review*, 5, 195–215

Trager, L. (1988) *The City Connection: Migration and Family Interdependence in the Philippines*, Ann Arbor: University of Michigan Press

Varshney, A. (ed.) (1993) *Beyond Urban Bias*, London: Frank Cass

Watson, W. (1958) *Tribal Cohesion in a Money Economy: A Study of the Mambwe of Northern Rhodesia*, Manchester: Manchester University Press; New York: Humanities Press

Young, K. (1982) 'The Creation of a Relative Surplus Population: A Case Study from Mexico', in L. Benería (ed.) *Women and Development: The Sexual Division of Labor in Rural Societies*, New York: Praeger, 149–77

WOMEN MIGRANTS: FROM MARGINAL
SUBJECTS TO SOCIAL ACTORS

GIOVANNA CAMPANI

Recent historical research in North America and Europe[1] suggests that women have always played an important social and economic role in the international migratory movements that shape the composition of populations across the world.

Researchers are now looking more closely at the socio-economic role of immigrant women in inter-European and transoceanic migration. They are interested not only in the unmarried women who left alone for employment purposes, but also in the women who formed part of the family reunification framework.[2]

Women have always worked for their families and for the market, often for both, and have made important contributions to family enterprises,[3] which have depended on them in both the sending and the receiving countries. Their social role in the decision to migrate and in accomplishing the migratory project has also been understimated, especially by European research on migration (Campani 1988); North American research has paid more attention to immigrant women (Schwartz-Seller 1981).

The tendency to assume that immigrant women are subordinate to men in the migratory process, that they are confined to the reproductive function and to a marginal position in the labour market has finally been abandoned. New migratory flows are no longer male dominated; there is a growing demand for female labour and new social needs have created a demand for services in which only immigrant women are prepared to work. The place immigrant women now occupy in the international labour market is determined by the structural character of a society that has changed considerably in recent years, a society defined by the yet ill-defined notions of 'post-modern' and 'post-industrial'.

Temporary migrations and settlement migrations

The socio-economic centrality of immigrant women in post-industrial society has recently been focused on by sociologists and economists (Morokvasic 1993; Vicarelli 1993). One of the reasons why migration studies has been 'gender blind' and has under-

estimated the importance of the socio-economic role of women for such a long time, particularly in Europe, is the predominance in the 1950s and 1960s of the model of 'temporary migration' in some of the most important immigration countries, such as Germany and Switzerland. According to this model, migration is planned and organized by state policies to provide a temporary and mobile labour force (mainly from southern Europe) to serve industry and construction. Women and children were supposed to stay in their country of origin, but if they did come, the women were supposed to follow their men and were accorded the dependent status of a 'migrant's partner', corresponding to their legal status under the family reunification laws.

These laws expressed and still express (not having being changed in the majority of countries) a patriarchal conception of gender relations. Women entering within the framework of family reunification are forced by the immigration laws into the role of a wife. Their professional lives are subject to certain constraints – for example, they have to wait for a given period of time before being accorded the legal right to work. On the other hand, women who enter as workers are often hindered in their family life, for they are forced to leave their families in the country of origin.

The model of settlement, i.e. the mobility of the whole family in response to demographic problems, has been more characteristic of transoceanic migration. Insofar as it existed in Europe, it was practised mainly in France. According to this model, women's migration is encouraged because of their reproductive function, and their insertion in the labour market is conditioned by the economic conjuncture of the receiving country.

Though the role and quantitative presence of women in migratory flows is, of course, different in the two models (temporary migrations and settlement), in both they support the reproduction of the labour force (whether in the country of origin or in the country of settlement).

However, economic roles carry their corresponding

social roles and, as Vicarelli (1993) notes, women who remain in the country of origin may have to defer more to the community, but they can also obtain a better position in their family and more autonomy in their own and in their children's lives.

Women who migrate with their families, however, do not suffer the difficulties and pain of separation and try for a while to carry on with their traditional model of life, but after a period of adaptation to the immigration country they tend to become elements of change inside the family.

The roles immigrant women play in cultural change – both in the sending and the receiving countries – depend on different factors. For example, segregation within the ethnic community favours tradition; entry into the labour market encourages socio-cultural change; active participation in ethnic networks and in associative life gives women autonomy and allows them to create 'all women' spaces, in which a sort of 'female ethnicity' can be produced (Campani 1993).

The most recent research shows that women can play an important socio-economic and cultural role in directing change in the migratory movements and among the settled immigrant population.

Parminder Bhachu, in her research on Asian women, who have a very active relationship with the labour market, in some cases a more active one than indigenous white women, shows that women are active 'manufacturers of their cultural values', which they generate by engaging with their cultural frameworks, while at the same time transforming them, in accordance with the class and local and regional niches they occupy in Britain (Bhachu 1985).

Immigrant women are *agents of cultural change*; moreover, according to some researchers (Taboada-Leonetti 1983), they have a greater capacity than men to adapt themselves to the new situation in the immigration country – this greater capacity has also to do with the specific position of men.

In cases of temporary migration, even if the man is suffering from social marginalization in the host country, he is economically responsible and retains his position as the head of his family, albeit at a distance. In cases of settlement migration, however, the wife and children who have migrated with the man are exposed to his economic and social difficulties, to his loss of power and status in the ethnic community (Vicarelli 1993).

The new context of international migrations
The model of temporary labour migration could not be maintained for a long time; processes of stabil-

ization could not be prevented. After the introduction of the 'stop policies' around the middle of the 1970s (Campani 1988), family reunification became an important means of getting into Europe for non-Community citizens. A consequence of the stabilization process was an increase in the number of women, arriving mainly through family reunification.

In the twelve main European Community countries the number of women increased between 1960 and 1980 from 30 per cent to 45 per cent of the immigrant population. Nowadays there are about 6 million migrant women in Europe, almost half the 12.8 million immigrants. Of these 5 million come from EC countries and the rest from outside the EC, and almost half are women (Eurostat 1992).

Despite growing unemployment in the Community since 1980, the percentage of active immigrant women has increased in almost all the European countries (France, Holland, Germany and Belgium) (OECD 1992).

During the 1970s there was a turning point in international migratory movements: the times and places of the new immigrations and their impact on a deeply transformed society changed (Calvanese and Pugliese 1990).

Contemporary international migration movements manifest certain characteristics that differentiate them from those that pertained in northern Europe in the 1950s and 1960s, before the introduction of 'stop policies' forced new migrants into behaving in a clandestine manner or into becoming refugees. The OECD's (1992) continous reporting system on migration describes an acceleration of the flows on a worldwide basis. In other words, both sending and receiving countries have been extended to formerly untouched or scarcely touched regions. For example, Asia (including countries like Japan where immigration was previously unknown) has become a whole continent of migration, and eastern Europe, after a long period of closed borders, has become one of the main emigration regions.

The composition of the new migratory flows has changed, with one of its new characteristics being the growing importance of women (along with urban, highly qualified, middle-class migrants). Women have become a more and more consistent part of the new flows, migrating not only for family reunification, but also for employment purposes. United Nations statistics in fact show that women make up half the world's migrant population (United Nations Population Division 1990).

The increase of women in present migratory flows

has to be understood within the general socio-economic context in which migrations take place. I shall consider the economic and social factors associated with female migrations in both sending and receiving countries.

The economic changes that have taken place in both the national and international labour markets of the receiving countries have brought industrial restructuring, increased flexibility in productive processes, the development of informal economies, tertiarization and the segmentation of the labour market (Palidda 1992; Reyneri 1992; Venturini 1990).

Venturini writes that migration flows are no longer attracted by an overall quantitative imbalance in the labour markets of the receiving countries, but rather by sectoral imbalances which may even arise in situations of unemployment, where they are the result of the 'segmentation' of the labour market and apply mainly to jobs at the lowest or higher rungs of the occupational ladder. In other words, despite the high unemployment of local populations there are areas in the labour markets of European countries with a demand for immigrant labour. The specificity of this demand particularly concerns the female labour force. The importance of women in the new migration flows is a highly significant trend and is associated with changes in the international labour market, which is witnessing a slackening in the demand for male manpower (Lim 1989; Weinert 1991) and a growing demand for traditionally female jobs (maids, nurses, entertainers) (Lim 1989).

The development of a demand in sectors such as domestic work and entertainment and in the labour-intensive sectors (mainly in the textile and garment industries) (Morokvasic 1988; Sassen-Koob 1984) has to do with the socio-economic changes taking place in industrialized countries – informalization, tertiarization (including the development of services to private persons) (Weinert 1991), loss of social security and of 'guaranteed' jobs, and the rise of new social needs. This creates new vacancies for the employment of immigrant women, both from the new flows and the established communities.

The employment of immigrant women in European and international labour markets reveals one of the main aspects of the new migratory process, i.e. a shift in the economic insertion of immigrants from the industrial to the service (including services to private persons) sector and to the informal economy.

Consequently, even traditional female jobs such as domestic work and prostitution, in which nowadays thousands of immigrant women are employed not only in Europe and the USA but also in the oil-rich monarchies and in Asia (Singapore, Hong Kong, Japan),[4] can no longer be considered as 'marginal' to the 'core' factory work of Marxist theory. These jobs have to be understood within the framework of a new economic context.

At a macro level of analysis, the work of immigrant women in Europe and in the world in the 1980s and 1990s accords with the logic of a society undergoing profound changes.

Immigrant women fit into the productive processes associated with the development of the informal economy and with the crisis of the industrial sector. They assist the elderly and the handicapped in the crumbling welfare state, or work as nurses; they find employment in restaurants, in tourism, in the sex industry and as maids for western women seeking their own autonomy.

But even if they are destined to work as live-in maids, as prostitutes, nurses or entertainers in traditionally female jobs, immigrant women are *not* – and I repeat it – they are *not* marginal economic subjects.

Immigrant women and social life

The economic position of immigrant women is not marginal because it is compatible with the economic developments of post-industrial society and responds to new social needs.

At the same time, through their social action, immigrant women are abandoning social marginality. As Tienda and Booth (1991) affirm, migration implies neither degradation nor improvement in women's position, but a restructuring of gender relations. This restructuring need not necessarily be expressed through a satisfactory professional life. It may take place through the assertion of autonomy in social life, through relations with the family of origin, or through participating in various networks and formal associations. The differential between earnings in the country of origin and the country of immigration may in itself create such autonomy, even if the job in the receiving country is one of a live-in maid or prostitute.

It must not be forgotten that women's migration is made possible by crises in the traditional community, village and family structures in the country of origin, and that within these structures women's roles are changing. Migration often occurs in a changing situation and the reasons for migration are often associated with a wish to become 'emancipated',[5] to gain autonomy and independence, to follow the model of Western women (Cruz and Paganoni 1989).

Immigrant women have to cope with a whole range of contradictory situations. These include the breakdown of traditional structures and dominant male roles in the immigrant community, ambitions being thwarted by finding it impossible to get out of domestic work, incongruence between class origins and social and professional status in the receiving country, and the difficulties of combining work for the family with work for the market.

A particularly interesting aspect of the social life of immigrant women is expressed through their increasingly active participation in associations. Immigrant women have traditionally developed informal networks (Andezian and Streiff-Fénart 1981): now they are becoming involved in associations, not only in countries like England, France or Germany where immigration is already established (Boumédienne 1988; Brah 1985; Gimetz and Wilpert 1987), but also in countries of recent immigration, like Italy, Spain or Portugal, where in some ethnic groups women are the majority of the immigrant population (Filipinas and Cape Verdians) (Campani 1993).

Notes

1. The migration history of women is a relatively new field of study in Europe (Liauzu 1994). In the USA, however, the history of women's migration has been included in academic courses for many years (Schwartz-Seller 1981).
2. From research on the activities of Italian migrant women between 1908 and 1918, developed by the Society for the Protection of Migrant Women and Children, it is possible to reconstruct the nature of work undertaken by Italian women who migrated either to other European countries or across the ocean. Young, unmarried women went to the industrial areas of nearby European countries, where they found lodgings in boarding houses run in a very authoritharian way by the employers or by religious organizations. The married women who went to the USA, however, tended to work in the 'family enterprise' once they had settled in the receiving country.
3. The notion of 'family enterprise' is pertinent in describing the efforts of families to realize the migratory project. The tendency to use the energies of the family to achieve self-employment is more developed in some ethnic groups (such as the Chinese and the Italians) than in others because of cultural traditions.
4. The number of immigrant women working as domestic helpers or in the sex industry is very high at the world level. There are 200,000 foreign maids in Italy, 25,000 in Spain (Weinert 1991), 60,000 in Great Britain, 86,000 Sri Lankan women in the Middle East (63,000 in Kuwait alone), 80,000 Filipina maids in Hong Kong and 35,000 in Singapore.
5. The word 'emancipation' is in fact a very ambiguous one, indicating the liberation of the slave by the will of the master (through the symbolic act of imposing a heavy hand). Feminist movements criticize this notion: not only do they want to obtain the same rights and opportunities as men, but they also want to create something new, something that expresses their difference.

References

Andezian, S. and J. Streiff-Fénart (1981) 'Les Réseaux sociaux des Femmes maghrébines immigrées en Provence-Côte d'Azur', doctoral thesis, University of Nice

Bhachu, P. K. (1985) *Twice Migrants*, London: Tavistock

Boumédienne, T. H. (1988) 'Work and Associative Life amongst North African Women in France', paper presented to the Conference, Women in International Migration, Social, Cultural and Occupational Issues, Berlin, Technische Universitat and UNESCO, October

Brah, A. (1985) 'Les Femmes du Sud-Est asiatique en Grande Bretagne: Questions concernant l'Emploi, l'Éducation et la Culture', Conseil de l'Europe, DECS/EGT

Calvanese F. and E. Pugliese (1990) 'I Tempi e gli Spazi della nuova Immigrazione in Europa', *Inchiesta*, October–December

Campani, G. (1988) 'Le Politiche di Stop', in Nino Sergi (ed.) *L'Immirazione straniera in Italia*, Rome: Edizioni Lavoro

(1993) 'I Reticoli sociali delle donne Immigrate in Italia', in M. Delle Donne, U. Melotti and S. Petilli (eds) *Immirazione straniera in Italia: Solidarieta e Conflitto*, Rome: CEDISS

Cruz, V. and A. Paganoni (1989) *Filipinas in Migration: Big Bills and Small Change*, New Manila, Quezon City: SMC Scalabrini Migration Center

Eurostat (1992) *Indaine sulle Forze lavoro*, Rome: Statistical Institute of the European Community

Gimetz, A. and C. Wilpert (1987) 'A Micro-Society or an Ethnic Community? Social Organization and Ethnicity among Turkish Migrants in Berlin', in J. Rex, D. Joly and C. Wilpert (eds) *Immigrant Associations in Europe*, Aldershot: Gower

Liauzu, C. (1994) 'Les Migrations dans l'Enseignement de l'Histoire en France', in G. Campani (ed.) *Educazione interculturale: Una Prospettiva internazionale*, Rome: Tecnodid

Lim, L. L. (1989) 'The Status of Women in International Migration: Background Paper for the Meeting on International Migration Policies and the Status of Female Migrants', United Nations

Morokvasic, M. (1988) 'Entreprendre au Féminin en Europe: Cas des Immigrées et des Minorités en France, Grande Bretagne, en Italie, au Portugal et en République Fédérale d'Allemagne. Motivations, Situations et Reccomandations pour Actions', Commission des Communautés Européennes, Direction Générale de l'Emploi, des Affaires Générales et de l'Education

(1993) 'Emerging Trends and Major Issues in Migration and Ethnic Relations in Western and Eastern Europe', paper presented at the International Seminar organized by UNESCO–CRER, University of Warwick, 5–8 November 1993, 400–83

OECD (1992) *Tendances des Migrations internationales*, Paris: OECD/OCDE/SOPEMI

Palidda, S. (1992) 'Eurocentrisme et Realités effectives des Migrations', *Migrations Sociétés*, 4 (24), November–December

Reyneri, E. (1992) 'L'Innovazione produttiva nella rete delle Relazioni sociali', *Stato e Mercato*, 23, August, 147–76

Sassen-Koob, S. (1984) 'Notes on the Incorporation of Third World Women into Wage Labour through Immigration and Offshore Production', *International Migration Review*, 4

Schwartz-Seller, M. (1981) *Immigrant Women*, Philadelphia: Temple University Press

Taboada-Leonetti, I. (1983) 'Le Role des Femmes migrantes

dans le Mantien ou la Déstruction des Cultures nationales du Groupe migrant', *Studi Emirazione*, 70

Tienda, M. and K. Booth (1991) 'Gender, Migration and Social Change', *International Sociology*, 6 (1), 51–72

United Nations Population Division (1990) 'Department of International Economic and Social Affairs Measuring the Extent of Female International Migration', paper prepared for the United Nations expert group meeting on International Migration Policies and the Status of Female Migrations, San Miniato, Italy, 27–30 March

Venturini, A. (1990), 'Un'Interpretazione economica delle Migrazioni mediterranee', in C. Maccheroni and A. Mauri (eds) *Le Migrazioni dall'Africa mediterranea verso l'Italia*, Milan, Giuffré

Vicarelli, G. (1993) 'Il Lavoro per il Mercato e il Lavoro per la Famiglia', paper presented at the Conference, Cittadine del Mondo, Le Donne migranti tra Identita e Mutamento, Ancona, 20–21 September 1993

Weinert, P. (1991) *Foreign Female Domestic Workers: HELP Wanted*, Geneva: International Labour Office, March

ETHICAL PROBLEMS OF IMMIGRATION CONTROL AND CITIZENSHIP

RAINER BAUBÖCK

Until recently, with a few significant exceptions, political and moral philosophers had little to say about migration. It was mostly taken for granted that state sovereignty implied the right to control movements of persons across borders (and quite often within borders as well). Free internal movement and choice of residence within a state and the freedom to leave any state have become accepted as universal human rights only since the Second World War (see article 13 of the 1948 Declaration of Human Rights). That there is, or ought to be, an equivalent right of free immigration is generally denied by scholars of international law but has become a controversial issue in a rapidly growing number of essays in normative political theory.

If free movement were a human right it ought to be guaranteed by states even if its consequences adversely affected certain collective interests. Arguments that appeal to universal principles of justice should therefore be examined before turning to consequentialist reasoning about the likely effects of such a right.

In his short treatise on 'Eternal Peace' Immanuel Kant (1984) proposed a world citizen right to free movement, which he grounded in mankind's common ownership of the earth. Originally nobody has a stronger right to be in any place than anybody else and the limited surface of the earth makes it impossible for mankind to avoid trans-societal contact by dispersing ever more over the globe. So all human beings must have a right to offer themselves for social contact with established inhabitants of any territory. Yet from these strong premises Kant derives only a right of 'hospitality', i.e. not to be treated in a hostile manner upon arriving. He seems to advocate a universal right to travel and to peaceful trade rather than to immigrate. For Kant the right to reject unwelcome immigrants is illustrated by the experience of societies invaded, colonized and exploited by Europeans. There is, however, one important proviso, which reads like an early formulation of the *non-refoulement* principle of Article 33 of the Geneva Refugee Convention – aliens can only be turned away if this does not lead to their perishing. Kant's vision

seems deeply embedded in pre-industrial capitalism. If trade is the major motive for people moving abroad then a visiting right is perfectly sufficient for their purposes. But when people migrate because they have to seek employment outside their societies of origin this will clearly not do. A right to immigration and to permanent residence will become necessary to secure their autonomy and to meet their needs. Yet such a right can hardly be derived from the original notion of man's common ownership of the earth's territories. Immigration rights of this kind cannot be conceived ahistorically as natural human rights but have to be grounded in the specific forms of mobility of modern society.

In a spirit of Kantian universalism Bruce Ackerman has gone much further in defending a *prima facie* right of immigration. For Ackerman (1980) citizenship in a liberal state is a valuable and scarce resource. People who claim that they want to share in enjoying such a resource can only be rejected if their exclusion can be defended in a dialogue under constraint of neutrality. Contestants are not allowed to base their cases on their own moral superiority. Contrary to communitarian philosophers like Michael Walzer (1983: 40ff.), Ackerman insists that a liberal state is not a private club. Ideally, '*all* people who fulfil the dialogic and behavioral conditions [i.e. their actions conform to their words] have an unconditional right to demand recognition as full citizens of a liberal state' (Ackerman 1980: 8, emphasis in original). Ackerman concedes that in the real world there may be justifiable limits to free access. Beyond a certain threshold immigration could provoke a backlash of anxiety among the native population and fascists could seize political power. But 'the *only* reason for restricting immigration is to protect the ongoing process of liberal conversation itself' (Ackerman 1980: 95, emphasis in original). This raises a number of puzzling questions. If, *prima facie*, citizenship is a resource that requires bounded political communities for its generation, how can there be a *prima facie* case for free access to such communities? When an association defends the special entitlements of its members against the claims of outsiders can it only do so by asserting the *moral inferiority* of non-members? If immigrants are admitted on a purely first-come first-served basis until a critical threshold has been reached, how can we make sure that special moral claims for entry such as those of refugees and family members will be given priority? Finally, if the threshold is determined by the threat of a political backlash will this not give opponents of liberal democracy a chance to pressurize liberal regimes into restricting immigration below levels that might be perfectly acceptable when measured by other criteria?

Although Ackerman does not fully succeed in arguing for free immigration, his approach can be used to defend an essential ethical principle. Even if states are entitled to restrict entry they may not reject immigrants *arbitrarily*. They must be able to provide reasons for non-admission which do not violate equal respect for immigrants as autonomous moral beings. Reasons that imply a moral inferiority of individuals or of their conceptions of the good cannot be accepted. All immigrants who have not shown by their personal deeds that they are hostile to a liberal democratic order must be attributed the *capacity* to become citizens of a liberal state, independently of their 'racial' or cultural origins.

Instead of arguing positively for a right of immigration one may as well deny that states are entitled to control it. The libertarian framework of justice developed by Robert Nozick (1974) seems to support this approach. Free movement is the prototypical negative liberty. Liberals generally share John Rawls's view that justice requires the most extensive system of liberties compatible with equal liberties for all (Rawls 1971).[1] Libertarians only accept restrictions on liberty incurred through voluntary contractual obligations, but not in the name of state or collective interests. While justly acquired property in land gives owners the right to deny entry to other persons, states according to this view would not be entitled to do the same. Nevertheless, as O'Neill poignantly observes, 'libertarians are known for advocating free trade, but not for advocating the dismantling of immigration laws. This may be because their stress on property rights entails an attrition of public space that eats into the freedom of movement and rights of abode of the unpropertied, even within national jurisdictions' (O'Neill 1991: 290). In spite of this inconsistency, libertarian reasoning could support the following conclusion. In a world of minimal states that used their monopoly of force only to defend basic civil rights, but which

developed neither democratic forms of collective decision-making nor extensive social redistribution, there would indeed be no good ethical reason for state restrictions on immigration.

If one attributes some ethical importance to political and social citizenship rights there is another challenge to be answered: why should the achievements of democratic welfare states be the exclusive property of those lucky enough to be born there? Some authors have suggested a global application of Rawls's theory of justice (Barry 1973; Beitz 1979). Behind a global 'veil of ignorance' about their own societal membership representatives of the 'original position' would vote for a right to free movement both because it extends the overall system of liberties and because it seems to follow from the 'different principle', namely that social inequalities should be arranged so that the least advantaged benefit most (Barry 1989: 189; Carens 1987).[2] The same inspiration has led many to demand free access in the First World for Third World immigrants to compensate for the failures of development aid. If the global distribution of resources is unjust and if resources cannot be brought to where people are, people should be allowed to go where the resources are (Goodin 1992: 8; Lichtenberg 1981: 92ff.). This is an argument about consequences rather than about natural liberty. But would the effects of free migration really be redistributive in this way? Research shows a rather ambiguous pattern of benefits and burdens. Sending countries might benefit during an initial period from remittances but will often suffer long-term costs as a result of losing the most active members of their populations. Instead of leading to a flow of resources towards the sending states, free labour immigration mostly opens up inequalities within the receiving countries. Overall, consumers would gain modestly from free immigration because of cheaper labour costs. Employers of immigrant labour will clearly profit and native workers competing within the same economic sectors will lose while the distribution of benefits will be inverse in other sectors of the economy. Immigrants themselves will benefit in economic terms, but at the same time the system of social security might be eroded by an abundant supply of additional labour. One may with good moral reason say that this is a price worth paying when confronted with global poverty. But then this cure might worsen the disease. Enforcing social redistribution within bounded political communities might be a more promising strategy (van Parijs 1992).

Arguing for free movement as a natural right or as a demand of universal justice is not the only strategy available. One can defend a disputed right that has not been widely granted by appealing to other well-established rights and by claiming that they imply the novel right by way of an analogy, symmetry or causal relation. A frequently heard analogy is that if money and goods can move freely between countries then people should be entitled to do so, too.[3] Another argument is that immigration and emigration are symmetrical phenomena and so should be rights corresponding to both kinds of movements. A consideration that appeals both to analogy and symmetry is that states are not entitled to restrict internal movement across administrative boundaries (of, for example, federal states) even when collective policy goals are affected negatively. So they should also not be allowed to control movement across international borders for similar reasons.

Mere analogy or symmetry can be criticized by showing that there is some ethically important difference between both sides of the equation. Goods and money do not have the same moral standing as people. Unlike people, goods are legitimately treated as mere means for satisfying the needs of other people. The analogy between both could be used to argue for free slave trade as well as for free migration. There is a utilitarian variation of this theme based on liberal economic theory that free movement for capital and labour will lead to the most efficient allocation of factors of production and will optimize aggregate wealth and welfare.[4] In this view migrants are conceived of as guest-workers who come voluntarily in search of economic opportunities. Yet in liberal democratic states individuals who are admitted into the country must be treated not only as economic agents but as bearers of fundamental rights and if they stay they ought to be treated as potential citizens. Thus immigrants can raise substantial claims to status and resources in receiving societies. If they are accepted as moral beings with morally relevant ties and rights towards both sending and receiving societies, considerations about aggregate economic welfare are insufficient to determine the rights and duties of both states and individuals involved.

The argument that emigration and immigration rights ought to be symmetrical seems a much stronger one in these respects. However, there are again some morally important differences. Voluntary associations generally allow their members to leave but do not admit everybody who wishes to become a member. States might not be voluntary associations but the analogy holds at least for emigration rights. Freedom of exit is a minimum test for consent in government.[5]

If states are seen as political communities entitled to redistribute resources and benefits among their members they seem to have good reasons to restrict access from outside. So, unless one can show why states *should* be different from voluntary associations in their admission policies, Walzer's conclusion seems to hold that 'immigration and emigration are morally asymmetrical' (Walzer 1983: 40).

However, even if there is no strict symmetry, the right of emigration may *imply* corresponding immigration rights. It does not matter whether a state closes its borders to emigrants or all its neighbouring states close their borders to entrants. In order to enjoy the right of emigration in a meaningful way, there must be other countries to which one can go (Zolberg 1987: 270). This is an important argument for immigration rights, but not for universal ones. While the obligation to permit emigration always falls on a single state of present residence, a corresponding right of immigration has to be guaranteed by no particular other state. Unallocated obligations such as this one may carry strong moral weight as reasons for voluntary commitments, but they cannot be enforced in the same way as more special ones can (O'Neill 1991).

The argument from analogy with internal freedom of movement draws attention to the fact that the establishment of zones of free migration has been an important achievement within modern liberal states. A general right to mobility becomes important only in a mobile society. In pre-modern society, mobility was mostly attached to the life either of social outcasts or of highly specialized elites. Neither the majority of the population, i.e. agricultural producers, nor the inhabitants of walled cities enjoyed or required mobility as a right. In an economy with a generalized labour market, the right to mobility becomes an urgent one. This does not mean that mobility as a *right* is a functional necessity of the economic system. Mobility need not be voluntary. If labour does not, or cannot, move freely to places of production, its mobility can also be enforced by evictions, slave trade, indentured labour and other forms of unfree labour (Cohen 1987). Invariably those who have been moved (rather than having chosen to move themselves) lack basic rights. However, political and union struggles of workers have set constraints on these forms of labour and industrial development within these constraints has made the forceful allocation of labour not only morally unacceptable but also more and more inefficient. Whereas the walls around ancient or late medieval city-states were a necessary condition for maintaining the liberties and privileges of urban citizenship, restrictions on mobility make for unequal citizenship in modern society. Internal freedom of movement has contributed to the equalization of citizenship within nation states, but state control over transnational movement has reinforced distinctions between aliens and citizens. Those who have to move across borders will only become full citizens when they also enjoy the *liberty* to move. Increasing transnational mobility in societies politically organized as territorial states thus provides a strong case for freedom of movement.

Yet the very achievement of substantial and equal rights of citizenship within a space of free movement might also require some form of external closure.[6] If objections along this line stand the test of moral scrutiny this will mean that universal freedom of movement has to be seen as a target for liberal democratic policies rather than as a moral right, which would constrain all existing political options. Adopting a universal right to immigration as a long-term target would still have an impact on the evaluation of today's policies. It means that immigration rights ought to be extended rather than restricted wherever possible. Extending citizenship rights beyond national memberships and territories creates the necessary preconditions for this and is therefore itself an ethical requirement of liberal democracy.

This line of argument makes sense only if one agrees that in an ideal world of modernity, freedom of movement would be established as a universal right. Brian Barry has recently opposed this view. He argues that 'an ideal world would be one in which the vast majority of people were content with conditions in their own countries' so that few would wish to migrate anyway. In a less ideal world, which would be like ours but where states were entirely motivated by moral considerations, migration would still be an activity subject to congestion, and regulation would therefore be necessary and justified (Barry 1992: 279ff.).

The fact that an activity requires some regulation because not everybody can engage in it at the same time in the same place is hardly an argument against conceiving of it as an unrestricted liberty or right (Rawls 1993a: 296). Not only internal free movement but also freedom of assembly and speech are regulated for such reasons. One could conceive of free immigration as a universal liberty even when a few areas are closed because of congestion or damage to the ecology and when there is some queuing for

access to permanent residence. This would still be a very different world compared with the present one where states defend their sovereign right to control, select or reject immigrants without a corresponding right to being admitted on the latter's part.

Furthermore, there are some difficulties with Barry's view that in the perfect world there would be little migration anyhow. Even if all countries were equally rich and democratic they need not in themselves contain a complete opportunity structure for all desires and needs that individuals should be free to satisfy. The principality of Luxembourg is too small to have its own university and therefore sends its students abroad. Is there something wrong with the existence of such states or with their inhabitants' wishes to get access to other country's resources? Only the world can be regarded as a complete opportunity structure for all the needs of humankind. An ideal world would be one in which all people would find roughly equal levels of resources in the places where they are born but where everybody would enjoy the right to search for better opportunities elsewhere without being impeded by the circumstances of his or her origins. Global markets, communication and mobility in modern society have turned the vision of self-sufficient nation states into a backward-looking utopia. Only a world that institutionalized the right to universal mobility could be called ideal in the sense of maximizing the opportunities for all individuals to satisfy their needs and interests by voluntary choices and actions.

If arguments for universal freedom are not strong enough to succeed in the present world proponents of liberal immigration policies can nevertheless make a strong case by focusing on ethical constraints on state regulation. The following are some principles that can be easily defended within any liberal democratic approach, but are far from being complied with in the current policies of western states:

- Individuals considered to be members of a society represented by a state ought to enjoy the right to enter that state and to stay in it without threat of expulsion. Where societal membership does not coincide with formal citizenship of a nation state, these rights must also be extended to aliens. This is a foundation for the rights of family reunification and of permanent residence.
- The universal right to emigrate implies a right to be admitted for those who have lost the protection of their own state. States specially responsible for admitting refugees are those that share some

responsibility for the causes of flight, those with whom refugees already have some personal or collective ties, or those in the best position to provide shelter. Ultimately, the universal right of exit implies a joint obligation of the community of states for refugees and therefore a more specific obligation for each state to contribute towards international solutions to refugee crises.

- The primary justification for imposing restrictions on immigration is the maintenance of a comprehensive system of civil, democratic and social rights of citizenship. Policies of protecting such systems within nation states ought to go hand in hand with extending them to transnational levels and thereby removing the major ethical reasons for immigration control.

- For those who are not exempted from control or who cannot claim priority in access there ought to be fair and non-discriminatory procedures for distributing places to applicants. Paying equal respect to non-entitled immigrants means that quantitative limitation should be more important in organizing such a scheme than qualitative selection.

- The costs of admitting more immigrants than the third criterion would permit must be balanced against the costs of deterring or rejecting those who want to come and of detecting and deporting those who have come illegally. Confronted with a big immigration push a liberal democratic state may face a dilemma in choosing which costs to minimize. Policies addressing root causes of poverty, unemployment, ecological disaster, mass disease, war and repression and policies of coordinating a gradual extension of receiving capacities among target states will be necessary if this dilemma is to be avoided.

Notes

1. Rawls now suggests instead that justice requires 'a fully adequate system of liberties' (Rawls 1993a: 331–4).
2. In a recent essay Rawls argues against these conclusions and for establishing only basic human rights as the standard of justice in international relations (Rawls 1993b).
3. This analogy structures the most comprehensive overview of political theory approaches to free movement so far edited by Brian Barry and Robin Goodin (1992).
4. As discussed above, in the real world an increase in aggregate utility achieved in this way will be hardly Pareto-optimal; there will be many losers.
5. A classical formulation is in Plato's *Crito* where Socrates imagines the Athenian laws arguing that 'any Athenian, on attaining to manhood and seeing for himself the political organization of the state and us laws, is permitted, if he is not satisfied with us, to take his property and go away wherever he likes. ... On the other hand, if any one of you stands his

ground when he can see how we administer justice and the rest of our public organization, we hold that by so doing he has in fact undertaken to do anything that we tell him' (Plato 1961: 36ff., Crito 51d). For excellent contemporary discussions of the right to leave see Whelan (1981) and Dowty (1987).
6. Hannah Arendt and Michael Walzer have strongly argued this point: 'Freedom, wherever it existed as a tangible reality, has always been spatially limited. This is especially clear for the greatest and most elementary of all negative liberties, the freedom of movement; the borders of national territory or the walls of the city-state comprehended and protected a space in which men could move freely. Treaties and international guarantees provide an extension of this territorially bound freedom for citizens outside their own country, but even under these modern conditions the elementary coincidence of freedom and a limited space remains manifest' (Arendt 1963: 279). In Walzer's view states cannot be as open as neighbourhoods: 'If states ever become large neighborhoods, it is likely that neighborhoods will become little states. ... Neighborhoods can be open only if countries are at least potentially closed' (Walzer 1983: 38).

References

Ackerman, Bruce A. (1980) *Social Justice in the Liberal State*, New Haven: Yale University Press

Arendt, Hannah (1963) *On Revolution*, London: Faber & Faber

Barry, Brian (1973) *The Liberal Theory of Justice*, Oxford: Clarendon Press

— (1989) *Theories of Justice: A Treatise on Social Justice*, vol. I, London: Harvester-Wheatsheaf

— (1992) 'The Quest for Consistency: A Sceptical View', in Brian Barry and Robert Goodin, *Free Movement: Ethical Issues in the Transnational Migration of People and of Money*, Pennsylvania: Pennsylvania State University Press

Barry, Brian and Robert Goodin (eds) (1992) *Free Movement: Ethical Issues in the Transnational Migration of People and of Money*, Pennsylvania: Pennsylvania State University Press

Beitz, Charles R. (1979) *Political Theory and International Relations*, Princeton, NJ: Princeton University Press

Carens, Joseph H. (1987) 'Aliens and Citizens: The Case for Open Borders', *The Review of Politics*, 49 (2), 251–73

Cohen, Robin (1987) *The New Helots: Migrants in the International Division of Labour*, Aldershot: Avebury

Dowty, Alan (1987) *Closed Borders: The Contemporary Assault on Freedom of Movement*, New Haven: Yale University Press

Goodin, Robert E. (1992) 'If People were Money...', in Brian Barry and Robert Goodin (eds) *Free Movement: Ethical Issues in the Transnational Migration of People and of Money*, Pennsylvania: Pennsylvania State University Press

Kant, Immanuel (1984) *Zum Ewigen Frieden*, Leipzig: Reclam, first published 1795

Lichtenberg, Judith (1981) 'National Boundaries and Moral Boundaries: A Cosmopolitan View', in P. G. Brown and H. Shue (eds) *Boundaries: National Autonomy and its Limits*, Totowa, NJ: Rowman & Littlefield

Nozick, Robert (1974) *Anarchy, State and Utopia*, Oxford: Basil Blackwell

O'Neill, Onora (1991) 'Transnational Justice', in David Held (ed.) *Political Theory Today*, Oxford: Polity Press, 276–304

Plato (1961) *The Collected Dialogues of Plato*, Princeton, NJ: Princeton University Press

Rawls, John (1971) *A Theory of Justice*, Oxford: Oxford University Press

— (1993a) *Political Liberalism*, New York: Columbia University Press

— (1993b) 'The Law of Peoples', in Stephen Shute and Susan Hurley, *On Human Rights: The Oxford Amnesty Lectures 1993*, New York: Basic Books

van Parijs, Philippe (1992) 'Commentary: Citizenship Exploitation, Unequal Exchange and the Breakdown of Popular Sovereignty', in Brian Barry and Robert Goodin (eds.) *Free Movement: Ethical Issues in the Transnational Migration of People and of Money*, Pennsylvania: Pennsylvania State University Press

Walzer, Michael (1983) *Spheres of Justice: A Defense of Pluralism and Equality*, New York: Basic Books

Whelan, Frederick G. (1981) 'Citizenship and the Right to Leave', *American Political Science Review*, 75: 53–63

Zolberg, Aristide (1987) 'Keeping Them Out: Ethical Dilemmas of Immigration Policy', in Robert J. Myers (ed.) *International Ethics in the Nuclear Age*, Boston: University Press of America

INTERNATIONAL SECURITY AND POPULATION MOVEMENTS

GIL LOESCHER

The end of the cold war has given rise to a new international context concerning forced migration. Refugees and displaced people are high on the list of international concerns today not only because of their humanitarian importance, but also because of their impact on peace and security (Loescher 1992).

It is no longer sufficient to discuss the subject of forced migration within a narrow national context or as a strictly humanitarian problem requiring humanitarian solutions. Despite this recognition of the underlying political nature of refugee movements and of the strategic effects of forced migration, surprisingly little systematic research has been carried out to explain the interrelationships among foreign policy factors and international security concerns and population movements. This chapter attempts to develop an analytical focus in order to link these previously disparate fields of enquiry.

National security in the post-cold war era

With the end of the cold war, the concept of what constitutes national security has changed dramatically and has acquired a new and complex significance. Considerations of national security have expanded from traditional military-political issues at the interstate level, such as protecting the inviolability of a country's borders or the continued existence of a state from external threats, to many new concerns, including refugee and migration flows (Azar and Moon 1988; Buzan 1991; Chipman 1992; Choucri 1992; Choucri and North 1990; Loescher 1993; Sayigh 1990; Ullman 1983; Weiner 1993).

In recent years, religious, ethnic or communal tensions in Africa, the former Soviet Union and the Balkans, and in the Middle East and parts of the Asian subcontinent frequently result in the spillover of conflict or of internal human rights crises into neighbouring countries, resulting not only in the outflow of refugees, but also in the exacerbation of interstate tensions and the destabilization and overthrow of governments. From this perspective, grievous human rights abuses are not solely an internal matter, particularly when neighbouring countries must bear the cost of repression by having refugees forced upon them.

Strategic causes of forced migration

Large-scale displacements are not just produced by external interventions or by random upheavals, conflicts and inequalities, but are frequently the result of officially instigated or organized state actions which often impel refugee movements (Weiner 1993). Certain kinds of government actions, ranging from decrees and overt use of force to more covert persecution, intimidation, discrimination and inducement of an unwanted group to leave, generate refugee flows.

Most states are ethnically plural societies in which individual national or communal groups have their own separate identities, rooted in common history and culture and often language (Scarritt and Gurr 1989). Mass displacements of people frequently occur when multinational governments seek to form or reconstitute homogeneous and united populations by forcible means. Sometimes a dominant group tries to marginalize further or expel minorities; sometimes a government seeks cultural and political homogeneity in the form of a new national identity; or sometimes ruling regimes impose a substitute ideology in place of nationalism in order to unite diverse peoples for state building (Keely 1991).

A large proportion of the world's displacements also occur as a direct result of political and social revolutions (Koehn 1991; Zolberg et al. 1989). Revolutions are uniquely powerful refugee-generating events because they involve a deliberate attempt to transform social and economic relations and to construct a radically different political system. Efforts to displace the governing elite, the occurrence of violent internal struggles to consolidate power, and the intolerance of domestic opposition characterize most contemporary revolutions and have been the source of many of the world's major refugee movements.

Forced migrants and security concerns of states

With the growth in recent years of mass movements of people, refugees are often viewed both as a challenge to the integrity and security of sending and receiving states and as a source of tension and conflict between states.

In some instances, forced migrants may present a military threat to a host country. Mass migrations are frequently employed as foreign policy tools and as instruments of warfare and military strategy. During the 1980s, the strategic and political interests of the West and its allies, to maintain pressure against and to destabilize revolutionary states in the Third World, and through them, to raise the costs to their patron, the Soviet Union, were served by the continued military use of refugees. The emergence of armed groups of exiles, the so-called 'refugee warriors' (Loescher and Monahan 1989; Zolberg et al. 1989), symbolized for the West the popular rejection of communist governments and served to legitimize the resistance movements. The former Soviet Union likewise allied itself with governments and opposition groups, providing them with arms and logistical support. An increase in military intervention in local Third World conflicts by other outside powers such as South Africa, Cuba, Israel, Vietnam, China, Syria, Iraq and India among others, was also evident, in some cases acting as proxies for the USA or the former Soviet Union, either supporting regimes causing major refugee flows or refugee warrior groups seeking to overthrow or destabilize governments.

The mass influx of refugees also influences domestic politics, particularly in the developing world. The presence of refugees accelerates existing internal conflicts in the host countries. During the 1980s, for example, the proliferation of arms following the influx of three million Afghans assisted a resurgence of Pathan unrest in Pakistan. Elsewhere, Palestinian refugees upset delicate domestic balances in Lebanon and Jordan. From Indochina to the Middle East to southern Africa to Central America, exiles agitated for changes in their home countries from within host countries: Cambodian guerrillas operating from Thailand; Afghan *mujaheddin* from Pakistan and Iran; Polisario from Algeria; Nicaraguan contras from Honduras; South Africans from black African frontline states; Palestinians from Arab radical states; Namibians from Angola, to mention only a few.

The presence of refugees in many Third World host states is further compounded by armed groups of exiles actively engaged in warfare with political objectives. Refugee warriors invite military retaliation, complicate relations with other states, and threaten the host states and the security of their citizens. As a result, host countries have often been unwillingly drawn into conflicts with their neighbours. Tensions between Rwanda and Zaire over the issue of sanctuary for Hutu militia, and the destruction wreaked on south Lebanon in Israeli reprisals for Palestinian raids are but two illustrations of the consequences for the security of host nations during the last decade. Even where guerrillas operated within their own national territory – as in the case of Eritrean and Salvadoran rebels – they depended on sanctuary and supply routes in neighbouring countries, again aggravating inter-state relations.

The great majority of refugees seek safety in the world's poorest states (the twenty countries with the highest ratio of refugees have an annual average per capita income of $700). Even when the international community provides assistance, forced migrants make demands on the host country's resources, in particular on water, food, fuel and arable land. The strain on a host population's social services and physical infrastructure and the distortion of local economic conditions can destabilize many weak developing states.

In countries with a precarious balance between ethnic or religious populations, the influx of people with ties to a particular group may change the population balance and pose a threat to the existing power structure. Countries like Malaysia or Turkey, with acute ethnic divisions, will not under any circumstances undermine their social and political order by a policy of unrestricted access for refugees from Vietnam or Kurdistan.

Even in the developed world population movements have become linked with security concerns. Western publics are concerned that mass migration will threaten communal identity and culture by directly altering the ethnic, cultural, religious and linguistic composition of the population and the integrity of their countries. These anxieties take various forms: the fear that western Europe may be flooded by refugees and immigrants from the former Soviet Union and eastern Europe; the fear that the establishment of a sectarian regime in Algeria and the spread of Islamic fundamentalism will unleash a flood of new refugees from North Africa; the fear that conflicts by migrant communities over support for political or religious struggles in their home countries will spill over into Europe; and the fear that refugees and immigrants are responsible for the rise of crime and drug traffic in western communities (Loescher 1991; Weiner 1993). In addition, there are increasing tensions between migrants and their host communities over education, religion and culture.

Population movements can also be perceived by governments to enhance their security and well-being. For example, sending states may use migration for the purposes of asserting either formal sovereignty or *de facto* control over a territory. This policy involves governmental encouragement of civilian rather than military movement into claimed territories for the purposes of establishing effective control. The Chinese policy of settling Han people in Singkiang province and Tibet, Israeli settlement of former Soviet Jewish immigrants on the West Bank and the highly publicized 'Green March' by Morocco of several hundred thousand of its own civilians into the territories of the former Spanish Sahara are explicit examples of using migration as a means to claim and occupy disputed territory.

Sending states can also actively use population movements or 'push-outs' as tools in their foreign policies (Teitlebaum 1985). Forced emigration is a policy instrument by which a state can project its economic and political influence, seek to affect the policies and politics of other states, and compel a neighbouring state to provide recognition, aid or credit in return for stemming or regularizing the flow.

The export of refugees can also be used as a bargaining chip in interstate negotiations over trade and bilateral political recognition. Typically in such situations the sending state possesses considerable leverage in the bargaining process. By pleading an inability to control the population outflow, or by demonstrating a willingness to manipulate it, the sending state is in a position to extract foreign policy and strategic concessions from the receiving state. In addition, the presence of refugees can lead to an inflow in aid either from international relief assistance or as permanent infrastructural benefits such as new roads and wells.

Some sending countries have come to see refugee exoduses as a national resource, to be exploited like any other. For sending countries, such as El Salvador, Vietnam or Morocco, to name only a few of the most obvious examples, the benefits of out-migration might include the export of their unemployed or underemployed population, the hope to maximize foreign currency earnings through remittances by its expatriate citizens, and the provision of an outlet or 'safety valve' for domestic dissidence and the relief of economic pressures. For example, remittances from overseas residents constitute an important source of El Salvador's and Vietnam's hard currency earnings and have helped compensate for the loss of earnings caused by long wars and economic disruption in these countries.

Some population movements are seen as contributing to the host state's power base, national self-confidence or dominant ethnic community. The large-scale influx of Jewish immigrants from the former Soviet Union to Israel, for example, is viewed by Tel Aviv as a demographic boost to the state, and stabilizes what was a steady decline of the Jewish people as a proportion of the population of 'Greater Israel'. Population influxes can also augment or increase the size of the receiving state's defence capabilities or military establishment. For example, Serbia recently incorporated refugees from Bosnia into its army.

Forced migration and changes in international relations

The recognition that security can no longer be viewed as an independent national problem based on limited self-interest, and that problems of forced migration can no longer be viewed from the limited humanitarian perspective has significantly broadened the agenda of international relations. The UN Security Council's Summit Declaration of 31 January 1992 acknowledged that threats to international peace and security can originate from 'non-military sources of instability in the economic, social, humanitarian and ecological fields', and that such conflicts fall within the Security Council's sphere of action. The declaration also welcomed 'election-monitoring, human rights verification, and the repatriation of refugees' as 'integral parts of the Security Council's efforts to maintain international peace and security'.

These expanded notions of what constitute threats to international security have resulted in new international actions to deal with human rights violations which generate forced migration on a large scale (Loescher 1993).

The most notorious recent example is Iraq's brutal treatment of its Kurdish population. UN Security Council Resolution 688 condemned Iraq's repression of its civilian population and argued that the consequences of this repression – the massive flow of refugees across international frontiers – threatened 'peace and security in the region'. The military intervention by the Allies in northern Iraq, and the subsequent emplacement of UN forces, was in effect a collective action authorized by the Security Council under Chapter 7 of the UN Charter to maintain and restore 'international peace and security'. Thus, a country that forces its citizens to flee or creates conditions that induce them to leave in a manner that threatens regional peace and security has in effect internationalized its internal affairs, and provides a cogent reason for policy makers to concern them-selves with internal conflicts and human rights conditions in other states.

This new thinking marks a break with the usual reluctance of the UN to intervene in the affairs of one of its member states and it means that the Security Council is more likely than it was previously to deal with mass repression when it can reasonably find a threat to international peace and security. While the notion of sovereignty is still recognized as a cardinal feature of the contemporary international political system, a variety of internal actions by states, particularly those that result in mass expulsions or refugee movements, are increasingly regarded as threats to others, particularly neighbouring states. In the future, 'active strategies of pre-emption, as opposed to passive strategies of absorption' are likely to be increasingly undertaken by both the United Nations and regional organizations (Chipman 1992).

Thus, in the post-cold war era, a convergence of the fields of security and forced migration is taking place. Because the causes and consequences of refugee movements are linked intimately to political issues, the international community needs to do more than simply forge a stronger humanitarian response. What is needed is nothing less than a working international security system that can help prevent refugee disasters from occurring in the first place.

References

Azar, E. and C. Moon (1988) *National Security in the Third World: The Management of Internal and External Threats*, Cheltenham: Edward Elgar

Buzan, B. (1991) 'New Patterns of Global Security in the Twenty-First Century', *International Affairs*, 67 (3), 431–51

Chipman, J. (1992) 'The Future of Strategic Studies: Beyond Even Grand Strategy', *Survival*, 117

Choucri, N. (1992) 'Population and Security: National Perspectives and Global Imperatives', in D. de Witt et al. (eds) *Emerging Trends in International Security*, London: Routledge, Chapman & Hall

Choucri, N. and R. North (1990) *War, Peace, Survival*, Boulder, CO: Westview Press

Keely, C. (1991) 'Filling a Critical Gap in the Refugee Protection Regime: The Internally Displaced', *World Refugee Survey 1991*, 22–7

Koehn, P. (1991) *Refugees from Revolution: US Policy and Third World Migration*, Boulder, CO: Westview Press

Loescher, G. (ed.) (1991) *Refugees and the Asylum Dilemma in the West*, University Park, PA: Pennsylvania State University Press

(1992) *Refugee Movements and International Security*, Adelphi Paper 268, London: Brassey's for IISS

(1993) *Beyond Charity: International Cooperation and the Global Refugee Crisis*, New York: Oxford University Press

Loescher, G. and Monahan, L. (eds) (1989) *Refugees and International Relations*, Oxford: Clarendon Press

Sayigh, Y. (1990) *Confronting the 1990s: Security in the Developing Countries*, Adelphi Paper 251, London: Brassey's for IISS

Scarritt, J. and T. R. Gurr (1989) 'Minority Rights at Risk: A Global Survey', *Human Rights Quarterly*, 11, 375–405

Teitlebaum, M. (1985) 'Immigration, Refugees and Foreign Policy', *International Organization*, 38, 429–50

Ullman, R. (1983) 'Redefining Security', *International Security*, 8 (1), 129–53

Weiner, M. (ed.) (1993) *International Migration and Security*, Boulder, CO: Westview Press

Zolberg, A. et al. (1989) *Escape from Violence: Conflict and the Refugee Crisis in the Developing World*, New York: Oxford University Press

Acknowledgements and credits

This book has been a labour of love for me, but perhaps a somewhat less joyous experience for those who have helped me. It is not difficult to find the person who has helped most. Selina Cohen, of Selro Publishing Services, has toiled her way through the copy-editing of 110 separate contributions before setting the book. As I was committed to ensuring a good representation of scholars outside Britain, the Commonwealth and the USA, there were inevitable problems in ironing out the language of those scholars who either sent mother-tongue contributions or had to have their colourful expressions rendered into more conventional English. Perhaps even more difficult a task was to persuade eminent scholars familiar with many different footnote and reference conventions to stick to the style sheet we provided. Drafts and redrafts arrived in a constant and bewildering stream of faxes, E-mail, snail-mail and diskettes – using every density, size and word-processing programme yet invented (or so it seemed). It would be an exaggeration to say that Selina Cohen maintained her equanimity throughout, but she stuck with it tenaciously which, as they say, is the important thing.

At Cambridge University Press, Jessica Kuper was a model editor – unobtrusive but supportive in every way. Others at the press, including Marigold Acland, Lyn Chatterton, Caroline Drake and Jane Williams were helpful. I am also grateful to Carol Fellingham Webb for her meticulous proofreading. Mandy Little arranged the contract in a painless way. Daily Information, a 'telecottage' in Oxford presided over by the redoubtable John Rose, and staffed *inter alia* by Cathy Brocklehurst, Jasper Smith and Chris Wiltshire, provided photo-copying, fax, scanning and computer facilities. Joanne Walton gave additional secretarial support. Lucy Jenkins translated the two contributions by Gérard Noiriel. Photographs were supplied by a variety of people, who are separately acknowledged in the credits below, but I would particularly like to thank Robert Mulder, a photo-journalist in the Netherlands, and Barry Moreno of the Ellis Island Museum library staff in New York for their open-hearted generosity.

One of the pleasures of editing this book was to initiate a correspondence with over 250 scholars of migration worldwide who, even if they could not contribute, suggested others who might and many of whom have continued to take an interest in the project. When we signed the contract, Cambridge University provided 1000 copies of headed note paper specially designed for the project. With the supply now finished and my having to move on to the photocopied version of the note paper, I can recall only one uncooperative letter. By contrast, scholars in many countries have become correspondents, then acquaintances and, often, friends. It is unfair to mention only a few, but I feel I need to acknowledge Kitty Calavita, Evelyn Hu-Dehart and Chan Kwok Bun for extraordinary services rendered. Hugh Tinker, whose pioneering work on migration from the Indian subcontinent remains unrivalled, completed his elegant contribution on the British colonies of settlement while seriously ill. If I thought he would not take the gesture as excessive, I would have dedicated this book to him and the inspiration he has given to his epigones. This little 'thank you' must serve as a substitute.

One note of sadness should be recorded. While this book was still being edited, one of our contributors, Laura Bigman, died in tragic circumstances.

Credits

The publisher, editor and contributors have made extensive efforts to trace copyright-holders for all the photographs, maps and figures that appear in this book. We believe that all permissions and copyrights have been properly accounted for, but undertake to make appropriate recompense to anyone whose rights may have been, wholly inadvertently, overlooked. Credits are listed below.

Plate 1: Scottish boys on Ellis Island, the Augustus Sherman Collection of the Ellis Island Museum, supplied by Barry Moreno ◆ Plate 2: Indian boys breakfasting on a 'coolie ship', first published in B. Lubbock *Coolie Ships and Oil Sailors*, Glasgow: Brown, Son and Ferguson, 1935, supplied by Steven Vertovec ◆ Plate 3: Indentured Indian women on a tea plantation in Natal, the Bhana Collection, Documentation Centre, University of Durban-Westville, supplied by Ravinder Thiara ◆ Plate 4: Indian women trenching and planting sugar cane, Natal, the Bhana Collection, Documentation Centre, University of Durban-Westville, supplied by Ravi Thiara ◆ Plate 5: Children on roof of Ellis Island, the Augustus Sherman Collection of the Ellis Island Museum, supplied by Barry Moreno ◆ Plate 6: Orphaned Jewish children, the Augustus Sherman Collection of the Ellis Island Museum, supplied by Barry Moreno ◆ Plate 7: German emigrants on board ship, courtesy of the Library of Congress library, Washington, DC, supplied by Walter Nugent ◆ Plate 8: Ukrainians detained in the Castle Mountain concentration camp, near Banff, Alberta, during the First World War, courtesy the G. W. H. Millican Collection at the Glenbow Museum, Calgary, Alberta, supplied by Lubomyr Luciuk ◆ Plate 9: Serbian gypsies c. 1904, the Augustus Sherman Collection of the Ellis Island Museum, supplied by Barry Moreno ◆ Plate 10: Miners enplane for the South African gold mines, courtesy of the South African Chamber of Mines library, supplied by Jonathan Crush ◆ Plate 11: A Moroccan grocery shop in Groningen, the Netherlands © Robert Mulder, Anna Paulownastraat 51-a, 9725 JS Groningen, Holland ◆ Plate 12: Returning from Africa at the end of the Portuguese empire, courtesy Maria Beatriz Rocha-Trinidade ◆ Plate 13: The docks at Lisbon, Portuguese repatriates from Africa look for their crates, courtesy of Maria Beatriz Rocha-Trinidade ◆ Plate 14: A reception centre for repatriates, Portugal, courtesy Maria Beatriz Rocha-Trinidade ◆ Plate 15: West Indian street carnival in the Netherlands © Robert Mulder, Anna Paulownastraat 51-a, 9725 JS Groningen, Holland ◆ Plate 16: Rohingya refugees arrive in Bangladesh from Burma © Robert Mulder, Anna Paulownastraat 51-a, 9725 JS Groningen, Holland ◆ Plate 17: Proud Greek-Australian proprietors outside their Refreshment Rooms in Singleton, NSW, 1911, courtesy Nell George © The Greek-Australian: In Their Own Image project archives, reproduced with permission and supplied by Gillian Bottomley ◆ Plate 18: Victoria Street, Darlinghurst, 1993 showing Italian cafés and influence © Effy Alexakis, reproduced with permission and supplied by Gillian Bottomley ◆ Plate 19: The grim mass housing of Gaza, home for many Palestinians, courtesy Howard Adelman and Orana Dell Penta, Centre for Refugee Studies, University of York, Toronto ◆ Plate 20: An Indian printer at work in Kuwait, courtesy the International Labour Office, Geneva/J. Maillard and supplied by Manolo Abella ◆ Plate 21: Egyptian migrant workers in Jordan, courtesy the International Labour Office, Geneva/J. Maillard and supplied by Manolo Abella ◆ Plate 22: Afghan women refugees weaving carpets in Surkhab, Baluchistan, 1982, courtesy the United Nations High Commissioner for Refugees, no. 12319/DA Giulianotti and supplied by Peter Marsden of the Refugee Council at the request of Dianne Cammack ◆ Plate 23: Village life among the Chakma in the Chittagong Hills, Bandarban, Bangladesh, 1990 © Robert Mulder, Anna Paulownastraat 51-a, 9725 JS Groningen, Holland.

Map 1: Regions of Italy showing key cities, cartographers at the University of Minnesota and Rudolph Vecoli ◆ Map 2: Volumes and destinations of migration flows from Italy, from Gianfausto Rosoli (ed.) *Un secolo di emigrazione italiana: 1876–1976* (Rome: Centro Studi Emigrazione,

1978) supplied by Rudolph Vecoli ◆ Map 3: Major migration routes to the South African gold mines, pre-1970, adapted from Francis Wilson, *Labour in the South African Gold Mines, 1911–1969* (Cambridge: Cambridge University Press, 1972) p. ix ◆ Map 4: East Africa. Major source and destination areas of migrants, drawn by cartographers at the University of Liverpool from data supplied by W. T. S. Gould ◆ Map 5: Seasonal labour migration in French North Africa, cartographer at the University of East Anglia from data supplied by Neil MacMaster ◆ Map 6: Distribution of 'ethnic Indians' born in East Africa in the UK, 1991 drawn and supplied by Vaughan Robinson ◆ Map 7: Population density in districts of Nepal and India's border districts, 1961, Censuses of Nepal and India, and Survey of India, supplied by David Seddon.

Figure 6.1: Pass law arrests in South Africa, adapted from Chamber of Mines data ◆ Figure 8.1: Landed immigrants to Canada, 1945–60, data from Employment and Immigration Canada drawn by Phil Armstrong after a chart supplied by Lawrence Lam and Anthony H. Richmond◆ Figure 9.1: Evolution of numbers of foreign nationals in France, drawn by the Geography Department cartographer at Queen Mary and Westfield College, adapted from data in INSEE, *Recensement de la populations de 1990/Nationalités. Résultants du sondage au quart* (Paris: INSEE, 1992) and supplied by Philip Ogden ◆ Figure 9.2: Evolution of foreign populations by nationality, France, 1946–90, drawn by the Geography Department cartographer at Queen Mary and Westfield College, London, adapted from data in INSEE, *Recensement de la populations de 1990/Nationalités. Résultants du sondage au quart* (Paris: INSEE, 1992) and supplied by Philip Ogden ◆ Figure 9.3: Annual arrivals of permanent foreign workers, France 1950–90, drawn by the Geography Department cartographer at Queen Mary and Westfield College, London, adapted from data in J. Costa-Lascoux, *De l'immigré au citoyen* (Paris: La Documentation Française, 1989: 38) and supplied by Philip Ogden ◆ Figure 9.4: Migration flows between Sweden and Finland, adapted from a graph in Borgegård m fl s. 55 eller Månglulturella Sverige s 98, drawn by Phil Armstrong, supplied by Tomas Hammar ◆ Figure 9.5: Age structure of the population with a Moroccan background, the Netherlands 1990, drawn by Phil Armstrong after a chart supplied by Hans van Amersfoort.

Index

This index is confined to the migrating groups listed by ethnicity and religion (Asians, British, Protestants, etc.) and to the region or country of destination (Asia, UK, etc.). Bold type indicates the principal entries.